## Financial Accounting Standards Board (FASB), Statements of Financial Accounting Standards (1973–1982)

*Refer to Index for page citations*

## Financial Accounting Standards Board (FASB), Interpretations (1974–1982)

*Refer to Index for page citations*

*(Listing continued on inside of back cover.)*

# INTERMEDIATE ACCOUNTING

## Accounting Textbooks from John Wiley and Sons

Arpan and Radebaugh:  INTERNATIONAL ACCOUNTING AND MULTINATIONAL ENTERPRISES

Bedford, Perry, and Wyatt:  ADVANCED ACCOUNTING, 4th

Buckley, Buckley, and Plank:  SEC ACCOUNTING

Burch and Sardinas:  COMPUTER CONTROL AND AUDIT

Burch, Strater, and Grudnitski:  INFORMATION SYSTEMS: THEORY AND PRACTICE, 3rd

Copeland and Dascher:  FINANCIAL ACCOUNTING

Copeland and Dascher:  MANAGERIAL ACCOUNTING, 2nd

DeCoster, Ramanathan, and Sundem:  ACCOUNTING FOR MANAGERIAL DECISION MAKING, 2nd

DeCoster and Schafer:  MANAGEMENT ACCOUNTING: A DECISION EMPHASIS, 3rd

Delaney and Gleim:  CPA EXAMINATION REVIEW – AUDITING

Delaney and Gleim:  CPA EXAMINATION REVIEW – BUSINESS LAW

Delaney and Gleim:  CPA EXAMINATION REVIEW – THEORY AND PRACTICE

Delaney and Gleim:  CPA EXAMINATION SOLUTIONS (Semi-annually, May and November)

Gleim and Delaney:  CPA EXAMINATION REVIEW, Volume I, OUTLINES AND STUDY GUIDE

Gleim and Delaney:  CPA EXAMINATION REVIEW, Volume II, PROBLEMS AND SOLUTIONS

Gross and Jablonsky:  PRINCIPLES OF ACCOUNTING AND FINANCIAL REPORTING
   FOR NONPROFIT ORGANIZATIONS

Guy:  STATISTICAL SAMPLING IN AUDITING

Haried, Imdieke, and Smith:  ADVANCED ACCOUNTING, 2nd

Helmkamp, Imdieke, and Smith:  PRINCIPLES OF ACCOUNTING

Kell and Ziegler:  MODERN AUDITING, 2nd

Kieso and Weygandt:  INTERMEDIATE ACCOUNTING, 4th

Loeb:  ETHICS IN THE ACCOUNTING PROFESSION

McCullers and Schroeder:  ACCOUNTING THEORY, 2nd

Mock and Grove:  MEASUREMENT, ACCOUNTING, AND ORGANIZATIONAL INFORMATION

Moscove and Simkin:  ACCOUNTING INFORMATION SYSTEMS

Ramanathan:  MANAGEMENT CONTROL IN NONPROFIT ORGANIZATIONS: TEXT AND CASES

Ramanathan and Hegstad:  READINGS IN MANAGEMENT CONTROL
   IN NONPROFIT ORGANIZATIONS

Sardinas, Burch, and Asebrook:  EDP AUDITING: A PRIMER

Stenzel:  APPROACHING THE CPA EXAMINATION: A PERSONAL GUIDE
   TO EXAMINATION PREPARATION

Taylor and Glezen:  AUDITING – INTEGRATED CONCEPTS AND PROCEDURES, 2nd

Taylor and Glezen:  CASE STUDY IN AUDITING, 2nd

Wilkinson:  ACCOUNTING AND INFORMATION SYSTEMS

# FOURTH EDITION
# INTERMEDIATE
# ACCOUNTING

**DONALD E. KIESO,** Ph.D., C.P.A.

Northern Illinois University
DeKalb, Illinois

**JERRY J. WEYGANDT,** Ph.D., C.P.A.

University of Wisconsin
Madison, Wisconsin

**JOHN WILEY & SONS**

New York   Chichester   Brisbane   Toronto   Singapore

Text and cover designer   Judith Fletcher Getman
Design supervisor   Sheila Granda
Copy editor   Romayne Ponleithner
Copy editing supervisor   Joan Knizeski
Senior production supervisor   Mary Halloran
Illustrator   John Balbalis, with the assistance of
    the Wiley Illustration Department

**Library of Congress Cataloging in Publication Data**

Kieso, Donald E.
    Intermediate accounting.

    Includes bibliographical references and index.
    1. Accounting.   I. Weygandt, Jerry J.   II. Title.
HF5635.K5   1983       657'.044      82-23819

ISBN: 0-471-08871-4
Printed in the United States of America
10   9   8   7   6   5   4   3

Dedicated to

**Our Parents and In-laws**

and to

| | |
|---|---|
| Donna, | Enid, |
| Douglas, | Matthew, |
| and Debra | Erin, |
| | and Lia |

# About the Authors

**Donald E. Kieso, Ph.D., CPA,** received his doctorate in accounting from the University of Illinois. He is currently Professor of Accountancy at Northern Illinois University. He has public accounting experience with Price Waterhouse & Co. (San Francisco and Chicago) and Arthur Andersen & Co. (Chicago) and research experience with the Research Division of the American Institute of Certified Public Accountants (New York). He has done post-doctorate work as a Visiting Scholar at the University of California at Berkeley and is a recipient of NIU's Teaching Excellence Award. Professor Kieso is the author of other accounting and business books and is a member of the American Accounting Association, the American Institute of Certified Public Accountants, the Financial Executives Institute, and the Illinois CPA Society. Most recently he has served as a member of the Board of Directors of the Illinois CPA Society, the Board of Governors of the American Accounting Association's Administrators of Accounting Programs Group, the Board of Directors of Aurora College, the State of Illinois Comptroller's Commission, and as Secretary-Treasurer of the Federation of Schools of Accountancy; currently, he is serving as Secretary-Treasurer of the American Accounting Association.

**Jerry J. Weygandt, Ph.D., CPA,** is Professor of Accounting at the University of Wisconsin—Madison. He holds a Ph.D. in accounting from the University of Illinois. Articles by Professor Weygandt have appeared in the *Accounting Review, Journal of Accounting Research,* the *Journal of Accountancy,* and other professional journals. These articles have examined such financial reporting issues as accounting for price-level adjustments, pensions, convertible securities, stock option contracts, and interim reports. He is a member of the American Accounting Association, the American Institute of Certified Public Accountants, and the Wisconsin Society of Certified Public Accountants. He has served on numerous committees of the American Accounting Association and as a member of the editorial board of the *Accounting Review.* In addition, he is actively involved with the American Institute of Certified Public Accountants and has been a member of the Accounting Standards Executive Committee (AcSEC) of that organization. He has served as a consultant to a number of businesses and state agencies on financial reporting issues. Currently, Professor Weygandt is serving on an FASB task force that is examining the problems of "accounting for income taxes."

# Preface

The fourth edition of *Intermediate Accounting* discusses in depth the traditional (intermediate) financial accounting topics as well as the recent developments in accounting valuation and reporting practices promulgated by the leading professional accounting organizations and applied by practitioners in public accounting and industry. Explanations and discussions of financial accounting theory are supported and illustrated by examples taken directly from practice and authoritative pronouncements.

Continuing to keep pace with the complexities of the modern business enterprise, we have added many new topics, clarified some of the existing coverage, added numerous illustrations, and updated all material where necessary. To provide the instructor with greater flexibility in choosing topics to cover or omit, we have continued the use of judiciously selected appendices. The sixteen appendices are concerned primarily with complex subjects, lesser used methods, or specialized topics.

The text is organized into six major parts.

1. Financial Accounting Functions and Basic Theory
   (Chapters 1 to 6)
2. Current Assets and Current Liabilities
   (Chapters 7 to 10)
3. Plant Assets and Long-Term Liabilities
   (Chapters 11 to 14)
4. Stockholders' Equity, Dilutive Securities, and Investments
   (Chapters 15 to 18)
5. Issues Related to Income Measurement
   (Chapters 19 to 23)
6. Preparation and Analysis of Financial Statements
   (Chapters 24 to 27)

Benefiting from the comments and recommendations of adopters of our third edition, we have made significant revisions. Explanations where necessary have been expanded, complicated discussions and illustrations have been simplified, realism has been integrated to heighten interest and relevancy, and new topics and coverage have been added to maintain currency.

We have attempted to balance our coverage so that the conceptual discussion and procedural presentation are mutually reinforcing. The study of concepts develops an understanding of procedures, and the performance of procedures enriches an understanding of the concepts. Accountants must act as well as think; therefore, we have given equal emphasis to *how* and to *why*.

We believe that individuals can account for events and phenomena best if they fully understand the nature of the phenomena and comprehend the economic consequences of the events. An appreciation for the behavioral and economic consequences of accounting and reporting alternatives is equally important. To this end, we have provided coverage that develops perspective as well as an understanding of the business transactions and other events for which enterprises account and report.

## REVISIONS AND NEW FEATURES

Some of the additions, significant revisions, and new features of this edition are as follows. In Chapter 1 we have added new coverage on the economic consequences of accounting standards and on setting standards in a political environment. In Chapter 2 we have integrated coverage of the FASB's conceptual framework project (including objectives, qualitative characteristics, and elements of financial statements) with prevailing accounting assumptions, principles, constraints, and industry practices. To both Chapters 4 and 5 we have added coverage on the implications of the FASB's conceptual framework project on the income statement and the balance sheet of the future. A new discussion on choosing an appropriate interest rate was added to Chapter 6.

The most significant change in Chapter 7 is the new presentation on accounts receivable and cash generation (including assignments and factoring of accounts receivable, with and without recourse) and the revision of our discussion on discounting receivables. To clarify our LIFO inventory presentation in Chapter 8, we have interjected a new section on "LIFO—A Pooled Approach" as a transition from item LIFO to dollar-value LIFO. A new presentation on "compensated absences" has been added to Chapter 10. In our plant asset chapters—Chapters 11 and 12—we have revised the presentation on "capitalization of interest" and the coverage on "declining-balance methods."

Our chapter on long-term liabilities has been updated through the integration of new debt instruments such as variable-rate and shared-appreciation mortgages, and deep-discount and commodity-backed bonds; new coverage has also been added on "unconditional long-term obligations" including "project financing arrangements" (take-or-pay contracts and through-put agreements). In Chapter 17 our presentation on stock compensation plans has been updated to include incentive stock options and performance-type plans; our comprehensive earnings-per-share illustration now presents the methodology used to rank order dilutive securities for computing EPS. Chapter 19 has been revised relative to revenue recognition criteria and terminology, expanded with new material on accounting for "losses incurred in long-term construction contracts," reorganized with franchise sales accounting integrated into the chapter and revenue from service sales transactions moved to an appendix, and condensed in its coverage of consignment sales and real estate sales.

Chapter 20, "Accounting for Income Taxes," has been completely reorganized, rewritten, and updated to incorporate the effects of the Economic Recovery Tax Act of 1981. New discussions on conceptual issues related to pensions have been added to Chapter 21. We have also expanded our coverage of the conceptual nature of lease transactions in Chapter 22, along with our coverage of guaranteed and unguaranteed residual values, and we have condensed our discussion of lease disclosures and leveraged leases. In Chapter 24 we placed greater emphasis on cash basis statements of changes in financial position. Finally, we have simplified and clarified our presentation in Chapter 25 on price-level accounting methods by placing the current cost/constant dollar discussion in an appendix and by developing clearer illustrations.

## QUESTIONS, CASES, EXERCISES, AND PROBLEMS

At the end of each chapter we have provided a comprehensive set of review and homework material consisting of questions, short cases, exercises, and problems. For this edition all exercises and problems have been revised, and the end-of-chapter material has been supplemented with many new cases and problems, nearly all of which have been class tested.

The questions are designed for review, self-testing, and classroom discussion purposes as well as homework assignments. The cases generally require essay as opposed to quantitative solutions; they are intended to confront the student with situations calling for conceptual analysis and the exercise of judgment in identifying problems and evaluating alternatives. Typically, an exercise covers a specific topic and requires less time and effort to solve than cases and problems. The problems are designed to develop a professional level of achievement and are more challenging to solve than the exercises.

Probably no more than one-fourth of the total case, exercise, and problem material must be used to cover the subject matter adequately; consequently, problem assignments may be varied from year to year.

## SUPPLEMENTARY MATERIALS

Accompanying this textbook is an improved and expanded package of supplements consisting of instructional aids for either students or instructors. The following supplements are available **for student use** (upon instructor approval): (1) a *Student Study Guide* (written by Raymond J. Clay); (2) a *Practice Set (Rockford Corporation),* revised edition; (3) a *Computer-Assisted Practice Set* (prepared by James H. Perkins); (4) ruled *Working Papers* for all problems; (5) a *Professional Examination Manual* (prepared by Max Rexroad); and (6) a selection of cases entitled *Cases: Intermediate Financial Theory and Practice* (prepared by Terry Campbell). The following supplements are available **for instructor use:** (1) a comprehensive *Solutions Manual* for all end-of-chapter assignment material; (2) a separate *Instructor's Manual* (by R. D. Nair); (3) overhead projector transparencies for all text problems; (4) an *Examination Booklet and Tests;* (5) a *Computerized Test Bank* for objective questions; (6) solutions to the practice sets; and (7) a "Checklist of Key Figures," available *free* in quantity.

## ACKNOWLEDGMENTS

We thank the many users of our third edition who contributed to this revision through their comments and constructive criticism. Special thanks are extended to the primary reviewers of our fourth edition manuscript: Thomas Barton, University of North Florida; Floyd A. Beams and Donald W. Hicks, Virginia Polytechnic Institute and State University; Louis F. Biagioni, Indiana University; Bruce P. Budge, University of Montana; Hussein Emin, Nassau Community College; Paula Harbecke, University of Maryland; Bernard H.

Newman, Pace University; W. Max Rexroad, Illinois State University; and Dorothy Steinsaper, Middlesex Community College. Three persons who contributed supplemental and special industry problem materials are: Mary M. Noble, University of Wisconsin—Madison; Mary Ellen Phillips, Oregon State University; and John Simon, Northern Illinois University.

Other colleagues in academe who have read portions of this work and made valuable suggestions include: John R. Cerepak, Fairleigh Dickinson University; Martin L. Gosman, Boston University; Jerry A. Leer, University of Wisconsin—Milwaukee; Thomas Buttars, Douglas Clarke, Lawrence Mohrweis, and Donald Moser, University of Wisconsin—Madison; John Borke, University of Wisconsin—Platteville; Patrick R. Delaney, Darrel Grove, Bambi Hora, Douglas W. Kieso, Curtis L. Norton, Kurt Reding, Doris Wang, Thomas Wetzel, and Thomas Yopst, Northern Illinois University; and M. Zafar Iqbal, California Polytechnic State University.

From the field of professional accountancy we owe thanks to the following practitioners for their technical advice: Arthur R. Wyatt, G. Michael Crooch, and John E. Stewart of Arthur Andersen & Co.; Curt Danekas of Ernst & Whinney; and Ray J. Clay, Jr., of Union Pacific Corporation.

We appreciate the exemplary support and professional commitment given us by our word processor operators Donna R. Kieso and Debra J. Kieso, by our typist Enid Weygandt, and by the production and editorial staffs, including Mary Halloran, Romayne Ponleithner, Serje Seminoff, Frank Burrows, and John Beresford, Judy Nolan, and the staff of Allservice Phototypesetting. We especially thank our editor, Don Ford, for his counsel, ingenuity, commitment and, most of all, his felicitous style.

We appreciate the cooperation of the American Institute of Certified Public Accountants and the Financial Accounting Standards Board in permitting us to quote from their pronouncements. We also acknowledge permission from the American Institute of Certified Public Accountants, the Institute of Management Accounting, and the Institute of Internal Auditors to adapt and use material from the Uniform CPA Examinations, the CMA Examinations, and the CIA Examinations, respectively.

If this book helps teachers instill in their students an appreciation for the challenges and limitations of accounting, if it encourages students to evaluate critically and understand financial accounting theory and practice, and if it prepares students for advanced study, professional examinations, and the successful pursuit of their careers in accounting or business, then we will have attained our objective.

Suggestions and comments from users of this book will be appreciated.

Donald E. Kieso
Jerry J. Weygandt

*DeKalb, Illinois*
*Madison, Wisconsin*
*January, 1983*

# Contents

# FINANCIAL ACCOUNTING FUNCTIONS AND BASIC THEORY

## 1

# CHAPTER 1

# The Environment of Financial Accounting and the Development of Accounting Standards

Is accounting a service activity, a descriptive/analytical discipline, or an information system? It is all three. **As a service activity,** accounting provides interested parties with quantitative financial information that helps them to make decisions about the deployment and use of resources in business and nonbusiness entities and in the economy. **As a descriptive/analytical discipline,** it identifies the great mass of events and transactions that characterize economic activity and, through measurement, classification, and summarization, reduces those data to relatively few, highly significant, and interrelated items that, when properly assembled and reported, describe the financial condition and results of operation of a specific economic entity. **As an information system,** it collects and communicates economic information about a business enterprise or other entity to a wide variety of persons whose decisions and actions are related to the activity.

Each of these three descriptions of accounting—different though they may seem—contains the three essential characteristics of accounting: (1) **identification, measurement, and communication of financial information about** (2) **economic entities to** (3) **interested persons.** These characteristics have been peculiar to accounting for hundreds of years. Yet, in the last fifty years economic entities have increased so greatly in size and complexity, and the interested persons have increased so greatly in number and diversity, that the responsibility placed on the accounting profession is greater today than ever before.

## NATURE AND ENVIRONMENT OF FINANCIAL ACCOUNTING

For purposes of study and practice the discipline of accounting is commonly divided into the following areas or subsets: financial accounting, managerial (cost) accounting, tax accounting, and nonprofit or fund accounting. This textbook concentrates on financial accounting. Financial accounting has been characterized as "the branch of accounting that focuses on the general-purpose reports on financial position and results of operations known as financial statements."[1] These statements provide "a continual history quantified in money terms of economic resources and obligations of a business enterprise and of

---

[1]"Basic Concepts and Accounting Principles Underlying Financial Statements of Business Enterprises," *Statement of the Accounting Principles Board No. 4* (New York: AICPA, 1970), par. 9.

economic activities that change these resources and obligations."[2] **Financial accounting** is the process that culminates in the preparation of financial reports relative to the enterprise as a whole for use by parties both internal and external to the enterprise. In contrast, **managerial accounting** is the process of identification, measurement, accumulation, analysis, preparation, interpretation, and communication of financial information used by management to plan, evaluate, and control within an organization and to assure appropriate use of, and accountability for, its resources.[3]

### Financial Statements and Financial Reporting

Financial statements are the principal means through which financial information is communicated to those outside an enterprise. The **financial statements** most frequently provided are (1) the balance sheet, (2) the income statement, (3) the statement of changes in financial position, and (4) the statement of changes in owners' or stockholders' equity. Appropriate footnote disclosures are an integral part of each of these four basic financial statements.

But some financial information is better provided, or can be provided only, by means of **financial reporting** other than formal financial statements, either because it is required by authoritative pronouncement, regulatory rule, or custom, or because management wishes to disclose it voluntarily. Financial reporting other than financial statements (and related footnotes) may take various forms and relate to various matters. Common examples are contained in corporate annual reports (for example, the president's letter or supplementary schedules), prospectuses, annual reports filed with government agencies, news releases, management's forecasts or plans or expectations, and descriptions of an enterprise's social or environmental impact.[4]

The primary but not exclusive focus of this textbook is on the development of financial information that is reported in the basic financial statements and the related disclosures.

### Environmental Factors that Influence Accounting

Accounting, like other social science disciplines and human activities, is largely a product of its environment. The environment of accounting consists of social-economic-political-legal conditions, restraints, and influences that vary from time to time. As a result, accounting objectives and practices are not the same today as they were in the past, because **accounting theory has evolved to meet changing demands and influences.** Modern financial accounting is the product of many influences and conditions, five of which deserve special consideration.

**First, accounting recognizes that people live in a world of scarce means and resources.** Because resources exist in limited supply, people try to conserve them, to use them effec-

---

[2]Ibid., par. 41.

[3]"Definition of Management Accounting," *Statements on Management Accounting No. 1A* (New York: NAA, 1981), p. 4.

[4]"Objectives of Financial Reporting by Business Enterprises," *Statement of Financial Accounting Concepts No. 1* (Stamford, Conn.: FASB, November 1978), pars. 5–8.

tively, and to identify and encourage those who can make efficient use of them. This stress on efficiency and effectiveness in economic activities leads to the use of income measurement as an indicator of success. Accounting measures and communicates the costs of efforts and resources that have been used or consumed in the production of goods and in the rendering of services. Similarly, accounting is involved with the distribution and disposition (consumption) of the values or other benefits represented by the goods and services. In short, the principal role of accounting is "to furnish the investor and lender with information useful to assess the prospective risks and returns associated with an investment."[5]

**Second, accounting recognizes and accepts society's current legal and ethical concepts of property and other rights as standards** in determining equity among the varying interests in the enterprise or entity. Accounting looks to its environment for its standards in regard to what property rights society protects, what society recognizes as value, and what society acknowledges as equitable and fair. In the United States, productive resources are generally privately owned rather than government owned. Therefore, markets (stock and commodities exchanges), free enterprise, and competition are significant factors in resource allocation in our economy. Yet government intervenes in many ways and for various purposes; that is, collecting taxes, borrowing money, paying subsidies, and regulating business activities.[6] The functioning of the markets and the protection of property rights are dependent upon the stability, continuity, and nature of government.

**Third, accounting recognizes that economic activity is conducted by separately identifiable units—business enterprises.** Enterprises consist of economic resources (assets), economic obligations (liabilities), and residual interests (owners' equity); these elements are increased or decreased by the economic activities of the enterprise. Accounting, therefore, accumulates and reports economic activity as it affects the elements of each business enterprise.

**Fourth, accounting recognizes that in highly developed, complex economic systems, some (owners and investors) entrust the custodianship of and control over property to others (managers).** One of the results of the corporate form of organization has been the tendency in large enterprises to divorce ownership from management. Thus, the function of measuring and reporting information to absentee investors, called the **stewardship function,** has been added to that of recording and presenting financial data for owner-manager use. This development greatly increased the need for accounting standards. The absentee owner, unlike the owner-operator, finds it prohibitively costly to combine reported information with first-hand knowledge of the conditions and activities of the enterprise. Accounting has become responsible for providing standards that ensure the relevance, reliability, and comparability of information reported to absentee owners. The public accountant (auditor) plays a major role in meeting this responsibility by attesting to the fairness of financial statements and their conformity to generally accepted accounting principles, thus enhancing confidence in the reliability of the statements.

**Fifth, accounting provides measures of the changes in economic resources, economic obligations, and residual interests of a business enterprise** as a basis for comparison and evaluation. In most economies, money serves as a measure of both qualitative and quantita-

---

[5]"Conceptual Framework for Financial Accounting and Reporting," *FASB Discussion Memorandum* (Stamford, Conn.: FASB, 1976), p. 5.

[6]Ibid., par. 14.

tive attributes of economic events, resources, and obligations.[7] Thus, the unit of measurement in accounting is expressed in terms of money.

These are some of the factors or conditions that constitute the environment of accounting and, therefore, influence it.

## Accounting Influences Its Environment

Accounting is not critical or important because it is a product of its environment, but rather because it shapes its environment and plays a significant role in the conduct of economic, social, political, legal, and organizational decisions and actions. **Accounting is a system that feeds back information to organizations and individuals, which they can use to reshape their environment.** It provides information for the reevaluation of social, political, and economic objectives as well as the relative costs and benefits of the alternative means of achieving these objectives.

More specifically, the effect of publicly reported accounting numbers is to influence the distribution of scarce resources. Resources are channeled where needed at returns commensurate with perceived risk. Accounting information is both by nature and design useful in assessing the prospective risks and returns associated with investments.

The **economic effects** of reported accounting numbers can directly and rapidly affect the transfer of resources among entities and individuals. Examples are: the amount of taxes paid based on accounting numbers (historical cost numbers produce a much different answer than numbers adjusted for inflation), the effects on existing contracts when a change in accounting rules impinges upon a restrictive covenant (a change to LIFO inventory accounting may reduce income sufficiently to cause a dividend restriction due to the violation of a bond covenant), and the rates allowed to utilities by regulatory agencies (permitting companies to expense certain capital assets may increase energy costs now rather than later). Other economic effects of accounting information may be indirect but no less critical because they affect people's perceptions of the enterprise's economic status and progress and, hence, their willingness to invest in it, subject it to regulation, work for it, enter into long-term supply contracts with it, purchase its products, etc.[8]

## Objectives of Financial Reporting

In a recent attempt to establish a foundation upon which financial accounting and reporting standards will be based, the accounting profession identified a set of **objectives of financial reporting by business enterprises.** Recognizing the characteristics of the environ-

---

[7]Qualitative attributes, as well as quantitative ones, are measurable (valued) in money terms. For instance, in August 1982, one ounce of gold measured $355 in money terms while one ounce of silver measured $7.50. The difference in price per ounce reflected differences in qualitative attributes. A doubling of the quantity would result in doubling the amount of money measurement. A dramatic example of qualitative attributes being reflected by money measurement was the recent sale at auction of one of Peter Paul Rubens' paintings (*Samson and Delilah*) for $5,400,000, while the author's brother had difficulty selling one of his paintings for $50 at an art fair. Monetary measurements reflect both quality and quantity.

[8]George J. Benston and Melvin A. Krasney, "The Economic Consequences of Financial Accounting Statements" (a paper prepared for the American Council of Life Insurance for submission to the FASB), presented in *Economic Consequences of Financial Accounting Standards,* Research Report (Stamford, Conn.: FASB, 1978).

ment, financial reporting should provide information:

(a) that is useful to present and potential investors and creditors and other users in making rational investment, credit, and similar decisions. The information should be comprehensible to those who have a reasonable understanding of business and economic activities and are willing to study the information with reasonable diligence.

(b) to help present and potential investors and creditors and other users in assessing the amounts, timing, and uncertainty of prospective cash receipts from dividends or interest and the proceeds from the sale, redemption, or maturity of securities or loans. Since investors' and creditors' cash flows are related to enterprise cash flows, financial reporting should provide information to help investors, creditors, and others assess the amounts, timing, and uncertainty of prospective net cash inflows to the related enterprise.

(c) about the economic resources of an enterprise, the claims to those resources (obligations of the enterprise to transfer resources to other entities and owners' equity), and the effects of transactions, events, and circumstances that change its resources and claims to those resources.[9]

In summary, the objectives of financial reporting are to provide (1) information that is useful in investment and credit decisions, (2) information that is useful in assessing cash flow prospects, and (3) information about enterprise resources, claims to those resources, and changes in them.

On first reading the objectives, the emphasis on "assessing cash flow prospects" might lead one to infer that the cash basis is being advocated over the accrual basis. This is not the case because accountants continue to believe that information about enterprise income based on **accrual accounting** generally provides a better indication of an enterprise's present and continuing ability to generate favorable cash flows than information limited to the financial effects of cash receipts and payments.[10]

The objective of **accrual basis accounting** (recognizing revenues when earned rather than when cash is received, and recognizing expenses when incurred rather than paid) is the measurement of income. Information about income is useful because it reveals relationships that are likely to be important in predicting future results. For example, under accrual accounting, revenues are recognized when sales are made, so they can be related to the economic environment of the period in which they occurred. Trends in revenues are thus more meaningful.

## THE DEVELOPMENT OF ACCOUNTING STANDARDS

Because accounting is influenced by, and simultaneously influences, its environment, there is a tremendous interest in the formulation of accounting standards and in the practice of accounting. The following discussion examines the manner in which accounting standards have been and are being developed. (The terms **principles** and **standards** are used interchangeably in practice and throughout this textbook.)

[9]*SFAC No. 1*, p. viii.

[10]*SFAC No. 1*, p. iv. As used here, cash flow means "cash generated and used in operations." The term cash flows is frequently used to also include cash obtained by borrowing and used to repay borrowing, cash used for investments in resources and obtained from the disposal of investments, and cash contributed by or distributed to owners.

## The Need to Develop Standards

The users of financial accounting statements have coinciding and conflicting needs for statements of various types. To meet these needs, and to satisfy the fiduciary reporting responsibility of management, accountants prepare a single set of **general-purpose financial statements.** These statements are expected to present fairly, clearly, and completely the economic facts of the existence and operations of the enterprise. **In preparing financial statements, accountants (like those involved in any communication process) are confronted with the potential dangers of bias, misinterpretation, inexactness, and ambiguity.** In order to minimize these dangers and to render financial statements that can be reasonably compared between enterprises and between accounting periods, the accounting profession has attempted to develop a body of theory that is generally accepted and universally practiced. Without this body of theory, each accountant or enterprise would have to develop its own theory structure and set of practices. If this happened, readers of financial statements would have to familiarize themselves with every company's peculiar accounting and reporting practices. As a result, it would be almost impossible to prepare statements that could be compared.

The accounting profession, therefore, has attempted to establish a body of theory and practice that acts as a general guide. Its efforts have resulted in the adoption of a common set of accounting concepts, standards, and procedures called **generally accepted accounting principles (GAAP).** Although the principles have provoked both debate and criticism, most accountants and members of the financial community recognize them as the theories, methods, and practices that, over time, have proved to be most useful.

## Historical Perspective

A historical perspective of the interaction between accounting and its environment would foster a greater appreciation of accounting's heritage and conventions. Because of space limitations, however, we shall confine our discussion to the development of the current generally accepted accounting principles in the United States, which are primarily a product of the years since 1930.

Before 1900 the economy of the United States required a relatively unsophisticated type of accounting function, and an accounting profession per se was virtually nonexistent. Before the beginning of this century, single ownership was the predominant form of business organization in our economy. Accounting reports emphasized solvency and liquidity and were limited to internal use and scrutiny by banks and other lending institutions. From 1900 to 1929 the growth of large corporations, with their absentee ownership and the increasing investment and speculation in corporate stocks, resulted in the demand for greater disclosure and a change in the concern with solvency to a concern with income-producing ability. The constitutional amendment in 1913 authorizing the federal government to impose an income tax on businesses and individuals intensified the emphasis on income measurement. As a result of the stock market crash of 1929, the Great Depression, and widespread dissatisfaction with accounting reports, the federal government, the stock exchanges, and the accounting profession all made efforts to improve accounting. Since that time, the environmental influences on the development of accounting principles have been primarily institutional (or organizational).

Although the needs of interested parties have been the focus in the development of accounting principles, certain professional organizations, governmental agencies, and legislative acts have exerted a significant influence also.

## Parties Involved in Standard-Setting

A number of organizations have been instrumental in the development of financial accounting standards (GAAP) in the United States. The major organizations are as follows:

1. American Institute of Certified Public Accountants (AICPA).
2. Financial Accounting Standards Board (FASB).
3. Securities and Exchange Commission (SEC).
4. American Accounting Association (AAA).
5. Other bodies such as the Financial Executives Institute (FEI) and National Association of Accountants (NAA).

**American Institute of CPAs (AICPA)**   The efforts of the **American Institute of Certified Public Accountants,** the national professional organization of practicing Certified Public Accountants (CPAs), have been vital to the development of GAAP. In 1905 the Institute began monthly publication of **The Journal of Accountancy,** which has been the most popular forum for the practicing CPA since then. In 1917 an Institute committee, at the request of the Federal Trade Commission, prepared a pamphlet on "Uniform Accounting," which suggested procedures for standardizing the preparation of financial statements. In 1930 the Institute appointed a special committee to cooperate with the New York Stock Exchange on matters of common interest to accountants, investors, and the Exchange. An outgrowth of this special committee was the Committee on Accounting Procedure.

**Committee on Accounting Procedure (CAP)**   During the years 1939 to 1959, the Committee on Accounting Procedure issued 51 **Accounting Research Bulletins** (see list on inside of front cover) dealing with a variety of timely accounting problems. These bulletins, however, were not directives to the members of the Institute. Their authority rested only on their general acceptance by the profession. Although these bulletins narrowed the range of alternative practices to some extent, this problem-by-problem approach of the Committee on Accounting Procedure failed to provide the well-defined and well-structured body of accounting principles that was so badly needed and desired. By the mid-1950s it was clear that the public believed that financial reporting was inadequate and that the profession should develop an overall conceptual framework to help resolve its problems.

**Accounting Principles Board (APB)**   In 1959 the AICPA created the **Accounting Principles Board** and a new Accounting Research Division as part of a program to advance the written expression of accounting principles, to determine appropriate practices, and to narrow the areas of difference and inconsistency in practice.[11] The objectives of this reorganization were fourfold: (1) to establish basic postulates,[12] (2) to formulate a set of broad principles, (3) to set up rules to guide the application of principles in specific situations, and (4) to base the entire program on research. Accordingly, a permanent accounting research staff was employed to carry on the research and to publish research studies.

---

[11]*Organization and Operation of the Accounting Research Program and Related Activities* (New York: AICPA, 1959), p. 9.

[12]Postulates are basic assumptions or self-evident propositions that are generally accepted as valid. Few in number and broad in nature, they provide the basis from which principles or standards may be deduced.

Research projects were conducted by independently employed consultants or by members of the research staff under the guidance of the Director of Accounting Research and a project advisory committee. Research usually was undertaken on a subject to be considered and acted on by the APB. The published **Accounting Research Studies** were not official pronouncements of the AICPA. Fifteen research studies were published between 1960 and 1973.

The APB had more authority and responsibility than did its predecessor, the Committee on Accounting Procedures. The Board's 18 to 21 members were selected primarily from public accounting but also included representatives from industry and the academic community. The Board's official pronouncements, called **APB Opinions,** were intended to be based mainly on research studies and to be supported by reasoning. Between its inception in 1959 and its dissolution in 1973, the APB issued 31 opinions (see complete list inside front cover).

APB Opinions were enforced primarily through the prestige of the AICPA, and its APB, which was recognized as the body that regulated the accounting profession and determined and enforced accounting principles. Probably the most critical and the most important enforcement pressure resulted from the Securities and Exchange Commission's willingness to recognize the AICPA and to support APB Opinions.

In 1964 the Council (the governing body) of the AICPA defined the long-used but officially undefined term **"generally accepted accounting principles."** In a document published as a Special Bulletin in 1964 and later as an appendix to *APB Opinion No. 6,* the Council adopted the following resolution:

1. "Generally accepted accounting principles" are those principles which have substantial authoritative support.
2. Opinions of the Accounting Principles Board constitute "substantial authoritative support."
3. "Substantial authoritative support" can exist for accounting principles that differ from Opinions of the Accounting Principles Board.
4. No distinction should be made between the Bulletins issued by the former Committee on Accounting Procedure on matters of accounting principles and Opinions of the Accounting Principles Board.

More important, the Council and the APB declared that all material departures by companies from APB Opinions and effective Accounting Research Bulletins must be disclosed and explained in the companies' published financial statements. Although the AICPA recognized other sources as constituting substantial authoritative support, the decision and burden of proof in these cases rested[13] with the reporting member. Because of this burden of proof and the related risk of liability from lawsuits, the pronouncements issued generally have been followed. Thus, the policy of strong **persuasion** gave way to a more effective one of professional (not legislative) **compulsion.**

**Financial Accounting Standards Board (FASB)**   The APB was beleaguered throughout its 13-year existence. It came under fire early, charged with lack of productivity and failing to

---

[13] Failure to follow generally accepted accounting principles may invoke the application of Rule 203 of the Rules of Conduct of the Code of Professional Ethics of the AICPA. Rule 203 prohibits a member of the AICPA from expressing an opinion that financial statements conform with generally accepted accounting principles if those statements contain a material departure from an accounting principle promulgated by the FASB, unless the member can demonstrate that because of unusual circumstances the financial statements otherwise would have been misleading.

act promptly to correct alleged accounting abuses. Later the APB tackled numerous thorny accounting issues, only to meet a buzz saw of industry and CPA firm opposition and occasional government interference. In 1971 the accounting profession's leaders, anxious to avoid governmental rule-making, responded by appointing a Study Group on Establishment of Accounting Principles (commonly known as the Wheat Committee) to examine the organization and operation of the Accounting Principles Board and determine what changes were necessary to attain better results faster. The Study Group's recommendations were submitted to the AICPA Council in the spring of 1972, adopted in total, and implemented by early 1973.

The Wheat Committee's recommendation caused the demise of the APB and the creation of the **Financial Accounting Standards Board.** There was widespread support for the creation of the unprecedented private, independent board. The expectations of success and support for the new FASB were based upon several significant differences between it and its predecessor APB:

1. **SMALLER MEMBERSHIP.** The FASB is composed of seven members, replacing the relatively large 18-member APB.
2. **FULL-TIME, REMUNERATED MEMBERSHIP.** FASB members are well-paid, full-time members appointed for renewable five-year terms, whereas the APB members were unpaid and part-time.
3. **GREATER AUTONOMY.** The APB was a senior committee of the AICPA, whereas the FASB is not an organ of any single professional organization. It is appointed by and answerable only to the Financial Accounting Foundation.[14]
4. **INCREASED INDEPENDENCE.** APB members retained their private positions with firms, companies, or institutions; FASB members must sever all such ties.
5. **BROADER REPRESENTATION.** All APB members were required to be CPAs and members of the AICPA; presently, it is not necessary to be a CPA to be a member of the FASB.

In recognition of the misconceptions caused by the term "principles," the FASB utilizes the term **financial accounting standards** in its pronouncements. Financial support for the new Board, averaging in excess of $7 million annually, is borne by the private sector (public accounting and industry) through contributions to the Financial Accounting Foundation.

Two basic premises of the FASB are that in establishing financial accounting standards: (1) it should be responsive to the needs and viewpoints of the entire economic community, not just the public accounting profession, and (2) it should operate in full view of the public through a "due process" system that gives interested persons ample opportunity to make their views known. To ensure the achievement of these goals, the following steps are taken in the evolution of a typical FASB Statement of Financial Accounting Standards:

1. A topic or project is identified and placed on the Board's agenda.
2. A task force of experts from various sectors is assembled to define problems, issues, and alternatives related to the topic.
3. Research and analysis are conducted by the FASB technical staff.
4. A **discussion memorandum** is drafted and released.

---

[14]The Financial Accounting Foundation members are appointed by representatives of the American Accounting Association, the American Institute of CPAs, the Financial Executives Institute, the National Association of Accountants, the Financial Analysts Federation, and the Securities Industry Association.

5. A public hearing is often held, usually 60 days after release of the memorandum.
6. The Board analyzes and evaluates the public response.
7. The Board deliberates on the issues and prepares an **exposure draft** (prepublication copy) for release.
8. After a 30-day (minimum) exposure period for public comment, the Board evaluates all of the responses received.
9. A committee studies the exposure draft in relation to the public responses, reevaluates its position, and revises the draft if necessary.
10. The full Board gives the revised draft final consideration and votes on issuance of a **Standards Statement.**

The passage of a new accounting standard in the form of an FASB Statement requires the support of four of the seven Board members. FASB Statements are considered GAAP and thereby binding in practice. All ARBs and APB Opinions that were in effect when the FASB became effective continue to be effective until amended or superseded by FASB pronouncements.

Sometimes in place of or before issuing a discussion memorandum the FASB will issue an **Invitation to Comment.** Initiated in 1978, Invitations to Comment are written either by an FASB or by an AICPA task force in an effort to stimulate research, gather information, and invite reactions to an existing but nonauthoritative pronouncement. An Invitation to Comment has not been deliberated by the FASB and has no authoritative status.

The major types of pronouncements that the FASB issues are:

1. Standards and Interpretations.
2. Financial Accounting Concepts.
3. Technical Bulletins.

STANDARDS AND INTERPRETATIONS   Financial accounting standards issued by the FASB are considered GAAP. In addition, the FASB also issues interpretations that represent modifications or extensions of existing standards. The interpretations have the same authority as standards and require the same majority votes for passage as standards. In the formulation of an interpretation, however, it is not considered necessary to operate in full view of the public through the due process system that is required for FASB Standards. It should be noted that during the time the APB was in operation, it also issued interpretations of APB Opinions. Both types of interpretations are now considered authoritative support for purposes of determining generally accepted accounting principles. Since replacing the APB in July 1973, the FASB has issued 68 standards and 36 interpretations (see list inside front cover).

FINANCIAL ACCOUNTING CONCEPTS   As part of a long-range effort to move away from the "problem-by-problem approach," the FASB in November 1978 issued the first in a series of **Statements of Financial Accounting Concepts** (see list inside back cover). The purpose of the series is to set forth fundamental objectives and concepts that the Board will use in developing future standards of financial accounting and reporting. Individual concept statements are issued serially; they are intended to form a cohesive set of interrelated concepts, a body of theory or a conceptual framework, that will serve as tools for solving existing and emerging problems in a consistent, sound manner. Unlike a Statement of Financial Accounting **Standards,** a Statement of Financial Accounting **Concepts** does not establish GAAP. Concepts statements, however, pass through the same due process system (discussion memo, public hearing, exposure draft, etc.) as do standards statements. The contents of *Concepts Statement No. 1* were presented earlier in this chapter. The contents of later concepts statements are presented in Chapter 2.

FASB TECHNICAL BULLETINS   The FASB receives many requests from various sources for guidelines on implementing or applying FASB Statements or Interpretations, APB Opinions, and Accounting Research Bulletins. Beginning in 1979, the FASB authorized its staff to issue FASB Technical Bulletins to provide guidance on financial accounting and reporting problems. *FASB Technical Bulletin No. 79-1,* "Purpose and Scope of FASB Technical Bulletins and Procedures for Issuance," describes the scope and purpose of the Bulletins. Interpretive in nature, these Bulletins do not establish new financial accounting and reporting standards or amend existing standards. Generally they are in question-and-answer format and are designed to provide prompt responses to specific questions. Unlike FASB Interpretations, they do not establish standards enforceable under the AICPA's Code of Professional Ethics. The Bulletins are not formally voted upon by the members of the FASB and are not expected to have a significant impact on financial accounting and reporting. To date, 29 Technical Bulletins, many of which deal with specialized topics, have been issued (see list inside front cover).

Since its inception in 1973, the FASB has undeniably been hard at work and quite productive. However, it is debatable whether the Board's effectiveness and productivity are any more free of criticism than were those of the APB. Like the APB, the FASB in its first ten years has generally adopted the "problem-by-problem approach" in establishing standards and has been under constant pressure to perform more expeditiously and be more responsive and productive. Recognizing that it must utilize the resources and talents of others, the FASB has consulted with numerous individuals and engaged them to develop materials and to research and draft Invitations to Comment, discussion memoranda, and follow-up studies.[15] Both critics and supporters agree that the FASB will have the best chance of survival if it deals with problems promptly, sets proper priorities, takes whatever action it thinks is right and in the public interest, and handles pressures responsibly without overreacting to them.

**The Securities and Exchange Commission**   The Great Depression of the 1930s, which resulted in the widespread collapse of businesses and the securities market, was the impetus for government intervention and regulation of business. This intervention and regulation involved a good deal of concern with financial statements and accounting standards. A direct result was the creation of the **Securities and Exchange Commission (SEC)** as an independent regulatory agency of the United States government to administer the Securities Act of 1933, the Securities Exchange Act of 1934, and several other acts. Companies that issue securities to the public or are listed on stock exchanges are required to file annual audited financial statements with the SEC. In addition, the SEC was given broad powers to prescribe, in whatever detail it desires, the accounting practices and standards to be

---

[15] Examples of special research projects conducted by academicians are: A. Rashad Abdel-khalik et al., *The Economic Effects on Lessees of FASB Statement No. 13,* Research Report (Stamford, Conn.: FASB, 1981); Yuji Ijiri, *Recognition of Contractual Rights and Obligations,* Research Report (Stamford, Conn.: FASB, 1980); Henry R. Jaenicke, *Survey of Present Practices in Recognizing Revenues, Expenses, Gains, and Losses,* Research Report (Stamford, Conn.: FASB, 1981); Paul A. Griffin, *Usefulness to Investors and Creditors of Information Provided by Financial Reporting,* Research Report (Stamford, Conn.: FASB, 1982).

employed by companies that fall within its jurisdiction. The SEC filing requirements[16] and accounting opinions are published in (1) its **Financial Reporting Releases (FRRs),**[17] of which more than 200 have been issued since 1937, (2) **Regulations S-X,** which contain instructions and forms for filing financial statements, and (3) decisions on cases coming before the SEC. Yet, the SEC until recently acted with remarkable restraint in the area of developing accounting standards. For the most part, until 1960 it relied on the AICPA to regulate the accounting profession and develop and enforce accounting standards.

During the APB era, however, the SEC took a more active interest in the development of accounting standards, pressing for quicker action, specific pronouncements, and eventually for the demise of the APB. During the past decade the SEC has interacted with the FASB as both a supporter and a prodder. Because it confronts the financial accounting and reporting practices of U.S. businesses on a daily basis, the SEC frequently identifies emerging problems for the FASB to address. The Commission communicates these problems to the FASB, responds to FASB drafts and exposures, and provides the FASB with counsel and advice upon request.

The SEC has reaffirmed its support for the FASB (in *ASR No. 150*) indicating "that financial statements conforming to standards set by the FASB will be presumed to have authoritative support." In addition, the SEC has indicated in its reports to Congress "that it continues to believe that the initiative for establishing and improving accounting standards should remain in the private sector, subject to Commission oversight."[18]

**The American Accounting Association**   The **American Accounting Association (AAA),** an organization of college professors and practicing accountants, seeks, as part of its stated objective, to influence the development of accounting theory by encouraging and sponsoring accounting research. Functioning through a series of committees, the Association has published numerous monographs and committee reports and a series of statements on accounting principles, standards, and theory. In 1936 the Association published "A Tentative Statement of Accounting Principles Underlying Corporate Financial Statements" as its first attempt to set forth a consistent, coordinated statement of accounting principles. This statement was first revised in 1941 and 1948, and then more extensively in 1957. A new approach to theory formulation was taken in the Association's 1966 extension in this series

---

[16]The Securities and Exchange Acts of 1933 and 1934 require that companies issuing securities file registration statements and periodic reports with the SEC. Most commercial and industrial companies file a *Form S-1* registration statement upon the initial issuance of securities. (Forms S-2 through S-18 are filed by companies in certain specialized industries.) *Form 10-K* is the annual report form required to be filed and *Form 10-Q* the report that must be filed for the first three quarters of each fiscal year. *Form 8-K* must be filed after the occurrence of a material event.

[17]In the past (prior to 1982) these pronouncements were referred to as Accounting Series Releases (ASRs). The SEC has changed the title of new releases to better reflect their nature and to differentiate FRRs (nonenforcement, nondisciplinary type releases) from the new AAERs (accounting and auditing enforcement releases—disciplinary in nature).

[18]One writer has described the relationship of the FASB and SEC and the development of financial reporting standards using the analogy of a pearl. The pearl (financial reporting standard) "is formed by the reaction of certain oysters (FASB) to an irritant (the SEC)—usually a grain of sand—that becomes embedded inside the shell. The oyster coats this grain with layers of nacre, and ultimately a pearl is formed. The pearl is a joint result of the irritant (SEC) and oyster (FASB); without both, it cannot be created." John C. Burton, "Government Regulation of Accounting and Information," the proceedings of the 1979 round table discussion at the University of Florida, Gainesville, edited by A. Rashad Abdel-khalik, 1980, Board of Regents of the State of Florida.

of statements entitled **A Statement of Basic Accounting Theory.** The authors determined four attributes that information must possess to be useful in accounting. These four attributes—relevance, verifiability, freedom from bias, and quantifiability—were presented, along with five guidelines to communication. The most recent publication in this AAA series is the 1978 **Statement on Accounting Theory and Theory Acceptance** which emphasizes the difficulty of developing a theory structure for accounting.

The AAA in its role as critic appraises accounting practice and recommends improvements through its quarterly publication, **The Accounting Review,** and the work of its committees. Its concern is more for "what should be, as opposed to what was, or what is." Unconcerned about immediate adoption of its proposals, the AAA takes a long-range point of view and attempts to lead practice rather than follow it.

During the past decade the AAA has given greater emphasis and encouragement to independent research in all areas of accounting through an ambitious program of financing research and sponsoring publication of the results. The first of the AAA **Studies in Accounting Research,** published in 1969, initiated a continuing series of contributions to accounting theory. The AAA also appoints from its membership ad hoc committees that draft responses to specific FASB discussion memorandums and exposure drafts.

**Other Influential Organizations**   Several other organizations also have been influential in the development of accounting theory. The **National Association of Accountants (NAA)** has been interested in research primarily in cost accounting and in managerial accounting since its origin in 1919. **Management Accounting** is the monthly publication of the NAA. In 1968 the NAA broadened its research program to "encompass the entire range of socio-economic information needed by those who manage a business and by those who provide its capital."[19]

The **Financial Executives Institute (FEI)** and its subsidiary, the Financial Executives Research Foundation, have published several interesting accounting and reporting studies. The FEI's monthly publication is **The Financial Executive.** The FEI has influenced the development of accounting standards through its Panel on Accounting Principles. This panel reviews the Discussion Memorandums and the exposure drafts of proposed pronouncements of the FASB and submits its views and recommendations. More recently the FEI established committees to parallel task forces of the FASB that are responsible for developing various standards.

The **state societies of CPAs** also provide sounding boards and forums for the airing of support and criticism of FASB exposure drafts on accounting statements. Comments and proposals are formally obtained by each state CPA society and submitted to the FASB, thus providing the Board with a grassroots reaction to its proposed standards.

The **Internal Revenue Service (IRS),** which derives its authority from the Internal Revenue Code and its amendments and legal interpretations, constitutes one of the strongest influences on accounting practice. In an effort to lessen the impact of taxes, and to avoid keeping two sets of books, business managers frequently adopt "acceptable" accounting procedures that minimize taxable income. Because the objectives of the tax law differ from the objectives of financial accounting, however, "good tax accounting" is not necessarily

---

[19]"Report and Recommendations of the Long-Range Objectives Committee of the NAA," *Management Accounting,* 1968, Section 3.

"good financial accounting." As noted throughout this textbook, tax laws and "tax effects" are a pervasive influence in business decision making and on the selection of accounting methods. Differences between tax accounting and financial accounting are generally permissible; however, in the preparation of financial statements, tax considerations must give ground to the requirements of sound accounting.

The **Cost Accounting Standards Board (CASB)** also has had influence on the development of accounting thought. The CASB was established in 1970 as an agency of the U.S. Congress to promote uniformity and consistency in cost accounting practices for defense contracts by establishing Cost Accounting Standards. Although our interest in this textbook is financial accounting rather than cost accounting, the CASB's interest in any cost that may be charged to a government contract necessarily overlaps topics relevant to financial accounting and reporting. Although Congress dissolved the CASB in 1980, the 17 standards that it issued remain in force.

## Changing Role of the AICPA

For several decades the AICPA provided the leadership in the development of accounting principles and rules; it regulated the accounting profession and developed and enforced accounting practice more than did any other professional organization. The Accounting Principles Board was a standing committee of the AICPA. When the APB was dissolved and replaced with the FASB, the AICPA established the Accounting Standards Division to act as its official voice on accounting and reporting issues. The **Accounting Standards Executive Committee (AcSEC)** was established within the Division and was designated as the senior technical committee authorized to speak for the AICPA in the area of financial accounting and reporting.

During the first five years of its operation, AcSEC (1) responded to pronouncements of both the FASB and the SEC and (2) through the issuance of **Statements of Position (SOP)** devoted attention to emerging problems not addressed by the FASB or the SEC. Unlike FASB pronouncements, the SOPs do not represent enforceable standards required of AICPA members (unless the FASB specifically gives one GAAP status); they are issued with the objective of influencing the development of accounting and reporting standards and of providing guidance where none exists.

Because of the numerous SOPs issued, the FASB in late 1978 publicly expressed concerns that the AICPA was evolving into a competing standard-setting body. The FASB proposed first to consolidate that work into a single standard-setting body—its own—by rewriting the SOPs into FASB style and format. After exposure to public comment they would be issued as final Statements of Financial Accounting Standards. Second, the FASB proposed to establish a new series of "FASB Technical Bulletins" that would offer timely guidance on preferred accounting and reporting practice. (As indicated earlier, 29 Technical Bulletins were issued between 1979 and 1982.)

The AICPA agreed in general with the FASB proposal, urging that the FASB adopt existing SOPs as authoritative just as it did Accounting Research Bulletins and APB Opinions. In 1979 "the FASB agreed to exercise responsibility for the specialized accounting and reporting principles and practices in AICPA Statements of Position and Guides on accounting and auditing matters by extracting those specialized principles and practices from those documents and issuing them as FASB Statements, after appropriate due process."[20] In the meantime, until due process is accomplished, the Board issued *Statement No. 32,* which designated a large number of SOPs and Guides on accounting and auditing as containing preferable accounting principles for purposes of justifying a change in accounting principles.

A major role of AcSEC, therefore, has become one of informing the FASB of financial reporting problems that are developing in practice through the development of issue papers. **Issue papers** identify current financial reporting problems, present alternative treatments of the issue, and recommend preferred solutions. This procedure provides the FASB with an early warning device to insure the timely issuance of FASB Standards, Interpretations, and Technical Bulletins.

The AICPA is still the leader in developing auditing standards through its **Auditing Standards Board,** in regulating accounting practice, in developing and enforcing professional ethics, and in providing continuing professional education programs. The AICPA also develops and grades the CPA examination, which is administered in all fifty states.

## Standard-Setting in a Political Environment

The earlier discussion of the environment of accounting disclosed some of the factors that shape and influence the nature and development of accounting standards and practice. Possibly the most influential environmental force flows from various user groups (Figure 1–1, page 18). User groups consist of the parties who are most interested in or affected by accounting standards, rules, and procedures. User groups play a significant role because the setting of accounting standards is a social decision; that is, **accounting standards are as much a product of political action as of careful logic or empirical findings.**[21]

User groups may want particular economic events accounted for or reported in a particular way, and they fight hard to get what they want. They know that the most effective way to influence the standards that dictate accounting practice is to participate in the formulation of these standards or to try to influence or persuade the formulator of them. Therefore, the FASB has become the target of many pressures and efforts to influence changes in the existing standards and the development of new ones.[22] Because of the accelerated rate of change in our economy, the increased complexity and interrelatedness of our economic activity, and the ever-increasing dependence on financial accounting, these pressures have been multiplying. Some influential groups demand that the accounting profession act more quickly and decisively to solve its problems and remedy its deficiencies; other groups resist such action, preferring to implement change more slowly, if at all.

The sources of influence are innumerable, but the most intense and continuous pressure comes from governmental agencies, financial analysts, bankers, industry associations, cli-

---

[20]"Specialized Accounting and Reporting Principles and Practices in AICPA Statements of Position and Guides on Accounting and Auditing Matters," *Statement of Financial Accounting Standards No. 32* (Stamford, Conn.: FASB, 1979).

[21]Charles T. Horngren, "The Marketing of Accounting Standards," *Journal of Accountancy* (October 1973), p. 61.

[22]Former FASB chairman Marshall S. Armstrong acknowledged that several of the Board's projects, including "Accounting for Contingencies," "Accounting for Changes in General Purchasing Power," and "Accounting for Certain Marketable Equity Securities," were targets of political pressure.

**FIGURE 1–1**    User groups that influence the formulation of accounting standards.

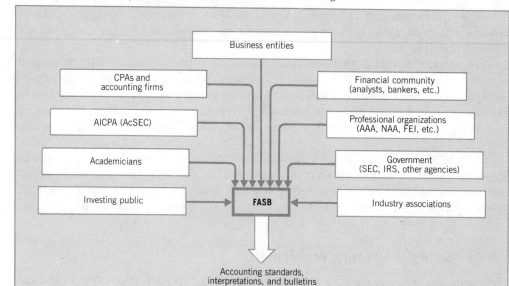

Accounting standards,
interpretations, and bulletins

ents of CPAs, individual companies, academicians, other accounting organizations, and public opinion. Several of these user groups significantly influence accounting standards.

Should there be politics in setting financial accounting and reporting standards? We have politics at home; at school; at the fraternity, sorority, and dormitory; at the office; at church; politics is everywhere! The FASB does not exist in a vacuum. Standard-setting is part of the real world and, as such, it cannot escape politics and political pressures. That is not to say that politics per se in standard-setting is evil. Considering the **economic conse-quences**[23] of many accounting standards, it is not surprising that special interest groups become vocal and critical (some supporting, some opposing) when these standards are being formulated. The Board must be attentive to the politics and economic consequences of its actions. What the Board should not do is issue pronouncements whose primary motivation is political. The politics of the day (contemporary wisdom) cannot be the guiding light in setting standards. While paying attention to its constituencies, the Board should base its standards on sound research and a conceptual framework that has its foundation in economic reality. Even so, the FASB can continue to expect politics and special interest pressures, since as T. S. Eliot said, "Humankind cannot bear very much reality."

A current illustration of an economic consequence is the depressed situation in the savings and loan industry (S&Ls). To acquire more liquidity, many S&Ls would like to sell off part of their investment portfolio. If they did so, however, large losses would be reported because the market value of these investments is considerably below their book

---

[23]"Economic consequences" in this context means the impact of accounting reports on the wealth positions of issuers and users of financial information and the decision-making behavior resulting from that impact. The resulting behavior of these individuals and groups could have detrimental financial effects on the providers (enterprises) of the financial information. For a more detailed discussion of this phenomenon, see Stephen A. Zeff, "The Rise of 'Economic Consequences,'" *Journal of Accountancy* (December 1978), pp. 56–63.

value. As a consequence, these losses would reduce stockholders' equity to such an extent that many S&Ls would be in violation of regulatory requirements. The S&Ls argue that they should be permitted to defer these losses and amortize them over an appropriate future period. The accounting profession, on the other hand, argues that under generally accepted accounting principles, a loss should be reported currently because the transaction is completed. We agree with the latter position. Such a situation demonstrates why certain industries will argue strongly for a position that does not appear in accord with the underlying substance of the transaction.

## Continued Interest in Standard-Setting

Since many interests may be affected by the implementation of an accounting standard, it is not surprising that there is much discussion about who should develop these standards and to whom they should apply. Some of the major issues are discussed below.

**Private Versus Public Sector**    All professions have come under increasing scrutiny by the government in the last ten years. Whether it be the legal profession because of Watergate, the medical profession because of high costs and medicare or medicaid frauds, or engineers because of their failure to consider environmental or societal consequences in their work, all have come under the attention of the government as it has assumed an increasingly active role in protecting the public interest. The accounting profession has not been ignored. Owing to some well-publicized instances of corporate fraud, domestic and foreign bribery, and sudden bankruptcies, critics of the accounting profession started to question its dedication and performance. Add to this society's general desire for more accountability from all institutions, and it is not surprising that Congress began to inquire into the structure and practices of the accounting profession, the accounting and auditing standard-setting process, and the role of the accounting profession in the business world.

In 1976, for example, a House of Representatives committee chaired by Representative John E. Moss (**Moss Committee**) issued a report critical of the FASB for not moving quickly enough to eliminate some of the alternative reporting practices in accounting. It recommended that the SEC take a more active role in establishing accounting principles and that a framework for uniform accounting principles be developed. Then, in 1977, a Senate committee chaired by Senator Lee Metcalf (**Metcalf Committee**) also examined the accounting profession and arrived at a number of conclusions that were not only critical but also inaccurate. The accounting profession was warned that, unless substantial changes were made in its self-regulation process, Congress would legislate (1) the setting of accounting and auditing standards for publicly held companies and (2) the regulation of CPA firms that audit financial statements of publicly held companies.

The AICPA's response was direct and immediate. Numerous task forces were constituted, recommendations were made, and many of these recommendations were implemented. For example, the AICPA established a new Accounting Firms Division (in addition to the existing division for individual AICPA members) with two sections: one for firms auditing SEC clients (called the **SEC Practice Section**) and the other for firms auditing privately owned, non-SEC clients (called the **Private Companies Section**).[24] And,

---

[24]CPA firms that audit SEC registered firms must join the SEC Practice Section and therefore must comply with more comprehensive practice requirements (such as compulsory peer practice review) than those of the Private Companies Section.

to help assure the public that the SEC Practice Section is meeting its responsibilities, the AICPA established as part of this structure an independent **Public Oversight Board.** The Board, composed of distinguished nonaccountants, has its own staff and is free to conduct its own inquiries and to report publicly as it wishes. The Private Companies Section also has its own quality control standards and peer review requirements.

**Competing Standard-Setting Bodies**   The right of the FASB to establish accounting principles for all entities continues to be challenged. For example, AcSEC started issuing SOPs because it believed that immediate guidance was needed for specific reporting problems and that the FASB was unable to respond in a timely fashion. More recently, the National Council on Governmental Accounting (NCGA) issued a report recommending that a separate standard-setting board patterned after the FASB be established to set accounting and reporting standards for governmental units. Proponents of such a board argue that there are sufficient differences in accounting and reporting requirements between governmental units and other entities to warrant establishment of a separate board. The Financial Accounting Foundation consented to support the proposal to establish a separate governmental accounting standards board (GASB) for state and local governments providing that GASB (1) be modeled after the FASB and (2) be under the Financial Accounting Foundation's oversight.

This development demonstrates the tenuousness of the ultimate authority of the FASB to establish accounting standards. Other groups may also decide to pursue such an approach. For example, trade associations and special industry organizations have become involved in issuing pronouncements on accounting matters. As a result, it is possible that someday there may be attempts to develop separate accounting standards boards for specific industries. Each of these competing standards-setters would represent a challenge to the FASB's authority.

## Summary

A delicate balance still exists between the private sector and the public sector. Some people in government, some in the financial community, and some in the profession itself are continually challenging the accounting profession to assume more responsibility and to be more responsive to the needs of its constituencies. At present, the accounting profession is reacting responsibly and effectively to remedy identified shortcomings. Because of its substantive resources and expertise, the private sector should be able to develop and maintain high standards. But it is a difficult process requiring time, logic, and diplomacy. By a judicious mix of these three ingredients, and a measure of luck, the profession may be able to continue to develop its own standards and regulate itself with minimal intervention.

## QUESTIONS

1. What is it in today's environment that places a greater responsibility upon accounting now than ever before?
2. Into what areas can the discipline of accounting be divided?
3. Differentiate broadly between financial accounting and managerial accounting.
4. Differentiate between "financial statements" and "financial reporting."
5. Accounting is an unchanging discipline independent of its environment and other influences. Comment.
6. Name several environmental conditions that shape financial accounting to a significant extent.
7. How are the current legal and ethical standards related to the basic nature of accounting?
8. Provide some examples of how accounting information influences its environment.
9. What are the major objectives of financial reporting?
10. Of what value is a common body of theory in financial accounting and reporting?
11. What is the likely limitation of "general-purpose financial statements"?
12. What are some of the developments or events that occurred between 1900 and 1930 that helped bring about changes in accounting theory or practice?
13. What was the Committee on Accounting Procedure and what were its accomplishments and failings?
14. For what purposes did the AICPA in 1959 create the Accounting Principles Board and a new Accounting Research Division?
15. Distinguish between Accounting Research Bulletins, Accounting Research Studies, Opinions of the Accounting Principles Board, and Statements of the Financial Accounting Standards Board.
16. If you had to explain or define "generally accepted accounting principles or standards" to a nonaccountant, what essential characteristics would you include in your explanation?
17. In what ways was it felt that the statements issued by the Financial Accounting Standards Board would carry greater weight than the opinions issued by the Accounting Principles Board?
18. How are FASB "discussion memorandums" and FASB "exposure drafts" related to FASB "statements"?
19. Distinguish between FASB "statements of financial accounting standards" and FASB "statements of financial accounting concepts."
20. What are "interpretations" of APB opinions and "interpretations" of FASB statements and how much authority do they have?
21. What is the purpose of FASB Technical Bulletins? How do FASB Technical Bulletins differ from FASB Interpretations?
22. In what way is the Securities and Exchange Commission concerned about and supportive of accounting principles and standards?
23. What is AcSEC and what is its relationship to the FASB? Include in your answer a discussion of AcSEC's apparent conflict with the FASB.
24. Explain how the Internal Revenue Code affects financial accounting standards and practices.
25. What are the sources of pressure that change and influence the development of accounting principles and standards?
26. Some individuals have indicated that the FASB must be cognizant of the economic consequences of its pronouncements. What is meant by economic consequences? What dangers exist if politics plays an important role in the development of financial reporting standards?
27. What are some possible reasons why another organization such as the National Council on Governmental Accounting (NCGA) should not issue financial reporting standards?
28. If you were given complete authority in the matter, how would you propose that accounting principles or standards should be developed and enforced?

## CASES

**C1-1** Presented below are a number of accounting organizations and the type of documents they have issued. Match the appropriate document to the organization involved. Note that more than one document may be issued by the same organization.

| Organization | Document |
| --- | --- |
| 1. ____ Financial Accounting Standards Board | (a) Financial Reporting Releases |
| 2. ____ Accounting Standards Executive Committee | (b) Financial Accounting Standards |
| | (c) Statements of Position |
| 3. ____ Securities and Exchange Commission | (d) Technical Bulletins |
| | (e) Discussion Memorandum |
| 4. ____ Accounting Principles Board | (f) Financial Accounting Concepts |
| 5. ____ Committee on Accounting Procedure | (g) Opinions |
| | (h) Invitations to Comment |
| | (i) Issue Papers |
| | (j) Accounting Research Bulletins |

**C1-2** At the completion of the Hamre Company's audit, the president, James Hamre, Sr., asks about the meaning of the phrase "in conformity with generally accepted accounting principles" that appears in your audit report on the management's financial statements. He observes that the meaning of the phrase must include more than what he thinks of as "principles."

**Instructions**

(a) Explain the meaning of the term "accounting principles" as used in the audit report. (Do **not** discuss in this part the significance of "generally accepted.")

(b) President Hamre wants to know how you determine whether or not an accounting principle is generally accepted. Discuss the sources of evidence for determining whether an accounting principle has substantial authoritative support. Do **not** merely list the titles of publications.

(c) President Hamre believes that diversity in accounting practice always will exist among independent entities despite continual improvements in comparability. Discuss the arguments that support his belief.

(AICPA adapted)

**C1-3** A press release announcing the appointment of the trustees of the new Financial Accounting Foundation stated that the Financial Accounting Standards Board (to be appointed by the trustees) "...will become the established authority for setting accounting principles under which corporations report to the shareholders and others" (AICPA news release, July 20, 1972).

**Instructions**

(a) No mention is made of the SEC in the press release. What role does the SEC play in setting accounting principles?

(b) How have accounting principles been set in the past ten years? In your answer identify the body performing this function, the sponsoring organization, and the method by which the body arrives at its decisions.

(c) What methods have management and management accountants used to influence the development of accounting principles in the past ten years?

(CMA adapted)

**C1-4** Some accountants have said that politicization in the development and acceptance of generally accepted accounting principles (i.e., standard-setting) is taking place. Some use the term "politicization" in a narrow sense to mean the influence by governmental agencies, particularly the Securities and Exchange Commission, on the development of generally accepted accounting principles. Others use it more broadly to mean the compromising that takes place in bodies responsible for developing generally accepted accounting principles because of the influence and pressure of interested groups (SEC, American Accounting Association, businesses through their various organizations, National Association of Accountants, financial analysts, bankers, lawyers, etc.).

**Instructions**

(a) The Committee on Accounting Procedures of the AICPA was established in the mid to late 1930s and functioned until 1959, at which time the Accounting Principles Board came into existence. In 1973, the Financial Accounting Standards Board was formed and the APB went out of existence. Do the reasons these groups were formed, their methods of operation while in existence, and the reasons for the demise of the first two indicate an increasing politicization (as the term is used in the broad sense) of accounting standard-setting? Explain your answer by indicating how the CAP, the APB and the FASB operated or operate. Cite specific developments that tend to support your answer.

(b) What arguments can be raised to support the "politicization" of accounting standard-setting?

(c) What arguments can be raised against the "politicization" of accounting standard-setting?

(CMA adapted)

**C1–5** Presented below are three models for setting accounting standards.

1. The purely political approach, where national legislative action decrees accounting standards.

2. The private, professional approach, where financial accounting standards are set and enforced by private professional actions only.

3. The public/private mixed approach, where standards are basically set by private sector bodies that behave as though they were public agencies and whose standards to a great extent are enforced through governmental agencies.

**Instructions**

(a) Which of these three models best describes standard setting in the United States? Comment on your answer.

(b) Why do companies, financial analysts, labor unions, industry trade associations, and others take such an active interest in standard setting?

(c) Cite an example of a group other than the FASB that attempts to establish accounting standards. Speculate as to why another group might wish to set its own standards.

# CHAPTER 2

# Conceptual Framework Underlying Financial Accounting

Accounting may appear to be primarily procedural in nature. The visible portion of accounting—record keeping and preparation of financial statements—too often suggests the application of a low-level skill in a mundane occupation that is devoid of challenge and imagination. In accounting a large body of theory does exist, however. Philosophical objectives, normative theories, interrelated concepts, precise definitions, and rationalized rules comprise this body of theory (conceptual framework), which may be unknown to many people in the business community.[1] Thus, **accountants philosophize, theorize, judge, create, and deliberate as a significant part of their professional practice.** The subjective aspects that are so critical to current accounting practice, such as searching for truth and fact, judging what is fair presentation, and considering the behavior induced by presentations, are often overshadowed by the appearance of exactitude, precision, and objectivity that accompanies the use of numbers to express the financial results of the enterprise.

The principles of accounting are unlike the principles of the natural sciences and mathematics, because they cannot be derived from or proved by the laws of nature, and they are not viewed as fundamental truths or axioms. **Accounting principles cannot be *discovered;* they are created, developed, or decreed. Accounting principles are supported and justified by intuition, authority, and acceptability.** Because it is difficult to substantiate accounting principles objectively or by experimentation, arguments concerning them can degenerate into quasi-religious dogmatism. As a result, the sanction for and credibility of accounting principles rest upon their general recognition and acceptance, which depend upon such criteria as usefulness, relevance, reliability, and cost-benefit considerations.

[1]Perhaps the most significant documents in this area are: Maurice Moonitz, *Accounting Research Study No. 1: The Basic Postulates of Accounting* (New York: AICPA, 1961); Robert T. Sprouse and Maurice Moonitz, *Accounting Research Study No. 3: A Tentative Set of Broad Accounting Principles for Business Enterprises* (New York: AICPA, 1962); *APB Statement No. 4:* Basic Concepts and Accounting Principles Underlying Financial Statements of Business Enterprises (New York: AICPA, 1970); "Conceptual Framework for Financial Accounting and Reporting: Elements of Financial Statements and Their Measurement," *FASB Discussion Memorandum,* (Stamford, Conn.: FASB, 1976); and subsequent related documents on the conceptual framework project. These studies provide useful reference material to those wishing to explore this area in greater depth.

In Chapter 1, we identified the environment of financial reporting and the objectives of financial reporting that have been developed by the FASB. The objectives represent a starting point in the development of a conceptual framework for financial accounting and reporting by the FASB. The conceptual framework has been the focus of much time, talent, and expense by the Board since its inception. Many have considered the Board's real contribution and even its continued existence to be dependent upon the quality and utility of a completed conceptual framework for financial reporting.

## NATURE OF A CONCEPTUAL FRAMEWORK

A conceptual framework is like a **constitution;** it is "a coherent system of interrelated objectives and fundamentals that can lead to consistent standards and that prescribes the nature, function, and limits of financial accounting and financial statements."[2]

Why is a conceptual framework necessary? First, to be useful, standard-setting should build on and relate to an established body of concepts and objectives. A soundly developed conceptual framework of concepts and objectives should enable the FASB to issue more useful and consistent standards in the future; **a coherent set of standards and rules should be the result,** because they would be built upon the same foundation. Second, new and emerging **practical problems should be more quickly soluble by reference to an existing framework** of basic theory. As an illustration of an emerging problem, unique types of debt instruments have been issued recently by companies as a response to high interest and inflation rates. Examples are: "shared appreciation mortgages" (debt in which the lender receives equity participation), "deep discount bonds" (debt with no stated interest rate), and "commodity-backed bonds" (debt that may be repaid in a commodity). Examining the commodity-backed bonds a little further, we find that companies are issuing debt that will be repaid either in cash or in some commodity, such as silver, oil, coal, and so on (also referred to as asset-linked bonds). For example, in 1980, Sunshine Mining (a silver mining company) sold two issues of bonds that it would redeem either with $1,000 in cash or with 50 ounces of silver (or the cash equivalent), whichever was greater at maturity. Both bond issues are due in 1995 and both have a low stated interest rate—8.5%. At what amounts should the bonds be recorded by Sunshine or the buyers of the bonds? What is the amount of the premium or discount on the bonds and how should it be amortized, if the bond redemption payments are to be made in silver (the future value of which is currently unknown)?

It is difficult, if not impossible, for the FASB to prescribe the proper accounting treatment quickly for situations like this. Practicing accountants, however, must resolve such problems on a day-to-day basis. Through the exercise of good judgment and with the help of a universally accepted conceptual framework, it is hoped that practitioners will be able to dismiss certain alternatives quickly because they fall outside the conceptual framework and then to focus upon a logical and acceptable treatment.

Third, a conceptual framework should **increase financial statement users' understanding of and confidence in financial reporting,** and fourth, such a framework should **enhance**

---

[2]"Conceptual Framework for Financial Accounting and Reporting: Elements of Financial Statements and Their Measurement," *FASB Discussion Memorandum* (Stamford, Conn.: FASB, 1976), page 1 of the "Scope and Implications of the Conceptual Framework Project" section.

**comparability among companies' financial statements.** Similar events and phenomena should be similarly accounted for and reported; dissimilar events properly should not be.

## DEVELOPMENT OF A CONCEPTUAL FRAMEWORK

Although numerous organizations, committees, and interested individuals have developed and published their own conceptual frameworks, no single framework is universally accepted and relied on in practice. Perhaps the most successful was *Accounting Principles Board Statement No. 4,* "Basic Concepts and Accounting Principles Underlying Financial Statements of Business Enterprises," which described existing practice but did not prescribe what practice ought to be.[3] Recognizing the need for a generally accepted framework, the FASB in 1976 issued a massive three-part Discussion Memorandum entitled *Conceptual Framework for Financial Accounting and Reporting: Elements of Financial Statements and Their Measurement.* It set forth the major issues that must be addressed in establishing a conceptual framework that would be a basis for setting accounting standards and for resolving financial reporting controversies. Since the publication of that document, the FASB has issued three Statements of Financial Accounting Concepts that relate to financial reporting for business enterprises.[4] They are:

1. *SFAC No. 1,* "Objectives of Financial Reporting by Business Enterprises," presents the goals and purposes of accounting.
2. *SFAC No. 2,* "Qualitative Characteristics of Accounting Information," examines the characteristics that make accounting information useful.
3. *SFAC No. 3,* "Elements of Financial Statements of Business Enterprises," provides definitions of items that financial statements comprise, such as assets, liabilities, revenues, and expenses.
4. The Board has issued an exposure draft on another concepts statement, "Reporting Income, Cash Flows and Financial Position of Business Enterprises," which recommends concepts to guide decisions about the display and disclosure of information about income, cash flows, and financial position.

Figure 2–1 provides an overview of the conceptual framework in accounting which is affected by the environmental aspects discussed in Chapter 1.[5] At the first level, the **objectives** identify the goals and purposes of accounting and are the building blocks for the conceptual framework. At the second level are the **qualitative characteristics** of accounting information and definitions of the **elements** of financial statements. The former are the characteristics that make accounting information useful and the latter are definitions of financial statement components (assets, liabilities, and so on). Together these two categories provide the foundation for developing operational guidelines to be used in practice. At the final or third level are the **operational guidelines** that the accountant uses in establishing and applying accounting standards. These operational guidelines comprise assumptions, principles, and constraints.

---

[3]"Basic Concepts and Accounting Policies Underlying Financial Statements of Business Enterprises," *APB Statement No. 4* (New York: AICPA, 1970).

[4]The FASB has also issued a Statement of Financial Accounting Concepts that relates to nonbusiness organizations: *Statement of Financial Accounting Concepts No. 4,* "Objectives of Financial Reporting by Nonbusiness Organizations," (December 1980).

[5]Adapted from William C. Norby, *The Financial Analysts Journal* (March–April, 1982), p. 22.

**FIGURE 2–1**   A conceptual framework for accounting.

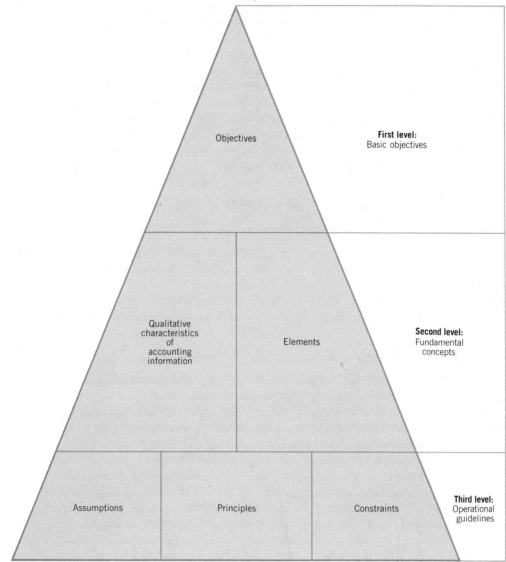

## FIRST LEVEL: BASIC OBJECTIVES

In Chapter 1, we discussed the objectives of financial reporting. The objectives of financial reporting are to provide information that is: (1) useful to those making investment and credit decisions who have a reasonable understanding of business and economic activities; (2) helpful to present and potential investors and creditors and other users in assessing the amount, timing, and uncertainty of future cash flows; and (3) about economic resources, the claims to those resources, and the changes in them.

The objectives, therefore, begin with a broad concern about information that is useful to investor and creditor decisions. They narrow that concern to the investors' and creditors' interest in the prospect of receiving cash from their investments in, or loans to, business enterprises. Finally, they focus on the financial statements that provide information useful in the assessment of prospective cash flows to the business enterprise, upon which, in turn, cash flows to investors and creditors depend.

In providing information to users of financial statements, the accounting profession has relied on general-purpose financial statements. The intent of general-purpose financial statements is to provide the most useful information possible to various user groups at minimal cost. Underlying these objectives is the notion that reasonable sophistication related to business and financial accounting matters is needed for users to understand the information contained in financial statements. This point is important because it means that in the preparation of financial statements accountants can assume a level of reasonable competence; this has an impact on the way and to the extent information is reported.

## SECOND LEVEL: FUNDAMENTAL CONCEPTS

The objectives (first level) are concerned with the goals and purposes of accounting. Later, we will discuss the ways these goals and purposes are implemented (third level). Between these two levels it is necessary to provide certain conceptual building blocks that explain the qualitative characteristics of accounting information and define the elements that financial statements comprise. These conceptual building blocks form a bridge between the **why** of accounting (the objectives) and the **how** of accounting (operational guidelines).

### Qualitative Characteristics of Accounting Information

How does one decide whether financial reports should provide information on an historical cost basis or on a current value basis? Or how does one decide whether the four main companies that constitute Sears, Roebuck & Co.—Sears (the retailer), Coldwell Banker (the real estate operation), Allstate (the insurance company), and Dean Witter (the brokerage firm)—should be combined and shown as one company or disaggregated and reported as four separate companies for financial reporting purposes? To answer such diverse yet basic questions, one looks to some criterion as a guide in choosing among alternatives.

Choosing an acceptable accounting method, the amount and types of information to be disclosed, and the format in which information should be presented involves determining which alternative provides the better (the most useful) information for decision-making purposes. Financial reporting is concerned in varying degrees with decision-making. As a consequence, **the overriding criterion by which accounting choices can be judged is that of decision usefulness,** that is, providing information that is the most useful for decision-making.

The FASB in *Concepts Statement No. 2* has identified the qualitative characteristics of accounting information that distinguish better (more useful) information from inferior (less useful) information for decision-making purposes.[6] In addition, the FASB has identified certain constraints (cost-benefit and materiality) as part of the conceptual framework. These are discussed later in the chapter. The characteristics may be viewed as a hierarchy, as illustrated in Figure 2–2 on page 29.

---

[6]"Qualitative Characteristics of Accounting Information," *Statement of Financial Accounting Concepts No. 2* (Stamford, Conn.: FASB, May 1980).

**FIGURE 2-2**  A hierarchy of accounting qualities.

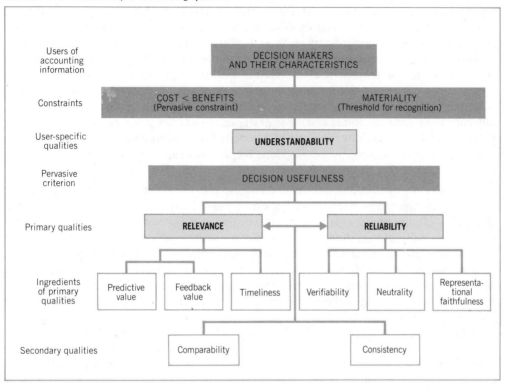

**Decision Makers (Users) and Understandability**  Decision makers vary widely in the types of decisions they make, the methods of decision-making they employ, the information they already possess or can obtain from other sources, and their ability to process the information. Consequently, for information to be useful there must be a connection (linkage) between these users and the decisions they make. This linkage is provided by communicating the appropriate information in an understandable fashion. This link, **understandability,** is the quality of information that permits reasonably informed users to perceive its significance. To illustrate the importance of this linkage, assume that IBM Corp. issues a three-months' earnings report (interim report) that provides relevant and reliable information for decision-making purposes. Unfortunately, certain users do not understand the content and significance of the interim report. Thus, although the information presented is highly relevant and reliable, it is useless to users who do not understand it.

**Primary Qualities**  The FASB has indicated that **relevance and reliability are the two primary qualities that make accounting information useful for decision-making.** As stated in *Concepts Statement No. 2*, "the qualities that distinguish 'better' (more useful) information from 'inferior' (less useful) information are primarily the qualities of relevance and reliability, with some other characteristics that those qualities imply."[7]

[7]Ibid., par. 15.

RELEVANCE    To be relevant, accounting information must be capable of making a difference in a decision.[8] If certain information is disregarded because it has no bearing on a decision, it is irrelevant to that decision. Relevant information helps users make predictions about the outcome of past, present, and future events (**predictive value**), or confirm or correct prior expectations (**feedback value**). For example, when IBM Corp. issues an interim report, this information is considered relevant because it provides a basis for forecasting annual earnings and provides feedback on past performance. It follows that for information to be relevant, it must also be available to decision makers before it loses its capacity to influence their decisions (**timeliness**). For example, if IBM Corp. did not report its interim results until six months after the end of the period, the information would be much less useful for decision-making purposes. Thus, **for information to be relevant, it should have predictive value and feedback value, and it must be presented on a timely basis.**

RELIABILITY    Accounting information is reliable to the extent that users can depend on it to represent the economic conditions or events that it purports to represent. **Reliability is the quality of information that gives assurance that it is reasonably free of error and bias and is a faithful representation.** To be reliable, accounting information must possess three key characteristics: verifiability, representational faithfulness, and neutrality.

**Verifiability** is a quality that is demonstrated when a high degree of consensus can be secured among independent measurers using the same measurement methods. **Representational faithfulness,** on the other hand, means correspondence or agreement between the accounting numbers and descriptions and the resources or events that these numbers and descriptions purport to represent. To illustrate, for the interim report of IBM to be considered reliable, it must be verifiable by outside parties. If outside parties using the same measurement methods arrive at different conclusions, the content of IBM's interim report is not verifiable. Similarly, if IBM's interim report presents cash sales of $1 billion when in fact it had cash sales of only $800 million, it would not represent what it purports to represent; that is, it would not be a faithful representation.

Reliability of information is a necessity for individuals who have neither the time nor the expertise to evaluate the factual content of the information. It is especially important to the independent audit process. Auditors would have a difficult time justifying their opinion about financial information if the information were not verifiable.

For information to be reliable, it must also be neutral. **Neutrality** means that in formulating or in implementing accounting standards, the primary concern should be the relevance and reliability of the information that results, not the economic consequence of the standard or rule. If information is reliable, it must be neutral; that is, it cannot be selected to favor one set of interested parties over another. For example, the applicability of a standard that requires a drug company to disclose in its footnotes that numerous lawsuits have been filed against it because of an inferior product should not be decided on the basis of the harm (or lack of) that such disclosure would inflict on the drug company.

**Secondary Qualities**    The use of different accounting methods makes financial comparisons among enterprises difficult. Information about an enterprise is more useful if it can be compared with similar information about another enterprise (**comparability**) and with similar information about the same enterprise at other points in time (**consistency**). Note that comparability and consistency are not qualities of information in the same sense that rele-

[8]Ibid., par. 47.

vance and reliability are. Information that is not reliable or that is not relevant will not be useful. Such may or may not be the case with comparability and consistency, because they do not have to be considered unless the information is both relevant and reliable.

COMPARABILITY   Information that has been measured and reported in a similar manner for different enterprises is considered comparable. Comparability enables users to identify the real similarities and differences in economic phenomena because these differences and similarities have not been obscured by the use of noncomparable methods of accounting. For example, if Company A prepares its information on an historical cost basis, but Company B uses a price-level adjusted basis, it becomes more difficult to compare and evaluate Companies A and B. Resource allocation decisions involve evaluations of alternatives, and a valid evaluation can be made only if comparable information is available.

CONSISTENCY   When an accounting entity applies the same accounting treatment from period to period to similar accountable events, the entity is considered to be consistent in its use of accounting standards. Consistency, therefore, means that a company applies the same methods to similar accountable events from period to period; it does not mean that companies cannot switch from one method of accounting to another. Companies can change methods, but the changes are restricted to situations in which it can be demonstrated that the newly adopted method is preferable to the old. Then the nature and effect of the accounting change, as well as the justification for it, must be disclosed in the financial statements for the period in which the change is made.

The standard opinion rendered by independent certified public accountants also refers to consistency. The relevant portion of this opinion is: "In our opinion, the accompanying financial statements present fairly the financial position and results of operations for the period under review in accordance with generally accepted accounting principles **applied on a basis consistent with that of the preceding year.**"

In summary, accounting reports for any given year are useful in themselves, but they are more useful if they can be compared with reports from other companies and with similar reports of the same entity for prior years. For example, if IBM is the only enterprise that prepares interim reports, the information is less useful because the user cannot relate it to interim reports for any other enterprise; that is, it lacks comparability. Similarly, if the measurement methods used to prepare IBM's interim report change from one interim period to another, the information is considered less useful because the user cannot relate it to previous interim periods; that is, it lacks consistency.

## Basic Elements

An important aspect of developing any theoretical structure is the establishment of a body of elements or definitions. FASB Chairman Donald Kirk noted that the establishment of definitions for such items as assets, liabilities, and so on, may be the most important phase of the FASB conceptual framework study.[9] At present, accounting uses many terms that have peculiar and specific meanings, terms that constitute the language of business or the jargon of accounting. One such term is **asset.** Is it something we own? If the answer is yes, can we assume that any asset leased would never be shown on the balance sheet? Is it something we have the right to use, or is it anything of value used by the enterprise to

---

[9]Speech by FASB Chairman Donald J. Kirk before the Financial Executives Institute International Conference, summarized in *FASB Viewpoints* (Stamford, Conn.: FASB, 1978), p. 3.

generate revenues? If the answer is yes, then why should the management of the enterprise not be considered an asset? It seems necessary, therefore, to develop basic definitions for the elements of accounting. *Concepts Statement No. 3* defines the ten interrelated elements that are most directly related to measuring the performance and financial status of an enterprise as follows:

---

### ELEMENTS OF FINANCIAL STATEMENTS

**ASSETS.** Probable future economic benefits obtained or controlled by a particular entity as a result of past transactions or events.

**LIABILITIES.** Probable future sacrifices of economic benefits arising from present obligations of a particular entity to transfer assets or provide services to other entities in the future as a result of past transactions or events.

**EQUITY.** Residual interest in the assets of an entity that remains after deducting its liabilities. In a business enterprise, the equity is the ownership interest.

**INVESTMENTS BY OWNERS.** Increases in net assets of a particular enterprise resulting from transfers to it from other entities of something of value to obtain or increase ownership interests (or equity) in it. Assets are most commonly received as investments by owners, but that which is received may also include services or satisfaction or conversion of liabilities of the enterprise.

**DISTRIBUTIONS TO OWNERS.** Decreases in net assets of a particular enterprise resulting from transferring assets, rendering services, or incurring liabilities by the enterprise to owners. Distributions to owners decrease ownership interests (or equity) in an enterprise.

**COMPREHENSIVE INCOME.** Change in equity (net assets) of an entity during a period from transactions and other events and circumstances from nonowner sources. It includes all changes in equity during a period except those resulting from investments by owners and distributions to owners.

**REVENUES.** Inflows or other enhancement of assets of an entity or settlement of liabilities (or a combination of both) during a period from delivering or producing goods, rendering services, or other activities that constitute the entity's ongoing major or central operations.

**EXPENSES.** Outflows or other using up of assets or incurrences of liabilities (or a combination of both) during a period from delivering or producing goods, rendering services, or carrying out other activities that constitute the entity's ongoing major or central operations.

**GAINS.** Increases in equity (net assets) from peripheral or incidental transactions of an entity and from all other transactions and other events and circumstances affecting the entity during a period except those that result from revenues or investments by owners.

**LOSSES.** Decreases in equity (net assets) from peripheral or incidental transactions of an entity and from all other transactions and other events and circumstances affecting the entity during a period except those that result from expenses or distributions to owners.[10]

---

Each of these elements will be explained and examined in more detail in subsequent chapters.

Two important points should be noted regarding these definitions. First, the term **comprehensive income** represents a new concept. Comprehensive income is more inclusive than our traditional notion of net income; if the FASB's definition is taken literally, it includes net income and all other changes in equity exclusive of owners' investments and distribu-

---

[10]"Elements of Financial Statements of Business Enterprises," *Statement of Financial Accounting Concepts No. 3* (Stamford, Conn.: FASB, December 1980), pp. xi and xii.

tions. Net income, therefore, is an intermediate amount that comprises part, but not all, of comprehensive income. For example, prior period adjustments (transactions that relate to previous periods, such as corrections of errors), which are currently excluded from net income, may be included under comprehensive income. Comprehensive income, therefore, is a very broad concept that gives the FASB flexibility in defining some intermediate components of this amount. This concept, which is not yet being applied in practice, is discussed in greater detail in Chapter 4.

Second, the FASB classifies the elements into two distinct groups. The first group of three elements—assets, liabilities, and equity—describes amounts of resources and claims to resources at a **moment in time.** The other seven elements (comprehensive income and its components—revenues, expenses, gains, and losses—as well as investments by owners and distributions to owners) describe transactions, events, and circumstances that affect an enterprise during a **period of time.** The first class—assets, liabilities, and equity—is changed by elements of the second class and at any time is the cumulative result of all changes. This interaction is referred to as "articulation." The articulation of the elements results in financial statements that articulate; that is, the financial statements are fundamentally interrelated so that statements (for example, balance sheet) that report elements of the first class depend on statements (for example, income statement) that report elements of the second class, and vice versa.

## THIRD LEVEL: OPERATIONAL GUIDELINES

The FASB has only recently issued pronouncements that present and explain the first two levels of this conceptual framework. The third level (operational guidelines) has not yet been fully developed by the FASB. Of necessity, however, the accounting profession has developed operational guidelines, which we have chosen to classify as assumptions, principles, and constraints. These guidelines are aids in developing rational responses to controversial financial reporting issues.

### Basic Assumptions

Four basic assumptions that seem to underlie the financial accounting structure are (1) **an economic entity assumption,** (2) **a going concern assumption,** (3) **a monetary unit assumption,** and (4) **a periodicity assumption.**

**Economic Entity Assumption**   **A major assumption in accounting is that economic activity can be identified with a particular unit of accountability.** In other words, the activity of a business enterprise can be kept separate and distinct from its owners and any other business unit.[11] If there were no meaningful way to separate all of the economic events that occur, no basis for accounting would exist. Accounting as a system for providing information for and about a given company simply would not exist. Imagine the results, for exam-

---

[11]Surprisingly, such a distinction is not always made in practice. A *Wall Street Journal* article, for example, noted that audit committees of six publicly held companies wanted their chief executive to reimburse the companies an additional $1 million in personal expenses for such items as company yachts, speedboats, refurbishing, and rent money on personal apartments. "Posners Asked to Repay Firms 1.1 Million More" (*Wall Street Journal,* November 27, 1978), p. 6.

ple, if the activities of General Motors could not be distinguished from those of Ford, Chrysler, or American Motors.

The entity concept does not apply solely to the segregation of activities among given business enterprises. Generally we think of entities as business enterprises; but an individual, a department or division, or an entire industry could be considered a separate entity if we chose to define the unit in such a manner. Thus **the entity concept is not necessarily a legal-entity concept;** a parent and its subsidiaries are separate **legal** entities, but merging their activities for accounting and reporting purposes is not a violation of the **economic entity** assumption.

**Going Concern Assumption** Most accounting methods are based on **the assumption that the business enterprise will have a long life.** Experience indicates that, in spite of numerous business failures, companies have a fairly high continuance rate, and it has proved useful to adopt a going concern or continuity assumption for accounting purposes. Although accountants do not believe that business firms will last indefinitely, they do expect them to last long enough to fulfill their objectives and commitments.

The implications of adopting this assumption are critical. Acceptance of this assumption provides credibility to the historical cost principle, which would be of limited usefulness if eventual liquidation were assumed. Under a liquidation approach, for example, asset values are better stated at net realizable value (sales price less costs of disposal) than at acquisition cost. **Only if we assume some permanence to the enterprise are depreciation and amortization policies justifiable and appropriate.** If a liquidation approach were adopted, the current-noncurrent classification of assets and liabilities would lose much of its significance. Labeling anything a fixed or long-term asset would be difficult to justify. The listing of the liabilities on the basis of priority in liquidation, for example, is more reasonable.

The going concern assumption is generally applicable in most business situations. **Only where liquidation appears imminent is the assumption inapplicable,** and in these cases a total revaluation of the assets and liabilities can provide information that closely approximates net realizable value of the entity. Most of the accounting problems related to an enterprise in liquidation are presented in advanced accounting.

**Monetary Unit Assumption** Accounting is based on the assumption that money is the common denominator by which economic activity is conducted, and that the monetary unit provides an appropriate basis for accounting measurement and analysis. This assumption implies that the monetary unit is the most effective means of expressing to interested parties changes in capital and exchanges of goods and services. Support for this assumption lies in the fact that **the monetary unit is relevant, simple, universally available, understandable, and useful.** Application of this assumption is dependent on the even more basic assumption that quantitative data are useful in communicating economic information and in making rational economic decisions.

In the United States, accountants have chosen generally to ignore the phenomenon of price-level change (inflation and deflation) by adopting the monetary unit assumption that **the unit of measure—the dollar—remains reasonably stable.** This second assumption about the monetary unit has traditionally been used by accountants to justify adding 1955 dollars to 1983 dollars without any adjustment.

**Periodicity Assumption** The most accurate way to measure the results of enterprise activity would be to measure them at the time of the enterprise's eventual liquidation. Business, government, investors, and various other user groups, however, cannot wait indefinitely for such information. If accountants did not provide financial information periodically, someone else would.

The periodicity or time period assumption simply implies that **the economic activities of an enterprise can be divided into artificial time periods.** These time periods vary, but the most common are monthly, quarterly, and yearly. Because accountants have to divide continuous operations into arbitrary time periods, they must determine the relevance of each business transaction or event to one specific accounting period. The shorter the time period, the more difficult it becomes to determine the proper net income for the period. Because of problems of allocation, a month's results are usually less reliable than a quarter's results, and a quarter's results are likely to be less reliable than a year's results. This phenomenon provides an interesting example of the trade-off between relevance and reliability in preparing financial data. Investors desire and demand that information be quickly processed and disseminated; yet the quicker the information is released, the more subject it is to error.

## Basic Principles of Accounting

In view of the basic assumptions of accounting, what are the principles or guidelines that the accountant follows in recording transaction data? These principles can be classified as (1) **the historical cost principle,** (2) **the revenue recognition principle,** (3) **the matching principle,** and (4) **the full disclosure principle.** The principles relate basically to how assets, liabilities, revenues, and expenses are to be identified, measured, recorded, and reported.

**Historical Cost**   Traditionally, preparers and users of financial statements have found that cost is generally the most useful basis for accounting measurement and reporting. As a result, existing GAAP requires that most assets and liabilities be accounted for and reported on the basis of acquisition price. This is often referred to as the **historical cost principle. Cost has an important advantage over other valuations: it is reliable.** To illustrate the importance of this advantage, let us consider the problems that would arise if we adopted some other basis for keeping records. If we were to select current selling price, for instance, we might have a difficult time in attempting to establish a sales value for a given item without selling it. Every member of the accounting department might have his or her own opinion of the proper valuation of the asset, and management might desire still another figure. And how often would we find it necessary to establish sales value? All companies close their accounts at least annually, and some compute their net income every month. These companies would find it necessary to place a sales value on every asset each time they wished to determine income—a laborious task and one that would result in a figure of net income materially affected by opinion on sales value of the many assets involved. Similar objections have been leveled against current cost (replacement cost, present value of future cash flows) and any other basis of valuation except cost.

Cost is definite and verifiable. Once established, it is fixed as long as the asset remains the property of the company. These two characteristics are of real importance to those who use accounting data. To rely on the information supplied, both internal and external parties must know that the information is accurate and based on fact. **By using cost as their basis for record keeping, accountants can provide objective and verifiable data in their reports.**

The question "What is cost?" is not always easy to answer because of other questions that follow in its wake. If fixed assets are to be carried in the accounts at cost, are cash discounts to be deducted in determining cost? Does cost include freight and insurance? Does it include cost of installation as well as the price of a machine itself? And what of the cost of reinstallation if the machine is later moved? When land purchased for a building site is occupied by old structures, is the cost of razing these structures part of the cost of the land? These and similar questions must be considered and answered in arriving at cost figures for assets purchased.

Furthermore, purchase is not the only method of acquiring assets. How do we determine the cost of items received as a gift? It is not unusual for a developing community to offer plant sites free as an inducement to companies to establish themselves in that locality. At what price should such assets be carried? Certain assets may be acquired by the issuance of the capital stock of the acquiring company or perhaps through the issuance of bonds or notes payable. Or assets may be exchanged for similar or dissimilar assets. If no money price is stated in the transaction, how is cost to be established? These questions are answered in later chapters; they are raised here only to point out some of the difficulties regularly encountered in accounting for costs.

The basic financial statements include liabilities and assets. We ordinarily think of cost as relating only to assets, and so it may seem strange that liabilities too are accounted for on a basis of cost. **If we convert the term "cost" to "exchange price," we will find that it applies to liabilities as well.** Liabilities, such as bonds, notes, and accounts payable, are issued by a business enterprise in exchange for assets, or perhaps services, upon which an agreed price has usually been placed. This price, established by the exchange transaction, is the "cost" of the liability and provides the figure at which it should be recorded in the accounts and reported in financial statements.

Many objections to the historical cost basis have been raised. Criticism is especially strong during a period when prices are changing substantially. At such times cost is said to go "out of date" almost as soon as it is recorded. In a period of rising or falling prices, the cost figures of the preceding years are viewed as not comparable with current cost figures. For example, assuming a rate of inflation of 1% per month, a McDonald's "quarter-pounder with cheese," which costs $1.45 today, will cost approximately $153.00 in 39 years. So much concern has been expressed about price-level information that the FASB issued *FASB Statement No. 33,* "Financial Reporting and Changing Prices," which requires supplemental price-level disclosures by certain large enterprises. Chapter 25 discusses the accounting problems and benefits of reporting price-level adjusted information.

**Revenue Recognition Principle**     Revenue is generally recognized when (1) **the earning process is virtually complete,** and (2) **an exchange transaction has occurred.** This approach has often been referred to as the **revenue recognition principle.** Generally, an objective test—confirmation by a sale to independent interests—is used to indicate the point at which revenue is recognized. Usually, only when an exchange transaction takes place is there an objective and verifiable measure of revenue—the sales price. Any basis for revenue recognition short of actual sale opens the door to wide variations in practice. Conservative individuals might wait until sale of their securities; more optimistic individuals could watch market quotations and take up gains as market prices increased; yet others might recognize increases that are only rumored; and unscrupulous persons could "write up" their investments as they pleased to suit their own purposes. To give accounting reports uniform meaning, a rule of revenue recognition comparable to the cost rule for asset valuation is essential. **Recognition through sale provides a uniform and reasonable test.**

There are, however, exceptions to the rule, and at times the basic rule is difficult to apply.

PERCENTAGE-OF-COMPLETION APPROACH     Recognition of revenue is allowed in certain long-term construction contracts before the contract is completed. The advantage of this method is that revenue is recognized periodically on the basis of the percentage that the job has been completed instead of only when the entire job has been finished. Although technically an exchange transaction has not occurred (transfer of ownership), the earning process is considered substantially completed at various stages as construction progresses. Naturally, if it is not possible to obtain dependable estimates of cost and progress, then the accountant should wait and record the revenue at the completion date.

END OF PRODUCTION     At times, revenue might be considered recognized before sale, but after the production cycle has ended. This is the case where the price is certain as well as the amount. An example would be the mining of certain minerals for which, once the mineral is mined, a ready market at a standard price exists. The same holds true for some artificial price supports set by the government in establishing agricultural prices.

RECEIPT OF CASH     Receipt of cash is another basis for revenue recognition. The cash basis approach should be used only when it is impossible to establish the revenue figure at the time of sale because of the uncertainty of collection. This approach is commonly referred to as the installment sales method where payment is required in periodic installments over a long period of time. Its most common use is in the retail field where all types of farm and home equipment and furnishings are sold on an installment basis. Use of the installment method is frequently justified on the basis that the risk of not collecting an account receivable may be so great that the sale is not sufficient evidence that recognition should take place. In some instances, this reasoning may be valid but not in a majority of such transactions. If a sale has been completed, it should be recognized; if bad debts are expected, they should be recorded as separate estimates of uncollectibles.

Revenue, then, is recorded in the period in which an exchange takes place and the earning process is virtually complete. Normally, this is the date of sale, but circumstances may dictate application of the percentage-of-completion approach, the end-of-production approach, or the receipt-of-cash approach.

Conceptually, the proper accounting treatment for revenue recognition should be apparent and should fit nicely into one of the conditions mentioned above, but often it does not. For example, how should motion picture companies such as Metro-Goldwyn-Mayer, Inc., Warner Bros., and United Artists account for the sale of rights to show motion picture films on television networks such as ABC, CBS, or NBC? Should the revenue from the sale of the rights be reported when the contract is signed, when the motion picture film is delivered to the network, when the cash payment is received by the motion picture company, or when the film is shown on television? The problem of revenue recognition is complicated because the TV networks are often restricted in regard to the number of times the film may be shown and over what period of time.

For example, Metro-Goldwyn-Mayer Film Co. (MGM) sold CBS the rights to show *Gone With The Wind* for $35 million. For this $35 million, CBS received the right to show this classic movie twenty times over a twenty-year period. MGM contended that revenue reporting should coincide with the right to telecast on first and subsequent showings as included in the license agreement. They argued that the right to show *Gone With The Wind* twenty times over a twenty-year period was a significant contract restriction and, therefore, revenue recognition should coincide with the showings. The accounting profession on the other hand argued that when (1) the sales price and cost of each film are known, (2) collectibility is assured, and (3) the film is available and accepted by the network, revenue recognition should occur. The restriction that *Gone With The Wind* be shown only once a year for twenty years was not considered significant enough or appropriate justification for deferring revenue recognition. It is interesting to note that MGM, Inc., in the first quarter of 1979, reported essentially the entire $35 million in revenue in one period as the following headline in the *Wall Street Journal* reported, "MGM's Net Tripled in the First Quarter that Ended Nov. 30."

The previous illustrations indicate the difficulty of determining when revenue should be recognized. What accountants have attempted to do in the past is to rely on the general procedure of recognizing revenue at the point of sale because at that time most uncertainties have been resolved and verifiable evidence, obtained through an exchange transaction, is available. There are transactions, however, in which delaying recognition until the point of sale does not remove all important uncertainties, as, for example, in cases when sales are made but a right of return exists. Determining when a sale is a sale can be difficult because the form of the transaction may misrepresent the substance. For example, in a sale to a third party that includes an agreement that the seller will buy back the goods in the next accounting period, a serious question arises as to whether a sale has occurred at all. As a result, accountants are still forced to develop revenue recognition guidelines when certain peculiar arrangements develop. It is hoped that the conceptual framework project will provide timely and consistent solutions to revenue recognition problems. The FASB is in the process of developing general guidelines as to when the rights and benefits of ownership have transferred and when no important uncertainties exist in regard to such transactions.

**Matching Principle**   In recognizing expenses, accountants attempt to follow the approach of "let the expense follow the revenues." Expenses are recognized not when wages are paid, or when the work is performed, or when a product is produced, but when the work (service) or the product actually makes its contribution to revenue. Thus, expense recognition is tied to revenue recognition. In some cases it is difficult to determine the period in which an expense contributes to the generation of revenues, but many expenses can be associated with particular revenues. This practice is referred to as the **matching principle** because it dictates that efforts (expenses) be matched with accomplishment (revenues) whenever it is reasonable and practicable to do so.

For those costs for which it is difficult to adopt some type of rational association with revenue, some other approach must be developed. Often, the accountant must develop a "rational and systematic" allocation policy that will approximate the matching principle. This type of expense recognition pattern involves assumptions about the benefits that are being received as well as the cost associated with those benefits. The cost of a long-lived asset, for example, must be allocated over all of the accounting periods during which the asset is used because the asset contributes to the generation of revenue throughout its useful life. Some costs are charged to the current period as expenses (or losses) simply because no future benefit is anticipated or no connection with revenue is apparent. Examples of these types of costs are officers' salaries and advertising and promotion expenses.

Summarizing, we might say that costs are analyzed to determine whether a relationship exists with revenue. Where this association holds, the costs are expensed and matched against the revenue in the period when the revenue is recognized. If no connection appears between costs and revenues, an allocation of cost on some systematic and rational basis might be appropriate. Where, however, this method does not seem desirable, the cost may be expensed immediately. Notice that costs are generally classified into two groups: **product costs and period costs.** Product costs such as material, labor, and overhead attach to the product and are carried into future periods if the revenue from the product is recognized in subsequent periods. Period costs such as officers' salaries and selling expenses are charged off immediately because no direct relationship between cost and revenue can be determined.

The problem of expense recognition is as complex as that of revenue recognition. For example, at one time a large oil company spent a considerable amount of money in an introductory advertising campaign in Hawaii. The company obviously hoped that this advertising campaign would attract new customers and develop brand loyalty. Over how many years, if any, should this outlay be expensed? For another example, Delta Air Lines depreciates its planes over 10 years, while American Airlines writes off its jet fleet over periods as long as 16 years. Does the revenue flow from these two fleets justify that much of a difference in the expense recognition?

The conceptual validity of the matching principle has been a subject of debate. A major concern is that matching permits certain costs to be deferred and treated as assets on the balance sheet when in fact these costs may not have future benefits. If abused, this principle permits the balance sheet to become a "dumping ground" for unmatched costs. In addition, there appears to be no objective definition of "systematic and rational." For example, Hartwig, Inc. purchased an asset for $100,000 that will last five years. Various depreciation methods (straight-line, accelerated, units of production, all considered systematic and rational) might be used to allocate this cost over the five-year period. What criteria should guide the accountant in determining what portion of the cost of the asset should be written off each period?[12] New solutions to the expense recognition issue are currently being studied by the FASB as part of the conceptual framework project.

**Full Disclosure Principle**   In deciding what information to report, accountants follow the general practice of providing information that is of sufficient importance to influence the judgment and decisions of an informed user. Often referred to as the **full disclosure principle,** this principle recognizes that the nature and amount of information included in financial reports reflects a series of judgmental trade-offs. These trade-offs strive for (1) sufficient detail to disclose matters that **make a difference** to users, and (2) sufficient combination and condensation to make the **information understandable,** keeping in mind costs of preparing and using it.[13] The accountant can place information about financial position, income, and cash flows in one of three places: (1) within the main body of financial statements, (2) in the notes to those statements, or (3) as supplementary information. Some broad guidelines for deciding where to place certain kinds of financial information are provided in the following paragraphs.

[12]Some would suggest that even that procedure is well nigh impossible, given that the revenue flow from any given asset is interrelated with the remaining asset structure of the enterprise. For example, see Arthur L. Thomas, "The Allocation Problem in Financial Accounting Theory," *Studies in Accounting Research No. 3* (Evanston, Ill.: American Accounting Association, 1969), and "The Allocation Problem: Part Two," *Studies in Accounting Research No. 9* (Sarasota, Fla.: American Accounting Association, 1974).

[13]"Reporting Income, Cash Flows, and Financial Position of Business Enterprises," Proposed *Statement of Financial Accounting Concepts* (Stamford, Conn.: FASB, 1982), p. viii.

The **financial statements** are a formalized, structured means of communicating. To be recognized in the main body of financial statements, an item should meet the definition of an element and meet other recognition conditions. The item must have been measured, recorded in the books, and passed through the double-entry system of accounting.

The **notes** to financial statements generally amplify or explain the items presented in the main body of the statements. If the information in the main body of the financial statements gives an incomplete picture of the performance and position of the enterprise, additional information that is needed to complete the picture should be included in the notes. Information in the notes does not have to be quantifiable, nor does it need to qualify as an element. Notes can be partially or totally narrative. Examples of notes are: descriptions of the accounting policies and methods used in measuring the elements reported in the statements; explanations of uncertainties and contingencies; and statistics and details too voluminous for inclusion in the statements. Information provided in the notes is not only helpful but also essential to an understanding of the performance and position of the enterprise.

**Supplementary information** may include information that presents a different perspective from that adopted in the financial statements. This may be quantifiable information that is high in relevance but low in reliability, or information that is helpful but not essential. The primary example of supplementary information is the data and schedules provided by certain companies on the effects of changing prices (constant dollar and current cost information). Supplementary information may also include management's explanation of the financial information and its discussion of the significance of that information. The full disclosure principle is not always easy to put into operation because the business environment is complicated and ever changing. For example, during the past decade many business combinations have produced innumerable conglomerate-type business organizations and financing arrangements that demand new and peculiar accounting and reporting practices and principles. Leases, investment credits, pension funds, franchising, stock options, and mergers have had to be studied, and proper reporting practices have had to be developed. In each of these situations, the accountant is faced with the problem of making sure that enough information is presented to ensure that the mythical **reasonably prudent investor** will not be misled.

A classic illustration of the problems of determining adequate disclosure guidelines is the past turmoil related to bribes and political gifts to foreign countries. How much disclosure, if any, is necessary in the financial statements for these types of expenditures?[14] On one hand, it is contended that payoffs are unavoidable in business abroad, and sometimes in the United States, and should be looked upon as a cost of doing business. In addition,

---

[14]The Foreign Corrupt Practices Act of 1977, which resulted from these developments, has been called by many the most significant piece of legislation affecting business enterprise in the last twenty years. This legislation requires business enterprises to keep books and records accurately to reflect accounting transactions and to maintain a system of internal accounting controls sufficient to provide reasonable assurance that transactions are handled properly. It establishes criminal penalties for making payments to foreign officials, political parties, or candidates in order to obtain or retain business. Such legislation provides guidance to accountants who, prior to this legislation, often were forced to make their own moral judgments on these questions. Additional guidance is now given to auditors in "The Independent Auditor's Responsibility for the Detection of Errors or Irregularities," *Statement on Auditing Standards No. 16* (New York: AICPA, 1977) and "Illegal Acts by Clients," *Statement on Auditing Standards No. 17* (New York: AICPA, 1977).

many of the transactions are small in comparison with the corporation's revenues and are not considered material in relation to the financial statements of the corporation. Conversely, others argue that these types of payoffs raise questions about the quality of management and the quality of earnings. It is contended that stockholders have the right to know if the continuation of a company's operations in a foreign country depends on making payoffs and what effect stopping the payoffs might have on the financial statements. The emergence of such a problem demonstrates the complexity and subjectivity of devising disclosure rules that meet the needs of society.[15]

The content, arrangement, and display of financial statements, along with other facets of full disclosure, are discussed in Chapters 4, 5, and 27.

## Constraints

In providing information with the qualitative characteristics that make it useful, two overriding constraints must be considered: (1) the **cost-benefit relationship** and (2) **materiality.** Two other less dominant yet important constraints that are part of the reporting environment are **industry practices** and **conservatism.**

**Cost-Benefit Relationship**    Too often, users assume that information is a cost-free commodity. But preparers and providers of accounting information know that it is not. The costs of providing the information must be weighed against the benefits that can be derived from using the information. Obviously the benefits should exceed the costs. Practicing accountants have traditionally applied this constraint through the notions of "expediency" ("it is or is not expedient") or "practicality" ("it is or is not practical"), but only recently have standard-setting bodies and governmental agencies resorted to cost-benefit analysis before making their informational requirements final. In order to justify requiring a particular measurement or disclosure, the benefits perceived to be derived from it must exceed the costs perceived to be associated with it.

The difficulty in cost-benefit analysis is that the costs and especially the benefits are not always evident or measurable. The costs are of several kinds, including costs of collecting and processing, costs of disseminating, costs of auditing, costs of potential litigation, costs of disclosure to competitors, and costs of analysis and interpretation. Benefits accrue both to preparers (that is, in terms of greater efficiency, control, and financing) and to users (in terms of allocation of resources, tax assessment, and rate regulation) but they are generally more difficult to quantify than are costs. Because the costs are immediately measurable but the benefits are not as readily apparent, an increasing number of individuals and organizations are urging that cost-benefit analysis be required as part of the accounting standards development process. Among both the providers and the users of accounting information there are those who believe that the cost associated with implementing certain standards is too high when compared with the benefits received.

**Materiality**    An item is material if its inclusion or omission would influence or change the judgment of a reasonable person. It is immaterial and, therefore, irrelevant if its inclusion

---

[15]Ibid., pars. 41 and 42.

or omission would have no impact on a decision maker. In short, **it must make a difference** or it need not be disclosed. The point involved here is one of **relative size and importance.** If the amount involved is significant when compared with the other revenues and expenses, assets and liabilities, or net income of the entity, sound and acceptable standards should be followed. If the amount is so small that it is quite unimportant when compared with other items, application of a particular standard may be considered of less importance. It is difficult to provide firm guides in judging when a given item is or is not material because materiality varies both with relative amount (the size of the item relative to the size of other items) and with relative importance (the nature of the item itself). The two sets of numbers presented below illustrate relative size.

| | Company A | Company B |
|---|---|---|
| Sales | $10,000,000 | $100,000 |
| Costs and expenses | 9,000,000 | 90,000 |
| Income from operations | $ 1,000,000 | $ 10,000 |
| Unusual gain | $ 20,000 | $ 5,000 |

During the period in question, the revenues and expenses and, therefore, the net incomes of Company A and Company B have been proportional. Each has had an unusual gain. In looking at the abbreviated income figures for Company A, it does not appear significant whether the amount of the unusual gain is set out separately or merged with the regular operating income. It is only 2% of the net income and, if merged, would not seriously distort the net income figure. Company B has had an unusual gain of only $5,000, but it is relatively much more significant than the larger gain realized by A. For Company B, an item of $5,000 amounts to 50% of its net income. Obviously, the inclusion of such an item in ordinary operating income would affect the amount of that income materially. Thus we see the importance of the **relative size** of an item in determining its materiality.

The **nature of the item may also be important.** For example, if a company is involved in a violation of a statute (Foreign Corrupt Practices Act or one of the antitrust laws), the amounts involved should be separately disclosed. Or, a misclassification of assets that would not be material in amount if it affected two categories of plant and equipment might be material if it changed the classification between a noncurrent and a current category.

Materiality is a difficult concept to grasp, as these practical examples indicate: (1) General Dynamics disclosed that at one time its Resources Group had improved its earnings by $5.8 million at the same time that its Stromberg Datagraphix subsidiary had taken write-offs of $6.7 million. Although both numbers were far larger than the $2.5 million that General Dynamics as a whole earned for the year, neither was disclosed as an unusual or nonrecurring item in the annual report; apparently the net effect on net income was not considered material. (2) In the first quarter, GAC's earnings rose from 76 cents to 77 cents a share. Nowhere did the annual report disclose that a favorable tax carry-forward of 4 cents a share prevented GAC's earnings from sliding to 73 cents a share. The company took the position that this carry-forward should not be shown as an extraordinary item because it was not material (6%). As one executive noted, "You know that accountants have a rule of thumb which says that anything under 10% is not material." The examples should illustrate one point: in practice, the answer to what is material is not clear-cut, and difficult decisions must be made each period.[16] Only by the exercise of good judgment and professional expertise can the accountant arrive at answers that are reasonable and appropriate.

Materiality is a factor in a great many accounting decisions, only some of which are concerned with reporting items in the financial statements. For example, the amount of classification required in a subsidiary expense ledger, the degree of accuracy required in prorating expenses among the departments of a business, and the extent to which adjustments should be made for accrued and deferred items, are examples of judgments which should finally be determined on a basis of reasonableness and practicability, which is the materiality constraint sensibly applied.

**Industry Practices**    Another practical consideration, which sometimes requires departure from basic theory, is **the peculiar nature of some industries and business concerns.** For example, banks often report certain investment securities at market value because these securities are traded frequently, and many believe a cash equivalent price provides more useful information. In the public utility industry, noncurrent assets are reported first on the balance sheet to highlight the capital intensive nature of the industry. In the agricultural industry, crops are often reported at market value because it is costly to develop accurate cost figures on individual crops. Such variations from basic theory are not many; yet they do exist, and so, whenever we find what appears to be a violation of basic accounting theory, it is well to determine whether it is explained by some peculiar feature of the type of business involved before being critical of the procedures followed.

**Conservatism**    Few conventions in accounting are as misunderstood as the constraint of conservatism. The practicing accountant must make many decisions, some of them very difficult. For example, in a particular case the accountant may be in doubt about whether a given purchase should be charged to an expense account or to an asset account. In reaching a decision he or she uses accounting theory as modified by cost-benefit considerations, materiality, industry practices, and the influence that this item will have on the financial statements. If this approach does not give the accountant a clear decision, he or she then tends to rely on the convention of conservatism which says, in effect: **when in doubt choose the solution that will be least likely to overstate assets and income.** Note that there is nothing in the conservatism convention urging the accountant to understate assets or income. Unfortunately it has been interpreted by some accountants to mean just that. All that conservatism does, properly applied, is to give the accountant a guide in difficult situations, and then the guide is a very reasonable one: refrain from overstatement of net income and net assets. Examples of conservatism in accounting are the use of the lower of cost or market approach in valuing inventories and the rule that accrued net losses should be recognized on firm purchase commitments for goods for inventory. If the issue is in doubt, it is better to understate than overstate. Of course, if there is no doubt, there is no need to apply this constraint.

[16]A search for a definition of materiality based upon interpretations by the courts in cases under the securities laws reveals differing concepts of materiality; see Kenneth R. Jeffries, "Materiality as Defined by the Courts," *The CPA Journal* (October 1981), pp. 13–17.

**FIGURE 2-3**    Conceptual framework — environmental aspects of financial reporting.

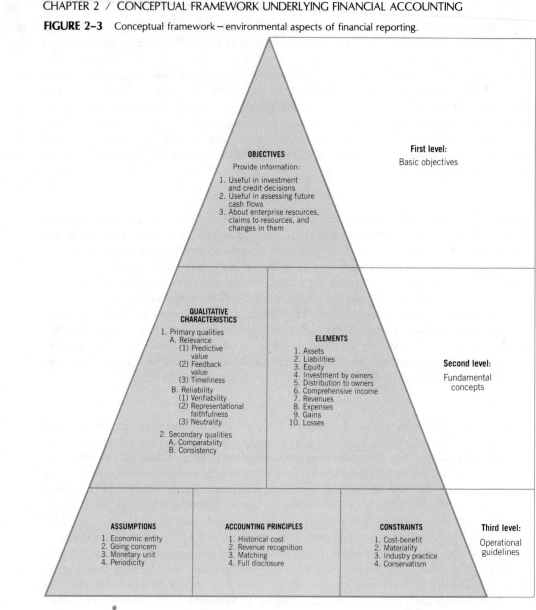

**OBJECTIVES**
Provide information:

1. Useful in investment and credit decisions
2. Useful in assessing future cash flows
3. About enterprise resources, claims to resources, and changes in them

**First level:**
Basic objectives

**QUALITATIVE CHARACTERISTICS**
1. Primary qualities
   A. Relevance
      (1) Predictive value
      (2) Feedback value
      (3) Timeliness
   B. Reliability
      (1) Verifiability
      (2) Representational faithfulness
      (3) Neutrality
2. Secondary qualities
   A. Comparability
   B. Consistency

**ELEMENTS**
1. Assets
2. Liabilities
3. Equity
4. Investment by owners
5. Distribution to owners
6. Comprehensive income
7. Revenues
8. Expenses
9. Gains
10. Losses

**Second level:**
Fundamental concepts

**ASSUMPTIONS**
1. Economic entity
2. Going concern
3. Monetary unit
4. Periodicity

**ACCOUNTING PRINCIPLES**
1. Historical cost
2. Revenue recognition
3. Matching
4. Full disclosure

**CONSTRAINTS**
1. Cost-benefit
2. Materiality
3. Industry practice
4. Conservatism

**Third level:**
Operational guidelines

## Summary of the Structure

Figure 2–3 above illustrates the conceptual framework discussed in this chapter. It is similar to Figure 2–1, except that it provides additional information for each level. We cannot overemphasize the usefulness of this conceptual framework in helping to understand many of the problem areas that are examined in subsequent chapters. As indicated earlier in the chapter, the FASB is now in the process of reexamining the third level (operational guidelines), with particular emphasis on the principles section. This reexamination of measurement (historical cost principle), recognition (revenue recognition principle and matching principle), and reporting (full disclosure principle) may lead to changes in financial reporting in the future. And, as the environment changes, so to some degree will the components of this theoretical structure. Nevertheless, the theoretical framework just presented provides you with insights into the basic components that comprise the existing body of financial accounting theory.

# APPENDIX A

# Approaches to Accounting Theory Formulation

As indicated in Chapter 2, accountants have attempted to develop a general theory (conceptual framework) to resolve the many financial accounting issues facing the accounting profession. In examining this framework, it is important to recognize that complete agreement on all aspects of a single conceptual framework is highly unlikely. Because accounting is influenced by its environment and affects its environment, the theory necessary to resolve accounting controversies will continue to be updated, modified, and at times completely changed.

The purpose of this appendix is to show that the proper approach to accounting theory formulation is very much a matter of debate and that different individuals have quite different perceptions about what approaches the profession should take to resolve financial accounting issues. The different views of accounting theory can be classified in the following manner:[1]

1. True income approach.
2. Decision model approach.
3. Individual user approach—behavioral.
4. Aggregate user approach—efficient markets.
5. Information economics approach.

## True Income Approach

Some accountants argue that if we search long enough, we will ultimately find the one proper method to account for various business transactions. This approach has been referred to as the **true income approach** because it implies that there is a single accounting method that will correctly identify the economic substance of a business transaction.

---

[1]The general approach to this section was heavily influenced by the AAA Committee on Concepts and Standards for External Financial Reports, *Statement on Accounting Theory and Theory Acceptance* (Sarasota: American Accounting Association, 1977).

Many of the writings in the early and mid-1900s, for example, seemed to adopt this position.[2] No consideration was given to the fact that information requirements might be different for different users of financial statements. These writers generally agreed that current values were superior to historical cost, although they differed as to how current values should be implemented. In short, the true income approach adopts the position that there is one correct reporting method and that research should be directed to finding this method.

## Decision Model Approach

In the **decision model** or **decision usefulness approach** to accounting theory formulation, an appropriate decision model based on the hypothesized needs of financial statement users is developed. For example, one theorist might argue that the greatest concern of users is that a company maintain its physical capacity. Using physical capacity as the economic attribute of interest to financial statement users, the theorist might then argue that replacement cost is the appropriate method for the valuation of business transactions. Conversely, another theorist might argue that command over consumer goods is the most important economic attribute of interest to financial statement users, and would suggest that selling prices or exit values are the appropriate bases for the valuation of business transactions. In other words, the decision model theorist establishes a set of normative assumptions about the goals, decisions, and information needs of users, and, given these assumptions, derives the accounting methods best suited for meeting these needs.

The decision model approach has been used to justify accounting methods based on (1) replacement cost, (2) selling price, and (3) present value of future cash flows.[3] The proponents of each accounting method argue forcefully that their method is correct, given their underlying assumptions as to what users of financial statements desire. Unlike the proponents of the true income approach, the decision model theorists acknowledge that different information may be needed for different users of the financial statements or for different kinds of decisions.

## Individual User Approach—Behavioral

Some accountants have suggested that accounting theory should be developed not by postulating a set of normative assumptions about how accounting information is used (decision model approach) but rather by examining actual user decision behavior. This approach has sometimes been referred to as the **individual user** or **behavioral approach** to accounting theory formulation.

To illustrate this approach, consider the current controversy over whether some form of price-level adjusted information should be reported in the financial statements. The behavioral/accounting theorist might solicit opinions from various financial statement users, primarily financial analysts and bankers, about the usefulness of price-level adjusted

[2]See, for example, John B. Canning, *The Economics of Accountancy* (New York: Ronald Press, 1929); Henry W. Sweeney, *Stabilized Accounting* (New York: Harper, 1936); Kenneth MacNeal, *Truth in Accounting,* (New York: Ronald Press, 1939).

[3]See, for example, Lawrence Revsine, *Replacement Cost Accounting* (Englewood Cliffs, N.J.: Prentice-Hall, 1973); Robert R. Sterling, *Theory of the Measurement of Enterprise Income* (Lawrence: University Press of Kansas, 1970); George J. Staubus, *A Theory of Accounting to Investors* (Berkeley: University of California Press, 1961).

information. If the majority of users indicated that price-level adjusted information would be useful, it would be argued that this information should be provided. Another technique used by behavioral theorists is to ask a group of financial statement users to make a series of investment or loan decisions based on some accounting information set, for example, conventional financial statements. Another group of users is then asked to make the same decisions on the basis of a different information set, for example, price-level adjusted financial statements. The decisions are then compared and the behavioral theorist attempts to infer which information set (conventional or price-level adjusted) is most useful.

## Aggregate User Approach—Efficient Markets

The **aggregate user** or **efficient market approach** holds that all publicly available information about a company is quickly incorporated into its stock price because of the sophistication of the many financial analysts and individual investors who comprise the stock market.[4] This approach does not say that the price of the stock is necessarily "correct" but rather that it reflects all publicly available information.

To illustrate the implications of the efficient market approach, suppose that we were concerned about whether price-level adjustments should be used to report financial information. Advocates of the efficient market approach would argue that, if reporting price-level adjusted information is a costless venture, both conventional and price-level adjusted information should be disclosed. Because the market is efficient, the marketplace will decide on what information to use. In other words, why be concerned about a specific reporting approach? Disclose the alternatives and the marketplace (aggregate users) will decide what information is useful.

Implicitly this approach suggests that if the information is publicly disclosed, the market as a whole cannot be fooled, although particular individual investors may be. For example, assume that two companies are exactly alike in all respects except that one company uses straight-line depreciation and the other accelerated depreciation. In such a case, one company will have higher reported profits than the other, but efficient market theorists would argue that the stock price would be the same as long as the alternative reporting methods are disclosed or can be computed from available financial information. The market is not fooled by this difference in accounting methods.

## Information Economics Approach

The **information economics approach** to accounting theory maintains that all accounting reporting decisions should be evaluated within a cost-benefit framework. Essentially this approach looks upon accounting information as a commodity, just as bread and butter are commodities, and asks what the costs of producing this commodity are and what the benefits are.[5] For example, comments are often made that a given reporting alternative is too costly in view of the benefits obtained, but few attempts have been made to measure the costs and benefits. Conversely, to say simply that a reporting method reflects the economic

---

[4]See, for example, William H. Beaver, "What Should Be the FASB Objectives?" *The Journal of Accountancy* (August 1973), for a simplified explanation of this approach.

[5]See, for example, Joel Demski, "Choice Among Financial Reporting Alternatives," *Accounting Review* (April 1974).

substance of a transaction and, therefore, should be used is equally inappropriate. What must be considered are all the possible ramifications (costs and benefits) of using this approach.[6]

To illustrate, the FASB mandated that ordinarily all research and development costs should be expensed as incurred. Assuming that this treatment reflects the economic substance of the situation, does it necessarily follow that we should adopt the FASB's mandate? One might argue that to report research and development expenditures in such a manner might incur social costs that far outweigh the benefits. For example, forcing companies to expense research and development costs as incurred might result in curtailment of their research and development projects, which might produce long-run social consequences that are undesirable.

In the FASB's study on foreign currency translation two studies were commissioned. The first tried to determine whether stock price behavior is significantly affected by the manner in which foreign exchange gains and losses are reported. This stock market study concluded that the method of reporting translation gains and losses had no significant effect on the stock price of the company involved. A second study attempted to determine whether companies would forgo profitable investments overseas or employ foreign exchange practices that might be considered uneconomical because of the way foreign currency translation gains and losses were reported. The conclusion was that the accounting standard was causing business enterprises to make bad economic decisions. Just recently the FASB changed the method of reporting foreign currency translations.[7]

## Concluding Remarks

We have tried to provide a brief overview of the alternative approaches to theory formulation currently being discussed in the accounting literature. Up until the late 1950s, the true income approach appeared to be the general theory used by most accountants to resolve accounting controversies. However, since that time, the emphasis has changed considerably. For example, *FASB Concepts No. 1,* "Objectives of Financial Reporting by Business Enterprises," appears to endorse a decision model approach whose objective is the prediction of future cash flows. In addition, there is evidence that the FASB has become more cognizant of other areas as well, such as the efficient markets and the information economics approaches. To illustrate, the FASB has become more willing to rely on disclosure standards rather than measurement standards to address certain reporting issues (this is in concert with aspects of the efficient market literature). Similarly, by incorporating cost-benefit considerations into the accounting policy-making area, aspects of information economics are utilized.

Although the descriptions of these various approaches are necessarily brief, it is hoped that they provide sufficient insight into the essence of each approach and a better understanding of our existing approach.

---

[6]Recently the FASB has been attempting to assess the economic consequences of accounting standards issued. To illustrate, studies were commissioned on *FASB Statement No. 5,* "Accounting for Contingencies;" *FASB Statement No. 8,* "Accounting for the Translation of Foreign Currency Transactions and Foreign Financial Statements;" and *FASB Statement No. 19,* "Financial Reporting by Oil and Gas Producing Companies."

[7]"Foreign Currency Translation," *Statement of Financial Accounting Standards No. 52* (Stamford, Conn.: 1982).

**Note:** All **asterisked** Questions, Cases, Exercises, and Problems relate to material contained in the appendix to each chapter.

## QUESTIONS

1. What is a conceptual framework? Why is a conceptual framework necessary in financial accounting?

2. What are the primary objectives of financial reporting as indicated in *Statement of Financial Accounting Concepts No. 1*?

3. What is meant by the term "qualitative characteristics of accounting information"?

4. Briefly describe the two primary qualities of useful accounting information.

5. What is the distinction between comparability and consistency?

6. Discuss whether the changes described in each of the cases below require recognition in the CPA's opinion as to consistency (assume that the amounts are material).
   (a) After three years of computing depreciation under the declining balance method for income tax purposes and under the straight-line method for reporting purposes, the company adopted the declining balance method for reporting purposes.
   (b) The company disposed of one of the two subsidiaries that had been included in its consolidated statements for prior years.
   (c) The estimated remaining useful life of plant property was reduced because of obsolescence.
   (d) The company is using an inventory valuation method that is different from all those used by other companies in its industry.

7. Why is it necessary to develop a definitional framework for the basic elements of accounting?

8. Expenses, losses, and distributions to owners are all decreases in net assets. What is the distinction among them?

9. Revenues, gains, and investments by owners are all increases in net assets. What is the distinction between them?

10. What are the four basic assumptions that underlie the financial accounting structure?

11. If the going-concern assumption is not made in accounting, what difference does it make in the amounts shown in the financial statements for the following items?
    (a) Land.
    (b) Unamortized bond premium.
    (c) Depreciation expense on equipment.
    (d) Long-term investments in common stocks of other companies.
    (e) Merchandise inventory.
    (f) Prepaid insurance.

12. The life of a business is divided into specific time periods, usually a year, to measure results of operations for each such time period and to portray financial conditions at the end of each period.
    (a) This practice is based on the accounting assumption that the life of the business consists of a series of time periods and that it is possible to measure accurately the results of operations for each period. Comment on the validity and necessity of this assumption.
    (b) What has been the effect of this practice on accounting? What is its relation to the accrual system? What influence has it had on accounting entries and methodology?

13. What is the basic accounting problem created by the monetary unit assumption when there is significant inflation?

14. The chairman of the board of directors of the company for which you are chief accountant has told you that he is entirely out of sympathy with accounting figures based on cost. He believes that replacement values are of far more significance to the board of directors than "out-of-date costs." Present some arguments to convince him that accounting data should still be based on cost.

15. Develop an argument supporting the adjustment of cost figures in financial statements for general price-level changes, or at least, the preparation of supplementary statements adjusted for changes in the general price level.

16. When is revenue generally recognized? Why has the date of sale been chosen as the point at which to recognize the revenue resulting from the entire producing and selling process?

17. What is the justification for the following deviations from recognizing revenue at the time of sale?
    (a) Installment sales method of recognizing revenue.
    (b) Recognition of revenue during production for certain agricultural products.
    (c) The percentage-of-completion basis in long-term construction contracts.

18. Bradley Company paid $81,000 for a machine in 1980. The Accumulated Depreciation account has a balance of $27,000 at the present time. The company could sell the machine today for $94,000. The company president believes that the company has a "right to this gain." What does the president mean by this statement? Do you agree?

19. Three expense recognition points (associating cause and effect, systematic and rational allocation, and immediate recognition) were discussed in the text under the matching principle. Indicate the basic nature of each of these types of expenses and give two examples of each.

20. Explain how you would decide whether to record each of the following expenditures as an asset or an expense.
    (a) Legal fees paid in connection with the purchase of land are $650.
    (b) Daley, Inc. paves the driveway leading to the office building at a cost of $9,000.
    (c) A meat market purchases a meat-grinding machine at a cost of $180.
    (d) On June 30, Smith and Johnson, medical doctors, pay six months' office rent to cover the month of June and the next five months.
    (e) The Logan Hardware Company pays $3,000 in wages to laborers for construction on a building to be used in the business.
    (f) Sally's Florists pays wages of $1,400 for November to an employee who serves as driver of their delivery truck.

21. Briefly describe the types of information concerning financial position, income, and cash flows that might be provided: (a) within the main body of the financial statements, (b) in the notes to the financial statements, or (c) as supplementary information.

22. In February 1984, Dain, Inc. doubled the amount of its outstanding stock by selling on the market an additional 10,000 shares to finance an expansion of the business. You propose that this information be shown by a footnote on the balance sheet as of December 31, 1983. The president objects, claiming that this sale took place after December 31, 1983 and, therefore, should not be shown. Explain your position.

23. Describe the two major constraints inherent in the presentation of accounting information.

24. What are some of the costs of providing accounting information? What are some of the benefits of accounting information? Describe the cost/benefit factors that should be considered when new accounting standards are being proposed.

25. How are materiality (and immateriality) related to the proper presentation of financial statements? What factors and measures should the CPA consider in assessing the materiality of a misstatement in the presentation of a financial statement?

26. The president of Egger Enterprises has heard that conservatism is a doctrine that is followed in accounting and, therefore, proposes that several policies be followed that are conservative in nature. State your opinion with respect to each of the policies listed below.
    (a) The inventory should be valued at "cost or market whichever is lower" because the losses from price declines should be recognized in the accounts in the period in which the price decline takes place.
    (b) The company gives a two-year warranty to its customers on all products sold. The estimated warranty costs incurred from this year's sales should be entered as an expense this year instead of an expense in the period in the future when the warranty is made good.
    (c) When sales are made on account, there is always uncertainty about whether the accounts are collectible. Therefore, the president recommends recording the sale when the cash is received from the customers.
    (d) A personal liability lawsuit is pending against the company. The president believes there is an even chance that the company will lose the suit and have to pay damages of $90,000 to

$150,000. The president recommends that a loss be recorded and a liability created in the amount of $150,000.

**\*27.** What is the difference between the true income and the decision model approach to resolving accounting controversies?

# CASES

**C2-1** Two students are discussing various aspects of the FASB's pronouncement, *Statement of Financial Accounting Concepts No. 1,* "Objectives of Financial Reporting by Business Enterprises." One student indicates that this pronouncement provides little, if any, guidance to the practicing professional in resolving accounting controversies. This student believes that the statement provides such broad guidelines that it would be impossible to apply the objectives to present-day reporting problems. The other student concedes this point, but indicates that objectives are still needed to provide a starting point for the FASB in helping to improve financial reporting.

**Instructions**

(a) Indicate the basic objectives established in *Statement of Financial Accounting Concepts No. 1.*

(b) What do you think is the meaning of the second student's statement that the FASB needs a starting point to resolve accounting controversies?

**C2-2** Accounting information provides useful information about business transactions and events. Those who provide and use financial reports must often select and evaluate accounting alternatives. *FASB Statement of Financial Accounting Concepts No. 2,* "Qualitative Characteristics of Accounting Information," examines the characteristics of accounting information that make it useful for decision making. It also points out that various limitations inherent in the measurement and reporting process may necessitate trade-offs or sacrifices among the characteristics of useful information.

(a) Describe briefly the following characteristics of useful accounting information:
1. Relevance.
2. Reliability.
3. Understandability.
4. Comparability.
5. Consistency.

(b) For each of the following pairs of information characteristics, give an example of a situation in which one of the characteristics may be sacrificed in return for a gain in the other:
1. Relevance and reliability.
2. Relevance and consistency.
3. Comparability and consistency.
4. Relevance and understandability.

(c) What criterion should be used to evaluate trade-offs between information characteristics?

**C2-3** The Financial Accounting Standards Board (FASB) has been working on a conceptual framework for financial accounting and reporting. The FASB has issued four *Statements of Financial Accounting Concepts.* These statements are intended to set forth objectives and fundamentals that will be the basis for developing financial accounting and reporting standards. The objectives identify the goals and purposes of financial reporting. The fundamentals are the underlying concepts of financial accounting—concepts that guide the selection of transactions, events, and circumstances to be accounted for; their recognition and measurement; and the means of summarizing and communicating them to interested parties.

The purpose of *Statement of Financial Accounting Concepts No. 2,* "Qualitative Characteristics of Accounting Information," is to examine the characteristics that make accounting information useful. The characteristics or qualities of information discussed in *Concepts No. 2* are the ingredients that make information useful and are the qualities to be sought when accounting choices are made.

**Instructions**

    (a) Identify and discuss the benefits which can be expected to be derived from the FASB's conceptual framework study.

    (b) What is the most important quality for accounting information as identified in *Statement of Financial Accounting Concepts No. 2* and explain why it is the most important.

    (c) *Statement of Financial Accounting Concepts No. 2* describes a number of key characteristics or qualities for accounting information. Briefly discuss the importance of any three of these qualities for financial reporting purposes.

(CMA adapted)

**C2–4** *FASB Concepts Statement No. 2* identifies the qualitative characteristics that make accounting information useful. Presented below are a number of questions related to these qualitative characteristics and underlying constraints.

    **1.** Rochester switches from FIFO to LIFO to FIFO over a two-year period. Which qualitative characteristic of accounting information is not followed?

    **2.** Assume that the profession permits the savings and loan industry to defer losses on investments it sells because immediate recognition of the loss may have adverse economic consequences on the industry. Which qualitative characteristic of accounting information is not followed? (Do not use reliability.)

    **3.** What are the two primary qualities that make accounting information useful for decision making?

    **4.** Cross, Inc. does not issue its second quarter report until after the third quarter's results are reported. Which qualitative characteristic of accounting is not followed? (Do not use relevance.)

    **5.** Predictive value is an ingredient of which of the two primary qualities that make accounting information useful for decision-making purposes?

    **6.** Leggett, Inc. is the only company in its industry to depreciate its plant assets on a straight-line basis. Which qualitative characteristic of accounting information may not be followed? (Do not use industry practices.)

    **7.** Laclede Company has attempted to determine the replacement cost of its inventory. Three different appraisers arrive at substantially different amounts for this value. The president, nevertheless, decides to report the middle value for external reporting purposes. Which qualitative characteristics of information are lacking in this data? (Do not use reliability or representational faithfulness.)

    **8.** What is the quality of information that enables users to confirm or correct prior expectations?

    **9.** Identify the two overall or pervasive constraints developed in *Statement of Financial Accounting Concepts No. 2*.

    **10.** The chairman of the SEC at one time noted that "if it becomes accepted or expected that accounting principles are determined or modified in order to secure purposes other than economic measurement—we assume a grave risk that confidence in the credibility of our financial information system will be undermined." Which qualitative characteristic of accounting information should ensure that such a situation will not occur? (Do not use reliability.)

**C2–5** Presented below is a statement that appeared about Weyerhaeuser Company in a financial magazine.

> The land and timber holdings are now carried on the company's books at a mere $422 million. The value of the timber alone is variously estimated at from $3 billion to $7 billion and is rising all the time. "The understatement of the company is pretty severe," conceded Charles W. Bingham, a senior vice-president. Adds Robert L. Schuyler, another senior vice-president: "We have a whole stream of profit nobody sees and there is no way to show it on our books."

**Instructions**

    (a) What does Schuyler mean when he says that "we have a whole stream of profit nobody sees and there is no way to show it on our books?"

    (b) If the understatement of the company's assets is severe, why does accounting not report this information?

**C2-6** On June 6, 1983, Burndy Corporation signed a contract with Mark Associates under which Mark agreed (1) to construct an office building on land owned by Burndy, (2) to accept responsibility for procuring financing for the project and finding tenants, and (3) to manage the property for 35 years. The annual net income from the project, after debt service, was to be divided equally between Burndy Corporation and Mark Associates. Mark was to accept its share of future net income as full payment for its services in construction, obtaining finances and tenants, and management of the project.

    By May 31, 1984, the project was nearly completed and tenants had signed leases to occupy 90% of the available space at annual rentals aggregating $3,000,000. It is estimated that, after operating expenses and debt service, the annual net income will amount to $1,100,000. The management of Mark Associates believed that the economic benefit derived from the contract with Burndy should be reflected on its financial statements for the fiscal year ended May 31, 1984 and directed that revenue be accrued in an amount equal to the commercial value of the services Mark had rendered during the year, that this amount be carried in contracts receivable, and that all related expenditures be charged against the revenue.

**Instructions**

    (a) Explain the main difference between the economic concept of business income as reflected by Mark's management and the measurement of income under generally accepted accounting principles.

    (b) Discuss the factors to be considered in determining when revenue should be recognized for the purpose of accounting measurement of periodic income.

    (c) Is the belief of Mark's management in accord with generally accepted accounting principles for the measurement of revenue and expense for the year ended May 31, 1984? Support your opinion by discussing the application to this case of the factors to be considered for asset measurement and revenue and expense recognition.

                                                               (AICPA adapted)

**C2-7** After the presentation of your report on the examination of the financial statements to the board of directors of the CCI Publishing Company, one of the new directors expresses surprise that the income statement assumes that an equal proportion of the revenue is earned with the publication of every issue of the company's magazine. She feels that the "crucial event" in the process of earning revenue in the magazine business is the cash sale of the subscription. She says that she does not understand why most of the revenue cannot be "recognized" in the period of the sale.

**Instructions**

    (a) List the various accepted methods for recognizing revenue in the accounts and explain when the methods are appropriate.

    (b) Discuss the propriety of timing the recognition of revenue in the CCI Publishing Company's account with:

        1. The cash sale of the magazine subscription.

        2. The publication of the magazine every month.

        3. Both events, by recognizing a portion of the revenue with cash sale of the magazine subscription and a portion of the revenue with the publication of the magazine every month.

                                                                (AICPA adapted)

**C2-8** A common objective of accountants is to prepare income statements that are as accurate as possible. A basic requirement in preparing accurate income statements is to match costs against revenues properly. Proper matching of costs against revenues requires that costs resulting from typical business operations be recognized in the period in which they expired.

**Instructions**

    (a) List three criteria that can be used to determine whether such typical costs should appear as charges in the income statement for the current period.

    (b) As generally presented in financial statements, the following items or procedures have been criticized as improperly matching costs with revenues. Briefly discuss each item from the viewpoint of matching costs with revenues and suggest corrective or alternative means of presenting the financial information.

        1. Receiving and handling costs.

        2. Valuation of inventories at the lower of cost or market.

        3. Cash discounts on purchases.

**C2-9** An accountant must be familiar with the concepts involved in determining earnings of a business entity. The amount of earnings reported for a business entity is dependent on the proper recognition, in general, of revenue and expense for a given time period. In some situations, costs are recognized as expenses at the time of product sale; in other situations, guidelines have been developed for recognizing costs as expenses or losses by other criteria.

**Instructions**

    (a) Explain the rationale for recognizing costs as expenses at the time of product sale.

    (b) What is the rationale underlying the appropriateness of treating costs as expenses of a period instead of assigning the costs to an asset? Explain.

    (c) In what general circumstances would it be appropriate to treat a cost as an asset instead of as an expense? Explain.

    (d) Some expenses are assigned to specific accounting periods on the basis of systematic and rational allocation of asset cost. Explain the underlying rationale for recognizing expenses on the basis of systematic and rational allocation of asset cost.

    (e) Identify the conditions in which it would be appropriate to treat a cost as a loss.

                                                (AICPA adapted)

**C2-10** Bassett Homes sells and erects shell houses, that is, frame structures that are completely finished on the outside but are unfinished on the inside except for flooring, partition studding, and ceiling joists. Shell houses are sold chiefly to customers who are handy with tools and who have time to do the interior wiring, plumbing, wall completion and finishing, and other work necessary to make the shell houses livable dwellings.

    Bassett buys shell houses from a manufacturer in unassembled packages consisting of all lumber, roofing, doors, windows, and similar materials necessary to complete a shell house. Upon commencing operations in a new area, Bassett buys or leases land as a site for its local warehouse, field office, and display houses. Sample display houses are erected at a total cost of from $3,600 to $7,700 including the cost of the unassembled packages. The chief element of cost of the display houses is the unassembled packages, inasmuch as erection is a short low-cost operation. Old sample models are torn down or altered into new models every three to seven years. Sample display houses have little salvage value because dismantling and moving costs amount to nearly as much as the cost of an unassembled package.

**Instructions**

    (a) A choice must be made between (1) expensing the costs of sample display houses in the periods in which the expenditure is made and (2) spreading the costs over more than one period. Discuss the advantages of each method.

    (b) Would it be preferable to amortize the cost of display houses on the basis of (1) the passage of time or (2) the number of shell houses sold? Explain.

                                                (AICPA adapted)

**C2-11** You are engaged in the audit of Prime Computer, Inc., which opened its first branch office in 1984. During the audit Sharon Walters, president, raises the question of the accounting treatment of the operating loss of the branch office for its first year, which is material in amount.

The president proposes to capitalize the operating loss as a "starting-up" expense to be amortized over a five-year period. She states that branch offices of other firms engaged in the same field generally suffer a first-year operating loss that is invariably capitalized, and you are aware of this practice. She argues, therefore, that the loss should be capitalized so that the accounting will be "conservative"; further, she argues that the accounting must be "consistent" with established industry practice.

**Instructions**

Discuss the president's use of the words "conservative" and "consistent" from the standpoint of accounting terminology. Discuss the accounting treatment you would recommend.

(AICPA adapted)

**C2–12** The general ledger of ABS, Inc., a corporation engaged in the development and production of television programs for commercial sponsorship, contains the following accounts before amortization at the end of the current year:

| Account | Balance (Debit) |
| --- | --- |
| LaVerne & Hirley | $60,000 |
| Superhero | 41,000 |
| The Badman | 21,500 |
| Spacetrack | 9,000 |
| Studio Rearrangement | 4,000 |

An examination of contracts and records revealed the following information:

1. The first two accounts listed above represent the total cost of completed programs that were televised during the accounting period just ended. Under the terms of an existing contract LaVerne & Hirley will be rerun during the next accounting period, at a fee equal to 50% of the fee for the first televising of the program. The contract for the first run produced $600,000 of revenue. The contract with the sponsor of Superhero provides that he may, at his option, rerun the program during the next season at a fee of 75% of the fee on the first televising of the program.

2. The balance in The Badman account is the cost of a new program that has just been completed and is being considered by several companies for commercial sponsorship.

3. The balance in the Spacetrack account represents the cost of a partially completed program for a projected series that has been abandoned.

4. The balance of the Studio Rearrangement account consists of payments made to a firm of engineers that prepared a report relative to the more efficient utilization of existing studio space and equipment.

**Instructions**

(a) State the general principle (or principles) of accounting that are applicable to the first four accounts.

(b) How would you report each of the first four accounts in the financial statements of ABS, Inc.? Explain.

(c) In what way, if at all, does the Studio Rearrangement account differ from the first four? Explain.

(AICPA adapted)

**\*C2–13** Two students in intermediate accounting are arguing about the merits of various theory approaches to resolving financial reporting controversies. The first student indicates that we should develop some type of normative criterion, such as prediction of cash flows, and then decide which accounting procedure or which reporting approach best meets this criterion. The second student believes that an analysis of the costs and the benefits of a proposed accounting alternative should be determined, and then, after assessing the costs and benefits, it can be determined whether or not this alternative should be selected.

**Instructions**

    (a) What general type of theory approach involves the establishment of some normative criterion, such as prediction of cash flows, to resolve accounting controversies? Discuss.

    (b) What general approach is employed when the costs and benefits of a proposed accounting standard are examined? Discuss.

# PROBLEMS

**P2–1** Each of the following statements represents a decision made by the controller of King Enterprises on which your advice is asked.

    **1.** Material included in the inventory that cost $90,000 has become obsolete. The controller contends that no loss can be recognized until the goods are sold, and so the material is included in the inventory at $90,000.

    **2.** Inasmuch as profits for the year appear to be extremely small, no depreciation of fixed assets is to be recorded as an expense this year.

    **3.** The company occupies the building in which it operates under a long-term lease requiring annual rental payments. It sublets certain office space not required for its own purposes. The controller credits rents received against rents paid to get net rent expense.

    **4.** A fire during the year destroyed or damaged a considerable amount of uninsured inventory. No entry was made for this loss because the controller reasons that the ending inventory will, of course, be reduced by the amount of the destroyed or damaged merchandise, and therefore its cost will be included in cost of goods sold and the net income figure will be correct.

    **5.** The company provides housing for certain employees and adjusts their salaries accordingly. The controller contends that the cost to the company of maintaining this housing should be charged to "Wages and Salaries."

    **6.** The entire cost of a new delivery truck is to be charged to an expense account.

    **7.** King Enterprises has paid a large sum for an advertising campaign to promote a new product that will not be placed on the market until the following year. The controller has charged this amount to a prepaid expense account.

    **8.** The company operates a cafeteria for the convenience of its employees. Sales made by the cafeteria are credited to the regular sales account for product sales; food purchased and salaries paid for the cafeteria operations are recorded in the regular purchase and payroll accounts.

    **9.** A customer leaving the building slipped on an icy spot on the stairway and wrenched his back. He immediately entered suit against the company for permanent physical injuries and claims damages in the amount of $110,000. The suit has not yet come to trial. The controller has made an entry charging a special loss account and crediting a liability account.

    **10.** A building purchased by the company five years ago at $75,000, including the land on which it stands, can now be sold for $115,000. The controller instructs that the new value of $115,000 be entered in the accounts.

**Instructions**

    You are to state (a) whether you agree with his decision and (b) the reasons supporting your position. Consider each decision independently of all others.

**P2–2** Presented below are a number of facts related to Standard Industries Co. Assume that no mention of these facts was made in the financial statements and the related footnotes.

    (a) The company changed its method of depreciating equipment from the double-declining balance to the straight-line method. No mention of this change was made in the financial statements.

(b) The company decided that, for the sake of conciseness, only net income should be reported on the income statement. Details as to revenues, cost of goods sold, and expenses were omitted.

(c) Equipment purchases of $90,000 were partly financed during the year through the issuance of a $60,000 notes payable. The company offset the equipment against the notes payable and reported plant assets at $30,000.

(d) The company is a defendant in a patent-infringement suit involving a material amount; you have received assurance from the company's counsel that the possibility of loss is remote.

(e) During the year, an assistant controller for the company embezzled $6,000. Standard's net income for the year was $1,600,000. The assistant controller and the money have not been found.

(f) Because of a recent gasoline shortage, it is possible that Standard may suffer a costly shutdown in the near future similar to those suffered by other companies both within and outside the industry.

(g) Standard has reported its ending inventory at $1,400,000 in the financial statements. No other information related to inventories is presented in the financial statements and related footnotes.

### Instructions

Assume that you are the auditor of Standard Industries, and that you have been asked to explain the appropriate accounting and related disclosure necessary for each of these items.

**P2-3** Presented below is information related to MacNeil, Inc.

(a) Depreciation expense on the building for the year was $23,000. Because the building was increasing in value during the year, the controller decided to charge the depreciation expense to retained earnings instead of to net income. The following entry is recorded.

| | | |
|---|---|---|
| Retained Earnings | 23,000 | |
|    Accumulated Depreciation—Buildings | | 23,000 |

(b) Materials were purchased on January 1, 1983 for $60,000 and this amount was entered in the Materials account. On December 31, 1983, the materials would have cost $72,000, so the following entry is made.

| | | |
|---|---|---|
| Inventory | 12,000 | |
|    Gain on Inventories | | 12,000 |

(c) An order for $16,000 has been received from a customer for products on hand. This order was shipped on January 10, 1984. The company made the following entry in 1983.

| | | |
|---|---|---|
| Accounts Receivable | 16,000 | |
|    Sales | | 16,000 |

(d) During the year, the company purchased equipment through the issuance of common stock. The stock had a par value of $70,000 and a fair market value of $300,000. The fair market value of the equipment was not easily determinable. The company recorded this transaction as follows:

| | | |
|---|---|---|
| Equipment | 70,000 | |
|    Common Stock | | 70,000 |

(e) During the year, the company sold certain equipment for $110,000, recognizing a gain of $7,000. Because the controller believed that new equipment would be needed in the near future, the controller decided to defer the gain and amortize it over the life of any new equipment purchased.

### Instructions

Comment on the appropriateness of the accounting procedures followed by MacNeil, Inc.

**P2–4** Each of the items below involves the question of materiality to Sanchez, Inc.

1. It is expected that purchase returns and allowances made in 1984 in the amount of $10,000 will represent returns and allowances on purchases made in 1983. This is a typical amount of returns and allowances made at the beginning of each year on sales made in the preceding year.

2. The company purchases hundreds of items of equipment each year that cost less than $80 each. Most of them are used for several years, but some of them last for less than a year. The total cost of these purchases is about the same each year.

3. The amount of $900 is paid during 1983 for an assessment of additional income taxes for the year 1981. The amount originally paid in 1981 was $24,000, and the amount of this year's income taxes will be $30,000.

4. Land that had originally been purchased for expansion is sold in 1984 at a gain of $7,000. Net income for the year is $53,000, including the gain of $7,000. The company has experienced similar types of gains in the past.

**Instructions**

State your recommendation as to how each item should be treated in the accounts and in the statements, giving proper consideration to materiality and practicability aspects.

**P2–5** A number of operational guidelines used by accountants are described below.

1. Shopko Discount Centers buys its merchandise by the truck and train-carload. Shopko does not defer any transportation costs in computing the cost of its ending inventory. Such costs, although varying from period to period, are always material in amount.

2. Dinner Bell, Inc., a fast-food company, sells franchises for $70,000, accepting a $500 down payment and a 50-year note for the remainder. Dinner Bell promises within 3 years to assist in site selection, building, and management training. Dinner Bell records the $70,000 franchise fee as revenue in the period in which the contract is signed.

3. Pogo Chemical Company "faces possible expropriation [i.e., take-over] of foreign facilities and possible losses on sums owed by various customers on the verge of bankruptcy." The company president has decided that these possibilities should not be noted on the financial statements because Pogo still hopes that these events will not take place.

4. The treasurer of Almadin Co. wishes to prepare financial statements only during downturns in their wine production, which occur periodically when the rhubarb crop fails. He states that it is at such times that the statements could be most easily prepared. In no event would more than 30 months pass without statements being prepared.

5. The RST Power & Light Company has purchased a large amount of property, plant, and equipment over a number of years. They have decided that because the general price level has changed materially over the years, they will issue only price-level adjusted financial statements.

6. Dixie Manufacturing Co. decided to manufacture its own widgets because it would be cheaper to do so than to buy them from an outside supplier. In an attempt to make their statements more comparable with those of their competitors, Dixie charged its inventory account for what they felt the widgets would have cost if they had been purchased from an outside supplier. (Do not use revenue recognition principle.)

7. Gerry Lobo, manager of University Bookstore, Inc., bought a computer for his own use. He paid for the computer by writing a check on the Bookstore checking account and charged the "Office Equipment" account.

8. Stevenson, Inc. recently completed a new 120-story office building which houses their home offices and many other tenants. All the office equipment for the building which had a per item or per unit cost of $1,000 or less was expensed as immaterial even though the office equipment has an average life of 10 years. The total cost of such office equipment was approximately $25 million. (Do not use the matching principle.)

9. A large lawsuit has been filed against Losso Corp. by Miller Co. Losso has recorded a loss and related estimated liability equal to the maximum possible amount it feels it might lose. They are confident, however, that either they will not lose the suit or they will owe a much smaller amount.

10. The AICPA, in an accounting guide for brokers and other dealers in securities, stated that "the trading and investment accounts...should be valued at market or fair value for financial reporting purposes...." The brokerage firm of Swab and Cummings, Inc. continues to value its trading and investment accounts at cost or market, whichever is lower.

**Instructions**

For each of the foregoing, list the assumption, principle, or constraint that has been violated. In each case, except where noted, list only one term.

**P2-6** Presented below are a number of operational guidelines and practices that have developed over time.

1. Price-level changes are not recognized in the accounting records.

2. Lower of cost or market is used to value inventories.

3. Financial information is presented so that reasonably prudent investors will not be misled.

4. Intangibles are capitalized and amortized over periods benefited.

5. Repair tools are expensed when purchased.

6. Brokerage firms use market value for purposes of valuation of all marketable securities.

7. Each enterprise is kept as a unit distinct from its owner or owners.

8. All significant postbalance sheet events are reported.

9. Revenue is recorded at point of sale.

10. All important aspects of bond indentures are presented in financial statements.

11. Rationale for accrual accounting is stated.

12. The use of consolidated statements is justified.

13. Reporting must be done at defined time intervals.

14. An allowance for doubtful accounts is established.

15. All payments out of petty cash are charged to Miscellaneous Expense. (Do not use conservatism.)

16. Anticipate no profits and recognize all possible losses.

17. Goodwill is recorded only at time of purchase.

**Instructions**

Select the assumption, principle, or constraint that most appropriately justifies these procedures and practices. (Do not use qualitative characteristics.)

**P2-7** Presented below are a number of business transactions that occurred during the current year for Bower, Inc.

1. The president of Bower, Inc. used his expense account to purchase a new automobile solely for personal use. The following entry was made:

| | | |
|---|---|---|
| Miscellaneous Expense | 8,000 | |
| Cash | | 8,000 |

2. Because of a "fire sale," equipment obviously worth $150,000 was acquired at a cost of $100,000. The following entry was made:

| | | |
|---|---|---|
| Equipment | 150,000 | |
| Cash | | 100,000 |
| Income | | 50,000 |

3. Merchandise inventory which cost $390,000 is reported on the balance sheet at $480,000, the expected selling price less estimated selling costs. The following entry was made to record this increase in value:

| | | |
|---|---|---|
| Merchandise Inventory | 90,000 | |
| Income | | 90,000 |

4. The company is being sued for $400,000 by a customer who claims damages for personal injury apparently caused by a defective product. Company attorneys feel extremely confident that the company will have no liability for damages resulting from the situation. Nevertheless, the company decides to make the following entry:

| | | |
|---|---|---|
| Loss from Lawsuit | 400,000 | |
| Liability for Lawsuit | | 400,000 |

5. Bower, Inc. has been concerned about whether intangible assets could generate cash in case of liquidation. As a consequence, goodwill arising from a purchase transaction during the current year and recorded at $700,000 was written off as follows:

| | | |
|---|---|---|
| Retained Earnings | 700,000 | |
| Goodwill | | 700,000 |

6. Because the general level of prices increased during the current year, Bower, Inc. determined that there was a $9,000 understatement of depreciation expense on its equipment and decided to record it in its accounts. The following entry was made:

| | | |
|---|---|---|
| Depreciation Expense | 9,000 | |
| Accumulated Depreciation | | 9,000 |

**Instructions**

In each of the situations above, discuss the appropriateness of the journal entries in accordance with generally accepted accounting principles.

**P2–8** You are engaged to review the accounting records of Bob Corporation prior to the closing of the revenue and expense accounts as of December 31, the end of the current fiscal year. The following information comes to your attention.

1. The company decided in October of the current fiscal year to start a massive advertising campaign to enhance the marketability of their product. In November, the company paid $500,000 for advertising time on a major television network to advertise their product during the next twelve months. The controller expensed the $500,000 in the current year on the basis that "once the money is spent, it can never be recovered from the television network."

2. In preparing the balance sheet, detailed information as to the amount of cash on deposit in each of several banks was omitted. Only the total amount of cash under a caption "Cash in banks" was presented.

3. On August 10 of the current year, Bob Corporation purchased an undeveloped tract of land at a cost of $285,000. The company spent $70,000 in subdividing the land and getting it ready for sale. An appraisal of the property at the end of the year indicated that the land was now worth $430,000. Although none of the lots were sold, the company recognized revenue of $145,000, less related expenses of $70,000, for a net income on the project of $75,000.

4. For a number of years the company had used the average cost method for inventory valuation purposes. During the current year, the president noted that all the other companies in their industry had switched to the LIFO method. The company decided not to switch to LIFO because net income would decrease $800,000.

5. During the current year, Bob Corporation changed its policy in regard to expensing purchases of small tools. In the past, these purchases had always been expensed because they amounted to less than 2% of net income, but the president has decided that capitalization and subsequent depreciation should now be followed. It is expected that purchases of small tools will not fluctuate greatly from year to year.

6. Bob Corporation constructed a warehouse at a cost of $400,000. The company had been depreciating the asset on a straight-line basis over ten years. In the current year, the controller doubled depreciation expense because the replacement cost of the warehouse had increased significantly.

**Instructions**

State whether or not you agree with the decisions made by Bob Corporation. Support your answers with reference, whenever possible, to the generally accepted principles and assumptions applicable in the circumstances.

# CHAPTER 3

# A Review of the Accounting Process

Accounting systems vary widely from one business to another, depending on the **nature of the business** and the transactions in which it engages, the **size of the firm,** the **volume of data** to be handled, and the **informational demands** that management and others place on the system.

The broadest definition of an accounting system includes all of the activities required to provide management with the quantified information needed for planning, controlling, and reporting the financial condition and operations of the enterprise. Managers and investors who are confronted with questions such as those listed below depend on the accounting system for the answers.

What is the composition of our asset structure?
What is the amount of invested and earned capital?
Did we make a profit last period?
What did it cost us to produce one unit of product?
Were our sales higher this period than last?
Are any of our product lines or divisions operating at a loss?
Can we safely increase our dividends to stockholders?
Is our rate of return on net assets increasing?

Many similar questions can be answered when there is an efficient accounting system to provide the data. A well-devised accounting system is a necessity for every business enterprise. For many companies, the matter of maintaining a set of accounting records is not optional. The Internal Revenue Service has long required that businesses prepare and retain a set of records and documents that are a financial history that can be audited. And, in 1977, the U.S. Congress enacted the Foreign Corrupt Practices Act which requires public companies to "... make and keep books, records, and accounts, which, in reasonable detail, accurately and fairly reflect the transactions and dispositions of the assets. ..." A company that does not keep an accurate record of its business transactions is likely to lose revenue and to operate inefficiently. Although most companies have satisfactory accounting systems, many companies are inefficient partly because of poor accounting procedures.

Consider, for example, the Long Island Railroad,[1] one of the nation's busiest commuter lines, which lost money at one time because its cash position was unknown; large amounts of money owed the railroad had not been billed; some payables were erroneously paid twice; and redemptions of bonds were not recorded. Although this situation is rare in large enterprises, it illustrates our point: accounts and detailed records must be kept by every business enterprise.

## PROCEDURES EMPLOYED IN ACCOUNTING

Financial accounting rests on a framework of rules for identifying, recording, classifying, and interpreting transactions and other events relating to enterprises. These rules are derived from the concepts discussed in Chapters 1 and 2. It is important that the accountant understand the **basic terminology employed in collecting accounting data.** The terms most commonly used are defined below.

### Basic Terminology

**EVENT.** A happening of consequence to an entity. An event generally is the source or cause of changes in assets, liabilities, and equity. Events may be categorized as external and internal.

**TRANSACTION.** An **external event** involving the transfer or exchange of something of value between two (or more) entities.

**ACCOUNT.** A systematic arrangement that shows the effect of transactions and other events on a specific asset or equity. A separate account is kept for each asset, liability, revenue, expense, and for capital (owners' equity).

**REAL AND NOMINAL ACCOUNTS.** Real accounts are asset, liability, and equity accounts and they appear on the balance sheet. Nominal (also called temporary) accounts are revenue and expense accounts; they appear on the income statement. Nominal accounts are periodically closed; real accounts are not.

**LEDGER.** The book (or computer printouts) containing the accounts. It usually has a separate page for each account. A **general ledger** is a collection of all the asset, liability, owners' equity, revenue, and expense accounts. A **subsidiary ledger** contains a group of accounts that constitute the details related to a specific general ledger account.

**JOURNAL.** The book of original entry where the essential facts and figures in connection with all transactions and selected other events are recorded initially. From the book of original entry the various amounts are transferred to the ledger.

**POSTING.** The mechanical (electronic) process of transferring the essential facts and figures from the book of original entry to the accounts in the ledger.

**TRIAL BALANCE.** A list of all open accounts in the ledger and their balances. A trial balance may be prepared at any time. A trial balance taken immediately after all adjustments have been posted is called an **adjusted trial balance.** A trial balance taken immediately after closing entries have been posted is designated an **after-closing** or **post-closing trial balance.**

**ADJUSTING ENTRIES.** Entries made at the end of an accounting period to bring all accounts up to date on an accrual accounting basis so that correct financial statements can be prepared.

**FINANCIAL STATEMENTS.** Statements that reflect the collection, tabulation, and final summarization of the accounting data. Basically four statements are involved: (1) the **balance sheet,**

---

[1]"Long Island Railroad is Said to Be Losing Revenue Due to 'Weak' Accounting System," *The Wall Street Journal* (February 19, 1971), p. 4.

which shows the financial condition of the enterprise at the end of a period, (2) the **income statement,** which measures the results of operations during the period, (3) the **statement of changes in financial position,** which measures the resources provided during the period and uses to which they are put, and (4) the **statement of retained earnings,** which reconciles the balance of the retained earnings account from the beginning to the end of the period.

**CLOSING ENTRIES.** The formal process by which all nominal accounts are reduced to zero and the net income or net loss is determined and transferred to the owners' equity is known as "closing the ledger," "closing the books," or merely "closing."

## DOUBLE-ENTRY ACCOUNTING RECORDING PROCESS

There are established rules for recording transactions and other events as they occur. These rules, often referred to as double-entry accounting, are the ones you probably learned in your basic principles course. Debit and credit in accounting simply mean left and right or, depending on the account, positive and negative. The left side of any account is the debit side; the right side, the credit side. In arithmetic, plus and minus signs indicate addition and subtraction; in accounting, addition or subtraction is indicated by the side of the account on which the amount is shown. All asset and expense accounts are increased on the left or debit side and decreased on the right or credit side. Conversely, all liability, revenue, and capital accounts are increased on the right or credit side and decreased on the left or debit side. The basic guidelines for an accounting system are presented below.

| Asset Accounts | | | | | Revenue Accounts | |
|---|---|---|---|---|---|---|
| Debit<br>+ (increase) | Credit<br>− (decrease) | | Owners' Equity | | Debit<br>− (decrease) | Credit<br>+ (increase) |
| Liability Accounts | | Debit<br>− (decrease) | Credit<br>+ (increase) | | Expense Accounts | |
| Debit<br>− (decrease) | Credit<br>+ (increase) | | | | Debit<br>+ (increase) | Credit<br>− (decrease) |

Assume a transaction in which service is rendered for cash. Two accounts are affected: both an asset account (Cash) and a revenue account (Sales) are increased. Cash is debited and Sales is credited. Therein are revealed the essentials of a **double-entry system**—for every debit there must be a credit and vice versa.

This leads us, then, to the basic equality in accounting:

$$\text{Assets} = \text{Liabilities} + \text{Owners' Equity}$$

Or simply:

$$\text{Assets} = \text{Equities}$$

Every time a transaction occurs, the elements of the equation change, but the basic equality remains. To illustrate, here are seven different transactions.

**1.** Investment by the owner of $30,000 for use in the business:

$$\text{Assets} = \text{Liabilities} + \text{Owners' Equity}$$
$$+30,000 \qquad\qquad +30,000$$

**2.** Disburses $600 cash for secretarial wages:

Assets = Liabilities + Owners' Equity

−600            −600 (expense)

**3.** Purchases office equipment priced at $5,200 giving a 10% promissory note in exchange:

Assets = Liabilities + Owners' Equity

+5,200    +5,200

**4.** Pays off a short-term liability of $7,000:

Assets = Liabilities + Owners' Equity

−7,000    −7,000

**5.** Declares a cash dividend of $5,000:

Assets = Liabilities + Owners' Equity

         +5,000     −5,000

**6.** Converts a long-term liability of $9,000 into common stock:

Assets = Liabilities + Owners' Equity

         −9,000     +9,000

**7.** Pays cash of $8,000 for a delivery van:

Assets = Liabilities + Owners' Equity

−8,000

+8,000

Revenue and expense accounts are elements of owners' equity. Revenues are increases or credits to owners' equity and expenses are decreases or debits. The difference between revenues and expenses for a period of time is the net increase (income) or net decrease (loss) in owners' equity.

## THE ACCOUNTING CYCLE

Using these definitions, accountants have established procedures for the periodic reporting of the effects of transactions and selected other events on an entity in the form of financial statements. The basic procedures normally used to ensure that the effects of transactions and selected other events are recorded correctly and transmitted to the user are often called the steps in the accounting cycle. The accounting cycle presented on page 67 (which is completed at least once each year) illustrates the necessary procedures followed from one accounting period to another.

## IDENTIFICATION AND RECORDING OF TRANSACTIONS AND OTHER EVENTS

The first step in the accounting cycle is analysis of transactions and selected other events. The problem is to determine what to record, that is, to **identify recordable events.** No simple rules exist that state whether an event should be recorded. For example, most accountants agree that changes in personnel, changes in managerial policies, and the value of human resources are important, but none of these items are recorded in the accounts. On the other hand, when the company makes a cash sale—no matter how small—we have no reservations about recording this transaction.

What makes the difference? Generally, two criteria are applied in determining whether an event or item should be recorded: Can the event or item **be measured objectively** (with reliability) in financial terms? And does this event or item **affect the financial position** of the company? If the answer to either question is no, the event should not be recorded.

**FIGURE 3–1**   The accounting cycle.

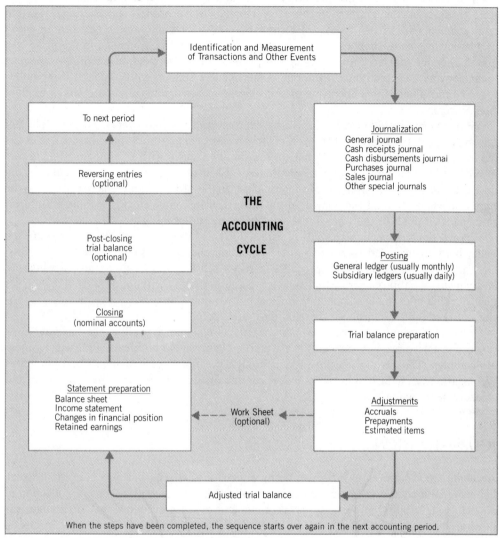

Events that can be measured and that directly affect the financial statements should be recorded. To illustrate, consider the problem of human resources. Should human resources be recognized on financial statements? R. G. Barry & Co., for example, at one time reported as supplemental data total assets of $14,055,926, including $986,094 for "net investments in human resources." Other companies, such as American Telephone and Telegraph and Mobil Oil Company, have also experimented with human resource accounting. Should accountants value employees for balance sheet purposes and also for income statement purposes? Certainly skilled employees are an important asset, but the problems of determining their value and measuring it objectively have not yet been solved. Consequently, human resources are not recorded; perhaps when measurement techniques become more sophisticated and accepted, such information will be presented, if only in supplemental form.

The phrase "transactions and other events and circumstances affecting an entity" is used to describe the sources or causes of changes in an entity's assets, liabilities, and equity.[2] **Events** are of two types: (1) **External events** involve interaction between an entity and its environment, such as a transaction with another entity, a change in the price of a good or service that an entity buys or sells, a flood or earthquake, or an improvement in technology by a competitor. (2) **Internal events** occur within an entity, such as using buildings and machinery in its operation or transferring or consuming raw materials in production processes.

Many events include elements of both external and internal events. For example, acquiring the services of employees or others involves exchange transactions, which are external events; using those services (labor), often simultaneously with their acquisition, is part of production, which is a series of internal events. Events may be initiated and controlled by an entity, such as the purchase of merchandise or the use of a machine, or they may be partly or wholly beyond the control of an entity and its management, such as an interest rate change, an act of theft or vandalism, or the imposition of taxes.[3]

**Transactions,** as particular kinds of external events, may be an exchange in which each entity both receives and sacrifices value, such as purchases and sales of goods or services. Or transactions may be nonreciprocal transfers (transfers in one direction) in which an entity incurs a liability or transfers an asset to another entity without directly receiving (or giving) value in exchange, such as investments by owners, distributions to owners, impositions of taxes, gifts, charitable contributions, and thefts.

In short, accountants record as many events as possible that affect the financial position of the enterprise, but some events are omitted because the problems of measuring them are complex. The accounting profession, through the efforts of individuals and numerous organizations, as indicated in Chapter 1, is continually working to refine its recognition and measurement techniques.

## JOURNALIZATION

**Accounts** are the means by which differing effects on the basic business elements (assets, liabilities, and equities) are categorized and collected. The **general ledger** is a collection of all the asset, liability, owners' equity, revenue, and expense accounts. A **"T" account** (as illustrated on page 70) is a convenient method of illustrating the effect of transactions on particular asset, liability, equity, revenue, and expense items.

In practice, transactions and selected other events are not recorded originally in the ledger because a transaction affects two or more different accounts, each of which is on a different page in the ledger. To circumvent this problem and to have a complete record of each transaction or other event in one place, a **journal** (the book of original entry) is employed. The simplest form of a journal is a chronological listing of transactions and selected other events expressed in terms of debits and credits to particular accounts. This type of journal is called a **general journal.** It is illustrated on page 69 for the following transactions.

---

[2]"Elements of Financial Statements of Business Enterprises," *Statement of Financial Accounting Concepts No. 3* (Stamford, Conn.: FASB, 1980), pars. 75–78.

[3]Ibid., pars. 75–78.

Nov.  1 Buys a new delivery truck on account from Yankee Motor Co., $14,700.

     3 Receives an invoice from the *Evening Journal* for advertising, $80.

     4 Returns merchandise to Ample Supply for credit, $175.

   16 Receives a $95 debit memo from Confederate Co., indicating that freight on a purchase from Confederate Co. was prepaid, terms f.o.b. shipping point.

Transactions and other events entered in the general journal record much the same data as are recorded in the "T" accounts. Each **general journal entry** consists of four parts: (1) the accounts and amounts to be debited (Dr.), (2) the accounts and amounts to be credited (Cr.), (3) a date, and (4) an explanation. The debit account titles and amounts are entered first, followed by the credit account titles and amounts, which are slightly indented to differentiate them from debits. The explanation is begun on the line below the name of the last account to be credited and may take one or more lines. The "Acct. No." column is completed at the time the accounts are posted.

| | GENERAL JOURNAL | | | Page 12 |
|---|---|---|---|---|
| Date 1983 | | Acct. No. | Amount Dr. | Cr. |
| Nov.  1 | Delivery Equipment | 8 | 14,700 | |
| |    Accounts Payable | 34 | | 14,700 |
| |    (Purchased delivery truck on account from Yankee Motor Co.) | | | |
| 3 | Advertising Expense | 65 | 80 | |
| |    Accounts Payable | 34 | | 80 |
| |    (Received invoice for advertising from *Evening Journal*) | | | |
| 4 | Accounts Payable | 34 | 175 | |
| |    Returned Purchases | 53 | | 175 |
| |    (Returned merchandise for credit to Ample Supply) | | | |
| 16 | Transportation-In | 55 | 95 | |
| |    Accounts Payable | 34 | | 95 |
| |    (Received debit memo for freight on merchandise purchased f.o.b. shipping point from Confederate Co.) | | | |

Most businesses use **special journals** in addition to the general journal. Special journals permit greater division of labor, reduce the time necessary to accomplish the various bookkeeping tasks, and summarize transactions possessing a common characteristic. Specialized journals are discussed in Appendix B at the end of this chapter.

## POSTING TO THE LEDGER

The items entered in a general journal must be transferred to the general ledger. This procedure, **posting,** is considered part of the summarizing and classifying activity of the accounting process. Because the debit and credit analysis of the transaction takes place as the entry is recorded in the general journal, posting consists of transferring to the proper ledger accounts the amounts entered in the general journal.

For example, the November 1 entry in the general journal expressed a debit to Delivery Equipment of $14,700 and a credit to Accounts Payable of $14,700. This entry indicates that the amount in the debit column is posted from the journal to the debit side of the ledger account, and that the amount in the credit column is posted from the journal to the credit side of the ledger account.

The numbers in the "Acct. No." column refer to the accounts in the ledger to which the respective items are posted. For example, the "8" to the right of the words "Delivery Equipment" means that Delivery Equipment is Account No. 8 in the ledger, to which the $14,700 was posted. Similarly, the "34" placed in the column to the right of "Accounts Payable" indicates that this $14,700 item was posted to Account No. 34 in the ledger. The posting of the general journal is completed when all of the posting reference numbers have been recorded opposite the account titles in the journal. Thus the number in the posting reference column serves two purposes: (1) to indicate the ledger account number of the account involved, and (2) to indicate that the posting has been completed for the particular item. Each business enterprise selects its own numbering system for its ledger accounts. One practice is to begin numbering with asset accounts and to follow with liabilities, owners' equities, revenue, and expense accounts, in that order.

The various ledger accounts affected by the journal entries in the preceding illustration appear below after the posting process is completed. The source of the data transferred to the ledger account is indicated by the reference GJ12 (General Journal, page 12).

| | | Delivery Equipment | | | No. 8 |
|---|---|---|---|---|---|
| Nov. 1 | GJ 12 | 14,700 | | | |
| | | Accounts Payable | | | No. 34 |
| Nov. 4 | GJ 12 | 175 | Nov. 1 | GJ 12 | 14,700 |
| | | | 3 | GJ 12 | 80 |
| | | | 16 | GJ 12 | 95 |
| | | Returned Purchases | | | No. 53 |
| | | | Nov. 4 | GJ 12 | 175 |
| | | Transportation-In | | | No. 55 |
| Nov. 16 | GJ 12 | 95 | | | |
| | | Advertising Expense | | | No. 65 |
| Nov. 3 | GJ 12 | 80 | | | |

## UNADJUSTED TRIAL BALANCE

At the end of a given period after the entries have been recorded in the journal and posted to the ledger, it is customary and desirable to prepare an unadjusted trial balance. A **trial**

**balance** is a list of all open accounts in the general ledger and their balances. The trial balance accomplishes two principal purposes:

1. It proves that debits and credits of an equal amount are in the ledger.
2. It supplies a listing of open accounts and their balances that is the basis for any adjustments and is used in preparing the financial statements and in supplying financial data about the concern.

The unadjusted trial balance for Ruddy Bros. Wholesale is illustrated below.

|  | | |
|---|---:|---:|
| Ruddy Bros. Wholesale<br>TRIAL BALANCE<br>December 31, 1983 | | |
| Cash | $ 13,000 | |
| Accounts Receivable | 14,650 | |
| Notes Receivable | 8,000 | |
| Inventory, January 1, 1983 | 89,500 | |
| Office Equipment | 16,000 | |
| Furniture and Fixtures | 12,300 | |
| Accounts Payable | | $ 14,100 |
| Notes Payable | | 24,000 |
| Ruddy Bros. Capital | | 91,240 |
| Sales | | 896,000 |
| Returned Sales | 3,760 | |
| Sales Allowances | 960 | |
| Purchases | 713,450 | |
| Returned Purchases | | 4,140 |
| Transportation-In | 6,570 | |
| Sales Salaries Expense | 65,700 | |
| Traveling Expenses | 4,900 | |
| Advertising Expense | 21,200 | |
| General Office Salaries | 39,800 | |
| Rent Expense | 18,000 | |
| Insurance Expense | 2,780 | |
| Utilities Expense | 4,310 | |
| Telephone Expense | 1,260 | |
| Auditing and Legal Expense | 2,780 | |
| Miscellaneous Administrative Expense | 2,200 | |
| Purchase Discounts | | 13,500 |
| Sales Discounts | 1,860 | |
| | $1,042,980 | $1,042,980 |

# ADJUSTMENTS

The employment of an accrual system means that numerous adjustments are necessary before financial statements are prepared because certain accounts are not accurately stated. For example, if we handle transactions on a cash basis, only cash transactions during the year are recorded. Consequently, if a company's employees are paid every two weeks and the end of an accounting period occurs in the middle of these two weeks, neither liability nor expense is shown for the last week. In order to bring the accounts up to date for the preparation of financial statements, both the wage expense and the wage liability accounts need to be increased. This change is accomplished by means of an adjusting entry.

A necessary step in the accounting process, then, is the adjustment of all accounts to an accrual basis and their subsequent posting to the general ledger. **Adjusting entries** are therefore necessary to achieve a proper matching of revenues and expenses in the determination of net income for the current period and to achieve an accurate statement of the assets and equities existing at the end of the period. Each adjusting entry affects both a real (asset, liability, or owners' equity) account and a nominal (revenue or expense) account.

Normally the adjustments are classified in the following manner:

> Prepaid (deferred) items:
>     Prepaid expenses (e.g., prepaid insurance)
>     Unearned revenues (e.g., rent received in advance)
> Accrued items:
>     Accrued liabilities (e.g., unpaid salaries)
>     Accrued assets (e.g., interest earned but not collected)
> Estimated items (e.g., depreciation)

## Prepaid Expenses

A prepaid expense is an item paid and recorded in advance of its use or consumption in the business, part of which properly represents expense of the current period and part of which represents an asset on hand at the end of the period. If a three-year insurance premium is paid in advance at the beginning of the current year, one-third of the amount paid represents expense of the current year and two-thirds is an asset at the end of the year, an amount properly to be deferred to and expensed in future years.

**ILLUSTRATION**   If insurance for three years is purchased for $1,200 on January 2, 1983, and the books are closed annually on December 31, the asset account appears as follows on December 31, 1983, before the adjusting entry is made:

| Unexpired Insurance | | | |
|---|---|---|---|
| 1983<br>Jan. 2 | Cash | 1,200 | |

Because one-third of the three-year period has now passed, one-third of the amount paid is reported as an expense for 1983, and the asset account is reduced by the same amount. The adjusting entry required on December 31, 1983, is:

**Dec. 31**

| | | |
|---|---|---|
| Insurance Expense | 400 | |
|    Unexpired Insurance | | 400 |
|    (To charge one-third of insurance premium to expense) | | |

The ledger now shows an expense for insurance of $400 and an asset, Unexpired Insurance, of $800.

| Unexpired Insurance | | | | | |
|---|---|---|---|---|---|
| 1983<br>Jan. 2 | Cash | 1,200 | 1983<br>Dec. 31 | To Insurance<br>Expense | 400 |
| Insurance Expense | | | | | |
| 1983<br>Dec. 31 | Insurance Expired | 400 | | | |

## Unearned Revenue

Unearned revenue is revenue received and recorded as a liability or as a revenue before the revenue has been earned by providing goods or services to customers. As dictated by the "revenue recognition principle" in accounting, revenue is reported in the period in which it is earned; therefore, when it is received in advance of its being earned, the amount applicable to future periods is deferred to future periods. The amount unearned is considered a liability because it represents an obligation to perform a service in the future arising from a past transaction.

Some common unearned revenue items are rent received in advance, interest received in advance on notes receivable, subscriptions and advertising received in advance by publishers, and deposits from customers in advance of delivery of merchandise.

ILLUSTRATION   Assume that a business rented part of a building for a three-year period from January 3, 1982, for $60,000 to a tenant who paid the full three years' rent in advance. The business made the following entry.

**Jan. 2**

| | | |
|---|---|---|
| Cash | 60,000 | |
| Unearned Rent Revenue | | 60,000 |
| (To record rent received for three years in advance) | | |

At the end of 1983 one-third of this amount is earned and, therefore, an adjusting entry is made.

**Dec. 31**

| | | |
|---|---|---|
| Unearned Rent Revenue | 20,000 | |
| Rent Revenue | | 20,000 |
| (To take up as revenue one-third of $60,000) | | |

The entry also records $20,000 in the Rent Revenue account, which represents the amount of revenue earned during the year. These two accounts now show the following balances after adjustment.

| Unearned Rent Revenue | | | | | |
|---|---|---|---|---|---|
| 1983<br>Dec. 31 | Adjusting | 20,000 | 1983<br>Jan. 2 | Cash | 60,000 |
| Rent Revenue | | | | | |
| | | | 1983<br>Dec. 31 | Adjusting | 20,000 |

For prepaid items, it makes no difference if an original transaction entry is recorded in a real account (asset or liability) or in a nominal account (revenue or expense). After adjusting entries, the balances of the respective accounts are the same, regardless of the original entry.

## Accrued Liabilities or Expenses

Accrued liabilities or accrued expenses are items of expense that have been incurred during the period, but have not yet been recorded or paid. As such, they represent liabilities at the end of the period. The related debits for such items are included in the income statement as expenses.

Some common accrued liabilities are interest payable, wages and salaries payable, and property taxes payable.

**ILLUSTRATION**   When employees are paid on a monthly basis on the last day of the month, there are no accrued wages and salaries at the end of the month or year because all employees will have been paid all amounts due them for the month or the year. When they are paid on a weekly or biweekly basis, however, it is usually necessary to make an adjusting entry for wages and salaries earned but not paid at the end of the fiscal period.

Assume that a business pays its sales staff every Friday for a five-day week, that the total weekly payroll is $8,000, and that December 31 falls on Thursday. On December 31, the end of the fiscal period, the employees have worked four-fifths of a week for which they have not been paid and for which no entry has been made. The adjusting entry on December 31 is:

**Dec. 31**

| | | |
|---|---|---|
| Sales Salaries Expense | 6,400 | |
| Salaries Payable | | 6,400 |
| (To record accrued salaries as of Dec. 31: 4/5 x $8,000) | | |

As a result of this entry, the income statement for the year includes the salaries earned by the sales staff during the last four days in December and the balance sheet shows as a liability salaries payable of $6,400.

| Sales Salaries Expense | | | | | |
|---|---|---|---|---|---|
| 1983 | | | | | |
| Paid in 1983 | | 409,600 | | | |
| Dec. 31 | Adjusting entry | 6,400 | | | |
| Total 1983 | | 416,000 | | | |
| **Salaries Payable** | | | | | |
| | | | 1983 | | |
| | | | Dec. 31 | Adjusting entry | 6,400 |

## Accrued Assets or Revenues

Items of revenue that have been earned during the period but that have not yet been collected are called accrued assets, accrued revenues, or revenues receivable. Adjusting entries must be made for these items to record the revenue that has been earned but not yet received and to record as an asset the amount receivable.

Some examples of accrued assets are rent receivable and interest receivable.

**ILLUSTRATION**    Assume that office space is rented to a tenant at $1,000 per month, that the tenant has paid the rent for the first 11 months of the year, and that the tenant has paid no rent for December. The adjusting entry on December 31 is:

**Dec. 31**

| | | |
|---|---|---|
| Rent Receivable | 1,000 | |
|   Rent Revenue | | 1,000 |
|   (To record December rent) | | |

As a result of this entry, an asset of $1,000, Rent Receivable, appears on the balance sheet disclosing the amount due from the tenant as of December 31. The income statement discloses rent revenue of $12,000, the $11,000 received for the first 11 months and the $1,000 for December entered by means of the adjusting entry. After adjustment the accounts appear as follows.

| Rent Revenue | | |
|---|---|---|
| | 1983 | |
| | Received in 1983 | 11,000 |
| | Dec. 31    Adjusting entry | 1,000 |
| | Total 1983 | 12,000 |

| Rent Receivable | |
|---|---|
| 1983 | |
| Dec. 31    Adjusting entry    1,000 | |

## Estimated Items

Uncollectible accounts and depreciation of fixed assets are ordinarily called estimated items because the amounts are not exactly determinable. In other words, an **estimated item** is a function of unknown future events and developments, which means that current period charges can be evaluated on a subjective basis only. It is known, for example, that some accounts receivable arising from credit sales will prove to be uncollectible. To prevent an understatement of expenses and losses of the period, it is necessary to estimate and record the bad debts that are expected to result.

Also, when a long-lived fixed asset is purchased, it is assumed that ultimately it will be scrapped or sold at a price much below the purchase price. This difference between an asset's cost and its scrap value represents an expense to the business that should be apportioned over the asset's useful life. We must estimate the probable life of the fixed asset and its scrap value to determine the expense that is charged in each period.

**Adjusting Entries for Bad Debts**    Proper matching of revenues and expenses dictates recording bad debts as an expense of the period in which the sale is made instead of the period in which the accounts or notes are written off. This method requires an adjusting entry.

At the end of each period an estimate is made of the amount of current period sales on account that will later prove to be uncollectible. The estimate is based on the amount of bad debts experienced in one or more past years, general economic conditions, the age of the receivables, and other factors that indicate the element of uncollectibility in the receivables outstanding at the end of the period. Usually it is expressed as a certain percent of the sales on account for the period, or it is computed by adjusting the account for Allowance for Doubtful Accounts to a certain percent of the trade accounts receivable and trade notes receivable at the end of the period.

Assume, for example, that experience reveals that bad debts usually approximate one-half of one percent of the net sales on account and that net sales on account for the year are $300,000. The adjusting entry for bad debts is:

**Dec. 31**

| | | |
|---|---|---|
| Bad Debts Expense | 1,500 | |
|    Allowance for Doubtful Accounts | | 1,500 |
|    (To record estimated bad debts for the year: $300,000 × .005) | | |

**Adjusting Entries for Depreciation**   Entries for depreciation are similar to those made for reducing the prepaid expenses in which the original amount was debited to an asset account. The principal difference is that for depreciation the credit is made to a separate account, Accumulated Depreciation, instead of to the asset account.

In estimating depreciation, the original cost of the property, its length of useful life, and its estimated salvage or trade-in value are used. Assume that a truck costing $18,000 has an estimated life of five years and an estimated trade-in value of $2,000 at the end of that period. Because the truck is expected to be worth $16,000 less at the time of its disposal than it was at the time of its purchase, the amount of $16,000 represents an expense that is apportioned over the five years of operations. It is neither logical nor good accounting practice to consider the $16,000 as an expense entirely of the period in which it was acquired or the period in which it was sold, inasmuch as the business receives the benefit of the use of the truck during the entire five-year period.

If the widely used straight-line method of depreciation is used, each year shows as an expense one-fifth of $16,000, or $3,200. Each full year the truck is used the following adjusting entry is made.

**Dec. 31**

| | | |
|---|---|---|
| Depreciation Expense—Delivery Equipment | 3,200 | |
|    Accumulated Depreciation—Delivery Equipment | | 3,200 |
|    (To record depreciation on truck for the year) | | |

## SUMMARY OF ADJUSTMENTS SECTION

As a review, we have summarized the basic adjustments and defined them individually:

> **PREPAID EXPENSE.** An expense paid in cash and recorded in an asset or expense account in advance of its use or consumption.
>
> **UNEARNED REVENUE.** A revenue received and recorded in a liability or revenue account before it is earned.
>
> **ACCRUED LIABILITIES** (expenses). Expense incurred but not yet paid.
>
> **ACCRUED ASSETS** (revenues). Revenue earned but not yet received.

ESTIMATED ITEMS. An expense recorded on the basis of subjective estimates because the expense is a function of unknown future events or developments.

As soon as these adjusting entries have been recorded and posted, another trial balance is prepared before closing. The second or **adjusted trial balance** is used to prepare the financial statements. The basic set of financial statements is discussed in the next two chapters.

## YEAR-END PROCEDURE FOR INVENTORY AND RELATED ACCOUNTS

When the inventory records are maintained on a **perpetual inventory system,** purchases and issues are recorded directly in the Inventory account as the purchases and issues occur. Therefore, the balance in the Inventory account should represent the ending inventory amount and no adjusting entries are needed. No Purchases account is used because the purchases are debited directly to the Inventory account. However, a Cost of Goods Sold account is used to accumulate the issuances from inventory.

When the inventory records are maintained on a **periodic inventory system,** a Purchases account is used and the Inventory account is unchanged during the period. The Inventory account represents the beginning inventory amount throughout the period. At the end of the accounting period the Inventory account must be adjusted by closing out the **beginning inventory** amount and recording the **ending inventory** amount. The ending inventory is determined by physically counting the items on hand and valuing them at cost or at the lower of cost or market. Under the periodic inventory system, cost of goods sold is, therefore, determined by adding the beginning inventory together with net purchases and deducting the ending inventory.

Computation of cost of goods sold under periodic inventory accounting has the characteristics of both an adjusting entry and a closing entry; thus, there is more than one way to prepare the entries that update inventory, record cost of goods sold, and close the other related nominal accounts. To illustrate, Collegiate Apparel Shop has a beginning inventory of $30,000; Purchases $200,000; Transportation-In $6,000; Returned Purchases $1,200; Purchase Allowances $800; Purchase Discounts $2,000; and the ending inventory is $26,000. One method of transferring the various merchandise accounts under a periodic inventory system into the Cost of Goods Sold account is to prepare a combination adjusting/ closing entry as follows:

|  | **Adjusting/Closing Entry** | | |
|---|---|---|---|
| Inventory (ending) | | 26,000 | |
| Purchase Discounts | | 2,000 | |
| Purchase Allowances | | 800 | |
| Returned Purchases | | 1,200 | |
| Cost of Goods Sold | | 206,000 | |
|    Inventory (beginning) | | | 30,000 |
|    Purchases | | | 200,000 |
|    Transportation-In | | | 6,000 |
|    (To transfer beginning inventory and net purchases to | | | |
|    Cost of Goods Sold and to record the ending inventory) | | | |

After the foregoing entry, only the Cost of Goods Sold account remains to be closed.

The following diagram illustrates in T-account form the process of adjusting the inventory balance, determining cost of goods sold, and closing the related nominal accounts.

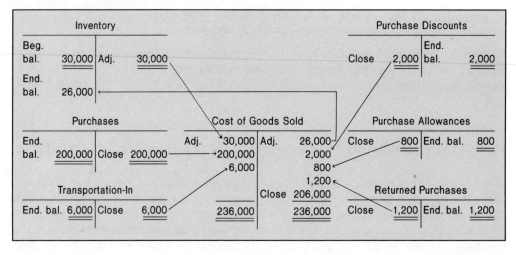

Alternatively, a second method consisting of the following series of entries could be prepared to adjust inventory, to close the accounts related to purchases, and to determine cost of goods sold under a periodic inventory system:

**Adjusting Entries**

| | | |
|---|---:|---:|
| Cost of Goods Sold | 30,000 | |
|    Inventory (beginning) | | 30,000 |
|      (To transfer beginning inventory to Cost of Goods Sold) | | |
| Inventory (ending) | 26,000 | |
|    Cost of Goods Sold | | 26,000 |
|      (To record the ending inventory balance) | | |

**Closing Entry**

| | | |
|---|---:|---:|
| Purchase Discounts | 2,000 | |
| Purchase Allowances | 800 | |
| Returned Purchases | 1,200 | |
| Cost of Goods Sold | 202,000 | |
|    Purchases | | 200,000 |
|    Transportation-In | | 6,000 |
|      (To transfer net purchases to Cost of Goods Sold) | | |

The first two entries adjusting the Inventory account are generally viewed as adjusting entries, while the third entry transferring net purchases to Cost of Goods Sold is viewed as a closing entry.

The balance of Cost of Goods Sold will be the same ($206,000) whether the method of its determination is considered a part of the adjusting process or a part of the closing process. Unless you are specifically directed to prepare separate adjusting entries for beginning and ending inventory amounts, you will be expected to prepare an entry similar to the first alternative above (combination adjusting and closing entry) and include it as part of the closing process when working the problems at the end of this chapter.

## CLOSING

The procedure generally followed to reduce the balance of nominal (temporary) accounts to zero in order to prepare the accounts for the next period's transactions is known as the

**closing process.** In the closing process all of the revenue and expense account balances (income statement items) are transferred to a clearing or suspense account called Income Summary, which is used only at the end of each accounting period. Revenues and expenses are matched in the Income Summary account and the net result of this matching, which represents the net income or net loss for the period, is then transferred to an owners' equity account (retained earnings for a corporation, and capital accounts normally for proprietorships and partnerships). Note that all closing entries are posted to the appropriate general ledger accounts.

For example, assume that revenue accounts of Collegiate Apparel Shop have the following balances, after adjustments, at the end of the year:

| | |
|---|---|
| Revenue from Sales | $280,000 |
| Rental Revenue | 27,000 |
| Interest Revenue | 5,000 |

These **revenue accounts** would be closed and the balances transferred through the following closing journal entry:

| | | |
|---|---|---|
| Revenue from Sales | 280,000 | |
| Rental Revenue | 27,000 | |
| Interest Revenue | 5,000 | |
| Income Summary | | 312,000 |
| (To close revenue accounts to Income Summary) | | |

Assume that the expense accounts, including Cost of Goods Sold, have the following balances, after adjustments, at the end of the year:

| | |
|---|---|
| Cost of Goods Sold | $206,000 |
| Selling Expenses | 25,000 |
| General and Adm. Expenses | 40,600 |
| Interest Expense | 4,400 |
| Income Tax Expense | 13,000 |

These **expense accounts** would be closed and the balances transferred through the following closing journal entry:

| | | |
|---|---|---|
| Income Summary | 289,000 | |
| Cost of Goods Sold | | 206,000 |
| Selling Expenses | | 25,000 |
| General and Adm. Expenses | | 40,600 |
| Interest Expense | | 4,400 |
| Income Tax Expense | | 13,000 |
| (To close expense accounts to Income Summary) | | |

The Income Summary account now has a credit balance of $23,000 which is net income. The **net income is transferred to owners' equity** by closing the Income Summary account to Retained Earnings as follows:

| | | |
|---|---|---|
| Income Summary | 23,000 | |
| Retained Earnings | | 23,000 |
| (To close Income Summary to Retained Earnings) | | |

After the closing process is completed, each income statement (that is, nominal) account is balanced out to zero and is ready for use in the next accounting period.

The following diagram illustrates in T-account form the closing process.

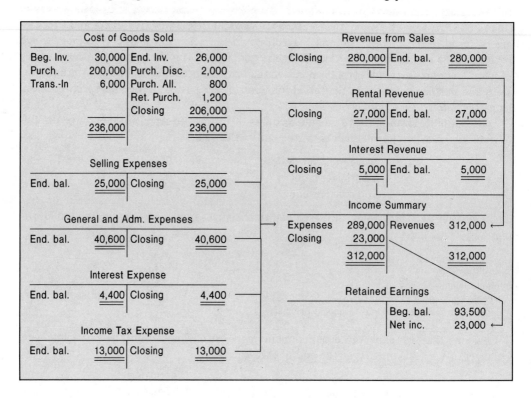

## POST-CLOSING TRIAL BALANCE

We already mentioned that a trial balance is taken after the regular transactions of the period have been entered and that a second trial balance (the adjusted trial balance) is taken after the adjusting entries have been posted. A third trial balance may be taken after posting the closing entries; the trial balance after closing, often called the **post-closing trial balance,** shows that equal debits and credits have been posted to the Income Summary. The post-closing trial balance consists only of asset, liability, and owners' equity (the real) accounts.

## REVERSING ENTRIES

After the financial statements have been prepared and the books closed, it is frequently helpful to reverse some of the adjusting entries before entering the regular transactions of the next period. Such entries are called reversing entries.

A **reversing entry** is the exact reverse, both in amount and in account titles, of an adjusting entry. Any adjusting entries that create an asset or a liability account should be reversed (all accruals and some prepaid items). Reversing entries are generally recorded at the beginning of the next accounting period. Such entries are optional. They are made only to simplify the recording of a subsequent transaction related to an adjusting entry. When an adjusting entry is reversed, the related subsequent transaction can be recorded as if the adjusting entry had never been recorded.

## Reversing Entries for Prepaid Items

Earlier in this chapter the adjusting entry for unexpired insurance (a prepaid expense) was illustrated. An asset account, Unexpired Insurance, was debited when the three-year premium of $1,200 was paid in advance. At the end of the year, one-third of that amount, $400, was transferred from the asset account to Insurance Expense, and Insurance Expense was then closed to the Income Summary account in the closing process. This adjusting entry does not require reversing; at the end of the next year the asset account is reduced by another $400 and that amount is debited to Insurance Expense.

Suppose, however, that the insurance premium was debited initially to the Insurance Expense account. In the adjusting entry Insurance Expense is credited and Unexpired (Prepaid) Insurance is debited for $800, the unexpired portion of the insurance coverage.

After the books are closed and before any transactions are recorded in the next period, a reversing entry is recorded.

**Jan. 1**

| | | |
|---|---|---|
| Insurance Expense | 800 | |
| Unexpired Insurance | | 800 |
| (To reverse the adjusting entry of Dec. 31) | | |

After we post this entry, the two accounts appear as below.

| Insurance Expense | | | | | | |
|---|---|---|---|---|---|---|
| First year | | | First year | | | |
| Jan. 2 | Cash paid | 1,200 | Dec. 31 | Adjusting entry | 800 | |
| | | | Dec. 31 | To Income | | |
| | | | | Summary | 400 | |
| | | 1,200 | | | 1,200 | |
| Second year | | | | | | |
| Jan. 1 | Reversing entry | 800 | | | | |

| Unexpired Insurance | | | | | |
|---|---|---|---|---|---|
| First year | | | Second year | | |
| Dec. 31 | Adjusting entry | 800 | Jan. 1 | Reversing entry | 800 |

Here a reversing entry was made to return to the expense account the cost of unexpired insurance at the beginning of the second year of the policy. The business continues to debit Insurance Expense for purchases of other insurance during the second year; to be consistent, the unexpired insurance at the beginning of the year is shown in the same account (Insurance Expense Account) as the insurance purchased. Reversing entries are also made for prepaid revenue transactions if the initial entry is made to the revenue account.

With respect to prepaid items, why are all such items not entered originally into real accounts (assets and liabilities), thus making reversing entries unnecessary? This practice is sometimes followed. It is particularly advantageous for items that need to be apportioned over several periods. However, items that do not follow this regular pattern and that may or may not involve two or more periods are ordinarily entered initially in revenue or expense accounts. The revenue and expense accounts may not require adjusting and are systematically closed to Income Summary.

## Accrued Items Are Reversed

Because each accrued item involves either a later receipt of cash for revenue or a later disbursement of cash for expense, a reversing entry is made to offset part of the credit to revenue or part of the debit to expense. In that way, the net balance that develops in the revenue or expense account in the later period represents the revenue earned or expense incurred for that period. To illustrate, we continue with the Sales Salaries account after the adjustment that was shown previously (page 74). The Sales Salaries Expense account, being an expense account, is closed to Income Summary on December 31. On January 1 this reversing entry is made.

**Jan. 1**

| | | |
|---|---|---|
| Salaries Payable | 6,400 | |
|    Sales Salaries Expense | | 6,400 |
|      (To reverse the adjusting entry of Dec. 31) | | |

This entry closes the Salaries Payable account and puts a credit balance of $6,400 in the Sales Salaries Expense account. On January 1, after we post the reversing entry the accounts appear as follows.

| Sales Salaries Expense | | | | | | |
|---|---|---|---|---|---|---|
| 1983 | | | | 1983 | | |
| Paid in 1983 | | 409,600 | | Dec. 31 | To Income | |
| Dec. 31 | Adjusting entry | 6,400 | | | Summary | 416,000 |
| Total 1983 | | 416,000 | | | | 416,000 |
| | | | | 1984 | | |
| | | | | Jan. 1 | Reversing entry | 6,400 |

| Salaries Payable | | | | | | |
|---|---|---|---|---|---|---|
| | | | | 1983 | | |
| | | | | Dec. 31 | Adjusting entry | 6,400 |
| 1984 | | | | | | |
| Jan. 1 | Reversing entry | 6,400 | | | | |

On Friday, January 1, the weekly payroll of $8,000 is paid, and the usual debit to Sales Salaries Expense and credit to Cash are recorded. The Sales Salaries Expense account now contains a debit of $8,000 and a credit of $6,400. The balance of $1,600 represents the expense incurred during the first day of January. This is illustrated below.

| Sales Salaries Expense | | | | | | |
|---|---|---|---|---|---|---|
| 1984 | | | | 1984 | | |
| Jan. 1 | Cash paid | 8,000 | | Jan. 1 | Reversing entry | 6,400 |

This item was reversed so that the entry for payment of salaries on the first Friday in 1984 is the same as that for any other payroll. If the entry had not been reversed, it would have been necessary to debit Salaries Payable for part of the amount, $6,400, and Sales Salaries Expense for $1,600. Analysis of this sort can be time-consuming and impractical.

**In general, all adjusting entries for prepaid items for which the original amount was entered in a revenue or expense account and for *all* accrued items should be reversed.** It follows, of course, that all other adjusting entries are not reversed; in other words, adjusting entries for prepaid items for which the original amount was entered in a real account and for estimated items are not reversed.

Some accountants avoid reversing entries entirely, but generally it is desirable to use them under the conditions described to ensure consistent treatment of the accounts and to establish standardized procedures for transactions that occur regularly.


## THE ACCOUNTING CYCLE SUMMARIZED

A summary of the steps in the accounting cycle shows a logical sequence of the accounting procedures used during a fiscal period. The process begins with the identification of transactions and other events for which business documents provide evidence of the accounts and amounts.

1. Enter the transactions of the period in appropriate journals.
2. Post from the journals to the ledger (or ledgers).
3. Take an unadjusted trial balance (first trial balance).
4. Prepare adjusting journal entries and post to the ledger(s).
5. Take a trial balance after adjusting (second trial balance).
6. Prepare the financial statements from the second trial balance.
7. Prepare closing journal entries and post to the ledger(s).
8. Take a trial balance after closing (third trial balance).
9. Prepare reversing entries (optional) and post to the ledger.

This list of procedures constitutes a complete accounting cycle that is normally performed in every fiscal period.


## USING A WORK SHEET TO PREPARE FINANCIAL STATEMENTS

To facilitate the end-of-period accounting and reporting process, accountants frequently use a work sheet. A **work sheet** is a columnar sheet of paper that may be used to help in adjusting the account balances and preparing the financial statements. Use of a work sheet aids in preparation of the financial statements on a more timely basis. It is not necessary to delay preparation of the financial statements until the adjusting and closing entries are journalized and posted. The **ten-column work sheet** illustrated in this chapter provides columns for the first trial balance, adjustments, adjusted trial balance, income statement, and balance sheet. The work sheet does not in any way replace the financial statements; instead, it is the accountant's informal device for accumulating and sorting the information that is needed for the financial statements. The satisfactory completion of the work sheet provides considerable assurance that all of the details related to the end-of-period accounting and statement preparation have been properly brought together.

Reliable Tire Corp.
TEN-COLUMN WORK SHEET
December 31, 1983

| Accounts | Trial Balance Dr. | Trial Balance Cr. | Adjustments Dr. | Adjustments Cr. | Adjusted Trial Balance Dr. | Adjusted Trial Balance Cr. | Income Statement Dr. | Income Statement Cr. | Balance Sheet Dr. | Balance Sheet Cr. |
|---|---|---|---|---|---|---|---|---|---|---|
| Cash | 1,200 | | | | 1,200 | | | | 1,200 | |
| Notes receivable | 16,000 | | | | 16,000 | | | | 16,000 | |
| Accounts receivable | 41,000 | | | | 41,000 | | | | 41,000 | |
| Allowance for doubtful accounts | | 2,000 | | (b) 1,000 | | 3,000 | | | | 3,000 |
| Inventory, Jan. 1, 1983 | 36,000 | | | | 36,000 | | 36,000 | | | |
| Unexpired insurance | 900 | | | (c) 360 | 540 | | | | 540 | |
| Furniture and equipment | 67,000 | | | | 67,000 | | | | 67,000 | |
| Accumulated depreciation of furniture and equipment | | 12,000 | | (a) 6,700 | | 18,700 | | | | 18,700 |
| Notes payable | | 20,000 | | | | 20,000 | | | | 20,000 |
| Accounts payable | | 13,500 | | | | 13,500 | | | | 13,500 |
| Bonds payable | | 30,000 | | | | 30,000 | | | | 30,000 |
| Common stock | | 50,000 | | | | 50,000 | | | | 50,000 |
| Retained earnings, Jan. 1, 1983 | | 14,200 | | | | 14,200 | | | | 14,200 |
| Sales | | 400,000 | | | | 400,000 | | 400,000 | | |
| Purchases | 320,000 | | | | 320,000 | | 320,000 | | | |
| Sales salaries expense | 20,000 | | | | 20,000 | | 20,000 | | | |
| Advertising expense | 2,200 | | | | 2,200 | | 2,200 | | | |
| Traveling expense | 8,000 | | | | 8,000 | | 8,000 | | | |
| Salaries, office and general | 19,000 | | | | 19,000 | | 19,000 | | | |
| Telephone and telegraph expense | 600 | | | | 600 | | 600 | | | |
| Rent expense | 4,800 | | | | 4,800 | | 4,800 | | | |
| Property tax expense | 3,300 | | (f) 2,000 | | 5,300 | | 5,300 | | | |
| Interest expense | 1,700 | | | (e) 500 | 1,200 | | 1,200 | | | |
| Totals | 541,700 | 541,700 | | | | | | | | |
| Depreciation expense— furniture and equipment | | | (a) 6,700 | | 6,700 | | 6,700 | | | |
| Bad debts expense | | | (b) 1,000 | | 1,000 | | 1,000 | | | |
| Insurance expense | | | (c) 360 | | 360 | | 360 | | | |
| Interest receivable | | | (d) 800 | | 800 | | | | 800 | |
| Interest revenue | | | | (d) 800 | | 800 | | 800 | | |
| Prepaid interest expense | | | (e) 500 | | 500 | | | | 500 | |
| Property tax payable | | | | (f) 2,000 | | 2,000 | | | | 2,000 |
| Totals | | | 11,360 | 11,360 | 552,200 | 552,200 | | | | |
| Inventory, Dec. 31, 1983 | | | | | | | | 40,000 | 40,000 | |
| Totals | | | | | | | 425,160 | 440,800 | | |
| Income before income taxes | | | | | | | 15,640 | | | |
| Totals | | | | | | | 440,800 | 440,800 | | |
| Income before income taxes | | | | | | | | 15,640 | | |
| Income tax expense | | | (g) 3,440 | | | | 3,440 | | | |
| Income tax payable | | | | (g) 3,440 | | | | | | 3,440 |
| Net income | | | | | | | 12,200 | | | 12,200 |
| Totals | | | | | | | 15,640 | 15,640 | 167,040 | 167,040 |

## Adjustments Entered on the Work Sheet

The information that serves as the basis for the adjusting entries made in the work sheet illustration on page 84 are items (a) through (f) below.

(a) Furniture and equipment is depreciated at the rate of 10% per year based on original cost.

(b) Estimated bad debts, one-quarter of 1% of sales.

(c) Insurance expired during the year, $360.

(d) Interest accrued on notes receivable as of December 31, $800.

(e) The Interest Expense account contains $500 interest paid in advance, which is applicable to next year.

(f) Property taxes accrued December 31, $2,000.

The adjusting entries shown on the work sheet are as follows:

(a)

| | | |
|---|---|---|
| Depreciation Expense—Furniture and Equipment | 6,700 | |
| Accumulated Depreciation of Furniture and Equipment | | 6,700 |

(b)

| | | |
|---|---|---|
| Bad Debts Expense | 1,000 | |
| Allowance for Doubtful Accounts | | 1,000 |

(c)

| | | |
|---|---|---|
| Insurance Expense | 360 | |
| Unexpired Insurance | | 360 |

(d)

| | | |
|---|---|---|
| Interest Receivable | 800 | |
| Interest Revenue | | 800 |

(e)

| | | |
|---|---|---|
| Prepaid Interest Expense | 500 | |
| Interest Expense | | 500 |

(f)

| | | |
|---|---|---|
| Property Tax Expense | 2,000 | |
| Property Tax Payable | | 2,000 |

These adjusting entries are transferred to the Adjustments columns of the work sheet, and each may be designated by letter. The accounts that are set up as a result of the adjusting entries and that are not already in the trial balance are listed below the totals of the trial balance, as illustrated on page 84. The Adjustments columns are then totaled and balanced.

The illustration does not include in the Adjustments columns the adjustments for cost of goods sold. Although these adjustments are sometimes included in these columns on a ten-column work sheet, this illustration assumes that these entries will be made during the closing process.

## Adjusted Trial Balance Columns

The amounts shown in the Trial Balance columns are combined with the amounts in the Adjustments columns and are extended to the Adjusted Trial Balance columns. For example, the amount of $2,000 shown opposite the Allowance for Doubtful Accounts in the Trial Balance Cr. column is added to the $1,000 in the Adjustments Cr. column, and the total of $3,000 is extended to the Adjusted Trial Balance Cr. column. Similarly, the $900 debit opposite Unexpired Insurance is reduced by the $360 credit in the Adjustments column, and the $540 is shown in the Adjusted Trial Balance Dr. column. The Adjusted Trial Balance columns are then totaled and determined to be in balance.

## Income Statement and Balance Sheet Columns

All the debit items in the Adjusted Trial Balance are extended into one of the two debit columns to the right, depending on the financial statement in which the items will appear. Similarly, all the credit items in the Adjusted Trial Balance are extended into one of the two credit columns to the right. It should be observed that the January 1 inventory, which was the inventory at the beginning of the year, is extended to the Income Statement Dr. column, because this item will appear as an addition in the cost of goods sold section of the income statement.

## Ending Inventory

The December 31 inventory, which is the inventory at the end of the year, is not in either of the trial balances but is listed as a separate item below the accounts already shown. In the illustration the amount of the ending inventory is assumed to be $40,000, and this amount is shown on the work sheet as both a debit and a credit. It is listed in the Balance Sheet Dr. column because it is an asset at the end of the year, and in the Income Statement Cr. column because it will be used as a deduction in the cost of goods sold section of the income statement.

## Income Taxes and Net Income

The next step is to total the Income Statement columns; the figure necessary to balance the debit and credit columns is the income or loss for the period before income taxes. In this illustration the income before income taxes of $15,640 is shown in the Income Statement Dr. column because the revenues exceeded the expenses by that amount.

The federal and state income tax expense and related tax liability are then computed (in this case an effective rate of 22% was applied). Because the Adjustments columns have been balanced, this adjustment is entered in the Income Statement Dr. column as Income Tax Expense $3,440 and in the Balance Sheet Cr. column as Income Tax Payable $3,440. Next the Income Statement columns are balanced with the income taxes included. The $12,200 difference between the debit and credit columns in this illustration represents net income. The net income of $12,200 is entered in the Income Statement Dr. column to achieve equality and in the Balance Sheet Cr. column as the increase in retained earnings. The following adjusting journal entry is recorded and posted to the general ledger as well as the work sheet.

(g)

| | | |
|---|---|---|
| Income Tax Expense | 3,440 | |
|     Income Tax Payable | | 3,440 |

## Eight-Column and Twelve-Column Work Sheets

An eight-column instead of a ten-column work sheet may be used to accumulate the same information. The only difference between the two is that the eight-column work sheet omits the Adjusted Trial Balance columns. The amounts shown in the Trial Balance columns (the first two columns) are combined with the amounts in the Adjustments columns and are extended directly into the Income Statement and Balance Sheet columns.

A twelve-column work sheet may be prepared to accommodate increases and decreases in retained earnings by adding Retained Earnings Dr. and Cr. columns. Dividends and net income would appear as adjustments to the beginning retained earnings.

## Preparation of Financial Statements from Work Sheet

The work sheet provides the information needed for preparation of the financial statements without reference to the ledger or other records. In addition, the data have been sorted into appropriate columns, which facilitates the preparation of the statements.

---

**Reliable Tire Corp.**
**INCOME STATEMENT**
**For the Year Ended December 31, 1983**

| | | | |
|---|---|---:|---:|
| Net sales | | | $400,000 |
| Cost of goods sold | | | |
|   Inventory, Jan. 1, 1983 | | $ 36,000 | |
|   Purchases | | 320,000 | |
|   Cost of goods available for sale | | 356,000 | |
|   Deduct inventory, Dec. 31, 1983 | | 40,000 | |
|     Cost of goods sold | | | 316,000 |
| Gross profit on sales | | | 84,000 |
| Selling expenses | | | |
|   Sales salaries expense | | 20,000 | |
|   Advertising expense | | 2,200 | |
|   Traveling expense | | 8,000 | |
|     Total selling expenses | | 30,200 | |
| Administrative expenses | | | |
|   Salaries, office and general | $19,000 | | |
|   Telephone and telegraph expense | 600 | | |
|   Rent expense | 4,800 | | |
|   Property tax expense | 5,300 | | |
|   Depreciation expense—furniture and equipment | 6,700 | | |
|   Bad debts expense | 1,000 | | |
|   Insurance expense | 360 | | |
|     Total administrative expenses | | 37,760 | |
|     Total selling and administrative expenses | | | 67,960 |
| Income from operations | | | 16,040 |
| Other revenues and gains | | | |
|   Interest revenue | | | 800 |
| | | | 16,840 |
| Other expenses and losses | | | |
|   Interest expense | | | 1,200 |
| Income before income taxes | | | 15,640 |
|   Income taxes | | | 3,440 |
| Net income | | | $ 12,200 |

The financial statements prepared from the ten-column work sheet illustrated are:

Statement of Income for the Year Ended December 31, 1983 (on page 87).
Statement of Retained Earnings for the Year Ended December 31, 1983 (below).
Balance Sheet as of December 31, 1983 (on page 89).

## Statement of Income

The income statement presented on page 87 is that of a trading or merchandising concern; if a manufacturing concern were illustrated, three inventory accounts would be involved: raw materials, work in process, and finished goods. When these accounts are used, a supplementary statement entitled cost of goods manufactured must be prepared.

## Statement of Retained Earnings

The net income earned by a corporation may be retained in the business or it may be distributed to stockholders by payment of dividends. In the illustration the net income earned during the year was added to the balance of retained earnings on January 1, thereby increasing the balance of retained earnings to $26,400 on December 31. No dividends were declared or paid during the year.

| Reliable Tire Corp.<br>STATEMENT OF RETAINED EARNINGS<br>For the Year Ended December 31, 1983 | |
| --- | ---: |
| Retained earnings, Jan. 1, 1983 | $14,200 |
| Add net income for 1983 | 12,200 |
| Retained earnings, Dec. 31, 1983 | $26,400 |

## Balance Sheet

The balance sheet prepared from the ten-column work sheet contains more new items resulting from year-end adjusting entries. Interest receivable, unexpired insurance, and prepaid interest expense are included as current assets, because these assets will be converted into cash or consumed in the ordinary routine of the business within a relatively short period of time. The amount of Allowance for Doubtful Accounts is deducted from the total of accounts, notes, and interest receivable because it is estimated that only $54,800 of the total of $57,800 will be collected in cash.

In the property, plant, and equipment section the accumulated depreciation is deducted from the cost of the furniture and equipment; the difference represents the book or carrying value of the furniture and equipment.

Property tax payable is shown as a current liability because it is an obligation that is payable within a year. Other short-term accrued liabilities would also be shown as current liabilities.

The bonds payable, due in 1988, are long-term or fixed liabilities and are shown in a separate section. (Interest on the bonds was paid on December 31.)

Reliable Tire Corp.
BALANCE SHEET
As of December 31, 1983

**Assets**

| | | |
|---|---:|---:|
| Current assets | | |
| Cash | | $ 1,200 |
| Notes receivable | $16,000 | |
| Accounts receivable | 41,000 | |
| Interest receivable | 800 | $57,800 |
| Less allowance for doubtful accounts | 3,000 | 54,800 |
| Merchandise inventory on hand | | 40,000 |
| Unexpired insurance | | 540 |
| Prepaid interest | | 500 |
| Total current assets | | 97,040 |
| Property, plant, and equipment | | |
| Furniture and equipment | 67,000 | |
| Less accumulated depreciation | 18,700 | |
| Total property, plant, and equipment | | 48,300 |
| Total assets | | $145,340 |

**Liabilities and Stockholders' Equity**

| | | |
|---|---:|---:|
| Current liabilities | | |
| Notes payable | | $ 20,000 |
| Accounts payable | | 13,500 |
| Property tax payable | | 2,000 |
| Income taxes payable | | 3,440 |
| Total current liabilities | | 38,940 |
| Long-term liabilities | | |
| Bonds payable, due June 30, 1988 | | 30,000 |
| Total liabilities | | 68,940 |
| Stockholders' equity | | |
| Common stock, $1.00 par value, issued and outstanding, 50,000 shares | $50,000 | |
| Retained earnings | 26,400 | |
| Total stockholders' equity | | 76,400 |
| Total liabilities and stockholders' equity | | $145,340 |

Reliable Tire Corp. is a corporation, and the capital section of the balance sheet, called the stockholders' equity section in the illustration, is somewhat different from the capital section for a proprietorship. The total capital or stockholders' equity consists of the common stock, which is the original investment by stockholders, and the earnings retained in the business.

## Closing and Reversing Entries

The entries for the closing process are as follows:

**General Journal**

| | | |
|---|---|---|
| Inventory (December 31) | 40,000 | |
| Cost of Goods Sold | 316,000 | |
| Inventory (January 1) | | 36,000 |
| Purchases | | 320,000 |
| (To record ending inventory balance and to determine cost of goods sold) | | |
| | | |
| Interest Revenue | 800 | |
| Sales | 400,000 | |
| Cost of Goods Sold | | 316,000 |
| Sales Salaries Expense | | 20,000 |
| Advertising Expense | | 2,200 |
| Traveling Expense | | 8,000 |
| Salaries, Office and General | | 19,000 |
| Telephone and Telegraph Expense | | 600 |
| Rent Expense | | 4,800 |
| Property Tax Expense | | 5,300 |
| Depreciation Expense—Furniture and Equipment | | 6,700 |
| Bad Debts Expense | | 1,000 |
| Insurance Expense | | 360 |
| Interest Expense | | 1,200 |
| Income Tax Expense | | 3,440 |
| Income Summary | | 12,200 |
| (To close revenues and expenses to Income Summary) | | |
| | | |
| Income Summary | 12,200 | |
| Retained Earnings | | 12,200 |
| (To close Income Summary to Retained Earnings) | | |

After the financial statements have been prepared, the enterprise may use reversing entries to facilitate the accounting next period. The following reversing entries would be made if a reversing system were used.

**(1)**

| | | |
|---|---|---|
| Interest Revenue | 800 | |
| Interest Receivable | | 800 |

**(2)**

| | | |
|---|---|---|
| Interest Expense | 500 | |
| Prepaid Interest Expense | | 500 |

**(3)**

| | | |
|---|---|---|
| Property Tax Payable | 2,000 | |
| Property Tax Expense | | 2,000 |

Reversing entries would not appear on the ten-column work sheet because they are recorded in the next year (1984). The main object of the work sheet is to obtain the correct balances at the end of the year for financial statement presentation for the current year (1983).

## Monthly Statements, Yearly Closing

**The use of a work sheet at the end of each month or quarter permits the preparation of** *interim financial statements* **even though the books are closed only at the end of each year.** For example, assume that a business closes its books on December 31 but that monthly financial statements are desired. At the end of January a work sheet similar to the one illustrated in this chapter can be prepared to supply the information needed for statements for January. At the end of February a work sheet can be used again. Because the accounts were not closed at the end of January, the income statement taken from the work sheet on February 28 will present the net income for two months. An income statement for the month of February can be obtained by subtracting the items in the January income statement from the corresponding items in the income statement for the two months of January and February.

A statement of retained earnings for February only also may be obtained by subtracting the January items. The balance sheet prepared from the February work sheet, however, shows the assets and equities as of February 28, the specific date for which a balance sheet is desired.

The March work sheet would show the revenues and expenses for three months, and the subtraction of the revenues and expenses for the first two months could be made to supply the amounts needed for an income statement for the month of March only.

# APPENDIX B

# Specialized Journals and Methods of Processing Accounting Data

## SPECIAL JOURNALS

Most businesses use special journals in addition to the general journal. Special journals permit greater division of labor, reduce the time necessary to accomplish the various bookkeeping tasks, and summarize transactions possessing a common characteristic. Therefore, the special journals used by any given business depend largely on the specific transactions common to that business. Most trading concerns have many transactions grouped into these categories:

Receipts of cash
Sales on account
Purchases on account
Payments of cash

A business that engages in many of these transactions is likely to use the following five journals.

1. **CASH RECEIPTS JOURNAL.** Receives entries for all cash received by the business.
2. **SALES JOURNAL.** Receives entries for all sales of merchandise on account.
3. **PURCHASES JOURNAL** (voucher register). Receives entries for all purchases of merchandise on account.
4. **CASH PAYMENTS JOURNAL** (check register). Receives entries for all cash paid.
5. **GENERAL JOURNAL.** Receives entries for all transactions that cannot be recorded in any of the special journals.

The general journal, special journals, and posting to the general and subsidiary ledgers are eliminated or altered in an automated or computerized system. The following discussion concerns a manual system normally used by smaller businesses.

## Cash Receipts Journal

Every transaction entered in the cash receipts journal represents a debit to cash and a credit to each of the accounts in the "account credited" column. In other words, the cash receipts journal is the book of original entry in which **all** receipts of cash are recorded before being posted to the ledger. Special columns are used in the cash receipts journal to save time in posting. Although all transactions entered in this journal are based on receipts of cash, not all cash receipts are necessarily from customers. Thus a one-column journal is not sufficient to accommodate all cash receipts transactions; columns must be provided for cash and the common sources of cash as illustrated below.

| CASH RECEIPTS JOURNAL | | | | | | | | Page 8 |
|---|---|---|---|---|---|---|---|---|
| Date 1984 | Acct. No. | Account Title | Explanation | Cash Dr. | Sales Discount Dr. | Accounts Receivable Cr. | Sales Cr. | Sundry Cr. |
| April 7 | 208 | Rex Road | In full | 182.28 | 3.72 | 186.00 | | |
| 8 | ✔ | Sales | Per cash register | 25.00 | | | 25.00 | |
| 9 | 16 | Notes Payable | 60-day, 12%, First Nat'l | 300.00 | | | | 300.00 |
| 16 | 206 | Joe Leo | On account | 200.00 | | 200.00 | | |
| 18 | 204 | Nita Doty | On account | 735.00 | 15.00 | 750.00 | | |
| 19 | ✔ | Sales | Per cash register | 185.00 | | | 185.00 | |
| | | | | 1,627.28 | 18.72 | 1,136.00 | 210.00 | 300.00 |
| | | | | (1) | (74) | (3) | (20) | ✔ |

The columns in the cash receipts journal indicate that the business receives cash from customers (credits to Accounts Receivable), sells goods for cash (credit Sales), and has miscellaneous sources of cash (credits entered in the Sundry column). Additional specific credit columns are used if business needs demand them. For example, if cash were borrowed from the bank frequently, a separate Notes Payable, Credit column could be used.

## Posting from Cash Receipts Journal

The posting procedures from a cash receipts journal are relatively simple. The totals of the columns for Cash, Sales Discount, Accounts Receivable, and Sales are posted to those general ledger accounts at the end of the month. Amounts entered in the Sundry Credit column must be posted to the general ledger as individual amounts to the accounts named in the Account Title column, because the ledger does not contain a Sundry account and because the purpose of this column in the journal is to provide a place to identify miscellaneous sources of cash receipts. The use of a Sundry column eliminates the need to have a column for every different credit account entered in the journal.

In addition to these general ledger postings, all amounts in the Accounts Receivable Credit column are posted to the credit side of the subsidiary ledger account named in the Account Title column. A **subsidiary ledger** is a group of accounts with a common characteristic (for example, all are accounts receivable) assembled together principally to facilitate the accounting process by freeing the general ledger from details concerning individual balances. Medium- and large-size business concerns frequently have accounts with thousands of customers and hundreds of creditors. A continuous record of the transactions affecting each customer and each creditor is necessary, and individual accounts with each customer and each creditor are better kept in ledgers separate from the ledger containing other asset, liability, and nominal accounts. Thus the average trading concern has one or more subsidiary ledgers containing nothing but accounts with customers, one or more subsidiary ledgers containing nothing but accounts with creditors, and one general ledger containing the other accounts of the business. The enterprise still maintains a **controlling account** in the general ledger that summarizes the same arithmetical results that the customers' or creditors' ledgers contain in detail. A general ledger is self-balancing (debit balances equal credit balances); subsidiary ledgers are not self-balancing.

The **advantages of subsidiary ledgers** are that they:

1. Permit the transactions affecting a single customer or single creditor to be shown in a single account.
2. Free the general ledger of details relating to accounts receivable and accounts payable.
3. Assist in locating errors in individual accounts by reducing the number of accounts combined in one ledger and by using controlling accounts.
4. Permit the division of labor by separating groups of accounts.

A business may establish and use controlling accounts and subsidiary ledgers for other than accounts receivable and accounts payable, such as for inventory, property, plant, and equipment, investments, general expenses, and selling expenses.

In the illustrated Cash Receipts Journal the page numbers in the "Acct. No." column opposite the names of individual customers refer to page numbers in the customer's subsidiary ledger. Care must be taken to post the amount appearing in the Accounts Receivable Credit column as a credit to the subsidiary ledger account. These postings are generally made on a daily basis, if possible, so that information on the status of any customer's account is up to date. Because each amount in the Accounts Receivable Cr. column is posted as a part of the column total to the Accounts Receivable (control account) in the general ledger and also to the individual customer account in the subsidiary ledger, each amount may be said to be **double posted.**

Check marks are used in the Acct. No. folio column opposite the two items titled "Sales." These check marks indicate that these items should not be posted individually to the Sales account because they are posted in total as a credit to the Sales account. Thus, individual postings would merely duplicate the amounts posted to Sales. Also, a check mark below the Sundry Credit total indicates that this total is not to be posted. Here the individual amounts that make up the total have been posted to the specific general ledger accounts identified in the entry.

The totals of the columns of the Cash Receipts Journal are posted at the end of the month to the account involved. Cash is posted to Account 1 in the general ledger; Sales Discount to Account 74; Accounts Receivable to Account 3; Sales to Account 20; and the Sundry total is not posted, because it was posted on a transaction-by-transaction basis. The total debited to various general ledger accounts equals the total credited.

### The Sales Journal

Entries in the sales journal are based on sales invoices or charge sales issued. Remember that the sales journal is used only for sales of merchandise on account. Sales of merchandise for cash are entered in the cash receipts journal.

The sales journal may take a variety of forms, depending on the specific needs of a business. In its simplest form it has an amount column on the right side of the page, with space for the date, account number, account title, and explanation to the left. If a business concern wishes to accumulate the sales according to the major types of merchandise sold, several amount columns are used, each denoting sales of one type of merchandise.

The following illustration shows the headings employed in a simple sales journal for a business concern that maintains only one Sales account.

| SALES JOURNAL | | | | | Page 6 |
|---|---|---|---|---|---|
| Date 1984 | Acct. No. | Account Debited | Explanation | Sales Invoice No. | Amount |
| April 1 | 208 | Rex Road | 2/10,n/30 | 62 | 186 |
| 2 | 202 | Ellen Odom | Net | 63 | 910 |
| 4 | 206 | Joe Leo | 2/10,n/30 | 64 | 816 |
| 6 | 204 | Nita Doty | 2/10,n/30 | 65 | 750 |
| | | | | | 2,662 |
| | | | | | 3/20 |

Notice that the sales journal follows basically the same procedure for posting as the cash receipts journal. The "T" accounts on page 96 illustrate how these postings are recorded in the general and subsidiary ledger.

## Purchases Journal (Voucher Register)

The purpose of a purchases journal is to record entries for all purchases of merchandise on account. Each invoice received for purchases of merchandise is the basis for an entry in the purchases journal. Transactions for purchases on account are entered in a separate journal in a manner similar to that described for the sales journal. The columns in a purchases journal are similar to those in a sales journal. If the business concern requires an analysis of purchases by product or department, the purchases journal is expanded to include a separate money column for each product or department. The headings for a purchases journal are shown in the illustration at the top of page 97.

Each entry in this journal is recorded on one line to show each purchase invoice received. The total of the items entered in the purchases journal represents the total purchases on account for the month or other accounting period. At the end of each accounting period, the purchases journal is totaled and posted to the purchases and accounts payable accounts in the general ledger. At frequent intervals during the accounting period, the accounts payable are posted to the individual accounts in the subsidiary ledger.

A **voucher register** is a book of original entry that often replaces the purchases journal. Entries in the voucher register are not limited to purchases of merchandise on account but include purchases of services, supplies, and fixed assets. In other words, purchases of all descriptions are properly entered in the voucher register. In a voucher system, a voucher is prepared for every payment. To voucher a payment it is necessary to make out a voucher form giving the facts about the amount to be paid. Vouchers are prepared and signed by a duly authorized person in the company. Not everyone would have the authority to prepare and sign a voucher. Such a restriction is an element of control. Furthermore, a check is

## GENERAL LEDGER

### Cash — No. 1

| 1984 | | | | | |
|------|------|------|---|---|---|
| March 31 | Balance | 600.00 | | | |
| April 30 | CR8 | 1,627.28 | | | |

### Accounts Receivable — No. 3

| 1984 | | | | | |
|------|------|------|----------|-----|----------|
| March 31 | Balance | 672.00 | April 30 | CR8 | 1,136.00 |
| April 30 | S6 | 2,662.00 | | | |

### Notes Payable — No. 16

| | | | 1984 | | |
|---|---|---|---------|-----|--------|
| | | | April 9 | CR8 | 300.00 |

### Sales — No. 20

| | | | 1984 | | |
|---|---|---|----------|---------|----------|
| | | | March 31 | Balance | 7,826.00 |
| | | | April 30 | S6 | 2,662.00 |
| | | | April 30 | CR8 | 210.00 |

### Sales Discount — No. 74

| 1984 | | | | | |
|------|-----|-------|---|---|---|
| April 30 | CR8 | 18.72 | | | |

## Accounts Receivable
## SUBSIDIARY LEDGER

### Ellen Odom — 202

| 1984 | | | | | |
|------|---------|-----|---|---|---|
| March 31 | Balance | 520 | | | |
| April 2 | S6 | 910 | | | |

### Nita Doty — 204

| 1984 | | | | | |
|------|---------|-----|----------|-----|-----|
| March 31 | Balance | 30 | April 18 | CR8 | 750 |
| April 6 | S6 | 750 | | | |

### Joe Leo — 206

| 1984 | | | | | |
|------|---------|-----|----------|-----|-----|
| March 31 | Balance | 122 | April 16 | CR8 | 200 |
| April 4 | S6 | 816 | | | |

### Rex Road — 208

| 1984 | | | | | |
|------|-----|-----|---------|-----|-----|
| April 1 | S6 | 186 | April 7 | CR8 | 186 |

| PURCHASES JOURNAL | | | | |
|---|---|---|---|---|
| Date 1984 | Acct. No. | Name of Creditor | Explanation | Amount |
| Nov. 1 | 105 | Battaglia Produce | Oct. 30, n/30 | 765.00 |

written only when there is a duly authorized and signed voucher presented. This procedure provides an important control feature over the disbursement of cash.

The types of columns generally employed in a voucher register are illustrated below.

| VOUCHER REGISTER | | | | | | | | | |
|---|---|---|---|---|---|---|---|---|---|
| Date 1984 | Voucher No. | Creditor | Payment Made | | Vouchers Payable Cr. | Purchases Dr. | Freight-In Dr. | Sundry Items Dr. | |
| | | | Check No. | Date | | | | Account Title | Amount |
| Jan. 2 | 200 | Bista Co. | 205 | Jan. 5 | 343.00 | 343.00 | | | |
| Jan. 3 | 201 | Steve Alton | 206 | Jan. 6 | 150.00 | | 150.00 | | |
| Jan. 4 | 202 | Lahey, Inc. | 208 | Jan. 9 | 200.00 | | 200.00 | | |
| Jan. 5 | 203 | Stoldt Corp. | 209 | Jan. 10 | 285.00 | 285.00 | | | |

Each voucher is numbered consecutively for control purposes and the entries are made in numerical order. Also, two columns are provided for Payment Made—one for the number of the check used to pay the voucher, and one for the date of payment. Because all entries made in the voucher register are for vouchers to be paid, the single credit money column needed is for Vouchers Payable. Also, because the vouchers are prepared for several different items, we find several money debit columns, as shown in the illustration.

The use of the voucher system assumes that all obligations are set up as liabilities in the form of vouchers payable, and that cash payments (by check) reduce liabilities thus set up. In other words, expressed in general journal form, the voucher system requires the following entries for every payment:

**In the Voucher Register**
| | | |
|---|---|---|
| Expense (or asset) | xxx | |
|   Vouchers Payable | | xxx |

**In the Cash Payments Journal (Check Register)**
| | | |
|---|---|---|
| Vouchers Payable | xxx | |
|   Cash | | xxx |

In this procedure a variety of items might appear in the cash payments journal, such as, a debit to Vouchers Payable, a credit to Cash, and a credit to Purchase Discounts.

## Cash Payments Journal (Check Register)

Every transaction entered in the cash payments journal represents a credit to Cash and a debit to each of the accounts named in the Account Debited column. Any transaction that does not stand this test of debits and credits cannot be entered in the cash payments journal. Here is the basic format of a cash payments journal (without a voucher system):

| | | | | | | | | |
|---|---|---|---|---|---|---|---|---|
| **CASH PAYMENTS JOURNAL** | | | | | | | | |
| Date 1984 | Acct. No. | Account Title | Explanation | Check No. | Cash Cr. | Purchase Discounts Cr. | Accts. Payable Dr. | Sundry Dr. |
| April 1 | 302 | Schieble Co. | In full | 501 | 514.50 | 10.50 | 525.00 | |
| April 3 | 65 | Advertising Exp. | Star Times | 502 | 173.00 | | | 173.00 |

The cash payments journal operates in principle much like the cash receipts journal. The totals of the Cash Cr., Purchase Discounts Cr., and Accounts Payable Dr. columns are posted at the end of the month. The items in the Sundry Dr. column are posted as individual items from time to time during the month. The amounts entered in the Accounts Payable Dr. column are posted daily, if possible, as debits to the individual accounts in the accounts payable subsidiary ledger.

Whenever a voucher system is employed, the enterprise replaces accounts payable with vouchers payable and adds another column to its cash payments journal (often called a check register in a voucher system) entitled Voucher Number to indicate which voucher is being paid. The column headings are illustrated below.

| | | | | | | | |
|---|---|---|---|---|---|---|---|
| **CASH PAYMENTS JOURNAL** (or check register) Entries for Vouchers Paid | | | | | | | |
| Date 1984 | Check No. | Payee | Voucher No. | Cash Cr. | Purchase Discounts Cr. | Vouchers Payable Dr. | Sundry Dr. |
| Jan. 5 | 205 | Bista Co. | 200 | 336.14 | 6.86 | 343.00 | |
| Jan. 6 | 206 | Steve Alton | 201 | 150.00 | | 150.00 | |
| Jan. 8 | 207 | Ehrlich Supply | 195 | 190.00 | | 190.00 | |
| Jan. 9 | 208 | Lahey, Inc. | 202 | 196.00 | 4.00 | 200.00 | |
| Jan. 10 | 209 | Stoldt Corp. | 203 | 280.00 | 5.00 | 285.00 | |

The totals of the Cash, Purchase Discounts, and Vouchers Payable columns are posted at the end of the month. The amounts entered in the Vouchers Payable column are posted daily, if possible, as debits to the individual accounts in the accounts payable (vouchers payable) subsidiary ledger.

## Flexibility in Selection of Journals

In addition to the journals described in this appendix, other specialized journals are required by various businesses. For example, if a business found that it had a large volume of returned sales or returned purchases, it could use a returned sales journal or a returned purchases journal. A notes receivable journal could be used by a business that regularly receives notes.

Each business decides on the appropriate journals to use after a study of the transactions in which it regularly engages. Most businesses have a general journal and the cash journals, whereas many trading companies also find a sales journal and a purchases journal necessary. A cash-and-carry grocery, on the other hand, has no need for a sales journal, because no sales are made on account. Thus, there is no established rule for a business to follow in choosing its books of original entry. It selects the books that result in the greatest convenience and saving of time in processing the many transactions in which it engages. The design of the journals and ledgers is part of the work involved in the design of an accounting system.

## Journals Not Always "Books"

Journals are usually called books of original entry, but some "books" of original entry are in reality not books at all; they are merely **files of business papers** preserved in an orderly manner in a filing or binding device.

For example, some concerns use carbon copies of sales invoices as a sales journal. These invoices give the essential facts about the sale, and a copy (usually a carbon) of each sales invoice for the period provides the data necessary to debit Accounts Receivable and credit Sales for the period. Thus the principle of the sales journal is applied in handling the sales transactions even though a journal is not used.

In a similar manner loose-leaf purchase invoice records, returned sales records, and purchase allowance records, for example, may take this form. Regardless of the arrangement used for the initial recording of transactions, all transactions are ultimately posted to the ledger accounts in accordance with the principles developed in this appendix for the several journals. These principles are fundamental; they do not change when a different means of recording and processing the data is used, whether it be loose-leaf records, adding machine tapes, bookkeeping machines, punched cards, or other mechanical or electrical devices.

# METHODS OF PROCESSING ACCOUNTING DATA

The principles of recording, classifying, and summarizing large quantities of accounting data described in this chapter are those applicable to a situation where sophisticated types of accounting machinery are not needed. In many business enterprises, the mass of data is so great that it is simply too time-consuming to post the entries manually, add the columns, update the files, and summarize the information. For this reason, accountants have resorted to more sophisticated devices to process the data quickly and efficiently. Our purpose now is to provide only a brief outline of the general types of equipment used for data processing, such as accounting machines, punched-card or tape systems, and EDP systems. No attempt is made to determine what machinery is best for a given situation because this question is complex and better left for an accounting systems course. Regardless of the devices used to process the data, the basic principles developed in this chapter apply.

### Accounting or Bookkeeping Machines

Accounting or bookkeeping machines are essentially posting machines operated by a clerk. They make it possible to post a transaction simultaneously to several different records. For example, a purchase invoice is recorded in the purchases journal and is posted to the subsidiary accounts payable ledger at the same time. Summary totals are then posted manually either daily or monthly to the purchases account and the accounts payable control account in the general ledger. The major benefits of an accounting or bookkeeping machine are that (1) the posting process is expedited, (2) the records are neater and easier to read, and (3) the equality of debits and credits is maintained.

### Punched-Card Equipment

A punched-card or tape system involves information that is punched onto various cards or tapes by means of holes arranged in a definite pattern. The punches identify the name of the customer, the item sold, the date, the amount, and other relevant data. For example, when a purchase order is received, the name of the customer, the type of item involved, and the dollar amount of the order are punched into a card. These cards are then processed through different types of machinery to arrive at the necessary grouped and summarized totals needed to determine the total purchases for the day, the various types and percentages of items sold in a given day, the percent of goods sold on a cash basis versus a credit basis, the geographical area where the goods were sold, and other pertinent information. Different types of machinery that reproduce, verify, collate, and tabulate the punched cards facilitate the analysis. The advantages of a punched-card or tape system are (1) flexibility, since many different procedures can be employed on this one card to develop different types of information, and (2) speed and accuracy, since this information can be summarized easily with little chance of error.

### Computers

A computer is a machine that can perform with amazing speed many internal operations from a specific set of instructions. The computer has revolutionized data processing not only because of its speed and accuracy in processing data, but also because it can be programmed to process the data in almost any manner desired by management. "Programmed" means that a data processor can write instructions to the computer to handle the data in a certain way. Essentially these instructions are all of a *yes* and *no* variety. For instance, if a certain sales level is achieved, a report might be issued warning of possible stockout on inventory items. One of the more interesting developments in the computer area has been the development of **on-line computer systems.** In this system, the transaction is recorded in the computer as it occurs without the use of any basic source document. The advantages of a computer are that it can take different courses of action depending on the results of data collected previously and can process data more quickly and efficiently than other types of business equipment.

Nearly every medium- or large-sized business owns or rents a computer, but until recently a computer was too expensive for a small business to own or rent. Small businesses generally avoided investing large sums of money yet gained the use of computers through **EDP service centers** or through **time-sharing arrangements.** However, with the recent emergence of **mini-computers** and **microprocessors,** even small businesses can own a computer and obtain the operating and record-keeping efficiencies provided by computers.

The growth in computers is nothing short of phenomenal. From the beginning of time through 1980, there were approximately 1 million computer systems. In 1982, one firm alone (Commodore International Ltd.) is expected to produce a half-million computers.[1] Worldwide, some 500,000 low-priced (under $5,000) computers were sold in 1980 at a total value of $730 million. By 1985, that total is expected to grow at least 40 percent annually to 3.7 million units, valued at $3.9 billion. The expected growth in sales of computers costing less than $10,000 by differing market segments is presented below:[2]

| Expected Sales of Computers Costing Less Than $10,000 | | | |
|---|---|---|---|
| Market | 1980 | (in millions) | 1985 |
| Home | $120 | | $ 475 |
| School | $ 35 | | $ 145 |
| Small business | $590 | | $2,700 |
| Office | $ 90 | | $1,450 |
| Scientific | $220 | | $1,020 |

What effect this growth in home, office, and small-business computers will have on accounting is anybody's guess. But because computers, of any size, are efficient and accurate at handling data, it is safe to say that more (if not most all) record keeping and accounting will be performed on and by computers. Present and future accountants and auditors would be wise to develop their computer competencies and skills in order to meet the challenges this growth brings.

[1] Andrew Pollack, "Next a Computer on Every Desk," *The New York Times* (August 23, 1981), Section 3, pp. 1 and 15.

[2] Ibid., p. 1.

# APPENDIX C

# Conversion of Cash Basis to Accrual Basis

Most companies use the **accrual basis of accounting,** recognizing revenue when it is earned and recognizing expenses in the period incurred, without regard to the time of receipt or payment of cash. Some small enterprises and the average individual taxpayer, however, use a strict or modified cash basis approach. Under the **strict cash basis,** revenue is recorded only when the cash is received and expenses are recorded only when the cash is paid. The determination of income on the cash basis rests upon the collection of revenue and the payment of expenses, and the matching principle is ignored. Consequently, cash basis financial statements are not in conformity with generally accepted accounting principles.

**FIGURE C-1**   Conversion of Cash Basis to Accrual Basis.

| Cash Basis ⟶ | ⟶ | ⟶ Accrual Basis |
|---|---|---|
| Receipts | − Beginning accounts receivable<br>+ Ending accounts receivable | = Net Sales |
| Rent receipts | + Beginning unearned rent<br>− Ending unearned rent<br>− Beginning rent receivable<br>+ Ending rent receivable | = Rent revenue |
| Payment for goods | + Beginning inventory<br>− Ending inventory<br>− Beginning accounts payable<br>+ Ending accounts payable | = Cost of goods sold |
| Payments for expenses | + Beginning prepaid expenses<br>− Ending prepaid expenses<br>− Beginning accrued expenses<br>+ Ending accrued expenses | = Operating expenses (except depreciation and similar write-offs) |
| Payments for property, plant, and equipment | − Cash payments for property, plant, and equipment<br>+ Periodic write-off of the asset cost through some formula(s) | = Depreciation or amortization expense |

The **modified cash basis,** a mixture of cash basis and accrual basis, is the method followed by service enterprises, such as lawyers, doctors, and public accountants. Expenditures having an economic life of more than one year are capitalized as assets and depreciated or amortized over future years. Prepaid expenses and accrued expenses are not treated in a consistent manner. Prepayments of expenses are deferred and deducted only in the year to which they apply, while expenses paid after the year of incurrence (accrued expenses) are deducted only in the year paid. Revenue is reported in the year of receipt. For tax purposes, however, any business in which inventory is a significant factor must use the accrual basis of accounting in reporting revenue from sales and cost of goods sold.

Not infrequently an accountant is required to convert a cash basis set of financial statements to the accrual basis for presentation and interpretation to a banker or for audit by an independent CPA. The simplified diagram on page 102 illustrates how cash basis financial data are converted to the accrual basis through various types of adjusting items.

In Figure C-1 cash receipts are converted to **net sales** by subtracting beginning accounts receivable and adding ending accounts receivable. By expanding the formula to include all of the accounts related to sales, cash receipts can be converted to **gross sales,** as shown below.

| | | |
|---|---:|---:|
| Cash receipts from customers | | xxx |
| Plus: Cash discounts | xx | |
|      Sales returns and allowances | xx | |
|      Accounts written off | xx | |
|      Ending accounts receivable | xx | xx |
| | | xxx |
| Less: Beginning accounts receivable | | xx |
| Gross sales | | xxx |

Cash receipts from customers can be converted to net sales also merely by adding or subtracting the change in the balance of accounts receivable from the beginning to the end of the year, as shown below.

Cash receipts from customers $\left\{ \begin{array}{l} + \text{ increase in accounts receivable} \\ \text{or} \\ - \text{ decrease in accounts receivable} \end{array} \right\}$ = Net sales

Similarly cash payments for goods can be converted to cost of goods sold by adding or deducting the change from the beginning to the end of the year in the accounts payable balance and in the inventory balance as follows.

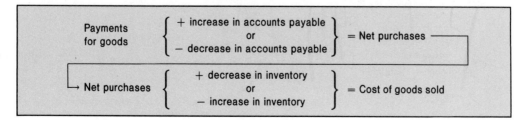

Payments for goods $\left\{ \begin{array}{l} + \text{ increase in accounts payable} \\ \text{or} \\ - \text{ decrease in accounts payable} \end{array} \right\}$ = Net purchases

Net purchases $\left\{ \begin{array}{l} + \text{ decrease in inventory} \\ \text{or} \\ - \text{ increase in inventory} \end{array} \right\}$ = Cost of goods sold

Figure C-1 presents the conversion of cash payments for *all* expenses to the accrual basis operating expenses in the aggregate and, therefore, involves both prepaid and accrued expenses in the conversion. Generally, each expense item is affected by a related accrual or a related prepayment, but not both. For example, the conversion of wages expense and the conversion of insurance expense are illustrated separately below.

$$\text{Wages paid during the year} \begin{cases} + \text{ Ending accrued wages} \\ - \text{ Beginning accrued wages} \end{cases} = \begin{array}{l} \text{Wages expense} \\ \text{for the year} \end{array}$$

$$\text{Insurance premiums paid during the year} \begin{cases} -\text{Ending prepaid insurance} \\ + \text{Beginning prepaid insurance} \end{cases} = \begin{array}{l} \text{Insurance expense} \\ \text{for the year} \end{array}$$

**ILLUSTRATION** Conversion of cash basis income statement data to the accrual basis will be illustrated for Diana Windsor, D.D.S., a dentist who keeps her accounting records on a cash basis. During 1983, Dr. Windsor collected $80,000 from her patients and paid $30,000 for operating expenses, resulting in a cash basis net income of $50,000. At January 1 and December 31, 1983, she has fees receivable, unearned fees, accrued expenses, and prepaid expenses as follows:

|  | January 1, 1983 | December 31, 1983 |
|---|---|---|
| Fees receivable | $12,000 | $5,000 |
| Unearned fees | –0– | 1,000 |
| Accrued expenses | 3,800 | 6,800 |
| Prepaid expenses | 2,000 | 3,000 |

Restatement of Diana Windsor's income statement data is presented in work sheet form below:

| Diana Windsor, D.D.S. Conversion of Income Statement from Cash Basis to Accrual Basis For the Year 1983 | | | | |
|---|---|---|---|---|
|  | Cash Basis | Adjustments Add | Adjustments Deduct | Accrual Basis |
| Revenue from fees: | $80,000 |  |  |  |
| — Fees receivable, Jan. 1 |  |  | $12,000 |  |
| + Fees receivable, Dec. 31 |  | $5,000 |  |  |
| — Unearned fees, Dec. 31 |  |  | 1,000 |  |
| Restated |  |  |  | $72,000 |
| Operating expenses: | 30,000 |  |  |  |
| — Accrued expenses, Jan. 1 |  |  | 3,800 |  |
| + Accrued expenses, Dec. 31 |  | 6,800 |  |  |
| + Prepaid expenses, Jan. 1 |  | 2,000 |  |  |
| — Prepaid expenses, Dec. 31 |  |  | 3,000 |  |
| Restated |  |  |  | 32,000 |
| Net income—cash basis | $50,000 |  |  |  |
| Net income—accrual basis |  |  |  | $40,000 |

The computation of income on the cash basis can result in a material misstatement when there is a lag in time between the exchange transactions and the related cash receipt or disbursement transactions.[1]

**Note:** All **asterisked** Questions, Cases, Exercises, or Problems relate to material contained in the appendix to each chapter.

## QUESTIONS

1. Why are revenue and expense accounts called temporary or nominal proprietorship accounts?

2. Do the following events represent business transactions? Explain your answer in each case.
   (a) The owner of the business withdraws cash from the business for personal use.
   (b) Merchandise is ordered for delivery next month.
   (c) A truck is purchased on account.
   (d) A customer returns merchandise and is given credit on account.
   (e) A prospective employee is interviewed.

3. Give an example of a transaction that results in
   (a) A decrease in one liability and an increase in another liability.
   (b) A decrease in one asset and an increase in another asset.
   (c) A decrease in an asset and a decrease in a liability.

4. Name the accounts debited and credited for each of the following transactions:
   (a) Purchase of office supplies on account.
   (b) Purchase of 10 gallons of gasoline for the delivery truck.
   (c) Billing a customer for work done.
   (d) Receipt of cash from customer on account.

5. Is it necessary that a trial balance be taken periodically? What purpose does it serve?

6. Indicate whether each of the items below is a real or nominal account and whether it appears in the balance sheet or the income statement.
   (a) Furniture.
   (b) Income from Services.
   (c) Office Salaries.
   (d) Supplies on Hand.
   (e) Prepaid Insurance Expense.
   (f) Wages Payable.
   (g) Merchandise Inventory.
   (h) Accumulated Depreciation.

7. Employees are paid every Saturday. If a balance sheet is prepared on Wednesday, December 31, what does the amount of wages earned during the first three days of the week (12/29, 12/30, 12/31) represent? Explain.

8. Why is the Purchases account debited both when merchandise is purchased for cash and when it is purchased on account? Why is the inventory amount as determined at the end of the fiscal period under a periodic inventory system deducted from the cost of goods available for sale?

9. What is the purpose of the Cost of Goods Sold account (assume a periodic inventory system)?

10. Under a periodic system is the amount shown for Inventory the same in a trial balance taken before closing as it is in a trial balance taken after closing? Why?

11. If the cost of a new typewriter ($850) purchased for office use were recorded as a debit to Purchases, what would be the effect of the error on the balance sheet and income statement in the period in which the error was made?

---

[1]The FASB in *Statement of Financial Accounting Concepts No. 1* acknowledges that accrual accounting provides a better indication of enterprise performance than does information about cash receipts and payments. Accrual accounting is an attempt to recognize the economic and financial effects of transactions and other events that have cash consequences to an enterprise in the periods in which those transactions and events occur rather than only in the periods in which cash is received or paid.

12. What differences are there between the trial balance before closing and the trial balance after closing with respect to the following?
    - (a) Revenue accounts.
    - (b) Retained earnings account.
    - (c) Cash.
    - (d) Expense accounts.
    - (e) Accounts payable.

13. What are "adjusting entries" and why are they necessary?

14. What are "closing entries" and why are they necessary?

15. What are "reversing entries" and why are they necessary?

*16. Why would a company use several journals instead of only a general journal? How would the company determine which special journals it should use?

*17. When the special journals illustrated in this chapter are used, how many monthly postings are made to the Cash account? Why?

*18. For each of the following transactions name the book of original entry and the accounts to be debited and credited, assuming that the five journals discussed in this chapter are used:
    - (a) Sale of merchandise for cash.
    - (b) Purchase of office equipment on account.
    - (c) Payment of cash to a creditor, no discount.
    - (d) Receipt of cash from customer on account.
    - (e) Loan from bank on a promissory note; interest payable at maturity date.
    - (f) Purchase of merchandise on account (periodic inventory system).
    - (g) Return of damaged merchandise to a supplier.

*19. What is a controlling account? What is its relationship to a subsidiary ledger?

*20. How does the use of controlling accounts and subsidiary ledgers affect (a) the taking of a trial balance, (b) the appearance of the trial balance, and (c) the equality of debits and credits in the trial balance?

*21. Differentiate between a purchase order, a purchase invoice, a voucher, and a check. What journal entry, if any, generally results from the issuance of each of these documents (assume a periodic inventory system)?

*22. List two types of transactions that would receive different accounting treatment using (a) strict cash basis accounting and (b) a modified cash basis.

*23. Why are beginning accrued wages subtracted from, and ending accrued wages added to, wages paid during the year when wages expense for the year is computed?

## EXERCISES

E3–1 The trial balance of the Sandy Knotts Company does not balance.

|  | | |
|---|---|---|
| | Sandy Knotts Co. | |
| | TRIAL BALANCE | |
| | April 30 | |
| Cash | $ 5,902 | |
| Accounts Receivable | 6,300 | |
| Supplies on Hand | 1,600 | |
| Furniture and Equipment | 5,200 | |
| Accounts Payable | | $ 4,500 |
| Sandy Knotts Co., Capital | | 10,000 |
| Income from Fees | | 4,700 |
| Office Expenses | 1,980 | |
| | $20,982 | $19,200 |

An examination of the ledger shows these errors.

1. Cash received from a customer on account was recorded (both debit and credit) as $1,400 instead of $1,120.

2. The purchase on account of a typewriter costing $780 was recorded as a debit to Office Expenses and a credit to Accounts Payable.

3. Services were performed on account for a client, $1,780, for which Accounts Receivable was debited $1,780 and Income from Fees was credited $178.

4. A payment of $80 for telephone charges was entered as a debit to Office Expenses and a debit to Cash.

5. The Income from Fees account was totaled at $4,700 instead of $4,720.

**Instructions**

From this information prepare a corrected trial balance.

**E3-2** Information concerning the first month of operations of Fran Rifkin Boutique is presented below (the periodic inventory system is used):

| | |
|---|---:|
| Transportation-in | $   900 |
| Total purchases on account | 18,000 |
| Purchase returns on account | 720 |
| Transportation-out | 540 |
| Total recorded as cash purchases | 8,280 |
| Purchase allowances on account | 1,260 |
| Inventory at the end of the month | 3,600 |
| Sales discounts | 585 |
| Refunds for defective items purchased for cash | 378 |
| Error made by bookkeeper debiting Supplies Expense, when in reality the item was a cash purchase of merchandise | 576 |

**Instructions**

(a) Compute the correct amount of cost of goods sold.
(b) Prepare the cost of goods sold section of the income statement.
(c) Indicate in which section of the income statement items not used in the cost of goods sold section of this exercise should appear.

**E3-3** When the accounts of S. Pritchett Donut Shoppe are examined, the adjusting data listed below are uncovered on December 31, the end of an annual fiscal period.

1. The unexpired insurance account shows a debit of $1,800, representing the cost of a 3-year fire insurance policy dated September 1 of the current year.

2. On November 1, Rental Income was credited for $1,200, representing income from a subrental for a 3-month period beginning on that date.

3. Purchase of advertising materials for $800 during the year was recorded in the advertising expense account. On December 31, advertising materials of $120 are on hand.

4. Interest of $180 has accrued on notes payable.

**Instructions**

Prepare in general journal form: (a) the adjusting entry for each item; (b) the reversing entry for each item where appropriate.

**\*E3-4** Presented below are the following transactions of the Mexicana Company.

Sept.  1  Purchases office equipment for cash, $1,412.

    3  Sells merchandise on account to Kelly Fritz, $1,063, f.o.b. shipping point.

    3  Pays freight on sale to Kelly Fritz, $56.

4 Receives a refund of $52 on office equipment because of a difference in the specifications of equipment ordered and received.

7 Purchases merchandise on account from M. B. Taylor, $1,500, 2/10, n/30, f.o.b. destination (record at gross amount).

9 M. B. Taylor has paid freight on shipment, $44.

13 Receives a check in full of account from Kelly Fritz.

18 Because of increased business, Mexicana Company purchases additional office equipment at a price of $600, giving in exchange shares of its own no-par stock having a total market price of $310, with the balance payable in 30 days.

21 Cash sales of $12,500 are made.

25 An invoice for heat, light, and water of $50 is received from Rural Utilities Inc.

27 Pays M. B. Taylor in full of account.

29 Office salaries of $876 and the utilities bill received on September 25 are paid.

**Instructions**

Prepare journal entries for each transaction and indicate in which journal they normally are recorded. (Mexicana Company uses a periodic inventory system.)

**\*E3–5** The general ledger of Doodle Company contains the following Accounts Payable control account. Also shown is the related subsidiary ledger.

### ACCOUNTS PAYABLE

| | | | | | | |
|---|---|---|---|---|---|---|
| Feb. 28 | General journal | 16,400 | Feb. | 1 | Balance | 56,000 |
| | 28 | 33,450 | | 5 | General journal | 360 |
| | | | | 11 | General journal | 106 |
| | | | | 28 | Cash receipts | 300 |
| | | | | 28 | General journal | 990 |
| | | | | 28 | Purchases | 21,750 |

### CREDITOR'S LEDGER

| J. Van Alstyne | Tammy Bridges | Cal Ulfsrud |
|---|---|---|
| Balance 4,783 | Balance 8,417 | Balance  ? |

**Instructions**

For the data above:
(a) Indicate the missing posting reference in the control account and the amount of the missing ending balance in the subsidiary ledger.
(b) Indicate the amounts in the control account that were double posted.
(c) What is meant by "double posting"? (Explain in full.)

**\*E3–6** On page 109 are selected records and documents for the voucher system of the Bob Penkowski Company.

**Instructions**

(a) Determine the balance in the control account.
(b) Prove the vouchers payable account by reconciling the voucher file with the detail in the register. Assume that the company's file of unpaid vouchers is correct.
(c) Determine the causes of any lack of agreement between the control account and subsidiary records. (Label all amounts.)
(d) What is the correct vouchers payable balance?

## VOUCHER REGISTER

| Date Feb. 1983 | Vou. No. | Creditor | Payment Made | | Vouchers Payable Cr. | Purchases Dr. | Sundry Items Dr. | |
|---|---|---|---|---|---|---|---|---|
| | | | Check No. | Date | | | Account Title | Amount |
| 2/5 | 300 | DeFlippo Supply | 113 | 2/7 | 1,800 | | Supplies | 1,800 |
| 2/9 | 301 | John Relias | 114 | 2/26 | 2,340 | 2,340 | | |
| 2/15 | 302 | Betts & Bore | 115 | 2/26 | 5,220 | 5,220 | | |
| 2/17 | 303 | Vrany Co. | 117 | 2/28 | 3,150 | | Furniture | 3,150 |
| 2/20 | 304 | Daily Courier | | | 450 | | Advertising | 450 |
| 2/24 | 305 | Lou Slezak | | | 126 | | Miscellaneous expenses | 126 |
| 2/25 | 306 | John Relias | | | 1,980 | 1,980 | | |
| 2/28 | 307 | Grigas Realty | 116 | 2/28 | 2,430 | | Rent | 2,430 |

### UNPAID VOUCHERS

| Voucher No. 304 | Voucher No. 305 |
|---|---|
| Date: 2/20   To:  Daily Courier | Date: 2/24   To:  Lou Slezak |
| Amount  $450 | Amount  $126 |
| Acct. Dr.  Advertising | Acct. Dr.  Miscellaneous Expenses |
| **Voucher No. 301** | **Voucher No. 299** |
| Date: 2/9   To:  John Relias | Date: 2/3   To:  Ruth Ann Meadow |
| Amount  $2,340 | Amount  $423 |
| Acct. Dr.  Purchases | Acct. Dr.  Repair Expenses |

### GENERAL LEDGER—CONTROL ACCOUNT
#### Vouchers Payable

| 1983 | | | | 1983 | | | |
|---|---|---|---|---|---|---|---|
| Feb. 28 | CP | | 14,580 | Feb. 28 | VR | | 17,496 |

**\*E3–7** No-nuke Company maintains its books on the accrual basis. The company reported insurance expense of $17,450 in its 1983 income statement. Prepaid insurance at December 31, 1983 amounted to $6,440; cash paid for insurance during the year 1983 totaled $19,800. There was no accrued insurance expense either at the beginning or at the end of 1983.

**Instructions**

What was the amount, if any, of prepaid insurance at January 1, 1983? Show computations.

**\*E3–8** Schimmle Corporation, which uses the accrual basis of accounting, reported interest expense of $90,280 in its 1983 income statement. Accrued interest at December 31, 1983 amounted to $15,000; cash paid for interest during 1983 totaled $84,400. There was no prepaid interest either at the beginning or at the end of 1983.

**Instructions**

What was the amount, if any, of accrued interest at January 1, 1983? Show computations.

**\*E3–9** Sip-N-Dip Corp. maintains its financial records on the cash basis of accounting. Interested in securing a long-term loan from its regular bank, Sip-N-Dip Corp. requests you as its independent CPA to convert its cash basis income statement data to the accrual basis. You are provided with the following summarized data covering 1981, 1982, and 1983.

|  | 1981 | 1982 | 1983 |
|---|---|---|---|
| Cash receipts from sales: | | | |
| On 1981 sales | $240,000 | $ 90,000 | $30,000 |
| On 1982 sales | -0- | 270,000 | 90,000 |
| Cash payments for expenses: | | | |
| On 1981 expenses | 150,000 | 21,000 | 18,000 |
| On 1982 expenses | 18,000[a] | 150,000 | 42,000 |
| On 1983 expenses | | 15,000[b] | |

[a]Prepayments of 1982 expense.
[b]Prepayments of 1983 expense.

**Instructions**

(a) Using the data above, prepare abbreviated income statements for the years 1981 and 1982 on the cash basis.

(b) Using the data above, prepare abbreviated income statements for the years 1981 and 1982 on the accrual basis.

## PROBLEMS

**P3–1** The accounts listed appeared in the December 31 trial balance of the Nodose Theater.

| | | |
|---|---|---|
| Equipment | 180,000 | |
| Accumulated Depreciation of Equipment | | 54,000 |
| Notes Payable | | 72,000 |
| Income from Admissions | | 378,000 |
| Income from Concessions | | 36,000 |
| Advertising Expense | 13,680 | |
| Salaries Expense | 57,600 | |
| Interest Expense | 1,080 | |

**Instructions**

(a) From the account balances listed above and the information given below prepare the adjusting entries necessary on December 31.

1. The equipment has an estimated life of 20 years and a trade-in value of $36,000 at the end of that time. (Use straight-line method.)

2. The note payable is a 90-day note given to the bank October 22 and bearing interest at 10%. (Use 360 days for denominator.)

3. In December 2,000 coupon admission books were sold at $18 each; they could be used for admission any time after January 1.

4. The concession stand is operated by a concessionaire who pays 10% of gross receipts for the privilege of selling popcorn, candy, and soft drinks in the lobby. Sales for December were $21,600, and the 10% due for December has not yet been received or entered.

5. Advertising expense paid in advance and included in Advertising Expense, $900.
6. Salaries accrued but unpaid, $3,100.

(b) What amounts should be shown for each of the following on the income statement for the year?

1. Interest expense.
2. Income from admissions.
3. Income from concessions.
4. Advertising expense.
5. Salaries expense.

**P3-2** Presented below are the trial balance and the other information related to Al E. Gator, a consulting engineer.

Al E. Gator, Consulting Engineer
TRIAL BALANCE
December 31, 1983

| | | |
|---|---:|---:|
| Cash | $ 37,800 | |
| Accounts Receivable | 13,100 | |
| Allowance for Doubtful Accounts | | $    972 |
| Engineering Supplies Inventory | 1,980 | |
| Unexpired Insurance | 666 | |
| Furniture and Equipment | 24,660 | |
| Accumulated Depreciation of Furniture and Equipment | | 3,960 |
| Notes Payable | | 5,400 |
| Al E. Gator, Capital | | 18,914 |
| Revenue from Consulting Fees | | 90,000 |
| Rent Expense | 9,360 | |
| Office Salaries | 29,880 | |
| Heat, Light, and Water | 1,080 | |
| Miscellaneous Office Expense | 720 | |
| | $119,246 | $119,246 |

1. Fees received in advance from clients, $5,400.

2. Services performed for clients that were not recorded by December 31, $3,600.

3. The Allowance for Doubtful Accounts account should be adjusted to 7% of the accounts receivable balance (adjusted).

4. Insurance expired during the year, $234.

5. Furniture and equipment is being depreciated at 10% per year.

6. Al E. Gator gave the bank a 90-day, 8% note for $5,400 on December 1, 1983.

7. Rent of the building is $720 per month. The rent for 1983 has been paid, as has that for January 1984.

8. Office salaries earned but unpaid December 31, 1983, $1,080.

**Instructions**

(a) From the trial balance and other information given, prepare adjusting entries as of December 31, 1983.

(b) Prepare a single-step income statement for 1983, a balance sheet, and a statement of owner's equity. Al E. Gator withdrew $18,000 cash for personal use during the year.

**P3-3** Following is the December 31 trial balance of Infocus TV Store.

Infocus TV Store
TRIAL BALANCE
December 31

| | | |
|---|---:|---:|
| Cash | $ 10,000 | |
| Accounts Receivable | 56,000 | |
| Allowance for Doubtful Accounts | | $ 4,000 |
| Inventory, January 1 | 70,000 | |
| Furniture and Equipment | 60,000 | |
| Accumulated Depreciation of Furniture and Equipment | | 24,000 |
| Prepaid Insurance | 3,600 | |
| Notes Payable | | 20,000 |
| Infocus, Capital | | 60,000 |
| Sales | | 600,000 |
| Purchases | 400,000 | |
| Sales Salaries | 40,000 | |
| Advertising Expense | 2,400 | |
| Administrative Salaries | 60,000 | |
| Office Expenses | 6,000 | |
| | $708,000 | $708,000 |

**Instructions**

(a) Construct "T" accounts and enter the balances shown.
(b) Prepare adjusting journal entries for the following and post to the "T" accounts. Open additional "T" accounts as necessary. (The books are closed yearly on December 31.)
   1. Adjust the Allowance for Doubtful Accounts to 10% of the accounts receivable.
   2. Furniture and equipment is depreciated at 10% per year.
   3. Insurance expired during the year, $1,600.
   4. Interest accrued on notes payable, $800.
   5. Sales salaries earned but not paid, $1,200.
   6. Advertising paid in advance, $600.
   7. Office supplies on hand, $1,000, charged to Office Expenses when purchased.
(c) Prepare closing entries and post to the accounts. The inventory on December 31 was $90,000.

**P3-4** Listed below are the transactions of E. Z. Pull, D.D.S., for the month of September:

Sept. 1  E. Z. Pull begins practice as a dentist and invests $12,000 cash.

2  Purchases furniture and dental equipment on account from Spaeth Co. for $17,280.

4  Pays rent for office space, $540 for the month.

4  Employs a receptionist, Daniella Ryan.

5  Purchases dental supplies for cash, $856.

8  Receives cash of $306 from patients.

10  Pays miscellaneous office expenses, $126.

14  Bills patients $1,620 for services performed.

18  Pays Spaeth Co. on account, $3,600.

19  Withdraws $2,000 cash from the business for personal use.

20  Receives $720 from patients on account.

25  Bills patients $1,530 for services performed.

30   Pays the following expenses in cash: office salaries, $900; miscellaneous office expenses, $72.

30   Dental supplies used during September, $150.

**Instructions**

(a)  Enter the transactions shown above in appropriate general ledger accounts. Allow 10 lines for the Cash account and five lines for each of the other accounts needed. Record depreciation using an 8-year life on the furniture and equipment, the straight-line method, and no salvage value. Do not use a drawing account.

(b)  Take a trial balance.

(c)  Prepare an income statement, a balance sheet, and a statement of capital.

(d)  Close the ledger.

(e)  Take a postclosing trial balance.

**P3–5**  The balance sheet of Remmers Company as of December 31, 1983, is presented below.

Remmers Company
BALANCE SHEET AS OF DECEMBER 31, 1983

| Assets | | Liabilities and Capital | |
|---|---|---|---|
| Cash | $ 3,900 | Accounts payable | $ 2,325 |
| Accounts receivable | 4,395 | Notes payable | 3,000 |
| Inventory | 3,000 | Total liabilities | $ 5,325 |
| Office equipment | 3,800 | | |
| Accum. depr. | (975) | | |
| Furniture and fixtures | 6,300 | | |
| Accum. depr. | (1,500) | Remmers, capital | 13,595 |
| Total assets | $18,920 | Total liabilities and capital | $18,920 |

The following transactions occurred during the month of January, 1984.

Jan. 2   Receives payment of $1,050 on accounts receivable.

3   Purchases merchandise on account from Norm & Jackie Co. for $1,875, 2/30, n/60 f.o.b. shipping point (record at gross amount).

4   Receives an invoice from *Eagle,* a trade magazine, for advertising, $24.

4   Sells merchandise on account to Dawna Co. for $825, 2/10, n/30 f.o.b. shipping point.

4   Makes a cash sale to Phillip Inc. for $1,613.

6   Sends a letter to Norm & Jackie Co. regarding a slight defect in one item of merchandise received.

9   Purchases merchandise on account from Heather's Novelty Company, $563.

11   Pays freight on merchandise received from Norm & Jackie Co., $53.

11   Receives a credit memo from Norm & Jackie Co. granting an allowance of $18 on defective merchandise (see transaction of January 6).

15   Receives $500 on account from Dawna Co..

19   Sells merchandise on account to Dan Urban, $713, 2/10, n/30.

21   Pays display clerk's salary of $488.

25   Sells merchandise for cash, $1,402.

27   Purchases office equipment on account, $750 (begin depreciating in February).

29   Pays Norm & Jackie Co. in full of account.

30   Receives a note from Dan Urban in full of account.

31   A count of the inventory on hand reveals $2,510 of salable merchandise.

**Instructions**

    (a) Open ledger accounts at January 1, 1984.

    (b) Enter the transactions into ledger accounts.

    (c) Take a trial balance after adjusting for depreciation; use 10-year life, straight-line method, and no salvage for all long-term assets.

    (d) Close the ledger for preparation of the monthly financial statements.

    (e) Prepare a balance sheet and income statement.

    (f) Take a postclosing trial balance.

**P3–6** On January 1, 1984, after reversing entries were made, the trial balance of Sharon Zima Co. contained the following account balances, all of which relate to prepaid or unearned items.

| | | |
|---|---:|---:|
| Interest Expense | $ 100 | |
| Prepaid Insurance ($480 was paid Oct. 1, 1983 for one year's premium) | 360 | |
| Subscription Income | | $2,200 |
| Newsprint on Hand (balance was $8,500 before adjusting) | 4,400 | |
| Stationery and Postage Expense | 1,220 | |
| Unearned Advertising Revenue (balance was $36,000 before adjusting) | | 6,000 |

**Instructions**

    (a) Give the December 31, 1983, adjusting entry that involved each of the accounts shown.

    (b) Which of the adjusting entries shown in (a) were probably reversed on January 1, 1984?

**P3–7** Presented below is information related to Ginnie Brown, realtor, at the close of the fiscal year ending December 31.

    **1.** She had paid the local newspaper $108 for an advertisement to be run in January of the next year, charging it to Advertising Expense.

    **2.** On November 1 she had her 90-day note for $3,000 discounted at the bank at 6% and received cash for the proceeds (Interest Expense was debited).

    **3.** Salaries and wages due and unpaid December 31: sales, $950; office clerks, $750.

    **4.** Interest accrued to date on Miller Company's note, which she holds, $300.

    **5.** Estimated loss on bad debts, $1,120 for the period.

    **6.** Stamps and stationery on hand, $180, charged to Stationery and Postage Expense account when purchased.

    **7.** She has not yet paid the December rent on the building her business occupies, $900.

    **8.** Insurance paid November 1 for one year, $648, charged to Unexpired Insurance when paid.

    **9.** Property taxes accrued, $2,300.

    **10.** On December 1 she gave Helen Buggert her 60-day, 6% note for $5,000 on account.

    **11.** On October 31 she received $2,040 from Bonnie Riggin in payment of six months' rent for office space occupied by her in the building and credited Unearned Rent Income.

    **12.** On September 1 she paid six months' rent in advance on a warehouse, $9,000, and debited the asset account Prepaid Rent Expense.

    **13.** The bill from the City Light & Power Company for December has been received but not yet entered or paid, $470.

    **14.** Estimated depreciation on furniture and equipment, $1,500.

**Instructions**

    (a) Prepare adjusting entries as of December 31.

    (b) List the numbers of the entries that would be reversed.

**P3–8** The following list of accounts and their balances represents the unadjusted trial balance of Omeomy Company at December 31, 1984.

| | Dr. | Cr. |
|---|---|---|
| Cash | $ 83,068 | |
| Accounts Receivable | 106,200 | |
| Allowance for Doubtful Accounts | | $ 3,060 |
| Merchandise Inventory | 59,400 | |
| Prepaid Insurance | 2,288 | |
| Investment in India Inc. Bonds (10%) | 22,000 | |
| Land | 27,000 | |
| Building | 121,500 | |
| Accumulated Depreciation—Building | | 13,500 |
| Equipment | 32,400 | |
| Accumulated Depreciation—Equipment | | 5,400 |
| Goodwill | 30,600 | |
| Accounts Payable | | 117,000 |
| Bonds Payable (20-year; 6%) | | 180,000 |
| Discount on Bonds Payable | 14,400 | |
| Common Stock | | 162,000 |
| Retained Earnings | | 36,211 |
| Sales | | 180,000 |
| Rental Income | | 4,860 |
| Advertising Expense | 33,750 | |
| Supplies Expense | 10,800 | |
| Purchases | 97,200 | |
| Purchase Discounts | | 1,800 |
| Office Salary Expense | 18,900 | |
| Sales Salary Expense | 35,550 | |
| Interest Expense | 8,775 | |
| | $703,831 | $703,831 |

Additional information:

1. Actual advertising costs amounted to $2,250 per month. The company has already paid for advertisements in *People Magazine* for the first quarter of 1985.

2. The building was purchased and occupied January 1, 1982 with an estimated life of 18 years. (The company uses straight-line depreciation.)

3. Prepaid insurance contains the premium costs of two policies: Policy A, cost of $840, 1-year term taken out on Sept. 1, 1983; Policy B, cost of $1,728, 3-year term taken out on April 1, 1984.

4. A portion of their building has been converted into a snack bar that has been rented to the Yummy Food Corp. since July 1, 1983 at a rate of $3,240 per year payable each July 1.

5. One of the company's customers declared bankruptcy December 30, 1984, and it has been definitely established that the $2,700 due from them will never be collected. This fact has not been recorded. In addition, Omeomy estimates that 4% of the Accounts Receivable balance on December 31, 1984 will become uncollectible.

6. Nine hundred dollars, which was advanced to a salesperson on December 31, 1984, was charged to Sales Salary Expense. Sales salaries are paid on the 1st and 16th of each month for the following half month.

7. When the company purchased a competing firm on July 1, 1982, it acquired goodwill in the amount of $36,000, which is being amortized.

8. On October 1, 1980, Omeomy issued 180 $1,000 bonds at 90% of par value. Interest payments are made semiannually on March 31 and September 30. (Use straight-line method for amortization of the bond discount.)

9. On August 1, 1984, Omeomy purchased 22 $1,000, 10% bonds maturing on August 31, 1989, at par value. Interest payment dates are July 31 and January 31.

10. The physical inventory on hand at December 31, 1984 was $84,000 per a physical inventory. Record the adjusting entry for inventory by using a "Cost of Goods Sold" account.

### Instructions

(a) Prepare adjusting and correcting entries in general journal form using the information above.

(b) Indicate which of the adjusting entries will probably be reversed.

**P3-9** The following list of accounts and their balances represents the unadjusted trial balance of Howat Co. at December 31, 1984:

|  | Dr. | Cr. |
|---|---|---|
| Cash | $ 5,000 | |
| Accounts Receivable | 46,000 | |
| Allowance for Doubtful Accounts | | $ 720 |
| Inventory | 55,000 | |
| Prepaid Insurance | 2,760 | |
| Prepaid Rent | 14,400 | |
| Investment in Cadalac Corp. Bonds | 10,000 | |
| Property, Plant, and Equipment | 104,000 | |
| Accumulated Depreciation | | 15,600 |
| Accounts Payable | | 10,930 |
| Bonds Payable | | 50,000 |
| Premium on Bonds Payable | | 950 |
| Capital Stock | | 100,000 |
| Retained Earnings | | 51,600 |
| Sales | | 216,000 |
| Rent Income | | 7,200 |
| Purchases | 170,000 | |
| Purchase Discounts | | 3,400 |
| Transportation-out | 10,000 | |
| Transportation-in | 4,400 | |
| Salaries and Wages | 32,000 | |
| Interest Expense | 1,950 | |
| Miscellaneous Expense | 890 | |
| | $456,400 | $456,400 |

Additional data:

1. On November 1, 1984, Howat received $7,200 rent from its lessee for a 12-month lease beginning on that date, crediting Rent Income.

2. Howat estimates that 4% of the Accounts Receivable balances on December 31, 1984, will become uncollectible. On December 28, 1984, the bookkeeper incorrectly credited Sales for a receipt on account in the amount of $1,000. This error had not yet been corrected on December 31.

3. Per a physical inventory, inventory on hand at December 31, 1984, was $57,000. Record the adjusting entry for inventory by using a cost of goods sold account.

4. Prepaid insurance contains the premium costs of two policies: Policy A, cost of $840, 1-year term, taken out on September 1, 1984; Policy B, cost of $1,920, 3-year term, taken out on April 1, 1984.

5. The regular rate of depreciation is 10% per year. Acquisitions and retirements during a year are depreciated at half this rate. There were no retirements during the year. On December 31, 1983, the balance of Property, Plant, and Equipment was $96,000.

6. On April 1, 1984, Howat issued 50 $1,000, 8% bonds, maturing on April 1, 1994, at 102% of par value. Interest payment dates are April 1 and October 1.

7. On August 1, 1984, Howat purchased 10 $1,000, 10% Cadalac Corp. bonds, maturing on August 31, 1986, at par value. Interest payment dates are July 31 and January 31.

8. On May 30, 1984, Howat rented a warehouse for $1,200 per month, paying $14,400 in advance, debiting Prepaid Rent.

**Instructions**

(a) Prepare adjusting and correcting entries in general journal form using the information above.

(b) Indicate the adjusting entries that would be reversed.

**P3-10** Following is the trial balance of the Exclusive Country Club as of December 31. The books are closed annually on December 31.

Exclusive Country Club
TRIAL BALANCE
December 31

| | | |
|---|---:|---:|
| Cash | $ 16,000 | |
| Dues Receivable | 13,200 | |
| Allowance for Doubtful Accounts | | $ 1,200 |
| Land | 400,000 | |
| Buildings | 120,000 | |
| Accumulated Depreciation of Buildings | | 40,000 |
| Equipment | 160,000 | |
| Accumulated Depreciation of Equipment | | 70,000 |
| Unexpired Insurance | 6,000 | |
| Capital | | 562,800 |
| Dues Income | | 180,000 |
| Income from Greens Fees | | 6,000 |
| Rent Income | | 13,200 |
| Utilities Expense | 54,000 | |
| Salaries Expense | 80,000 | |
| Maintenance | 24,000 | |
| | $873,200 | $873,200 |

**Instructions**

(a) Enter the balances in ledger accounts. Allow five lines for each account.

(b) From the trial balance and the information given, prepare adjusting entries and post to the ledger accounts.

1. The buildings have an estimated life of 40 years with no salvage value (straight-line method).

2. The equipment is depreciated at 10% per year.

3. Insurance expired during the year, $2,500.

4. The rent income represents the amount received for 11 months for dining facilities. The December rent has not yet been received.

5. It is estimated that 20% of the dues receivable will be uncollectible.

6. Salaries earned but not paid by December 31, $2,400.

7. Dues paid in advance by members, $7,500.

(c) Prepare an adjusted trial balance.

(d) Prepare closing entries and post.

(e) Prepare reversing entries and post.

(f) Prepare a trial balance.

**P3–11** Presented below is the trial balance for Tom Hanson, proprietor.

Tom Hanson
**TRIAL BALANCE**
December 31, 1984

| | | |
|---|---:|---:|
| Cash | $ 11,100 | |
| Accounts Receivable | 64,800 | |
| Allowance for Doubtful Accounts | | $ 2,000 |
| Inventory, January 1 | 76,000 | |
| Land | 27,000 | |
| Building | 90,000 | |
| Accumulated Depreciation of Building | | 14,400 |
| Furniture and Fixtures | 17,300 | |
| Accumulated Depreciation of Furniture and Fixtures | | 5,700 |
| Unexpired Insurance | 7,800 | |
| Accounts Payable | | 32,400 |
| Notes Payable | | 27,000 |
| Mortgage Payable | | 36,000 |
| Tom Hanson, Capital | | 79,380 |
| Sales | | 720,000 |
| Sales Returns and Allowances | 3,600 | |
| Purchases | 558,000 | |
| Purchase Returns and Allowances | | 5,900 |
| Transportation-in | 14,800 | |
| Sales Salaries | 21,600 | |
| Advertising | 4,700 | |
| Salaries, Office and General | 16,200 | |
| Heat, Light, and Water | 4,300 | |
| Telephone and Telegraph | 1,600 | |
| Miscellaneous Office Expenses | 2,000 | |
| Purchase Discounts | | 9,600 |
| Sales Discounts | 9,500 | |
| Interest Expense | 2,080 | |
| | $932,380 | $932,380 |

**Instructions**

(a) Copy the trial balance above in the first two columns of a ten-column work sheet.

(b) Prepare adjusting entries in journal form from the following information. (The fiscal year ends December 31.)

1. Estimated bad debts, one-quarter of 1% of sales less returns and allowances.
2. Depreciation on building, 2% per year; on furniture and fixtures, 10% per year.
3. Insurance expired during the year, $3,500.
4. Interest at 12% is payable on the mortgage on January 1 of each year.
5. Sales salaries accrued, December 31, $2,000.
6. Advertising expenses paid in advance, $700.
7. Office supplies on hand December 31, $2,000. (Charged to Miscellaneous Office Expenses when purchased.)
8. Interest accrued on notes payable December 31, $1,500.

(c) Transfer the adjusting entries to the work sheet and complete it. Merchandise inventory on hand December 31, $60,000.

(d) Prepare an income statement, a balance sheet, and a statement of retained earnings.

(e) Prepare closing journal entries.

(f) Indicate the adjusting entries that would be reversed.

**P3-12** Spelunker Company closes its books only once a year on December 31 but prepares monthly financial statements by estimating month-end inventories and by using work sheets.

The company's trial balance on January 31, 1983, is presented below. Selling Expenses and Administrative Expenses are controlling accounts.

Spelunker Company
TRIAL BALANCE
January 31, 1983

| | | |
|---|---:|---:|
| Cash | $ 1,150 | |
| Accounts Receivable | 10,000 | |
| Notes Receivable | 2,000 | |
| Allowance for Doubtful Accounts | | $ 650 |
| Inventory, Jan. 1, 1983 | 15,000 | |
| Furniture and Fixtures | 25,000 | |
| Accumulated Depreciation of Furniture and Fixtures | | 5,000 |
| Unexpired Insurance | 600 | |
| Supplies on Hand | 1,050 | |
| Accounts Payable | | 6,000 |
| Notes Payable | | 5,000 |
| Common Stock | | 20,000 |
| Retained Earnings | | 10,125 |
| Sales | | 101,600 |
| Sales Returns and Allowances | 1,600 | |
| Purchases | 70,000 | |
| Transportation-in | 2,000 | |
| Selling Expenses | 11,000 | |
| Administrative Expenses | 9,000 | |
| Interest Revenue | | 125 |
| Interest Expense | 100 | |
| | $148,500 | $148,500 |

**Instructions**

(a) Copy the trial balance in the first two columns of an eight-column work sheet.
(b) Prepare adjusting entries in journal form (administrative expenses includes bad debts, depreciation, insurance, supplies, and office salaries).
   1. Estimated bad debts, .3% of net sales.
   2. Depreciation of furniture and fixtures, 12% per year.
   3. Insurance expired in January, $60.
   4. Supplies used in January, $250.
   5. Office salaries accrued, $400.
   6. Interest accrued on notes payable, $220.
   7. Interest unearned on notes receivable, $65.
(c) Transfer the adjusting entries to the work sheet.
(d) Estimate the January 31 inventory and enter it on the work sheet. The average gross profit earned by the company is 35% of net sales.
(e) Complete the work sheet.
(f) Prepare a balance sheet, an income statement, and a statement of retained earnings. Dividends of $4,000 were paid on the common stock during the month.

**P3-13** Phillips Wholesale Distributors, Inc. operates on a fiscal year ending on January 31. The agreement with the First Federal Bank of Albany, Oregon, for its loan to Phillips requires that Phillips submit quarterly financial statements to the bank.

You have just been hired by Phillips Wholesale Distributors, Inc. as their accountant, and your first responsibility is to prepare financial statements for the quarter ended April 30,

1984, for submission to the bank. The following is the trial balance at April 30, 1984 prepared by the bookkeeper.

Phillips Wholesale Distributors, Inc.
TRIAL BALANCE
April 30, 1984

| | | |
|---|---:|---:|
| Cash | $ 37,540 | |
| Accounts Receivable | 124,700 | |
| Allowance for Doubtful Accounts | 700 | |
| Notes Receivable | 25,000 | |
| Interest Receivable | 700 | |
| Inventory, February 1, 1984 | 47,600 | |
| Unexpired Insurance | 1,600 | |
| Supplies on Hand | 3,700 | |
| Land | 40,000 | |
| Building | 135,000 | |
| Accumulated Depreciation—Building | | $ 19,600 |
| Equipment | 90,000 | |
| Accumulated Depreciation—Building | | 45,400 |
| Delivery Truck | 24,000 | |
| Accumulated Depreciation—Delivery Truck | | 5,000 |
| Accounts Payable | | 64,500 |
| Salaries and Wages Payable | | -0- |
| Interest Payable | | -0- |
| Payroll Taxes Payable (including withholding) | | -0- |
| Income Taxes Payable | | -0- |
| Notes Payable, 16%, due March 31, 1985 | | 70,000 |
| Mortgage Payable, 12%, due January 1, 2002 | | 126,300 |
| Common Stock, $100 par | | 100,000 |
| Paid-In Capital in Excess of Par | | 14,700 |
| Retained Earnings | | 54,020 |
| Dividends Declared | 5,000 | |
| Sales | | 324,600 |
| Sales Discounts | 4,600 | |
| Purchases | 216,300 | |
| Purchase Discounts | | 470 |
| Purchase Returns and Allowances | | 1,300 |
| Transportation In | 6,300 | |
| Executive Salary Expense | 10,000 | |
| Wages Expense | 42,000 | |
| Payroll Tax Expense | 1,700 | |
| Utilities Expense | 2,400 | |
| Supplies Expense | -0- | |
| Truck Expense | 3,100 | |
| Depreciation Expense | -0- | |
| Bad Debt Expense | -0- | |
| Miscellaneous Expense | 390 | |
| Interest Expense | 3,560 | |
| Interest Revenue | | -0- |
| Gain or Loss on Sale of Assets | | -0- |
| Income Tax Expense | -0- | |
| | $825,890 | $825,890 |

You determine the following information about the ledger accounts which may need adjustment or correction. Phillips does *not* use reversing entries.

1. The accounts receivable consist of $104,200 of current accounts and $20,500 of past due accounts. In estimating bad debts, the balance in the allowance account is determined by using 1% of current accounts and 10% of past due accounts.

2. The notes receivable consist of the following:
   (a) Able Sales Co., $10,000 face dated June 30, 1983, interest at 12%, interest and principal due June 30, 1984.
   (b) Caraco Retailers, $15,000 face dated February 15, 1984, interest at 16%, interest and principal due June 15, 1984.
   (c) Phillips computes interest using 30-day months, 360-day years.

3. The land has a fair market value of $60,000 and the building has a fair market value of $150,000.

4. The building, which was purchased February 1, 1982, has an estimated useful life of 25 years and an estimated salvage value of $5,000. Phillips uses the sum-of-the-year's-digits method of depreciation for the building.

5. The equipment consists of three forklifts. In your discussions with the bookkeeper, you learn that on February 1, 1984 forklift Number 2 was sold for $7,000 and the selling price was credited to accumulated depreciation, and a new forklift purchased.

| | Date Acquired | Cost | Salvage Value |
|---|---|---|---|
| Forklift No. 1 | February 1, 1982 | $20,000 | $1,000 |
| Forklift No. 2 | February 1, 1982 | 20,000 | 1,000 |
| Forklift No. 3 | February 1, 1982 | 20,000 | 1,000 |
| Forklift No. 5 | February 1, 1984 | 30,000 | 2,000 |

The forklifts are depreciated on the double-declining-balance method of depreciation over 5 years.

6. The delivery truck was purchased on February 1, 1982 for $24,000. The truck has a useful life of 4 years, estimated life in miles of 200,000, and a salvage value of $4,000. On January 31, 1984, the truck had been driven 50,000 miles. You ascertain the truck has been driven 6,000 miles since January 31, 1984, and that Phillips depreciates the truck on the basis of miles driven.

7. The unexpired insurance consists of a combination policy that covers the building, the equipment, and the trucks. The 3-year policy was purchased February 1, 1982 for $4,800 (Debit Miscellaneous Expense).

8. The estimate of supplies on hand at April 30, 1984 is $2,900.

9. The company pays its employees once a month on the fifth day of the month for the prior month. The payroll for April 1984 consists of the following:

| | Gross Pay | Taxes to be Withheld | Net Pay |
|---|---|---|---|
| Executives | $ 5,000 | $1,000 | $ 4,000 |
| Other employees | 23,000 | 3,700 | 19,300 |
| | $28,000 | $4,700 | $23,300 |

Phillips also will pay for April payroll taxes totaling $900.

10. The three notes payable at 16%, due March 31, 1985, were taken out on January 31, 1982 to finance the purchase of the forklifts and delivery truck. The interest is payable every January 31, and the principal is due at maturity.

11. The mortgage payable of $130,000 was for the purchase of the land and building. The mortgage is payable over 20 years with $1,375 monthly payments, including principal and interest at 12% due at month end. All payments have been made and recorded.

12. You discover that the company estimates inventory for quarterly financial statements. The company has had a gross margin equal to 40% of net sales since it started in business on February 1, 1982.

13. The company's average tax rate is 30%. Compute to the nearest dollar.

**Instructions**

(a) Prepare a 12-column work sheet for preparation of the quarterly financial statements.

(b) Prepare a combined statement of income and retained earnings for the three months ended April 30, 1984 and the balance sheet at April 30, 1984.

*P3–14 Presented below is information related to McGinnis Company.

### Journals

| | |
|---|---|
| Sales journal | Page 17 |
| Purchases journal | Page 8 |
| Cash receipts journal | Page 43 |
| Cash payments journal | Page 44 |
| General journal | Page 12 |

### Ledger Accounts

| Title | Balance July 1 | Acct. No. |
|---|---|---|
| Cash | $6,000 | 2 |
| Accounts Receivable | 8,000 | 5 |
| Delivery Equipment | 7,000 | 8 |
| Sales Equipment | 1,000 | 21 |
| Accounts Payable | 5,000 | 35 |
| Advertising Expense | 0 | 65 |
| Purchases | 0 | 52 |
| Purchase Returns | 0 | 53 |
| Sales | 0 | 69 |
| Transportation-in | 0 | 70 |

The following transactions occurred during the month of July.

July   1   Sells merchandise for cash, $9,000.

3   Buys a new delivery truck on account from Flemal Motors, $12,000.

3   Receives an invoice from the *Daily Advertiser* for a full-page advertisement, $150, which appeared in the paper on July 2.

5   Receives a purchase requisition for display equipment from the sales manager; the equipment sells for $1,130.

6   Returns merchandise for credit of $130 on a cash purchase.

7   Sells merchandise on account to Peggy Graham, $15,000.

8   Purchases merchandise on account from Joanne Grometer, $9,000, f.o.b. shipping point.

10   Receives cash of $130 for merchandise returned July 6.

11   Receives a debit memo for $140 from Joanne Grometer, indicating that the merchandise purchased July 8 was shipped with freight prepaid.

13   Purchases display equipment for $1,130; the invoice is paid immediately. (See July 5 information.)

17   Sells merchandise on account to Laz Gardin, $1,000.

20   Pays Joanne Grometer in full of account.

24   Purchases merchandise on account from Mary Ann Strain, $3,400.

28   Pays the *Daily Advertiser.*

31   Receives full payment from Peggy Graham.

**Instructions**

Complete the following:

(a) Open ledger accounts and enter the July 1 balances.

(b) Record the July transactions in appropriate journals.

(c) Post from the journals to the ledger with posting references in good form (omit subsidiary ledger postings).

**\*P3–15** The E. T. Elsner Company maintains a voucher register with debit columns for Purchases, Office Salaries, Sales Salaries, Advertising Expense, Office Supplies Expense, and Sundry, and a credit column for Vouchers Payable. The check register contains a debit column for Vouchers Payable and credit columns for Cash and Purchase Discounts.

May 3  Purchases merchandise from the J. Lankford Company for $10,800, terms 1/10, n/30 (purchases are recorded at gross amount).

6  Purchases merchandise from Doreen Chase for $6,300, 2/10, n/30.

9  Pays office payroll of $2,160 and sales payroll of $4,500.

11  Purchases office equipment for $3,600 from Spaeth Equipment Company, terms 1/15, n/45.

12  Returns damaged merchandise of $800 to J. Lankford Company and pays the balance due.

15  Receives an invoice from the Power and Light Company for utilities of $82.

17  Pays Spaeth Equipment Company the full amount due.

20  Purchases office supplies of $1,500 from Office Equipment Company, making immediate payment by check.

21  Receives an invoice for advertising from WGSN Radio Station, $270.

23  Pays Doreen Chase in full of account.

27  Pays the telephone bill of $47 received from the telephone company.

28  Pays the invoices for utilities and advertising.

31  Supplies on hand are valued at $558.

**Instructions**

Record the transactions in the books of original entry of the E. T. Elsner Company beginning with voucher no. 1 and check no. 101.

**\*P3–16** On January 2, 1983, Alschuler-Roesch Inc. was organized with two stockholders, Ben Alschuler and Shirley Roesch. Alschuler purchased 500 shares of $100 par value common stock for $50,000 cash; Roesch received 600 shares of common stock in exchange for the assets and liabilities of a men's clothing shop that she had operated as a sole proprietorship. The trial balance immediately after incorporation appears on the work sheet.

No formal books have been kept during 1983. The following information has been gathered from the checkbooks, deposit slips, and other sources:

1. Most balance sheet account balances at December 31, 1983 have been determined and recorded on the work sheet.

2. Cash receipts for the year are summarized as follows:

| | |
|---|---:|
| Advances from customers | $    800 |
| Cash sales and collections on accounts receivable (after sales discounts of $1,520 and sales returns and allowances of $1,940) | 126,540 |
| Sale of equipment costing $5,000 on which $1,000 of depreciation had accumulated | 4,500 |
| | $131,840 |

3. During 1983, the depreciation expense on the building was $800; the depreciation expense on the equipment was $1,750.

**4.** Cash disbursements for the year are summarized as follows:

| | |
|---|---:|
| Insurance premiums | $ 900 |
| Purchase of equipment | 18,000 |
| Addition to building | 4,600 |
| Cash purchases and payments on accounts payable (after purchase discounts of $1,150 and purchase returns and allowances of $1,800) | 82,050 |
| Salaries paid to employees | 39,820 |
| Utilities | 1,850 |
| Total cash disbursements | $147,220 |

**5.** Bad debts are estimated to be 1.2% of total sales for the year. The ending accounts receivable balance of $18,700 has been reduced by $650 for specific accounts that were written off as uncollectible.

### Instructions

Complete the work sheet for the preparation of accrual basis financial statements. Formal financial statements and journal entries are not required.

(AICPA adapted)

Alschuler-Roesch, Inc.
WORK SHEET FOR PREPARATION OF ACCRUAL BASIS
FINANCIAL STATEMENTS
For the Year 1983

| | Trial Balance January 2, 1983 | | Adjustments | | Income Statement 1983 | | Balance Sheet December 31, 1983 | |
|---|---|---|---|---|---|---|---|---|
| | Debit | Credit | Debit | Credit | Debit | Credit | Debit | Credit |
| Cash | $ 60,000 | | | | | | | |
| Accounts receivable | 12,400 | | | | | | 18,700 | |
| Merchandise inventory | 23,000 | | | | | | 24,500 | |
| Unexpired insurance | 350 | | | | | | 200 | |
| Land | 15,000 | | | | | | 15,000 | |
| Buildings | 20,000 | | | | | | | |
| Accumulated depreciation— buildings | | $ 7,000 | | | | | | |
| Equipment | 8,000 | | | | | | | |
| Accumulated depreciation— equipment | | 2,400 | | | | | | |
| Accounts payable | | 17,850 | | | | | | 9,229 |
| Advances from customers | | 900 | | | | | | 550 |
| Salaries payable | | 600 | | | | | | 1,595 |
| Capital stock | | 110,000 | | | | | | 110,000 |
| | $138,750 | $138,750 | | | | | | |

(Prepare your own work sheet, because you will need additional accounts.)

# CHAPTER 4

# Statement of Income and Retained Earnings

The statement of income, or statement of earnings as it is frequently called,[1] is the report that measures the success of enterprise operations for a given period of time. The business and investment community uses this report to determine investment value, credit worthiness, and income success, for instance. Whether existing confidence in the income statement is well founded is a matter of conjecture. Because the derived income is at best a rough estimate, the reader of the statement should take care not to give it more significance than it deserves.

As indicated in Chapter 2, the measurement of income in accounting is a reflection of the many assumptions and principles (standards) established over the years by accountants, such as the periodicity assumption, the revenue recognition principle, and the matching principle. If for any reason the assumptions and principles are ill-founded, weaknesses will appear in the income statement.

## MEASUREMENT AND PRESENTATION OF INCOME

Economists have often criticized accountants for their definition of income, because accountants do not include many items that contribute to the general growth and well-being of an enterprise. For example, the noted economist, J. R. Hicks, has defined income as the maximum value a person can consume during a period and still be as well off at the end as at the beginning.[2] This definition provides the essential elements of measuring an individual's income. Any effort to measure how well-off an individual is at any point in time, however, will prove fruitless unless certain restrictive assumptions are developed and applied.

For example, what was your net income for last year? Let us suppose that you worked during the summer and earned $3,600. Because you paid taxes and incurred tuition and living expenses for school, your income statement may show a loss for the year, if measured

---

[1]*Accounting Trends and Techniques—1981* (New York: AICPA), p. 255, indicates that for the 600 companies surveyed in 1980 the term *income* is employed in the title of 367 income statements. The term *earnings* is second in acceptance with 175, while the term *operations* is used by 56 companies.

[2]J. R. Hicks, *Value and Capital* (Oxford: Clarendon Press, 1946), p. 172.

in terms of straight dollar value. But have you sustained a loss? How do you value the education obtained during this one year? One interpretation of Hicks's definition states that you would measure not only monetary income but also psychic income. Psychic income is defined as a measure of increase in net wealth arising from qualitative features, in this case the value of your educational experience.

Accountants undoubtedly recognize that a measurement of such experiences might be useful, but the problem of measurement has not been solved. Items that cannot be quantified with any degree of reliability have been discarded as impractical to measure.

## Capital Maintenance Approach Versus Transaction Approach

Hicks's definition of income assumes that net income is measured by subtracting beginning net assets (assets minus liabilities) from ending net assets and adjusting for any additional investments during the period. When income is calculated in this manner, accountants state that a capital maintenance approach to income measurement is employed. The **capital maintenance approach** (sometimes referred to as the change in equity approach) takes the net assets or capital values based on some valuation (for example, historical cost, discounted cash flows, current cost, or fair market value) and measures income by the difference in capital values at two points in time.[3] Here is an illustration assuming the use of historical costs.

Suppose that a corporation had beginning net assets of $10,000 and end of the year net assets of $18,000, and that during this same period additional owners' investments of $5,000 were made. Calculation of the net income for the period, employing the capital maintenance approach, is shown below.

| | |
|---|---:|
| Net assets, December 31, 1983 | $18,000 |
| Net assets, January 1, 1983 | 10,000 |
| | 8,000 |
| Less: | |
| Owners' investments during the year | 5,000 |
| Net income for 1983 | $ 3,000 |

With the capital maintenance approach we compute the net income for the period, but there is one important drawback. Detailed information concerning the composition of the income is not evident because the revenue and expense amounts are not presented to the financial statement reader.

An alternative procedure measures the basic income-related transactions that occur during a period and summarizes them in an income statement. This method is normally called the **transaction approach.** This approach focuses on the activities that have occurred during a given period; instead of presenting only a net change, the components that comprise the change are disclosed. Income may be classified by customer, product line, or

[3]The Internal Revenue Service uses the capital maintenance approach to identify unreported income and refers to its approach as a "net worth check." See Joseph Karasyk, "The Net Worth Method in Tax Evasion Cases," *The CPA Journal* (Vol. XLIX, No. 4, April 1979), pp. 35–40.

function. In addition, classification into groupings such as regular and irregular[4] is developed to aid user groups. The transaction approach to income measurement is the method that you learned in your basic accounting course.

## Elements of the Income Statement

The transaction approach to income measurement is superior to the capital maintenance approach because it provides information on the elements of income. As indicated in Chapter 2, the major elements of the income statement are as follows:

---

### ELEMENTS OF THE INCOME STATEMENT

**REVENUES.** Inflows or other enhancements of assets of an entity or settlements of its liabilities (or a combination of both) during a period from delivering or producing goods, rendering services, or other activities that constitute the entity's ongoing major or central operations.

**EXPENSES.** Outflows or other using up of assets or incurrences of liabilities (or a combination of both) during a period from delivering or producing goods, rendering services, or carrying out other activities that constitute the entity's ongoing major or central operations.

**GAINS.** Increases in equity (net assets) from peripheral or incidental transactions of an entity and from all other transactions and other events and circumstances affecting the entity during a period except those that result from revenues or investments by owners.

**LOSSES.** Decreases in equity (net assets) from peripheral or incidental transactions of an entity and from all other transactions and other events and circumstances affecting the entity during a period except those that result from expenses or distributions to owners.[5]

---

Revenues take many forms, such as sales, fees, interest, dividends, and rents. Expenses also take many forms, such as cost of goods sold, depreciation, interest, rent, salaries and wages, and taxes. Gains and losses also are of many types, such as gains or losses resulting from the sale of investments, sale of plant assets, settlement of liabilities, write-offs of assets due to obsolescence or casualty, and theft.

The distinction between revenues and gains and the distinction between expenses and losses depend to a great extent on the typical activities of the enterprise. For example, the sales price of investments sold by an insurance company such as Mutual of Omaha would generally be classified as revenues, whereas the sales price less book value on the sale of an investment by a manufacturing enterprise (such as General Motors Corp.) would be classified as a gain or loss. The different treatment results because the sale of investments by an insurance company is part of its regular operations, whereas in a manufacturing enterprise it is not.

The importance of reporting these elements should not be underestimated. For most decision makers, the parts of a financial statement will often be more useful than the whole. As indicated earlier, investors and creditors are interested in predicting the amounts, timing, and uncertainty of future income and cash flows. Revenues, expenses, gains, and losses occur as a result of numerous events and activities that vary in their

---

[4]**Irregular** encompasses transactions and other events that are derived from developments outside the normal operations of the business.

[5]"Elements of Financial Statements of Business Enterprises," *Statement of Financial Accounting Concepts No. 3* (Stamford, Conn.: FASB, 1980), p. xii.

stability, risk, and predictability. By reporting these income statement elements in some detail and in comparative form with prior years' data, decision makers are better able to assess future income and cash flows.

## Single-Step Income Statements

In reporting revenues, gains, expenses, and losses, many accountants prefer a format known as the **single-step** income statement.

In this single-step statement, two groups exist: revenues on the one hand, and cost and expenses on the other. The expenses are deducted from the revenues to arrive at the net income or loss; the expression "single-step" is derived from the single subtraction necessary to arrive at net income. Frequently, however, income taxes are reported separately as the last item to indicate their relationship to income before taxes.

For example, here is the income statement of Ehrlich, Inc.

| Ehrlich, Inc. INCOME STATEMENT For the Year Ended December 31, 1983 | |
|---|---:|
| Net sales revenue | $343,000 |
| Other revenue | 6,000 |
| Total revenue | 349,000 |
| Expenses | |
| Cost of goods sold | 258,000 |
| Selling and administrative expenses | 49,000 |
| Interest on long-term debt | 3,961 |
| Other expenses | 1,104 |
| Total expenses | 312,065 |
| Income before taxes | 36,935 |
| Income taxes | 16,000 |
| Net income | $ 20,935 |
| Earnings per share | $1.36 |

Today the single-step form of income statement is used predominantly in business reporting, although in recent years, the multiple-step form which is described below, has regained some of its former popularity.[6]

The primary advantage of the single-step format lies in the simplicity of presentation and the absence of any implication that one type of revenue or expense item has priority over another. Potential classification problems are thus eliminated.

## Multiple-Step Income Statements

Some accountants contend that other important relationships exist in revenue and expense data and that the income statement becomes more informative and more useful when it

---

[6]*Accounting Trends and Techniques—1981.* Of the 600 companies surveyed, 346 employed the single-step form and 254 employed the multiple-step income statement format.

Siska Company
INCOME STATEMENT
For the Year Ended December 31, 1983

| | | | |
|---|---:|---:|---:|
| **Sales Revenue** | | | |
| Sales | | | $3,053,081 |
| Less: Sales discounts | | $ 44,241 | |
| Sales returns and allowances | | 36,427 | 80,668 |
| Net sales revenue | | | 2,972,413 |
| **Cost of Goods Sold** | | | |
| Merchandise inventory, Jan. 1, 1983 | | 461,219 | |
| Purchases | $1,989,693 | | |
| Less purchase discounts | 19,270 | | |
| Net purchases | 1,970,423 | | |
| Freight and transportation-in | 40,612 | 2,011,035 | |
| Total merchandise available for sale | | 2,472,254 | |
| Less merchandise inventory, Dec. 31, 1983 | | 489,713 | |
| Cost of goods sold | | | 1,982,541 |
| Gross profit on sales | | | 989,872 |
| **Operating Expenses** | | | |
| Selling expenses | | | |
| Sales salaries and commissions | 202,644 | | |
| Sales office salaries | 59,200 | | |
| Travel and entertainment | 48,940 | | |
| Advertising expense | 38,315 | | |
| Freight and transportation-out | 41,209 | | |
| Shipping supplies and expense | 24,712 | | |
| Postage and stationery | 16,788 | | |
| Depreciation of sales equipment | 9,005 | | |
| Telephone and telegraph | 12,215 | 453,028 | |
| Administrative expenses | | | |
| Officers' salaries | 186,000 | | |
| Office salaries | 61,200 | | |
| Legal and professional services | 23,721 | | |
| Utilities expense | 23,275 | | |
| Insurance expense | 7,029 | | |
| Depreciation of building | 8,059 | | |
| Depreciation of office equipment | 6,000 | | |
| Stationery, supplies, and postage | 2,875 | | |
| Miscellaneous office expenses | 2,612 | 320,771 | 773,799 |
| Income from operations | | | 216,073 |
| **Other Revenues and Gains** | | | |
| Dividend revenue | | 8,500 | |
| Rental revenue | | 2,910 | 11,410 |
| | | | 227,483 |
| **Other Expenses and Losses** | | | |
| Interest on bonds and notes | | | 26,060 |
| Income before taxes | | | 201,423 |
| Income taxes | | | 102,000 |
| Net income for the year | | | $ 99,423 |
| Earnings per share | | | $3.06 |

*(margin notes, handwritten)* operating section → ; nonoperating section →

shows these relationships. Further classification and association of data within the statement make it more useful. Among the features are:

1. A separation of results achieved through regular operations from those obtained through the subordinate or nonoperating activities of the company. This separation is helpful because it provides a sound basis for evaluating the results of nonoperating activities as well as those of regular activities. For example, enterprises often present an income from operations figure and then a section entitled other revenues and gains or other expenses and losses that includes interest revenue and expense and sales of miscellaneous items and dividends received.

2. A classification of expenses by functions, such as merchandising or manufacturing (cost of goods sold), selling, and administration. This presentation of the total expense of each activity permits immediate comparison with costs of previous years and with the cost of other departments during the same year.

Accountants who show these additional relationships in the operating data favor what is called a **multiple-step** income statement over the single-step statement. In a multiple-step statement the basic division is between operating and nonoperating activities, and both revenues and expenses are separated into these two groups. And, whenever practicable, costs and expenses are classified and grouped within each major division. This statement is recommended because it recognizes a separation of operating transactions from nonoperating transactions and matches costs and expenses with related revenues to provide more information to the financial statement reader. The multiple-step format highlights certain intermediate components of income that are used for the computation of ratios used to assess the performance of the enterprise. To illustrate, the Siska Company's multiple-step statement of income is presented on page 129.

For a manufacturing company, the section concerned with the cost of goods manufactured and sold is usually too extensive to include in the income statement. Normally, a separate schedule is required for the presentation of this data, if it is presented at all.

## Intermediate Components of the Income Statement

The development of the intermediate components (often referred to as sections or subsections) within the income statement is described below.

1. **Operating section.** A report of the revenues and expenses of the company's principal operations. (This section may or may not be presented on a departmental basis.)

    (a) **Sales or revenue section.** A subsection within the operating section to present the pertinent facts about sales, discounts, allowances, returns, and other related information, and to arrive at the net amount of sales revenue.

    (b) **Cost of goods sold section.** A subsection within the operating section that shows the cost of goods that were sold to produce the sales, and that shows in adequate detail the components of this cost figure.

    (c) **Selling expenses.** A subsection within the operating section that states expenses resulting from the company's efforts to make sales.

    (d) **Administrative or general expenses.** A subsection within the operating section reporting expenses of general administration of the company's operations.

2. **Nonoperating section.** A report of the revenues and expenses resulting from secondary or auxiliary activities of the company. In addition, special gains and losses that are infrequent or unusual, but not both, are normally reported in this section. Generally these items break down into two main subsections:

    (a) **Other revenues and gains.** A list of the revenues earned or gains incurred, generally net of related expenses, from nonoperating transactions.

    (b) **Other expenses and losses.** A list of the expenses, or losses incurred, generally net of any related incomes, from nonoperating transactions.

3. **Income taxes.** A short section to report as a separate item the amount of federal and state taxes levied on income.

4. **Discontinued operations.** Material gains or losses resulting from the disposition of a segment of the business.

5. **Extraordinary items.** Unusual and infrequent gains and losses of material amounts.

6. **Cumulative effect of a change in accounting principle.**

7. **Earnings per share.**[7]

Although the content of the operating section is always the same, the organization of the material need not be as described above. The breakdown above uses a **natural expense classification** and is commonly used for manufacturing concerns and for merchandising companies in the wholesale trade. Another classification of operating expenses recommended for retail stores uses a **functional expense classification** of administrative, occupancy, publicity, buying, and selling expenses. Thus any reasonable classification that serves to inform those who use the statement is satisfactory. The present tendency in statements prepared for management is to present considerable detailed expense data grouped along lines of responsibility. This permits evaluation of the effectiveness of the work of individuals and departments according to work done and amounts expended.

Whether a single-step or a multiple-step income statement is used, irregular transactions such as discontinued operations, extraordinary items, and cumulative effect of changes in accounting principles should be reported separately following income from continuing operations.

Refer to the income statement of Tenneco, Inc., Appendix D, p. 195, for an illustration of an income statement from practice.

## Condensed Income Statements

In some cases it is impossible to present in a single report of convenient size all of the detailed expenses that are desirable in the statement of income. This problem is solved by including only the totals of expense groups in the statement of income and preparing supplementary schedules of expenses to support the totals in the statement. When this is done, the income statement proper may be reduced to a few lines on a single sheet. For this reason, readers who study all the reported data on operations must give their attention to the supporting schedules of expenses as well. The income statement on page 132 for Siska Company is a condensed version of the more detailed statement presented earlier and is more representative of the type found in practice. If the condensed version is used, it should be accompanied by supporting schedules to present as much detail as desirable.

How much detail to include in the financial statements is always a problem. On the one hand, we want to present a simple, summarized statement so that a reader can readily discover the facts of importance. On the other hand, we want to disclose the results of all activities and to provide more than just a skeleton report. Hopefully, the conceptual framework will provide some guidelines to use in determining the level of disclosure necessary for the components of the income statement.[8]

[7]The profession requires that earnings per share or net loss per share be included on the face of the income statement except for certain nonpublic companies.

[8]As discussed later in this chapter, the FASB has issued a proposed statement of concepts which offers some guidance on this topic "Reporting Income, Cash Flows, and Financial Position of Business Enterprises," *Proposed Statement of Financial Accounting Concepts No. 5* (Stamford, Conn.: FASB, 1982). p. ix.

Siska Company
INCOME STATEMENT
For the Year Ended December 31, 1983

| | | |
|---|---:|---:|
| Net sales | | $2,972,413 |
| Cost of goods sold | | 1,982,541 |
| Gross profit | | 989,872 |
| Selling expense | $453,028 | |
| Administrative expense | 320,771 | 773,799 |
| Income from operations | | 216,073 |
| Other revenues and gains | | 11,410 |
| | | 227,483 |
| Other expenses and losses | | 26,060 |
| Income before taxes | | 201,423 |
| Income taxes | | 102,000 |
| Net income for the year | | $   99,423 |
| Earnings per share | | $3.06 |

## Professional Pronouncements and the Income Statement

The profession has not taken a position on whether the single-step or the multiple-step income statement should be employed. Flexibility in the presentation of the components of the income statement data has been permitted. There are two important areas, however, where guidelines have been developed. These two areas relate to what should be included in income and how certain unusual or irregular items should be reported.

What should be included in net income has been a controversy for many years. For example, should irregular gains and losses and corrections of revenues and expenses of prior years be closed directly to Retained Earnings and therefore not be reported in the income statement (current operating performance concept)? Or should they first be presented in the income statement and then carried to Retained Earnings along with the net income or loss for the period (all-inclusive concept)? When all the items are first presented in the income statement, the Retained Earnings account normally includes for any given year only the net income (or loss) for the year and any dividends declared.

Advocates of the **current operating performance income statement** argue that the net income figure should show the regular, recurring earnings of the business based on its normal operations. Irregular gains and losses are neither representative nor reflective of an enterprise's future earning power. Therefore, they should not be included in computing net income but should be carried directly to Retained Earnings as special items. In addition, they note that many readers are not trained to differentiate between regular and irregular items and, therefore, would be confused if such items were included in computing net income.

Advocates of the **all-inclusive income statement** insist that such items be included in net income because they reflect the long-range income-producing ability of the enterprise. They state that any gain or loss experienced by the concern, whether directly or indirectly related to operations, contributes to its long-run profitability and should be included in the computation of net income. They point out that irregular gains and losses can be separated from the results of regular operations to arrive at a figure of income from operations, but that in determining the net income for the year, all transactions should be included. They believe that when judgment is allowed to determine irregular items, differences develop in treatment of questionable items and, as a result, a danger of manipulating income data arises. For example, at one time American Standard wrote off $17.9 million in losses from discontinued operations directly to Retained Earnings. This enabled the company to report earnings per share of $1.01; if the write-off had been charged against revenue, American Standard would have reported a loss of 78 cents per share. It could be to the advantage of the corporation to run losses through Retained Earnings, but gains through income. Supporters of the all-inclusive concept argue that this flexibility should not be allowed because it leads to poor financial reporting practices. In other words, Gresham's law applies; poor accounting practices drive out good ones.

The most convincing arguments must have been given by those who favor the all-inclusive concept. *APB Opinion No. 9,* issued in 1967, **adopted the all-inclusive concept and requires application of this approach in practice with a few exceptions.** Subsequently, a number of pronouncements were issued that directly or indirectly involved the classification of unusual items. For purposes of discussion, we will classify these items into six general categories:

1. Extraordinary items.
2. Unusual gains and losses.
3. Prior period adjustments.
4. Normal, recurring corrections and adjustments.
5. Changes in accounting principle.
6. Discontinued operations.

**Extraordinary Items**   These are defined as **material** items "of a character significantly different from the typical or customary business activities of the entity" and "which would not be expected to recur frequently and which would not be considered as recurring factors in any evaluation of the ordinary operating processes of the business."

In *Opinion No. 30* the following criteria for extraordinary items were developed:

Extraordinary items are events and transactions that are distinguished by their unusual nature **and** by the infrequency of their occurrence. Thus, **both** of the following criteria should be met to classify an event or transaction as an extraordinary item:

(a) **UNUSUAL NATURE.** The underlying event or transaction should possess a high degree of abnormality and be of a type clearly unrelated to, or only incidentally related to, the ordinary and typical activities of the entity, taking into account the environment in which the entity operates.

(b) **INFREQUENCY OF OCCURRENCE.** The underlying event or transaction should be of a type that would not reasonably be expected to recur in the foreseeable future, taking into account the environment in which the entity operates.[9]

---

[9]"Reporting the Results of Operations," *Opinions of the Accounting Principles Board No. 30* (New York: AICPA, 1973), par. 20.

For further clarification, the Board specified that the following gains and losses do not constitute extraordinary items:

(a) Write-down or write-off of receivables, inventories, equipment leased to others, deferred research and development costs, or other intangible assets.

(b) Gains or losses from exchange or translation of foreign currencies, including those relating to major devaluations and revaluations.

(c) Gains or losses on disposal of a segment of a business.

(d) Other gains or losses from sale or abandonment of property, plant, or equipment used in the business.

(e) Effects of a strike, including those against competitors and major suppliers.

(f) Adjustment of accruals on long-term contracts.[10]

The items listed above do not constitute extraordinary items in an ongoing business "because they are usual in nature and may be expected to recur as a consequence of customary and continuing business activities." Only in rare situations will an event or transaction occur that clearly meets the criteria specified in *Opinion 30* and thus gives rise to an extraordinary gain or loss.[11] In these circumstances, gains or losses such as (a) and (d) above should be classified as extraordinary if they are a **direct result of a major casualty** (such as an earthquake), **an expropriation,** or **a prohibition under a newly enacted law or regulation** that clearly meets the criteria of unusual and infrequent. A good example of an extraordinary item is the approximately $36 million loss incurred by Weyerhaeuser Company (forest and lumber) as a result of volcanic activity at Mount St. Helens. Standing timber, logs, buildings, equipment, and transportation systems covering 68,000 acres were destroyed by the volcanic eruption.

In determining whether an item is an extraordinary item, **the environment in which the entity operates is of primary importance.** The environment of an entity includes such factors as the characteristics of the industry or industries in which it operates, the geographical location of its operations, and the nature and extent of governmental regulations. Thus, extraordinary item treatment is accorded the loss arising from hail damages to a tobacco grower's crops because severe damage from hailstorms in the locality is rare. On the other hand, frost damage to a citrus grower's crop in Florida does not qualify as extraordinary because frost damage is normally experienced every three or four years. In this environment, the criterion of infrequency is not met. Similarly, when a company sells the only security investment it has ever owned, the gain or loss meets the criteria of an extraordinary item. Another company, however, that has a portfolio of securities which it has acquired for investment purposes, would not have an extraordinary item upon the sale of such securities. Because the company owns several securities for investment purposes, sale of such securities is considered part of its ordinary and typical activities in the environment in which it operates.

It should be noted that there are **exceptions** to the general rules provided above. As

---

[10] Ibid., par. 23.

[11] Some accountants have concluded that the extraordinary item classification is so restrictive that only such items as a single chemist who knew the secret formula for an enterprise's mixing solution but was eaten by a tiger on a big game hunt or a plant facility that was smashed by a meteor would qualify for extraordinary item treatment.

indicated earlier, the disposal of a segment of a business [item (c), page 134], which is not an extraordinary item, requires special accounting treatment unlike any of the other items resulting in a gain or loss. In addition, **material gains and losses from early extinguishment of debt** ordinarily should be reported as an extraordinary item even though these gains or losses do not meet the criteria mentioned above for extraordinary items.[12] The rationale for this position will be discussed in Chapter 14. In addition, the **tax benefits of loss carry-forwards** recognized in periods subsequent to the loss must be reported as an extraordinary item in those periods (discussed in Chapter 20).[13]

Unfortunately, it is often difficult to determine what is extraordinary because accountants have never clearly defined materiality. As indicated in Chapter 2, firm guidelines to follow in judging when an item is or is not material have not been established. For example, companies have shown as extraordinary gains or losses items that accounted for less than 1% of income before extraordinary items. Our point is that as long as the definition of materiality is not sharply outlined, it will be difficult in some cases to differentiate an ordinary from an extraordinary item.[14] In determining whether an extraordinary gain or loss is material in relation to income before extraordinary items, to the trend of earnings, or by other appropriate criteria, items should be considered individually and not in the aggregate.[15]

In addition, considerable judgment must be exercised in determining whether an item should be reported as extraordinary. For example, some paper companies have had their forest lands condemned by the government for state or national parks or forests. Is such an event extraordinary or is it part of normal operations? Such determination is not easy; much depends on the frequency of previous condemnations, the expectation of future condemnations, materiality, etc.

Extraordinary items are to be shown net of taxes in a separate section in the income statement, usually just before net income. After listing the usual revenues, costs and expenses, and income taxes, the remainder of the statement shows:

Income before extraordinary items
Extraordinary items (less applicable income taxes of $ _____ )
Net income

[12]"Reporting Gains and Losses from Extinguishment of Debt," *Statement of Financial Accounting Standard No. 4* (Stamford, Conn.: FASB, 1975), par. 8.

[13]"Accounting for Income Taxes," *Opinions of the Accounting Principles Board No. 11* (New York: AICPA, 1967), par. 45.

[14]For an interesting discussion of some of the weaknesses of earlier pronouncements, see Leopold A. Bernstein, "Reporting the Results of Operations—A Reassessment of APB *Opinion No. 9*," *The Journal of Accountancy* (July 1970), pp. 57–61. Another problem deals with what is referred to as the "big-bath" approach. Many companies, if they see that a large loss is inevitable, write off as much as possible on the theory that investors do not make that great a distinction between a small loss and a larger one. Future statements are also relieved of these charges and provide a company with a quick earnings injection.

[15]"Reporting the Results of Operations," *op. cit.*, par. 24.

For example, Keystone Consolidated Industries, Inc. presented its extraordinary loss in this manner:

| Keystone Consolidated Industries, Inc. | |
|---|---|
| Income before extraordinary item | $11,638,000 |
| Extraordinary item—flood loss (Note E) | 1,216,000 |
| Net income | $10,422,000 |

Note E. *Extraordinary Item*. The Keystone Steel and Wire Division's Steel Works experienced a flash flood on June 22. The extraordinary item represents the estimated cost, net of related income taxes of $1,279,000, to restore the steel works to full operation.

**Unusual Gains and Losses** Because of the profession's restrictive criteria for extraordinary items, financial statement users now must examine carefully the financial statements for items that are **unusual or infrequent but not both.** As indicated earlier, items such as write-downs of inventories and gains and losses from fluctuation of foreign exchange should be reflected in the determination of income before extraordinary items. Thus, these items are shown with the normal, recurring revenues, costs, and expenses. If they are not material in amount, they are combined with other items in the statement. If they are material, they must be disclosed separately, but are shown above "income (loss) before extraordinary items."

For example, Cosco, Inc. presented an unusual charge in the following manner:

| Net sales | $56,961,631 |
|---|---|
| Cost and expenses | |
| Cost of sales | 43,254,687 |
| Marketing, general and administrative | 13,876,172 |
| Unusual charges (Note 4) | 685,931 |
| Interest | 1,686,669 |
| | 59,503,459 |
| Loss from operations before income taxes | ( 2,541,828) |

Note 4. *Unusual charges.* Cost of businesses acquired in excess of values assigned to assets was written down by $685,931 representing amounts applicable to businesses, which, in management's opinion, no longer have significant intangible value.

When a multiple-step income statement is being prepared for homework purposes, unusual gains and losses should be reported in the other revenues and gains or expenses and losses section unless otherwise stated.

In dealing with events that are either unusual or nonrecurring but not both, the profession attempted to prevent a practice that many accountants believed was misleading. Companies often reported these transactions on a net-of-tax basis and prominently displayed the earnings per share effect of these items. Although not captioned extraordinary items, they were presented in the same manner as extraordinary items. Some had referred to these as "first cousins" to extraordinary items. As a consequence, the Board specifically **prohibited a net-of-tax treatment for such items** to insure that users of financial statements can easily differentiate extraordinary items from material items that are unusual or infrequent, but not both.

**Prior Period Adjustments**  The accounting treatment for prior period adjustments is relatively straightforward. *FASB Statement No. 16* requires that items of profit and loss related to the following shall be accounted for and reported as prior period adjustments and excluded from the determination of net income for the current period:

(a) Correction of an error in the financial statements of a prior period and
(b) Adjustments that result from realization of income tax benefits of pre-acquisition operating loss carry forwards of purchased subsidiaries.

In addition, certain accounting changes required or permitted by an FASB Statement, an FASB Interpretation, or an APB Opinion are required to be accounted for retroactively and reported similar to prior period adjustments.[16]

Prior period adjustments (net of tax) should be charged or credited to the opening balance of retained earnings net of tax and, thus, excluded from the determination of net income for the current period. To illustrate, in 1984, Nevin Enterprises determined that it had overstated its depreciation expense in 1983 by $75,000 owing to an error in computation. The error affected both the income statement and the tax return for 1983. Adjustment for this error is presented in the financial statements for 1984 as follows (all other figures are assumed):

| | |
|---|---:|
| Retained earnings, January 1, 1984, as previously reported | $130,000 |
| Correction of an error in depreciation in prior period (net of $35,000 tax) | 40,000 |
| Adjusted balance of retained earnings at January 1, 1984 | 170,000 |
| Net income | 27,000 |
| Retained earnings, December 31, 1984 | $197,000 |

As a practical illustration, the annual report of Lafayette Radio Electronics Corporation presented a revised balance sheet, a revised income statement, and a revised statement of changes in financial position with the accompanying footnote explaining the nature of the prior period adjustment that necessitated the revised statements.

Note 6—*Revision of 1977 Financial Statements:* Subsequent to the issuance of its financial statements the Company discovered a computational error in the amount of $1,046,000 in the calculation of its July 2, 1977 inventory used to determine cost of sales for the year then ended. Accordingly, the 1977 statements have been restated. The effect of the correction of the error resulted in an increase in the 1977 net loss from $3,101,000 to $3,621,000 or from $1.42 to $1.65 per share.

The accounting treatment for prior period adjustments provides an interesting illustration of the evolutionary nature of accounting principle formulation. In 1966, *Opinion No. 9* identified certain criteria that had to be met before an item could be classified as a prior period adjustment.[17] These criteria permitted, for example, settlements of law suits in

---

[16]"Prior Period Adjustments," *Statement of Financial Accounting Standards Board No. 16* (Stamford, Conn.: FASB, 1977), pars. 11 and 12.

[17]"Reporting the Results of Operations," *Opinions of the Accounting Principles Board No. 9* (New York: AICPA, 1966).

litigation to be reported as prior period adjustments but did not permit such treatment of corrections of errors. After considerable concern had been expressed about how corrections of errors should be handled, *Opinion No. 20,* "Accounting Changes," was issued in 1971; it required that corrections of errors related to a previous period be reported as prior period adjustments.[18]

Subsequently, the SEC began to challenge prior period classification for litigation settlements, arguing that the outcome of litigation could not have been determined in a prior period and, therefore, these items should be run through the current year's income statement. The real concern was that adverse effects on net income could be partially hidden by direct charges to retained earnings. The FASB then reconsidered this issue, but only four of the seven members voted in late 1976 to eliminate litigative suits as prior period adjustments. According to the then existing by-laws of the FASB, five votes were required to establish a new standard; therefore, no change in the accounting for prior period adjustments was made. In early 1977, the trustees of the Financial Accounting Foundation in reviewing their operating procedures, decided that a simple majority vote of the FASB was sufficient to establish a new standard and that this change in the by-laws should be retroactive. Thus, what did not become an accounting standard in late 1976 did become an accounting standard in early 1977 **because of a change in the voting rules.** As a result, the number of prior period adjustments will be reduced, because generally only corrections of errors related to a prior period are accorded this treatment. The foregoing narrative illustrates the tenuous nature of accounting standard-setting.

**Normal, Recurring Corrections and Adjustments**   Adjustments that grow out of the use of estimates in accounting are not classified as prior period adjustments and, therefore, are used in the determination of income for the current period and future periods and not charged or credited directly to Retained Earnings. Items resulting from changes in the estimated lives of fixed assets, adjustment of the costs, realizability of inventories believed to be obsolete in preceding years, and similar items are accounted for in the period of the change if they affect only that period, or in the period of change and future periods if the change affects both. Note that **changes in estimate should not be treated as extraordinary items nor are they considered errors.**

**Changes in Accounting Principle**   As just indicated, changes in accounting occur frequently in practice, because at the statement date important events or conditions may be in dispute or uncertain. One type of accounting change, therefore, comprises the normal recurring corrections and adjustments that are made by every business enterprise. Another accounting change is a change in accounting principle that results when an accounting principle is adopted that is different from the one previously used. Changes in accounting principle are, for example, a change in the method of inventory pricing from FIFO to average cost or a change in depreciation from the double-declining to the straight-line method.[19]

---

[18]"Accounting Changes," *Opinions of the Accounting Principles Board No. 20* (New York: AICPA, 1971).

[19]Ibid., par. 18. Chapter 23 examines in greater detail the problems related to accounting changes; our purpose now is to provide general guidance for the major types of transactions affecting the income statement.

These types of changes are recognized generally by including in the income statement of the current year net of tax the cumulative effect, based on a retroactive computation, of changing to a new accounting principle. **The effect on net income of adopting the new accounting principle should be disclosed as a separate item following extraordinary items in the income statement.**

To illustrate, Halin, Inc. decided at the beginning of 1984 to change from the sum-of-the-years'-digits method of computing depreciation on its plant assets to the straight-line method. The assets originally cost $100,000 in 1982 and have a service life of four years. Here are the data assumed for this illustration and the manner of reporting the change.

| Year | Sum-of-the-Years'-Digits Depreciation | Straight-Line Depreciation | Excess of Sum-of-the-Years'-Digits over Straight-Line Method |
|------|---------------------------------------|----------------------------|--------------------------------------------------------------|
| 1982 | $40,000 | $25,000 | $15,000 |
| 1983 | 30,000 | 25,000 | 5,000 |
| Total | | | $20,000 |

The information is shown on the 1984 financial statements as follows (tax rate, 30%):

| | |
|---|---|
| Income before extraordinary item and cumulative effect of a change in accounting principle | $120,000 |
| Extraordinary item—casualty loss (net of $12,000 tax) | (28,000) |
| Cumulative effect on prior years of retroactive application of new depreciation method (net of $6,000 tax) | 14,000 |
| Net income | $106,000 |

**Discontinued Operations**   One of the most common types of irregular items has been the disposal of a business or a product line. Because of the increasing importance of this type of event, *Opinion No. 30* developed a set of classification and disclosure requirements to provide the information necessary to assess the impact of discontinued operations on the business enterprise.[20] Discontinued operations refer to those of a separate line of business or class of customers.

A separate income statement category for the gain or loss from **disposal of a segment of a business** must be provided. In addition, the **results of operations of a segment that has been or will be disposed of** is reported in conjunction with the gain or loss on disposal and separated from the results of continuing operations. The effects of discontinued operations are shown net of tax as a separate category in the income statement after continuing operations but before extraordinary items.

To illustrate, Zoe, Inc., a highly diversified company, decides to discontinue its electronics division. During the current year, the electronics division lost $300,000 (net of tax)

---

[20]The reporting requirements for discontinued operations are complex; only the major provisions are discussed here.

and was sold at the end of the year at a loss of $500,000 (net of tax). The information is shown on the current year's income statement as follows:

| | | |
|---|---:|---:|
| Income from continuing operations (after related taxes) | | $20,000,000 |
| Discontinued operations | | |
|   Loss from operation of discontinued electronics | | |
|     division (net of tax) | $300,000 | |
|   Loss from disposal of electronics division (net of tax) | 500,000 | 800,000 |
| Net income | | $19,200,000 |

The assets, results of operations, and activities of a segment of a business must be clearly distinguishable, physically, operationally, and for financial reporting purposes, from the other assets, results of operations and activities of the entity to qualify for discontinued operations treatment. Disposal of assets incidental to the evolution of the entity's business is not considered to be disposal of a segment of the business. **Disposals of assets that do *not* qualify as disposals of a segment** of a business include the following:

1. Disposal of *part* of a line of business.
2. Shifting of production or marketing activities for a particular line of business from one location to another.
3. Phasing out of a product line or class of service.
4. Other changes occasioned by a technological improvement.

Examples that would qualify as a disposal of a segment of a business are: (1) sale by a meat-packing company of a 53% interest in a professional football team, or (2) sale by a communications company of all of its radio stations but none of its television stations or publishing houses.

Conversely, examples that would not qualify are (1) discontinuance by a children's wear manufacturer of its operations in Italy but not elsewhere, or (2) sale by a diversified company of one furniture-manufacturing subsidiary but not all furniture-manufacturing subsidiaries. Note that judgment must be exercised in defining a disposal of a segment of a business because the criteria in some cases are difficult to apply.

## Summary

The public accounting profession now tends to accept a modified all-inclusive income concept instead of the current operating performance concept. The only items ordinarily charged or credited directly to Retained Earnings are **prior period adjustments** that are essentially error corrections, and certain accounting changes that require restatement of prior period financial statements. All other irregular gains or losses or nonrecurring items are closed to Income Summary and are included in the income statement. Of these, the **unusual, material, non-recurring items** that are significantly different from the typical or customary business activities are shown in a separate section for "extraordinary items" in the income statement just before net income. Other items of a material amount that are of an **unusual or nonrecurring** nature and are **not considered extraordinary** are separately disclosed. In addition, the cumulative adjustment that occurs when a change in accounting principles develops is disclosed as a separate item before net income. Finally **discontinued operations of a segment** of a business are classified as a separate item in the income statement after continuing operations but before extraordinary items.

The following chart summarizes the basic concepts previously examined. Although the chart is simplified, it provides a useful framework for determining the proper treatment of special items affecting the income statement.

### SUMMARY OF APB OPINIONS AND FASB STANDARDS[a]

| Type of Situation | Criteria | Examples | Placement on Financial Statements |
|---|---|---|---|
| Extraordinary items | Material, and both unusual and infrequent (nonrecurring). | Gains or losses resulting from casualties, an expropriation, or a prohibition under a new law.[b] | Separate section in the income statement entitled extraordinary items. (Shown net of tax) |
| Unusual gains or losses, not considered extraordinary | Material; character typical of the customary business activities; unusual or infrequent but not both. | Write-downs of receivables, inventories; adjustments of accrued contract prices; gains or losses from fluctuations of foreign exchange; gains or losses from sales of assets used in business. | Separate section in income statement above income before extraordinary items. Often reported in other revenues and gains or other expenses and losses section. (Not shown net of tax) |
| Prior period adjustments and accounting changes that require restatement | Material corrections of errors applicable to prior periods or accounting changes required or permitted by an FASB Statement or an APB Opinion to be handled retroactively. | Corrections of errors; retroactive restatements per *APB Opinion No. 20* or other authoritative pronouncements. | Adjust the beginning balance of retained earnings. (Shown net of tax) |
| Changes in estimates | Normal, recurring corrections and adjustments. | Changes in the realizability of receivables and inventories; changes in estimated lives of equipment, intangible assets; changes in estimated liability for warranty costs, income taxes, and salary payments. | Change in income statement only in the account affected. (Not shown net of tax) |
| Changes in principle[c] | Change from one generally accepted principle to another. | Changing the basis of inventory pricing from FIFO to average cost; change in the method of depreciation from accelerated to straight-line. | Cumulative effect of the adjustment is reflected in the income statement between the captions extraordinary items and net income. (Shown net of tax) |
| Discontinued operations | Disposal of a segment of a business constituting a separate line of business or class of customer. | Sale by diversified company of major division that represents only activities in electronics industry. Food distributor that sells wholesale to supermarket chains and through fast-food restaurants decides to discontinue the division that sells to one of two classes of customers. | Shown in separate section of the income statement after continuing operations but before extraordinary items. (Shown net of tax) |

[a]This summary provides only the general rules to be followed in accounting for the various situations described above. Exceptions do exist in some of these situations.
[b]Material gains and losses from extinguishment of debt and tax benefits of loss carry forwards are considered extraordinary, even though criteria for extraordinary items may not be met.
[c]The general rule per *APB Opinion No. 20* is to use the cumulative effect approach. However, all the recent FASB pronouncements require or permit the retroactive method whenever a new standard is adopted for the first time.

## INTRAPERIOD TAX ALLOCATION

Whenever an extraordinary item, prior period adjustment, change in accounting principle, or discontinued operation occurs, most accountants believe that the resulting income tax effect should be directly associated with that event or item. In other words, the tax expense for the year should be related, where possible, to **specific** items on the income statement to provide a more informative disclosure to statement users. This procedure is called **intraperiod tax allocation,** that is, allocation within a period. Its main purpose is to relate the income tax expense of the fiscal period to the following items that affect the amount of the tax provisions: (1) income from continuing operations, (2) discontinued operations, (3) extraordinary items, (4) changes in accounting principle, and (5) prior period adjustments. The general concept is "let the tax follow the income."

The income tax expense attributable to "income from continuing operations" is simply computed by ascertaining the income tax expense related to revenue and to expense transactions entering into the determination of this income. In this computation, no effect is given to the tax consequences of the items excluded from the determination of "income from continuing operations." The income tax expense attributable to other items is determined by the tax consequences of transactions involving these items. Because all these items are ordinarily material in amount, the applicable tax effect is also material and is disclosed separately and in close association with the related items.

### Extraordinary Losses

For example, assume that a company has income before extraordinary items of $250,000 and an extraordinary loss from a major casualty of $100,000. Because the casualty is not expected to recur frequently, has a material effect, and is not considered a recurring factor in any evaluation of the ordinary operating processes of the business, it is reported as an extraordinary item. The loss is deductible for tax purposes, however. Therefore, if the income tax rate is assumed to be 35%, the income tax payable for the year will be calculated as follows:

| | |
|---|---:|
| Income before loss deduction | $250,000 |
| Less loss from casualty | 100,000 |
| Taxable income | $150,000 |
| Income tax payable at 35% | $ 52,500 |

The income tax expense applicable to the $250,000 income before extraordinary items is $87,500, and the tax reduction applicable to the loss of $100,000 from the major casualty is $35,000. If the tax reduction of $35,000 is **not** associated with the extraordinary loss, the income statement would appear incorrectly as follows:

| | |
|---|---:|
| Income before tax and extraordinary item | $250,000 |
| Income tax | 52,500 |
| Income before extraordinary item | 197,500 |
| Extraordinary item—loss from casualty | (100,000) |
| Net income | $ 97,500 |

The previous report does not disclose an appropriate relationship between the income tax expense, the "income before extraordinary item," and the "loss." Without the tax benefit of the loss, the $250,000 of operating income would have been taxed at the 35% rate for an income tax of $87,500. The income before extraordinary item then would have appeared as $162,500 instead of $197,500. Thus we have the paradoxical situation of a loss of $100,000 making the income before extraordinary item appear larger by $35,000 instead of smaller.

To avoid such a misleading presentation, we report the tax effect in the income statement along with the loss in the following way.

| | | |
|---|---:|---:|
| Income before tax and extraordinary item | | $250,000 |
| Income tax | | 87,500 |
| Income before extraordinary item | | 162,500 |
| Extraordinary item—loss from casualty | $100,000 | |
| Less applicable income tax reduction | 35,000 | (65,000) |
| Net income | | $ 97,500 |

Or the extraordinary item may be reported "net of tax" with footnote disclosure as illustrated below.

| | |
|---|---:|
| Income before tax and extraordinary item | $250,000 |
| Income tax | 87,500 |
| Income before extraordinary item | 162,500 |
| Extraordinary item, less applicable income tax (note 1) | (65,000) |
| Net income | $ 97,500 |

Note 1. During the year the Company suffered a major casualty loss of $65,000 net of applicable income tax reduction of $35,000.

An example of a comprehensive footnote accompanying an "Extraordinary Charge ... $262,000" reported by Conemaugh Company in its annual report is presented below.

*Note 11—Extraordinary Charge:* On July 20, 1981 a flash flood in the Johnstown, Pennsylvania area damaged the Company's milk processing and ice cream manufacturing plant and its largest department store. The resultant extraordinary charge is computed as follows:

| | | |
|---|---:|---:|
| Physical damage and other losses (net) | | $2,039,000 |
| Business interruption | | 525,000 |
| Flood loss | | 2,564,000 |
| Less: Insurance proceeds | $2,000,000 | |
| Income tax benefits | 302,000 | 2,302,000 |
| Extraordinary charge | | $ 262,000 |

Following the flood, the Company suspended all retail operations in the downtown area. The Company currently owns the building formerly used for the department store (239,700 square feet) and a supporting warehouse building (41,300 square feet). Disposition or alternative use of the two buildings is presently being investigated. The Company's milk and ice cream manufacturing plant was back in operation by September 1981.

### Extraordinary Gains

If a company realizes an extraordinary gain, the tax expense is allocated between the gain and the income before extraordinary gain. If we assume a $100,000 extraordinary gain, the income statement disclosure is as follows.

| | | |
|---|---:|---:|
| Income before tax and extraordinary item | | $250,000 |
| Income tax (35%) | | 87,500 |
| Income before extraordinary item | | 162,500 |
| Extraordinary gain | $100,000 | |
| Less applicable income tax | 35,000 | 65,000 |
| Net income | | $227,500 |

### Prior Period Adjustments

The possibility of misleading reports resulting from carrying prior period adjustments directly to retained earnings also results unless the related tax effect is reported with the adjustment. Again, "let the tax follow the income" expresses the basic idea. A prior period adjustment having a current tax effect is disclosed in this statement of retained earnings as follows.

| | | |
|---|---:|---:|
| Retained earnings at beginning of year: | | |
| As previously reported | | $2,000,000 |
| Correction of an error | $200,000 | |
| Less applicable income tax reduction | 70,000 | (130,000) |
| Adjusted balance of retained earnings at beginning of year | | 1,870,000 |
| Net income | | 420,000 |
| Retained earnings at end of year | | $2,290,000 |

Under this arrangement the net income for the year shows the income tax expense related to the revenue and expense transactions that determine such income.

## EARNINGS PER SHARE

The results of a company's operations are customarily summed up in one important figure: net income. As if this condensation were not enough of a simplification of a complex operation, the financial world has widely accepted an even more distilled and compact figure as its most significant business indicator—"earnings per share."

The computation of earnings per share is usually straightforward. Net income minus preferred dividends (income available to common stockholders) is divided by the weighted average of shares outstanding to arrive at earnings per share. To illustrate, assume that Lancer, Inc. reports net income of $350,000 and declares and pays preferred dividends of $50,000 for the year; the weighted average number of shares outstanding during the year is 100,000 shares. The earnings per share is $3.00, as computed on the next page.

$$\frac{\text{Net Income} - \text{Preferred Dividends}}{\text{Weighted Average of Shares Outstanding}} = \text{Earnings per share}$$

$$\frac{\$350,000 - \$50,000}{100,000} = \$3.00$$

"Net income per share" or "earnings per share" is a ratio commonly used in prospectuses, proxy material, and annual reports to stockholders, and in the compilation of business earnings data for the press and other statistical services. Because of the inherent dangers of focusing attention on earnings per share by itself, the profession concluded that **earnings per share must be disclosed on the face of the income statement.** In addition to net income per share, per share amounts should be shown for "income from continuing operations," "income before extraordinary items and cumulative effect of accounting changes," and "cumulative effect of changes in accounting principles." Reporting per share amounts for gain or loss on discontinued operations and gain or loss on extraordinary items is optional.

To illustrate comprehensively both the income statement order of presentation and the earnings per share data, assume that Juarez Industries, Inc. had the condensed income statement shown on page 146 and that 100,000,000 shares of stock have been outstanding for the entire year.

The earnings per share data also may be disclosed parenthetically by a corporation, as illustrated below (this form is especially applicable when only one per share amount is involved):

| | |
|---|---|
| Net Income (per share $4.02) | $804,000 |

As indicated earlier, amounts for discontinued operations and extraordinary items need not be stated on a per share basis. These per share amounts can be determined simply by subtraction if not reported as separate per share amounts. For example, General Mills reported $1.77 earnings per share before an extraordinary item and net income of $1.83. This means it had an extraordinary gain of $.06 per share net of income tax. It should be emphasized that the Juarez illustration is highly condensed, and that items such as the "Unusual Charge," "Discontinued Operation," "Extraordinary Item," and the "Change in Accounting Principle" would have to be described fully and appropriately in the statement or related footnotes. Additional earnings per share computations are also required for certain types of accounting changes which will be discussed in Chapter 23.

Many corporations have simple capital structures that include only common stock. For these companies, a presentation such as "earnings per common share" is appropriate on the income statement. In an increasing number of instances, however, companies' earnings per share are subject to dilution (reduction) in the future because existing contingencies permit the further issuance of common shares.[21] Examples of such instances are (1) outstanding preferred stock or debt that is convertible into common shares, (2) outstanding stock

---

[21]"Earnings Per Share," *Opinions of the Accounting Principles Board No. 15* (New York: AICPA, 1969), pars. 14 and 15.

Juarez Industries, Inc.
INCOME STATEMENT
For the Year Ended December 31, 1983
(000 omitted)

| | | |
|---|---:|---:|
| Sales revenue | | $1,480,000 |
| Cost of goods sold | | 600,000 |
| Gross profit | | 880,000 |
| Selling and administrative expenses | | 320,000 |
| Income from operations | | 560,000 |
| Other revenues and gains | | |
|   Interest revenue | | 10,000 |
| Other expenses and losses | | |
|   Loss on disposal of part of Steel Division | (5,000) | |
|   Unusual charge—loss on sale of investments | (45,000) | (50,000) |
| Income from continuing operations before income taxes | | 520,000 |
| Income taxes | | 208,000 |
| Income from continuing operations | | 312,000 |
| Discontinued operations | | |
|   Income from operations of Hartley Division, less | | |
|     applicable income taxes of $36,000 | 54,000 | |
|   Loss on disposal of Hartley Division, less | | |
|     applicable income taxes of $60,000 | (90,000) | (36,000) |
| Income before extraordinary item and cumulative | | |
|     effect of accounting change | | 276,000 |
| Extraordinary item—loss from earthquake, less | | |
|     applicable income taxes of $30,000 | | (45,000) |
| Cumulative effect in prior years of retroactive application of new | | |
|     depreciation method, less applicable income taxes of $40,000 | | (60,000) |
| Net income | | $ 171,000 |
| | | |
| Per share of common stock | | |
|   Income from continuing operations | | $3.12 |
|   Income from operations of discontinued division, net of tax | | .54 |
|   Loss on disposal of discontinued operation, net of tax | | (.90) |
|   Income before extraordinary item and cumulative effect | | 2.76 |
|   Extraordinary loss, net of tax | | (.45) |
|   Cumulative effect of change in accounting principle, net of tax | | (.60) |
|   Net income | | $1.71 |

options or warrants, and (3) agreements for the issuance of common shares for little or no consideration in the satisfaction of certain conditions (for example, the attainment of specified levels of earnings following a business combination). The computational problems involved in accounting for these dilutive securities in earnings per share computations are discussed in Chapter 17.

In summary, the simplicity and availability of figures for per-share earnings lead inevitably to their widespread use. Because of the undue importance that the public, even the well-informed public, attaches to earnings per share, accountants have an obligation to make the earnings per share figure as meaningful as possible.

# STATEMENT OF RETAINED EARNINGS

A statement of retained earnings is generally included, together with an income statement, a balance sheet, and a statement of changes in financial position in the financial statements of an enterprise. Actually, instead of being a statement that reports related data, **it is a reconciliation of the balance of the retained earnings account from the beginning to the end of the year.**

Every effort should be made to prepare as useful and informative a statement of retained earnings as possible. If the retained earnings account is to receive direct charges and credits for certain prior period adjustments, the income statement will not reveal all the necessary information about income. The statement of retained earnings must be studied in conjunction with the income statement; otherwise, important components of the results of operations may be overlooked. Therefore, the statement of retained earnings makes full use of descriptive terminology so that readers can relate the appropriate items to the income statement.

## Items Disclosed

Some of the significant relationships and data recorded in the account for retained earnings that should be clearly disclosed in the statement are:

1. **PRIOR PERIOD ADJUSTMENTS.** Any adjustment that relates to prior periods indicates that one or more income statements for prior years was incorrect, and that the amounts shown as prior period adjustments do not appear in any prior income statement. Such items should be described clearly. Prior period adjustments normally require the restatement of prior period financial statements that are presented for comparative purposes.
2. **THE RELATIONSHIP OF DIVIDEND DISTRIBUTIONS TO NET INCOME FOR THE PERIOD.** An association of these two items indicates whether management is distributing all earnings, is "plowing" part of the earnings back into the business, or is distributing not only current income but also the accumulated earnings of prior years.
3. **TRANSFERS TO AND FROM RETAINED EARNINGS.** Transfers to and from retained earnings may be made in accordance with contract requirements, a continuing policy, or the apparent necessity of the moment. In any case, the amounts of retained earnings appropriated for stated reasons and the amounts returned should be clearly arranged for evaluation by the user of the statement.

An example of a statement of retained earnings is as follows:

|  |  |  |
|---|---:|---:|
| Fieldcrest Corporation<br>STATEMENT OF RETAINED EARNINGS<br>For the Year Ended December 31, 1983<br>(000 omitted) | | |
| Retained earnings January 1, 1983 | | $ 21,159 |
| Add net income for the year | | 99,423 |
| | | 120,582 |
| Deduct dividends declared on: | | |
| Preferred stock, at $5 per share | $15,000 | |
| Common stock, at $7 per share | 28,000 | 43,000 |
| Retained earnings December 31, 1983 | | $ 77,582 |

### Combined Statement of Income and Retained Earnings

Some accountants believe that the statements of income and retained earnings are so closely related that they present both statements in one combined report. The principal advantage of a combined statement is that all items affecting income, including operating items and prior period adjustments, appear in one statement. On the other hand, the figure of net income for the year is "buried" in the body of the statement, a feature that some find objectionable. There once was a definite trend toward this method of presentation, but at present it is no longer gaining in favor. When a combined statement is prepared, the income statement is presented as if it were to be issued as an independent report but, instead of closing that statement with the amount of net income, the reconciliation of retained earnings is stated as below.

| The Magnavox Company<br>COMBINED STATEMENT OF INCOME<br>AND RETAINED EARNINGS<br>(lower portion only) | |
| --- | ---: |
| Net income for the year | $ 42,290,385 |
| Retained earnings at beginning of year | 106,734,310 |
| | 149,024,695 |
| Cash dividends declared and paid | 15,764,250 |
| Retained earnings at end of year | $133,260,445 |

If the company has other capital accounts such as Additional Paid-In Capital, a good practice is to present a statement of these accounts reconciling the beginning and ending balances. *APB Opinion No. 12,* for example, indicates that when both a balance sheet and an income statement are presented, disclosure of changes in the separate accounts comprising stockholders' equity (such as Additional Paid-In Capital) is required to make the financial statements sufficiently informative. Disclosure of such changes may be made in separate statements, in the basic financial statements, or in the footnotes.

An example of a retained earnings statement combined with additional paid-in capital sections is presented in Appendix D (page 199) of Chapter 5.

## THE CONCEPTUAL FRAMEWORK—ITS IMPLICATION

As the conceptual framework progresses, future standards involving the measurement and reporting of income should flow from an integrated set of soundly developed concepts and criteria. To date, as indicated in earlier chapters, the FASB has identified the objectives of financial reporting, the qualitative characteristics of information, and provided definitions for the elements of financial statements. It has defined income, referred to as **comprehensive income,** as the increase in the amount of net assets resulting from transactions and other events and circumstances occurring during a period of time (excluding the effects of investments and distributions to owners). Comprehensive income is an "all-inclusive" concept of income, under which all changes in net assets (except certain transactions with owners) would be reported as part of income.

How will the conceptual framework affect the income statement and statement of retained earnings? Although it is difficult to predict, a recently proposed statement of concepts provides some clues to possible changes. The FASB's proposal depicts comprehensive income as comprising (1) the basic elements (revenues, expenses, gains, and losses) and (2) various intermediate components (in effect, subtotals of comprehensive income) that result from combining the basic elements.[22] The general criteria for disclosing components are relevancy (with special emphasis on predictive value), reliability, and cost effectiveness. Specifically, "a component should be shown separately if it has a special significance for the assessment of some aspect of enterprise performance and for users' assessments of future income and cash flows."[23]

Under this approach the income statement consists of the major subsections called **components** which are made up of the **elements** (revenues, expenses, gains, and losses), which in turn when described and reported in detail are called **items.** In order to predict the future, the amounts of individual items that make up the component may have to be reported. For example, if "income from continuing operations" is significantly lower this year and is reported as a single amount, users would not know whether to attribute the decrease to a temporary increase in an expense item (for example, an unusually large bad debt), a structural change (for example, a change in the relationship between variable and fixed expenses), or some other factor. Another example is income data that are distorted because of large discretionary expenses. Discretionary expenses are those that management can vary in amount within a relatively wide range without affecting current revenues. Examples of discretionary expenses are research and development expense, repair and maintenance costs, and certain sales promotion expenses. If these items are not disclosed separately when material in amount, users will be less likely to assess correctly the relationship between current revenues and expenses and, therefore, less able to assess future income and cash flows. To help users in these kinds of situations, the proposed statement recommends (1) that the amount of a significant item should be reported separately in any year in which its amount is unusual, and (2) that the corresponding amount for the previous year also be reported, so that the difference will be readily identifiable.[24]

The proposed statement provides the following guides as a basis for decisions about the display of elements and items in the income statement:

1. Report separately items that are unusual in amount as judged by the experience of previous periods.
2. Distinguish between items that are affected in different ways by changes in economic conditions.
3. Provide enough detail to enable the users to understand the main relationships among the items. In particular, it is relevant to report separately (1) expenses that vary with volume of activity or other components of income, (2) expenses that are discretionary, and (3) expenses that are stable over time or that depend on other factors, such as the level of interest rates and rates of taxation.
4. Distinguish between items whose measurement is subject to different levels of reliability.
5. Distinguish between items, the amounts of which must be known, for the calculation of summary indicators (such as earnings per share and rate of return on assets) that users are known to use frequently.[25]

---

[22]"Reporting Income, Cash Flows, and Financial Position of Business Enterprises," *Proposed Statement of Financial Accounting Concepts* (Stamford, Conn.: FASB, 1982).

[23]Ibid., par. 46.

[24]Ibid., par. 161.

[25]Ibid., par. 48.

Moreover, the usefulness of these display criteria is increased by consistent application from period to period and by comparable application by other enterprises.

In summary, it appears that some changes in the content of the income statement may occur. For example, more emphasis will be placed on the reasons for changes in items from period to period. At present, information on changes is limited. In addition, it appears that the profession will continue with the all-inclusive concept of income. Given the FASB's definition of comprehensive income, it suggests that even prior period adjustments will be reported in the income statement in the future. As a consequence, the statement of retained earnings will probably change in accordance with this new approach to the computation of income.

## QUESTIONS

1. Why should caution be exercised in the use of the income figure derived in an income statement? What are the objectives of generally accepted accounting principles in their application in the income statement?

2. What is the difference between the capital maintenance approach to income measurement and the transaction approach? Is the final income figure the same under both approaches?

3. What are the advantages and disadvantages of the "single-step" income statement?

4. What is the major distinction (a) between revenues and gains and (b) between expenses and losses?

5. What are the advantages and disadvantages of a combined statement of income and retained earnings? What is the basis for distinguishing between operating and nonoperating items?

6. Distinguish between the "all-inclusive" income statement and the "current operating performance" income statement. According to present generally accepted accounting principles, which is recommended? Explain.

7. What is the significance of the materiality of an item in deciding the proper placement of a nonrecurring item in the statement of retained earnings or in the income statement? Explain.

8. How should prior period adjustments be reported in the financial statements? Give an example of a prior period adjustment.

9. Discuss the appropriate treatment in the financial statements of each of the following:
   (a) An amount of $71,000 realized in excess of the cash surrender value of an insurance policy on the life of one of the founders of the company who died during the year.
   (b) A profit-sharing bonus to employees computed as a percentage of net income.
   (c) Additional depreciation on factory machinery because of an error in computing depreciation for the previous year.
   (d) Rent received from subletting a portion of the office space.
   (e) A patent infringement suit, brought two years ago against the company by another company, was settled this year by a cash payment of $132,000.
   (f) A reduction in the Allowance for Doubtful Accounts balance, because the account appears to be considerably in excess of the probable loss from uncollectible receivables.

10. Give the section of a multiple-step income statement in which each of the following is shown.
    (a) Gain on sale of machinery.               (e) Loss on inventory writedown.
    (b) Interest revenue.                         (f) Loss from strike.
    (c) Depreciation expense.                     (g) Bad debt expense.
    (d) Material write-offs of notes receivable.  (h) Loss on disposal of a segment of the business.

11. Indicate where the following items would ordinarily appear on the financial statements of D. Spangler, Inc. for the year 1983:
    (a) D. Spangler, Inc. changed its depreciation from double-declining to straight-line on machinery in 1983. The cumulative effect of the change was $300,000 (net of tax).

(b) In 1980, a supply warehouse with an expected useful life of seven years was erroneously expensed.

(c) An income tax refund related to the 1980 tax year was received.

(d) In 1983 the company wrote off one million dollars of inventory that was considered obsolete.

(e) In 1983 a flood destroyed a warehouse that had a book value of $400,000. Floods are rare in this locality.

(f) The service life of certain equipment was changed from eight to five years. If a five-year life had been used previously, additional depreciation of $41,000 would have been charged.

12. What is meant by "tax allocation within a period?" What is the justification for such practice?

13. When does tax allocation within a period become necessary? How should this allocation be handled?

14. During 1983, Matkovcik Company earned income of $400,000 before federal income taxes and realized a gain of $250,000 on a government-forced condemnation sale of a division plant facility. The income is subject to federal income taxation at the rate of 46%; the gain on the sale of the plant is taxed at 25%. Proper accounting suggests that the unusual gain be reported as an extraordinary item. Illustrate an appropriate presentation of these items in the income statement.

15. Recently Scott Paper Company decided to close two small pulp mills in Oconto Falls, Wisconsin and Anacortes, Washington. Would these closings be reported in a separate section entitled Discontinued Operations after Income from Continuing Operations? Discuss.

16. On January 30, 1981, a suit was filed against Olin Corporation under the Environmental Protection Act. On August 6, 1982, Olin Corporation agreed to settle the action and pay $180,000 in damages to certain current and former employees. How should this settlement be reported in the 1982 financial statements? Discuss.

17. What major types of items are reported in the retained earnings statement?

18. The controller for B. Flanigan, Inc. is discussing the possibility of presenting a combined statement of income and retained earnings for the current year. Indicate a possible advantage and disadvantage of this presentation format.

19. Generally accepted accounting principles usually require the use of accrual accounting to "fairly present" income. If the cash receipts and disbursements method of accounting will "clearly reflect" taxable income, why does this method not usually also "fairly present" income?

20. State some of the more serious problems encountered in seeking to achieve the ideal measurement of periodic net income. Explain what accountants do as a practical alternative.

21. What is meant by the terms *components, elements,* and *items* as they relate to the income statement? Why might items have to be disclosed in the income statement?

22. Given the profession's definition of comprehensive income, does it appear likely that a current operating or all-inclusive concept of income will be employed in the future?

# CASES

**C4-1** Duce Company was incorporated and began business on January 1, 1983. It has been successful and now requires a bank loan for additional working capital to finance expansion. The bank has requested an audited income statement for the year 1983. The bookkeeper for Duce Company provides you with the following income statement which Duce plans to submit to the bank:

| INCOME STATEMENT | |
|---|---:|
| Sales | $902,000 |
| Dividends | 32,300 |
| Gain on recovery of insurance proceeds from earthquake loss (extraordinary) | 38,500 |
| | 972,800 |

| | | |
|---|---:|---:|
| Less: | | |
| Selling expenses | $101,100 | |
| Cost of goods sold | 532,200 | |
| Advertising expense | 13,700 | |
| Loss on obsolescence of inventories | 34,000 | |
| Loss on discontinued operations | 48,600 | |
| Administrative expense | 73,400 | 803,000 |
| Income before income taxes | | 169,800 |
| Income taxes | | 80,000 |
| Net income | | $ 89,800 |

**Instructions**

Indicate the deficiencies in the income statement presented above. Assume that the company desires a single-step income statement.

C4–2 Information concerning the operations of a corporation is presented in an income statement or in a combined "statement of income and retained earnings." Income statements are prepared on a "current operating performance" basis ("earning power concept") or an "all-inclusive" basis ("historical concept"). Proponents of the two types of income statements do not agree upon the proper treatment of material nonrecurring charges and credits.

**Instructions**

(a) Define "current operating performance" and "all-inclusive" as used above.
(b) Explain the differences in content and organization of a "current operating performance" income statement and an "all-inclusive" income statement. Include a discussion of the proper treatment of material nonrecurring charges and credits.
(c) Give the principal arguments for the use of each of the three statements, "all-inclusive" income statement, "current operating performance" income statement, and a combined "statement of income and retained earnings."

(AICPA adapted)

C4–3 Stimack, Inc. is a real estate firm which derives approximately 30% of its income from the Executive Management Division, which manages apartment complexes. As auditor for Stimack, Inc., you have recently overheard the following discussion between the controller and financial vice-president.

VICE-PRESIDENT: If we sold the Executive Management Division, it seems ridiculous to seg-
regate the results of the sale in the income statement. Separate categories tend to be absurd and confusing to the stockholders. I believe that we should simply report gain on the sale as other income or expense without detail.

CONTROLLER: Professional pronouncements would require that we disclose this informa-
tion separately in the income statement. If a sale of this type is considered unusual and infrequent, it must be reported as an extraordinary item.

VICE-PRESIDENT: What about the walkout we had last month when our employees were upset about their commission income? Would this situation not also be an extraordinary item?

CONTROLLER: I am not sure whether this item would be reported as extraordinary or not.

VICE-PRESIDENT: Oh well, it doesn't make any difference because the net effect of all these items is immaterial, so no disclosure is necessary.

**Instructions**

(a) On the basis of the foregoing discussion, answer the following questions: Who is correct about handling the sale? What would be the income statement presentation for the sale of the Executive Management Division?

(b) How should the walkout by the employees be reported?

(c) What do you think about the vice-president's observation on materiality?

(d) What facts can you give the group about the earnings per share implications of these topics?

**C4–4** Lars Ewell, vice-president of finance for Axleson, Inc., has recently been asked to discuss with the company's division controllers the proper accounting for extraordinary items. Lars Ewell prepared the factual situations presented below as a basis for discussion.

1. A company experiences a material loss in the repurchase of a large bond issue that has been outstanding for three years. The company regularly repurchases bonds of this nature.

2. A railroad experiences an unusual flood loss to part of its track system. Flood losses normally occur every three or four years.

3. A machine tool company sells the only land it owns. The land was acquired ten years ago for future expansion, but shortly thereafter the company abandoned all plans for expansion but decided to hold the land for appreciation.

4. An earthquake destroys one of the oil refineries owned by a large multinational oil company. Earthquakes are rare in this geographical location.

5. A publicly held company has incurred a substantial loss in the unsuccessful registration of a bond issue.

6. A large portion of a cigarette manufacturer's tobacco crops are destroyed by a hailstorm. Severe damage from hailstorms is rare in this locality.

7. A large diversified company sells a block of shares from its portfolio of securities acquired for investment purposes.

8. A company sells a block of common stock of a publicly traded company. The block of shares, which represents less than 10% of the publicly held company, is the only security investment the company has ever owned.

9. A company that operates a chain of warehouses sells the excess land surrounding one of its warehouses. When the company buys property to establish a new warehouse, it usually buys more land than it expects to use for the warehouse with the expectation that the land will appreciate in value. Twice during the past five years the company sold excess land.

10. A textile manufacturer with only one plant moves to another location and sustains relocation costs of $400,000.

**Instructions**

Determine whether the foregoing items should be classified as extraordinary items. Present a rationale for your position.

**C4–5** The following financial statement was prepared by employees of the Avery Corporation.

Avery Corporation
STATEMENT OF INCOME AND RETAINED EARNINGS
Year Ended December 31, 1984

| | |
|---|---:|
| Revenues | |
| Gross sales, including sales taxes | $887,900 |
| Less returns, allowances, and cash discounts | 29,800 |
| Net sales | 858,100 |
| Dividends, interest, and purchase discounts | 30,250 |
| Recoveries of accounts written off in prior years | 13,850 |
| Total revenues | 902,200 |

| Costs and expenses | |
|---|---|
| Cost of goods sold, including sales taxes | 415,900 |
| Salaries and related payroll expenses | 60,500 |
| Rent | 19,100 |
| Freight-in and freight-out | 3,400 |
| Bad debt expense | 24,000 |
| Addition to reserve for possible inventory losses | 3,800 |
| Total costs and expenses | 526,700 |
| Income before extraordinary items | 375,500 |
| Extraordinary items | |
| Loss on discontinued styles (note 1) | 37,000 |
| Loss on sale of marketable securities (note 2) | 39,050 |
| Loss on sale of warehouse (note 3) | 86,350 |
| Retroactive settlement of federal income taxes for 1983 and 1982 (note 4) | 34,600 |
| Total extraordinary items | 197,000 |
| Net income | 178,500 |
| Retained earnings at beginning of year | 310,700 |
| Total | 489,200 |
| Less: Federal income taxes | 120,000 |
| Cash dividends on common stock | 31,900 |
| Total | 151,900 |
| Retained earnings at end of year | $337,300 |
| Net income per share of common stock | $1.81 |

Notes to the Statement of Income and Retained Earnings:

1. New styles and rapidly changing consumer preferences resulted in a $37,000 loss on the disposal of discontinued styles and related accessories.

2. The corporation sold an investment in marketable securities at a loss of $39,050. The corporation normally sells securities of this nature.

3. The corporation sold one of its warehouses at an $86,350 loss.

4. The corporation was charged $34,600 retroactively for additional income taxes resulting from a settlement in 1984. Of this amount, $17,000 was applicable to 1983, and the balance was applicable to 1982. Litigation of this nature is recurring for this company.

**Instructions**

Identify and discuss the weaknesses in classification and disclosure in the single-step Statement of Income and Retained Earnings above. You should explain why these treatments are weaknesses and what the proper presentation of the items would be in accordance with recent professional pronouncements.

C4–6 Mike Moluf, controller for Silverman, Inc., has recently prepared an income statement for 1984. Mr. Moluf admits that he has not examined any recent professional pronouncements, but believes that the following presentation presents fairly the financial progress of this company during the current period.

Silverman, Inc.
INCOME STATEMENT
For the Year Ended December 31, 1984

| | |
|---|---|
| Sales | $357,852 |
| Less: sales returns and allowances | 16,320 |
| Net sales | 341,532 |

Cost of goods sold:

| | | |
|---|---:|---:|
| Inventory, January 1, 1984 | | $ 50,235 |
| Purchases | $182,143 | |
| Less: purchase discounts | 3,142 | 179,001 |
| Cost of goods available for sale | | 229,236 |
| Inventory, December 31, 1984 | | 37,124 |
| Cost of goods sold | | 192,112 |
| Gross profit | | 149,420 |
| Selling expenses | 41,850 | |
| Administrative expenses | 32,142 | 73,992 |
| Income before taxes | | 75,428 |
| Other revenues and gains | | |
| Dividends received | | 40,000 |
| | | 115,428 |
| Income taxes | | 41,342 |
| Net income | | $ 74,086 |

Silverman, Inc.
STATEMENT OF RETAINED EARNINGS
For the Year Ended December 31, 1984

| | | | |
|---|---:|---:|---:|
| Retained earnings, January 1, 1984 | | | $176,000 |
| Add | | | |
| Net income for 1984 | $74,086 | | |
| Gain from casualty (net of tax) | 10,000 | | |
| Gain on sale of plant assets | 21,400 | $105,486 | |
| Deduct | | | |
| Loss on expropriation (net of tax) | 8,000 | | |
| Cash dividends declared on common stock | 30,000 | | |
| Correction of mathematical error in depreciating plant assets in 1982 (net of tax) | 7,186 | (45,186) | 60,300 |
| Retained earnings, December 31, 1984 | | | $236,300 |

## Instructions

(a) Determine whether these statements are prepared under the "current operating" or "all-inclusive" concept of income. Cite specific details.

(b) Which method do you favor and why?

(c) Which method must be used, and how should the information be presented? Common shares outstanding for the year are 100,000 shares.

For questionable items, use the classification that ordinarily would be appropriate.

C4–7 As audit partner for Foot and Crossfoot, you are in charge of reviewing the classification of unusual items that have occurred during the current year. The following items have come to your attention:

1. An automobile dealer sells for $96,000 an extremely rare 1926 Type 37 Bugatti which it purchased for $15,000 ten years ago. The Bugatti is the only such display item the dealer owns.

2. A drilling company during the current year extended the estimated useful life of certain drilling equipment from 9 to 15 years. As a result, depreciation for the current year was materially lowered.

3. A merchandising company incorrectly overstated its ending inventory two years ago by a material amount. Inventory for all other periods is correctly computed.

4. A retail outlet changed its computation for bad debt expense from 1% to ½ of 1% of sales because of changes in its customer clientele.

5. A mining concern sells a foreign subsidiary engaged in uranium mining, although it (the seller) continues to engage in uranium mining in other countries.

6. A steel company changes from straight-line depreciation to accelerated depreciation in accounting for its plant assets.

7. A construction company, at great expense, prepares a major proposal for a government loan. The loan is not approved.

8. A water pump manufacturer has had large losses resulting from a strike by its employees early in the year.

9. Depreciation for a prior period was incorrectly understated by $58,000. The error was discovered in the current year.

10. A large sheep rancher suffered a major loss because the state required that all sheep in the state be killed to halt the spread of a rare disease. Such a situation has not occurred in the state for twenty years.

11. A food distributor that sells wholesale to supermarket chains and to fast-food restaurants (two major classes of customers) decides to discontinue the division that sells to one of the two classes of customers.

**Instructions**

From the foregoing information, indicate in what section of the income statement or retained earnings statement these items should be classified. Provide a brief rationale for your position.

## EXERCISES

**E4–1** Presented below are changes in the account balances of Pac-Man Manufacturing Co. during the current year, except for retained earnings.

|  | Increase (Decrease) |  | Increase (Decrease) |
|---|---|---|---|
| Cash | $ 70,000 | Accounts payable | $ (26,000) |
| Accounts receivable (net) | 24,000 | Bonds payable | 80,000 |
| Inventory | 126,000 | Common stock | 120,000 |
| Investments | (42,000) | Additional paid-in capital | 11,000 |

**Instructions**

Compute the net income for the current year, assuming that there were no entries in the retained earnings account except for a dividend declaration of $30,000 which was paid in the current year.

**E4–2** Presented below is certain information pertaining to the Quest Medical Company:

| | |
|---|---|
| Cash balance, January 1, 1984 | $ 7,000 |
| Accounts receivable, January 1, 1984 | 20,000 |
| Collections from customers in 1984 | 180,000 |
| Capital account balance, January 1, 1984 | 39,000 |
| Total assets, January 1, 1984 | 60,000 |
| Cash investment added, July 1, 1984 | 4,000 |
| Total assets, December 31, 1984 | 68,000 |
| Cash balance, December 31, 1984 | 10,000 |
| Accounts receivable, December 31, 1984 | 27,000 |
| Merchandise taken for personal use during 1984 | 10,000 |
| Total liabilities, December 31, 1984 | 28,000 |

**Instructions**

Compute the net income for 1984.

**E4-3** Presented below are certain account balances of Cricket, Inc.

| | | | |
|---|---|---|---|
| Ending inventory | $ 55,000 | Sales returns | $ 7,200 |
| Rental revenue | 8,400 | Sales discounts | 18,100 |
| Interest expense | 10,300 | Selling expenses | 98,800 |
| Purchase allowances | 8,200 | Sales | 372,400 |
| Beginning retained earnings | 105,300 | Income taxes | 33,000 |
| Ending retained earnings | 124,100 | Beginning inventory | 44,400 |
| Freight-in | 10,100 | Purchases | 184,200 |
| Dividends earned | 75,000 | Purchase discounts | 17,300 |
| | | Administrative expenses | 82,000 |

**Instructions**

From the foregoing, compute the following: (a) Net revenue; (b) Cost of goods sold; (c) Net income; (d) Dividends declared during the current year.

**E4-4** The financial records of Wirlwind, Inc. were destroyed by fire at the end of the current year. Fortunately the controller had kept certain statistical data related to the income statement as presented below.

1. The beginning merchandise inventory was $88,000 and decreased 25% during the current year.

2. Sales discounts amount to $18,500.

3. 20,000 shares of common stock were outstanding for the entire year.

4. Interest expense was $28,000.

5. The income tax rate is 48%.

6. Cost of goods sold amounts to $460,000.

7. Administrative expenses are 20% of cost of goods sold but only 8% of gross sales.

8. Four-fifths of the operating expenses relate to sales activities.

**Instructions**

From the foregoing information prepare an income statement for the current year in single-step form.

**E4-5** The bookkeeper of Cat-Nip Co. has compiled the following information from the company's records as a basis for an income statement for the year ended 12/31/84.

| | |
|---|---|
| Rental revenues | $ 23,000 |
| Interest on notes payable | 10,000 |
| Market appreciation on temporary investments | 18,000 |
| Merchandise purchases | 389,000 |
| Transportation-in—merchandise | 45,000 |
| Wages and salaries—sales | 104,000 |
| Materials and supplies—sales | 29,500 |
| Common stock outstanding (no. of shares) | 10,000[a] |
| Income taxes | 53,300 |
| Wages and salaries—administrative | 142,000 |
| Other administrative expense | 45,750 |
| Merchandise inventory, 1/1/84 | 85,000 |
| Merchandise inventory, 12/31/84 | 70,000 |
| Purchase returns and allowances | 9,000 |
| Net sales | 952,000 |

| | |
|---|---:|
| Depreciation on plant assets | |
| (75% selling, 25% administrative) | 52,000 |
| Dividends declared | 22,000 |

a Remained unchanged all year.

**Instructions**

(a) Prepare a multiple-step income statement.
(b) Prepare a single-step income statement.
(c) Which format do you prefer? Discuss.

**E4-6** Two accountants for the firm of Check and Doublecheck are arguing about the merits of presenting an income statement on the basis of a multiple-step versus a single-step format. The discussion involves the following information related to Lutherman Company.

| | |
|---|---:|
| Administrative expense | |
| Officers' salaries | $ 6,000 |
| Depreciation of office furniture and equipment | 4,250 |
| Purchase returns | 6,150 |
| Purchases | 51,250 |
| Rental revenue | 16,650 |
| Selling expense | |
| Transportation-out | 4,450 |
| Sales commissions | 7,320 |
| Depreciation of sales equipment | 5,850 |
| Merchandise inventory, beginning inventory | 12,550 |
| Merchandise inventory, ending inventory | 14,150 |
| Sales | 87,650 |
| Transportation-in | 2,280 |
| Income taxes | 13,360 |
| Interest expense on bonds payable | 2,950 |

**Instructions**

(a) Prepare an income statement for the year 1984 using the multiple-step form. Common shares outstanding for 1984 are 50,000 shares.
(b) Prepare an income statement for the year 1984 using the single-step form.
(c) Which one do you prefer? Discuss.

**E4-7** Presented below is information related to Spanish Imports, Inc. for the year 1984. There were 20,000 shares of common stock outstanding during 1984. Assume that the loss due to damage from flood is an extraordinary item.

| | |
|---|---:|
| Administrative expenses | $ 11,000 |
| Income tax expense | 12,000 |
| Inventory, January 1, 1984 | 4,000 |
| Inventory, December 31, 1984 | 7,500 |
| Cash dividend paid ($5,000 declared) | 4,000 |
| Loss due to uninsured flood loss (net of tax) | 10,000 |
| Accrued rent payable | 2,000 |
| Appropriation for contingencies | 12,000 |
| Purchases | 26,000 |
| Interest revenue | 6,000 |
| Selling expense | 20,000 |
| Sales | 100,000 |
| Transportation-in | 8,000 |

**Instructions**

(a) Prepare a multiple-step income statement.
(b) Prepare a single-step income statement.
(c) Which format do you prefer? Discuss.

**E4–8** Presented below is income statement information related to Egyptian Corporation for the year 1984.

| | |
|---|---:|
| Administrative expenses: | |
|   Officers' salaries | $ 45,000 |
|   Depreciation expense—building | 12,600 |
|   Office supplies expense | 7,000 |
| Income tax applicable to uninsured flood | 12,500 |
| Inventory (ending) | 140,000 |
| Flood damage (pretax extraordinary item, tax rate 25%) | 50,000 |
| Purchases | 575,000 |
| Sales | 850,000 |
| Transportation-in | 10,000 |
| Purchase discounts | 7,000 |
| Inventory (beginning) | 135,000 |
| Sales returns and allowances | 17,000 |
| Selling expenses: | |
|   Sales salaries | 55,000 |
|   Depreciation expense—store equipment | 12,000 |
|   Store supplies expense | 9,000 |

In addition, the corporation has other revenue from dividends received of $35,000 and other expense of interest on notes payable of $9,000. There are 13,000 shares of common stock outstanding for the year. The tax rate on income is 45%.

**Instructions**

    (a) Prepare a multiple-step income statement for 1984.
    (b) Prepare a single-step income statement for 1984.
    (c) Discuss the relative merits of the two income statements.

**E4–9** The following balances were taken from the books of the Health Foods Corp. on December 31, 1984:

| | |
|---|---:|
| Interest revenue | $ 80,000 |
| Sales | 1,200,000 |
| Sales returns and allowances | 200,000 |
| Sales discount | 30,000 |
| Inventory 1/1/84 | 225,000 |
| Inventory 12/31/84 | 320,000 |
| Purchases | 700,000 |
| Purchases returns and allowances | 125,000 |
| Purchase discounts | 55,000 |
| Selling expenses | 150,000 |
| Administrative and general expenses | 100,000 |
| Interest expense | 40,000 |
| Loss from earthquake damage (extraordinary item) | 150,000 |

    Income tax rates are:
      (1) 50% on ordinary income.
      (2) 25% on extraordinary gains and losses.

**Instructions**

    Prepare a multiple-step income statement. Assume that 75,000 shares of common stock were outstanding during the year.

**E4–10** Presented below is information related to Disseldorf, Inc. for the year 1984.

| | |
|---|---:|
| Net sales | $2,000,000 |
| Cost of goods sold | 1,300,000 |
| Selling expenses | 110,000 |
| Administrative expenses | 60,000 |

| | |
|---|---:|
| Dividend revenue | 15,000 |
| Interest revenue | 6,000 |
| Write-off of inventory due to obsolescence | 60,000 |
| Depreciation expenses omitted by accident in 1983 | 25,000 |
| Casualty loss (extraordinary item) | 20,000 |
| Dividends declared | 30,000 |
| Retained earnings at December 31, 1983 | 2,500,000 |
| Federal tax rate of 40% on all items | |

### Instructions

(a) Prepare a multiple-step income statement for 1984. Assume that 100,000 shares of common stock are outstanding.

(b) Prepare a separate statement of retained earnings for 1984.

**E4-11** During 1984 Entertainment Enterprises had pretax earnings of $500,000 exclusive of a realized and tax deductible loss of $200,000 from the condemnation of properties (extraordinary item). In addition, the company discovered that depreciation expense was overstated by $90,000 in 1979. Retained earnings at January 1, 1984, amounted to $1,000,000; dividends of $150,000 were declared on common stock during 1984. One hundred thousand shares of common stock were outstanding during 1984.

Assume that the income tax rate on income is 45% for both 1979 and 1984.

### Instructions

Prepare a combined statement of income and retained earnings beginning with income before taxes and extraordinary item.

**E4-12** The stockholders' equity section of Stoakheld Corporation appears below as of December 31, 1984:

| | | |
|---|---:|---:|
| 8% cumulative preferred stock, $50 par value, authorized | | |
|    100,000 shares, outstanding 90,000 shares | | $  4,500,000 |
| Common stock, $1.00 par, authorized and issued | | |
|    10 million shares | | 10,000,000 |
| Additional paid-in capital | | 20,000,000 |
| Retained earnings Dec. 31, 1983 | $200,000,000 | |
|    Net income for 1984 | 20,000,000 | 220,000,000 |
| | | $254,500,000 |

Net income for 1984 reflects a tax rate of 50%. Included in the net income figure is a loss of $10,000,000 (before tax) as a result of a major casualty loss (extraordinary item).

### Instructions

Compute earnings per share data as it should appear on the financial statements of the Stoakheld Corporation.

**E4-13** The following information was taken from the records of Bachrach, Inc. for the year 1984. Income tax applicable to income from continuing operations, $250,000; income tax applicable to loss on discontinued operations, $60,000; income tax applicable to extraordinary gain, $40,000; income tax applicable to extraordinary loss, $20,000.

| | |
|---|---:|
| Extraordinary gain | $ 90,000 |
| Loss on discontinued operations | 100,000 |
| Administrative expenses | 110,000 |
| Rent revenue | 35,000 |
| Extraordinary loss | 50,000 |
| Cash dividends declared | 46,000 |
| Retained earnings January 1, 1984 | 500,000 |

| Cost of goods sold | 800,000 |
|---|---|
| Selling expenses | 200,000 |
| Sales | 1,600,000 |

Shares outstanding during 1984 were 18,000.

**Instructions**

(a) Prepare a single-step income statement for 1984. Include per share data.
(b) Prepare a combined single-step income and retained earnings statement.
(c) Which one do you prefer? Discuss.

# PROBLEMS

**P4–1** The president of Sock-a-Rue Corporation provides you with the following selected account balances as of 12/31/84.

| | Dr. | Cr. |
|---|---|---|
| Sales | | $2,750,000 |
| Sales office salaries | $ 180,000 | |
| Officers' salaries | 195,000 | |
| Building depreciation (50% of building is directly related to sales) | 90,000 | |
| Freight-out | 50,000 | |
| Cost of goods sold | 1,050,000 | |
| Dividends declared and paid | 75,000 | |
| Dividends received | | 40,000 |
| Interest expense—10% bonds | 60,000 | |
| Retained earnings—1/1/84 | | 250,000 |
| Expropriation of foreign holdings (extraordinary item) | 500,000 | |
| Damages payable from litigation ~~other exp~~ | | 75,000 |
| Federal income taxes paid | 295,000 | |

The president informs you that the damages payable from litigation arose in 1984 out of a lawsuit initiated in 1980, and the bookkeeper debited retained earnings for $75,000. Assume that the company is continually involved in litigation of this nature. The bookkeeper had also credited cash for $295,000 in payment of the federal income taxes for 1984. The president requests your help in constructing an income statement. She advises you that the corporation had 100,000 shares of common stock outstanding, and was taxed at a straight rate of 50% on all income-related items.

**Instructions**

(a) Prepare a combined statement of income and retained earnings in multiple-step form.
(b) Prepare a combined statement of income and retained earnings in single-step form.

**P4–2** Selected accounts and related amounts appearing in the income statement and balance sheet columns of Elastic Corporation's worksheet at December 31 are as follows:

| | | | |
|---|---|---|---|
| Purchase discounts | $ 13,000 | Administrative expenses (total) | $105,000 |
| Rent income | 22,000 | Capital stock | 300,000 |
| Retained earnings (1/1) | 230,000 | Dividends declared and paid | 50,000 |
| Salaries payable | 18,000 | Freight-in | 10,500 |
| Sales | 960,000 | Gain on sale of land | 15,000 |
| Sales discounts | 7,500 | Merchandise inventory (1/1) | 87,500 |
| Sales returns | 13,500 | Merchandise inventory (12/31) | 92,500 |
| Selling expenses (total) | 186,000 | Purchases | 587,500 |

The gain on sale of land is not an extraordinary item. All income is taxed at a uniform rate of 45% except for the gain on sale of land, which is taxed at a 30% rate.

**Instructions**

Prepare a combined statement of income and retained earnings using the single-step form. Assume that the only change in the unappropriated retained earnings balance during the current year was for dividends. Ten thousand shares of common stock were outstanding during the entire year.

**P4-3** The following account balances were included in the trial balance of the Brown Toaster Corporation at June 30, 1984.

| | |
|---|---:|
| Sales | $1,495,625 |
| Sales discounts | 28,352 |
| Purchases | 895,450 |
| Freight-in | 20,500 |
| Purchase returns | 5,150 |
| Purchase discounts | 18,670 |
| Sales salaries | 31,750 |
| Sales commissions | 88,700 |
| Travel expense—salespersons | 23,650 |
| Freight-out | 19,500 |
| Entertainment expense | 15,150 |
| Telephone and telegraph—sales | 8,700 |
| Depreciation of sales equipment | 4,980 |
| Building expense—prorated to sales | 6,200 |
| Miscellaneous selling expenses | 2,980 |
| Office supplies | 3,450 |
| Telephone and telegraph—administration | 2,820 |
| Depreciation of office furniture and equipment | 5,340 |
| Real estate and other local taxes | 6,525 |
| Bad debt expense—selling | 4,315 |
| Building expense—prorated to administration | 8,210 |
| Miscellaneous office expenses | 6,000 |
| Sales returns | 22,450 |
| Dividends received | 25,000 |
| Bond interest expense | 14,000 |
| Income taxes | 162,190 |
| Depreciation understatement due to error—1981 (net of tax) | 6,680 |
| Dividends declared on preferred stock | 9,000 |
| Dividends declared on common stock | 32,000 |
| Merchandise inventory—July 1, 1983 | 225,000 |

The merchandise inventory at June 30, 1984 amounted to $260,000. The Unappropriated Retained Earnings account had a balance of $195,000 at June 30, 1984, before closing; the only entry in that account during the year was a debit of $35,000 to establish an Appropriation for Bonded Indebtedness. There are 70,000 shares of common stock outstanding.

**Instructions**

(a) Using the multiple-step form, prepare a combined statement of income and unappropriated retained earnings for the year ended June 30, 1984.

(b) Using the single-step form, prepare a combined statement of income and unappropriated retained earnings for the year ended June 30, 1984.

**P4-4** Presented below is information related to Halloran Company for 1984.

| | |
|---|---:|
| Retained earnings balance, January 1, 1984 | $ 980,000 |
| Sales for the year | 25,000,000 |
| Cost of goods sold | 17,000,000 |
| Interest revenue | 50,000 |
| Selling and administrative expenses | 5,000,000 |
| Write-off of goodwill (not tax deductible) | 500,000 |

| | |
|---|---:|
| Federal income taxes for 1984 | 1,100,000 |
| Assessment for additional 1981 income taxes (normally recurring) | 250,000 |
| Gain on the sale of investments (normal recurring) | 90,000 |
| Loss due to flood damage—extraordinary item (net of tax) | 120,000 |
| Loss on the disposition of the wholesale division (net of tax) | 450,000 |
| Loss on sale of the wholesale division (net of tax) | 350,000 |
| Dividends declared on common stock | 250,000 |
| Dividends declared on preferred stock | 75,000 |

**Instructions**

Prepare a combined statement of income and retained earnings using the multiple-step form. Halloran Company decided to discontinue its entire wholesale operations and to retain their manufacturing operations. On September 15, Halloran sold the wholesale operations to J. R. Philip Co. During 1984, there were 300,000 shares of common stock outstanding all year.

**P4–5** Below is the Retained Earnings account for the year 1984 for Huffy, Inc.

| | | |
|---|---:|---:|
| Retained earnings, January 1, 1984 | | $274,155 |
| Add: | | |
| Gain on sale of investments (net of tax) | $33,400 | |
| Net income | 61,800 | |
| Refund on litigation with government, related to the year 1981 (net of tax) | 12,750 | |
| Recognition of income earned in 1983, but omitted from income statement in that year (net of tax) | 9,100 | 117,050 |
| | | 391,205 |
| Deduct | | |
| Loss on discontinued operations (net of tax) | 20,000 | |
| Write-off of goodwill | 48,000 | |
| Cumulative effect on income in changing from straight-line depreciation to accelerated depreciation in 1984 (net of tax) | 15,470 | |
| Cash dividends declared | 12,000 | 95,470 |
| Retained earnings, December 31, 1984 | | $295,735 |

**Instructions**

(a) Prepare a statement of Retained Earnings. Huffy, Inc. normally sells investments of the type mentioned above.

(b) State where the items that do not appear in the Retained Earnings statement should be shown.

**P4–6** Mercy Company has 100,000 shares of common stock outstanding. In 1984, the company reports income from continuing operations before taxes of $1,570,000. Additional transactions not considered in the $1,570,000 are as follows:

1. In 1984 the company reviewed its accounts receivable and wrote off as an expense of that year $19,200 of accounts receivable that had been carried for years and appeared unlikely to be collected.

2. An internal audit discovered that amortization of intangible assets was understated by $41,000 (net of tax) in a prior period. The amount was charged against retained earnings.

3. The company sold its only investment in common stock during the year at a gain of $130,000. The gain is taxed at a rate of 25%. Assume that the transaction meets the requirements of an extraordinary item.

4. In 1984, Mercy Company sold equipment for $40,000. The machine had originally cost $68,000 and had accumulated depreciation of $26,000. The gain or loss (considered ordinary) is taxed at the rate of 40%.

5. The company discontinued operations of one of its subsidiaries during the current year at a loss of $190,000 before taxes. Assume that this transaction meets the criteria for discontin-

ued operations. The loss on operations of the discontinued subsidiary was $90,000 before taxes; the loss from disposal of the subsidiary was $100,000 before taxes.

6. The sum of $90,000, applicable to a breached 1980 contract, was received as a result of a lawsuit. Prior to the award, legal counsel was uncertain about the outcome of the suit and had not established a receivable.

**Instructions**

Prepare an income statement for the year 1984 starting with income from continuing operations before taxes. Compute earnings per share as it should be shown on the face of the income statement. (Assume a tax rate of 40% on all items, unless indicated otherwise.)

**P4–7** Richmond, Inc. reported income from continuing operations before taxes during 1984 of $750,000. Additional transactions occurring in 1984 but not considered in the $750,000 are as follows:

1. The corporation experienced an uninsured flood loss (extraordinary) in the amount of $50,000 during the year. The tax rate on this item is 48%.

2. At the beginning of 1982, the corporation purchased a machine for $72,000 (salvage value of $6,000) that had a useful life of six years. The bookkeeper uses straight-line depreciation, but failed to deduct the salvage value in computing the depreciation base.

3. Securities sold as a part of its portfolio resulted in a loss of $93,000 (pretax).

4. When its president died, the corporation realized $92,000 from an insurance policy. The cash surrender value of this policy had been carried on the books as an investment in the amount of $53,000 (the gain is nontaxable).

5. The corporation disposed of its recreational division at a loss of $90,000 before taxes. Assume that this transaction meets the criteria for discontinued operations.

6. The corporation decided to change its method of inventory pricing from average cost to the FIFO method. The effect of this change on prior years is to increase 1982 income by $50,000 and decrease 1983 income by $10,000 before taxes. The FIFO method has been used for 1984. The tax rate on these items is 40%.

**Instructions**

Prepare an income statement for the year 1984 starting with income from continuing operations before taxes. Compute earnings per share as it should be shown on the face of the income statement. Common shares outstanding for the year are 24,000 shares. (Assume a tax rate of 40% on all items, unless indicated otherwise.)

**P4–8** The Ludlow Corp. commenced business on January 1, 1981. Recently the corporation has had several unusual accounting problems related to the presentation of their income statement for financial reporting purposes.

You have been the CPA for Ludlow Corp. for several years and have been asked to examine the following data.

Ludlow Corp.
STATEMENT OF INCOME
For the Year Ended December 31, 1984

| | |
|---|---:|
| Sales | $9,500,000 |
| Cost of goods sold | 6,000,000 |
| Gross profit | 3,500,000 |
| Selling and administrative expense | 1,300,000 |
| Income before income taxes | 2,200,000 |
| Income tax (45%) | 990,000 |
| Net income | $1,210,000 |

In addition, this information was provided:

1. The controller mentioned that the corporation has had difficulty in collecting on several of their receivables. For this reason, the bad debt write-off was increased from 1% to 1½% of sales. The controller estimates that if this rate had been used in past periods, an additional $25,000 worth of expense would have been charged. The bad debt expense for the current period was calculated and is part of selling and administrative expense.

2. Common shares outstanding at the end of 1984 totaled 1,000,000. No additional shares were purchased or sold during 1984.

3. Ludlow noted also that
   (a) Inventory in the amount of $48,000 was obsolete.
   (b) The major casualty loss suffered by the corporation was partially uninsured and cost $55,000, net of tax (extraordinary item).

4. Retained earnings as of January 1, 1984 was $3,600,000. Cash dividends of $500,000 were paid in 1984.

5. In January, 1984, Ludlow Corp. changed its method of accounting for plant assets from the straight-line method to the accelerated method (double-declining balance). The controller has prepared a schedule indicating what depreciation expense would have been in previous periods if the double-declining method had been used. (The effective tax rate for 1981, 1982, and 1983 was 30%.)

|  | Depreciation Expense under Straight-Line | Depreciation Expense under Double-Declining | Difference |
|---|---|---|---|
| 1981 | $ 90,000 | $140,000 | $50,000 |
| 1982 | 90,000 | 121,000 | 31,000 |
| 1983 | 90,000 | 105,000 | 15,000 |
|  | $270,000 | $366,000 | $96,000 |

6. In 1984, Ludlow discovered that two errors were made in previous years. First, when it took a physical inventory at the end of 1981, one of the count sheets was apparently lost. The ending inventory for 1981 was therefore understated by $80,000. The inventory was correctly taken in 1982, 1983, and 1984. Also, the corporation found that in 1983 it had failed to record $16,000 as an expense for sales commissions. The effective tax rate for 1981, 1982, and 1983 was 30%. The sales commissions for 1983 are included in 1984 expenses.

**Instructions**

Prepare the income statement for Ludlow Corp. in accordance with professional pronouncements. Do not prepare footnotes.

**P4–9** A condensed statement of income and retained earnings of the Sioux Company for the year ended December 31, 1984 is presented on page 166.

Also presented are three unrelated situations involving accounting changes and classification of certain items as ordinary or extraordinary. Each situation is based upon the condensed statements of income and retained earnings of the Sioux Company and requires revisions of these statements.

The Sioux Company
CONDENSED STATEMENTS OF INCOME
AND RETAINED EARNINGS
For The Year Ended 1984

| | |
|---|---|
| Sales | $5,000,000 |
| Cost of goods sold | 2,800,000 |
| Gross margin | 2,200,000 |
| Selling, general, and administrative expenses | 1,500,000 |
| Income before extraordinary item | 700,000 |
| Extraordinary item | (450,000) |
| Net income | 250,000 |
| Retained earnings, January 1 | 900,000 |
| Retained earnings, December 31 | $1,150,000 |

## Situation A

During the latter part of 1984, the company discontinued its retail and apparel fabric divisions. The results of such operations and the loss on sale of these two discontinued divisions amounted to a total loss of $440,000. This amount was considered part of selling, general, and administrative expenses. The transaction meets the criteria for discontinued operations.

The extraordinary item in the condensed statement of income and retained earnings for 1984 relates to a loss sustained as a result of damage to the company's merchandise caused by a tornado that struck its main warehouse in Michigan City. This natural disaster was considered an unusual and infrequent occurrence for that section of the country.

## Situation B

At the end of 1984, the Sioux management decided that the estimated loss rate on uncollectible accounts receivable was too low. The loss rate used for the years 1983 and 1984 was 1.2% of total sales, and owing to an increase in the write-off of uncollectible accounts, the rate has been raised to 3% of total sales. The amount recorded in bad debt expense under the heading of selling, general, and administrative expenses for 1984 was $60,000 and for 1983 was $30,000.

The extraordinary item in the condensed statement of income and retained earnings for 1984 relates to a loss incurred in the abandonment of outmoded equipment formerly used in the business.

## Situation C

On January 1, 1982, Sioux acquired machinery at a cost of $400,000. The Company adopted the double-declining balance method of depreciation for this machinery, and had been recording depreciation over an estimated life of ten years, with no residual value. At the beginning of 1984, a decision was made to adopt the straight-line method of depreciation for this machinery. Owing to an oversight, however, the double-declining balance method was used for 1984. For financial reporting purposes, depreciation is included in selling, general, and administrative expenses.

The extraordinary item in the condensed statement of income and retained earnings relates to shutdown expenses incurred by the company during a major strike by its operating employees during 1984.

### Instructions

For each of the three unrelated situations, prepare a revised condensed statement of income and retained earnings of the Sioux Company. Ignore income tax considerations and earnings per share computations.

(AICPA adapted)

**P4-10** Presented below is a combined single-step statement of income and retained earnings for Jefferson Company for 1983.

|  | (000 omitted) |
|---|---|
| Net sales | $600,000 |
| Cost and expenses: | |
| Cost of goods sold | 480,000 |
| Selling, general and administrative expenses | 66,000 |
| Other, net | 17,000 |
|  | 563,000 |
| Income before income taxes | 37,000 |
| Income taxes | 16,800 |
| Net income | 20,200 |
| Retained earnings at beginning of period, as previously reported | 141,000 |
| Adjustment required for correction of error | (7,000) |
| Retained earnings at beginning of period, as restated | 134,000 |
| Dividends on common stock | (12,200) |
| Retained earnings at end of period | $142,000 |

Additional facts are as follows:

1. "Selling, general and administrative expenses" for 1983 included a usual but infrequently occurring charge of $9,000,000.

2. "Other, net" for 1983 included an extraordinary item (charge) of $10,000,000. If the extraordinary item (charge) had not occurred, income taxes for 1983 would have been $21,800,000 instead of $16,800,000.

3. "Adjustment required for correction of an error" was a result of a change in estimate (useful life of certain assets reduced to 7 years and a catch-up adjustment made).

4. Jefferson Company disclosed earnings per common share for net income in the Notes to the Financial Statements.

**Instructions**

Determine from these additional facts whether the presentation of the facts in the above Jefferson Company Statements of Income and Retained Earnings is appropriate. If the presentation is not appropriate, describe the appropriate presentation and discuss its theoretical rationale.

# CHAPTER 5

# Balance Sheet and Statement of Changes in Financial Position

Investors have often focused their attention primarily on the income statement and earnings per share to the virtual exclusion of the balance sheet and statement of changes in financial position. However, the recent high inflation rates, coupled with the related credit "crunches of the 1970s and early 1980s," have taught investors an important lesson—many surprises in earnings per share could have been anticipated if these financial statements had not been overlooked. Liquidity and financial flexibility are necessary conditions for any profitable enterprise, and only through careful analysis of balance sheets and statements of changes in financial position can information about these conditions be obtained.

## SECTION 1   BALANCE SHEET

### USEFULNESS OF THE BALANCE SHEET[1]

The balance sheet provides information about the nature and amounts of investments in enterprise resources, obligations to enterprise creditors, and the owners' equity in net enterprise resources. That information not only complements information about the components of income, but also contributes to financial reporting by providing a basis for (1) computing rates of return, (2) evaluating the capital structure of the enterprise, and (3) assessing the liquidity and financial flexibility of the enterprise. In order to make certain judgments

[1]*Accounting Trends and Techniques—1981* indicates that 91% of the companies surveyed used the term "balance sheet." The term "statement of financial position" is used infrequently, although it is conceptually appealing.

**168**

about enterprise risk[2] and assessments of future cash flows, one must analyze the balance sheet and determine enterprise liquidity and financial flexibility.

**Liquidity** describes "the amount of time that is expected to elapse until an asset is realized or otherwise converted into cash or until a liability has to be paid."[3] Both short-term and long-term credit grantors are interested in such short-term measures as cash or near cash to current liabilities to assess the enterprise's ability to meet current and maturing obligations. Similarly, present and prospective equity holders study the liquidity of an enterprise to assess the likelihood of continuing or increased cash dividends or the possibility of expanded operations. Generally, the greater the liquidity, the lower the risk of enterprise failure.

**Financial flexibility** is the "ability of an enterprise to take effective actions to alter the amounts and timing of cash flows so it can respond to unexpected needs and opportunities."[4] For example, a company may become so loaded with debt that its sources of monies to finance expansion or to pay off maturing debt are limited or nonexistent; thus, it lacks financial flexibility. An enterprise with a high degree of financial flexibility is better able to survive bad times, to recover from unexpected setbacks, and to take advantage of profitable and unexpected investment opportunities. Generally, the greater the financial flexibility, the lower the risk of enterprise failure.

The serious effects of a lack of liquidity and inadequate financial flexibility are illustrated in the experience of the airline industry in the United States today. Pan Am, American, Eastern, United, and TWA all reported 1980 or 1981 quarterly operating losses that stemmed primarily from high interest rates, deregulation and increased competition, increased fuel costs, and price cutting. Because of operating losses and lowered liquidity, some airlines asked their employees to sign labor contracts that provided no wage increases. Other airlines, already heavily in debt and lacking financial flexibility and liquidity, had to cancel orders for new, more efficient aircraft of the 757 and 767 variety. They were not able even to generate cash through the sale of their old aircraft because of lowered air traffic (controllers' strike and layoff) and the lower fuel efficiency of the older aircraft. Pan Am was forced to sell its Manhattan skyscraper for $400 million to maintain its liquidity. The problem has become so acute that one of the major airlines (Braniff) has declared bankruptcy. An examination of the airlines' balance sheets reveals their financial inflexibility and low liquidity.

## LIMITATIONS OF THE BALANCE SHEET

As indicated in earlier chapters the balance sheet **does not reflect current value** because accountants have adopted a historical cost basis in valuing and reporting the assets and liabilities. When a balance sheet, for example, is prepared in accordance with generally accepted accounting principles, most assets are stated at cost; exceptions are receivables, marketable securities, and some long-term investments. Many accountants believe that all the assets should be restated in terms of current values; there are, however, widely different opinions about the exact type of valuation basis to be employed. Some contend that

[2]Risk is an expression of the unpredictability of future events, transactions, circumstances, and results of the enterprise.

[3]"Reporting Income, Cash Flows, and Financial Position of Business Enterprises," *Proposed Statement of Financial Accounting Concepts* (Stamford, Conn.: FASB, 1981), par. 29.

[4]Ibid., par. 25.

historical statements should be adjusted for constant dollars (general price-level changes) when inflation is significant; others believe that a current cost concept (specific price-level changes) is more useful; still others believe that a net realizable value concept or some variant should be adopted. Regardless of the method favored, all are significantly different from the historical cost approach. Each approach has the advantage over the historical cost basis of presenting a more accurate assessment of the current value of the enterprise, although the question of whether reliable valuations can be obtained is still unresolved. These issues are discussed further in Chapter 25.

Another basic limitation of historical cost statements is that **judgments must be used.** Even if significant changes in the price level do not occur, the determination of the collectibility of receivables, the salability of inventory, and the useful life of long-term tangible and intangible assets are difficult to determine. Although the process of depreciating long-term assets is a generally accepted practice, the recognition of accretion and enhancement in value is generally ignored by accountants for similar fixed assets.

In addition, the balance sheet necessarily **omits many items that are of financial value to the business** but cannot be recorded objectively. As indicated earlier, the value of a company's human resources is certainly significant, but it is omitted because such assets are difficult to quantify as a result of the uncertainty surrounding their ultimate value. Such omissions are understandable and excusable. But many items that could and should appear on the balance sheet (most are of a liability or commitment nature) are reported in an "off balance sheet" manner, if reported at all.[5] Several of these omitted items (such as, sales of receivables with recourse, leases, through-put arrangements, and take-or-pay contracts) are discussed in later chapters.

## CLASSIFICATION IN THE BALANCE SHEET

In the balance sheet accounts are classified so that similar items are grouped together to arrive at significant subtotals; furthermore, the material is arranged so that important relationships are shown and attention is focused on the most important items.

The three general classes of items included in the balance sheet are assets, liabilities, and equity. Here is how we defined them in Chapter 2, as excerpted from *Concepts Statement No. 3.*

---

**ELEMENTS OF THE BALANCE SHEET**

1. **ASSETS.** Probable future economic benefits obtained or controlled by a particular entity as a result of past transactions or events.
2. **LIABILITIES.** Probable future sacrifices of economic benefits arising from present obligations of a particular entity to transfer assets or provide services to other entities in the future as a result of past transactions or events.
3. **EQUITY.** Residual interest in the assets of an entity that remains after deducting its liabilities. In a business enterprise, the equity is the ownership interest.[6]

---

[5] For a discussion of various methods that businesses have devised to remove debt from the balance sheet, read: "Get It Off the Balance Sheet," Richard Dieter and Arthur R. Wyatt, *Financial Executive* (Vol. 48, June 1980), pp. 42, 44–48.

[6] "Elements of Financial Statements of Business Enterprises," *Statement of Financial Accounting Concepts No. 3* (Stamford, Conn.: FASB, 1980), p. xi.

These items are then divided into several subclassifications that provide the reader with additional information. The table below indicates the general format of balance sheet presentation.

| BALANCE SHEET | |
| --- | --- |
| Assets | Liabilities and Owners' Equity |
| Current assets | Current liabilities |
| Long-term investments | Long-term debt |
| Property, plant and equipment | Owners' equity |
| Intangible assets | Capital stock |
| Other assets | Additional paid-in capital |
| | Retained earnings |

The balance sheet may be classified in some other manner, but these are the major subdivisions, and there is very little departure from them in practice. If a proprietorship or partnership is involved, the classifications within the owners' equity section are presented a little differently.

## Current Assets

Current assets are cash and other assets that are expected to be converted into cash, sold, or consumed either in one year or in the operating cycle, whichever is longer. For this purpose, the operating cycle of any given enterprise is considered to be the average time between the acquisition of materials and supplies and the realization of cash through sales of the product for which the materials and supplies were acquired. Thus the time it takes to process the material, to sell the product, and to collect from customers is included in the operating cycle. The cycle operates from cash through inventory and receivables back to cash. This definition ignores the arbitrary one-year period except when there are several operating cycles within one year; then the one-year period is used. If the operating cycle is more than one year, the longer period is used.

Current assets are presented in the balance sheet in the order of their liquidity. The five major items found in the current section are cash, marketable securities, receivables, inventories, and prepayments. **Cash** is included at its stated value; **marketable securities** are valued at cost or the lower of cost or market; **accounts receivable** are stated at the estimated amount collectible; **inventories** generally are included at cost or the lower of cost or market; and **prepaid items** are valued at cost.

These items are not considered current assets if they are not expected to be realized in one year or in the operating cycle, whichever is longer. For example, cash restricted for purposes other than payment of current obligations or for use in current operations is excluded from the current asset section. **Generally, the rule is that if an asset is to be turned into cash or is to be used to pay a current liability within a year or the operating cycle, whichever is longer, it is classified as current.** This requirement is subject to exceptions. Marketable securities, for example, pose a problem. Depending on the intent of management, an investment in common stock is classified as either a current asset or a noncurrent asset. The problem is especially difficult when a company has small holdings of common stocks or bonds of another company. Should these assets be classified as current? At this point, the differentiation can be made only on the basis of intent: What does the company plan to do with these securities?

Note also that although a current asset is well defined, certain theoretical problems develop. One problem is justifying the inclusion of prepaid expense in the current asset section. The normal justification is that if these items had not been paid in advance, they would require the use of current assets during the operating cycle. If we follow this logic to its ultimate conclusion, however, any asset purchased previously saves the use of current assets during the operating cycle and is considered current. Prepaid expenses are not ordinarily material in amount, however, and their placement on the balance sheet has been of little concern.

Another problem occurs in the current asset definition when fixed assets are consumed during the operating cycle. A literal interpretation of the accounting profession's position on this matter would indicate that an amount equal to the current depreciation and amortization charges on the noncurrent assets should be placed in the current asset section at the beginning of the year, because they will be consumed in the next operating cycle. This conceptual problem is generally ignored, which illustrates that the formal distinction made between current and noncurrent assets is, nonetheless, "flexible."[7]

**Cash**   Any restrictions on the general availability of cash or any commitments on its probable disposition must be disclosed.

| Current assets | | |
|---|---|---|
| Cash | | |
| Restricted in accordance with terms of the purchase contract | $48,500.00 | |
| Unrestricted—available for current use | 14,928.92 | $63,428.92 |

In the example above, it was assumed that the necessary amount of cash ($48,500) was restricted to meet an obligation due currently and, therefore, the restricted cash was included under current assets. If cash is restricted for purposes other than current obligations, it is excluded from the current assets, as shown below:

| Current assets | | |
|---|---|---|
| Cash | $78,327.45 | |
| Less cash restricted for additions to plant | 45,000.00 | $33,327.45 |
| Long-term assets | | |
| Cash restricted for additions to plant in accordance with action of the board of directors | | $45,000.00 |

---

[7]For an interesting discussion of the shortcomings of the current and noncurrent classification framework, see Loyd Heath, "Financial Reporting and the Evaluation of Solvency," *Accounting Research Monograph No. 3* (New York: AICPA, 1978), pp. 43–69. The principal recommendation

**Short-Term Investments**  The basis of valuation and any differences between cost and current market value should be included in the balance sheet presentation of short-term investments. The generally accepted method for accounting for short-term investments, often referred to as marketable securities, is cost or market, whichever is lower.[8]

| Current assets | |
|---|---|
| Marketable securities—at cost which<br>approximates market | $26,342.00 |

**Receivables**  Any anticipated loss due to uncollectibles, the amount and nature of any nontrade receivables, and any amounts pledged or discounted should be clearly stated.

| Current assets | | |
|---|---|---|
| Notes and accounts receivable | | |
| Customers— | | |
| Notes | $ 35,000.00 | |
| Accounts (of which $40,000 are pledged as<br>security for a note payable) | 146,528.75 | |
| Subsidiary company | 18,247.12 | |
| Officers and employees | 17,912.11 | |
| | 217,687.98 | |
| Less allowance for doubtful accounts | 11,200.00 | $206,487.98 |

**Inventories**  For a proper presentation of inventories, the basis of valuation, the method of pricing, and, for a manufacturing concern, the stage of completion of the inventories are disclosed.

| Current assets | | |
|---|---|---|
| Inventories—at the lower of cost (determined<br>by the first-in, first-out method) or market | | |
| Finished goods | $ 47,258.91 | |
| Work in process | 12,246.88 | |
| Raw materials | 188,764.21 | $248,270.00 |

Some accountants contend that, in a company that assembles a final product from both purchased and manufactured parts and also sells some of these parts, a distinction among

---

is that the current and noncurrent classification be abolished, and that assets and liabilities simply be listed without classification in their present order. This approach is justified on the basis that any classification scheme is arbitrary and that users of the financial statements can assemble the data in the manner they believe most appropriate.

[8]Special rules that apply for both short-term and long-term marketable securities are discussed in Chapters 7 and 18. "Accounting for Certain Marketable Securities," *Statement of Financial Accounting Standards No. 12* (Stamford, Conn.: FASB, 1975).

work in process, finished goods, and raw materials is arbitrary and misleading. They prefer a classification that indicates the source or nature of the inventory amount as shown below.

| Current assets | | |
|---|---:|---:|
| Inventories—at the lower of cost (determined by the first-in, first-out method) or market | | |
| Materials | $103,856.18 | |
| Direct labor | 74,212.11 | |
| Manufacturing overhead | 70,201.71 | $248,270.00 |

## Current Liabilities

Current liabilities are the obligations that are reasonably expected to be liquidated either through the use of current assets or the creation of other current liabilities.

This concept includes:

1. Payables resulting from the acquisition of goods and services: accounts payable, wages payable, taxes payable, and so on.

2. Collections received in advance for the delivery of goods or performance of services; for example, prepaid rent revenue or prepaid subscriptions revenue.

3. Other liabilities whose liquidation will take place within the operating cycle. This includes long-term liabilities such as bonds to be paid in the current period, or short-term obligations arising from purchase of equipment.

At times, even though a liability will be paid next year, it is not included in the current liability section. This occurs either when the debt is expected to be refinanced through another long-term issue,[9] or when the debt is retired out of noncurrent assets. This approach is used because liquidation does not result from the use of current assets or the creation of other current liabilities. Current liabilities frequently are reported on the balance sheet in the order they will be paid.

Here is an example of a current liability section.

| Current liabilities | | |
|---|---:|---:|
| Notes payable to bank (secured by pledge of raw materials inventory) | | $ 45,000.00 |
| Accounts payable | | |
| Trade | $185,917.18 | |
| Customers' deposits and advances | 32,412.81 | |
| Employees' payroll deductions | 18,912.88 | 237,242.87 |
| Bank overdraft | | 7,245.12 |
| Current maturities of installment note payable, secured by lien against land and buildings | | 50,000.00 |
| Dividend payable | | 18,000.00 |
| Income taxes | | 23,000.00 |
| Miscellaneous accrued liabilities | | 17,245.86    $397,733.85 |

[9]A detailed discussion of accounting for debt expected to be refinanced is found in Chapter 10 and in "Classification of Short-term Obligations Expected to Be Refinanced," *Statement of Financial Accounting Standards No. 6* (Stamford, Conn.: FASB, 1975).

Current liabilities include such items as trade payables, nontrade notes and accounts payable, advances received from customers, and current maturities of long-term debt. Income taxes and other accrued items are classified separately, if material. Any secured liability, for example, stock held as collateral on notes payable, is fully described so that the assets providing the security can be determined.

## Long-Term Investments

Long-term investments, often referred to simply as investments, normally consist of one of three types:

1. Investments in securities such as bonds, common stock, or long-term notes.
2. Investments in tangible fixed assets not currently used in operations, such as land held for speculation.
3. Investments set aside in special funds such as a sinking fund, pension fund, or plant expansion fund. The cash surrender value of life insurance is included here.

Long-term investments are to be held for many years, and are not acquired with the intention of disposing of them in the near future. Long-term investments are usually presented on the balance sheet just below Current Assets in a separate section called Investments. Many securities that are properly shown among the long-term investments are readily marketable but should not be included as current assets if they were not acquired or are not held with the intention of converting them to cash in a year or in the operating cycle, whichever is longer.

| Investments | | | | |
|---|---|---|---|---|
| Investments in subsidiary companies—at equity | | | | |
| Leelco, Inc. | | | | |
| 1,000 shares (45%) of | | | | |
| capital stock | $86,425 | | | |
| Cash advance | 10,000 | $96,425 | | |
| Career Co., Inc. | | | | |
| 2,000 shares (40%) of capital stock | | 42,000 | $138,425 | |
| Miscellaneous other investments— | | | | |
| at cost, which is approximately | | | | |
| $13,500 below current market value[10] | | | 84,600 | $223,025 |

## Property, Plant, and Equipment, and Intangible Assets

Property, plant, and equipment are properties of a durable nature used in the regular operations of the business. These assets consist of physical property such as land, buildings, machinery, furniture, tools, and wasting resources (timberland, minerals). With the exception of land, most assets are either depreciable (such as buildings) or consumable (such as timberlands).

---

[10]Noncurrent investments in marketable equity securities are required to be reported at the lower of cost or market unless the equity method of accounting is used. See discussion of *FASB Statement No. 12* in Chapter 18.

| | | | |
|---|---:|---:|---:|
| **Property, plant, and equipment** | | | |
| Land | | $ 80,000 | |
| Buildings | $420,000 | | |
| Less accumulated depreciation | 176,000 | 244,000 | |
| Buildings in process of construction— at cost to date (subject to the first mortgage lien of $200,000) | | 230,000 | $554,000 |
| **Intangible assets** | | | |
| Franchise— at cost less amortization of $4,712 | | 8,244 | |
| Licenses, trademarks, and patents— at cost less amortization of $12,444 | | 16,556 | |
| Goodwill—at cost less amortization of $10,000 | | 70,000 | 94,800 |

Intangible assets lack physical substance and usually have a high degree of uncertainty concerning the future benefits that are to be received from their employment. They include, for example, patents, copyrights, franchises, goodwill, trademarks, trade names, and secret processes. Generally, all of these intangibles are written off (amortized) to expense. Intangibles can represent significant economic resources, yet financial analysts often ignore them, and accountants write them down or off arbitrarily because valuation is difficult. Intangibles are not generally capitalized and amortized unless acquired in arm's-length transactions.

The basis of valuing the property, plant, and equipment, and intangible assets, any liens against the properties, and accumulated depreciation should be shown. It is seldom advisable to show a detailed classification of the property, plant, and equipment in the balance sheet; a supplementary schedule or analysis generally provides a better means of presenting such information.

## Other Assets

The items included in the section "Other Assets" vary widely in practice. Some of the items commonly included are deferred charges (long-term prepaid expenses), noncurrent receivables, intangible assets, assets in special funds, and advances to subsidiaries. Such a section unfortunately is too general a classification. Instead, this classification should be restricted to unusual items sufficiently different from assets included in the categories above. Some deferred costs such as organization costs incurred during the early life of the business are commonly classified here. Even these costs, however, are more properly placed in the intangible asset section.[11]

---

[11]Some of these items may not be assets at all. We can only hope that, as the recommendations of the FASB's conceptual framework project are implemented, some of these unusual deferred costs will be critically examined.

## Long-Term Liabilities

Long-term liabilities are obligations that are not reasonably expected to be liquidated within the normal operating cycle of the business but, instead, are payable at some date beyond that time. Bonds payable, notes payable, deferred income taxes, lease obligations, and pension obligations are the most common long-term liabilities. Generally, a great deal of supplementary disclosure is needed for this section because most long-term debt is subject to various covenants and restrictions for the protection of the lenders. Long-term liabilities that mature within the current operating cycle are classified as current liabilities if their liquidation requires the use of assets included in the current asset group.

Generally, long-term liabilities are of three types:

1. Obligations arising from specific financing situations where additional assets are acquired, such as the issuance of bonds, long-term lease obligations, and long-term notes payable.
2. Obligations arising from the ordinary operations of the enterprise such as pension obligations and deferred income taxes.
3. Obligations that are dependent upon the occurrence or nonoccurrence of one or more future events to confirm the amount payable, or the payee, or the date payable, such as service or product warranties.

For issued bonds payable it is desirable to report any premium or discount separately as an addition to or subtraction from the bonds payable. The terms of all long-term liability agreements including maturity date or dates, rates of interest, nature of obligation, and any security pledged to support the debt should be described as illustrated below.

| Long-term liabilities | | | |
|---|---|---|---|
| First mortgage 10% notes payable in semiannual installments of $25,000 | $500,000 | | |
| Less current maturities | 50,000 | $450,000 | |
| Bond payable 14½% (due in 1989) | | 850,000 | $1,300,000 |

Notes in the amount of $50,000, which mature currently and have been deducted above, are shown as current liabilities.

## Owners' Equity

The complexity of capital stock agreements and the various restrictions on residual equity imposed by state corporation laws, liability agreements, and voluntary actions of boards of directors make the owners' equity (stockholders' equity) section one of the most difficult sections to prepare and understand. The section is usually divided into three parts:

1. CAPITAL STOCK. The par or stated value of the shares issued.
2. ADDITIONAL PAID-IN CAPITAL. Primarily the excess of the amounts paid in over the par or stated value.
3. RETAINED EARNINGS. The undistributed earnings of the corporation.

The major requirements for reporting the capital stock account are that the par value amounts authorized, issued, and outstanding be disclosed. In addition, any capital stock reacquired (treasury stock) is shown as a reduction of stockholders' equity. The additional paid-in capital is usually presented in one amount, although breakdowns are informative if the sources of additional capital obtained are varied and material. The retained earnings section may be divided between the unappropriated (the amount that is usually available for dividend distribution) and any amounts that are restricted (such as for future plant expansion).

The ownership or stockholders' equity accounts in a corporation are considerably different from those in a partnership or proprietorship. Partners' permanent capital accounts and the balance in their temporary accounts (drawing accounts) are shown separately. Proprietorships ordinarily use a single capital account that handles all of the owners' equity transactions.

Presented below are illustrations of various owners' equity sections.

| Capital investment | | |
|---|---:|---:|
| Capital stock, par value $5 | | |
| Authorized and issued, 100,000 shares | $500,000 | |
| Additional paid-in capital | 40,000 | |
| Earnings reinvested in the business | | |
| (of which $16,500 is not available | | |
| for dividends on capital stock under | | |
| terms of the bank loan payable) | 27,200 | $567,200 |

| Investment of stockholders, represented by | | | |
|---|---:|---:|---:|
| Cumulative 11% preferred stock, par value $25 | | | |
| Authorized and issued 10,000 shares | | $250,000 | |
| Common stock, par value $1.00 | | | |
| Authorized 500,000 shares; | | | |
| issued and outstanding, | | | |
| 450,000 shares | | 450,000 | |
| Premium on common stock | | 33,000 | |
| Earnings retained in the business: | | | |
| Appropriated for future inventory losses | $20,000 | | |
| Unappropriated | 15,000 | 35,000 | $768,000 |

| Stockholders' equity | | |
|---|---:|---:|
| Paid in on capital stock: | | |
| 10% cumulative preferred— | | |
| Authorized, 2,500 shares of $50 | | |
| par value; issued 2,000 shares | $100,000 | |
| (Aggregate involuntary liquidation | | |
| value, $105,000)[12] | | |
| Less 200 shares reacquired | | |
| and held in treasury | 10,000 | |
| | 90,000 | |

[12]"Omnibus Opinion—1966," *Opinions of the Accounting Principles Board, No. 10* (New York: AICPA, 1966), par. 10, recommends that the liquidation value of preferred stock be disclosed in the equity section of the balance sheet in the aggregate.

| | | |
|---|---|---|
| Common— | | |
| Authorized, 60,000 shares without par value; issued and outstanding, 50,000 shares at a stated value of $2.50 a share | 125,000 | |
| Excess of issue price over stated value of common stock | 45,000 | $260,000 |
| Retained earnings: | | |
| Restricted by purchase of treasury stock | 10,000 | |
| Appropriated in accordance with terms of 15% sinking fund bonds | 87,000 | |
| Appropriated for plant expansion | 50,000 | |
| Unrestricted | 107,314 | 254,314   $514,314 |

## ADDITIONAL INFORMATION REPORTED

The balance sheet is not complete simply because a listing of the assets, liabilities, and owners' equity accounts has been presented. Great importance is given to supplemental information that is completely new or is an elaboration or qualification of items in the balance sheet. There are normally four types of information that are supplemental to account titles and amounts presented in the balance sheet.

1. **CONTINGENCIES.** Events that have an uncertain outcome that may have a material effect on financial position.
2. **VALUATIONS AND ACCOUNTING POLICIES.** Explanations of the valuation methods used or the basic assumptions made concerning, for example, inventory valuations, depreciation methods, investments in subsidiaries.
3. **CONTRACTUAL SITUATIONS.** Explanations of certain restrictions or covenants attached either to specific assets or, more likely, to liabilities.
4. **POST-BALANCE SHEET DISCLOSURES.** Disclosures of certain events that have occurred after the balance sheet date but before the financial statements have been issued.

Chapter 27 on full disclosure discusses these subjects and additional topics on disclosure.

### Gain Contingencies

The term **gain contingencies** designates claims or rights to receive assets (or have a liability reduced) whose existence is uncertain but which may become valid property rights eventually.

The typical gain contingencies are:

1. Possible receipts of monies from gifts, donations, bonuses, and so on.
2. Possible refunds from the government in tax disputes.
3. Pending court cases where the probable outcome is favorable.

Accountants have adopted a conservative policy in this area. Gain contingencies are not recorded and are disclosed only when the probabilities are high that a gain contingency will become reality. As a result, it is unusual to find information of this type in the financial statements and related reports.

### Loss Contingencies

*FASB Statement No. 5* requires that an estimated loss from loss contingencies be accrued by a charge to expense and the recording of a liability or a contra asset if both of the following conditions are met:

1. Information available prior to issuance of the financial statements indicates that it is **probable** that a liability had been incurred at the date of the financial statements.
2. The amount of loss can be **reasonably estimated.**[13]

As indicated earlier, the establishment of a liability for service or product warranties would ordinarily meet the two conditions mentioned above and thus qualify as a loss contingency that should be accrued.

In most loss contingency cases, however, one or both of the conditions are not present. For example, assume that a company is involved in a lawsuit with one of its competitors. The company's lawyer indicates that there is a reasonable possibility that they may lose. In such a case, there is only a **reasonable possibility** of loss rather than a **probable** one and, therefore, a liability and the related loss should not be recorded. The nature of the contingency and, where possible, the amount involved, however, should be disclosed. If a reasonable estimate of the amount of the contingency is not possible, disclosure is made in general terms, describing the loss contingency and explaining that no estimated amount is determinable. Because these types of contingencies are only possibilities, they should not enter into the determination of net income.

Diversity in practice exists in accounting for contingencies because varied interpretations are made of the words "probable" and "reasonably possible." As a result, the contingencies reported and disclosed vary somewhat. This area of practice requires that the accountant use professional judgment because the determination of what constitutes full and proper accounting and disclosure is accompanied by a high element of subjectivity.

Some of the more common sources of **loss contingencies that ordinarily will not be accrued as liabilities are:**

1. Guarantees of indebtedness of others.
2. Obligations of commercial banks under "stand-by letters of credit" (commitments to finance projects under certain circumstances).
3. Guarantees to repurchase receivables (or any related property) that have been sold or assigned.
4. Disputes over additional income taxes for prior years.
5. Pending lawsuits whose outcome is uncertain.

It should be noted that the reporting rules for loss contingencies are complex and are presented here only in general terms. In Chapter 10 the subject is discussed at great length. **General risk contingencies** that are inherent in business operations, such as the possibility of war, strike, losses from catastrophes not ordinarily insured against, or a business recession, are not reflected in financial statements either by incorporation in the accounts or by other disclosure.

---

[13]"Accounting for Contingencies," *Statement of Financial Accounting Standards No. 5* (Stamford, Conn.: FASB, 1975), par. 8.

## Valuations and Accounting Policies

As subsequent chapters of this textbook indicate, accountants utilize many different methods and bases in valuing assets and allocating costs. For instance, inventories can be computed under several flow assumptions (such as LIFO and FIFO), plant and equipment can be depreciated under several accepted methods of cost allocation (such as double-declining balance and straight line), and investments can be carried at different valuations (such as cost, equity, and market). Many users of financial statements know of these possibilities and examine the statements closely to determine the methods used.

Generally, specific requirements have been established to make certain that these valuation methods are disclosed either in the statement itself or in the footnotes to the statements. *APB Opinion No. 22* recommends that all significant accounting principles and methods that involve selection from among alternatives and/or those that are peculiar to a given industry be specifically identified and described in the annual report.[14] Disclosure is particularly useful if given in a separate **Summary of Significant Accounting Policies** preceding the footnotes to the financial statement or as the initial footnote. See the specimen financial statements in Appendix D following this chapter for an example of such a summary (pages 200–201) and further discussion of this topic in Chapter 27.

## Contracts and Negotiations

In addition to the contingencies and different methods of valuation disclosed as supplementary data to the financial statements, any contracts and negotiations of significance should be disclosed in the footnotes to the statements.

It is mandatory, for example, that the essential provisions of lease contracts, pension obligations, and stock option plans be clearly stated in the footnotes to the financial statements. The analyst who examines a set of financial statements wants to know not only the amount of the liabilities, but also how the different contractual provisions of these debt obligations affect the company at present and in the future.

As just indicated, the profession has spelled out exacting disclosure requirements for certain obligations. In addition, many other items may have an important and significant effect on the enterprise, and this information should be disclosed. It is here that the accountant must exercise considerable judgment about whether omission of such information is misleading to the financial statement user. The axiom "When in doubt, disclose" is appropriate here; it seems better to disclose a little too much information than not enough.

## Post-Balance Sheet Events

Footnotes to the financial statements should include adequate explanations of any significant financial events taking place after the formal date of the balance sheet, but before it is finally issued.

A period of several weeks, and sometimes months, may elapse after the end of the year before the financial statements are issued. Problems involved in taking and pricing the inventory, reconciling subsidiary ledgers with controlling accounts, preparing necessary adjusting entries, assuring that all transactions for the period have been entered, obtaining

---

[14]"Disclosure of Accounting Policies," *Opinions of the Accounting Principles Board No. 22* (New York: AICPA, 1972).

an audit of the financial statements by independent certified public accountants, and printing the annual report all take time. During the period between the balance sheet date and its distribution to stockholders and creditors, important transactions or other events may have occurred that materially affect the company's financial position or operating situation.

Those who read a balance sheet (if it is fairly recent) may think of the balance sheet condition as remaining constant and project it into the future. Numerous events or transactions may make this projection inappropriate, however. If the company has sold one of its plants, acquired a subsidiary, suffered extraordinary losses, settled significant litigation, or experienced any other important event in the post-balance sheet period, such an event should be brought to the attention of financial statement readers. Without an explanation of such an occurrence in a footnote, the reader (not knowing of its existence) might easily be misled and might make conclusions that could be avoided if all the facts were disclosed.

Two types of events or transactions occurring after the balance sheet date (commonly referred to as **subsequent events**) may have a material effect on the financial statements or may need to be considered to interpret these statements accurately.

**The first type of event or transaction consists of events that provide additional evidence about conditions that existed at the balance sheet date, affect the estimates that are used in preparing financial statements, and, therefore, result in adjustments of the financial statements.** The accountant is obliged to use all of the information that is available prior to the issuance of the financial statements in evaluating estimates previously made. To ignore these subsequent events is to pass up an opportunity to improve the accuracy of the financial statements. This first type encompasses information that would have been recorded in the accounts had it been available at the balance sheet date: for example, subsequent events that affect the realization of assets such as receivables and inventories or the settlement of estimated liabilities. Such events typically represent the culmination of conditions that existed for some time.

**The second type consists of the events that provide evidence about conditions that did not exist at the balance sheet date but arise subsequent to that date and do not require adjustment of the financial statements.** Some of these events may have to be disclosed to keep the financial statements from being misleading. These disclosures take the form of footnotes, supplemental schedules, or even pro forma (as if) financial data that make it appear as if the event had occurred on the date of the balance sheet. Below are examples of such events that require disclosure (but do not result in adjustment):

(a) Sale of bonds or capital stock.

(b) Purchase of a business.

(c) Settlement of litigation when the event giving rise to the claim took place subsequent to the balance sheet date.

(d) Loss of plant or inventories as a result of fire or flood.

(e) Losses on receivables resulting from conditions (such as a customer's major casualty) arising subsequent to the balance sheet date.

(f) Gains or losses on certain marketable securities.[15]

Identifying events that require adjustment of or disclosure in the financial statements under the criteria stated above calls for the exercise of judgment and knowledge of the

---

[15]"Subsequent Events," *Statement on Auditing Standards No. 1* (New York: AICPA, 1973), pp. 123–124, and "Accounting for Certain Marketable Securities," *op. cit.,* par. 17.

facts and circumstances. For example, if a loss on an uncollectible trade account receivable results from a customer's deteriorating financial condition, leading to bankruptcy subsequent to the balance sheet date, the financial statements are adjusted before their issuance because the event (bankruptcy) indicates conditions existing at the balance sheet date. A similar loss resulting from a customer's major casualty, such as a fire or flood, after the balance sheet date is not indicative of conditions existing at that date, however, and adjustment of the financial statements is not necessary; the materiality of the loss determines whether it should be disclosed. The same criterion applies to settlements of litigation. If the events that gave rise to the litigation, such as personal injury or patent infringement, took place prior to the balance sheet date, adjustment of the financial statements is necessary. If the event giving rise to the claim took place subsequent to the balance sheet date, no adjustment is necessary but disclosure is. Subsequent events such as changes in the quoted market prices of securities ordinarily do not result in adjustment of the financial statements because such changes typically reflect a concurrent evaluation of new conditions.

In addition to the events noted above, **many subsequent events or developments are not likely to require either adjustment of or disclosure in the financial statements.** These are nonaccounting events or conditions that managements normally communicate by other means. These events include legislation, product changes, management changes, strikes, unionization, marketing agreements, and loss of important customers.

## TECHNIQUES OF DISCLOSURE

The effect of various contingencies on financial condition, the methods of valuing assets, and the companies' contracts and agreements should be disclosed as completely and as intelligently as possible in the balance sheet. These methods of disclosing pertinent information are available:

> Parenthetical explanations
> Footnotes
> Supporting schedules
> Cross reference and contra items

Appendix D contains specimen financial statements that illustrate these methods.

### Parenthetical Explanations

Additional information or description is often given by means of parenthetical explanations following the item. For example, investments in common stock are shown on the balance sheet under Investments as follows.

---

Investments in Common Stock (market value, $330,586)—at cost $280,783

---

This device permits disclosure of additional pertinent information that adds clarity and completeness to the balance sheet. It has an advantage over a footnote because it brings the additional information into the body of the statement where it is less likely to be overlooked. Of course, lengthy parenthetical explanations that might distract the reader from, or even appear to contradict, the balance sheet information must be used with care.

## Footnotes

If additional explanations or descriptions cannot be shown conveniently as parenthetical explanations, footnotes are used. For example, inventories are shown in this balance sheet as follows:

| | |
|---|---|
| Inventories—See Note 2 | $8,380,576 |

On the same page as the balance sheet or on the following page Note 2 appears:

Note 2. Inventories were priced at cost of $8,380,576. The market price, or cost to replace the inventory as of the balance sheet date, was $8,780,635. The Company has consistently followed a policy of determining cost on the basis of specific lots on hand, and this policy was followed in arriving at the cost of $8,380,576, shown on the balance sheet.

Footnotes are commonly used to present other information such as the existence and amount of any preferred stock dividends in arrears, the terms of or obligations imposed by purchase commitments, special financial arrangements, depreciation policies, any changes in the application of accounting principles, and the existence of contingencies. The following footnotes indicate a common method of presenting such information.

Note 3. The Company has entered into a loan agreement with certain banks, which agreement makes available to the Company until January 31, 1988, sums not to exceed $5,000,000 outstanding at any one time. Borrowings may be made to mature, at the Company's option, before January 31, 1984, or in five equal annual installments commencing on that date. The Company pays interest at 15% on all amounts borrowed under this agreement and pays a commitment fee of ¾ of 1% annually on all the unused amount available. As of December 31, 1984, $1,800,000 has been borrowed under this agreement.

Note 4. During the year ended December 31, 1984 the Company changed from the first-in, first-out method of pricing inventories to the last-in, first-out method. This reduced the December 31, 1984, inventory valuation from approximately $18,275,800 under the first-in, first-out method to $16,935,250 under the last-in, first-out method, thereby reducing net income for the year by approximately $1,340,550.

Note 5. Provisions for depreciation of plant facilities and equipment charged to cost of goods sold amounted to $386,520 in 1984 and $327,840 in 1983.

In the preparation of footnotes, we must be sure that they present all essential facts as completely and succinctly as possible. Careless wording may result in misleading instead of aiding readers. Footnotes should add to the total information made available in the financial statements, not raise unanswered questions or contradict other portions of the statements.

## Cross Reference and Contra Items

A direct relationship between an asset and a liability is called to the attention of the balance sheet reader by use of cross-referencing. For example, on December 31, 1984, among the current assets this might be shown:

| | |
|---|---|
| Cash on deposit with sinking fund trustee for redemption of bonds payable—see current liabilities | $800,000 |

Included among the current liabilities is the amount of bonds payable to be redeemed currently:

| | |
|---|---|
| Bonds payable to be redeemed in 1985—see current assets | $2,300,000 |

This cross reference points out that $2,300,000 of bonds payable are to be redeemed currently, for which only $800,000 in cash has been set aside; therefore the additional amount of cash needed must come from the general cash, from sales of investments, or from some other source. The same information can be shown parenthetically, if this device is preferred.

Another procedure that is often used is to establish contra or adjunct accounts. A **contra account** is an account that reduces either an asset, liability, or owners' equity account on a balance sheet. As examples, Accumulated Depreciation is considered a contra account; Discount on Bonds Payable also is a contra account. Contra accounts provide the accountant with some flexibility in presenting the financial information. With the use of the Accumulated Depreciation account, for example, a reader of the statement can see the original cost of the asset as well as the depreciation to date.

An **adjunct account,** on the other hand, increases either an asset, a liability, or owners' equity account. An example is Premium on Bonds Payable which, when added to the Bonds Payable account, provides a picture of the total liability of the enterprise.

## Supporting Schedules

Often a separate schedule is needed to present more detailed information about certain assets or liabilities. Here is a single item in the balance sheet for long-term tangible assets that might be appropriate:

| Property, plant, and equipment | |
| --- | --- |
| Land, building, equipment, and other fixed assets (see Schedule 3) | 643,300 |

A separate schedule then might be presented as follows:

**Schedule 3**
**LAND, BUILDINGS, EQUIPMENT, AND OTHER FIXED ASSETS**

| | Total | Land | Buildings | Equip. | Other Fixed Assets |
| --- | --- | --- | --- | --- | --- |
| Balance January 1, 1984 | $740,000 | $46,000 | $358,000 | $260,000 | $76,000 |
| Additions in 1984 | 161,200 | | 120,000 | 38,000 | 3,200 |
| | 901,200 | 46,000 | 478,000 | 298,000 | 79,200 |
| Assets retired or sold in 1984 | 31,700 | | | 27,000 | 4,700 |
| Balance December 31, 1984 | 869,500 | 46,000 | 478,000 | 271,000 | 74,500 |
| Depreciation taken to January 1, 1984 | 196,000 | | 102,000 | 78,000 | 16,000 |
| Depreciation taken in 1984 | 56,000 | | 28,000 | 24,000 | 4,000 |
| | 252,000 | | 130,000 | 102,000 | 20,000 |
| Depreciation on assets retired in 1984 | 25,800 | | | 22,000 | 3,800 |
| Depreciation accumulated December 31, 1984 | 226,200 | | 130,000 | 80,000 | 16,200 |
| Book value of assets | $643,300 | $46,000 | $348,000 | $191,000 | $58,300 |

## BALANCE SHEET FORM

One common arrangement followed in the presentation of the balance sheet is called the **account form.** It lists the assets by sections on the left side and the liabilities and stockholders' equity by sections on the right side. Refer to the financial statements of Tenneco, Inc., Appendix D, pages 196 and 197 for a practical illustration of a balance sheet presentation in account form. To avoid the use of facing pages, another arrangement lists the liabilities and stockholders' equity directly below the assets and on the same page, in what is often called the **report form.**[16] This arrangement is illustrated on page 187. Other presentations have infrequently been used in practice. For example, current liabilities are sometimes deducted from current assets to arrive at the amount of working capital, or all liabilities are deducted from all assets.

---

[16]*Accounting Trends and Techniques—1981* indicates that practically all of the companies surveyed use the "report or account form," sometimes collectively referred to as the "customary form."

## Ecological Management, Inc.
## BALANCE SHEET
### December 31, 1984

**Assets**

Current assets

| | | |
|---|---|---|
| Cash | | $ 42,485 |
| Marketable securities—at cost which approximates market value | | 28,250 |
| Accounts receivable | $165,824 | |
| Less allowance for doubtful accounts | 1,850 | 163,974 |
| Notes receivable | | 23,000 |
| Inventories—at average cost | | 489,713 |
| Supplies on hand | | 9,780 |
| Prepaid expenses | | 16,252 |
| Total current assets | | $ 773,454 |

Long-term investments

| | | |
|---|---|---|
| Securities at cost (market value $94,000) | | 87,500 |

Property, plant, and equipment

| | | |
|---|---|---|
| Land—at cost | | 125,000 |
| Buildings—at cost | 975,800 | |
| Less accumulated depreciation | 341,200 | 634,600 |
| Total property, plant, and equipment | | 759,600 |

Intangible assets

| | | |
|---|---|---|
| Goodwill | | 100,000 |
| Total assets | | $1,720,554 |

**Liabilities and Stockholders' Equity**

Current liabilities

| | | |
|---|---|---|
| Notes payable to banks | | $ 50,000 |
| Accounts payable | | 197,532 |
| Accrued interest on notes payable | | 500 |
| Income taxes payable | | 62,520 |
| Accrued salaries, wages, and other liabilities | | 9,500 |
| Deposits received from customers | | 420 |
| Total current liabilities | | $ 320,472 |

Long-term debt *voucher of debt*

| | | |
|---|---|---|
| Twenty-year 12% debentures, due January 1, 1998 | | 500,000 |
| Total liabilities | | 820,472 |

Stockholders' equity

| | | |
|---|---|---|
| Paid in on capital stock | | |
| Preferred, 7%, cumulative | | |
| Authorized and outstanding, 30,000 shares of $10 par value | $300,000 | |
| Common | | |
| Authorized, 500,000 shares of $1.00 par value; issued and outstanding, 400,000 shares | 400,000 | |
| Additional paid-in capital | 37,500 | 737,500 |
| Earnings retained in the business | | |
| Appropriated | 85,000 | |
| Unappropriated | 77,582 | 162,582 |
| Total stockholders' equity | | 900,082 |
| Total liabilities and stockholders' equity | | $1,720,554 |

## QUESTIONS ON TERMINOLOGY

The account titles in the general ledger do not necessarily represent the best terminology for balance sheet purposes. Account titles are often brief and include technical terms that are understood only by those keeping the records and by other accountants who are familiar with such technical expressions. Balance sheets are examined by many persons who are not acquainted with the technical vocabulary of accounting and, therefore, should contain descriptions that will be generally understood and not be subject to misinterpretation. Accountants are becoming aware of the need for better terminology in financial statements. This awareness is evident in the helpful descriptions used in recent published financial statements and in the attention given this subject by professional groups, periodicals, and textbooks.

For example, the profession recommended that the word "reserve" be used only to describe an appropriation of retained earnings. This term had been used in several ways: to describe amounts deducted from assets (contra accounts such as accumulated depreciation, and allowance for doubtful accounts), as a part of the title of contingent liabilities, and to describe certain charges in the income statement. Because of the different meanings attached to this term, its significance in the balance sheet was questionable, and misinterpretation often resulted from its use. The use of "reserve" only to describe appropriated retained earnings has resulted in a better understanding of its significance when it appears in a balance sheet. Perhaps the use of the word should be discontinued entirely, because to the nonaccountant a reserve is something quite different from what is signified by a reserve on a balance sheet. The term "appropriated" appears more logical and its use should be encouraged.

For years the profession has recommended that the use of the word "surplus" be discontinued in balance sheet presentations of owners' equity. This term has a connotation outside accounting that is quite different from its meaning in the accounts or in the balance sheet. The use of the terms capital surplus, paid-in surplus, and earned surplus is confusing to the nonaccountant and leads to misinterpretation. Although condemned by the profession, these terms appear all too frequently in current financial statements and in current literature. We have discussed these terms only to enable you to understand them when you encounter them in practice.

The profession's recommendations relating to changes in terminology have been directed primarily to the balance sheet presentation of stockholders' equity so that the words or phrases used for these unique accounts describe more accurately the nature of the amounts shown.

---

# SECTION 2    STATEMENT OF CHANGES IN FINANCIAL POSITION

If you were asked to determine the additions to or dispositions of property, plant and equipment for the past year at B. F. Goodrich Company or the amount of money borrowed or capital stock issued by General Electric Company during the year, you would best proceed by analyzing their **statements of changes in financial position.** The statement of changes in financial position provides the answers to these questions because it (1) summarizes information concerning the **financing** and **investing** activities of the company and (2) completes the **disclosure of changes** in financial position during the period.[17]

Although the income statement, balance sheet, and statement of retained earnings contain information on financing and investing activities, they present this information only in a partial, fragmented manner. Only the statement of changes in financial position indicates where the resources (funds) came from during the period and how they were used. Since 1971 (*APB Opinion No. 19*), the statement of changes in financial position has been a mandatory accompaniment to the balance sheet and statement of income and retained earnings, which means that it can be considered as **a basic financial statement.**

The statement of changes in financial position summarizes the changes between the beginning and ending balance sheets in addition to the changes summarized by the income statement. The financing and investing activities are usually summarized on the basis of either **changes in cash and cash equivalents** or **changes in working capital**[18] (current assets minus current liabilities). Regardless of the basis used in preparation of the statement, significant financing and investing activities must be incorporated in the statement even though neither cash nor working capital was directly affected: this is referred to as the **all-financial resources concept.** Examples of transactions that must be reflected although they do not affect cash or working capital are: acquisition of property in exchange for other property, issuance of stock for property, and conversion of long-term debt to common stock.

When the all-financial resources concept is employed concurrently with the working capital approach, the major resources provided and applied transactions are classified as follows:

| **Resources provided by** | **Resources applied to** |
| --- | --- |
| Income from operations | Loss from operations |
| Sale of noncurrent assets | Purchase of noncurrent assets |
| Increase in long-term debt | Retirement of long-term debt |
| Issuance of additional capital stock | Retirement of capital stock |
| | Dividends on capital stock |

The statement of changes in financial position for Morreale Candy Company on page 190 illustrates the typical form and content.

Note that the statement of changes in financial position begins with resources provided from operations. In the operations section, income is the usual starting point (unless there is an extraordinary item, in which case income before extraordinary item is the starting point) to which nonworking capital items are added or deducted. For example, depreciation is added back to income before extraordinary item in arriving at working capital from operations exclusive of extraordinary item because depreciation expense is a nonworking

---

[17]"Reporting Changes in Financial Position," *Opinions of the Accounting Principles Board No. 19* (New York: AICPA, 1971), par. 4. Procedures for preparing this statement are discussed in more detail in Chapter 24. The major purpose of this discussion is to focus on the content and use of the statement.

[18]Note that the financial reporting environment is changing regarding the presentation of the statement of changes in financial position. Recently, the Financial Executives Institute recommended that companies use the cash basis instead of the working capital basis in preparing this statement. Furthermore, the Financial Accounting Standards Board seems ready to adopt a cash basis orientation. It appears likely, therefore, that the cash basis may soon become the more popular basis for preparing the statement of changes in financial position, possibly replacing and eliminating the working capital based statement.

Morreale Candy Company
STATEMENT OF CHANGES IN FINANCIAL POSITION
For the Year 1983
(000 omitted)

| | | |
|---|---:|---:|
| Resources provided by: | | |
| Operations: | | |
| Income before extraordinary item | | $55,458 |
| Add (or deduct) items not affecting working capital: | | |
| Depreciation expense | $11,250 | |
| Bond discount amortization | 486 | |
| Equity in earnings of 25%-owned company | (5,880) | 5,856 |
| Working capital provided by operations, | | |
| exclusive of extraordinary item | | 61,314 |
| Extraordinary item—Condemnation of land, including | | |
| extraordinary gain of $8,500 (net of $3,000 tax) | | 21,300 |
| Sale of bonds | | 63,560 |
| Issuance of common stock to | | |
| retire preferred stock (Note 5) | | 30,000 |
| Total resources provided | | $176,174 |
| Resources applied to: | | |
| Purchase of equipment | | 81,500 |
| Cash dividends | | 8,000 |
| Payment on long-term note | | 21,674 |
| Preferred stock retired by issuance | | |
| of common stock (Note 5) | | 30,000 |
| Total resources applied | | 141,174 |
| Increase in working capital | | $ 35,000 |

SCHEDULE OF WORKING CAPITAL CHANGES
For the Year 1983

| | Working Capital Change | |
|---|---:|---:|
| | Increase | Decrease |
| **Current Assets** | | |
| Increase in cash | $35,426 | |
| Decrease in marketable securities | | $ 9,200 |
| Increase in accounts receivable | 25,000 | |
| Increase in inventory | 17,500 | |
| **Current Liabilities** | | |
| Decrease in accounts payable | 3,890 | |
| Increase in dividends payable | | 8,000 |
| Increase in income taxes payable | | 29,616 |
| Totals | 81,816 | 46,816 |
| Increase in working capital | | 35,000 |
| | $81,816 | $ 81,816 |

Notes to the financial statements.
Note 5. All of the 8% preferred stock was retired through the issuance of two shares of common stock ($1.00 par) for each share of preferred. Retirement required the issuance of 18,000 shares of common stock. No cash was paid or received incidental to this retirement.

capital charge. After the operations section is completed, extraordinary items and all other financing and investing transactions should be disclosed individually when material. As shown in the Morreale Candy Company statement, additional resources are provided by the sale of bonds and the issuance of common stock to retire preferred stock. The statement then shows that resources were applied to the purchase of equipment, cash dividends, payment on long-term debt, and to the retirement of the preferred stock. The arrangement of these items is kept somewhat flexible so that any significant changes that might develop in a particular year can be highlighted. The statement generally ends with an increase or decrease in working capital for the year. A schedule detailing the changes in the individual items comprising working capital is also reported in the statement or in a separate tabulation accompanying the statement.

Appendix D, page 198, provides an illustration of Tenneco, Inc.'s statement of changes in financial position as presented in its 1981 annual report. Chapter 24 presents a comprehensive discussion of this subject and illustrates the techniques of preparing the statement of changes in financial position on both the cash and the working capital basis.

The statement of changes in financial position provides information about the flow of funds into and out of the business enterprise during a period. This type of information is useful for assessing the amount, timing, and uncertainty of future cash flows. For example, by establishing different sources and applications of resources, such as resources provided by operations, resources obtained by borrowing, resources applied to dividends, and so on, the user has a better understanding of the **liquidity** and **financial flexibility** of the enterprise. Similarly, these reports are useful in **providing feedback** about the flow of enterprise resources. This information should help users make more accurate predictions of future cash flows. In addition, some individuals have expressed concern about the "quality of the earnings" because the measurement of income depends on a number of accruals and estimates which may be somewhat subjective. As a result, the higher the ratio of resources provided by operations to income, the more comfort some users have in the reliability of the earnings.[19]

## CONCEPTUAL FRAMEWORK PROJECT—ITS IMPLICATIONS

How will the conceptual framework project affect the balance sheet and statement of changes in financial position? At this time it is not possible to determine its effects entirely (particularly on the balance sheet) because the recognition and measurement parts of the conceptual framework project are not completed. An FASB proposed statement of concepts, however, contains some recommendations relative to the content and format of these two statements.

---

[19]Numerous empirical studies have been made regarding the usefulness of the funds statement. Some of these studies are: Morton Backer and Martin L. Gosman, "Financial Reporting and Business Liquidity" (New York: National Association of Accountants, 1978); they show that the ratio of resources provided by operations to total debt is useful in assessing credit-worthiness for intermediate- and long-term debt. Similarly William H. Beaver, "Alternative Accounting Measures as Predictors of Failure," *The Accounting Review* (January 1968), found the same types of information useful in assessing bankruptcy. David F. Hawkins and Walter J. Campbell, "Equity Valuation: Models, Analysis and Implications," *Financial Executive* (New York: Financial Executives Research Institute, 1978), found that institutional investors and research firms used resource flow information to determine a company's ability to fund capital expenditures and dividends internally, and that a comparison of cash flows to earnings was used as a basis for evaluating the quality of earnings.

As indicated earlier, the position of the FASB is that for users the parts and subsections of financial statements can be more informative than the whole. Therefore, as one would expect, the reporting of summary accounts (total assets, net assets, total liabilities, etc.) alone is discouraged. Individual items should be separately reported and classified in sufficient detail to permit users to assess the amounts, timing, and uncertainty of future cash flows. In the preparation of a balance sheet, emphasis should be placed on providing information that permits the evaluation of liquidity and financial flexibility. In the words of the FASB in its proposed statement of concepts, "The main basis for deciding the number of classes and the content of each is that the result should help users to assess the nature, amounts, and liquidity of available resources, including management's intentions regarding their function in use, and the amounts and timing of obligations that require liquid resources for settlement."[20] The following guides provide a basis for decisions on the optimal number of asset and liability items to be reported.[21]

1. Assets that differ in their **type or expected function** in the central operations or other activities of the enterprise should be reported as separate items; for example, merchandise inventories should be reported separately from property, plant, and equipment.
2. Assets and liabilities with **different implications for the financial flexibility** of the enterprise should be reported as separate items; for example, assets used in operations, assets held for investment, and assets subject to restrictions such as leased equipment.
3. Assets and liabilities with **different general liquidity characteristics** should be reported as separate items. For example, cash should be separately reported from inventories.
4. Assets and liabilities with **different measurement bases** should be reported in separate categories; for example, inventories measured at historical cost and inventories measured at net realizable value.

Given the emphases indicated above, it appears that the form, content, and classifications of the balance sheet will not change significantly. We already prepare balance sheets that provide information about the function of assets, the types of claims on assets, the bases of measuring assets and liabilities, and about liquidity and financial flexibility.

Regarding the statement of changes in financial position, it appears that more substantive changes may occur. Specifically, the proposed statement of concepts indicates that reporting meaningful components of cash flow is generally more useful than changes in working capital. The components of this type of statement of changes in financial position (referred to as the "cash flow statement") probably would be:

1. Cash generated and used in operations.
2. Cash obtained by borrowing and used to repay borrowing.
3. Cash used for investments in resources and obtained from the disposal of investments.
4. Cash contributed by or distributed to owners.

What this recommendation suggests is that an emphasis on cash flow rather than working capital flow provides a better predictor of future cash flows and enhances the user's evaluation of liquidity and financial flexibility.

---

[20]"Reporting Income, Cash Flows, and Financial Position of Business Enterprises," *op. cit.*, par. 50.

[21]Ibid., par. 51.

# APPENDIX D

# Specimen Financial Statements

**To the student—**
The following 18 pages contain the financial statements and accompanying notes of a complex industrial conglomerate—Tenneco, Inc. Because of the diversity and worldwide scope of its operation in many industries, Tenneco's accounting and reporting practices are affected by most accounting topics covered in this text and by nearly every facet of generally accepted accounting principles, as well as many specialized industry accounting requirements. Of all U.S. companies, Tenneco, Inc. is the 16th largest in sales dollars (15.5 billion), 19th largest in terms of net income ($813 million), 14th largest in dollars of assets ($16.8 billion), and 21st largest with 103,000 employees in 1981.

We do not expect that you will comprehend Tenneco, Inc.'s financial statements and the accompanying notes in their entirety at your first reading. But we expect that by the time you complete the coverage of the material in this text your level of understanding and interpretive ability will have grown enormously.

At this point we recommend that you take 20 to 30 minutes to scan the statements and notes to familiarize yourself with the contents and accounting elements. Throughout the following twenty-two chapters when you are asked to refer to specific parts of Tenneco's financials, do so! Then, when you have completed reading this book, we challenge you to reread Tenneco's financials to see how much greater and more sophisticated is your understanding of them.

# Tenneco Inc 37th Annual Report Summary

## Financial Highlights    (Millions Except Per Share Amounts)

| CONSOLIDATED RESULTS | 1981 | 1980 | Percent Change |
|---|---|---|---|
| Net sales and operating revenues | $15,462 | $13,226 | +17% |
| Net income | 813 | 726 | +12 |
| Preferred and preference stock dividends | 63 | 52 | +21 |
| Net income to common stock | 750 | 674 | +11 |
| Earnings per average share of common stock | 6.01 | 5.95 | + 1 |
| Average number of shares outstanding | 125 | 113 | +11 |
| Capital expenditures | 2,359 | 1,825 | +29 |
| Total assets | 16,808 | 13,853 | +21 |
| Return on average common stockholders' equity | 16.3% | 18.0% | |

| RESULTS BY MAJOR BUSINESS | Net Sales and Operating Revenues | | | | Income Before Interest and Federal Income Taxes | | | |
|---|---|---|---|---|---|---|---|---|
| | 1981 | | 1980 | | 1981 | | 1980 | |
| Oil exploration and production | $ 2,290 | 15% | $ 1,424 | 11% | $ 1,055 | 54% | $ 740 | 46% |
| Natural gas pipelines | 4,276 | 28 | 3,440 | 26 | 334 | 17 | 304 | 19 |
| Oil processing and marketing, chemicals | 4,542 | 29 | 3,992 | 30 | 181 | 9 | 282 | 18 |
| Manufacturing | 4,392 | 28 | 4,106 | 31 | 210 | 11 | 153 | 10 |
| Life insurance* | — | — | — | — | 96 | 5 | 71 | 4 |
| Fiber, food, land and other | 972 | 6 | 938 | 7 | 78 | 4 | 46 | 3 |
| Intergroup sales | (1,010) | (6) | (674) | (5) | — | — | — | — |
| Total | $15,462 | 100% | $13,226 | 100% | $ 1,954 | 100% | $ 1,596 | 100% |

*Equity in earnings of unconsolidated life insurance subsidiaries is included on an after-tax basis.

# Financial Statements

## Tenneco Inc. and Consolidated Subsidiaries
Year Ended December 31, 1981, 1980 and 1979       STATEMENT OF INCOME

| (Millions Except Per Share Amounts) | 1981 | 1980 | 1979 |
|---|---|---|---|
| Revenues: | | | |
| Net sales and operating revenues— | | | |
| Oil exploration and production.......................... | $ 2,290 | $ 1,424 | $ 1,008 |
| Natural gas pipelines ................................. | 4,276 | 3,440 | 2,670 |
| Oil processing and marketing, chemicals ................. | 4,542 | 3,992 | 3,277 |
| Manufacturing ....................................... | 4,392 | 4,106 | 3,913 |
| Fiber, food, land and other .......................... | 972 | 938 | 830 |
| Intergroup sales .................................... | (1,010) | (674) | (489) |
| | 15,462 | 13,226 | 11,209 |
| Other income, net..................................... | 133 | 120 | 71 |
| | 15,595 | 13,346 | 11,280 |
| Costs and Expenses: | | | |
| Cost of sales (exclusive of depreciation shown below)......... | 7,650 | 7,032 | 6,231 |
| Operating expenses .................................. | 3,739 | 2,903 | 2,135 |
| Excise tax on oil production .......................... | 225 | 92 | — |
| Selling, general and administrative ...................... | 1,360 | 1,246 | 1,063 |
| Depreciation, depletion and amortization .................... | 849 | 619 | 549 |
| Interest— | | | |
| Incurred .......................................... | 896 | 617 | 492 |
| Capitalized ....................................... | (213) | (142) | (28) |
| | 14,506 | 12,367 | 10,442 |
| Income Before Federal Income Taxes and Equity in Net Income of Affiliated Companies........................... | 1,089 | 979 | 838 |
| Federal Income Taxes ..................................... | 458 | 395 | 325 |
| Equity in Net Income of Affiliated Companies................... | 182 | 142 | 58 |
| Net Income | 813 | 726 | 571 |
| Preferred, Second Preferred and Preference Stock Dividends ..... | 63 | 52 | 32 |
| Net Income to Common Stock ............................. | $ 750 | $ 674 | $ 539 |
| Average Number of Shares of Common Stock Outstanding ....... | 124,922,481 | 113,208,029 | 101,621,499 |
| Earnings Per Average Share of Common Stock ................. | $6.01 | $5.95 | $5.30 |
| Cash Dividends Per Share of Common Stock .................. | $2.60 | $2.45 | $2.25 |

(The accompanying notes to financial statements are an integral part of this statement of income.)

## Tenneco Inc. and Consolidated Subsidiaries
December 31, 1981 and 1980

**BALANCE SHEET**

| (Millions Except Share Amounts) | 1981 | 1980 |
|---|---|---|
| **ASSETS** | | |
| Current Assets: | | |
| Cash | $ 53 | $ 49 |
| Temporary cash investments | 23 | 25 |
| Notes and accounts receivable— | | |
| Customers | 1,569 | 1,300 |
| Affiliated companies | 119 | 59 |
| Other | 353 | 314 |
| Allowance for doubtful accounts | (40) | (48) |
| Shipbuilding contracts in progress, less billings | 60 | 97 |
| Inventories— | | |
| Raw materials, work in process and finished products | 1,597 | 1,770 |
| Materials and supplies | 300 | 194 |
| Prepayments and other | 460 | 231 |
| | 4,494 | 3,991 |
| | | |
| Investments and Other Assets: | | |
| Investment in affiliated companies | 1,792 | 1,459 |
| Other investments, at cost | 91 | 136 |
| Long-term receivables | 75 | 128 |
| Advances to secure future natural gas pipeline supply | 70 | 131 |
| Investment in consolidated subsidiaries in excess of net assets at date of acquisition, less amortization | 77 | 80 |
| Unamortized debt and preferred stock expense | 31 | 24 |
| Other | 99 | 87 |
| | 2,235 | 2,045 |
| | | |
| Plant, Property and Equipment, at cost: | | |
| Oil exploration and production (full-cost method) | 7,029 | 4,796 |
| Natural gas pipelines | 3,304 | 3,070 |
| Oil processing and marketing, chemicals | 2,105 | 1,805 |
| Manufacturing | 2,003 | 1,846 |
| Fiber, food, land and other | 915 | 853 |
| | 15,356 | 12,370 |
| Less—Reserves for depreciation, depletion and amortization | 5,277 | 4,553 |
| | 10,079 | 7,817 |
| | $16,808 | $13,853 |

(The accompanying notes to financial statements are an integral part of this balance sheet.)

## BALANCE SHEET

| (Millions) | 1981 | 1980 |
|---|---:|---:|
| **LIABILITIES AND STOCKHOLDERS' EQUITY** | | |
| Current Liabilities: | | |
| Current maturities on long-term debt | $ 149 | $ 122 |
| Commercial paper | 276 | 71 |
| Notes payable— | | |
| Affiliated companies | 41 | 37 |
| Other | 612 | 601 |
| Accounts payable— | | |
| Trade | 1,849 | 1,629 |
| Affiliated companies | 255 | 232 |
| Deferred federal income taxes | 321 | 317 |
| Interest accrued | 127 | 104 |
| Natural gas pipeline revenue refund reservation | 152 | 77 |
| Other | 364 | 342 |
| | 4,146 | 3,532 |
| Long-term Debt | 5,089 | 4,161 |
| Deferred Federal Income Taxes | 1,562 | 982 |
| Deferred Credits and Other Liabilities | 359 | 402 |
| Commitments and Contingencies | | |
| | | |
| Preferred and Preference Stock With Mandatory Redemption Provisions: | | |
| Preferred stock, par value $100 per share, authorized 3,324,500 and 3,424,500 shares, issued and outstanding 1,717,500 and 1,817,500 shares at the respective dates (less—par value of 14,700 and 49,500 shares held for sinking fund at the respective dates) | 170 | 177 |
| Preference stock, no par value, authorized 10,000,000 shares, issued and outstanding 4,986,807 shares, mandatory redemption value $499 million | 437 | 435 |
| | 607 | 612 |
| Common and Other Stockholders' Equity: | | |
| Common stock, par value $5 per share, authorized 350,000,000 and 150,000,000 shares, issued and outstanding 130,095,457 and 118,416,083 shares at the respective dates | 650 | 592 |
| Premium on capital stock and other capital surplus | 1,747 | 1,330 |
| Retained earnings | 2,675 | 2,269 |
| | 5,072 | 4,191 |
| Less—980,157 shares of common stock held by a subsidiary, at cost | 27 | 27 |
| | 5,045 | 4,164 |
| | $16,808 | $13,853 |

**Tenneco Inc. and Consolidated Subsidiaries**
Year Ended December 31, 1981, 1980 and 1979

STATEMENT OF CHANGES
IN FINANCIAL POSITION

| (Millions) | 1981 | 1980 | 1979 |
|---|---|---|---|
| **SOURCE OF FUNDS:** | | | |
| Net income | $ 813 | $ 726 | $ 571 |
| Items which did not affect working capital: | | | |
| Depreciation, depletion and amortization | 865 | 633 | 561 |
| Deferred federal income taxes | 586 | 191 | 18 |
| Undistributed earnings of affiliated companies | (127) | (21) | (47) |
| Other | (2) | 2 | 3 |
| Total funds provided from operations | 2,135 | 1,531 | 1,106 |
| Long-term debt incurred | 1,138 | 1,406 | 594 |
| Short-term debt refinanced | (200) | 200 | (225) |
| Common stock issued | 475 | 424 | 197 |
| Preference stock issued | — | 260 | — |
| Investments and other assets | 26 | (268) | (45) |
| | 3,574 | 3,553 | 1,627 |
| **USE OF FUNDS:** | | | |
| Natural gas pipeline cash refund | 45 | 260 | 87 |
| Amount reflected in other working capital accounts | (45) | (260) | (87) |
| | — | — | — |
| Capital expenditures for plant, property and equipment— | | | |
| Oil exploration and production | 1,498 | 1,014 | 858 |
| Natural gas pipelines | 242 | 219 | 109 |
| Oil processing and marketing, chemicals | 345 | 286 | 199 |
| Manufacturing | 199 | 250 | 246 |
| Fiber, food, land and other | 75 | 56 | 65 |
| | 2,359 | 1,825 | 1,477 |
| Net assets purchased in acquisitions— | | | |
| Net tangible assets | 419 | 17 | 137 |
| Investment in affiliated companies accounted for on an equity basis | — | 653 | 36 |
| | 419 | 670 | 173 |
| Working capital of acquired companies | (14) | — | (8) |
| Reduction of long-term debt | 463 | 630 | 322 |
| Dividends | 387 | 329 | 259 |
| Preferred and preference stock reacquired or exchanged for common stock | 6 | 9 | 32 |
| Other (net) | 65 | (86) | (180) |
| | 3,685 | 3,377 | 2,075 |
| Increase (Decrease) in Working Capital | $ (111) | $ 176 | $ (448) |
| **CHANGES IN COMPONENTS OF WORKING CAPITAL:** | | | |
| Current Assets— | | | |
| Cash | $ 4 | $ (41) | $ — |
| Temporary cash investments | (2) | (2) | (4) |
| Notes and accounts receivable | 376 | 17 | 330 |
| Shipbuilding contracts in progress, less billings | (37) | (22) | (59) |
| Inventories | (67) | 80 | 233 |
| Prepayments and other | 229 | 14 | 57 |
| Current Liabilities— | | | |
| Current maturities on long-term debt | (27) | 47 | 65 |
| Commercial paper | (205) | 82 | (153) |
| Notes payable | (15) | (44) | (91) |
| Accounts payable | (243) | (269) | (491) |
| Deferred federal income taxes | (4) | (151) | (50) |
| Interest accrued | (23) | 2 | (36) |
| Natural gas pipeline revenue fund reservation | (75) | 153 | (71) |
| Other | (22) | 310 | (178) |
| Increase (Decrease) in Working Capital | $ (111) | $ 176 | $ (448) |

(The accompanying notes to financial statements are an integral part of this statement of changes in financial position.)

| (Millions Except Share Amounts) | 1981 | | 1980 | | 1979 | |
|---|---|---|---|---|---|---|
| | Shares | Amount | Shares | Amount | Shares | Amount |
| **COMMON STOCK:** | | | | | | |
| Balance January 1 | 118,416,083 | $ 592 | 106,313,488 | $ 532 | 98,612,441 | $ 493 |
| Conversion of securities | 62,566 | — | 63,874 | | 2,877,750 | 14 |
| Issued to employee benefit plans and the | | | | | | |
| Dividend Reinvestment Plan | 1,570,297 | 8 | 679,221 | 3 | 863,971 | 5 |
| Exercise of warrants | — | — | — | — | 2,575,529 | 13 |
| Issued to acquire Houston Oil & | | | | | | |
| Minerals Corporation | 10,046,511 | 50 | — | — | — | — |
| Issued to acquire Southwestern Life | | | | | | |
| Corporation | — | — | 11,359,500 | 57 | — | — |
| Issued to acquire East Tennessee Natural | | | | | | |
| Gas Company | — | — | — | — | 97,547 | 1 |
| Sale of common stock | — | — | — | — | 1,250,000 | 6 |
| Exercise of options | — | — | — | — | 36,250 | — |
| Balance December 31 | 130,095,457 | 650 | 118,416,083 | 592 | 106,313,488 | 532 |
| **PREMIUM ON CAPITAL STOCK** | | | | | | |
| **AND OTHER CAPITAL SURPLUS:** | | | | | | |
| Balance January 1 | | 1,330 | | 966 | | 830 |
| Premium on common stock issued: | | | | | | |
| Upon conversion of securities | | 1 | | 1 | | 31 |
| To employee benefit plans and the | | | | | | |
| Dividend Reinvestment Plan | | 49 | | 26 | | 26 |
| Upon exercise of warrants | | — | | — | | 64 |
| To acquire Houston Oil | | | | | | |
| & Minerals Corporation | | 367 | | — | | — |
| To acquire Southwestern Life Corporation | | — | | 336 | | — |
| To acquire East Tennessee Natural Gas | | | | | | |
| Company | | — | | — | | 3 |
| Upon sale of common stock | | — | | — | | 29 |
| Other | | — | | 1 | | (17) |
| Balance December 31 | | 1,747 | | 1,330 | | 966 |
| **RETAINED EARNINGS:** | | | | | | |
| Balance January 1— | | | | | | |
| As previously reported | | 2,269 | | 1,874 | | 1,575 |
| Prior periods effect of change in accounting | | | | | | |
| for compensated absences and revenue | | | | | | |
| recognition when right of return exists | | | | | | |
| (no significant effect in any single | | | | | | |
| prior year) | | (18) | | — | | — |
| | | 2,251 | | 1,874 | | 1,575 |
| Net income | | 813 | | 726 | | 571 |
| Dividends— | | | | | | |
| Preferred stock | | (13) | | (13) | | (13) |
| Preference stock | | (48) | | (37) | | (17) |
| Common stock | | (326) | | (279) | | (229) |
| Other | | (2) | | (2) | | (13) |
| Balance December 31 | | 2,675 | | 2,269 | | 1,874 |
| Less—Common Stock held by a Subsidiary, | | | | | | |
| at cost: | | | | | | |
| Balance January 1 | 980,157 | 27 | 980,157 | 27 | 1,083,891 | 30 |
| Issued in acquisition | — | — | — | — | (103,734) | (3) |
| Balance December 31 | 980,157 | 27 | 980,157 | 27 | 980,157 | 27 |
| Total | | $5,045 | | $4,164 | | $3,345 |

(The accompanying notes to financial statements are an integral part of this statement of changes in common and other stock-holders' equity.)

# Notes to Financial Statements

## Tenneco Inc. and Consolidated Subsidiaries

### (1) SUMMARY OF ACCOUNTING POLICIES
#### Consolidation

The consolidated financial statements include all majority-owned subsidiaries other than finance, insurance and inactive subsidiaries. Reference is made to Note 11 for summarized financial information of J I Case Credit Corporation, an unconsolidated wholly-owned finance subsidiary, and unconsolidated wholly-owned life insurance subsidiaries.

Unconsolidated majority-owned subsidiaries and companies in which at least a 20% voting interest is owned are carried at cost plus equity in undistributed earnings since date of acquisition. Such equity in undistributed earnings amounted to approximately $327 million and $200 million at December 31, 1981 and 1980, respectively.

Equity in net income of and dividends received from companies accounted for on an equity basis were as follows:

| | (Millions) Year Ended December 31, | | |
|---|---|---|---|
| | 1981 | 1980 | 1979 |
| Equity in net income— | | | |
| J I Case Credit Corporation . . . . . . | $ 48 | $ 31 | $19 |
| Philadelphia Life . . . . . . . . . . . . . . | 35 | 28 | 25 |
| Southwestern Life . . . . . . . . . . . . . | 63 | 46 | — |
| Other . . . . . . . . . . . . . . . . . . . . . . | 36 | 37 | 14 |
| | $182 | $142 | $58 |
| Dividends and distributions received— | | | |
| J I Case Credit Corporation . . . . . . | $ — | $ 90 | $— |
| Philadelphia Life . . . . . . . . . . . . . . | 5 | — | — |
| Southwestern Life . . . . . . . . . . . . . | 31 | — | — |
| Other . . . . . . . . . . . . . . . . . . . . . . | 19 | 31 | 11 |
| | $ 55 | $121 | $11 |

All significant intercompany items have been eliminated in consolidation.

The excess of investment in consolidated subsidiaries and unconsolidated subsidiaries which are accounted for on an equity basis over net assets at date of acquisition is being amortized over a 40 year period. Such amortization for 1981, 1980 and 1979 amounted to approximately $19 million, $12 million and $5 million, respectively. At December 31, 1981, the unamortized balance applicable to unconsolidated subsidiaries which are accounted for on an equity basis was approximately $676 million.

#### Temporary Cash Investments

Temporary cash investments are carried at cost, which closely approximates market.

#### Currency Translation and Foreign Operations

Foreign currency transactions and foreign currency financial statements are translated into U.S. dollars using applicable current and historical rates. The resulting gains or losses are included in the determination of net income for the period in which the exchange rate changes. Deferred income taxes are provided for unrealized translation gains and losses of companies included in the Tenneco Inc. consolidated federal income tax return. These gains and losses, when realized, are included in the U.S. federal income tax return.

Foreign exchange gains and losses included in income were as follows:

| | (Millions) Year Ended December 31, | | |
|---|---|---|---|
| | 1981 | 1980 | 1979 |
| Exchange gains (losses) reflected in cost of sales . . . . . . . . | $74 | $ 9 | $(19) |
| Tax benefit (expense) associated with exchange gains (losses). . . . . . | (14) | 4 | 3 |
| Exchange gains (losses) reflected on an after-tax basis in equity in net income of affiliated companies . . . . | 21 | 9 | 1 |
| Net income increase (decrease). . . . . . . . . . . . . . . . . . . . | $81 | $22 | $(15) |

At December 31, 1981, the combined net assets of subsidiaries and branches engaged in foreign operations were as follows:

| | (Millions) |
|---|---|
| Assets . . . . . . . . . . . . . . . . . . . . . . . . . . . . . . . . . . . . . . . . | $3,132 |
| Liabilities . . . . . . . . . . . . . . . . . . . . . . . . . . . . . . . . . . . . . | 2,167 |
| Net Assets . . . . . . . . . . . . . . . . . . . . . . . . . . . . . . . . . . . . | $ 965 |

Net sales from such operations were approximately $3.0 billion, $2.9 billion and $2.6 billion for 1981, 1980 and 1979, respectively. Corresponding net income was $7 million, $77 million and $89 million, respectively.

#### Acquisitions

On May 1, 1980, Tenneco acquired the assets of Southwestern Life Corporation through the exchange of 11,359,500 shares of Tenneco Inc.'s common stock and 3,029,200 shares of Tenneco Inc.'s $11.00 preference stock (such stock had a market value at date of issuance of approximately $653 million). If Southwestern Life had been acquired as of January 1, 1980, there would not have been a significant effect on net income for 1980.

On April 24, 1981, Tenneco Inc. acquired all of the outstanding common stock of Houston Oil & Minerals Corporation ("Houston Oil") in exchange for 10,046,511 shares of Tenneco Inc.'s common stock (market value at date of issuance of approximately $417 million). Houston Oil is primarily engaged in the exploration of oil and natural gas on undeveloped properties and the development of production upon discovery. Prior to the merger, Houston Oil created a royalty trust consisting of a 75% net profits interest in its presently productive domestic oil and gas properties, a 5% overriding royalty in its domestic exploratory oil and gas properties and varying net profits interests in certain foreign exploratory oil and gas properties and distributed units in such trust to its stockholders. This acquisition has been accounted for on the "purchase" basis of accounting, and accordingly, the accompanying financial statements include approximately $200 million in net sales of Houston Oil since date of acquisition. If Houston Oil had been acquired as of January 1, 1981, there would not have been a significant effect on net income for 1981.

#### Federal Income Taxes

The companies follow deferred tax accounting for timing differences in the recognition of revenues and expenses for tax and financial reporting purposes, except for unremitted earnings of foreign subsidiaries.

No provision has been made for U.S. income taxes on unremitted earnings of foreign subsidiaries (approximately $327 million at December 31, 1981) since it is the present intention of management to reinvest a major portion of such unremitted earnings in foreign operations.

The companies follow the flow-through method of accounting whereby the benefit of the investment tax credit is currently recognized in the income statement. At December 31, 1981, the companies had investment tax credits of approximately $93 million which could not be utilized as a reduction to current year federal income taxes but which could be utilized as a carryback to prior years. Accordingly, this amount is included as investment tax credit in the Statement of Income for the year ended December 31, 1981. All investment tax credits generated during the year were utilized either against current year income taxes payable or as carrybacks to prior years. Accordingly, at December 31, 1981, the companies had no unused investment tax credits.

For additional information, reference is made to Note 2.

## Oil and Gas Accounting and Depreciation, Depletion and Amortization

Tenneco and its subsidiaries follow the full-cost method of accounting whereby all productive and non-productive costs incurred in connection with the acquisition, exploration and development of oil and gas reserves are capitalized and amortized over the companies' estimate of proved oil and gas reserves using the unit-of-production method. Cost centers for amortization purposes are determined on a country-by-country basis. Certain unevaluated properties are excluded for amortization purposes until the properties have been evaluated. When a lease is abandoned, all costs incurred in connection with its acquisition, exploration and development are charged to the reserve for depreciation, depletion and amortization.

Reference is made to Note 12 for additional financial data for oil and gas producing activities, Note 13 for unaudited information relative to oil and gas reserve data and Note 14 for unaudited information prepared on the basis of Reserve Recognition Accounting.

Depreciation of the other properties is provided on a straight-line basis in amounts which, in the opinion of management, are adequate to allocate the cost of properties over their estimated useful lives.

## Long-Term Shipbuilding Contracts

Newport News Shipbuilding and Dry Dock Company ("Newport"), a subsidiary, reports profits on its long-term shipbuilding contracts on the percentage-of-completion method of accounting, determined on the basis of a comparison of costs incurred to date to estimated final costs. Newport reports losses on such contracts when first estimated. The performance of such contracts may extend over several years; thereforce, periodic reviews of estimated final revenues and costs are necessary during the term of the contracts. Final contract settlements and periodic reviews may result in revisions to estimated final contract profits or losses which have the effect of including cumulative adjustments of income in the period the revisions are made.

## Inventories

A substantial portion of inventories are valued at "last-in, first-out" ("LIFO") cost, which is not in excess of market. All other inventories are valued at the lower of cost, determined on the "first-in, first-out" ("FIFO") or "average" methods, or market, determined on the basis of estimated realizable value.

If the FIFO or average method of inventory accounting had been used by Tenneco Inc., inventories would have been approximately $321 million, $320 million and $157 million higher than reported at December 31, 1981, 1980 and 1979, respectively.

During 1981, certain LIFO based quantities were reduced. This reduction resulted in a liquidation of LIFO inventory quantities carried at lower costs prevailing in prior years as compared with the cost of 1981 purchases, the effect of which increased net income by approximately $50 million.

Inventories used in the computation of cost of sales at each year-end were approximately $1.6 billion in 1981, $1.8 billion in 1980, $1.7 billion in 1979 and $1.5 billion in 1978.

## Interest Capitalized

Interest is capitalized on regulated gas transmission construction projects in accordance with established regulatory practices which permit the companies to earn a fair return on such costs and to recover them in rates charged to customers. Prior to 1980 the companies capitalized interest on borrowed funds utilized in acquiring and carrying offshore oil and gas leases until development was substantially completed, in acquiring and carrying real estate held for resale and in the construction of major capital additions. Effective January 1, 1980, the companies commenced capitalizing interest in accordance with Financial Accounting Standard No. 34.

## (2) PROVISION FOR FEDERAL INCOME TAXES

The components of income before federal income taxes are as follows:

| | (Millions) Year Ended December 31, | | |
| --- | --- | --- | --- |
| | 1981 | 1980 | 1979 |
| Consolidated companies— | | | |
| U.S. income before income taxes ... | $1,017 | $ 922 | $750 |
| Foreign income before income taxes | 72 | 57 | 88 |
| Income before federal income taxes and equity in net income of affiliated companies . . . . . . . . | 1,089 | 979 | 838 |
| Equity in net income of affiliated companies (net of tax) . . . . . . . . . . . | 182 | 142 | 58 |
| | $1,271 | $1,121 | $896 |

Following is an analysis of the components of consolidated federal income tax expense:

| | (Millions) Year Ended December 31, | | |
| --- | --- | --- | --- |
| | 1981 | 1980 | 1979 |
| Current before investment tax credit— | | | |
| U.S. companies included in the consolidated tax return . . . . . . . . | $ (57) | $ 86 | $225 |
| Less—Tax expense of companies accounted for on an equity basis | 42 | 25 | 16 |
| U.S. consolidated tax expense . . . . . | (99) | 61 | 209 |
| Foreign . . . . . . . . . . . . . . . . . . . . . . . | 64 | 43 | 51 |
| | (35) | 104 | 260 |
| Investment tax credit . . . . . . . . . . . . . . | (102) | (55) | (43) |

| Deferred— | | | |
|---|---|---|---|
| U.S. | 577 | 382 | 150 |
| Foreign | 18 | (21) | (5) |
| Reversal of deferred taxes applicable to U.K. stock relief* | — | (15) | (37) |
| | 595 | 346 | 108 |
| | $458 | $395 | $325 |

| Foreign exchange gain (loss) for financial purposes not included in taxable income until realized | 48 | (3) | 2 |
|---|---|---|---|
| Other | 7 | (25) | (10) |
| | $595 | $346 | $108 |

*The United Kingdom stock relief legislation permits enterprises to deduct, for the purpose of determining taxable income, increases in the carrying amount of inventories. Prior to 1979, such deduction was accounted for as a timing difference since it is subject to recapture for tax purposes if inventories decrease in future years. Pursuant to U.K. legislation enacted in 1979, $15 million and $37 million of the related deferred tax previously provided was reversed in 1980 and 1979, respectively, because in the opinion of Tenneco Inc., such deductions will not be recaptured.

Following is a reconciliation of the U.S. federal income tax rate to the effective tax rate reflected in the Statement of Income:

| | Year Ended December 31, | | |
|---|---|---|---|
| | 1981 | 1980 | 1979 |
| U.S. federal income tax rate | 46% | 46% | 46% |
| Increases (reductions) in tax rate resulting from: | | | |
| Investment tax credit | (8) | (5) | (5) |
| Equity in earnings of unconsolidated subsidiaries included in income on an after-tax basis | (6) | (6) | (3) |
| Foreign income taxed at different rates | 5 | — | — |
| Reversal of deferred taxes applicable to U.K. stock relief | — | (1) | (4) |
| Other | (1) | 1 | 2 |
| Effective federal income tax rate | 36% | 35% | 36% |

Deferred federal income tax expense results from timing differences in the recognition of revenues and expenses for tax and financial reporting purposes. A description of the differences and the related tax effect were as follows:

| | (Millions) Year Ended December 31, | | |
|---|---|---|---|
| | 1981 | 1980 | 1979 |
| Excess of tax over financial deductions for oil and gas exploration and development costs | $229 | $130 | $ 82 |
| Difference in timing of recognition of income on long-term contracts | 70 | 80 | 57 |
| Difference in timing of recognition of income and expense relative to operations regulated by the FERC | (22) | 40 | 13 |
| Excess of tax depreciation over book depreciation applicable to operations not regulated by the FERC | 57 | 50 | 26 |
| Transactions reported on the installment basis for tax purposes | 55 | 31 | 14 |
| Reversal of deferred taxes applicable to U.K. stock relief | — | (15) | (37) |
| Decrease (increase) in reserves not deductible until incurred | 40 | (31) | (40) |
| Mining development costs capitalized | 19 | 31 | 1 |
| Interest capitalized | 92 | 58 | — |

## (3) FEDERAL ENERGY REGULATORY COMMISSION ("FERC") RATE MATTERS

In May 1981, Tenneco Inc. refunded approximately $36 million (including interest) to its regulated natural gas pipeline customers under a FERC settlement agreement and at December 31, 1981, has an obligation to refund approximately $59 million (including interest) under another settlement agreement. The latter settlement agreement resolved substantially all prior contested issues except for rate of return and depreciation rates applicable to a rate increase placed into effect November 1, 1980.

At December 31, 1981, Tenneco Inc. was collecting revenues pursuant to an application for a rate increase which was placed in effect, subject to refund on November 1, 1981. This increase is designed, as amended, to provide increased annual revenues of $184 million above the pre-filing level. Revenues have been reserved to reflect probable adverse regulatory decisions and Tenneco believes the ultimate resolution of these matters will have no significant effect on its consolidated financial position or reported net income.

On November 30, 1981, Tenneco Inc. filed an application which proposed rates designed to increase annual revenues by approximately $122 million above the prefiling level. Such proposed increase was based upon an overall rate of return of 15.72% and increases in other costs of doing business. The new rates will become conditionally effective on June 1, 1982.

## (4) LONG-TERM DEBT, INTERIM FINANCING AND SHORT-TERM DEBT
### Long-Term Debt

A summary of long-term debt outstanding at December 31, 1981, is set forth in the following tabulation:

| | (Millions) |
|---|---|
| Tenneco Inc.— | |
| First mortgage pipeline bonds due 1983 through 1991, average interest rate 7.36% | $ 182 |
| Debentures due 1982 through 2011, average interest rate 11.54% (net of $243 million of unamortized discount) | 1,602 |
| Notes due 1983 through 1999, average interest rate 11.4% (net of $26 million of unamortized discount) | 1,753 |
| | 3,537 |
| Tenneco Corporation— | |
| Debentures due 1990 through 1993, average interest rate 6.56% | 103 |
| Notes due 1984, average interest rate 12.48% | 400 |
| Tenneco International N.V.— | |
| 7.75% Debentures due 1987 (net of $1 million of unamortized discount) | 120 |
| Notes due 1984 through 1989, average interest rate 14.96% (net of $2 million of unamortized discount) | 238 |
| Tenneco International Inc.— | |
| 13.19% Eurodollar loan due 1985 | 65 |
| Tenneco United Kingdom Holdings Ltd.— | |
| 16% Note due 1984 | 72 |

| | |
|---|---:|
| Other subsidiaries due 1982 through 2008, average interest rate 10.37% ................... | 703 |
| | 5,238 |
| Less—Current maturities ......................... | 149 |
| | $5,089 |

At December 31, 1981, approximately $3.6 billion of gross plant, property and equipment was pledged as collateral to secure $335 million principal amount of long-term debt.

The aggregate maturities and sinking fund requirements applicable to the issues outstanding at December 31, 1981, are $149 million, $367 million, $834 million, $267 million and $212 million for 1982, 1983, 1984, 1985 and 1986, respectively.

## Interim Financing

Tenneco Inc. has arranged two Revolving Credit and Term Loan Agreements which provide for borrowings up to an aggregate principal amount of $1,250 million. These funds are available to Tenneco Inc., Tenneco Corporation or any designated wholly-owned subsidiary through various dates in 1984 and 1985, at which time all or any part of such funds not then outstanding as term loans will be available as term loans which would mature at various dates in 1989 and 1990. As of December 31, 1981, $288 million was outstanding as a Eurodollar term loan and is included in the foregoing table as long-term debt. Borrowings, whether on a revolving credit basis or a term loan basis, are available as either domestic loans generally at the prime rate of interest or as Eurodollar loans at LIBOR plus a margin. The Agreements provide for commitment fees on the unused portion plus, in one agreement, a fee on the total commitment until August 31, 1984, and thereafter on the unpaid balance of the term loans.

## Short-Term Debt

The companies have lines of credit with various banks and also sell commercial paper to provide short-term financing. The credit agreements provide for borrowings at various rates, and commitment fees on the unused amount of the commitments are required on certain lines. Information for 1981 regarding the lines of credit and commercial paper issued follows:

| | (Millions) | |
|---|---|---|
| | Lines of Credit* | Commercial Paper |
|---|---|---|
| Outstanding borrowings at end of year ... | $ 510 | $276 |
| Average interest rate on outstanding borrowings at end of year ............ | 13.4% | 11.8% |
| Approximate maximum month-end outstanding borrowings during year .... | $ 604 | $650 |
| Approximate average month-end outstanding borrowings during year .... | $ 551 | $438 |
| Weighted average interest rate on approximate average month-end outstanding borrowings during year .... | 15.6% | 15.4% |
| Approximate unused portion of lines of credit at end of year— | | |
| Tenneco Inc. (available for direct borrowings or support of commercial paper) ............... | $ 762 | |
| Subsidiary companies................ | 260 | |
| | $1,022 | |

*Excluding $400 million of outstanding borrowings from credit agreements classified as long-term debt in the accompanying balance sheet at December 31, 1981.

Included in the lines of credit existing at December 31, 1981, are approximately $1,171 million which expire in 1982 and may be extended annually at the election of the participating banks and approximately $761 million which expire subsequent to December 31, 1982. Additionally, at December 31, 1981, the companies had other short-term borrowings of $102 million.

At December 31, 1981, approximately $2 million of compensating balances, all subject to legal withdrawal, were maintained in connection with lines of credit.

## (5) PREFERRED AND PREFERENCE STOCK WITH MANDATORY REDEMPTION PROVISIONS
### Preferred Stock

At December 31, 1981, there were ten series of cumulative preferred stock outstanding with annual dividend rates ranging from 4.90% to 8.52% (average dividend rate of 7.21%). The aggregate redemption value was $177 million which declines at various future dates. The preference in involuntary liquidation is the par value of each issue. Tenneco Inc. is required to retire a portion of the outstanding preferred stock each year. Sinking fund requirements, net of shares held at December 31, 1981, are approximately $7 million, $9 million, $10 million, $10 million and $9 million for 1982, 1983, 1984, 1985 and 1986, respectively.

### Preference Stock

At December 31, 1981, there were outstanding 1,957,607 shares designated as $7.40 preference stock and 3,029,200 shares designated as $11.00 preference stock having a mandatory redemption value of $100 per share ($499 million at December 31, 1981). Tenneco Inc. has the option of redeeming the $7.40 preference stock from March 1, 1988, until March 1, 1993, for $101 per share and from March 1, 1993, until March 1, 1998, for $100 per share. Within each twelve-month period commencing with the twelve-month period ending on March 1, 1989, Tenneco Inc. must redeem at $100 per share, plus accrued and unpaid dividends, 10% of the number of shares of $7.40 preference stock originally issued. Tenneco Inc. has the option of redeeming the $11.00 preference stock at the following redemption prices per share, plus accrued and unpaid dividends: from May 1, 1985, until May 1, 1990, for $102 per share; from May 1, 1990, until May 1, 1995, for $101 per share and $100 per share thereafter. Within each twelve-month period commencing with the twelve-month period ending on May 1, 1990, Tenneco Inc. must redeem at $100 per share, plus accrued and unpaid dividends, 6.25% of the number of shares of $11.00 preference stock originally issued.

Tenneco Inc. has recorded the preference stock at its fair value at date of issue (approximately $430 million) and is making periodic accretions of the excess of the redemption value over the fair value at date of issue. Such accretions are included in preference stock dividends as a reduction of net income to arrive at net income to common stock.

## (6) SECOND PREFERRED STOCK WITHOUT MANDATORY REDEMPTION PROVISIONS

At December 31, 1981, there were 2,000,000 shares of second preferred stock authorized. At such date, there were 33,065 shares outstanding consisting of four series of cumulative second preferred stock with annual dividend rates ranging from 4.50% to 5.00% (average dividend rate of 4.87%). The aggregate redemption value was $3 million which declines at various future dates. The conversion privileges on these shares

Changes in the Preferred and Preference Stock

| | 1981 | | 1980 | | 1979 | |
| --- | --- | --- | --- | --- | --- | --- |
| | Shares | Amount | Shares | Amount | Shares | Amount |
| Preferred Stock: | | | | | | |
| Balance January 1 . . . . . . . . . . . . . . . . . . . . . . . . . . . . . . | 1,768,000 | $177 | 1,849,365 | $185 | 1,894,676 | $190 |
| Acquired for sinking fund . . . . . . . . . . . . . . . . . . . . . . | (65,200) | (7) | (81,365) | (8) | (45,311) | (5) |
| Balance December 31 . . . . . . . . . . . . . . . . . . . . . . . . . . | 1,702,800 | 170 | 1,768,000 | 177 | 1,849,365 | 185 |
| Preference Stock: | | | | | | |
| Balance January 1 . . . . . . . . . . . . . . . . . . . . . . . . . . . . . . | 4,968,807 | 435 | 1,957,607 | 173 | 1,955,289 | 172 |
| Issued to acquire Southwestern Life Corporation . . . . . . | — | — | 3,029,200 | 260 | — | — |
| Stock options . . . . . . . . . . . . . . . . . . . . . . . . . . . . . . . | — | — | — | — | 2,318 | — |
| Accretions of the excess of liquidating value over fair value at date of issue . . . . . . . . . . . . . . . . . . . . . | — | 2 | — | 2 | — | 1 |
| Balance December 31 . . . . . . . . . . . . . . . . . . . . . . . . . . | 4,986,807 | 437 | 4,986,807 | 435 | 1,957,607 | 173 |
| | | $607 | | $612 | | $358 |

(Millions Except Share Amounts)

has expired and Tenneco Inc. has no obligation to redeem these shares. Due to the immaterial amount involved, the carrying value of the shares outstanding (approximately $3 million) has been included in the caption "Premium on capital stock and other capital surplus" in the accompanying financial statements.

## (7) COMMON STOCK
### Reserved
At December 31, 1981, the shares of Tenneco Inc. common stock reserved for issuance were as follows:

| | |
| --- | --- |
| Stock Option Plan . . . . . . . . . . . . . . . . . . . . . . . . . . . . . . | 3,500,000 |
| Performance Unit Plan . . . . . . . . . . . . . . . . . . . . . . . . . . | 2,000,000 |
| Thrift Plan . . . . . . . . . . . . . . . . . . . . . . . . . . . . . . . . . . . | 1,216,074 |
| Conversion of Tenneco Inc. 10% loan stock through December 21, 1995 . . . . . . . . . . . . . . . . . . . . | 372,502 |
| Dividend Reinvestment Plan . . . . . . . . . . . . . . . . . . . . . . | 150,557 |
| Other . . . . . . . . . . . . . . . . . . . . . . . . . . . . . . . . . . . . . . . | 8,000 |
| | 7,247,133 |

### Stock Option Plan and Performance Unit Plan
In September 1981, the Tenneco Inc. Board of Directors (the "Board") adopted the 1981 Tenneco Inc. Key Employee Stock Option Plan (the "Plan"), subject to the approval of the Plan by the Company's shareholders at their April 1982 annual shareholder meeting. The total number of shares of common stock which can be issued under the Plan cannot exceed 3,500,000 shares, subject to certain adjustments. Stock options will be granted at the fair market value of a share of common stock at the date of grant, become exercisable 25% per year on a cumulative basis beginning one year from the date of grant and lapse ten years from the date of grant. The Plan also provides for the granting of stock appreciation rights in tandem with the stock options so that the exercise of a right or option causes a corresponding reduction in the option or right respectively. The amount of the Company's payment, upon the exercise of a stock appreciation right, will be the excess of the fair market value of the stock at the time of exercise over the stock option price, but not to exceed the amount of the underlying option price. Payment will be in shares of common stock, cash or a combination of both at the discretion of the Company. In September 1981, subject to approval of the Plan by shareholders, the Company granted 332,200 stock options and a corresponding num-

ber of stock appreciation rights at the market price of $36.875 per share. In December 1981, 850 stock options and corresponding stock appreciation rights were granted at the market price of $33.69 per share. No compensation expense was recorded by the Company in 1981 in connection with the stock appreciation rights which had been granted because the market price of the Company's common stock at December 31, 1981 was less than the option exercise prices.

In December 1981, the Board adopted the Tenneco Inc. Performance Unit Plan (the "Plan"), to become effective January 1, 1982, subject to approval of the Plan by the Company's shareholders at their April 1982 annual shareholder meeting. The total number of shares of common stock which can be issued under the Plan cannot exceed 2,000,000 shares. This Plan will terminate December 31, 1992. Performance units will be awarded to certain key employees at the beginning of each year. The value of a performance unit will be determined by established schedules based on the achievement of specific earnings performance objectives over the performance period, which is three years from award date. Upon completion of a performance period, and based upon the financial objectives achieved, the value of the performance unit will be paid in shares of common stock, cash or a combination of both at the discretion of the Company.

### Earnings Per Share
Earnings per share of common stock are based on the average number of shares of common stock outstanding during each period. Convertible or exchangeable securities outstanding during each of the three years ended December 31, 1981, were not materially dilutive.

## (8) RESTRICTIONS ON PAYMENT OF DIVIDENDS
At December 31, 1981, under its most restrictive dividend provision contained in indentures under which certain series of debentures have been issued, Tenneco Inc. had approximately $850 million of retained earnings available for the payment of dividends on common stock. The liquidating value of Tenneco Inc.'s preference stock does not impose a restriction on retained earnings.

Certain of Tenneco Inc.'s consolidated subsidiaries and unconsolidated subsidiaries which are accounted for on an equity basis have provisions under financing arrangements and statutory requirements which limit the amount of their related earnings available for dividends. The payment of unrestricted amounts by such subsidiaries would not affect the amount of retained earnings of Tenneco Inc. available for dividends on common stock.

## (9) PENSION PLANS

The companies have several retirement plans which cover substantially all of their employees. Costs of all plans are actuarially determined, and it is the companies' policy to fund all pension costs accrued. Total pension expense was approximately $106 million, $114 million and $96 million for 1981, 1980 and 1979, respectively, which includes amortization of unfunded prior service cost over periods ranging from 10 to 40 years.

A statement of accumulated plan benefits and plan net assets for the companies' domestic defined benefit plans determined as of the latest actuarial valuations (primarily January 1, 1981 and 1980, respectively) is presented below:

| | (Millions) | |
| --- | --- | --- |
| | 1981 | 1980 |
| Actuarial present value of accumulated plan benefits: | | |
| Vested | $613 | $589 |
| Nonvested | 81 | 70 |
| | $694 | $659 |
| Net assets available for benefits | $620 | $517 |

The weighted average assumed rate of return used in determining the actuarial present value of accumulated plan benefits was approximately 7.0 percent and 6.3 percent for 1981 and 1980, respectively. Changes in actuarial assumptions in 1981, primarily an increase in the assumed rate of return, reduced the present value of benefits by approximately $77 million.

The companies' foreign pension plans are not required to report to the United States' government agencies pursuant to the Employee Retirement Income Security Act and do not determine the actuarial value of the accumulated benefits or net assets available for benefits on bases consistent with amounts calculated and disclosed above. Based on available information, Tenneco Inc. believes that the difference between actuarially computed vested benefits and funded amounts and accruals for such plans was not significant at December 31, 1981 and 1980, respectively.

## (10) COMMITMENTS AND CONTINGENCIES
### Capital Commitments

Tenneco Inc. estimates that expenditures aggregating approximately $1.7 billion will be required after December 31, 1981 to complete facilities and projects authorized at such date, and substantial commitments have been made in connection therewith.

### Lease Commitments

At December 31, 1981, the companies had long-term leases covering certain of their facilities and equipment. The minimum rental commitments under noncancellable operating leases with lease terms in excess of one year are approximately $70 million, $59 million, $54 million, $47 million and $38 million for 1982, 1983, 1984, 1985 and 1986, respectively, and $105 million for subsequent years. Commitments under capital leases were not significant to the accompanying financial statements. Total rental expense for 1981, 1980 and 1979 was approximately $142 million, $116 million and $103 million, respectively, including minimum rentals under noncancellable operating leases of $83 million, $62 million and $59 million, respectively.

### Litigation

Certain purchases of natural gas by Channel Industries Gas Company ("Channel"), a subsidiary of Tenneco Inc., are being investigated by the FERC, successor to the Federal Power Commission (the "FPC"), as a result of a petition filed by Tenneco Inc. in 1977 with the FPC for a determination as to whether additional regulatory authorization was required in connection with certain volumes of natural gas purchased by Channel which were produced from acreage or reservoirs which were, or may have been, at one time dedicated to interstate commerce under contracts between various producers and Tenneco Inc.'s interstate pipeline division. Such gas was released from dedication to interstate commerce under a variety of procedures, some of which involve transactions which may have failed to meet all regulatory requirements therefor under the Natural Gas Act. The transactions in question were initiated a number of years ago, one dating back as far as 1958. Tenneco Inc. has conducted an investigation of these transactions and on the basis of its review presently estimates that Channel's purchases of gas in such transactions have amounted to an aggregate of approximately 400 billion cubic feet over a period commencing in 1965. Counsel for Tenneco Inc. are unable to express an opinion as to the ultimate outcome of this investigation or the nature or extent of any charges or claims which might be asserted in connection therewith or as a result thereof. However, based upon information available to date, Tenneco Inc. believes that the resolution of this matter will have no material effect on Tenneco Inc. and its consolidated subsidiaries' financial position or results of operations.

In 1977, the Federal Trade Commission (the "FTC") commenced an administrative proceeding to determine if the acquisition by Tenneco Inc. of Monroe Auto Equipment Company ("Monroe") violated the federal antitrust laws. The administrative law judge in such proceeding issued an initial decision in May 1980, finding such acquisition did not violate federal antitrust law. In September 1981, the FTC issued a final order reversing the initial decision of the administrative law judge, and ordered Tenneco Inc., subject to prior FTC approval, to divest its ownership of Monroe within one year and to refrain from acquiring any interest in a shock absorber firm for a period of ten years. Tenneco Inc. has appealed the FTC final order to the United States Court of Appeals for the Second Circuit.

Tenneco Inc. and its subsidiaries are parties to numerous other legal proceedings arising from their operations. Tenneco Inc. believes that the outcome of these proceedings as well as those described above, individually and in the aggregate, will have no material effect on Tenneco Inc. and its consolidated subsidiaries' financial position or results of operations.

## (11) UNCONSOLIDATED SUBSIDIARIES

Summarized financial information of J I Case Credit Corporation, an unconsolidated wholly-owned finance subsidiary, and unconsolidated wholly-owned life insurance subsidiaries, at December 31, 1981, 1980 and 1979, and for the years then ended is as follows:

J I Case Credit Corporation

|  | (Millions) | | |
| --- | --- | --- | --- |
|  | 1981 | 1980 | 1979 |
| Assets . . . . . . . . . . . . . . . . . . . . . . . . . | $1,894 | $1,383 | $992 |
| Liabilities . . . . . . . . . . . . . . . . . . . . . . . | 1,621 | 1,158 | 860 |
| Equity in net assets . . . . . . . . . . . . . . . . | 273 | 225 | 132 |
| Net income . . . . . . . . . . . . . . . . . . . . . . | 48 | 31 | 19 |

Combined Life Insurance Subsidiaries*

|  | 1981 | 1980 | 1979 |
| --- | --- | --- | --- |
| Assets . . . . . . . . . . . . . . . . . . . . . . . . . | $3,288 | $3,199 | $907 |
| Liabilities . . . . . . . . . . . . . . . . . . . . . . . | 2,250 | 2,206 | 651 |
| Equity in net assets . . . . . . . . . . . . . . . . | 1,038 | 993 | 256 |
| Net income . . . . . . . . . . . . . . . . . . . . . . | 98 | 74 | 25 |

*Includes Southwestern Life since date of acquisition, May 1, 1980.

**(Notes 12, 13 and 14 have been omitted.)**

## (15) QUARTERLY FINANCIAL DATA

Unaudited quarterly financial data for 1981 and 1980 is presented on page 210.

## (16) SEGMENT AND GEOGRAPHIC AREA INFORMATION

Segment and geographic area information is presented separately.

## (17) PRICE LEVEL ADJUSTED DATA

Unaudited price level adjusted data is presented on pages 207 and 288.

## (18) SUBSEQUENT EVENT

Tenneco Inc. is negotiating the sale of its interests in Canadian oil and gas properties. Such Canadian oil and gas properties contributed approximately $14 million to net income in 1981. Tenneco will retain its 49% interest in the Athabasca tar sands project as well as its investment in an Arctic Islands project.

(The above notes are an integral part of the foregoing financial statements.)

---

ARTHUR ANDERSEN & CO.

To the Stockholders and Board of Directors,
Tenneco Inc.:

We have examined the balance sheet of Tenneco Inc. (a Delaware corporation) and consolidated subsidiaries as of December 31, 1981 and 1980, and the related statements of income, changes in common and other stockholders' equity, and changes in financial position for each of the three years in the period ended December 31, 1981. Our examinations were made in accordance with generally accepted auditing standards and, accordingly, included such tests of the accounting records and such other auditing procedures as we considered necessary in the circumstances. We did not examine the 1981, 1980 and 1979 financial statements of certain consolidated subsidiaries and certain other subsidiaries reflected in the accompanying consolidated financial statements utilizing the equity method of accounting. Earnings of such subsidiaries comprise approximately 8%, 10% and 13% of consolidated net income for the years ended December 31, 1981, 1980 and 1979, respectively. The financial statements of such subsidiaries were examined by other auditors whose reports thereon have been furnished to us, and our opinion expressed herein, insofar as it relates to the amounts included for such subsidiaries, is based solely upon the reports of the other auditors.

In our opinion, based upon our examinations and the reports of other auditors referred to above, the aforementioned financial statements present fairly the financial position of Tenneco Inc. and consolidated subsidiaries as of December 31, 1981 and 1980, and the results of their operations and the changes in their financial position for each of the three years in the period ended December 31, 1981, in conformity with generally accepted accounting principles applied on a consistent basis.

Houston, Texas
February 9, 1982

ARTHUR ANDERSEN & CO.

# Price Level Adjusted Data    (Unaudited)

## INTRODUCTION

The following schedules provide certain information with respect to the effects of inflation on Tenneco's operations. Although Tenneco believes that the data have been developed in a reasonable manner, the methods utilized inherently involve the use of assumptions, approximations, and subjective judgments and, therefore, the resulting measurements should be viewed as estimates of the approximate effects of inflation rather than as precise measures.

## ADJUSTMENTS FOR GENERAL INFLATION (MEASURED BY THE CONSUMER PRICE INDEX FOR ALL URBAN CONSUMERS)

Revenues and all other income and expenses except cost of sales and depreciation, depletion and amortization were considered to reflect the average price levels for the year and, accordingly, were not adjusted. The adjustment for inflation to cost of sales is relatively small because of Tenneco's extensive use of the LIFO method of accounting for inventories which already reflects current costs in the historical financial statements. Such cost of sales has been adjusted for the liquidation of certain LIFO inventory quantities. Depreciation, depletion and amortization expense was calculated using the same methods and rates of depreciation as used in the historical financial statements.

Although the adjustments for general inflation to cost of sales and depreciation, depletion and amortization expense affect pretax income, no adjustments were made to the provision for income taxes since only historical costs are deductible for income tax purposes.

The unrealized gain from excess of amounts owed over cash, securities and receivables was calculated by measuring the decline in purchasing power for the year attributable to general inflation having taken into account net balances of monetary liabilities at the beginning and end of the year and transactions for the year.

Except for Tenneco's natural gas pipeline properties, net assets is a restatement of total assets less total liabilities at year-end as reported in the historical financial statements adjusted to reflect the increase in inflation adjusted amounts for inventories and plant, property and equipment resulting from the effects of general inflation. Similar adjustments were made to historical cost of sales and depreciation, depletion and amortization expense in arriving at net income and earnings per common share adjusted for general inflation.

Tenneco's natural gas pipeline properties and the related depreciation expense were included in net assets and net income, respectively, at historical cost rather than on an inflation adjusted basis since the recovery through depreciation is limited under current rate making procedures to historical cost. Pipeline historical net plant was $1,453 million, $1,363 million and $1,279 million at December 31, 1981, 1980 and 1979, respectively; historical depreciation expense was $146 million, $130 million and $126 million for the respective year-end periods and historical additions to plant in 1981 and 1980 were $236 million and $214 million, respectively. Additional depreciation expense computed on a constant dollar basis but not included in net income adjusted for general inflation was $224

## STATEMENT OF INCOME ADJUSTED FOR CHANGING PRICES
Year Ended December 31, 1981

| (Dollars in millions) | As Reported in the Historical Financial Statements (Historical Cost) | Adjusted for General Inflation (Average 1981 Dollars) | Adjusted for Changes in Specific Prices (Current Cost) |
|---|---|---|---|
| Net sales and operating revenues | $15,462 | $15,462 | $15,462 |
| Equity in net income of affiliated companies and other income (net) | 315 | 315 | 315 |
| | 15,777 | 15,777 | 15,777 |
| Costs and expenses: | | | |
| Cost of sales | 7,650 | 7,875 | 7,895 |
| Operating expenses | 3,964 | 3,964 | 3,964 |
| Selling, general and administrative | 1,360 | 1,360 | 1,360 |
| Depreciation, depletion and amortization | 849 | 1,110 | 1,227 |
| Interest | 683 | 683 | 683 |
| Federal income taxes | 458 | 458 | 458 |
| | 14,964 | 15,450 | 15,587 |
| Net Income | $ 813 | $ 327 | $ 190 |
| Unrealized gain from excess of amounts owed over cash, securities and receivables, resulting from decline in purchasing power | | $ 668 | $ 668 |
| Excess of the increase in the specific prices of inventories and plant, property and equipment held during the year over the increase in the general price level | | | $ 219 |

At December 31, 1981, inventories and net plant, property and equipment restated on a current cost basis were $2,215 million and $13,942 million, respectively, which includes natural gas pipelines properties at historical cost of $1,453 million.

million, $205 million and $189 million for 1981, 1980 and 1979, respectively.

## ADJUSTMENTS FOR CHANGES IN SPECIFIC PRICES

Except for Tenneco's natural gas pipeline properties, net assets adjusted for changes in specific prices is a restatement of total assets less total liabilities at year-end as reported in the historical financial statements reflecting adjustments to inventories and plant, property and equipment based on specific asset class indices. Similar adjustments were made to cost of sales and depreciation, depletion and amortization expense in arriving at net income and earnings per common share adjusted for specific prices. The methodology used in computing income statement item adjustments is the same as explained under "Adjustments for General Inflation" above.

Tenneco's natural gas pipeline properties and the related depreciation expense were included in net assets and net income, respectively, at historical cost rather than on a current cost basis since the recovery through depreciation is limited

under current rate making procedures to historical cost. Additional depreciation expense computed on a current cost basis but not included in net income adjusted for changes in specific prices was $274 million, $269 million and $268 million for 1981, 1980 and 1979, respectively.

Timberlands and income-producing real estate and the related depreciation, depletion and amortization expenses were included in net assets and net income, respectively, on a historical cost basis adjusted for changes in the general price level.

## SUMMARY

Tenneco believes that comparisons of data adjusted for changing prices are most meaningful when interpreted in terms of trends and relationships among the periods and that the absolute dollar amounts have little meaning. Comparisons of adjusted to unadjusted data can be significantly impacted through the choice of alternative base periods. Accordingly, caution should be employed whenever such comparisons are made.

## COMPARISON OF SELECTED DATA ADJUSTED FOR EFFECTS OF CHANGING PRICES
Year Ended December 31,

| (Millions except per share amounts) | 1981 | 1980 | 1979 | 1978 | 1977 |
|---|---|---|---|---|---|
| Net sales and operating revenues: | | | | | |
| As reported | $15,462 | $13,226 | $11,209 | $ 8,762 | $ 7,408 |
| Adjusted for general inflation | 15,462 | 14,598 | 14,045 | 12,215 | 11,118 |
| Net income: | | | | | |
| As reported | $ 813 | $ 726 | $ 571 | | |
| Adjusted for general inflation | 327 | 337 | 345 | | |
| Adjusted for changes in specific prices | 190 | 237 | 175 | | |
| Earnings per average share of common stock: | | | | | |
| As reported | $ 6.01 | $ 5.95 | $ 5.30 | | |
| Adjusted for general inflation | 2.11 | 2.47 | 2.98 | | |
| Adjusted for changes in specific prices | 1.02 | 1.59 | 1.33 | | |
| Net assets at year-end: | | | | | |
| As reported | $ 5,652 | $ 4,776 | $ 3,703 | | |
| Adjusted for general inflation | 9,155 | 8,390 | 7,199 | | |
| Adjusted for changes in specific prices | 9,563 | 9,320 | 7,927 | | |
| Unrealized gain from excess of amounts owed over cash, securities and receivables, resulting from decline in purchasing power | $ 668 | $ 811 | $ 814 | | |
| Excess of the increase in the specific prices of inventories and plant, property and equipment held during the year over the increase in the general price level | $ 219 | $ 238 | $ 117 | | |
| Cash dividends per common share: | | | | | |
| As reported | $ 2.60 | $ 2.45 | $ 2.25 | $ 2.05 | $ 1.94 |
| Adjusted for general inflation | 2.60 | 2.70 | 2.82 | 2.86 | 2.91 |
| Market price per common share at year-end: | | | | | |
| As reported | $ 33½ | $ 51⅝ | $ 38¾ | $ 30¼ | $ 30¾ |
| Adjusted for general inflation | 32⅜ | 54⅜ | 46 | 40⅝ | 45 |
| Average Consumer Price Index | 272.4 | 246.8 | 217.4 | 195.4 | 181.5 |

Adjusted data expressed in average 1981 dollars.

# Management's Discussion and Analysis

## Financial Condition

During the past three years Tenneco has accelerated the trend of increasing capital expenditures in its energy businesses. Energy expenditures were $2.0 billion in 1981 compared to $695 million in 1978, an increase of 187% or a 42% annual compound growth rate per year. Overall capital expenditures increased 134%, assets rose 68%, common stockholders' equity was up 76% and net income increased 80% during this three year period. Funds required to support this major expansion program were generated through a combination of internally generated funds, short and long-term borrowings and equity financings. Tenneco has continued to employ leverage in its capital structure to meet its expansion requirements. During this growth period, Tenneco's debt ratio as a percent of capitalization did show slight improvement as shown in the following table:

| | December 31, | | | |
| --- | --- | --- | --- | --- |
| | 1978 | 1979 | 1980 | 1981 |
| Long-Term Debt . . . . . . . . . . . | 49.0% | 46.1% | 46.6% | 47.4% |
| Preferred and Preference Stock | 5.7 | 5.2 | 6.8 | 5.6 |
| Common Stockholders' Equity | 45.3 | 48.7 | 46.6 | 47.0 |
| Capitalization. . . . . . . . . . . . . . | 100.0% | 100.0% | 100.0% | 100.0% |
| Short-Term Debt to Capitalization (Including Short-Term Debt) . . . . . . . . . | 10.4% | 11.8% | 8.5% | 9.1% |

In addition to the issuance of equity securities, which were used primarily in major acquisitions, common stockholders' equity increased $1.1 billion over this three-year period due to the reinvestment of earnings in the business.

Tenneco's funds from operations increased from $1.0 billion in 1978 to $2.1 billion in 1981 or 112%. This increase is primarily attributable to the expanding energy operations. As shown in the following table, external funds were required to supplement funds provided from operations to meet the requirements of the capital expenditure and acquisition programs:

| | (Millions) | | | |
| --- | --- | --- | --- | --- |
| | Year Ended December 31, | | | Cumulative Total |
| | 1979 | 1980 | 1981 | |
| Long-Term Debt-Incurred . . . . . | $369 | $1,606 | $938 | $2,913 |
| -Retired . . . . . . | (322) | (630) | (463) | (1,415) |
| Net Long-Term Debt . . . . . . . . . | 47 | 976 | 475 | 1,498 |
| Preference Stock Issued . . . . . | — | 260 | — | 260 |
| Common Stock Issued . . . . . . . | 197 | 424 | 475 | 1,096 |
| Equity Financing . . . . . . . . . . . | 197 | 684 | 475 | 1,356 |
| Net Financings . . . . . . . . . . | $244 | $1,660 | $990 | $2,854 |

Long-term debt financings of $2.9 billion consisted of bank borrowings, public offerings and private placements. In addition to the above, $473 million of long-term debt was assumed in the Houston Oil & Minerals acquisition.

Equity financings of $1.4 billion were utilized for major acquisitions. In May 1980, Southwestern Life Corporation was acquired in consideration for $260 million of preference stock and $393 million of common stock. In April 1981, Houston Oil & Minerals Corporation was acquired for $417 million of common stock. The remaining common stock issued resulted principally from sales to the employee benefit plans, the shareholder reinvestment plan and the exercise of warrants and associated stock sales.

Working capital at year-end 1981, 1980, and 1979 totaled $348 million, $459 million, and $283 million, respectively. During this period minimum levels were maintained through improved management controls and the reliance on short-term borrowings to fund day-to-day operations. Working capital decreased $111 million in 1981, increased $176 million in 1980, and decreased $448 million in 1979, for an aggregate reduction of $383 million over the last three years. During this three year period, the most significant working capital changes were (i) an increase in inventories ($246 million) due principally to an increase in the cost of oil field materials and supplies and the lack of demand for construction and farm equipment; (ii) an increase in natural gas storage volumes and prepayments for natural gas ($300 million); (iii) an increase in notes and accounts receivable ($723 million) resulting from higher oil and gas prices; (iv) an increase in accounts payable ($1,003 million) primarily due to the rise in cost of purchased gas by the pipeline companies and increased other costs from inflation as well as expanded operations; (v) an increase in deferred federal income taxes ($205 million) due to increased installment sales of construction and farm equipment and progress on shipbuilding contracts; and (vi) an increase in short-term debt ($341 million).

Tenneco's estimated capital expenditures for 1982 are approximately $2.4 billion. The major portion of these expenditures will continue to be applied to energy-related businesses with the majority of funds provided from operations. Funds generated from the sale of certain assets, including Tenneco's Canadian oil and gas properties will also be available for use in the capital program. Approximately $1.7 billion will be required over the next several years to complete projects authorized at December 31, 1981, and substantial commitments have been made in connection with these projects. Of this amount, approximately $700 million is included in the 1982 capital expenditure program.

## Results of Operations

### Years 1981 and 1980

**Revenues.** Net sales and operating revenues for 1981 totaled $15.5 billion, a 17% increase over the $13.2 billion recorded in 1980. Tenneco's energy divisions recorded a $2.3 billion increase during that period, of which oil exploration and production operations contributed $866 million. Of that amount $549 million resulted principally from increased prices of natural gas and crude oil. Production of crude oil increased 11% which led to an increase of $90 million in revenues from such production. Additionally, the 1981 revenue increase included $200 million from the Houston Oil & Minerals acquisition.

Tenneco's natural gas pipeline business reported increased revenues of $836 million due primarily to the recovery of higher gas costs and higher rates. Revenues from the oil processing and marketing, chemicals business rose $550 million due primarily to higher prices for refined products. Increased revenue of $286 million was reported by Tenneco's manufacturing business due primarily to an increase in the volume of ship construction contracts and greater progress on existing contracts. Revenues from the Company's fiber, food, land and other operations increased $34 million.

**Income (Before Interest and Federal Income Taxes).** Income was $1,954 million for 1981 compared to $1,596 million for 1980, an increase of 22%. Although income was up $358 million, benefits derived from reductions in LIFO inventory quantities (approximately $90 million) and foreign currency exchange gains ($95 million) made significant contributions to this improvement. Income from Tenneco's energy businesses was $1,542 million, up $298 million from 1980's $1,244 million. Oil exploration and production operations contributed to the most significant improvement with an increase of $315 million over

last year. Income from new production and higher price realizations from crude oil and natural gas contributed to the majority of the increase. Revenues from higher volumes and prices of these products were partially offset by increased operating expenses of $549 million, including increased excise tax on oil production of $133 million.

Natural gas pipelines income increased $30 million from $304 million in 1980 to $334 million. The increase was primarily a result of higher rates. The oil processing and marketing, chemicals business income was down $101 million due primarily to lower profit margins on refined products partly offset by a benefit derived from a reduction in LIFO inventory quantities and lower prices for chemical products.

Income from manufacturing, insurance, and Tenneco's fiber, food, land and other businesses increased over last year. Improved income from manufacturing of $57 million was due primarily to higher profit margins and volumes of business for shipbuilding and automotive operations. While construction and

# Quarterly Data    (Unaudited)

QUARTERLY FINANCIAL DATA

| Quarter | Net sales and operating revenues | Income before interest and federal income taxes | Net income | Earnings per average share of common stock |
|---|---|---|---|---|
| **1981** | | | | |
| 1st | $ 3,809 | $  446 | $194 | $1.51 |
| 2nd | 3,776 | 462 | 203 | 1.50 |
| 3rd | 3,585 | 452 | 156 | 1.09 |
| 4th | 4,292 | 594 | 260 | 1.91 |
| | 15,462 | 1,954 | 813 | 6.01 |
| **1980** | | | | |
| 1st | 3,316 | 416 | 178 | 1.62 |
| 2nd | 3,201 | 406 | 186 | 1.52 |
| 3rd | 3,068 | 359 | 162 | 1.25 |
| 4th | 3,641 | 415 | 200 | 1.56 |
| | $13,226 | $1,596 | $726 | $5.95 |

QUARTERLY PER SHARE MARKET PRICES AND DIVIDENDS

| | Common Stock | | | $7.40 Preference Stock | | | $11.00 Preference Stock | | |
|---|---|---|---|---|---|---|---|---|---|
| | Market Prices | | | Market Prices | | | Market Prices | | |
| Quarter | High | Low | Dividends | High | Low | Dividends | High | Low | Dividends |
| **1981** | | | | | | | | | |
| 1st | $51⅞ | $44¼ | $.65 | $66¼ | $63 | $1.85 | $88 | $81 | $2.75 |
| 2nd | 48 | 36¾ | .65 | 65 | 58 | 1.85 | 86¼ | 79 | 2.75 |
| 3rd | 43⅝ | 30¾ | .65 | 60 | 52 | 1.85 | 80¾ | 71 | 2.75 |
| 4th | 35¼ | 29⅞ | .65 | 61 | 50¾ | 1.85 | 85 | 71½ | 2.75 |
| **1980** | | | | | | | | | |
| 1st | 44¾ | 31¼ | .60 | 78 | 56½ | 1.85 | * | * | * |
| 2nd | 41⅝ | 32½ | .60 | 77¾ | 56⅝ | 1.85 | * | * | * |
| 3rd | 44¾ | 39 | .60 | 74 | 61 | 1.85 | 97¼ | 87 | 2.75 |
| 4th | 58⅜ | 41½ | .65 | 65½ | 60⅝ | 1.85 | 90¼ | 81 | 2.75 |

*$11.00 Preference Stock was issued May 1, 1980.
Source of Market Prices: National Quotation Bureau Incorporated          Principal Market: New York Stock Exchange

farm equipment sales volumes continued to decline in 1981, income increased slightly due to cost reduction programs, foreign currency gains and the reduction in LIFO inventory quantities. Income from insurance operations increased $25 million as a result of higher sales and the inclusion of Southwestern Life Insurance results for a full year in 1981. Income from the Company's fiber, food, land and other businesses rose $32 million due principally to investment gains from foreign currency hedge transactions and reacquiring long-term debt at a discount.

**Foreign Operations.** Tenneco's international businesses continued to face adverse business conditions in 1981. Net sales from foreign operations were approximately $3.0 billion and $2.9 billion for 1981 and 1980, respectively. Corresponding net income was $7 million and $77 million, respectively. The 1981 decline in income from operations was partially offset by foreign currency exchange gains of $81 million, mostly related to construction and farm equipment operations.

**Interest Expense.** Interest incurred was $279 million greater in 1981 than 1980 due principally to substantially higher interest rates ($88 million), increased borrowings ($139 million), and debt assumed in the Houston Oil & Minerals acquisition ($52

million). Partially offsetting this rise was an increase in interest capitalized of $71 million resulting primarily from a greater number of oil and gas properties under development and an increase in the capitalization rate.

**Federal Income Taxes.** The total federal income tax provision increased $63 million in 1981 due primarily to a higher level of income in the United States. Current taxes declined $139 million due primarily to the increased deduction for intangible oil and gas drilling costs which were offset by increased deferred tax expense. Investment tax credit increased $47 million over 1980 to $102 million, substantially all of which will be utilized through a carryback claim for refund of prior years tax payments. While foreign operations were basically in a break-even position, operating losses in certain foreign countries could not be utilized for tax purposes in 1981. The effective tax rate was 36% in 1981 compared to 35% in 1980.

**Earnings Per Share.** Net income to common stock increased 11% over 1980 but earnings per share increased 1%, from $5.95 in 1980 to $6.01 in 1981. The additional shares issued in the Houston Oil & Minerals acquisition increased the average shares outstanding 6%, and had a dilutive effect on 1981 results.

# QUESTIONS

1. How does information from the balance sheet help users of the financial statements?
2. A recent financial magazine indicated that a drug company had good financial flexibility. What is meant by financial flexibility and why is it important?
3. What are the major limitations of the balance sheet as a source of information?
4. State the generally accepted accounting principle (standard) applicable to the balance sheet valuation of each of the following assets.
   (a) Marketable securities.
   (b) Prepaid expenses.
   (c) Trade accounts receivable.
   (d) Land.
   (e) Inventories.
5. In what section of the balance sheet should the following items appear, and what balance sheet terminology would you use?
   (a) Investment in copyrights.
   (b) Employees' pension fund (consisting of cash and securities).
   (c) Premium on capital stock.
   (d) Long-term investments (pledged against bank loans payable).
   (e) Treasury stock (entered at cost, which is below par).
   (f) Checking account at bank.
   (g) Land (held as an investment).
   (h) Reserve for sinking fund.
   (i) Unamortized premium on bonds payable.
6. Where should the following items be shown on the balance sheet, if shown at all?
   (a) Merchandise out on consignment.
   (b) Pension fund on deposit with a trustee (under a trust revocable at depositor's option).
   (c) Goodwill.
   (d) Accumulated depreciation of plant and equipment.

(e) Materials in transit—f.o.b. destination.

(f) Allowance for doubtful accounts receivable.

(g) Merchandise held on consignment.

(h) Advances received on sales contract.

(i) Cash surrender value of life insurance.

(j) Accommodation endorsement on note.

7. What is the relationship between a current asset and a current liability?

8. The creditors of Marco company agree to accept promissory notes for the amount of its indebtedness with a proviso that two-thirds of the annual profits must be applied to their liquidation. How should these notes be reported on the balance sheet of the issuing company? Give a reason for your answer.

9. What are some of the techniques of disclosure for the balance sheet?

10. The president of your company has recently read an article that disturbs him greatly. The author of this article stated that "although the balance sheet and income statement balance to the penny, they are full of estimates and subject to material error." Indicate items found in these statements that are based on estimates and explain why you must resort to "guessing" these amounts.

11. What are the major types of subsequent events? Indicate how each of the following "subsequent events" would be reported.

(a) Death of the company's chief executive officer (CEO).

(b) Settlement of a four-week strike at additional wage costs.

(c) Settlement of a federal income tax case at considerably more tax than anticipated at year-end.

(d) Change in the product mix from consumer goods to industrial goods.

(e) Collection of a note written off in a prior period.

(f) Issuance of a large preferred stock offering.

(g) Acquisition of a company in a different industry.

(h) Destruction of a major plant in a flood.

12. What is a gain contingency? A loss contingency? Give two examples of each.

13. What is the difference between the report form and the account form for the purpose of balance sheet presentation?

14. What is a "Summary of Significant Accounting Policies"?

15. What types of contractual obligations must be disclosed in great detail in the footnotes to the balance sheet? Why do you think these detailed provisions should be disclosed?

16. What is the purpose of the statement of changes in financial position? How does it differ from a balance sheet or income statement?

17. The net income for the year for Sundance Company is $810,000, but the statement of changes in financial position indicates that the resources provided by operations is $880,000. What might account for the difference?

18. Each of the following items must be considered in preparing a statement of changes in financial position. State where each item is to be reported in the statement, if at all.

(a) Uncollectible accounts receivable in the amount of $14,000 were written off against the Allowance for Doubtful Accounts.

(b) During the year, 1,000 shares of preferred stock with a stated value of $5 a share were issued at $40 per share.

(c) The company had a net income for the year of $80,000. Depreciation expense amounted to $16,000 and bond premium amortization to $6,000.

19. What is the profession's recommendation in regard to the use of the term "surplus"? Explain.

20. One benefit of the conceptual framework is that users will better understand the criteria employed to report information in a certain way. What guides might accountants use to provide a basis for decisions on the optimal number of asset and liability items to be reported?

21. What major change in the statement of changes in financial position may occur in the near future? Explain.

# CASES

**C5–1** The assets of Blair, Inc. are presented below:

Blair, Inc.
BALANCE SHEET
December 31, 1984

**Assets**

Current Assets

| | | |
|---|---|---|
| Cash | | $ 70,000 |
| Unclaimed payroll checks | | 17,500 |
| Marketable securities (cost $20,000) at market | | 24,500 |
| Accounts receivable (less bad debt reserve) | | 75,000 |
| Inventories—at lower of cost (determined by the next-in, first-out method) or market | | 250,000 |
| Total current assets | | 437,000 |

Tangible Assets

| | | |
|---|---|---|
| Land (less accumulated depreciation) | | 80,000 |
| Buildings and equipment | $800,000 | |
| Less accumulated depreciation | 300,000 | 500,000 |
| Net tangible assets | | 580,000 |

Long-Term Investments

| | | |
|---|---|---|
| Stocks and bonds | | 100,000 |
| Treasury stock | | 40,000 |
| Total long-term investments | | 140,000 |

Other Assets

| | | |
|---|---|---|
| Discount on bonds payable | | 14,200 |
| Claim against U.S. government (pending in 3rd Dist.) | | 975,000 |
| Total other assets | | 989,200 |
| Total Assets | | $2,146,200 |

**Instructions**

Indicate the deficiencies, if any, in the foregoing assets of Blair, Inc.

**C5–2** Presented below is the balance sheet of Lockstep Corporation:

Lockstep Corporation
BALANCE SHEET
December 31, 1984

**Assets**

| | | |
|---|---|---|
| Current assets: | | |
| Cash | $10,000 | |
| Marketable securities | 8,000 | |
| Accounts receivable | 25,000 | |
| Merchandise inventory | 20,000 | |
| Supplies inventory | 4,000 | |
| Stock investment in Subsidiary Company | 20,000 | $ 87,000 |

| | | |
|---|---:|---:|
| Investments: | | |
| Treasury stock | | 26,000 |
| Property, plant, and equipment: | | |
| Buildings and land | 71,000 | |
| Less: Reserve for depreciation | 20,000 | 51,000 |
| Other assets: | | |
| Cash surrender value of life insurance | | 18,000 |
| | | $182,000 |

### Liabilities and Capital

| | | |
|---|---:|---:|
| Current liabilities: | | |
| Accounts payable | $12,000 | |
| Reserve for income taxes | 14,000 | |
| Customers' accounts with credit balances | 1 | $ 26,001 |
| Deferred credits: | | |
| Unamortized premium on bonds payable | | 2,000 |
| Long-term liabilities: | | |
| Bonds payable | | 46,000 |
| Total liabilities | | 74,001 |
| Capital stock: | | |
| Capital stock, par $5 | 75,000 | |
| Earned surplus | 24,999 | |
| Cash dividends declared | 8,000 | 107,999 |
| | | $182,000 |

## Instructions

Indicate your criticism of the balance sheet presented above. State briefly the proper treatment of the item criticized.

**C5–3** In an examination of the Dandy Corporation as of December 31, 1984, you have learned that the following situations exist. No entries have been made in the accounting records.

1. The corporation erected its present factory building in 1969. Depreciation was calculated by the straight-line method, using an estimated life of 35 years. Early in 1984, the board of directors conducted a careful survey and estimated that the factory building had a remaining useful life of 25 years as of January 1, 1984.

2. An additional assessment of 1983 income taxes was levied and paid in 1984.

3. When calculating the accrual for officers' salaries at December 31, 1984, it was discovered that the accrual for officers' salaries for December 31, 1983, had been overstated.

4. On December 15, 1984, the Dandy Corporation declared a common stock dividend of 1,000 shares per 100,000 of its common stock outstanding, payable February 1, 1985, to the common stockholders of record December 31, 1984.

5. Dandy Corporation, which is on a calendar-year basis, changed its inventory method as of January 1, 1984. The inventory for December 31, 1983, was costed by the average method, and the inventory for December 31, 1984, was costed by the FIFO method.

6. Dandy Corporation has guaranteed the payment of interest on the 20-year first mortgage bonds of the Hesston Company, an affiliate. Outstanding bonds of the Hesston Company amount to $150,000 with interest payable at 10% per annum, due June 1 and December 1 of each year. The bonds were issued by the Hesston Company on December 1, 1980, and all interest payments have been met by the company with the exception of the payment due December 1, 1984. The Dandy Corporation states that it will pay the defaulted interest to the bondholders on January 15, 1985.

7. During the year 1984, the Dandy Corporation was named as a defendant in a suit for damages by the Short Company for breach of contract. The case was decided in favor of Short Company, and it was awarded $80,000 damages. At the time of the audit, the case was under appeal to a higher court.

**Instructions**

Describe fully how each of the items above should be reported in the financial statements of Dandy Corporation for the year 1984.

**C5–4** The following items were brought to your attention during the course of the year-end audit:

1. The client expects to recover a substantial amount in connection with a pending refund claim for a prior year's taxes. Although the claim is being contested, counsel for the company has confirmed this expectation.

2. Your client is a defendant in a patent infringement suit involving a material amount; you have received from the client's counsel a statement that the loss can be reasonably estimated and that a reasonable possibility of a loss exists.

3. Cash includes a substantial sum specifically set aside for immediate reconstruction of plant and renewal of machinery.

4. Because of a general increase in the number of labor disputes and strikes, both within and outside the industry, it is very likely that the client will suffer a costly strike in the near future.

5. Trade accounts receivable include a large number of customers' notes, many of which had been renewed several times and may have to be renewed continually for some time in the future. The interest is settled on each maturity date and the makers are in good credit standing.

6. At the beginning of the year the client entered into a ten-year nonrenewable lease agreement. Provisions in the lease require the client to make substantial reconditioning and restoration expenditures at the termination of the lease.

7. Inventory includes retired equipment, some at regularly depreciated book value, and some at scrap or sale value.

**Instructions**

For each of the situations above describe the accounting treatment you recommend for the current year. Justify your recommended treatment for each situation.

**C5–5** At December 31, 1983, Jemco, Inc. has assets of $9,000,000, liabilities of $6,000,000, common stock of $2,000,000 (representing 2,000,000 shares of $1.00 par common stock), and retained earnings of $1,000,000. Net sales for the year 1983 were $18,000,000 and net income was $800,000. As auditors of this company, you are making a review of subsequent events of this company on February 13, 1984 and find the following.

1. On February 3, 1984, one of Jemco's customers declared bankruptcy. At December 31, 1983, this company owed Jemco $200,000, of which $20,000 was paid in January, 1984.

2. On January 18, 1984, one of the three major plants of the client burned.

3. On January 23, 1984, a strike was called at one of Jemco's largest plants which halted 30% of its production. As of today (February 13) the strike has not been settled.

4. A major electronics enterprise has introduced a line of products that would compete directly with Jemco's primary line, now being produced in a specially designed new plant. Because of manufacturing innovations, the competitor has been able to achieve quality similar to that of Jemco's products, but at a price 50% lower. Jemco officials say they will meet the lower prices, which are high enough to cover variable manufacturing and selling costs but which permit recovery of only a portion of fixed costs.

5. Merchandise traded in the open market is recorded in the company's records at $1.40 per unit on December 31, 1983. This price had prevailed for two weeks, after release of an official market report that predicted vastly enlarged supplies; however, no purchases were

made at $1.40. The price throughout the preceding year had been about $2.00, which was the level experienced over several years. On January 18, 1984, the price returned to $2.00, after public disclosure of an error in the official calculations of the prior December, correction of which destroyed the expectations of excessive supplies. Inventory at December 31, 1983 was on a cost or market basis.

**6.** On February 1, 1984, the board of directors adopted a resolution accepting the offer of an investment banker to guarantee the marketing of $1,000,000 of preferred stock.

**Instructions**

State in each case what notice, if any, you would make in your report affecting the year 1983.

**C5–6** The financial statement below was prepared by employees of your client, Schroeder Manufacturing Company. The statement is unaccompanied by footnotes.

Schroeder Manufacturing Company
BALANCE SHEET
As of November 30, 1984

| | Cost | Depreciation | Value | |
|---|---|---|---|---|
| **Current assets** | | | | |
| Cash | | | $ 100,000 | |
| Accounts receivable (less allowance of $15,000 for doubtful accounts) | | | 319,900 | |
| Inventories | | | 2,554,000 | $2,973,900 |
| **Less current liabilities** | | | | |
| Accounts payable | | | 206,400 | |
| Accrued payroll | | | 8,260 | |
| Accrued interest on mortgage note | | | 12,000 | |
| Estimated taxes payable | | | 66,000 | 292,660 |
| Net working capital | | | | 2,681,240 |
| **Property, plant, and equipment (at cost)** | | | | |
| Land and buildings | $ 983,300 | $310,000 | 673,300 | |
| Machinery and equipment | 1,135,700 | 568,699 | 567,001 | |
| | $2,119,000 | $878,699 | | 1,240,301 |
| **Deferred charges** | | | | |
| Prepaid taxes and other expenses | | | 11,700 | |
| Unamortized discount on mortgage note | | | 10,800 | 22,500 |
| Total net working capital and noncurrent assets | | | | 3,944,041 |
| **Less deferred liabilities** | | | | |
| Mortgage note payable | | | 300,000 | |
| Unearned revenue | | | 1,898,000 | 2,198,000 |
| Total net assets | | | | $1,746,041 |
| **Stockholders' equity** | | | | |
| 10% Preferred stock at par value | | | | $ 400,000 |
| Common stock at par value | | | | 697,000 |
| Paid-in surplus | | | | 210,000 |
| Retained earnings | | | | 483,641 |
| Treasury stock at cost (400 shares) | | | | (44,600) |
| Total stockholders' equity | | | | $1,746,041 |

**Instructions**

Indicate the deficiencies, if any, in the balance sheet above.

**C5-7** Below are the account titles of a number of debit and credit accounts as they might appear on the balance sheet of Garden Products Corp. as of October 31, 1984.

| Debits | Credits |
|---|---|
| Interest accrued on U.S. government securities | Capital stock—preferred |
| Notes receivable | 11% first mortgage bonds due in 1991 |
| Petty cash fund | Preferred stock dividend, payable Nov. 1, 1984 |
| U.S. government securities | Allowance for doubtful accounts receivable |
| Treasury stock | Provision for federal income taxes |
| Unamortized bond discount | Customers advances (on contracts to be |
| Cash in bank | completed in 1985) |
| Land | Appropriation for possible decline in value of |
| Inventory of operating parts and supplies | raw materials inventory |
| Inventory of raw materials | Premium on bonds redeemable in 1984 |
| Patents | Officers' 1984 bonus accrued |
| Cash and U.S. government bonds set aside for | Accrued payroll |
| property additions | Provision for renegotiation of U.S. government |
| Investment in subsidiary | contracts |
| Accounts receivable | Notes payable |
| U.S. government contracts | Accrued interest on bonds |
| Regular | Accumulated depreciation |
| Installments—due in 1984 | Accounts payable |
| Installments—due in 1985-1986 | Capital in excess of par |
| Goodwill | Accrued interest on notes payable |
| Inventory of finished goods | 8% first mortgage bonds to be redeemed in |
| Inventory of work in process | 1984 out of current assets |
| Deficit | |

**Instructions**

Select the current asset and current liability items from among these debits and credits. If there appear to be certain borderline cases that you are unable to classify without further information, mention them and explain your difficulty, or give your reasons for making questionable classifications, if any.

(AICPA adapted)

**C5-8** The following year-end financial statements were prepared by the Advanced Micro Corporation's bookkeeper. Advanced Micro Corporation operates a chain of retail stores.

Advanced Micro Corporation
BALANCE SHEET
June 30, 1984

**Assets**

| | |
|---|---|
| Current assets | |
| Cash | $ 150,000 |
| Notes receivable | 50,000 |
| Accounts receivable, less reserve for | |
| doubtful accounts | 75,000 |
| Inventories | 395,500 |
| Investment securities (at cost) | 100,000 |
| Total current assets | 770,500 |

| | | |
|---|---:|---:|
| Property, plant, and equipment | | |
| Land (at cost) (note 1) | $180,000 | |
| Buildings, at cost less accumulated depreciation of $350,000 | 500,000 | |
| Equipment, at cost less accumulated depreciation of $180,000 | 400,000 | 1,080,000 |
| Intangibles | | 450,000 |
| Other assets | | |
| Prepaid expenses | | 16,405 |
| Total assets | | $2,316,905 |

### Liabilities and Owners' Equity

| | | |
|---|---:|---:|
| Current liabilities | | |
| Accounts payable | | $    35,500 |
| Estimated income taxes payable | | 160,000 |
| Contingent liability on discounted notes receivable | | 75,000 |
| Total current liabilities | | 270,500 |
| Long-term liabilities | | |
| 15% serial bonds, $50,000 due annually on December 31 | | |
| Maturity value | $865,000 | |
| Less unamortized discount | 35,000 | 830,000 |
| Total liabilities | | 1,100,500 |
| Owners' equity | | |
| Common stock, stated value $10 (authorized and issued, 75,000 shares) | 750,000 | |
| Retained earnings | | |
| Appropriated (note 2) | $120,000 | |
| Free | 346,405 | 466,405 | 1,216,405 |
| Total liabilities and owners' equity | | $2,316,905 |

---

**Advanced Micro Corporation**
**INCOME STATEMENT**
**As at June 30, 1984**

| | | | |
|---|---:|---:|---:|
| Sales | | | $2,500,000 |
| Interest revenue | | | 6,000 |
| Total revenue | | | 2,506,000 |
| Cost of goods sold | | | 1,780,000 |
| Gross margin | | | 726,000 |
| Operating expenses | | | |
| Selling expenses | | | |
| Salaries | $ 95,000 | | |
| Advertising | 85,000 | | |
| Sales returns and allowances | 50,000 | $230,000 | |
| General and administrative expenses | | | |
| Wages | 84,000 | | |
| Property taxes | 38,000 | | |
| Depreciation and amortization | 86,000 | | |
| Rent (note 3) | 75,000 | | |
| Interest on serial bonds | 48,000 | 331,000 | 561,000 |
| Income before income taxes | | | 165,000 |
| Income taxes | | | 80,000 |
| Net income | | | $    85,000 |

Notes to financial statements:
Note 1. Includes a future store site acquired during the year at a cost of $90,000.
Note 2. Retained earnings in the amount of $120,000 have been set aside to finance expansion.
Note 3. During the year the corporation acquired certain equipment under a long-term lease.

**Instructions**

Identify and discuss the defects in the financial statements above with respect to terminology, disclosure, and classification. Your discussion should explain why you consider them to be defects. Do not prepare revised statements.

(AICPA adapted)

# EXERCISES

**E5–1** Presented below are a number of balance sheet accounts of Jill Castleberry Inc.:

1. Investment in Preferred Stock
2. Treasury Stock
3. Common Stock Distributable
4. Accumulated Depreciation
5. Warehouse in Process of Construction
6. Petty Cash
7. Deficit

8. Marketable Securities (short-term)
9. Income Taxes Payable
10. Accrued Interest on Notes Payable
11. Unearned Subscription Revenue
12. Work in Process
13. Accrued Vacation Pay
14. Cash Dividends Payable

**Instructions**

For each of the accounts above, indicate the proper balance sheet classification. In the case of borderline items, indicate the additional information that would be required to determine the proper classification.

**E5–2** Presented below are the captions of a balance sheet:

A. Current assets
B. Investments
C. Property, plant, and equipment
D. Intangible assets
E. Other assets

F. Current liabilities
G. Noncurrent liabilities
H. Capital stock
I. Additional paid-in capital
J. Retained earnings

**Instructions**

Indicate by letter where each of the following items would be classified:

1. Preferred stock
2. Goodwill
3. Wages payable
4. Trade accounts payable
5. Buildings
6. Marketable securities
7. Current portion of long-term debt
8. Premium on bonds payable
9. Allowance for doubtful accounts
10. Appropriation for contingencies

11. Cash surrender value of life insurance
12. Notes payable (due next year)
13. Common stock
14. Land
15. Bond sinking fund
16. Merchandise inventory
17. Office supplies
18. Prepaid insurance
19. Bonds payable
20. Taxes payable

**E5–3** Assume that Peterose, Inc. has the following accounts at the end of the current year.

1. Common Stock

2. Discount on Bonds Payable

3. Treasury Stock (at cost)
4. Common Stock Subscribed
5. Raw Materials
6. Preferred Stock Investments—Long-term
7. Unearned Rent Income
8. Appropriation for Plant Expansion
9. Work in Process
10. Copyrights
11. Buildings
12. Notes Receivable (short-term)
13. Cash
14. Accrued Salaries Payable
15. Accumulated Depreciation—Buildings
16. Notes Receivable Discounted
17. Cash Restricted for Plant Expansion
18. Land Held for Future Plant Site
19. Allowance for Doubtful Accounts—Accounts Receivable
20. Retained Earnings—Unappropriated
21. Discount on Common Stock
22. Unearned Subscription Income
23. Receivables—Officers (due in one year)
24. Finished Goods
25. Accounts Receivable
26. Bonds Payable (due in four years)
27. Stocks Subscriptions Receivable

**Instructions**

Prepare a balance sheet in good form (no monetary amounts are necessary).

**E5–4** Assume that Safeway Enterprises uses the following headings on its balance sheet:

A. Current assets
B. Investments
C. Property, plant, and equipment
D. Intangible assets
E. Other assets
F. Current liabilities
G. Long-term liabilities
H. Capital stock
I. Paid-in capital in excess of par
J. Retained earnings

**Instructions**

Indicate by letter how each of the following usually should be classified. If an item should appear in a note to the financial statements, use the letter "N" to indicate this fact. If an item need not be reported at all on the balance sheet, use the letter "X."

1. Advances to suppliers.
2. Unearned rental income.
3. Treasury stock.
4. Unexpired insurance.
5. Stock owned in affiliated companies.
6. Unearned subscriptions revenue.
7. Premium on preferred stock.
8. Copyrights.
9. Petty cash fund.
10. Sale of large issue of common stock 15 days after balance sheet date.
11. Accrued interest on notes receivable.
12. Twenty-year issue of bonds payable which will mature within the next year. (No sinking fund exists and refunding is not planned.)
13. Machinery retired from use and held for sale.
14. Fully depreciated machine still in use.
15. Organization costs.
16. Salaries which company budget shows will be paid to employees within the next year.
17. Company is a defendant in a lawsuit for $1 million (possibility of loss is reasonably possible).
18. Discount on bonds payable. (Assume related to bonds payable in No. 12.)
19. Accrued interest on bonds payable.
20. Accumulated depreciation.

**E5–5** O'Reilly Company has decided to expand their operations. The bookkeeper recently completed the balance sheet presented below in order to obtain additional funds for expansion.

O'Reilly Company
BALANCE SHEET
For the Year Ended 1984

| | |
|---|---:|
| Current assets | |
| Cash (net of bank overdraft of $40,000) | $180,000 |
| Accounts receivable (net) | 325,000 |
| Inventories at lower of average cost or market | 420,000 |
| Marketable securities—at market (cost $110,000) | 125,000 |
| Property, plant, and equipment | |
| Building (net) | 460,000 |
| Office equipment (net) | 185,000 |
| Land held for future use | 210,000 |
| Intangible assets | |
| Goodwill | 75,000 |
| Cash surrender value of life insurance | 64,000 |
| Prepaid expenses | 2,200 |
| Current liabilities | |
| Accounts payable | 95,000 |
| Notes payable (due next year) | 100,000 |
| Pension obligation | 71,000 |
| Rent payable | 85,000 |
| Premium on bonds payable | 68,000 |
| Long-term liabilities | |
| Bonds payable | 500,000 |
| Appropriation for plant expansion | 75,000 |
| Stockholders' equity | |
| Common stock, $1.00 par, authorized | |
| 400,000 shares, issued 305,000 | 305,000 |
| Additional paid-in capital | 70,000 |
| Retained earnings | ? |

### Instructions

Prepare a revised balance sheet given the available information. Assume that the accumulated depreciation balance for the buildings is $95,000 and for the office equipment, $55,000. The allowance for doubtful accounts has a balance of $25,000. The pension obligation is considered a long-term liability.

**E5–6** The bookkeeper for Pet Food Company has prepared the following balance sheet as of July 31, 1984:

Pet Food Company
BALANCE SHEET
As of July 31, 1984

| | | | |
|---|---:|---|---:|
| Cash | $ 64,000 | Notes and accounts payable | $ 41,000 |
| Accounts receivable (net) | 38,000 | Long-term liabilities | 64,000 |
| Inventories | 50,000 | Stockholders' equity | 141,000 |
| Equipment (net) | 73,000 | | |
| Patents | 21,000 | | |
| | $246,000 | | $246,000 |

The following additional information is provided:

1. Cash includes $800 in a petty cash fund and $10,000 in a bond sinking fund.

2. The net accounts receivable balance is comprised of the following three items: (a) accounts receivable—debit balances $45,000; (b) accounts receivable—credit balances $5,000; (c) allowance for doubtful accounts $2,000.

3. Merchandise inventory costing $2,400 was shipped out on consignment on July 31, 1984. The ending inventory balance does not include the consigned goods. Receivables in the amount of $3,200 were recognized on these consigned goods.

4. Equipment had a cost of $95,000 and an accumulated depreciation balance of $22,000.

5. Taxes payable of $4,000 were accrued on July 31. The Pet Food Company, however, had set up a cash fund to meet this obligation. This cash fund was not included in the cash balance, but was offset against the taxes payable amount.

**Instructions**

Prepare a corrected balance sheet as of July 31, 1984 from the available information.

**E5-7** The current asset and liability sections of the balance sheet of Serenity, Inc. appear as follows:

| | | Serenity, Inc. PARTIAL BALANCE SHEET December 31, 1984 | | | |
|---|---|---|---|---|---|
| Cash | | $ 30,000 | Accounts payable | $48,000 |
| Accounts receivable | $80,000 | | Notes payable | 70,000 |
| Less allowance for doubtful acounts | 6,000 | 74,000 | | |
| Inventories | | 170,000 | | |
| Prepaid expenses | | 10,000 | | |
| | | $284,000 | | $118,000 |

The following errors in the corporation's accounting have been discovered:

1. January 1985 cash disbursements entered as of December 1984 included payments of accounts payable in the amount of $37,000, on which a cash discount of 2% was taken.

2. The inventory included $24,000 of merchandise that had been received at December 31 but for which no purchase invoices had been received or entered. Of this amount, $12,000 had been received on consignment; the remainder was purchased f.o.b. destination, terms 2/10, n/30.

3. Sales for the first four days in January 1985 in the amount of $26,000 were entered in the sales book as of December 31, 1984. Of these, $20,000 were sales on account and the remainder were cash sales.

4. Cash, not including cash sales, collected in January 1985 and entered as of December 31, 1984, totaled $30,384. Of this amount, $20,384 was received on account after cash discounts of 2% had been deducted; the remainder represented the proceeds of a bank loan.

**Instructions**

(a) Restate the current asset and liability sections of the balance sheet in accordance with good accounting practice. (Assume that both accounts receivable and accounts payable are recorded gross.)

(b) State the net effect of your adjustments on Serenity, Inc.'s retained earnings balance.

**E5-8** Condensed financial data of Ceremony Company for the years ended December 31, 1983 and December 31, 1984, are presented on page 223.

Ceremony Company
Comparative Balance Sheet Data
As of December 31, 1983 and 1984

|  | 1983 | 1984 |
|---|---|---|
| Cash | $ 18,400 | $129,800 |
| Receivables, net | 49,000 | 83,200 |
| Inventories | 61,900 | 92,500 |
| Investments | 100,000 | 90,000 |
| Plant assets | 220,000 | 240,000 |
|  | $449,300 | $635,500 |
| Accounts payable | $ 67,300 | $100,000 |
| Mortgage payable | 73,500 | 50,000 |
| Accumulated depreciation | 50,000 | 30,000 |
| Common stock | 125,000 | 175,000 |
| Retained earnings | 133,500 | 280,500 |
|  | $449,300 | $635,500 |

Ceremony Company
INCOME STATEMENT
For the Year Ended December 31, 1984

| Sales | $300,000 | |
|---|---|---|
| Interest and other revenue | 10,000 | $310,000 |
| Less: | | |
| Cost of goods sold | $100,000 | |
| Selling and administrative expenses | 10,000 | |
| Depreciation | 22,000 | |
| Income taxes | 5,000 | |
| Interest charges | 3,000 | |
| Loss on sale of plant assets | 8,000 | 148,000 |
| Net income | | $162,000 |
| Dividends declared | | 15,000 |
| Income retained in business | | $147,000 |

Additional information:
    New plant assets costing $80,000 were purchased during the year. Investments were sold at book value.

**Instructions**
    From the foregoing information, prepare a statement of changes in financial position (working capital approach).

**E5–9** Presented below is a condensed version of the balance sheet for Pana Corporation for the last two years:

|  | 1984 | 1983 |
|---|---|---|
| Current assets | $320,000 | $245,000 |
| Investments | 60,000 | 71,000 |
| Equipment | 305,000 | 260,000 |
| Less accumulated depreciation | (110,000) | (98,000) |
| Current liabilities | 140,000 | 142,000 |
| Capital stock | 130,000 | 130,000 |
| Retained earnings | 305,000 | 206,000 |

Additional information:

Investments were sold at a loss (not extraordinary) of $3,000; no equipment was sold; cash dividends declared were $31,000; and net income was $130,000.

**Instructions**

Prepare a statement of changes in financial position for 1984 for Pana Corporation.

## PROBLEMS

**P5–1** Presented below is a list of accounts in alphabetical order.

| | |
|---|---|
| Accounts Receivable | Interest Receivable |
| Accrued Wages | Inventory—Beginning Inventory |
| Accumulated Depreciation—Buildings | Inventory—Ending Inventory |
| Accumulated Depreciation—Equipment | Land for Future Plant Site |
| Advances to Employees | Notes Payable |
| Advertising | Patent |
| Allowance for Doubtful Accounts | Pension Fund |
| Appropriation for Possible Inventory Price Declines | Pension Obligations |
| | Petty Cash |
| Appropriation for Plant Expansion | Preferred Stock |
| Bond Sinking Fund | Premium on Bonds Payable |
| Bonds Payable | Premium on Preferred Stock |
| Buildings | Prepaid Expenses |
| Cash in Bank | Purchases |
| Cash on Hand | Purchase Returns and Allowances |
| Cash Surrender Value of Life Insurance | Retained Earnings—Unappropriated |
| Commission Expense | Sales |
| Common Stock | Sales Discounts |
| Copyright | Sales Salaries |
| Dividends Payable | Temporary Investments |
| Equipment | Transportation-in |
| FICA Taxes Payable | Treasury Stock (at cost) |
| Gain on Sale of Equipment | Unearned Subscription Income |

**Instructions**

Prepare a balance sheet in good form (no monetary amounts are to be shown).

**P5–2** Presented below are a number of balance sheet items for Chortle, Inc. for the current year, 1984.

| | | | |
|---|---|---|---|
| Accumulated depreciation— | | Goodwill | $ 124,263 |
| equipment | $272,084 | Payroll taxes payable | 168,000 |
| Inventories | 225,468 | Bonds payable | 240,000 |
| Rent payable—short-term | 33,600 | Discount on bonds payable | 12,000 |
| Taxes payable | 70,541 | Cash | 240,000 |
| Long-term rental obligations | 460,296 | Land | 300,000 |
| Common stock, $.10 par value | 156,162 | Notes receivable | 627,905 |
| Preferred stock, $10 par value | 160,000 | Notes payable to banks | 241,652 |
| Prepaid expenses | 110,000 | Accounts payable | 701,244 |

| Equipment | $1,766,874 | Retained earnings | $ ? |
| Marketable securities | | Refundable federal and state | |
| (short-term) | 96,000 | income taxes | 92,632 |
| Accumulated depreciation— | | Unsecured notes payable | |
| building | 80,800 | (long term) | 1,633,154 |
| Building | 1,802,823 | | |

**Instructions**

Prepare a balance sheet in good form. Common stock authorized was 35,000,000 shares and preferred stock authorized was 30,000 shares. Assume that notes receivable and notes payable are short-term, unless stated otherwise.

**P5-3** Presented below is the balance sheet of Charity Corporation as of December 31, 1984:

Charity Corporation
BALANCE SHEET
December 31, 1984

**Assets**

| Building (note 1) | $1,425,000 |
| Land | 823,500 |
| Treasury stock (50,000 shares, no par) | 91,500 |
| Cash on hand | 187,500 |
| Assets allocated to trustee for plant expansion | |
| Cash in bank | 60,000 |
| U.S. Treasury notes, at cost | 165,000 |
| Accounts receivable | 130,500 |
| Inventories | 158,300 |
| Goodwill (note 2) | 108,000 |
| | $3,149,300 |

**Equities**

| Common stock, authorized and issued, 1,000,000 shares, no par | $1,650,000 |
| Notes payable (note 3) | 480,000 |
| Federal income taxes payable | 46,500 |
| Reserve for repairs of machinery (note 4) | 39,000 |
| Reserve for contingencies | 67,500 |
| Reserve for depreciation of building | 315,000 |
| Appreciation capital (note 1) | 288,000 |
| Retained earnings (unappropriated) | 263,300 |
| | $3,149,300 |

Note 1. Buildings are stated at cost, except for one building that was recorded at appraised value. The excess of appraisal value over cost was $288,000.

Note 2. Goodwill in the amount of $108,000 was recognized because the company believed that their book value was not an accurate representation of the fair market value of the company.

Note 3. Notes payable are long-term except for the current installment due of $15,000.

Note 4. A reserve for repairs was set up by a charge to expense. Upon consultation with the company's auditors, it was determined that this contingency did not meet the criteria of a loss contingency. The company still wishes to show this amount in stockholders' equity.

**Instructions**

Prepare a corrected balance sheet in good form.

**P5-4** Presented below is the balance sheet of Charlatan Corporation for the current year, 1984.

Charlatan Corporation
BALANCE SHEET
December 31, 1984

| | | | |
|---|---|---|---|
| Current assets | $ 435,000 | Current liabilities | $ 380,000 |
| Investments | 640,000 | Long-term liabilities | 1,040,000 |
| Property, plant, and equipment | 1,720,000 | Stockholders' equity | 1,680,000 |
| Intangible assets | 305,000 | | |
| | $3,100,000 | | $3,100,000 |

The following information is presented:

1. The current asset section includes: cash $100,000, accounts receivable $170,000 less $10,000 for allowance for doubtful accounts, inventories $180,000, and prepaid revenue $5,000. The cash balance is comprised of $116,000, less a bank overdraft of $16,000. Inventories are stated on the lower of FIFO cost or market.

2. The investments section includes the cash surrender value of a life insurance contract $40,000, investments in common stock, short-term $80,000 and long-term $140,000, bond sinking fund $200,000, and organization costs $180,000.

3. Property, plant, and equipment includes buildings $1,040,000 less accumulated depreciation $360,000, equipment $420,000 less accumulated depreciation $180,000, land $500,000, and land held for future use $300,000.

4. Intangible assets include a franchise $165,000, goodwill $100,000, and discount on bonds payable $40,000.

5. Current liabilities include accounts payable $90,000, notes payable—short-term $120,000 and long-term $80,000, taxes payable $40,000, and appropriation for short-term contingencies $50,000.

6. Long-term liabilities are comprised solely of 10% bonds payable due 1995.

7. Stockholders' equity has preferred stock, no par value, authorized 300,000 shares, issued 150,000 shares for $450,000, and common stock, $1.00 par value, authorized 400,000 shares, issued 100,000 shares at an average price of $10. In addition, the corporation has unappropriated retained earnings of $230,000.

**Instructions**

Prepare a balance sheet in good form.

**P5-5** The trial balance of Skyscraper Construction Co. and other related information for the year 1984 is presented on page 227.

Skyscraper Construction Co.
TRIAL BALANCE
December 31, 1984

| | | |
|---|---:|---:|
| Cash | $ 33,700 | |
| Accounts Receivable | 144,000 | |
| Allowance for Doubtful Accounts | | $ 5,940 |
| Prepaid Expenses | 1,820 | |
| Inventory | 270,000 | |
| Long-term Investments | 324,000 | |
| Land | 72,000 | |
| Construction Work in Progress | 108,000 | |
| Patents | 18,000 | |
| Equipment | 360,000 | |
| Accumulated Depreciation of Equipment | | 108,000 |
| Unamortized Discount on Bonds Payable | 7,200 | |
| Accounts Payable | | 162,000 |
| Accrued Expenses | | 3,600 |
| Notes Payable | | 72,000 |
| Bonds Payable | | 360,000 |
| Capital Stock | | 540,000 |
| Premium on Capital Stock | | 23,400 |
| Retained Earnings | | 37,280 |
| Reserve for Future Plant Expansion | | 26,500 |
| | $1,338,720 | $1,338,720 |

Additional information is given as follows:

1. The inventory has a replacement market value of $320,400. The LIFO method of inventory value is used.

2. The market value of the long-term investments that consist of stocks and bonds is $350,000.

3. The amount of the Construction Work in Progress account represents the costs expended to date on a building in the process of construction. (The company rents factory space at the present time.) The land on which the building is being constructed cost $72,000, as shown in the trial balance.

4. The patents were purchased by the company at a cost of $28,800 and are being amortized on a straight-line basis.

5. Of the unamortized discount on bonds payable, $600 will be amortized in 1985.

6. The notes payable represent bank loans that are secured by long-term investments carried at $144,000. These bank loans are due in 1985.

7. The bonds payable bear interest at 11% and are due January 1, 1995.

8. Six hundred thousand shares of common stock of a par value of $1.00 were authorized, of which 540,000 shares were issued and are outstanding.

9. The Reserve for Future Plant Expansion was created by action of the board of directors.

**Instructions**

Prepare a balance sheet as of December 31, 1984 so that all important information is fully disclosed.

P5–6 You have been engaged to examine the financial statements of Momentous Corporation for the year 1984. The bookkeeper who maintains the financial records has prepared all the unaudited financial statements for the corporation since its organization on January 2, 1978. The client provides you with the information below.

Momentous Corporation
BALANCE SHEET
As of December 31, 1984

| Assets | | Liabilities | |
|---|---|---|---|
| Current assets | $2,073,130 | Current liabilities | $ 951,765 |
| Other assets | 6,481,657 | Long-term liabilities | 1,500,000 |
| | | Capital | 6,103,022 |
| | $8,554,787 | | $8,554,787 |

An analysis of current assets discloses the following:

| | |
|---|---|
| Cash (restricted in the amount of $730,000 for plant expansion) | $1,363,195 |
| Investments in land | 106,500 |
| Accounts receivable less allowance of $48,000 | 118,710 |
| Inventories (LIFO flow assumption) | 484,725 |
| | $2,073,130 |

Other assets include

| | |
|---|---|
| Prepaid expenses | $ 48,730 |
| Plant and equipment less accumulated depreciation of $1,506,000 | 5,123,490 |
| Cash surrender value of life insurance policy | 90,198 |
| Unamortized bond discount | 47,130 |
| Notes receivable (short term) | 182,148 |
| Goodwill, at cost less amortization of $4,500 | 347,100 |
| Land | 642,861 |
| | $6,481,657 |

Current liabilities include

| | |
|---|---|
| Accounts payable | $ 480,000 |
| Notes payable (due, 1986) | 183,513 |
| Estimated income taxes payable | 150,000 |
| Premium on common stock | 138,252 |
| | $ 951,765 |

Long-term liabilities include

| | |
|---|---|
| Unearned revenue | $ 527,730 |
| Dividends payable (cash) | 222,270 |
| 6% Serial bonds payable ($150,000 maturing annually 1985–1989) | 750,000 |
| | $1,500,000 |

Capital includes

| | |
|---|---|
| Retained earnings (unappropriated) | $2,131,657 |
| Capital stock, par value $10; authorized 200,000 shares, 175,000 shares issued | 1,750,000 |
| Reserve for contingencies | 2,221,365 |
| | $6,103,022 |

The supplementary information below is also provided.

1. On May 1, 1984, the corporation issued $750,000 of bonds to finance plant expansion. The long-term bond agreement provided for the annual payment of principal and interest over five years. The existing plant was pledged as security for the loan.

2. The bookkeeper made the following mistakes:
   (a) In 1982, the ending inventory was overstated by $183,000. The ending inventories for 1983 and 1984 were correctly computed.

(b) In 1984, accrued wages in the amount of $330,000 were omitted from the balance sheet and these expenses were not charged on the income statement.

(c) In 1984, a gain of $175,000 (net of tax) on the sale of certain plant assets was credited directly to retained earnings.

3. A major competitor has introduced a line of products that will compete directly with Momentous' primary line, now being produced in a specially designed new plant. Because of manufacturing innovations, the competitor's line will be of comparable quality but priced 50% below the client's line. The competitor announced its new line on January 14, 1985. The client indicates that the company will meet the lower prices that are high enough to cover variable manufacturing and selling expenses, but permit recovery of only a portion of fixed costs.

4. You learned on January 28, 1985, prior to completion of the audit, of heavy damage because of a recent fire to one of the client's two plants; the loss will not be reimbursed by insurance. The newspapers described the event in detail.

**Instructions**

Prepare the balance sheet for Momentous Corporation in accordance with proper accounting principles. Describe the nature of any footnotes that might need to be prepared.

**P5–7** Olson, Inc. had the following condensed balance sheet at the end of operations for 1983:

Olson, Inc.
BALANCE SHEET
December 31, 1983

| | | | |
|---|---|---|---|
| Current assets | $ 37,500 | Current liabilities | $ 15,000 |
| Investments | 20,000 | Long-term notes payable | 16,500 |
| Plant assets (net) | 67,500 | Bonds payable | 25,000 |
| Land | 31,000 | Capital stock | 75,000 |
| | | Retained earnings | 24,500 |
| | $156,000 | | $156,000 |

During 1984 the following occurred:

1. Olson, Inc. sold part of its investment portfolio for $10,300. This transaction resulted in a gain of $300 for the firm. The company often sells and buys securities of this nature.

2. A tract of land was purchased for $6,000.

3. Bonds payable in the amount of $5,000 were retired at par.

4. An additional $10,000 in capital stock was issued at par.

5. Dividends totaling $7,500 were declared and paid to stockholders.

6. Net income for 1984 was $21,000 after allowing for depreciation of $9,000.

7. Land was purchased through the issuance of $18,000 in bonds.

**Instructions**

(a) Prepare a statement of changes in financial position (working capital approach) for 1984. A supporting schedule of working capital changes need not be prepared.

(b) Prepare the condensed balance sheet for Olson, Inc. as it would appear at December 31, 1984. Assume that current liabilities remained at $15,000.

(c) How might the statement of changes in financial position help the user of the financial statements?

# CHAPTER 6

# Accounting and the Time Value of Money

Would you like to be a millionaire? If you are 20 years old now, can save $100 every month, and can invest those savings to earn an after-tax rate of return of 1% per month (over 12% per year), you can be a millionaire before you're 59 years old. Or if you could invest just $10,000 today at that same interest rate, you would have over a million dollars by age 59. Such is the power of **interest,** especially when it is energized with a generous dosage of **time.** With interest rates in double digits, interest becomes one of the most significant factors affecting business decisions.

Business enterprises both invest and borrow large sums of money. The common characteristic in these two types of transactions is the **time value of the money** (that is, the interest factor) involved. The timing of the returns on the investment has an important effect on the worth of the investment (asset), and the timing of debt repayments has an effect on the value of the commitment (liability). Business people have become acutely aware of this timing factor and invest and borrow only after carefully analyzing the relative values of the cash outflows and inflows.

The accountant also is expected to make value measurements and to understand their implications. To do so, the accountant must understand and be able to measure the present value of future cash inflows and outflows. This measurement requires an understanding of compound interest, annuities, and present value concepts.

## ACCOUNTING APPLICATIONS

Compound interest, annuities, and present value concepts and procedures are relevant to accounting and to understanding much of the information in succeeding chapters of this text. Some of the applications involving accounting topics are:

1. **NOTES.** Valuing receivables and payables that carry no stated interest rate or a lower than market interest rate.
2. **LEASES.** Valuing assets to be capitalized under long-term leases and measuring the amount of the lease payments and annual leasehold amortization.
3. **AMORTIZATION OF PREMIUMS AND DISCOUNTS.** Measuring amortization of premium or discount on both bond investments and bonds payable.

**230**

4. **PENSIONS.** Measuring amortization, accruals, and interest equivalents relative to unfunded past or prior service cost.

5. **CAPITAL ASSETS.** Evaluating alternative investments by discounting cash flows. Determining the value of assets acquired under deferred payment contracts.

6. **SINKING FUNDS.** Determining the contributions necessary to accumulate a fund for debt retirements.

7. **BUSINESS COMBINATIONS.** Determining the value of receivables, payables, liabilities, accruals, and commitments acquired or assumed in a "purchase."

8. **DEPRECIATION.** Measuring depreciation charges under the sinking fund and the annuity methods.

9. **INSTALLMENT CONTRACTS.** Measuring periodic payments on long-term purchase contracts.

This chapter discusses the essentials of compound interest and annuities. This coverage is introduced early in this textbook to provide you with enough knowledge of the subject to understand and to apply present value techniques to topics in Chapters 7, 11, 13, 14, 18, 19, 21, and 22.

## NATURE OF INTEREST

**Interest** is the payment for the use of money. It represents an excess in cash exchanged over and above the principal amount lent or borrowed. For example, if the Corner Bank lends you $1,000 with the understanding that you will repay $1,150, the excess over $1,000, or $150, represents interest.

The amount of interest to be paid is generally stated as a rate over a specific period of time. For example, if you used the $1,000 for one year before repaying $1,150, the rate of interest would be 15% per year. That is, the interest is 15% of the principal each year. The custom of expressing interest as a rate is an established business practice.[1] In fact, business managers make investing and borrowing decisions on the basis of the rate of interest involved rather than on the actual dollar amount of interest to be received or paid.

The rate of interest is commonly applied to the time interval of one year. Interest of 12% represents a rate of 12% per year unless stipulated otherwise. The statement that a corporation will pay bond interest of 12%, payable semiannually, means a rate of 6% every six months, not 12% every six months.

### Simple Interest

**Simple interest** is the term used to describe interest that is computed on the amount of the principal only. It is the return on (or growth of) the principal for one time period or for each period in a succession of periods at a given rate per period applied to the principal at the beginning of the series. For example, if the $1,000 you borrowed in the previous illustration were for a five-year period, with a simple interest rate of 15% per year, the total interest you would pay would be $750 ($150 times five years).

[1] Federal law requires the disclosure of interest rates on an **annual basis** in all contracts. That is, instead of stating the rate as "1% per month," it must be stated as "12% per year" if it is simple interest or "12.68% per year" if it is compounded monthly.

Simple interest[2] is commonly expressed as:

$$\text{Interest} = P \times i \times n$$

where

$P$ = principal
$i$ = rate of interest for a single period
$n$ = number of periods

## Compound Interest

**Compound interest** is the term used to describe interest that is computed on principal *and* on any interest earned that has not been paid. It is the return on (or growth of) the principal for two or more time periods, assuming that the growth (the interest) in each time period is added to the principal at the end of the period and earns a return in all subsequent periods. Compounding calculates interest not only on the principal but also on the interest earned to date on that principal, assuming the interest is left on deposit.[3] To illustrate the difference between simple interest and compound interest, assume that you deposit $1,000 in the Last National Bank, where it will earn simple interest of 9% per year, and you deposit another $1,000 in the First State Bank, where it will earn compound interest of 9% per year compounded annually. Also assume that in both cases you will not withdraw any interest until three years from the date of deposit. The calculation of interest to be received would be as indicated below.

|  |  | Simple Interest Last National | Compound Interest First State |
|---|---|---|---|
| First year | ($1,000 × 9%) | $ 90.00 | $ 90.00 |
| Second year | ($1,000 × 9%) | 90.00 | 90.00 |
|  | ($90 × 9%) | -0- | 8.10 |
| Third year | ($1,000 × 9%) | 90.00 | 90.00 |
|  | ($188.10 × 9%) | -0- | 16.93 |
| Total interest, three-year period |  | $270.00 | $295.03 |

Obviously if you had a choice between investing your money at simple interest or at compound interest, you would choose compound interest, all other things—especially risk—being equal. The interests received from the two banks differ because of the calcula-

---

[2]Simple interest is traditionally expressed in textbooks in business mathematics or business finance as: $i$(interest) = $P$(principal) × $R$(rate) × $T$(time).

[3]Here is an illustration of the power of *time* and *compounding* interest on money. In 1626, Peter Minuit bought Manhattan Island from the Manhattoe Indians for $24 worth of trinkets and beads. If the Indians had taken a boat to Holland, invested the $24 in Dutch securities returning just 6% per year, and kept the money and interest invested at 6%, by 1971 they would have had $13 billion, enough to buy back all the land on the island and still have a couple of billion dollars left for doodads (*Forbes*, Vol. 107, #11, June 1, 1971). By 1981, 355 years after the trade, the $24 would have grown to $23 billion. An annual increase in the interest rate of only 2% from 6% to 8% would have caused the $24 to have grown to over $17 trillion by 1981.

tion of interest on interest in the case of the compound interest. For practical purposes in computing compound interest, it may be assumed that unpaid interest earned becomes a part of the principal and is entitled to interest. In the previous illustration, the computation of compound interest in the third year—9% times $1,188.10 ($1,000 plus $90 plus $98.10)—is illustrated below.

| Year | Annual Amount of Interest | Cumulative Amount of Interest | Principal End of Year |
|---|---|---|---|
| 0 | — | — | $1,000.00 |
| 1 ($1,000 × .09) | $ 90.00 | $ 90.00 | 1,090.00 |
| 2 ($1,090 × .09) | 98.10 | 188.10 | 1,188.10 |
| 3 ($1,188.10 × .09) | 106.93 | 295.03 | 1,295.03 |

Compound interest is the typical interest computation applied in business situations, particularly in our economy where large amounts of long-lived capital are used productively and financed over long periods of time. Financial managers view and evaluate their investment opportunities in terms of a series of periodic returns, each of which can be reinvested to yield additional returns. Simple interest is usually applicable only to short-term investments and debts that involve a time span of one year or less.

The remainder of the chapter is organized to cover the following six major time value of money concepts using both formula and interest table approaches in the solution of problems:

1. Amount (future value) of 1.
2. Present value of 1.
3. Amount (future value) of an ordinary annuity.
4. Present value of an ordinary annuity.
5. Amount (future value) of an annuity due.
6. Present value of an annuity due.

## Compound Interest Tables

Five different types of compound interest tables are presented at the end of this chapter. These tables are to be used by you in the study of this chapter and throughout this book in solving problems involving interest. The titles of these five tables and their contents are:

1. **"Amount of 1"** table. Contains the amounts to which 1 will accumulate if deposited now at a specified rate and left for a specified number of periods. (Table 6–1)
2. **"Present value of 1"** table. Contains the amounts that must be deposited now at a specified rate of interest to amount to 1 at the end of a specified number of periods. (Table 6–2)
3. **"Amount of an ordinary annuity of 1"** table. Contains the amounts to which periodic rents of 1 will accumulate if the rents are invested at the **end** of each period at a specified rate of interest and are continued for a specified number of periods. This table may also be used as a basis for converting to the amount of an annuity due of 1. (Table 6–3)
4. **"Present value of an ordinary annuity of 1"** table. Contains the amounts that must be deposited now at a specified rate of interest to permit withdrawals of 1 at the **end** of regular periodic intervals for the specified number of periods. This table may also be used as a basis for converting to the present value of an annuity due of 1. (Table 6–4)

5. **"Present value of an annuity due of 1"** table. Contains the amounts that must be deposited now at a specified rate of interest to permit withdrawals of 1 at the **beginning** of regular periodic intervals for the specified number of periods. (Table 6–5)

The excerpt below illustrates the general format and content of these tables. This excerpt of Table 6–1 is an "amount of 1" table that indicates how much principal plus interest a dollar accumulates to (the amount of 1) at the end of each of five periods at three different rates of compound interest.

| | AMOUNT OF 1 AT COMPOUND INTEREST (Excerpt from Table 6-1, page 251) | | |
|---|---|---|---|
| Period | 9% | 10% | 11% |
| 1 | 1.09000 | 1.10000 | 1.11000 |
| 2 | 1.18810 | 1.21000 | 1.23210 |
| 3 | 1.29503 | 1.33100 | 1.36763 |
| 4 | 1.41158 | 1.46410 | 1.51807 |
| 5 | 1.53862 | 1.61051 | 1.68506 |

Interpreting the table, if $1.00 is invested for three periods at a compound interest rate of 9% per period, the $1.00 will amount to $1.30 (1.29503 $\times$ $1.00), the **compound amount;** if the investment were for five periods, it would amount to $1.54. If $1.00 were invested at 11%, at the end of four periods it would amount to $1.52; at the end of five periods it would equal $1.69. If the investment were $1,000 instead of $1.00, the respective amounts would be:

If invested for 3 periods at 9% ($1,000 $\times$ 1.29503) = $1,295.03
If invested for 5 periods at 9% ($1,000 $\times$ 1.53862) = $1,538.62
If invested for 4 periods at 11% ($1,000 $\times$ 1.51807) = $1,518.07
If invested for 5 periods at 11% ($1,000 $\times$ 1.68506) = $1,685.06

Throughout the foregoing discussion of "compound interest tables" (and most of the discussion that follows) the use of the term **periods** instead of **years** is intentional. Interest is generally expressed in terms of an annual rate but in many business circumstances the compounding period is less than one year. In such circumstances the annual interest rate must be converted to correspond to the length of the period. The process is to convert the "annual interest rate" into the "compounding period interest rate" by **dividing the annual rate by the number of compounding periods per year.** In addition, the number of periods is determined by **multiplying the number of years involved by the number of compounding periods per year.** To illustrate, assume that $1.00 is invested for six years at 8% annual interest compounded **quarterly.** Using Table 6–1, page 250, we can determine the amount to which this $1.00 will accumulate by reading the factor that appears in the 2% column on the 24th row, namely 1.60844, or approximately $1.61. Thus, the term **periods** not **years** is used in all compound interest tables to express the quantity of $n$.

As another point on the frequency of compounding, because interest is theoretically earned (accruing) every second of every day, it is possible to calculate interest that is **compounded continuously.** Computations involving continuous compounding are facilitated through the use of the natural, or Napierian, system of logarithms. In spite of the soundness of continuous compounding, most business situations involving interest are resolved through discrete compounding techniques as illustrated in this chapter.

Problems involving compound interest must be carefully analyzed to determine which table to use and which procedures to apply. Frequently, problems are encountered that represent a combination of elements. Then each dissimilar element must be identified and separated before deciding which procedure to follow in reaching a solution. Deferred annuities, as illustrated later for example, may require the application of a combination of these tables.

Present value tables deal with dollars as dollars, without allowance for the likely differences in purchasing power. Therefore, the answers obtained by the use of the tables make no allowance for inflation or deflation. If you need to consider the changes in dollar purchasing power, you have to do so outside the present value framework or by adjusting the interest rate to reflect inflation.

## AMOUNT OF 1 PROBLEMS

### Computation of Future Amount

For any sum invested, the amount to which 1 (one) would accumulate (the compound amount) may be multiplied by the amount invested to determine the amount to which the sum invested would accumulate. For example, if $50,000 is invested for five years at a compound interest rate of 11%, the investment will grow to $84,253 ($50,000 $\times$ 1.68506) by the end of the fifth year.

The amount to which 1 (one) will accumulate may be expressed as a formula:

$$a_{\overline{n}|i} = (1 + i)^n$$

where

$a_{\overline{n}|i}$ = compound amount of 1
$i$ = rate of interest for a single period
$n$ = number of periods

The symbol $a_{\overline{n}|i}$ is expressed as "lowercase $a$ angle $n$ at $i$." It is the amount to which $1.00 will accumulate at $i$ rate of interest per period for $n$ periods.

To illustrate, assume that $1.00 is invested at 9% interest for three periods. The amounts to which the $1.00 will accumulate at the end of each period are:

$$a_{\overline{1}|9\%} = (1 + .09)^1 \text{ for the end of the first period}$$
$$a_{\overline{2}|9\%} = (1 + .09)^2 \text{ for the end of the second period}$$
$$a_{\overline{3}|9\%} = (1 + .09)^3 \text{ for the end of the third period}$$

Illustrated diagrammatically, these compound amounts accumulate as follows:

| Period | Beginning-of-Period Amount | Multiplier (1 + i) | End-of-Period Amount | Formula (1 + i)ⁿ |
|--------|-----------------|--------------|-----------------|---------------|
| 1 | 1.00000 | 1.09 | 1.09000 | $(1.09)^1$ |
| 2 | 1.09000 | 1.09 | 1.18810 | $(1.09)^2$ |
| 3 | 1.18810 | 1.09 | 1.29503 | $(1.09)^3$ |
| 4 | 1.29503 | 1.09 | 1.41158 | $(1.09)^4$ |

When tables are available, there is no need to apply the formula because, as shown above, the formula is the basis for the construction of the table.

### Computation of the Number of Periods

If the future amount to which a given investment will accumulate at a given interest rate is known, the number of interest periods involved can be calculated. In other words, three of the four values (original investment, interest rate, periods, future amount) must be known. For example, assume that the sum to be invested at 11% is $50,000 and the desired future amount is $84,253. The number of interest periods is calculated by dividing the future amount of $84,253 by $50,000 to give 1.68506, the amount $1.00 would accumulate to at 11% for the unknown number of interest periods. The factor 1.68506 or its approximate can be located in the amount of 1 table, page 251, by reading down the 11% column **to the 5-period line;** thus 5 is the unknown number of periods.

### Computation of the Interest Rate

If the future amount to which a given investment will accumulate over a specified number of interest periods is known, the rate of interest can be calculated. For example, again assume that the sum to be invested is $50,000 for five years to accumulate to $84,253. The interest rate required is again calculated by dividing the future amount of $84,253 by $50,000 to give 1.68506, the amount $1.00 would accumulate to in five periods at an unknown interest rate. The factor 1.68506 or its approximate can be located in the amount of 1 table, page 251, by reading across the 5-period line **to the 11% column;** thus, 11% is the unknown interest rate.

## PRESENT VALUE

The example on page 235 showed that $50,000 invested at a compound interest rate of 11% will be worth $84,253 at the end of five years. It follows then that $84,253 five years from now is worth $50,000 now; that is, $50,000 is the present value of $84,253. The **present value** is the amount that must be invested now to produce the known future value. In the compound amount illustrations, it was the future value of a known present value that was determined; in present-value problems, it is the present value of a known future value that must be determined. The present value is always a smaller amount than the known future amount because interest will be earned and accumulated on the present value to the future date.

The present value of an amount may be computed by dividing 1 by the amount of 1 for a given number of periods and a given rate of interest and then multiplying the result by the known future amount (this process is known as "discounting"). To illustrate, assume that $1,000 is needed in five years and that funds can be invested currently at 12% per year. Using the "amount of 1" table on page 251, we see that $1.00 invested for five periods at 12% will equal $1.76234. If $1.00 is divided by this amount (1.76234), the result will equal the present value of 1 due in five years if invested at 12% per year, or $0.56743. This means that an investment of approximately $0.57 now at 12% compounded annually will equal approximately $1.00 in five years. Because $1,000 is needed, the amount to be invested would be 1,000 times $0.56743 or $567.43.

## PRESENT VALUE OF 1 TABLES

Quick computations of present values are frequently needed. As a result, tables have been developed showing how much must be invested at various compound interest rates for various periods of time to equal 1 at a future date. A "present value of 1 table" appears at the end of this chapter. The excerpt below illustrates the nature of such a table by indicating the present value of 1 for five different periods at three different rates of interest.

| PRESENT VALUE OF 1 AT COMPOUND INTEREST (Excerpt from Table 6-2, page 253) | | | |
|---|---|---|---|
| Period | 10% | 11% | 12% |
| 1 | 0.90909 | 0.90090 | 0.89286 |
| 2 | 0.82645 | 0.81162 | 0.79719 |
| 3 | 0.75132 | 0.73119 | 0.71178 |
| 4 | 0.68301 | 0.65873 | 0.63552 |
| 5 | 0.62092 | 0.59345 | 0.56743 |

"Present value of 1" tables are constructed from the following general formula.

$$p_{\overline{n}|i} = 1 \div a_{\overline{n}|i}$$

where

$$p_{\overline{n}|i} = \text{present value of 1}$$
$$a_{\overline{n}|i} = \text{compound amount of 1}$$

The symbol $p_{\overline{n}|i}$ is expressed as "lowercase $p$ angle $n$ at $i$." Assume that you need to determine the present value of $1.00 at compound interest of 10% for four periods. Referring to the amount of 1 on page 251, the amount of 1 at 10% compound interest for four periods is 1.46410. To determine the present value, the formula above becomes:

$$p_{\overline{4}|10\%} = \frac{1}{1.46410} = \$0.68301$$

or the amount that must be invested now to equal $1.00 in four years at 10% compound interest. A simpler method is to refer to a "present value of 1" table, where this same amount, 0.68301, may be found in the 10% column on the fourth period line.

### Computation of Investment

To illustrate the use of the table, assume that your rich uncle proposes to give you $2,000 for a trip to Europe when you graduate from college three years from now. He proposes to finance the trip by investing a sum of money now at 12% compound interest that will provide you with $2,000 upon your graduation. The only conditions are that you graduate and that you tell him how much to invest now. By referring to the "present value of 1" table, 12% column and 3 period row, you find that approximately $0.71 (0.71178) invested now at 12% will yield $1.00 in three years. Because you are promised $2,000 instead of $1.00, you must multiply the 0.71178 by $2,000. The multiplication indicates that your uncle should invest $1,423.56 now to provide you with $2,000 upon graduation. To satisfy his other condition, you must pass this course and many more.

If any *three* of the *four* values (amount, rate, periods, and present value) are known, the unknown one can be derived.

### Computation of the Number of Periods

Given (1) the present investment, (2) the future amount, and (3) the rate of interest, the **number of required periods** can be approximated by reference to the appropriate tables. To illustrate, Rockerfeller Foundation has $80,000 to invest now at 12% for future scholarships to disadvantaged children totaling $140,987. How many years will it take for the $80,000 to accumulate enough to pay for these scholarships? By dividing the future amount of $140,987 by the present value of $80,000, the compound amount of $1.00 is computed to be 1.76234 ($140,987 ÷ $80,000). The factor 1.76234 or its approximate can be located in the "amount of 1" table (6–1, page 251) in the 12% interest column; by reference to the periods row in which it appears, the unknown number of periods can be determined to be 5.

In a similar manner, by dividing the present value of $80,000 by the future amount of $140,987, the present value of $1.00 is computed to be .56743 ($80,000 ÷ $140,987). The factor .56743 or its approximate can be located in the "present value of 1" table (6–2, page 253) in the 12% interest column; by reference to the periods row in which it appears, the unknown number of periods can be determined to be 5.

The exact factors as computed above are not always found in the tables, but for most business decisions the nearest approximate factor suffices. If the situation demands more exact answers, interpolation (as illustrated on pages 247–248) can be used with the tables, or logarithms may be used.

### Computation of the Interest Rate

Given (1) the present investment, (2) the future amount, and (3) the number of periods, the **required interest rate** can be approximated by reference to the appropriate tables. To illustrate, using the data in the preceding illustration, the amount of 1 factor, 1.76234, is computed similarly ($140,987 ÷ $80,000) as is the present value of 1 factor, .56743 ($80,000 ÷ $140,987). The 1.76234 factor can be found in the "amount of 1" table (6–1, page 251) by reading across the 5-periods (known) row; by reference to the interest column in which it appears, the unknown rate of 12% can be determined. Likewise, the .56743 factor can be found in the "present value of 1" table (6–2, page 253) by reading across the 5-periods (known) row; by reference to the corresponding interest column, the unknown interest rate of 12% can be determined.

## ANNUITIES

The preceding discussion has involved only the accumulation or discounting of a single principal sum. Individuals frequently encounter situations in which a series of dollar amounts are to be paid or received periodically, such as loans or sales to be repaid in installments, invested funds that will be partially recovered at regular intervals, and cost savings that are realized repeatedly. A life insurance contract is probably the most common and most familiar type of transaction involving a series of equal payments made at equal intervals of time. Such a process of periodic saving represents the accumulation of a sum of money through an annuity. An **annuity** by definition requires that the periodic payments or receipts (called **rents**) always be the **same amount** and that **the interval** between such rents always be the same. It is also assumed that **interest is compounded** once each time period.

The **amount of an annuity** is the sum (future value) of all the rents (payments or receipts) plus the accumulated compound interest on them. It should be noted that the rents may occur at either the beginning or the end of the periods (not necessarily January 1 or December 31). To distinguish annuities under these two alternatives, an annuity is classified as an **ordinary annuity** if the rents occur at the end of the period, and as an **annuity due** if the rents occur at the beginning of the period.

To illustrate the difference between an ordinary annuity and an annuity due, assume an annuity of $1,000 a year earning compound interest at 9%.

|  | Ordinary Annuity | Annuity Due |
|---|---|---|
| First year's investment: |  |  |
|   (at the beginning of the year) |  | $1,000.00 |
|   (at the end of the year) | $1,000.00 |  |
| First year's interest | -0- | 90.00 |
| Balance at end of first year | 1,000.00 | 1,090.00 |
| Second year's investment | 1,000.00 | 1,000.00 |
| Second year's interest: |  |  |
|   $1,000 @ 9% | 90.00 |  |
|   $2,090 @ 9% |  | 188.10 |
| Balance at end of second year | 2,090.00 | 2,278.10 |
| Third year's investment | 1,000.00 | 1,000.00 |
| Third year's interest: |  |  |
|   $2,090 @ 9% | 188.10 |  |
|   $3,278.10 @ 9% |  | 295.03 |
| Balance at end of third year | $3,278.10 | $3,573.13 |

As illustrated above, the amount to which an annuity of $1,000 a year for three years at 9% will accumulate will depend on whether it is an ordinary annuity or an annuity due. The difference is that with an annuity due all deposits receive one more period of compounding. In the above illustration, the ordinary annuity consists of three investment payments and two interest periods while the annuity due consists of three investment payments and three interest periods.

The amount of an ordinary annuity of 1 may be expressed by the following formula.

$$A_{\overline{n}|i} = \frac{(1 + i)^n - 1}{i}$$

where

$A_{\overline{n}|i}$ = amount of an ordinary annuity of 1
$n$ = number of periods
$i$ = rate of interest

The symbol $A_{\overline{n}|i}$ is expressed "capital $A$ angle $n$ at $i$"; for example, $A_{\overline{5}|9\%}$ is expressed "capital $A$ angle 5 at 9%" and refers to the amount to which an ordinary annuity of 1 will accumulate in five periods at 9% interest.

## Amount of an Ordinary Annuity of 1 Table

One approach to the problem of determining the future amount to which an annuity will accumulate is to compute the amount to which each of the rents in the series will accumulate and then aggregate their individual future amounts. Assuming an interest rate of 12%, the future amount in 5 years of an ordinary annuity of 1 can be computed as follows using the "amount of 1" table (6–1, page 251).

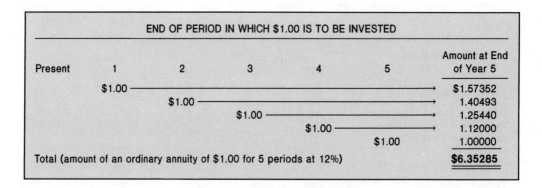

| END OF PERIOD IN WHICH $1.00 IS TO BE INVESTED | | | | | | |
|---|---|---|---|---|---|---|
| Present | 1 | 2 | 3 | 4 | 5 | Amount at End of Year 5 |
| | $1.00 ———————————————→ | | | | | $1.57352 |
| | | $1.00 ———————————→ | | | | 1.40493 |
| | | | $1.00 ———————→ | | | 1.25440 |
| | | | | $1.00 ———→ | | 1.12000 |
| | | | | | $1.00 | 1.00000 |
| Total (amount of an ordinary annuity of $1.00 for 5 periods at 12%) | | | | | | **$6.35285** |

However, tables have been developed similar to those used for the "amount of 1" and the "present value of 1" for both an ordinary annuity and an annuity due. Because annuity due factors are easily converted from an ordinary annuity table, ordinary annuity tables are more commonly found in reference books, textbooks, and in practice. Therefore, we have provided an explanation of the process of converting an amount of 1 table into ordinary annuity data. The table below is an excerpt from the "amount of an ordinary annuity of 1" table.

| AMOUNT OF AN ORDINARY ANNUITY OF 1 (Excerpt from Table 6-3, page 255) | | | |
|---|---|---|---|
| Period | 10% | 11% | 12% |
| 1 | 1.00000 | 1.00000 | 1.00000 |
| 2 | 2.10000 | 2.11000 | 2.12000 |
| 3 | 3.31000 | 3.34210 | 3.37440 |
| 4 | 4.64100 | 4.70973 | 4.77933 |
| 5 | 6.10510 | 6.22780 | **6.35285\*** |

*Note that this annuity table factor is the same as the sum of the future amounts of 1 factors shown in the previous schedule.

**Computation of the Future Amount**   Interpreting the table, if $1.00 is invested at the end of each year for four years at 11% interest compounded annually, the amount of the annuity at the end of the fourth year will be $4.71 (4.70973 × $1.00). By multiplying the figures from the appropriate line and column of the table on page 240 by the dollar amount of one rent involved in an ordinary annuity, the accumulated sum of the rents and the compound interest to the date of the last rent may be determined. For example, if $7,500 is deposited in a bank account at the end of each year for five years at 12% interest compounded annually, the amount on deposit at the end of the fifth year will be $47,646.38 (6.35285 × $7,500).

In the foregoing example three values were known (amount of one rent, interest rate, and number of periods) and used to determine the fourth value, future amount, which was unknown. Obviously, if any three of these four values are known, the unknown one can be derived.

**Computation of Each Rent**   The ordinary annuity table (or the formula) may be used to **compute the amount of the periodic rents** when the desired future amount of the annuity is known. To illustrate, assume that you wish to accumulate $14,000 for a down payment on a condominium apartment five years from now; for the next five years you can earn an annual return of 8% compounded semiannually. How much should your deposit at the end of each six-month period be? The amount of each deposit is simply determined by dividing the future amount of $14,000 by the "amount of an ordinary annuity of 1" (Table 6–3, page 254) for ten (5 × 2) periods at 4% (8% ÷ 2), or 12.00611. Each six months' deposit must be approximately $1,166 ($14,000 ÷ 12.00611) to accumulate to $14,000 in five years.

**Computation of the Number of Periodic Rents**   If you wish to accumulate $117,332 by making periodic rents of $20,000 at the end of each period that will earn 8% each period while accumulating, how many rent payments must be made? To derive the required number of rents, divide the future amount of $117,332 by the amount of each rent, $20,000, to obtain 5.86660, the "amount of an ordinary annuity of 1" at 8% for the unknown number of periods. By reference to Table 6–3, 8% interest column, we find 5.86660 **at the 5-period line;** thus, 5 is the unknown number of periodic rents.

**Computation of the Interest Rate**   In the example above, if the number of periodic rents were known to be 5 and the interest rate were unknown, the rate would be determined by making the same computation ($117,332 ÷ $20,000 = 5.86660) and reading across the 5-period line of Table 6–3 until we find 5.86660 **in the 8% interest column.**

## Amount of an Annuity Due

The preceding analysis of an ordinary annuity was based on the fact that the periodic rents occur at the end of each period. An annuity due is based on the fact that the periodic rents occur at the **beginning** of each period. This means an annuity due will accumulate interest on the first year's rent in the first year, whereas an ordinary annuity rent will earn no interest during the first year because the rent is not received or paid until the end of the period. In other words, the significant difference between the two types of annuities is in the number of interest accumulation periods involved.

If rents occur at the end of a period, in determining the **amount of an annuity,** there will be one less interest period than if the rents occur at the beginning of the period. The distinction is shown graphically below.

The generalization that "the periodic interest earnings under an ordinary annuity will always be lower by one period's interest than the interest earned by an annuity due" suggests the basis for converting an ordinary annuity table to an annuity due table. **If the last rent in an ordinary annuity is deducted from the end-of-period accumulation, the remainder will represent the amount of an annuity due for one less period.** For example, if one rent is deducted from the ordinary annuity of five periods at 12%, in the illustration above, the result will be the amount of an annuity due of four periods at 12%.

| | |
|---|---|
| 1. Amount of ordinary annuity of $1,000 a period for five periods at 12% | $6,352.85 |
| 2. Deduct last payment | −1,000.00 |
| 3. Amount of annuity due of $1,000 per period for four periods at 12% | $5,352.85 |

In the case of an ordinary annuity, there is one rent (the last) on which no interest is involved. That is the reason for subtracting the last payment as shown above. The annuity due has one more interest period than the ordinary annuity.

To illustrate the use of the ordinary annuity tables in converting to an annuity due, assume that Hank Lotadough plans to deposit $800 a year on each birthday of his son Howard, starting today, his fifth birthday, at 12% interest compounded annually. Hank wants to know the amount he will have accumulated for college expenses by his son's eighteenth birthday.

If the first deposit is made on his son's fifth birthday, Hank will make a total of 13 deposits over the life of the annuity (assume no deposit on the eighteenth birthday). Because all the deposits will be made at the beginning of the periods, they represent an annuity due. Referring to the "amount of an ordinary annuity of 1" table for 14 periods at 12% and deducting 1, [(factor for $n + 1$ rents) $- 1$], to arrive at the annuity due for 13 periods, the solution may be computed as follows.

| | |
|---|---|
| **1.** Amount of an ordinary annuity of 1 for 14 periods at 12% (Table 6-3) | 32.39260 |
| **2.** Deduct one rent | $-1.00000$ |
| **3.** Amount of annuity due of 1 for 13 periods at 12% | 31.39260 |
| **4.** Periodic deposit | $\times$   $800 |
| **5.** Accumulated amount on son's eighteenth birthday | $25,114.08 |

The same solution can be arrived at in the following manner.

| | |
|---|---|
| **1.** Amount of an ordinary annuity of $800 per period at 12% for 14 periods (32.39260 $\times$ $800) | $25,914.08 |
| **2.** Deduct last payment | $-$   800.00 |
| **3.** Amount of an annuity due of $800 a period at 12% for 13 periods | $25,114.08 |

## Present Value of an Ordinary Annuity

The present value of an annuity may be viewed as **the single sum** that, if invested at compound interest now, would provide for an annuity (a series of withdrawals) of a certain amount per period for a certain number of future periods. In other words, the present value of an ordinary annuity is the present value of a series of rents to be made at equal intervals in the future.

One approach to the problem of valuing at the present an annuity consisting of a series of future rents is to determine the present value of each of the rents in the series and then aggregate their individual present values. For example, an annuity of $1.00 to be received at the end of each period for five periods may be viewed as separate amounts and the present value of each computed from the table of present values (see pages 252–253). Assuming an interest rate of 12%, the present value can be computed:

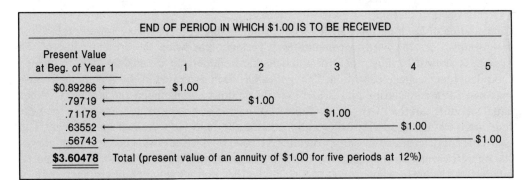

END OF PERIOD IN WHICH $1.00 IS TO BE RECEIVED

| Present Value at Beg. of Year 1 | 1 | 2 | 3 | 4 | 5 |
|---|---|---|---|---|---|
| $0.89286 ← | $1.00 | | | | |
| .79719 ← | | $1.00 | | | |
| .71178 ← | | | $1.00 | | |
| .63552 ← | | | | $1.00 | |
| .56743 ← | | | | | $1.00 |
| **$3.60478** | Total (present value of an annuity of $1.00 for five periods at 12%) | | | | |

This computation tells us that if we invest $3.60 today at 12% interest for five periods, we will be able to withdraw $1.00 at the end of each period for five periods.

Such a procedure could become quite cumbersome and subject to error if the annuity consisted of many rents. The formula for which convenient tables of the "present values of ordinary annuities of 1" are prepared is expressed:

$$P_{\overline{n}|i} = \frac{1 - \dfrac{1}{(1 + i)^n}}{i}$$

The symbol $P_{\overline{n}|i}$ is expressed "capital $P$ angle $n$ at $i$"; for example $P_{\overline{5}|12\%}$ is expressed "capital $P$ angle 5 at 12%" and refers to the present value of an ordinary annuity of 1 for five periods at 12% interest. An excerpt from a present value of an ordinary annuity of 1 table is illustrated below.

PRESENT VALUE OF AN ORDINARY ANNUITY OF 1
(Excerpt from Table 6-4, page 257)

| Period | 10% | 11% | 12% |
|---|---|---|---|
| 1 | 0.90909 | 0.90090 | 0.89286 |
| 2 | 1.73554 | 1.71252 | 1.69005 |
| 3 | 2.48685 | 2.44371 | 2.40183 |
| 4 | 3.16986 | 3.10245 | 3.03735 |
| 5 | 3.79079 | 3.69590 | **3.60478*** |

*Note that this annuity table factor is equal to the sum of the present value of 1 factors shown in the previous schedule.

**Computation of the Present Value of the Periodic Rents** Interpreting the table, if $1.00 is due at the end of each period for five periods, compounded annually at 12% interest, the present value of the five rents of $1.00 each is $3.60. The figures in the table above are discount factors that, when multiplied by any series of equal rents due at regular intervals in the future, produce the present equivalent (discounted amount) of that series of rents. For example, to produce $3,000 at the end of each period for the next five periods at 10% interest compounded annually, $3,000 × 3.79079, or $11,372.37, must be deposited now.

**Computation of Each Periodic Rent** The "present value of an ordinary annuity table" (or the formula) may be used to **compute each periodic rent** when the present value of the annuity is known. To illustrate, Norm and Jackie Remmers have saved $12,000 to finance their daughter's college education. The money has been deposited in the Bloomington Savings and Loan Association and is earning 10% interest compounded semiannually. What equal amounts can their daughter withdraw at the end of every six months during the next four years while she attends college and exhaust the fund with the last withdrawal? The answer is not determined by simply dividing $12,000 by 8 withdrawals because that ignores the interest earned on the money on deposit. The amount of each withdrawal is computed by dividing the present investment of $12,000 by the "present value of an ordinary annuity of 1" (Table 6–4) for eight (4 × 2) periods at 5% (10% ÷ 2), or 6.46321. Starting six months from the date of the deposit, she can withdraw $1,856.66 ($12,000 ÷ 6.46321) every six months for four years.

**Computation of the Interest Rate or the Number of Periodic Rents**   If the present value of an annuity and the amount of the periodic rents are known, the unknown interest rate or the unknown number of periods can be determined either through formula or tables. To illustrate, if Song Kim wants to invest $42,567.80 today to provide $5,000 payments to his daughter at the end of each year for the next twenty years, what is the **rate of interest** which must be earned on the investment? The present value of $1.00 per period can be calculated by dividing the known present value ($42,567.80) by the known amount of the rents ($5,000).

$$\$42,567.80 \div \$5,000 = 8.51356$$

Referring to the present value of an ordinary annuity table (6–4, page 257), 8.51356 or its approximate can be located in the 20-period row; by reference to the column in which it appears, the interest rate is determined to be 10%.

    If the interest rate were known but the number of periods unknown, the number of $5,000 annual withdrawals that would be provided Song Kim's daughter would be determined in a similar manner using the same table.

## Present Value of an Annuity Due

In the discussion of the present value of an ordinary annuity, the value now was discounted back one period from the first rent; the number of rents and the number of discount periods were the same. A diagram for finding the present value of an ordinary annuity for five periods follows.

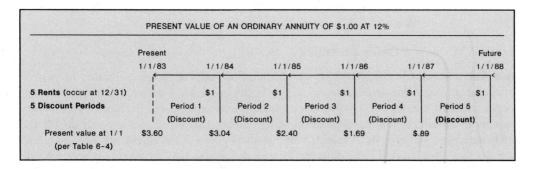

This diagram illustrates that in an ordinary annuity where the rents occur at the end of the period, the first rent can be discounted for one period. In an annuity due where the rents occur at the beginning of the periods, there is no opportunity for discounting the first rent because no time period exists relative to it. In order to see this distinction, compare the diagram on page 246 with the one above.

    We could compute the present value of an annuity due by simply adding together the present value of each of the periodic rents, but we can use the present value tables for

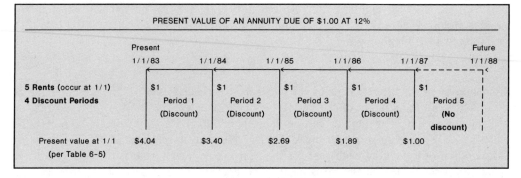

ordinary annuities to simplify the computation. The diagrams in this section illustrate that **in an ordinary annuity the number of discount periods and the number of rents are the same, whereas in an annuity due, the number of discount periods is always one less than the number of rents.** The basis then for converting a table of present value of an ordinary annuity of 1 to a table of present value of an annuity due of 1 involves adding one rent to the present value of an ordinary annuity **of one less period** $[(n - 1 \text{ rents}) + 1]$ than that of the annuity due. Referring to the table of "present value of an ordinary annuity of 1," this can be illustrated as follows:

| | |
|---|---|
| **1.** Present value of an ordinary annuity of 1 for four rents at 12% (Table 6-4) | 3.03735 |
| **2.** Add 1 | 1.00000 |
| **3.** Present value of an annuity due of 1 for five rents at 12% (Table 6-5) | 4.03735 |

Because the payment and receipt of rentals at the beginning of periods (such as leases, insurance, and subscriptions) are as common as those at the end of the periods (referred to as "in arrears"), we have provided annuity due factors in the form of Table 6–5.

### Present Value of a Deferred Annuity

A **deferred annuity** is an annuity in which the rents begin a specified number of periods after the arrangement or contract is made. In other words, a deferred annuity does not begin to produce rents until two or more periods have expired. For example, "an **ordinary annuity** of six annual rents deferred four years" means that no rents will occur during the first four years, and that the first of the six rents will occur at the end of the fifth year. "An **annuity due** of six annual rents deferred four years" means that no rents will occur during the first four years, and that the first of six rents will occur at the beginning of the fifth year.

In computing the present value of a deferred annuity, recognition must be given to the interest that accrues on the original investment during the deferral period, which is one period less than the number of periods prior to the first payment, assuming an ordinary annuity.

To compute the present value of a deferred annuity, we compute the present value of an ordinary annuity of 1 as if the rents had occurred for the entire period, and then subtract the present value of those rents not received during the deferral period. We are then left with the present value of the rents actually received subsequent to the deferred period.

To illustrate, Buccaneer Corp. purchases an ordinary annuity of six annual rents of $5,000 each, the rents deferred four years from today, with interest accruing at the rate of 8%. What is the present value of the six rents? The present value is $16,989.75 as calculated below using Table 6–4:

| | |
|---|---|
| **1.** Each periodic rent | $5,000 |
| **2.** Present value of an ordinary annuity of 1 for total periods (10) involved [number of rents (6) plus number of deferred periods (4)] at 8% | 6.71008 |
| **3.** Less: Present value of an ordinary annuity of 1 for the number of deferred periods (4) at 8% | −3.31213 |
| **4.** Difference (times amount of periodic rents) | ×3.39795 |
| **5.** Present value of six rents of $5,000 | $16,989.75 |

The subtraction of the present value of an annuity of 1 for the deferred periods eliminates the nonexistent rents during the deferral period and converts the present value of an ordinary annuity of $1.00 for 10 periods to the present value of 6 rents of $1.00, deferred 4 periods.

Alternatively, the present value of the 6 rents could be computed as follows using Table 6–2:

| Period of Rent | Present Value of 1 at 8% | | Amount of Rent | | Present Value |
|---|---|---|---|---|---|
| 5 | .68058 | X | $5,000 | = | $ 3,402.90 |
| 6 | .63017 | X | 5,000 | = | 3,150.85 |
| 7 | .58349 | X | 5,000 | = | 2,917.45 |
| 8 | .54027 | X | 5,000 | = | 2,701.35 |
| 9 | .50025 | X | 5,000 | = | 2,501.25 |
| 10 | .46319 | X | 5,000 | = | 2,315.95 |
| | | | Total | | $16,989.75 |

In the case of **the amount of a deferred annuity** there is no accumulation or investment on which interest may accrue, so the amount of a deferred annuity is the same as the amount of an annuity not deferred. The deferral period does not affect the amount.

## INTERPOLATION OF TABLES TO DERIVE INTEREST RATES

Throughout the previous discussion our illustrations were designed to produce interest rates and factors that could be found in the tables. Frequently it is necessary to **interpolate** to derive the exact or required interest rate. Interpolation is useful in finding a particular unknown value that lies between two given table values. The following examples illustrate the method of interpolation using the tables on pages 250–257.

**EXAMPLE 1.**    If $2,000 accumulates to $5,900 after being invested for 20 years, what is the annual interest rate that the investment paid?

By dividing the future amount of $5,900 by the investment of $2,000, we obtain the amount to which $1.00 would have grown if invested for 20 years, that is, $2.95. Referring to Table 6–1 and reading across the 20-period line, we find that the value under 5% is 2.65330 and the value under 6% is 3.20714. The factor 2.95 is between 5% and 6%, which means that the interest rate is also between 5% and 6%. By interpolation the rate is determined more precisely as follows ($i$ = unknown rate and $d$ = difference between 5% and $i$):

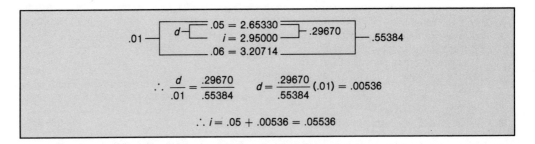

$$\therefore \frac{d}{.01} = \frac{.29670}{.55384} \qquad d = \frac{.29670}{.55384} (.01) = .00536$$

$$\therefore i = .05 + .00536 = .05536$$

The approximate interest rate is 5.536%, or 5.5% rounded.

**EXAMPLE 2.**    You are offered an annuity of $1,000 a year beginning one year from now for 25 years for investing $15,000 cash. What rate of interest is your investment earning?

By dividing the investment of $15,000 by the annuity of $1,000 we obtain 15, which is the "present value of an ordinary annuity of 1" for 25 years at an unknown interest rate.

Referring to Table 6–4 and reading across the 25-period line, we find that the value under 4% is 15.62208 and the value under 5% is 14.09394. The factor 15 is between 4% and 5%, which means that the unknown interest rate is also between 4% and 5%. By interpolation the rate is determined more precisely as follows ($i$ = unknown rate and $d$ = difference between 4% and $i$):

```
        ┌── .04 = 15.62208 ─┐
 .01 ──┤ d ┤  i = 15.00000 ──┼─ .62208 ── 1.52814
        └── .05 = 14.09394 ─┘
```

$$\therefore \frac{d}{.01} = \frac{.62208}{1.52814} \qquad d = \frac{.62208}{1.52814} (.01) = .00407$$

$$\therefore i = .04 + d = .04 + .004 = .04407$$

The approximate interest rate is 4.407%, or 4.4% rounded.

Interpolation assumes that the change between any two values in the table is linear. Although such an assumption is not correct, if the table value ranges are not too wide, the margin of error is generally insignificant.

## CHOOSING AN APPROPRIATE INTEREST RATE

Up to this point, we have assumed a known or given interest rate; therefore, only the mechanics of computing accumulated values and present values have been illustrated.

However, one of the more perplexing problems facing the accountant is the selection of an appropriate interest rate. Consider the following debates that have taken place in practice.

1. In pension accounting, the amount payable to pension claimants in the future **does not** factor in an inflation expectation. The interest rate used to determine present value of the amount payable in the future, however, is a market rate of interest that **does** reflect inflation. Some argue, therefore, that the present value of estimated benefits payable is understated because the smaller the estimate of benefits payable in the future, and the larger the interest rate used as a discount factor, the smaller the computed present value of the pension obligation will be.

2. In oil and gas accounting, the Securities and Exchange Commission at one time recommended that the fair value of oil and gas reserves in the ground be computed at the present value of the future revenues discounted at a flat 10% rate. The SEC argued that the use of one rate leads to comparability and that a rate of this magnitude provides a reasonable representation of the present value of future oil and gas reserves. Others disagree, noting that a 10% rate was unrealistic for two reasons. First, in many cases the rate should be much higher than 10%, considering the existing prime rate. Second, not all companies and situations deserve the same rate because of differences in risk.

3. In trying to resolve the problem of capitalizing interest cost incurred during construction, the profession encountered support for two different bases to the measurement of interest cost. Some accountants favored capitalizing the interest cost associated with the specific borrowing. Others disagreed, arguing that a weighted average is preferable because the borrowing on any specific project affects the borrowing costs of the entire company as it relates to other projects.

These are just a few examples of the problems that are encountered in practice regarding the selection of an appropriate discount (interest) rate.

How then should we select an interest rate for purposes of present value computations? In the past, interest rates have often been selected on the basis of expediency (availability), regulatory stipulations, the application of traditional principles of interest rate determination, and ease of auditability. No consistent approach has been adopted. This is not surprising, given the wide variety of rates from which to choose, such as the general borrowing rate (prime rate), a specific borrowing rate for a given company, opportunity cost rate, investment rate of return, cost-of-capital rate on a weighted-average basis, and so on.

The appropriate interest rate is not always obvious. This is so because an interest rate generally has three components:

1. **PURE RATE OF INTEREST** (2 to 4 percent). This would be the amount a lender would charge if there were no possibilities of default and no expectation of inflation.

2. **CREDIT RISK RATE OF INTEREST** (0 to 5 percent). The government has little or no credit risk (i.e., risk of nonpayment) when it issues bonds; a business enterprise, however, depending upon its financial stability, profitability, etc., can have a low or a high credit risk.

3. **EXPECTED INFLATION RATE OF INTEREST** (0 to ?). Lenders recognize that in an inflationary economy, they are being paid back with less valuable dollars. As a result, they increase their interest rate to compensate for this loss in purchasing power. When inflationary expectations are high, interest rates are high.

Identifying and mixing the three components above in the appropriate ratio for any given company or investor at any given moment is not easy. But because double-digit rates are the rule rather than the exception in today's environment, the relevance and reliability of accounting information is becoming more and more dependent on the selection of appropriate interest rates.

**TABLE 6-1** AMOUNT OF 1

$$a_{\overline{n}|i} = (1 + i)^n$$

| (n) Periods | 2% | 2½% | 3% | 4% | 5% | 6% |
|---|---|---|---|---|---|---|
| 1 | 1.02000 | 1.02500 | 1.03000 | 1.04000 | 1.05000 | 1.06000 |
| 2 | 1.04040 | 1.05063 | 1.06090 | 1.08160 | 1.10250 | 1.12360 |
| 3 | 1.06121 | 1.07689 | 1.09273 | 1.12486 | 1.15763 | 1.19102 |
| 4 | 1.08243 | 1.10381 | 1.12551 | 1.16986 | 1.21551 | 1.26248 |
| 5 | 1.10408 | 1.13141 | 1.15927 | 1.21665 | 1.27628 | 1.33823 |
| 6 | 1.12616 | 1.15969 | 1.19405 | 1.26532 | 1.34010 | 1.41852 |
| 7 | 1.14869 | 1.18869 | 1.22987 | 1.31593 | 1.40710 | 1.50363 |
| 8 | 1.17166 | 1.21840 | 1.26677 | 1.36857 | 1.47746 | 1.59385 |
| 9 | 1.19509 | 1.24886 | 1.30477 | 1.42331 | 1.55133 | 1.68948 |
| 10 | 1.21899 | 1.28008 | 1.34392 | 1.48024 | 1.62889 | 1.79085 |
| 11 | 1.24337 | 1.31209 | 1.38423 | 1.53945 | 1.71034 | 1.89830 |
| 12 | 1.26824 | 1.34489 | 1.42576 | 1.60103 | 1.79586 | 2.01220 |
| 13 | 1.29361 | 1.37851 | 1.46853 | 1.66507 | 1.88565 | 2.13293 |
| 14 | 1.31948 | 1.41297 | 1.51259 | 1.73168 | 1.97993 | 2.26090 |
| 15 | 1.34587 | 1.44830 | 1.55797 | 1.80094 | 2.07893 | 2.39656 |
| 16 | 1.37279 | 1.48451 | 1.60471 | 1.87298 | 2.18287 | 2.54035 |
| 17 | 1.40024 | 1.52162 | 1.65285 | 1.94790 | 2.29202 | 2.69277 |
| 18 | 1.42825 | 1.55966 | 1.70243 | 2.02582 | 2.40662 | 2.85434 |
| 19 | 1.45681 | 1.59865 | 1.75351 | 2.10685 | 2.52695 | 3.02560 |
| 20 | 1.48595 | 1.63862 | 1.80611 | 2.19112 | 2.65330 | 3.20714 |
| 21 | 1.51567 | 1.67958 | 1.86029 | 2.27877 | 2.78596 | 3.39956 |
| 22 | 1.54598 | 1.72157 | 1.91610 | 2.36992 | 2.92526 | 3.60354 |
| 23 | 1.57690 | 1.76461 | 1.97359 | 2.46472 | 3.07152 | 3.81975 |
| 24 | 1.60844 | 1.80873 | 2.03279 | 2.56330 | 3.22510 | 4.04893 |
| 25 | 1.64061 | 1.85394 | 2.09378 | 2.66584 | 3.38635 | 4.29187 |
| 26 | 1.67342 | 1.90029 | 2.15659 | 2.77247 | 3.55567 | 4.54938 |
| 27 | 1.70689 | 1.94780 | 2.22129 | 2.88337 | 3.73346 | 4.82235 |
| 28 | 1.74102 | 1.99650 | 2.28793 | 2.99870 | 3.92013 | 5.11169 |
| 29 | 1.77584 | 2.04641 | 2.35657 | 3.11865 | 4.11614 | 5.41839 |
| 30 | 1.81136 | 2.09757 | 2.42726 | 3.24340 | 4.32194 | 5.74349 |
| 31 | 1.84759 | 2.15001 | 2.50008 | 3.37313 | 4.53804 | 6.08810 |
| 32 | 1.88454 | 2.20376 | 2.57508 | 3.50806 | 4.76494 | 6.45339 |
| 33 | 1.92223 | 2.25885 | 2.65234 | 3.64838 | 5.00319 | 6.84059 |
| 34 | 1.96068 | 2.31532 | 2.73191 | 3.79432 | 5.25335 | 7.25103 |
| 35 | 1.99989 | 2.37321 | 2.81386 | 3.94609 | 5.51602 | 7.68609 |
| 36 | 2.03989 | 2.43254 | 2.89828 | 4.10393 | 5.79182 | 8.14725 |
| 37 | 2.08069 | 2.49335 | 2.98523 | 4.26809 | 6.08141 | 8.63609 |
| 38 | 2.12230 | 2.55568 | 3.07478 | 4.43881 | 6.38548 | 9.15425 |
| 39 | 2.16474 | 2.61957 | 3.16703 | 4.61637 | 6.70475 | 9.70351 |
| 40 | 2.20804 | 2.68506 | 3.26204 | 4.80102 | 7.03999 | 10.28572 |

TABLE 6-1   AMOUNT OF 1   **251**

AMOUNT OF 1   **TABLE 6-1**

| 8% | 9% | 10% | 11% | 12% | 15% | (n)<br>Periods |
|---|---|---|---|---|---|---|
| 1.08000 | 1.09000 | 1.10000 | 1.11000 | 1.12000 | 1.15000 | 1 |
| 1.16640 | 1.18810 | 1.21000 | 1.23210 | 1.25440 | 1.32250 | 2 |
| 1.25971 | 1.29503 | 1.33100 | 1.36763 | 1.40493 | 1.52088 | 3 |
| 1.36049 | 1.41158 | 1.46410 | 1.51807 | 1.57352 | 1.74901 | 4 |
| 1.46933 | 1.53862 | 1.61051 | 1.68506 | 1.76234 | 2.01136 | 5 |
| 1.58687 | 1.67710 | 1.77156 | 1.87041 | 1.97382 | 2.31306 | 6 |
| 1.71382 | 1.82804 | 1.94872 | 2.07616 | 2.21068 | 2.66002 | 7 |
| 1.85093 | 1.99256 | 2.14359 | 2.30454 | 2.47596 | 3.05902 | 8 |
| 1.99900 | 2.17189 | 2.35795 | 2.55803 | 2.77308 | 3.51788 | 9 |
| 2.15892 | 2.36736 | 2.59374 | 2.83942 | 3.10585 | 4.04556 | 10 |
| 2.33164 | 2.58043 | 2.85312 | 3.15176 | 3.47855 | 4.65239 | 11 |
| 2.51817 | 2.81267 | 3.13843 | 3.49845 | 3.89598 | 5.35025 | 12 |
| 2.71962 | 3.06581 | 3.45227 | 3.88328 | 4.36349 | 6.15279 | 13 |
| 2.93719 | 3.34173 | 3.79750 | 4.31044 | 4.88711 | 7.07571 | 14 |
| 3.17217 | 3.64248 | 4.17725 | 4.78459 | 5.47357 | 8.13706 | 15 |
| 3.42594 | 3.97031 | 4.59497 | 5.31089 | 6.13039 | 9.35762 | 16 |
| 3.70002 | 4.32763 | 5.05447 | 5.89509 | 6.86604 | 10.76126 | 17 |
| 3.99602 | 4.71712 | 5.55992 | 6.54355 | 7.68997 | 12.37545 | 18 |
| 4.31570 | 5.14166 | 6.11591 | 7.26334 | 8.61276 | 14.23177 | 19 |
| 4.66096 | 5.60441 | 6.72750 | 8.06231 | 9.64629 | 16.36654 | 20 |
| 5.03383 | 6.10881 | 7.40025 | 8.94917 | 10.80385 | 18.82152 | 21 |
| 5.43654 | 6.65860 | 8.14028 | 9.93357 | 12.10031 | 21.64475 | 22 |
| 5.87146 | 7.25787 | 8.95430 | 11.02627 | 13.55235 | 24.89146 | 23 |
| 6.34118 | 7.91108 | 9.84973 | 12.23916 | 15.17863 | 28.62518 | 24 |
| 6.84847 | 8.62308 | 10.83471 | 13.58546 | 17.00000 | 32.91895 | 25 |
| 7.39635 | 9.39916 | 11.91818 | 15.07986 | 19.04007 | 37.85680 | 26 |
| 7.98806 | 10.24508 | 13.10999 | 16.73865 | 21.32488 | 43.53532 | 27 |
| 8.62711 | 11.16714 | 14.42099 | 18.57990 | 23.88387 | 50.06561 | 28 |
| 9.31727 | 12.17218 | 15.86309 | 20.62369 | 26.74993 | 57.57545 | 29 |
| 10.06266 | 13.26768 | 17.44940 | 22.89230 | 29.95992 | 66.21177 | 30 |
| 10.86767 | 14.46177 | 19.19434 | 25.41045 | 33.55511 | 76.14354 | 31 |
| 11.73708 | 15.76333 | 21.11378 | 28.20560 | 37.58173 | 87.56507 | 32 |
| 12.67605 | 17.18203 | 23.22515 | 31.30821 | 42.09153 | 100.69983 | 33 |
| 13.69013 | 18.72841 | 25.54767 | 34.75212 | 47.14252 | 115.80480 | 34 |
| 14.78534 | 20.41397 | 28.10244 | 38.57485 | 52.79962 | 133.17552 | 35 |
| 15.96817 | 22.25123 | 30.91268 | 42.81808 | 59.13557 | 153.15185 | 36 |
| 17.24563 | 24.25384 | 34.00395 | 47.52807 | 66.23184 | 176.12463 | 37 |
| 18.62528 | 26.43668 | 37.40434 | 52.75616 | 74.17966 | 202.54332 | 38 |
| 20.11530 | 28.81598 | 41.14479 | 58.55934 | 83.08122 | 232.92482 | 39 |
| 21.72452 | 31.40942 | 45.25926 | 65.00087 | 93.05097 | 267.86355 | 40 |

**TABLE 6-2**    PRESENT VALUE OF 1

$$p_{\overline{n}|i} = \frac{1}{(1+i)^n} = (1+i)^{-n}$$

| (n) Periods | 2% | 2½% | 3% | 4% | 5% | 6% |
|---|---|---|---|---|---|---|
| 1 | .98039 | .97561 | .97087 | .96154 | .95238 | .94340 |
| 2 | .96117 | .95181 | .94260 | .92456 | .90703 | .89000 |
| 3 | .94232 | .92860 | .91514 | .88900 | .86384 | .83962 |
| 4 | .92385 | .90595 | .88849 | .85480 | .82270 | .79209 |
| 5 | .90573 | .88385 | .86261 | .82193 | .78353 | .74726 |
| 6 | .88797 | .86230 | .83748 | .79031 | .74622 | .70496 |
| 7 | .87056 | .84127 | .81309 | .75992 | .71068 | .66506 |
| 8 | .85349 | .82075 | .78941 | .73069 | .67684 | .62741 |
| 9 | .83676 | .80073 | .76642 | .70259 | .64461 | .59190 |
| 10 | .82035 | .78120 | .74409 | .67556 | .61391 | .55839 |
| 11 | .80426 | .76214 | .72242 | .64958 | .58468 | .52679 |
| 12 | .78849 | .74356 | .70138 | .62460 | .55684 | .49697 |
| 13 | .77303 | .72542 | .68095 | .60057 | .53032 | .46884 |
| 14 | .75788 | .70773 | .66112 | .57748 | .50507 | .44230 |
| 15 | .74301 | .69047 | .64186 | .55526 | .48102 | .41727 |
| 16 | .72845 | .67362 | .62317 | .53391 | .45811 | .39365 |
| 17 | .71416 | .65720 | .60502 | .51337 | .43630 | .37136 |
| 18 | .70016 | .64117 | .58739 | .49363 | .41552 | .35034 |
| 19 | .68643 | .62553 | .57029 | .47464 | .39573 | .33051 |
| 20 | .67297 | .61027 | .55368 | .45639 | .37689 | .31180 |
| 21 | .65978 | .59539 | .53755 | .43883 | .35894 | .29416 |
| 22 | .64684 | .58086 | .52189 | .42196 | .34185 | .27751 |
| 23 | .63416 | .56670 | .50669 | .40573 | .32557 | .26180 |
| 24 | .62172 | .55288 | .49193 | .39012 | .31007 | .24698 |
| 25 | .60953 | .53939 | .47761 | .37512 | .29530 | .23300 |
| 26 | .59758 | .52623 | .46369 | .36069 | .28124 | .21981 |
| 27 | .58586 | .51340 | .45019 | .34682 | .26785 | .20737 |
| 28 | .57437 | .50088 | .43708 | .33348 | .25509 | .19563 |
| 29 | .56311 | .48866 | .42435 | .32065 | .24295 | .18456 |
| 30 | .55207 | .47674 | .41199 | .30832 | .23138 | .17411 |
| 31 | .54125 | .46511 | .39999 | .29646 | .22036 | .16425 |
| 32 | .53063 | .45377 | .38834 | .28506 | .20987 | .15496 |
| 33 | .52023 | .44270 | .37703 | .27409 | .19987 | .14619 |
| 34 | .51003 | .43191 | .36604 | .26355 | .19035 | .13791 |
| 35 | .50003 | .42137 | .35538 | .25342 | .18129 | .13011 |
| 36 | .49022 | .41109 | .34503 | .24367 | .17266 | .12274 |
| 37 | .48061 | .40107 | .33498 | .23430 | .16444 | .11579 |
| 38 | .47119 | .39128 | .32523 | .22529 | .15661 | .10924 |
| 39 | .46195 | .38174 | .31575 | .21662 | .14915 | .10306 |
| 40 | .45289 | .37243 | .30656 | .20829 | .14205 | .09722 |

TABLE 6-2   PRESENT VALUE OF 1   **253**

PRESENT VALUE OF 1   **TABLE 6-2**

| 8% | 9% | 10% | 11% | 12% | 15% | (n) Periods |
|---|---|---|---|---|---|---|
| .92593 | .91743 | .90909 | .90090 | .89286 | .86957 | 1 |
| .85734 | .84168 | .82645 | .81162 | .79719 | .75614 | 2 |
| .79383 | .77218 | .75132 | .73119 | .71178 | .65752 | 3 |
| .73503 | .70843 | .68301 | .65873 | .63552 | .57175 | 4 |
| .68058 | .64993 | .62092 | .59345 | .56743 | .49718 | 5 |
| .63017 | .59627 | .56447 | .53464 | .50663 | .43233 | 6 |
| .58349 | .54703 | .51316 | .48166 | .45235 | .37594 | 7 |
| .54027 | .50187 | .46651 | .43393 | .40388 | .32690 | 8 |
| .50025 | .46043 | .42410 | .39092 | .36061 | .28426 | 9 |
| .46319 | .42241 | .38554 | .35218 | .32197 | .24719 | 10 |
| .42888 | .38753 | .35049 | .31728 | .28748 | .21494 | 11 |
| .39711 | .35554 | .31863 | .28584 | .25668 | .18691 | 12 |
| .36770 | .32618 | .28966 | .25751 | .22917 | .16253 | 13 |
| .34046 | .29925 | .26333 | .23199 | .20462 | .14133 | 14 |
| .31524 | .27454 | .23939 | .20900 | .18270 | .12289 | 15 |
| .29189 | .25187 | .21763 | .18829 | .16312 | .10687 | 16 |
| .27027 | .23107 | .19785 | .16963 | .14564 | .09293 | 17 |
| .25025 | .21199 | .17986 | .15282 | .13004 | .08081 | 18 |
| .23171 | .19449 | .16351 | .13768 | .11611 | .07027 | 19 |
| .21455 | .17843 | .14864 | .12403 | .10367 | .06110 | 20 |
| .19866 | .16370 | .13513 | .11174 | .09256 | .05313 | 21 |
| .18394 | .15018 | .12285 | .10067 | .08264 | .04620 | 22 |
| .17032 | .13778 | .11168 | .09069 | .07379 | .04017 | 23 |
| .15770 | .12641 | .10153 | .08170 | .06588 | .03493 | 24 |
| .14602 | .11597 | .09230 | .07361 | .05882 | .03038 | 25 |
| .13520 | .10639 | .08391 | .06631 | .05252 | .02642 | 26 |
| .12519 | .09761 | .07628 | .05974 | .04689 | .02297 | 27 |
| .11591 | .08955 | .06934 | .05382 | .04187 | .01997 | 28 |
| .10733 | .08216 | .06304 | .04849 | .03738 | .01737 | 29 |
| .09938 | .07537 | .05731 | .04368 | .03338 | .01510 | 30 |
| .09202 | .06915 | .05210 | .03935 | .02980 | .01313 | 31 |
| .08520 | .06344 | .04736 | .03545 | .02661 | .01142 | 32 |
| .07889 | .05820 | .04306 | .03194 | .02376 | .00993 | 33 |
| .07305 | .05340 | .03914 | .02878 | .02121 | .00864 | 34 |
| .06763 | .04899 | .03558 | .02592 | .01894 | .00751 | 35 |
| .06262 | .04494 | .03235 | .02335 | .01691 | .00653 | 36 |
| .05799 | .04123 | .02941 | .02104 | .01510 | .00568 | 37 |
| .05369 | .03783 | .02674 | .01896 | .01348 | .00494 | 38 |
| .04971 | .03470 | .02430 | .01708 | .01204 | .00429 | 39 |
| .04603 | .03184 | .02210 | .01538 | .01075 | .00373 | 40 |

**TABLE 6-3** AMOUNT OF AN ORDINARY ANNUITY OF 1

$$A_{\overline{n}|i} = \frac{(1 + i)^n - 1}{i}$$

| (n) Periods | 2% | 2½% | 3% | 4% | 5% | 6% |
|---|---|---|---|---|---|---|
| 1 | 1.00000 | 1.00000 | 1.00000 | 1.00000 | 1.00000 | 1.00000 |
| 2 | 2.02000 | 2.02500 | 2.03000 | 2.04000 | 2.05000 | 2.06000 |
| 3 | 3.06040 | 3.07563 | 3.09090 | 3.12160 | 3.15250 | 3.18360 |
| 4 | 4.12161 | 4.15252 | 4.18363 | 4.24646 | 4.31013 | 4.37462 |
| 5 | 5.20404 | 5.25633 | 5.30914 | 5.41632 | 5.52563 | 5.63709 |
| 6 | 6.30812 | 6.38774 | 6.46841 | 6.63298 | 6.80191 | 6.97532 |
| 7 | 7.43428 | 7.54743 | 7.66246 | 7.89829 | 8.14201 | 8.39384 |
| 8 | 8.58297 | 8.73612 | 8.89234 | 9.21423 | 9.54911 | 9.89747 |
| 9 | 9.75463 | 9.95452 | 10.15911 | 10.58280 | 11.02656 | 11.49132 |
| 10 | 10.94972 | 11.20338 | 11.46338 | 12.00611 | 12.57789 | 13.18079 |
| 11 | 12.16872 | 12.48347 | 12.80780 | 13.48635 | 14.20679 | 14.97164 |
| 12 | 13.41209 | 13.79555 | 14.19203 | 15.02581 | 15.91713 | 16.86994 |
| 13 | 14.68033 | 15.14044 | 15.61779 | 16.62684 | 17.71298 | 18.88214 |
| 14 | 15.97394 | 16.51895 | 17.08632 | 18.29191 | 19.59863 | 21.01507 |
| 15 | 17.29342 | 17.93193 | 18.59891 | 20.02359 | 21.57856 | 23.27597 |
| 16 | 18.63929 | 19.38022 | 20.15688 | 21.82453 | 23.65749 | 25.67253 |
| 17 | 20.01207 | 20.86473 | 21.76159 | 23.69751 | 25.84037 | 28.21288 |
| 18 | 21.41231 | 22.38635 | 23.41444 | 25.64541 | 28.13238 | 30.90565 |
| 19 | 22.84056 | 23.94601 | 25.11687 | 27.67123 | 30.53900 | 33.75999 |
| 20 | 24.29737 | 25.54466 | 26.87037 | 29.77808 | 33.06595 | 36.78559 |
| 21 | 25.78332 | 27.18327 | 28.67649 | 31.96920 | 35.71925 | 39.99273 |
| 22 | 27.29898 | 28.86286 | 30.53678 | 34.24797 | 38.50521 | 43.39229 |
| 23 | 28.84496 | 30.58443 | 32.45288 | 36.61789 | 41.43048 | 46.99583 |
| 24 | 30.42186 | 32.34904 | 34.42647 | 39.08260 | 44.50200 | 50.81558 |
| 25 | 32.03030 | 34.15776 | 36.45926 | 41.64591 | 47.72710 | 54.86451 |
| 26 | 33.67091 | 36.01171 | 38.55304 | 44.31174 | 51.11345 | 59.15638 |
| 27 | 35.34432 | 37.91200 | 40.70963 | 47.08421 | 54.66913 | 63.70577 |
| 28 | 37.05121 | 39.85980 | 42.93092 | 49.96758 | 58.40258 | 68.52811 |
| 29 | 38.79223 | 41.85630 | 45.21885 | 52.96629 | 62.32271 | 73.63980 |
| 30 | 40.56808 | 43.90270 | 47.57542 | 56.08494 | 66.43885 | 79.05819 |
| 31 | 42.37944 | 46.00027 | 50.00268 | 59.32834 | 70.76079 | 84.80168 |
| 32 | 44.22703 | 48.15028 | 52.50276 | 62.70147 | 75.29883 | 90.88978 |
| 33 | 46.11157 | 50.35403 | 55.07784 | 66.20953 | 80.06377 | 97.34316 |
| 34 | 48.03380 | 52.61289 | 57.73018 | 69.85791 | 85.06696 | 104.18376 |
| 35 | 49.99448 | 54.92821 | 60.46208 | 73.65222 | 90.32031 | 111.43478 |
| 36 | 51.99437 | 57.30141 | 63.27594 | 77.59831 | 95.83632 | 119.12087 |
| 37 | 54.03425 | 59.73395 | 66.17422 | 81.70225 | 101.62814 | 127.26812 |
| 38 | 56.11494 | 62.22730 | 69.15945 | 85.97034 | 107.70955 | 135.90421 |
| 39 | 58.23724 | 64.78298 | 72.23423 | 90.40915 | 114.09502 | 145.05846 |
| 40 | 60.40198 | 67.40255 | 75.40126 | 95.02552 | 120.79977 | 154.76197 |

TABLE 6-3   AMOUNT OF AN ORDINARY ANNUITY OF 1   **255**

| 8% | 9% | 10% | 11% | 12% | 15% | (n) Periods |
|---|---|---|---|---|---|---|
| 1.00000 | 1.00000 | 1.00000 | 1.00000 | 1.00000 | 1.00000 | 1 |
| 2.08000 | 2.09000 | 2.10000 | 2.11000 | 2.12000 | 2.15000 | 2 |
| 3.24640 | 3.27810 | 3.31000 | 3.34210 | 3.37440 | 3.47250 | 3 |
| 4.50611 | 4.57313 | 4.64100 | 4.70973 | 4.77933 | 4.99338 | 4 |
| 5.86660 | 5.98471 | 6.10510 | 6.22780 | 6.35285 | 6.74238 | 5 |
| 7.33592 | 7.52334 | 7.71561 | 7.91286 | 8.11519 | 8.75374 | 6 |
| 8.92280 | 9.20044 | 9.48717 | 9.78327 | 10.08901 | 11.06680 | 7 |
| 10.63663 | 11.02847 | 11.43589 | 11.85943 | 12.29969 | 13.72682 | 8 |
| 12.48756 | 13.02104 | 13.57948 | 14.16397 | 14.77566 | 16.78584 | 9 |
| 14.48656 | 15.19293 | 15.93743 | 16.72201 | 17.54874 | 20.30372 | 10 |
| 16.64549 | 17.56029 | 18.53117 | 19.56143 | 20.65458 | 24.34928 | 11 |
| 18.97713 | 20.14072 | 21.38428 | 22.71319 | 24.13313 | 29.00167 | 12 |
| 21.49530 | 22.95339 | 24.52271 | 26.21164 | 28.02911 | 34.35192 | 13 |
| 24.21492 | 26.01919 | 27.97498 | 30.09492 | 32.39260 | 40.50471 | 14 |
| 27.15211 | 29.36092 | 31.77248 | 34.40536 | 37.27972 | 47.58041 | 15 |
| 30.32428 | 33.00340 | 35.94973 | 39.18995 | 42.75328 | 55.71747 | 16 |
| 33.75023 | 36.97371 | 40.54470 | 44.50084 | 48.88367 | 65.07509 | 17 |
| 37.45024 | 41.30134 | 45.59917 | 50.39593 | 55.74972 | 75.83636 | 18 |
| 41.44626 | 46.01846 | 51.15909 | 56.93949 | 63.43968 | 88.21181 | 19 |
| 45.76196 | 51.16012 | 57.27500 | 64.20283 | 72.05244 | 102.44358 | 20 |
| 50.42292 | 56.76453 | 64.00250 | 72.26514 | 81.69874 | 118.81012 | 21 |
| 55.45676 | 62.87334 | 71.40275 | 81.21431 | 92.50258 | 137.63164 | 22 |
| 60.89330 | 69.53194 | 79.54302 | 91.14788 | 104.60289 | 159.27638 | 23 |
| 66.76476 | 76.78981 | 88.49733 | 102.17415 | 118.15524 | 184.16784 | 24 |
| 73.10594 | 84.70090 | 98.34706 | 114.41331 | 133.33387 | 212.79302 | 25 |
| 79.95442 | 93.32398 | 109.18177 | 127.99877 | 150.33393 | 245.71197 | 26 |
| 87.35077 | 102.72314 | 121.09994 | 143.07864 | 169.37401 | 283.56877 | 27 |
| 95.33883 | 112.96822 | 134.20994 | 159.81729 | 190.69889 | 327.10408 | 28 |
| 103.96594 | 124.13536 | 148.63093 | 178.39719 | 214.58275 | 377.16969 | 29 |
| 113.28321 | 136.30754 | 164.49402 | 199.02088 | 241.33268 | 434.74515 | 30 |
| 123.34587 | 149.57522 | 181.94343 | 221.91317 | 271.29261 | 500.95692 | 31 |
| 134.21354 | 164.03699 | 201.13777 | 247.32362 | 304.84772 | 577.10046 | 32 |
| 145.95062 | 179.80032 | 222.25154 | 275.52922 | 342.42945 | 644.66553 | 33 |
| 158.62667 | 196.98234 | 245.47670 | 306.83744 | 384.52098 | 765.36535 | 34 |
| 172.31680 | 215.71076 | 271.02437 | 341.58955 | 431.66350 | 881.17016 | 35 |
| 187.10215 | 236.12472 | 299.12681 | 380.16441 | 484.46312 | 1014.34568 | 36 |
| 203.07032 | 258.37595 | 330.03949 | 422.98249 | 543.59869 | 1167.49753 | 37 |
| 220.31595 | 282.62978 | 364.04343 | 470.51056 | 609.83053 | 1343.62216 | 38 |
| 238.94122 | 309.06646 | 401.44778 | 523.26673 | 684.01020 | 1546.16549 | 39 |
| 259.05652 | 337.88245 | 442.59256 | 581.82607 | 767.09142 | 1779.09031 | 40 |

**TABLE 6-4** PRESENT VALUE OF AN ORDINARY ANNUITY OF 1

$$P_{\overline{n}|i} = \frac{1 - \dfrac{1}{(1 + i)^n}}{i} = \frac{1 - p_{\overline{n}|i}}{i}$$

| (n) Periods | 2% | 2½% | 3% | 4% | 5% | 6% |
|---|---|---|---|---|---|---|
| 1 | .98039 | .97561 | .97087 | .96154 | .95238 | .94340 |
| 2 | 1.94156 | 1.92742 | 1.91347 | 1.88609 | 1.85941 | 1.83339 |
| 3 | 2.88388 | 2.85602 | 2.82861 | 2.77509 | 2.72325 | 2.67301 |
| 4 | 3.80773 | 3.76197 | 3.71710 | 3.62990 | 3.54595 | 3.46511 |
| 5 | 4.71346 | 4.64583 | 4.57971 | 4.45182 | 4.32948 | 4.21236 |
| 6 | 5.60143 | 5.50813 | 5.41719 | 5.24214 | 5.07569 | 4.91732 |
| 7 | 6.47199 | 6.34939 | 6.23028 | 6.00205 | 5.78637 | 5.58238 |
| 8 | 7.32548 | 7.17014 | 7.01969 | 6.73274 | 6.46321 | 6.20979 |
| 9 | 8.16224 | 7.97087 | 7.78611 | 7.43533 | 7.10782 | 6.80169 |
| 10 | 8.98259 | 8.75206 | 8.53020 | 8.11090 | 7.72173 | 7.36009 |
| 11 | 9.78685 | 9.51421 | 9.25262 | 8.76048 | 8.30641 | 7.88687 |
| 12 | 10.57534 | 10.25776 | 9.95400 | 9.38507 | 8.86325 | 8.38384 |
| 13 | 11.34837 | 10.98319 | 10.63496 | 9.98565 | 9.39357 | 8.85268 |
| 14 | 12.10625 | 11.69091 | 11.29607 | 10.56312 | 9.89864 | 9.29498 |
| 15 | 12.84926 | 12.38138 | 11.93794 | 11.11839 | 10.37966 | 9.71225 |
| 16 | 13.57771 | 13.05500 | 12.56110 | 11.65230 | 10.83777 | 10.10590 |
| 17 | 14.29187 | 13.71220 | 13.16612 | 12.16567 | 11.27407 | 10.47726 |
| 18 | 14.99203 | 14.35336 | 13.75351 | 12.65930 | 11.68959 | 10.82760 |
| 19 | 15.67846 | 14.97889 | 14.32380 | 13.13394 | 12.08532 | 11.15812 |
| 20 | 16.35143 | 15.58916 | 14.87747 | 13.59033 | 12.46221 | 11.46992 |
| 21 | 17.01121 | 16.18455 | 15.41502 | 14.02916 | 12.82115 | 11.76408 |
| 22 | 17.65805 | 16.76541 | 15.93692 | 14.45112 | 13.16300 | 12.04158 |
| 23 | 18.29220 | 17.33211 | 16.44361 | 14.85684 | 13.48857 | 12.30338 |
| 24 | 18.91393 | 17.88499 | 16.93554 | 15.24696 | 13.79864 | 12.55036 |
| 25 | 19.52346 | 18.42438 | 17.41315 | 15.62208 | 14.09394 | 12.78336 |
| 26 | 20.12104 | 18.95061 | 17.87684 | 15.98277 | 14.37519 | 13.00317 |
| 27 | 20.70690 | 19.46401 | 18.32703 | 16.32959 | 14.64303 | 13.21053 |
| 28 | 21.28127 | 19.96489 | 18.76411 | 16.66306 | 14.89813 | 13.40616 |
| 29 | 21.84438 | 20.45355 | 19.18845 | 16.98371 | 15.14107 | 13.59072 |
| 30 | 22.39646 | 20.93029 | 19.60044 | 17.29203 | 15.37245 | 13.76483 |
| 31 | 22.93770 | 21.39541 | 20.00043 | 17.58849 | 15.59281 | 13.92909 |
| 32 | 23.46833 | 21.84918 | 20.38877 | 17.87355 | 15.80268 | 14.08404 |
| 33 | 23.98856 | 22.29188 | 20.76579 | 18.14765 | 16.00255 | 14.23023 |
| 34 | 24.49859 | 22.72379 | 21.13184 | 18.41120 | 16.19290 | 14.36814 |
| 35 | 24.99862 | 23.14516 | 21.48722 | 18.66461 | 16.37419 | 14.49825 |
| 36 | 25.48884 | 23.55625 | 21.83225 | 18.90828 | 16.54685 | 14.62099 |
| 37 | 25.96945 | 23.95732 | 22.16724 | 19.14258 | 16.71129 | 14.73678 |
| 38 | 26.44064 | 24.34860 | 22.49246 | 19.36786 | 16.86789 | 14.84602 |
| 39 | 26.90259 | 24.73034 | 22.80822 | 19.58448 | 17.01704 | 14.94907 |
| 40 | 27.35548 | 25.10278 | 23.11477 | 19.79277 | 17.15909 | 15.04630 |

TABLE 6-4   PRESENT VALUE OF AN ORDINARY ANNUITY OF 1   **257**

PRESENT VALUE OF AN ORDINARY ANNUITY OF 1   **TABLE 6-4**

| 8% | 9% | 10% | 11% | 12% | 15% | (n) Periods |
|---|---|---|---|---|---|---|
| .92593 | .91743 | .90909 | .90090 | .89286 | .86957 | 1 |
| 1.78326 | 1.75911 | 1.73554 | 1.71252 | 1.69005 | 1.62571 | 2 |
| 2.57710 | 2.53130 | 2.48685 | 2.44371 | 2.40183 | 2.28323 | 3 |
| 3.31213 | 3.23972 | 3.16986 | 3.10245 | 3.03735 | 2.85498 | 4 |
| 3.99271 | 3.88965 | 3.79079 | 3.69590 | 3.60478 | 3.35216 | 5 |
| 4.62288 | 4.48592 | 4.35526 | 4.23054 | 4.11141 | 3.78448 | 6 |
| 5.20637 | 5.03295 | 4.86842 | 4.71220 | 4.56376 | 4.16042 | 7 |
| 5.74664 | 5.53482 | 5.33493 | 5.14612 | 4.96764 | 4.48732 | 8 |
| 6.24689 | 5.99525 | 5.75902 | 5.53705 | 5.32825 | 4.77158 | 9 |
| 6.71008 | 6.41766 | 6.14457 | 5.88923 | 5.65022 | 5.01877 | 10 |
| 7.13896 | 6.80519 | 6.49506 | 6.20652 | 5.93770 | 5.23371 | 11 |
| 7.53608 | 7.16073 | 6.81369 | 6.49236 | 6.19437 | 5.42062 | 12 |
| 7.90378 | 7.48690 | 7.10336 | 6.74987 | 6.42355 | 5.58315 | 13 |
| 8.24424 | 7.78615 | 7.36669 | 6.98187 | 6.62817 | 5.72448 | 14 |
| 8.55948 | 8.06069 | 7.60608 | 7.19087 | 6.81086 | 5.84737 | 15 |
| 8.85137 | 8.31256 | 7.82371 | 7.37916 | 6.97399 | 5.95424 | 16 |
| 9.12164 | 8.54363 | 8.02155 | 7.54879 | 7.11963 | 6.04716 | 17 |
| 9.37189 | 8.75563 | 8.20141 | 7.70162 | 7.24967 | 6.12797 | 18 |
| 9.60360 | 8.95012 | 8.36492 | 7.83929 | 7.36578 | 6.19823 | 19 |
| 9.81815 | 9.12855 | 8.51356 | 7.96333 | 7.46944 | 6.25933 | 20 |
| 10.01680 | 9.29224 | 8.64869 | 8.07507 | 7.56200 | 6.31246 | 21 |
| 10.20074 | 9.44243 | 8.77154 | 8.17574 | 7.64465 | 6.35866 | 22 |
| 10.37106 | 9.58021 | 8.88322 | 8.26643 | 7.71843 | 6.39884 | 23 |
| 10.52876 | 9.70661 | 8.98474 | 8.34814 | 7.78432 | 6.43377 | 24 |
| 10.67478 | 9.82258 | 9.07704 | 8.42174 | 7.84314 | 6.46415 | 25 |
| 10.80998 | 9.92897 | 9.16095 | 8.48806 | 7.89566 | 6.49056 | 26 |
| 10.93516 | 10.02658 | 9.23722 | 8.54780 | 7.94255 | 6.51353 | 27 |
| 11.05108 | 10.11613 | 9.30657 | 8.60162 | 7.98442 | 6.53351 | 28 |
| 11.15841 | 10.19828 | 9.36961 | 8.65011 | 8.02181 | 6.55088 | 29 |
| 11.25778 | 10.27365 | 9.42691 | 8.69379 | 8.05518 | 6.56598 | 30 |
| 11.34980 | 10.34280 | 9.47901 | 8.73315 | 8.08499 | 6.57911 | 31 |
| 11.43500 | 10.40624 | 9.52638 | 8.76860 | 8.11159 | 6.59053 | 32 |
| 11.51389 | 10.46444 | 9.56943 | 8.80054 | 8.13535 | 6.60046 | 33 |
| 11.58693 | 10.51784 | 9.60858 | 8.82932 | 8.15656 | 6.60910 | 34 |
| 11.65457 | 10.56682 | 9.64416 | 8.85524 | 8.17550 | 6.61661 | 35 |
| 11.71719 | 10.61176 | 9.67651 | 8.87859 | 8.19241 | 6.62314 | 36 |
| 11.77518 | 10.65299 | 9.70592 | 8.89963 | 8.20751 | 6.62882 | 37 |
| 11.82887 | 10.69082 | 9.73265 | 8.91859 | 8.22099 | 6.63375 | 38 |
| 11.87858 | 10.72552 | 9.75697 | 8.93567 | 8.23303 | 6.63805 | 39 |
| 11.92461 | 10.75736 | 9.77905 | 8.95105 | 8.24378 | 6.64178 | 40 |

**TABLE 6-5** PRESENT VALUE OF AN ANNUITY DUE OF 1

$$PD_{\overline{n}|i} = 1 + \frac{1 - \dfrac{1}{(1+i)^{n-1}}}{i} = (1+i)\left(\frac{1 - p_{\overline{n}|i}}{i}\right) = (1+i)\,P_{\overline{n}|i}$$

| (n) Periods | 2% | 2½% | 3% | 4% | 5% | 6% |
|---|---|---|---|---|---|---|
| 1 | 1.00000 | 1.00000 | 1.00000 | 1.00000 | 1.00000 | 1.00000 |
| 2 | 1.98039 | 1.97561 | 1.97087 | 1.96154 | 1.95238 | 1.94340 |
| 3 | 2.94156 | 2.92742 | 2.91347 | 2.88609 | 2.85941 | 2.83339 |
| 4 | 3.88388 | 3.85602 | 3.82861 | 3.77509 | 3.72325 | 3.67301 |
| 5 | 4.80773 | 4.76197 | 4.71710 | 4.62990 | 4.54595 | 4.46511 |
| 6 | 5.71346 | 5.64583 | 5.57971 | 5.45182 | 5.32948 | 5.21236 |
| 7 | 6.60143 | 6.50813 | 6.41719 | 6.24214 | 6.07569 | 5.91732 |
| 8 | 7.47199 | 7.34939 | 7.23028 | 7.00205 | 6.78637 | 6.58238 |
| 9 | 8.32548 | 8.17014 | 8.01969 | 7.73274 | 7.46321 | 7.20979 |
| 10 | 9.16224 | 8.97087 | 8.78611 | 8.43533 | 8.10782 | 7.80169 |
| 11 | 9.98259 | 9.75206 | 9.53020 | 9.11090 | 8.72173 | 8.36009 |
| 12 | 10.78685 | 10.51421 | 10.25262 | 9.76048 | 9.30641 | 8.88687 |
| 13 | 11.57534 | 11.25776 | 10.95400 | 10.38507 | 9.86325 | 9.38384 |
| 14 | 12.34837 | 11.98319 | 11.63496 | 10.98565 | 10.39357 | 9.85268 |
| 15 | 13.10625 | 12.69091 | 12.29607 | 11.56312 | 10.89864 | 10.29498 |
| 16 | 13.84926 | 13.38138 | 12.93794 | 12.11839 | 11.37966 | 10.71225 |
| 17 | 14.57771 | 14.05500 | 13.56110 | 12.65230 | 11.83777 | 11.10590 |
| 18 | 15.29187 | 14.71220 | 14.16612 | 13.16567 | 12.27407 | 11.47726 |
| 19 | 15.99203 | 15.35336 | 14.75351 | 13.65930 | 12.68959 | 11.82760 |
| 20 | 16.67846 | 15.97889 | 15.32380 | 14.13394 | 13.08532 | 12.15812 |
| 21 | 17.35143 | 16.58916 | 15.87747 | 14.59033 | 13.46221 | 12.46992 |
| 22 | 18.01121 | 17.18455 | 16.41502 | 15.02916 | 13.82115 | 12.76408 |
| 23 | 18.65805 | 17.76541 | 16.93692 | 15.45112 | 14.16300 | 13.04158 |
| 24 | 19.29220 | 18.33211 | 17.44361 | 15.85684 | 14.48857 | 13.30338 |
| 25 | 19.91393 | 18.88499 | 17.93554 | 16.24696 | 14.79864 | 13.55036 |
| 26 | 20.52346 | 19.42438 | 18.41315 | 16.62208 | 15.09394 | 13.78336 |
| 27 | 21.12104 | 19.95061 | 18.87684 | 16.98277 | 15.37519 | 14.00317 |
| 28 | 21.70690 | 20.46401 | 19.32703 | 17.32959 | 15.64303 | 14.21053 |
| 29 | 22.28127 | 20.96489 | 19.76411 | 17.66306 | 15.89813 | 14.40616 |
| 30 | 22.84438 | 21.45355 | 20.18845 | 17.98371 | 16.14107 | 14.59072 |
| 31 | 23.39646 | 21.93029 | 20.60044 | 18.29203 | 16.37245 | 14.76483 |
| 32 | 23.93770 | 22.39541 | 21.00043 | 18.58849 | 16.59281 | 14.92909 |
| 33 | 24.46833 | 22.84918 | 21.38877 | 18.87355 | 16.80268 | 15.08404 |
| 34 | 24.98856 | 23.29188 | 21.76579 | 19.14765 | 17.00255 | 15.23023 |
| 35 | 25.49859 | 23.72379 | 22.13184 | 19.41120 | 17.19290 | 15.36814 |
| 36 | 25.99862 | 24.14516 | 22.48722 | 19.66461 | 17.37419 | 15.49825 |
| 37 | 26.48884 | 24.55625 | 22.83225 | 19.90828 | 17.54685 | 15.62099 |
| 38 | 26.96945 | 24.95732 | 23.16724 | 20.14258 | 17.71129 | 15.73678 |
| 39 | 27.44064 | 25.34860 | 23.49246 | 20.36786 | 17.86789 | 15.84602 |
| 40 | 27.90259 | 25.73034 | 23.80822 | 20.58448 | 18.01704 | 15.94907 |

TABLE 6-5   PRESENT VALUE OF AN ANNUITY DUE OF 1   **259**

PRESENT VALUE OF AN ANNUITY DUE OF 1   **TABLE 6-5**

| 8% | 9% | 10% | 11% | 12% | 15% | (n) Periods |
|---|---|---|---|---|---|---|
| 1.00000 | 1.00000 | 1.00000 | 1.00000 | 1.00000 | 1.00000 | 1 |
| 1.92593 | 1.91743 | 1.90909 | 1.90090 | 1.89286 | 1.86957 | 2 |
| 2.78326 | 2.75911 | 2.73554 | 2.71252 | 2.69005 | 2.62571 | 3 |
| 3.57710 | 3.53130 | 3.48685 | 3.44371 | 3.40183 | 3.28323 | 4 |
| 4.31213 | 4.23972 | 4.16986 | 4.10245 | 4.03735 | 3.85498 | 5 |
| 4.99271 | 4.88965 | 4.79079 | 4.69590 | 4.60478 | 4.35216 | 6 |
| 5.62288 | 5.48592 | 5.35526 | 5.23054 | 5.11141 | 4.78448 | 7 |
| 6.20637 | 6.03295 | 5.86842 | 5.71220 | 5.56376 | 5.16042 | 8 |
| 6.74664 | 6.53482 | 6.33493 | 6.14612 | 5.96764 | 5.48732 | 9 |
| 7.24689 | 6.99525 | 6.75902 | 6.53705 | 6.32825 | 5.77158 | 10 |
| 7.71008 | 7.41766 | 7.14457 | 6.88923 | 6.65022 | 6.01877 | 11 |
| 8.13896 | 7.80519 | 7.49506 | 7.20652 | 6.93770 | 6.23371 | 12 |
| 8.53608 | 8.16073 | 7.81369 | 7.49236 | 7.19437 | 6.42062 | 13 |
| 8.90378 | 8.48690 | 8.10336 | 7.74987 | 7.42355 | 6.58315 | 14 |
| 9.24424 | 8.78615 | 8.36669 | 7.98187 | 7.62817 | 6.72448 | 15 |
| 9.55948 | 9.06069 | 8.60608 | 8.19087 | 7.81086 | 6.84737 | 16 |
| 9.85137 | 9.31256 | 8.82371 | 8.37916 | 7.97399 | 6.95424 | 17 |
| 10.12164 | 9.54363 | 9.02155 | 8.54879 | 8.11963 | 7.04716 | 18 |
| 10.37189 | 9.75563 | 9.20141 | 8.70162 | 8.24967 | 7.12797 | 19 |
| 10.60360 | 9.95012 | 9.36492 | 8.83929 | 8.36578 | 7.19823 | 20 |
| 10.81815 | 10.12855 | 9.51356 | 8.96333 | 8.46944 | 7.25933 | 21 |
| 11.01680 | 10.29224 | 9.64869 | 9.07507 | 8.56200 | 7.31246 | 22 |
| 11.20074 | 10.44243 | 9.77154 | 9.17574 | 8.64465 | 7.35866 | 23 |
| 11.37106 | 10.58021 | 9.88322 | 9.26643 | 8.71843 | 7.39884 | 24 |
| 11.52876 | 10.70661 | 9.98474 | 9.34814 | 8.78432 | 7.43377 | 25 |
| 11.67478 | 10.82258 | 10.07704 | 9.42174 | 8.84314 | 7.46415 | 26 |
| 11.80998 | 10.92897 | 10.16095 | 9.48806 | 8.89566 | 7.49056 | 27 |
| 11.93518 | 11.02658 | 10.23722 | 9.54780 | 8.94255 | 7.51353 | 28 |
| 12.05108 | 11.11613 | 10.30657 | 9.60162 | 8.98442 | 7.53351 | 29 |
| 12.15841 | 11.19828 | 10.36961 | 9.65011 | 9.02181 | 7.55088 | 30 |
| 12.25778 | 11.27365 | 10.42691 | 9.69379 | 9.05518 | 7.56598 | 31 |
| 12.34980 | 11.34280 | 10.47901 | 9.73315 | 9.08499 | 7.57911 | 32 |
| 12.43500 | 11.40624 | 10.52638 | 9.76860 | 9.11159 | 7.59053 | 33 |
| 12.51389 | 11.46444 | 10.56943 | 9.80054 | 9.13535 | 7.60046 | 34 |
| 12.58693 | 11.51784 | 10.60858 | 9.82932 | 9.15656 | 7.60910 | 35 |
| 12.65457 | 11.56682 | 10.64416 | 9.85524 | 9.17550 | 7.61661 | 36 |
| 12.71719 | 11.61176 | 10.67651 | 9.87859 | 9.19241 | 7.62314 | 37 |
| 12.77518 | 11.65299 | 10.70592 | 9.89963 | 9.20751 | 7.62882 | 38 |
| 12.82887 | 11.69082 | 10.73265 | 9.91859 | 9.22099 | 7.63375 | 39 |
| 12.87858 | 11.72552 | 10.75697 | 9.93567 | 9.23303 | 7.63805 | 40 |

## SUMMARY OF FUNDAMENTAL TERMS AND CONCEPTS

The following list of terms and their definitions is provided as a summarization and review of the essential items presented in this chapter.

---

### FUNDAMENTAL TERMS AND CONCEPTS

1. **SIMPLE INTEREST.** Interest on principal only, regardless of interest that may have accrued in the past.

2. **COMPOUND INTEREST.** Interest accrues on the unpaid interest of past periods as well as on the principal.

3. **RATE OF INTEREST.** Interest is usually expressed as an annual rate, but when the interest period is shorter than one year, the interest rate for the shorter period must be determined.

4. **ANNUITY.** A series of payments or receipts (called rents) which occur at equal intervals of time.
   Types of annuities:
   (a) **ORDINARY ANNUITY.** Each rent is payable (receivable) at the **end** of a period.
   (b) **ANNUITY DUE.** Each rent is payable (receivable) at the **beginning** of the period.

5. **AMOUNT.** Value at a later date of a given sum that is invested at compound interest.
   (a) **AMOUNT OF 1** (or amount of a given sum). The future value of $1.00 (or a single given sum), $a$, at the end of $n$ periods at $i$ compound interest rate (Table 6–1).
   (b) **AMOUNT OF AN ANNUITY.** The amount of a series of rents invested at compound interest; in other words, it is the accumulated total that results from a series of equal deposits at regular intervals invested at compound interest. Both deposits and interest increase the accumulation.
   
   (1) **AMOUNT OF AN ORDINARY ANNUITY.** The future value **on** the date of the last rent (hence, there is one less interest period than rents—this is taken into account in the computation of Table 6–3).
   (2) **AMOUNT OF AN ANNUITY DUE.** The future value **one period after** the date of the last rent (hence, there are the same number of interest periods as rents). When an annuity due table is not available, use Table 6–3 with the following formula:

   Amount of annuity due of 1 for $n$ rents =
   Amount of ordinary annuity for $(n + 1$ rents$) - 1$.

6. **PRESENT VALUE.** The value at an earlier date (usually now) of a given sum in the future discounted at compound interest.
   (a) **PRESENT VALUE OF 1** (or present value of a single sum). The present value (worth) of $1.00 (or a given sum) due $n$ periods hence, discounted at $i$ compound interest (Table 6–2).
   (b) **PRESENT VALUE OF AN ANNUITY.** The present value (worth) of a series of rents discounted at compound interest; in other words, it is the sum when invested at compound interest that will permit a series of equal withdrawals at regular intervals.
   
   (1) **PRESENT VALUE OF AN ORDINARY ANNUITY.** The value now of $1.00 to be received or paid at the end of each period (rents) for $n$ periods, discounted at $i$ compound interest (Table 6–4).
   (2) **PRESENT VALUE OF AN ANNUITY DUE.** The value now of $1.00 to be received or paid at the beginning of each period (rents) for the $n$ periods, discounted at $i$ compound interest; thus there is one less discount period than rents (Table 6–5). To use Table 6–4 for an annuity due, apply this formula:

   Present value of annuity due of 1 for $n$ rents =
   Present value of an ordinary annuity of $(n - 1$ rents$) + 1$.

# QUESTIONS

1. What is the time value of money? Why should accountants have an understanding of compound interest, annuities, and present value concepts?

2. What is the nature of interest? Distinguish between "simple interest" and "compound interest."

3. Presented below are a number of values taken from compound interest tables involving the same number of periods and the same rate of interest. Indicate what each of these four values represent.
   - (a) .10367
   - (b) 7.46944
   - (c) 9.64629
   - (d) 72.05244

4. Thomas Linsmeier deposited $15,000 in a money market certificate that provides interest of 12% compounded quarterly if the amount is maintained for three years. How much will Linsmeier have at the end of three years?

5. Thomas Buttars will receive $25,000 on December 31, 1988 (five years from now) from a trust fund established by his father. Assuming the appropriate interest rate for discounting is 12% (compounded semiannually), what is the present value of this amount today?

6. What are the primary characteristics of an annuity? Differentiate between an "ordinary annuity" and an "annuity due."

7. Hillside, Inc. owes $25,000 to Lowery Company. How much would Hillside have to pay each year if the debt is retired through four equal payments (made at the end of the year) given an interest rate on the debt of 15%? (Round to two decimal places.)

8. The Hogans are planning for a retirement home. They estimate they will need $100,000 four years from now to purchase this home. Assuming an interest rate of 10%, what amount must be deposited at the end of each of the four years to fund the home price?

9. Assume the same situation as in question 8, except that the four equal amounts are deposited at the beginning of the period rather than at the end. In this case, what amount must be deposited at the beginning of each period?

10. Explain how the amount of an ordinary annuity interest table is converted to the amount of an annuity due table.

11. Explain how the present value of an ordinary annuity interest table is converted to the present value of an annuity due interest table.

12. Albrecht Enterprises leases property to Erin, Inc. Because Erin, Inc. is experiencing financial difficulty, Albrecht agrees to receive five rents of $8,000 at the end of each year, with the rents deferred three years and interest accruing at the rate of 12%. What is the present value of the five rents?

13. Warner, Inc. invests $20,000 initially, which accumulates to $38,000 at the end of five years. What is the annual interest rate of the investment paid? (Hint: Interpolation will be needed.)

14. What are the components that comprise an interest rate? Why is it important for accountants to understand these components?

15. Answer the following questions:
    - (a) On May 1, 1983, Sanchez Company sold some machinery to Hargrove Company on an installment contract basis. The contract required five equal annual payments, with the first payment due on May 1, 1983. What present value concept is appropriate for this situation?
    - (b) On June 1, 1983, Sunset, Inc. purchased a new machine that it does not have to pay for until May 1, 1985. The total payment on May 1, 1985 will include both principal and interest. Assuming interest at a 15% rate, the cost of the machine would be the total payment multiplied by what time value of money concept?
    - (c) Fortune, Inc. wishes to know how much monies it will have available in five years if five equal amounts of $20,000 are invested, with the first amount invested immediately. What interest table is appropriate for this situation?
    - (d) El Cerro invests in a "jumbo" $100,000 three-year certificate of deposit at City Bank. What table would be used to determine the amount accumulated at the end of three years?

## EXERCISES

(Interest rates are per annum unless otherwise indicated.)

**E6–1** Joanie Schmidt invests $2,000 at 8% annual interest, leaving the money invested without withdrawing any of the interest for ten years. At the end of the ten years, Joanie withdrew the accumulated amount of money.

**Instructions**

(a) Compute the amount Joanie would withdraw assuming the investment earns **simple interest.**
(b) Compute the amount Joanie would withdraw assuming the investment earns **interest compounded annually.**
(c) Compute the amount Joanie would withdraw assuming the investment earns **interest compounded semiannually.**

**E6–2** For each of the following cases, indicate (a) to what rate columns and (b) to what number of periods you would refer in looking up the interest factor.

**1.** In an amount of 1 table

| Annual Rate | Number of Years Invested | Compounded |
|---|---|---|
| a.  6% | 15 | Annually |
| b.  10% | 6 | Quarterly |
| c.  8% | 15 | Semiannually |

**2.** In a present value of an annuity of 1 table

| Annual Rate | Number of Years Involved | Number of Rents Involved | Frequency of Rents |
|---|---|---|---|
| a.  12% | 20 | 20 | Annually |
| b.  10% | 5 | 10 | Semiannually |
| c.  8% | 4 | 16 | Quarterly |

**E6–3** Merriment Company recently signed a lease for a new office building, for a lease period of 25 years. Under the lease agreement, a security deposit of $10,000 is made, with the deposit to be returned at the expiration of the lease, with interest compounded at 10% per year.

**Instructions**

What amount will the company receive at the time the lease expires?

**E6–4** Under the terms of his salary agreement, President Joe Leo has an option of receiving either an immediate bonus of $20,000, or a deferred bonus of $40,000, payable in 20 years. Ignoring tax considerations, and assuming a relevant interest rate of 6%, which form of settlement should President Leo accept?

**E6–5** Determine the amount that must be deposited now at compound interest to provide the desired sum at the end of the following designated periods at the interest rate specified.

(a) Dollars to be invested and held for 5 years at 8% per year to amount to $1,500.
(b) Dollars to be invested and held for 8 years at 6% per year, then invested at 8% per year and held for another 5 years to amount to $10,000.
(c) Dollars to be invested now at 12% per year and held for 30 years to have $100,000 at retirement.

**E6–6** Using the appropriate interest table, compute the amounts to be invested now at compound interest in order to provide the following sums at the end of the designated periods.
  (a) Amount invested for 5 periods at 6% to amount to $15,000.
  (b) Amount invested for 15 periods at 10% to amount to $15,000.
  (c) Amount invested for five years at 6%, then at 8% for another five years to amount to $15,000.

**E6–7** Using the appropriate interest table, compute the amounts to which the following periodic investments would accumulate at compound interest by the end of the last period in which an investment is made (end-of-period payments).
  (a) $12,000 each period for ten periods at 8%.
  (b) $12,000 each period for thirty periods at 6%.
  (c) $12,000 each period for ten periods at 8% and then $12,000 each period for the eleventh through the twentieth periods at 10%.

**E6–8** Musical Corporation, having recently issued a $10 million, 10-year bond issue, is committed to make annual sinking fund deposits of $600,000. The deposits are made on the last day of each year, and yield a return of 10%. Will the fund at the end of 10 years be sufficient to retire the bonds? If not, what will the deficiency be?

**E6–9** Determine the amount that Zaf Iqbal would have at the end of 1991 if investments were made under the following conditions:
  (a) $1,000 is to be invested at the end of each year, 1982 through 1991, at 9% interest compounded annually.
  (b) $1,000 is to be invested at the beginning of each year, 1982 through 1991, at 9% interest compounded annually.

**E6–10** Using the appropriate interest table, answer each of the following questions (each case is independent of the others).
  (a) What is the future amount of $2,500 at the end of 10 periods at 8% compounded interest?
  (b) What is the present value of $2,500 due 8 periods hence, discounted at 10%?
  (c) What is the future amount of 15 periodic payments of $2,500 each made at the end of each period and compounded at 6%?
  (d) What is the present value of $2,500 to be received at the end of each of 30 periods, discounted at 5% compound interest?

**E6–11** Using the appropriate interest table, answer the following questions (each case is independent of the others).
  (a) What is the future amount of 15 periodic payments of $1,200 each made at the beginning of each period and compounded at 10%?
  (b) What is the present value of $1,000 to be received at the beginning of each of thirty periods, discounted at 9% compound interest?
  (c) What is the future amount of 10 deposits of $500 each made at the beginning of each period and compounded at 8%? (Future amount as of the end of the tenth period.)
  (d) What is the present value of eight receipts of $900 each received at the beginning of each period, discounted at 10% compounded interest?

**E6–12** What would you pay for a $10,000 debenture bond that matures in 30 years and pays $1,000 a year in interest if you wanted to earn a yield of:
  (a) 8%?
  (b) 10%?
  (c) 12%?

**E6–13** Mr. Greg Garious, a super salesman contemplating retirement on his fifty-fifth birthday, decides to create a fund on a 10% basis that will enable him to withdraw $5,000 per year on June 30, beginning in 1988, and continuing through 1991. To develop this fund, Greg intends to make equal contributions on June 30 of each of the years 1984–1987.

**Instructions**

(a) How much must the balance of the fund equal on June 30, 1987, in order for Greg Garious to satisfy his objective?

(b) What are each of Greg's contributions to the fund?

**E6–14** Using the appropriate interest table, compute the present values of the following periodic amounts due at the end of the designated periods.

(a) $18,500 receivable at the end of each period for ten periods compounded at 8%.

(b) $18,500 payments to be made at the end of each period for sixteen periods at 10%.

(c) $18,500 payable at the end of the seventh, eighth, ninth, and tenth periods at 8%.

**E6–15** Leslie Topple wishes to invest $10,000 on July 1, 1983 and have it accumulate to $22,000 by July 1, 1993.

**Instructions**

At what exact annual rate of interest must Leslie invest the $10,000? (Interpolation is required.)

**E6–16** On July 17, 1982, Eric Stottrup borrowed $40,000 from his grandfather to open a clothing store. Starting July 17, 1983, Eric has to make five equal annual payments of $10,500 each to repay the loan.

**Instructions**

What interest rate is Eric Stottrup paying? (Interpolation is required.)

**E6–17** As the purchaser of a new house, Sara Silverman has signed a mortgage note to pay the Honorable National Bank and Trust Co. $5,000 every six months for 15 years, at the end of which time she will own the house. At the date the mortgage is signed the cash value of the house is $60,000. The first payment will be made six months after the date the mortgage is signed.

**Instructions**

Compute the exact rate of interest earned on the mortgage by the bank. (Interpolate if necessary.)

**E6–18** Laura Vessely intends to invest $16,000 in a trust on January 10 of every year, 1984 to 1998, inclusive. She anticipates that interest rates will change during that period of time as follows:

| | |
|---|---|
| 1/10/84–1/10/87 | 5% |
| 1/10/87–1/10/94 | 6% |
| 1/10/94–1/10/98 | 8% |

How much will Laura have in trust on January 10, 1998?

# PROBLEMS

(Interest rates are per annum unless otherwise indicated.)

**P6–1** Using the appropriate interest table, provide the solution to each of the following four questions by computing the unknowns.

(a) Scott Marks has $15,000 to invest today at 8% to pay a debt of $25,707.30. How many years will it take him to accumulate enough to liquidate the debt?

(b) Geneen Deutsch has an $8,500 debt which she wishes to repay five years from today; she has $5,524.43 which she intends to invest for the five years. What rate of interest will she need to earn annually in order to accumulate enough to pay the debt?

(c) What is the amount of the payments that Steve Robinson must make at the end of each of eight years to accumulate a fund of $30,000 by the end of the eighth year, if the fund earns 8% interest, compounded annually?

(d) Maria Resch wishes to accumulate $200,000 by her fifty-fifth birthday so she can retire to her summer place on Lake Holiday. She wishes to accumulate this amount by equal deposits on each of her next twenty-five birthdays, her thirtieth through her fifty-fourth. What annual deposit must Maria make if the fund will earn 12% interest compounded annually?

**P6–2** Answer each of these unrelated questions.

1. Electric Corporation bought a new machine and agreed to pay for it in equal annual installments of $5,000 at the end of each of the next five years. Assuming that a prevailing interest rate of 15% applies to this contract, how much should Electric record as the cost of the machine?

2. Electric Corporation purchased a special tractor on December 31, 1983. The purchase agreement stipulated that Electric should pay $10,000 at the time of purchase and $10,000 at the end of each of the next five years. The tractor should be valued on December 31, 1983 at what amount, assuming an appropriate interest rate of 12%?

3. Electric Corporation wants to withdraw $30,000 (including principal) from an investment fund at the end of each year for five years. What should be the required initial investment at the beginning of the first year if the fund earns 10%?

4. On January 1, 1983, Electric Corporation sold a building that cost $190,000 and that had accumulated depreciation of $80,000 on the date of sale. Gray received as consideration a $200,000 noninterest-bearing note due on January 1, 1986. There was no established exchange price for the building, and the note had no ready market. The prevailing rate of interest for a note of this type on January 1, 1983 was 10%. At what amount should the revenue from the sale of the building be reported?

5. On January 1, 1983, Electric Corporation purchased 100 of the $1,000 face value, 8% ten-year bonds of Ruth, Inc. The bonds mature on January 1, 1993, and pay interest annually beginning January 1, 1984. Electric Corporation purchased the bonds to yield 12%. How much did Electric pay for the bonds? (Hint: Payment for bonds must consider both principal and interest.)

**P6–3** Mack Aroni, a bank robber, is worried about his retirement. He decides to start a savings account. Mack deposits annually his net share of the "loot," which consists of $50,000 per year, for three years beginning January 1, 1976. Mack is arrested on January 4, 1978 (after making the third deposit) and spends the rest of 1978 and most of 1979 in jail. He escapes in September of 1979. He resumes his savings plan with semiannual deposits of $15,000 each beginning January 1, 1980. Assume that the bank's interest rate was 5% compounded annually from January 1, 1976 through January 1, 1979, and 6% annual rate compounded semi-annually thereafter.

**Instructions**

When Mack retires on January 1, 1983 (six months after his last deposit), what is the balance in his savings account?

**P6–4** John Sanford borrowed $40,000 on March 1, 1982. This amount plus accrued interest at 8% compounded semiannually is to be repaid March 1, 1992. To retire this debt, John plans to contribute to a debt retirement fund five equal amounts starting on March 1, 1987 and for the next four years. The fund is expected to earn 10% per annum.

**Instructions**

How much must be contributed each year by John Sanford to provide a fund sufficient to retire the debt on March 1, 1992?

**P6–5** Your client, Lowrental Leasing Company, is preparing a contract to lease a machine to Neverown Corporation for a period of 20 years. Lowrental has an investment cost of $249,245 in the machine, which has a useful life of 20 years and no salvage value at the end of that time.

Your client is interested in earning a 12% return on its investment and has agreed to accept 20 equal rental payments at the end of each of the next 20 years.

**Instructions**

You are requested to provide Lowrental with the amount of each of the 20 rentals that will render a 12% return on investment.

**P6-6** Your client, Universal, Inc., has acquired Brockabrella Manufacturing Company in a business combination that is to be accounted for as a purchase transaction (at fair market value). Along with the assets and business of Brockabrella, Universal assumed an outstanding debenture bond issue having a principal amount of $5,000,000 with interest payable semiannually at a stated rate of 7%. Brockabrella received $4,800,000 in proceeds from the issuance five years ago. The bonds are currently 15 years from maturity. Equivalent securities command a 10% current market rate of interest.

**Instructions**

Your client requests your advice regarding the amount to record for the acquired bond issue.

**P6-7** Hardhat, Inc., has decided to surface and maintain for ten years a vacant lot next to one of its discount retail outlets to serve as a parking lot for customers. Management is considering the following bids involving two different qualities of surfacing for a parking area of 10,000 square yards:

**Bid A.** A surface that costs $8.00 per square yard to install. This surface has a probable useful life of 10 years and will require annual maintenance in each year except the last year, at an estimated cost of 3 cents per square yard.

**Bid B.** A surface that costs $4.50 per square yard to install. This surface will have to be replaced at the end of five years. The annual maintenance cost on this surface is estimated at 12 cents per square yard for each year but the last year of its service. The replacement surface will be similar to the initial surface.

**Instructions**

Prepare computations showing which bid should be accepted by Hardhat, Inc. You may assume that the cost of capital is 10%, that the annual maintenance expenditures are incurred at the end of each year, and that prices are not expected to change during the next ten years.

**P6-8** Terry & Melissa Corporation has outstanding a contractual debt. The corporation has available two means of settlement: It can either make immediate payment of $750,000, or it can make annual payments of $115,000 for 10 years, each payment due on the last day of the year. Which method of payment do you recommend, assuming an expected effective interest rate of 10% during the future period?

**P6-9** Assuming the same facts as those in Problem 6-8 except that the payments must begin now and be made on the first day of each of the 10 years, what payment method would you recommend?

**P6-10** Solve for the unknowns in each of the following three situations using the interest tables.
   (a) On June 1, 1983, Rich Cushing purchases twenty acres of farm land from his neighbor, Nita Doty, and agrees to pay the purchase price in five payments of $12,000 each, the first payment to be payable June 1, 1987, with interest compounded annually at the rate of 15%. What is the purchase price of the twenty acres?
   (b) Ruth Washington wishes to invest $45,201 today to insure $8,000 payments to her son at the end of each year for the next ten years. At what interest rate must the $45,201 be invested?
   (c) Mr. and Mrs. Greg Taylor have decided to provide for their handicapped son by investing $230,000 today in an annuity at 10% interest, compounded annually. They feel their son should receive approximately $25,400 per year beginning one year from today. The in-

vestment of the $230,000 will provide approximately $25,400 per year for how many years before being depleted?

**P6–11** Paul Bearer died, leaving to his wife Mona an insurance policy contract that provides that the beneficiary (Mona) can choose any one of the following four options.
(a) $40,000 immediate cash.
(b) $1,600 every three months payable at the end of each quarter for 10 years.
(c) $20,000 immediate cash and $800 every three months for eight years, payable at the beginning of each three-month period.
(d) $2,800 every three months for three years and $800 each quarter for the following 25 quarters, all payments payable at the end of each quarter.

**Instructions**

If money is worth 2% per quarter, compounded quarterly, which option would you recommend that Mona exercise?

**P6–12** Provide a solution to each of the following situations by computing the unknowns (use the interest tables).
(a) Jean Isham owes a debt of $15,000 from the purchase of her new sports car. The debt bears interest of 12% payable annually. Jean wishes to pay the debt and interest in four annual installments, beginning one year hence. What equal annual installments will pay the debt and interest?
(b) On January 1, 1984, Willie Hayseed offers to buy Barney Olfield's used combine for $18,000, payable in five equal installments, which are to include 10% interest on the unpaid balance and a portion of the principal with the first payment to be made on January 1, 1984. How much will each payment be?
(c) Evelyn Reed invests in a $50,000 annuity insurance policy at 5% compounded annually on February 8, 1984. The first of 20 receipts from the annuity is payable to Evelyn ten years after the annuity is purchased, or on February 8, 1994. What will be the amount of each of the 20 equal annual receipts?

**P6–13** During the past year Edward Chablis planted a new vineyard on 100 acres of land which he leases for $15,000 a year. He has asked you as his accountant to assist him in determining the value of his vineyard operation.

The vineyard will bear no grapes for the first five years (1–5). In the next five years (6–10), Edward estimates that the vines will bear grapes that can be sold for $40,000 each year. For the next 20 years (11–30) he expects the harvest will provide annual revenues of $60,000. But during the last 10 years (31–40) of the vineyard's life he estimates that revenues will decline to $50,000 per year.

During the first five years the annual cost of pruning, fertilizing, and caring for the vineyard is estimated at $4,000; during the years of production, 6–40, these costs will rise to $6,000 per year. The relevant market rate of interest for the entire period is 8%. Assume that all receipts and payments are made at the end of each year.

**Instructions**

Dolores Hass has offered to buy Edward's vineyard business by assuming the 40-year lease. On the basis of the current value of the business what is the mimimum price Edward should accept?

**P6–14** Mary Ann Wetzel plans to establish an annuity arrangement whereby her three children would each receive $5,000 on December 25 of the years 1986 to 2000, inclusive. Variations in the interest rates during that period of time are estimated as follows:

|  |  |
|---|---|
| 12/26/85-12/25/90 | 12% |
| 12/26/90-12/25/96 | 10% |
| 12/26/96-12/25/00 | 8% |

**Instructions**

Compute the amount that Mrs. Wetzel must invest on December 26, 1985 to assure these annual payments to her children.

**P6–15** Answer the following questions related to Hadley, Inc.

1. Hadley, Inc. loans money to Fairchild Corporation in the amount of $100,000. Hadley accepts a note due in five years at 10% compounded semiannually. After two years (and receipt of interest for two years), Hadley needs money and therefore sells the note to First National Bank, which demands interest on the note of 16% compounded semiannually. What is the amount Hadley will receive on the sale of the note?

2. Hadley, Inc. wishes to accumulate $500,000 by December 31, 1993, to retire bonds outstanding. The company deposits $100,000 on December 31, 1983, which will earn interest at 8% compounded quarterly, to help in the retirement of this debt. In addition, the company wants to know how much should be deposited at the end of each quarter for 10 years to insure that $500,000 is available at the end of 1993. (The quarterly deposits will also earn at a rate of 8%, compounded quarterly.) Round to even dollars.

3. Hadley, Inc. has $80,000 to invest. The company is trying to decide between two alternative uses of the funds. One alternative provides $15,000 at the end of each year for 10 years, and the other is to receive a single lump-sum payment of $200,000 at the end of the 10 years. Which alternative should Hadley select? Assume the interest rate is constant over the entire investment.

4. Hadley, Inc. has completed the purchase of a new IBM computer. The fair market value of the equipment is $452,500. The purchase agreement specifies an immediate down-payment of $100,000 and semiannual payments of $71,685 beginning at the end of six months for three years. What is the interest rate, to the nearest percent, used in discounting this purchase transaction?

# CURRENT ASSETS AND CURRENT LIABILITIES

2

# CHAPTER 7

# Cash, Temporary Investments, and Receivables

The primary liquid assets of most business enterprises are cash, temporary investments, and receivables. Accounting for cash presents few problems because the questions of valuation and classification are easily answered. Accounting for temporary investments and receivables, however, can be somewhat more complex.

## SECTION 1  CASH AND CASH EQUIVALENTS

### NATURE AND COMPOSITION OF CASH

Cash is the standard medium of exchange and provides the basis for measuring and accounting for all other items. It is generally classified as a current asset. To be reported as **"cash,"** it must be readily available for the payment of current obligations, and it must be free from any contractual restriction that limits its use in satisfying debts.

Cash consists of coin, currency, and available funds on deposit at the bank. Negotiable instruments such as money orders, certified checks, cashiers' checks, personal checks, and bank drafts are also viewed as cash.

Savings accounts are usually classified as cash, although the bank has the legal right to demand notice before withdrawal. But the privilege of prior notice is rarely exercised by banks, so savings accounts are considered cash.

Money market funds, money market savings certificates, certificates of deposit (CDs), and similar types of deposits and "short-term paper"[1] that provide small investors with an opportunity to earn high rates of interest are more appropriately classified as temporary

---

[1]A variety of "short-term paper" is available for investment. **Certificates of deposit** (CDs) represent formal evidence of indebtedness, issued by a bank, subject to withdrawal under the specific terms of the instrument. Issued in $10,000 and $100,000 denominations, they mature in 30 to 360 days and generally pay interest at the short-term interest rate in effect at date of issuance. **Money market savings certificates** are issued by banks and savings and loan associations in denominations of $10,000 or more for six-month periods (6 to 48 months). The interest rate is tied to the 26-week treasury bill rate. In **money market funds,** a relatively recent variation of the mutual fund, the yield is

investments than as cash. The logic for this classification is that these securities usually contain restrictions or penalties on their conversion to cash. Money market funds that provide checking account privileges are usually classified as cash, however.

Items that present classification problems are postdated checks, I.O.U.s, travel advances, postage stamps, and special cash funds. **Postdated checks and I.O.U.s** are treated as receivables. **Travel advances** are properly treated as receivables if the advances are to be collected from the employees or deducted from their salaries. Otherwise, classification of the travel advance as a prepaid expense is more appropriate. **Postage stamps on hand** are classified as part of office supplies inventory or as a prepaid expense. **Petty cash funds and change funds** are included in current assets as cash because these funds are used to meet current operating expenses and to liquidate current liabilities.

Cash that is restricted or in escrow is segregated from the general cash account. The **restricted cash** is classified either in the current asset or in the long-term asset section, depending on the date of availability or disbursement. If the cash is to be used (within a year or the operating cycle, whichever is longer) for payment of existing or maturing obligations, classification in the current section is appropriate. On the other hand, if the cash is to be held for a longer period of time, the restricted cash is shown in the long-term section of the balance sheet. Generally, cash to be held for long periods is invested and not held in the form of cash.

*legal agreement handled by 3rd party until conditions are fulfilled*

Cash classified in the long-term section is frequently set aside either for plant expansion or retirement of long-term debt. For example, an annual report of American Can Company contained this item:

| American Can Company | |
| --- | --- |
| Long-term assets | |
| Funds held by trustee for construction | $28,157,000 |

In summary, cash includes the medium of exchange and most negotiable instruments. If the item cannot be converted immediately to coin or currency, it is separately classified as an investment, as a receivable, or as a prepaid expense. Cash that is not available for payment of currently maturing liabilities is segregated and classified in the long-term asset section.

## COMPENSATING BALANCES

In recent years it has become common for banks and other lending institutions to require the maintenance of minimum cash balances on deposit of those customers to whom they

---

determined by the mix of treasury bills and commercial paper making up the fund's portfolio. Most money market funds require an initial minimum investment of $5,000; many allow withdrawal by check or wire transfer. **Treasury bills** are U.S. government obligations generally having 91- and 182-day maturities; they are sold on a discount basis in $10,000 denominations at weekly government auctions. **Commercial paper** is a short-term note (30 to 270 days) issued by corporations with good credit ratings. Issued in $5,000 and $10,000 denominations, these notes generally yield a higher rate than treasury bills.

lend money or extend credit. These minimum balances, called **compensating balances,** are defined by the SEC as: "that portion of any demand deposit (or any time deposit or certificate of deposit) maintained by a corporation which constitutes support for existing borrowing arrangements of the corporation with a lending institution. Such arrangements would include both outstanding borrowings and the assurance of future credit availability."[2] Compensating balances may be payment for bank services rendered to the company for which there is no direct fee, for example, check processing and lockbox management. By requiring a compensating balance, the bank achieves an effective interest rate on a loan that is higher than the stated rate because of the restricted amount that must remain on deposit.

The need for the disclosure of compensating balances was highlighted in the early 1970s when a number of companies were involved in a liquidity crisis. Many investors believed that the cash reported on the balance sheet was fully available to meet recurring obligations, but these funds were restricted because of the need for these companies to maintain minimum cash balances at various lending institutions.

The SEC recommends that legally **restricted deposits** held as compensating balances against short-term borrowing arrangements be stated separately among the "cash and cash items" in current assets. Restricted deposits held as compensating balances against long-term borrowing arrangements should be separately classified as noncurrent assets in either the "investments" or "other assets" sections, using a caption such as "Cash on deposit maintained as compensating balance."

In cases where compensating balance arrangements exist without agreements that restrict the use of cash amounts shown on the balance sheet, the arrangements and the amounts involved should be described in footnotes to the financial statements. Compensating balances that are maintained under an agreement to assure future credit availability also must be disclosed separately in the footnotes together with the amount and duration of such agreement.

## CASH—MANAGEMENT AND CONTROL

Cash presents special management and control problems not only because it enters into a great many transactions but also for these reasons:

1. Cash is the single asset readily convertible into any other type of asset. It is easily concealed and transported, and it is almost universally desired. Correct accounting for cash transactions therefore requires that controls be established to insure that cash belonging to the enterprise is not improperly converted to personal use by someone in or connected with the enterprise.

2. The amount of cash owned by an enterprise should be regulated carefully so that neither too much nor too little is available at any time. An adequate supply must always be maintained without tying up too much of the firm's resources. As the medium of exchange, cash is required to pay for all assets and services purchased by the company and to meet all its obligations as they mature. The disbursement of cash is thus a daily occurrence, and a

---

[2]*Accounting Series Release No. 148,* "Amendments to Regulations S-X and Related Interpretations and Guidelines Regarding the Disclosure of Compensating Balances and Short-Term Borrowing Arrangements," Securities and Exchange Commission (November 13, 1973). The SEC defines 15% of liquid assets (current cash balances, whether restricted or not, plus marketable securities) as being material.

sufficient fund of cash must be kept on hand to meet these needs. On the other hand, cash, as such, is not a productive asset; it earns no return. Hence it is undesirable to keep on hand a supply of cash any larger than that necessary to meet day-by-day needs, with a reasonable margin for emergencies. Cash in excess of what is needed should be invested either in income-producing securities or in other productive assets.

Two problems of accounting for cash transactions face the accounting department: (1) proper controls must be established to insure that no unauthorized transactions are entered into by officers or employees; (2) information necessary to the proper management of cash on hand and cash transactions must be provided. Most companies fix the responsibility for obtaining proper record control over cash transactions in the accounting department. Record control, of course, is not possible without adequate physical control; therefore the accounting department must take an interest in preventing intentional or unintentional mistakes in cash transactions. It should be emphasized that even with sophisticated control devices errors can and do happen. The *Wall Street Journal* ran a story entitled "A $7.8 Million Error Has a Happy Ending for a Horrified Bank," which described how Manufacturers Hanover Trust Co., one of the nation's largest banks, mailed about $7.8 million too much in cash dividends to its stockholders. Happily most of the monies were subsequently returned.

Regulating the amount of cash on hand is primarily a management problem, but accountants must be able to provide the information required by management for regulating cash on hand through the special transactions of borrowing or investing.

## Using Bank Accounts

A company can vary the number and location of banks and the types of bank accounts to obtain desired control objectives. For large companies operating in multiple locations, the location of bank accounts can be important. Establishing collection accounts in strategic locations can accelerate the flow of cash into the company by shortening the time between a customer's mailing of a payment and the company's having the use of the cash. Multiple collection centers generally are used to reduce the size of a company's **collection float,** which is the difference between the amount on deposit according to the company's records and the amount of collected cash according to the bank record.

The **general checking account** is the principal bank account in most companies and frequently the only bank account in small businesses. Cash is deposited in and disbursed from this account as all transactions are cycled through it. Deposits from and disbursements to all other bank accounts are made through the general checking account.

**Imprest bank accounts** are used to make a specific amount of cash available for a limited purpose. The account acts as a clearing account for a large volume of checks or for a specific type of check. The specific and intended amount to be cleared through the imprest account is deposited therein by transferring that amount from the general checking account or other source. Imprest bank accounts are often used for disbursing payroll checks, dividends, commissions, bonuses, confidential expenses (for example, officers' salaries), and travel expenses.

**Lockbox accounts** are frequently used by large, multilocation companies to make collections in cities within areas of heaviest customer billing. The company rents a local post office box and authorizes a local bank to pick up the remittances mailed to that box number. The bank empties the box at least once a day and immediately credits the company's account for collections. The greatest advantage of a lockbox is that it accelerates the availability of collected cash. Generally, in a lockbox arrangement the bank microfilms the checks for record purposes and provides the company with a deposit slip, a list of collections, and any other correspondence mailed by the customer. If the control over cash is improved and if the income generated from accelerating the receipt of funds exceeds the cost of the lockbox system, it is considered worth undertaking.

### Electronic Funds Transfer (EFT)

Businesses and individuals use about 35 billion checks annually to pay their bills. This process is not without its cost. Preparing, issuing, receiving, and clearing a check through the banking system is estimated to cost between 55 cents and $1.00 and the cost is rising rapidly with inflation.[3] It is not surprising, therefore, that in this electronic age new methods are being developed to transfer funds among parties without the use and movement of paper. We are entering the age of **electronic funds transfer (EFT),** a process that uses wire, telephone, telegraph, computer (maybe even satellite), or other electronic device rather than paper to make instantaneous transfers of funds.

America's major banks are now in the process of developing national automated teller machine (ATM) networks. The pace of development has been so hectic that greater strides were made in the first six months of 1982 than in the whole decade of the 1970s. It is expected that before the end of 1983 most banks will be affiliated with one of about six national electronic banking networks that consolidate most retail banking services in much the same way that Visa and MasterCard unified consumer credit services.

But the new ATM electronic networks will be far more powerful than the credit card networks of Visa and MasterCard because they will operate with the **debit card,** which can give access to all of a customer's accounts within a bank. Using an ATM, customers are able to withdraw cash and make deposits to both their checking and savings accounts, as well as to transfer funds between accounts and make balance inquiries. By linking ATMs nationally, the new networks are building the first electronic funds transfer system capable of processing large-volume retail fund transfers between computers at different banks. Already the use of checks has disappeared for certain funds transfers. For example, neither author of this book receives a formal payroll check from his employer university; the universities send our banks a magnetic tape that transfers money from the university's account to our account. Within a short time the services provided by these ATM networks will accommodate electronic transfers from home and retail point-of-sale terminals. When this occurs, the banks will have the power to replace with electronic transactions many of those 35 billion checks.

Safeguards and controls must be built into these electronic systems to reduce the exposure to massive fraud that comes from heavy reliance on computer technology, which transfers funds without personal intervention.

### The Imprest Petty Cash System

Almost every company finds it necessary to pay small amounts for a great many things such as employees' lunches and carfare, purchases of minor office supply items, and small expense payments. It is frequently impractical to require that such disbursements be made

[3]Alfred Hunt, *Corporate Cash Management Including Electronic Funds Transfer* (New York: AMACOM, 1978), p. 142.

by check, yet some control over them is important. A common method of obtaining reasonable control, simplicity of operation, and general adherence to the rule of disbursement by check is the **imprest system** for petty cash disbursements.

This is how the system works:

1. Some individual is designated as the petty cash custodian and given a small amount of currency as a fund from which to make small payments.

| | | |
|---|---|---|
| Petty Cash Fund | 300 | |
| Cash | | 300 |

2. As disbursements are made, the petty cash custodian obtains signed receipts from each individual to whom cash is paid. If possible, evidence of the disbursement should be attached to the petty cash receipt.

   (Petty cash transactions are not recorded until the fund is reimbursed and, then, such entries are recorded by someone in accounting, not the petty cash custodian.)

3. When the supply of cash runs low, the custodian presents to the general cashier a request for reimbursement supported by the petty cash receipts and other evidence that has been obtained for all disbursements and receives a company check drawn to "Cash" or "Petty Cash" to replenish the fund.

| | | |
|---|---|---|
| Office Supplies Expense | 42 | |
| Postage Expense | 53 | |
| Entertainment Expense | 76 | |
| Cash Over and Short | 2 | |
| Cash | | 173 |

4. If it is decided that the amount of cash in the petty cash fund is excessive, an adjustment may be made as follows (lowering the fund balance from $300 to $250):

| | | |
|---|---|---|
| Cash | 50 | |
| Petty Cash | | 50 |

Entries are made to the Petty Cash account only to increase or decrease the size of the fund or to adjust the petty cash account balance and related expenses if not replenished at year end. The reimbursement entry does not affect the Petty Cash account, but it does affect the amount of petty cash on hand.

A **Cash Over and Short** account is used when the fund fails to prove out. If cash proves out short (that is, the sum of the vouchers and cash in the fund is less than the imprest amount), the shortage is debited to the Cash Over and Short account. If it proves out over, the overage is credited to Cash Over and Short. This account is left open until the end of the year, when it is closed and generally shown on the income statement as a miscellaneous expense or income.

There are usually expense items in the fund except immediately after reimbursement; therefore, if accurate financial statements are desired, the funds must be reimbursed at the end of each accounting period and also when nearly depleted.

Under the imprest system the petty cash custodian is responsible at all times for the amount of the fund on hand either as cash or in the form of signed vouchers. These vouchers provide the evidence required by the disbursing officer to issue a reimbursement check. Two additional procedures are followed to obtain more complete control over the petty cash fund:

1. Surprise counts of the fund are made from time to time by a superior of the petty cash custodian to determine that the fund is being accounted for satisfactorily.

**2.** Petty cash vouchers are canceled or mutilated after they have been submitted for reimbursement, so that they cannot be used to secure a second and improper reimbursement.

## Physical Protection of Cash Balances

Not only must cash receipts and cash disbursements be safeguarded through internal control measures, but also the cash on hand and in banks must be protected. Because receipts become cash on hand and disbursements are made from cash in banks, adequate control of receipts and disbursements is a part of the protection of cash balances. Certain other procedures, however, should be given some consideration.

Physical protection of cash is so elementary a necessity that it requires little discussion. Every effort should be made to hold to a minimum the cash on hand in the office. A petty cash fund, perhaps change funds, and the current day's receipts should be all that is on hand at any one time, and these funds should be kept, insofar as possible, in a vault, safe, or locked cash drawer. Each day's receipts should be transmitted intact to the bank as soon as practicable.

Related to the problem of protecting cash balances is the problem of accurately stating the amount of available cash both in internal reports for management and in financial statements for external use.

Every company has, in its cash books and cash account, a record of all cash received and disbursed and the balance. Because of the many cash transactions, however, errors or omissions may be made in keeping this record. Therefore, it is necessary to prove periodically the balance shown in the general ledger. Cash actually present in the office—petty cash, change funds, and undeposited receipts—can be counted and the amount determined in that way, for comparison with the company records. Cash on deposit with a bank is not available for count and is proved through the **preparation of a bank reconciliation,** that is, a reconciliation of the company's record of cash in the bank and the bank's record of the company's cash that is on deposit.

## Reconciliation of Bank Balances

Generally, at the end of each calendar month the bank supplies each customer with a **bank statement** (a copy of the bank's account with the customer) together with the customer's withdrawal checks that have been paid by the bank during the month. If no errors were made by the bank or the customer, if all deposits made and all checks drawn by the customer reached the bank within the same month, and if no other transactions occurred that affected either the company's or the bank's record of cash, the balance of cash reported by the bank to the customer should be the same as that shown in the customer's own records as of the same point in time. Thus, comparison of the balance shown on the bank statement with the balance shown in the customer's own records should verify the latter.

For various reasons this condition seldom occurs. In most cases checks issued by the customer near the end of the month do not reach the bank within the same month; deposits made by the customer on the last day of the month may not be recorded by the bank until about the first day of the following month; and such items as service charges by the bank are not brought to the attention of the customer until the bank statement is received by the customer. Hence, there regularly are differences between the customer's record of cash and the bank's record, and the two must be reconciled to determine the nature of the differences between the two amounts.

A **bank reconciliation,** then, is a schedule indicating and explaining any differences between the bank's and the company's records of cash. If the difference results only from transactions with customers not yet recorded by the bank, the company's record of cash is considered correct. But if some part of the difference arises from other items, either the bank's records or the customer's records or both must be adjusted.

Two general forms of bank reconciliation are in common use. One form starts with the bank balance and, then, by adding or subtracting the various items making up the difference, works to the book balance. This form is entitled **Reconciliation of Bank and Book Balances** or simply "Bank to Books" and is illustrated below.

---

**Reconciliation of Bank and Book Balances:**

Nugget Mining Company
BANK RECONCILIATION
Denver National Bank, November 30, 1983

| | | |
|---|---:|---:|
| Balance per bank statement, Nov. 30, 1983 | | $22,365.30 |
| Add | | |
| Bank charge not recorded by the company | $    8.10 | |
| Receipts of Nov. 30 on hand, not in bank's balance | 3,680.43 | 3,688.53 |
| | | 26,053.83 |
| Deduct | | |
| Outstanding checks | | |
| #7327 | $   150.47 | |
| #7348 | 4,820.00 | |
| #7349 | 30.64 | 5,001.11 |
| Interest on Sequoia bonds collected by bank on | | |
| Nov. 30 for the company, not recorded | | |
| by the company | 600.00 | 5,601.11 |
| Balance per books, Nov. 30, 1983 | | $20,452.72 |

---

The other widely used form, entitled **Reconciliation of Bank and Book Balances to Corrected Balance,** is composed of two distinct sections. One section begins with the balance as shown on the bank statement and works to a correct (actual) balance, that is, the balance the bank statement would show if all transactions were recorded. The second section starts with the balance shown by the company records and also works to a correct (actual) balance, the balance that should be shown in the records after all transactions are recorded properly. This form is shown on page 278, with the same facts as those given in the previous illustration.

Both forms of reconciliation account for and itemize any differences between the bank and book amounts, but the second form is preferable for the following reasons.

1. It reconciles to the correct (actual) cash balance. The correct balance of $21,044.62 in the reconciliation on page 278 is the amount carried to the balance sheet.
2. All of the reconciling items that require adjusting journal entries for book purposes are grouped in the section devoted to the book balance.
3. The additions and subtractions appear more logical. It avoids adding back items that were properly deducted (note the difference in the handling of the bank charge).

**Reconciliation of Bank and Book Balances to Corrected Balance:**

Nugget Mining Company
BANK RECONCILIATION
Denver National Bank, November 30, 1983

| | | |
|---|---:|---:|
| Balance per bank statement, Nov. 30, 1983 | | $22,365.30 |
| Add | | |
| Receipts of Nov. 30 on hand, not in bank's balance | | 3,680.43 |
| | | 26,045.73 |
| Deduct | | |
| Outstanding checks | | |
| #7327 | $  150.47 | |
| #7348 | 4,820.00 | |
| #7349 | 30.64 | 5,001.11 |
| Correct balance, Nov. 30, 1983 | | $21,044.62 |
| | | |
| Balance per books, Nov. 30, 1983 | | $20,452.72 |
| Add | | |
| Interest on Sequoia Co. bonds collected by bank on Nov. 30 | | |
| for the company, not recorded by the company | | 600.00 |
| | | 21,052.72 |
| Deduct | | |
| Bank charge not recorded by the company | | 8.10 |
| Correct balance, Nov. 30, 1983 | | $21,044.62 |

Adjusting entries are required to record items properly recognized by the bank but not yet recorded per the books as illustrated below for the Nugget Mining Company:

| | | |
|---|---:|---:|
| **November 30** | | |
| Cash | 600.00 | |
| Interest Revenue | | 600.00 |
| (To record semiannual interest on Sequoia bonds, | | |
| collected by bank) | | |
| **November 30** | | |
| Office Expense—Bank Charges | 8.10 | |
| Cash | | 8.10 |
| (To record bank charges for November) | | |

The correct cash balance on November 30 is $21,044.62, or $20,452.72 per books increased by $600.00 and decreased by $8.10, as per the entries above. In the second method the correct cash balance is shown as the final figure in each of the two sections. The first method requires a simple calculation to arrive at the corrected cash figure. In general, the second method is favored by internal and industrial accountants, the first method by auditors.

Another widely used form of bank reconciliation is the **four-column reconciliation** ("proof of cash"), which is discussed and illustrated in Appendix E to this chapter.

# SECTION 2   TEMPORARY INVESTMENTS

## NATURE OF TEMPORARY (SHORT-TERM) INVESTMENTS

Transactions involving investments are infrequent for some enterprises, but for others they occur during every fiscal period. Sound financial management requires not only that cash and other assets be available when needed in the business, but also that cash and near cash assets not immediately needed in the conduct of regular operations be employed advantageously. In many cases, transactions involving investments result in a considerable amount of revenue in addition to that derived from regular operations.

A distinction is made in accounting between temporary investments and long-term investments. Temporary investments ordinarily consist of **short-term paper** (certificates of deposit, treasury bills, and commercial paper), **marketable debt securities** (government and corporate bonds), and **marketable equity securities** (preferred and common stock) acquired with cash not immediately needed in operations. The investments are held temporarily in place of cash and can be readily converted to cash when current financing needs make such conversion desirable. A temporary investment must be:

1. Readily marketable.
2. Intended to be converted into cash as needed within one year or the operating cycle, whichever is longer.

Readily marketable means that the security can be sold quite easily. For example, if the stock is closely held (not publicly traded), there may be no market or a limited market at best for the security and its classification as a long-term investment may be more appropriate. Intent to convert is an extremely difficult principle to apply in practice. Generally, intention to convert is substantiated when the invested cash is considered a contingency fund to be used whenever a need arises or when investment is made from cash temporarily idle because of the seasonality of the business.

Long-term investments, on the other hand, are purchased as a part of some long-range program or plan such as long-term appreciation in the price of the security, ownership for control purposes, or maintaining or increasing supplier or customer relationships. Long-term investments are discussed in Chapter 18.

## MARKETABLE SECURITIES

At one time, there was considerable diversity in practice relative to the carrying value of temporary investments. Some enterprises carried marketable securities at cost, some at market, some at lower of cost or market, and some applied more than one of these methods to different classes of securities. Accentuated by severe stock market fluctuations during 1974–1975, this problem of diversity in accounting practice was addressed by the FASB and partially resolved through the issuance of *Statement of Financial Accounting Standards No. 12,* "Accounting for Certain Marketable Securities." The "certain" marketable securities referred to are **marketable equity securities.**

An **equity security** is "any instrument representing ownership shares (for example, common, preferred, and other capital stock) or the right to acquire (for example, warrants, rights, and call options) or dispose of (for example, put options) ownership shares in an enterprise at fixed or determinable prices."[4] Treasury stock, redeemable preferred stock, and convertible bonds are excluded. **Marketable** means readily tradeable equity securities; restricted stock or "thin market" stock does not qualify.[5]

## Acquisition of Marketable Equity Securities

Investments in marketable equity securities, like other assets, are recorded at cost when acquired. Cost includes the purchase price and incidental acquisition costs such as brokerage commissions and taxes. According to *Statement No. 12*, "cost refers to the original cost of a marketable equity security unless a new cost basis has been assigned based on recognition of an impairment that was deemed other than temporary or as the result of a transfer between current and noncurrent classifications." In such cases the new cost basis (that is, after adjustment for impairment of value) shall be the cost.

## Accounting for Changes in Market Value—Marketable Equity Securities

A single share or unit of a marketable equity security has a **market price,** which when multiplied by the number of shares or units of that specific security produces the aggregate market price referred to as the **market value.** The market price generally changes as transactions involving the security occur. The central issue for many years has been: To what extent should the financial statements reflect the changes in market value of marketable securities?

The FASB resolved this issue in relation to marketable equity securities by requiring that **the carrying amount of a marketable equity securities portfolio be reported at the lower of its aggregate cost or market value determined at the balance sheet date.**[6] (Lower of cost or market is not acceptable for tax purposes.) The amount by which aggregate cost exceeds market value (the net unrealized loss) of the short-term marketable equity securities portfolio should be accounted for as the "valuation allowance" and the unrealized loss reported in the determination of net income for the period. Further, the FASB requires that realized gains and losses and changes in the valuation allowance for a marketable equity securities portfolio included in current assets should be used in the determination of net income of the period in which they occur. These valuation adjustments are recorded as part of the adjustment process whenever statements are to be prepared. In subsequent periods, recoveries of market value are recognized to the extent that the market valuation does not exceed original cost. In substance, the FASB says "adjust to market at each reporting date, down and up, but not in excess of acquired cost." Thus, **unrealized losses and recoveries on short-term marketable equity securities flow through the income statement.**[7]

The following discussion illustrates application of the lower of cost or market method to marketable equity securities classified as current assets.

[4]"Accounting for Certain Marketable Securities," *Statement of Financial Accounting Standards No. 12* (Stamford, Conn.: FASB, 1975), par. 7(a).

[5]Investments accounted for by the equity method (as discussed in Chapter 18) are excluded from the requirements of *Statement No. 12*. "Thin market" stocks trade so infrequently that they do not have a quoted market price.

[6]The carrying amount of marketable equity securities is the amount at which the portfolio of marketable equity securities is reported in the financial statements of an enterprise.

[7]Specialized industries (investment companies, brokers and dealers in securities, stock life insurance companies, and fire and casualty insurance companies) which carry marketable equity securities at market do not have to follow lower of cost or market. *Statement No. 12* (like the SEC in *ASR No. 166*) specifically permits the insurance industry (and other specialized industries that have used

Republic Service Corporation made the following purchases of marketable equity securities as temporary investments during the year 1981, which is the first year in which Republic invested in marketable equity securities:

February 23, 1981—Purchased 10,000 shares of Northwest Industries, Inc. common stock at a market price of $51.50 per share plus brokerage commissions[8] of $4,400 (total cost, $519,400).

April 10, 1981—Purchased 10,000 shares of Campbell Soup Co. common stock at a market price of $31.50 per share plus brokerage commissions of $2,500 (total cost, $317,500).

August 3, 1981—Purchased 5,000 shares of St. Regis Pulp Co. common stock at a market price of $28 per share plus brokerage commissions of $1,350 (total cost, $141,350).

Each of the purchases above is recorded at total acquisition cost (market price plus commissions) by a debit to "Marketable Equity Securities" and a credit to Cash.

During the year Republic made the following security sale:

September 23, 1981—Sold 5,000 shares of Northwest Industries, Inc. common stock at a market price of $58 per share less brokerage commissions, taxes, and fees of $2,780 (proceeds, $287,220).

On December 31, 1981, Republic Service Corporation determined the carrying amount of its portfolio in short-term marketable equity securities to be:

| Short-term marketable equity securities | December 31, 1981 | | |
| --- | --- | --- | --- |
| | Cost | Market | Unrealized Gain (Loss) |
| Northwest Industries, Inc. | $259,700 | $275,000 | $ 15,300 |
| Campbell Soup Co. | 317,500 | 304,000 | (13,500) |
| St. Regis Pulp Co. | 141,350 | 104,000 | (37,350) |
| Total of portfolio | $718,550 | $683,000 | $(35,550) |
| Balance required in the valuation allowance | | | $(35,550) |

Applying the lower of cost or market method to Republic's securities portfolio results in a carrying value of $683,000. The net unrealized loss of $35,550 represents the aggregate excess of cost over the market value of Republic's portfolio of marketable equity securities classified as current assets. The unrealized loss of $35,550 is recorded as follows:

**December 31, 1981**

| | | |
| --- | --- | --- |
| Unrealized Loss on Valuation of Marketable Equity Securities | 35,550 | |
| Allowance for Excess of Cost of Marketable Equity Securities over Market Value | | 35,550 |
| (To recognize a loss equal to the excess of cost over market value of marketable equity securities) | | |

market) to carry equity securities at market, with unrealized gains and losses being classified in the equity accounts. As indicated earlier, the accounting treatment for noncurrent marketable equity securities is different and is discussed in Chapter 18.

[8]Brokerage commissions are incurred both when buying and selling securities; such commissions generally range between 1% and 3% of trade value on lots of 1,000 or less and $12.50 to $30.00 per hundred shares on lots between 1,000 and 100,000 shares. State transfer taxes (New York) and SEC fees are incurred only by the seller of securities.

The loss account appears on the income statement in the "Other Expenses and Losses" section and therefore would be included in income before extraordinary items in Republic's 1981 financial statements. The allowance account appears on the balance sheet among current assets as an asset valuation (contra account) deducted from the portfolio cost of $718,550 to produce a carrying amount of its portfolio of $683,000.

During 1982, Republic made the following sale and purchase of marketable equity securities:

*realized loss*

March 22, 1982—Sold 5,000 shares of St. Regis Pulp Co. common stock at a market price of $17.50 per share less brokerage commissions, taxes, and fees of $1,590 (proceeds, $85,910).

July 2, 1982—Purchased 10,000 shares of Pacific Gas & Electric common stock at a market price of $20.25 per share plus brokerage commissions of $2,300 (total cost, $204,800).

On December 31, 1982, Republic Service Corporation determined the carrying amount of its portfolio in short-term marketable equity securities to be:

| | December 31, 1982 | | |
| --- | --- | --- | --- |
| Short-term marketable equity securities | Cost | Market | Unrealized Gain (Loss) |
| Northwest Industries, Inc. | $259,700 | $312,500 | $52,800 |
| Campbell Soup Co. | 317,500 | 327,500 | 10,000 |
| Pacific Gas & Electric | 204,800 | 202,500 | (2,300) |
| Total of portfolio | $782,000 | $842,500 | $60,500 |
| Balance required in the valuation allowance | | | $ -0- |

Applying the lower of cost or market method to Republic's portfolio at December 31, 1982, results in a carrying amount of $782,000 and elimination of the balance in the valuation allowance account of $35,550. The adjustment of the valuation allowance is recorded as follows:

**December 31, 1982**

| | | |
| --- | --- | --- |
| Allowance for Excess of Cost of Marketable Equity Securities over Market Value | 35,550 | |
| Recovery of Unrealized Loss on Valuation of Marketable Equity Securities | | 35,550 |
| (To record a reduction in the valuation allowance due to increase in market value of the marketable equity securities portfolio classified as current assets) | | |

The Recovery of Unrealized Loss on Valuation of Marketable Equity Securities of $35,550 is reported in the "Other Revenues and Gains" section and therefore would be included in income before extraordinary items on Republic's 1982 income statement.

Note that **the recovery is recognized only to the extent that unrealized losses were previously recognized.** That is, the write-down of $35,550 in 1981, representing net unrealized losses, may be reversed but only to the extent that the resulting carrying amount of the portfolio does not exceed original cost or, in other words, to the extent that a balance exists in the valuation allowance account at the date of write-up. Also, note that **the valuation is applied to the total portfolio and not to individual securities.**

The profession does not regard the reversal of the write-down as representing recognition of an unrealized gain. The unrealized gain is the excess of market value over cost, or the $60,500 net difference between aggregate cost and aggregate market value of Republic's portfolio on December 31, 1982. The profession views the write-down as establishing a valuation allowance representing the estimated reduction in the realizable value of the portfolio, and it views the subsequent market increase as having reduced or eliminated the requirements for such an allowance. In the FASB's view, the reversal of the write-down represents a change in an accounting estimate of an unrealized loss.[9]

If Republic's investment portfolio of short-term marketable equity securities had suffered an additional loss of market value during 1982 instead of the increase described above, a loss would have been charged to 1982 expense and the valuation allowance would have been increased (credited) by the amount of the additional write-down.

If a marketable equity security is **transferred from the current to the noncurrent portfolio,** or vice versa, the security must be transferred at the lower of its cost or market value at the date of transfer. If market value is less than cost, the market value becomes the new cost basis, and the difference is accounted for as if it were a realized loss and included in the determination of net income.[10] This procedure has the effect of accounting for an unrealized loss at the date of transfer in the same manner as if it had been realized, thus reducing the incentive to manipulate income by transferring securities between the current and noncurrent portfolios.

## Disposition of Marketable Equity Securities

Marketable securities are sold when cash needs develop or when good investment management dictates a change in the securities held. The owner who sells the securities incurs costs of brokerage commissions, state transfer taxes, and SEC fees, receiving only the net proceeds for the sale. The difference between the net proceeds from the sale of a marketable equity security and its cost represents the **realized gain or loss.** At the date of sale no regard is given to unrealized losses or recoveries or the amount accumulated in the valuation allowance account because the valuation allowance relates to the total portfolio and not to specific security holdings.

For example, in the previous illustration Republic Service Corporation sold 5,000 shares of Northwest Industries, Inc. common stock on September 23, 1981 for $58 per share, incurring $2,780 in brokerage commissions, taxes, and fees. The gain on the sale is computed as follows:

| | |
|---|---:|
| Gross selling price of 5,000 shares @ $58 | $290,000 |
| Less commissions, taxes, and fees | 2,780 |
| Net proceeds from sale | 287,220 |
| Cost of 5,000 shares ($519,400 ÷ 2) | 259,700 |
| Gain on sale | $ 27,520 |

[9]*FASB Statement No. 12,* par. 29(c).
[10]Ibid., par. 10.

The sale is recorded as follows:

**September 23, 1981**

| | | |
|---|---|---|
| Cash | 287,220 | |
| Marketable Equity Securities | | 259,700 |
| Realized Gain on Sale of Marketable Equity Securities | | 27,520 |
| (To record sale of 5,000 shares of Northwest Industries common stock held as a temporary investment at a gain) | | |

Republic Service Corporation also sold 5,000 shares of St. Regis Pulp Co. on March 22, 1982, for $17.50 per share, incurring $1,590 in brokerage commissions, taxes, and fees. The loss on the sale is computed as follows:

| | | |
|---|---|---|
| Cost of 5,000 shares | 5000 × 17.50 | $141,350 |
| Gross proceeds from sale | $87,500 | |
| Less commissions, taxes, and fees | 1,590 | |
| Net proceeds from sale | | 85,910 |
| Loss on sale | | $ 55,440 |

As in the 1981 security sale, the amount of net proceeds from the 1982 sale of securities is compared with the original cost to determine the gain or loss and recorded as follows:

**March 22, 1982**

| | | |
|---|---|---|
| Cash | 85,910 | |
| Realized Loss on Sale of Marketable Equity Securities | 55,440 | |
| Marketable Equity Securities | | 141,350 |
| (To record the sale of 5,000 shares of St. Regis Pulp Co. common stock held as a temporary investment) | | |

The presence or absence of realized gains or losses recorded since the last portfolio valuation as a result of sales of marketable equity securities has no effect upon the method of computing the lower of cost or market for the remaining portfolio at the end of the period.

## Valuation at Market

The accounting profession's requirement of the use of the lower of cost or market and discontinuance of original cost as the carrying amount of a current asset portfolio of marketable equity securities was long awaited. Using original cost as the basis when the market value of the portfolio is lower has the effect of deferring unrealized losses on the basis of the expectation of a future recovery in market value, which may or may not occur.

However, many accountants are unhappy with *FASB Statement No. 12*. They argue that market value, whether higher or lower than cost, should be recognized in the accounts. It is considered inconsistent to reduce the carrying amount of the securities to an amount below cost without increasing their carrying amount when market value is above cost. **Market value proponents indicate that gains or losses develop when the value of the investments change and not when the investments are sold.** Recognition of losses only is conservative and does not reflect the underlying economics when prices increase. Because of this situation, management can to some extent manipulate net income by determining when securities are sold to realize gains. For example, an enterprise whose earnings are low in one year might sell some securities that have appreciated in past years to offset the low income figure from current operations.

A major objection to the use of market value is that fluctuations in earnings result as the market price of the equity securities changes. To illustrate, Leaseway Transportation estimated that in the mid-1970s bear market, the use of market value would have reduced earnings 28%, but that the use of market value a year later would have increased earnings approximately 21%. Most companies dislike these types of fluctuations in earnings because they have little control over these changes.

Recognition of impairment as opposed to improvement in the carrying amount of a securities portfolio is still the dominant attitude of accounting. As a result, it is not surprising that the profession adopted a compromise position (lower of cost or market). The following rationale was given for not using market value alone as the determinant of carrying value: "Consideration of that alternative would raise pervasive issues concerning the valuation of other types of assets, including the concept of historic cost versus current or realizable value."[11]

## Accounting for Marketable Debt (Nonequity) Securities

Because the FASB in *Statement No. 12* addressed itself only to "marketable equity securities," temporary investments in **marketable debt (nonequity) securities** (securities not qualifying under its definition of marketable equity securities) have continued to be accounted for at cost. *Accounting Research Bulletin No. 43* prescribed cost as the carrying basis for marketable securities except that "where market value is less than cost by a substantial amount and it is evident that the decline in market value is not due to a mere temporary condition, the amount to be included as a current asset should not exceed the market value."[12] Under the cost basis if a permanent decline in the market value of debt securities occurs, the write-down from cost to market is charged to expense in the period of recognition but there is no later recognition for subsequent market value increases (no valuation allowance account is utilized).

During the past decade, however, some companies have adopted the **lower of cost or market** method for debt securities that are readily marketable and are classified as current assets. Since the issuance of *Statement No. 12,* this practice has become more acceptable. Marketable debt securities, such as bonds, may be carried at lower of cost or market, and any unrealized loss may be charged to expense and a valuation allowance used to carry the credit. The unrealized loss can be recovered and credited to revenue in the same manner as that accorded the marketable equity securities. Marketable debt securities, therefore, are carried either at cost or at the lower of cost or market bases.

The acquisition of debt securities is recorded at cost. If the debt securities are bonds purchased between interest dates, the accrued interest at the date of purchase is segregated

---

[11] *FASB Statement No. 12,* par. 29(a).

[12] Committee on Accounting Procedure, "Restatement and Revision of Accounting Research Bulletins," *ARB No. 43* (New York: AICPA, 1953), Ch. 3A, par. 9; originally adopted as *ARB No. 30* in 1947.

from the acquisition cost and classified appropriately. For example, Western Publishing Company invested some of its excess cash in the bond market. Western purchased at 86 on April 1, 1982, 100 bonds (face value $1,000 and stated interest rate 10%) of Burlington-Northern, Inc., interest payable semiannually on July 1 and January 1. The brokerage commissions associated with this purchase were $1,720. The cash outlay is:

| | |
|---|---:|
| Purchase price of bonds | $86,000 |
| Commission | 1,720 |
| Cost of bonds acquired | 87,720 |
| Accrued interest January 1 to April 1 ($100,000 × 10% × 3/12) | 2,500 |
| Cash payment | $90,220 |

The journal entry to record this transaction is:

**April 1, 1982**

| | | |
|---|---:|---:|
| Marketable Debt Securities | 87,720 | |
| Interest Revenue (or Accrued Interest Receivable) | 2,500 | |
| Cash | | 90,220 |

Generally, the discount or premium on temporary investments is not recorded in the accounts and not amortized because the investment is ordinarily held for only a short time.

The journal entry to record the receipt of interest as of July 1 is as follows, assuming that Interest Revenue was originally debited at the time of purchase:

**July 1, 1982**

| | | |
|---|---:|---:|
| Cash | 5,000 | |
| Interest Revenue | | 5,000 |

When marketable debt securities are sold, the difference between the cost (or carrying amount if a permanent-type write-down has occurred) and the selling price is recorded as a gain or loss. For example, if Western Publishing Company on November 1, 1982, sold at 98 plus accrued interest the Burlington-Northern, Inc. bonds (purchased above on April 1, 1982), the computation of the gain would be as follows (assume that commission and taxes associated with the sale are $1,870):

| | |
|---|---:|
| Selling price of bonds (100 × $980) | $98,000 |
| Less commissions and taxes | (1,870) |
| Net proceeds | 96,130 |
| Carrying value of bonds | 87,720 |
| Gain on sale of bonds | $ 8,410 |

The journal entry to record this transaction is:

**November 1, 1982**

| | | |
|---|---:|---:|
| Cash | 99,463 | |
| Interest Revenue (100,000 × .10 × 4/12) | | 3,333 |
| Marketable Debt Securities | | 87,720 |
| Gain on Sale of Temporary Investment | | 8,410 |

The gain on sale enters into the determination of income from continuing operations and before extraordinary items. In cases where there are numerous purchases of similar securities, some flow assumption must be applied to match the proper cost with the proceeds of sale. For financial reporting purposes, specific identification, FIFO, or average cost may be employed. The Internal Revenue Service will accept only specific identification or FIFO for tax purposes.[13]

## Financial Statement Disclosure

**Cash,** the most liquid asset, is listed first in the current asset section of the balance sheet. All unrestricted cash, whether on hand (including petty cash) or on deposit at a financial institution, is presented as a single item using the caption "Cash."

**Marketable equity securities** usually rank next to cash in liquidity and should be listed in the current asset section of the balance sheet (assuming that they are held as temporary investments) immediately after cash. Marketable equity securities that are held for other than liquidity and temporary investment purposes should not be classified as current assets.

As of the date of **each balance sheet** presented, the aggregate cost and the aggregate market value of marketable equity securities must be disclosed either in the body of the financial statements or in the accompanying footnotes. When classified balance sheets are presented, the aggregate cost and the aggregate market value should be disclosed, segregated between current and noncurrent assets.

In addition, for the **latest balance sheet,** disclosures are required of (1) gross unrealized gains and (2) gross unrealized losses. For **each** period for which an **income statement** is presented, disclosures relating to marketable equity securities are required of (1) the net realized gain or loss included in net income, (2) the basis on which cost was determined in computing realized gain or loss, and (3) the change in the valuation allowance included in net income.

Further, **significant** net realized and net unrealized gains and losses arising **after** the date of the financial statements, but prior to their issuance, that are applicable to marketable equity securities in the portfolio at the date of the most recent balance sheet should be disclosed.

To illustrate, we will use the data from Republic Service Corporation's December 31, 1981 and December 31, 1982 portfolio valuations presented on pages 281 and 282, respectively. Republic's marketable equity securities might be presented in the financial statements and the footnotes thereto as shown on page 288.

Temporary investments that do not conform to the criteria of marketable equity securities should be listed after marketable equity securities among the current assets under a classification such as "Debt Securities" or "Other Temporary Investments." If these temporary investments are less liquid than other current asset items such as receivables and inventories, they should be listed as the last item in the current asset section.

---

[13]LIFO can be duplicated, however, simply by selling the most recent certificates first and following specific identification.

### BALANCE SHEET

| | December 31 | |
| --- | --- | --- |
| | 1982 | 1981 |
| Current assets: | | |
| Marketable equity securities, carried at lower of cost or market (Note 2) | $782,000 | $683,000 |

### INCOME STATEMENT

| | Year Ended December 31 | |
| --- | --- | --- |
| | 1982 | 1981 |
| Income from operations | $    XXX | $    XXX |
| Other revenues and gains | | |
| Realized gain on sale of marketable equity securities | | 27,520 |
| Recovery of unrealized loss on valuation of marketable equity securities | 35,550 | |
| Other expenses and losses | | |
| Realized loss on sale of marketable equity securities | (55,440) | |
| Unrealized loss on valuation of marketable equity securities | | (35,550) |
| Income before extraordinary items | $ XXXXX | $ XXXXX |

Note 2—*Marketable Equity Securities.* Marketable equity securities are carried at the lower of cost or market at the balance sheet date; that determination is made by aggregating all current marketable equity securities. Marketable equity securities included in current assets had a market value at December 31, 1982 of $842,500 and a cost at December 31, 1981 of $718,550.

At December 31, 1982, there were gross unrealized gains of $62,800 and gross unrealized losses of $2,300 pertaining to the current portfolio.

A net realized loss of $55,440 on the sale of marketable equity securities was included in the determination of net income for 1982. A net realized gain of $27,520 on the sale of marketable equity securities was included in the determination of net income in 1981. The cost of the securities sold was based on the first-in, first-out method in both years. A reduction of $35,550 in the valuation allowance for net unrealized losses was included in income during 1982. The valuation allowance was established in 1981 by a charge to expense of $35,550.

# SECTION 3  RECEIVABLES

## SHORT-TERM RECEIVABLES

Short-term receivables are defined as claims held against others for money, goods, or services collectible within a year or the operating cycle, whichever is longer. For financial statement purposes, receivables are generally classified into two categories: (1) trade receivables and (2) nontrade receivables. Trade receivables are amounts owed by customers for goods and services sold as part of the normal operations of the business. They are usually the most significant receivables an enterprise possesses and are commonly called "accounts receivable." Trade receivables are oral as opposed to written commitments by others and are normally collectible within 30 to 60 days. They are represented by "open accounts" resulting from short-term extensions of credit.

Nontrade or special receivables arise from a variety of transactions and are oral or written promises to pay or deliver. Here are some examples of nontrade receivables:

1. Advances to officers and employees.
2. Advances to subsidiaries.
3. Deposits to cover potential damages or losses.
4. Deposits as a guarantee of performance or payment.
5. Dividends and interest receivable.
6. Stock subscriptions receivable.
7. Claims against:
    (a) Insurance companies for casualties sustained.
    (b) Defendants under suit.
    (c) Governmental bodies for tax refunds.
    (d) Common carriers for damaged or lost goods.
    (e) Creditors for returned, damaged, or lost goods.
    (f) Customers for returnable items (crates, containers, etc.).

The basic problems in accounting for receivables relate to (1) their valuation and (2) their classification in the balance sheet. Short-term receivables are valued at **net realizable value,** which is the net amount expected to be received in cash within a year or the operating cycle, whichever is longer.

Once the receivable transactions and their dates of occurrence have been identified, the appropriate amount to record must be determined. The accountant must consider (1) the face value of the receivable, (2) the probability of future collection, and (3) the length of time the receivable will be outstanding.

## Determination of Face Value

**Trade Discount**   Customers are often quoted prices on the basis of list or catalog prices that may be subject to a trade or quantity discount. Trade discounts are used to avoid frequent changes in catalogs, or to quote different prices for different quantities purchased, or to hide the true invoice price from competitors. They are commonly quoted in percentages. For example, if your textbook has a list price of $30.00 and the publisher sells it to college book stores for list less a 30% trade discount, the receivable recorded by the publisher is $21.00 per textbook. The normal practice is simply to deduct the trade discount from the list price and bill the customer net.

**Cash Discounts (Sales Discounts)**   Cash discounts (sales discounts) are offered as an inducement for prompt payment and communicated in terms that read 2/10, n/30 (two percent if paid within 10 days, gross amount due in 30 days), or 2/10, E.O.M. (end of month). Companies that fail to take sales discounts are usually not employing their money advantageously. An enterprise that receives a 1% reduction in the sales price for payment within 10 days, total payment due within 30 days, is effectively earning 18.25%, (.01 ÷ 20/365), or at least avoiding that rate of interest cost. For this reason, it is usual for companies to take the discount unless their cash is severely limited.

The easiest and most commonly used method of recording sales and related sales discount transactions is to enter the receivable and sale at the gross amount. Under this method, sales discounts are recognized in the accounts only when payment is received within the discount period. Sales discounts would then be shown in the income statement as a deduction from sales to arrive at net sales.

Some accountants contend that sales discounts are not actually discounts but penalties added to an established price to encourage prompt payment. That is, the seller offers sales on account at a slightly higher price than if selling for cash, and the increase is offset by the cash discount offered. Thus, customers who pay within the discount period purchase at the cash price; those who pay after expiration of the discount period are penalized because they must pay an amount in excess of the cash price. If this approach is adopted, sales and receivables are recorded net, and any discounts not taken are subsequently debited to Accounts Receivable and credited to Sales Discounts Forfeited. To illustrate the difference between the gross and net methods, assume the following transactions.

**Entries Under Gross and Net Methods**

| Gross Method | | | Net Method | | |
|---|---|---|---|---|---|
| **Sale of $10,000, terms 2/10, n/30:** | | | | | |
| Accounts Receivable | 10,000 | | Accounts Receivable | 9,800 | |
| Sales | | 10,000 | Sales | | 9,800 |
| **Payment of $4,000 received within discount period:** | | | | | |
| Cash | 3,920 | | Cash | 3,920 | |
| Sales Discount | 80 | | Accounts Receivable | | 3,920 |
| Accounts Receivable | | 4,000 | | | |
| **Payment of $6,000 received after discount period:** | | | | | |
| Cash | 6,000 | | Accounts Receivable | 120 | |
| Accounts Receivable | | 6,000 | Sales Discounts | | |
| | | | Forfeited | | 120 |
| | | | Cash | 6,000 | |
| | | | Accounts Receivable | | 6,000 |

As noted earlier, if the gross method is employed, sales discounts should be reported as a deduction from sales in the income statement. If the net method is used, Sales Discounts Forfeited should be considered as an other revenue item. Theoretically, the recognition of Sales Discounts Forfeited is correct because the receivable is stated at its realizable value and the net sale figure measures the revenue earned from the sale. As a practical matter, the net method is seldom used because it requires additional analysis and bookkeeping. For example, adjusting entries are required under the net method to record sales discounts forfeited on accounts receivable that have passed the discount period.

## Probability of Uncollectible Accounts Receivable

As one accountant so aptly noted: "The credit manager's idea of heaven probably would envisage a situation in which everybody (eventually) paid his debts."[14] Sales on any basis other than for cash make subsequent failure to collect the account a real possibility. An

---

[14]William J. Vatter, *Managerial Accounting* (Englewood Cliffs, N.J.: Prentice-Hall, 1950), p. 60.

uncollectible account receivable is a loss of revenue that requires, through proper entry in the accounts, a decrease in the asset accounts receivable and a related decrease in income and stockholders' equity.

The chief problem in recording uncollectible accounts receivable is establishing the time at which to record the loss. Two general procedures are in use.

1. No entry is made until a specific account has definitely been established as uncollectible. Then the loss is recorded by crediting Accounts Receivable and debiting Bad Debt Expense. This is normally referred to as the "direct write-off" method for receivables.

2. An estimate is made of the expected uncollectible accounts from all sales made on account or from the total of outstanding receivables. This estimate is entered as an expense and a reduction in accounts receivable (via an increase in the allowance account) in the period in which the sale is recorded. This is usually called the "allowance" method.

The direct write-off method records the bad debt in the year it is determined that a specific receivable cannot be collected; the allowance method enters the expense on an estimated basis in the accounting period that the sales on account are made. Either method is acceptable for tax purposes as long as it is consistently applied.

Supporters of the **direct write-off method** contend that facts, not estimates, are recorded. It assumes that a good account receivable resulted from each sale, and that later events proved certain accounts to be uncollectible and worthless. From a practical standpoint this method is simple and convenient to apply, although we must recognize that receivables do not generally become worthless at an identifiable moment of time. The direct write-off method is theoretically deficient because it usually does not match costs with revenues of the period, nor does it result in receivables being stated at estimated realizable value on the balance sheet. As a result, its use is not considered appropriate, except when the amount uncollectible is immaterial.

Advocates of the **allowance method** believe that bad debt expense should be recorded in the same period as the sale to obtain a proper matching of expenses and revenues and to achieve a proper carrying value for accounts receivable at the end of a period. They support the position that although estimates are involved, the percentage of receivables that will not be collected can be predicted from past experiences, present market conditions, and an analysis of the outstanding balances.

Because the collectibility of receivables is considered a loss contingency, the allowance method is appropriate only in situations where it is probable that an asset has been impaired and that the amount of the loss can be reasonably estimated.[15] Accountants, for the most part, have accepted the challenge of estimating the proportion of uncollectible accounts. A receivable is a prospective cash inflow, and the probability of its collection must be considered in valuing this inflow. These estimates normally are made either (1) on the basis of percentage of sales or (2) on the basis of outstanding receivables.

**Percentage of Sales**   When the percentage-of-sales approach is employed, a company's past experience with uncollectible accounts is analyzed. If there is a fairly stable relationship between previous years' charge sales and bad debts, that relationship can be turned into a percentage and used to determine this year's bad debt expense.

The percentage-of-sales method matches costs with revenues because it relates the charge to the period in which the sale is recorded. To illustrate, assume that E. T. Elsner's,

---

[15]"Accounting for Contingencies," *Statement of the Financial Accounting Standards No. 5* (Stamford, Conn.: FASB, 1975), par. 8.

Inc. estimates from past experience that about 2% of charge sales become uncollectible. If E. T. Elsner's, Inc. had charge sales of $400,000 in 1983, the entry to record bad debt expense using the percentage-of-sales method is as follows:

| | | |
|---|---|---|
| Bad Debt Expense | 8,000 | |
| Allowance for Doubtful Accounts | | 8,000 |

The Allowance for Doubtful Accounts is a valuation account (i.e., contra asset) and is subtracted from the trade receivables on the balance sheet. The amount of bad debt expense and the related credit to the allowance account is unaffected by any balance currently existing in the allowance account. Because the bad debt expense is related to a nominal account (Sales), any balance in the allowance is ignored. A proper matching of cost and revenues is therefore achieved.

**Percentage of Outstanding Receivables**   Using past experience, a company can estimate the percentage of its outstanding receivables that will become uncollectible, without identifying specific accounts. This procedure provides a reasonably accurate estimate of the realizable value of the receivables at any time, but does not fit the concept of matching cost and revenues. Rather, its objective is to report receivables in the balance sheet at net realizable values and it accomplishes that objective reasonably well.

The percentage of receivables may be applied using one **composite rate** that reflects an estimate of the uncollectible receivables. Another approach that is more sensitive to the actual status of the accounts receivable is achieved by setting up an **aging schedule** and applying a different percentage to the various age categories established. The percentages used are developed from past experience. An aging schedule is a method frequently used in practice. This schedule indicates which accounts require special attention by providing the age of such accounts receivable. The following schedule of Wilson & Co. is an example.

**Wilson & Co.**
**AGING SCHEDULE**

| Name of Customer | Balance Dec. 31 | Under 60 days | 61–90 days | 91–120 days | Over 120 days |
|---|---|---|---|---|---|
| Western Stainless Steel Corp. | $ 98,000 | $ 80,000 | $18,000 | $ | $ |
| Brockway Steel Company | 320,000 | 320,000 | | | |
| Freeport Sheet & Tube Co. | 55,000 | | | | 55,000 |
| Allegheny Iron Works | 74,000 | 60,000 | | 14,000 | |
| | $547,000 | $460,000 | $18,000 | $14,000 | $55,000 |

**Summary**

| Age | Amount | Percentage Estimated to be Uncollectible | Required Balance in Allowance |
|---|---|---|---|
| Under 60 days old | $460,000 | 1% | $ 4,600 |
| 61–90 days old | 18,000 | 5% | 900 |
| 91–120 days old | 14,000 | 10% | 1,400 |
| Over 120 days | 55,000 | 20% | 11,000 |
| Year-end balance of allowance for doubtful accounts | | | $17,900 |

The amount $17,900 would be the bad debt expense to be reported for this year, assuming that no balance existed in the allowance account. To change the illustration slightly, assume that the allowance account had a credit balance of $800 before adjustment. In this case, the amount to be added to the allowance account is $17,100 ($17,900 − $800), and the following entry is made.

| | | |
|---|---|---|
| Bad Debt Expense | 17,100 | |
| Allowance for Doubtful Accounts | | 17,100 |

The balance in the Allowance account is therefore correctly stated at $17,900. If the Allowance balance before adjustment had a debit balance of $200, then the amount to be recorded for bad debt expense would be $18,100 ($17,900 desired balance + $200 debit balance). In the percentage of outstanding receivables method, the balance in the allowance account cannot be ignored because the percentage is related to a real account (accounts receivable).

An aging schedule is usually not prepared to determine the bad debt expense but as a control device to determine the composition of receivables and to identify delinquent accounts. The estimated loss percentage developed for each category is based on previous loss experience and the advice of credit department personnel. Regardless of whether a composite rate or an aging schedule is employed, the primary objective of the percentage of outstanding receivables method for financial statement purposes is to report receivables in the balance sheet at net realizable value. However, it is deficient in that it may not match the bad debt expense to the period in which the sale takes place.

As indicated above, the allowance for doubtful accounts as a percentage of receivables will vary, depending upon the industry and the economic climate. To illustrate, companies such as Eastman Kodak, General Electric, and Monsanto have recorded allowances of $3 to $6 per $100 of accounts receivable. Others such as CPC International ($1.48), Texaco ($1.23), and U.S. Steel ($.78) are examples of large enterprises that have had bad debt allowances of less than $1.50 per $100.

In summary, the percentage-of-sales method results in a direct entry to an expense account and the allowance account because the amount calculated is related to the year's sales and not to the balance remaining in accounts receivable. Generally, the percentage-of-sales approach provides the best results from a matching viewpoint. If no consistent pattern of uncollectibles to sales is established, other approaches might be desirable. The account description employed for the allowance account is usually "Allowance for Doubtful Accounts" or simply "Allowance."[16]

**Collection of Accounts Receivable Written Off**    If a collection is made on a receivable that was previously written off, the procedure to be followed is first to reestablish the receivable by debiting Accounts Receivable and crediting Allowance for Doubtful Accounts. An entry is then made to debit Cash and credit the customer's account in the amount of the remittance received.

---

[16]*Accounting Trends and Techniques (1981),* for example, indicates that approximately 73% of the companies surveyed used "allowance" in their description. Approximately 10%, in addition to deducting an allowance for doubtful accounts from receivables, also deducted amounts for unearned discounts or finance charges or sale returns.

If the direct write-off approach is employed, the amount collected is debited to Cash and credited to a revenue account entitled Uncollectible Amounts Recovered, with proper notation in the customer's account.

## Special Allowance Accounts

To properly match expenses against sales revenues, it is sometimes necessary to establish allowance accounts. These allowance accounts are reported as contra accounts to accounts receivable and establish the receivables at **net realizable value.** The most common allowances are:

1. Allowance for sales returns and allowances.
2. Allowance for freight.
3. Allowance for collection expenses.

**Sales Returns and Allowances**   Many accountants question the soundness of recording returns and allowances in the current period when they are derived from sales made in the preceding period. Normally, however, the amount of mismatched returns and allowances is not material, if such items are handled consistently from year to year. Yet, if a company completes a few special orders involving large amounts near the end of the accounting period, returns and allowances should be anticipated in the period of the sale to avoid distorting the income statement of the current period.

As an example, Astro Turf Corporation recognizes that approximately 5% of its $1,000,000 trade receivables outstanding are returned or some adjustment made to the sale price. Omission of a $50,000 charge could have a material effect on net income for the period.

The entry to reflect this anticipated sales return and allowance is:

| | | |
|---|---|---|
| Sales Returns and Allowances | 50,000 | |
| Allowance for Sales Returns and Allowances | | 50,000 |

· Sales returns and allowances are reported as an offset to sales revenue in the income statement. Returns and allowances are accumulated separately instead of debited directly to the sales account simply to let the business manager and the statement reader know the magnitude of the returns and allowances. The allowance is an asset valuation account (contra asset) and is deducted from total accounts receivable; the receivables are stated at realizable value.

In most cases, the inclusion in the income statement of all returns and allowances made during the period, whether or not they resulted from the current period's sales, is an acceptable accounting procedure justified on the basis of practicality and immateriality.[17]

**Freight**   A seller may ship goods f.o.b. destination with the understanding that the purchaser will pay for the freight charges and deduct that amount from the remittance. In

---

[17]An interesting sidelight to the entire problem of returns and allowances has developed in recent years. Determination of when a sale is a sale has become difficult, because in certain circumstances the seller is exposed to such a high risk of ownership through possible return of the property that the entire transaction is nullified and the sale not recognized. Such situations have developed particularly in sales to related parties. This subject is discussed in more detail in Chapters 8 and 19.

such cases, the seller may record the receivable gross with a corresponding freight allowance to offset the accounts receivable. This allowance is deducted from accounts receivable with the debit either offsetting sales or being set up as a freight charge (selling expense); the latter treatment is correct.

**Collection Expense**    A similar concept holds true for collection expense. If a significant handling and service charge is incurred to collect the open accounts receivables at the end of the year, an allowance for collection expenses should be recorded. For example, Sears, Roebuck and Company reports its receivables net, with an attached schedule indicating the types of receivables outstanding. Sears' contra account is entitled "Allowance for Collection Expenses and Losses on Customer Accounts" as shown below.

| Sears, Roebuck and Company | |
| --- | --- |
| **Receivables** | |
| Customer installment accounts receivable | |
| Easy payment accounts | $2,221,017,167 |
| Revolving charge accounts | 1,372,874,725 |
| | 3,593,891,892 |
| Other customer accounts | 101,904,882 |
| Miscellaneous accounts and notes receivable | 96,446,334 |
| | 3,792,243,108 |
| Less allowance for collection expenses and losses on customer accounts | 236,826,866 |
| | $3,555,416,242 |

## Nonrecognition of Interest Element

Receivables should be valued in terms of the discounted value of the cash to be received in the future. When expected cash receipts require a waiting period, the receivable currently is not worth the amount that is ultimately received. To illustrate, assume that a company makes a sale on account for $1,000 with payment due in 120 days. Also assume that the applicable rate of interest in this case is 12% and that payment is made at the end of the 120th day. The present value of that receivable is not $1,000 but $961.54 ($1,000 × present value factor of .96154). In other words, $1,000 to be received 120 days from now is not the same as $1,000 received today.

Any revenue after the period of sale is interest revenue (actual or implicit). Accountants have chosen to ignore this for the most part in connection with accounts receivable, because the amount of the discount is not usually material in relation to the net income for the period. Unearned discounts, finance charges, and interest included in the face amount of a receivable are shown as deductions from the related receivables, whenever they are material.[18] The profession, however, specifically excludes from the present value consider-

---

[18]"Status of Accounting Research Bulletins," *Opinions of the Accounting Principles Board No. 6* (New York: AICPA, 1965), par. 14.

ations "receivables arising from transactions with customers in the normal course of business which are due in customary trade terms not exceeding approximately one year."[19]

## ACCOUNTS RECEIVABLE AND CASH GENERATION

The net realizable value of accounts receivable as reported on the balance sheet represents the amount expected to be collected in cash at some near-term future date. In order to advance the timing of the cash receipt from these receivables, the owner may transfer the receivables to a third party for cash. In this way, accounts receivable can be an immediate source of cash.

The transfer of accounts receivable to a third party for cash is generally accomplished in one of two ways:

1. Assignment of accounts receivable (pledging a security interest in accounts receivable).
2. Factoring (sale of accounts receivable).

### Assignment of Accounts Receivable

In an assignment of accounts receivable, the owner of the receivables (the assignor) borrows cash from a lender (the assignee) by writing a promissory note that contains a provision designating the accounts receivable as collateral. If the note is not paid when due, the assignee has the right to convert the collateral to cash, that is, to collect the receivables. The term pledging is sometimes used instead of assignment to describe this transaction.

**General Assignment**  If the assignment is general, all the receivables serve as collateral for the note. New receivables can be substituted for the ones collected. To illustrate, Machlin Motor Company assigns its accounts receivable to First City Finance Company as collateral for a loan of $90,000. The entry to record this transaction is as follows:

| | | |
|---|---|---|
| Cash | 90,000 | |
| Notes Payable | | 90,000 |

No special entries are made to the receivable accounts to record the assignment. Information concerning the assigned receivables is disclosed in a note or in a parenthetical explanation. To illustrate, United Air Industries, Inc. reports its general assignment in the following manner:

---

**United Air Industries, Inc.**

**Current Assets**

| | |
|---|---|
| Trade accounts, notes, and other receivables, less allowance of $95,000 in 1981 and $75,000 in 1980 for doubtful accounts (Note B) | $8,695,372 |

Note B. *Other Notes Payable.* Under the terms of the amended revolving credit agreement with a commercial finance company, the corporation may borrow up to 90% of eligible trade accounts receivable and 60% of certain inventories. The maximum that may be borrowed under this agreement is $7,000,000. The corporation's trade accounts, notes, and other receivables and inventories are pledged as collateral.

---

[19]"Interest on Receivables and Payables," *Opinions of the Accounting Principles Board No. 21* (New York: AICPA, 1971), par. 3(a).

**Specific Assignment**  In a specific assignment, the borrower and lender enter into an agreement as to (1) who is to receive the collections—the borrower or the lender, (2) the finance charges (which are in addition to the interest on the note), (3) the specific accounts that serve as security, and (4) notification or non-notification of account debtors. In this case the total of the specifically assigned accounts should be transferred to a special general ledger control account and the individual accounts in the subsidiary ledger should be segregated or clearly marked as assigned. Collections on the assigned accounts are generally made by the assignor. To illustrate, on March 1, 1983, Crest Textiles, Inc. assigns a group of its accounts receivable totaling $700,000 to Citizens Bank as collateral for a $500,000 note. Crest Textiles will continue to make collections of the accounts receivable; the account debtors are not notified of the assignment. Citizens Bank assesses a finance charge of 1% of the accounts receivable assigned and interest on the note of 12%. Settlement is to be made monthly for all cash collected on the assigned receivables.

---

### Entries for Assignment of Specific Accounts Receivable

| Crest Textiles, Inc. | | | Citizens Bank | | |
|---|---|---|---|---|---|
| **Assignment of accounts receivable and issuance of note on March 1, 1983:** | | | | | |
| Cash | 493,000 | | Notes Receivable | 500,000 | |
| Finance Charge | 7,000* | | Finance Revenue | | 7,000* |
| Accounts Rec. Assigned | 700,000 | | Cash | | 493,000 |
|   Notes Payable | | 500,000 | | | |
|   Accounts Rec. | | 700,000 | | | |
| *(1% × $700,000) | | | | | |

**Collection in March of $440,000 of assigned accounts less cash discounts of $6,000. In addition, sales returns of $14,000 were received:**

| Crest Textiles, Inc. | | | Citizens Bank | | |
|---|---|---|---|---|---|
| Cash | 434,000 | | | | |
| Sales Discounts | 6,000 | | | | |
| Sales Returns | 14,000 | | (No entry) | | |
|   Accts. Rec. Assigned | | 454,000 | | | |
|     ($440,000 + $14,000 = $454,000) | | | | | |

**Remitted March collections plus accrued interest to the bank on April 1:**

| Crest Textiles, Inc. | | | Citizens Bank | | |
|---|---|---|---|---|---|
| Interest Expense | 5,000* | | Cash | 439,000 | |
| Notes Payable | 434,000 | | Interest Revenue | | 5,000 |
|   Cash | | 439,000 | Notes Receivable | | 434,000 |
| *($500,000 × .12 × 1/12) | | | | | |

**Collection in April of the balance of assigned accounts less $2,000 written off as uncollectible:**

| Crest Textiles, Inc. | | | Citizens Bank | | |
|---|---|---|---|---|---|
| Cash | 244,000 | | | | |
| Allow. for Doubtful | | | | | |
|     Accts. | 2,000 | | (No entry) | | |
|   Accts. Rec. Assigned | | 246,000* | | | |
| *($700,000 − $454,000) | | | | | |

**Remitted the balance due of $66,000 ($500,000 − $434,000) on the note plus interest on May 1:**

| Crest Textiles, Inc. | | | Citizens Bank | | |
|---|---|---|---|---|---|
| Interest Expense | 660* | | Cash | 66,660 | |
| Notes Payable | 66,000 | | Interest Revenue | | 660* |
|   Cash    A/r    A/R assigned | | 66,660 | Notes Receivable | | 66,000 |
| *($66,000 × .12 × 1/12) | | | | | |

If the account debtors had been notified to make remittance directly to Citizens Bank, the bank would have communicated monthly the amount of collections and sales discount on the assigned accounts and the amount of interest due. A liability account ("Payable to Crest Textiles, Inc.") would be used by the bank to record cash collections during the period. The bank would not record the assigned accounts receivable as an asset of the bank. Upon full payment of principal and interest on the note, the bank would remit to Crest Textiles any cash collections in excess of the note along with any uncollected accounts.

Specifically assigned accounts receivable should be reported in the financial statements by Crest Textiles as a separate asset account if material. The assignor's equity in the assigned accounts should be disclosed. For instance, Crest Textiles, Inc. has equity of $200,000 in its assigned receivables at March 1 ($700,000 − $500,000).

### Factoring Accounts Receivable

Factoring is the sale of accounts receivable. Factors are finance companies or banks that buy receivables from businesses for a fee and then collect the remittances directly from the customers. Factoring, traditionally associated with the textiles, apparel, footwear, furniture, and home furnishing industries, has now spread to many other types of businesses and represents a $28 billion business in this country. As an illustration, Sears, Roebuck & Co. recently arranged to sell $550 million of customer accounts receivable at 99.015% of face value. MasterCard, VISA, Diners Club, and American Express Card are a type of factoring arrangement.

Factoring arrangements vary widely, but typically the factor charges a commission of from ¾ to 1½% of the net amount of receivables purchased (except for the credit card factoring which costs the retailer or restaurateur 4 to 5 percent). The following diagram illustrates in sequential process the basic procedures in factoring.

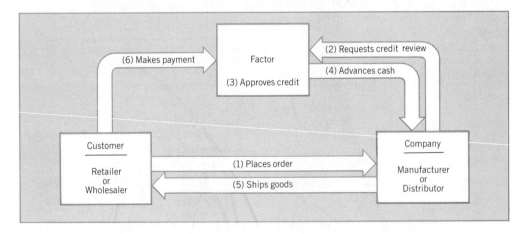

Although in most factoring transactions the factor buys the receivables without recourse, receivables can be factored with recourse.[20]

---

[20]**Recourse** is the contractual right of a transferee of receivables to demand payment from the transferor of those receivables in the event of default or late payment by debtors. See "Accounting and Reporting by Transferors for Transfers of Receivables with Recourse," *Proposed Statement of Financial Accounting Standards* (Stamford, Conn.: FASB, 1982), par. 1.

**Factoring Without Recourse**    When a factor buys receivables **without recourse,** the factor assumes the risk of collectibility and absorbs any credit losses. The transfer of accounts receivable in a nonrecourse transaction is both in form (transfer of title) and substance (transfer of the risk and reward) an outright sale of the receivables. No loan is created when receivables are sold to factors without recourse. In nonrecourse transactions, as in any sale of assets, Cash is debited for the proceeds, Accounts Receivable is credited for the carrying value of the receivables, and the difference, reduced by any provision for probable adjustments (discounts, returns, allowances, etc.), is recognized as a Loss on the Sale of Receivables.[21] A "Due from Factor" account is used by the seller to account for the amount of proceeds retained by the factor to cover the probable adjustments in the form of sales discounts, sales returns, and sales allowances.

To illustrate, Crest Textiles, Inc. factors $500,000 of accounts receivable with Commercial Factors, Inc. on a **without recourse** basis. On May 1 the receivable records are transferred to Commercial Factors, Inc., which will receive the collections. Commercial Factors assesses a finance charge of 3% of the amount of accounts receivable and retains an amount equal to 5% of the accounts receivable. Crest Textiles handles returned goods, claims for defective goods (allowances), and disputes concerning shipments. The factor handles the sales discounts and absorbs the credit losses.

---

**Entries for Factored Receivables Without Recourse**

Crest Textiles, Inc.                                    Commercial Factors, Inc.

**Sale of accounts receivable without recourse on May 1:**

| Crest Textiles, Inc. | | | Commercial Factors, Inc. | | |
|---|---|---|---|---|---|
| Cash | 460,000 | | Accounts Receivable | 500,000 | |
| Due from Factor | 25,000* | | Due to Crest Textile | | 25,000* |
| Loss on Sale of Rec. | 15,000** | | Financing Revenue | | 15,000** |
| Accounts Receivable | | 500,000 | Cash | | 460,000 |

*(5% × $500,000)    **(3% × $500,000)

**Transactions in May—collections of $340,000; returned merchandise of $8,000; sales discounts taken of $2,600; sales allowances of $1,500; and uncollectibles of $900:**

| | | | | | |
|---|---|---|---|---|---|
| Sales Returns | 8,000 | | Cash | 340,000 | |
| Sales Allowances | 1,500 | | Due to Crest Textiles | 2,600 | |
| Due from Factor | | 9,500 | Bad Debt Expense | 900 | |
| | | | Accounts Receivable | | 343,500* |

*($340,000 + $2,600 + $900)

**Monthly settlement between Crest Textiles and Commercial Factors (no further discounts, allowances, or returns are expected):**

| | | | | | |
|---|---|---|---|---|---|
| Cash | 12,900 | | Due to Crest Textiles | 22,400* | |
| Sales Discounts | 2,600 | | Accounts Receivable | | 9,500 |
| Due from Factor | | 15,500* | Cash | | 12,900 |

*($25,000 − $9,500)                          *($25,000 − $2,600)

---

**Factoring with Recourse**    If the factor buys receivables with recourse, the seller guarantees payment to the factor in the event the debtor does not pay. The question is: Is the sale of receivables on a with recourse basis a **borrowing transaction,** in which the difference between the proceeds and the receivables is a financing cost (interest) that should be amortized over the term of the receivables? Or, is it a **sale transaction,** in which a gain or loss should be recognized immediately? The FASB has proposed that the transfer of receiv-

[21] Ibid., par. 8.

ables with recourse be accounted for and reported as a sale only if certain criteria are met,[22] but it has not obtained sufficient agreement on the criteria to issue a standard. Until a standard is issued on the sale of receivables with recourse, such transactions will be accounted for inconsistently. We recommend that unless the with recourse transaction can be shown to be in substance a sale, it be treated as a borrowing transaction and the financing cost be accounted for as an interest cost over the life of the receivables.

### Conceptual Issues Related to the Transfer of Receivables

As indicated from the above discussion, the transfer of receivables to a third party for cash takes one of three forms:[23]

1. One form is to borrow from a third party and **assign or pledge the receivables** as collateral. Both the form of this transaction and its substance suggest that it be accounted for and reported as a **borrowing.**

2. A second form is to **transfer the receivables** to a third party in exchange for cash and in a manner whereby the third party is **without recourse** to the transferor in connection with the receivables. Both the form of this transaction and its substance suggest that it be accounted for and reported as a **sale.**

3. A third form is to **transfer the receivables** to a third party in exchange for cash but in a manner whereby the third party has full or partial recourse (**with recourse**) to the transferor in connection with the receivables. In this case the form of the transaction may either be a sale or a borrowing, depending on the facts.

The essence of a transfer of receivables in a **borrowing transaction** is that the transferor retains the same risks of collectibility on the receivables after the transaction that it had before the transaction. This is the situation in the first and in some cases the third form presented above. In the second form, where the receivables are transferred without recourse, the transferor has substantially eliminated its risks on the receivables transferred. The transferee assumes the risk of uncollectibles. As is required in other sale transactions, the substantial (or complete) risk transfer test has been met.

The third form of transfer has been the cause of greatest concern to accountants because it leads to what is referred to as **"off-balance-sheet financing."** Under the third form of transfer the asset, accounts receivable, is sometimes removed from the balance sheet as if it has been sold for cash and the transaction is treated as complete. The question is: Has a liability been created because of the transfer with recourse? It is hoped that the FASB will resolve this issue in the near future.

## NOTES RECEIVABLE

A note receivable involves a formal promissory note, whereas an account receivable is only an informal promise to pay. In addition, notes frequently carry a provision for interest on the face amount of debt. Except in some businesses that regularly accept notes from cus-

---

[22]"Accounting and Reporting by Transferors for Transfers of Receivables with Recourse," *op. cit.*, par. 7.

[23]Understanding these transactions is made more difficult by the inconsistent use of terms to describe these transactions in practice. When you encounter such transactions in practice, we recommend that you attempt to classify them in accordance with their basic nature as one of the foregoing three types.

tomers (installment sales usually require signed installment notes), most companies have relatively few trade notes receivable.

## Discounting Notes Receivable

Notes receivable, because of their greater negotiability, are readily converted to cash through discounting at a bank. The bank accepts the note and pays the holder cash in an amount equal to the note's maturity value less a discount which represents the bank's financing (interest) charge. At maturity the bank collects the face value of the note plus interest from the maker.

Notes may be discounted with or without recourse. In those rare instances when a note is discounted **without recourse** (a qualified endorsement), the notes receivable account is credited as in an outright sale. The transferor conveys all the risks and benefits of ownership to the transferee in discounting a note without recourse. Having transferred all the risks and benefits of ownership, the transferor no longer has an asset. In a nonrecourse transfer the difference between the book carrying value of the note and the cash proceeds is recorded as a gain or loss on sale.

The more common transaction is the discounting of a note at a bank **with recourse.** If the maker fails to pay at maturity, the bank presents the note to the transferor (endorser), who is then liable for payment. In most discounting transactions, the bank will insist on having recourse. Is the discounting of a note a sale with a gain or loss to be recognized and a contingent liability to be disclosed? Or is it a borrowing transaction that is accounted for by retaining the notes receivable in the accounts, reporting the endorser's obligation among the current liabilities, and recognizing interest expense or interest revenue? Whichever it is, accounting for a discounted note receivable is a six-step process:

1. Compute the maturity value of the note (face value plus interest to maturity).
2. Compute the discount (the bank's discount rate times the maturity value times the time to maturity).
3. Compute the proceeds (maturity value minus the bank's discount).
4. Compute the book carrying value of the note (face value plus interest accrued to date of discounting).
5. Compute the gain or loss, if a sale, or the interest revenue or expense, if a borrowing, (proceeds minus the book carrying value).
6. Record the journal entry.

To illustrate, on July 30, the Reliable Appliance Co. discounts at the bank a customer's 3-month $10,000 note receivable dated June 30 and bearing interest at 12%; the bank accepts the note **with recourse** and discounts it at 15%. The maturity value, discount, proceeds, book carrying value, and interest element are computed as follows:

| **Discounting with Recourse** | |
|---|---:|
| Face value of note | $10,000.00 |
| Plus interest ($10,000 × .12 × 3/12) | 300.00 |
| Step 1. Maturity value | 10,300.00 |
| Step 2. Less discount ($10,300 × .15 × 2/12) | 257.50 |
| Step 3. Proceeds | 10,042.50 |
| Step 4. Book carrying value ($10,000 + [$10,000 × .12 × 1/12]) | 10,100.00 |
| Step 5. Interest expense or loss on sale | $ 57.50 |

**Entries for Sale or Borrowing**

| Discounting A Sale | | Discounting A Borrowing | |
|---|---|---|---|

**Receipt of a 3-month note from an overdue customer, June 30:**

| Notes Receivable | 10,000.00 | | Notes Receivable | 10,000.00 | |
|---|---|---|---|---|---|
| Accts. Receivable | | 10,000.00 | Accts. Receivable | | 10,000.00 |

**Interest accrued (June 30–July 30) at date of discounting, July 30:**

| Interest Receivable | 100.00 | | Interest Receivable | 100.00 | |
|---|---|---|---|---|---|
| Interest Revenue | | 100.00 | Interest Revenue | | 100.00 |

**Discounting of notes receivable with recourse, July 30:**

| Cash | 10,042.50 | | Cash | 10,042.50 | |
|---|---|---|---|---|---|
| Loss on Sale of Note | 57.50 | | Interest Expense | 57.50 | |
| Notes Receivable | | 10,000.00 | Liability on Discounted | | |
| Interest Receivable | | 100.00 | Notes Receivable | | 10,000.00 |
| | | | Interest Receivable | | 100.00 |

**If payment of note by the maker at maturity date, September 30:**

| (No entry) | | | Liability on Discounted | | |
|---|---|---|---|---|---|
| | | | Notes Receivable | 10,000.00 | |
| | | | Notes Receivable | | 10,000.00 |

**If maker defaults and endorser pays note the following day with interest of $300 plus a bank protest fee of $25, October 1:**

| Notes Rec.— | | | Notes Rec.— | | |
|---|---|---|---|---|---|
| Past Due* | 10,325.00 | | Past Due* | 10,325.00 | |
| Cash | | 10,325.00 | Cash | | 10,325.00 |
| | | | Liability on Discounted | | |
| | | | Notes Receivable | 10,000.00 | |
| | | | Notes Receivable | | 10,000.00 |

*Accounts Receivable is frequently used as the account to reinstate the default.

In the above discounting transaction that is a sale, the endorser would disclose its contingent liability on the discounted notes with recourse by reporting the contingency in a note to the financial statements. Alternatively, the endorser could credit Notes Receivable Discounted, instead of Notes Receivable, for $10,000 and report it as a contra asset deducted from Notes Receivable in the current asset section of the balance sheet. This would serve to disclose the endorser's contingent liability for default by the maker of the note.

## Dishonored Notes

Notes receivable that are not paid at maturity (whether discounted or not) remain notes receivable and are considered notes receivable past due. Defaulted notes should be separately classified on the balance sheet. If all efforts to collect fail, the note is written off as a loss. Whether the loss is charged to the allowance for doubtful accounts or directly to a loss account depends on (1) whether the company has an allowance for doubtful accounts and (2) whether the periodic provisions cover losses only on accounts receivable or on both accounts and notes receivable.

## Determining the Present Value of Long-Term Notes Receivable

In a transaction involving the receipt of a long-term note, the objective is to record the note at its present value. Establishing the present value permits the determination of the real or effective interest involved irrespective of the stated interest rate or the absence of any stipulated interest rate.

If a noninterest-bearing note is received solely for cash, it is presumed to have a present value measured by the cash proceeds received by the borrower. The difference between the face amount and the proceeds (present value) is recorded as a discount or premium. This discount or premium is amortized to interest revenue or interest expense over the life of the note.

When a note is exchanged for property, goods, or services in a bargained transaction entered into at arm's length, the stated interest rate is presumed to be fair unless:[24]

1. No interest rate is stated, or
2. The stated interest rate is unreasonable, or
3. The stated face amount of the note is materially different from the current cash sales price for the same or similar items or from the current market value of the debt instrument.

In these circumstances the present value of the note is measured by the fair value of the property, goods, or services or by an amount that reasonably approximates the market value of the note.[25]

**Imputing an Interest Rate**  If the fair value of the property, goods, or services is not determinable and if the note has no ready market, the problem of determining the present value of the note is more difficult. To estimate the present value of a note under such circumstances, an applicable interest rate is approximated that may differ from the stated interest rate. This process of interest-rate approximation is called **imputation,** and the resulting interest rate is called an **imputed interest rate.** The imputed interest rate is used to establish the present value of the note by discounting, at that rate, all future receipts (interest and principal) on the note.

*Opinion No. 21* provides the following general guidelines for imputing the appropriate interest rate:

> The prevailing rates for similar instruments of issuers with similar credit ratings will normally help determine the appropriate interest rate for determining the present value of a specific note at its date of issuance. In any event, the rate used for valuation purposes will normally be at least equal to the rate at which the debtor can obtain financing of a similar nature from other sources at the date of the transaction. The objective is to approximate the rate which would have resulted if an independent borrower and an independent lender had negotiated a similar transaction under comparable terms and conditions with the option to pay the cash price upon purchase or to give a note for the amount of the purchase which bears the prevailing rate of interest to maturity.[26]

The choice of a rate may be affected specifically by the credit standing of the issuer, restrictive covenants, the collateral, payment, and other terms pertaining to the debt, and

---

[24]"Interest on Receivables and Payables," *Opinions of the Accounting Principles Board No. 21* (New York: AICPA, 1971), par. 12.

[25]Ibid.

[26]Ibid., par. 13.

the existing prime interest rate. Determination of the imputed interest rate is made when the note is received; any subsequent changes in prevailing interest rates are ignored.

**Accounting for Imputed Interest**  On December 31, 1983, Brown Interiors Company rendered architectural services and accepted in exchange a long-term promissory note with a face value of $550,000, a due date of December 31, 1988, and a stated interest rate of 2%, interest receivable at the end of each year. The fair value of the services is not readily determinable and the note is not readily marketable. When the credit rating of the maker of the note, the absence of collateral, the prime interest rate at that date, and the prevailing interest on the maker's outstanding debt are considered, an 8% interest rate is imputed as appropriate in this circumstance. The present value of the note is determined as follows.

| | | |
|---|---|---|
| Face value of the note | | $550,000 |
| Present value of $550,000 due in 5 years at 8%—$550,000 × .6806 (Table 6-2) | $374,330 | |
| Present value of $11,000 ($550,000 × .02) payable annually for 5 years at 8%— $11,000 × 3.9927 (Table 6-4) | 43,920 | |
| Present value of the note | | 418,250 |
| Discount | | $131,750 |

The receipt of the note in exchange for the services is recorded as follows:

**December 31, 1983**

| | | |
|---|---|---|
| Notes Receivable | 550,000 | |
|     Discount on Notes Receivable | | 131,750 |
|     Revenue from Services | | 418,250 |

The five-year amortization schedule appears below.

| SCHEDULE OF NOTE DISCOUNT AMORTIZATION<br>EFFECTIVE INTEREST METHOD<br>2% NOTE DISCOUNTED AT 8% (IMPUTED) | | | | | |
|---|---|---|---|---|---|
| Date | Cash<br>Interest<br>(2%) | Effective<br>Interest<br>(8%) | Discount<br>Amortized | Unamortized<br>Discount<br>Balance | Present Value<br>of Note |
| 12/31/83 | | | | $131,750 | $418,250 |
| 12/31/84 | $11,000[a] | $ 33,460[b] | $ 22,460[c] | 109,290[d] | 440,710[e] |
| 12/31/85 | 11,000 | 35,257 | 24,257 | 85,033 | 464,967 |
| 12/31/86 | 11,000 | 37,197 | 26,197 | 58,836 | 491,164 |
| 12/31/87 | 11,000 | 39,293 | 28,293 | 30,543 | 519,457 |
| 12/31/88 | 11,000 | 41,543[f] | 30,543 | -0- | 550,000 |
| | $55,000 | $186,750 | $131,750 | | |

[a]$550,000 × 2% = $11,000  
[b]$418,250 × 8% = $33,460  
[c]$33,460 − $11,000 = $22,460  

[d]$131,750 − $22,460 = $109,290  
[e]$418,250 + $22,460 = $440,710  
[f]$14 adjustment to compensate for rounding.

Receipt of the annual interest and amortization of the discount (unearned interest) is recorded as follows:

**December 31, 1984**

| | | |
|---|---|---|
| Cash | 11,000 | |
| Discount on Notes Receivable | 22,460 | |
| Interest Revenue | | 33,460 |

In the case of a **noninterest-bearing note** where a reasonable rate must be imputed, the periodic cash receipt for interest would be zero; therefore, the entry would be simply for the imputed interest—debit Discount on Notes Receivable and credit Interest Revenue.

**Financial Statement Presentation of Discount or Premium**    Any discount or premium resulting from the determination of present value in such transactions is not an asset or a liability separable from the note that gives rise to it. Therefore, the discount or premium is reported in the balance sheet as a direct deduction from or addition to the face amount of the note. It is not classified as a deferred charge or deferred credit. The face amount of the note is disclosed in the balance sheet or in the footnotes, and the description of the note should include the effective interest rate. The balance sheet presentation of discounted notes may assume two different forms: (1) presentation of the discount in caption form and (2) presentation of the discount separately.[27] Using the data from the Interiors Company illustration, we see how these two forms would appear, on December 31, 1984, one year after receipt of the note:

| Presentation of the Discount in Caption Form | | |
|---|---|---|
| | 12/31/84 | 12/31/83 |
| Note receivable from services rendered: | | |
| $550,000 face amount, due December 31, 1988, bearing 2% stated interest (less unamortized discount based on imputed interest rate of 8%—1984, $109,290; 1983, $131,750) | $440,710 | $418,250 |
| **Presentation of the Discount Separately** | | |
| | 12/31/84 | 12/31/83 |
| Note receivable from services rendered: | | |
| Note due December 31, 1988, bearing stated interest of 2% | $550,000 | $550,000 |
| Less unamortized discount based on imputed interest rate of 8% | 109,290 | 131,750 |
| Note receivable less unamortized discount | $440,710 | $418,250 |

If several notes are involved, the principal amount of such notes and the balance of total unamortized discount are presented in the balance sheet with the details of each note disclosed individually in a footnote or separate schedule to the balance sheet.

Amortization of discounts or premiums resulting from imputed interest on notes receivable are reported as interest in the statement of income.

---

[27]Ibid., par. 16.

## Accounts and Notes Receivable: Balance Sheet Presentation

The general rules in classifying the typical transactions in the receivable section are: (1) segregate the different receivables that an enterprise possesses, if material; (2) insure that the valuation accounts are appropriately offset against the proper receivable accounts; (3) determine that receivables classified in the current asset section will be converted into cash within the year or the operating cycle, whichever is longer; (4) disclose any loss contingencies that exist on the receivables; and (5) disclose any receivables assigned or pledged as collateral.

The following asset sections of Colt Corporation illustrate many of these concepts.

**Colt Corporation**
**As of December 31, 1983**

| | | |
|---|---:|---:|
| Current Assets | | |
| | | |
| Accounts receivable (Note 1) | $3,767,798 | |
| Less allowance for doubtful accounts | (226,500) | |
| | 3,541,298 | |
| Advances to subsidiaries due 9/30/84 | 980,000 | |
| Dividends receivable | 57,000 | |
| Notes receivable | 253,000 | |
| Other receivables and claims (includes | | |
| debit balances in accounts payable) | 120,000 | |
| Total current assets—receivables | | $4,951,298 |
| Long-Term Receivables | | |
| | | |
| Notes receivable from officers and key | | |
| employees for purchase of common | | |
| stock of company | | 333,000 |
| Claims receivable (refers to litigation | | |
| settlement to be collected over four years) | | 125,000 |
| Total receivables | | $5,409,298 |

Note 1. In June 1983, the company arranged with a finance company to refinance a part of their indebtedness. The loans are evidenced by a 12% note payable. The notes are payable on demand and are secured by substantially all the accounts receivable.

As illustrated, many different types of receivables can arise and are classified in accordance with the definition of current and noncurrent receivables.

# APPENDIX E

# Four-Column Bank Reconciliation

## RECONCILIATION OF RECEIPTS AND DISBURSEMENTS

In addition to the forms presented in this chapter, another form of reconciliation, frequently used by auditors and typically illustrated in auditing textbooks, is the so-called **proof of cash** or "four-column bank reconciliation" as shown below.

| | Balance October 31 | November Receipts | November Disbursements | Balance Nov. 30 |
|---|---|---|---|---|
| Nugget Mining Company PROOF OF CASH FOR NOVEMBER 1983 Denver National Bank | | | | |
| Per bank statement | $17,520 | $96,450 | $91,605 | $22,365 |
| Deposits in transit | | | | |
| at Oct. 31 | 4,200 | (4,200) | | |
| at Nov. 30 | | 3,680 | | 3,680 |
| Outstanding checks | | | | |
| at Oct. 31 | (3,700) | | (3,700) | |
| at Nov. 30 | | | 5,001 | (5,001) |
| Other reconciling items | | | | |
| Unrecorded bank charge | | | (8) | 8 |
| Unrecorded interest collected by bank | | (600) | | (600) |
| Per books | $18,020 | $95,330 | $92,898 | $20,452 |

This form of reconciliation is actually four reconciliations in one:

1. Reconciliation of the **beginning** of the period bank balance to the beginning of the period book balance (first column).
2. Reconciliation of **receipts** per the bank statement to receipts per books (second column).
3. Reconciliation of **disbursements** per the bank statement to disbursements per books (third column).
4. Reconciliation of the **end** of the period bank balance to the end of the period book balance (fourth column).

The top line across the four-column reconciliation is a summary of the transactions for the period covered as taken from the bank statement or statements. The beginning and ending bank balances are shown on the bank statement as are the bank receipts (as shown in the "deposits" column) and the bank disbursements (as shown in the "charges" or "checks cashed" column).

The bottom line, "Per books," is a summary of the cash transactions as recorded in the books. These totals should be taken directly from the books, preferably from the Cash account itself, which should, of course, show receipts and disbursements as debit and credit entries and the beginning and ending cash balances.

The left-hand and right-hand columns are simply **end-of-the-prior-period** and **end-of-the-current-period** reconciliations, the preparation of which was illustrated on page 277. The two center columns, receipts and disbursements, tie the left-hand column and right-hand column reconciliations together. With few exceptions, the amounts needed to complete these center columns may be found in the figures included in either the top or bottom lines or in the left- and right-hand columns; no new data need be added. The exceptions consist of such items as a bank error corrected by the bank within the month in which it was made so that bank transactions but not balances are affected. A customer's check deposited, returned N.S.F., and redeposited without entry in the same period would have the same effect. Each of the reconciling items must be analyzed carefully to determine whether an addition or subtraction from the top of the column "Per bank" figure is the logical reconciliation treatment.

The four-column reconciliation is preferred by auditors as a means of identifying differences between the books and the bank statement during the period covered by the reconciliation.

As indicated earlier, an alternative procedure for preparing a bank reconciliation involves reconciling the bank and the book balances to the correct (actual) balance. This same alternative can also be applied to the four-column reconciliation, as illustrated on page 309.

This alternative form of reconciliation is preferable because it (1) reconciles to the correct (actual) cash balance, (2) groups all of the reconciling items that require adjusting journal entries in the section devoted to the book balance, and (3) results in a more logical handling of the reconciling items.

Nugget Mining Company
PROOF OF CASH FOR NOVEMBER 1983
Denver National Bank

| | Balance October 31 | November Receipts | November Disbursements | Balance Nov. 30 |
|---|---|---|---|---|
| Per bank statement | $17,520 | $96,450 | $91,605 | $22,365 |
| Deposits in transit | | | | |
| at October 31 | 4,200 | (4,200) | | |
| at November 30 | | 3,680 | | 3,680 |
| Outstanding checks | | | | |
| at October 31 | (3,700) | | (3,700) | |
| at November 30 | | | 5,001 | (5,001) |
| Correct balance | $18,020 | $95,930 | $92,906 | $21,044 |
| Per books | $18,020 | $95,330 | $92,898 | $20,452 |
| Unrecorded bank charge | | | 8 | (8) |
| Unrecorded interest | | | | |
| collected by bank | | 600 | | 600 |
| Correct balance | $18,020 | $95,930 | $92,906 | $21,044 |

**Note:** All **asterisked** Questions, Cases, Exercises or Problems relate to material contained in the appendix to each chapter.

## QUESTIONS

1. What may be included under the heading of "cash"?

2. Distinguish among the following: (1) certificates of deposit, (2) money market savings certificates, (3) money market funds, (4) treasury bills, and (5) commercial paper.

3. Define a "compensating balance." How should a compensating balance be reported?

4. Distinguish among the following: (1) a general checking account, (2) an imprest bank account, and (3) a lockbox account.

5. What is electronic funds transfer, and what effect is its widespread use likely to have on record-keeping and accounting?

6. In what accounts should the following items be classified?
   (a) Travel advances.
   (b) Cash (to be used for retirement of long-term bonds).
   (c) Three shares of IBM stock (intention is to sell in one year or less).
   (d) Savings and checking accounts. cash
   (e) Petty cash.
   (f) Cash in a bank that is in receivership.
   (g) Deposits in transit.
   (h) Coins and currency.
   (i) Certificate of deposit.
   (j) U.S. Treasury (Government) bonds.
   (k) Postdated checks. AR
   (l) NSF check (returned with bank statement).
   (m) Deposit in foreign bank (exchangeability limited).
   (n) Stamps. cash

7. Distinguish between the nature of temporary investments and long-term investments. Give two examples of each type of investment. Is it possible for securities of the same kind to be carried by one company as a temporary investment and to be carried by another company as a long-term investment? Explain.

8. Define "marketable equity securities" and explain how to account for them when they are a current asset.

9. What disclosure is required for current marketable equity securities in either the financial statements or the accompanying footnotes?

10. Why is market value proposed as a substitute for cost in valuing marketable securities?

11. In what way may the accounting treatment of marketable debt securities differ from that accorded marketable equity securities (both classified as current assets)?

12. What is the difference between trade receivables and nontrade receivables? Give two examples of each type.

13. What are the basic problems that occur in the valuation of accounts receivable?

14. What are the reasons that a company gives trade discounts? Why are trade discounts not recorded in the accounts like cash discounts?

15. What are two methods of recording accounts receivable transactions when a cash discount situation is involved? Which is the most theoretically correct? Which is used in practice most of the time? Why?

16. Why is the account "Allowance for Sales Returns and Allowances" sometimes used? What other types of allowance accounts (similar to Allowance for Sales Returns and Allowances) are employed? What is their purpose?

17. What is the normal procedure for handling the collection of accounts receivable previously written off using the direct write-off method? The allowance method?

18. Because of calamitous earthquake losses, Pelican Company, one of your client's oldest and largest customers, suddenly and unexpectedly became bankrupt. Approximately 25% of your client's total sales have been made to Pelican Company during each of the past several years. The amount due from Pelican Company—none of which is collectible—equals 20% of total accounts receivable, an amount that is considerably in excess of what was determined to be an adequate provision for doubtful accounts at the close of the preceding year. How would your client record the write-off of the Pelican Company receivable if it is using the allowance method of accounting for bad debts? Justify your suggested treatment.

19. What is the theoretical justification of the allowance method as contrasted with the direct write-off method of accounting for bad debts?

20. Indicate how well the percentage-of-sales method and the aging method accomplish the objectives of the allowance method of accounting for bad debts.

21. Of what merit is the contention that the allowance method lacks the objectivity of the direct write-off method? Discuss in terms of accounting's measurement function.

22. Mesmerism Shop shows a balance in Accounts Receivable on December 31, 1984 of $150,000. Of this amount $80,000 is assigned to the Security Finance Co. as security for a loan of $60,000. Illustrate three satisfactory methods for showing this information on the balance sheet for December 31, 1984.

23. The Pinnacle Company includes in its trial balance for December 31 an item for "Accounts Receivable, $477,000." This balance consists of the following items:

| | |
|---|---:|
| Due from regular customers | $301,000 |
| Refund receivable on prior year's income taxes (an established claim) | 10,000 |
| Loans to officers | 22,000 |
| Loan to wholly owned subsidiary | 45,500 |
| Advances to creditors for goods ordered | 61,000 |
| Accounts receivable assigned as security for loans payable | 31,500 |
| Notes receivable past due plus interest on these notes | 6,000 |
| Total | $477,000 |

Illustrate how these items should be shown in the balance sheet as of December 31.

24. Differentiate between assigning and factoring accounts receivable.

25. Identify three forms by which receivables can be transferred to a third party for cash. Conceptually, what is the nature or substance of each form?

26. Identify the different methods of disclosing the loss contingency for notes receivable discounted with recourse.

27. What is "imputed interest"? In what situations is it necessary to impute an interest rate for notes receivable? What are the considerations in imputing an appropriate interest rate?

28. On January 1, 1984, Pipedream, Inc. sells property for which it had paid $500 to Seltzer Company receiving in return Seltzer's noninterest-bearing note for $1,000 payable in five years. What entry would Pipedream make to record the sale, assuming that Pipedream frequently sells similar items of property for a cash sales price of $600?

## CASES

**C7–1** Penguin Company has followed the practice of valuing its temporary investments in marketable equity securities at the lower of cost or market. At December 31, 1983, its account Investment in Marketable Equity Securities had a balance of $40,000, and the account Allowance for Excess of Cost of Marketable Equity Securities over Market Value had a balance of $2,000. Analysis disclosed that on December 31, 1982, the facts relating to the securities were as follows:

| | Cost | Market | Allowance Required |
|---|---|---|---|
| Robin Corp. Stock | $20,000 | $19,000 | $1,000 |
| Batman Co. Stock | 10,000 | 9,000 | 1,000 |
| Joker Company Stock | 20,000 | 20,400 | 40 0 |
| | $50,000 | 48,400 | $2,000 |

During 1983 Batman Company stock was sold for $9,100, the difference between the $9,100 and the "new adjusted basis" of $9,000 being recorded as a "Gain on Sale of Securities." The market price of the stock on December 31, 1983, was: Robin Corp. stock—$19,900; Joker Company stock—$20,500.

### Instructions

(a) What justification is there for the use of the lower of cost or market in valuing marketable equity securities?

(b) Did Penguin Company properly apply this rule on December 31, 1982? Explain.

(c) Did Penguin Company properly account for the sale of the Batman Company stock? Explain.

(d) Are there any additional entries necessary for Penguin Company at December 31, 1983, to reflect the facts on the balance sheet and income statement in accordance with generally accepted accounting principles? Explain.

(AICPA adapted)

**C7–2** The president of Cedar Closet Co. is concerned about a proposed accounting change related to investments in marketable securities. The proposal is that all marketable securities be presented at market value on the balance sheet and the changes that occur in market value be reflected in income in the current period. The president agrees that market value on the balance sheet may be more useful to the investor, but he sees no reason why changes in market value should be reflected in income of the current year.

Teresa Chavez, controller of Cedar Closet Co., is also unhappy about the proposal and has recommended the following alternatives.

"Recognize realized gains and losses from changes in market value in income, and report unrealized gains and losses in a special balance sheet account on the equity side of the balance sheet."

"Report realized and unrealized gains and losses from market value changes in a statement separate from the income statement or as direct charges and credits to a stockholders' equity account."

"Recognize gains and losses from changes in market value in income based on long-term yield; for example, use the past performance of the enterprise over several years (a 10-year period has been suggested) to determine an average annual rate of yield because of an increase in value."

To the president of Cedar Closet Co. these recommendations seem more reasonable.

**Instructions**

(a) Is the use of a market value or fair value basis of accounting for all marketable securities a desirable and feasible practice? Discuss.

(b) Do you believe the president is correct in stating that one of the alternatives is a better approach to recognition of income in accounting for marketable securities?

**C7–3** Cwynar Supply, Inc. conducts a wholesale merchandising business that sells approximately 5,000 items per month with a total monthly average sales value of $150,000. Its annual bad debt ratio has been approximately 1½% of sales. In recent discussions with his bookkeeper, Mr. Cwyner has become confused by all the alternatives apparently available in handling the Allowance for Doubtful Accounts balance. The following information has been shown.

1. An allowance can be set up (a) on the basis of a percentage of sales or (b) on the basis of a valuation of all past due or otherwise questionable accounts receivable—those considered uncollectible being charged to such allowance at the close of the accounting period; or specific items are charged off directly against (c) gross sales, or to (d) bad debt expense in the year in which they are determined to be uncollectible.

2. Collection agency and legal fees, and so on, incurred in connection with the attempted recovery of bad debts can be charged to (a) bad debt expense, (b) allowance for doubtful accounts, (c) legal expense, or (d) general expense.

3. Debts previously written off in whole or in part but currently recovered can be credited to (a) other revenue, (b) bad debt expense, or (c) allowance for doubtful accounts.

**Instructions**

Which of the foregoing methods would you recommend to Mr. Cwyner in regard to (1) allowances and charge-offs, (2) collection expenses, and (3) recoveries? State briefly and clearly the reasons supporting your recommendations.

**C7–4** Malone, Inc. operates a full-line department store that is dominant in its market area, is easily accessible to public and private transportation, has adequate parking facilities, and is near a large permanent military base. The president of the company, Gordon Graham, seeks your advice on a recently received proposal.

A local bank in which your client has an account recently affiliated with a popular national credit card plan and has extended an invitation to your client to participate in the plan. Under the plan affiliated banks mail credit card applications to persons in the community who have good credit ratings regardless of whether they are bank customers. If the recipients wish to receive a credit card, they complete, sign, and return the application and installment credit agreement. Holders of cards thus activated may charge merchandise or services at any participating establishment throughout the nation.

The bank guarantees payment to all participating merchants on all presented invoices that have been properly completed, signed, and validated with the impression of credit cards that have not expired or been reported stolen or otherwise canceled. Local merchants including your client may turn in all card-validated sales tickets or invoices to their affiliated local bank at any time and receive immediate credits to their checking accounts of 96.5% of the face value of the invoices. If card users pay the bank in full within 30 days for amounts billed, the bank levies no added charges against the customer. If they elect to make their payments under a deferred payment plan, the bank adds a service charge that amounts to an effective interest rate of 18% per annum on unpaid balances. Only the local affiliated banks and the franchiser of the credit card plan share in these revenues.

The 18% service charge approximates what your client has been billing customers who pay their accounts over an extended period on a schedule similar to that offered under the credit card plan. Participation in the plan does not prevent your client from continuing to carry on its credit business as in the past.

**Instructions**

(a) What are (1) the positive and (2) the negative financial and accounting-related factors that Malone, Inc. should consider in deciding whether to participate in the described credit card plan? Explain.

(b) If Malone, Inc. does participate in the plan, which income statement and balance sheet accounts may change materially as the plan becomes fully operative? (Such factors as market position, sales mix, prices, markup, etc., are expected to remain about the same as in the past.) Explain.

(AICPA adapted)

**C7-5** You have just started work for Magnolia, Inc. as part of the controller's group involved in current financial reporting problems. The controller for Magnolia is interested in your accounting background because the company has experienced a series of financial reporting surprises over the last few years. Recently, the controller has learned from its auditors that an FASB *Statement* may apply to its investment in securities. He assumes that you are familiar with this pronouncement and asks how the following situations should be reported in the financial statements.

*Situation I*

A marketable equity security, whose market value is currently less than cost, is classified as noncurrent but is to be reclassified as current.

*Situation II*

A company's current portfolio of marketable equity securities consists of the common stock of one company. At the end of the prior year the market value of the security was 50% of original cost, and this reduction in market value was properly reflected in a valuation allowance account. However, at the end of the current year the market value of the security had appreciated to twice the original cost. The security is still considered current at year-end.

*Situation III*

A marketable equity security whose market value is currently less than cost is classified as current but is to be reclassified as noncurrent.

*Situation IV*

Marketable debt securities in the current asset section have a market value of $3,000 lower than cost.

*Situation V*

The company has purchased some convertible debentures that it plans to hold for less than a year. The market value of the convertible debenture is $5,000 below its cost.

**Instructions**

What is the effect upon classification, carrying value, and earnings for each of the situations above? Assume that these situations are unrelated.

**C7-6** Soon after beginning the year-end audit work on March 10 at the Medicate Company, the auditor has the following conversation with the controller.

CONTROLLER: The year ended March 31st should be our most profitable in history, and, as a consequence, the Board of Directors has just awarded the officers generous bonuses.

AUDITOR: I thought profits were down this year in the industry, according to your latest interim report.

CONTROLLER: Well, they were down but 10 days ago we closed a deal that will give us a substantial increase for the year.

AUDITOR: Oh, what was it?

CONTROLLER: Well, you remember a few years ago our former president bought stock in Meek Enterprises because he had those grandiose ideas about becoming a conglomerate. For six years we have not been able to sell this stock, which cost us $1,500,000 and has not paid a nickel in dividends. Thursday we sold this stock to Casino, Inc. for $2,000,000. So, we will have a gain of $350,000 ($500,000 pretax) which will increase our net income for the year to $2,000,000, compared with last year's $1,900,000. As far as I know, we'll be the only company in the industry to register an increase in net income this year. That should help the market value of the stock!

AUDITOR: Do you expect to receive the $2,000,000 in cash by March 31st, your fiscal year-end?

CONTROLLER: No. Although Casino, Inc. is an excellent company, they are a little tight for cash because of their rapid growth. Consequently, they are going to give us a $2,000,000 noninterest-bearing note due $200,000 per year for the next 10 years. The first payment is due on March 31 of next year.

AUDITOR: Why is the note noninterest-bearing?

CONTROLLER: Because that's what everybody agreed to. Since we don't have any interest-bearing debt, the funds invested in the note do not cost us anything and besides, we were not getting any dividends on the Meek Enterprises stock.

### Instructions

Do you agree with the way the controller has accounted for the transaction? If not, how should the transaction be accounted for?

# EXERCISES

**E7-1** The following information was available from Letzkus Corporation's books:

| 1983 | Purchases | Sales |
|------|-----------|-------|
| Jan. | $42,000 | $72,000 |
| Feb. | 48,000 | 66,000 |
| Mar. | 36,000 | 60,000 |
| Apr. | 54,000 | 78,000 |

Collections from customers are normally 70% in the month of sale, 20% in the month following the sale, and 9% in the second month following the sale. The balance is expected to be uncollectible. Letzkus takes full advantage of the 2% discount allowed on purchases paid for by the tenth of the following month. Purchases for May are budgeted at $60,000, while sales for May are forecasted at $66,000. Cash disbursements for expenses are expected to be $14,400 for the month of May. Letzkus' cash balance at May 1 was $22,000.

### Instructions

Prepare the following schedules:
(a) Expected cash collections during May.
(b) Expected cash disbursements during May.
(c) Expected cash balance at May 31.

(AICPA adapted)

**E7-2** The petty cash fund of Tim's Auto Repair Service, a sole proprietorship, contains the following:

| | | |
|---|---:|---:|
| 1. Coins and currency | | $ 15.46 |
| 2. Fourteen, 20¢ stamps | | 2.80 |
| 3. An IOU from Mary Mechanic, an employee, for cash advance | | 50.00 |
| 4. Check payable to Tim's Auto Repair from John Brakeshoe, an employee, marked NSF | | 30.00 |
| 5. Vouchers for the following: | | |
| Stamps | $20.00 | |
| Two Rose Bowl tickets for Tim | 70.00 | |
| Typewriter repairs | 9.85 | 99.85 |
| | | $198.11 |

The general ledger account Petty Cash has a balance of $200.00.

**Instructions**

Prepare the journal entry to record the reimbursement of the petty cash fund.

**E7-3** Golfpro Company has just received the August 31, 1983 bank statement, which is summarized below:

| County National Bank | Disbursements | Receipts | Balance |
|---|---:|---:|---:|
| Balance, August 1 | | | $ 8,600 |
| Deposits during August | | $28,000 | 36,600 |
| Note collected for depositor, including $24 interest | | 924 | 37,524 |
| Checks cleared during August | $32,200 | | 5,324 |
| Bank service charges | 15 | | 5,309 |
| Balance, August 31 | | | 5,309 |

The general ledger Cash account contained the following entries for the month of August:

| Cash | | | |
|---|---:|---|---:|
| Balance, August 1 | 8,200 | Disbursements in August | 32,500 |
| Receipts during August | 31,000 | | |

Deposits in transit at August 31 are $3,000 and checks outstanding at August 31 are determined to total $900. Cash on hand at August 31 is $190. The bookkeeper improperly entered one check in the books at $155.39 which was written for $165.39 for supplies; it cleared the bank during the month of August.

**Instructions**

(a) Prepare a bank reconciliation dated August 31, 1983, proceeding to a corrected balance.
(b) Prepare any entries necessary to make the books correct and complete.
(c) What amount of cash should be reported in the August 31 balance sheet?

**E7-4** Hamsmith Company deposits all receipts and makes all payments by check. The following information is available from the cash records.

### June 30 BANK RECONCILIATION

| | |
|---|---:|
| Balance per bank | $4,610 |
| Add: Deposits in transit | 1,200 |
| Deduct: Outstanding checks | (1,500) |
| Balance per books | $4,310 |

Month of July Results

|  | Per Bank | Per Books |
|---|---|---|
| Balance July 31 | $7,000 | $6,600 |
| July deposits | 4,100 | 4,590 |
| July checks | 2,500 | 2,300 |
| July note collected (not included in July deposits) | 1,000 | -0- |
| July bank service charge | 10 | -0- |
| July NSF check of a customer returned by the bank (recorded by bank as a charge) | 200 | -0- |

**Instructions**

(a) Prepare a bank reconciliation going from balance per bank and balance per book to corrected cash balance.

(b) Prepare the general journal entry to correct the cash account.

**E7–5** Stafseth Company has the following securities in its short-term portfolio of marketable equity securities on December 31, 1983:

|  | Cost | Market |
|---|---|---|
| 1,000 shares of General Motors, Common | $ 34,250 | $ 29,025 |
| 5,000 shares of GTE, Common | 128,750 | 128,750 |
| 500 shares of AT&T, Preferred | 26,250 | 28,000 |
|  | $189,250 | $185,775 |

All of the securities were purchased in 1983.

In 1984, Myers completed the following securities transactions:

March 1   Sold 1,000 shares of General Motors, Common, @ $30 less fees of $900.

April 1   Bought 500 shares of U.S. Steel, Common, @ $40 plus fees of $550.

August 1   Transferred the AT&T, Preferred, from the short-term portfolio to the long-term portfolio when the stock was selling at $50 per share.

Stafseth Company's short-term portfolio of marketable equity securities appeared as follows on December 31, 1984:

|  | Cost | Market |
|---|---|---|
| 5,000 shares of GTE, Common | $128,750 | $145,500 |
| 500 shares of U.S. Steel, Common | 20,550 | 20,500 |
|  | $149,300 | $166,000 |

**Instructions**

Prepare the general journal entries for Stafseth Company for:

(a) The 1983 adjusting entry.

(b) The sale of the GM stock.

(c) The purchase of the U.S. Steel stock.

(d) The transfer of the AT&T stock from the short-term to the long-term portfolio.

(e) The 1984 adjusting entry for the short-term portfolio.

**E7–6** Krenek, Inc. purchased marketable equity securities at a cost of $250,000 on March 1, 1982. When the securities were purchased, the company intended to hold the investment for more than one year. Therefore, the investment was classified as a noncurrent asset in the company's annual report for the year ended December 31, 1982 and stated at its then market value of $200,000.

On September 30, 1983, when the investment had a market value of $215,000, management reclassified the investment as a current asset because the company intended to sell the securities within the next twelve months. The market value of the investment was $225,000 on December 31, 1983.

**Instructions**

    (a) The consequence of management's decision to recognize the investment in marketable equity securities as short-term and reclassify it as a current asset was recorded in the accounts. At what amount would the investment be recorded on September 30, 1983, the date of this decision?

    (b) How would the investment in the marketable equity securities be reported in the financial statements of Krenek, Inc. as of December 31, 1983 so that the company's financial position and operations for the year 1983 would reflect and report properly the reclassification of the investment from a noncurrent asset to a current asset? Be sure to indicate the affected accounts and the related dollar amounts and the note disclosures, if any.

(CMA adapted)

**E7-7** The following information relates to the temporary debt investments of the Reindeer Sleigh Company.

    **1.** On February 1, the company purchased 10% marketable bonds of Capitol Co. having a par value of $300,000 at 98 plus accrued interest. Interest is payable April 1 and October 1.

    **2.** On April 1, semiannual interest is received.

    **3.** On July 1, 12% marketable bonds of Quincy, Inc. were purchased. These bonds with a par value of $400,000 were purchased at 100 plus accrued interest. Interest dates are June 1 and December 1.

    **4.** On September 1, bonds of a par value of $100,000, purchased on February 1, are sold at 99 plus accrued interest.

    **5.** On October 1, semiannual interest is received.

    **6.** On December 1, semiannual interest is received.

    **7.** On December 31, the market value of the bonds purchased February 1 and July 1 are 94 and 96, respectively.

**Instructions**

    (a) Prepare any journal entries you consider necessary, including year-end entries (Dec. 31), assuming that the cost basis is used.

    (b) If Reindeer Sleigh used the lower of cost or market basis, how would the entries prepared in part (a) differ?

**E7-8** Regulator Company frequently invests in marketable debt securities cash that is not immediately needed for operations. These temporary investments are generally held for a period of several months. The company has adopted the lower of cost or market method on an aggregate basis in accounting for its marketable debt securities.

    The following transactions occurred over a period of two years.

May  1  12% marketable bonds of a par value of $150,000, with interest payable June 1 and Dec. 1, are purchased at 98 plus accrued interest.

June  1  Semiannual interest is received.

Aug.  1  Bonds of a par value of $20,000, purchased on May 1, are sold at 96½ plus accrued interest.

Dec.  1  Semiannual interest is received.

      31  Entry is made to accrue the proper amount of interest.

      31  The bonds are listed on the market at 93.

June  1  Semiannual interest is received (assume that reversing entries were made on 1/1).

Nov. 15  The remaining bonds of a par value of $130,000 are sold at 97 plus accrued interest.

Dec. 31  The allowance is closed out because no temporary securities are now held.

**Instructions**

Prepare entries to record the transactions above.

**E7-9** Rectifier Company shows a balance of $134,250 in the accounts receivable account on December 31, 1983. The balance consists of the following:

| | |
|---|---:|
| Due from regular customers, of which $30,000 represents accounts pledged as security for a bank loan | $75,000 |
| Advances to employees | 700 |
| Advance to subsidiary company (made in 1979) | 24,000 |
| Installment accounts due in 1984 | 15,000 |
| Installment accounts due after 1984 | 18,000 |
| Overpayments to creditors | 1,550 |

**Instructions**

Illustrate how the information above should be shown on the balance sheet of the Rectifier Company on December 31, 1983.

**E7-10** Your accounts receivable clerk, Mr. Robby Morley, to whom you pay a salary of $950 per month, has just purchased a new Cadillac. You decided to test the accuracy of the accounts receivable balance of $60,200 as shown in the ledger.

The following information is available for your *first year* in business:

| | |
|---|---:|
| (1) Collections from customers | $225,000 |
| (2) Merchandise purchased | 300,000 |
| (3) Ending merchandise inventory | 80,000 |
| (4) Goods are marked to sell at 40% above cost | |

**Instructions**

Compute an estimate of the ending balance of accounts receivable from customers that should appear in the ledger and any apparent shortages. Assume that all sales are made on account.

**E7-11** On June 3, Rotunda Company sold to Karen Deeman merchandise having a sale price of $2,000 with terms of 2/10, n/60, f.o.b. shipping point. An invoice totaling $90, terms n/30, was received by Karen Deeman on June 8 from the Madsen Transport Service for the freight cost. On receipt of the goods, June 5, Karen Deeman notified the Rotunda Company that merchandise costing $200 contained flaws that rendered it worthless; the same day Rotunda Company issued a credit memo covering the worthless merchandise and asked that it be returned at company expense. The freight on the returned merchandise was $20, paid by Rotunda Company on June 7. On June 12, the company received a check for the balance due from Karen Deeman.

**Instructions**

(a) Prepare journal entries on the Rotunda Company books to record all the events noted above under each of the following bases:
1. Sales and receivables are entered at gross selling price.
2. Sales and receivables are entered at net of cash discounts.
(b) Prepare the journal entry under basis 2, assuming that Karen Deeman did not remit payment until July 29.

**E7-12** At January 1, 1984, the credit balance in the allowance for doubtful accounts of the Ackerman Company was $400,000. For 1984, the provision for doubtful accounts is based on a percentage of net sales. Net sales for 1984 were $60,000,000. On the basis of the latest available facts, the 1984 provision for doubtful accounts is estimated to be 0.7% of net sales. During 1984, uncollectible receivables amounting to $450,000 were written off against the allowance for doubtful accounts.

**Instructions**

Prepare a schedule computing the balance in Ackerman's allowance for doubtful accounts at December 31, 1984.

**E7-13** The trial balance before adjustment of Rick Meier Auto Parts shows the following balances:

| | Dr. | Cr. |
|---|---|---|
| Accounts Receivable | 60,000 | |
| Allowance for Doubtful Accounts | | 750 |
| Sales (all on credit) | | 581,200 |
| Sales Returns and Allowances | 15,000 | |

*bad debts exp. 2100    2100*
*all DA*

**Instructions**

Give the entry for estimated bad debts assuming that the allowance is to provide for doubtful accounts on the basis of (a) 4% of gross accounts receivable and (b) 3% of net sales. *p 290*

**E7-14** The Reding Company includes the following account among its trade receivables.

Missy Mecklenburg

| | | | | | |
|---|---|---|---|---|---|
| 1/1 | Balance forward | 500 | 1/28 | Cash (#1710) | 1,300 |
| 1/20 | Invoice #1710 | 1,300 | 4/2 | Cash (#2116) | 890 |
| 3/14 | Invoice #2116 | 890 | 4/10 | Cash | 125 |
| 4/12 | Invoice #2412 | 1,420 | 4/30 | Cash (#2412) | 1,000 |
| 9/5 | Invoice #3614 | 490 | 9/20 | Cash (#3614 and | |
| 10/17 | Invoice #4912 | 860 | | part of #2412) | 790 |
| 11/18 | Invoice #5681 | 2,300 | 10/31 | Cash (#4912) | 860 |
| 12/20 | Invoice #6347 | 630 | 12/1 | Cash (#5681) | 1,700 |
| | | | 12/29 | Cash (#6347) | 630 |

**Instructions**

Age the balance and specify any items that apparently require particular attention.

**E7-15** The chief accountant for the Robinson Corporation provides you with the following list of accounts receivable written off in the current year.

| Date | Customer | Amount |
|---|---|---|
| Mar. 31 | GLC Designs | $7,600 |
| June 30 | Harley Associates | 5,700 |
| Sept. 30 | Susan's Dress Shop | 6,120 |
| Dec. 31 | Drew Corporation | 4,800 |

Robinson Corporation follows the policy of debiting Bad Debt Expense as accounts are written off. The chief accountant maintains that this procedure is appropriate for financial statement purposes because the Internal Revenue Service will not accept other methods for recognizing bad debts.

All of Robinson Corporation's sales are on a 30-day credit basis. Sales for the current year total $1,500,000 and research has determined that bad debt losses approximate 2% of sales.

**Instructions**

(a) Do you agree or disagree with the Robinson Corporation policy concerning recognition of bad debt expense? Why or why not?

(b) By what amount would net income differ if bad debt expense was computed using the percentage-of-sales approach?

**E7-16** Presented below is information related to Bambi Corp.

June 1          Bambi Corp. sold to Moat Co. merchandise having a sales price of $6,000 with terms 2/10, net/60. Bambi records its sales and receivables net.

| | |
|---|---|
| June 3 | Moat Co. returned merchandise having a sales price of $600 which was defective. |
| June 5 | Accounts receivable of $8,000 are factored with Mohr Credit Corp. without recourse at a financing charge of 10%. Cash is received for the proceeds; collections are handled by the finance company. (These accounts were all past the discount period.) |
| June 9 | Specific accounts receivable of $9,000 are assigned to Chase Credit Corp. as security for a loan of $6,000 at a finance charge of 6% of the amount of the loan. The finance company will make the collections. (All the accounts receivable are past the discount period.) |
| December 30 | Moat Co. notifies Bambi that it is bankrupt and will pay only 10% of its account. Give the entry to write off the uncollectible balance using the allowance method. (Note: First record the increase in the receivable on June 11 when the discount period passed.) |

**Instructions**

Prepare all necessary entries in general journal form for Bambi Corp.

**E7-17** Presented below is information related to Stringency Whlse., Inc.

1. Customers' accounts in the amount of $36,000 are assigned to the Macks Finance Company as security for a loan of $20,000. The finance charge is 3% of the amount borrowed.

2. Cash collections on assigned accounts amount to $12,600.

3. Collections on assigned accounts to date, plus a $300 check for interest on the loan, are forwarded to Macks Finance Company.

4. Additional collections on assigned accounts amount to $14,200.

5. The loan is paid in full plus additional interest of $100.

6. Uncollected balances of the assigned accounts are returned to the regular customers' ledger.

**Instructions**

Prepare entries in journal form for Stringency Whlse., Inc.

**E7-18** The trial balance before adjustment for the Leather Goods Company shows the following balances:

| | Dr. | Cr. |
|---|---|---|
| Accounts Receivable | $64,800 | |
| Allowance for Doubtful Accounts | 1,080 | |
| Sales | | $373,000 |
| Sales Returns and Allowances | 1,800 | |

**Instructions**

Using the data above, give the journal entries required to record each of the following cases (each situation is independent):

1. The company wants to maintain the Allowance for Doubtful Accounts at 4% of gross accounts receivable.

2. The company wishes to increase the allowance by 1½% of net sales.

3. To obtain additional cash, Leather factors, without recourse, $18,000 of Accounts Receivable with Tri-County Finance. The finance charge is 10% of the amount factored.

4. To obtain a one-year loan of $45,000, Leather assigns $54,000 of specific receivable accounts to Blair Financial. The finance charge is 9% of the loan; the cash is received and the accounts turned over to Blair.

**E7-19** Steg, Inc. factors receivables with a carrying amount of $173,120 to Lisa Company for $140,000 on a with recourse basis.

**Instructions**

(a) Assuming that this transaction should be reported as a sale, prepare the appropriate journal entry.

(b) Assuming that this transaction should be reported as a borrowing, prepare the appropriate journal entry.

**E7-20** The Guide Company requires additional cash for its business. Guide has decided to use its accounts receivable to raise the additional cash as follows:

1. On July 1, 1983, Guide assigned $200,000 of accounts receivable to the Cell Finance Company. Guide received an advance from Cell of 85% of the assigned accounts receivable less a commission on the advance of 3%. Prior to December 31, 1983, Guide collected $150,000 on the assigned accounts receivable, and remitted $160,000 to Cell, $10,000 of which represented interest on the advance from Cell.

2. On December 1, 1983, Guide sold $300,000 of net accounts receivable to the Factoring Company for $260,000. The receivables were sold outright on a nonrecourse basis.

3. On December 31, 1983, an advance of $100,000 was received from the Domestic Bank by pledging $120,000 of Guide's accounts receivable. Guide's first payment to Domestic is due on January 30, 1984.

**Instructions**

Prepare a schedule showing the income statement effect for the year ended December 31, 1983, as a result of the above facts. Show supporting computations in good form.

(AICPA adapted)

**E7-21** Presented below is information related to Nofftz Co. and Truemper, Inc.

May 1 Nofftz Co. gave Truemper, Inc. a $5,400, 60-day, 10% note in payment of its account of the same amount.

 16 Truemper, Inc. discounted the note at the bank at an 11% discount rate.

June 30 On the maturity date of the note, Nofftz Co. paid the amount due.

**Instructions**

(a) Record the transactions above on both the books of Nofftz Co. and the books of Truemper, Inc. (Assume it is a borrowing transaction.)

(b) Assume that Nofftz Co. dishonored its note and the bank notified Truemper, Inc., that it had charged the maturity value plus a protest fee of $25 to the Truemper, Inc. bank account. What entry(ies) should Truemper, Inc. make upon receiving this notification?

**E7-22** On July 1, 1984, Greek Company made two sales:

(a) It sold land having a fair market value of $500,000 in exchange for a four-year noninterest-bearing promissory note in the face amount of $786,760. The land is carried on Greek Company's books at a cost of $425,000.

(b) It rendered services in exchange for a 3%, eight-year promissory note having a maturity value of $200,000 (interest payable annually).

  Greek Company recently had to pay 8% interest for monies that it borrowed from Georgia National Bank. The customers in these two transactions have credit ratings that require them to borrow money at 12% interest.

**Instructions**

Record the two journal entries that should be recorded by Greek Company for the sales transactions above that took place on July 1, 1984.

**E7-23** On December 31, 1984, Tulip Company sold some of its product to Three M Company, accepting a $210,000 noninterest-bearing note, receivable in full on December 31, 1987. Tulip Company enjoys a high credit rating and, therefore, borrows funds from its several lines of credit at 10%. Three M Company, however, pays 15% for its borrowed funds. The product sold is carried on the books of Tulip Company at a manufactured cost of $110,000. Assume that the effective interest method is used for amortization payments.

**Instructions**

(a) Prepare the journal entry to record the sale on December 31, 1984, by the Tulip Company. Assume that a perpetual inventory system is used.

(b) Prepare the journal entries on the books of Tulip Company for the year 1985 that are necessitated by the sales transaction of December 31, 1984.

(c) Prepare the journal entries on the books of Tulip Company for the year 1986 that are necessitated by the sale on December 31, 1984.

**\*E7-24** Following is the general format of a four-column bank reconciliation with the various categories and operations numbered (1) through (8):

|  | Balance 10/31 | November Receipts | November Disbursements | Balance 11/30 |
|---|---|---|---|---|
| Per Bank Statement | $ XXXXX | $ XXXXX | $ XXXXX | $ XXXXX |
| Items to be *added:* | (1) | (3) | (5) | (7) |
| Items to be *deducted:* | (2) | (4) | (6) | (8) |
| Per Books | $ XXXXX | $ XXXXX | $ XXXXX | $ XXXXX |

**Instructions**

(a) For each of the following items indicate in which columns the reconciling items would appear. Question 1 is answered as an example.

| 6 | 7 | 1. November service charge of $15 is included on bank statement. |
|---|---|---|
| — | — | 2. October service charge of $15 is included in book disbursements for November. |
| — | — | 3. A $6,000 deposit in transit is included in book receipts for November. |
| — | — | 4. All $10,000 of checks written in October, which had not cleared the bank at October 31, cleared the bank in November. |
| — | — | 5. The bank collected a $600 note receivable for the firm in November plus $50 interest. The firm has not yet recorded this receipt. |
| — | — | 6. An "NSF" check in the amount of $250 was returned with the November bank statement. This check will be redeposited in December. The firm has not yet made an entry for this "NSF" check. |
| — | — | 7. The bank, in error, credited the firm's account for $500 in November for another firm's deposit. |
| — | — | 8. A check written in November for $700 was written in the check register in error in the amount of $770. This check cleared the bank in November for $700. Both the debit to Utilities Expense and the credit were overstated as a result of this error in the books. |
| — | — | 9. $10,000 of checks written in November have not cleared the bank by November 30. |
| — | — | 10. The initial $4,500 deposit shown on the November bank statement was included in October's book receipts. |

(b) Prepare the entries that should be recorded to make the books complete and accurate at November 30.

# PROBLEMS

**P7-1** Gaffknee Foundry closes its books regularly on December 31, but at the end of 1983 it held its cash book open so that a more favorable balance sheet could be prepared for credit purposes. Cash receipts and disbursements for the first 10 days of January were recorded as December transactions. The following information is given.

1. January cash receipts recorded in the December cash book totaled $32,730, of which $18,000 represents cash sales and $14,730 represents collections on account for which cash discounts of $270 were given.

2. January cash disbursements recorded in the December check register liquidated accounts payable of $21,750 on which discounts of $512 were taken.

3. The ledger has not been closed for 1983.

4. The amount shown as inventory was determined by physical count on December 31, 1983.

**Instructions**

(a) Prepare any entries you consider necessary to correct Gaffknee Foundry Company's accounts at December 31.

(b) To what extent was Gaffknee Foundry Company able to show a more favorable balance sheet at December 31 by holding its cash book open? Assume that the balance sheet that was prepared by the company showed the following amounts:

|  | Dr. | Cr. |
|---|---|---|
| Cash | $45,000 | |
| Receivables | 30,000 | |
| Inventories | 75,000 | |
| Accounts payable | | $45,000 |
| Other current liabilities | | 15,000 |

**P7-2** Presented below is information related to Hoosier Products Company.

Balance per books at October 31, $32,965.58; receipts, $164,834.34; disbursements, $159,225.68. Balance per bank statement November 30, $45,328.44.

The following checks were outstanding at November 30:

| 1224 | $1,600.34 |
|---|---|
| 1230 | 3,335.78 |
| 1232 | 2,285.60 |
| 1233 | 391.18 |

Included with the November bank statement and not recorded by the company were a bank debit ticket for $33.60 covering bank charges for the month, a debit ticket for $375.60 for a customer's check returned and marked NSF, and a credit ticket for $1,200.00 representing bond interest collected by the bank in the name of Hoosier Products Company. Cash on hand at November 30 recorded and awaiting deposit amounted to $1,649.50.

**Instructions**

(a) Prepare a bank reconciliation (bank balance to book balance) at November 30, 1983, for Hoosier Products Company from the information above.

(b) Prepare any journal entries required to adjust the cash account at November 30.

(c) State the amount of cash available for disbursement at November 30.

**P7-3** The cash account of Badger Co. showed a ledger balance of $4,112.78 on June 30, 1983. The bank statement as of that date showed a balance of $3,278.85. Upon comparing the statement with the cash records, the following facts were determined:

(a) The bank had charged the Badger Co.'s account for a customer's uncollectible check amounting to $505.20 on June 29.

(b) A 60-day, 6%, $1,000 customer's note dated April 25, and discounted by Badger on June 12, remained unpaid by the customer on the due date. On June 28 the bank charged the Badger Co. for $1,012.90, which included a protest fee of $2.90 (Badger discloses discounted notes receivable by use of a footnote.)

(c) A customer's check for $90 had been entered as $70 in the cash receipts journal by Badger on June 15.

(d) Check no. 742 in the amount of $392 had been entered in the cashbook as $329, and check no. 747 in the amount of $47.10 had been entered as $471. Both checks had been issued to pay for purchases of equipment.

(e) There were bank service charges for June of $25.00.

(f) A bank memo stated that W. W. Briscoe's note for $600 and interest of $24 had been collected on June 29, and the bank had made a charge of $5.50 on the collection. (No entry had been made on Badger's books when Briscoe's note was sent to the bank for collection.)

(g) Receipts for June 30 for $1,735 were not deposited until July 2.

(h) Checks outstanding on June 30 totaled $1,444.77.

**Instructions**

(a) Prepare a bank reconciliation dated June 30, 1983, proceeding to a corrected cash balance.

(b) Prepare any entries necessary to make the books correct and complete.

**P7-4** Presented below is information related to Hawkeye Company.

**Hawkeye Company**
**BANK RECONCILIATION**
**May 31, 1983**

| | | |
|---|---:|---:|
| Balance per bank statement | | $30,928.46 |
| Less outstanding checks | | |
| No. 6124 | $2,125.00 | |
| No. 6138 | 932.65 | |
| No. 6139 | 960.57 | |
| No. 6140 | 1,420.00 | 5,438.22 |
| | | 25,490.24 |
| Add deposit in transit | | 4,710.56 |
| Balance per books | | $30,200.80 |

**CHECK REGISTER—JUNE**

| Date | Payee | No. | V. Pay | Discount | Cash |
|---|---|---|---:|---:|---:|
| June 1 | Lund Mfg. | 6141 | $ 237.50 | | $ 237.50 |
| 1 | Geo Bates Mfg. | 6142 | 915.00 | $ 9.15 | 905.85 |
| 8 | Office Supply Co., Inc. | 6143 | 122.90 | 2.45 | 120.45 |
| 9 | Lund Mfg. | 6144 | 306.40 | | 306.40 |
| 10 | Petty Cash | 6145 | 89.93 | | 89.93 |
| 17 | Allservice Photo | 6146 | 706.00 | 14.12 | 691.88 |
| 22 | Linda Elbert Publishing | 6147 | 447.50 | | 447.50 |
| 23 | Payroll Account | 6148 | 4,130.00 | | 4,130.00 |
| 25 | Warren Tools, Inc. | 6149 | 390.75 | 3.91 | 386.84 |
| 28 | American Insurance Agency | 6150 | 1,050.00 | | 1,050.00 |
| 28 | Riley Construction | 6151 | 2,250.00 | | 2,250.00 |
| 29 | S. Hargrove, Inc. | 6152 | 750.00 | | 750.00 |
| 30 | Wixon Bros. | 6153 | 295.25 | 5.90 | 289.35 |
| | | | $11,691.23 | $35.53 | $11,655.70 |

STATEMENT
First State Bank of Iowa
General Checking Account of Hawkeye Co.—June 1983

| Debits | | | Date | Credits | Balance |
|---|---|---|---|---|---|
| | | | | | $30,928.46 |
| $2,125.00 | $237.50 | $ 905.85 | June 1 | $4,710.56 | 32,370.67 |
| 932.65 | 120.45 | | 12 | 1,507.06 | 32,824.63 |
| 1,420.00 | 447.50 | 306.40 | 23 | 1,458.55 | 32,109.28 |
| 4,130.00 | | 11.05 (BC) | | | 27,968.23 |
| 89.93 | 2,250.00 | 1,050.00 | 28 | 4,157.48 | 28,735.78 |

Cash received June 29 and 30 and deposited in the mail for the general checking account June 30 amounted to $4,407.96. Because the cash account balance at June 30 is not given, it must be calculated from other information in the problem.

### Instructions

From the information above, prepare a bank reconciliation (bank balance to book balance) as of June 30, 1983, for the Hawkeye Company.

**P7-5** Ohio Corp. invested its excess cash in temporary investments during 1982. As of December 31, 1982, the portfolio of short-term marketable equity securities consisted of the following common stocks:

| Security | Quantity | Per Share Cost | Market |
|---|---|---|---|
| Tinkers, Inc. | 1,000 shares | $12 | $15 |
| Evers Corp. | 3,000 shares | 25 | 19 |
| Chance Aircraft | 2,000 shares | 34 | 29 |

### Instructions

(a) What descriptions and amounts should be reported on the face of Ohio's December 31, 1982, balance sheet relative to temporary investments?

On December 31, 1983, Ohio's portfolio of short-term marketable equity securities consisted of the following common stocks:

| Security | Quantity | Per Share Cost | Market |
|---|---|---|---|
| Tinkers, Inc. | 1,000 shares | $12 | $19 |
| Tinkers, Inc. | 2,000 shares | 18 | 19 |
| Lakeshore Company | 1,000 shares | 15 | 12 |
| Chance Aircraft | 2,000 shares | 34 | 10 |

During the year 1983, Ohio Corp. sold 3,000 shares of Evers Corp. at a loss of $10,000 and purchased 2,000 more shares of Tinkers, Inc. and 1,000 shares of Lakeshore Company.

(b) What descriptions and amounts should be reported on the face of Ohio's December 31, 1983, balance sheet? What descriptions and amounts should be reported to reflect the data in Ohio's 1983 income statement?

On December 31, 1984, Ohio's portfolio of short-term marketable equity securities consisted of the following common stocks:

| | | Per Share | |
| Security | Quantity | Cost | Market |
|---|---|---|---|
| Chance Aircraft | 2,000 shares | $34 | $42 |
| Lakeshore Company | 500 shares | 15 | 13 |

During the year 1984, Ohio Corp. sold 3,000 shares of Tinkers, Inc. at a gain of $12,000 and 500 shares of Lakeshore Company at a loss of $2,300.

(c) What descriptions and amounts should be reported on the face of Ohio's December 31, 1984, balance sheet? What descriptions and amounts should be reported to reflect the above in Ohio's 1984 income statement?

(d) Assuming that comparative financial statements for 1983 and 1984 are presented, draft the footnote necessary for full disclosure of Ohio's transactions and position in marketable equity securities.

**P7-6** Nevada Casino Co. invests its excess idle cash on March 2, 1983, in the following short-term marketable securities:

| Security | Quantity | Per Share Cost |
|---|---|---|
| Mableleen Corporation, preferred stock | 1,600 shares | $90 |
| Seattle Cement Co., common stock | 2,500 shares | 30 |
| Pacific Electric Co., common stock | 1,000 shares | 40 |

The following data related to the years 1983 and 1984:

For year 1983—Cash dividends received: Mableleen, $5.00 per share
Seattle Cement, $.80 per share
Pacific Electric, $2.00 per share

December 31, 1983—Market values per share: Mableleen, $84
Seattle Cement, $32
Pacific Electric, $33

February 12, 1984—Sold all shares of Seattle Cement at $35 per share.

November 30, 1984—Purchased 1,500 shares of Mobil Company common stock for $55 per share.

For year 1984—Cash dividends received: Mableleen $5.00 per share
Seattle Cement, $.20 per share
Pacific Electric, $2.30 per share
Mobil Company, $.40 per share

December 31, 1984—Market values per share: Mableleen, $100
Pacific Electric, $34
Mobil Company, $61

**Instructions**

(a) Prepare all of the journal entries to reflect the transactions above and data in accordance with professional pronouncements.

(b) Prepare the descriptions and amounts that should be reported on the face of Nevada Casino's comparative financial statements for 1983 and 1984.

(c) Draft the footnote that should accompany the 1983–84 comparative statements relative to the marketable equity securities.

**P7-7** Pro Fit Company has a policy of investing any cash not needed for immediate use in marketable securities. Pro Fit usually invests in debt securities, but occasionally invests in high yield stocks. On December 31, 1984, the portfolio of marketable securities contained the following:

| | Cost | Market |
|---|---|---|
| 100—9½% City of Albany Serial Sewer Bonds, maturity date July 1, 1985, interest payable January 1 and July 1 (Face value, $1,000). | 97½ | 96⅝ |
| 200—12% Evans Produce Bonds, interest payable March 1 and September 1 (Face value, $1,000). | 87½ | 84¼ |

|  | Cost | Market |
|---|---|---|
| 50—16% Sure Grow Lawn Turf Bonds, interest payable February 1 and August 1 (Face value, $1,000). | 100¼ | 99¾ |

Pro Fit had the following transactions in marketable securities during 1985.

| | |
|---|---|
| January 1 | Received the semiannual interest on City of Albany Sewer Bonds. |
| February 1 | Received the semiannual interest on Sure Grow Lawn Turf Bonds. |
| February 10 | Purchased 500 shares, $100 par value common stock, of Northwest Bell Co. at 26 plus $135 of brokerage fees. |
| March 1 | Received the semiannual interest on Evans Produce Bonds. |
| March 15 | Sold the Sure Grow Lawn Turf Bonds at 102½ plus accrued interest less brokerage fees of $147. |
| March 31 | Received the first quarterly dividend of $1.25 per share from Northwest Bell Co. |
| April 24 | Purchased 1,000 shares of Hydro Power Co., 8%, $50 par, preferred stock, at 51 plus brokerage fees of $180. |
| June 30 | Received the semiannual dividend on Hydro Power Co. preferred stock, and quarterly dividend of $1.25 per share from Northwest Bell Co. |
| July 1 | Received the semiannual interest on the City of Albany Sewer Bonds and the maturity value. |
| July 15 | Purchased 300, 15% City of Bend School District #6 Serial Bonds, with a maturity date of May 15, 1990, at 96½ plus brokerage fees of $348. The bonds pay interest semiannually on May 15 and November 15 (Face value, $1,000). |
| July 31 | Purchased 300 shares of Uranium Unlimited Inc. common stock at 63 plus brokerage fees of $212. |
| August 7 | Sold 200 shares of the Northwest Bell Co. common stock at 25 less brokerage fees of $80. |
| September 1 | Received the semiannual interest payment on Evans Produce Bonds. |
| September 30 | Received the quarterly dividend of $1.30 from Northwest Bell Co. |
| November 15 | Received the semiannual interest payment on City of Bend School District #6 Serial Bonds. |
| December 10 | Received a 15% common stock dividend from Uranium Unlimited Co. |
| December 31 | You determine the closing market values to be: |

| | |
|---|---|
| City of Albany Serial Sewer Bonds | 98 |
| Evans Produce Bonds | 81½ |
| Sure Grow Lawn Turf Bonds | 103 |
| City of Bend School District #6 Serial Bonds | 96⅞ |
| Hydro Power Co. $50 Preferred Stock | 50 |
| Northwest Bell Co. Common Stock | 24¼ |
| Uranium Unlimited Inc. Common Stock | 60 |

**Instructions**

(a) Prepare general journal entries for the transactions listed above in marketable securities and year-end adjusting entries, assuming Pro Fit Company reports all securities at the lower of cost or market in the aggregate. Pro Fit does *not* use reversing entries. (All computations should be to the nearest dollar.)

(b) If Pro Fit only reports the equity securities at lower of cost or market in the aggregate and debt securities at cost, how would your journal entries in part (a) be different?

(c) If Pro Fit reports equity securities at lower of cost or market in the aggregate and debt securities at lower of cost or market individually, how would your journal entries in part (a) be different?

(d) Prepare the balance sheet presentation of marketable securities at December 31, 1985 for part (c).

**P7-8** The balance sheet of Rooster, Inc. at December 31, 1983 includes the following:

| | | |
|---|---:|---:|
| Notes receivable | $ 43,000 | |
| Less: Notes receivable discounted | 15,000 | $28,000 |
| Accounts receivable | $166,400 | |
| Less: Allowance for doubtful accounts | 12,400 | 154,000 |

Transactions in 1984 include the following:

1. Notes receivable discounted at 12/31/83 matured and were paid with the exception of a $3,000 note for which the company had to pay $3,050, which included $50 interest and protest fees. Recovery is expected in 1984. (Use Notes Receivable Past Due account.)

2. Cash collected on accounts receivable totaled $135,000 including accounts of $25,000 on which 2% sales discounts were allowed.

3. $4,200 was received in payment of an account which was written off the books as worthless in 1981. (Hint: Reestablish the receivable account.)

4. Customer accounts of $14,400 were written off during the year.

5. At year-end the allowance for doubtful accounts was estimated to need a balance of $18,000. This estimate is based on an analysis of aged accounts receivable.

6. Rooster, Inc. discounted a $12,000, 90-day note dated Nov. 1, 1984 on Dec. 1, 1984. The note bears a 12% interest rate and was discounted at 10%. (Treat as a sale.)

**Instructions**

Prepare all journal entries necessary to reflect the transactions above.

**P7-9** Presented below is information related to the accounts receivable accounts of Wayout Creations, Inc. during the current year 1984.

1. The accounts receivable control account has a debit balance of $366,500 on December 31, 1984.

2. Two entries were made in the Bad Debt Expense account during the year: (1) a debit on December 31 for the amount credited to Allowance for Doubtful Accounts, and (2) a credit for $1,810 on November 3, 1984 because of a bankruptcy.

3. The Allowance for Doubtful Accounts is as follows for 1984:

Allowance for Doubtful Accounts

| Nov. 3 | Uncollectible accounts written off | 1,810 | Jan. 1 | Beginning balance | 6,660 |
|---|---|---:|---|---|---:|
| | | | Dec. 31 | 5% of $366,500 | 18,325 |

4. An aging schedule of the accounts receivable as of December 31, 1984 is as follows:

| Age | Net debit balance | % to be applied after correction made |
|---|---:|---|
| Under 60 days | $164,664 | 1% |
| 61–90 days | 139,140 | 3% |
| 91–120 days | 39,924* | 6% |
| Over 120 days | 22,772 | $3,600 definitely uncollectible; estimated remainder collectible is 75% |
| | $366,500 | |

*The $1,810 write-off of receivables is related to the 91 to 120 day category.

5. A credit balance exists in the Accounts Receivable (61–90 days) of $3,960, which represents an advance on a sales contract.

**Instructions**

Assuming that the books have not been closed for 1984, make the necessary correcting entries.

**P7-10** From inception of operations in 1978, Summit carried no allowance for doubtful accounts. Uncollectible receivables were expensed as written off and recoveries were credited to income as collected. On March 1, 1982 (after the 1981 financial statements were issued), management recognized that Summit's accounting policy with respect to doubtful accounts was not correct, and determined that an allowance for doubtful accounts was necessary. A policy was established to maintain an allowance for doubtful accounts based on Summit's historical bad debt loss percentage applied to year-end accounts receivable. The historical bad debt loss percentage is to be recomputed each year based on all available past years up to a maximum of five years.

Information from Summit's records for five years is as follows:

| Year | Credit Sales | Accounts Written Off | Recoveries |
|------|------|------|------|
| 1978 | $1,500,000 | $15,000 | $0 |
| 1979 | 2,250,000 | 38,000 | 2,700 |
| 1980 | 2,950,000 | 52,000 | 2,500 |
| 1981 | 3,300,000 | 65,000 | 4,800 |
| 1982 | 4,000,000 | 83,000 | 5,000 |

Accounts receivable balances were $1,250,000 and $1,460,000 at December 31, 1981, and December 31, 1982, respectively.

**Instructions**

(a) Prepare the journal entry, with appropriate explanation, to set up the allowance for doubtful accounts as of January 1, 1982. Show supporting computations in good form.
(b) Prepare a schedule analyzing the changes in the Allowance for Doubtful Accounts account for the year ended December 31, 1982. Show supporting computations in good form.

(AICPA adapted)

**P7-11** Farina Corporation operates in an industry that has a high rate of bad debts. On December 31, 1983, before any year-end adjustments, the balance in Farina's accounts receivable account was $505,000 and the allowance for doubtful accounts had a balance of $25,000. The year-end balance reported in the statement of financial position for the allowance for doubtful accounts will be based on the aging schedule shown below.

| Days Account Outstanding | Amount | Probability of Collection |
|------|------|------|
| Less than 15 days | $300,000 | .98 |
| Between 16 and 30 days | 100,000 | .90 |
| Between 31 and 45 days | 50,000 | .80 |
| Between 46 and 60 days | 30,000 | .70 |
| Between 61 and 75 days | 10,000 | .60 |
| Over 75 days | 15,000 | .00 |

**Instructions**

(a) What is the appropriate balance for the allowance for doubtful accounts on December 31, 1983?
(b) Show how accounts receivable would be presented on the balance sheet prepared on December 31, 1983.
(c) What is the dollar effect of the year-end bad debt adjustment on the before-tax income for 1983?

(CMA adapted)

**P7-12** Hendricks Company finances some of its current operations by assigning accounts receivable to a finance company. On July 1, 1984, it assigned, under guarantee, specific accounts amounting to $50,000, the finance company advancing to Hendricks 80% of the accounts assigned (20% of the total to be withheld until the finance company has made its full recovery), less a finance charge of ½% of the total accounts assigned.

On July 31, Hendricks Company received a statement that the finance company had collected $24,000 of these accounts, and had made an additional charge of ½% of the total accounts outstanding as of July 31, this charge to be deducted at the time of the first remittance due Hendricks Company from the finance company. (Hint: Make entries at this time.) On August 31, 1984, Hendricks Company received a second statement from the finance company, together with a check for the amount due. The statement indicated that the finance company had collected an additional $19,000 and had made a further charge of ½% of the balance outstanding as of August 31.

### Instructions

(a) Make all entries on the books of Hendricks Company that are involved in the transactions above.
(b) Explain how these accounts should be presented in the financial statements of Hendricks Company at July 31 and at August 31.

(AICPA adapted)

**P7–13** Douglas Sports Company produces soccer, football, and track shoes. The treasurer has recently completed negotiations in which Douglas Sports agrees to loan Ehrlich Company, a leather supplier, $500,000. Ehrlich Company will issue a noninterest-bearing note due in five years (a 15% interest rate is appropriate), and has agreed to furnish Douglas Sports with leather at prices that are 10% lower than those usually charged.

### Instructions

(a) Prepare the accounting entry to record this transaction on Douglas Sports Company's books.
(b) Determine the balances at the end of each year the note is outstanding for the following accounts for Douglas Sports Company:
Notes receivable
Unamortized discount
Interest revenue

**P7–14** On December 31, 1984, Rexroad Company rendered services to ISU Corporation at an agreed price of $80,000, accepting $20,000 down and agreeing to accept the balance in four equal installments of $15,000 receivable each December 31. An assumed interest rate of 12% is implicit in the agreed price.

### Instructions

Prepare the journal entries that would be recorded by the Rexroad Company for the sale and for the receipts and interest on the following dates (Assume that the effective interest method is used for amortization purposes.):
(a) December 31, 1984.
(b) December 31, 1985.
(c) December 31, 1986.
(d) December 31, 1987.
(e) December 31, 1988.

**P7–15** You are engaged in your fifth annual examination of the financial statements of NIU Corporation. Your examination is for the year ended December 31, 1984. The client prepared the following schedules of Trade Notes Receivable and Interest Receivable for you at December 31, 1984. You have agreed the opening balances to your prior year's audit workpapers.

NIU Corporation
TRADE NOTES RECEIVABLE AND RELATED INTEREST RECEIVABLE
**Trade Notes Receivable**

| Maker | Issue Date | Terms | Interest Rate | Bal. Dec. 31, 1983 | 1984 Debits | 1984 Credits | Bal. Dec. 31, 1984 |
|---|---|---|---|---|---|---|---|
| Morley Co. | 4/1/83 | One year | 12% | $60,000 | | $ 60,000 | |
| Ekberg Co. | 5/1/84 | 90 days after date | — | | $ 20,000 | 19,625 | $ 375 |
| Kennedy Ind. | 7/1/84 | 60 days after date | 12% | | 4,000 | | 4,000 |
| J. Schmidt | 8/3/84 | Demand | 12% | | 10,000 | | 10,000 |
| Morreale Corp. | 10/2/84 | 60 days | | | 40,000 | 40,000 | |
| | | after date | 12% | | 40,000 | | 40,000 |
| Slezak, Inc. | 11/1/84 | 90 days after date | 8% | | 42,000 | 35,000 | 7,000 |
| Alton Co. | 11/1/84 | 90 days after date | 14% | | 24,000 | | 24,000 |
| | | Totals | | $60,000 | $180,000 | $154,625 | $85,375 |

**Interest Receivable**

| Due From | Bal. Dec. 31, 1983 | 1984 Debits | 1984 Credits | Bal. Dec. 31, 1984 |
|---|---|---|---|---|
| Morley Co. | $5,400 | $1,800 | $7,200 | |
| Kennedy Ind. | | 80 | | $ 80 |
| J. Schmidt | | 400 | | 400 |
| Morreale Corp. | | 800 | 460 | 340 |
| Slezak, Inc. | | 560 | | 560 |
| Alton Co. | | 560 | | 560 |
| Totals | $5,400 | $4,200 | $7,660 | $1,940 |

Your examination reveals this information.

1. Interest is computed on a 360-day basis. In computing interest, it is the corporation's practice to exclude the first day of the note's term and to include the due date.

2. The Ekberg Company's 90-day non-interest bearing note was discounted on May 16 at 9%, and the proceeds were credited to the Trade Notes Receivable account. The note was paid at maturity.

3. Kennedy Industries became bankrupt on August 31, and the corporation will recover 75 cents on the dollar. The corporation uses the direct write-off method for recording bad debt expense. All of NIU Corporation's notes receivable provide for interest at a rate of 12% on the maturity value of a dishonored note.

4. Jeannie Schmidt, president of NIU Corporation, confirmed that she owed NIU Corporation $10,000 and that she expected to pay the note within six months. You are satisfied that the note is collectible.

5. Morreale Corporation's 60-day note was discounted on November 1 at 10%, and the proceeds were credited to the Trade Notes Receivable and Interest Receivable accounts. On December 2, NIU Corporation received notice from the bank that Morreale Corporation's note was not paid at maturity and that it had been charged against NIU's check-

ing account by the bank. Upon receiving the notice from the bank, the bookkeeper recorded the note and the accrued interest in the Trade Notes Receivable and Interest Receivable accounts. Morreale Corporation paid NIU Corporation the full amount due in January, 1985.

6. Slezak, Inc., 90-day note was pledged as collateral for $35,000, 60-day, 10% loan from the First National Bank on December 1.

7. On November 1, the corporation received four, $6,000, 90-day notes from Alton Co. On December 1, the corporation received payment from Alton Co. for one of the $6,000 notes with accrued interest. Prepayment of the notes is allowed without penalty. The bookkeeper credited the Alton Company Accounts Receivable account for the cash received.

**Instructions**

Prepare the adjusting journal entries that you would suggest at December 31, 1984, for the transactions above. Reclassify all past due notes and related carrying costs to accounts receivable.

(AICPA adapted)

**P7-16** Minnesota Woolens, Inc. factors $1,000,000 of accounts receivable with Dundee Credit Corp. on a without-recourse basis. On June 1, the receivable records are transferred to Dundee Credit which will make the collections. Dundee Credit assesses a finance charge of 4% of the total accounts receivable factored and retains an amount equal to 5% of the total receivables to cover sales discounts, returns, and allowances. Minnesota Woolens handles any returned goods, claims and allowances for defective goods, and disputes concerning shipments. Dundee handles the sales discounts and absorbs the credit losses.

During the month of June, the factor collects $680,000; merchandise totaling $13,500 is returned; sales discounts of $9,500 are taken; and allowances of $4,300 are granted.

During the month of July, the factor collects $279,000; merchandise totaling $1,700 is returned; no sales discounts are allowed; and allowances of $2,100 for defective goods are granted.

On August 1, Minnesota Woolens and Dundee Credit agree that any further returns, discounts, and allowance will be absorbed by Minnesota Woolens; Dundee therefore returns the balance of the retainer held for such events. Uncollectibles are estimated to be $4,800.

**Instructions**

(a) Prepare the entries on Minnesota Woolens' books at June 1, for the June transactions, for the July transactions, and at August 1.

(b) Prepare the entries on Dundee Credit's books at June 1, for the June transactions, for the July transactions, and at August 1.

**\*P7-17** You have been hired as the new assistant controller of Woodcraft, Inc. and assigned the task of proving the cash account balance. As of December 31, 1983, you have obtained the following information relative to the December cash operations.

1. Balance per bank

| | |
|---|---|
| 11/30/83 | $114,050 |
| 12/31/83 | 105,893 |

2. Balance per books

| | |
|---|---|
| 11/30/83 | 82,413 |
| 12/31/83 | 88,800 |

3. Receipts for the month of December, 1983

| | |
|---|---|
| per bank | 679,175 |
| per books | 694,223 |

4. Outstanding checks

| | |
|---|---|
| 11/30/83 | 31,762 |
| 12/31/83 | 37,523 |

5. Dishonored checks returned by the bank and recorded by Woodcraft, Inc. amounted to $3,125 during the month of December 1983; according to the books $2,500 was redeposited. Dishonored checks, recorded on the bank statement but not on the books until the following months, amounted to $125 at November 30, 1983, and $1,150 at December 31, 1983.

6. On December 31, 1983, a $1,162 check of the Northside Company was charged to the Woodcraft, Inc. account by the bank in error.

7. Proceeds of a note of the Bryant Company collected by the bank on December 10, 1983, were not entered on the books:

|  |  |
|---|---|
| Principal | $1,000 |
| Interest | 10 |
|  | 1,010 |
| Less collection charge | 3 |
|  | $1,007 |

8. Interest on a bank loan for the month of December charged by the bank but not recorded on the books amounted to $3,070.

9. Deposit in transit:

| 12/31/83 | $16,055 |
|---|---|

**Instructions**

Prepare bank reconciliations as of November 30, 1983, and December 31, 1983, using a four-column "proof of cash" with the following column headings for amounts:

| 11/30/83 Beginning Reconciliation | Receipts | Disbursements | 12/31/83 Ending Reconciliation |
|---|---|---|---|

Proceed from "balance per bank statement" to "balance per books."

**\*P7–18** Using the data given in Problem 7–17, prepare (a) a four-column bank reconciliation proceeding from "balance per bank statement" to "correct balance" and "balance per books" to "correct balance," and (b) accompanying entries to adjust the books.

**\*P7–19** You have been hired by the Blackwell Manufacturing Company as an internal auditor. One of your first assignments is to reconcile the bank account for the Burns Division.

The bank statement shows the following:

| | |
|---|---|
| Beginning Balance, August 1, 1984 | $ 72,327 |
| Deposits—(20) | 867,408 |
| Checks—(64) plus debit memos | (786,539) |
| Service charges—new checks | (39) |
| Ending Balance, August 31, 1984 | $153,157 |

The cash account on the books of the Burns Division is as follows:

Cash

| | | | |
|---|---|---|---|
| July 1, | 49,628 | July 31—Cash Disbursements | 665,441 |
| July 31—Cash Receipts | 682,429 | August 1—Bank Reconciliation | 227 |
| August 31—Cash Receipts | 871,546 | August 31—Cash Disbursements | 791,654 |

Your review of last month's bank reconciliation and the current bank statement reveals the following:

1. Outstanding checks

| | |
|---|---|
| July 31, 1984 | $20,619 |
| August 31, 1984 | 28,746 |

**2.** Deposits in transit

| | |
|---|---|
| July 31, 1984 | 14,681 |
| August 31, 1984 | 18,819 |

**3.** Check #216 for office furniture was written for $234 but recorded in the cash disbursements journal as $324. The bank deducted the check as $234.

**4.** A check written on the account of the Barnes Manufacturing Co. for $627 was deducted by the bank from the Burns Division account.

**5.** Included with the bank statement was a debit memorandum dated August 31 for $2,475 for interest on a note taken out by the Burns Division on July 30th.

**6.** The service charge for new checks has not been recorded.

**7.** The July 31, 1984 bank reconciliation showed as reconciling items a service charge of $12 and an NSF check for $215.

**Instructions**

(a) Prepare a four-column proof of cash reconciling the balance per bank to the balance per book.

(b) Prepare a four-column proof of cash reconciling balance per bank to the "correct balance" and balance per books to the "correct balance."

(c) Prepare any adjusting journal entries necessary to correct the cash account per the books of the Burns Division.

**P7-20** Allservice Photosetting Co. holds Wiley Company's $20,000, 6-month, note receivable, dated July 31, 1983, payable on January 31, 1984, and bearing interest at 15%. On October 31, Allservice discounts with recourse Wiley's note at 10% at the Phoenix National Bank.

**Instructions**

(a) Prepare journal entries on Allservice's books on the following dates treating the discounting as a sale transaction:

1. July 31, 1983—receipt of the note.
2. October 31, 1983—discounted note with recourse.
3. January 31, 1984—Wiley pays principal and interest to Phoenix National Bank.
4. Assume that, instead of paying off the note on February 1, 1984, Wiley defaults and Allservice pays the note, interest, and a bank protest fee of $85.

(b) Prepare journal entries on Allservice's books on each of the four dates listed in part (a) treating the discounting as a borrowing transaction.

# CHAPTER 8

# Valuation of Inventories: A Cost Basis Approach

The description and measurement of inventory demand careful attention because inventories are one of the most significant assets of many enterprises. The sale of inventory at a price greater than total cost is the primary source of revenue for manufacturing and retail business enterprises. Matching inventory cost against revenue is necessary for the proper determination of net income. Inventories are particularly significant because they may materially affect both the income statement and the balance sheet.

**Inventories are asset items held for sale in the ordinary course of business or goods that will be used or consumed in the production of goods to be sold.** Assets specifically excluded from inventory because they are not normally sold in the course of business include such items as plant and equipment awaiting final disposition and securities being held for sale. The accounting problems associated with inventory valuation are complex; Chapters 8 and 9 discuss the basic issues involved in recording, valuing, and reporting inventoriable items.

## MAJOR CLASSIFICATIONS OF INVENTORY

Inventories commonly are considered in the context of trading concerns. A **trading concern** ordinarily purchases its merchandise in a form ready for sale to customers and reports the cost assigned to unsold units left on hand at the end of the period as merchandise inventory. Only one inventory account, Merchandise Inventory, appears in the financial statements of a trading concern. Many large businesses, however, are manufacturing concerns whose function is to produce goods to be sold to the merchandising firms (either wholesale or retail). A **manufacturing firm** normally has three inventory accounts—Raw Materials, Work in Process, and Finished Goods. The cost assigned to goods and materials on hand but not yet placed into production is reported as **raw materials inventory.** Raw materials include items such as the wood to make a baseball bat or the steel to make a car. These materials ultimately can be traced directly to the end product. At any point in time in a continuous production process some units generally are not completely processed. The cost of the raw material on which production has been started but not completed, plus the cost of direct labor applied specifically to this material and a ratable share of manufacturing overhead costs, constitute the **work in process inventory.** The costs identified with the completed but unsold units on hand at the end of the fiscal period are reported as **finished goods inventory.** The relationship of these inventory accounts and the flow of costs through a manufacturing company are illustrated on page 336 and contrasted to that of a merchandising firm.

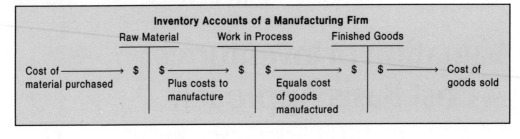

It is, therefore, common to see three inventory accounts on the balance sheet of a manufacturer: (1) Raw Materials, (2) Work in Process, and (3) Finished Goods. A **manufacturing** or **factory supplies inventory** account might also be included. This account includes items like machine oils, nails, cleaning materials, and the like that are used in production but are not the primary materials being processed. An annual report of Scott Paper Company illustrates the reporting of these accounts.

| Scott Paper Company | |
| --- | --- |
| Current assets | (Thousands of dollars) |
| Inventories | |
| Finished products | $401,966 |
| Work in process | 15,231 |
| Pulp, logs, and pulpwood | 22,412 |
| Other materials and supplies | 29,836 |

## MANAGEMENT INTEREST IN ACCOUNTING FOR INVENTORIES

From the standpoint of management, inventories constitute an extremely important asset. The investment in inventories is frequently the largest current asset in manufacturing and retail establishments, and also may be a material portion of the company's total assets. If unsalable items have accumulated in the inventory, a potential loss exists. If products ordered by customers are not available in the desired style, quality, and quantity, sales and customers may be lost. An inefficient purchasing procedure, faulty manufacturing techniques, or inadequate sales efforts all result in excessive and unsalable inventories. Also, in the current environment of high interest rates, it becomes even more important for businesses to monitor inventory levels carefully to limit the financing costs of carrying large inventories.

In many respects inventories are more sensitive to general business fluctuations than are other assets. In periods of prosperity when sales are high, merchandise can be disposed of readily, and quantities on hand may not appear excessive. But with even a slight downward trend in the business cycle, many lines of merchandise begin to move slowly, stocks pile up, and obsolescence becomes a real possibility.

For these and other reasons, management (and therefore the accounting department) is vitally interested in inventory planning and control. One essential of inventory control is an accounting system with accurate, up-to-date records, containing the information needed by management to implement its manufacturing, merchandising, and financial policies. This degree of control usually requires a perpetual inventory system.

## DETERMINING INVENTORY QUANTITIES

As indicated in Chapter 3, inventory records may be maintained on a perpetual or periodic inventory system basis. In a **perpetual inventory system,** purchases and issues of goods are recorded directly in the inventory account as the purchases and issues occur. No Purchases account is used because the purchases are debited directly to the inventory account. A Cost of Goods Sold account is used to accumulate the issuances from inventory. The balance in the inventory account at the end of the year should represent the ending inventory amount. For example, in the case of a manufacturing enterprise, separate inventory accounts may be used for raw materials, work in process, and finished goods, while only one inventory account is used by a merchandising enterprise.

When the inventory records are maintained on a **periodic inventory system,** a Purchases account is used and the beginning inventory is unchanged during the period. At the end of the accounting period the inventory account must be adjusted by closing out the beginning inventory amount and recording the ending inventory amount. Cost of goods sold is therefore determined by adding the beginning inventory together with the net purchases and deducting the ending inventory.

In the past, few companies maintained inventory records in both quantities and dollars. However, with the advent of computers and in particular the new mini and micro computers (Apples, TRS-80's, IBMs, etc.), small as well as large businesses today maintain perpetual inventories that report both quantities and dollars, and much more. The additional data might consist of such items as catalogue or reference number, supplier, location, and reorder points. Perpetual inventory systems are used extensively whenever high-cost items are involved such as automobiles and appliances. Conversely, enterprises such as hardware and drug stores that sell a large variety of low-cost items rely heavily on the periodic inventory system.

When a periodic system is employed, how is the ending inventory computed? One method is to take a **physical inventory count** once a year. However, most companies need more current information on the quantities of their inventory items to protect against stockouts, overpurchasing, and to aid in the preparation of monthly or quarterly financial data. As a consequence, many companies use a **modified perpetual inventory system** in which increases and decreases in quantities are kept in a detailed inventory record. The detailed inventory record does not include dollar amounts and is therefore merely an informational memorandum device outside the double entry system which helps in determining the level of inventory at any point in time.

Whether a company maintains a perpetual inventory in quantities and dollars, quantities only, or has no perpetual inventory record at all, it probably takes a physical inventory once a year. No matter what type of inventory records are in use or how well organized the procedures for recording purchases and requisitions, the danger of error is always present.

Waste, breakage, theft, improper entry, failure to prepare or record requisitions, and any number of similar possibilities may cause the inventory records to differ from the actual inventory on hand. This requires periodic verification of the inventory records by actual count, weight, or measurement of the inventory items. These counts are compared with the detail inventory records and the records corrected to agree with the quantities actually on hand.

As indicated above, most companies take a physical inventory count only once a year.[1] More frequent counts are desirable in businesses that deal in extremely costly merchandise, but in general an annual physical inventory is sufficient to assure reasonable accuracy of the records. Insofar as possible, the physical inventory should be taken close to the end of the concern's fiscal year so that correct inventory quantities are available for use in preparing annual accounting reports and statements. Because this is not always possible, however, physical inventories taken within two or three months of the year's end are quite satisfactory, if the detail inventory records are maintained with a fair degree of accuracy.

To illustrate the difference between a perpetual and a periodic system, assume that Katt, Inc. had the following transactions during the current year:

| | |
|---|---|
| Sales | 600 units at $12 = $7,200 |
| Beginning inventory | 100 units at $ 6 = $  600 |
| Purchases | 900 units at $ 6 = $5,400 |
| Ending inventory | 400 units at $ 6 = $2,400 |

The entries to record these transactions during the current year are as follows:

**Entries Under Perpetual and Periodic Inventory Systems**

| Perpetual Inventory System | | | Periodic Inventory System | | |
|---|---|---|---|---|---|
| **Purchase merchandise for resale:** | | | | | |
| Inventory (900 at $6) | 5,400 | | Purchases (900 at $6) | 5,400 | |
| Accounts Payable | | 5,400 | Accounts Payable | | 5,400 |
| **Record sale:** | | | | | |
| Accounts Receivable | 7,200 | | Accounts Receivable | 7,200 | |
| Sales (600 at $12) | | 7,200 | Sales (600 at $12) | | 7,200 |
| Cost of Goods Sold | | | | | |
| (600 at $6) | 3,600 | | (no entry necessary) | | |
| Inventory | | 3,600 | | | |
| **Closing entries:** | | | | | |
| | | | Cost of Goods Sold | 600 | |
| | | | Inventory (beginning) | | 600 |
| (No entry) | | | Inventory (ending) | 2,400 | |
| | | | Cost of Goods Sold | | 2,400 |
| | | | Cost of Goods Sold | 5,400 | |
| | | | Purchases | | 5,400 |

[1] In recent years, some companies have developed inventory controls or methods of determining inventories, including statistical sampling, that are highly effective in determining inventory quantities and sufficiently reliable to make unnecessary an annual physical count of each item of inventory.

## BASIC ISSUES IN INVENTORY VALUATION

Because the goods sold or used during an accounting period seldom correspond exactly to the goods bought or produced during that period, the physical inventory either increases or decreases. Accounting for these increases or decreases requires that the cost of all the goods available for sale or use be allocated between the goods that were sold or used and those that are still on hand. The **cost of goods available for sale or use** is the sum of (1) the cost of the goods on hand at the beginning of the period and (2) the cost of the goods acquired or produced during the period. The cost of goods sold is the difference between the cost of goods available for sale during the period and the cost of goods on hand at the end of the period.

| | |
|---|---:|
| Beginning inventory, Jan. 1 | $100,000 |
| Cost of goods acquired or produced during the year | 800,000 |
| Total cost of goods available for sale | 900,000 |
| Ending inventory, Dec. 31 | 200,000 |
| Cost of goods sold during the year | $700,000 |

Inventory accounting involves the proper determination of each of the items listed above, but the focus is generally on the valuation of the ending inventory.

The valuation of inventories can be a complex process that requires determination of:

1. The physical goods to be included in inventory.
2. The costs to be included in inventory.
3. The cost flow assumption to be adopted.

## PHYSICAL GOODS TO BE INCLUDED IN INVENTORY

Technically, purchases should be recorded when legal title to the goods passes to the buyer. General practice, however, is to record acquisitions when the goods are received, because it is difficult for the buyer to determine the exact time of legal passage of title for every purchase and because no material error is likely to result from such a practice if it is consistently applied.

### Goods in Transit

Even though the legal rule is not followed in day-to-day transactions, purchased merchandise in transit at the end of a fiscal period, to which legal title has passed, should be recorded as purchases of the fiscal period. This means that ordinarily all goods shipped f.o.b. (free on board) shipping point that are in transit at the end of the period belong to the buyer and should be shown in the buyer's records, because legal title to these goods passed to the buyer when the goods were shipped. To disregard such purchases would result in

---

See *Codification of Statements on Auditing Standards,* "Evidential Matter for Receivables and Inventories" (New York: AICPA, 1980), Section 331.

an understatement of inventories and accounts payable in the balance sheet and an understatement of purchases and ending inventories in the income statement.

The accountant normally prepares a purchase cut-off schedule or worksheet at the end of the period and analyzes the transactions near the end of the year to ensure that the purchases and inventories are recorded in the proper period. Preparation of a purchase cut-off requires application of the "passage of title" rule in the following manner: if the goods are shipped **f.o.b. shipping point,** title passes to the buyer when the seller delivers the goods to the common carrier who acts as an agent for the buyer; if the goods are shipped **f.o.b. destination,** title does not pass until the buyer receives the goods from the common carrier. "Shipping point" and "destination" are designated by a particular location, for example, f.o.b. Denver. When the terms are f.o.b. shipping point, the transportation cost generally must be borne by the buyer, and such liability arises when the common carrier completes the delivery. When the terms are f.o.b. destination, the transportation cost generally is the expense of the seller. It should also be noted that **goods produced on special order** are ordinarily considered sold as soon as segregated from the regular inventory. In such a case, title is considered to have passed, even though delivery has not taken place.

In cases where there is some question as to whether title has passed, the accountant should exercise judgment, taking into consideration the practices common to the industry, the intent of the sales agreement, the policies of the parties involved, and any other available evidence of intent.

### Consigned Goods

A specialized method of marketing certain types of products makes use of a device known as a consignment shipment. Under this arrangement, one party, the consignor, ships merchandise to another, the consignee, who is to act as an agent for the consignor in selling the goods. The consignee agrees to accept the goods without any liability, except to exercise due care and reasonable protection from loss or damage, until the goods are sold to a third party. When the goods are sold by the consignee, the revenue less a selling commission and expenses incurred in accomplishing the sale is remitted to the consignor.

Goods out on consignment remain the property of the consignor and must be included in the consignor's inventory at purchase price or production cost plus the cost of handling and shipping involved in the transfer to the consignee. Occasionally, the inventory out on consignment is shown as a separate item, but unless the amount is large there is little need for this. No entry to adjust the inventory account is made by the consignee for goods received because they are the property of the consignor. The consignee should be extremely careful not to include any of the goods consigned as a part of inventory. Accounting for consignments by both the consignor and the consignee is covered in Chapter 19.

### Special Sale Agreements

As indicated earlier, transfer of legal title is the general guideline that accountants follow in determining whether an item should be included in inventory. Unfortunately, transfer of legal title and the underlying economics of the situation often do not match, and therefore considerable professional judgment must be exercised. For example, it is possible that legal title has passed to the purchaser but that the economic substance of the transaction is such that the seller of the goods still retains the risks of ownership. Conversely, transfer of legal title may not occur, but the economic substance of the transaction is that the seller no longer retains the risks of ownership. Three special sale situations are illustrated here to indicate the types of problems encountered in practice. These are as follows:

1. Product financing arrangements.
2. Sales with high rates of return.
3. Installment sales.

**Product Financing Arrangements** A variety of approaches have been used in practice whereby an enterprise finances its inventory without reporting on its balance sheet the liability or the inventory. To illustrate, Hill Enterprises transfers ("sells") inventory to Chase, Inc. and as part of the same transaction agrees to repurchase this merchandise at a specified price over a specified period in the future. Chase, Inc. then uses the inventory as collateral and borrows against the value of the product from a bank and remits the proceeds to Hill Enterprises as "payment" for the inventory. Hill Enterprises then repurchases the inventory in the future and Chase, Inc. employs the proceeds from repayment to meet its loan obligation.

The essence of this transaction is that Hill Enterprises is financing its inventory even though technical legal title to the merchandise was transferred to Chase, Inc. The advantage to Hill Enterprises for structuring a transaction in this manner is the avoidance of personal property taxes in certain states, the removal of the current liability from its balance sheet, and the ability to manipulate income. The advantages to Chase, Inc. are that the purchase of the goods may solve a LIFO liquidation problem (discussed later), or that it may be interested in a reciprocal agreement at a later date.

Legal title has transferred in this situation, but the economic substance of the transaction is that the risks of ownership are retained by Hill Enterprises (seller). These transactions are often described as **"parking transactions"** in practice, because the seller simply parks the inventory on another enterprise's balance sheet for a short period of time. The profession has taken steps to curtail this practice by requiring that when a repurchase agreement exists at a set price and this price covers all costs of the inventory plus related holding costs, the inventory and related liability remain on the seller's books.[2]

**Sales with High Rates of Return** Formal or informal agreements often exist in such industries as publishing, records and tapes, and toys and sporting goods that permit goods to be returned for a full refund or that allow for an adjustment to be made to the amount owed. To illustrate, MEM Publishing Company sells textbooks to University Bookstores with an agreement that any books not sold may be returned for full credit. In the past, approximately 25% of the textbooks sold to University Bookstores were returned. How should MEM Publishing report its sales transactions? One alternative is to record the sale at the full amount and establish an estimated sales returns and allowances account. A second possibility is to not record any sale until circumstances indicate that the buyer will not return the inventory. The key question is: Under what circumstances should the inventory be considered sold and removed from MEM's inventory? According to the profession, when the amount of returns can be reasonably estimated, the goods should be considered

---

[2]"Accounting for Product Financing Arrangements," *Statement of Financial Accounting Standards No. 49* (Stamford, Conn.: FASB, 1981).

sold. Conversely, if returns are unpredictable, removal of these goods from inventory does not appear to be warranted.[3]

**Installment Sales** "Goods sold on installment" describes any type of sale in which payment is required in periodic installments over an extended period of time. Because the risk of loss from uncollectibles is higher in installment sale situations than in other sale transactions, the seller often asks for protection in the form of a conditional sales contract that withholds legal title to the merchandise until all the payments have been made. The question is whether the inventory should be considered sold, even though legal title has not passed. The economic substance of the transaction is that the goods should be excluded from the seller's inventory if the percentage of bad debts can be reasonably estimated. Chapter 19 covers in detail the accounting for installment sales. Installment sales are discussed here to show that in some cases, although legal title may not have passed, the goods should be removed from inventory.

### Effect of Inventory Errors

If items are incorrectly included or excluded for inventory purposes, there will be errors in the financial statements. To illustrate, suppose that certain goods in transit that we owned were not recorded as a purchase or counted in ending inventory. To disregard such purchases would result in an understatement of inventories and accounts payable in the balance sheet and an understatement of purchases and ending inventories in the income statement. The net income for the period would not be affected by the omission of such purchases, since purchases and ending inventory would both be understated by the same amount, the error thereby offsetting itself in cost of goods sold. Total working capital would be unchanged, but the **current ratio** would be overstated because of the omission of equal amounts from inventory and accounts payable.

To illustrate the effect on working capital items, Barker, Inc. reports the following at the end of a fiscal period:

| | |
|---|---|
| Current assets | $120,000 |
| Current liabilities | 40,000 |
| Current ratio $\left(\dfrac{\$120,000}{\$\ 40,000}\right)$ | 3 to 1 |

If Barker, Inc. should have included goods in transit of $40,000 in ending inventory, then the following would be presented:

| | |
|---|---|
| Current assets | $160,000 |
| Current liabilities | 80,000 |
| Current ratio $\left(\dfrac{\$160,000}{\$\ 80,000}\right)$ | 2 to 1 |

---

[3]"Revenue Recognition When Right of Return Exists," *Statement of Financial Accounting Standards No. 48 (Stamford, Conn.: FASB, 1981).*

The correct current ratio is 2 to 1 instead of 3 to 1 because the goods in transit should be reported in both the inventory and accounts payable.

What would happen if the beginning inventory and the goods purchased are recorded correctly, but some items on hand are not included in ending inventory? In this situation, ending inventory, net income, current ratio, and working capital are all understated. Net income is understated because cost of goods sold is larger than it should be; the current ratio and working capital are understated because a portion of ending inventory is omitted.

To illustrate the effect on net income, assume that the ending inventory of Antonio, Inc. is understated by $10,000 and that all other items are correctly stated. The effect of this error will be to decrease net income in the current year and to increase net income in the following year. The error will be counterbalanced (offset) in the next period because the beginning inventory will be understated and net income will be overstated. In other words, both net income figures are misstated, but the total for the two years is correct as illustrated below.

**Antonio, Inc.**
**Effect of Inventory Error on Two Periods**
**(All figures assumed)**

|  | 1983 | | 1984 | |
|---|---|---|---|---|
|  | Correct | Incorrect | Incorrect | Correct |
| Revenues | $100,000 | $100,000 | $100,000 | $100,000 |
| Cost of goods sold |  |  |  |  |
| Beginning inventory | 25,000 | 25,000 | 20,000 | 30,000 |
| Purchased or produced | 45,000 | 45,000 | 60,000 | 60,000 |
| Goods available for sale | 70,000 | 70,000 | 80,000 | 90,000 |
| Less ending inventory | 30,000 | 20,000 | 40,000 | 40,000 |
| Cost of goods sold | 40,000 | 50,000 | 40,000 | 50,000 |
| Gross profit | 60,000 | 50,000 | 60,000 | 50,000 |
| Administrative and |  |  |  |  |
| selling expenses | 40,000 | 40,000 | 40,000 | 40,000 |
| Net income | $ 20,000 | $ 10,000 | $ 20,000 | $ 10,000 |

Total income for two
years correct

If a purchase is not recorded, but is included in ending inventory, the reverse effect occurs. Net income, the current ratio, and working capital are all overstated. The effect of the error on net income will be counterbalanced in the subsequent year (assuming that purchases are recorded in the next year), but both years' financial statements will be misstated. These illustrations indicate that an accurate computation of purchases and inventory is needed to assure that proper income and asset figures are presented.

## COSTS TO BE INCLUDED IN INVENTORY

One of the most important problems in dealing with inventories concerns the amount at which the inventory should be carried in the accounts and stated in the accounting reports. Inventories, like other assets, are generally accounted for on a basis of cost (other bases are discussed in Chapter 9). In defining cost as it applies to inventories, it becomes necessary to define inventoriable costs (product costs), that is, those costs that are said to attach to the inventory and are considered to be a part of the total inventory valuation. Charges directly connected with the bringing of goods to the place of business of the buyer and converting such goods to a salable condition are accepted as proper inventoriable costs. Such charges would include freight and hauling charges on goods purchased, other direct costs of acquisition, and labor and other production costs incurred in processing the goods up to the time of sale.

It would seem proper also to allocate to inventories a share of any buying costs or expenses of a purchasing department, storage costs, and other costs incurred in storing or handling the goods before they are sold. Because of the practical difficulties involved in allocating such costs and expenses, however, these items are not ordinarily included in valuing inventories.

## Period Expenses

**Selling expenses** and, under ordinary circumstances, **general and administrative expenses** are not considered to be directly related to the acquisition or production of goods and, therefore, are not considered to be a part of the inventories. Such costs are period costs rather than product costs. Conceptually, these expenses are as much a cost of the product as the initial purchase price and related freight charges attached to the product. Why then are these costs not considered inventoriable items?

In some industries these charges are not material and no real purpose is served by making an allocation of these costs to inventory. In other cases, especially where selling expenses are significant, the cost is more directly related to the cost of goods sold than to the unsold inventory. In most cases the costs, especially administrative expenses, are so unrelated or indirectly related to the immediate production process that any allocation is purely arbitrary. One guideline that may be followed is to charge to inventory those costs that bear a fairly direct relationship to the quantity produced. If, for example, an increase in administrative expenses occurs, without a subsequent increase in inventories, some justification exists for treating the cost as a period charge on the basis that the inventory quantities were not affected.

**Interest costs** associated with getting inventories ready for sale usually are expensed as incurred. A major argument for this approach is that interest costs are a cost of financing and should not be considered a cost of the asset. Others have argued, however, that interest costs incurred to finance activities associated with bringing inventories to a condition and place ready for sale are as much a cost of the asset as materials, labor, and overhead and, therefore, should be capitalized.[4] Recently the FASB indicated that interest cost related to assets constructed for internal use or assets produced as discrete projects (such as ships or real estate projects) for sale or lease should be capitalized.[5] It is emphasized that these discrete projects should take considerable time, entail substantial expenditures, and be likely to involve significant amounts of interest cost. Interest costs should not be capitalized for

---

[4]The reporting rules related to interest cost capitalization have their greatest impact in accounting for long-term assets and, therefore, are discussed in detail in Chapter 11. This brief overview provides the basic issues when inventories are involved.

[5]"Capitalization of Interest Cost," *Statement of Financial Accounting Standards No. 34* (Stamford, Conn.: FASB, 1979).

inventories that are routinely manufactured or otherwise produced in large quantities on a repetitive basis because the informational benefit does not justify the cost of doing so. The interest cost eligible for capitalization is based on the rates of the enterprise's specific borrowings to finance the purchase of the inventory or in some cases on a weighted average of interest rates incurred on all outstanding debt.

## Treatment of Purchase Discounts

In accordance with practice, purchase discounts have been treated in the accounts either as a financial revenue or as a reduction of purchases. From a theoretical standpoint, the arguments for a reduction of purchases are stronger than those usually presented in support of financial revenue. If discounts received for prompt payment of purchase invoices are shown as revenue, this may result in recognizing revenue even before the goods have been sold, at least to the extent that such purchases are still in the inventory at the end of the accounting period. It is generally held that a business does not recognize revenue by buying goods and paying bills; it recognizes revenue by selling them, and the sale transaction is an essential step in the revenue recognition process.

The treatment of purchase discounts as financial revenue has been supported by the argument that it is similar to interest earned in that it represents a reduction allowed by the seller so that cash may be obtained promptly. This argument has little merit; it may be countered by the statement that the buyer is not in any sense lending money to the seller; the buyer is merely paying a bill for purchases, and the amount paid is the cost of such purchases.

The use of a Purchase Discounts account indicates that the company is reporting its purchases and accounts payable at the gross amount. A more appropriate approach is to record the purchases and accounts payable at an amount net of the cash discounts. This treatment is often considered more appropriate because the net amount (1) provides a correct reporting of the cost of the asset and related liability and (2) presents the opportunity to measure the inefficiency of financial management if the discount is not taken. In the net approach, the failure to take a purchase discount within the discount period is recorded in a Purchase Discounts Lost account. To illustrate the difference between the gross and net method, assume the following transactions:

| **Entries Under Gross and Net Methods** | | | | |
|---|---|---|---|---|
| Gross Method | | | Net Method | |
| **Purchase cost $10,000, terms 2/10, net 30:** | | | | |
| Purchases | 10,000 | | Purchases | 9,800 | |
| Accounts Payable | | 10,000 | Accounts Payable | | 9,800 |
| **Invoices of $4,000 are paid within discount period:** | | | | |
| Accounts Payable | 4,000 | | Accounts Payable | 3,920 | |
| Purchase Discounts | | 80 | Cash | | 3,920 |
| Cash | | 3,920 | | | |
| **Invoices of $6,000 are paid after discount period:** | | | | |
| Accounts Payable | 6,000 | | Accounts Payable | 5,880 | |
| Cash | | 6,000 | Purchase Discounts Lost | 120 | |
| | | | Cash | | 6,000 |

As indicated earlier, if the gross method is employed, purchase discounts should be reported as a deduction from purchases on the income statement. If the net method is used, purchase discounts lost should be considered a financial expense and reported in the other expense section of the income statement. In addition, when purchases are recorded net, beginning and ending inventories are reported on the same basis. Many believe, however, that the difficulty involved in using the somewhat more complicated net method is not justified by the resulting benefits, which may account for the widespread use of the less logical but simpler gross method illustrated. In addition, some contend that management is reluctant to report the amount of purchase discounts lost in the financial statements.

## Manufacturing Costs

As previously indicated, a business that manufactures goods, utilizes three inventory accounts—raw materials, work in process, and finished goods. Work in process and finished goods include raw materials, direct labor, and manufacturing overhead costs. Manufacturing overhead costs include all manufacturing costs except direct materials and direct labor. Items included in manufacturing overhead are indirect material, indirect labor, and such items as depreciation, taxes, insurance, heat, and electricity, incurred in the manufacturing process. To illustrate how these different costs affect the inventory accounts, a **cost of goods manufactured statement** is presented below.

| | | | |
|---|---|---:|---:|
| | Leonard, Inc. | | |
| | STATEMENT OF COST OF GOODS MANUFACTURED | | |
| | Year Ended December 31, 1984 | | |
| Raw materials consumed | | | |
|   Raw materials Inventory, Jan. 1, 1984 | | | $ 14,000 |
|   Add net purchases: | | | |
|     Purchases | | $126,000 | |
|     Less: Purchase returns and allowances | $1,800 | | |
|       Purchase discounts | 1,200 | 3,000 | 123,000 |
|   Raw materials available for use | | | 137,000 |
|   Less raw materials inventory, Dec. 31, 1984 | | | 17,000 |
| | | | 120,000 |
| Direct labor | | | 200,000 |
| Manufacturing overhead | | | |
|   Supervisors' salaries | | 52,000 | |
|   Indirect labor | | 20,000 | |
|   Factory supplies used | | 18,000 | |
|   Taxes | | 15,000 | |
|   Heat, light, power, and water | | 13,000 | |
|   Depreciation on building and equipment | | 12,000 | |
|   Factory rent | | 11,000 | |
|   Tools expense | | 2,000 | |
|   Patent expense | | 1,000 | |
|   Miscellaneous factory expenses | | 6,000 | 150,000 |
| Total manufacturing costs for the period | | | 470,000 |
| Work in process inventory, Jan. 1, 1984 | | | 33,000 |
| Total manufacturing costs | | | 503,000 |
| Less work-in-process inventory, Dec. 31, 1984 | | | 28,000 |
| Cost of goods manufactured during the year | | | $475,000 |

The cost of raw materials consumed section is presented in a format similar to that used for reporting cost of goods sold in the income statement. Cost of goods manufactured statements are prepared primarily for internal use; such details are rarely disclosed in published financial statements. The cost of goods sold section in the income statement for a manufacturing firm is similar to the cost of goods sold section for a trading concern. The principal difference is the substitution of cost of goods manufactured during the year for the details related to purchases of merchandise.

If the inventory of finished goods was $16,000 at the beginning of the year and $10,000 at the end of the year, the cost of goods sold section of the income statement would appear as follows:

| Cost of goods sold | |
| --- | --- |
| Finished goods inventory, Jan. 1, 1984 | $ 16,000 |
| Cost of goods manufactured during 1984 | 475,000 |
| Cost of goods available for sale | 491,000 |
| Finished goods inventory, Dec. 31, 1984 | 10,000 |
| Cost of goods sold | $481,000 |

The principles applied in classifying inventory amounts on the income statement and on the balance sheet are the same for a manufacturing firm as for a trading concern.

## Variable Costing Versus Absorption Costing

Fixed manufacturing overhead costs present a special problem in costing inventories because two concepts exist relative to the costs that attach to the product as it flows through the manufacturing process. These two concepts are (1) **variable costing,** frequently called **direct costing,** and (2) **absorption costing,** also called **full costing.**

In a variable cost system all costs must be classified as variable or fixed. **Variable costs** are those that fluctuate in direct proportion to changes in output, and **fixed costs** are those that remain constant in spite of changes in output. Under variable costing only costs that vary directly with the volume of production are charged to products as manufacturing takes place. Only direct material, direct labor, and the variable costs in manufacturing overhead are charged to work-in-process and finished goods inventories and appear as cost of goods sold. Fixed overhead costs such as property taxes, insurance, depreciation on plant building, and salaries of supervisors are considered to be **period costs.** All fixed costs are charged as expenses to the current period under variable costing. Because the fixed costs are not viewed as costs of the products being manufactured, they are not associated with inventories.

Under **absorption costing,** all manufacturing costs, variable and fixed, direct and indirect, incurred in the factory or production process attach to the product and are included in the cost of inventory. Direct material, direct labor, and all manufacturing overhead—fixed as well as variable—are charged to output and allocated to cost of goods sold and inventories. The profession's position on inventory costing is that "cost means in principle the sum of the applicable expenditures and charges directly or indirectly incurred in bringing an article to its existing condition and location."[6] It went on to say that "it should also be

---

[6]"Restatement and Revision of Accounting Research Bulletins," *Accounting Research Bulletin No. 43* (New York: AICPA, 1953), Ch. 4, par. 4.

recognized that the exclusion of all overhead from inventory costs does not constitute an acceptable accounting procedure."

Proponents of the **variable costing** system believe that it provides data that are more useful to management in formulating pricing policies and in controlling costs than are data prepared under conventional absorption costing methods. Information for marginal income analysis, for fixed and variable expense analysis, and for cost-volume-profit analysis is readily available. Variable costing is not acceptable for income tax purposes or for use in published financial reports (external reporting) because it is claimed that it understates inventories as a reasonable representation of a firm's investment in this asset. In spite of this alleged deficiency, because variable costing is so useful to management in decision making, cost control, and budget preparation, it is widely used internally. Relatively simple adjustments at the end of each accounting period can be made to convert variable costed inventory and cost of goods sold to a basis acceptable for income tax and financial reporting purposes.

## WHAT COST FLOW ASSUMPTION SHOULD BE ADOPTED?

During any given fiscal period it is very likely that merchandise will be purchased at several different prices. If inventories are to be priced at cost and numerous purchases have been made at different unit costs, the question arises as to which of the various cost prices should be used. Conceptually, a specific identification of the given items sold and unsold seems optimal, but this measure is often not only difficult but impossible to achieve. Consequently, for practical reasons and in the interests of reliable financial reporting, the accountant must turn to the consistent application of one of several cost selection methods that are based on differing but systematic inventory cost flow assumptions. Therefore, the actual physical flow of goods and the cost flow assumption are often quite different. There is no requirement that the cost flow assumption adopted be consistent with the physical movement of goods.

To illustrate, assume that Ceco, Inc. had the following transactions in its first month of operations.

| Date | Purchases | Sold or Issued | Balance |
|------|-----------|----------------|---------|
| March 2 | 2,000 @ $4.00 | | 2,000 units |
| March 15 | 6,000 @ $4.40 | | 8,000 units |
| March 19 | | 4,000 units | 4,000 units |
| March 30 | 2,000 @ $4.15 | | 6,000 units |

From this information, the ending inventory of 6,000 units and the cost of goods available for sale (beginning inventory + purchases) of $42,700 ([2,000 @ $4.00] + [6,000 @ $4.40] + [2,000 @ $4.15]) can be computed. The question is, "Which price or prices should be assigned to the 6,000 units of ending inventory?" The answer depends on which cost flow assumption is employed.

## Specific Identification

Specific identification calls for identifying each item sold and each item in inventory. The costs of the specific items sold are included in the cost of goods sold, while the costs of the specific items on hand are included in the inventory. This method may be used only in instances where it is practical to separate physically the different purchases made. Any goods on hand may then be identified as quantities remaining from specific purchases, and the invoice cost of each lot or item may be separately determined. Obviously this method has a very limited application because of the impossibility or impracticability of segregating separate purchases in most instances. It can be successfully applied, however, in situations where a relatively small number of costly, easily distinguishable items are handled. In the retail trade this includes some types of jewelry, fur coats, automobiles, and some furniture. In manufacturing it includes special orders and many products manufactured under a job cost system.

To illustrate the specific identification method, assume that Ceco, Inc.'s 6,000 units of inventory comprised 1,000 units from the March 2 purchase, 3,000 from the March 15 purchase, and 2,000 from the March 30 purchase. The ending inventory and cost of goods sold would be computed as follows:

| Specific Identification Method | | | |
|---|---|---|---|
| Date | No. of Units | Unit Cost | Total Cost |
| March 2 | 1,000 | $4.00 | $ 4,000 |
| March 15 | 3,000 | 4.40 | 13,200 |
| March 30 | 2,000 | 4.15 | 8,300 |
| **Ending inventory** | **6,000** | | **$25,500** |
| Cost of goods available for sale (computed in previous section) | | $42,700 | |
| Deduct ending inventory | | 25,500 | |
| **Cost of goods sold** | | **$17,200** | |

Conceptually, this method appears ideal because actual costs are matched against actual revenue and ending inventory is reported at actual cost. In other words, the cost flow matches the physical flow of the goods. On closer observation, however, deficiencies can be found in using this method as a basis for inventory valuation and income measurement. One argument against specific identification is that it makes it possible to manipulate net income. For example, assume that a wholesaler purchases plywood early in the year at three different prices. When the plywood is sold, the wholesaler can, if desired, select either the lowest or the highest price to charge to expense simply by selecting the plywood from a specific lot for delivery to the customer. A business manager is, therefore, afforded the opportunity to manipulate net income simply by delivering to the customer the higher- or lower-priced item, depending on whether higher or lower reported earnings are desired for the period.

Another problem relates to the arbitrary allocation of costs that sometimes occurs with specific inventory items. In certain circumstances, it is difficult to relate adequately, for example, shipping charges, storage costs, and discounts directly to a given inventory item.

The alternative, then, is to allocate these costs somewhat arbitrarily, which leads to a "breakdown" in the preciseness of the specific identification method.[7]

## Average Cost

As the name implies, the **average cost method** prices items in the inventory on the basis of the average cost of all similar goods available during the period. If perpetual inventory records are not kept, the cost of the inventory is computed only at the end of the period. The periodic average cost method is often referred to as the **weighted-average method** and is another periodic inventory technique for valuing inventories.

To illustrate, assuming that Ceco, Inc. used the periodic method, the ending inventory and cost of goods sold would be computed as follows:

| **Periodic Inventory—Weighted-Average Method** | | | |
|---|---|---|---|
| Date of Invoice | No. Units | Unit Cost | Total Cost |
| Mar. 2 | 2,000 | $4.00 | $ 8,000 |
| Mar. 15 | 6,000 | 4.40 | 26,400 |
| Mar. 30 | 2,000 | 4.15 | 8,300 |
| Total goods available | 10,000 | | $42,700 |

Weighted-average cost per unit $\dfrac{\$42,700}{10,000} = \$4.27$

Inventory in units     6,000 units

**Ending inventory**     6,000 × $4.27 = **$25,620**

| | |
|---|---|
| Cost of goods available for sale | $42,700 |
| Deduct ending inventory | 25,620 |
| **Cost of goods sold** | **$17,080** |

As implied in this computation, any beginning inventory is included both in the total units available and in the total cost of goods available in computing the average cost per unit.

Another average cost method is the **moving-average method,** which is used with perpetual inventory records. The application of the average cost method for perpetual records is shown below:

| **Perpetual Inventory—Moving-Average Method** | | | | | |
|---|---|---|---|---|---|
| Date | Purchased | | Sold or Issued | Balance | |
| Mar. 2 | (2,000 @ $4.00) | $ 8,000 | | (2,000 @ $4.00) | $ 8,000 |
| Mar. 15 | (6,000 @ 4.40) | 26,400 | | (8,000 @ 4.30) | 34,400 |
| Mar. 19 | | | (4,000 @ $4.30) $17,200 | (4,000 @ 4.30) | 17,200 |
| Mar. 30 | (2,000 @ 4.15) | 8,300 | | (6,000 @ 4.25) | **25,500** |

[7]A good illustration of the cost allocation problem arises in the motion picture industry. Often actors and actresses receive a percentage of net income for a given movie or television program. Some actors such as James Garner and Fess Parker, who have these arrangements, have alleged that their

As indicated above, a new average unit cost is computed each time a purchase is made. On March 15, after 6,000 units are purchased for $26,400, 8,000 units costing $34,400 ($8,000 plus $26,400) are on hand. The average unit cost is $34,400 divided by 8,000, or $4.30. This unit cost is used in costing withdrawals until another purchase is made, when a new average unit cost is computed. Accordingly, the cost of the 4,000 units withdrawn on March 19 is shown at $4.30, a total cost of goods sold of $17,200, and on March 30 a new unit cost of $4.25 is determined for an ending inventory of $25,500.

The use of the average cost methods is usually justified on the basis of practical rather than conceptual reasons. They are simple to apply, objective, and not as subject to income manipulation as some of the other inventory pricing methods. In addition, proponents of the average cost methods argue that it is often impossible to measure a specific physical flow of inventory and therefore it is better to cost items on an average price basis. This argument is particularly persuasive when the inventory involved is relatively homogeneous in nature. A moving average is probably more representative of the costs to be associated with the product, although a weighted average can give approximately the same results.

## First-In, First-Out (FIFO)

Under the **FIFO** method, costs are allocated between inventory on hand and goods sold, on the assumption that goods are used in the order in which they are purchased; in other words, the first goods purchased are the first used (in a manufacturing concern) or sold (in a trading concern). The inventory remaining must therefore represent the most recent purchases.

To illustrate, assume that Ceco, Inc. uses the periodic inventory system, such that the amount of inventory is computed only at the end of the month. The cost of the ending inventory is computed by taking the most recent purchase and working back until all units in the inventory are accounted for. The ending inventory and cost of goods sold are determined below:

| Date | No. Units | Unit Cost | Total Cost |
|------|-----------|-----------|------------|
| **Periodic Inventory—FIFO Method** | | | |
| Mar. 30 | 2,000 | $4.15 | $ 8,300 |
| Mar. 15 | 4,000 | 4.40 | 17,600 |
| **Ending inventory** | **6,000** | | **$25,900** |
| | Goods available for sale | $42,700 | |
| | Deduct ending inventory | 25,900 | |
| | **Cost of goods sold** | **$16,800** | |

If a perpetual inventory system in quantities and dollars is used, a cost figure is attached to each withdrawal. Then the cost of the 4,000 units removed on March 19 would be

---

programs have been extremely profitable to the motion picture studios but they have received little in the way of profit sharing. Actors contend that the studios allocate additional costs to successful projects to insure that there will be no profits to share.

made up of the items purchased on March 2 and March 15. The inventory on a FIFO basis perpetual system for Ceco, Inc. would be as follows:

| | Perpetual Inventory—FIFO Method | | | |
|---|---|---|---|---|
| Date | Purchased | | Sold or Issued | Balance |
| Mar. 2 | (2,000 @ $4.00) | $ 8,000 | | 2,000 @ $4.00    $ 8,000 |
| Mar. 15 | (6,000 @ 4.40) | 26,400 | | 2,000 @ 4.00 ⎫<br>6,000 @ 4.40 ⎭  34,400 |
| Mar. 19 | | | 2,000 @ $4.00 ⎫<br>2,000 @ 4.40 ⎭<br>($16,800) | 4,000 @ 4.40    17,600 |
| Mar. 30 | (2,000 @ 4.15) | 8,300 | | 4,000 @ 4.40 ⎫<br>2,000 @ 4.15 ⎭  25,900 |

The ending inventory in this situation is $25,900 and the cost of goods sold is $16,800 ([2,000 @ $4.00] + [2,000 @ $4.40]). In all cases where FIFO is used, the inventory and cost of goods sold would be the same at the end of the month whether a perpetual or periodic system is used.

One objective of FIFO is to follow an approximation of the physical flow of goods. When the physical flow of goods is actually first-in, first-out, the FIFO method very nearly represents specific identification. At the same time, it does not permit manipulation of income because the enterprise is not free to pick a certain cost item to be charged to expense.

A major advantage of the FIFO method is that the ending inventory is stated in terms of an approximate current cost figure. Because the first goods in are the first goods out, the ending inventory amount will be composed of the most recent purchases. This is particularly true where the inventory turnover is rapid. This approach generally provides a reasonable approximation of replacement cost when price changes have not occurred since the most recent purchases.

The basic disadvantage of this method is that current costs are not matched against current revenues. The oldest costs are charged against the more current revenue, which can lead to distortions in the operating data.

## Last-in, First-Out (LIFO)

The LIFO method allocates costs on the assumption that the cost of the last goods purchased are matched against revenue first. If a periodic inventory is used, then it would be assumed that the total quantity sold or issued during the month would have come from the most recent purchases. The ending inventory would be priced by using the total units as a basis of computation and disregarding the exact dates involved. The assumption would be made that the 4,000 units withdrawn absorbed the 2,000 units purchased on March 30 and 2,000 of the 6,000 units purchased on March 15. The inventory and related cost of goods sold would then be computed as shown at the top of page 353.

If a perpetual inventory record is kept in quantities and dollars, application of the last-in, first-out method will result in different ending inventory and cost of goods sold amounts as shown in the second exhibit on page 353.

### Periodic Inventory—LIFO Method

| Date of Invoice | No. Units | Unit Cost | Total Cost |
|---|---|---|---|
| Mar. 2 | 2,000 | $4.00 | $ 8,000 |
| Mar. 15 | 4,000 | 4.40 | 17,600 |
| **Ending inventory** | **6,000** | | **$25,600** |

| | | |
|---|---|---|
| Goods available for sale | $42,700 | |
| Deduct ending inventory | 25,600 | |
| **Cost of goods sold** | **$17,100** | |

### Perpetual Inventory—LIFO Method

| Date | Purchased | | Sold or Issued | Balance | | |
|---|---|---|---|---|---|---|
| Mar. 2 | (2,000 @ $4.00) | $ 8,000 | | 2,000 @ $4.00 | $ 8,000 | |
| Mar. 15 | (6,000 @ 4.40) | 26,400 | | 2,000 @ 4.00 }<br>6,000 @ 4.40 } | 34,400 | |
| Mar. 19 | | | (4,000 @ $4.40)<br>**$17,600** | 2,000 @ 4.00 }<br>2,000 @ 4.40 } | 16,800 | |
| Mar. 30 | (2,000 @ 4.15) | 8,300 | | 2,000 @ 4.00 }<br>2,000 @ 4.40 }<br>2,000 @ 4.15 } | **25,100** | |

The month-end computation illustrated first (inventory $25,600 and cost of goods sold $17,100) shows a different amount from the perpetual inventory computation immediately below it (inventory $25,100 and cost of goods sold $17,600) because the former matches the total withdrawals for the month with the total purchases for the month in applying the last-in, first-out method, but the latter matches each withdrawal with the immediately preceding purchases. In effect, the first computation assumed that goods that were not purchased until March 30 were included in the sale or issue of March 19.

## Last-In, First-Out—A Pooled Approach

Up to this point, we have emphasized a single goods approach to costing LIFO inventories. Such an assumption is unrealistic with LIFO because most enterprises have numerous goods in inventory at the end of a period and costing (pricing) them on a single goods basis is extremely expensive and time consuming.

As a consequence, goods are often combined into natural groups, or **pools.** Each pool is then assumed to be one unit for purposes of costing. For example, all the units contained in each pool of the opening inventory are considered as having been acquired at the same time for the same price so that the unit cost is obtained by dividing the beginning amount by the total number of units in the pool. Any increment in inventory is usually priced at the average cost of goods purchased during the year, although other variants are possible.

To illustrate, assume that Mary Lane Cosmetics in its first year of operations has four raw materials, musk, wax, lavender, and gum, that comprise the basic ingredients for its cosmetics manufacturing process. Mary Lane's beginning inventory is comprised of the following:

| Raw Materials | Beginning Inventory | | |
|---|---|---|---|
| | Quantity | Price | Total |
| Musk | 24,000 lbs. | $4.00 | $ 96,000 |
| Wax | 36,000 | 6.10 | 219,600 |
| Lavender | 22,000 | 9.00 | 198,000 |
| Gum | 8,000 | 3.30 | 26,400 |
| | 90,000 lbs. | | $540,000 |
| | | Average cost/lb. $6.00 | |

Assuming that the raw materials are one pool, the average cost for this pool is $6.00 ($540,000 ÷ 90,000 lbs.). The following transactions for Mary Lane Cosmetics occurred in the next period:

| Raw Materials | Beginning Inventory Quantity | Transactions | | | | |
|---|---|---|---|---|---|---|
| | | Purchases | | | Requisitions | Ending Inventory Quantity |
| | | Quantity | Price | Total | (Quantities Used) | |
| Musk | 24,000 lbs. | 30,000 lbs. | $ 4.50 | $135,000 | 30,000 lbs. | 24,000 lbs. |
| Wax | 36,000 | 40,000 | 6.40 | 256,000 | 42,000 | 34,000 |
| Lavender | 22,000 | 35,000 | 10.00 | 350,000 | 30,000 | 27,000 |
| Gum | 8,000 | 15,000 | 5.00 | 75,000 | 15,000 | 8,000 |
| | 90,000 lbs. | 120,000 lbs. | | $816,000 | 117,000 lbs. | 93,000 lbs. |
| | | | Average cost/lb. $6.80 | | | |

The average cost computation of purchases made during the current month is $6.80 per pound ($816,000 ÷ 120,000 lbs.). The average cost figure of $6.80 per pound would be used to value any inventory increase that occurred in the current month. Because the total ending inventory was higher than the total beginning inventory by 3,000 pounds (93,000 − 90,000), the ending inventory is computed as follows:

| Pooled LIFO Cost of Ending Inventory | | | |
|---|---|---|---|
| | Quantity | Price | Total |
| Beginning inventory | 90,000 lbs. | $6.00 | $540,000 |
| Increase during the year | 3,000 | 6.80 | 20,400 |
| | 93,000 lbs. | | $560,400 |

The beginning inventory cost and the cost of the increase during the year were computed using an average cost basis. Increases in inventory quantities from period to period form **inventory layers.** If the ending inventory is never lower than the quantity on hand at the beginning of the period, the original unit costs remain intact in inventory. When the inventory is decreased, the most recently added inventory layer is the first layer eliminated. This is in accordance with the concept that the last goods purchased are the first goods sold. For example, Mary Lane's 3,000 pound ($6.80) layer, as the most recent increment, would be the layer first reduced if a decrease in the number of units on hand took place in the next period.

As indicated earlier, the pooled approach reduces recordkeeping and clerical costs. In addition, it is more difficult to erode the layer because the reduction of one quantity in the pool may be offset by an increase in another. For example, Mary Lane had a decrease in the quantity of wax from the beginning to the end of the period, but in the aggregate the pool increased, so no adjustment in the quantity of the layer was necessary.

## Dollar-Value LIFO

As indicated above, the pooled approach eliminates some of the disadvantages of the single good approach to accounting for LIFO inventories. The pooled approach using quantities as its measurement basis, however, creates other types of problems. First, most companies are continually changing the mix of their products, materials, and production methods. A business once engaged in manufacturing train locomotives may now be involved in the automobile or aircraft business. A business that had used cotton fabric in its clothing now uses synthetic fabric (dacron, nylon, etc.). If a pooled approach using quantities is employed, it means that the pools must be continually redefined; this can be time consuming and costly. Second, even when such an approach is practical, an erosion of the base layers often results, thereby losing much of the LIFO costing benefits.

An erosion of the layers results because a specific good or material in the pool may be replaced by another good or material either temporarily or permanently. This replacement may occur for competitive reasons or simply because a shortage of a certain material exists. Whatever the reason, the new item may not be similar enough to be treated as part of the old pool, and therefore any inflationary profit deferred in the old goods may have to be recognized as the old goods are replaced.

To overcome these problems, the dollar-value LIFO method was developed. The important feature of the dollar-value LIFO method is that increases and decreases in a pool are determined and measured in terms of total dollar value, not the physical quantity of the goods in the inventory pool. Such an approach has two important advantages over the regular LIFO pool approach. First, a broader range of goods may be included in a dollar-value LIFO pool than in a regular LIFO pool. Second, in a dollar-value LIFO pool, replacement is permitted if it is similar as to type of material, or similarity in use, or interchangeability. (In a regular LIFO pool, the replacement of any item must be with an item that is substantially identical.) As a result, changes in quantities and product mix are often ignored. Thus, it is more difficult to erode the LIFO layers using dollar-value LIFO techniques than with a regular LIFO pool concept. It follows that the dollar-value LIFO method has all the advantages of the regular LIFO pool approach and more and therefore is widely used in practice. Only in situations where few goods are employed and little change in product mix is predicted would the more traditional LIFO approaches be utilized.

Under the dollar-value LIFO method, it is possible to have the entire inventory in only one pool, although several pools are usually employed. In general, the more goods included in a pool, the more likely that decreases in the quantities of some goods will be offset by increases in others in the same pool; thus liquidation of the LIFO layers is avoided. It follows that fewer pools means less cost and less chance of a reduction of a LIFO layer.

**Basic Dollar-Value LIFO Illustration**    To illustrate how the dollar-value LIFO method works, assume that dollar-value LIFO was first adopted (base period) on December 31, 1982, that the inventory at current prices on that date was $20,000, and that the inventory on December 31, 1983 at current prices is $26,400. We should not conclude that the quantity has increased 32% during the year ($26,400 ÷ $20,000 = 132%). First, we need to ask: What is the value of the ending inventory in terms of beginning of the year prices? Assuming that prices have increased 20% during the year, the ending inventory at beginning of the year prices amounts to $22,000 ($26,400 ÷ 120%). Therefore, the inventory quantity has increased 10%, or from $20,000 to $22,000 in terms of beginning of the year prices.

The next step is to price this real dollar quantity increase. This real dollar quantity increase of $2,000 valued at year-end prices is $2,400 (120% × $2,000). This increment (layer) of $2,400, when added to the beginning inventory of $20,000, gives a total of $22,400 for the December 31, 1983 inventory, as shown below:

| | |
|---|---:|
| First layer—(beginning inventory) in terms of 100 | $20,000 |
| Second layer—(1983 increase) in terms of 120 | 2,400 |
| Dollar-value LIFO inventory, December 31, 1983 | $22,400 |

It should be emphasized that a layer is formed only when the ending inventory at base-year prices exceeds the beginning inventory at base-year prices.

**Complex Dollar-Value LIFO Illustration**    To illustrate the use of the dollar-value LIFO method in a more complex situation, assume that Boston Company develops the following information:

| | Dec. 31 | Inventory at End-of-Year Prices | ÷ | Price Index (percentage) | = | End-of-Year Inventory at Base-Year Prices |
|---|---|---|---|---|---|---|
| (Base year) | 1980 | $200,000 | | 100 | | $200,000 |
| | 1981 | 299,000 | | 115 | | 260,000 |
| | 1982 | 300,000 | | 120 | | 250,000 |
| | 1983 | 351,000 | | 130 | | 270,000 |

At December 31, 1980, the ending inventory under dollar-value LIFO is simply the $200,000 computed as follows:

| Computation of 1980 Inventory | | | | | | |
|---|---|---|---|---|---|---|
| Ending Inventory at Base-Year Prices | Layer at Base-Year Prices | | Price Index (percentage) | | Ending Inventory at LIFO Cost | |
| $200,000 | $200,000 | × | 100 | = | $200,000 | |

At December 31, 1981, a comparison of the ending inventory at base-year prices ($260,000) with the beginning inventory at base-year prices ($200,000), indicates that the quantity of goods has increased $60,000 ($260,000 − $200,000). This increment (layer) is then priced at the 1981 index of 115% to arrive at a new layer of $69,000. Ending inventory for 1981 is $269,000, comprised of the beginning inventory of $200,000 and the new layer of $69,000. The following schedule illustrates these computations:

| Computation of 1981 Inventory | | | | | | |
|---|---|---|---|---|---|---|
| Ending Inventory at Base-Year Prices | Layers at Base-Year Prices | | | Price Index (percentage) | | Ending Inventory at LIFO Cost |
| $260,000 | 1980 | $200,000 | × | 100 | = | $200,000 |
|  | 1981 | 60,000 | × | 115 | = | 69,000 |
|  |  | $260,000 |  |  |  | $269,000 |

At December 31, 1982, a comparison of the ending inventory at base-year prices ($250,000) with the beginning inventory at base-year prices ($260,000) indicates that the quantity of goods has decreased $10,000 ($250,000 − $260,000). If the ending inventory at base-year prices is less than the beginning inventory at base-year prices, the decrease must be subtracted from the most recently added layer. When a decrease occurs, previous layers must be "peeled off" at the prices in existence when the layers were added. In Boston Company's situation, this means that $10,000 in base-year prices must be removed from the 1981 layer of $60,000 at base-year prices. The balance of $50,000 ($60,000 − $10,000) at base-year prices must be valued at the 1981 price index of 115% so that this 1981 layer now is valued at $57,500 ($50,000 × 115%). The ending inventory is therefore computed at $257,500, comprising the beginning inventory of $200,000 and the second layer, $57,500. The computations are illustrated below:

| Computation of 1982 Inventory | | | | | | |
|---|---|---|---|---|---|---|
| Ending Inventory at Base-Year Price | Layers at Base-Year Prices | | | Price Index (percentage) | | Ending Inventory at LIFO Cost |
| $250,000 | 1980 | $200,000 | × | 100 | = | $200,000 |
|  | 1981 | 50,000 | × | 115 | = | 57,500 |
|  |  | $250,000 |  |  |  | $257,500 |

It should be noted that if a layer or base (or portion thereof) has been eliminated, it cannot be rebuilt in future periods; that is, it is gone forever.

At December 31, 1983, a comparison of the ending inventory at base-year prices ($270,000) with the beginning inventory at base-year prices ($250,000) indicates that the dollar quantity of goods has increased $20,000 ($270,000 − $250,000) in terms of base-year prices. After converting the $20,000 increase to the 1983 price index, the ending inventory is $283,500, comprised of the beginning layer of $200,000, a 1981 layer of $57,500, and a 1983 layer of $26,000, ($20,000 × 130%). This computation is shown below:

| | Computation of 1983 Inventory | | | |
|---|---|---|---|---|
| Ending Inventory at Base-Year Prices | Layers at Base-Year Prices | | Price Index (percentage) | Ending Inventory at LIFO Cost |
| | 1980 $200,000 | × | 100 | = $200,000 |
| $270,000 | 1981 50,000 | × | 115 | = 57,500 |
| | 1983 20,000 | × | 130 | = 26,000 |
| | $270,000 | | | $283,500 |

The ending inventory at base-year prices must always equal the total of the layers at base-year prices; checking that this situation exists will help to insure that the dollar-value computation is made correctly.

**Selecting a Price Index**    One question that has not been answered concerning dollar-value LIFO is: How are the price indexes determined? Although different methods of computation might be used, the general approach is to price the ending inventory at the most current cost. Current cost is ordinarily determined by referring to the actual cost of goods most recently purchased. The price index is then a measurement of the change of price or cost levels between the base year and the current year. An index is computed for each year after the base year. The general formula for computing the index is as follows:

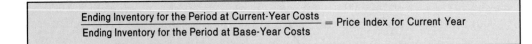

$$\frac{\text{Ending Inventory for the Period at Current-Year Costs}}{\text{Ending Inventory for the Period at Base-Year Costs}} = \text{Price Index for Current Year}$$

Computation of the index becomes difficult where certain goods are in only one of the two inventory figures or where damaged or obsolete merchandise is involved. However, procedures are available to handle these difficulties such as computing the current index on the basis of sample prices at both current and base year costs or using existing indexes that are relevant to the inventories of the enterprise.[8]

In summary, dollar-value LIFO is a method employed by many companies that currently use a LIFO system. Although the approach appears complex, the logic and the computations are deceptively simple, once an appropriate index is determined. Basically the

---

[8]A more thorough discussion of the development and use of price indexes and other problems related to LIFO are discussed in Appendix F of Chapter 9.

dollar-value method is a more practical way of valuing a complex, multiple-item inventory than the traditional LIFO method.

This is not to suggest that problems do not exist with the dollar-value LIFO method. For example, the selection of the items to be put in a pool can be subjective and difficult. Such a determination, however, is extremely important because manipulation of the items in the pool with little conceptual justification can affect reported net income. In addition, because of changes in product mix, items in the ending inventory may not be in the beginning inventory. Thus the base year is often adjusted; this can be costly and it leads to additional management discretion in determining inventory valuations.

## Evaluation of LIFO

In certain situations the LIFO cost flow may approximate the physical flow of the goods in and out of inventory. For instance, in the case of a coal pile, it can be shown that in some situations the last goods in are the first goods out because the coal remover is not going to take the coal from the bottom of the pile. The coal that is going to be taken first is the coal that was placed on the pile last.

Because the coal pile situation is one of only a few situations where the actual physical flow corresponds to LIFO, most adherents of LIFO use other arguments for its widespread employment, as follows:

### MAJOR ADVANTAGES OF LIFO

**Matching** In LIFO, the more recent costs are matched against current revenues to provide a better measure of current earnings. With the present inflationary trend, which is expected to continue, many accountants have challenged the quality of non-LIFO earnings, noting that by failing to match current costs against current revenues, transitory or "paper" profits ("inventory profits") are created. Inventory profits occur when the inventory costs matched against sales are less than the replacement cost of the inventory. The cost of goods sold therefore is understated and profit is considered overstated. By using LIFO (rather than some method such as FIFO), current costs are matched against revenues and inventory profits are thereby reduced.

**Tax Benefits** Tax benefits are the major reason why LIFO has become popular. As long as the price level increases and inventory quantities do not decrease, a deferral of income tax occurs, because the items most recently purchased at the higher price level are matched against revenues. For example, when Fuqua Industries decided to switch to LIFO, it had a resultant tax savings of 3 to 4 million dollars. Even if the price level later decreases, the company has been given a temporary deferral of its income taxes. It should be noted that if LIFO is used for tax purposes, it must also be used for financial reporting purposes.[9] This requirement is often referred to as the **LIFO conformity rule.** Other inventory valuation methods do not have this requirement.

---

[9]Management often selects an accounting procedure because a lower tax results from its use; an accounting method that is conceptually more appealing therefore is ignored. Throughout this textbook, an effort has been made to identify accounting procedures that provide income tax benefits to the user.

**Improved Cash Flow**    This advantage is related to the tax benefits, because taxes must be paid in cash. As a consequence, some companies are forced to borrow to finance replacement of existing inventory levels, and interest costs can be staggering. Fuqua Industries, for example, expected to save approximately $400,000 in interest costs by switching to LIFO. A side effect of this situation is that given a prolonged period of inflation, the cumulative effect of LIFO cash savings, when reinvested, could increase profit more than would be attainable using FIFO inventory.[10]

**Future Earnings Hedge**    With LIFO, a company's future reported earnings will not be affected substantially by future price declines. LIFO eliminates or substantially minimizes write-downs to market as a result of price decreases because the inventory value ordinarily will be much lower than net realizable value, which is in sharp contrast to the FIFO method, which ordinarily has a higher inventory value than LIFO. Inventory costed under FIFO is more vulnerable to price declines, which can reduce net income substantially.

## MAJOR DISADVANTAGES OF LIFO

**Reduced Earnings**    Many corporate managers view the lower profits reported under the LIFO method as a distinct disadvantage and would rather have higher reported profits than lower taxes. This view assumes that prices are increasing; in some industries where prices are declining, the opposite effect may occur. Some fear that an accounting change to LIFO may be misunderstood and that, as a result of the lower profits, the price of the company's stock will fall. It should be noted that there is some evidence to refute this contention, however, and, in fact, non-LIFO earnings are now highly suspect and may be severely penalized as a result.

**Inventory Understated**    The inventory valuation on the balance sheet is normally outdated because the oldest costs remain in inventory. This understatement presents several problems, but manifests itself most directly in evaluating the working capital position of the company. The magnitude and direction of this variation between the carrying amount of inventory and its current price depend on the degree and direction of the changes in price and the amount of inventory turnover.

**Physical Flow**    LIFO does not approximate the physical flow of the items except in peculiar situations. Originally LIFO could be used only in certain circumstances. This situation has changed over the years to the point where physical flow characteristics no longer play an important role in determining whether LIFO may be employed.

**Current Cost Income Not Measured**    LIFO falls short of measuring current cost (replacement cost) income. In order to measure current cost income, as opposed to monetary income, the cost of goods sold should consist not of the most recently incurred costs but rather of the cost that will be incurred to replace the goods that have been sold. Using

---

[10]Note that, even though some would receive substantial tax benefits if they switched to LIFO, they have chosen not to. Some of the reasons for not changing to LIFO are presented in the following article. See Gary C. Biddle, "Accounting Methods and Management Decisions: The Case of Inventory Costing and Inventory Policy," *The Journal of Accounting Research,* Supplement 1980, for the rationale of why managers select one inventory method over another.

replacement cost is referred to as the next-in, first-out method, a method not currently acceptable for purposes of inventory valuation.

**Involuntary Liquidation**   LIFO also faces the involuntary liquidation problem. If the base or layers of old costs are eliminated, strange results can occur because old, irrelevant costs can be matched against current revenues. A distortion in reported income for a given period may result, as well as consequences that are detrimental from an income tax point of view.

For example, Interlake, Inc. reported $5.6 million income from liquidation of LIFO inventories in 1980, which provided almost all of its profit increase to $19.4 million from $13.7 million in the previous year. The income tax problem is particularly severe when the involuntary liquidation results from a strike or a shortage of materials. In these situations, companies may incur high tax bills when they can least afford to pay taxes.

**Poor Buying Habits**   LIFO may cause poor buying habits because of this liquidation problem. A company may simply purchase more goods and match these goods against revenue to ensure that the old costs are not charged to expense. Furthermore, the possibility always exists with LIFO that a company will attempt to manipulate its net income at the end of the year simply by altering its pattern of purchases. For example, one reason why General Tire and Rubber accelerated raw material purchases at the end of 1980 was to minimize the book profit from a liquidation of LIFO inventories and to minimize income taxes for the year.

Because price rises have been the way of life in the U.S. economy during the last four decades, LIFO has provided a tax advantage over FIFO. During periods of continuing price decreases, this tax advantage could become a disadvantage. And during periods of stable prices, FIFO and LIFO methods of inventory costing produce identical results (assuming that at the beginning of the period of price stability the inventory values are equal).

## OTHER COST-BASED METHODS

The inventory costing methods previously illustrated are widely employed in practice. In addition, two other approaches (base stock and standard costs) merit attention.

### Base Stock

The **base stock method** is founded on the assumption that a minimum normal stock of goods is required at all times to carry on normal business activity, and that such normal stock should be carried at a long-run "normal" price, which may be, and often is, the lowest cost experienced or likely to be experienced. The lowest cost is used to avoid showing an "unrealized" inventory profit. Proponents of this method contend that the minimum inventory quantity is similar to a fixed asset and should not be affected by fluctuations in purchase prices; the costs of maintaining and replenishing this normal stock are charged to operations. The cost of any excess on hand above the base quantity is considered as a temporary increment and is priced at current costs by the application of the LIFO, FIFO, average cost, or any other suitable method selected. Any shortage in the base stock compared with units on hand is also considered temporary and is charged against revenue at current replacement cost.

If the base stock inventory is assumed to be 5,000 units at $3.80 per unit, then the inventory on hand of 6,000 units on March 31 might be computed as follows (using the data from the prior section and assuming that the excess over the normal stock is to be priced on a first-in, first-out basis):

| | |
|---|---|
| Base stock (5,000 units @ $3.80) | $19,000 |
| Excess above base quantity (1,000 units @ $4.15) | 4,150 |
| Inventory, March 31 | $23,150 |

If the base stock is assumed to be 7,000 units at $3.80 per unit, then the inventory on hand of 6,000 units on March 31 is computed:

| | |
|---|---|
| Base stock (7,000 units @ $3.80) | $26,600 |
| Temporary deficiency (1,000 units @ $4.15, current replacement cost) | 4,150 |
| Inventory, March 31 | $22,450 |

The application of the base stock method represents a departure from the cost principle as applied to assets, because the base stock quantity is carried at an amount that has no necessary relationship to the cost of units now in inventory. Like the LIFO method, the base stock method matches current costs with current revenues. It also is subject to some of the same objections as the LIFO method; in addition, the "normal" quantity is subject to manipulation. It is not a widely used method of inventory pricing because it is difficult to determine a normal quantity, and it is not acceptable for tax purposes; similar results can be obtained by using LIFO.

## Standard Costs

A manufacturing concern that uses a **standard cost system** predetermines the unit costs for material, labor, and manufacturing overhead. Usually the standard costs used are determined on the basis of the costs that should be incurred per unit of finished goods when the plant is operating at normal capacity. The approximate ideal or expected costs are useful to management in its objective of controlling actual costs. Deviations from standard costs are reflected in variance accounts that may be analyzed to determine the reasons for such deviations so that management may take appropriate action to achieve greater control over manufacturing costs.

Under a standard cost system, the raw materials, work-in-process, and finished goods inventories may be valued at standard costs. For financial reporting purposes the pricing of inventories at standard costs is considered acceptable if there is no significant difference between actual and standard. If there is a significant difference, the inventory amounts should be adjusted to actual cost. Otherwise the net income will be misstated in the income statement, and both the assets and the retained earnings will be misstated in the balance sheet.

Some accountants disagree with the notion that actual costs are the only acceptable costs for inventory purposes. They believe that standard costs are more representative of the appropriate cost of the product than actual costs. This group argues that variances are measures of abnormal inefficiencies and should be immediately recognized in determining net income of the period rather than prorated to inventories and cost of goods sold. Thus, the costs attached to the product are the costs that should have been incurred, not the costs that were incurred. The profession takes the position that **"standard costs are acceptable if adjusted at reasonable intervals to reflect current conditions so that at the balance sheet date standard costs reasonably approximate costs computed under one of the recognized bases."**[11] The recognized bases are specific identification, average cost, FIFO, and LIFO.

## BASIS FOR SELECTION

As indicated in Chapter 1, the primary objectives of financial reporting are to provide (1) information useful in investment and credit decisions, (2) information that is useful in assessing cash flow prospects, and (3) information about enterprise resources, claims to these resources, and changes in them. The inventory valuation method(s) that leads to the accomplishment of these objectives should be the one selected. However, attempting to implement these objectives is extremely difficult because operational guidelines are not developed that distinguish better (more useful) information from other unnecessary (less useful) information.

One thing is certain: Although FIFO has always been the most popular inventory method, a tremendous shift from FIFO and average cost to the LIFO method took place during the 1970s. For example, according to one survey of 600 firms, the number using LIFO for part or all of their inventory increased from 146 in 1970 to 396 in 1980.[12] During the mid-1970s at least 8 of the 100 largest industrial corporations had changed to LIFO, their change alone reducing reported earnings by approximately $500 million. As noted earlier, the major reason for the shift to LIFO is the tax benefits associated with such a move.

Although no absolute rules can be stated, preferability for LIFO can ordinarily be established if: (1) selling prices and revenues have been increasing, whereas costs have lagged, to such a degree that an unrealistic earnings picture is presented, and (2) in situations where LIFO has been traditional, such as department stores and industries such as refining, chemicals, and glass where a fairly constant "base stock" is present. Conversely, LIFO would probably not be appropriate: (1) where prices tend to lag behind costs; (2) in situations where specific identification is traditional, such as in the sale of automobiles, farm equipment, art, and antique jewelry; and (3) where unit costs tend to decrease as production increases, thereby nullifying the tax benefit that LIFO might provide. Note that where inventory turnover is high, the difference between inventory methods is usually negligible.

It should be noted that switching from FIFO to LIFO usually results in an immediate tax benefit. On the other hand, switching from LIFO to FIFO can result in a substantial tax burden. For example, in 1971 when Chrysler changed from LIFO to FIFO, it became responsible for an additional $53 million in taxes that had been deferred over the preceding 14 years of LIFO inventory valuation. Given that this period (1957–1971) was a period of mild inflation as compared with present inflation rates, it is easy to see the tremendous tax burden a company may face if a switch is made. The major reason why companies like

---

[11] Accounting Research and Terminology Bulletins, Final Edition (New York: AICPA, 1961), Ch. 4, p. 30.

[12] *Accounting Trends and Techniques—1981* reports that of 1,073 inventory method disclosures, 396 used LIFO, 382 used FIFO, 238 used average cost, and 57 used other methods.

Chrysler changed to FIFO in the late 1960s and early 1970s was the profit crunch of that era. For example, although Chrysler showed a loss of $7.6 million dollars after the switch, the loss would have been $20 million more if the company had not changed its inventory valuation back to FIFO from LIFO.

Whether companies should switch from LIFO to FIFO for the sole purpose of increasing reported earnings is questionable. Intuitively one would assume that companies with higher reported earnings would have a higher share (common stock price) valuation. Some studies have indicated, however, that the users of financial data exhibit a much higher sophistication than might be expected and, as a consequence, share prices are the same and, in some cases, even higher under LIFO in spite of lower reported earnings.[13]

The concern about reduced income through adoption of LIFO has even less substance now because the IRS has relaxed the LIFO conformity rule. As indicated earlier, the old LIFO conformity rule required a company that employed LIFO for tax purposes to use LIFO for book purposes as well. In addition, it severely restricted any attempt to provide non-LIFO income numbers as supplementary information. However, the IRS has recently relaxed these requirements. Companies using LIFO are now permitted to present inventory valuation on a basis other than LIFO in the balance sheet, in the notes to the financial statements, and in management's discussion and analysis section. Income, gross profit, or income per share amounts reported on a basis other than LIFO cannot be disclosed on the income statement, but they can be disclosed in the notes or in the discussion and analysis section of the annual report. For example, J. C. Penney, Inc. (a LIFO user) in a recent annual report presented the following information.

| Some companies in the retail industry use the FIFO method in valuing part or all of their inventories. Had J. C. Penney used the FIFO method and made no other assumptions with respect to changes in income resulting therefrom, income and income per share from continuing operations would have been: | | | |
| --- | --- | --- | --- |
| | 1980 | 1979 | 1978 |
| Income from continuing operations (in millions) | $325 | $308 | $295 |
| Income from continuing operations per share | $4.63 | $4.45 | $4.40 |

Relaxation of the LIFO conformity rule will probably lead more companies to select LIFO as their inventory valuation method because companies will be able to disclose FIFO income numbers in the financial reports if they so desire.[14]

Often the inventory methods are used in combination with other methods. For example, most companies never use LIFO totally, but often use it in combination with other valu-

[13]See, for example, Shyam Sunder, "Relationship Between Accounting Changes and Stock Prices: Problems of Measurement and Some Empirical Evidence," *Empirical Research in Accounting: Selected Studies, 1973* (Chicago: University of Chicago), pp. 1–40; but see Robert Moren Brown, "Short-Range Market Reaction to Changes to LIFO Accounting Using Preliminary Earnings Announcement Dates," *Journal of Accounting Research* (Spring 1980), which found that companies that do change to LIFO suffer a short-run decline in the price of their stock.

[14]Note that a company can use one variation of LIFO for financial reporting purposes and another for tax without violating the LIFO conformity rule. Such a relaxation will undoubtedly involve many problems for accountants because the general approach to accounting for LIFO has been "whatever is good for tax is good for financial reporting." As a result, the authoritative accounting literature provides little guidance regarding the LIFO method, and what is available states only the conceptual basis for acceptance without providing implementation guidelines.

ation approaches. The reason for adoption of the average cost method is simply the difficulty of trying to approximate a flow assumption. Some of the other approaches, such as standard costs and base stock, are used infrequently.

This variety of inventory methods has been devised to assist accurate computation of net income rather than to permit manipulation of reported income. Hence, it is recommended that the pricing method most suitable to a company be selected and, once selected, be applied consistently thereafter. If conditions indicate that the inventory pricing method in use is unsuitable, serious consideration should be given to all other possibilities before selecting another method. Any change should be clearly explained and its effect disclosed in the financial statements.

## Inventory Valuation Method—Summary Analysis

A number of inventory valuation methods are described in the preceding sections of this chapter. A brief summary of the three major inventory methods is presented below and on page 366 to show the differing effects these valuation methods have on the financial statements. The first schedule provides selected data for the comparison as follows:

| Selected Data | | |
|---|---|---|
| Given | | |
| Beginning cash balance | | $ 7,000 |
| Beginning retained earnings | | $10,000 |
| Beginning inventory | 4,000 units @ | $ 3 |
| Purchases | 6,000 units @ | $ 4 |
| Sales | 5,000 units @ | $ 12 |
| Operating expenses (40% tax rate) | | $10,000 |

The comparative results of using average cost, FIFO, and LIFO, on net income are computed as follows:

| Comparative Results of Average Cost, FIFO, and LIFO | | | |
|---|---|---|---|
| | Average Cost | FIFO | LIFO |
| Sales | $60,000 | $60,000 | $60,000 |
| Cost of goods sold | 18,000[a] | 16,000[b] | 20,000[c] |
| Gross profit | 42,000 | 44,000 | 40,000 |
| Operating expenses | 10,000 | 10,000 | 10,000 |
| Income before taxes | 32,000 | 34,000 | 30,000 |
| Income taxes (40%) | 12,800 | 13,600 | 12,000 |
| Net income | $19,200 | $20,400 | $18,000 |

[a]4,000 @ $3 = $12,000
6,000 @ $4 = 24,000
$36,000

[b]4,000 @ $3 = $12,000
1,000 @ $4 = 4,000
$16,000

[c]5,000 @ $4 = $20,000

$36,000 ÷ 10,000 = $3.60
$3.60 × 5,000 = $18,000

The table below then shows the final balances of selected items at the end of the period:

| | Inventory | Gross Profit | Taxes | Net Income | Retained Earnings | Cash |
|---|---|---|---|---|---|---|
| | | | | **Balances of Selected Items** | | |
| Average Cost | $18,000 (5,000 × $3.60) | $42,000 | $12,800 | $19,200 | $29,200 ($10,000 + $19,200) | $20,200[a] |
| FIFO | $20,000 (5,000 × $4) | $44,000 | $13,600 | $20,400 | $30,400 ($10,000 + $20,400) | $19,400[a] |
| LIFO | $16,000 (4,000 × $3) (1,000 × $4) | $40,000 | $12,000 | $18,000 | $28,000 ($10,000 + $18,000) | $21,000[a] |

| [a]Cash at year end | = | Beg. balance | + | sales | − | purchases | − | operating expenses | − | taxes |
|---|---|---|---|---|---|---|---|---|---|---|
| Average cost—$20,200 | = | $7,000 | + | $60,000 | − | $24,000 | − | $10,000 | − | $12,800 |
| FIFO—$19,400 | = | $7,000 | + | $60,000 | − | $24,000 | − | $10,000 | − | $13,600 |
| LIFO—$21,000 | = | $7,000 | + | $60,000 | − | $24,000 | − | $10,000 | − | $12,000 |

Note that the use of the LIFO inventory valuation method results in the lower net income but the higher cash balance. However, this example assumes that prices are rising; if prices are decreasing, the opposite effect occurs.

# QUESTIONS

1. In what ways are the inventory accounts of a retailing concern different from those of a manufacturing enterprise?

2. What is the difference between a perpetual inventory and a physical inventory? If a company maintains a perpetual inventory, should its physical inventory at any date be equal to the amount indicated by the perpetual inventory records? Why?

3. Why should inventories be included (a) in a statement of financial position and (b) in the computation of net income?

4. Define "cost" as applied to the valuation of inventories.

5. Where, if at all, should the following items be classified on a balance sheet?
   (a) Raw materials.
   (b) Goods received on consignment.
   (c) Manufacturing supplies.
   (d) Goods out on approval to customers.
   (e) Goods in transit that were recently purchased f.o.b. shipping point.
   (f) Land held by a realty firm for sale.

6. Briefly indicate the arguments pro and con for variable costing. Indicate how each of the following conditions would affect the amounts of net income reported under conventional absorption costing and variable costing.
   (a) Sales and production are in balance at a standard volume.
   (b) Sales exceed production.
   (c) Production exceeds sales.

7. At the balance sheet date the Wiglet Company held title to goods in transit amounting to $48,110. This amount was omitted from the purchases figure for the year and also from the ending inventory. What is the effect of this omission on the net income for the year as calculated when the books are closed? On the company's financial position as shown in its balance sheet? Is materiality a factor in determining whether an adjustment for this item should be made?

8. What is the difference beween variable costing and conventional absorption costing? Is variable costing acceptable for external financial reporting and for income tax purposes? Why?

9. Senbet purchases 300 units of an item at an invoice cost of $2,700. What is the cost per unit? If the goods are shipped f.o.b. shipping point and the freight bill was $300, what is the cost per unit if Senbet pays the freight charges? If these items were bought on 2/10, n/30 terms and the invoice and the freight bill were paid within the 10-day period, what would be the cost per unit?

10. What is a product financing arrangement? How should product financing arrangements be reported in the financial statements?

11. Specific identification is sometimes said to be the ideal method of assigning cost to inventory and to cost of goods sold. Briefly indicate the arguments for and against this method of inventory valuation.

12. First-in, first-out; weighted average; and last-in, first-out methods are often used instead of specific identification for inventory valuation purposes. Compare these methods with the specific identification method, discussing the theoretical propriety of each method in the determination of income and asset valuation.

13. In what respects is the LIFO method of costing inventories similar to the base stock method? In what respects is it dissimilar? Is the base stock method acceptable for either external financial reporting purposes or income tax purposes?

14. What is the LIFO conformity rule? How has the LIFO conformity rule been relaxed?

15. What is the advantage of combining inventory goods into natural groups, or pools? What is the distinction between a LIFO pool and a dollar-value LIFO pool? What are the advantages of a dollar-value LIFO pool?

16. In a recent article that appeared in the *Wall Street Journal,* the phrases "phantom (paper) profits" and "high LIFO profits" through involuntary liquidation were used. Explain these phrases.

17. As compared with the FIFO method of costing inventories, does the LIFO method result in a larger or smaller net income in a period of rising prices? What is the comparative effect on net income in a period of falling prices?

18. What is the dollar-value method of LIFO inventory valuation? What advantage does the dollar-value method have over the quantity method of LIFO inventory valuation? Why will the LIFO inventory costing method and the dollar-value LIFO inventory costing method produce different inventory valuations if the composition of the inventory base changes? What are the similarities and differences between the dollar-value LIFO inventory method and the base stock method?

19. On December 31, 1983, the inventory of Crucible Steel Company amounts to $800,000. During 1984, the company decides to use the dollar-value method of costing inventories. On December 31, 1984, the inventory is $927,500 at December 31, 1984 prices. Using the December 31, 1983, price level of 100 and the December 31, 1984, price level of 106, compute the inventory value at December 31, 1984, under the dollar-value method.

20. Define standard costs. What are the advantages of a standard cost system? Present arguments in support of each of the following three methods of treating standard cost variances (actual costs—standard costs) for purposes of financial reporting:
    (a) They may be carried as deferred charges or credits on the balance sheet.
    (b) They may appear as charges or credits on the income statement.
    (c) They may be allocated between inventories and cost of goods sold.

# CASES

C8-1 Shelly Johnson, the controller for Hitech Enterprises, has recently hired you as assistant controller. She wishes to determine your expertise in the area of inventory accounting and therefore requests that you **answer the following unrelated situations:**

(a) A company is involved in the wholesaling and retailing of automobile tires for foreign cars. Most of the inventory is imported, and it is valued on the company's records at the actual inventory cost plus freight-in. At year-end, the warehousing costs are prorated over cost of goods sold and ending inventory. Are warehousing costs considered to be a product cost or a period cost?

(b) A certain portion of a company's "inventory" is composed of obsolete items. Should obsolete items that are not currently consumed in the production of "goods or services to be available for sale" be classified as part of inventory?

(c) A company purchases airplanes for sale to others. However, until they are sold, the company charters and services the planes. What is the proper way to report these airplanes in the company's financial statements?

(d) A competitor uses standard costs for valuing inventory. Is this permissible?

(e) A company wants to buy coal deposits but does not want the financing for the purchase to be reported on its financial statements. The company therefore establishes a trust to acquire the coal deposits. The company agrees to buy the coal over a certain period of time at specified prices. The trust is able to finance the coal purchase and pay off the loan as it is paid by the company for the minerals. How should this transaction be reported?

(f) A company has decided that part of its inventory is similar to a long-term asset in that a portion must always be available for potential stockout problems. The company therefore decides to use the base stock method of inventory valuation. Is this permissible? Discuss.

C8-2 Max Hillery, an inventory control specialist, is interested in better understanding the accounting for inventories. Although Max understands the more sophisticated computer inventory control systems, he has little knowledge of how inventory cost is determined. In studying the records of Harmon Enterprises which sells normal brand name goods from its own store and on consignment through Darien, Inc., he asks you to answer the following questions.

**Instructions**

    (a) Should Harmon Enterprises include in its inventory normal brand name goods purchased from its suppliers but not yet received if the terms of purchase are f.o.b. shipping point (manufacturer's plant)? Why?

    (b) Should Harmon Enterprises include freight-in expenditures as an inventory cost? Why?

    (c) Harmon Enterprises purchased cooking utensils for sale in the ordinary course of business three times during the current year, each time at a higher price than the previous purchase. What would have been the effect on ending inventory and cost of goods sold had Harmon used the weighted average cost method instead of the FIFO method?

    (d) What are products on consignment? How should they be treated in the financial records?

                                               (AICPA adapted)

**C8-3** Graphic Sales Company has been growing rapidly, but during this period of rapid growth the accounting records have not been properly maintained. You were recently employed to correct the accounting records and to assist in the preparation of the financial statements for the fiscal year ended February 28, 1984. One of the accounts you have been analyzing is entitled "Merchandise." That account in summary form follows. Numbers in parentheses following each entry correspond to related numbered explanations and additional information that you have accumulated during your analysis.

Merchandise

| | | | |
|---|---|---|---|
| Balance, March 1, 1983 | (1) | Merchandise sold | (5) |
| Purchases | (2) | Consigned merchandise | (6) |
| Freight-in | (3) | | |
| Insurance | (4) | | |
| Freight-out on consigned merchandise | (7) | | |
| Freight-out on merchandise sold | (8) | | |

**Explanations and Additional Information**

    **1.** You have satisfied yourself that the March 1, 1983, inventory balance represents the approximate cost of the few units in inventory at the beginning of the year. Graphic employs the FIFO method of accounting for inventories.

    **2.** The merchandise purchased was recorded in the account at the sellers' catalog list price, which is the price appearing on the face of each vendor's invoice. All purchased merchandise is subject to a trade (chain) discount of 20%-10%. These discounts have been accounted for as revenue when the merchandise was paid for.

        All merchandise purchased was also subject to cash terms of 2/15, n/30. During the fiscal year Graphic recorded $3,500 in purchase discounts as revenue when the merchandise was paid for. Some purchase discounts were lost because payment was made after the discount period ended. All purchases of merchandise were paid for in the fiscal year they were recorded as purchased.

    **3.** All merchandise is purchased f.o.b. sellers' business locations. The freight-in amount is the cost of transporting the merchandise from the sellers' business locations to Graphic.

    **4.** The insurance charge is for an all-perils policy to cover merchandise in transit to Graphic from sellers.

    **5.** The credit to this account for merchandise sold represents the sellers' catalog list price of merchandise sold plus the cost of the beginning inventory; the debit side of the entry was made to the cost of goods sold account.

    **6.** Consigned merchandise represents goods that were shipped to M. Burke Co. during January 1984, priced at the sellers' catalog list price. The offsetting debit was made to accounts receivable when the merchandise was shipped to M. Burke Co..

    **7.** The freight-out on consigned goods is the cost of trucking the consigned goods to M. Burke Co. from Graphic.

    **8.** Freight-out on merchandise sold is the amount paid trucking companies to deliver merchandise sold to Graphic's customers.

**Instructions**

Consider each of the eight (8) numbered items independently and explain specifically how and why each item should have (if correctly accounted for) affected

(a) The amount of cost of goods sold to be included in Graphic's earnings statement, and

(b) The amount of any other account to be included in Graphic's February 28, 1984, financial statements.

Organize your answer in the following format:

| Item Number | How and Why the Amount of Cost of Goods Sold Should Have been Affected | How and Why the Amount of Any Other Account Should Have been Affected |
| --- | --- | --- |

**C8–4** In February, 1984, Lumber Products, Inc. requested and secured permission from the Commissioner of Internal Revenue to compute inventories under the last-in, first-out (LIFO) method and elected to determine inventory cost under the dollar-value method. Lumber Products, Inc. satisfied the Commissioner that cost could be accurately determined by use of an index number computed from a representative sample selected from the company's single inventory pool.

**Instructions**

(a) Why should inventories be included in (1) a balance sheet and (2) the computation of net income?

(b) The **Internal Revenue Code** allows some accountable events to be considered differently for income tax reporting purposes and financial accounting purposes, while other accountable events must be reported the same for both purposes. Discuss why it might be desirable to report some accountable events differently for financial accounting purposes than for income tax reporting purposes.

(c) Discuss the ways and conditions under which the FIFO and LIFO inventory costing methods produce different inventory valuations. Do not discuss procedures for computing inventory cost.

(AICPA adapted)

**C8–5** You are asked to travel to Portland to observe and verify the inventory of the Portland branch of one of your clients. You arrive on Thursday, December 30, and find that the inventory procedures have just been started. You note that there is a railway car spotted on the sidetrack at the unloading door and ask the warehouse superintendent Chris Dillman how he plans to inventory the contents of the car. Chris responds: "We are not going to include the contents in the inventory."

Later in the day, you ask the bookkeeper for the invoice on the carload and the related freight bill. The invoice lists the various items, prices, and extensions of the goods in the car. You note that the carload was shipped December 24 from Chicago f.o.b. Chicago, and that the total invoice price of the goods in the car was $30,300. The freight bill called for a payment of $1,150. Terms were net 30 days. The bookkeeper affirms the fact that this invoice is to be held for recording in January.

**Instructions**

(a) Does your client have a liability which should be recorded at December 31? Discuss.

(b) Prepare a journal entry(ies), if required, to reflect any audit adjustment required.

(c) For what possible reason(s) might your client wish to postpone recording the transaction?

**C8–6** Heimerdinger Pipe Co. is a manufacturing business with relatively heavy fixed costs and large inventories of finished goods. These inventories constitute a very material item on the balance sheet. The company has a departmental cost accounting system that assigns all manufacturing costs to the product each period.

Reneé D. Allen, controller of the company, has informed you that the management is giving serious consideration to the adoption of direct costing as a method of accounting for

plant operations and inventory valuation. The management wishes to have your opinion of the effect, if any, that such a change would have on:
(1) the year-end financial position, (2) the net income for the year.

**Instructions**

State your reply to the request and the reasons for your conclusions.

(AICPA adapted)

C8–7 Paula L. Brown, president of Kreidle, Inc. recently read an article that claimed that at least 100 of the country's largest 500 companies were either adopting or considering adopting the last-in, first-out (LIFO) method for valuing inventories. The article stated that the firms were switching to LIFO to (1) neutralize the effect of inflation in their financial statements, (2) eliminate inventory profits, and (3) reduce income taxes. Ms. Brown wonders if the switch would benefit her company.

Kreidle, Inc. currently uses the first-in, first-out (FIFO) method of inventory valuation in its periodic inventory system. The company has a high inventory turnover rate, and inventories represent a significant proportion of the assets.

In discussing this trend toward LIFO inventory with business friends, she has been told that the LIFO system is more costly to operate and will provide little benefit to companies with high turnover. Ms. Brown intends to use the inventory method that is best for the company in the long run rather than selecting a method just because it is the current fad.

**Instructions**

(a) Explain to Ms. Brown what "inventory profits" are and how the LIFO method of inventory valuation could reduce them.
(b) Explain to Ms. Brown the conditions that must exist for Kreidle to receive tax benefits from a switch to the LIFO method.

C8–8 Sanchez Company is a medium-sized manufacturing company with two divisions and three subsidiaries, all located in the United States. The Metallic Division manufactures metal castings for the automotive industry, and the Plastic Division produces small plastic items for electrical products and other uses. The three subsidiaries manufacture various products for other industrial users.

Sanchez Company plans to change from the lower of first-in, first-out (FIFO) cost or market method of inventory valuation to the last-in, first-out (LIFO) method of inventory valuation to obtain tax benefits. To make the method acceptable for tax purposes, the change also will be made for its annual financial statements.

**Instructions**

(a) Describe the establishment of and subsequent pricing procedures for each of the following LIFO inventory methods:
1. LIFO applied to units of product when the periodic inventory system is used.
2. Application of the dollar-value method to LIFO units of product.
(b) Discuss the specific advantages and disadvantages of using the dollar-value LIFO application as compared to traditional LIFO methods. Ignore income tax considerations.
(c) Discuss the general advantages and disadvantages claimed for LIFO methods.

## EXERCISES

E8–1 How would you recommend that the following items be reported on the balance sheet?

(a) Janitorial supplies  _____
(b) Unsold goods in the hands
    of consignees  _____
(c) Raw materials pledged by
    means of warehouse receipts
    on notes payable to bank  _____

(d) Raw materials in transit
from suppliers _____

(e) An allowance to reduce the
inventory cost to market _____

(f) An appropriation of
retained earnings for
possible inventory declines _____

(g) Materials received from
a customer for processing _____

(h) Merchandise produced by
special order and set aside
to be picked up by
customer _____

**E8-2** The net income per books was determined without knowledge of the errors indicated.

| Year | Net Income per Books | Error in Ending Inventory | |
|------|------|------|------|
| 1979 | $41,000 | Overstated | $ 3,000 |
| 1980 | 44,000 | Overstated | 6,000 |
| 1981 | 42,000 | Understated | 10,000 |
| 1982 | 44,600 | No error | |
| 1983 | 43,800 | Understated | 2,000 |
| 1984 | 46,000 | Overstated | 9,000 |

**Instructions**

Prepare a work sheet to show the adjusted net income figure for each of the six years after taking into account the inventory errors.

**E8-3** Two or more items are omitted in each of the following tabulations of income statement data. Fill in the amounts that are missing.

| | 1982 | 1983 | 1984 |
|------|------|------|------|
| Sales | $245,000 | $320,000 | $ _____ |
| Sales Returns | _____ | 7,500 | 12,500 |
| Net Sales | _____ | _____ | 340,000 |
| Beginning Inventory | _____ | 15,000 | _____ |
| Ending Inventory | _____ | _____ | 22,500 |
| Purchases | 119,000 | _____ | 175,000 |
| Purchase Returns and Allowances | 4,000 | 5,000 | 7,500 |
| Transportation-In | 5,000 | 7,000 | 5,000 |
| Cost of Goods Sold | 125,000 | 150,000 | _____ |
| Gross Profit on Sales | 110,000 | _____ | 160,000 |

**E8-4** Penobscot Co. has a calendar-year accounting period. The following errors have been discovered in 1984.

1. The December 31, 1982, merchandise inventory had been understated by $15,000.

2. Merchandise purchased on account during 1983 was recorded on the books for the first time in February 1984, when the original invoice for the correct amount of $2,750 arrived. The merchandise had arrived December 28, 1983 and was included in the December 31, 1983 merchandise inventory. The invoice arrived late because of a mixup on the wholesaler's part.

3. Accrued interest of $315 at December 31, 1983, on notes receivable had not been recorded until the cash for the interest was received in March, 1984.

**Instructions**

    (a) Compute the effect each error had on the 1983 net income.

    (b) Compute the effect, if any, each error had on the December 31, 1983 balance sheet items.

**E8-5** The following purchase transactions occurred during the last few days of Rusty Dunn Company's business year, which ends October 31, or in the first few days after that date. A periodic inventory system is used.

    **1.** An invoice for $2,500, terms f.o.b. shipping point, was received and entered November 1. The invoice shows that the material was shipped October 29, but the receiving report indicates receipt of goods on November 3.

    **2.** An invoice for $1,800, terms f.o.b. destination, was received and entered November 2. The receiving report indicates that the goods were received October 29.

    **3.** An invoice for $2,840, terms f.o.b. shipping point, was received October 15 but never entered. Attached to it is a receiving report indicating that the goods were received October 18. Across the face of the receiving report is the following notation: "Merchandise not of same quality as ordered—returned for credit October 19."

    **4.** An invoice for $3,600, terms f.o.b. shipping point, was received and entered October 27. The receiving report attached to the invoice indicates that the shipment was received October 27 in satisfactory condition.

    **5.** An invoice for $5,100, terms f.o.b. destination, was received and entered October 28. The receiving report indicates that the merchandise was received November 2.

Before preparing financial statements for the year, you are instructed to review these transactions and to determine whether any correcting entries are required and whether the inventory of $77,500 determined by physical count on October 31 should be changed.

**Instructions**

Complete the following schedule, and state the correct inventory at October 31. Assume that the books have not been closed.

| Transaction | Purchase and Related Payable Should be Recognized in (month) | Purchase and Related Payable Were Recognized in (month) | Correcting Journal Entries Needed | Should Inventory Be Included in October Ending Inventory? | Was Inventory Included in October Ending Inventory? | Dollar Adjustments Needed to October Ending Inventory |
|---|---|---|---|---|---|---|
| | | | | | | |

**E8-6** Presented below are the following transactions related to Urbana, Inc.

    May 10   Purchased goods billed at $12,450 subject to cash discount terms of 2/10, n/60.

        11   Purchased goods billed at $9,500 subject to terms of 1/15, n/30.

        19   Paid invoice of May 10.

        22   Purchased goods billed at $9,000 subject to cash discount terms of 2/10, n/30.

**Instructions**

    (a) Prepare general journal entries for the transactions above under the assumption that purchases are to be recorded at net amounts after cash discounts and that discounts lost are to be treated as financial expense.

    (b) Assuming no purchase or payment transactions other than those given above, prepare the adjusting entry required on May 31 if financial statements are to be prepared as of that date.

**E8-7** Peoria Manufacturing Company maintains a general ledger account for each class of inventory, debiting such accounts for increases during the period, and crediting them for decreases. The transactions below relate to the Raw Materials inventory account, which is debited for materials purchased and which is credited for materials requisitioned for use.

1. An invoice for $8,600, terms f.o.b. destination, was received and entered January 2, 1984. The receiving report shows that the materials were received December 28, 1983.

2. Materials costing $32,000, shipped f.o.b. destination, were not entered by December 31, 1983, "because they were in a railroad car on the company's siding on that date and had not been unloaded."

3. Materials costing $3,600 were returned on December 29, 1983, to the creditor, and were shipped f.o.b. shipping point. They were entered on that date, even though they are not expected to reach the creditor's place of business until January 6, 1984.

4. An invoice for $7,300, terms f.o.b. shipping point, was received and entered December 30, 1983. The receiving report shows that the materials were received January 4, 1984, and the bill of lading shows that they were shipped January 2, 1984.

5. Materials costing $18,000 were received December 30, 1983, but no entry was made for them because "they were ordered with a specified delivery of no earlier than January 10, 1984."

**Instructions**

Prepare correcting general journal entries required December 31, 1983, assuming that the books have not been closed.

**E8–8** In an annual audit of Lathe Mfg. Company at December 31, 1984, you find the following transactions near the closing date.

1. A special machine, fabricated to order for a customer, was finished and specifically segregated in the back part of the shipping room on December 31, 1984. The customer was billed on that date and the machine excluded from inventory although it was shipped on January 4, 1985.

2. Merchandise costing $991 was received on January 3, 1985, and the related purchase invoice recorded January 5. The invoice showed the shipment was made on December 29, 1984, f.o.b. destination.

3. Merchandise costing $355 was received on December 28, 1984, and the invoice was not recorded. You located it in the hands of the purchasing agent; it was marked on consignment.

4. A packing case containing a product costing $804 was standing in the shipping room when the physical inventory was taken. It was not included in the inventory because it was marked "Hold for shipping instructions." Your investigation revealed that the customer's order was dated December 18, 1984, but that the case was shipped and the customer billed on January 10, 1985. The product was a stock item of your client.

5. Merchandise received on January 6, 1985, costing $380 was entered in the purchase journal on January 7, 1985. The invoice showed shipment was made f.o.b. supplier's warehouse on December 31, 1984. Because it was not on hand at December 31, it was not included in inventory.

**Instructions**

Assuming that each of the amounts is material, state whether the merchandise should be included in the client's inventory and give your reason for your decision on each item.

**E8–9** The board of directors of Remarkable Computer Corporation is considering whether or not it should instruct the accounting department to shift from a first-in, first-out (FIFO) basis of pricing inventories to a last-in, first-out (LIFO) basis. The following information is available.

| | |
|---|---|
| Sales | 20,000 units @ $50 |
| Inventory Jan. 1 | 4,000 units @ 30 |
| Purchases | 2,000 units @ 30 |
| | 12,000 units @ 33 |
| | 8,000 units @ 35 |
| Inventory Dec. 31 | 6,000 units @ ? |
| Operating expenses | $100,000 |

**Instructions**

Prepare a condensed income statement for the year on both bases for comparative purposes.

**E8-10** The following accounts, among others, appear on the trial balance of the El Paso Corporation at the end of the year 1984:

| | |
|---|---:|
| Raw Materials Inventory 1/1/84 | $ 30,000 |
| Goods in Process Inventory 1/1/84 | 40,000 |
| Finished Goods Inventory 1/1/84 | 50,000 |
| Raw Materials Purchased | 66,000 |
| Direct Labor | 76,000 |
| Manufacturing Overhead | 55,000 |
| Sales | 200,000 |
| General and Administrative Expense | 50,000 |

**Instructions**

Assuming that no other nominal accounts existed, give the adjusting and closing entries that would be made at the end of the year. Inventories on December 31, 1984, are: raw materials, $26,000; goods in process, $36,000; finished goods, $40,000. Ignore income tax effects.

**E8-11** The following is a record of Micro Company's transactions for transistor radios for the month of January, 1984:

| | | |
|---|---|---|
| Jan. 1 | Balance 400 units @ $18.00 | Jan. 10 Sale 300 units @ $28.00 |
| 12 | Purchase 200 units @ $20.00 | 30 Sale 200 units @ $32.00 |
| 28 | Purchase 200 units @ $22.00 | |

(a) Assuming that perpetual inventories are **not** maintained and that a physical count at the end of the month shows 300 units to be on hand, what is the cost of the ending inventory using (1) FIFO? (2) LIFO?

(b) Assuming that perpetual records are maintained and they tie into the general ledger, calculate the ending inventory using (1) FIFO; (2) LIFO.

**E8-12** The Frate Company was formed on December 1, 1982. The following information is available from Frate's inventory records for Product Ply:

| | Units | Unit Cost |
|---|---:|---:|
| January 1, 1983 (beginning inventory) | 800 | $ 9.00 |
| Purchases: | | |
| January 5, 1983 | 1,500 | $10.00 |
| January 25, 1983 | 1,200 | $10.50 |
| February 16, 1983 | 600 | $11.00 |
| March 26, 1983 | 900 | $11.50 |

A physical inventory on March 31, 1983, shows 1,600 units on hand.

**Instructions**

Prepare schedules to compute the ending inventory at March 31, 1983, under each of the following inventory methods:

(a) FIFO.

(b) LIFO.

(c) Weighted average.

(AICPA adapted)

**E8-13** Inventory information for Part 311 of Krummery Corp. discloses the following information for the month of June:

| | | | | | |
|---|---|---|---|---|---|
| June 1: | Balance | 300 units @ $10 | June 10: | Sold | 200 units @ $24 |
| 11: | Purchased | 500 units @ $16 | 23: | Sold | 400 units @ $22 |
| 20: | Purchased | 400 units @ $14 | 27: | Sold | 200 units @ $20 |

**Instructions**

(a) Assuming that the periodic inventory method is used, compute the cost of goods sold and ending inventory under (1) LIFO; (2) FIFO.

(b) Assuming that the perpetual inventory record is kept in dollars, and costs are computed at the time of each withdrawal, what is the value of the ending inventory at LIFO?

(c) Assuming that the perpetual inventory record is kept in dollars, and costs are computed at the time of each withdrawal, what is the gross profit if the inventory is valued at FIFO?

(d) Why is it stated that LIFO usually produces a lower gross profit than FIFO?

**E8–14** Beawinner Sports Shop began operations on January 1, 1984. The following stock record card for footballs was taken from the records at the end of the year.

| Date | Voucher | Terms | Units Received | Unit Invoice Cost | Gross Invoice Amount |
|------|---------|-------|----------------|-------------------|----------------------|
| 1/15 | 10624 | Net 30 | 60 | $16.00 | $ 960.00 |
| 3/15 | 11437 | 1/5, net 30 | 24 | 14.00 | 336.00 |
| 6/20 | 21332 | 1/10, net 30 | 120 | 13.00 | 1,560.00 |
| 9/12 | 27644 | 1/10, net 30 | 84 | 12.00 | 1,008.00 |
| 11/24 | 31269 | 1/10, net 30 | 96 | 11.00 | 1,056.00 |
| | Totals | | 384 | | $4,920.00 |

A physical inventory on December 31, 1984 reveals that 150 footballs were in stock. The bookkeeper informs you that all the discounts were taken. Assume that Beawinner uses the invoice price less discount for recording purchases.

**Instructions**

(a) Compute the 12/31/84 inventory using the FIFO method.

(b) Compute the 1984 cost of goods sold using the LIFO method.

(c) What method would you recommend to the owner to minimize income taxes in 1984, using the inventory information for footballs as a guide?

**E8–15** Pocket Calculator Company's record of transactions for the month of May was as follows:

| Purchases | | Sales | |
|-----------|-----|-------|-----|
| May 1 (balance on hand) | 1,400 @ $5.00 | May 3 | 800 @ $9.00 |
| 4 | 600 @ 5.20 | 9 | 1,000 @ 8.50 |
| 8 | 600 @ 5.20 | 11 | 600 @ 8.20 |
| 13 | 2,000 @ 5.10 | 23 | 1,200 @ 8.60 |
| 21 | 800 @ 5.50 | 27 | 1,600 @ 8.70 |
| 29 | 600 @ 5.60 | | 5,200 |
| | 6,000 | | |

**Instructions**

(a) Assuming that perpetual inventory records are kept in units only, compute the inventory at May 31 using (1) LIFO; (2) average cost.

(b) Assuming that perpetual inventory records are kept in dollars, determine the inventory using (1) FIFO; (2) LIFO.

(c) Compute cost of goods sold assuming periodic inventory procedures and inventory priced at FIFO.

(d) In an inflationary period, which of the following inventory methods (FIFO, LIFO, average cost, or base stock) will show the highest net income?

**E8–16** Rorry Halverson, the vice president of finance of Swimsuit Corporation, a retail company, made two different schedules of gross margin for the first quarter ended March 31, 1984.

These schedules appear below.

| | Sales ($5 per unit) | Cost of Goods Sold | Gross Margin |
|---|---|---|---|
| Schedule 1 | $140,000 | $115,700 | $24,300 |
| Schedule 2 | 140,000 | 116,900 | 23,100 |

The computation of cost of goods sold in each schedule is based on the following data:

| | Units | Cost per Unit | Total Cost |
|---|---|---|---|
| Beginning inventory, January 1 | 10,000 | $4.10 | $41,000 |
| Purchase, January 10 | 8,000 | 4.20 | 33,600 |
| Purchase, January 30 | 5,000 | 4.16 | 20,800 |
| Purchase, February 11 | 7,000 | 4.30 | 30,100 |
| Purchase, March 17 | 12,000 | 4.00 | 48,000 |

Doreen Chase, the president of the corporation, cannot understand how two different gross margins can be computed from the same set of data. As the vice-president of finance you have explained to Ms. Chase that the two schedules are based on different assumptions concerning the flow of inventory costs; i.e., first-in, first-out; and last-in, first-out. Schedules 1 and 2 were not necessarily prepared in this sequence of cost-flow assumptions.

**Instructions**

Prepare two separate schedules computing cost of goods sold and supporting schedules showing the composition of the ending inventory under both cost-flow assumptions.

**E8–17** Presented below is information related to Renae Tolf Company.

| Date | Ending Inventory (End of Year Prices) | Price Index |
|---|---|---|
| December 31, 1981 | $ 72,000 | 100 |
| December 31, 1982 | 117,000 | 130 |
| December 31, 1983 | 150,000 | 150 |
| December 31, 1984 | 105,600 | 120 |
| December 31, 1985 | 99,750 | 105 |
| December 31, 1986 | 81,400 | 110 |

**Instructions**

Compute the ending inventory for Renae Tolf Company for 1981 through 1986 using the dollar-value LIFO method.

**E8–18** The dollar-value LIFO method was adopted by Kevin Meier Company on January 1, 1984. Its inventory on that date was $160,000. On December 31, 1984, the inventory at prices existing on that date amounted to $143,000. The price level at January 1, 1984, was 100, and the price level at December 31, 1984, was 110.

**Instructions**

(a) Compute the amount of the inventory at December 31, 1984, under the dollar-value LIFO method.
(b) On December 31, 1985, the inventory at prices existing on that date was $185,000, and the price level was 125. Compute the inventory on that date under the dollar-value LIFO method.

# PROBLEMS

**P8–1** Layne Corporation, a manufacturer of small tools, provided the following information from its accounting records for the year ended December 31, 1983:

Inventory at December 31, 1983 (based on physical count of goods
  in Layne's plant at cost on December 31, 1983)        $1,750,000
Accounts payable at December 31, 1983        1,200,000
Net sales (sales less sales returns)        8,500,000

Additional information is as follows:

1. Included in the physical count were tools billed to a customer f.o.b. shipping point on December 31, 1983. These tools had a cost of $28,000 and were billed at $35,000. The shipment was on Layne's loading dock waiting to be picked up by the common carrier.

2. Goods were in transit from a vendor to Layne on December 31, 1983. The invoice cost was $50,000, and the goods were shipped f.o.b. shipping point on December 29, 1983.

3. Work-in-process inventory costing $20,000 was sent to an outside processor for plating on December 30, 1983.

4. Tools returned by customers and held pending inspection in the returned goods area on December 31, 1983, were not included in the physical count. On January 8, 1984, the tools costing $26,000 were inspected and returned to inventory. Credit memos totaling $40,000 were issued to the customers on the same date.

5. Tools shipped to a customer f.o.b. destination on December 26, 1983, were in transit at December 31, 1983, and had a cost of $25,000. Upon notification of receipt by the customer on January 2, 1984, Layne issued a sales invoice for $42,000.

6. Goods, with an invoice cost of $30,000, received from a vendor at 5:00 p.m. on December 31, 1983, were recorded on a receiving report dated January 2, 1984. The goods were not included in the physical count, but the invoice was included in accounts payable at December 31, 1983.

7. Goods received from a vendor on December 26, 1983, were included in the physical count. However, the related $60,000 vendor invoice was not included in accounts payable at December 31, 1983, because the accounts payable copy of the receiving report was lost.

8. On January 3, 1984, a monthly freight bill in the amount of $4,000 was received. The bill specifically related to merchandise purchased in December 1983, one-half of which was still in the inventory at December 31, 1983. The freight charges were not included in either the inventory or in accounts payable at December 31, 1983.

### Instructions

Using the format shown below, prepare a schedule of adjustments as of December 31, 1983, to the initial amounts per Layne's accounting records. Show separately the effect, if any, of each of the eight transactions on the December 31, 1983 amounts. If the transactions would have no effect on the initial amount shown, state NONE.

|  | Inventory | Accounts Payable | Net Sales |
|---|---|---|---|
| Initial amounts | $1,750,000 | $1,200,000 | $8,500,000 |
| Adjustments—increase (decrease) |  |  |  |
| 1 |  |  |  |
| 2 |  |  |  |
| 3 |  |  |  |
| 4 |  |  |  |
| 5 |  |  |  |
| 6 |  |  |  |
| 7 |  |  |  |
| 8 |  |  |  |
| Total adjustments |  |  |  |
| Adjusted amounts | $ | $ | $ |

(AICPA adapted)

**P8–2** The Plug Company is a wholesale distributor of automotive replacement parts. Initial amounts taken from Plug's accounting records are as follows:

Inventory at December 31, 1984 (based on physical count of goods in Plug's
warehouse on December 31, 1984)      $1,250,000

Accounts payable at December 31, 1984:

| Vendor | Terms | Amount |
|---|---|---|
| L. Poe Company | 2% 10 days, net 30 | $ 280,000 |
| Joy Corporation | Net 30 | 210,000 |
| Chestnut Company | Net 30 | 300,000 |
| Vanessa Enterprises | Net 30 | 225,000 |
| Firefox Products | Net 30 | — |
| R. Casey Company | Net 30 | — |
| | | $1,015,000 |

Sales in 1984      $9,000,000

Additional information is as follows:

1. Parts received on consignment from Joy Corporation by Plug, the consignee, amounting to $160,000, were included in the physical count of goods in Plug's warehouse on December 31, 1984, and in accounts payable at December 31, 1984.

2. $20,000 of parts that were purchased from Firefox and paid for in December 1984 were sold in the last week of 1984 and appropriately recorded as sales of $28,000. The parts were included in the physical count of goods in Plug's warehouse on December 31, 1984, because the parts were on the loading dock waiting to be picked up by customers.

3. Parts in transit on December 31, 1984, to customers, shipped f.o.b. shipping point, on December 28, 1984, amounted to $34,000. The customers received the parts on January 6, 1985. Sales of $44,000 to the customers for the parts were recorded by Plug on January 2, 1985.

4. Retailers were holding $215,000 at cost ($260,000 at retail), of goods on consignment from Plug, the consignor, at their stores on December 31, 1984.

5. Goods were in transit from Casey to Plug on December 31, 1984. The cost of the goods was $30,000, and they were shipped f.o.b. shipping point on December 29, 1984.

6. A quarterly freight bill in the amount of $2,500 specifically relating to merchandise purchases in December 1984, all of which was still in the inventory at December 31, 1984, was received on January 3, 1985. The freight bill was not included in the inventory or in accounts payable at December 31, 1984.

7. All of the purchases from Poe occurred during the last seven days of the year. These items have been recorded in accounts payable and accounted for in the physical inventory at cost before discount. Plug's policy is to pay invoices in time to take advantage of all cash discounts, adjust inventory accordingly, and record accounts payable, net of cash discounts.

**Instructions**

Prepare a schedule of adjustments to the initial amounts using the format shown on the following page. Show the effect, if any, of each of the transactions separately and if the transactions would have no effect on the amount shown, state **NONE.**

| | Inventory | Accounts Payable | Sales |
|---|---|---|---|
| Initial amounts | $1,250,000 | $1,015,000 | $9,000,000 |
| Adjustments-increase (decrease) | | | |
| 1 | | | |
| 2 | | | |
| 3 | | | |
| 4 | | | |
| 5 | | | |
| 6 | | | |
| 7 | | | |
| Total adjustments | | | |
| Adjusted amounts | $ | $ | $ |

(AICPA adapted)

**P8–3** Some of the transactions of Thorn Bird Company during August are listed below.

August 10   Purchased merchandise on account, $8,000, terms 2/10, n/30.

      13   Returned part of the purchase of August 10, $500, and received credit on account.

      15   Purchased merchandise on account, $12,000, terms 1/10, n/60.

      25   Purchased merchandise on account, $6,000, terms 2/10, n/30.

      28   Paid invoice of August 15 in full.

**Instructions**

(a) Assuming that purchases are recorded at gross amounts and that discounts are to be recorded when taken:
1. Prepare general journal entries to record the transactions.
2. Describe how the various items would be shown in the financial statements.

(b) Assuming that purchases are recorded at net amounts and that discounts lost are treated as financial expenses:
1. Prepare general journal entries to enter the transactions.
2. Prepare the adjusting entry necessary on August 31 if financial statements are to be prepared at that time.
3. Describe how the various items would be shown in the financial statements.

(c) Which of the two methods do you prefer and why?

**P8–4** The books of Dana Bethard Corporation on December 31, 1984, are in agreement with the following balance sheet:

---

Dana Bethard Corporation
BALANCE SHEET AS OF DECEMBER 31, 1984

---

**Assets**

| | |
|---|---|
| Cash | $ 30,000 |
| Accounts and notes receivable | 40,000 |
| Inventory | 80,000 |
| | $150,000 |

**Liabilities and Capital**

| | |
|---|---|
| Accounts and notes payable | $ 24,000 |
| Common stock | 100,000 |
| Retained earnings | 26,000 |
| | $150,000 |

The following errors were made by the corporation on December 31, 1983 and were not corrected: the inventory was overstated $8,000, prepaid expense of $1,500 was omitted, and accrued income of $1,000 was omitted. On December 31, 1984, the inventory was understated $12,000, prepaid expense of $1,200 was omitted, accrued expense of $800 was omitted, and unearned income of $1,400 was omitted.

The net income shown by the books for 1984 was $15,000.

**Instructions**

(a) Compute the corrected net income for 1984.
(b) Prepare a corrected balance sheet for December 31, 1984.

**P8-5** Teddy Bear Manufacturing Company manufactures two products: Andy Panda and Cuddly Cub. At December 31, 1984, Teddy used the first-in, first-out (FIFO) inventory method. Effective January 1, 1985, Teddy changed to the last-in, first-out (LIFO) inventory method. The cumulative effect of this change is not determinable and, as a result, the ending inventory of 1984 for which the FIFO method was used, is also the beginning inventory for 1985 for the LIFO method. Any layers added during 1985 should be costed by reference to the first acquisitions of 1985 and any layers liquidated during 1985 should be considered a permanent liquidation.

The following information was available from Teddy's inventory records for the two most recent years:

| | Andy Panda | | Cuddly Cub | |
|---|---|---|---|---|
| | Units | Unit Cost | Units | Unit Cost |
| **1984 purchases** | | | | |
| January 7 | 5,000 | $4.00 | 22,000 | $2.00 |
| April 16 | 12,000 | 4.50 | | |
| November 8 | 17,000 | 5.50 | 18,500 | 3.00 |
| December 13 | 10,000 | 6.00 | | |
| **1985 purchases** | | | | |
| February 11 | 3,000 | 7.00 | 23,000 | 3.50 |
| May 20 | 8,000 | 7.50 | | |
| October 15 | 20,000 | 8.00 | | |
| December 23 | | | 15,500 | 4.00 |
| **Units on hand** | | | | |
| December 31, 1984 | 15,000 | | 14,500 | |
| December 31, 1985 | 17,000 | | 13,000 | |

**Instructions**

Compute the effect on income before income taxes for the year ended December 31, 1985, resulting from the change from the FIFO to the LIFO inventory method.

(AICPA adapted)

**P8-6** Summarized below are certain quarterly data relative to the Beresford Company. Assume that there was no inventory on hand at the beginning of the first quarter.

|  | Purchases | Sales |
|---|---|---|
| First quarter | 10,000 @ $3.00 | 8,000 @ $3.70 |
|  | 4,000 @ 3.10 | 3,000 @ 3.80 |
| Second quarter | 8,000 @ 3.10 | 5,000 @ 3.90 |
|  | 4,000 @ 3.25 | 4,000 @ 4.00 |
| Third quarter | 9,000 @ 3.30 | 10,000 @ 4.05 |
|  | 4,000 @ 3.40 | 2,000 @ 4.10 |
| Fourth quarter | 5,000 @ 3.40 | 4,000 @ 4.20 |
|  | 8,000 @ 3.50 | 6,000 @ 4.25 |

**Instructions**

(a) Compute the gross profit for the Beresford Company by quarters under each of the following methods of inventory pricing, assuming that inventory costs are determined only at the end of each quarter.
1. First-in, first-out (FIFO).
2. Last-in, first-out (LIFO).
3. Average cost (carry unit costs to the nearest cent).
(b) Evaluate the effect of each of these three methods on gross profit in a period of rising prices as presented above.

**P8-7** Eileen Scudder Company's record of transactions concerning Part 453 for the month of April was as follows:

| **Purchases** |  | **Sales** | |
|---|---|---|---|
| Apr. 1 (balance on hand) | 100 @ $4.00 | Apr. 5 | 300 |
| Apr. 4 | 300 @ 4.10 | Apr. 12 | 200 |
| Apr. 11 | 400 @ 4.00 | Apr. 27 | 800 |
| Apr. 18 | 200 @ 3.80 | Apr. 28 | 100 |
| Apr. 26 | 500 @ 3.50 | | |
| Apr. 30 | 300 @ 3.40 | | |

**Instructions**

(a) Compute the inventory at April 30 on each of the following bases. Assume that perpetual inventory records are kept in units only. Carry unit costs to the nearest cent.
1. First-in, first-out (FIFO).
2. Last-in, first-out (LIFO).
3. Average cost.
(b) If the perpetual inventory record is kept in dollars, and costs are computed at the time of each withdrawal, what amount would be shown as ending inventory in 1, 2, and 3 above? Carry unit costs to the neatest cent.

**P8-8** Here is some of the information found on a detail inventory card for Kurt Reding, Inc. for the first month of operations.

| Date | Received No. of Units | Received Unit Cost | Issued, No. of Units | Balance, No. of Units |
|---|---|---|---|---|
| Jan. 2 | 1,200 | $3.00 | | 1,200 |
| 7 | | | 700 | 500 |
| 10 | 500 | 3.20 | | 1,000 |
| 13 | | | 600 | 400 |
| 18 | 1,500 | 3.20 | 300 | 1,600 |
| 20 | | | 1,000 | 600 |
| 23 | 1,000 | 3.40 | | 1,600 |
| 26 | | | 900 | 700 |
| 28 | 1,500 | 3.50 | | 2,200 |
| 31 | | | 1,200 | 1,000 |

**Instructions**

(a) From these data compute the ending inventory on each of the following bases (assume that perpetual inventory records are kept in units only; carry unit costs to the nearest cent):

1. First-in, first-out (FIFO).
2. Last-in, first-out (LIFO).
3. Average cost.
4. Base stock (assume 500 units at $3.00 to be the base stock with receipts and issues over that figure to be priced on a first-in, first-out basis).

(b) If the perpetual inventory record is kept in dollars, and costs are computed at the time of each withdrawal, would the amounts shown as ending inventory in 1, 2, and 3 above be the same? Explain.

**P8–9** On January 1, 1979, Grover Company changed its inventory cost flow method to the LIFO cost method from the FIFO cost method for its raw materials inventory. The change was made for both financial statement and income tax reporting purposes. Grover uses the multiple-pools approach under which substantially identical raw materials are grouped into LIFO inventory pools; weighted average costs are used in valuing annual incremental layers. The composition of the December 31, 1981, inventory for the Class F inventory pool is as follows:

|  | Units | Weighted Average Unit Cost | Total Cost |
|---|---|---|---|
| Base year inventory—1979 | 9,000 | $10.00 | $ 90,000 |
| Incremental layer—1980 | 3,000 | 11.00 | 33,000 |
| Incremental layer—1981 | 2,000 | 12.50 | 25,000 |
| Inventory, December 31, 1981 | 14,000 | | $148,000 |

Inventory transactions for the Class F inventory pool during 1982 were as follows:

**1.** On March 1, 1982, 4,800 units were purchased at a unit cost of $13.50 for $64,800.

**2.** On September 1, 1982, 7,200 units were purchased at a unit cost of $14.00 for $100,800.

**3.** A total of 15,000 units were used for production during 1982.

The following transactions for the Class F inventory pool took place during 1983:

**1.** On January 10, 1983, 7,500 units were purchased at a unit cost of $14.50 for $108,750.

**2.** On May 15, 1983, 5,500 units were purchased at a unit cost of $15.50 for $85,250.

**3.** On December 29, 1983, 7,000 units were purchased at a unit cost of $16.00 for $112,000.

**4.** A total of 16,000 units were used for production during 1983.

**Instructions**

(a) Prepare a schedule to compute the inventory (units and dollar amounts) of the Class F inventory pool at December 31, 1982. Show supporting computations in good form.

(b) Prepare a schedule to compute the cost of Class F raw materials used in production for the year ended December 31, 1982.

(c) Prepare a schedule to compute the inventory (units and dollar amounts) of the Class F inventory pool at December 31, 1983. Show supporting computations in good form.

(AICPA adapted)

**P8–10** The management of Ron Knutson Wire Company has asked its accounting department to describe the effect upon the company's financial position and its income statements of accounting for inventories on the LIFO rather than the FIFO basis during 1984 and 1985. The accounting department is to assume that the change to LIFO would have been effective on January 1, 1984, and that the initial LIFO base would have been the inventory value on December 31, 1983. Presented below are the company's financial statements and other data for the years 1984 and 1985 when the FIFO method was in fact employed.

| Financial Position as of | 12/31/83 | 12/31/84 | 12/31/85 |
|---|---|---|---|
| Cash | $ 67,700 | $121,300 | $167,050 |
| Accounts receivable | 40,000 | 54,000 | 61,750 |
| Inventory | 69,000 | 75,000 | 87,000 |
| Other assets | 114,000 | 114,000 | 114,000 |
| Total assets | $290,700 | $364,300 | $429,800 |
| Accounts payable | $ 23,000 | $ 30,000 | $ 36,400 |
| Other liabilities | 40,000 | 40,000 | 40,000 |
| Common stock | 140,000 | 140,000 | 140,000 |
| Retained earnings | 87,700 | 154,300 | 213,400 |
| Total equities | $290,700 | $364,300 | $429,800 |

| Income for Years Ended | 12/31/84 | 12/31/85 |
|---|---|---|
| Sales | $540,000 | $617,500 |
| Less: Cost of goods sold | $294,000 | $365,000 |
| Other expenses | 135,000 | 154,000 |
| | $429,000 | $519,000 |
| Net income before income taxes | $111,000 | $ 98,500 |
| Income taxes (40%) | 44,400 | 39,400 |
| Net income | $ 66,600 | $ 59,100 |

Other data:
1. Inventory on hand at 12/31/83 consisted of 30,000 units valued at $2.30 each
2. Sales (all units sold at the same price in a given year):
   1984—120,000 units @ $4.50 each    1985—130,000 units @ $4.75 each
3. Purchases (all units purchased at the same price in given year):
   1984—120,000 units @ $2.50 each    1985—130,000 units @ $2.90 each
4. Income taxes at the effective rate of 40 percent are paid on December 31 each year.

**Instructions**

Name the account(s) presented in the financial statement that would have different amounts for 1985 if LIFO rather than FIFO had been used and state the new amount for each account that is named. Show computations.

(CMA adapted)

**P8-11** Presented below is information related to P. Harbecke Corp. for the last three years:

| Item | Quantities in Ending Inventories | Base-Year Cost Unit Cost | Base-Year Cost Amount | Current Year Cost Unit Cost | Current Year Cost Amount |
|---|---|---|---|---|---|
| December 31, 1982 | | | | | |
| A | 10,000 | $1.00 | $10,000 | $1.20 | $12,000 |
| B | 2,000 | 2.00 | 4,000 | 2.50 | 5,000 |
| C | 1,000 | 5.00 | 5,000 | 5.80 | 5,800 |
| | | TOTALS | $19,000 | | $22,800 |
| December 31, 1983 | | | | | |
| A | 9,200 | $1.00 | $ 9,200 | $1.30 | $11,960 |
| B | 3,000 | 2.00 | 6,000 | 2.67 | 8,010 |
| C | 800 | 5.00 | 4,000 | 6.25 | 5,000 |
| | | TOTALS | $19,200 | | $24,970 |

December 31, 1984

| | | | | | |
|---|---|---|---|---|---|
| A | 8,000 | $1.00 | $ 8,000 | $1.40 | $11,200 |
| B | 2,400 | 2.00 | 4,800 | 2.75 | 6,600 |
| C | 1,600 | 5.00 | 8,000 | 7.20 | 11,520 |
| | | TOTALS | $20,800 | | $29,320 |

**Instructions**

Compute the ending inventories under the dollar-value method as illustrated in the textbook for 1982, 1983, and 1984. The base period is January 1, 1982 and the beginning inventory cost at that date was $18,000. Compute indexes to two decimal places.

**P8–12** As the controller of Nessinger Farms, Inc., a retail company, you made three different schedules of gross margin for the third quarter ended September 30, 1984. These schedules appear below.

| | Sales ($10 per Unit) | Cost of Goods Sold | Gross Margin |
|---|---|---|---|
| Schedule A | $560,000 | $234,700 | $325,300 |
| Schedule B | 560,000 | 233,386 | 326,614 |
| Schedule C | 560,000 | 231,030 | 328,970 |

The computation of cost of goods sold in each schedule is based on the following data:

| | Units | Cost per Unit | Total Cost |
|---|---|---|---|
| Beginning inventory, July 1 | 10,000 | $4.00 | $ 40,000 |
| Purchase, July 25 | 15,000 | 4.20 | 63,000 |
| Purchase, August 15 | 33,000 | 4.13 | 136,290 |
| Purchase, September 5 | 6,000 | 4.30 | 25,800 |
| Purchase, September 25 | 20,000 | 4.25 | 85,000 |

Tom Nessinger, president of the corporation, cannot understand how three different gross margins can be computed from the same set of data. As controller, you have explained that the three schedules are based on three different assumptions concerning the flow of inventory costs, i.e., first-in, first-out; last-in, first-out; and weighted average. Schedules A, B, and C were not necessarily prepared in this sequence of cost-flow assumptions.

**Instructions**

Prepare three separate schedules computing cost of goods sold and supporting schedules showing the composition of the ending inventory under each of the three cost-flow assumptions.

**P8–13** Austermiller Company cans two food commodities that it stores at various warehouses. The company employs a perpetual inventory accounting system under which the finished goods inventory is charged with production and credited for sales at standard cost. The detail of the finished goods inventory is maintained on punched cards by the tabulating department in units and dollars for the various warehouses.

Company procedures call for the accounting department to receive copies of daily production reports and sales invoices. Units are then extended at standard cost and a summary of the day's activity is posted to the Finished Goods Inventory general ledger control account. Next the sales invoices and production reports are sent to the tabulating department for processing. Every month the control account and detailed tab records are reconciled and adjustments recorded. The last reconciliation and adjustments were made at November 30, 1984.

Your CPA firm, Tick & Check, observed the taking of the physical inventory at all locations on December 31, 1984. The inventory count began at 3:00 P.M. and was completed at 8:00 P.M. The company's figure for the physical inventory is $323,550. The general ledger control account balance at December 31 was $381,200 and the final "tab" run of the inventory punched cards showed a total of $395,800.

Unit cost data for the company's two products are as follows:

| Product | Standard Cost |
|---------|---------------|
| A | $3.00 |
| B | 4.00 |

A review of December transactions disclosed the following:

1. Sales invoice #1603, 12/2/84, was priced at standard cost for $12,100 but was listed on the accounting department's daily summary at $11,200.

2. A production report for $23,900, 12/15/84, was processed twice in error by the tabulating department.

3. Sales invoice #1481, 12/9/84, for 1,200 units of product A, was priced at a standard cost of $1.50 per unit by the accounting department. The tabulating department noticed and corrected the error but did not notify the accounting department of the error.

4. A shipment of 3,400 units of product A was invoiced by the billing department as 3,000 units on sales invoice #1703, 12/27/84. The error was discovered by your review of transactions.

5. On December 27 the Memphis warehouse notified the tabulating department to remove 2,200 unsalable units of product A from the finished goods inventory, which it did without receiving a special invoice from the accounting department. The accounting department received a copy of the Memphis warehouse notification on December 29 and made up a special invoice that was processed in the normal manner. The units were not included in the physical inventory.

6. A production report for the production on January 3 of 2,500 units of product B was processed for the Omaha plant as of December 31.

7. A shipment of 300 units of product B was made from the Portland warehouse to Bill's Markets, Inc. at 8:30 P.M. on December 31 as an emergency service. The sales invoice was processed as of December 31. The client prefers to treat the transactions as a sale in 1984.

8. The working papers of the auditor observing the physical count at the Chicago warehouse revealed that 600 units of product B were omitted from the client's physical count. The client concurred that the units were omitted in error.

9. A sales invoice for 500 units of product A shipped from the Newark warehouse was mislaid and was not processed until January 5. The units involved were shipped on December 30.

10. The physical inventory of the St. Louis warehouse excluded 350 units of product A that were marked "reserved." Upon investigation it was ascertained that this merchandise was being stored as a convenience for Beu's Grocery, a customer. This merchandise, which has not been recorded as a sale, is billed as it is shipped.

11. A shipment of 10,000 units of product B was made on December 27 from the Newark warehouse to the Chicago warehouse. The shipment arrived on January 6 but had been excluded from the physical inventories.

## Instructions

Prepare a work sheet to reconcile the balances for the physical inventory, Finished Goods Inventory general ledger control account, and tabulating department's detail of finished goods inventory ("Tab Run").

The following format is suggested for the work sheet.

| | Physical Inventory | General Ledger Control Account | Tabulating Department's Detail of Inventory |
|---|---|---|---|
| Balance per client | $323,550 | $381,200 | $395,800 |

(AICPA adapted)

# CHAPTER 9

# Inventories: Additional Valuation Problems

In Chapter 8, different methods for computing the unit cost for inventories were explained by examining the various flow assumptions used in accounting. Other possibilities will be explored now. For example, what happens if the value of the inventory increases or decreases after the initial purchase date? Does the accountant recognize these increases or decreases in value before the point of sale? What happens if there is a fire and a physical count cannot be made? How does the accountant determine the ending inventory for insurance purposes? Or, what happens in large department stores where monthly inventory figures are needed, but monthly physical counts are not feasible?

These questions involve the development and use of estimation techniques to value the ending inventory without a physical count. Estimation methods that are widely used are discussed in this chapter.

## LOWER OF COST OR MARKET

A major departure from adherence to the historical cost principle is made in the area of inventory valuation. If the inventory declines in value below its original cost for whatever reason (for example, obsolescence, price-level changes, or damaged goods), the inventory should be written down to reflect this loss. **The general rule is that the historical cost principle is abandoned when the future utility (revenue-producing ability) of the asset is no longer as great as its original cost.** A departure from cost is justified on the basis that a loss of utility should be reflected as a charge against the revenues in the period in which it occurs. Inventories are valued therefore on the basis of the lower of cost or market instead of on an original cost basis. The term **"market"** in the phrase "the lower of cost or market" generally means the cost to replace the item (by purchase or reproduction). "Market," however, is limited to an amount that should not exceed the net realizable value (that is, estimated selling price in the ordinary course of business less reasonably predictable costs of completion and disposal) and "should not be less than net realizable value reduced by an allowance for an approximately normal profit margin."[1]

---

[1]"Restatement and Revision of Accounting Research Bulletins," *Accounting Research Bulletin No. 43* (New York: AICPA, 1953), Ch. 4, par. 8.

Basically the accountant determines the replacement cost of the inventory, and when it is lower than cost, uses that valuation for pricing the inventory unless it either exceeds net realizable value or is less than net realizable value less a normal profit margin. These concepts are illustrated below.

| | |
|---|---:|
| Inventory—sales value | $1,000 |
|     Less: Estimated cost of completion and disposal | 300 |
| Net realizable value | 700 |
|     Less: Allowance for normal profit margin (10% of sales) | 100 |
| Net realizable value less normal profit margin | $  600 |

## How Lower of Cost or Market Works

The lower of cost or market rule requires that the inventory be valued at cost unless "market" is lower than cost, in which case the inventory is valued at "market." In retailing, **the term "market" as used in this rule refers to the market in which the goods were purchased, not the market in which they are sold; in manufacturing, the term refers to the cost to reproduce.** Thus the rule really means that goods are to be valued at cost or cost to replace, whichever is lower. For example, material that cost $1.00 a unit when purchased, which can now be sold for $1.15, and which can be replaced for $0.90, should be priced at $0.90 for inventory purposes under the lower of cost or market rule.

To understand the rationale for the use of replacement cost, assume that a buyer and seller are negotiating on the price of a unit of merchandise and agree that the regular selling price should be reduced. It would seem logical that the replacement cost of that unit of merchandise either has decreased or will decrease because the expected revenue-producing ability of that unit has been reduced. In attempting to measure the decrease in value of the unit of merchandise, the accountant employs replacement cost, because changes in replacement cost usually reflect or predict a decline in selling price and they are easy to identify. Therefore, to insure that the company continues to obtain the same rate of gross profit margin, the inventory is reduced to replacement cost.

Note that in some cases replacement cost and selling price might not move together; therefore, additional safeguards are needed to insure that a proper inventory value is obtained. Thus **"market" is further limited to an amount that "should not exceed the net realizable value** (that is, estimated selling price in the ordinary course of business less reasonably predictable costs of completion and disposal)" **and "should not be less than net realizable value reduced by an allowance for an approximately normal profit margin."** These restrictions cover rather unusual circumstances or cases. The first, "not to exceed the net realizable value (ceiling)," covers obsolete, damaged, or shopworn material. For example, an item that cost $1.00 when purchased, and that could be replaced for $0.90, may have a realizable value of only $0.70 because it is becoming obsolete. In this case, the item is priced at $0.70 for inventory purposes because to price the inventory at replacement cost would be an overstatement of the value of that item.

The second limitation, "not be less than net realizable value reduced by an allowance for an approximately normal profit margin," is a deterrent to serious understatement of inventory. In effect, it establishes a floor or minimum below which the inventory should not be priced regardless of replacement costs. For example, assume that an inventory item that originally cost $1.00 has a replacement cost of only $0.75. Because of firm sales contracts at firm prices, this item will be sold at $1.15 per unit; however, the net realizable value after deducting the normal profit margin will be $0.90 per unit. In this case the item would be priced in the inventory at $0.90 per unit.

Note that the appropriate market value (replacement cost, net realizable value, or net realizable value less a normal markup) should first be designated and then the **designated market value** should be compared with cost as determined by an acceptable historical cost method. Note that the "designated market value" is always the middle value of: replacement cost, net realizable value, or net realizable value less a normal markup. The following cases illustrate how the inventory value is determined under the lower of cost or market approach.

| | | **Illustration of Lower of Cost or Market Approach** | | | |
| | | Market | | | |
| Case | Cost | Replacement Cost | Net Realizable Value | Net Realizable Value Less a Normal Markup | Final Inventory Value |
|---|---|---|---|---|---|
| 1 | $1.00 | $1.10 | $1.50 | $1.20 | $1.00 |
| 2 | 1.00 | .90 | 1.00 | .70 | .90 |
| 3 | 1.00 | .95 | .80 | .56 | .80 |
| 4 | 1.00 | .40 | .80 | .56 | .56 |
| 5 | 1.00 | 1.05 | .95 | .80 | .95 |

**CASE 1.** Cost selected because it is lower than designated market.

**CASE 2.** Replacement cost selected because it is lower than cost and within the constraints imposed by the rule.

**CASE 3.** Net realizable value (ceiling) selected because replacement cost, while lower than cost, is higher than net realizable value. Future utility is limited to net realizable value.

**CASE 4.** Net realizable value less a normal margin (floor) is selected because replacement cost is below this figure, which is the lower constraint for market.

**CASE 5.** Net realizable value (ceiling) is selected because replacement cost is above this upper constraint. Cost is not selected because it is higher than designated market.

Only losses in inventory value that occur in the normal course of business from such causes as style changes, shift in demand, or regular shop wear result from the application of the lower of cost or market rule. Damaged and deteriorated goods are reduced to net realizable value; such goods are carried in separate inventory accounts when significant in amount.

## Recording "Market" Instead of Cost

In those cases in which "market" rather than cost is used as the inventory price, many accountants consider it undesirable accounting procedure merely to substitute the replacement cost figure for cost when pricing the new inventory. This procedure increases the cost of goods sold by the difference between cost and market and thus fails to reflect this loss separately. This objection may be overcome by first determining and recording the inventory at cost in the adjusting or closing process and then making a separate entry to reduce the inventory to market. For a situation in which the inventory cost $82,000 but which must be reduced to $70,000 under the lower of cost or market rule, the entries are:

| | | |
|---|---|---|
| Inventory | 82,000 | |
| Cost of Goods Sold (Income Summary) | | 82,000 |
| (To record inventory for the year) | | |
| | | |
| Loss Due to Market Decline of Inventory | 12,000 | |
| Inventory | | 12,000 |
| (To write down inventory to market) | | |

The loss is then shown as a separate item in the income statement, but not as an extraordinary item, and the cost of the sales for the year is not distorted by its inclusion. Also, the rate of gross profit for the year is not affected by the loss due to market decline.

The advantage of recording a market decline in this manner is indicated in the following comparison.

---

**Inventory Priced at Market**

| | | |
|---|---|---|
| Sales | | $200,000 |
| Cost of goods sold | | |
| Inventory Jan. 1 | $ 65,000 | |
| Purchases | 125,000 | |
| Goods available | 190,000 | |
| Inventory Dec. 31 (at market which is lower than cost) | 70,000 | |
| Cost of goods sold | | 120,000 |
| Gross profit on sales | | $ 80,000 |

**Inventory Priced at Cost and Reduced to Market by Separate Journal Entry**

| | | |
|---|---|---|
| Sales | | $200,000 |
| Cost of goods sold | | |
| Inventory Jan. 1 | $ 65,000 | |
| Purchases | 125,000 | |
| Goods available | 190,000 | |
| Inventory Dec. 31 (at cost) | 82,000 | |
| Cost of goods sold | | 108,000 |
| Gross profit on sales | | 92,000 |
| Loss due to market decline of inventory | | 12,000 |
| | | $ 80,000 |

---

The second presentation is preferable, because it clearly discloses the loss resulting from the market decline of inventory prices, which is "buried" in the cost of goods sold figure in the first presentation. Although this presentation is preferred to direct pricing of the inventory at market because the loss due to market decline is shown separately, it does include an inconsistency: the inventory is shown at $82,000 in the income statement but it is included in the balance sheet at only $70,000. In overcoming this inconsistency, some accountants have advocated the use of a special account to receive the credit for such an inventory write-down. Instead of the inventory account being credited directly, the entries to write down the inventory from cost to the lower of cost or market are modified as follows:

| | | |
|---|---|---|
| Inventory | 82,000 | |
| Cost of Goods Sold (Income Summary) | | 82,000 |
| (To record inventory for the year) | | |

| | | |
|---|---|---|
| Loss Due to Market Decline of Inventory | 12,000 | |
| Reduction of Inventory to Market | | 12,000 |
| (To write down inventory to market) | | |

The Reduction of Inventory to Market (contra asset) would be reported on the balance sheet as a deduction from the inventory of $82,000, thereby reducing it to the lower of cost or market. This deduction permits both the income statement and the balance sheet to show the amount of $82,000, although the inventory extension in the balance sheet is a net amount of $70,000. It also keeps subsidiary inventory ledgers and records in correspondence with the control account without changing unit prices.

Although this device permits disclosure on the balance sheet of the amount of inventory both at cost and at the lower of cost or market, it raises the additional problem of how to dispose of the balance of the new account in the following period. If the merchandise in question is still on hand, the account may be retained, but if it is assumed that the goods that suffered the decline have been sold, this account should be removed from the books. Because the inventory account is currently stated at cost, the beginning inventory and thus the cost of goods sold in the next period are overstated if the allowance balance is not closed. **Closing the allowance account against beginning inventory** (or to Cost of Goods Sold if beginning inventory has already been removed from the accounts) **corrects the misstatement.** A "new" allowance account is then established for the decline in inventory value that has taken place in the current period. Another possibility justified on the basis that the item is immaterial is to close the allowance account to the Income Summary account.

**Some accountants leave this account on the books and merely adjust the balance at the next year end to agree with the discrepancy between cost and the lower of cost or market at that balance sheet date.** Thus, if prices are falling, a loss is recorded and if prices are increasing, a loss recorded in prior years is recovered and a gain is recorded, as illustrated in the example below.

| Date | Inventory at Cost | Inventory at Market | Amount Required in Valuation Account | Adjustment of Valuation Account Balance | Effect on Net Income |
|---|---|---|---|---|---|
| Dec. 31, 1981 | $188,000 | $176,000 | $12,000 | $12,000 inc. | Loss |
| Dec. 31, 1982 | 194,000 | 187,000 | 7,000 | 5,000 dec. | Gain |
| Dec. 31, 1983 | 173,000 | 174,000 | 0 | 7,000 dec. | Gain |
| Dec. 31, 1984 | 182,000 | 180,000 | 2,000 | 2,000 inc. | Loss |

This net "gain" can be thought of as the excess of the credit effect of closing the beginning allowance balance over the debit effect of setting up the current year-end allowance account. Recognition of gain or loss has the same effect on net income as closing the allowance balance to beginning inventory or to cost of goods sold.

This discussion indicates some of the basic presentation problems surrounding the lower of cost or market approach. It also illustrates the complications that arise when deviations are made from basic accounting theory. To the alert student of business one conclusion seems inevitable. As long as a number of treatments and practices are followed, real understanding of accounting reports requires some knowledge of all the possibilities and their effect on the reported data.

## Methods of Applying Cost or Market

The cost or market rule may be "applied either directly to each item or to the total of the inventory (or, in some cases, to the total of the components of each major category). The method should be the one that most clearly reflects periodic income."[2] Ordinarily the application of the rule to the total of the inventory, or to the total components of each major category, results in an amount that more nearly approaches cost than it would if the rule were applied to each item. Under the first two methods, increases in market prices offset, to some extent, the decreases in market prices, as illustrated below.

| | Cost | Market | Lower of Cost or Market by: Individual Items | Lower of Cost or Market by: Major Categories | Lower of Cost or Market by: Total Inventory |
|---|---|---|---|---|---|
| Radios | | | | | |
| Type A | $ 800 | $ 750 | $ 750 | | |
| B | 1,500 | 1,600 | 1,500 | | |
| C | 900 | 800 | 800 | | |
| Total | 3,200 | 3,150 | | $ 3,150 | |
| TV Sets | | | | | |
| Type X | 3,000 | 3,400 | 3,000 | | |
| Y | 4,500 | 4,300 | 4,300 | | |
| Z | 2,000 | 1,900 | 1,900 | | |
| Total | 9,500 | 9,600 | | 9,500 | |
| Total Inventory | $12,700 | $12,750 | $12,250 | $12,650 | $12,700 |

If the lower of cost or market rule is applied to individual items, the amount of inventory is $12,250. If applied to major categories, it is $12,650 and, if applied to the total inventory, it is $12,700.

The most common practice is to price the inventory on an item-by-item basis. Companies favor the individual item approach because tax rules require that an individual item basis be used unless it involves practical difficulties. In addition, the individual item approach gives the most conservative valuation for balance sheet purposes.[3]

Whichever method is selected, it should be applied consistently from one period to the next. **As soon as the inventory is written down to market, this new basis is considered to be the cost basis for future periods.** A rise in the market prices of the inventory after it has been written down generally should not be recognized.[4]

[2]*Accounting Research Bulletin No. 43, op. cit.*, par. 10.

[3]Note that marketable equity securities illustrated in Chapter 7 use the aggregate cost or market approach; the item by item or variant thereof is not permitted.

[4]Accounting for financial statement purposes can be different than accounting for income tax purposes in the area of inventories. For example, the lower of cost or market rule cannot be used with LIFO for tax purposes. There is nothing, however, to prevent the use of the lower of cost or market and LIFO for financial accounting purposes. In addition, for financial accounting purposes, companies often write down slow-moving inventory because experience indicates that some of it will not be sold for many years, if at all. However, to be deductible for tax purposes a writedown in inventory value resulting from the application of lower of cost or market rule can be taken only in the year in which the actual decline in the sale prices of the item occurs, and the writedown must be computed

## Evaluation of Lower of Cost or Market Rule

Conceptually, the lower of cost or market rule has some deficiencies. First, if the inventory is written down because of a loss in utility, does it not seem appropriate to write up the value of the inventory when the utility of the asset increases? Decreases in the value of the asset and the charge to expense are recognized in the period in which the loss in utility occurs—not in the period of sale. On the other hand, increases in the value of the asset are recognized only at the point of sale. This situation is inconsistent and can lead to distortions in the presentation of income data.

Even if we accept this inconsistency, another problem arises in defining market. **Basically, three different types of valuation can be used: replacement cost, net realizable value, and net realizable value less a normal markup.** Replacement cost was chosen as the initial value to employ because changes in replacement cost usually reflect or predict declines in the selling price, and changes in replacement cost are easy to identify. Sometimes, however, a reduction in the replacement cost of an item does not indicate a corresponding reduction in the utility of the item. To illustrate, assume that a retailer has several shirts that were bought at $8.00 per shirt. The replacement cost of these shirts falls to $7.80, but the selling price remains the same. Has the retailer suffered a loss? To recognize a loss in this period misstates this year's income and also that of future periods, because when the shirts are sold subsequently, the full price for the shirts is received.

The second valuation approach—net realizable value—is the most logical method for valuing inventory. The net realizable value reflects the future service potential of the asset and, for that reason, it is conceptually sound. Unfortunately, net realizable value cannot often be measured with any certainty. Therefore, we revert to replacement cost, because net realizable value less a normal markup is even more uncertain than net realizable value. With net realizable value less a normal markup, for example, we face the difficult problem of determining a normal profit. In addition, under this approach a large loss occurs in one period, yet part of this loss is booked as profit in a future period. To illustrate, assume that an item costing $10 has a net realizable value of $8.00 and that the normal markup is 30% of the cost price. Those who use net realizable value simply indicate that a loss of $2.00 occurs ($10 − $8.00); those who advocate net realizable value less a normal markup show a loss of $5.00 ($10 − [$8.00 − $3.00]) and then later record a gain of $3.00 ($8.00 −

---

on an individual item basis rather than on classes of inventory or on the inventory as a whole. The important tax case *Thor Power Tool Company* v. *Commissioner of Internal Revenue* provides guidelines. In this case, the IRS negated Thor's practice of writing down the value of its spare parts inventory which it held to cover future warranty commitments. Thor contended that, although the sales price on the individual parts did not decline over the years, the probability of all the parts being sold decreased as time passed, and thus so did the net realizable value of the inventory as a whole. The IRS contended that a decline in inventory values for tax purposes must await actual decline in the sales price of the individual parts. The Supreme Court indicated that for tax purposes, the lower of cost or market method was to be applied on an individual item basis and that if no decline in sales price occurred, no loss should be permitted. The Court did indicate that for financial accounting purposes, the write-down to lower of cost or market for the parts inventory is consistent with the accounting principle of matching current costs and revenues.

The importance of the Thor Tool case should not be underestimated. Many businesses that maintain large inventories over extended periods of time, such as book publishers and auto and applicance replacement part distributors, are complaining that they may be forced to destroy their inventory to receive their tax deductions. Such a situation then would lead to less inventory of old books and replacement parts.

$5.00), assuming the item is sold for $8.00. The purpose of the latter approach is to show a normal profit margin in the period of sale.

From the standpoint of accounting theory there is little to justify the lower of cost or market rule. Although conservative from the balance sheet point of view, it permits the income statement to show a larger net income in future periods than would be justified if the inventory were carried forward at cost. The rule is applied only in those cases where strong evidence indicates that market declines in inventory prices have occurred that will result in losses when such inventories are disposed of. Net realizable value and not replacement cost appears to be the appropriate basis of valuation in these circumstances.[5]

## PURCHASE ORDERS AND CONTRACTS

Usually it is neither necessary nor proper for the buyer to make any entries to reflect commitments for purchases of goods that have not been shipped by the seller. Ordinary orders, for which the prices are determined at the time of shipment and **which are subject to cancellation** by the buyer or seller, do not represent either an asset or a liability to the buyer and need not be reported in the books or in the financial statements.

Formal purchase contracts for which a firm price has been established, however, if of material amount, should be disclosed in the balance sheet of the buyer by means of a footnote. The following is such a footnote.

---

Note 1. Contracts for the purchase of raw materials in 1984 have been executed in the amount of $600,000. The market price of such raw materials on December 31, 1983, is $640,000.

---

In the foregoing illustration we assumed that the contracted price was less than the market price at the date of the balance sheet. If the contracted price is in excess of the purchase market price and it is expected that losses will occur when the purchase is effected, losses should be recognized in the accounts in the period during which such declines in prices take place.[6] For example, if purchase contracts for delivery in 1984 have been executed at a firm price of $800,000 and the market price of the materials on December 31, 1983 is $750,000, the following entry is made:

| | | |
|---|---|---|
| Loss on Purchase Commitments | 50,000 | |
|   Accrued Loss on Purchase Commitments | | 50,000 |

This loss would be closed out to Income Summary and shown on the income statement; the Accrued Loss on Purchase Commitments is shown in the liability section of the balance sheet. When the goods are delivered in 1984, the entry will be:

[5] *Accounting Research Study No. 13*, "The Accounting Basis of Inventories" (New York: AICPA, 1973) recommends that net realizable value be adopted. It also should be noted that a literal interpretation of the rules of lower of cost or market is frequently not applied in practice. For example, the lower limit, net realizable value less a normal markup, is rarely computed and applied because it results in an extremely conservative inventory valuation approach. In addition, inventory is often not reduced to market unless its disposition is expected to result in a loss. Furthermore, if the net realizable value of finished goods exceeds cost, it is usually assumed that both work in process and raw materials do as well. In practice, therefore, *ARB No. 43* is considered a guide, and professional judgment is often exercised in lieu of following this pronouncement literally.

[6] *Accounting Research Bulletin No. 43, op. cit.,* par. 16.

| | | |
|---|---|---|
| Purchases | 750,000 | |
| Accrued Loss on Purchase Commitments | 50,000 | |
| Accounts Payable | | 800,000 |

This procedure represents a departure from the basic theory that assets should be accounted for on a basis of cost. Those who advocate this procedure contend that the desirability of recognizing the loss in the period during which the price decline takes place justifies departing from the cost principle.

If the price is partially or fully recovered before the inventory is received, the Accrued Loss on Purchase Commitments would be reduced. A resulting gain would then be reported in the period of the price increase for the amount of the partial or full recovery. Accounting for purchase commitments (and for that matter all commitments) is controversial. Some argue that these contracts should be reported as assets and liabilities at the time the contract is signed; others believe that our present recognition at the delivery date is most appropriate. It is hoped that the conceptual framework will provide additional guidance in this area.[7]

## VALUATION AT SELLING PRICE

Under certain circumstances, support exists for **recording inventory at selling price less estimated costs to complete and sell.** For example, an exception to the normal recognition rule is permitted where (1) there is a controlled market with a fixed price applicable to all quantities and (2) no significant costs of disposal are involved. Inventories of certain minerals, for example, are ordinarily reflected at selling prices because there is often a controlled market without significant costs of disposal. A similar treatment is given agricultural products that are immediately marketable at fixed prices.

Another reason for allowing this method of valuation is that often the cost figures are too difficult to obtain. Meat packing provides a classic illustration. In a manufacturing plant, various raw materials and purchased parts are put together to create a finished product. Because the cost of each individual component part is known, the various items in inventory, whether completely or partially finished, can be accounted for on a basis of cost as required by basic theory. In a meat-packing house a different situation prevails. The "raw material" consists of cattle, hogs, or sheep, each unit of which is purchased as a whole and then divided into parts that are the products. Instead of one product out of many parts, many products are made from one "unit" of raw material. To allocate the cost of the animal "on the hoof" into the cost of ribs, chucks, and shoulders, for instance, is a practical impossibility. It is much easier and more useful to determine the market price of the various products and value them in the inventory at selling price less the various costs, such as shipping and handling, necessary to get them to market. Hence, because of a peculiarity of the industry, **inventories are sometimes carried at sales price less distribution costs in the meat-packing industry.** The same type of problem faces agricultural producers who often would rather report market value information than become involved in complex cost allocation problems. Note that recognition of inventories at selling price less cost of disposal

---

[7]See, for example, Yuji Ijiri, *Recognition of Contractual Rights and Obligations, Research Report* (Stamford, Conn.: FASB, 1980), who argues that firm purchase commitments might be capitalized. "Firm" means that it is unlikely that performance under the lease can be avoided without a severe penalty.

means that income is usually recognized before the goods are transferred to an outside party. If this approach is adopted, the use of such basis should be fully disclosed in the financial statements.

Accounting for inventories at market value is limited currently. For the most part, market value is used for inventories only to avoid complex cost allocation problems. As the conceptual framework progresses on the measurement and recognition issues, it will be interesting to see whether any significant changes in our present historical cost system will occur.

## RELATIVE SALES VALUE METHOD

A special problem of pricing inventory items arises when a group of varying units is purchased at a single lump sum price. For example, a lot consisting of 400 melons is purchased at a total cost of $100. These melons are of different weights and grades but can be sorted roughly into three groups graded A, B, and C. As melons are sold, it becomes necessary to apportion the purchase cost of $100 between the melons sold and the melons remaining on hand.

It is unfair to divide 400 melons into the total cost of $100 to get a cost of $0.25 for each melon, because they vary in size and grade. When such a situation is encountered—and it is not at all unusual—the common and most logical practice is to allocate the total cost among the various units on the basis of their relative sales value. For the example given, the allocation works out as follows:

| | | | | Allocation of Cost | | | |
|---|---|---|---|---|---|---|---|
| Grade | Number of Melons | Sales Price per Melon | Total Sales Price | Relative Sales Price | Total Cost | Cost Allocated to Grade | Cost per Melon |
| A | 100 | $1.00 | $100.00 | 100/250 | $100 | $ 40.00 | $.40 |
| B | 100 | .60 | 60.00 | 60/250 | 100 | 24.00 | .24 |
| C | 200 | .45 | 90.00 | 90/250 | 100 | 36.00 | .18 |
| | | | $250.00 | | | $100.00 | |

The cost of melons sold can be computed by using the amounts given in the column for "Cost Per Melon," and the gross profit is determined as follows:

| | | Determination of Gross Profit | | | |
|---|---|---|---|---|---|
| Grade | Number of Melons Sold | Cost Per Melon | Cost of Melons Sold | Sales | Gross Profit |
| A | 77 | $.40 | $30.80 | $ 77.00 | $ 46.20 |
| B | 80 | .24 | 19.20 | 48.00 | 28.80 |
| C | 100 | .18 | 18.00 | 45.00 | 27.00 |
| | | | $68.00 | $170.00 | $102.00 |

This information may be applied in a slightly different way. The ratio of the cost to the selling price of all the melons is $100 divided by $250, or 40%. Accordingly, if the total sales price of melons sold is, say, $170, then the cost of these melons sold is 40% of $170, or $68. The inventory of melons on hand is $100 less $68, or $32.

## THE GROSS PROFIT METHOD OF ESTIMATING INVENTORY

The basic purpose in taking a physical inventory is to verify the accuracy of the inventory records or, if no records exist, to arrive at an inventory amount. Sometimes substitute measures are used to arrive at the same answer. One substitute method of verifying or determining the inventory amount is called the gross profit method. This method is widely used by auditors in situations where only an estimate of the amount of the company's inventory is needed (for example, for determining monthly or quarterly inventory amounts) or where both inventory and inventory records have been destroyed by fire or other catastrophe.

The **gross profit method** is based on the assumptions that (1) the beginning inventory plus purchases equal total goods to be accounted for; (2) goods not sold must be on hand; and (3) if the sales, reduced to cost, are deducted from the sum of the opening inventory plus purchases, the result is the goods on hand or, in other words, the inventory.

To illustrate, assume that a department has a beginning inventory of $60,000 and purchases of $200,000, both at cost. Sales at selling price amount to $280,000. The average rate of gross margin on selling price for that department is 30%. The gross profit method is applied as follows:

| | | |
|---|---:|---:|
| Beginning inventory (at cost) | | $ 60,000 |
| Purchases (at cost) | | 200,000 |
| Goods available (at cost) | | 260,000 |
| Sales (at selling price) | $280,000 | |
| Less gross margin (30% of $280,000) | 84,000 | |
| Sales (at cost) | | 196,000 |
| Approximate inventory (at cost) | | $ 64,000 |

When the inventory is approximated by this method, care must be taken in applying a blanket rate of gross margin. Frequently a store or department handles merchandise with widely varying rates of gross margin. In these situations the gross profit method may have to be applied by subsections, lines of merchandise, or a similar basis that classifies merchandise according to rates of gross margin.

The gross profit method is not normally acceptable for financial reporting purposes, because it is only an estimate, and a physical inventory is needed as additional verification that the inventory indicated in the records is on hand. The gross profit method also uses past percentages for determination of the markup, and although the past can often provide answers to the future, a current rate is more appropriate. The gross profit percentage is an average rate, and whenever several different items are sold, it is best to make separate gross profit calculations for each line of items. If a composite approach is used, a change in the quantity of one line relative to another, or a change in the markup of one line could lead to an inaccurate final inventory value.

## Calculation of Gross Margin Percentage

In most situations, the gross margin percentage is given as a percentage of selling price. The previous illustration indicated that a 30% gross margin on sales was used. Gross margin on selling price is the common method for quoting the margin because (1) most goods are stated on a retail basis, not a cost basis, and (2) a margin quoted on selling price is lower than one based on cost, and this lower rate gives a favorable impression to the consumer, and (3) the gross margin based on selling price can never exceed 100%.

To see how gross margin is computed, assume that an article cost $15.00 and sells for $20.00, a gross margin of $5.00. This markup is ¼ or 25% of retail and ⅓ or 33⅓% of cost.

$$\frac{\text{Markup}}{\text{Retail}} = \frac{\$\ 5.00}{\$20.00} = 25\% \text{ at retail} \qquad \frac{\text{Markup}}{\text{Cost}} = \frac{\$\ 5.00}{\$15.00} = 33\tfrac{1}{3}\% \text{ on cost}$$

Although it is normal to compute the gross margin on the basis of selling price, the accountant should understand the basic relationship between markup on cost and markup on selling price. For example, again assume that an item sells for $20.00 and costs $15.00, generating a $5.00 gross margin. As illustrated above, this gross margin is 25% when based on selling price, but is 33⅓% when based on cost. The accountant must be able to convert from one base to another. The following diagram shows these relationships.

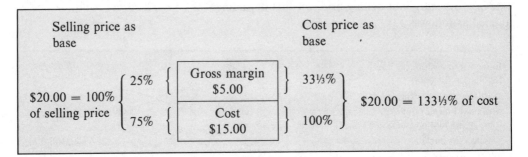

Retailers use the following formulas to express these relationships:

**1.** Percentage markup on selling price = $\dfrac{\text{percentage markup on cost}}{100\% + \text{percentage markup on cost}}$

**2.** Percentage markup on cost = $\dfrac{\text{percentage markup on selling price}}{100\% - \text{percentage markup on selling price}}$

To illustrate how these formulas are employed, let us assume that the markup on cost is 25% and that the accountant wishes to determine the markup on the selling price. Using formula (1) we get

$$\frac{25\%}{100\% + 25\%} = 20\%$$

A markup of 50% on selling price is translated to a markup on cost by formula (2):

$$\frac{50\%}{100\% - 50\%} = 100\%$$

The gross margin on cost is naturally higher than the gross margin on selling price. It should be emphasized that sales may not be multiplied by a cost-based gross margin percentage; the gross margin percentage must be converted to a percentage based on selling price.

### Appraisal of Gross Profit Method

The gross profit method suffers from the disadvantage that the percentages used are based on data from past periods. When these percentages are fair representations of the current year's gross margin, no problem of valuation occurs. Whenever significant fluctuations have occurred, however, it is the accountant's function to adjust the percentage as appropriate.

Regardless of whether the gross profit method is used for estimating inventory values, a physical inventory should be taken once a year to verify the inventory actually on hand. When a physical inventory is not possible (such as when a catastrophe occurs), the accountant must seriously consider developing a representative gross profit percentage; the accountant must also insure that the goods in inventory are representative of the goods that were available for sale.

## RETAIL INVENTORY METHOD

Retailers with certain types of inventory may use the specific identification method for valuation of their inventories. For example, when individual inventory units are significant, such as automobiles, pianos, or fur coats, such an approach makes sense. However, imagine attempting to use such an approach with K-Mart, True-Value Hardware, or Sears—retailers that have many different types of merchandise at low unit costs and also have a large volume of transactions. In such situations, it would be extremely difficult to determine the cost of each sale, enter cost codes on the tickets, change the codes to reflect declines in value of the merchandise, allocate costs such as transportation, and so on. As a result, any type of unit cost method would be unsatisfactory in most department stores selling enormous numbers of items in a huge volume of transactions. An alternative is to compile the inventories at retail prices. In most retail concerns, an observable pattern between cost and sales price lends itself to the computation of inventory on hand through the use of retail prices. These retail prices can then be converted to cost through an adjustment process.

This method, called **the retail inventory method, requires that a record be kept of (1) the total cost and retail value of goods purchased, (2) the total cost and retail value of the goods available for sale, and (3) the sales for the period.** The sales for the period are deducted from the retail value of the goods available for sale to produce an estimated inventory at retail. The ratio of cost to retail for all goods passing through a department or firm is then determined by dividing the total goods available for sale at cost by the total goods available at retail. The inventory valued at retail is reduced to approximate cost by applying the cost to retail ratio. The retail inventory method is illustrated for Marshy Field, Inc. on page 400.

|  | Cost | Retail |
|---|---|---|
| Marshy Field, Inc. RETAIL INVENTORY METHOD (current period) | | |
| Beginning inventory | $14,000 | $ 20,000 |
| Purchases | 63,000 | 90,000 |
| Goods available | $77,000 | 110,000 |
| Deduct sales | | 85,000 |
| Ending inventory, at retail | | $ 25,000 |
| Ratio of cost to retail ($77,000 ÷ $110,000) | | 70% |
| Ending inventory at cost (70% of $25,000) | | $ 17,500 |

This calculation is based on the equation that the total goods available for sale (at retail) less the goods sold (at retail) equals the goods on hand (at retail). The goods on hand at retail are then converted to goods on hand at cost by application of the cost to retail ratio. To avoid a potential overstatement of the inventory, periodic inventory counts are made, especially in retail operations where loss due to shoplifting and breakage is common.

The retail method is sanctioned by the IRS, various retail associations, and the accounting profession. One advantage of the retail inventory method is that the inventory balance **can be approximated without a physical count.** This method is particularly useful for any type of interim report, because a fairly quick and reliable measure of the inventory value can be made. Insurance adjusters often use this approach when estimates of the inventory are needed because of a fire, flood, or other type of casualty. This method also acts as a **control device** because any deviations from a physical count at the end of the year have to be explained. In addition, the retail method also **expedites the physical inventory count** at the end of the year. The inventory crew need only record the retail prices of each item. There is no need to look up each item's invoice cost, thereby saving time and expense.

## Retail Method Terminology

The amounts shown in the Retail column of the preceding illustration represent the original retail prices, assuming no other price changes up or down. Sales prices are frequently changed from the original retail prices, being marked up or marked down. For retailers, **markup** is considered in the context of an additional markup on original selling price; normally, we think of markup on the basis of cost. **Markup cancellations** are decreases in prices of merchandise that had been marked up above the original retail price.

**Markdowns** below the original sale prices may be necessary because of a decrease in the general level of prices, special sales, soiled and damaged goods, overstocking, and competition, for instance. Markdowns are by far the more common phenomenon. **Markdown cancellations** occur when the markdowns are partially offset at a later date by increases in the prices of goods that had been marked down below the original sales price. Neither a markup cancellation nor a markdown cancellation can exceed the original markup or markdown.

To illustrate these different concepts, assume that the Hub Clothing Store recently purchased 100 high-fashion dress shirts from Marroway, Inc. The cost for these shirts was $800 or $8.00 a shirt. Hub Clothing established the selling price on these shirts at $17.00

a shirt. The manager noted that the shirts were selling quickly, so he added a markup of $1.50 per shirt. This markup made the price too high so sales lagged; the manager then reduced the price to $17.50. At this point we would say that Hub Clothing has had a markup of $1.50 and a markup cancellation of $1.00. As soon as the major marketing season passed, the manager marked the remaining shirts down to a sales price of $14.50. At this point, an additional markup cancellation of $.50 has taken place and a $2.50 markdown has occurred. If the shirts are later written up to $15.50, a markdown cancellation of $1.00 will develop.

## Retail Inventory Method with Markups and Markdowns

Retailers use these concepts in developing the proper inventory valuation at the end of the accounting period. To obtain the appropriate inventory figures, proper treatment must be given to markups, markup cancellations, markdowns, and markdown cancellations. To illustrate the different possibilities, assume the following conditions for Donovan Stores, Inc.

|  | Cost | Retail |
|---|---|---|
| Beginning inventory | $ 500 | $ 1,000 |
| Purchases (net) | 20,000 | 35,000 |
| Markups | | 3,000 |
| Markup cancellations | | 1,000 |
| Markdowns | | 2,500 |
| Markdown cancellations | | 2,000 |
| Sales (net) | | 25,000 |

Donovan Stores, Inc.
RETAIL INVENTORY METHOD

|  | Cost | Retail |  |
|---|---|---|---|
| Beginning inventory | $ 500 | $ 1,000 | |
| Purchases (net) | 20,000 | 35,000 | |
| Merchandise available for sale | 20,500 | 36,000 | |
| Cost ratio $\dfrac{\$20,500}{\$36,000} = 56.9\%$ .......................... | | | (A) |
| Add: | | | |
| Markups | $3,000 | | |
| Less markup cancellations | (1,000) | | |
| Net markups | | 2,000 | |
| | 20,500 | 38,000 | |
| Cost ratio $\dfrac{\$20,500}{\$38,000} = 53.9\%$ .......................... | | | (B) |
| Deduct: | | | |
| Markdowns | 2,500 | | |
| Less markdown cancellations | (2,000) | | |
| Net markdowns | | 500 | |
| | $20,500 | 37,500 | |
| Cost ratio $\dfrac{\$20,500}{\$37,500} = 54.7\%$ .......................... | | | (C) |
| Deduct sales (net) | | 25,000 | |
| Ending inventory at retail | | $12,500 | |

Computation of ending inventory at cost under different assumptions:

A $12,500 × 56.9% = $7,112.50
B  12,500 × 53.9% =  6,737.50
C  12,500 × 54.7% =  6,837.50

The first percentage (A) considers only the sum of the beginning inventory and net purchases and represents a cost percentage before markups or markdowns. The second percentage (B) reflects a cost percentage after the additional markups but before the markdowns. Finally, the third percentage (C) is computed after both the markups and the markdowns. Which percentage should be employed to compute the ending inventory valuation?

**The conventional retail inventory method is designed to approximate the lower of average cost or market.** We will simply refer to this approach as the lower of cost or market approach or the conventional retail inventory method. Thus the accountant computes the cost percentage after the markups but before the markdowns. To understand why the markups but not the markdowns are considered in the cost percentage, we must understand how a retail outlet operates. When a company has an additional markup, it normally indicates that the market value of that item has increased. On the other hand, if the company has a net markdown, it means that a decline in the utility of that item has occurred. Therefore, if we attempt to approximate the lower of cost or market, markdowns are considered a current loss and are not involved in the calculation of the cost to retail ratio. For example, two items were purchased for $5.00 apiece, and the original sales price was established at $10.00 each. One item was subsequently written down to $2.00. Assuming no sales for the period, if markdowns are considered in the cost to retail ratio, we compute the ending inventory in the following manner.

| | Cost Method<br>Markdowns Considered in Cost Ratio | | |
| --- | --- | --- | --- |
| | | Cost | Retail |
| Purchases | | $10.00 | $20.00 |
| Deduct markdowns | | | 8.00 |
| Ending inventory, at retail | | | $12.00 |

Cost to retail ratio $\dfrac{\$10.00}{\$12.00}$ = 83.3%

Ending inventory at cost ($12.00 × .833) = $10.00

This approach reflects an average cost of the two items of the commodity without considering the loss on the one item. If a lower of cost or market approach is adopted, the calculation is made as shown at the top of page 403.

Under the conventional retail inventory method when markdowns are **not** considered in computing the cost to retail ratio, the ratio would be 50% ($10/20) and ending inventory would be $6.00 ($12 × .50), the same as lower of cost or market.

**Conventional Method**
**Lower of Cost or Market**

|  | Cost | Retail |
|---|---|---|
| Purchases | $10.00 | $20.00 |
| Cost to retail ratio $\dfrac{\$10.00}{\$20.00} = 50\%$ |  |  |
| Deduct markdown |  | 8.00 |
| Ending inventory, at retail |  | $12.00 |
| Ending inventory, at cost ($12 × .50) = $6.00 |  |  |

The inventory valuation of $6.00 reflects two inventory items, one inventoried at $5.00, the other at $1.00. Basically, the sale price was reduced from $10.00 to $2.00 and the cost reduced from $5.00 to $1.00.[8] To approximate the lower of cost or market, therefore, the **cost to retail ratio** must be established by dividing the cost of goods available by the sum of the original retail price of these goods plus the net markups; the markdowns and markdown cancellations are excluded. The basic format for the retail inventory method using the lower of cost or market approach is illustrated below using the Donovan Stores information.

Donovan Stores
RETAIL METHOD—LOWER OF COST OR MARKET APPROACH

|  | Cost | | Retail |
|---|---|---|---|
| Beginning inventory | $ 500.00 | | $ 1,000.00 |
| Purchases (net) | 20,000.00 | | 35,000.00 |
| Totals | 20,500.00 | | 36,000.00 |
| Add net markups— | | | |
| Markups | | $3,000.00 | |
| Markup cancellations | | 1,000.00 | 2,000.00 |
| Totals | $20,500.00 | | 38,000.00 |
| Deduct net markdowns— | | | |
| Markdowns | | 2,500.00 | |
| Markdown cancellations | | 2,000.00 | 500.00 |
| Sales price of goods available | | | 37,500.00 |
| Deduct sales | | | 25,000.00 |
| Ending inventory, at retail | | | $12,500.00 |

Cost-to-retail ratio $= \dfrac{\text{cost of goods available}}{\text{original retail price of goods available, plus net markups}}$

$= \dfrac{\$20,500}{\$38,000} = 53.9\%$

| Ending inventory at lower of cost or market (53.9% × $12,500.00) | $ 6,737.50 |
|---|---|

[8]This figure is really not market (replacement cost), but is net realizable value less the normal margin that is allowed. In other words, the sale price of the goods written down is $2.00, but subtracting a normal margin of 100%, the figure becomes $1.00. The normal margin is 100% based on cost (a markup of $5.00 on a cost of $5.00).

Because an averaging effect occurs, an exact lower of cost or market inventory valuation is ordinarily not obtained, but an adequate approximation can be achieved. By computing the cost ratio from the totals after adding net markups **and** deducting net markdowns, it is possible to arrive at **approximate cost** instead of approximating the lower of cost or market.

## LIFO Retail

Many retailers and accounting theorists have argued that the conventional retail method follows a flow assumption that does not match current cost against current revenues and, therefore, large fluctuations in profit can occur. It is not surprising that many individuals suggest that a LIFO assumption be adopted to obtain a better matching of costs and revenues. In addition, once the LIFO method was accepted for income tax purposes, many retail establishments changed from the more conventional treatment to the LIFO retail approach simply for the tax advantages associated with valuing inventories on a LIFO basis. The application of LIFO retail is made under two assumptions: (1) stable prices and (2) fluctuating prices.

**Stable Prices**   The computation of the final inventory balance assuming a LIFO flow is much more complex than the calculation related to the conventional retail method. Because the LIFO method is a cost method, not a cost or market approach, both the markups **and** the markdowns must be considered in obtaining the proper cost to retail percentage. Furthermore, since the LIFO method is concerned only with the additional layer that is added, or the amount that should be subtracted from the previous layer, the beginning inventory should be excluded from the cost to retail percentage. **A major assumption of the LIFO retail method is that the markups and markdowns apply only to the goods purchased during the current period and not to the beginning inventory.** Although this assumption may not be true in reality, the LIFO retail procedure assumes that it is true. This assumption can be viewed as a limitation to the LIFO retail procedure. In addition, we have assumed that the price level has remained unchanged. The concepts are illustrated below.

| Retail LIFO Method (Stable Prices) | Cost | Retail |
|---|---|---|
| Beginning inventory | $ 27,000 | $ 45,000 |
| Net purchases during the period | 346,500 | 480,000 |
| Net markups | | 20,000 |
| Net markdowns | | (5,000) |
| Total (excluding beginning inventory) | 346,500 | 495,000 |
| Total (including beginning inventory) | $373,500 | 540,000 |
| Net sales during the period | | (484,000) |
| Ending inventory at retail | | $ 56,000 |
| Establishment of cost to retail percentage under assumptions of LIFO retail ($346,500 ÷ $495,000) | | 70% |

| | | |
|---|---|---|
| Ending inventory at cost | | |
| Beginning inventory ($45,000 @ 60%[a]) | | $27,000 |
| Additional increment | | |
| Ending inventory | $ 56,000 | |
| Beginning inventory | (45,000) | |
| Additional increment at retail | 11,000 | |
| Cost to retail percentage | 70% | 7,700 |
| Ending inventory at LIFO cost (stable prices) | | $34,700 |

[a]$\dfrac{\$27,000}{\$45,000}$ (prior year's cost to retail percentage)

The illustration indicates that the inventory is composed of two layers: the beginning inventory and the additional increase that occurred in the inventory this period. If we start the next period, the beginning inventory will be composed of two layers, and if an increase in inventory occurs again, an additional layer will be added. If, however, the final inventory figure is below the beginning inventory, it is necessary to reduce the beginning inventory starting with the most recent (second) layer. For example, assume that the ending inventory for the next period at retail is $50,000. The computation of the ending inventory at cost is shown below.

| | |
|---|---|
| Ending inventory at retail | $50,000 |
| Composed of: | |
| First layer    $45,000 × 60% | $27,000 |
| Second layer $ 5,000 × 70% | 3,500 |
| Ending inventory at cost | $30,500 |

When a layer concept is involved, as in a LIFO situation, previous layers must be reduced in a LIFO flow starting with the last layer added, whenever the ending inventory is smaller than the beginning inventory.

**Fluctuating Prices**  The computation of the LIFO retail method was simplified in the previous illustration because changes in the selling price of the inventory were ignored. Let us now assume that a change in the price level of the inventories occurs (as is usual). If the price level does change, the price change must be eliminated because we are measuring the real increase in inventory, not the dollar increase. To illustrate, assume that the beginning inventory had a retail market value of $10,000 and the ending inventory a retail market value of $15,000. If the price level has risen from 100 to 125, it is inappropriate to suggest that a real increase in inventory of $5,000 has occurred. Instead, the ending inventory at retail should be deflated as indicated by the computation shown at the top of page 406.

This approach is essentially the dollar-value method previously discussed in Chapter 8. In computing the LIFO inventory under a dollar-value LIFO approach, the dollar increase in inventory is found and deflated to beginning of the year prices to determine whether actual increases or decreases in quantity have occurred. If an increase in quantities develops, this increase is priced at the new index to find the new layer to be added to the previous layers. If a decrease in quantities develops, it is subtracted from the most recent layers to the extent necessary to find the proper valuation. In deflating the retail inventory figures, an appropriate index representative of the industry involved is employed.

| | | |
|---|---|---|
| Ending inventory at retail (deflated) $15,000 × $\frac{100}{125}$ | $12,000 | |
| Beginning inventory at retail | 10,000 | |
| Real increase in inventory at retail | $ 2,000 | |
| Ending inventory at retail on LIFO basis: | | |
| First layer | $10,000 | |
| Second layer ($2,000 × 1.25) | 2,500 | $12,500 |

The following computations, taken from our previous illustration, illustrate the differences between the dollar-value LIFO retail method and the regular LIFO retail approach. Assume that the current price index is 112 (prior year = 100) and that the inventory ($56,000) has remained unchanged. (See illustration below.)

The inventory is computed as shown below before adjustment. Note that the computations below involved in finding the cost to retail percentage are exactly the same as they are under the LIFO approach presented in the preceding section (pages 404–405). At this point the two approaches differ, however, because the dollar-value method, shown below, determines the real increase that has occurred in the inventory.

| Dollar-Value LIFO Method (Fluctuating Prices) | | |
|---|---|---|
| | Cost | Retail |
| Beginning inventory—1983 | $ 27,000 | $ 45,000 |
| Net purchases during the period | 346,500 | 480,000 |
| Net markups | | 20,000 |
| Net markdowns | | (5,000) |
| Total (excluding beginning inventory) | 346,500 | 495,000 |
| Total (including beginning inventory) | $373,500 | 540,000 |
| Net sales during the period at retail | | (484,000) |
| Ending inventory at retail | | $ 56,000 |
| Establishment of cost to retail percentage under assumptions of LIFO retail ($346,500 ÷ $495,000) | 70% | |
| A. Ending inventory at retail prices deflated to base year prices | | |
| $56,000 × $\frac{100}{112}$ = | | $50,000 |
| B. Beginning inventory (retail) at base-year prices | | 45,000 |
| C. Inventory increase (retail) from beginning of period | | $ 5,000 |
| D. Increment (retail) now priced in terms of end-of-year prices | | |
| $5,000 × $\frac{112}{100}$ = | | $ 5,600 |

From this information, we compute the appropriate inventory amount at cost:

| | |
|---|---:|
| First layer—beginning inventory in terms of 100 | $27,000 |
| Second layer—(remainder of 1983 increase at new price level times cost to retail percentage) $5,600 × 70% — see (D) above | 3,920 |
| Ending inventory at LIFO cost (fluctuating prices) | $30,920 |

As is illustrated above, layers of a particular year must be restated to the prices in effect in the year when the layer was added before the conversion to cost takes place.

Note the difference between the LIFO approach (stable prices) and the dollar-value LIFO method as indicated below:

| | LIFO (stable prices) | LIFO (fluctuating prices) |
|---|---:|---:|
| Beginning inventory | $27,000 | $27,000 |
| Increment | 7,700 | 3,920 |
| Ending inventory | $34,700 | $30,920 |

The difference of $3,780 ($34,700 — $30,920) is a result of an increase in the price of goods, but is not representative of an increase in the quantity of goods.

## Special Items Relating to Retail Method

The retail inventory method becomes more complicated when such items as freight-in, purchase returns and allowances, and purchase discounts are involved. **Freight costs** are treated as a part of the cost of the purchase; **purchase returns and allowances** are ordinarily considered both as a reduction of the cost price and the retail price; **purchase discounts** usually are considered as a reduction of the cost of purchases. When the purchase allowance is not reflected by a reduction in the selling price, no adjustment is made to the retail column. In short, the treatment for the items affecting the cost column of the retail inventory approach follows the computation for cost of goods available for sale. Note also that **sales returns and allowances** are considered as proper adjustments to gross sales; **sales discounts,** however, are not recognized when sales are recorded gross. To adjust for the sales discount account in such a situation would provide an ending inventory figure at retail that would be overvalued.

In addition, a number of special items require careful analysis. **Transfers-in** from another department, for example, should be reported in the same way as purchases. Instead of purchasing from an outside enterprise, a department is purchasing from another department in the same entity. **Normal spoilage** (breakage, damage, theft) should reduce the retail column because these goods are no longer available for sale. Because a certain amount of spoilage is considered normal in a retail enterprise, these costs are reflected in the selling price. As a result, this amount is not considered in computing the cost to retail percentage but is shown as a deduction similar to sales to arrive at ending inventory at retail. **Abnormal spoilage** should be deducted from both the cost and retail columns and reported as a special inventory amount or as a loss. To do otherwise distorts the cost to retail ratio and overstates ending inventory. Finally, companies often provide their employees with special discounts to encourage loyalty, better performance, and so on. **Employee discounts** should be deducted from the retail column in the same way as sales. These discounts should not be considered in the cost to retail percentage because they do not reflect an overall change in the selling price.

## Appraisal of Retail Inventory Method

The retail inventory method of computing inventory is used widely (1) to permit the computation of net income without a physical count of inventory, (2) as a control measure in determining inventory shortages, (3) in regulating quantities of merchandise on hand, and (4) as a basis for information needed for insurance purposes.

The advantages and disadvantages of the lower of cost or market method (conventional retail) versus LIFO retail are the same for retail as for nonretail operations. As a practical matter, the selection of the retail inventory method to be used often involves determining which method provides a lower taxable income. Although it might appear that retail LIFO will provide the lowest taxable income in a period of rising prices, such is not always the case. LIFO will provide an approximate current cost matching, but the ending inventory is stated at cost. The conventional retail method may have a large write-off because of the use of the lower of cost or market approach which may offset the LIFO current cost matching.

One characteristic of the retail inventory method is that it **has an averaging effect on varying rates of gross margin.** When applied to the operations of an entire business where rates of gross margin vary among departments, no allowance is made for possible distortion of results because of the differences in rates of gross margin. Some concerns use a refinement of the retail method under such conditions by computing the inventory separately by departments or by classes of merchandise with similar rates of gross margin. In addition, the reliability of this method rests on the assumption that the distribution of items in the inventory is roughly the same as the "mix" in the total collection of goods available for sale.

# FINANCIAL STATEMENT PRESENTATION OF INVENTORIES

Inventories are one of the most significant assets of industrial business enterprises; therefore, the accounting profession has adopted standards to be followed in reporting inventory on financial statements. These standards require that information be reported relative to the composition of the inventory, the inventory financing, the inventory costing methods employed, and the consistent application of costing methods from one period to another. Also, in recent years the disclosure of price-level information has become increasingly important.

Manufacturers should report the inventory composition either in the balance sheet or in a separate schedule in the notes, that is, raw materials, work in process, and finished goods. The relative mix of raw materials, work in process, and finished goods is important in assessing liquidity and in computing the stage of completion of the inventories.

Unusual or significant financing arrangements relating to inventories that may require disclosure are: transactions with related parties, product financing arrangements, firm purchase commitments, involuntary liquidation of LIFO inventories, and pledging of inventories as collateral. Inventories pledged as collateral for a loan should be presented in the current asset section rather than as an offset to the liability.

The basis upon which inventory amounts are stated (lower of cost or market) and the method used in determining cost (LIFO, FIFO, average cost, etc.) should also be reported.

The annual report of Mumford of Wyoming contains the following disclosures.

| Note A—Significant Accounting Policies | |
| --- | --- |
| Live feeder cattle and feed—last-in, first-out (LIFO) cost, which is below approximate market | $ 854,800 |
| Live range cattle—lower of principally identified cost or market | $1,240,500 |
| Live sheep and supplies—lower of first-in, first-out (FIFO) cost or market | $ 674,000 |
| Dressed meat and by-products—principally at market less allowances for distribution and selling expenses | $ 362,630 |

The illustration above indicates that a company can use different pricing methods for different elements of its inventory. If Mumford of Wyoming changes the method of pricing any of its inventory elements, a change in accounting principle must be reported. For example, if Mumford changes its method of accounting for live sheep from FIFO to average cost, this change, along with the effect on income, should be separately reported in the financial statements. Changes in accounting principle require a consistency exception in the auditor's report. The methods of reporting accounting changes are discussed in detail in Chapter 23.

As indicated in Chapter 2, the inflation rates of the 1970s have necessitated reporting price-level information related to inventory as supplementary data in the financial statements for certain large publicly held business enterprises. These disclosures basically involve reporting income from continuing operations on a current cost (replacement cost) and a constant dollar basis.[9] In addition, inventories on a current cost basis also must be reported. For example, selected data from Johnson & Johnson illustrate this disclosure.

| Johnson & Johnson (in millions) | Historical Cost | Constant Dollars | Current Cost |
| --- | --- | --- | --- |
| Income from Continuing Operations | $352 | $298 | $289 |
| At the end of the year, the current cost of inventories was $843 million estimated on the FIFO or full absorption cost basis. | | | |

This reporting requirement is highly controversial, because many companies contend that the high cost of preparing this information is not warranted by the benefits received. Others disagree, noting that historical cost income numbers are misleading in a period of rising prices because inventory profits result. As indicated earlier, inventory profits arise when inventory costs that are matched against current revenues are less than the replacement cost of these inventories. Many accountants believe these profits to be illusory because the company must replace that inventory at a higher price. Thus, it is argued, to better assess the quality of enterprise income, disclosure of changing price information is necessary. The detailed computational aspects related to reporting changes in price are discussed in Chapter 25.

[9]"Financial Reporting and Changing Prices," *Statement of Financial Accounting Standards No. 33* (Stamford, Conn.: FASB, 1979).

# APPENDIX F

# Special LIFO Reporting Problems

The LIFO discussion in the last two chapters has emphasized the basic issues and procedures related to this inventory valuation technique. The purpose of this appendix is to introduce a number of special LIFO reporting problems that may occur. They are generally classified as follows:

1. Initial adoption of LIFO.
2. LIFO reserve.
3. Interim reporting problems.
4. Index determination for dollar-value LIFO.

## INITIAL ADOPTION OF LIFO

The initial adoption of LIFO presents a reporting problem because it is difficult if not impossible to reconstruct the accounting records to determine what net income would have been in prior years had LIFO been used. As a result, **when changing to LIFO neither a cumulative effect nor a retroactive adjustment can be made.** The base-year inventory for all subsequent LIFO computations is the opening inventory of the year the method is adopted. The effect that the change to LIFO has on current net income must be disclosed in a footnote.

Revere Copper and Brass Incorporated's annual report provides a good example of the type of information disclosed:

INVENTORY PRICING. In the fourth quarter of 1980 the Company expanded, effective January 1, 1980, its use of the last-in, first-out (LIFO) method of inventory valuation to a substantial additional portion of its inventories in order to more closely match current costs with current revenues. The effect of this change was to reduce net income for the year 1980 by $2,804,000 or $.49 per share. It is not practicable to restate prior years or determine the cumulative effect of the change. As of December 31, 1980, inventories valued on a LIFO basis amounted to $74,166,000 ($22,071,000 at December 31, 1979). If valued on a first-in, first-out basis, such inventories would be increased to $90,551,000 ($84,017,000 at December 31, 1979).

Formal journal entries are not required in adopting LIFO except when the inventory is restored to a cost basis from the lower of cost or market approach. Because LIFO is considered a cost approach, the inventory must be restated to a cost basis if market is lower than cost at the time of LIFO adoption. To illustrate, assume that Ramos, Inc. decided to switch **from FIFO to LIFO** for purposes of valuing its inventory. The inventory under FIFO has a cost basis of $100,000 but is reported at $90,000 because market is lower than cost. The following entry is made to restate the inventory to a cost basis (ignoring tax effects):

| | | |
|---|---|---|
| Inventory | 10,000 | |
| Adjustment to Record Inventory at Cost | | 10,000 |

The Adjustment to Record Inventory at Cost should be reported on the income statement in the other revenues and gains section.

The same type of problem arises when the company changes **from the conventional retail method to LIFO retail.** Because conventional retail is a lower of cost or market approach, the beginning inventory must be restated to a cost basis. The usual approach is to compute the cost basis from the purchases of the prior year, adjusted for both markups and markdowns.[1] To illustrate, assume that Clark Clothing Store employs the conventional retail method but wishes to change to the LIFO retail method beginning in 1984. The amounts shown by the firm's books are as follows:

| | At Cost | At Retail |
|---|---|---|
| Inventory January 1, 1983 | $ 5,210 | $ 15,000 |
| Net purchases in 1983 | 47,250 . | 100,000 |
| Net markups in 1983 | | 7,000 |
| Net markdowns in 1983 | | 2,000 |
| Sales in 1983 | | 95,000 |

Ending inventory under the **conventional retail method for 1983** is computed as follows:

| Conventional Retail | | |
|---|---|---|
| | Cost | Retail |
| Inventory January 1, 1983 | $ 5,210 | $ 15,000 |
| Net purchases | 47,250 | 100,000 |
| Net additional markups | | 7,000 |
| | $52,460 | 122,000 |
| Net markdowns | | (2,000) |
| Sales | | (95,000) |
| Ending inventory at retail | | $ 25,000 |
| Establishment of cost to retail percentage ($52,460 ÷ $122,000) | 43% | |
| December 31, 1983 inventory at cost | | |
| Inventory at retail | | $ 25,000 |
| Cost to retail ratio | | 43% |
| Inventory at cost under conventional retail | | $ 10,750 |

[1]A logical question to ask is, "Why are only the purchases considered from the prior period and not also the beginning inventory?" Apparently the IRS believes that "the purchases only approach" provides a more reasonable cost basis. The IRS position is debatable and litigation has ensued on this matter. For our purposes, it seems appropriate to use the purchases only approach.

The ending inventory for 1983 under the **LIFO retail method** can then be quickly approximated in the following way.

---

**LIFO Retail**
**(December 31, 1983 inventory at LIFO cost)**

|  | Retail | Ratio | LIFO |
|---|---|---|---|
| Ending inventory | $25,000 | × 45%[a] = | $11,250 |

[a]The cost to retail ratio was computed as follows:

$$\frac{\text{Net purchases at cost}}{\text{Net purchases plus markups less markdowns at retail}} = \frac{\$47,250}{\$100,000 + \$7,000 - \$2,000} = 45\%$$

---

The difference of $500 ($11,250 − $10,750) between the LIFO retail method and the conventional retail method in the ending inventory for 1983 is the amount by which the beginning inventory for 1984 must be adjusted. The entry to adjust the inventory to a cost basis is as follows:

| | | |
|---|---|---|
| Inventory | 500 | |
|    Adjustment to Record Inventory at Cost | | 500 |

## LIFO RESERVE

Many companies use LIFO for tax and external reporting purposes, but they usually maintain a FIFO, average cost, or standard cost system for internal reporting purposes. The reasons for this procedure are that (1) companies often base their pricing decisions on a FIFO, average, or standard cost assumption, rather than on a LIFO basis; (2) record-keeping is easier because the LIFO assumption usually does not approximate the physical flow of the product; (3) profit-sharing and other bonus arrangements are often not based on a LIFO inventory assumption; and (4) the use of a pure LIFO system is troublesome for interim periods where estimates must be made of year-end quantities and prices.

The difference between the inventory method used for internal reporting purposes and LIFO is referred to as the Allowance to Reduce Inventory to LIFO or the LIFO reserve. The change in the allowance balance from one period to the next is called the **LIFO effect.** The LIFO effect is the adjustment that must be made to the accounting records in a given year. To illustrate, assume that Kroger Company uses the FIFO method for internal reporting purposes and LIFO for external reporting purposes. At January 1, 1984, the Allowance to Reduce Inventory to LIFO balance was $20,000 and the ending balance should be $50,000. The LIFO effect is, therefore, $30,000 and the following entry is made at year end.

| | | |
|---|---|---|
| Cost of Goods Sold | 30,000 | |
|    Allowance to Reduce Inventory to LIFO | | 30,000 |

The Allowance to Reduce Inventory to LIFO would be deducted from inventory to insure that the inventory is stated on a LIFO basis at year-end.

# INTERIM REPORTING PROBLEMS

The use of LIFO in interim periods is complicated because LIFO is an annual, not an interim, computation. *APB Opinion No. 28,* however, specifies that accounting principles must be consistently applied among interim periods and that the same principles used for annual purposes must be used for interim periods.[2] This situation presents difficulties because at an interim period the future prices of the inventory and the quantity on hand at year-end are not known. The accountant, therefore, must estimate the total LIFO effect and allocate this LIFO effect in some reasonable and consistent fashion. This is not an easy task and it is one that often results in substantial fourth-quarter adjustments. The LIFO effect may be allocated on the basis of estimated sales or estimated production costs, or it may be allocated equally over the four periods.

A special problem develops in interim periods when the temporary liquidation of a LIFO layer occurs. A temporary liquidation occurs when a layer would be liquidated for interim purposes but is expected to be replaced by year-end. In such a situation, the inventory at the interim period should not give effect to the LIFO liquidation. Instead, the cost of goods sold for the interim period affected should include the expected cost of the replacement of the liquidated LIFO layer. To illustrate, assume that in the second quarter Trident Manufacturing Co. experiences a temporary reduction in its LIFO inventory of 1,000 units that cost $40.00 per unit. Trident expects to replace the entire reduction in the third quarter at a cost of $55.00 per unit. The entry to record the second-quarter reduction is as follows:

| | | |
|---|---|---|
| Cost of Goods Sold | 55,000 | |
| Inventory | | 40,000 |
| Excess of Replacement Cost of | | |
| LIFO Temporarily Liquidated | | 15,000 |

When the inventory is replenished in the third quarter, the following entry is made:

| | | |
|---|---|---|
| Inventory | 40,000 | |
| Excess of Replacement Cost of | | |
| LIFO Temporarily Liquidated | 15,000 | |
| Accounts Payable (Cash) | | 55,000 |

The Excess of Replacement Cost of LIFO Temporarily Liquidated is reported as a current liability and **is reported only in interim reports.**

If any part of the LIFO base is liquidated at year-end, it represents a permanent reduction. Because a permanent reduction may have a substantive impact on net income when low-cost items are matched against current revenues, disclosure is required in the annual report. Brunswick Corporation recently reported a year-end LIFO liquidation:

> During 1980, certain inventory quantities, valued using the last-in, first-out (LIFO) method of accounting, were substantially decreased. This caused results of operations to be charged with prior years' inventory costs which are lower than current costs. The effect of the liquidation of LIFO inventory quantities increased 1980 net earnings by approximately $6.4 million, or $.32 per share.

[2]"Interim Financial Reporting," *APB Opinion No. 28* (New York: AICPA, 1973).

## Index Determination for Dollar Value LIFO

In Chapter 8, the development of the indexes used in the dollar-value LIFO method was briefly discussed. The general formula for computing the index is as follows:

$$\frac{\text{Ending Inventory for the Period at Current Cost}}{\text{Ending Inventory for the Period at Base-Year Cost}} = \text{Price Index for Current Year}$$

This approach is generally referred to as the **double-extension method** in that the inventory is extended at both base-year prices and current-year prices. To illustrate this computation, assume that Hartford, Inc.'s base-year inventory (January 1, 1983) was composed of the following:

| Items | Quantity | Cost Per Unit | Total Cost |
|-------|----------|---------------|------------|
| A | 1,000 | $6 | $ 6,000 |
| B | 2,000 | $20 | 40,000 |
| (January 1, 1983 inventory at base year costs) | | | $46,000 |

Examination of the ending inventory indicates that 3,000 units of Item A and 6,000 units of Item B are held on December 31, 1983. The most recent actual purchases related to these items were as follows:

| Items | Purchase Date | Quantity Purchased | Cost Per Unit |
|-------|---------------|--------------------|---------------|
| A | December 1, 1983 | 4,000 | $ 7 |
| B | December 15, 1983 | 5,000 | 25 |
| B | November 16, 1983 | 1,000 | 22 |

We double extend the inventory as follows:

| Items | 12/31/83 inventory at base-year costs — Units | Cost Per Unit | Total | 12/31/83 inventory at current-year costs — Units | Cost Per Unit | Total |
|-------|-------|-------|-------|-------|-------|-------|
| A | 3,000 | $6 | $ 18,000 | 3,000 | $7 | $ 21,000 |
| B | 6,000 | $20 | 120,000 | 5,000 | $25 | 125,000 |
| | | | | 1,000 | $22 | 22,000 |
| | | | $138,000 | | | $168,000 |

After the inventories are double-extended, the formula above is used to develop the index for the current year as follows:

$$\frac{\text{Ending Inventory for the Period at Current Cost}}{\text{Ending Inventory for the Period at Base-Year Cost}} = \frac{\$168,000}{\$138,000} = 121.74\%$$

This index (121.74%) is then applied to the layer added in 1983. Note in this illustration that Hartford, Inc. used the most recent actual purchases to determine current cost; other approaches such as FIFO and average cost may also be used. Whichever flow assumption is adopted, consistent use from one period to another is required.

Use of the double-extension method is time consuming and difficult where substantial technological change has occurred or where a large number of items is involved. Another approach, often referred to as the **index method,** is used to simplify the analysis. Under this method, an index is obtained by reference to an outside source or by double-pricing only a sample portion of the inventory. An example of an acceptable outside source for an index is the Bureau of Labor Statistics—Department Store Inventory Price Indexes, published semiannually in the *Internal Revenue Bulletin.* Generally, the IRS frowns on the use of an outside index except by retail department stores. If a sample is employed, statistical methods, judgment, or a combination of the two is utilized to determine the index. Once the index is obtained, the ending inventory at current costs is divided by the index to find the base-year cost.[3]

Note: All **asterisked** Questions, Cases, Exercises, or Problems relate to material contained in the appendix to each chapter.

## QUESTIONS

1. Where there is evidence that the utility of inventory goods, as part of their disposal in the ordinary course of business, will be less than cost, what is the proper accounting treatment?

2. Why are inventories valued at the lower of cost or market? What are the arguments against the use of the lower of cost or market method of valuing inventories?

3. (a) Determine the ending inventory under the conventional retail method for the Paint Department of the Sunspot Energy Co. from the following data.

|  | Cost | Retail |
|---|---|---|
| Inventory Jan. 1 | $ 94,500 | $ 141,750 |
| Purchases | 720,000 | 1,080,000 |
| Freight-in | 35,000 | |
| Markups, net | | 46,000 |
| Markdowns, net | | 24,000 |
| Sales | | 1,122,000 |

(b) If the results of a physical inventory indicated an inventory at retail of $120,000, what inferences would you draw?

4. In some instances accounting principles require a departure from valuing inventories at cost alone. Determine the proper unit inventory price in the following cases:

| | Cases | | | | |
|---|---|---|---|---|---|
| | 1 | 2 | 3 | 4 | 5 |
| Cost | $4.00 | $4.00 | $4.00 | $4.00 | $4.00 |
| Net realizable value | 3.60 | 4.80 | 3.80 | 2.60 | 4.10 |
| Net realizable value less normal profit | 3.20 | 4.40 | 3.40 | 2.20 | 3.70 |
| Market (replacement cost) | 3.70 | 4.30 | 3.20 | 2.40 | 4.20 |

[3]Another approach to finding an index is the *link-chain method.* It is not discussed here because it is permitted only in limited circumstances where the double-extension and index methods are impractical. For a more detailed discussion of the link-chain method, read Raymond A. Hoffman and Henry Gunders, *Inventories,* 2nd ed. (New York: The Ronald Press, 1970).

5. What method(s) might be used in the accounts to record a loss due to a price decline in the inventories? Discuss.

6. What approaches may the accountant employ in applying the lower of cost or market procedure? Which approach is normally used and why?

7. At December 31, 1984, Bernard Newman Co. has outstanding purchase commitments for purchase of 75,000 gallons, at $3.10 per gallon, of a raw material to be used in its manufacturing process. The company prices its raw material inventory at cost or market, whichever is lower. Assuming that the market price as of December 31, 1984 is $2.90, how would you treat this situation in the accounts?

8. What factors might call for inventory valuation at sales prices?

9. Distinguish between gross profit as a percentage of cost and gross profit as a percentage of sales price. Convert the following gross profit percentages based on cost to gross profit percentages based on sales price: 20% and 33⅓%. Convert the following gross profit percentages based on sales price to gross profit percentages based on cost: 33⅓% and 60%.

10. What are the major uses of the gross profit method?

11. Lopez, Inc. with annual net sales of $3 million maintains a markup of 25% based on cost. Lopez's expenses average 15% of net sales. What is Lopez's gross margin and net profit in dollars?

12. What conditions must exist for the retail inventory method to provide valid results?

13. The retail inventory method yields results that are essentially the same as those yielded by the lower of cost or market method. Explain. Prepare an illustration of how the retail inventory method reduces inventory to market.

14. What modifications to the conventional retail method are necessary to approximate a LIFO retail flow?

15. G. Gregory Gardner, Inc. provides the following information with respect to its inventories:

Inventories    $9,620,000

What additional disclosure is necessary to present the inventory fairly?

*16. Saluki, Inc. switched from the FIFO to the LIFO method of inventory valuation. As a result, the beginning inventory was increased $14,600 in order to report it on the cost basis. What is the appropriate journal entry to record this adjustment?

*17. Your instructor has noted that some special problems are associated with the use of LIFO. In particular, in interim reports, the allocation of LIFO reserves and the possibility of temporary liquidation present difficulties. Why do these items present difficulties in interim reports?

*18. Romayne Company is considering the use of the dollar-value LIFO method for inventory valuation purposes. The auditor for Romayne Company notes that the double-extension method should be employed. Explain the double-extension method. When might the double-extension method not be appropriate?

*19. Companies using LIFO sometimes establish an "Excess of Replacement Cost of LIFO Temporarily Liquidated" account. Explain why and how this account is established and where it should be reported on the balance sheet.

## CASES

C9–1 You have just been hired as a new accountant for the accounting firm of Ketchum and Stingem. The manager of the office is interested in your formal education and provides you with the following factual situations that were recently encountered in their practice.

1. One of our client's major business activities is the purchase and resale of used heavy mining and construction equipment, including trucks, cranes, shovels, conveyors, crushers, etc. The company was organized in 1975. In its earlier years it purchased individual items of heavy equipment and resold them to customers throughout the United States. In the early 1980s, the company began negotiating the "package" purchase of all the existing

equipment at mine sites, concurrent with the closing down of several of the large iron mines in North Dakota and exhausted coal mines in Illinois. The mine operators preferred to liquidate their mine assets on that basis rather than holding auctions or leaving the mine site open until all of the equipment could be liquidated. As there were numerous pieces of equipment in these package purchases, the client found it difficult to assign costs to each individual item. As a result, the company followed the policy of valuing these "package" purchases by the cost recovery method. Under this method, the company recognized no income until the entire cost had been recovered through sales revenues. This produced a desirable tax answer by deferring income to later periods and represented, for financial reporting purposes, a "conservative" valuation of inventories in what was essentially a new field for the company where its level of experience had not been demonstrated.

**Instructions**

Comment on the propriety of this approach.

2. In December 1982, one of our clients underwent a major management change and a new president was hired. After reviewing the various policies of the company, the president's opinion was that prior systems employed by the company did not allow for adequate testing of obsolescence (including discontinued products) and overstocks in inventories. Accordingly, the president changed the mechanics of the procedures of reviewing for obsolete and excess stock and determining the amount. These reviews resulted in a significant increase between years in the amount of inventory that was written off. You are satisfied that these procedures are accurate and provide reliable results. The amounts charged against operations for excess and obsolete stock for the last three years were: 1982—$440,000; 1981—$114,000; and 1980—$113,000. Net income for 1982 before adjustment for these additional obsolescence charges was $540,000.

**Instructions**

How should these charges be reported in the financial statements, if at all?

3. Another of our clients, Scott Rongey Foods, was upset because we forced them to write down their inventory on an item-by-item basis. For example, our computation resulted in a write-down of approximately $300,000 as follows:

|                  | Frozen    | Cans      |
|------------------|-----------|-----------|
| Spinach          | 183,000   | 8,000     |
| Carrots          | 12,000    | 7,000     |
| Cut beans        | —         | 25,000    |
| Peas             | —         | 45,000    |
| Mixed vegetables | 5,000     | 15,000    |
|                  | $200,000  | $100,000  |

The company argued that the products are sold on a line basis (frozen or canned) with customers taking all varieties, and only rarely are sales made on an individual product basis. As a result, they argued that the application of the lower of cost or market rule to the total product line would result in the proper determination of income (loss). A pricing of the inventory on this basis would result in a $60,000 write-off.

**Instructions**

Why do you believe our accounting firm argued for the item-by-item approach? Which method should be used, given the information in this case?

C9–2 Dorothy Swanson Company manufactures and sells four products, the inventories of which are priced at cost or market, whichever is lower. A normal profit margin rate of 30% is usually maintained on each of the four products.

The following information was compiled as of December 31, 1983.

| Product | Original Cost | Cost to Replace | Estimated Cost to Dispose | Expected Selling Price[a] |
|---------|--------------|-----------------|--------------------------|--------------------------|
| A | $17.50 | $15.00 | $ 5.00 | $ 30.00 |
| B | 45.00 | 46.00 | 26.00 | 100.00 |
| C | 35.00 | 42.00 | 15.00 | 80.00 |
| D | 47.50 | 45.00 | 20.50 | 95.00 |

[a]Normal margin is 30% of selling price.

**Instructions**

(a) Why are expected selling prices important in the application of the lower of cost or market rule?

(b) Prepare a schedule containing unit values (including "floor" and "ceiling") for determining the lower of cost or market on an individual-product basis. The last column of the schedule should contain for each product the unit value for the purpose of inventory valuation resulting from the application of the lower of cost or market rule.

**C9-3** You are in charge of the audit of Spandex Hosiery, Incorporated. The following items were in Spandex's inventory at November 30, 1984 (fiscal year end).

| Product number | 075936 | 078310 | 079104 | 081111 |
|----------------|--------|--------|--------|--------|
| Selling price per unit November 30, 1984 | $15.00 | $23.00 | $28.00 | $13.00 |
| Standard cost, per unit, as included in inventory at November 30, 1984 | $ 8.00 | $11.25 | $14.26 | $ 7.40 |

In discussions with Spandex's marketing and sales personnel you were told that there will be a general 9% (rounded to the next highest nickel) increase in selling prices, effective December 1, 1984. This increase will affect all garments except those that have 081 as the first three digits of the product code. The 081 codes are assigned to new apparel introductions, and for product code 081111, the selling price will be $9.00 effective December 1, 1984.

In addition, you were told by the controller that Spandex attempts to earn a 50% gross profit on selling price for all their hosiery.

From the cost department you obtained the following standard costs, which will be used for fiscal 1985:

| Product number | 1985 Standard |
|----------------|---------------|
| 075936 | $ 8.25 |
| 078310 | $10.75 |
| 079104 | $14.71 |
| 081111 | $ 7.51 |

Sales commissions and estimates of other costs of disposal approximate 25% of fiscal 1985 standard costs to manufacture. Assume that standard costs for fiscal 1985 provide an accurate assessment of the replacement cost of the product.

**Instructions**

(a) Compute the value at which each of the items should be reported in the November 30, 1984, inventory.

(b) When should inventories be reported at market?

(c) Does the literal interpretation of the rule of lower of cost or market always apply? Could you cite in this case where a possible exception to the lower of cost or market might be employed?

**C9-4** Dri-Fast Company, your client, manufactures paint. The company's president, Ms. Ruth Kalamarides, has decided to open a retail store to sell Dri-Fast paint as well as wallpaper and other supplies that would be purchased from other suppliers. She has asked you for information about the retail method of pricing inventories at the retail store.

**Instructions**

Prepare a report to the president explaining the retail method of pricing inventories. Your report should include these points:

(a) Description and accounting features of the method.
(b) The conditions that may distort the results under the method.
(c) A comparison of the advantages of using the retail method with those of using cost methods of inventory pricing.
(d) The accounting theory underlying the treatment of net markdowns and net markups under the method.

(AICPA adapted)

C9–5 Presented below are a number of items that may be encountered in computing the cost to retail percentage when using the conventional retail method or the LIFO retail method.

| | |
|---|---|
| **1.** Markdowns | **8.** Cost of beginning inventory |
| **2.** Markdown cancellations | **9.** Retail value of beginning inventory |
| **3.** Cost of items transferred in from other departments | **10.** Cost of purchases |
| **4.** Retail value of items transferred in from other departments | **11.** Retail value of purchases |
| | **12.** Markups |
| **5.** Sales discounts | **13.** Markup cancellations |
| **6.** Purchases discounts (purchases recorded gross) | **14.** Employee discounts (sales recorded net) |
| **7.** Estimated retail value of goods broken or stolen | |

**Instructions**

For each of the items listed above, indicate whether this item would be considered in the cost to retail percentage under (1) conventional retail, (2) LIFO retail.

# EXERCISES

**E9–1** The inventory of Hamsmith Company on December 31, 1984, consists of these items:

| Part No. | Quantity | Cost per Unit | Cost to Replace per Unit |
|---|---|---|---|
| 110 | 200 | $100 | $110 |
| 111 | 500 | 60 | 52 |
| 112 | 1,500 | 80 | 76 |
| 113 | 100 | 160 | 180 |
| 120 | 300 | 205 | 208 |
| 121ᵃ | 2,000 | 16 | 14 |
| 122 | 100 | 240 | 244 |

ᵃPart No. 121 is obsolete and has a realizable value of $0.20 each as scrap.

**Instructions**

(a) Determine the inventory as of December 31, 1984, by the method of cost or market, whichever is lower, applying this method directly to each item.
(b) Determine the inventory by cost or market, whichever is lower, applying the method to the total of the inventory.

**E9–2** Iqbal Company follows the practice of pricing its inventory at the lower of cost or market, on an individual-item basis.

| Item No. | Quantity | Cost per Unit | Cost to Replace | Estimated Selling Price | Cost of Completion and Disposal | Normal Profit |
|---|---|---|---|---|---|---|
| 1320 | 1,000 | $3.00 | $3.05 | $4.50 | $.35 | $1.25 |
| 1333 | 1,100 | 2.50 | 2.40 | 3.50 | .50 | .50 |
| 1426 | 600 | 4.00 | 3.90 | 5.00 | .40 | 1.00 |
| 1437 | 1,000 | 3.60 | 3.10 | 3.00 | .25 | .90 |
| 1510 | 900 | 2.25 | 2.00 | 3.25 | .70 | .60 |
| 1522 | 400 | 3.00 | 2.50 | 3.50 | .40 | .50 |
| 1573 | 3,200 | 1.60 | 1.50 | 2.50 | .75 | .50 |
| 1626 | 1,000 | 4.50 | 5.25 | 6.00 | .50 | 1.00 |

**Instructions**

From the information above, determine the amount of Iqbal Company inventory.

**E9–3** Presented below is information related to Appalachian Enterprises.

| | Jan. 31 | Feb. 28 | Mar. 31 | Apr. 30 |
|---|---|---|---|---|
| Inventory | $16,000 | $15,500 | $17,000 | $13,000 |
| Inventory at the lower of cost or market | 15,000 | 13,500 | 15,500 | 12,500 |
| Purchases for the month | | 20,000 | 24,000 | 22,000 |
| Sales for the month | | 28,000 | 35,000 | 30,000 |

**Instructions**

(a) From the information prepare (as far as the data permit) monthly income statements in columnar form for February, March, and April. The inventory is to be shown in the statement at cost, the profit or loss due to market fluctuations is to be shown separately, and a valuation account is to be set up for the difference between cost and the lower of cost or market.

(b) Prepare the journal entry required to establish the valuation account at January 31 and entries to adjust it monthly thereafter.

**E9–4** Oshkosh Boat Company has been having difficulty obtaining key raw materials for its manufacturing process. The company therefore signed a long-term noncancelable purchase commitment with its largest supplier of this raw material on November 30, 1984 at an agreed price of $380,000. At December 31, 1984, the raw material had declined in price to $350,000, and it was further anticipated that the price would drop another $15,000, so that at the date of delivery the value of the inventory would be $335,000.

**Instructions**

What entries would you make on December 31, 1984 to recognize these facts?

**E9–5** At December 31, 1984, Whitewater Company has outstanding purchase commitments for 50,000 gallons, at $3.00 per gallon, of raw material to be used in its manufacturing process. The company prices its raw material inventory at cost or market, whichever is lower.

**Instructions**

(a) Assuming that the market price as of December 31, 1984, is $3.10, how would this matter be treated in the accounts and statements? Explain.

(b) Assuming that the market price as of December 31, 1984, is $2.75, instead of $3.10, how would you treat this situation in the accounts and statements?

(c) Give the entry in January, 1985, when the 50,000-gallon shipment is received, assuming that the situation given in (b) above existed at December 31, 1984. Give an explanation of your treatment.

**E9–6** Romesh Sood Corporation began business on January 1, 1983. Information about its inventories under different valuation methods is presented below.

**Inventory**

|  | LIFO Cost | FIFO Cost | Replacement Cost | Lower of Cost or Market |
|---|---|---|---|---|
| December 31, 1983 | $20,400 | $20,000 | $19,200 | $17,800 |
| December 31, 1984 | 18,200 | 18,000 | 17,600 | 17,000 |
| December 31, 1985 | 20,600 | 22,000 | 24,000 | 21,800 |

**Instructions**

(a) Indicate the inventory basis that will show the highest net income in (1) 1983; and (2) 1984.

(b) Indicate whether the FIFO cost basis would provide a higher or lower profit than the lower of cost or market basis in 1984.

**E9–7** Hallam Furniture Company purchases, during 1984, a carload of wicker chairs at a cost of $43,200. The manufacturer sells the chairs to Hallam for a lump sum of $43,200, because it is discontinuing manufacturing operations and wishes to dispose of its entire stock. Three types of chairs are included in the carload. The three types and the estimated selling price for each are listed below.

| Type | No. of Chairs | Estimated Selling Price Each |
|---|---|---|
| Lounge chairs | 500 | $90 |
| Armchairs | 300 | 60 |
| Straight chairs | 200 | 45 |

During 1984 Hallam sells 150 lounge chairs, 80 armchairs, and 110 straight chairs.

**Instructions**

What is the amount of gross profit realized during 1984? What is the amount of inventory of unsold wicker chairs on December 31, 1984?

**E9–8** Barbara Masseri Realty Corporation purchased a tract of unimproved land for $38,140. This land was improved and subdivided into building lots at an additional cost of $15,200. These building lots were all of the same size but owing to differences in location were offered for sale at different prices as follows:

| Group | No. of Lots | Price per Lot |
|---|---|---|
| 1 | 12 | $2,500 |
| 2 | 18 | 2,000 |
| 3 | 6 | 1,700 |

Operating expenses for the year allocated to this project total $13,500. Lots unsold at the year-end were as follows:

| | |
|---|---|
| Group 1 | 4 lots |
| Group 2 | 6 lots |
| Group 3 | 1 lot |

**Instructions**

At the end of the fiscal year Barbara Masseri Realty Corporation instructs you to arrive at the net income realized on this operation to date.

**E9–9** A fire destroys all of the merchandise of the Arizona Company on February 10, 1984. Presented below is information compiled up to the date of the fire.

| | |
|---|---|
| Inventory January 1, 1984 | $ 250,000 |
| Sales to February 10, 1984 | 1,500,000 |

| | |
|---|---|
| Purchases to February 10, 1984 | 1,250,000 |
| Freight-in to February 10, 1984 | 50,000 |
| Rate of gross profit on selling price | 40% |

**Instructions**

From the information above, compute the approximate inventory on that date.

**E9–10** Presented below is information related to Oceanside Corporation for the current year:

| | | |
|---|---|---|
| Beginning inventory | $ 300,000 | |
| Purchases | 1,200,000 | |
| Total goods available for sale | | $1,500,000 |
| Sales | | 2,000,000 |

**Instructions**

Compute the ending inventory, assuming that (1) gross margin is 30% of sales; (2) gross margin is 33⅓% of cost; (3) gross margin is 50% of cost; and (4) gross margin is 25% of sales.

**E9–11** Vanessa Van Bougart requires an estimate of the cost of goods lost by fire on March 9. Merchandise on hand on January 1 was $32,000. Purchases since January 1 were $22,500; freight-in, $2,500; purchase returns and allowances, $1,500. Sales are made at 25% above cost and totaled $28,000 to March 9. Goods costing $6,125 were left undamaged by the fire; remaining goods were destroyed.

**Instructions**

(a) Compute the cost of goods destroyed.

(b) Compute the cost of goods destroyed, assuming that the gross profit is 25% of sales.

**E9–12** Rozanski Lumber Company handles three principal lines of merchandise with these varying rates of gross profit on cost:

| | |
|---|---|
| Lumber | 40% |
| Millwork | 25% |
| Hardware and fittings | 30% |

On August 18 a fire destroyed the office, lumber shed, and a considerable portion of the lumber stacked in the yard. To file a report of loss for insurance purposes, the company must know what the inventories were immediately preceding the fire. No detail or perpetual inventory records of any kind were maintained. The only pertinent information you are able to obtain are the following facts from the general ledger, which was kept in a fireproof vault and thus escaped destruction.

| | Lumber | Millwork | Hardware |
|---|---|---|---|
| Inventory, Jan. 1, 1984 | $ 187,500 | $ 67,500 | $ 27,750 |
| Purchases to Aug. 18, 1984 | 1,470,000 | 375,000 | 117,750 |
| Sales to Aug. 18, 1984 | 1,875,000 | 510,000 | 180,000 |

**Instructions**

Submit your estimate of the inventory amounts immediately preceding the fire.

**E9–13** You are called by Gary Fish of Cycle Co. on July 16 and asked to prepare a claim for insurance as a result of a theft that took place the night before. You suggest that an inventory be taken immediately. The following data are available:

| | |
|---|---|
| Inventory, July 1 | $32,000 |
| Purchases—goods placed in stock July 1-15 | 18,600 |
| Sales—goods delivered to customers (gross) | 34,000 |
| Sales returns—goods returned to stock | 2,500 |

Your client reports that the goods on hand on July 16 cost $30,000, but you determine that this figure includes goods of $9,000 received on a consignment basis. Your past records show that sales are made at approximately 50% over cost.

**Instructions**

Compute the claim against the insurance company.

**E9-14** Presented below is information related to John Simmons Company.

|  | Cost | Retail |
|---|---|---|
| Beginning inventory | $ 150,000 | $ 200,000 |
| Purchases | 1,350,000 | 1,800,000 |
| Markups |  | 75,000 |
| Markup cancellations |  | 15,000 |
| Markdowns |  | 37,500 |
| Markdown cancellations |  | 7,500 |
| Sales |  | 1,950,000 |

**Instructions**

Compute the inventory by the conventional retail inventory method.

**E9-15** The records of The Clothes Horse report the following data for the month of September.

| | |
|---|---|
| Sales | $50,000 |
| Sales returns | 1,000 |
| Additional markups | 10,000 |
| Markup cancellations | 1,500 |
| Markdowns | 7,500 |
| Markdown cancellations | 2,500 |
| Freight on purchases | 1,000 |
| Purchases (at cost) | 20,000 |
| Purchases (at sales price) | 30,000 |
| Purchase returns (at cost) | 1,000 |
| Purchase returns (at sales price) | 1,500 |
| Beginning inventory (at cost) | 40,000 |
| Beginning inventory (at sales price) | 60,000 |

**Instructions**

Compute the ending inventory by the conventional retail inventory method.

**E9-16** Graumitz Company began operations on January 1, 1982, adopting the conventional retail inventory system. None of its merchandise was marked down in 1982 and, because there was no beginning inventory, its ending inventory for 1982 of $21,740 would have been the same under either the conventional system or the LIFO system. On December 31, 1983, the store management considers adopting the LIFO system, and desires to know how the December 31, 1983 inventory would appear under both systems. All pertinent data regarding purchases, sales, markups, and markdowns are shown below. There has been no change in the price level.

|  | Cost | Retail |
|---|---|---|
| Inventory, Jan. 1, 1983 | $ 21,740 | $ 32,000 |
| Markdowns (net) |  | 12,000 |
| Markups (net) |  | 20,000 |
| Purchases (net) | 132,000 | 200,000 |
| Sales (net) |  | 148,000 |

**Instructions**

Determine the cost of the 1983 ending inventory under both (1) the conventional retail method and (2) the LIFO method.

**E9–17** You assemble the following information for Hudson Department Store, which computes its inventory under the dollar-value LIFO method.

| | Cost | Retail |
|---|---|---|
| Inventory on January 1, 1984 | $210,600 | $270,000 |
| Purchases | 360,000 | 450,000 |
| Increase in price level for year | | 7% |

**Instructions**

Compute the cost of the inventory on December 31, 1984, assuming that the inventory at retail is (1) $267,500, (2) $310,300.

**E9–18** Presented below is information related to Mustang Enterprises:

| | Price Index | LIFO Cost | Retail |
|---|---|---|---|
| Inventory on December 31, 1984 when dollar-value LIFO is adopted | 100 | $13,080 | $44,000 |
| Inventory, December 31, 1985 | 105 | ? | 54,600 |

**Instructions**

Compute the ending inventory under the dollar-value LIFO method at December 31, 1985. The cost to retail ratio for 1985 was 45%.

**\*E9–19** Prange Stores has just experienced a large fire loss to its inventories. Fortunately, the records for the years 1982–1984 have been salvaged. The conventional retail method was in use during 1982. The corporation switched to the LIFO retail method for the year ending 1983. You have been hired to reconstruct the divisional financial statements for the years 1982–1984 and are currently engaged in recomputing the final inventory figures as originally stated in the financial statements of the respective years. The following data are available for your examination.

| | 1982 | 1983 | 1984 |
|---|---|---|---|
| Beginning inventory @ retail | $135,000 | $250,000 | $318,000 |
| Ending inventory @ retail | 250,000 | 318,000 | 297,000 |
| Ending inventory @ cost (Conventional) | ? | 225,780 | 213,840 |
| Ending inventory @ cost (LIFO) | ? | ? | ? |
| Price index | 100 | 106 | 110 |
| Cost ratio—conventional retail | 72 | 71 | 72 |
| Cost ratio—LIFO retail | 74 | 75 | 76 |

**Instructions**

(a) Compute the ending inventory under the (1) conventional retail method for 1982, and (2) the LIFO retail method for the years 1983–1984. Round to the nearest dollar.

(b) Prepare the entry that was necessary when the change was made from the conventional retail to the LIFO retail method.

**\*E9–20** Finn's, Ltd., a local retailing concern, has decided to change from the conventional retail inventory method to the LIFO retail method starting on January 1, 1984. The company recomputed its ending inventory for 1983 in accordance with the procedures necessary to switch to LIFO retail. The inventory computed was $178,500.

**Instructions**

Assuming that Finn's ending inventory for 1983 under the conventional retail inventory method was $175,000, prepare the appropriate journal entry on January 1, 1984.

## PROBLEMS

**P9-1** Biagioni Company manufactures desks. Most of the company's desks are standard models and are sold on the basis of catalog prices. At December 31, 1984, the following finished desks appear in the company's inventory:

| Finished desks | A | B | C | D |
|---|---|---|---|---|
| 1984 catalog selling price | $440 | $470 | $870 | $1,040 |
| FIFO cost per inventory list 12/31/84 | 450 | 440 | 840 | 980 |
| Estimated current cost to manufacture (at December 31, 1984 and early 1985) | 460 | 430 | 710 | 1,000 |
| Sales commissions and estimated other costs of disposal | 40 | 70 | 120 | 160 |
| 1985 catalog selling price | 480 | 520 | 1,000 | 1,200 |

The 1984 catalog was in effect through November, 1984 and the 1985 catalog is effective as of December 1, 1984. All catalog prices are net of the usual discounts. Generally, the company attempts to obtain a 25% gross margin on selling price and has usually been successful in doing so.

**Instructions**

At what amount should each of the four desks appear in the company's December 31, 1984 inventory, assuming that the company has adopted a lower of FIFO cost or market approach for valuation of inventories on an individual item basis?

**P9-2** Liverpool Leather Co. follows the practice of valuing its inventory at the lower of cost or market. The following information is available from the company's inventory records as of December 31, 1984.

| Item | On Hand Quantity | Unit Cost | Replacement Cost/Unit | Estimated Unit Selling Price | Completion & Disposal Costs/Unit | Normal Unit Profit |
|---|---|---|---|---|---|---|
| A | 1,500 | $4.50 | $5.50 | $ 7.50 | $1.50 | $1.40 |
| B | 1,200 | 7.20 | 8.00 | 8.00 | .90 | .90 |
| C | 800 | 4.20 | 4.00 | 6.00 | 1.10 | .60 |
| D | 200 | 8.20 | 9.00 | 8.00 | .60 | 2.00 |
| E | 800 | 4.80 | 7.40 | 10.00 | 3.20 | 3.70 |

**Instructions**

(a) Indicate the inventory price that should be used for each item under the lower of cost or market rule.

(b) Liverpool applies the lower of cost or market rule directly to each item in the inventory and uses a perpetual inventory system to account for the items above. Give the adjusting entry, if one is necessary, to write down the ending inventory from cost to market.

(c) If Liverpool applies the lower of cost or market rule to the total of the inventory, what is the proper dollar amount for inventory as of 12/31/84?

**P9-3** Kenny Company is a food wholesaler that supplies independent grocery stores in the immediate region. The company has a perpetual inventory system for all of its food products. The first-in, first-out (FIFO) method of inventory valuation is used to determine the cost of the inventory at the end of each month. Transactions and other related information regarding two of the items (instant coffee and sugar) carried by Kenny are given below for October 1983, the last month of Kenny's fiscal year.

|  | Instant Coffee | Sugar |
|---|---|---|
| Standard unit of packaging: | Case containing 24, one-pound jars | Baler containing 12, five-pound bags |
| Inventory, 10/1/83: | 1,200 cases @ $53.22 per case | 600 balers @ $6.50 per baler |
| Purchases: | **1.** 10/10/83—1,600 cases @ $56.40 per case plus freight of $480. | **1.** 10/5/83—640 balers @ $5.76 per baler plus freight of $320. |
|  | **2.** 10/20/83—1,600 cases @ $57.00 per case plus freight of $480. | **2.** 10/16/83—640 balers @ $5.40 per baler plus freight of $320. |
|  |  | **3.** 10/24/83—640 balers @ $5.04 per baler plus freight of $320. |
| Purchase terms: | 2/10, net/30, f.o.b. shipping point | Net 30 days, f.o.b. shipping point |
| October sales: | 3,400 cases @ $76.00 per case | 2,200 balers @ $7.80 per baler |
| Returns and allowances: | A customer returned 50 cases that had been shipped by error. The customer's account was credited for $3,800. | As the October 16 purchase was unloaded, 20 balers were discovered as damaged. A representative of the trucking firm confirmed the damage and the balers were discarded. Credit of $108 for the merchandise and $10 for the freight was received by Kenny. |
| Inventory values including freight and net of purchase discounts— 10/31/83: |  |  |
| • Most recent quoted price | $56.65 per case | $5.30 per baler |
| • Net realizable value | $60.80 per case | $5.20 per baler |
| • Net realizable value less a normal markup of 12½% | $53.20 per case | $4.55 per baler |

Kenney's sales terms are 1/10, net/30, f.o.b. shipping point. Kenny records all purchases net of purchase discounts and takes all purchase discounts.

**Instructions**

(a) Calculate the number of units in inventory and the FIFO unit cost for instant coffee and sugar as of October 31, 1983.

(b) Kenny Company applies the lower of cost or market rule in valuing its year-end inventory. Calculate the total dollar amount of the inventory for instant coffee and sugar applying the lower of cost or market rule on an individual product basis.

(c) Could Kenny Company apply the lower of cost or market rule to groups of products or the inventory as a whole rather than on an individual product basis? Explain your answer.

(CMA adapted)

**P9–4** Luoma, Inc. lost most of its inventory in a fire in December just before the year-end physical inventory was taken. The corporation's books disclosed the following:

| | | | |
|---|---|---|---|
| Beginning inventory | $120,000 | Sales | $440,000 |
| Purchases for the year | 360,000 | Sales returns | 10,000 |
| Purchase returns | 34,000 | Rate of gross profit on sales | 20% |

Merchandise with a selling price of $12,000 remained undamaged after the fire. Damaged merchandise with an original selling price of $8,000 had a net realizable value of $2,000.

**Instructions**

Compute the amount of the loss as a result of the fire, assuming that the corporation had no insurance coverage.

**P9–5** Borke Products Corporation, which began operations in 1981, always values its inventories at the current replacement cost. Its annual inventory figure is arrived at by taking a physical inventory and then pricing each item in the physical inventory at current prices determined from recent vendors' invoices or catalogs. Here is the condensed income statement for this company for the last four years.

|  | 1981 | 1982 | 1983 | 1984 |
|---|---|---|---|---|
| Sales | $800,000 | $840,000 | $920,000 | $900,000 |
| Cost of goods sold | 580,000 | 610,000 | 650,000 | 660,000 |
| Gross profit | 220,000 | 230,000 | 270,000 | 240,000 |
| Operating expenses | 150,000 | 164,000 | 180,000 | 178,000 |
| Income before income taxes | $ 70,000 | $ 66,000 | $ 90,000 | $ 62,000 |

**Instructions**

(a) Do you see any objections to their procedure for valuing inventories?

(b) Assuming that the inventory at cost and as determined by the corporation at the end of each of the four years is as follows, restate the condensed income statements, using cost for inventories.

| Ending Inventory | At Cost | As Determined By Company |
|---|---|---|
| 1981 | $120,000 | $102,000 |
| 1982 | 130,000 | 104,000 |
| 1983 | 125,000 | 98,000 |
| 1984 | 135,000 | 115,000 |

**P9–6** Rashad Research, Inc. lost most of its inventory in a fire in December just before the year-end physical inventory was taken. Corporate records disclose the following:

| | | | |
|---|---|---|---|
| Inventory (beginning) | $ 85,000 | Sales | $350,000 |
| Purchases | 240,000 | Sales returns | 8,000 |
| Purchase returns | 15,000 | Gross profit % based on | |
| | | selling price | 25% |

Merchandise with a selling price of $20,000 remained undamaged after the fire, and damaged merchandise has a salvage value of $3,750. Rashad does not carry fire insurance on its inventory. It is estimated that the year-end inventory would have been subject to a normal 10% write-down for obsolescence.

**Instructions**

Prepare a formal labeled schedule computing the fire loss incurred by Rashad Research, Inc. (Do not use the retail inventory method.)

**P9–7** On June 30, 1984, a flash flood damaged the warehouse and factory of J. Cerepak Corporation, completely destroying the work-in-process inventory. There was no damage to either the raw materials or finished goods inventories. A physical inventory taken after the flood revealed the following valuations:

| | |
|---|---|
| Raw materials | $ 50,000 |
| Work-in-process | -0- |
| Finished goods | 125,000 |

The inventory on January 1, 1984, consisted of the following:

| | |
|---|---|
| Raw materials | $ 30,000 |
| Work-in-process | 120,000 |
| Finished goods | 140,000 |
| | $290,000 |

A review of the books and records disclosed that the gross profit margin historically approximated 25% of sales. The sales for the first six months of 1984 were $360,000. Raw material purchases were $115,000. Direct labor costs for this period were $80,000 and manufacturing overhead has historically been applied at 50% of direct labor.

**Instructions**

Compute the value of the work-in-process inventory lost at June 30, 1984.

**P9–8** The records for the Shoe Department of the Kathryn Siska Store are summarized below for the month of January.

Inventory, January 1, at retail, $12,000; at cost, $8,400
Purchases in January, at retail, $90,000; at cost, $60,000
Freight-in, $5,000
Purchase returns, at retail, $3,000; at cost, $2,000
Purchase allowances, $1,500
Transfers in from Department B, at retail, $3,000; at cost, $2,100
Net markups, $8,000
Net markdowns, $3,000
Inventory losses due to normal breakage, etc., at retail, $600
Sales at retail, $60,000
Sales returns, $1,600

**Instructions**

Compute the inventory for this department as of January 31, at (1) sales price, and (2) lower of average cost or market.

**P9–9** Presented below is information related to McComb's, Inc.

| | Cost | Retail |
|---|---|---|
| Inventory 12/31/1983 | $195,000 | $ 300,000 |
| Purchases | 900,000 | 1,350,000 |
| Purchase returns | 60,000 | 90,000 |
| Purchase discounts | 15,000 | — |
| Gross sales (after employee discounts) | — | 1,325,000 |
| Sales returns | — | 97,500 |
| Markups | — | 90,000 |
| Markup cancellations | — | 50,000 |
| Markdowns | — | 30,000 |
| Markdown cancellations | — | 15,000 |
| Freight-in | 80,000 | — |
| Employee discounts granted | — | 6,000 |
| Loss from breakage (normal) | — | 1,500 |

**Instructions**

Assuming that McComb's, Inc. uses the conventional retail inventory method, compute the cost of their ending inventory at December 31, 1984.

**P9–10** Bloomington Department Store, Inc. uses the retail inventory method to estimate ending inventory for its monthly financial statements. The following data pertain to a single department for the month of October, 1984.

| | |
|---|---|
| Inventory, October 1, 1984 | |
| At cost | $ 40,000 |
| At retail | 60,000 |
| Purchases (exclusive of freight and returns): | |
| At cost | 245,000 |
| At retail | 350,000 |
| Freight-in | 13,660 |

| Purchase returns | |
|---|---|
| At cost | 4,900 |
| At retail | 7,000 |
| Additional markups | 6,500 |
| Markup cancellations | 1,500 |
| Markdowns (net) | 1,600 |
| Normal spoilage and breakage | 9,000 |
| Sales | 282,500 |

**Instructions**

(a) Using the conventional retail method, prepare a schedule computing estimated lower of cost or market inventory for October 31, 1984.

(b) A department store using the conventional retail inventory method estimates the cost of its ending inventory as $58,000. An accurate physical count reveals only $44,000 of inventory at lower of cost or market. List the factors that may have caused the difference between the computed inventory and the physical count.

**P9–11** As of January 1, 1984, Roller Skate Store installed the retail method of accounting for its merchandise inventory.

To prepare the store's financial statements at June 30, 1984, you obtain these data.

| | Cost | Selling Price |
|---|---|---|
| Inventory, January 1 | $28,350 | $ 45,000 |
| Markdowns | | 10,500 |
| Markups | | 12,900 |
| Markdown cancellations | | 7,500 |
| Markup cancellations | | 3,450 |
| Purchases | 91,000 | 137,880 |
| Sales | | 125,000 |
| Purchase returns and allowances | 1,700 | 2,575 |
| Sales returns and allowances | | 6,000 |

**Instructions**

(a) Prepare a schedule to compute the Roller Skate Store's June 30, 1984, inventory under the conventional retail method of accounting for inventories.

(b) Without prejudice to your solution to part (a), assume that you computed the June 30, 1984 inventory to be $73,500 at retail and the ratio of cost to retail to be 74%. The general price level has increased from 100 at January 1, 1984 to 105 at June 30, 1984. Prepare a schedule to compute the June 30, 1984 inventory at the June 30 price level under the dollar-value LIFO method.

(AICPA adapted)

**\*P9–12** LaCrosse Department Store converted from the conventional retail method to the LIFO retail method on January 1, 1983, and is now considering converting to the dollar-value LIFO inventory method. During your examination of the financial statements for the year ended December 31, 1984, management requested that you furnish a summary showing certain computations of inventory cost for the past three years.

Here is the available information.

**1.** The inventory at January 1, 1982, had a retail value of $50,000 and cost of $30,000 based on the conventional retail method.

**2.** Transactions during 1982 were as follows:

| | Cost | Retail |
|---|---|---|
| Gross purchases | $280,000 | $489,000 |
| Purchase returns | 4,500 | 9,000 |
| Purchase discounts | 5,000 | |

| | | |
|---|---:|---:|
| Gross sales | | 492,000 |
| Sales returns | | 6,000 |
| Employee discounts | | 4,000 |
| Freight-in | 21,500 | |
| Net markups | | 30,000 |
| Net markdowns | | 10,000 |

3. The retail value of the December 31, 1983, inventory was $68,640, the cost ratio for 1983 under the LIFO retail method was 62%, and the regional price index was 104% of the January 1, 1983, price level.

4. The retail value of the December 31, 1984, inventory was $58,300, the cost ratio for 1984 under the LIFO retail method was 61%, and the regional price index was 106% of the January 1, 1983, price level.

**Instructions**

(a) Prepare a schedule showing the computation of the cost of inventory on hand at December 31, 1982, based on the conventional retail method.

(b) Prepare a schedule showing the recomputation of the inventory to be reported on December 31, 1982, in accordance with procedures necessary to convert from the conventional retail method to the LIFO retail method beginning January 1, 1983. Assume that the retail value of the December 31, 1982, inventory was $60,000.

(c) Without prejudice to your solution to part (b) assume that you computed the December 31, 1982, inventory (retail value $60,000) under the LIFO retail method at a cost of $36,000. Prepare a schedule showing the computations of the cost of the store's 1983 and 1984 year-end inventories under the dollar-value LIFO method.

(AICPA adapted)

**P9–13**  Eau Claire Corporation is an importer and wholesaler. Its merchandise is purchased from several suppliers and is warehoused by Eau Claire Corporation until sold to consumers.

In conducting her audit for the year ended June 30, 1984, the corporation's CPA determined that the system of internal control was good. Accordingly, she observed the physical inventory at an interim date, May 31, 1984, instead of at year-end.

The following information was obtained from the general ledger.

| | |
|---|---:|
| Inventory, July 1, 1983 | $ 97,500 |
| Physical inventory, May 31, 1984 | 95,000 |
| Sales for 11 months ended May 31, 1984 | 900,000 |
| Sales for year ended June 30, 1984 | 980,000 |
| Purchases for 11 months ended May 31, 1984 (before audit adjustments) | 668,000 |
| Purchases for year ended June 30, 1984 (before audit adjustments) | 800,000 |

The CPA's audit disclosed the following information.

| | |
|---|---:|
| Shipments received in May and included in the physical inventory but recorded as June purchases | 7,500 |
| Shipments received in unsalable condition and excluded from physical inventory; credit memos had not been received nor had chargebacks to vendors been recorded: | |
| Total at May 31, 1984 | 1,000 |
| Total at June 30, 1984 (including the May unrecorded chargebacks) | 1,500 |
| Deposit made with vendor and charged to purchases in April, 1984. Product was shipped in July, 1984. | 2,000 |
| Deposit made with vendor and charged to purchases in May, 1984. Product was shipped, f.o.b. destination, on May 29, 1984, and was included in May 31, 1984, physical inventory as goods in transit | 5,500 |
| Through the carelessness of the receiving department, a June shipment was damaged by rain. This shipment was later sold in June at its cost of $10,000. | |

**Instructions**

In audit engagements in which interim physical inventories are observed, a frequently used auditing procedure is to test the reasonableness of the year-end inventory by the application of gross profit ratios.

Prepare in good form the following schedules:
(a) Computation of the gross profit ratio for 11 months ended May 31, 1984.
(b) Computation by the gross profit method of cost of goods sold during June, 1984.
(c) Computation by the gross profit method of June 30, 1984, inventory.

(AICPA adapted)

**P9-14** On April 15, 1984, fire damaged the office and warehouse of Kenosha Tool Corporation. The only accounting record saved was the general ledger, from which the trial balance below was prepared.

|  | Kenosha Tool Corporation TRIAL BALANCE March 31, 1984 | |
|---|---|---|
| Cash | $ 9,000 | |
| Accounts receivable | 30,000 | |
| Inventory, December 31, 1983 | 60,000 | |
| Land | 20,000 | |
| Building and equipment | 120,000 | |
| Accumulated depreciation | | $ 37,200 |
| Other assets | 3,600 | |
| Accounts payable | | 23,700 |
| Other expense accruals | | 10,200 |
| Capital stock | | 100,000 |
| Retained earnings | | 47,700 |
| Sales | | 90,400 |
| Purchases | 40,000 | |
| Other expenses | 26,600 | |
| | $309,200 | $309,200 |

The following data and information have been gathered:

1. The fiscal year of the corporation ends on December 31.

2. An examination of the April bank statement and canceled checks revealed that checks written during the period April 1–15 totaled $11,600: $5,700 paid to accounts payable as of March 31, $2,000 for April merchandise shipments, and $3,900 paid for other expenses. Deposits during the same period amounted to $10,700, which consisted of receipts on account from customers with the exception of a $500 refund from a vendor for merchandise returned in April.

3. Correspondence with suppliers revealed unrecorded obligations at April 15 of $9,000 for April merchandise shipments, including $1,500 for shipments in transit on that date.

4. Customers acknowledged indebtedness of $28,000 at April 15, 1984. It was also estimated that customers owed another $5,000 that will never be acknowledged or recovered. Of the acknowledged indebtedness, $600 will probably be uncollectible.

5. The companies insuring the inventory agreed that the corporation's fire-loss claim should be based on the assumption that the overall gross profit ratio for the past two years was in effect during the current year. The corporation's audited financial statements disclosed this information:

| | Year Ended December 31 | |
| --- | --- | --- |
| | 1983 | 1982 |
| Net sales | $440,000 | $360,000 |
| Net purchases | 264,000 | 226,000 |
| Beginning inventory | 45,000 | 50,000 |
| Ending inventory | 60,000 | 45,000 |

6. Inventory with a cost of $6,500 was salvaged and sold for $3,000. The balance of the inventory was a total loss.

## Instructions

Prepare a schedule computing the amount of inventory fire loss. The supporting schedule of the computation of the gross profit margin should be in good form.

(AICPA adapted)

*P9–15 College Book Store uses the conventional retail method and is now considering converting to the retail LIFO method for the period beginning 1/1/1984. Available information consists of the following:

| | 1983 | | 1984 | |
| --- | --- | --- | --- | --- |
| | Cost | Retail | Cost | Retail |
| Inventory 1/1/1983 | $ 12,600 | $ 22,500 | $ ? | $ ? |
| Purchases (net) | 266,400 | 360,000 | 245,000 | 345,000 |
| Net additional markups | — | 5,000 | — | 10,000 |
| Net markdowns | — | 2,500 | — | 5,000 |
| Sales (net) | — | 342,000 | — | 340,000 |
| Loss from breakage | — | 1,000 | — | -0- |
| Applicable price index | — | 100 | — | 104 |

Following is a schedule showing the computation of the cost of inventory on hand at 12/31/1983 based on the conventional retail method.

| | Cost | Retail |
| --- | --- | --- |
| Inventory 1/1/1983 | $ 12,600 | $ 22,500 |
| Purchases (net) | 266,400 | 360,000 |
| Net additional markups | — | 5,000 |
| Goods available | $279,000 | 387,500 |
| (Ratio: $279,000 ÷ $387,500 = 72%) | | |
| Less: | | |
| Sales | | 342,000 |
| Net markdowns | | 2,500 |
| Loss from breakage | | 1,000 |
| Inventory 12/31/1983 at retail | | $ 42,000 |
| Inventory 12/31/1983 at lower of cost or market Cost ($42,000 × 72%) | $ 30,240 | |

## Instructions

(a) Prepare a schedule showing the recomputation of the inventory on hand at 12/31/1983 in accordance with the procedures necessary to convert from the conventional retail method to the LIFO retail method beginning January 1, 1984.

(b) Prepare the journal entry necessary to restate the 1/1/84 inventory to LIFO retail.

(c) Prepare a schedule showing the computation of the 12/31/1984 inventory by the LIFO retail method as adjusted for fluctuating prices. Without prejudice to your answers to parts (a) or (b) above, assume that you computed the 12/31/1983 inventory (retail value $42,000) under the LIFO retail method at a cost of $29,400. Round your answer to the nearest dollar.

**\*P9–16** Lansirs, Inc., which uses the conventional retail inventory method, wishes to change to the LIFO retail method beginning with the accounting year ending December 31, 1984.

Amounts as shown below appear on the firm's books before adjustment:

|  | At Cost | At Retail |
|---|---|---|
| Inventory, January 1, 1984 | $ 5,120 | $ 9,000 |
| Purchases in 1984 | 90,000 | 147,000 |
| Markups in 1984 |  | 8,000 |
| Markdowns in 1984 |  | 5,000 |
| Sales in 1984 |  | 124,000 |

You are to assume that all markups and markdowns apply to 1984 purchases, and that it is appropriate to treat the entire inventory as a single department.

**Instructions**

Compute the inventory at December 31, 1984, under:

(a) Conventional retail method.

(b) Last-in, first-out retail method, effecting the change in method as of January 1, 1984. Assume that the cost to retail percentage for 1983 was recomputed correctly in accordance with procedures necessary to change to LIFO. This ratio was 62%.

(AICPA adapted)

# CHAPTER 10

# Current Liabilities

In recent years the concept of liabilities apparently has been undergoing a change. One reason for the increased attention being paid to liabilities is that financial statements have become more complicated because of the increase in special financing and sales agreements, new labor contract formulas and provisions, and more complex tax laws. Also, most accounting thought and analysis have been directed toward the determination of the debit, the valuation of the assets, or the charge to expense, with the related liabilities being handled as an afterthought and as expediently as possible. Although it is true that all liabilities have credit balances, it is debatable whether all credits appearing above the stockholders' equity section in published balance sheets are liabilities, or even that all liabilities have been recorded.

## WHAT IS A LIABILITY?

The question, "What is a liability?" is not easy to answer. It seems clear that liabilities include more than debts arising from borrowings. The acquisition of goods or services on credit terms gives rise to liabilities and is much like borrowing. Less similar are liabilities resulting from the imposition of taxes, withholdings from employees' wages and salaries, dividend declarations, and product warranties.

To illustrate the complexity of this issue, one might ask whether preferred stock is a liability or an ownership claim. The first reaction is to say that preferred stock is in fact an ownership claim and should be reported as part of stockholders' equity. But, assuming that the preferred stock is cumulative, nonparticipating, and callable by the issuer at any time, is it a liability or part of stockholders' equity? Or, to go even one step further—assume that the preferred stock is cumulative, nonparticipating, and is callable by *either* issuer or holder on demand. Would the preferred stock now be a liability?[1] This question and others

---

[1] It should be noted that this illustration is not just a theoretical exercise. In practice, there are a number of preferred stock issues that have all the characteristics of a debt instrument, except that they are called and legally classified preferred stock. In some cases, for example, the IRS has even permitted the dividend payments to be treated as interest expense for tax purposes. This issue is discussed further in Chapter 15.

similar to it are difficult to answer in the absence of concise definitions. For decades the official definitions of liabilities have been stated in terms of the rules and procedures of accounting, and they have been conceptually deficient. As a result, the liability section of the balance sheet has degenerated into a catchall for all leftover credit balances, some of them ill-conceived.

Recently, the FASB, as part of its conceptual framework study, defined liabilities as **"probable future sacrifices of economic benefits arising from present obligations of a particular entity to transfer assets or provide services to other entities in the future as a result of past transactions or events."**[2] The Board further stated that a liability has three essential characteristics: (1) it is a present obligation that entails settlement by probable future transfer or use of cash, goods, or services; (2) it must be an unavoidable obligation of a particular enterprise; and (3) the transaction or other event obligating the enterprise must have already happened. Although this definition may be subject to different interpretations, it is a welcome addition to the professional literature, and it is hoped that it will replace the varied definitions offered by differing authorities in the past.[3]

Because liabilities involve future disbursements of assets or services, one of the most important features is the date on which they are payable. Currently maturing obligations represent a demand on the current assets of the enterprise—a demand that must be satisfied promptly and in the ordinary course of business if operations are to be continued. Liabilities with a more distant due date do not, as a rule, represent a claim on the enterprise's current resources, and they are in a slightly different category. This feature gives rise to the basic division of liabilities into (1) current liabilities and (2) long-term debt.

## NATURE OF CURRENT LIABILITIES

For many years payment within one year was the characteristic that distinguished a current liability from a long-term debt. This one-year rule, although simple and easy to follow, produced some unreasonable results when the operating cycle of a business exceeded one year. Under currently acceptable practice, both current liabilities and current assets are defined in terms of the operating cycle of the individual enterprise. The **operating cycle** is the period of time elapsing between the acquisition of goods and services involved in the manufacturing process and the final cash realization resulting from sales and subsequent collections. Industries that manufacture products requiring an aging process and certain capital intensive industries have an operating cycle of considerably more than one year; on the other hand, some processing and most retail and service establishments have several operating cycles within a year.

Current assets are those assets which can reasonably be expected to be converted into cash or consumed in operations within a single operating cycle or within a year if more than one cycle is completed each year. **Current liabilities are "obligations whose liquidation is reasonably expected to require use of existing resources properly classified as current**

---

[2]"Elements of Financial Statements of Business Enterprises," *Statement of Financial Accounting Concepts No. 3* (Stamford, Conn.: FASB, 1980), pars. 28 and 29.

[3]For definitions that are similar to the new FASB definition: see Maurice Moonitz, "The Changing Concept of a Liability," *The Journal of Accountancy* (May, 1960), pp. 41–46; Eldon S. Hendricksen, *Accounting Theory,* 3rd edition (Homewood, Ill.: Richard D. Irwin, Inc. 1977), p. 451; and American Accounting Association, *Accounting and Reporting Standards for Corporate Financial Statements* (Sarasota, Fla.: AAA, 1957), p. 16.

**assets, or the creation of other current liabilities.**[4] This definition has gained wide acceptance because it recognizes operating cycles of varying lengths in different industries and takes into consideration the important relationship between current assets and current liabilities. The FASB affirmed this concept of **"maturity within one year or the operating cycle whichever is longer"** in its definition of short-term obligations in *Statement No. 6.*[5]

## VALUATION OF CURRENT LIABILITIES

Theoretically, liabilities should be measured by the present value of the future outlay of cash required to liquidate them. But, in practice, current liabilities are usually recorded in accounting records and reported in financial statements at their full maturity amount. Because of the short time periods involved, frequently less than one year, the difference between the present value of a current liability and the maturity value is not usually large. The slight overstatement of liabilities that results from carrying current liabilities at maturity value is accepted on the grounds of immateriality. *APB Opinion No. 21,* "Interest on Receivables and Payables," specifically exempts from present value measurements those payables arising from transactions with suppliers in the normal course of business that do not exceed approximately one year.[6]

## DIFFERENCES IN CURRENT LIABILITIES

We have concluded that liabilities are probable future sacrifices arising from obligations resulting from past transactions. But within this sphere of similarity, liabilities possess characteristics that lend themselves to categorization. All liabilities, because they are probable future sacrifices, involve an element of uncertainty. The differences in degrees of uncertainty related to liabilities are the dissimilarities that allow us to discuss current liabilities under the following categories.

1. Determinable current liabilities.
2. Contingent current liabilities.

## DETERMINABLE CURRENT LIABILITIES

The types of liabilities discussed in this category are susceptible to precise measurement. The amount of cash that will be needed to discharge the obligation and the date of payment or discharge are reasonably certain. There is nothing uncertain about (1) the fact that the obligation has been incurred and (2) the amount of the obligation. The existence of written or implied contracts or the imposition of legal statutes minimizes the uncertainty in amount, risk, and timing of these liabilities. The primary problem is one of discovery, which arises from the possibility of omitting these liabilities. In contrast to long-term debts,

[4]Committee on Accounting Procedure, American Institute of Certified Public Accountants, "Accounting Research and Terminology Bulletins," Final Edition (New York: AICPA, 1961), p. 21.

[5]"Classification of Short-term Obligations Expected to be Refinanced," *Statement of Financial Accounting Standards No. 6* (Stamford, Conn.: FASB, 1975), par. 2.

[6]"Interest on Receivables and Payables," *Opinions of the Accounting Principles Board No. 21* (New York: AICPA, 1971), par. 3.

which are normally large in amount and supported by documentary evidence consisting of contracts, authorization, and correspondence, current liabilities may result from unwritten extensions of credit or unrecorded accruals, and they may be small. Once these liabilities are discovered, however, the amount is readily determinable.

## Accounts Payable

Accounts payable, or **trade accounts payable,** are balances owed to others for goods, supplies, and services purchased on open account. Accounts payable arise because of the time lag between the receipt of services or acquisition of title to assets and the payment for them. This period of extended credit is usually found in the terms of the sale (for example, 2/10, n/30 or 1/10, E.O.M.) and is commonly 30 to 60 days.

Most accounting systems are designed to record liabilities for purchase of goods when the goods are received or, practically, when the invoices are received. Frequently there is some delay in recording the goods and the related liability on the books. In addition, if title has passed to the purchaser before the goods are received, the transaction should be recorded at the time of title passage. As a result, the accountant must pay particular attention to transactions occurring near the end of one accounting period and at the beginning of the next to ascertain that the record of goods received (the inventory) is in agreement with that of the liability (accounts payable) and that both are recorded in the proper period.

Measuring the amount of an account payable poses no particular difficulty because the invoice received from the creditor specifies the due date and the exact outlay in money that is necessary to settle the account. The only calculation that may be necessary concerns the amount of cash discount. See Chapter 8 for illustrations of entries related to accounts payable and purchase discounts.

## Notes Payable

Obligations in the form of written promissory notes that are classified as current liabilities are usually either (1) trade notes, (2) short-term loan notes, or (3) current maturities of long-term debts.

**Trade Notes**   Trade notes payable represent the unpaid face amount of promissory notes owed to suppliers of goods, services, and equipment. In some industries and for certain classes of customers, promissory notes are required as part of the transaction in lieu of the normal extension of open account or verbal credit. Normally, both the due date and the amount of the outlay necessary to discharge the note are contained on the note. The only calculation that is commonly involved is the calculation of interest if the note is interest bearing.

**Short-Term Loan Notes**   Short-term promissory notes payable to banks or loan companies represent a current liability and generally arise from cash loans. When these notes are interest bearing, it is necessary to record and report in financial statements any accrued interest payable and to carry the note payable as a liability in the amount of its **face value** (also called **principal amount**).

If a **noninterest-bearing note** is issued, the bank or loan company **discounts** the note and remits the proceeds to the borrower. This discounting practice may lead to an inaccurate recording of the transaction. To illustrate, on October 1 the Airfrate Company has its

$100,000 one-year noninterest-bearing note discounted at 9% at the Corner National Bank. The Airfrate Company receives the proceeds of $91,000 and assumes the obligation to pay $100,000 to the bank in 12 months. It should be apparent that the Airfrate Company has borrowed $91,000 for a period of one year at a cost of $9,000. Although the **stated discount rate** was 9%, the **effective interest rate** was 9.89% ($9,000/$91,000), because the full $100,000 is not available to the Airfrate Company during the year. A loan under these circumstances is recorded on the date the loan is completed in the following manner:

| | | |
|---|---|---|
| Cash | 91,000 | |
| Discount on Notes Payable | 9,000 | |
| Notes Payable | | 100,000 |

The balance in the Discount on Notes Payable account would be deducted on the balance sheet from Notes Payable. Interest expense would be recorded in monthly increments of $750 by reducing Discount on Notes Payable through the following entry (assuming straight-line amortization approximates the effective interest method of amortization):

| | | |
|---|---|---|
| Interest Expense $(9,000 \div 12)$ | 750 | |
| Discount on Notes Payable | | 750 |

Thus, a balance sheet prepared at December 31 would show:

| | | |
|---|---|---|
| Current liabilities | | |
| Notes payable | $100,000 | |
| Less: Discount on notes payable | 6,750 | |
| | | $93,250 |

The interest expense of $2,250 for the three-month period would be reported in the income statement.

**Current Maturities of Long-Term Debts**   The portion of bonds, mortgage notes, and other long-term indebtedness that matures within the next fiscal year is reported as a current liability. When only a part of a long-term debt is to be paid within the next 12 months, as in the case of serial bonds that are to be retired through a series of annual installments, the maturing portion of the debt is reported as a current liability, the balance as a long-term debt. Long-term debts maturing currently should not be included as current liabilities if they are (1) to be retired by assets accumulated for this purpose that properly have not been shown as current assets, (2) to be refinanced, or retired from the proceeds of a new debt issue (see next topic below), or (3) to be converted into capital stock. The plan for liquidation of such a debt should be disclosed either parenthetically or by a footnote to the financial statements.

## Short-Term Obligations Expected to be Refinanced

Short-term obligations are those debts that are scheduled to mature within one year after the date of an enterprise's balance sheet or within an enterprise's operating cycle, which-ever is longer. Some short-term obligations are expected to be refinanced on a long-term basis and, therefore, are not expected to require the use of working capital during the next year (or operating cycle).[7] Before 1975, the accounting profession generally supported the exclusion of short-term obligations from current liabilities if they are "expected to be refinanced." Because the profession provided no specific guidelines, however, determination of whether a short-term obligation was "expected to be refinanced" was usually based solely on management's **intent** to refinance on a long-term basis. A company may sell short-term commercial paper to finance new plant and equipment, intending eventually to refinance it on a long-term basis. Or it may obtain a five-year bank loan but, because the bank prefers it, handle the actual financing with 90-day notes, which it must keep turning over (renewing). So what is it, long-term debt or current liabilities? To illustrate this problem of classification, the Penn Central Railroad (before it went bankrupt) was deep into short-term debt and commercial paper but classified it as long-term debt. Why? Because the railroad believed it had commitments by lenders to keep refinancing the short-term debt. When those commitments suddenly disappeared, it was good-bye Pennsy. As the Greek philosopher Epictetus once said, "Some things in this world are not and yet appear to be."

**Refinancing Criteria.**   In 1975 the FASB issued *Statement No. 6,* in which it set forth authoritative criteria for determining the circumstances under which short-term obligations may properly be excluded from current liabilities. An enterprise is required to exclude a short-term obligation from current liabilities only if both of the following conditions are met:

1. It must **intend to refinance** the obligation on a long-term basis, and
2. It must **demonstrate an ability** to consummate the refinancing.[8]

Intention to refinance on a long-term basis means the enterprise intends to refinance the short-term obligation so that the use of working capital will not be required during the ensuing fiscal year or operating cycle, if longer. The ability to consummate the refinancing may be demonstrated by:

(a) **Actually refinancing** the short-term obligation by issuance of a long-term obligation or equity securities after the date of the balance sheet but before it is issued; or
(b) Entering into a **financing agreement** that clearly permits the enterprise to refinance the debt on a long-term basis on terms that are readily determinable.

If an actual refinancing occurs, the portion of the short-term obligation to be excluded from current liabilities may not exceed the proceeds from the new obligation or equity securities issued that are applied to retire the short-term obligation. For example, Montavon Winery with $3,000,000 of short-term debt issued 100,000 shares of common stock subsequent to the date of the balance sheet but before the balance sheet was issued, intending to use the proceeds to liquidate the short-term debt at its maturity. If the net proceeds from the sale of the 100,000 shares totaled $2,000,000, only that amount of the short-term debt could be excluded from current liabilities.

When a financing agreement is relied upon to demonstrate ability to refinance a short-term obligation on a long-term basis, the agreement must meet all of the following conditions:

---

[7] *Refinancing a short-term obligation on a long-term basis* means either replacing it with a long-term obligation or with equity securities, or renewing, extending, or replacing it with short-term obligations for an uninterrupted period extending beyond one year (or the operating cycle, if longer) from the date of the enterprise's balance sheet.

[8] "Classification of Short-term Obligations Expected to be Refinanced," *Statement of Financial Accounting Standards No. 6* (Stamford, Conn.: FASB, 1975), pars. 10 and 11.

(a) The agreement must be noncancelable as to all parties and must extend beyond the normal operating cycle of the company or one year, whichever is longer.

(b) At the balance sheet date and at the date of its issuance, the company must not be in violation of the agreement.

(c) The lender or investor is expected to be financially capable of honoring the agreement.

The amount of short-term debt that can be excluded from current liabilities:

1. Cannot exceed the amount available for refinancing under the agreement.
2. Must be adjusted for any limitations or restrictions in the agreement that indicate that the full amount obtainable will not be available to retire the short-term obligations.
3. Cannot exceed a reasonable estimate of the minimum amount expected to be available, if the amount available for refinancing will fluctuate (that is, the most conservative estimate must be used).

If any of these three amounts cannot be reasonably estimated, the entire amount of the short-term debt must be included in current liabilities.

As an illustration of a fluctuating amount situation (item 3 above), consider the following:

Chicago Casket Company enters into an agreement with Continental Bank to borrow up to 80% of the amount of its trade receivables. During the next fiscal year, the receivables are expected to range between a low of $900,000 in the first quarter and a high of $1,700,000 in the third quarter. The minimum amount expected to be available to refinance the short-term obligations that mature during the first quarter of the next year is $720,000 (80% of the expected low for receivables during the first quarter). Consequently, no more than $720,000 of short-term obligations may be excluded from current liabilities at the balance sheet date.

An additional question relates to whether a short-term obligation should be excluded from current liabilities if it is paid off after the balance sheet date and then subsequently replaced by long-term debt before the balance sheet is issued (for example, the balance sheet date might be December 31, 1983; the short-term debt repayment date January 17, 1984; the long-term debt issuance date February 3, 1984; and the balance sheet issuance date March 1, 1984). Because the repayment of a short-term obligation **before** funds are obtained through a long-term refinancing requires the use of current assets, the profession requires that:

. . . if a short-term obligation is repaid after the balance sheet date and subsequently a long-term obligation or equity securities are issued whose proceeds are used to replenish current assets before the balance sheet is issued, the short-term obligation shall not be excluded from current liabilities at the balance sheet date.[9]

## Disclosure of Short-Term Obligations Expected to be Refinanced

*FASB Statement No. 6* specifies that "a total of current liabilities shall be presented in classified balance sheets."[10] If a short-term obligation is excluded from current liabilities

---

[9]"Classification of a Short-Term Obligation Repaid Prior to Being Replaced by a Long-term Security" (an interpretation of *FASB Statement No. 6*), *FASB Interpretation No. 8* (Stamford, Conn.: FASB, 1976), par. 3.

[10]A "classified" balance sheet shows separate classifications of current assets and current liabilities permitting ready determination of working capital. *Statement No. 6* does not apply to enterprises in several specialized industries (including broker-dealers and finance, real estate, and stock life insurance companies) for which unclassified balance sheets are prepared because the current/noncurrent distinction is deemed in practice to have little or no relevance.

because of refinancing, the footnote to the financial statements should include:

1. A general description of the financing agreement.
2. The terms of any new obligation incurred or to be incurred.
3. The terms of any equity security issued or to be issued.

When refinancing on a long-term basis is expected to be accomplished through the issuance of equity securities, it is not appropriate to include the short-term obligation in owners' equity. The obligation is a liability and not owners' equity at the date of the balance sheet.

| Actual Refinancing | |
| --- | --- |
| Current liabilities: | December 31, 1982 |
| Accounts payable | $ 3,600,000 |
| Accrued payables | 2,500,000 |
| Income taxes payable | 1,100,000 |
| Current portion of long-term debt | 1,000,000 |
| Total current liabilities | $ 8,200,000 |
| Long-term debt: | |
| Notes payable refinanced in January 1983—Footnote 1 | $ 2,000,000 |
| 8% bonds due serially through 1996 | 15,000,000 |
| Total long-term debt | $17,000,000 |

*Footnote 1.* On January 19, 1983, the Company issued 50,000 shares of Common Stock and received proceeds totaling $2,385,000 of which $2,000,000 was used to liquidate notes payable that matured on February 1, 1983. Accordingly, such notes payable have been classified as long-term debt at December 31, 1982.

| Financing Agreement | |
| --- | --- |
| Current liabilities: | December 31, 1982 |
| Accounts payable | $ 3,600,000 |
| Accrued payables | 2,500,000 |
| Income taxes payable | 1,100,000 |
| Current portion on long-term debt | 1,000,000 |
| Total current liabilities | $ 8,200,000 |
| Long-term debt: | |
| Notes payable expected to be refinanced in 1983—Footnote 1 | $ 2,000,000 |
| 8% bonds due serially through 1996 | 15,000,000 |
| Total long-term debt | $17,000,000 |

*Footnote 1.* Under a financing agreement with a major New York bank the Company may borrow up to $4,000,000 at any time through 1984. Amounts borrowed under the agreement bear interest at 1% above the bank's prime interest rate and mature three years from the date of the loan. The agreement requires the Company to maintain a working capital level of $9,000,000 and prohibits the payment of dividends on common stock without prior approval of the bank. The notes have been classified as long-term debt because the Company intends to borrow $2,000,000 under the agreement to liquidate its notes payable which mature on May 1, 1983.

Short-term obligations expected to be refinanced may be shown in captions distinct from both current liabilities and long-term debt, such as "Interim Debt," "Short-term Debt Expected to be Refinanced," and "Intermediate Debt."

The disclosure requirements are illustrated on page 441 for an actual refinancing situation and a financing agreement situation.

## Dividends Payable

A **cash dividend payable** is an amount owed by a corporation to its stockholders as a result of a distribution that the board of directors has formally authorized. At the date of declaration the corporation assumes a liability that places the stockholders in the position of creditors relative to the amount of dividends declared. Because cash dividends are always paid within one year of declaration (generally within three months), they are classified as current liabilities.

Accumulated but undeclared dividends on cumulative preferred stock are not a recognized liability because **preferred dividends in arrears** are not an obligation until formal action is taken by the board of directors authorizing the distribution of earnings. Nevertheless, the amount of cumulative dividends unpaid should be disclosed as a footnote or it may be shown parenthetically in the capital stock section following a description of the stock.

Dividends payable in the form of additional shares of stock are not recognized as a liability because **stock dividends** do not require future outlays of assets or services and they are revocable by the board of directors at any time prior to issuance. Even so, such undistributed stock dividends are generally reported in the stockholders' equity section because they represent retained earnings in the process of transfer to paid-in capital.

## Returnable Deposits

Current liabilities of a company may include returnable deposits (monies) received from customers and employees. Deposits may be received from customers to guarantee performance of a contract or service or as guarantees to cover payment of expected future obligations. For example, telephone companies often require a deposit upon installation of a phone. Deposits may also be received from customers as guarantees for possible damage to property left with the customer. Some companies require their employees to make deposits for the return of keys or other company property or for locker privileges. The classification of these items as current or noncurrent liabilities is dependent on the time involved between the date of the deposit and the termination of the relationship that required the deposit.

## Liability on the Advance Sale of Tickets, Tokens, and Certificates

Transportation companies may issue tickets or tokens that can be exchanged or used to pay for future fares, or restaurants may issue meal tickets that can be exchanged or used to pay for future meals, or retail stores may issue gift certificates that are redeemable in merchandise. In such cases, the businesses have received cash in exchange for promises to perform services or to furnish goods at some indefinite future date.

The balance sheet should reflect the obligation for any outstanding instruments that are redeemable in goods or services; the income statement should reflect the revenues earned as a result of performances during the period. The sale of these tickets, tokens, and certificates is recorded by a debit to Cash and a credit to a current liability account usually described as Deferred or Unearned Revenue. As the claims are redeemed, the liability account is debited and an appropriate revenue account is credited.

Because these advances are usually small in amount and relatively numerous, some are not presented to the issuing company for redemption. If these claims are rendered void by lapse of time or some other reason as defined by the sales agreement, the amount of forfeited claims may be easily measured. If the offer is of indefinite duration, however, it is necessary to reduce the liability balance by an estimate of the claims that will not be redeemed and to credit an appropriate account for the gain that results from forfeitures.

## Collections for Third Parties

A common current liability results from a company collecting taxes from customers for a governmental unit and withholding taxes from employees' payrolls.

**Sales Taxes**   Sales taxes on transfers of tangible personal property and on certain services must be collected from customers and remitted to the proper governmental authority. A liability must be set up to provide for the taxes collected from customers but as yet unremitted to the tax authority. If the actual sales total and the sales tax collections are recorded separately at the time of the sale, the sales tax payable account should reflect the liability for sales taxes due the government. The entry below is the proper one for a sale of $3,000 when a 4% sales tax is in effect.

| | | |
|---|---|---|
| Cash or Accounts Receivable | 3,120 | |
| Sales | | 3,000 |
| Sales Taxes Payable | | 120 |

When the sales tax collections credited to the liability account are not equal to the liability as computed by the governmental formula, an adjustment of the liability account may be made by recognizing a gain or a loss on sales tax collections.

In many companies, however, the sales tax and the amount of the sale are not segregated at the time of sale; both are credited in total in the sales account. To reflect correctly the actual amount of sales and the liability for sales taxes, the sales account must be debited for the amount of the sales taxes due the government on these sales and the sales taxes payable account credited for the same amount. As an illustration, assume that the sales account balance of $150,000 includes sales taxes of 4%. Because the amount recorded in the sales account is equal to sales plus 0.04 of sales, or 1.04 times the sales total, the sales are $150,000 ÷ 1.04, or $144,230.77. The sales tax liability is $5,769.23 ($144,230.77 × 0.04; or $150,000 − $144,230.77) and the following entry would be made to record the amount due the taxing unit:

| | | |
|---|---|---|
| Sales | 5,769.23 | |
| Sales Taxes Payable | | 5,769.23 |

**Social Security Taxes**   Since January 1, 1937, social security legislation has provided federal old-age, survivor, and disability insurance (O.A.S.D.I.) benefits for certain individuals and their families through the imposition of taxes on both the employer and the employee. All employers covered are required to collect the employee's share of this tax, by deducting it from the employee's gross pay, and to remit it to the government along with the employer's share. Both the employer and the employee are taxed at the same rate, currently 6.7% (1982) based on the employee's gross pay up to a $32,400 annual limit.

In 1965 Congress passed the first federal health insurance program for the aged—popularly known as Medicare. It is a two-part program designed to alleviate the high cost of medical care for those over 65. The Basic Plan, which provides hospital and other institutional services, is financed by a separate Hospital Insurance tax paid by both the employee and the employer on the employee's first $32,400 of annual compensation. The Voluntary Plan takes care of the major part of doctors' bills and other medical and health services and is financed by monthly payments from all who enroll plus matching funds from the Federal government.

The combination of the O.A.S.D.I. tax, more commonly called Federal Insurance Contribution Act (F.I.C.A.) tax, and the federal Hospital Insurance Tax is commonly referred to as the **social security tax.** The combined rate for these taxes is changed intermittently by acts of Congress.

The amount of unremitted employee and employer social security tax on gross wages paid should be reported by the employer as a current liability.

**Income Tax Withholding**   Federal and some state income tax laws require employers to withhold from the pay of each employee an amount approximating the applicable income tax due on those wages. The amount of income tax withheld is computed by the employer according to a government-prescribed formula or a government provided withholding tax table and is dependent on the length of the pay period and each employee's taxable wages, marital status, and claimed dependents.

If the income tax withheld plus the employee and the employer social security taxes exceeds specified amounts per month, the employer is required to make remittances to the government during the month. Monthly deposits are not required if the employer's liability for the calendar quarter is less than $500. Instead, the tax liability is remitted with the employer's quarterly payroll tax return.

**Other Payroll Deductions**   In addition to the payroll tax deductions, employers frequently deduct insurance premiums, employee savings, and union dues that must be recognized as liabilities to third parties to the extent that the amounts deducted are still among the employer's assets.

## Accrued Liabilities

Accrued liabilities (sometimes called **accrued expenses**) arise through accounting recognition of unpaid costs that come into existence as the result of past contractual commitments, past services received, or by operation of a tax law. The matching principle requires that incurred but unpaid expenses and the related liabilities be estimated as of the financial statement date, recorded in the accounts, and reported in the financial statements on an accrual basis. In published financial statements these accruals, with the exception of accrued taxes, are often conveniently combined under one heading. But, in recording these liabilities, appropriate account titles should be used, such as Wages Payable, Interest Payable, Property Taxes Payable, Payroll Taxes Payable, Bonuses Payable, and Income Taxes Payable. Payroll taxes payable, liability for compensated absences, and property taxes payable are three accrued expenses, common to every business, that deserve special mention. Income taxes payable and bonuses payable are accrued liabilities accorded special attention in the discussion of conditional payments that follows this section.

**Accrued Payroll Taxes**   As wages and salaries are earned by employees, the employer's share of F.I.C.A. (social security) tax accrues. The employer incurs a tax expense on each employee's earnings up to an annual maximum (6.7% on $32,400 in 1982). The employer is required to remit to the government its share of F.I.C.A. tax along with the amount of F.I.C.A. tax deducted from each employee's gross compensation. All unremitted employer F.I.C.A. taxes on employee earnings should be recorded as payroll tax expense and payroll tax payable.

Another payroll tax levied by the federal government in cooperation with state governments provides a system of unemployment insurance. All employers who (1) paid wages of $1,500 or more during any calendar quarter in the year or preceding year or (2) employed at least one individual on at least one day in each of 20 weeks during the current or preceding calendar year are subject to the Federal Unemployment Tax Act (F.U.T.A.). This tax is levied only on the employer at a rate of 3.4% (1982) on the first $6,000 of compensation paid to each employee during the calendar year. The employer is allowed a tax credit not to exceed 2.7% for contributions paid to a state plan for unemployment compensation. Thus, if an employer is subject to a state unemployment tax of 2.7% or more, only 0.7% tax is due the federal government.

State unemployment compensation laws differ from the federal law and differ among various states. Therefore, employers must be familiar with the unemployment tax laws in each state in which they pay wages and salaries. Although the normal state tax may be 2.7% or higher, all states provide for some form of merit rating under which a reduction in the state contribution rate is allowed. Employers who display by their benefit and contribution experience that they have provided steady employment are entitled to this reduction—if the size of the state fund is adequate to provide the reduction. In order not to penalize an employer who has earned a reduction in the state contribution rate, the federal law allows a credit of 2.7% even though the state contribution rate is less than 2.7%.

To illustrate the application of the federal and state unemployment compensation tax laws, assume that the Alpine Lodge Co. has a taxable payroll of $100,000. The federal rate is 3.4% and the state contribution rate is 2.7%, but because of good employment experience, the company's rate has been reduced by the state to 1%. The computation of the federal and state unemployment taxes for Alpine Lodge Co. is:

| | | | |
|---|---:|---:|---:|
| State tax payment (1% of $100,000) | | | $1,000 |
| Federal tax before credit (3.4% of $100,000) | | $3,400 | |
| Less: Credit for state tax payment | $1,000 | | |
| Additional credit (difference between $2,700 and $1,000) | 1,700 | 2,700 | |
| Net federal tax | | | 700 |
| Total federal and state tax | | | $1,700 |

The federal unemployment tax is paid annually on or before January 31, following the taxable calendar year, and state contributions generally are required to be paid quarterly. Because both the federal and the state unemployment taxes accrue on earned compensation, the amount of accrued but unpaid employer contributions should be recorded as an operating expense and as a current liability as financial statements are prepared at year end.

Accounting for employee payroll deductions and employer's payroll taxes is illustrated below. Assume a weekly payroll of $10,000 entirely subject to F.I.C.A. (6.7%), federal

(0.7%) and state (2.7%) unemployment taxes with income tax withholding of $1,320 and union dues of $88 deducted.

The entry to record the wages and salaries paid and the employee payroll deductions would be:

| | | |
|---|---|---|
| Wages and Salaries | 10,000 | |
| Withholding Taxes | | 1,320 |
| F.I.C.A. Taxes Payable | | 670 |
| Union Dues Payable to Local No. 257 | | 88 |
| Cash | | 7,922 |

The entry to record the employer payroll taxes would be:

| | | |
|---|---|---|
| Payroll Tax Expense | 1,010 | |
| F.I.C.A. Taxes Payable | | 670 |
| Federal Unemployment Tax Payable | | 70 |
| State Unemployment Tax Payable | | 270 |

The entries above illustrate the recording of the liabilities associated with withholdings from employees' wages and the employer's share of payroll taxes and fringe benefits. In a manufacturing enterprise, the cost side of this problem is commonly refined to the extent that all of the payroll costs (wages, payroll taxes, and fringe benefits) are allocated to appropriate cost accounts such as Direct Labor, Indirect Labor, Sales Salaries, Administrative Salaries, and the like.

This abbreviated and somewhat simplified discussion of payroll costs and deductions is not indicative of the volume of records and clerical work that may be involved in maintaining a sound and accurate payroll system or of its importance.

**Compensated Absences** Compensated absences are absences from employment, such as vacation, illness, and holidays, for which it is expected that employees will be paid. Prior to the issuance of *FASB Statement No. 43*, "Accounting for Compensated Absences," employers used alternative methods to account for compensated absences, varying from accrual of the cost over some period before payment to recognition of the cost in the period when paid. *FASB No. 43* was issued to eliminate the latter alternative and to reduce the potential for significant unrecorded or understated liabilities. It requires that a liability be accrued for the cost of compensation for future absences if **all** of the following conditions are met:[11]

(a) The employer's obligation relating to employees' rights to receive compensation for future absences is attributable to employee's services already rendered.

(b) The obligation relates to the rights that vest or accumulate.

(c) Payment of the compensation is probable, and

(d) The amount can be reasonably estimated.

If an employer meets conditions (a), (b), and (c), but does not accrue a liability because of a failure to meet condition (d), that fact should be disclosed.

**Vested rights** exist when an employer has an obligation to make payment to an employee even if his or her employment is terminated; thus, vested rights are not contingent

---

[11]"Accounting for Compensated Absences," *Statement of Financial Accounting Standards No. 43* (Stamford, Conn.: FASB, 1980), par. 6.

on an employee's future service. **Accumulated rights** are those that can be carried forward to future periods if not used in the period in which earned. For example, assume that you have earned four days of vacation pay as of December 31, the end of your employer's fiscal year, and that you will be paid for this vacation time even if you terminate employment. In this situation, your four days of vacation pay are considered vested and must be accrued. Now assume that your vacation days are not vested, but that you can carry the four days over into later periods. Although the rights are not vested, they are rights that accumulated, and the employer must provide an accrual, allowing for estimated forfeitures due to turnover.

A modification of the general rules relates to the issue of sick pay. If sick pay benefits vest, an accrual should be made. If sick pay benefits accumulate but do not vest, accrual is permitted but not required. The reason for this distinction is that compensation which is designated as "sick pay" may be administered in one of two ways. In some companies, employees are allowed to accumulate unused sick pay and take compensated time off from work even though they are not ill. In other companies, employees receive sick pay only if they are absent because of illness. A liability must be accrued for the first type of sick pay, because it will be paid whether or not employees are ill in the future. Accrual of a liability is permitted but not required for the second type of sick pay, because its payment is contingent upon future employee illnesses.

The expense and related liability for compensated absences should be recognized in the year in which earned by employees. For example, if new employees receive rights to two weeks' paid vacation at the beginning of their second year of employment, the vacation pay is considered to be earned during the first year of employment. After it is determined in what period the employee earned the right to the vacation, an issue arises as to what rate should be used to accrue the compensated absence cost—the current rate or an estimated future rate. *Statement No. 43* is silent on this subject; therefore, it is likely that companies will use the current rate rather than the future rate, which is less certain and raises issues concerning the discounting of the future amount. To illustrate, assume that Mark Walters, Inc. began operations on January 1, 1983. The company employs ten individuals who are paid $280 per week. Vacation weeks earned by all employees in 1983 were 20 weeks, but none were used during this period. In 1984, the vacation weeks were used when the current rate of pay was $300 per week for each employee. The entry at December 31, 1983 to accrue the accumulated vacation pay is as follows:

| | | |
|---|---|---|
| Wages Expense | 5,600 | |
| Vacation Wages Payable | | 5,600* |
| *($280 × 20) | | |

At December 31, 1983 the company would report on its balance sheet a liability of $5,600. In 1984, the vacation pay related to 1983 would be recorded as follows:

| | | |
|---|---|---|
| Vacation Wages Payable | 5,600 | |
| Wages Expense | 400 | |
| Cash | | 6,000* |
| *($300 × 20) | | |

In 1984 the vacation weeks were used; therefore, the liability is extinguished. Note that the difference between the amount of cash paid and the reduction in the liability account is recorded as an adjustment to wages expense in the period when paid. This difference arises because the liability account was accrued at the rates of pay in effect during the period when compensated time was earned. The cash paid, however, is based on the rates in effect during the period compensated time is used. If the future rates of pay had been used to compute the accrual in 1983, then the cash paid in 1984 would have been equal to the liability.

**Accrued Property Taxes** Local governmental units generally depend on property taxes as their primary source of revenue. Such taxes are based on the assessed value of both real and personal property and become a lien against the property at a date determined by law, usually the assessment date. This lien is a liability of the property owner and is a cost of the services of such property. The accounting questions that arise from property taxes are: (1) When should the property owner record the liability? (2) To which period should the cost be charged?

The date that the tax becomes a lien against the property is frequently used as the date to recognize and record the liability. But the lien date may not coincide with or occur in the period when the taxpayer pays or benefits from the taxes. Therefore, some businesses record the liability as the expense is accrued (up to the date of payment).

The accounting profession in considering the various periods to which property taxes might be charged contends that "generally, the most acceptable basis of providing for property taxes is monthly accrual on the taxpayer's books during the fiscal period of the taxing authority for which the taxes are levied."[12] Charging the taxes to the period subsequent to the levy would relate the expense to the period in which the taxes were used by the governmental unit to provide benefits to the property owner.

Assume that Seaboard Company, which closes its books each year on December 31, receives its property tax bill in May each year. The fiscal year for the city and county in which Seaboard Company is located begins on May 1 and ends on the following April 30. Property taxes of $36,000 are assessed against Seaboard Company property on January 1, 1983, and become a lien on May 1, 1983. However, tax bills are sent out in May and are payable in equal installments on July 1 and September 1.

One alternative is to record the property tax liability on the lien date of May 1, 1983, and amortize the deferred tax expense monthly throughout the fiscal year of the governmental taxing unit. A second alternative is not to recognize the full property tax liability at the lien date of May 1, 1983, but to accrue the liability monthly during the fiscal year of the governmental taxing unit May 1 to April 30. Entries to record the liability, monthly tax charges, and the tax payments for taxes becoming a lien on May 1, 1983 are shown on page 449 under both alternatives.

Under both alternatives deferred property taxes of $12,000 will be reported as a current asset on the December 31, 1983 balance sheet, and this amount will be amortized at the rate of $3,000 per month during January, February, March, and April of the following calendar year (1984). Under the first method the deferral is set up when the payable is recorded, whereas under the second method the deferral is set up when the payment is made. Under both alternatives the expense is accrued monthly during the fiscal year of the governmental taxing unit.

---

[12]Possible alternatives are: (a) Year in which paid. (b) Year ending on assessment (or lien) date. (c) Year beginning on assessment (or lien) date. (d) Calendar or fiscal year of taxpayer prior to assessment (or lien) date. (e) Calendar or fiscal year of taxpayer including assessment (or lien) date. (f) Calendar or fiscal year of taxpayer prior to payment date. (g) Fiscal year of governing body levying the tax. (h) Year appearing on tax bill. Committee on Accounting Procedure, American Institute of Certified Public Accountants, *Accounting Research and Terminology Bulletin, Final Edition* (New York: AICPA, 1961), chapter 10, sec. A, par. 10.

Some accountants advocate accruing property taxes by charges to expense during the fiscal year ending on the lien date, rather than during the fiscal year beginning on the lien date or the fiscal year of the tax authority. In such instances the property tax for the coming fiscal year must be estimated and charged monthly to Property Tax Expense and must be credited to Property Tax Payable. Under this method the entire amount of the tax is accrued by the lien date and the expense is charged to the fiscal period preceding payment of the tax. Justification for this method exists when the assessment date precedes the lien date by a year or more, as is the case in some taxing units. Since, in such instances, the amount is estimated and accrued by the property owner before receipt of the tax bill, it is proper theoretically to categorize property taxes as an estimated current liability rather than as a determinable current liability.

Recognizing that special circumstances may suggest the use of alternative accrual periods, the profession supports the view that "consistency of application from year to year is the important consideration and selection of any of the periods mentioned is a matter for individual judgment."[13]

---

**Entries to Accrue Property Tax Expense**

| Record Liability on Lien Date | | | Accrue Liability Monthly | | |
|---|---|---|---|---|---|
| **May 1 (lien date):** | | | | | |
| Deferred Property Taxes | 36,000 | | No entry | | |
|   Property Taxes Payable | | 36,000 | | | |
| **May 31 and June 30 (monthly expense accrual):** | | | | | |
| Property Tax Expense | 3,000 | | Property Tax Expense | 3,000 | |
|   Deferred Property Taxes | | 3,000 |   Property Taxes Payable | | 3,000 |
| **July 1 (First tax payment):** | | | | | |
| Property Taxes Payable | 18,000 | | Property Taxes Payable | 6,000 | |
|   Cash | | 18,000 | Deferred Property Taxes | 12,000 | |
| | | |   Cash | | 18,000 |
| **July 31 and August 31 (monthly expense accrual):** | | | | | |
| Property Tax Expense | 3,000 | | Property Tax Expense | 3,000 | |
|   Deferred Property Taxes | | 3,000 |   Deferred Property Taxes | | 3,000 |
| **September 1 (Second tax payment):** | | | | | |
| Property Tax Payable | 18,000 | | Deferred Property Taxes | 18,000 | |
|   Cash | | 18,000 |   Cash | | 18,000 |
| **Sept. 30, Oct. 31, Nov. 30, and Dec. 31 (monthly expense accrual):** | | | | | |
| Property Tax Expense | 3,000 | | Property Tax Expense | 3,000 | |
|   Deferred Property Taxes | | 3,000 |   Deferred Property Taxes | | 3,000 |

---

## Conditional Payments

The amount of certain determined liabilities is dependent on annual income, which cannot be known for certain until the end of an accounting period. At the end of the year, items such as income taxes, bonuses, and profit-sharing payments, even though dependent on the

[13]Ibid., par. 13.

results of operations, can be readily measured. For interim monthly or quarterly financial statements, however, the amounts of these obligations must be viewed as estimates in advance of the final determination of annual income.

**Income Taxes Payable**   Any federal or state income tax is a conditional liability because the amount of this tax varies in proportion to the amount of annual income. Some accountants consider the amount of income tax on annual income as an estimate because the computation of income (and the tax thereon) is subject to the review and the approval of the Internal Revenue Service. The meaning and application of numerous tax rules, especially new ones, are debatable and often dependent on a court's interpretation. Using the best information and advice available, a business must prepare an income tax return and compute the income tax payable resulting from the operations of the current period. The taxes payable on the income of a corporation, as computed per the tax return, should be classified as a current liability. Unlike the corporation, the proprietorship and the partnership are not taxable entities. Because the individual proprietor and the members of a partnership are subject to personal income taxes on their share of the business's taxable income, income tax liabilities do not appear on the financial statements of proprietorships and partnerships.[14]

Corporations whose tax liabilities for the tax year are reasonably expected to be $40 or more are required to estimate the amount of annual tax payable. This **estimated tax** is payable in equal installments on the fifteenth day of the fourth, sixth, ninth, and twelfth months of the tax year. A corporation must deposit income taxes in an authorized commercial bank depository or a Federal Reserve bank; failure to make proper payments may result in a penalty assessed at 20% of the underpayment. If, after computing and making payments of estimated income tax, a corporation determines that the original estimate is substantially too low, or too high, it should recompute the estimated tax before the next installment and increase or decrease the amount of each remaining installment to reflect the change.

If in a later year an additional tax is assessed on the income of an earlier year, Income Taxes Payable should be credited. The related debit should be charged to current operations.

Differences between taxable income under the tax laws and accounting income under generally accepted accounting principles have become greater in recent years. Because of these differences and the high income tax rates on corporations, the amount of income tax payable to the government in any given year, based on taxable income, may differ substantially from the amount of income tax that relates to the income before income taxes, as

---

[14]The Economic Recovery Tax Act of 1981 imposes the following five-step progressive tax rate structure on corporate income:

| Corporate Taxable Income | 1983 and After |
| --- | --- |
| $0 to $25,000 | 15% |
| $25,000 to $50,000 | 18 |
| $50,000 to $75,000 | 30 |
| $75,000 to $100,000 | 40 |
| Over $100,000 | 46 |

reported on the published financial statements. The accounting procedure recommended by the profession to reconcile properly these differences and to reflect business income correctly is called **interperiod income tax allocation.** Chapter 20 is devoted solely to income tax matters and presents an extensive discussion of this complex and controversial problem.

**Bonus Agreements**  For various reasons, many companies give bonuses to certain or all officers and employees in addition to their regular salary or wage. Frequently the amount of the bonus is dependent on the company's profits for the year so that in effect the employees who are included in the bonus plan participate in the profits of the enterprise.

From the standpoint of the enterprise, **bonus payments to employees** may be considered additional wages and should be included as a deduction in determining the net income for the year.

Because the amount of a bonus to employees is an expense of the business, the problem of computing the amount of bonus to be paid becomes more difficult. To illustrate, assume a situation in which a company has income of $100,000 determined before considering the bonus as an expense. According to the terms of the bonus agreement, 20% of the income is to be set aside for distribution among the employees. Now if the bonus were not itself an expense to be deducted in determining income, the amount of the bonus could be computed very simply as 20% of the net income of $100,000. The bonus is an expense, however, that must be deducted in arriving at the amount of income on which the bonus is to be based. Hence, $100,000 reduced by the amount of the bonus is the figure on which the bonus is to be computed. That is, the bonus is equal to 20% of $100,000 less the bonus. Stated algebraically:

$$
\begin{aligned}
B &= 0.20\,(\$100,000 - B) \\
B &= \$20,000 - 0.2B \\
1.2\,B &= \$20,000 \\
B &= \$16,666.67
\end{aligned}
$$

A similar problem results from the relationship of bonus payments to federal income taxes. Assume the same situation as before with the income of $100,000 computed without subtracting either the employees' bonus or taxes on income. The bonus is to be based on income after deducting income taxes but before deducting the bonus. The rate of income tax is 40% and the bonus of 20% is a deductible expense for tax purposes. The bonus is, therefore, equal to 20% of $100,000 minus the tax, and the tax is equal to 40% of $100,000 minus the bonus. Thus we have two simultaneous equations that, using $B$ as the symbol for the bonus and $T$ for the tax, may be stated algebraically as follows:

$$
\begin{aligned}
B &= 0.20\,(\$100,000 - T) \\
T &= 0.40\,(\$100,000 - B)
\end{aligned}
$$

These may be solved by substituting the value of $T$ as indicated in the second equation for $T$ in the first equation.

$$B = 0.20 \ (\$100,000 - 0.40 \ [\$100,000 - B])$$
$$B = 0.20 \ (\$100,000 - \$40,000 + 0.4B)$$
$$B = 0.20 \ (\$60,000 + 0.4B)$$
$$B = \$12,000 + 0.08B$$
$$0.92B = \$12,000$$
$$B = \$13,043.48$$

Substituting this value for $B$ into the second equation allows us to solve for $T$:

$$T = 0.40 \ (\$100,000 - \$13,043.48)$$
$$T = 0.40 \ (\$86,956.52)$$
$$T = \$34,782.61$$

To prove these amounts, both should be worked back into the original equation.

$$B = 0.20 \ (\$100,000 - T)$$
$$\$13,043.48 = 0.20 \ (\$100,000 - \$34,782.61)$$
$$\$13,043.48 = 0.20 \ (\$65,217.39)$$
$$\$13,043.48 = \$13,043.48$$

If the terms of the agreement provide for deducting both the tax and the bonus to arrive at the income figure on which the bonus is computed, the equations would be:

$$B = 0.20 \ (\$100,000 - B - T)$$
$$T = 0.40 \ (\$100,000 - B)$$

Substituting the value of $T$ from the second equation into the first equation enables us to solve for $B$:

$$B = 0.20 \ (\$100,000 - B - 0.40 \ [\$100,000 - B])$$
$$B = 0.20 \ (\$100,000 - B - \$40,000 + 0.4B)$$
$$B = 0.20 \ (\$60,000 - 0.6B)$$
$$B = \$12,000 - 0.12B$$
$$1.12B = \$12,000$$
$$B = \$10,714.29$$

The value for $B$ may then be substituted in the second equation above, and that equation solved for $T$:

$$T = 0.40 \, (\$100,000 - \$10,714.29)$$
$$T = 0.40 \, (\$89,285.71)$$
$$T = \$35,714.28$$

If these values are then substituted in the original bonus equation, they prove themselves as follows:

$$B = 0.20 \, (\$100,000 - B - T)$$
$$\$10,714.29 = 0.20 \, (\$100,000 - \$10,714.29 - \$35,714.28)$$
$$\$10,714.29 = 0.20 \, (\$53,571.43)$$
$$\$10,714.29 = \$10,714.29$$

Drawing up a legal document such as a bonus agreement is a task for a lawyer, not an accountant, although accountants are frequently called on to express an opinion on the feasibility of the provisions of the agreement. In this respect, one should always insist that the agreement state specifically whether income taxes and the bonus itself are expenses deductible in determining the income for purposes of the bonus computation.

It should be apparent from the preceding paragraphs that no entry can be made for a profit-sharing bonus until all other adjusting entries, except the one for accrued taxes on income, have been made and the income before bonus and tax has been calculated. This calculation can be accomplished through the use of a work sheet or by some other method. Once the income before bonus has been calculated, it is possible to make the bonus calculation and to record it by means of an adjusting entry.

| | | |
|---|---|---|
| Employees' Bonus Expense | 10,714.29 | |
| Accrued Profit-Sharing Bonus Payable | | 10,714.29 |

Later when the bonus is paid, the journal entry would be:

| | | |
|---|---|---|
| Accrued Profit-Sharing Bonus Payable | 10,714.29 | |
| Cash | | 10,714.29 |

The expense account should appear in the income statement as an operating expense. The liability, accrued profit-sharing bonus payable, is usually payable within a short period, and should be included as a current liability in the balance sheet.

Similar to bonus arrangements are contractual agreements covering rents or royalty payments that are conditional on the amount of revenues earned or the quantity of product produced or extracted. Conditional expenses based on revenues or units produced are usually less difficult to compute than the bonus arrangements just illustrated. For example, if a lease calls for a fixed rent payment of $500 per month and 1% of all sales over $300,000 per year, the annual rent obligation would amount to $6,000 plus $.01 of each dollar of revenue over $300,000. Or, a royalty agreement may accrue to the patent owner $1.00 for every ton of product resulting from the patented process, or accrue to the owner of the mineral rights $.50 on every barrel of oil extracted. As each additional unit of product is produced or extracted, an additional obligation, usually a current liability, is created.

# CONTINGENCIES

**Contingent liabilities** are obligations that are dependent upon the occurrence or nonoccurrence of one or more future events to confirm either the amount payable, or the payee, or the date payable, or its existence; that is, determination of one or more of these factors is dependent upon a contingency. A **contingency** is defined in *FASB Statement No. 5* "as an existing condition, situation, or set of circumstances involving uncertainty as to possible gain (**gain contingency**) or loss (**loss contingency**) to an enterprise that will ultimately be resolved when one or more future events occur or fail to occur."[15] A liability incurred as a result of a "loss contingency" is by definition a **contingent liability.**

## Accounting for Contingent Liabilities

When a loss contingency exists, the likelihood that the future event or events will confirm the incurrence of a liability can range from probable to remote. The FASB uses the terms **probable, reasonably possible,** and **remote** to identify three areas within that range and assigns the following meanings:

PROBABLE. The future event or events are likely to occur.

REASONABLY POSSIBLE. The chance of the future event or events occurring is more than remote but less than likely.

REMOTE. The chance of the future event or events occurring is slight.

An estimated loss from a loss contingency should be accrued by a charge to expense and a liability recorded only if both of the following conditions are met:

1. Information available prior to the issuance of the financial statements indicates that it is **probable that a liability had been incurred** at the date of the financial statements.
2. The amount of the loss can be **reasonably estimated.**

Only those loss contingencies that result in the incurrence of a liability are relevant to the discussion in this chapter. Loss contingencies that result in the impairment of an asset (for example, collectibility of receivables or threat of expropriation of assets) are discussed more fully in other appropriate sections of this textbook.

It is implicit in the first condition that it must be **probable** that one or more future events confirming the fact of the loss will occur. Neither the exact payee nor the exact date payable need be known to record a liability. **What must be known is whether it is probable that a liability has been incurred.** The second criterion indicates that an amount for the liability can be reasonably determined; otherwise it should not be accrued as a liability. To determine a reasonable estimate of the liability, such evidence may be based on the company's own experience, experience of other companies in the industry, engineering or research studies, legal advice, or educated guesses of personnel in the best position to know.

Obviously the application of these terms (probable, reasonably possible, and remote) as guidelines for differentiating or classifying economic events or conditions for accounting purposes involves judgment and subjectivity. The following items are examples of loss contingencies and the general accounting treatment accorded them.[16]

---

[15]"Accounting for Contingencies," *Statement of Financial Accounting Standards No. 5* (Stamford, Conn.: FASB, 1975), par. 1.

[16]Adapted from Ernst & Ernst, *Financial Reporting Developments*—No. 38353 (August 1975), p. 4.

| Accounting Treatment of Loss Contingencies | | | |
|---|---|---|---|
| | Usually Accrued | Not Accrued | Maybe Accrued* |
| Loss Related to | | | |
| 1. Collectibility of receivables | X | | |
| 2. Obligations related to product warranties and product defects | X | | |
| 3. Premiums offered to customers | X | | |
| 4. Risk of loss or damage of enterprise property by fire, explosion, or other hazards | | X | |
| 5. General or unspecified business risks | | X | |
| 6. Risk of loss from catastrophes assumed by property and casualty insurance companies including reinsurance companies | | X | |
| 7. Threat of expropriation of assets | | | X |
| 8. Pending or threatened litigation | | | X |
| 9. Actual or possible claims and assessments** | | | X |
| 10. Guarantees of indebtedness of others | | | X |
| 11. Obligations of commercial banks under "standby letters of credit" | | | X |
| 12. Agreements to repurchase receivables (or the related property) that have been sold | | | X |

*Should be accrued when both criteria are met (probable and reasonably estimable).
**Estimated amounts of losses incurred prior to the balance sheet date but settled subsequently should be accrued as of the balance sheet date.

The following excerpt from the annual report of Quaker State Oil Refining Corp. is an example of an accrual recorded for a loss contingency.

Quaker State Oil Refining Corp.
Notes to Financial Statements
Note 5: Contingencies
During the period from November 13 to December 23, 1980, a change in an additive component purchased from one of its suppliers caused certain oil refined and shipped to fail to meet the Company's low-temperature performance requirements. The Company has recalled this product and has arranged for reimbursement to its customers and the ultimate consumers of all costs associated with the product. Estimated cost of the recall program, net of estimated third party reimbursement, in the amount of $3,500,000 has been charged to 1980 operations.

The accounting concepts and procedures relating to contingent items are relatively new and unsettled. Practicing accountants express concern over the diversity that now exists in the interpretation of "probable," "reasonably possible," and "remote." Current practice relies heavily on the exact language used in responses received from lawyers (such language is necessarily biased and protective rather than predictive). As a result, accruals and disclosures of contingencies vary considerably in practice.

## Guarantee and Warranty Costs

A warranty (product guarantee) is a promise made by a seller to a buyer to make good on a deficiency of quantity, quality, or performance in a product. It is commonly used by manufacturers as a sales promotion technique. Chrysler Corp., for instance, recently hyped its sales by extending its new-car warranty to five years or 50,000 miles. For a specified period of time following the date of sale to the consumer, the manufacturer may promise to bear all or part of the cost of replacing defective parts, to perform any necessary repairs or servicing without charge, to refund the purchase price, or even to "double your money back." Warranties and guarantees entail future costs, frequently significant additional costs, which are sometimes called "after costs," or "post-sale costs." Although the future cost is indefinite as to amount, due date, and even customer, a liability is probable in most cases and should be recognized in the accounts if it can be reasonably estimated. The amount of the liability is an estimate of all the costs that will be incurred after sale and delivery and that are incident to the correction of defects or deficiencies required under the warranty provisions.

There are two basic methods of accounting for warranty costs: (1) the cash basis method and (2) the accrual method. Under the **cash basis method,** warranty costs are charged to expense as they are incurred; in other words, warranty costs are charged to the period in which the seller or manufacturer performs in compliance with the warranty. No liability is recorded for future costs arising from warranties, nor is the period in which the sale is recorded necessarily charged with the costs of making good on outstanding warranties. Use of this method, the only one recognized for income tax purposes, is frequently justified for accounting on the basis of expediency when warranty costs are immaterial or when the warranty period is relatively short.

Also, the cash basis method is required in accounting for warranty costs when no warranty liability is accrued in the year of the sale because (1) it is not probable that a liability has been incurred or (2) the amounts of the liability cannot be reasonably estimated.

If, on the basis of available information, it is probable that customers will make claims under warranties relating to goods or services that have been sold and a reasonable estimate of the costs involved can be made, the accrual method must be used.

Under the **accrual method,** a provision for warranty costs is made in the year of sale or in the year that the productive activity takes place. The accrual method may be divided further into two different accounting treatments: (1) expense warranty treatment (accrual method) and (2) sales warranty treatment (deferral method). The **expense warranty treatment** charges the estimated future warranty costs to operating expense in the year of sale or in the year services were performed. It is the generally accepted method and should be used whenever the warranty is an integral and inseparable part of the sale and is viewed as a loss contingency. The **sales warranty treatment** defers a certain percentage of the original sales price until some future time when actual costs are incurred or the warranty expires. The following example illustrates the accrual method of accounting for warranty costs and the difference between the accrual and deferral treatments.

The Denson Machinery Company begins production on a new machine in July 1983, and sells 100 units at $5,000 each by its year end, December 31, 1983. Each machine is under warranty for one year and the company has estimated, from past experience with a similar machine, that the warranty cost will probably average $200 per unit. Further, as a result of parts replacements and services rendered in compliance with machinery warranties, the company incurs $4,000 in warranty costs in 1983 and $16,000 in 1984.

**Entries Under Accrual Method of Accounting for Warranties**

| Expense Warranty Treatment | | Sales Warranty Treatment | |
|---|---|---|---|

**Sale of 100 machines at $5,000 each, July through December, 1983:**

| Cash or Accts. Rec. | 500,000 | | Cash or Accts. Rec. | 500,000 | |
|---|---|---|---|---|---|
| Sales | | 500,000 | Sales | | 480,000 |
| | | | Unearned Warranty Rev. | | 20,000 |

**Recognition of warranty expense, July through December, 1983:**

| Warranty Expense | 20,000 | | Warranty Expense | 4,000 | |
|---|---|---|---|---|---|
| Estimated Liability | | | Cash, Inventory, or | | |
| Under Warranties | | 20,000 | Accrued Payroll | | 4,000 |
| ($200 × 100 machines) | | | (Warranty costs incurred) | | |
| Estimated Liability | | | Unearned Warranty Rev. | 4,000 | |
| Under Warranties | 4,000 | | Revenue from Warranties | | 4,000 |
| Cash, Inventory, or | | | (Warranty revenue earned) | | |
| Accrued Payroll | | 4,000 | | | |
| (Warranty costs incurred) | | | | | |

The 12/31/83 balance sheet would report Estimated Liability Under Warranties as a current liability of $16,000, and the income statement for 1983 would report Warranty Expense of $20,000.

The 12/31/83 balance sheet would report Unearned Warranty Revenue as a current liability of $16,000. (Note that the $4,000 of Warranty Expense offsets the $4,000 of Warranty Revenue.)

**Recognition of warranty costs incurred in 1984 (on 1983 machinery sales):**

| Estimated Liability | | | Warranty Expense | 16,000 | |
|---|---|---|---|---|---|
| Under Warranties | 16,000 | | Cash, Inventory, or | | |
| Cash, Inventory, or | | | Accrued Payroll | | 16,000 |
| Accrued Payroll | | 16,000 | (Warranty costs incurred) | | |
| (Warranty costs incurred) | | | Unearned Warranty Rev. | 16,000 | |
| | | | Revenue from Warranties | | 16,000 |
| | | | (Warranty revenue earned) | | |

Although the net income in both 1983 and 1984 is the same under both methods, the 1983 income statement would report $16,000 less revenues and $16,000 less operating expenses under the sales warranty method, and the 1984 income statement would report $16,000 more revenues and $16,000 more operating expenses. Notice that the sales warranty treatment above assumes that at the time of sale two items are sold, the product and the warranty. Accordingly, a portion of the total sales price is deferred until the warranty revenue is earned through the replacement of parts and the performance of repairs, that is, as the costs are incurred.

The illustration above assumed a zero profit from the sale of the warranty. This illustration also assumed that the revenue recognition was a function of costs incurred during the period. Other criteria for revenue recognition for "service sales type transactions" similar to this are discussed in Appendix K (Chapter 19).

The sales warranty treatment is applicable to companies that sell warranty contracts separately from the product. For instance, if the Denson Machinery Company had sold each machine for $4,750 and each warranty contract separately for $250, the sales warranty method clearly would be appropriate. A liability in the form of unearned revenue would be recorded at the time of the sale, and the warranty revenues, costs, and any income would be recognized in the periods in which the services, repairs, and replacements under the warranty were performed.

Business managers commonly view warranty costs simply as additional expenses of selling or manufacturing the product rather than as additional sales. It is normally assumed that the selling price of a product covers costs of warranty, not that the warranty is something to be sold separately. Many accountants believe that the revenues must be recognized in the period the sale is made rather than when the cost of repair or replacement is incurred. Neither the expensed warranty nor the sales warranty treatment is allowable for income tax purposes.

If the cash basis method were applied to the facts in the Denson Machinery Company example, $4,000 would be recorded as warranty expense in 1983 and $16,000 as warranty expense in 1984 with all of the sale price being recorded as revenue in 1983. In many instances, application of the cash basis method does not match the warranty costs relating to the products sold during a given period with the revenues derived from such products. Where ongoing warranty policies exist year after year, the differences between the cash and the accrual basis probably would not be so great.

## Premiums Offered to Customers

Numerous companies offer (either on a limited or on a continuing basis) premiums to customers in return for boxtops, certificates, coupons, labels, or wrappers. The premium may be silverware, dishes, a small appliance, a toy, or other goods. These premium offers are made to stimulate sales, and their costs should be charged to expense in the period of the sale that benefits from the premium plan. At the end of the accounting period many of these premium offers may be outstanding and, when presented in subsequent periods, must be redeemed. The number of outstanding premium offers that will be presented for redemption must be estimated in order to reflect the existing current liability and to match costs with revenues. The cost of premium offers should be charged to Premium Expense, and the outstanding obligations should be credited to an account titled Estimated Premium Claims Outstanding.

Although the FASB did not include premium offers in its list of loss contingencies, the authors believe that premium offers result in the probable existence of a liability at the date of the financial statements, can be reasonably estimated in amount, are contingent upon the occurrence of a future event (redemption), and, therefore, are a loss contingency within the guidelines of *FASB Statement No. 5*.

The following example illustrates the accounting treatment accorded a premium offer. The Fluffy Cakemix Company offered its customers a large nonbreakable mixing bowl in exchange for 25 cents and 10 boxtops. The mixing bowl costs the Fluffy Cakemix Company 75 cents, and the company estimates that 60% of the boxtops will be redeemed. The premium offer began in June 1983 and resulted in the following transactions and entries during 1983.

1. To record purchase of 20,000 mixing bowls

| | | |
|---|---|---|
| Inventory of Premium Mixing Bowls | 15,000 | |
| Cash | | 15,000 |

2. To record sales of 300,000 boxes of cake mix at 80 cents

| | | |
|---|---|---|
| Cash | 240,000 | |
| Sales | | 240,000 |

**3.** To record redemption of 60,000 boxtops

| | | |
|---|---|---|
| Cash [(60,000 ÷ 10) × $0.25] | 1,500 | |
| Premium Expense  *6,000 × (.75 − .25)* | 3,000 | |
|    Inventory of Premium Mixing Bowls | | 4,500 |
|    (Computation: [60,000 ÷ 10] × $0.75 = $4,500) | | |

**4.** To record estimated liability for outstanding premium offers

| | | |
|---|---|---|
| Premium Expense  *1,200 (.75 − .25)* | 6,000 | |
|    Estimated Premium Claims Outstanding | | 6,000 |

Computation:

| | |
|---|---|
| Total boxtops sold in 1983 | 300,000 |
| Total estimated redemptions (60%) | 180,000 |
| Boxtops redeemed in 1983 | 60,000 |
| Estimated future redemptions | 120,000 |

Cost of estimated claims outstanding
(120,000 ÷ 10) × ($0.75 − $0.25) = $6,000

The December 31, 1983, balance sheet of Fluffy Cakemix Company will report an Inventory of Premium Mixing Bowls of $10,500 as a current asset and Estimated Premium Claims Outstanding of $6,000 as a current liability. The 1983 income statement will report a $9,000 Premium Expense among the selling expenses.

In the illustration above, the company establishes its own premium plan, issues its own boxtops, and assumes complete redemption responsibilities. Another very common premium plan, also used to stimulate sales, is the issuance of trading stamps. Generally the trading stamp company sells its stamps to consumer-type businesses (commonly grocery stores and gasoline stations) and assumes full responsibility for the redemption of the stamps. The trading stamp company records the sale of stamps, the purchase of premiums (all sorts of consumer articles), the distribution of the premiums at gift centers, and the estimated premium claims outstanding. For instance, the Sperry and Hutchinson Company (licensor of S & H Green Stamps) reported "Liability for Stamp Redemptions—$117,599,000" as a current liability with a like amount as a long-term liability and made the following footnote disclosure:

*Liability for Stamp Redemptions*—The Company records stamp service revenue and provides for cost of redemptions at the time stamps are furnished to licensees. The liability for stamp redemptions is adjusted each year based upon current operating experience and includes the cost of merchandise and related redemption service expenses required to redeem 95% of the stamps issued.

Company studies have indicated that approximately 50% of the stamps outstanding are not presented for redemption within one year; consequently this portion of the liability for stamp redemptions is classified as a long-term liability.

The businesses that buy the trading stamps merely record the purchase and the issuance of the stamps; stamps on hand are reported as an asset and stamps issued as a selling expense.

## Risk of Loss Due to Lack of Insurance Coverage

Uninsured risks may arise in a number of ways, including **noninsurance** of certain risks or **coinsurance** or **deductible clauses** in an insurance contract. But the absence of insurance (frequently referred to as self-insurance) does not mean that a liability has been incurred at the date of the financial statements. For example, fires, explosions, and other similar events that may cause damage to a company's own property are random in occurrence and unrelated to the activities of the company prior to their occurrence. The conditions for accrual stated in *Statement No. 5* are not satisfied prior to the occurrence of the event because until that time there is no diminution in the value of the property. And, unlike an insurance company, which has contractual obligations to reimburse policyholders for losses, a company can have no such obligations to itself and, hence, no liability either before or after the occurrence of damage.[17]

Exposure to risks of loss resulting from uninsured past injury to others, however, is an existing condition involving uncertainty about the amount and timing of losses that may develop, in which case a contingency exists. For example, a company with a fleet of vehicles would have to accrue uninsured losses resulting from injury to others or damage to the property of others that took place prior to the date of the financial statements (if the experience of the company or other information enables it to make a reasonable estimate of the liability). Of course, it should not establish a liability for expected future injury to others or damage to the property of others even if the amount of losses is reasonably estimable.

## Litigation, Claims, and Assessments

The following factors, among others, must be considered in determining whether a liability should be recorded with respect to **pending or threatened litigation** and actual or possible claims and assessments:

1. The period in which the underlying cause for action occurred.
2. The degree of probability of an unfavorable outcome.
3. The ability to make a reasonable estimate of the amount of loss.

To report a loss and a liability in the financial statements, the cause for litigation must have occurred on or before the date of the financial statements. It does not matter that the company does not become aware of the existence or possibility of the lawsuit or claims until after the date of the financial statements but before they are issued. Among the factors the profession recommended be considered in **evaluating the probability of an unfavorable outcome** are: the nature of the litigation; the progress of the case; the opinion of legal counsel; the experience of the company in similar cases; the experience of other companies; and any decision of management as to how the company intends to respond to the lawsuit.

The outcome of pending litigation, however, can seldom be predicted with any assurance. And, even if the evidence available at the balance sheet date does not favor the defendant company, it is hardly reasonable to expect the company to publish in its financial statements a dollar estimate of the probable negative outcome. Such specific disclosures could weaken the company's position in the dispute and encourage the plaintiff to intensify its efforts.

With respect to **unfiled suits** and **unasserted claims and assessments,** a company must determine (1) the degree of **probability** that a suit may be filed or a claim or assessment may be asserted and (2) the **probability** of an unfavorable outcome. For example, assume that Nawtee Company is being investigated by the Federal Trade Commission for prac-

---

[17]"Accounting for Contingencies," *FASB Statement No. 5, op. cit.*, par. 28.

tices in restraint of trade, and enforcement proceedings have been instituted. Such proceedings are often followed by private claims of triple damages for redress. In this case, Nawtee Company must determine the probability of the claims being asserted **and** the probability of triple damages being awarded. If both are probable, the loss reasonably estimable, and the cause for action dated on or before the date of the financial statements, the liability should be accrued.

## Disclosure of Loss Contingencies

If no accrual is made for a loss contingency and a liability is not recorded because one or both conditions necessary for accrual are not met, *Statement No. 5* requires the following disclosure via footnote when there is at least **a reasonable possibility** that a liability may have been incurred:

1. The nature of the contingency.
2. An estimate of the possible loss or range of loss or a statement that an estimate cannot be made.[18]

Presented below is the disclosure of a possible loss contingency as contained in the footnotes to the financial statements of Eagle-Pitcher Industries, Inc.

---

**EAGLE-PITCHER INDUSTRIES, INC.**
Notes to Financial Statements

*Litigation*—As of November 30, 1980 the Company is one of a number of companies involved in approximately 6,100 claims involving injuries allegedly caused by contact with asbestos-containing insulation products of the various companies. The Company last manufactured such products in 1971. Approximately 800 claims, some of which have been covered by insurance, were disposed of through November 30, 1980. The Company's average cost per claim, including legal fees, has been approximately $7,000. Charges to operations for expenses of asbestos litigation amounted to approximately $2,400,000 in 1980 compared with $1,500,000 in 1979. Expenses of disposing of such claims in the future, and the period of time over which such expenses will be incurred are not reasonably predictable. However, it is the opinion of management that such costs will not have a materially adverse effect upon the financial condition of the Company.

---

Contingencies involving an unasserted claim or assessment need not be disclosed when there has not been any manifestation by a potential claimant of an awareness of a possible claim or assessment unless (1) it is considered **probable** that a claim will be asserted **and** (2) there is a **reasonable possibility** that the outcome will be unfavorable.

Certain other contingent liabilities that should be disclosed even though the possibility of loss may be remote are as follows:

---

[18]The FASB pronouncements on this topic require that, when some amount within the range appears at the time to be a better estimate than any other amount within the range, that amount is accrued. When no amount within the range is a better estimate than any other amount, the dollar amount at the low end of the range is **accrued** and the dollar amount of the high end of the range is **disclosed.** See *FASB Interpretation No. 14,* "Reasonable Estimation of the Amount of a Loss" (Stamford, Conn.: FASB, 1976), par. 3, and *FASB Statement No. 5,* "Accounting for Contingencies" (Stamford, Conn.: FASB, 1975).

1. Guarantees of indebtedness of others.
2. Obligations of commercial banks under "stand-by letters of credit."
3. Guarantees to repurchase receivables (or any related property) that have been sold or assigned.

Disclosure should include the nature and amount of the guarantee and, if estimable, the amount that could be recovered from outside parties. Cities Service Company disclosed its guarantees of indebtedness of others in the following footnote:

---

**CITIES SERVICE COMPANY**
*Note 10: Contingent Liabilities*

The Company and certain subsidiaries have guaranteed debt obligations of approximately $62 million of companies in which substantial stock investments are held. Also, under long-term agreements with certain pipeline companies in which stock interests are held, the Company and its subsidiaries have agreed to provide minimum revenue for product shipments. The Company has guaranteed mortgage debt ($80 million) incurred by a 50 percent owned tanker affiliate for construction of tankers which are under long-term charter contracts to the Company and others. It is not anticipated that any loss will result from any of the above described agreements.

---

## DISCLOSURE IN THE FINANCIAL STATEMENTS

The current liability accounts are commonly presented as the top or first classification in the "liabilities and stockholders' equity" section of the balance sheet. In some instances, current liabilities are presented as a group immediately below current assets with the total of the current liabilities deducted from the total current assets to obtain "working capital" or "current assets in excess of current liabilities."

Within the current liability section the accounts may be listed in order of maturity, according to amount (largest to smallest), or in order of liquidation preference. The authors' review of published financial statements in 1980–81 disclosed that a significant majority of the companies examined listed "notes payable" first, regardless of relative amount, followed most often with "accounts payable," and ended the current liability section with "current portion of long-term debt." However, see Tenneco, Inc.'s current liability section on page 197; it begins with "current maturities of long-term debt."

Detail and supplemental information concerning current liabilities should be sufficient to meet the requirement of full disclosure. Secured liabilities should be identified clearly, and the related assets pledged as collateral indicated. If the due date of any liability can be extended, the details should be disclosed. Current liabilities should not be offset against assets that are to be applied to their liquidation. Current maturities of long-term debt should be classified as current liabilities. A major exception exists when a currently maturing obligation is to be paid from assets classified as long-term. For example, if payments to retire a bond payable are made from a bond sinking fund classified as a long-term asset, the bonds payable should be reported in the long-term liability section. Presentation of this debt in the current liability section would distort the working capital position of the enterprise.

Existing commitments that will result in obligations in succeeding periods that are material in amount may require disclosure. For example, commitments to purchase goods or services, and for the construction, purchase, or lease of equipment or properties may require disclosure in footnotes accompanying the balance sheet.

Presented below is an excerpt of the Dresser Industries, Inc. 1981 published financial statements which is a representative presentation of the current liabilities as found in the reports of large corporations:

| DRESSER INDUSTRIES (DRESSER) | | | |
| In Millions of Dollars—October 31, | 1981 | 1980 | 1979 |
| --- | --- | --- | --- |
| Current Liabilities | | | |
| Short-term debt | $ 84.5 | $ 72.2 | $ 53.3 |
| Accounts payable | 275.5 | 243.3 | 190.7 |
| Advances from customers on contracts | 83.5 | 66.6 | 63.4 |
| Accrued compensation | 83.3 | 74.8 | 75.8 |
| Accrued taxes, interest and other expenses | 189.2 | 175.0 | 152.1 |
| Accrued warranty costs | 66.5 | 56.8 | 55.0 |
| Federal, state and foreign income taxes | 96.0 | 72.9 | 27.1 |
| Current portion of long-term debt | 31.7 | 19.9 | 18.3 |
| Total Current Liabilities | 910.2 | 781.5 | 635.7 |

## QUESTIONS

1. Assume that your friend, who is an engineering major, asks you to define and discuss the nature of a liability. Assist him or her by preparing a definition of a liability and by explaining to him or her what you believe are the elements or factors inherent in the concept of a liability.

2. Distinguish between a current liability and a long-term debt.

3. Why is the liability section of the balance sheet of primary significance to bankers?

4. How are current liabilities related by definition to current assets?

5. How are current liabilities related to a company's operating cycle?

6. How is present value related to the concept of a liability?

7. What is the nature of a "discount" on notes payable?

8. Under what conditions should a short-term obligation be excluded from current liabilities?

9. (a) What evidence is necessary to demonstrate the ability to consummate the refinancing of short-term debt?
   (b) When a financing agreement is relied upon to demonstrate ability to consummate refinancing, what amount of short-term debt may be excluded from current liabilities?

10. Discuss the accounting treatment or disclosure that should be accorded a declared but unpaid cash dividend; an accumulated but undeclared dividend on cumulative preferred stock; a stock dividend payable.

11. How does deferred or unearned revenue arise? Why can it be classified properly as a current liability? Give several examples of business activities that result in unearned revenues.

12. What are compensated absences?

13. Under what conditions must an employer accrue a liability for the cost of compensated absences?

14. Under what conditions is an employer required to accrue a liability for sick pay? Under what conditions is an employer permitted but not required to accrue a liability for sick pay?

15. Over which two periods of time is the property tax most commonly allocated? Under what circumstances might each of these periods be justified as the period of expense?

16. What is the nature of a "conditional payment"? How is a conditional payment unlike the other liabilities presented under the classification of determinable current liabilities? List three examples of conditional payment liabilities.

17. Define (a) a contingency and (b) a contingent liability.

18. Under what conditions should a contingent liability be recorded?

19. Distinguish between a "determinable current liability" and a "contingent current liability." Give two examples of each type.

20. How are the terms "probable," "reasonably possible," and "remote" related to contingent liabilities?

21. Contrast the "cash basis method" and the "accrual method" of accounting for warranty costs.

22. How does the "expense warranty treatment" differ from the "sales warranty method"?

23. Should a liability be recorded for risk of loss due to lack of insurance coverage? Discuss.

24. What factors must be considered in determining whether or not to record a liability for pending litigation? For threatened litigation?

25. Within the current liability section, how do you believe the accounts should be listed? Defend your position.

26. When should liabilities for each of the following items be recorded on the books of an ordinary business corporation?
    (a) Dividends.
    (b) Purchase commitments.
    (c) Acquisition of goods by purchase on credit.
    (d) Officers' salaries.
    (e) Special bonus to employees.

## CASES

**C10-1** Iowa Corporation issued $6,000,000 of short-term commercial paper during the year 1982 to finance construction of a plant. At December 31, 1982, the corporation's year-end, Iowa intends to refinance the commercial paper by issuing long-term debt. However, because the corporation temporarily has excess cash, in January 1983 it liquidates $2,000,000 of the commercial paper as the paper matures. In February 1983, Iowa completes a $12,000,000 long-term debt offering. Later during the month of February, it issues its December 31, 1982, financial statements. The proceeds of the long-term debt offering are to be used to replenish $2,000,000 in working capital, to pay $4,000,000 of commercial paper as it matures in March 1983, and to pay $6,000,000 of construction costs expected to be incurred later that year to complete the plant.

**Instructions**

(a) How should the $6,000,000 of commercial paper be classified on the December 31, 1982; January 31, 1983; and February 29, 1983, balance sheets? Give support for your answer and also consider the cash element.

(b) What would your answer be if, instead of a completed financing at the date of issuance of the financial statements, a financing agreement existed at that date?

**C10-2** The following items are listed as liabilities on the balance sheet of Baker Industrial Co. on December 31, 1983:

| | |
|---|---|
| Accounts payable | $ 280,000 |
| Notes payable | 420,000 |
| Bonds payable | 1,460,000 |

The accounts payable represent obligations to suppliers that were due in January 1984. The notes payable mature on various dates during 1984. The bonds payable mature on July 1, 1984.

These liabilities must be reported on the balance sheet in accordance with generally accepted accounting principles governing the classification of liabilities as current and noncurrent.

**Instructions**

(a) What is the general rule for determining whether a liability is classified as current or noncurrent?

(b) Under what conditions may any of Baker Industrial Co.'s liabilities be classified as noncurrent? Explain your answer.

(CMA adapted)

**C10-3** PRD Corporation reflects in the current liability section of its balance sheet at December 31, 1983 (its year-end), short-term obligations of $12,000,000, which includes the current portion of 12% long-term debt in the amount of $8,000,000 (mature in March 1984). Management has stated its intention to refinance the 12% debt whereby no portion of it will mature during 1984. The date of issuance of the financial statements is March 25, 1984.

**Instructions**

(a) Is management's intent enough to support long-term classification of the obligation in this situation?

(b) Assume that PRD Corporation issues $10,000,000 of 10-year debentures to the public in January 1984 and that management intends to use the proceeds to liquidate the $8,000,000 debt maturing in March 1984. Furthermore, assume that the debt maturing in March 1984 is paid from these proceeds prior to the issuance of the financial statements. Will this have any impact on the balance sheet classification at December 31, 1983? Explain your answer.

(c) Assume that PRD Corporation issues common stock to the public in January and that management intends to entirely liquidate the $8,000,000 debt maturing in March 1984 with the proceeds of this equity securities issue. In light of these events, should the $8,000,000 debt maturing in March 1984 be included in current liabilities at December 31, 1983?

(d) Assume that PRD Corporation, on February 15, 1984, entered into a financing agreement with a commercial bank that permits PRD Corporation to borrow at any time through 1985 up to $12,000,000 at the bank's prime rate of interest. Borrowings under the financing agreement mature three years after the date of the loan. The agreement is not cancelable except for violation of a provision with which compliance is objectively determinable. No violation of any provision exists at the date of issuance of the financial statements. Assume further that $8,000,000 representing the current portion of long-term debt does not mature until August 1984. In addition, management intends to refinance the $8,000,000 obligation under the terms of the financial agreement with the bank, which is expected to be financially capable of honoring the agreement.

1. Given these facts, should the $8,000,000 be classified as current on the balance sheet at December 31, 1983?

2. Is disclosure of the refinancing method required?

**C10-4** (a) What is the meaning of the term "contingency" as used in accounting? pg 454

(b) Distinguish between accounting for a "gain contingency" and accounting for a "loss contingency." pg 454

(c) How should the following situations be recognized in the calendar year-end financial statements of Adams Labs Inc.? Explain.

1. Pending in a federal district court is a suit against Adams Labs. The suit, which asks for token damages, alleges that Adams has infringed on a 15-year-old patent. Briefs will be heard on March 31.

2. The TUF Union, sole bargaining agent of Adams Labs' production employees, has threatened a strike unless Adams agrees to a proposed profit-sharing plan. Negotiations begin on March 1.

3. A recently completed (during the calendar year in question) government contract

is subject to renegotiation. Although Adams suspects that a refund of approximately $125,000 may be required by the government, the company does not wish, for obvious reasons, to publicize this fact.

4. Adams has a $170,000, 9% note receivable due next May 1 from Carver Coil Co., its largest customer. Adams discounted the note on December 20, with recourse, at the bank to raise needed cash. Carver Coil Co. has never defaulted on a debt and possesses a high credit rating. (Treated as a sale on December 20.)

**C10-5** On February 1, 1984, one of the huge storage tanks of the Scientific Chemical Company exploded. Windows in houses and other buildings within a one-mile radius of the explosion were severely damaged, and a number of people were injured. As of February 15, 1984 (when the December 31, 1983 financial statements were completed and sent to the publisher for printing and public distribution), no suits had been filed or claims asserted against the company as a consequence of the explosion. The company fully anticipates that suits will be filed and claims asserted for injuries and damages. Because the casualty was uninsured and the company considered at fault, Scientific Chemical will have to cover the damages from its own resources.

**Instructions**

Discuss fully the accounting treatment and disclosures that should be accorded the casualty and related contingent losses in the financial statements dated December 31, 1983.

**C10-6** The following three independent sets of facts relate to (1) the possible accrual or (2) the possible disclosure by other means of a loss contingency.

### Situation I

A company offers a one-year warranty for the product that it manufactures. A history of warranty claims has been compiled and the probable amount of claims related to sales for a given period can be determined.

### Situation II

Subsequent to the date of a set of financial statements, but prior to the issuance of the financial statements, a company enters into a contract that will probably result in a significant loss to the company. The amount of the loss can be reasonably estimated.

### Situation III

A company has adopted a policy of recording self-insurance for any possible losses resulting from injury to others by the company's vehicles. The premium for an insurance policy for the same risk from an independent insurance company would have an annual cost of $2,500. During the period covered by the financial statements, there were no accidents involving the company's vehicles that resulted in injury to others.

**Instructions**

Discuss the accrual or type of disclosure necessary (if any) and the reason(s) why such disclosure is appropriate for each of the three independent sets of facts above.

Complete your response to each situation before proceeding to the next situation.

(AICPA adapted)

**C10-7** The two basic requirements for the accrual of a loss contingency are supported by several basic concepts of accounting. Three of these concepts are: periodicity (time periods), measurement, and objectivity.

**Instructions**

Discuss how the two basic requirements for the accrual of a loss contingency relate to the three concepts listed above.

(AICPA adapted)

# EXERCISES

**E10–1** On December 31, 1983, Catch-up Co. had $1,200,000 of short-term debt in the form of notes payable due February 2, 1984. On January 21, 1984, the company issued 100,000 shares of its common stock for $9 per share, receiving $875,000 proceeds after brokerage fees and other costs of issuance. On February 2, 1984, the proceeds from the stock sale, supplemented by an additional $325,000 cash, are used to liquidate the $1,200,000 debt. The December 31, 1983, balance sheet is issued on February 23, 1984.

**Instructions**

Show how the $1,200,000 of short-term debt should be presented on the December 31, 1983, balance sheet, including footnote disclosure.

**E10–2** During the month of June, Jamaican Imports had cash sales of $180,760 and credit sales of $80,000, both of which include the 6% sales tax that must be remitted to the state by July 15.

**Instructions**

Prepare the adjusting entry that should be recorded to fairly present the June 30 financial statement.

**E10–3** The payroll of the Tropaz Company for September 1982 is as follows:

Total payroll was $425,000, of which $225,000 represented amounts paid in excess of $32,400 to certain employees. The amount paid to employees in excess of $6,000 was $400,000. Income taxes in the amount of $90,000 were withheld, as was $9,000 in union dues. The state unemployment tax is 2.7%, but the Tropaz Company is allowed a credit of 1.7% by the state for its unemployment experience. Also, assume that the current F.I.C.A. tax is 7% and the federal unemployment tax rate is .5% after state credit.

**Instructions**

Prepare the necessary journal entries if the wages and salaries paid and the employer payroll taxes are recorded separately.

**E10–4** American Jewelry Company's payroll for August, 1983, is summarized below.

| | | | Amount Subject to Payroll Taxes | |
| | | | Unemployment Tax | |
| Payroll | Wages Due | F.I.C.A. | Federal | State |
|---|---|---|---|---|
| Factory | $120,000 | $112,000 | $40,000 | $40,000 |
| Sales | 44,000 | 32,000 | 4,000 | 4,000 |
| Administrative | 36,000 | 12,000 | — | — |
| Total | $200,000 | $156,000 | $44,000 | $44,000 |

At this point in the year some employees have already received wages in excess of those to which payroll taxes apply. Assume that the state unemployment tax is 2.5%. The F.I.C.A. rate is 7% for both employee and employer, and the federal unemployment tax rate is .6% after credits. Income tax withheld amounts to $14,000 for factory, $6,000 for sales, and $7,000 for administrative.

**Instructions**

(a) Prepare a schedule showing the employer's total cost of wages for August.
(b) Prepare the journal entries to record the factory, sales, and administrative payrolls including the employer's payroll taxes.

**E10–5** D. Skorton Company began operations on January 2, 1982. It employs 7 individuals who work 8-hour days and are paid hourly. Each employee earns 10 paid vacation days and 6 paid sick days annually. Vacation days may be taken after January 15 of the year following the year in which they are earned. Sick days may be taken as soon as they are earned. Additional information is as follows:

| Actual Hourly Wage Rate | | Vacation Days Used by Each Employee | | Sick Days Used by Each Employee | |
|---|---|---|---|---|---|
| 1982 | 1983 | 1982 | 1983 | 1982 | 1983 |
| $6.00 | $6.75 | 0 | 9 | 4 | 5 |

D. Skorton Company has chosen to accrue the cost of compensated absences at rates of pay in effect during the period when earned and to accrue sick pay when earned.

**Instructions**

(a) Prepare journal entries to record transactions related to compensated absences during 1982 and 1983.
(b) Compute the amounts of any liability for compensated absences that should be reported on the balance sheet at December 31, 1982 and 1983.

**E10-6** Assume the facts in the preceding exercise, except that D. Skorton Company has chosen not to accrue paid sick leave until used, and has chosen to accrue vacation time at expected future rates of pay without discounting. The company used the following projected rates to accrue vacation time:

| Year in Which Vacation Time Was Earned | Projected Future Pay Rates Used to Accrue Vacation Pay |
|---|---|
| 1982 | $6.70 |
| 1983 | 7.50 |

**Instructions**

(a) Prepare journal entries to record transactions related to compensated absences during 1982 and 1983.
(b) Compute the amounts of any liability for compensated absences that should be reported on the balance sheet at December 31, 1982 and 1983.

**E10-7** Dave Durkee, president of the Durkee Music Company, has a bonus arrangement with the company under which he receives 20% of the net income (after deducting taxes and bonuses) each year. For the current year, the net income before deducting either the provision for income taxes or the bonus is $162,000. The bonus is deductible for tax purposes, and the effective tax rate may be assumed to be 40%.

**Instructions**

(a) Compute the amount of Dave Durkee's bonus.
(b) Compute the appropriate provision for federal income taxes for the year.

**E10-8** The incomplete income statement of a glue company appears below:

Sticky Glue Company
INCOME STATEMENT
For the Year 1983

| | | |
|---|---|---|
| Revenue | | $5,000,000 |
| Cost of goods sold | | 3,400,000 |
| Gross profit | | 1,600,000 |
| Administrative and selling expenses | $500,000 | |
| Profit-sharing bonus to employees | ? | ? |

| | | |
|---|---|---|
| Income before income taxes | | ? |
| Income taxes | | ? |
| Net income | $ | ? |

The employee profit-sharing plan requires that 20% of all profits remaining after the deduction of the bonus and income taxes be distributed to the employees by the first day of the fourth month following each year-end. The federal income tax is 40%, and the bonus is tax-deductible.

**Instructions**

Complete the condensed income statement of the Sticky Glue Company for the year 1983.

**E10–9** Platteville Mfg. Company sold 200 copymaking machines in 1983 for $4,000 apiece, together with a one-year warranty. Maintenance on each machine during the warranty period averages $300.

**Instructions**

(a) Prepare entries to record the sale of the machines and the subsequent expenditure of $59,400 to service the machines during the guarantee period, assuming that the expensed warranty accrual method is used.

(b) On the basis of the data above, prepare the appropriate entries, assuming that the cash basis (i.e., "tax") method is used and that $28,000 was expended to service the machines in 1983.

**E10–10** Crimson Tide Co. includes 1 coupon in each box of soap powder that it packs, and 10 coupons are redeemable for a premium (a kitchen utensil). In 1983, Crimson Tide Co. purchased 5,000 premiums at 80 cents each and sold 80,000 boxes of soap powder @ $2.50 per box. 20,000 coupons were presented for redemption in 1983. It is estimated that 60% of the coupons will eventually be presented for redemption.

**Instructions**

Prepare all the entries that would be made relative to sales of soap powder and to the premium plan in 1983.

**E10–11** How would each of the following items be reported on the balance sheet?

(a) Current maturities of long-term debts to be paid from current assets.
(b) Discount on notes payable.
(c) Notes receivable discounted.
(d) Cash dividends declared but unpaid.
(e) Deposit received from customer to guarantee performance of a contract.
(f) Dividends in arrears on preferred stock.
(g) Loans from officers.
(h) Accommodation endorsement.
(i) Estimated taxes payable.
(j) Employee payroll deductions unremitted.
(k) Unpaid bonus to officers.
(l) Gift certificates sold to customers but not yet redeemed.
(m) Accrued vacation pay.
(n) Premium offers outstanding.
(o) Personal injury claim pending.
(p) Service warranties on appliance sales.

# PROBLEMS

**P10–1** Described below are certain transactions of Huron Corporation.

1. On February 2, the corporation purchased goods from Becker Company for $40,000 subject to cash discount terms of 2/10, n/30. Purchases and accounts payable are recorded by the corporation at net amounts after cash discounts. The invoice was paid on February 26.

2. On April 1, the corporation bought a truck for $15,800 from the Elite Company, paying $1,800 in cash and signing a one-year, 12% note for the balance of the purchase price.

**3.** On May 1, the corporation borrowed $50,000 from the Huntley National Bank by signing a $57,500 note due one year from May 1.

**4.** On June 30 the corporation partially refunded $40,000 of its outstanding 10% note payable made one year ago to the Sycamore State Bank by paying $40,000 plus interest of $4,000, having obtained the $44,000 by using $18,500 of its own cash and signing a new one-year, $30,000 note discounted at 15% by the bank.

**5.** On August 1, the Board of Directors declared a $150,000 cash dividend that was payable on September 10 to stockholders of record on August 31.

**Instructions**

(a) Make all the journal entries necessary to record the transactions above using appropriate dates.

(b) Huron Corporation's year-end is December 31. Assuming that no adjusting entries relative to the transactions above have been recorded at year-end, prepare any adjusting journal entries concerning interest that are necessary to present fair financial statements at December 31. Assume straight-line amortization of discounts.

**P10-2** Listed below are selected transactions of Drier's Department Store for the current year ending December 31.

**1.** On December 5, the store received $400 from the Townhouse Players as a deposit to be returned after certain furniture to be used in stage production was returned on January 15.

**2.** During December, sales totaled $936,000, which includes the 4% sales tax that must be remitted to the state by the fifteenth day of the following month.

**3.** On December 10, the store purchased for cash three delivery trucks for $45,000. The trucks were purchased in a state that applies no sales tax, but the store is located in and must register the trucks in a state that applies a use tax of 5% to nonsalable goods bought outside of its sales tax authority.

**4.** The store follows the practice of recording its property tax liability on the lien date and amortizing the tax over the subsequent 12 months. Property taxes of $54,000 became a lien on May 1 and were paid in two equal installments on July 1 and October 1.

**5.** During the year the store estimated that its annual federal income tax would be $675,000. At year-end, income tax expense (for both accounting and tax return purposes) was determined to be $650,000. (Estimated taxes paid quarterly.)

**Instructions**

Prepare all the journal entries necessary to record the transactions noted above as they occurred and any adjusting journal entries relative to the transactions that would be required to present fair financial statements at December 31. Date each entry.

**P10-3** On December 31, 1983, Doritos Company has $4,000,000 of short-term debt in the form of notes payable to Chase National Bank due periodically in 1984. On January 28, 1984, Doritos enters into a refinancing agreement with Chase which will permit it to borrow up to 60% of the gross amount of its accounts receivable. Receivables are expected to range between a low of $3,000,000 in May to a high of $3,500,000 in October during the year 1984. The interest cost of the maturing short-term debt is 15%, and the new agreement calls for a fluctuating interest at 1% above the prime rate on notes due in 1991. Doritos' December 31, 1983, balance sheet is issued on February 15, 1984.

**Instructions**

Prepare a partial balance sheet for Doritos at December 31, 1983, showing how its $4,000,000 of short-term debt should be presented, including footnote disclosures.

**P10-4** This is a payroll sheet for E-Z Rider Company for the month of Sept. 1983. The company is allowed a 1% unemployment compensation rate by the state; the federal unemployment tax rate is .6% and the maximum for both is $6,000. Assume a 10% federal income tax rate for all employees and a 7% F.I.C.A. tax on employee and employer on a maximum of $32,400 per employee.

| Name | Earnings to Aug. 31 | September Earnings | Income Tax Withholding | F.I.C.A. | State U.C. | Federal U.C. |
|------|------|------|------|------|------|------|
| B. Morris | $ 1,200 | $ 600 | | | | |
| H. Remmers | 2,800 | 400 | | | | |
| B. Harris | 5,400 | 900 | | | | |
| V. Odom | 12,600 | 1,700 | | | | |
| A. Scaperlanda | 38,000 | 3,200 | | | | |
| E. Wunderlich | 30,700 | 2,700 | | | | |

**Instructions**

(a) Complete the payroll sheet and make the necessary entry to record the payment of the payroll.
(b) Make the entry to record the payroll tax expenses of E-Z Rider Company.
(c) Make the entry to pay the payroll liabilities created. Assume that the company pays all payroll liabilities at the end of each month.

**P10–5** Knickerbocker Company pays its office employee payroll weekly. Below is a partial list of employees and their payroll data for August. Because August is their vacation period, vacation pay is also listed.

| Employee | Earnings to July 31 | Weekly Pay | Vacation Pay To Be Received in August |
|------|------|------|------|
| Minnie Sotta | $2,900 | $100 | — |
| Brent Grometer | 2,465 | 85 | $170 |
| Susan Robinson | 6,300 | 210 | 420 |
| Wes Konsin | 3,770 | 130 | — |
| Ken Tucki | 7,000 | 240 | 480 |

Assume that the federal income tax collected is 10% of wages. Union dues collected are 3% of wages. Vacations are taken the second and third weeks of August by Grometer, Robinson, and Tucki. The state unemployment tax rate is 2% and the federal is .6%, both on a $6,000 maximum. The F.I.C.A. rate is 7% on employee and employer on a maximum of $32,400 per employee.

**Instructions**

Make the journal entries necessary for each of the four August payrolls. The entries for the payroll and for the company's liability are made separately. Also make the entry to record the monthly payment of accrued payroll liabilities.

**P10–6** Elevator Company has a contract with its president, Ann Short, to pay her a bonus during each of the years 1982, 1983, 1984, and 1985. The federal income tax rate is 40% during the four years. The profit before deductions for bonus and federal income taxes was $200,000 in 1982, $200,000 in 1983, $400,000 in 1984, and $300,000 in 1985. The president's bonus of 15% is deductible for tax purposes in each year and is to be computed as follows:

(a) In 1982 the bonus is to be based on profit before deductions for bonus and income tax.
(b) In 1983 the bonus is to be based on profit after deduction of bonus but before deduction of income tax.
(c) In 1984 the bonus is to be based on profit before deduction of bonus but after deduction of income tax.
(d) In 1985 the bonus is to be based on profit after deductions for bonus and income tax.

**Instructions**

Compute the amounts of the bonus and the income tax for each of the four years.

**P10–7** Midwest Herbicide Company has a profit-sharing agreement with its employees that provides for deposit in a pension trust for the benefit of the employees 20% of the net income after deducting (1) federal taxes on income, (2) the amount of the annual pension contribution, and (3) a return of 8% on the stockholders' equity as of the end of the year 1983.

**Instructions**

Compute the amount of the pension contribution under the assumption that the stockholders' equity at the end of the year before adding the net income for the year is $1,000,000; that net income for the year before either the pension contribution or tax is $250,000; and that the pension contribution is deductible for tax purposes. Use 45% as the applicable rate of tax.

**P10–8** During 1984, Magic Motor Company sells 60,000 high-compression engines under a three-year warranty that requires the company to replace all defective parts during the warranty period at no cost to the purchaser. These engines constitute nearly all of the company's 1984 business.

**Instructions**

(a) Name two basic methods of accounting for the warranty costs.
(b) What accounts would be used for each of the two methods?
(c) What effect would each method have on net income during the period of the warranties?
(d) In your opinion, which of the two methods is more appropriate for Magic Motor Company?

**P10–9** The Potts Products Company sells electric typewriters for $750 each and offers to each customer a three-year warranty contract for $75 that requires the company to perform periodic services and to replace defective parts. During 1983, the company sold 300 typewriters and 250 warranty contracts for cash. It estimates the three-year warranty costs as $20 for parts and $35 for labor and accounts for warranties on the sales warranty accrual method. Assume sales occurred on December 31, 1983, profit is recognized on the warranties, and straight-line recognition of revenues occurs.

**Instructions**

(a) Record any necessary journal entries in 1983.
(b) What amounts relative to these transactions would appear on the December 31, 1983, balance sheet and how would they be classified?
   In 1984, the Potts Company incurred actual costs relative to 1983 typewriter warranty sales of $1,800 for parts and $3,000 for labor.
(c) Record any necessary journal entries in 1984 relative to 1983 typewriter warranties.
(d) What amounts relative to the 1983 typewriter warranties would appear on the December 31, 1984, balance sheet and how would they be classified?

**P10–10** Khatan-Jamir Corporation sells portable computers under a two-year warranty contract that requires the corporation to replace defective parts and to provide the necessary repair labor. During 1983 the corporation sells for cash 250 computers at a unit price of $6,000. On the basis of past experience, the two-year warranty costs are estimated to be $150 for parts and $105 for labor per unit. (For simplicity, assume that all sales occurred on December 31, 1983.)

**Instructions**

(a) Record any necessary journal entries in 1983, applying the cash basis method.
(b) Record any necessary journal entries in 1983, applying the expense warranty accrual method.
(c) What amounts relative to these transactions would appear on the December 31, 1983 balance sheet and how would they be classified if the cash basis method is applied?
(d) What amounts relative to these transactions would appear on the December 31, 1983 balance sheet and how would they be classified if the expense warranty accrual method is applied?

In 1984 the actual warranty costs to Khatan-Jamir Corporation were $16,700 for parts and $11,650 for labor.

(e) Record any necessary journal entries in 1984, applying the cash basis method.

(f) Record any necessary journal entries in 1984, applying the expensed warranty accrual method.

**P10–11** The Elexio Adono Company sells a machine for $4,500 under a 12-month warranty agreement that requires the company to replace all defective parts and to provide the repair labor at no cost to the customers. With sales being made evenly throughout the year, the company sells 1,400 machines in 1984 (warranty expense is incurred ½ in 1984 and ½ in 1985). As a result of product testing, the company estimates that the warranty cost is $150 per machine ($60 parts and $90 labor).

**Instructions**

Assuming that actual warranty costs are incurred exactly as estimated, what journal entries would be made relative to these facts:

(a) Under application of the expense warranty accrual method for:
1. Sale of machinery in 1984?
2. Warranty expense charged against 1984 revenues?
3. Warranty costs incurred in 1984?
4. Warranty costs incurred in 1985?

(b) Under application of the cash basis method for:
1. Sale of machinery in 1984?
2. Warranty expense charged against 1984 revenues?
3. Warranty costs incurred in 1984?
4. Warranty costs incurred in 1985?

(c) What amount, if any, is disclosed in the balance sheet as a liability for future warranty cost as of December 31, 1984, under each method?

(d) Which method best reflects the income in 1984 and 1985 of the Elexio Adono Company? Why?

**P10–12** To stimulate the sales of its Banana-Nuts breakfast cereal, the Hitching Post Company places 1 coupon in each box. Five coupons are redeemable for a premium consisting of a children's hand puppet. In 1984, the company purchases 25,000 puppets at 40 cents each and sells 200,000 boxes of Banana-Nuts at 90 cents a box. From its experience with other similar premium offers, the company estimates that 40% of the coupons issued will be mailed back for redemption. During 1984, 40,000 coupons are presented for redemption.

**Instructions**

Prepare the journal entries that should be recorded in 1984 relative to the premium plan.

**P10–13** Sweet Candy Company offers a stereo record as a premium for every five candy bar wrappers presented by customers together with 75 cents. The candy bars are sold by the company to distributors for 30 cents each. The purchase price of each record to the company is 80 cents; in addition it costs 25 cents to mail each record. The results of the premium plan for the years 1983 and 1984 are as follows (all purchases and sales are for cash):

|  | 1983 | 1984 |
| --- | --- | --- |
| Stereo records purchased | 240,000 | 250,000 |
| Candy bars sold | 2,861,420 | 2,647,500 |
| Wrappers redeemed | 924,600 | 1,350,000 |
| 1983 wrappers expected to be redeemed in 1984 | 360,000 | |
| 1984 wrappers expected to be redeemed in 1985 | | 240,000 |

**Instructions**

(a) Prepare the journal entries that should be made in 1983 and 1984 to record the transactions related to the premium plan of the Sweet Candy Company.

(b) Indicate the account names, amounts, and classifications of the items related to the premium plan that would appear on the balance sheet and the income statement at the end of 1983 and 1984.

**P10-14** Borke Company must make computations and adjusting entries for the following independent situations at December 31, 1983:

1. Its line of amplifiers carries a three-year warranty against defects. On the basis of past experience the estimated warranty costs related to dollar sales are: first year after sale—1% of sales; second year after sale—2% of sales; and third year after sale—4% of sales. Sales and actual warranty expenditures for the first three years of business were:

| | Sales | Warranty Expenditures |
|---|---|---|
| 1981 | $ 800,000 | $ 3,800 |
| 1982 | 1,040,000 | 17,400 |
| 1983 | 1,200,000 | 46,000 |

**Instructions**

Compute the amount that Borke Company should report as a liability in its December 31, 1983, balance sheet. Assume that all sales are made evenly throughout each year with warranty expenses also evenly spaced relative to the rates above.

2. Borke Company's profit-sharing plan provides that the company will contribute to a fund an amount equal to one-third of its net income after taxes each year. Income before taxes and before deducting the profit-sharing contribution for 1983 is $900,000. The applicable income tax rate is 40%, and the profit-sharing contribution is deductible for tax purposes.

**Instructions**

Compute the amount to be contributed to the profit-sharing fund for 1983.

3. With some of its products, Borke Company includes coupons that are redeemable in merchandise. The coupons have no expiration date and, in the company's experience, 40% of them are redeemed. The liability for unredeemed coupons at December 31, 1982, was $9,000. During 1983, coupons worth $22,000 were issued, and merchandise worth $8,000 was distributed in exchange for coupons redeemed.

**Instructions**

Compute the amount of the liability that should appear on the December 31, 1983, balance sheet.

(AICPA adapted)

**P10-15** On November 24, 1983, 26 passengers on Flypaper Airlines Flight No. 901 were injured upon landing when the plane skidded off the runway. Personal injury suits for damages totaling $3,000,000 were filed on January 11, 1984 against the airline by 18 injured passengers. The airline carries no insurance. Legal counsel has studied each suit and advised Flypaper that it can reasonably expect to pay 60% of the damages claimed. The financial statements for the year ended December 31, 1983 were issued February 27, 1984.

**Instructions**

(a) Prepare any disclosures and journal entries required by the airline in preparation of the December 31, 1983 financial statements.
(b) Ignoring the Nov. 24, 1983 accident, what liability due to the risk of loss from lack of insurance coverage should Flypaper Airlines record or disclose? During the past decade the company has experienced at least one accident per year and incurred average damages of $2,500,000. Discuss fully.

**P10-16** Universal, Inc., in preparation of its December 31, 1983 financial statements, is attempting to determine the proper accounting treatment for each of the following situations:

1. As a result of uninsured accidents during the year, personal injury suits for $300,000 and $50,000 have been filed against the company. It is the judgment of Universal's legal counsel that an unfavorable outcome is unlikely in the $50,000 case but that an unfavorable verdict approximating $180,000 will probably result in the $300,000 case.

2. Universal, Inc. owns a subsidiary in a foreign country that has a book value of $6,780,000 and an estimated fair value of $9,500,000. The foreign government has communicated to Universal its intention to expropriate the assets and business of all foreign investors. On the basis of settlements other firms have received from this same country, Universal expects to receive 40% of the fair value of its properties as final settlement.

3. Universal's chemical product division consisting of five plants is uninsurable because of the special risk of injury to employees and losses due to fire and explosion. The year 1983 is considered one of the safest (luckiest) in the division's history because no loss due to injury or casualty was suffered. Having suffered an average of three casualties a year during the rest of the past decade (ranging from $45,000 to $800,000), management is certain that next year the company will probably not be so fortunate.

## Instructions

(a) Prepare the journal entries that should be recorded as of December 31, 1983, to recognize each of the situations above.

(b) Indicate what should be reported relative to each situation in the financial statements and accompanying notes. Explain why.

**P10-17** Seminoff Inc., a publishing company, is preparing its December 31, 1983, financial statements and must determine the proper accounting treatment for each of the following situations:

1. Seminoff sells subscriptions to several magazines for a one-year, two-year, or three-year period. Cash receipts from subscribers are credited to magazine subscriptions collected in advance, and this account had a balance of $2,400,000 at December 31, 1983. Outstanding subscriptions at December 31, 1983, expire as follows:

> During 1984 — $600,000
> During 1985 —  900,000
> During 1986 —  400,000

2. On January 2, 1983, Seminoff discontinued collision, fire, and theft coverage on its delivery vehicles and became self-insured for these risks. Actual losses of $45,000 during 1983 were charged to delivery expense. The 1982 premium for the discontinued coverage amounted to $100,000, and the controller wants to set up a reserve for self-insurance by a debit to delivery expense of $55,000 and a credit to the reserve for self-insurance of $55,000.

3. A suit for breach of contract seeking damages of $1,000,000 was filed by an author against Seminoff on July 1, 1983. The company's legal counsel believes that an unfavorable outcome is probable. A reasonable estimate of the court's award to the plaintiff is in the range between $100,000 and $500,000. No amount within this range is a better estimate of potential damages than any other amount.

4. During December 1983 a competitor company filed suit against Seminoff for industrial espionage claiming $2,000,000 in damages. In the opinion of management and company counsel, it is reasonably possible that damages will be awarded to the plaintiff. However, the amount of potential damages awarded to the plaintiff cannot be reasonably estimated.

## Instructions

For each of the situations above, prepare the journal entry that should be recorded as of December 31, 1983, or explain why an entry should not be recorded. Show supporting computations in good form.

(AICPA adapted)

# PLANT ASSETS AND LONG-TERM LIABILITIES

3

# CHAPTER 11

# Acquisition and Disposition of Property, Plant, and Equipment

Almost every business enterprise of any size or activity uses assets of a durable nature in its operations. Such assets, commonly referred to as **property, plant, and equipment; plant assets;** or **fixed assets,** include land, building structures (offices, factories, warehouses), and equipment (machinery, furniture, tools). These terms are used interchangeably throughout this textbook. The major characteristics of property, plant, and equipment are:

1. **They are acquired for use in operations and not for resale.** Only assets used in the normal operations of the business should be classified as property, plant, and equipment. An idle building is more appropriately classified separately as an investment; land held by land developers or subdividers is classified as inventory.

2. **They are long-term in nature and usually subject to depreciation.** Property, plant, and equipment yield services over a number of years. The investment in these assets is assigned to future periods through periodic depreciation charges. The exception is land, which is not depreciated, except where a material decrease in value occurs, such as a loss in fertility of agricultural land because of poor crop rotation, drought, or soil erosion.

3. **They possess physical substance.** Property, plant, and equipment are characterized by physical existence or substance and thus are differentiated from intangible assets, such as patents or goodwill. Unlike raw material, however, property, plant, and equipment do not physically become part of the product held for resale.

This chapter discusses the basic accounting problems associated with (1) the incurrence of costs related to property, plant, and equipment and (2) the accounting methods used to retire or dispose of these costs. The methods of allocating costs of property, plant, and equipment to accounting periods are presented in Chapter 12.

## ACQUISITION OF PROPERTY, PLANT, AND EQUIPMENT

Historical cost is the usual basis for valuing property, plant, and equipment. **Historical cost is measured by the cash or cash equivalent price of obtaining the asset and bringing it to the location and condition necessary for its intended use.** The purchase price, freight costs, and installation costs of a productive asset are considered part of the cost of the asset. These costs are allocated to future periods through the depreciation process. Any costs related to the asset that are incurred after its acquisition, such as additions, improvements, or replacements, are added to the cost of the asset if they provide future service potential; otherwise they are expensed in the period of incurrence.

Accountants agree that cost should be the basis used at the date of acquisition because the cash or cash equivalent price best measures the value of the asset at that time. Disagreement does exist concerning accounting recognition of substantial differences arising subsequent to acquisition between historical cost and other valuation methods such as current replacement cost or fair market value. Current standards as stated in *APB Opinion No. 6* are that "property, plant, and equipment should not be written up by an entity to reflect appraisal, market, or current values which are above cost to the entity." Although minor exceptions are noted, current standards indicate that departures from historical cost should be rare.

Currently, the profession for the most part has taken the position that property, plant, and equipment should be reported at historical cost. The main reasons for this position are (1) at the date of acquisition, cost reflects fair value; (2) historical cost involves actual, not hypothetical, transactions, and as a result is extremely reliable; and (3) gains and losses should not be anticipated but should be recognized when the asset is sold. As indicated earlier, there are several other concepts of valuation that might be used to value property, plant, and equipment such as (1) constant dollar accounting (adjustments for general price-level changes), (2) current cost accounting (adjustments for specific price-level changes), (3) net realizable value, or (4) a combination of constant dollar accounting and current cost or net realizable value. These alternative valuation concepts are discussed in Chapter 25.

## Cost of Land

All expenditures made to acquire land and to ready it for use should be considered as part of the land cost. Land costs typically include (1) the purchase price, (2) costs incurred in "closing," such as title to the land, attorney's fees, and recording fees, (3) costs incurred in getting the land in condition for its intended use, such as grading, filling, draining, and clearing, (4) assumption of any liens or mortgages or encumbrances on the property, and (5) any additional land improvements that have an indefinite life.

When land has been purchased for the purpose of constructing a building, all costs incurred up to the excavation for the new building are considered land costs. Removal of old buildings, clearing, grading, and filling are considered costs of the land because these costs are necessary to get the land in condition for its intended purpose. Any proceeds obtained in the process of getting the land ready for its intended use, such as salvage receipts on the demolition of an old building or the sale of timber that has been cleared, are treated as reductions in the price of the land.

In some cases, the purchaser of land has to assume certain obligations on the land such as back taxes or possible liens on the property. In such situations, the cost of the land is the cash paid for it, plus the encumbrances. In other words, if the purchase price of the land is $50,000 cash, but accrued property taxes of $5,000 on the land are assumed, the cost of the land is $55,000.

**Special assessments** for local improvements, such as pavements, street lights, sewers, and drainage systems, are usually charged to the Land account because they are relatively permanent in nature and are maintained and replaced by the local government body. In addition, if the improvement made by the owner is rather permanent in nature, such as landscaping, then the item is properly chargeable to the Land account. **Improvements with**

**limited lives,** such as private driveways, walks, fences, and parking lots, are best recorded separately as Land Improvements so they can be depreciated over their estimated lives.

Generally, land is considered part of property, plant, and equipment. If the major purpose of acquiring and holding land is speculative, however, it is more appropriately classified as an investment. If the land is held by a real estate concern for resale, it should be classified as part of inventory. In cases where land is held as an investment, a question develops regarding the accounting treatment that should be given taxes, insurance, and other direct costs incurred while holding the land. Many accounting theorists believe these costs should be capitalized because the revenue from the investment still has not been received. This approach is reasonable and seems justified except in cases where the asset is currently producing revenue (such as rental property).

## Cost of Buildings

The cost of buildings should include all expenditures related directly to their acquisition or construction. These costs include (1) materials, labor, and overhead costs incurred during construction and (2) fees, such as attorney's and architect's, and building permits. Generally, companies contract to have their buildings constructed. All costs incurred starting with excavation to completion of the building are considered part of the building costs.

One accounting problem in determining building costs is deciding what to do about an old building that is on the site of a newly proposed building. Is the cost of removal of the old building a cost of the land or a cost of the building? Accountants take the position that if land is purchased with an old building on it, the cost of demolition of the old building less its salvage value is a cost of getting the land ready for the intended use and relates to the land rather than to the construction of the new building. As indicated earlier, the general rule is that all costs of getting the asset ready for its intended use are costs of that asset.

## Cost of Equipment

The term equipment in accounting includes delivery equipment, office equipment, machinery, furniture and fixtures, furnishings, factory equipment, and similar fixed assets. The cost of such assets includes the purchase price, freight and handling charges incurred, insurance on the equipment while in transit, cost of special foundations if required, assembling and installation costs and costs of conducting trial runs. Costs thus include all expenditures incurred in acquiring the equipment and preparing it for use.

## Self-Constructed Assets

Determining the cost of machinery and other fixed assets is a problem when companies (particularly in the railroad and utility industries) construct their own assets. Without a purchase price or contract price, the company must allocate costs and expenses to arrive at the construction cost to be entered in the property records. Materials and direct labor used in construction pose no problem because these costs can be traced directly to work and material orders related to the fixed assets constructed.

The assignment of indirect costs of manufacturing creates special problems, however. These indirect costs, called overhead or burden, consist of such items as power, heat, light, insurance, property taxes on factory buildings and equipment, factory supervisory labor, depreciation of fixed assets, and supplies.

These costs may be handled three ways.

1. **Assign no fixed overhead to the cost of the constructed asset.** The major reason for this treatment is that indirect overhead is generally fixed in nature and does not increase as a result of constructing one's own plant or equipment. This approach assumes that the company will have the same costs regardless of whether the company constructs the asset or not, so to charge a portion of the overhead costs to the equipment will normally relieve current expenses and consequently overstate income of the current period. Variable overhead costs that increase as a result of the construction should be assigned to the cost of the asset.

2. **Assign a portion of all overhead to the construction process.** This approach, a full costing concept, is appropriate if one believes that costs attach to all products and assets manufactured or constructed. This procedure assigns overhead costs to construction as it would to normal production. This method is employed extensively because most accountants believe a better matching of costs with revenues is obtained. Advocates of this approach indicate that failure to allocate overhead costs understates the initial cost of the equipment and results in an inaccurate allocation in the future.

3. **Allocate on basis of lost production.** A third alternative is to allocate to the construction project the cost of any curtailed production that occurs because the asset is built instead of purchased. This method is conceptually appealing, but is based on "what might have occurred," which is essentially an opportunity cost concept. The practicality of this approach is questionable because valuation problems would be extremely difficult.

Given the assumptions and principles currently used in accounting, such as going-concern, matching, and historical cost, a pro rata portion of the fixed overhead should be assigned to the asset to obtain its cost. If the allocated overhead results in recording construction costs in excess of the costs that would be charged by an outside independent producer, the excess overhead should be recorded as a period loss rather than capitalized to avoid capitalizing the asset at more than its probable market value.

## Interest Costs

The proper accounting for interest costs has been a long-standing controversy in accounting. Three approaches have been suggested to account for the interest incurred in financing the construction or acquisition of property, plant, and equipment:

1. **Capitalize no interest charges during construction.** Under this approach interest is considered a cost of financing and not a cost of construction. It is contended that if the company had used stock financing rather than debt financing, this expense would not have developed. The major arguments against this approach are that an implicit interest cost is associated with the use of cash regardless of its source; if stock financing is employed, a real cost exists to the stockholders although a contractual claim does not develop.

2. **Capitalize only the actual interest costs incurred during construction.** This approach relies on the historical cost concept that only actual transactions are recorded. It is argued that interest incurred is as much a cost of acquiring the asset as the cost of the materials, labor, and other resources used. As a result, a company that uses debt financing will have an asset of higher cost than an enterprise that uses stock financing. The results achieved by this approach are held to be unsatisfactory by some because the cost of an asset should be the same whether cash, debt financing, or stock financing is employed.

3. **Charge construction with all costs of funds employed, whether identifiable or not.** This method is an economic cost approach that maintains that one part of the cost of construction is the cost of financing, whether by debt, cash, or stock financing. An asset should be charged with all costs necessary to get it ready for its intended use. Interest, whether actual or imputed, is a cost of building, just as labor, materials, and overhead are costs. A major criticism of this approach is that imputation of a cost of equity capital is subjective and outside the framework of an historical cost system.

The profession has established standards for capitalizing interest cost as part of the historical cost of acquiring certain assets.[1] To qualify for interest capitalization, assets must require a period of time to get them ready for their intended use. However, interest capitalization is required for these assets only if its effect, compared with the effect of expensing interest, is material.[2]

Interest costs are capitalized starting with the first expenditure related to the asset, and capitalization continues until the asset is substantially completed and ready for its intended use. The amount of interest to be capitalized is the **actual interest incurred** on an enterprise's debt obligations and does not include a **cost of capital charge** for stockholders' equity. Assets that qualify for interest cost capitalization include assets under construction for an enterprise's own use, including buildings, plants, and large machinery; and assets intended for sale or lease that are constructed or otherwise produced as discrete projects (for example, ships or real estate developments). Examples of assets that do not qualify for interest capitalization are (1) assets that are in use or ready for their intended use, and (2) assets that are not being used in the earnings activities of the enterprise and that are not undergoing the activities necessary to get them ready for use (such as land that is not being developed and assets not being used because of obsolescence, excess capacity or need for repair).

In *Statement No. 34*, the FASB specified that the amount of interest to be capitalized for qualifying assets is that portion of total interest cost incurred during the period that theoretically could have been avoided if expenditures for the assets had not been made. To apply this concept, the potential amount of interest that may be capitalized during an accounting period is determined by multiplying an interest rate(s) by the weighted-average amount of accumulated expenditures (**average accumulated expenditures**) for qualifying assets during the period. For our purposes we will refer to this amount as **avoidable interest.** The interest rates to be used are:

1. For the portion of average accumulated expenditures that is less than or equal to any amounts borrowed specifically to finance construction of the assets, use the interest rate incurred on the specific borrowings.
2. For the portion of average accumulated expenditures that is greater than any debt incurred specifically to finance construction of the assets, use a weighted average of interest rates incurred on all outstanding debt during the period.

The capitalization period (that is, period of time during which interest must be capitalized) begins when three conditions are present:

1. Expenditures for the asset have been made.
2. Activities that are necessary to get the asset ready for its intended use are in progress.
3. Interest cost is being incurred.

Interest capitalization continues as long as those three conditions are present. The capitalization period ends when the asset is substantially complete and ready for its intended use.

The amount of interest cost to be capitalized is the "avoidable interest," explained above, or total actual interest cost incurred, whichever is less. Interest cost that is capitalized should be written off over the useful lives of the assets involved and not over the term

---

[1]"Capitalization of Interest Costs," *Statement of Financial Accounting Standards No. 34* (Stamford, Conn.: FASB, 1979).

[2]Ibid., summary paragraph.

of the debt. Disclosure should be made of the total interest cost incurred during the period, indicating the portion charged to expense and the portion capitalized.

To illustrate, assume that on November 1, 1982 Gardner Company contracted with Wesleyan Construction Co. to have a building constructed for $1,500,000 on land Gardner purchased years earlier. Gardner made the following payments to the construction company during 1983:

| March 1 | May 1 | December 31 | Total |
|---|---|---|---|
| $510,000 | $540,000 | $450,000 | $1,500,000 |

Construction was completed and the building was ready for occupancy on December 31, 1983. Gardner Company had the following debt outstanding at December 31, 1983:

1. 15% three-year note to finance construction of the building,
   dated March 31, 1983, with interest payable annually on March 31     $750,000
2. 10% five-year note payable, dated December 31, 1979,
   with interest payable annually on December 31     $550,000
3. 12% ten-year bonds issued December 31, 1978, with interest
   payable annually on December 31     $600,000

The average accumulated expenditures during 1983 and the avoidable interest that is potentially capitalizable during 1983 is computed as follows:

| Date | Expenditures | × | Capitalization Period* | = | Average Accumulated Expenditures |
|---|---|---|---|---|---|
| March 1 | 510,000 | | 10/12 | | $425,000 |
| May 1 | 540,000 | | 8/12 | | 360,000 |
| Dec. 31 | 450,000 | | 0 | | 0 |
| | $1,500,000 | | | | $785,000 |

*Months elapsing between the date expenditures were made and the date interest capitalization stops (Dec. 31, 1983).

**Average accumulated expenditures: $785,000**

| Average Accumulated Expenditures | × | Interest Rate | = | Avoidable Interest |
|---|---|---|---|---|
| $750,000 | | .15 (construction note) | | $112,500 |
| 35,000 | | .1104 (weighted average of other debt)* | | 3,864 |
| $785,000 | | | | $116,364 |

*Weighted-average interest rate computation:

| | Principal | Interest |
|---|---|---|
| 10%, Five-year note | $ 550,000 | $ 55,000 |
| 12%, Ten-year bonds | 600,000 | 72,000 |
| | $1,150,000 | $127,000 |

$$\frac{\text{Total interest}}{\text{Total principal}} = \frac{\$127,000}{\$1,150,000} = 11.04\%$$

**Avoidable interest: $116,364**

The actual interest cost, that represents the maximum amount of interest that may be capitalized during 1983, is computed as follows:

| | | | |
|---|---|---|---|
| Construction note | $750,000 × .15 × 9/12 | = | $ 84,375 |
| Five-year note | $550,000 × .10 | = | 55,000 |
| Ten-year bonds | $600,000 × .12 | = | 72,000 |
| | | | $211,375 |
| | **Actual interest: $211,375** | | |

The interest cost to be capitalized is the lesser of $116,364 (avoidable interest) and $211,375 (actual interest), which is **$116,364.**

The journal entries to be made by Gardner Company during 1983 would be as follows:

**March 1**

| | | |
|---|---|---|
| Building | 510,000 | |
|    Cash | | 510,000 |

**March 31**

| | | |
|---|---|---|
| Cash | 750,000 | |
|    Notes Payable | | 750,000 |

**May 1**

| | | |
|---|---|---|
| Building | 540,000 | |
|    Cash | | 540,000 |

**December 31**

| | | |
|---|---|---|
| Building | 450,000 | |
|    Cash | | 450,000 |

| | | |
|---|---|---|
| Building | 116,364 | |
| Interest Expense ($211,375 − $116,364) | 95,011 | |
|    Interest Payable ($750,000 × .15 × 9/12) | | 84,375 |
|    Cash ($55,000 + $72,000) | | 127,000 |

At December 31, 1983, Gardner should disclose the following in the footnotes to its financial statements:

During 1983 total interest cost was $211,375 of which $116,364 was capitalized and $95,011 was charged to expense.

Two additional points should be noted regarding interest capitalization. First, when interest cost is incurred in connection with the purchase of land that will be used as a building site, the interest to be capitalized should be debited to the building account and not to the land account. Second, companies frequently borrow money to finance construction of assets and temporarily invest the excess borrowed funds in interest-bearing securities until the funds are needed to pay for construction. During the early stages of construction, interest revenue earned may exceed the interest cost incurred on the borrowed funds. Some accountants have wondered whether it is appropriate to offset interest revenue against interest cost when determining the amount of interest to be capitalized as a part of the construction cost of assets. To clarify this issue, the FASB issued *Technical Bulletin No. 81-5,* "Offsetting Interest to be Capitalized with Interest Income." It provides that **interest revenue should not be netted or offset against interest cost.** Temporary or short-term investment decisions are not related to the interest incurred as part of the acquisition cost of assets. Therefore, the interest incurred on qualifying assets should be capitalized whether or not excess funds are temporarily invested in short-term securities. Some accountants are critical of this accounting because a company is able to defer the interest cost, but is permitted to report the interest revenue in the current period.

The requirement of interest capitalization could have a substantive impact on the financial statements of business enterprises. To illustrate, public utilities have been permitted to capitalize interest during construction (whether actual or imputed) for many years.[3] For example, at one time it was estimated that Duke Power's net income of $58.5 million would be reduced by more than 85% if interest costs were shown as an expense. In addition, compare the results of different methods of handling interest adopted by two large utilities.

| | Comparison of Earnings Between Companies That Follow Different Practices Concerning Capitalization of Interest During Construction | |
|---|---|---|
| | Reported Net Income Regulatory | Adjusted for Capitalized Interest |
| | (In millions) | |
| Wisconsin Electric Power | $78.1 | $78.1 |
| Public Service Company of Colorado | 78.3 | 71.1 |
| Difference | $ (0.2) | $ 7.0 |
| Percentage Differences | ( .3%) | 9.0% |

The difference between the methods of presentation (approximately 9.3%) is significant and illustrates the necessity for appropriate guidelines in this area.

The interest capitalization requirement is controversial. From a conceptual viewpoint, many believe that either no interest cost should be capitalized or all interest costs, actual or imputed, should be capitalized for the reasons mentioned earlier in this section. In addition, some practical problems exist. For example, capitalization is supposed to take place only when the benefits of the information provided exceed the costs of providing the information, a difficult concept to operationalize. As a result, it appears that this topic will continue to be debated.

---

[3]Non-utility companies traditionally had not capitalized any interest cost during construction, whether actual or imputed. In the early 1970s, however, a number of companies decided to do so. The reason for this switch was to prevent the decline in earnings that resulted when an enterprise expensed these interest costs. In 1974, the SEC in *ASR No. 163* declared a moratorium on the capitalization of interest costs for most non-utility companies, indicating that practices in this area were leading to noncomparability of financial data. The FASB standard is an attempt to develop guidelines in accounting for interest costs during construction.

## ACQUISITION AND VALUATION

**An asset should be recorded at the fair market value of what is given up to acquire it or at its own fair market value, whichever is more clearly evident.** Fair market value, however, is sometimes obscured by the process through which the asset is acquired. As an example, assume that land and buildings are bought together for one price. How are separate values for the land and building determined? A number of accounting problems of this nature are examined in the following sections.

### Cash Discount

When plant assets are purchased subject to cash discounts for prompt payment, the question of how the discount should be handled arises. If the discount is taken, it should be considered a reduction in the purchase price of the asset. What is not clear, however, is whether a reduction in the asset cost should occur if the discount is not taken. Two points of view exist on this matter. Under one approach, the discount, whether taken or not, is considered a reduction in the cost of the asset. The rationale for this approach is that the real cost of the asset is the cash or cash equivalent price of the asset. In addition, some argue that the terms of cash discounts are so attractive that failure to take a discount is a loss because management was inefficient. On the other hand, some argue that the discount should not be considered a loss because the terms may be unfavorable or because it would not be prudent for the company to take the discount. At present, both methods are employed in practice. The former method is generally preferred because it represents the current cash equivalent price to acquire the asset at the date of acquisition.

### Deferred Payment Contracts

Plant assets are purchased frequently on long-term credit contracts through the use of notes, mortgages, bonds, or equipment obligations. **Assets purchased on long-term credit contracts should be accounted for at the present value of the consideration exchanged between the contracting parties at the date of the transaction to properly reflect cost.** An asset, therefore, that requires five annual payments of $1,000, with no interest specified in the contract, should not be recorded originally at $5,000. The present value of these payments, at an appropriate interest rate, should be used to determine the purchase price of the asset. If the asset in the situation above was purchased on a basis that required the payment of $1,000 per year for five years, including an interest element stated at 8% annually, the cost of the asset would be $3,992.71 ($1,000 × 3.99271; see Table 6–4).

Determining the purchase price becomes more complex when a specific interest rate does not appear on the obligation or if the specified rate is unreasonable. To estimate the present value of a note under such circumstances, an appropriate interest rate is imputed. The objective is to approximate the interest rate that the buyer and seller would negotiate at arm's length in a similar transaction. If an interest rate is not imputed, the asset will be recorded at an amount greater than its fair value. In addition, interest expense would be incorrectly projected in future periods. In determining the interest rate, the cash exchange price of the asset acquired might indicate the value.

To illustrate, assume that Sutter, Inc., decides to purchase a specially built metal cutter to help in the preparation of some new molding designs. The company issues a $100,000, 20-year, noninterest-bearing note to T & R Metalcutters for the new equipment when the prevailing market rate of interest for obligations of this nature is 10%. The company will pay off the note in twenty $5,000 installments at the end of each period over the life of the note. The fair market value of this particular metal cutter cannot be established in the market place and is thus approximated by determining the market value of the note. The entries at date of purchase and subsequently are:

**At date of purchase**

| | | |
|---|---|---|
| Equipment ($5,000 × 8.514 — Table 6-4) | 42,570 | |
| Discount on Notes Payable | 57,430 | |
| Notes Payable | | 100,000 |

**At end of first year**

| | | |
|---|---|---|
| Interest Expense | 4,257 | |
| Notes Payable | 5,000 | |
| Cash | | 5,000 |
| Discount on Notes Payable | | 4,257 |

Interest expense under the effective interest approach is $4,257, ($100,000 − $57,430) × 10%; if straight-line amortization is used, interest expense would be $2,871.50, ($57,430 ÷ 20). The entry at the end of the second year to record interest and to pay off a portion of the note employing the effective interest approach is as follows:

**At end of second year**

| | | |
|---|---|---|
| Interest Expense | 4,183 | |
| Notes Payable | 5,000 | |
| Cash | | 5,000 |
| Discount on Notes Payable | | 4,183 |

Interest expense in the second year under the effective interest approach is $4,183, [($100,000 − $57,430) − ($5,000 − $4,257)] × 10%.

## Exchanges of Property, Plant, and Equipment (Nonmonetary Assets)

The proper accounting for exchanges of nonmonetary assets (such as inventories and property, plant, and equipment) is controversial.[4] Some accountants argue that the accounting for these types of exchanges should be based on the fair value of the asset given up with a gain or loss recognized; others believe that the accounting should be based on the recorded amount (book value) of the asset given up with no gain or loss recognized; and still others favor an approach that would recognize losses in all cases, but defer gains in special situations.

Ordinarily accounting for the exchange of nonmonetary assets should be based on **the fair value of the asset given up or the fair value of the asset received, whichever is clearly more evident.**[5] If the fair value of either asset is not reasonably determinable, the book value of the asset given up is usually used as the basis for recording the nonmonetary exchange. Thus, any gains or losses on the exchange should be recognized immediately. The rationale for this approach is that **the earnings process related to these assets is completed**

---

[4]Nonmonetary assets are items whose price in terms of the monetary unit may change over time, whereas monetary assets are fixed in terms of units of currency by contract or otherwise, for example, cash and short- or long-term accounts and notes receivable.

[5]"Accounting for Nonmonetary Transactions," *Opinions of the Accounting Principles Board No. 29* (Stamford, Conn.: FASB, 1973), par. 18.

and, therefore, a gain or loss should be recognized. This approach is always employed when the assets are **dissimilar** in nature, such as the exchange of land for a building, or the exchange of equipment for inventory.

The general rule is modified when exchanges of **similar nonmonetary** assets occur. For example, when a company exchanges inventory items with inventory of another company because of color, size, etc. to facilitate sale to an outside customer, the earnings process is not considered completed and a **gain** should not be recognized. Likewise if a company trades **similar productive assets** (assets held for or used in the production of goods or services) such as land for land or equipment for equipment, the enterprise is not considered to have completed the earnings process and, therefore, **a gain should not be recognized.** However, if the exchange transaction involving **similar assets** would result in a loss, **the loss is recognized immediately.**

In certain situations, gains on exchange of similar nonmonetary assets may be involved where **monetary consideration** (**boot**) is received. When monetary consideration such as cash is received in addition to the nonmonetary asset, it is assumed that a portion of the earnings process is completed and, therefore, a partial gain is recognized.

In summary, losses on nonmonetary transactions are always recognized whether the exchange involves dissimilar or similar assets. Gains on nonmonetary transactions are recognized if the exchange involves dissimilar assets; gains are deferred if the exchange involves similar assets, unless cash or some other form of monetary consideration is received, in which case a partial gain is recognized. Any gain or loss on disposal of nonmonetary assets is computed by comparing the book value of the asset given up with the fair value of the asset given up.

To illustrate the accounting for these different types of transactions, the discussion is divided into three sections as follows:

1. Accounting for dissimilar assets.
2. Accounting for similar assets—loss situation.
3. Accounting for similar assets—gain situations.

**Dissimilar Assets**  The cost of a nonmonetary asset acquired in exchange for a dissimilar nonmonetary asset is usually recorded at the **fair value of the asset given up,** and a gain or loss is recognized. The **fair value of the asset received** should be used only if it is more clearly evident than the fair value of the asset given up.

To illustrate, Newbold Transportation Company exchanged a number of used trucks plus cash for vacant land that might be used for a future plant site. The trucks have a combined book value of $42,000 (cost $64,000 less $22,000 accumulated depreciation). Newbold's purchasing agent, who has had previous dealings in the second-hand market, indicates that the trucks have a fair market value of $49,000. In addition to the trucks, Newbold must pay $17,000 cash for the land. The cost of the land is $66,000 computed as follows:

| | Computation of Land Cost |
|---|---|
| Fair value of trucks exchanged | $49,000 |
| Cash paid | 17,000 |
| Cost of land | $66,000 |

The journal entry to record the exchange transaction is:

| | | |
|---|---|---|
| Land | 66,000 | |
| Accumulated Depreciation—Trucks | 22,000 | |
|    Trucks | | 64,000 |
|    Gain on Disposal of Trucks | | 7,000 |
|    Cash | | 17,000 |

The gain is the difference between the fair value of the trucks and their book value. It is verified as follows:

| | Computation of Gain | |
|---|---|---|
| Fair value of trucks | | $49,000 |
| Cost of trucks | $64,000 | |
| Less accumulated depreciation | 22,000 | |
| Book value of trucks | | 42,000 |
| Gain on disposal of used trucks | | $ 7,000 |

It follows that if the fair value of the trucks was $39,000 instead of $49,000, a loss on the exchange of $3,000 ($42,000 − $39,000) would be reported. In either case, as a result of the exchange of dissimilar assets, the earnings process on the used trucks has been completed and a gain **or** loss should be recognized.

**Similar Assets—Loss Situation**    Similar nonmonetary assets are those that are of the same general type, or that perform the same function, or that are employed in the same line of business. When similar nonmonetary assets are exchanged and a loss results, the loss should be recognized immediately. For example, Information Processing, Inc. trades its used accounting machine for a new model. The accounting machine given up has a book value of $8,000 (original cost $12,000 less $4,000 accumulated depreciation) and a fair value of $6,000. It is traded for a new model that has a list price of $16,000. In negotiations with the seller, a trade-in allowance of $9,000 is finally agreed on for the used machine. The cash payment that must be made for the new asset and the cost of the new machine are computed as follows:

| | Cost of New Machine |
|---|---|
| List price of new machine | $16,000 |
| Less trade-in allowance for used machine | 9,000 |
| Cash payment due | 7,000 |
| Fair value of used machine | 6,000 |
| Cost of new machine | $13,000 |

The journal entry to record this transaction is:

| | | |
|---|---|---|
| Equipment | 13,000 | |
| Accumulated Depreciation—Equipment | 4,000 | |
| Loss on Disposal of Equipment | 2,000 | |
|    Equipment | | 12,000 |
|    Cash | | 7,000 |

The loss on the disposal of the used machine can be verified as follows:

| | Computation of Loss |
|---|---|
| Fair value of used machine | $6,000 |
| Book value of used machine | 8,000 |
| Loss on disposal of used machine | $2,000 |

Why was the trade-in allowance or the book value of the old asset not used as a basis for the new equipment? The trade-in allowance is not employed because it included a price concession (similar to a price discount) to the purchaser. For example, few individuals pay list price for a new car. Trade-in allowances on the used car are often so inflated that actual selling prices are below list prices. In short, the list price of a new car is usually inflated and to record the car at list price would state it at an amount in excess of its cash equivalent price. Use of book value in this situation would overstate the value of the new accounting machine by $2,000. Because assets should not be valued at more than their cash equivalent price, the loss should be recognized immediately rather than added to the cost of the newly acquired asset.

**Similar Assets—Gain Situation (no cash received)**   The accounting treatment for exchanges of **similar** nonmonetary assets when a gain develops is more complex. If the exchange does not complete the earnings process, then any **gain should be deferred.** The real estate industry provides a good example of why the profession decided not to recognize gains on exchanges of similar nonmonetary assets. In the early 1970s when the real estate business was booming, it was common practice for companies to "swap" real estate holdings. To illustrate, Landmark Company and Hillfarm, Inc. each had undeveloped land on which they intended to build shopping centers. Appraisals indicated that the land of both companies had increased significantly in value. The companies decided to exchange (swap) their undeveloped land, record a gain, and report their new parcels of land at current fair values. But, should gains be recognized at this point? The profession's position was that the earnings process is not completed because the companies remain in the same economic position after the swap as before; therefore, the asset acquired should be recorded at book value with no gain recognized. If, however, the book value exceeds fair value, a loss should be recognized.

To illustrate, Davis Rent-A-Car has a rental fleet of automobiles that are primarily Ford Motor Company products. Davis's management is interested in increasing the variety of automobiles in its rental fleet by adding numerous models of General Motors products. During a long delay in delivery from the manufacturer, Davis arranges with Nertz Rent-A-Car to exchange a group of Ford Fairmonts and Futuras with a fair value of $160,000 and a book value of $135,000 (cost $150,000 less accumulated depreciation $15,000) for a number of Chevy Citations and Pontiac Phoenixes. The fair value of the automobiles received from Nertz is $170,000; Davis, therefore, pays $10,000 in cash in addition to the Ford automobiles exchanged. The total gain to Davis Rent-A-Car is computed as shown in the first schedule at the top of page 491.

Because the earnings process is not considered completed in this transaction, the total gain is deferred and the basis of the General Motors automobiles is reduced via two different but acceptable computations as shown in the second illustration on page 491:

|  | Computation of Gain |
|---|---|
| Fair value of Ford automobiles exchanged | $160,000 |
| Book value of Ford automobiles exchanged | 135,000 |
| Total gain (unrecognized) | $ 25,000 |

| Basis of New Automobiles to Davis | | | | |
|---|---|---|---|---|
| Fair value of GM automobiles | $170,000 | | Book value of Ford automobiles | $135,000 |
| Less gain deferred | (25,000) | OR | Cash paid | 10,000 |
| Basis of GM automobiles | $145,000 | | Basis of GM automobiles | $145,000 |

The entry by Davis to record this transaction is as follows:

| | | |
|---|---|---|
| Automobiles (GM) | 145,000 | |
| Accumulated Depreciation—Automobiles | 15,000 | |
| Automobiles (Ford) | | 150,000 |
| Cash | | 10,000 |

The gain that reduced the basis of the new automobiles will be recognized when those automobiles are sold to an outside party. If these automobiles are held for an extended period of time, depreciation charges will be lower and net income higher in subsequent periods because of the reduced basis.

**Similar Assets—Gain Situation (some cash received)**    The accounting issue of gain recognition becomes more difficult if monetary consideration such as cash is **received** in an exchange of similar nonmonetary assets. When cash is received, part of the nonmonetary asset is considered sold and part exchanged; therefore, only a portion of the gain is deferred.[6] The general formula for gain recognition when some cash is received is as follows:

$$\frac{\text{Cash Received (Boot)}}{\text{Cash Received (Boot)} + \text{Fair Value of Asset Received}} \times \text{Total Gain} = \frac{\text{Recognized}}{\text{Gain}}$$

For example, consider recording the foregoing exchange of automobiles on the books of Nertz Rent-A-Car. If the book value of Nertz's Chevy and Pontiac automobiles exchanged is $136,000 (cost $200,000 less accumulated depreciation $64,000), the total gain on the exchange to Nertz would be computed as follows:

---

[8]The part-sold, part-exchanged treatment is applicable to exchanges of similar nonmonetary assets respective of the amount of monetary consideration involved in the transaction. See James B. Hubbs and D. R. Bainbridge, "Nonmonetary Exchange Transactions: Clarification of APB Opinion No. 29," *The Accounting Review* (January, 1982), pp. 171–175.

|  | Computation of Total Gain to Nertz |
|---|---|
| Fair value of GM automobiles exchanged | $170,000 |
| Book value of GM automobiles exchanged | 136,000 |
| Total gain | $ 34,000 |

But, because Nertz received $10,000 in cash, the recognized gain on this transaction is computed as follows using the formula at the bottom of page 491:

$$\frac{\$10,000}{\$10,000 + \$160,000} \times \$34,000 = \$2,000$$

The ratio of monetary assets ($10,000) to the total consideration received ($10,000 + $160,000) is the portion of the total gain ($34,000) to be recognized, that is, $2,000. Because only a gain of $2,000 is recognized on this transaction, the remaining $32,000 ($34,000 − $2,000) is deferred and reduces the basis of the new automobiles. The computation of the basis is as follows:

| Basis of New Automobiles to Nertz | | | | |
|---|---|---|---|---|
| Fair value of Ford automobiles | $160,000 |  | Book value of GM automobiles | $136,000 |
| Less gain deferred | (32,000) | OR | Portion of book value | |
| Basis of Ford automobiles | $128,000 |  | presumed sold | (8,000)* |
|  |  |  | Basis of Ford automobiles | $128,000 |

$$\frac{*\$10,000}{\$170,000} \times \$136,000 = \$8,000$$

The entry by Nertz to record this transaction is as follows:

| | | |
|---|---|---|
| Cash | 10,000 | |
| Automobiles (Ford) | 128,000 | |
| Accumulated Depreciation—Automobiles (GM) | 64,000 | |
| Automobiles (GM) | | 200,000 |
| Gain on Disposal of GM Automobiles | | 2,000 |

The profession's rationale for this treatment is as follows: Before the exchange, Nertz Rent-A-Car had an unrecognized gain of $34,000, as evidenced by the difference between the book value ($136,000) and the fair value ($170,000) of its GM automobiles. When the exchange occurred, a portion ($10,000/$170,000 or 1/17) of the fair value was converted to a more liquid asset. The ratio of this liquid asset ($10,000) to the total consideration received ($160,000 + $10,000) is the portion of the gain ($34,000) realized. Thus, a gain of $2,000 (1/17 × $34,000) is recognized and recorded.

Presented below in summary form are the accounting requirements for recognizing gains and losses on exchanges of nonmonetary assets.[7]

1. Compute the total gain or loss on the transaction, which is equal to the difference between the fair value of the asset given up and the book value of the asset given up.
2. If a loss is computed in 1, always recognize the entire loss.
3. If a gain is computed in 1,
   (a) and the earnings process is considered completed, the entire gain is recognized (dissimilar assets).
   (b) and the earning process is not considered completed (similar assets),
      (1) and no cash is involved, no gain is recognized.
      (2) and some cash is given, no gain is recognized.
      (3) and some cash is received, the following portion of the gain is recognized:

$$\frac{\text{Cash Received (Boot)}}{\text{Cash Received (Boot)} + \text{Fair Value of Assets Received}} \times \text{Total Gain}$$

An enterprise that engages in one or more nonmonetary exchanges during a period should disclose in financial statements for the period the nature of the transactions, the basis of accounting for the assets transferred, and gains or losses recognized on transfers.[8]

## Lump Sum Purchase

A special problem of pricing fixed assets arises when a group of plant assets is purchased at a single lump sum price. When such a situation occurs, and it is not at all unusual, the practice is to allocate the total cost among the various assets on the basis of their relative fair market values. The assumption is that costs will vary in direct proportion to sales value.

Although the accountant may not be an expert in this area, responsibility for determining that the valuations associated with the different assets are reasonable and that they can be verified to some degree must be accepted. Generally, an appraisal for insurance purposes, the assessed valuation for property taxes, or simply an independent appraisal by an engineer or other appraiser might be used. Normally, the seller's book value used should not be employed as a basis for allocation.

To illustrate, Norduct Heating, Inc., decides to purchase several assets of a small heating concern, Harker Heating, for $80,000. Harker Heating is in the process of liquidation, and its assets sold are:

|  | Book Value | Fair Market Value |
|---|---|---|
| Inventory | $30,000 | $ 25,000 |
| Land | 20,000 | 25,000 |
| Building | 35,000 | 50,000 |
|  | $85,000 | $100,000 |

[7]Adapted from an article by Robert Capettini and Thomas E. King, "Exchanges of Nonmonetary Assets: Some Changes," *The Accounting Review* (January, 1976).

[8]"Accounting for Nonmonetary Transactions," *op. cit.,* par. 28.

The $80,000 purchase price would be allocated on the basis of the relative fair market values (assuming specific identification of costs is not practicable) in the following manner:

| | |
|---|---|
| Inventory | $\dfrac{\$\ 25{,}000}{\$100{,}000} \times \$80{,}000 = \$20{,}000$ |
| Land | $\dfrac{\$\ 25{,}000}{\$100{,}000} \times \$80{,}000 = \$20{,}000$ |
| Building | $\dfrac{\$\ 50{,}000}{\$100{,}000} \times \$80{,}000 = \$40{,}000$ |

## Issuance of Stock

When property is acquired by issuance of securities, such as common stock, the cost of the property is not properly measured by the par or stated value of such stock. If the stock is being actively traded, **the market value of the stock issued is a fair indication of the cost of the property acquired because the stock is a good measure of the current cash equivalent price.**

For example, Coyle-Lukkin decides to purchase some adjacent land for expansion of its carpeting and cabinet operation. In lieu of paying cash for the land, the company issues to Starret Company 5,000 shares of common stock (par value $10) that have a fair market value of $12 per share. Coyle-Lukkin would make the following entry.

| | | |
|---|---|---|
| Land (5,000 × $12) | 60,000 | |
| Common Stock | | 50,000 |
| Additional Paid-In Capital | | 10,000 |

If the market value of the common stock exchanged is not determinable, the market value of the property should be established and used as the basis for recording the asset and issuance of the common stock.[9]

## Acquisition and Disposition by Donation or Gift

An enterprise may be both the recipient of donations and the maker of donations. Such exchanges are referred to as **nonreciprocal transfers** because they are transfers of assets in one direction. Many agricultural and transportation enterprises, for example, have received substantial donations (in the form of rebates and subsidies) from the federal government. When assets are acquired in this manner, a strict cost concept dictates that the valuation of

[9]When the fair market value of the stock is used as the basis of valuation, careful consideration must be given to the effect that the issuance of additional shares will have on the existing market price. Where the effect on market price appears significant, an independent appraisal of the asset received should be made. This valuation should be employed as the basis for valuation of the asset as well as for the stock issued. In the unusual case where the fair market value of the stock or the fair market value of the asset cannot be determined objectively, the board of directors of the corporation may set the value.

the asset should be zero. A departure from the cost principle seems justified, however, because the only costs incurred, legal fees and other relatively minor expenditures, do not constitute a reasonable basis of accounting for the assets acquired. To record nothing, we believe, is to ignore the economic realities of an increase in wealth and asset utility. Therefore, **the appraisal or fair market value of the asset should be used to establish a reasonable basis of asset valuation for purposes of enterprise accountability.**

The classification of the offsetting credit to the asset received, however, is controversial. Some believe the credit should be to Donated Capital (an additional paid-in capital account) because these donations increase the amount of assets and, therefore, stockholders' equity available to the enterprise. To illustrate, Max Wayer Meat Packing, Inc. has recently accepted a donation of land with a fair value of $150,000 from the city of Burke in return for a promise to build a packing plant in Burke. Max Wayer's entry is:

| | | |
|---|---|---|
| Land | 150,000 | |
| Donated Capital | | 150,000 |

Others argue that capital is contributed only by the owners of the business and that donations are benefits to the enterprise which should be reported as revenue. An issue related to the revenue approach is whether the revenue should be reported immediately or over the period that the asset is employed. For example, to attract new industry a city may offer land, but the receiving enterprise may incur additional costs in the future (transportation, higher state income taxes, etc.) because the location is not the most desirable.

As a consequence, some argue that the revenue should be deferred and recognized as the costs mentioned above are incurred. It should be noted that whether the donated capital approach, the immediate recognition of revenue approach, or the deferred revenue approach is used, if the donation is contingent upon some performance (such as building a plant), this contingency should be reported in the footnotes.

In practice, enterprises permit cash donations in the form of subsidies, rebates, and tax credits to flow through the income statement, while noncash donations are generally credited to donated capital. The general guidelines used in practice should be followed in solving homework problems.

When a nonmonetary asset is donated, that is, given away, the amount of the donation should be recorded at the fair market value of the donated asset. If a difference exists between the fair market value of the asset and its book value, a gain or loss should be recognized.[10] To illustrate, Kline Industries donates land which cost $80,000 and has a fair market value of $110,000 to the City of Los Angeles for a city park. The entry to record this donation would be:

| | | |
|---|---|---|
| Donation | 110,000 | |
| Land | | 80,000 |
| Gain on Disposition of Land | | 30,000 |

The donation cost would ordinarily be classified in the other expenses and losses section of the income statement. Note that sometimes a real estate developer will donate certain property in a development to a municipality to enhance the value of the development. In this case, the cost of the donation would be added to the cost of development rather than treated as an expense.

---

[10]"Accounting for Nonmonetary Transactions," *op. cit.,* par. 18.

## COSTS SUBSEQUENT TO ACQUISITION

After plant assets are installed and ready for use, additional costs are incurred that range from ordinary repair costs to significant additions. The major problem in this area is allocating these costs to individual periods. Accountants for the most part have adopted the position that costs incurred to achieve greater future benefits should be capitalized (debited to an asset account), whereas expenditures that simply maintain a given level of services should be expensed. In order for costs to be capitalized (capital expenditures), one of three conditions must be present: (1) **the useful life of the asset must be increased;** (2) **the quantity of units produced from the asset must be increased; or** (3) **the quality of the units produced must be enhanced.**

Expenditures (revenue expenditures) that do not increase the service benefits of the assets are expensed. Ordinary repairs, for example, are expenditures that maintain the existing condition of the asset or restore it to normal operating efficiency and should be expensed immediately. In addition, most expenditures below an established arbitrary minimum amount are expensed rather than capitalized. For example, many enterprises have adopted the rule that expenditures below a certain arbitrarily selected amount, say, $100 or $500, should always be expensed. Although conceptually this treatment may not be correct, expediency demands that this approach be followed; otherwise, accountants would have to set up depreciation schedules for such things as wastepaper baskets and ash trays.

The distinction between a **capital (asset)** and **revenue (expense)** expenditure is not always clear-cut. For example, determination of the **property unit** with which costs should be associated is critical. If a fully equipped steamship is considered a property unit, then replacement of the engine might be considered an expense, whereas if the ship's engine is considered a property unit, then its replacement would be capitalized. As another illustration, AT&T recently argued that it should be permitted to expense its station connectors (wires which connect your telephone to the outside wall). In the past, these wires were capitalized and depreciated over an eight-year period. AT&T argued that continual changes in home occupancy resulted in so much rewiring that expensing these wires was more appropriate. The Federal Communications Commission approved this request and, therefore, the cost of wiring will be expensed as installation charges rather than spread over an eight-year period. This decision is significant—it was recently estimated that the cost of phone installation in Illinois will go from $36 to $109 as a result of this accounting change.[11] It follows that the disposition and treatment of many items require considerable analysis and judgment before the proper distinction can be made. In most cases, consistent application of a capital/expense policy is justified as more important than attempting to provide general theoretical guidelines.

Generally, four major types of expenditures are incurred relative to existing assets.

1. **ADDITIONS.** Increase or extension of existing assets.
2. **IMPROVEMENTS AND REPLACEMENTS.** Substitution of an improved asset for an existing one.
3. **REINSTALLATION AND REARRANGEMENT.** Movement of assets from one location to another.
4. **REPAIRS.** Expenditures that maintain assets in condition for operation.

---

[11]*Forbes* (October 26, 1981), p. 44.

## Additions

Additions should present no major accounting problems. By definition, any addition to plant assets is capitalized because a new asset has been created. The addition of a wing to a hospital or the addition of an air conditioning system to an office, for example, increases the service potential of that facility and should be capitalized and matched against the revenues that will result in future periods.

The most difficult problem that develops in this area is accounting for any changes related to the existing structure as a result of the addition. Is the cost that is incurred to tear down a wall of the old structure to make room for the addition a cost of the addition or an expense or loss of the period? The answer is that it depends on the original intent. If the company had anticipated that an addition was going to be added later, then this cost of removal is a proper cost of the addition. But if the company had not anticipated this development, it should properly be reported as a loss in the current period on the basis that the company was inefficient in its planning. Normally, the carrying amount of the old wall remains in the accounts, although theoretically it should be removed.

## Improvements and Replacements

Improvements (often referred to as betterments) and replacements are substitutions of one asset for another. The distinguishing feature between an improvement and a replacement is that an improvement is the substitution of a better asset for the one currently used (say, a concrete floor for a wooden floor). A replacement, on the other hand, is the substitution of a similar asset (a wooden floor for a wooden floor).

Many times improvements and replacements occur as the result of a general policy to modernize or rehabilitate an older building or piece of equipment. The problem lies in differentiating these types of expenditure from normal repairs. The accountant should ask: Does the expenditure increase the **future** service potential of the asset, or does it merely maintain the existing level of service? Many times the answer is not clear-cut, and good judgment must be used in order to classify these expenditures.

If it is determined that the expenditure increases the future service potential of the asset and, therefore, should be capitalized, this capitalization is handled in one of three ways, depending on the circumstances.

1. **SUBSTITUTION APPROACH.** Conceptually, the substitution approach is the correct procedure if the carrying amount of the old asset is available. If the carrying amount of the old asset can be determined, it is a simple matter to remove the cost of the old asset and replace it with the cost of the new asset.

    To illustrate, Instinct Enterprises decides to replace the pipes in its plumbing system. A plumber suggests that in place of the cast iron pipes and copper tubing, a newly developed plastic tubing be used. The old pipe and tubing have a book value of $15,000 (cost of $150,000 less accumulated depreciation of $135,000), and a scrap value of $1,000. The plastic tubing system has a cost of $125,000. Assuming that Instinct has to pay $124,000 for the new tubing after exchanging the old tubing, the entry is:

| | | |
|---|---|---|
| Plumbing System | 125,000 | |
| Accumulated Depreciation | 135,000 | |
| Loss on Disposal of Plant Assets | 14,000 | |
| Plumbing System | | 150,000 |
| Cash ($125,000 minus $1,000) | | 124,000 |

The problem with this approach is determining the book value of the old asset. Generally, the components of a given asset depreciate at different rates, but no separate accounting is made of each component. As an example, the tires, motor, and body of a truck depreciate at different rates, but most concerns use only one depreciation rate for the truck. Separate depreciation rates could be set for each component, but practicality precludes the use of this approach. If the carrying amount of the old asset cannot be determined, one of two other approaches is adopted.

2. **CAPITALIZING THE NEW COST.** The justification for capitalizing the cost of the improvement or replacement is that even though the carrying amount of the old asset is not removed from the accounts, sufficient depreciation was taken on the item to reduce the carrying amount almost to zero. Although this assumption may not be true in every case, in many situations the differences would not be significant. Improvements especially are handled in this manner.

3. **CHARGING TO ACCUMULATED DEPRECIATION.** There are times when the quantity or quality of the asset itself has not been improved, but its useful life has been extended. Replacements, particularly, may extend the useful life of the asset, yet they may not improve the quality or quantity of service or product produced in a given period. In these circumstances, the expenditure may be debited to Accumulated Depreciation rather than to an asset account on the theory that the replacement extends the useful life of the asset and thereby recaptures some or all of the past depreciation. The main justification for this approach is that it is a recovery of past depreciation charges. The carrying amount of the asset is the same whether the asset is charged or the accumulated depreciation is charged—it is only in the manner of presentation that a difference arises.

## Reinstallation and Rearrangement

Reinstallation and rearrangement costs are expenditures that are intended to benefit future periods but do not represent either additions, replacements, or improvements. An example is the reinstallation or rearrangement of a group of machines to facilitate future production. If the original installation cost can be estimated along with the accumulated depreciation taken to date, the reinstallation cost might properly be handled as a replacement. If not, which is generally the case, the new costs should be carried forward as an asset to be amortized against future revenue.[12]

## Repairs

**Ordinary repairs** are expenditures made to maintain plant assets in operating condition; they are charged to an expense account in the period in which they are incurred on the basis that it is the only period benefited. Replacement of minor parts, lubricating and adjusting of equipment, repainting, and cleaning are examples of the type of maintenance charges that occur regularly and are treated as ordinary operating expenses. It is often difficult to distinguish a repair from an improvement or replacement. The major consider-

---

[12]Another cost of this nature is relocation costs. For example, when Shell Oil moved its headquarters from New York to Houston, it amortized the cost of relocating over four years. Conversely, estimated relocation costs of $15 million were charged to revenue at GAF Corp. The point is that no definitive guidelines have been established in this area, and generally costs are deferred over some arbitrary period in the future. Some writers have argued that these costs should generally be expensed as incurred. See, for example, Charles W. Lamden, Dale L. Gerboth, and Thomas W. McRae, "Accounting for Depreciable Assets," *Accounting Research Monograph No. 1* (New York: AICPA, 1975), pp. 54–61.

ation is whether the expenditure benefits more than one year or one operating cycle, whichever is longest. If a **major repair,** such as an overhaul, occurs, several periods will benefit and the cost should be handled as an addition, improvement, or replacement, depending on the type of repair made.

If operating and income statements are prepared for short periods of time, say, monthly or quarterly, the same principles must be applied to accounting for repair costs. Ordinary repairs and other regular maintenance charges for an annual period may benefit several quarters, and allocation of the cost among the periods concerned might be required. For example, a concern will often find it advantageous to concentrate its repair program at a certain time of the year, perhaps during the period of least activity or when the plant is shut down for vacation. Short-term comparative statements might be misleading if such expenditures were shown as expenses of the quarter in which they were incurred. To give comparability to monthly or quarterly income statements, an account such as Allowance for Repairs might be used so that repair costs could be better assigned to periods benefited.

To illustrate, Cricket Tractor Company estimated that its total repair expense for the year would be $720,000. It decided to charge each quarter for a portion of the repair cost even though the total cost for the year would occur only in two quarters.

**End of first quarter (zero repair costs incurred):**

| | | |
|---|---|---|
| Repair Expense | 180,000 | |
|   Allowance for Repairs (¼ × $720,000) | | 180,000 |

**End of second quarter ($344,000 repair costs incurred):**

| | | |
|---|---|---|
| Allowance for Repairs | 344,000 | |
|   Cash, Wages Payable, Inventory, etc. | | 344,000 |
| Repair Expense | 180,000 | |
|   Allowance for Repairs (¼ × $720,000) | | 180,000 |

**End of third quarter (zero repair costs incurred):**

| | | |
|---|---|---|
| Repair Expense | 180,000 | |
|   Allowance for Repairs (¼ × $720,000) | | 180,000 |

**End of fourth quarter ($380,800 repair costs incurred):**

| | | |
|---|---|---|
| Allowance for Repairs | 380,800 | |
|   Cash, Wages Payable, Inventory, etc. | | 380,800 |
| Repair Expense | 184,800 | |
|   Allowance for Repairs | | 184,800 |
|     ($344,000 + $380,800 − $180,000 − $180,000 − $180,000) | | |

Ordinarily, no balance should be carried over to the following year in the Allowance for Repairs account, and the fourth quarter would normally absorb the variation from estimates. If balance sheets are prepared during the year, the Allowance account should be added to or subtracted from the property, plant, and equipment section to obtain a proper valuation during the year.

Some accountants advocate the accrual of estimated repair costs beyond one year. This approach is based on the assumption that the allocation of asset cost via depreciation charges does not take into consideration the incurrence of repair costs. For example, in aircraft overhaul and open hearth furnace rebuilding, an allowance for repairs is sometimes established because the amount of repairs can be established with a high degree of certainty. Although conceptually this approach may be appealing, it has many drawbacks. First, it is difficult to justify the Allowance for Repairs account as a liability because one might ask, Whom do you owe? Placement in the stockholders' equity section is also illogical because no addition to the stockholders' investment has taken place. One possibility might be to treat allowance for repairs as an addition to or subtraction from the asset on the basis that the value has increased or decreased, depending on when the repairs were made. The fact is that expenses should not be anticipated before they arise unless estimates of the future are predictable within a reasonable range.

## DISPOSITIONS OF PLANT ASSETS

Plant assets may be retired voluntarily or disposed of by sale, exchange, involuntary conversion, or abandonment. Regardless of the time of disposal, depreciation must be taken up to the date of disposition, and all accounts related to the retired asset should be removed from the accounts. Ideally, the book value of the specific plant asset would be equal to its disposal value. This is generally not the case, however, and a resulting gain or loss occurs.

This gain or loss develops because depreciation is a process of cost allocation and not a process of valuation. The gain or loss in most situations is in reality a correction of net income for the years during which the fixed asset was used. If it had been possible at the time of acquisition to forecast the exact date of disposal and the amount to be realized at disposition, then a more accurate estimate of depreciation could have been recorded and no gain or loss would have developed.

Gains or losses on the retirement of plant assets should be shown in the income statement along with other items that arise from customary business activities. If, however, the "operations of a segment of a business" are sold, abandoned, spun off, or otherwise disposed of, the profession requires that the results of "continuing operations" should be reported separately from "discontinued operations" and that any gain or loss from disposal of a segment of a business should be reported in conjunction with the related results of discontinued operations and not as an extraordinary item. To be reported as discontinued operations, however, the segment of a business must represent a separate line of business or class of customers. Reporting requirements were discussed in Chapter 4.

### Sale of Plant Assets

The problems related to the outright sale of a plant asset are relatively simple. Depreciation must be recorded for the period of time between the date of the last depreciation entry and the date of retirement. To illustrate, assume that depreciation on a machine costing $18,000 has been recorded for nine years at the rate of $1,200 per year. If the machine is sold in the middle of the tenth year for $7,000, the entry to record depreciation to the date of sale is:

| | | |
|---|---|---|
| Depreciation Expense | 600 | |
|   Accumulated Depreciation of Machinery | | 600 |

This separate entry ordinarily is not made because most companies enter all depreciation, including this amount, in one entry at the end of the year. In either case the entry for the sale of the asset is:

| | | |
|---|---|---|
| Cash | 7,000 | |
| Accumulated Depreciation of Machinery | 11,400 | |
| ($1,200 × 9 plus $600) | | |
|   Machinery | | 18,000 |
|   Gain on Disposal of Plant Assets | | 400 |

The book value of the machinery at the time of the sale is $6,600 ($18,000 − $11,400); because it is sold for $7,000, the amount of the gain on the sale is $400.

## Involuntary Conversion

Sometimes, an asset's service is terminated through some type of involuntary conversion such as fire, flood, theft, condemnation, and so on. The accounting problems in this area are not difficult, inasmuch as the gains or losses are no different from those in any other type of disposition except that they are often reported in the extraordinary items section of the income statement.

To illustrate, Camel Transport Corp. was forced to sell a plant located on company property that stood directly in the path of an interstate highway. For a number of years the state had sought to purchase the land on which the plant stood but the company resisted. The state ultimately exercised its right of eminent domain and was upheld by the courts. In settlement, Camel received $500,000, which was substantially in excess of the $200,000 book value of the plant and land (cost of $400,000 less accumulated depreciation of $200,000). The following entry was made:

| | | |
|---|---|---|
| Cash | 500,000 | |
| Accumulated Depreciation of Plant Assets | 200,000 | |
| Plant Assets | | 400,000 |
| Gain on Disposal of Plant Assets | | 300,000 |

There has been some objection to the recognition of a gain or loss in certain involuntary conversion situations. For example, the federal government is continually condemning forests for national parks; as a result, the paper companies who owned these forests are required to report a gain or loss on the condemnation. However, companies such as Georgia Pacific contend that because they must replace this condemned forest land immediately, they are in the same economic position as they were before and no gain or loss should be reported. The issue is whether the condemnation and subsequent purchase should be viewed as one or two transactions. *FASB Interpretation No. 30* requires "that gain or loss be recognized when a nonmonetary asset is involuntarily converted to monetary assets even though an enterprise reinvests or is obligated to reinvest the monetary assets in replacement nonmonetary assets."[13]

The gain or loss that develops on these types of unusual, nonrecurring transactions should normally be shown as an extraordinary item in the income statement. Similar treatment would be given to other types of involuntary conversions such as those resulting from a major casualty (such as an earthquake) or an expropriation, assuming that it meets the conditions for extraordinary item treatment. The difference between the amount recovered (condemnation award or insurance recovery), if any, and the book value of the asset would be reported as a gain or loss. The determination of the insurance proceeds to be received in a casualty situation is sometimes quite complex; it is discussed in the appendix to this chapter.

## Miscellaneous Problems

If an asset is scrapped or abandoned without any cash recovery, a loss should be recognized in the amount of the asset's book value. If scrap value exists, the gain or loss that occurs is

---

[13]"Accounting for Involuntary Conversions of Nonmonetary Assets to Monetary Assets," *FASB Interpretation No. 30* (Stamford, Conn.: FASB, 1979), summary paragraph.

the difference between the asset's scrap value and its book value. If an asset still can be used even though it is fully depreciated, either the asset may be kept on the books at historical cost less its related depreciation or the asset may be carried at scrap value. If the asset is written up or down to scrap value, the gain or loss could be recognized, although many accountants believe that recognition of the gain violates the revenue recognition principle. Footnote disclosure of the amount of fully depreciated assets in service should be made in the financial statements.

## OTHER ASSET VALUATION METHODS

We have generally assumed that accountants have used cost as the basis for valuing assets at acquisition. The major exception has been the acquisition of plant assets through donation. Another approach that is sometimes allowed and not considered a violation of historical cost is a concept often referred to as **prudent cost.** This concept states that if for some reason you were ignorant about a certain price and paid too much for the asset originally, it is theoretically preferable to charge a loss immediately. As an example, assume that a company constructs an asset at a cost substantially in excess of its present economic usefulness. In this case, an appropriate procedure would be to charge these excess costs as a loss to the current period, rather than capitalize them as part of the cost of the asset. This problem seldom develops because at the outset individuals either use good reasoning in paying a given price or fail to recognize any such errors. On the other hand, a purchase that is obtained at a bargain, or a piece of equipment internally constructed at what amounts to a cost savings, should not result in immediate recognition of a gain under any circumstances. Although immediate recognition of a gain is conceptually appealing, the implications of such a treatment would be to change completely the entire basis of accounting.

The general accounting standard of **lower of cost or market does not apply to property, plant, and equipment.** And, even when property, plant, and equipment has suffered partial obsolescence, accountants are reluctant to write it down to net realizable value. This reluctance stems from the fact that it is difficult to arrive at a net realizable value that is not subjective and arbitrary for property, plant, and equipment, unlike inventories, for which values can be more easily obtained. For example, Falconbridge Nickel Mines was recently faced with a decision as to whether all or a part of its property, plant, and equipment in a nickel-mining operation in the Dominican Republic should be written off. The project has been incurring losses because nickel prices are low and operating costs are high. Only if nickel prices increase by approximately 33⅓% would the company be reasonably profitable. Whether a write-off is appropriate therefore, depends on the future price of nickel which places the accountant in the difficult position of predicting future prices. Even if a write-off is deemed appropriate, another important question is: How much should be written off? In addition to this problem, many argue that depreciation is a method of cost allocation and, therefore, should not be concerned with valuation. Finally, there is some concern that permitting write-offs of this type may lead companies to make unreasonable write-offs in bad years to insure that future periods will be relieved of these costs (the "big bath" phenomenon). We are not sympathetic with these arguments and believe that whenever a permanent impairment in the revenue-producing ability of property, plant, and equipment occurs, a loss should be recognized.

# APPENDIX G

# Casualty Insurance

Business enterprises constantly face the risk of loss of assets by fire, storm, theft, accident, or other casualties. Generally companies shift the burden of such losses by entering into a casualty insurance contract whereby an insurance company in consideration for a premium payment assumes the risk of all or a portion of these losses. The premium, a charge per $100 of insurance carried, is paid in advance. Because a premium discount is given when the term of the policy exceeds one year, many companies pay insurance premiums in advance, creating the asset **prepaid insurance.**

When an insured asset is damaged, destroyed, or lost, the relevant accounts must be adjusted and settlement with the insurance company must be completed. The maximum amount recoverable is the **fair market value** of the property at the date of loss and is referred to as the **insurable value.** Although the book value is irrelevant in determining the amount recoverable from the insurance company, it is used for accounting purposes to measure the loss (or gain) resulting from the casualty and any insurance settlement. For example, if $40,000 is recovered under an insurance policy after the complete destruction of an asset having a book value of $34,000, a gain of $6,000 would be recognized. In some instances the amount recoverable is limited by some special feature such as a **deductible clause** in the case of automobile insurance ($100 or $200 deductible) or a **coinsurance clause** in the case of fire insurance.

## COINSURANCE

Because most assets are only partially destroyed by any casualty, companies would take out only enough insurance to cover a fraction of the value of the asset and receive full reimbursement of most losses if they were not encouraged through a coinsurance clause to do otherwise. Most casualty insurance policies therefore contain a **coinsurance clause** which provides that if the property is insured for less than a certain percentage (frequently 80%) of its fair market value (insurable value) at the time of the loss, the insurance company will be liable for only a portion of any loss, that is, the owner becomes a **coinsurer** with the insurance company.

Stated proportionately, coinsurance means that the amount recoverable is to the loss as the face value of the policy (amount of insurance carried) is to the coinsurance requirement (amount of insurance that should be carried). As a formula, coinsurance may be stated as follows:

$$\frac{\text{Face value of policy}}{\text{Coinsurance requirement}} \times \text{Loss} = \text{Amount Recoverable}$$

The following examples illustrate the use of the formula in determining the amount recoverable using an 80% coinsurance clause.

| Amount Recoverable Under Coinsurance | | | | |
|---|---|---|---|---|
| | Case 1 | Case 2 | Case 3 | Case 4 |
| Fair market value | $10,000 | $10,000 | $10,000 | $10,000 |
| Face value of policy | 7,000 | 5,000 | 9,000 | 8,000 |
| Coinsurance requirement | 8,000 | 8,000 | 8,000 | 8,000 |
| Amount of loss | 6,000 | 6,000 | 6,000 | 9,000 |
| Amount recoverable | 5,250[a] | 3,750[b] | 6,000[c] | 8,000[d] |

[a] $\dfrac{\$7,000}{\$8,000} \times \$6,000 = \$5,250$

[b] $\dfrac{\$5,000}{\$8,000} \times \$6,000 = \$3,750$

[c] $\dfrac{\$9,000}{\$8,000} \times \$6,000 = \$6,750*$

[d] $\dfrac{\$8,000}{\$8,000} \times \$9,000 = \$9,000**$

*Amount recoverable limited to amount of loss.
**Amount recoverable limited to face value of policy.

As illustrated above, **the amount recoverable from the insurance company is the lowest of (1) the amount of the loss, (2) the face value of the policy, or (3) the coinsurance formula amount.**

## RECOVERY FROM MULTIPLE POLICIES

If an asset is insured under two or more insurance policies, all of which have the same or **no coinsurance** requirement, recovery of a loss is obtained from the different policies in proportion to the face value of each policy. If the policies have **different coinsurance** requirements, the amount recoverable under each of the policies is computed by multiplying the loss by a fraction, the numerator of which is the face value of the individual policy, and the denominator of which is the higher of (1) the total face value of all policies, or (2) the amount required under the coinsurance requirement of the particular policy. To illustrate, assume that an asset having a fair market value of $100,000 is insured under policies presented on the next page, and that a fire loss of $72,000 is suffered.

If the policies contain the same (90%) coinsurance requirement, recovery from each policy would be as follows:

| | | Amount Recoverable Under Multiple Policies with Identical Coinsurance | | | |
|---|---|---|---|---|---|
| Policy | Face Value | Coinsurance Requirement | Fraction | Loss | Amount Collectible |
| A | $30,000 | $90,000 | 30/90 | $72,000 | $24,000 |
| B | 40,000 | 90,000 | 40/90 | 72,000 | 32,000 |
| C | 10,000 | 90,000 | 10/90 | 72,000 | 8,000 |
| | $80,000 | | | | $64,000 |

If the policies contain different (70%, 85%, and 90%) coinsurance requirements, recovery from each policy would be as follows:

| | | Amount Recoverable Under Multiple Policies with Different Coinsurance | | | |
|---|---|---|---|---|---|
| Policy | Face Value | Coinsurance Requirement | Fraction | Loss | Amount Collectible |
| A | $30,000 | $70,000 | 30/80 | $72,000 | $27,000 |
| B | 40,000 | 85,000 | 40/85 | 72,000 | 33,882 |
| C | 10,000 | 90,000 | 10/90 | 72,000 | 8,000 |
| | $80,000 | | | | $68,882 |

## ACCOUNTING FOR CASUALTY LOSSES

In the event of a casualty loss the accounting records as maintained or as reconstructed (if destroyed in the casualty) must be adjusted as of the date of the casualty. The loss may be summarized in a casualty loss account, charging such account for the book value of the assets destroyed or damaged and crediting it for amounts recoverable from salvage and from insurance companies. The total amount recoverable (receivable) from the insurance companies would be classified as a current asset if current settlement is anticipated. If the casualty loss is material and the consequence of an unusual and infrequent event or circumstance, it would be classified as an extraordinary item.

Because the amount recovered under insurance policies is based upon fair market and appraised values, the insurance proceeds may exceed the book value of the assets destroyed or damaged. The excess of insurance proceeds over the book value should be presented as a book gain. For example, the tragic DC-10 aircraft crash in Chicago in 1979 increased American Airlines income per share by 88 cents because the plane's replacement value (in this case insurable value) was higher than its book value.

**Note:** All **asterisked** Questions, Cases, Exercises, or Problems relate to material contained in the appendix to each chapter.

## QUESTIONS

1. What are the major characteristics of plant assets?
2. Indicate where the following items would be shown on a balance sheet.
   (a) A parking lot servicing employees in the building.

(b) The cost of demolishing an old building that was on the land when purchased.

(c) A lien that was attached to the land when purchased.

(d) Landscaping costs.

(e) Attorney's fees and recording fees related to purchasing land.

(f) Variable overhead related to construction of machinery.

(g) Cost of temporary building for workers during construction of building.

(h) Interest expense on bonds payable incurred during construction of a building.

(i) Sidewalks that are maintained by the city.

3. Once equipment has been installed and placed in operation, subsequent expenditures relating to this equipment are frequently thought of as being in the nature of repairs or general maintenance and, hence, chargeable to operations in the period in which the expenditure is made. Actually, determination of whether such an expenditure should be charged to operations or capitalized involves a much more careful analysis of the character of the expenditure. What are the factors that should be considered in making such a decision? Discuss fully.

4. What accounting treatment is normally given to the following items in accounting for plant assets?

(a) Additions.

(b) Major repairs.

(c) Improvements and replacements.

5. Name the items, in addition to the amount paid to the former owner or contractor, that may be properly included as part of the acquisition cost of the following plant assets:

(a) Land.

(b) Machinery and equipment.

(c) Buildings.

6. Three positions have normally been taken with respect to the recording of fixed manufacturing overhead as an element of the cost of plant assets constructed by a company for its own use:

(a) It should be excluded completely.

(b) It should be included at the same rate as is charged to normal operations.

(c) It should be allocated on the basis of the lost production that occurs from normal operations.

What are the circumstances or rationale that support or deny the application of these methods?

7. What interest rates should be used in determining the amount of interest to be capitalized? How should the amount of interest to be capitalized be determined?

8. How should the amount of interest capitalized be disclosed in the footnotes to the financial statements? How should interest revenue from temporarily invested excess funds borrowed to finance the construction of assets be accounted for?

9. Expenditures may be divided into two general categories: (1) capital expenditures and (2) revenue expenditures.

(a) Distinguish between these two categories of expenditures and between their treatments in the accounts.

(b) Discuss the impact on both present and future balance sheets and income statements of improperly distinguishing between capital and revenue expenditures.

(c) What criteria do accountants generally use in establishing a policy for classifying expenditures under these two general categories?

10. The Hunt Trucking Company purchased a heavy-duty truck on July 1, 1977, for $30,000. It was estimated that it would have a useful life of 10 years and then would have a trade-in value of $6,000. It was traded on October 1, 1981, for a similar truck costing $38,000; $14,000 was allowed as trade-in value (also fair value) on the old truck and $24,000 was paid in cash. What is the entry to record the trade-in? The company uses the straight-line method.

11. The Buildings account of a corporation includes the following items that were used in determining the basis for depreciating the cost of a building:

(a) Organization and promotion expenses.

(b) Architect's fees.

(c) Interest and taxes during construction.

(d) Commission paid on the sale of capital stock.

(e) Bond discount and expenses.

Do you agree with these charges? If not, how would you deal with each of the items above in the corporation's books and in its annual financial statements?

**12.** New machinery, which replaced a number of employees, was installed and put in operation in the last month of the fiscal year. The employees had been dismissed after payment of an extra month's wages and this amount was added to the cost of the machinery. Discuss the propriety of the charge and, if it was improper, describe the proper treatment.

**13.** To what extent do you consider the following items to be proper costs of the fixed asset? Give reasons for your opinions.

(a) Freight on equipment returned before installation, for replacement by other equipment of greater capacity.

(b) Cost of moving machinery to a new location.

(c) Cost of plywood partitions erected as part of the remodeling of the office.

(d) Replastering of a section of the building.

(e) Cost of a new motor for one of the trucks.

(f) Overhead of a business that builds its own equipment.

(g) Cost of constructing new models of machinery.

(h) Cash discounts on purchases of equipment.

(i) Interest paid during construction of a building.

(j) Cost of a safety device installed on a machine.

**14.** Discuss the basic accounting problem that arises in handling each of the following situations.

(a) Assets purchased by issuance of capital stock.

(b) Acquisition of plant assets by gift or donation.

(c) Purchase of a plant asset subject to a cash discount.

(d) Assets purchased on a long-term credit basis.

(e) A group of assets acquired for a lump sum.

(f) An asset traded in or exchanged for another asset.

**15.** Recently, Porter Manufacturing Co. presented the account "Allowance for Repairs" in the long-term liability section. Evaluate this procedure.

**16.** Segoe Enterprises has a number of fully depreciated assets that are still being used in the main operations of the business. Because the assets are fully depreciated, the president of the company decides not to show them on the balance sheet or disclose this information in the footnotes. Evaluate this procedure.

**17.** Recently, Gremlin, Inc. decided to discontinue production of one of its product lines because demand for it had fallen substantially. Although it is highly unlikely that the plant may be used for this type of production in the future, the controller is reluctant to write the plant down to its net realizable value. Why might the controller be reluctant to write the asset down?

**\*18.** What is the objective of a coinsurance clause in a casualty insurance policy?

## CASES

**C11-1** Wetzel Medical, Inc. began operations five years ago producing stetrics, a new type of instrument it hoped to sell to doctors, dentists, and hospitals. The demand for stetrics far exeeded initial expectations, and the company was unable to produce enough stetrics to meet demand.

The company was manufacturing its product on equipment that it built at the start of its operations. To meet demand, more efficient equipment was needed. The company decided to design and build the equipment since the equipment currently available on the market was unsuitable for producing stetrics.

In 1983 a section of the plant was devoted to development of the new equipment and a special staff of personnel was hired. Within six months a machine was developed at a cost of $420,000 which successfully increased production and reduced labor costs substantially. Sparked by the success of the new machine, the company built three more machines of the same type at a cost of $260,000 each.

**Instructions**

(a) In general, what costs should be capitalized for self-constructed plant?

(b) Discuss the propriety of including in the capitalized cost of self-constructed assets:

1. The increase in overhead caused by the self-construction of fixed assets.

2. A proportionate share of overhead on the same basis as that applied to goods manufactured for sale.

(c) Discuss the proper accounting treatment of the $160,000 ($420,000 − $260,000) by which the cost of the first machine exceeded the cost of the subsequent machines. This additional cost should not be considered research and development costs.

**C11–2** Your client, Vestpocket Co., found three suitable sites, each having certain unique advantages, for a new plant facility. In order to thoroughly investigate the advantages and disadvantages of each site, one-year options were purchased for an amount equal to 6% of the contract price of each site. The costs of the options cannot be applied against the contracts. Before the options expired, one of the sites was purchased at the contract price of $180,000. The option on this site had cost $10,800. The two options not exercised had cost $7,000 each.

**Instructions**

Present arguments in support of recording the cost of the land at each of the following amounts.

(a) $180,000.

(b) $190,800.

(c) $204,800.

(AICPA adapted)

**C11–3** You have recently been hired as a junior accountant in the firm of Tickim and Checkum. Mr. Tickim is an alumnus of the same school from which you graduated and, therefore, is quite interested in your accounting training. He therefore presents the following situations and asks for your response.

### Situation I

Recently a construction company agreed to construct a new hospital for its client at the construction company's cost; that is, the contractor was to realize no profit. The construction company was interested in performing this service because it had substantial interests in the community and wanted to make the community more attractive. The building was completed in 1983, and the costs of the hospital were $17,000,000. An appraisal firm indicated, however, that the fair market value of the properties was $18,500,000, the difference due to the $1,500,000 that the company did not charge the hospital.

**Instructions**

At what amount should the hospital value the asset? A related question is whether the donated profit on the hospital should be reported as revenue or as a capital contribution. What is your answer to this question?

### Situation II

Recently, one of our clients asked whether it would be appropriate to capitalize a portion of the salaries of the corporate officers for time spent on construction activities. During construction, one of the officers devotes full time to the supervision of construction projects. His activities are similar to those of a construction superintendent for a general contractor. During periods of heavy construction activity, this officer also employs several assistants to help with administrative matters related to construction. All other officers are general corporate officers.

The compensation and other costs related to the construction officer are not dependent upon the level of construction activity in a particular period (except to the extent that additional assistants are employed on a short-term basis). These expenses would continue to be incurred even if there was no construction activity unless the company decided to discontinue permanently, or for the foreseeable future, all construction activity. In that case, it could well reach the decision to terminate the construction officer. The company has, however, aggressive expansion plans which anticipate continuing construction of shopping center properties.

**Instructions**

What salary costs, if any, should be capitalized to the cost of properties?

*Situation III*

Every few years one of our clients publishes a new catalog for distribution to its sales outlets and customers. The latest catalog was published in 1979. Periodically, current price lists and new product brochures are issued. The company is now contemplating the issue of a new catalog during the latter part of 1982. The cost of the new catalog has been accounted for as follows:

(a) Estimated total cost of the catalog is accounted for over a period beginning with the initial planning (1980) and is expected to end at time of publication.

(b) Estimated costs are accumulated in an accrued liability account through monthly charges to selling expenses.

(c) Monthly charges were based upon the estimated total cost of the guide and the estimated number of months remaining before publication; periodic revisions were made to the estimates as current information became available.

(d) Actual costs were recorded as charges to the accrued liability account as they were accrued.

In summary, the company accrues the entire estimated cost (including anticipated costs to be incurred) of a contemplated catalog through charges to operations prior to the expected publication date.

**Instructions**

Comment on the propriety of this treatment.

C11–4 You have been engaged to examine the financial statements of Blackjack Corporation for the year ending December 31, 1984. Blackjack Corporation was organized in January, 1984, by Messrs. Moses and Price, original owners of options to acquire oil leases on 5,000 acres of land for $700,000. They expected that first the oil leases would be acquired by the corporation and subsequently 180,000 shares of the corporation's common stock would be sold to the public at $12 per share. In February 1984, they exchanged their options, $300,000 cash, and $100,000 of other assets for 75,000 shares of common stock of the corporation. The corporation's board of directors appraised the leases at $1,200,000, basing its appraisal on the price of other acreage recently leased in the same area. The options were therefore recorded at $500,000 ($1,200,000 − $700,000 option price).

The options were exercised by the corporation in March, 1984, prior to the sale of common stock to the public in April, 1984. Leases on approximately 500 acres of land were abandoned as worthless during the year.

**Instructions**

(a) Why is the valuation of assets acquired by a corporation in exchange for its own common stock sometimes difficult?

(b) 1. What reasoning might Blackjack Corporation use to support valuing the leases at $1,200,000, the amount of the appraisal by the board of directors?

    2. Assuming that the board's appraisal was sincere, what steps might Blackjack Corporation have taken to strengthen its position to use the $1,200,000 value and to provide additional information if questions were raised about possible overvaluation of the leases?

(c) Discuss the propriety of charging one-tenth of the recorded value of the leases to expense at December 31, 1984, because leases on 500 acres of land were abandoned during the year.

(AICPA adapted)

**C11–5** The invoice price of a machine is $30,000. Various other costs relating to the acquisition and installation of the machine including transportation, electrical wiring, special base, and so on amount to $5,000. The machine has an estimated life of 10 years, with no residual value at the end of that period.

The owner of the business suggests that the incidental costs of $5,000 be charged to expense immediately for the following reasons:

1. If the machine should be sold, these costs cannot be recovered in the sales price;

2. The inclusion of the $5,000 in the machinery account on the books will not necessarily result in a closer approximation of the market price of this asset over the years, because of the possibility of changing demand and supply levels; and

3. Charging the $5,000 to expense immediately will reduce federal income taxes.

**Instructions**

Discuss **each** of the points raised by the owner of the business.

(AICPA adapted)

**C11–6** Bluyonder Airline is converting from piston-type planes to jets. Delivery time for the jets is three years, during which period substantial progress payments must be made. The multimillion-dollar cost of the planes cannot be financed from working capital; Bluyonder must borrow funds for the payments.

Because of high interest rates and the large sum to be borrowed, management estimates that interest costs in the second year of the period will be equal to one-third of income before interest and taxes, and one-half of such income in the third year.

After conversion, Bluyonder's passenger-carrying capacity will be doubled with no increase in the number of planes, although the investment in planes would be substantially increased. The jet planes have a seven-year service life.

**Instructions**

Give your recommendation concerning the proper accounting for interest during the conversion period. Support your recommendation with reasons **and** suggested accounting treatment. (Disregard income tax implications.)

(AICPA adapted)

# EXERCISES

**E11–1** Ramrod Company, a newly formed corporation, incurred the following expenditures related to Land, to Buildings, and to Machinery and Equipment.

| | | |
|---|---:|---:|
| Architect's fees | | $ 2,200 |
| Cash paid for land and dilapidated building thereon | | 66,000 |
| Removal of old building | $9,000 | |
| Less salvage | 1,200 | 7,800 |
| Abstract company's fee for title search | | 270 |
| Surveying before construction | | 450 |
| Interest on short-term loans during construction | | 6,500 |
| Excavation before construction for basement | | 13,700 |
| Machinery purchased (subject to 3% cash discount, which was not taken); record net | | 44,000 |
| Freight on machinery purchased | | 750 |
| Storage charges on machinery, necessitated by noncompletion of building when machinery was delivered | | 1,070 |
| New building constructed (building construction took 6 months from date of purchase of land and old building) | | 400,000 |
| Assessment by city for drainage project | | 900 |
| Hauling charges for delivery of machinery from storage to new building | | 300 |

| | |
|---|---:|
| Trees, shrubs, and other landscaping after completion of building (permanent in nature) | 4,500 |
| Installation of machinery | 1,400 |

**Instructions**

Determine the amounts that should be debited to Land, to Buildings, and to Machinery and Equipment accounts. Assume the benefits of capitalizing interest during construction exceed the cost of implementation.

**E11–2** Reichenbacher Co. purchased land as a factory site for $300,000. The process of tearing down two old buildings on the site and constructing the factory required six months.

The company paid $12,000 to raze the old buildings and sold salvaged lumber and brick for $2,100. Legal fees of $1,560 were paid for title investigation and drawing the purchase contract. Payment to an engineering firm was made for a land survey, $1,800, and for drawing the factory plans, $60,000. The land survey had to be made before definitive plans could be drawn. Title insurance on the property cost $1,500, and a liability insurance premium paid during construction was $600. The contractor's charge for construction was $2,250,000. The company paid the contractor in two installments: $1,200,000 at the end of three months and $1,050,000 upon completion. Interest costs of $45,000 were incurred to finance the construction.

**Instructions**

Determine the cost of the land and the cost of the building as they should be recorded on the books of the Reichenbacher Co. Assume that the land survey was for the building.

**E11–3** Triple Value Construction Company started construction of a combination office and warehouse building for their own use at an estimated cost of $3,500,000 on October 1, 1984. Triple Value expects to complete the building by June 30, 1985. Triple Value has the following debt obligations during the construction period.

| | Balance October 1, 1984 |
|---|---:|
| Construction loan—15%, interest payable monthly, principal due one month after completion of the new building. | $1,200,000 |
| Short-term loan—20%, interest and principal payable at maturity on September 30, 1985. | 500,000 |
| Long-term loan—10%, interest payable on January 1st of each year. Principal payable on January 1, 1990. | 900,000 |

**Instructions**

(a) If Triple Value Construction completed the office and warehouse building on June 30, 1985 as planned at a total cost of $3,600,000 and the average accumulated expenditures were $1,900,000, compute the avoidable interest on this project. (Round all decimals to four places.)

(b) Assuming the actual interest incurred exceeded the avoidable interest, compute the depreciation expense for the year ended December 31, 1985. Triple Value elected to depreciate the building on a straight-line method and determined that the asset has a useful life of 10 years and a salvage value of $23,000.

**E11–4** On July 31, 1983, the Downing Company engaged the Collins Machine Tooling Company to construct a special-purpose piece of factory machinery. Construction was begun immediately and was completed on November 1, 1983. To help finance construction, on July 31 Downing discounted a $160,000, 3-year non-interest bearing note payable at Hudson National Bank. Interest on the note should be imputed at 12%, and the discount is to be amortized using the straight-line method. (Hint: Present value the note to find the proceeds received by Downing.) $75,000 of the proceeds of the note was paid to Collins on July 31. The remainder of the proceeds was temporarily invested in short-term marketable securities at 10% until November 1. On November 1, Downing made a final $75,000 payment to Collins. Other than the note to Hudson, Downing's only outstanding liability at December 31, 1983 is a $20,000, 8%, 6-year note payable, dated January 1, 1980, on which interest is payable each December 31.

**Instructions**

(a) Calculate the interest revenue, average accumulated expenditures, avoidable interest, and total interest cost to be capitalized during 1983. Round all computations to the nearest dollar.

(b) Prepare the journal entries needed on the books of Downing Company at each of the following dates:
  1. July 31, 1983.
  2. November 1, 1983 (capitalize interest at year end).
  3. December 31, 1983 (ignore depreciation entry).

**E11-5** Shirley's Machine Shop builds machines for its regular manufacturing department. During 1983, the company built a machine that had the following costs associated with it:

|  | Machinery Cost |
|---|---|
| Material and purchased parts | $ 6,000 |
| Freight on material and parts | 600 |
| Insurance in transit | 75 |
| Implicit interest on tied-up working capital | 120 |
| Labor to build | 9,000 |
| Labor to test | 2,000 |
| Overhead | 5,000 |
|  | $22,795 |

The machine immediately after construction has a fair market value of $30,000.

**Instructions**

What dollar amount should appear in Shirley's balance sheet for this machinery?

**E11-6** Prozit, Inc. has decided to purchase equipment from Tillie Industries on January 2, 1983, to expand its production capacity to meet customers' demand for its product. Prozit issues a $600,000, five-year, noninterest-bearing note to Tillie for the new equipment when the prevailing market rate of interest for obligations of this nature is 12%. The company will pay off the note in five $120,000 installments due at the end of each year over the life of the note.

**Instructions**

(a) Prepare the journal entry(ies) at the date of purchase. (Round to nearest dollar in all computations.)

(b) Prepare the journal entry(ies) at the end of the first year to record the payment and interest, assuming that the company employs the effective interest method.

(c) Prepare the journal entry(ies) at the end of the second year to record the payment and interest.

(d) Assuming that the equipment had a 10-year life and no salvage value, prepare the journal entry necessary to record depreciation in the first year. (Straight-line depreciation is employed.)

**E11-7** Wasco, Inc. purchased a computer on December 31, 1982, for $40,000, paying $10,000 down and agreeing to pay the balance in four equal installments of $7,500 payable each December 31 beginning in 1983. An assumed interest of 12% is implicit in the purchase price.

**Instructions**

(a) Prepare the journal entry(ies) at the date of purchase. (Round to two decimal places.)

(b) Prepare the journal entry(ies) at December 31, 1983, to record the payment and interest (effective interest method employed).

(c) Prepare the journal entry(ies) at December 31, 1984, to record the payment and interest (effective interest method employed).

**E11-8** The Rocket Corporation, which manufactures shoes, hired a recent college graduate to work in their accounting department. On the first day of work, the accountant was assigned to total a batch of invoices with the use of an adding machine. Before long, the accountant, who had never before seen such a machine, managed to break the machine. The Rocket Corporation gave the machine plus $620 to the Cricket Business Machine Company in exchange for a new machine. Assume the following information about the machines:

|  | Rocket Corp. (Old Machine) | Cricket Co. (New Machine) |
|---|---|---|
| Machine cost | $550 | $600 |
| Accumulated depreciation | 300 | -0- |
| Fair value | 150 | 770 |

**Instructions**

For each company, prepare the necessary journal entry to record the exchange.

**E11-9** Doreen Company exchanged equipment used in its manufacturing operations plus $3,000 in cash for similar equipment used in the operations of Atle Sutland Company. The following information pertains to the exchange:

|  | Doreen Co. | Atle Sutland Co. |
|---|---|---|
| Equipment (cost) | $25,000 | $23,000 |
| Accumulated depreciation | 21,000 | 6,000 |
| Fair value of equipment | 12,000 | 15,000 |
| Cash given up | 3,000 | |

**Instructions**

Prepare the journal entries to record the exchange on the books of both companies.

**E11-10** Jackie Kiss Inc. has negotiated the purchase of a new piece of automatic equipment at a price of $36,000, f.o.b. factory. Kiss Inc. paid $7,500 cash, gave an installment note calling for monthly payments of $2,100 for 10 months plus interest at 8% on the unpaid balance, and traded in used equipment. The used equipment had originally cost $30,000; it had a book value of $9,000 and a second-hand market value of $5,250, as indicated by recent transactions involving similar equipment. Freight and installation charges for the new equipment amounted to $1,200.

**Instructions**

(a) Prepare the general journal entry to record this transaction, assuming that the assets Kiss Inc. exchanged are similar in nature.

(b) Assuming the same facts as in (a) except that the asset traded in has a fair market value of $11,000, prepare the general journal entry to record this transaction.

**E11-11** Wicks Company purchased an electric wax melter on 6/30/84 by trading in their old gas model and paying the balance in cash. The following data relate to the purchase:

| | |
|---|---|
| List price of new melter | $12,000 |
| Cash paid | 5,960 |
| Cost of old melter (eight-year life, $500 residual value) | 10,100 |
| Accumulated depreciation—old melter (straight-line) | 5,900 |
| Second-hand market value of old melter | 5,320 |

**Instructions**

Prepare the journal entry(ies) necessary to record this exchange, assuming that the melters exchanged are (1) similar in nature; (2) dissimilar in nature. Wicks' fiscal year ends on 12/31 and depreciation has been recorded through 12/31/83.

**E11–12** On October 1, Steg's, a local entertainment establishment, acquired a new piano that had a list price of $2,700. Steg received a trade-in allowance of $1,200 on its old piano, which had a book value of $900 (original cost $1,400). The fair market value of the old piano was $800. The remainder owed by Steg was paid in cash.

**Instructions**

(a) Prepare the journal entry to record this transaction.

(b) What significance does the list price have for this computation?

**E11–13** Presented below is information related to Readyrite Company.

1. On July 6 Readyrite Company acquired the plant assets of Tom Yopst Company, which had discontinued operations. The appraised value of the property is:

| | |
|---|---|
| Land | $ 200,000 |
| Building | 1,200,000 |
| Machinery and Equipment | 400,000 |
| Total | $1,800,000 |

Readyrite Company gave 12,000 shares of its $100 par value common stock in exchange. The stock had a market value of $120 per share on the date of the purchase of the property.

2. Readyrite Company expended the following amounts in cash between July 6 and December 15, the date when it first occupied the building.

| | |
|---|---|
| Repairs to building | $ 75,000 |
| Construction of bases for machinery to be installed later | 120,000 |
| Driveways and parking lots | 110,000 |
| Remodeling of office space in building, including new partitions and walls | 160,000 |
| Special assessment by city | 12,000 |

3. On December 20, the company paid cash for machinery, $200,000, subject to a 2% cash discount, and freight on machinery of $7,000.

**Instructions**

Prepare entries on the books of Readyrite Company for these transactions.

**E11–14** Below are transactions related to McDonald Manufacturing Company.

1. On March 10, 1984, McDonald Manufacturing Company purchases land with an appraised value of $12,000 and buildings with an appraised value of $30,000 for $37,800.

2. Between March 10, 1984, and September 1, 1984, the date of occupancy, the company expends the following amounts in cash.

| | |
|---|---|
| Additional wing constructed | $22,000 |
| Replastering | 3,600 |
| Additional windows and doors | 2,500 |
| Repairs to roof | 2,640 |
| Brick pointing and masonry repairs | 4,540 |
| Painting and decorating | 4,920 |

**Instructions**

(a) Prepare entries on the books of the McDonald Manufacturing Company to reflect the information given above.

(b) Prepare entries to record depreciation on a straight-line basis at December 31, 1984, assuming a 20-year life.

**E11–15** Below are transactions related to Lindbergh Company.

(a) The City of Malta gives the company five acres of land as a plant site. The market value of this land is determined to be $45,000.

(b) 10,000 shares of common stock with a par value of $40 per share are issued in exchange for land and buildings. The property has been appraised at a fair market value of $560,000, of which $200,000 has been allocated to land and $360,000 to buildings. The stock of the Lindbergh Company is not listed on any exchange, but a block of 100 shares was sold by a stockholder 12 months ago at $60 per share, and a block of 200 shares was sold by another stockholder 18 months ago at $55 per share.

(c) No entry has been made to remove from the accounts for Materials, Factory Supplies, Direct Labor, and Overhead the amounts properly chargeable to plant asset accounts for machinery constructed during the year. The following information is given relative to costs of the machinery constructed.

| | |
|---|---:|
| Materials used | $ 9,000 |
| Factory supplies used | 800 |
| Direct labor incurred | 10,000 |
| Additional overhead (over regular) caused by construction of machinery | 1,800 |
| Fixed overhead rate applied to regular manufacturing operations | 50% of direct labor cost |
| Cost of similar machinery if it had been purchased from outside suppliers | $31,000 |

**Instructions**

Prepare journal entries on the books of the Lindbergh Company to record these transactions.

**E11–16** The following transactions occurred during 1984. Assume that depreciation of 12½% per year is charged on all machinery and 5% per year on buildings, on a straight-line basis, with no estimated salvage value. Depreciation is charged for a full year on all fixed assets acquired during the year, and no depreciation is charged on fixed assets disposed of during the year.

Jan. 30  A building that cost $45,000 in 1966 is torn down to make room for a new building. The wrecking contractor was paid $3,000 and was permitted to keep all materials salvaged.

Mar. 10  Machinery that was purchased in 1977 for $12,000 is sold for $1,350 cash, f.o.b. purchaser's plant. Freight of $300 is paid on this machinery.

Mar. 20  A gear breaks on a machine that cost $9,000 in 1978 and the gear is replaced at a cost of $400.

May 18  A special base installed for a machine in 1979 when the machine was purchased has to be replaced at a cost of $4,500 because of defective workmanship on the original base. The cost of the machinery was $10,500 in 1979; the cost of the base was $3,300, and this amount was charged to the Machinery account in 1979.

June 23  One of the buildings is repainted at a cost of $4,500. It had not been painted since it was constructed in 1980.

**Instructions**

Prepare general journal entries for the transactions. (Round to nearest dollar.)

**E11–17** Cain Corporation purchased conveyor equipment with a list price of $6,000. The vendor's credit terms were 2/10, n/30. Presented below are three independent cases related to the equipment. Assume that the purchases of equipment are recorded gross.

(a) Cain paid cash for the equipment eight days after the purchase.

(b) Cain traded in equipment with a book value of $300, and paid $5,700 in cash one month after the purchase. The old equipment could have been sold for $300 at the date of trade.

(c) Cain gave the vendor a $6,050 noninterest-bearing note for the equipment on the date of purchase. The note was due in one year and was paid on time. Assume that the effective interest rate in the market was 10%. (Round to the nearest dollar.)

**Instructions**

Prepare the general journal entries required to record the acquisition and payment in each of the independent cases above.

**E11–18** Presented below is information related to Perfecto Gusto Company.

1. In January, 1980, Perfecto Gusto Company built a loading dock to accommodate heavy tractor- and trailer-type trucks at a cost of $19,000 as follows:

| | |
|---|---|
| Labor | $8,000 |
| Materials | 7,000 |
| Estimated overhead | 4,000 |

It is estimated that this structure will have a useful life of 20 years.

2. During 1982 several planks in the loading platform split and were weakened to such an extent that they had to be replaced at a cost of $150.

3. In July, 1983, the entire dock was repainted at a cost of $325.

4. An inexperienced driver backed into the end of the dock and damaged it in February, 1984. The company for which he worked was insured against such accidents, and a settlement of $1,800 was obtained. Cost to Perfecto Gusto Company of repairing the damage was: labor, $700, and materials, $500 and overhead, $350.

5. In June, 1984, a hailstorm damaged the roof. A settlement of $1,500 was obtained from the insurance company. It was decided, however, that a new roof would soon be needed and repairs were not worthwhile. Therefore nothing was done until October, when a roofing contractor was engaged to reroof the loading dock at a price of $4,000.

**Instructions**

State how each of the items above should be recorded in the accounts and support your conclusions.

**\*E11–19** Presented below are data for three independent cases involving coinsurance coverage.

| | Case 1 | Case 2 | Case 3 |
|---|---|---|---|
| Fair market value at date of loss | $66,000 | $54,000 | $60,000 |
| Face value of policy | 39,600 | 47,520 | 36,000 |
| Coinsurance requirement (80%) | 52,800 | 43,200 | 48,000 |
| Amount of loss | 33,000 | 32,400 | 60,000 |

**Instructions**

For each of the cases above compute the amount recoverable.

## PROBLEMS

**P11–1** Selected accounts included in the property, plant, and equipment section of the Kingston Corporation's balance sheet at December 31, 1982, had the following balances:

| | |
|---|---|
| Land | $175,000 |
| Land improvements | 90,000 |
| Buildings | 900,000 |
| Machinery and equipment | 850,000 |

During 1983 the following transactions occurred:

1. A tract of land was acquired for $125,000 as a potential future building site.   *Investment*

2. A plant facility consisting of land and building was acquired from the Nostrand Company in exchange for 10,000 shares of Kingston's common stock. On the acquisition date, Kingston's stock had a closing market price of $45 per share on a national stock exchange. The plant facility was carried on Nostrand's books at $89,000 for land and $130,000 for the building at the exchange date. Current appraised values for the land and building, respectively, are $120,000 and $240,000.

3. Items of machinery and equipment were purchased at a total cost of $300,000. Additional costs were incurred as follows:

|                      |          |
|----------------------|----------|
| Freight and unloading | $ 5,000  |
| Sales and use taxes   | 12,000   |
| Installation          | 25,000   |

4. Expenditures totaling $75,000 were made for new parking lots, streets, and sidewalks at the corporation's various plant locations. These expenditures had an estimated useful life of fifteen years.

5. A machine costing $50,000 on January 1, 1975, was scrapped on June 30, 1983. Double-declining-balance depreciation has been recorded on the basis of a ten-year life.

6. A machine was sold for $20,000 on July 1, 1983. Original cost of the machine was $36,000 on January 1, 1980, and it was depreciated on the straight-line basis over an estimated useful life of seven years and a salvage value of $1,000.

**Instructions**

(a) Prepare a detailed analysis of the changes in each of the following balance sheet accounts for 1983:

   Land

   Land improvements

   Buildings

   Machinery and equipment

   (Hint: Disregard the related accumulated depreciation accounts.)

(b) List the items in the fact situation that were not used to determine the answer to (a), showing the pertinent amounts and supporting computations in good form for each item. In addition, indicate where, or if, these items should be included in Kingston's financial statements.

(AICPA adapted)

**P11–2** At December 31, 1982, certain accounts included in the property, plant, and equipment section of the McCartney Company's balance sheet had the following balances:

|                          |           |
|--------------------------|-----------|
| Land                     | $100,000  |
| Buildings                | 850,000   |
| Leasehold improvements   | 500,000   |
| Machinery and equipment  | 725,000   |

During 1983 the following transactions occurred:

Land site number 621 was acquired for $1,125,000. In addition, to acquire the land McCartney paid a $60,000 commission to a real estate agent. Costs of $20,000 were incurred to clear the land. During the course of clearing the land, timber and gravel were recovered and sold for $7,000.

A second tract of land (site number 622) with a building was acquired for $350,000. The closing statement indicated that the land value was $250,000 and the building value was $100,000. Shortly after acquisition, the building was demolished at a cost of $30,000. A new building was constructed for $150,000 plus the following costs:

| | |
|---|---:|
| Excavation fees | $11,000 |
| Architectural design fees | 9,000 |
| Building permit fee | 1,000 |
| Imputed interest on funds used during construction (stock financing) | 6,000 |

The building was completed and occupied on September 30, 1983.

A third tract of land (site number 623) was acquired for $700,000 and was put on the market for resale.

During December 1983 costs of $70,000 were incurred to improve leased office space. The related lease will terminate on December 31, 1985, and is not expected to be renewed. (Hint: Leasehold improvements should be handled in the same manner as land improvements.)

A group of new machines was purchased under a royalty agreement which provides for payment of royalties based on units of production for the machines. The invoice price of the machines was $75,000, freight costs were $2,500, unloading charges were $1,500, and royalty payments for 1983 were $14,000.

**Instructions**

(a) Prepare a detailed analysis of the changes in each of the following balance sheet accounts for 1983:

  Land

  Buildings

  Leasehold improvements

  Machinery and equipment

  Disregard the related accumulated depreciation accounts.

(b) List the items in the fact situation that were not used to determine the answer to (a) above, and indicate where, or if, these items should be included in McCartney's financial statements.

(AICPA adapted)

**P11-3** Presented below is a schedule of property dispositions for Albert Camper Co.

### SCHEDULE OF PROPERTY DISPOSITIONS

| | Cost | Accumulated Depreciation | Cash Proceeds | Fair Market Value | Nature of Disposition |
|---|---:|---:|---:|---:|---|
| Land | $22,000 | — | $19,000 | $19,000 | Condemnation |
| Building | 6,800 | — | 1,800 | — | Demolition |
| Warehouse | 60,000 | $7,978 | 61,000 | 61,000 | Destruction by fire |
| Machine | 4,000 | 1,700 | 500 | 3,300 | Trade-in |
| Furniture | 8,200 | 6,560 | — | 2,000 | Contribution |
| Automobile | 6,000 | 2,250 | 3,100 | 3,100 | Sale |

The following additional information is available:

**LAND.** On February 15, a condemnation award was received as consideration for unimproved land held primarily as an investment, and on March 31, another parcel of unimproved land to be held as an investment was purchased at a cost of $21,500.

**BUILDING.** On April 2, land and building were purchased at a total cost of $34,000, of which 20% was allocated to the building on the corporate books. The real estate was acquired with the intention of demolishing the building, and this was accomplished during the month of November. Cash proceeds received in November represent the net proceeds from demolition of the building.

**WAREHOUSE.** On June 30, the warehouse was destroyed by fire. The warehouse was purchased January 2, 1973, and had depreciated $7,978. On December 27, part of the insurance proceeds was used to purchase a replacement warehouse at a cost of $57,000.

**MACHINE.** On December 26, the machine was exchanged for another machine having a fair market value of $2,800 and cash of $500 was received. (Round to nearest dollar.)

**FURNITURE.** On August 15, furniture was contributed to a qualified charitable organization. No other contributions were made or pledged during the year.

**AUTOMOBILE.** On November 3, the automobile was sold to Jeff Light, a stockholder.

**Instructions**

Indicate how these items would be reported on the income statement of Albert Camper Co.

(AICPA adapted)

**P11-4** During 1984, Curt See Company manufactured a machine for its own use. At December 31, 1984, the account related to that machine is as follows:

Machinery

| | | | |
|---|---|---|---|
| Machine cost | $ 4,800 | Old machine—cost | $4,800 |
| Cost of dismantling old machine | 900 | Cash proceeds from sale of old machine | 500 |
| Raw materials used in construction of new machine | 18,000 | Depreciation for 1984, 10% of $44,400 | 4,440 |
| Labor in construction of new machine | 12,600 | | |
| Cost of installation | 2,040 | | |
| Materials used in trial runs | 960 | | |
| Profit on construction | 10,400 | | |

An analysis of the detail in the account discloses the following:

1. The old machine, which was removed during installation of the new one, has been fully depreciated.

2. Cash discounts received on the payments for materials used in construction totaled $500 and were reported in the "purchases discount" account.

3. The factory overhead account shows a balance of $300,000, which includes variable overhead and total fixed overhead, for the year ended December 31, 1984. $3,600 of the variable overhead is attributable to the production of the machine. Fixed overhead is normally priced to operations at $2 per man-hour of labor. 980 man-hours of labor were consumed in the production of the machine.

4. A profit was recognized on construction for the difference between costs incurred and the price at which the machine could have been purchased. The profit was credited to "self-construction gains."

5. Machinery has an estimated life of 10 years with no salvage value. The new machine was used for production beginning July 1, 1984.

**Instructions**

Prepare the entries necessary to correct the Machinery account as of December 31, 1984, and to record depreciation expense for the year 1984.

**P11-5** The Brinkley Furniture Company was incorporated on January 2, 1984, but was unable to begin manufacturing activities until July 1, 1984, because new factory facilities were not completed until that date.

The Land and Building account at December 31, 1984, was as follows:

| | | |
|---|---|---:|
| January 31, 1984 | Land and building | $ 98,000 |
| February 28, 1984 | Cost of removal of building | 1,700 |
| May 1, 1984 | Partial payment of new construction | 35,000 |
| May 1, 1984 | Legal fees paid | 2,000 |
| June 1, 1984 | Second payment on new construction | 30,000 |
| June 1, 1984 | Insurance premium | 1,800 |
| June 1, 1984 | Special tax assessment | 1,900 |
| June 30, 1984 | General expenses | 12,000 |
| July 1, 1984 | Final payment on new construction | 35,000 |
| December 31, 1984 | Asset write-up | 12,600 |
| | | $230,000 |
| December 31, 1984 | Depreciation—1984 at 1% | 2,300 |
| | Account balance | $227,700 |

The following additional information is to be considered.

1. To acquire land and building the company paid $48,000 cash and 500 shares of its 5% cumulative preferred stock, par value $100 per share. Fair market value of the stock is $105 per share.

2. Cost of removal of old buildings amounted to $1,700, and the demolition company retained all materials of the building.

3. Legal fees covered the following:

| | |
|---|---:|
| Cost of organization | $ 400 |
| Examination of title covering purchase of land | 900 |
| Legal work in connection with construction contract | 700 |
| | $2,000 |

4. Insurance premium covered the building for two-year term beginning May 1, 1984.

5. General expenses covered the following for the period from January 2, 1984, to June 30, 1984.

| | |
|---|---:|
| President's salary | $ 7,000 |
| Plant superintendent covering supervision of new building | 3,800 |
| Office salaries | 1,200 |
| | $12,000 |

6. The special tax assessment covered street improvements that are permanent in nature.

7. Because of a general increase in construction costs after entering into the building contract, the board of directors increased the value of the building $12,600, believing that such an increase was justified to reflect the current market at the time the building was completed. Retained earnings was credited for this amount.

8. Estimated life of building—50 years.
Write-off for 1984—1% of asset value (1% of $230,000, or $2,300).

**Instructions**

(a) Prepare entries to reflect correct land, building, and depreciation allowance accounts at December 31, 1984.

(b) Show the proper presentation of land, building, and depreciation on the balance sheet at December 31, 1984.

(AICPA adapted)

**P11-6** Kemp Corporation wishes to exchange a machine used in its operations. Kemp has received the following offers from other companies in the industry:

1. The Fisk Company offered to exchange a similar machine plus $15,000.

2. The Baines Company offered to exchange a similar machine.

3. The Edmonton Company offered to exchange a similar machine, but wanted $20,000 in addition to Kemp's machine.

In addition, Kemp contacted the Park Corporation, a dealer in machines. To obtain a new machine, Kemp must pay $150,000 in addition to trading in its old machine.

| | Kemp | Fisk | Baines | Edmonton | Park |
|---|---|---|---|---|---|
| Machine cost | $175,000 | $115,000 | $275,000 | $180,000 | $185,000 |
| Accumulated depreciation | 85,000 | 40,000 | 225,000 | 108,000 | -0- |
| Fair value | 75,000 | 60,000 | 75,000 | 95,000 | 225,000 |

**Instructions**

For each of the four independent situations, prepare the journal entries to record the exchange on the books of each company. (Round to nearest dollar.)

**P11-7** On August 1, 1984, Harrison, Inc. exchanged productive assets with Clapton, Inc. Harrison's asset is referred to below as "Asset A" and Clapton's is referred to as "Asset B." The following facts pertain to these assets:

| | Asset A | Asset B |
|---|---|---|
| Original cost | $96,000 | $110,000 |
| Accumulated depreciation (to date of exchange) | 40,000 | 52,000 |
| Fair market value at date of exchange | 60,000 | 75,000 |
| Cash paid by Harrison, Inc. | 15,000 | |
| Cash received by Clapton, Inc. | | 15,000 |

**Instructions**

(a) Assume that Assets A and B are similar, and record the exchange for both Harrison, Inc. and Clapton, Inc. in accordance with generally accepted accounting principles.

(b) Assume that Assets A and B are dissimilar, and record the exchange for both Harrison, Inc. and Clapton, Inc. in accordance with generally accepted accounting principles.

**P11-8** Presented below are unrelated transactions related to the acquisition of plant assets for Starlight Corp. for the current year.

1. Starlight Corp. acquired a machine with a list price of $130,000 on May 1 of the current year. To acquire this machine, Starlight Corp. exchanged 5,000 shares of its $2.00 par common stock, and paid cash of $40,000. The stock of Starlight Corp. was selling for $15 per share on May 1.

2. A used truck costing $13,000 with a book value of $4,000 is exchanged for a new truck with a fair market value of $8,000 and $5,000 cash is given. Assume that the assets exchanged are similar productive assets.

3. Used machinery having a fair market value of $12,000 and cash of $4,000 is received in exchange for a newer piece of machinery having a book value of $10,000 (original cost $10,500 less accumulated depreciation of $500). Assume that the assets exchanged are similar productive assets.

4. Starlight Corporation purchased plant assets which included land and building for cash of $90,000. Starlight Corp. borrowed $40,000 in cash at 11% interest (principal and interest are due in one year) to finance part of the purchase. The property was appraised for tax purposes as follows: land, $20,000, and building, $60,000. It is decided to use the tax appraisals to allocate cost between the land and the building because the relative tax values appear reasonable.

5. An old computer has a book value of $41,000 (original cost $100,000 less $59,000 accumulated depreciation), and a fair market value of $56,000. A new computer having a fair market value of $140,000 is obtained by paying $84,000 cash and trading in the old computer. Assume that the assets exchanged are considered similar in nature.

**Instructions**

(a) Prepare the general journal entries necessary to record these transactions during the current year.

(b) Assume that the assets exchanged in the foregoing transactions were dissimilar in nature, and prepare the general journal entries necessary to record these transactions during the current year.

**P11-9** During the current year, Condo Construction trades an old crane that has a book value of $96,000 (original cost $120,000 less accumulated depreciation $24,000) for a new crane from Bombay Manufacturing Co. The new crane cost Bombay $140,000 to manufacture. The following information is also available.

|  | Condo Const. | Bombay Mfg. Co. |
|---|---|---|
| Fair market value of old crane | $84,000 | |
| Fair market value of new crane | | $180,000 |
| Cash paid | 96,000 | |
| Cash received | | 96,000 |

**Instructions**

(a) Assume that this exchange is considered to involve dissimilar assets (culmination of the earnings process), and prepare the journal entries on the books of (1) Condo Construction, and (2) Bombay Manufacturing.

(b) Assume that this exchange is considered to involve similar assets (no culmination of the earnings process), and prepare the journal entries on the books of (1) Condo Construction, and (2) Bombay Manufacturing.

(c) Assuming the same facts as those in (a), except that the fair market value of the old crane is $102,000 and the cash paid $78,000, prepare the journal entries on the books of (1) Condo Construction, and (2) Bombay Manufacturing.

(d) Assuming the same facts as those in (b), except that the fair market value of the old crane is $108,000 and the cash paid $72,000, prepare the journal entries on the books of (1) Condo Construction, and (2) Bombay Manufacturing.

**P11-10** On March 1, 1983, Wheeler Corporation acquired a tract of land as a plant site. Wheeler paid $20,000 cash and gave a $50,000, 3-year, 12% note payable, on which interest is payable annually. Construction was begun immediately on the plant, and it was completed on October 31, 1983. Expenditures for construction were $300,000 monthly for 8 months beginning on March 1. In order to help finance construction, Wheeler borrowed $2,000,000 on March 1 on a 10%, 2-year note payable. Interest on this note is payable at maturity. Excess funds which are not needed to pay construction costs were invested in temporary securities at 14%. Other than these two notes, Wheeler had no outstanding debt during 1983.

**Instructions**

(a) Calculate interest revenue, average accumulated expenditures, avoidable interest, total interest cost incurred, and interest cost to be capitalized during 1983. In computing avoidable interest, start with the specific borrowing on the land. Round all computations to the nearest dollar.

(b) Prepare the journal entry needed on the books of Wheeler at December 31, 1983 to record interest cost incurred and interest cost capitalized.

**P11-11** Napa Winery Co. received a $535,000 low bid from a reputable manufacturer for the construction of special production equipment needed by Napa in an expansion program. Because the company's own plant was not operating at capacity, Napa decided to construct the equipment there and recorded the following production costs related to the construction:

| | |
|---|---:|
| Services of consulting engineer | $ 20,000 |
| Work subcontracted | 30,000 |
| Materials | 265,000 |
| Plant labor normally assigned to production | 80,000 |
| Plant labor normally assigned to maintenance | 130,000 |
| Total | $525,000 |

Management prefers to record the cost of the equipment under the incremental cost method. Approximately 40% of the corporation's production is devoted to government supply contracts which are all based in some way on cost. The contracts require that any self-constructed equipment be allocated its full share of all costs related to the construction.

The following information is also available:

(a) The production labor was for partial fabrication of the equipment in the plant. Skilled personnel were required and were assigned from other projects. The maintenance labor would have been idle time of nonproduction plant employees who would have been retained on the payroll whether or not their services were utilized.

(b) Payroll taxes and employee fringe benefits are approximately 30% of labor cost and are included in manufacturing overhead cost. Total manufacturing overhead for the year was $6,969,000, including the $130,000 maintenance labor used to construct the equipment.

(c) Manufacturing overhead is approximately 50% variable and is applied on the basis of production labor cost. Production labor cost for the year for the corporation's normal products totaled $8,420,000.

(d) General and administrative expenses include $30,000 of allocated executive salary cost and $12,500 of postage, telephone, supplies, and miscellaneous expenses identifiable with this equipment construction.

**Instructions**

(a) Prepare a schedule computing the amount that should be reported as the full cost of the constructed equipment to meet the requirements of the government contracts. Any supporting computations should be in good form.
(b) Prepare a schedule computing the incremental cost of the constructed equipment.
(c) What is the greatest amount that should be capitalized as the cost of the equipment? Why?

(AICPA adapted)

**\*P11-12** Jimmy Cricket, Inc. has two fire insurance policies. Policy A covers the office building at a face value of $720,000 and the furniture and fixtures at a face value of $182,400. Policy B covers only the office building at an additional face value of $345,600. Each policy is with a different insurance company. A fire caused losses to the office building and the furniture and fixtures. The relevant data are summarized below:

| | Furniture and Fixtures | Office Building | |
|---|---|---|---|
| Insurance policy | A | A | B |
| Fair market value of the property before fire | $240,000 | $1,440,000 | $1,440,000 |
| Fair market value of the property after fire | $ 20,000 | $ 880,000 | $ 880,000 |
| Face of insurance policy | $182,400 | $ 720,000 | $ 345,600 |
| Co-insurance requirement | 80% | 80% | 80% |

**Instructions**

Compute the amount due from each insurance company for the loss on each asset category. Show computations in good form.

(AICPA adapted)

# CHAPTER 12

# Depreciation and Depletion

Accountants, engineers, lawyers, and economists all define depreciation differently, and they probably will continue to do so because each group uses depreciation in a different context. All agree, however, that most assets are on an inevitable "march to the rubbish heap," and some type of write-down or write-off of cost is needed to indicate that the usefulness of an asset has declined. **Depreciation** is the term most often employed to indicate that tangible plant assets have declined in service potential. Where natural resources, such as timber, gravel, oil, and coal, are involved, the term **depletion** is employed. The expiration of intangible assets, such as patents or goodwill, is called **amortization.**

## DEPRECIATION—A METHOD OF COST ALLOCATION

Most individuals at one time or another are party to the trade-in and purchase of an automobile. In discussions with the automobile dealer, depreciation is a consideration on two points. First, how much has the old car "depreciated"? That is, how much is the trade-in value? Second, how fast will the new car depreciate? That is, what will its trade-in value be? In both cases the concept of depreciation is viewed as a valuation issue; depreciation is thought of as a loss in value.

To accountants, depreciation is not a matter of valuation but a means of cost allocation. Assets are not depreciated on the basis of a decline in their fair market value, but on the basis of systematic charges of cost to expense.

This approach is employed because between the time the asset is purchased and the time it is sold or junked, the value of the asset may fluctuate. Attempts to measure these interim value changes have not been well received by accountants because values are difficult to measure objectively. Therefore, accountants charge the cost of the asset to depreciation expense over its estimated life, making no attempts to value the asset at fair market value between acquisition and disposition. The cost allocation approach is used because a matching of costs with revenues occurs and because fluctuations in market value are tenuous and difficult to measure.

# FACTORS INVOLVED IN THE DEPRECIATION PROCESS

Before a pattern of charges to revenue can be established, three basic questions must be answered:

1. What depreciation base is to be used for the asset?
2. What is the asset's useful life?
3. What method of cost apportionment is best for this asset?

The answers to these questions involve the distillation of several estimates into one single figure. Keep in mind that the depreciation charge is not a measurement of value changes; **it is an allocation of the cost of the asset.** The calculations on which it is based assume perfect knowledge of the future, which is never attainable.

## Depreciation Base for the Asset

The base established for depreciation is a function of two factors: the original cost and salvage or disposal value. In the previous chapter, the procedures used in establishing a cost basis for plant assets were illustrated; little attention was given to salvage value. Salvage value is the estimated amount that will be received at the time the asset is sold or removed from service. The salvage value is the amount to which the asset must be written down or depreciated during its useful life. To illustrate, if an asset has a cost of $10,000 and a salvage value of $1,000, the depreciation base is $9,000.

| | |
|---|---:|
| Original cost | $10,000 |
| Less salvage value | 1,000 |
| Depreciation base | $ 9,000 |

From a practical standpoint, salvage value is often considered to be zero because the valuation is small. Some long-lived assets, however, have substantial residual values.

Companies also differ as to their estimate of salvage value. For example, at one time Leasco, Greyhound Corp., and Boothe Computer all depreciated the same IBM computer equipment on a straight-line basis, but Leasco and Greyhound assumed a 10% salvage value, whereas Boothe assumed zero.

## Estimation of Service Lives

There is a basic difference between the service life of an asset and its physical life. A piece of machinery may be physically capable of producing a given product for many years beyond its service life, but the equipment is not used for all of those years because the cost of producing the product in later years may be too high. For example, the old Slater cotton mill in Pawtucket, Rhode Island is preserved in remarkable physical condition as an historic landmark in American industrial development, although its service life was terminated many years ago.[1]

---

[1] Taken from J. D. Coughlan and W. K. Strand, *Depreciation Accounting, Taxes and Business Decisions* (New York: The Ronald Press, 1969), pp. 10–12.

Assets are retired for two reasons: **physical factors** (such as casualty or expiration of physical life) and **economic factors** (obsolescence). Physical factors are the wear and tear, decay, and casualties that make it difficult for the asset to perform indefinitely. These physical factors set the outside limit for the service life of an asset.

Economic or functional factors are other constraints that develop to shorten the service life of an asset. The reasons why an asset is scrapped before its physical life expires are varied. New processes or techniques or improved machines, for example, may provide the same service at lower costs and with higher quality. Changes in the product may also shorten the service life of the asset. Public requirements may also demand that the asset be retired. Ecological factors, for instance, often play a role in a decision to retire a given asset.

The economic or functional factors can be classified into three categories: inadequacy, supersession, and obsolescence. **Inadequacy** results when an asset ceases to be useful to a given enterprise because the demands of the firm have increased: for example, the need for a larger building to handle increased production. Although the old building may still be sound, it may have become inadequate for that enterprise's purposes. **Supersession** is the replacement of one asset with another more efficient and economical asset: for example, the replacement of a second-generation computer (transistor type) with a third-generation computer (integrated circuit type) or the replacement of the Boeing 727 with the Boeing 767. **Obsolescence** is the catchall for situations not involving inadequacy and supersession. Because the distinction between these categories appears artificial, it is probably best to consider economic factors totally instead of trying to make distinctions that are not clear-cut.

To illustrate the above-mentioned concepts, consider a new nuclear power plant. What do you think would be the most important factors in determining its useful life: physical factors or economic factors? An answer may not be possible on the basis of the limited data provided, but some observations seem valid. The limiting factors seem to be (1) ecological considerations, (2) competition from other power sources (nonnuclear), and (3) safety concerns.

In this situation, the physical life does not appear to be the primary factor affecting useful life. Although the plant's physical life may be far from over, the plant may become obsolete in 10 years. For a house, physical factors undoubtedly supersede the economic or functional factors relative to useful life. Whenever the physical nature of the asset is the primary determinant of useful life, maintenance plays an extremely vital role. The better the maintenance, the longer the life of the asset.[2]

The problem of estimating service life is difficult; estimation and judgment are the primary means of developing service lives. In some cases, arbitrary lives are selected; in others, fairly sophisticated statistical methods are employed to establish a useful life for accounting purposes. In many cases, the primary basis for estimating the useful life of an asset is the enterprise's past experience with the same or similar assets. In a highly industrial economy such as that of the United States, where research and innovation are so prominent, economic and technological factors have as much, if not more, effect on the service lives of tangible plant assets as physical factors do.

---

[2]The airline industry also illustrates the type of problem involved in estimation. In the past, aircraft were assumed not to wear out—they just became obsolete. However, some jets have been in service as long as twenty years, and maintenance of these aircraft has become increasingly expensive. As a result, some airlines are finding it necessary to replace aircraft not because of obsolescence but because of their physical deterioration.

The problem related to the estimation of service lives has been accentuated by the Economic Recovery Tax Act of 1981. This act established the **accelerated cost recovery system (ACRS),** which usually permits companies to depreciate assets over a considerably shorter period of time than their estimated useful life. The ACRS was designed to encourage investment in productive assets by allowing faster write off of the cost of an asset. GAAP, however, requires that the cost of a depreciable asset be allocated to expense over the expected useful life of the asset in a systematic and rational manner. Some argue that from a cost-benefit consideration it would be better for the accounting profession to adopt the ACRS approach to eliminate the maintenance of two different sets of records. Given the different objectives of the two approaches, we believe that adoption of this approach would be unfortunate.

## METHODS OF COST APPORTIONMENT (DEPRECIATION)

The determination of the depreciation charge also depends on the selection of an appropriate method. The profession requires that the depreciation method employed be "systematic and rational." The arbitrary assignment of cost to accounting periods without regard to the probable pattern of losses in an asset's services is not acceptable.

Depreciation methods may be classified as follows:[3]

1. Activity method (units of use or production)
2. Straight-line method
3. Decreasing charge methods
   (a) Sum-of-the-years'-digits
   (b) Double-declining balance
4. Special depreciation methods
   (a) Inventory method
   (b) Retirement and replacement methods
   (c) Group and composite-life methods
   (d) Compound interest methods

To illustrate, Barek Coal Mines recently purchased an additional crane for digging purposes. Pertinent data concerning the purchase of the crane are:

| | |
|---|---|
| Cost of crane | $500,000 |
| Estimated useful life | 5 years |
| Estimated salvage value | $ 50,000 |
| Productive life in hours | 30,000 hours |

[3]*Accounting Trends and Techniques—1981* reports that of its 600 surveyed companies various depreciation methods were used for financial reporting purposes by the following number of companies: straight-line, 562; declining-balance, 65; sum-of-the-years'-digits, 26; accelerated method (not specified), 69; units of production, 51. No utility or transportation companies (the ones that use the "special depreciation methods") are included in the AICPA's survey.

### Activity Method

The activity method (often called the variable charge approach) assumes that depreciation is a function of use or productivity instead of the passage of time. The life of the asset is considered in terms of either the output it provides (units it produces), or the number of hours it works. Conceptually, the proper cost association is established in terms of output instead of hours used, but often the output is not homogeneous. In such cases, an **input measure** such as machine hours is a more appropriate method of measuring the dollar amount of depreciation charges for a given accounting period.

The crane poses no particular problem because the usage (hours) is relatively easy to measure. If we assume that the crane is used 4,000 hours the first year, the depreciation charge is:

$$\frac{(\text{Cost less salvage}) \times \text{Hours this year}}{\text{Total estimated hours}} = \text{Depreciation charge}$$

$$\frac{(\$500,000 - \$50,000) \times 4,000}{30,000} = \$60,000$$

The major limitation of this method is that it is not appropriate in situations in which depreciation is a function of time instead of activity. For example, a building is subject to a great deal of steady deterioration from the elements (a function of time) regardless of its use. In addition, where an asset is subject to economic or functional factors, independent of its use, the activity method loses much of its significance. For example, if a company is expanding rapidly, a particular building may soon become obsolete for its intended purposes, without activity playing any role in its loss of utility.

Another problem in using an activity method is that an estimate of units of output or service hours received are often difficult to measure. Data are more frequently available concerning estimated lives of given assets in relation to time than on the number of units of output that will be achieved.

### Straight-Line Method

The straight-line method overcomes some objections directed at the activity method, because depreciation is considered a function of time instead of a function of usage. This method is widely employed in practice because of its simplicity. The straight-line procedure is often justified on a more theoretical basis as well. When creeping obsolescence is the primary reason for a limited service life, a decline in usefulness may be constant from period to period. In this situation, the straight-line method is appropriate. The depreciation charge for the crane is computed as follows:

$$\frac{\text{Cost less salvage}}{\text{Estimated service life}} = \text{Depreciation charge}$$

$$\frac{\$500,000 - \$50,000}{5} = \$90,000$$

The major objection to the straight-line method is that it rests on tenuous assumptions that in most situations are not realistic. The major assumptions are that (1) the asset's economic usefulness is the same each year, and (2) the repair and maintenance expense is essentially the same each period (given constant revenue flows).

One additional problem that occurs in using the straight-line method is that distortions in the rate of return analysis (income/assets) develop. For example, Table 12–1 indicates how the rate of return increases, given constant revenue flows.

**TABLE 12–1**   DEPRECIATION AND RATE OF RETURN ANALYSIS—CRANE EXAMPLE

| Year | Depreciation Expense | Undepreciated Asset Balance (book value) | Income Flow (after depreciation expense) | Rate of Return (income ÷ book value) |
|---|---|---|---|---|
| 0 | $ | $500,000 | $ | |
| 1 | 90,000 | 410,000 | 100,000 | 24.4% |
| 2 | 90,000 | 320,000 | 100,000 | 31.2% |
| 3 | 90,000 | 230,000 | 100,000 | 43.5% |
| 4 | 90,000 | 140,000 | 100,000 | 71.4% |
| 5 | 90,000 | 50,000 | 100,000 | 200.0% |

This illustration indicates that the rate of return analysis can be misleading when the straight-line method is employed because the income flow remains the same, whereas the book value of the asset decreases. With the exception of the compound interest methods, the rate of return analysis is similarly distorted by other depreciation methods that systematically allocate cost. A student of accounting soon realizes that any cost allocation procedure has several limiting assumptions and that simplicity and ease of understanding are valid considerations in making the final selection.

## Decreasing Charge Methods

The decreasing charge methods (often called accelerated depreciation) provide for a higher depreciation cost in the earlier years and lower charges in later periods. The main justification for this approach is that inasmuch as the asset is more efficient or suffers the greatest loss of services in the earlier years, more depreciation should be charged in those years. Another argument presented is that repair and maintenance costs are often higher in the later periods, and the accelerated methods thus provide a constant cost because the depreciation charge is lower in the later periods. Generally, one of two methods is employed in the decreasing charge method: the sum-of-the-years'-digits method or the declining balance method.

**Sum-of-the-Years'-Digits**   The sum-of-the-years'-digits method results in a decreasing depreciation charge based on a decreasing fraction of depreciable cost (original cost less salvage value). Each fraction uses the sum of the years as a denominator (5 + 4 + 3 + 2 + 1 = 15) and the number of years of estimated life remaining as of the beginning of the year as a numerator. In this method, the numerator decreases year by year although the denominator remains constant (5/15, 4/15, 3/15, 2/15, and 1/15). At the end of the asset's useful life, the balance remaining should be equal to the salvage value. The example (Table 12–2) involving a crane shows this method of computation.[4]

**TABLE 12–2**    SUM-OF-THE-YEARS'-DIGITS: DEPRECIATION SCHEDULE—CRANE EXAMPLE

| Year | Depreciation Base | Remaining Life in Years | Depreciation Fraction | Depreciation Expense | Book Value, End of Year |
|------|------|------|------|------|------|
| 1 | $450,000 | 5 | 5/15 | $150,000 | $350,000 |
| 2 | 450,000 | 4 | 4/15 | 120,000 | 230,000 |
| 3 | 450,000 | 3 | 3/15 | 90,000 | 140,000 |
| 4 | 450,000 | 2 | 2/15 | 60,000 | 80,000 |
| 5 | 450,000 | 1 | 1/15 | 30,000 | 50,000[a] |
| | | 15 | 15/15 | $450,000 | |

[a]Salvage value.

**Declining-Balance Methods**    Another decreasing charge method is the declining balance method which utilizes a depreciation rate (expressed as a percentage) that is some multiple of the straight-line method. For example, the double-declining rate for a 10 year asset would be 20% (double the straight-line rate which is 1/10 or 10%). The declining balance rate remains constant and is applied to the reducing book value each year. Unlike other methods, in the declining-balance method the salvage value is not deducted in computing the depreciation base. The declining balance rate is multiplied by the book value of the asset at the beginning of each period. Since the book value of the asset is reduced each period by the depreciation charge, the constant declining balance rate is applied to a successively lower book value that results in lower depreciation charges each year. This process continues until the book value of the asset is reduced to its estimated salvage value at which time depreciation is discontinued. As indicated above, various multiples are used in

**TABLE 12–3**    DOUBLE-DECLINING DEPRECIATION SCHEDULE—CRANE EXAMPLE

| Year | Book Value of Asset First of Year | Rate on Declining Balance[a] | Debit Depreciation Expense | Balance Accumulated Depreciation | Book Value, End of Year |
|------|------|------|------|------|------|
| 1 | $500,000 | 40% | $200,000 | $200,000 | $300,000 |
| 2 | 300,000 | 40% | 120,000 | 320,000 | 180,000 |
| 3 | 180,000 | 40% | 72,000 | 392,000 | 108,000 |
| 4 | 108,000 | 40% | 43,200 | 435,200 | 64,800 |
| 5 | 64,800 | 40% | 14,800[b] | 450,000 | 50,000 |

[a]Based on twice the straight-line rate of 20% ($90,000/$450,000 = 20%; 20% × 2 = 40%).
[b]Limited to $14,800 because book value should not be less than salvage value.

[4]What happens if the estimated service life of the asset is, let us say, 51 years? How would you calculate the sum-of-the-years'-digits? Fortunately the mathematicians have developed a formula that permits easy computation as follows. It is:

$$\frac{n(n+1)}{2} = \frac{51(51+1)}{2} = 1326.$$

practice, such as twice the straight-line rate (double-declining balance method) and 150% of the straight-line rate. Using the double-declining approach in the crane example, Barek Coal Mines would have the depreciation charges shown in Table 12–3 (page 530).

Enterprises often switch from the declining-balance methods to the sum-of-the-years'-digits or straight-line methods near the end of the asset's useful life to insure that the asset is depreciated only to its salvage value.[5]

As indicated earlier, for tax purposes the IRS has adopted a different system referred to as the **accelerated cost recovery system (ACRS)**. ACRS eliminates the need to determine each asset's useful life. The selection of a depreciation method and a salvage value is also unnecessary under ACRS. The taxpayer determines the recovery deduction for an asset by applying a statutory percentage to the historical cost of the property. ACRS is discussed more fully in Chapter 20.

## SPECIAL DEPRECIATION SYSTEMS

Sometimes an enterprise does not select one of the more popular depreciation methods because the assets involved have unique characteristics, or the nature of the industry dictates that a special depreciation method be adopted. Generally, these systems can be classified into four groups:

1. Inventory systems.
2. Retirement and replacement systems.
3. Group and composite methods.
4. Compound interest methods.

### Inventory Systems

The inventory method (often called the appraisal system) is used to value small tangible assets such as hand tools or utensils. A tool inventory, for example, might be taken at the beginning and the end of the year; the value of the beginning inventory plus the cost of tools acquired for the year less the value of the ending inventory provides the amount of depreciation expense for the year. Separate depreciation schedules for the assets in use are impractical; consequently, this method is appealing.

The major objection to this depreciation method is that it is not "systematic and rational." No set formula is involved, and a great deal of subjectivity may be involved in the valuations presented. In many situations, a market or liquidation value is used as the basis for valuation, a practice that is criticized as a violation of the historical cost principle.

---

[5]A pure form of the declining-balance method (sometimes appropriately called the "fixed percentage of book value method") has also been suggested as a possibility. This approach finds a rate that depreciates the asset exactly to salvage value at the end of its expected useful life. The formula for determination of this rate is as follows:

$$\text{Depreciation rate} = 1 - \sqrt[n]{\frac{\text{Salvage value}}{\text{Acquisition cost}}}$$

The life in years is $n$. Once the depreciation rate is computed, it is applied on the declining book value of the asset from period to period, which means that depreciation expense will be successively lower period by period. This method is not used extensively in practice, because the computations are cumbersome and it is not permitted for tax purposes.

## Retirement and Replacement Systems

The retirement and replacement methods are used principally by public utilities and railroads that own many similar units of small value such as poles, ties, conductors, telephones, and so on. The purpose of these approaches is to avoid elaborate depreciation schedules for the individual assets. The distinction between the two methods is that **the retirement system charges the cost of the retired asset (less salvage value) to depreciation expense,** and **the replacement system charges the cost of units purchased as replacements less salvage value from the units replaced to depreciation expense.** In the replacement method the original cost (sometimes called aboriginal cost) of the old asset is maintained in the accounts indefinitely. For example, railroad companies, which only recently switched to a more traditional method of depreciating railroad track, have track costs in their accounts from as early as 1887.

To illustrate these two methods, let us assume that the transmission lines of Hi-Test Utility, Inc. originally cost $1,000,000 and that eight years later lines costing $150,000 are replaced with lines having a cost of $200,000.

| Entries Under Retirement and Replacement System | | | | | |
|---|---|---|---|---|---|
| Retirement System | | | Replacement System | | |
| **Installation of lines — 1983:** | | | | | |
| Plant Assets—Lines | 1,000,000 | | Plant Assets | 1,000,000 | |
| Cash | | 1,000,000 | Cash | | 1,000,000 |
| **Retirement of old asset — 1991:** | | | | | |
| Depreciation Expense | 150,000 | | (no entry) | | |
| Plant Assets—Lines | | 150,000 | | | |
| **Cost of new asset — 1991:** | | | | | |
| Plant Assets—Lines | 200,000 | | Depreciation Expense | 200,000 | |
| Cash | | 200,000 | Cash | | 200,000 |

Any salvage value from the old transmission lines is considered a reduction of the depreciation expense in the period of retirement or replacement under both methods. Note that neither makes use of an accumulated depreciation account.

Both systems are subject to the criticism that a proper allocation of costs to all periods does not occur, particularly in the early years. To overcome this objection, a special allowance account may be established in the earlier years so that an assumed depreciation charge can be provided. The probability of retirements or replacements being fairly constant is essential to the validity of this concept; otherwise, depreciation is simply a function of when retirement and replacement occur.

## Group and Composite Systems

Depreciation methods are usually applied to a single asset. In certain circumstances, however, multiple-asset accounts are depreciated using one rate. For example, an enterprise such as American Telephone and Telegraph Co. might depreciate by equipment groups, such as telephone poles, microwave systems, or switchboards. Two methods of depreciating multiple-asset accounts are employed: the group method and the composite method. The term **group refers to a collection of assets that are similar in nature; composite refers to a collection of assets that are dissimilar in nature.** The group method is frequently used where the assets are fairly homogeneous and have approximately the same useful lives. The composite approach is used when the assets are heterogeneous and have different lives. The group method more closely approximates a single-unit cost procedure because the dispersion from the average is not as great. The method of computation for either group or composite is essentially the same: find an average and depreciate on that basis.

To illustrate, Smart Motors depreciates its fleet of cars, trucks, and campers on a composite basis. The depreciation rate is established in this manner:

| Asset | Original Cost | Residual Value | Depreciable Cost | Estimated Life (yrs.) | Depreciation Per Year (straight-line) |
|-------|--------------|---------------|-----------------|----------------------|--------------------------------------|
| Cars | $145,000 | $25,000 | $120,000 | 3 | $40,000 |
| Trucks | 44,000 | 4,000 | 40,000 | 4 | 10,000 |
| Campers | 35,000 | 5,000 | 30,000 | 5 | 6,000 |
| | $224,000 | $34,000 | $190,000 | | $56,000 |

$$\text{Depreciation or composite rate} = \frac{\$56,000}{\$224,000} = 25\%$$

Composite life = 3.39 years ($190,000 ÷ $56,000)

If there are no changes in the asset account, the group will be depreciated to the residual or salvage value at the rate of $56,000 ($224,000 × .25) a year for 3.39 years. This system simplifies the procedure for keeping depreciation records when there are a multitude of assets.

The differences between the group or composite method and the single-unit depreciation methods become accentuated in the area of asset retirements. If an asset is retired before, or after, the average service life of the group is reached, the resulting gain or loss is buried in the accumulated depreciation account. This practice is justified because some assets will be retired before the average service life and others after the average life. For this reason, the debit to Accumulated Depreciation is the difference between original cost and cash received. No gain or loss on disposition is recorded. To illustrate, suppose that one of the campers with a cost of $5,000 was sold for $2,600 at the end of the third year. The entry is:

| | | |
|---|---|---|
| Accumulated Depreciation | 2,400 | |
| Cash | 2,600 | |
|    Cars, Trucks, and Campers | | 5,000 |

If a new type of asset is purchased (mopeds, for example), a new depreciation rate must be computed and applied in subsequent periods.

## Compound Interest Methods

The compound interest methods are not discussed in this chapter. Conceptually, the interest methods have much to offer, but they have found limited acceptance. At the present time, their use is limited to companies primarily in the public utility industry. Other industries, such as the real estate industry, also have argued for such an approach. Unlike most depreciation methods, the compound interest methods ("sinking fund method" and "annuity method") are **increasing charge methods** that result in lower depreciation charges in the early years and higher depreciation charges in the later years.

## SELECTION OF DEPRECIATION METHOD

Which depreciation method should be selected? Conceptually, the answer (as with the selection of an inventory method) is to determine which method best meets the objectives of financial reporting as indicated in *FASB Concepts Statement No. 1*. In attempting to achieve these objectives, many believe that the **matching** of revenues and cost best meets these objectives. For example, if revenues generated by the asset are constant over the asset's useful life, straight-line depreciation is employed, whereas if revenues are higher (or lower) at the beginning, some form of decreasing (or increasing) charge method of depreciation appears justified. Others argue that it is difficult in most cases to develop projections of future revenues and therefore **simplicity** should govern. In such cases, it might be argued that the straight-line method of depreciation should be used. In similar fashion, others argue that whatever is used for tax purposes should be used for book purposes because it **eliminates some record-keeping costs.**

Because it is difficult to defend one approach as more useful than another on a conceptual basis, the selection of the depreciation method is often made on more practical grounds. For example, many companies adopt some type of accelerated depreciation method for tax purposes but use the straight-line method for book purposes. This practice provides the best of both worlds—a **lower tax** and usually a **higher net income** for financial reporting purposes. For example, in the late 1960s, U.S. Steel changed its method of depreciation from an accelerated to a straight-line method for financial reporting purposes. Many observers note that the reason for the change was to report higher income so that it would be less susceptible to takeover by another enterprise. In effect, U.S. Steel wanted to report higher income so that the market value of its stock would rise.[6]

As another illustration, the real estate industry is frustrated with depreciation accounting because it is argued that real estate often does not decline in value. In addition, because real estate is highly leveraged, most real estate concerns report losses in earlier years when

---

[6]This assumption is highly tenuous. It is based on the belief that stock market analysts will not be able to recognize that the change in depreciation methods is purely cosmetic and therefore will give more value to the stock after the change. In fact, research in this area reports just the opposite. For example, one study showed that companies that switched from accelerated to straight-line (which increased income) experienced declines in stock value after the change; see Robert J. Kaplan and Richard Roll, "Investor Evaluation of Accounting Information: Some Empirical Evidence," *The Journal of Business* (April, 1972), pp. 225–257. Similarly, others have noted that switches to more liberal accounting policies (generating higher income numbers) have resulted in lower stock market performance. One rationale for such an occurrence is that such changes signal the market that the company is in trouble and also leads to skepticism about managements' attitudes and behavior. See, for example, David F. Hawkins and Walter J. Campbell, "Equity Valuation: Models, Analysis, and Implications," *Research Study and Report* (New York: Financial Executives Research Foundation, 1978); and Tom Harrison, "Different Market Reactions to Discretionary and Nondiscretionary Accounting Changes," *Journal of Accounting Research* (Spring 1977), pp. 84–107.

the sum of depreciation and interest charges exceed the revenues from the real estate project. The industry argues for some form of increasing charge method of depreciation (lower depreciation at the beginning and higher depreciation at the end), so that higher total assets and net income are reported in the earlier years of the project. Some even use an economic consequences argument that Canadian real estate companies (which may use an increasing charge method) have a competitive edge over U.S. real estate companies. In support of this view, they point to the increasing number of acquisitions by Canadian real estate companies of U.S. real estate companies and U.S. real estate properties.

**Tax policy** also has an effect. To illustrate, most railroads recently changed from the retirement-replacement method of accounting for railroad tracks to the more traditional method of capitalizing these track costs and depreciating them. Although the railroads had argued for the traditional method for many years, they were reluctant to switch because higher tax deductions were achieved through the retirement-replacement approach. The railroads feared that changing to a more traditional method of depreciating for financial reporting purposes might suggest to Congress that this method be used for tax purposes. Recently, Congress provided favorable tax legislation to the industry and the concern with dollars lost to taxes was alleviated. As a result, many companies have since changed to more traditional methods of depreciation.

It is hoped that the conceptual framework will be able to provide more operational guidelines than those existing at present. As indicated above, the selection of a depreciation method involves factors such as the nature and uncertainty of revenue flows, matching costs and revenues, effect on income and asset book values, tax considerations, and record-keeping costs.

## SPECIAL DEPRECIATION ISSUES

Several special issues related to depreciation remain to be discussed. Although it is difficult to classify these issues in special categories, the major issues are:

1. How should depreciation be computed for partial periods?
2. Does depreciation provide for the replacement of assets?
3. How are revisions in depreciation rates handled?

### Depreciation and Partial Periods

Plant assets are seldom purchased on the first day of a fiscal period or disposed of on the last day of a fiscal period. A practical question is: How much depreciation should be charged for the partial periods involved? Assume, for example, that an asset with a five-year life is purchased for $4,500 (no salvage value) on June 10 and the company's fiscal year ends December 31; depreciation is charged for $6\frac{2}{3}$ months during that year. In other words, the total depreciation for a full year (assuming straight-line depreciation) is $900 ($4,500/5), and the depreciation for the fraction of the year is:

$$\frac{6\frac{2}{3}}{12} \times \$900 = \$500$$

In some cases, the previous method is modified to handle acquisitions and disposals of plant assets more simply. For example, depreciation is computed for the full period on the opening balance in the asset account and no depreciation is charged on acquisitions during the year. Another variation is to charge a full year's depreciation on assets used for a full year and to charge one-half year's depreciation in the year of acquisition and in the year of disposal.

These are examples of modifications that are acceptable if they are applied consistently. Depreciation, however, is normally computed on the basis of the nearest whole month unless otherwise stipulated.

What happens when an accelerated method such as sum-of-the-years'-digits or double-declining balance is used when partial periods are involved? As an illustration, assume that an asset was purchased for $10,000 on July 1, 1983, with an estimated useful life of five years; the depreciation figures for 1983, 1984, and 1985 are as below.

|  | Sum-of-the-Years'-Digits | Double-Declining Balance |
|---|---|---|
| 1st Full Year | (5/15 × $10,000) = $3,333.33 | (40% × $10,000) = $4,000 |
| 2nd Full Year | (4/15 × 10,000) = 2,666.67 | (40% × 6,000) = 2,400 |
| 3rd Full Year | (3/15 × 10,000) = 2,000.00 | (40% × 3,600) = 1,440 |
| **Depreciation from July 1, 1983 to December 31, 1983** | | |
| 1/2 × $3,333.33 = | $1,666.67 | 1/2 × $4,000 = $2,000 |
| **Depreciation for 1984** | | |
| 1/2 × $3,333.33 = | $1,666.67 | 1/2 × $4,000 = $2,000 |
| 1/2 × 2,666.67 = | 1,333.33 | 1/2 × 2,400 = 1,200 |
| | $3,000.00 | $3,200 |
| | or ($10,000 − $2,000) × 40% = | $3,200 |
| **Depreciation for 1985** | | |
| 1/2 × 2,666.67 = | $1,333.33 | 1/2 × $2,400 = $1,200 |
| 1/2 × 2,000.00 = | 1,000.00 | 1/2 × 1,440 = 720 |
| | $2,333.33 | $1,920 |
| | or ($10,000 − $5,200) × 40% = | $1,920 |

In computing depreciation expense for partial periods, it is necessary to determine the depreciation expense for the full year and then to prorate this depreciation expense between the two periods involved. This process should continue throughout the useful life of the asset.

## Depreciation and Replacement of Fixed Assets

A common misconception about depreciation is that it provides funds for the replacement of fixed assets. Depreciation is similar to any other expense, in that it reduces net income and differs from most other expenses in that it does not involve a current cash outflow.

To illustrate why depreciation does not provide funds for replacement of plant assets, assume that a business starts operating with plant assets of $500,000, which have a useful life of five years. The company's balance sheet at the beginning of the period is:

| Plant Assets | $500,000 | | Owner's Equity | $500,000 |

Now if we assume that the enterprise earned no revenue over the five years, the income statements are:

| | Year 1 | Year 2 | Year 3 | Year 4 | Year 5 |
|---|---|---|---|---|---|
| Revenue | -0- | -0- | -0- | -0- | -0- |
| Depreciation | (100,000) | (100,000) | (100,000) | (100,000) | (100,000) |
| Loss | (100,000) | (100,000) | (100,000) | (100,000) | (100,000) |

The balance sheet at the end of the five years is:

| Plant Assets | -0- | | Owner's Equity | -0- |

This extreme illustration points out that depreciation in no way provides funds for the replacement of assets. The funds for the replacement of the assets come from the revenues; without the revenues no income materializes and no cash inflow results.

## Revision of Depreciation Rates

When a plant asset is purchased, depreciation rates are determined as accurately as possible; the necessary estimates are based on past experience with similar assets and all other pertinent information available. The provisions for depreciation are only estimates, however, and it may be necessary to revise them during the life of the asset. Unexpected physical deterioration or unforeseen obsolescence may indicate that the useful life of the asset is less than originally estimated. Improved maintenance procedures, revision of operating procedures, or similar developments may prolong the life of the asset beyond the expected period.

For example, assume that machinery costing $90,000 and originally estimated to have a life of 20 years with no salvage value at the end of that time has been used for 10 years when it is estimated that it will be used an additional 20 years. It, therefore, will have a total life of 30 years instead of 20 years. Depreciation has been recorded at the rate of 1/20 of $90,000, or $4,500 per year by the straight-line method. On the basis of a 30-year life, depreciation should have been 1/30 of $90,000, or $3,000 per year. Depreciation, therefore, has been overestimated, and net income has been less in the amount of $1,500 for each of the past 10 years, or a total amount of $15,000. The amount of the difference can be computed as shown at the top of page 538.

Changes in estimate should be handled in the current and prospective periods; that is, no changes should be made in previously reported results. Opening balances are not adjusted and no attempt is made to "catch up" for prior periods. The reason for this requirement is that changes in estimates are a continual process, an inherent part of any estimation process, and continual restatement would occur for revisions of estimates unless they are handled prospectively. Therefore, no entry is made at the time the change in esti-

|  | Per Year | For 10 Years |
|---|---|---|
| Depreciation charged per books (1/20 × $90,000) | $4,500 | $45,000 |
| Depreciation based on a 30-year life (1/30 × $90,000) | 3,000 | 30,000 |
| Excess depreciation charged | $1,500 | $15,000 |

mate occurs, and charges for depreciation in subsequent periods are based on dividing the remaining book value less any salvage value by the remaining estimated life:

| Machinery |  | $90,000 |
|---|---|---|
| Less: Accumulated depreciation |  | 45,000 |
| Book value of machinery at end of 10th year |  | $45,000 |

The entry to record depreciation for each of the remaining twenty years is:

| Depreciation Expense | 2,250 | |
|---|---|---|
| Accumulated Depreciation—Machinery | | 2,250 |
| ($45,000 ÷ 20 years) | | |

## DISCLOSURE OF PROPERTY, PLANT, AND EQUIPMENT, AND DEPRECIATION

The basis of valuation for property, plant, and equipment should be stated; it is usually historical cost. Pledges, liens, and other commitments related to these assets should be disclosed also. Any liability secured by property, plant, and equipment should not·be offset against these assets, but should be reported in the liability section. Property, plant, and equipment not currently employed as producing assets in the business, such as idle facilities and land held as an investment, should be segregated from assets being used in operations. When assets are depreciated, a valuation account normally called Accumulated Depreciation or Allowance for Depreciation results. The employment of an Accumulated Depreciation account permits the reader of the financial statements to determine the original cost of the asset and provides the reader with information concerning the amount of depreciation that has been charged to expense in past years.

In the presentation of depreciation, the following disclosures should be made in the financial statements or in notes thereto:

(a) Depreciation expense for the period.
(b) Balances of major classes of depreciable assets, by nature and function, at the balance sheet date.
(c) Accumulated depreciation, either by major classes of depreciable assets or in total, at the balance sheet date, and
(d) A general description of the method or methods used in computing depreciation with respect to major classes of depreciable assets.[7]

[7]"Omnibus Opinion—1967," *Opinions of the Accounting Principles Board No. 12* (New York: AICPA, 1967), par. 5.

The financial report of General Electric Company illustrates an acceptable disclosure (also see Tenneco's financials in Appendix D of Chapter 5).

| General Electric Company STATEMENT OF FINANCIAL POSITION (in millions) | 1981 | 1980 |
|---|---|---|
| Property, plant, and equipment—net (note 10) | $ 6,844 | $ 5,780 |

**Summary of Significant Accounting Policies**

Property, plant, and equipment—

Manufacturing plant and equipment includes the original cost of land, buildings and equipment less depreciation, which is the estimated cost consumed by wear and obsolescence. An accelerated depreciation method, based principally on a sum-of-the-years digits formula, is used to record depreciation of the original cost of manufacturing plant and equipment in the U.S. Most manufacturing plant and equipment located outside the U.S. is depreciated on a straight-line basis. If manufacturing plant and equipment is subject to abnormal economic conditions or obsolescence, additional depreciation is provided. Expenditures for maintenance and repairs of manufacturing plant and equipment are charged to operating costs as incurred.

**Notes to Financial Statements**

10. Property, plant and equipment

| (in millions) | 1981 | 1980 |
|---|---|---|
| Major classes at December 31: | | |
| Manufacturing plant and equipment | | |
| Land and improvements | $    164 | $    139 |
| Buildings, structures, and related equipment | 2,581 | 2,329 |
| Machinery and equipment | 7,121 | 6,197 |
| Leasehold costs and manufacturing plant under construction | 576 | 453 |
| Mineral property, plant, and equipment | 2,263 | 1,917 |
| | $12,705 | $11,035 |
| Cost at January 1 | $11,035 | $ 9,365 |
| Additions | 2,025 | 1,948 |
| Dispositions | (355) | (278) |
| Cost at December 31 | $12,705 | $11,035 |
| **Accumulated depreciation, depletion, and amortization** | | |
| Balance at January 1 | $ 5,255 | $ 4,752 |
| Current-year provision | 882 | 707 |
| Dispositions | (267) | (214) |
| Other changes | (9) | 10 |
| Balance at December 31 | $ 5,861 | $ 5,255 |
| **Property, plant, and equipment less depreciation, depletion, and amortization at December 31** | $ 6,844 | $ 5,780 |

Many individuals argue that the disclosure requirements are still not sufficient. For example, some accountants believe that the average useful life of the assets or the range of years for asset life is significant information that should be disclosed.[8]

[8]Charles W. Lamden, Dale L. Gerboth, and Thomas W. McRae, "Accounting for Depreciable Assets," *Accounting Research Monograph No. 1* (New York: AICPA, 1975), p. 111. Also, one

The effects of inflation on property, plant, and equipment are substantial. At one time the Commerce Department noted that if depreciation based on the replacement cost of aging assets were correctly measured, corporate net income for U.S. companies would decrease $18 billion. The FASB, recognizing the need for price-level information, now requires the disclosure of this type of information for certain companies. One such requirement is that supplementary information on income from continuing operations on a current cost basis (replacement cost) and on increases (decreases) in specific prices of property, plant, and equipment net of inflation be reported. This means (1) reporting current cost information on property, plant, and equipment and depreciation expense and (2) computing and disclosing increases (decreases) that arise from the difference between the current cost of property, plant, and equipment and its historical cost adjusted for inflation. The detailed computational aspects related to price-level information are discussed in Chapter 25.

## INVESTMENT CREDIT

In recent years, Congress has attempted to stimulate the economy by granting special tax advantages to enterprises that invest in capital assets. One special tax advantage that has occurred intermittently over the past 15 years is the investment credit. The investment credit allows a taxpayer to reduce taxes payable by an amount up to 10% of the cost of qualified depreciable property purchased. For example, suppose that an enterprise purchases an asset for $100,000 in 1984 that qualifies for the investment credit. If the company has a tax liability of $30,000 before the credit, the company's final tax liability is:

| | |
|---|---:|
| Taxes payable for 1984 prior to investment credit | $30,000 |
| Less: investment credit ($100,000 × 10%) | 10,000 |
| Final tax liability | $20,000 |

A vigorous controversy has developed within the accounting profession about how the investment credit should be reported for financial reporting purposes. Many believe that the investment credit is a government reduction in the cost of qualified property similar to a purchase discount and should be accounted for over the same period as that of the related asset (cost reduction or deferred approach). Others believe that the investment credit is a selective reduction in the taxes payable for the year of the purchase and should be handled similarly for financial reporting purposes (tax reduction or flow-through approach). The arguments for the two approaches are presented below.

### Cost Reduction or Deferral Method

Advocates for this position argue that earnings (or reduction in tax expense) do not arise from the purchase of qualified property. Instead, the use of the asset creates the benefits to be received from the investment credit. Additional support is given to this argument on the

---

writer found that variances in useful life had a greater impact on the variation among companies than the depreciation methods selected. See Robert R. Sterling, "A Test of the Uniformity Hypothesis," *Abacus* (September 1969), pp. 39–47.

basis that if the property is not kept a given number of years, part or all of the investment credit must be refunded to the government.

Another position taken is that the true cost of the asset is not the invoice cost but the invoice cost less the investment credit. Many believe that a company would not buy the property unless the credit were available, and the invoice cost of the asset should be reduced accordingly.

## Tax Reduction or Flow-Through Method

In the tax reduction method the investment credit is a selective tax reduction in the period of the purchase and, therefore, tax expense for that period should be reduced by the credit. Advocates of this approach indicate that realization of the credit is not dependent on future use of the property, and the benefits of the credit should therefore not be deferred. The investment credit is earned by the act of investment. Except for a minimum holding period, the credit is not affected by the use or nonuse, retention or nonretention, of the asset.

## Comparison of Deferral Versus Flow-Through

The example below illustrates the way the investment credit is handled under the two approaches. Kane, Inc. purchases railroad tank cars on January 1, 1984 for $100,000 that qualifies for the 10% investment credit. The tank cars have a useful life of ten years and no salvage value. The company intends to use straight-line depreciation for both book and tax purposes, and net taxable income before income taxes but after depreciation is $25,000. The tax rate is 50%. Assume that yearly revenues are $35,000 for the next ten years.

| Entries Under Cost Reduction and Tax Reduction Bases | | | | | |
|---|---|---|---|---|---|
| Cost Reduction (Deferral) | | | Tax Reduction (Flow-Through) | | |
| **At time of purchase:** | | | | | |
| Machinery | 100,000 | | Machinery | 100,000 | |
| Cash | | 100,000 | Cash | | 100,000 |
| **Recognition and Payment of Taxes:** | | | | | |
| Income Tax Expense | 12,500 | | Income Tax Expense | 2,500 | |
| Cash | | 2,500 | Cash | | 2,500 |
| Deferred Investment | | | | | |
| Credit | | 10,000 | | | |
| Deferred Investment | | | | | |
| Credit | 1,000 | | | | |
| Income Tax Expense | | 1,000 | | | |
| **Recognition of Depreciation:** | | | | | |
| Depreciation Expense | 10,000 | | Depreciation Expense | 10,000 | |
| Accumulated Depr. | | 10,000 | Accumulated Depr. | | 10,000 |
| **Annual Entries in Subsequent Periods, Assuming Taxable Income of $25,000:** | | | | | |
| Income Tax Expense | 11,500 | | Income Tax Expense | 12,500 | |
| Deferred Investment | | | Cash | | 12,500 |
| Credit | 1,000 | | | | |
| Cash | | 12,500 | | | |
| Depr. Expense | 10,000 | | Depr. Expense | 10,000 | |
| Accumulated Depr. | | 10,000 | Accumulated Depr. | | 10,000 |

*(handwritten annotation next to Income Tax Expense 1,000: (100,000 ÷ 10 yrs) × 10%)*

The effects on the income statement and the balance sheet for 1984 and the ten years combined are illustrated below.

---

**INCOME STATEMENT AND BALANCE SHEET UNDER COST REDUCTION AND TAX REDUCTION METHODS OF RECORDING INVESTMENT CREDIT**

**Income Statement**

| | 1984 | | Ten Years Combined | |
|---|---|---|---|---|
| | Cost Reduction | Tax Reduction | Cost Reduction | Tax Reduction |
| Sales | $35,000 | $35,000 | $350,000 | $350,000 |
| Depreciation expense | 10,000 | 10,000 | 100,000 | 100,000 |
| Income before income taxes | 25,000 | 25,000 | 250,000 | 250,000 |
| Income taxes | 11,500 | 2,500 | 115,000 | 115,000 |
| Net income | $13,500 | $22,500 | $135,000 | $135,000 |

**Balance Sheet**

| | 1984 | | At End of Ten Years | |
|---|---|---|---|---|
| | Cost Reduction | Tax Reduction | Cost Reduction | Tax Reduction |
| Machinery | $100,000 | $100,000 | $100,000 | $100,000 |
| Accumulated depreciation | (10,000) | (10,000) | (100,000) | (100,000) |
| | $ 90,000 | $ 90,000 | -0- | -0- |
| Deferred investment credit (liability) | $ 9,000 | -0- | -0- | -0- |

---

Given a choice, most companies prefer the tax reduction or flow-through method for financial reporting purposes because the earnings in the year of the purchase of qualified property can be substantially increased.[9] Currently either method is acceptable for financial reporting purposes. The APB attempted to resolve the controversy but was unsuccessful. In 1962, the APB issued *Opinion No. 2,* "Accounting for the Investment Credit," which permitted only the cost reduction method to be used.[10] Such strong resistance to this Opinion resulted that *APB Opinion No. 4* (amended No. 2), "Accounting for the Investment Credit," was issued. *Opinion No. 4* indicated that the cost reduction method was the preferred approach but that the tax reduction method could be used.[11]

In 1971 the APB considered the matter again, but the question became academic when the Treasury Department, with the support of Congress, included a provision in tax legisla-

---

[9] *Accounting Trends and Techniques—1981* reports that 88% of the companies surveyed used the flow-through method. As indicated earlier, in our discussion on selection of depreciation methods, higher earnings resulting from accounting changes that are merely cosmetic may decrease the stock price rather than increase it.

[10] "Accounting for the Investment Credit," *Opinions of the Accounting Principles Board No. 2* (New York: AICPA, 1962).

[11] "Accounting for the Investment Credit," *Opinions of the Accounting Principles Board No. 4* (Amended No. 2) (New York: AICPA, 1964).

tion that no taxpayer is required to use any particular method of accounting for the credit in reports subject to the jurisdiction of any federal agency. This pronouncement permits complete flexibility in accounting for the investment credit.

The accounting profession is concerned about this legislation because the establishment of accounting principles for financial reports to investors has been largely the responsibility of the accounting profession and the Securities and Exchange Commission. This action by Congress is paradoxical and one that is particularly disconcerting because Congress and others have complained about the numerous alternatives existing in financial reporting, yet they have chosen to continue one themselves.

# DEPLETION

Natural resources, often called wasting assets, include petroleum, minerals, and timber. Natural resources are characterized by two main features: (1) the complete removal (consumption) of the asset, and (2) replacement of the asset only by an act of nature. Unlike plant and equipment, natural resources are consumed physically over the period of use and do not maintain their physical characteristics. For the most part, the accounting problems associated with natural resources are similar to those encountered in the plant asset area. The questions to be answered are:

1. How is the cost basis for write-off (depletion) established?
2. What pattern of allocation should be employed?

## Establishment of Depletion Base

How do we determine the proper cost for an oil well? Rather large expenditures are needed to find these natural resources, and for every successful discovery there are many "dry holes." Furthermore, long delays are encountered between the time the costs are initially incurred and the benefits are obtained from the extracted resources. As a result, a conservative policy frequently is adopted in accounting for the expenditures incurred in finding and extracting natural resources.

The **costs of natural resources** can be divided into three categories: (1) acquisition cost of deposit, (2) exploration costs, and (3) development costs. The **acquisition cost of the deposit** is the price paid to obtain the property right to search and find an undiscovered natural resource or the price paid for an already discovered resource. In some cases, property is leased and special royalty payments paid to the lessor if a productive natural resource is found and is commercially profitable. Generally, the acquisition cost is placed in an account titled Undeveloped Property and assigned to the natural resource if exploration efforts are successful. If they are unsuccessful, the cost is written off as a loss.

As soon as the enterprise has the right to use the property, considerable **exploration costs** are entailed in finding the resource. The accounting treatment for these costs varies: some firms expense all exploration costs; others capitalize only those costs that are directly related to successful projects (**successful efforts approach**); and others adopt a **full-cost approach** (capitalization of all costs whether related to successful or unsuccessful projects).

Conceptually, the question is whether the unsuccessful exploration costs are a cost of those that are successful. At first glance, the full-cost approach appears to have much validity, but at present most companies have not adopted it. The prevalent practice is to capitalize all exploration costs that result in the discovery of profitable natural resources and to expense all other costs. The large international oil companies such as Exxon, Mobil, and Gulf use such an approach. Full-cost accounting is used by most of the smaller, exploration-oriented companies. The differences in net income figures under the two methods can be staggering. For example, until Texaco switched to the successful efforts approach in 1975, it was estimated that full-cost accounting increased Texaco's reported profits by $500 million over a ten-year period.

Proponents of the full-cost concept believe that unsuccessful ventures are a cost of those that are successful, because the cost of drilling a dry hole is a cost that is needed to find the commercially profitable wells. Those who believe that only the costs of successful projects should be capitalized contend that the unsuccessful companies will end up capitalizing many costs that will make an unsuccessful company over a short period of time show no less income than does one that is successful. In addition, it is contended that to measure accurately cost and effort for a single property unit, the only measure is in terms of the cost directly related to that unit. The remainder of the costs should be allocated as period charges similar to such period costs as advertising, which at present are not assigned to inventory.

The final costs that are incurred in finding natural resources are **development costs,** which are classified in two ways: (1) tangible equipment, and (2) intangible development costs. Tangible equipment includes all of the transportation and other heavy equipment necessary to extract the resource and get it ready for production or shipment. **Tangible equipment costs are normally not considered in the depletion base;** instead, separate depreciation charges are employed because the asset can be moved from one drilling or mining site to another. Depreciation expense is, therefore, based on a service life relevant to its total usefulness. Tangible assets that cannot be moved should be depreciated over their useful life or the life of the resource, whichever is shorter. **Intangible development costs, on the other hand, are considered part of the depletion base.** These costs are for such items as the drilling costs, tunnels, shafts, and wells, which have no tangible characteristics, but are needed for the production of the natural resource.

## Write-off of Resource Cost

As soon as the depletion base is established, the next problem is determining how the natural resource cost should be allocated to accounting periods. Normally, depletion is computed on the unit of production method (activity approach), which means that depletion is a function of the number of units withdrawn during the period. In adopting this approach, the total cost of the natural resource is divided by the number of units estimated to be in the resource deposit to obtain a cost per unit of product. This cost per unit is multiplied by the number of units extracted to compute the depletion.

For example, MaClede Oil Co. has acquired the right to use 1,000 acres of land in northern Texas to explore for oil. The lease cost is $50,000; the related exploration costs for a discovered oil deposit on the property are $100,000; and intangible development costs incurred in erecting and drilling the well are $850,000. Total costs related to the oil deposit before the first gallon is extracted are, therefore, $1,000,000. It is estimated that the well will provide approximately 1,000,000 barrels of oil. The depletion rate established is computed in the following manner:

$$\frac{\text{Total cost}}{\text{Total estimated units available}} = \text{Depletion charge per unit}$$

$$\frac{\$1,000,000}{1,000,000} = \$1.00 \text{ per barrel}$$

If 250,000 barrels are withdrawn in the first year, then the depletion charge for the year is $250,000 (250,000 barrels at $1.00). The entry to record the depletion is:

| | | |
|---|---|---|
| Depletion Expense | 250,000 | |
| Accumulated Depletion | | 250,000 |

In some instances an Accumulated Depletion account is not used, and the credit goes directly to the natural resources asset account. In the income statement the depletion cost is part of the cost of producing the product. The balance sheet presents the cost of the property and the amount of depletion entered to date as follows:

| | | |
|---|---|---|
| Oil deposit (at cost) | $1,000,000 | |
| Less accumulated depletion | 250,000 | $750,000 |

The tangible equipment used in extracting the oil may also be depreciated on a unit of production basis, especially if the estimated lives of the equipment can be directly assigned to one given resource deposit. If the equipment is utilized in more than one job, other cost allocation methods such as straight-line or accelerated depreciation methods would be more appropriate.

## Controversy Concerning Oil and Gas Accounting

As indicated, either the successful efforts approach or the full costing approach is permitted in accounting for costs in the oil and gas industry. The FASB has attempted to narrow the available accounting alternatives but has met with little success. In 1977, the FASB issued *Statement No. 19,* which would have required oil and gas companies to follow a form of successful efforts accounting.[12] However, as soon as this standard was issued, the smaller oil and gas producers voiced strong objections and lobbied extensively in Congress for relief from this type of accounting. As a result, governmental agencies assessed the implications of *FASB Statement No. 19* from a public interest standpoint and reacted contrary to the FASB's position. For example, the Department of Energy indicated that companies now using the full cost method would reduce their exploration activities because of the unfavorable earnings impact associated with successful efforts accounting. The Justice Department asked the SEC to postpone adoption of one uniform method of accounting in the oil and gas industry until the SEC could determine whether the information reported to investors would be enhanced and whether competition would be constrained by adoption of the successful efforts method.

[12]"Financial Accounting and Reporting by Oil and Gas Producing Companies," *FASB Statement No. 19* (Stamford, Conn.: FASB, 1977).

In response, the SEC in 1978 issued three pronouncements on the subject of oil and gas accounting in which it first adopted the form of successful efforts approach recommended by *FASB Statement No. 19,* then adopted a unique form of full costing, and ultimately stated that it found both successful efforts and full cost accounting inadequate because neither reflects the economic substance of oil and gas exploration in a meaningful way.[13] As a substitute, the SEC argued in favor of a yet-to-be developed method, **Reserve Recognition Accounting (RRA),** which it believed would provide more useful information. As a result of SEC action in this area, in 1979 the FASB issued *Statement No. 25,* which suspended *FASB Statement No. 19,* except for certain disclosure provisions.[14]

Under RRA, as soon as a company discovers oil, its value is reported on the balance sheet and in the income statement. Thus, RRA is a current value approach as opposed to full costing and successful efforts, which are historical cost approaches. To illustrate the differences in these methods, assume that Allied Oil Company has spent $2,000,000 on each of two oil fields. On the one field Allied discovers oil; the other is a dry hole. Under successful efforts accounting, the $2,000,000 associated with the producing well is capitalized, while the $2,000,000 related to the dry hole is expensed. Under full costing, the entire $4,000,000 is capitalized and amortized over the life of the reserves because the cost of the unsuccessful wells is considered a cost of the successful wells. Once RRA is in effect, the fair value of the reserves will have to be determined and reported as assets. If the value of the oil reserve is $15,000,000, an asset ("oil deposits") is reported on the balance sheet at $15,000,000. On the income statement, income of $11,000,000 ($15,000,000 − $4,000,000) would be reported.

The use of RRA would make a substantial difference in the balance sheets and income statements of oil companies. For example, Atlantic Richfield Co. at one time reported net producing property of $2.6 billion. If RRA were adopted, the same properties would be valued at $11.8 billion. Similarly, Standard Oil of Ohio, which reported net producing properties of $1.7 billion, would have reported approximately $10.7 billion under RRA.

Conceptually there is merit for writing the asset upward, particularly where a significant disparity exists. For example, assume that $50,000 was paid for land on which an oil deposit worth $10 million is discovered. Should the oil deposit not be reported or at least disclosed in the financial statements? In the past, the accounting treatment has ranged from complete silence to actual reporting in the financial statements. However, **there are numerous practical problems, in estimating (1) the amount of the reserves, (2) the future production costs, (3) the periods of expected disposal, (4) the discount rate, and (5) the selling price.** An estimate for each of these elements is necessary to arrive at an accurate valuation of the existing oil or gas reserve. If the oil or gas reserve is not to be extracted and sold for several years, estimating the future selling price, the appropriate discount rate, and the future costs of extraction and delivery can each be a formidable task.

In 1982, the SEC announced that it had abandoned RRA as a potential accounting method in the primary financial statements of oil and gas producers. Because of the inher-

[13]"Adoption of Requirements for Financial Accounting and Reporting Practices for Oil and Gas Producing Activities," *Accounting Series Release No. 253* (Washington, D.C.: SEC, August 1978); "Requirements for Financial Accounting and Reporting Practices for Oil and Gas Producing Activities," *Accounting Series Release No. 257* (Washington, D.C.: SEC, December 1978); and "Oil and Gas Producers—Full Cost Accounting Practices," *Accounting Series Release No. 258* (Washington, D.C.: SEC, 1978).

[14]"Suspension of Certain Accounting Requirements for Oil and Gas Producing Companies," *Statement of Financial Accounting Standards No. 25* (Stamford, Conn.: FASB, 1979).

ent uncertainty of determining recoverable quantities of proved oil and gas reserves, the SEC indicated that RRA does not currently possess the required degree of reliability for use as a primary method of financial reporting. However, the SEC continued to stress that some form of value-based disclosure is needed for oil and gas reserves, and it encouraged the FASB to develop a comprehensive package of disclosures for oil and gas producers.

What will become the accepted accounting method for the oil and gas industry is difficult to predict. Either the full-cost approach or the successful efforts approach is currently acceptable. It appears that some form of value-based disclosure of oil and gas reserves eventually will be required. It does seem ironic that it was Congress that mandated the FASB to develop one method of accounting for the oil and gas industry, and when the FASB did so, the government chose not to accept it. Subsequently, the government (SEC) attempted to develop a new approach, failed, and now wishes the FASB to develop the disclosure requirements in this area. As a result, alternatives still exist in the oil and gas industry.

These events in the oil and gas industry provide a number of lessons to the student in accounting. First, this controversy (and for that matter the investment credit situation) demonstrates the strong influence that federal agencies have in financial reporting matters. Second, the concern for economic consequences places considerable pressure on the FASB to weigh the economic effects of any required standard. Third, the experience with RRA highlights the problems that are encountered when a change from a historical cost to a current value approach is proposed. Fourth, this controversy illustrates the difficulty of establishing standards when affected groups have differing viewpoints. And finally, it reinforces the need for a conceptual framework with carefully developed guidelines for recognition, measurement, and reporting, so that issues of this nature may be more easily resolved in the future.

## Special Problems in Depletion Accounting

Accounting for natural resources has some interesting problems that are uncommon to most other types of assets. For purposes of discussion we have divided these problems into four categories:

1. Difficulty of estimating recoverable reserves.
2. Problems of discovery value.
3. Tax aspects of natural resources.
4. Accounting for liquidating dividends.

**Estimating Recoverable Reserves**  Not infrequently the estimate of recoverable reserves has to be changed either because new information has become available or because production processes have become more sophisticated.

Natural resources such as oil and gas deposits and some rare metals have recently provided the greatest challenges. Estimates of these reserves are in large measure "knowledgeable guesses." And these estimates change frequently in today's environment where marginal projects are undertaken because of price escalations.

This problem is the same as that faced in accounting for changes in estimates of the useful lives of plant and equipment. The procedure is to revise the depletion rate on a prospective basis by dividing the remaining cost by the estimate of the new recoverable reserves. This approach has much merit in this field because the required estimates are quite tenuous.

**Discovery Value** Discovery value accounting and reserve recognition accounting are essentially similar. RRA is specifically related to the oil and gas industry, whereas discovery value is a broader term associated with the whole natural resources area. As indicated earlier, general practice has not recognized discovery values in the general ledger accounts. If discovery value is recorded, an asset account would be debited and usually an Unrealized Appreciation account would be credited. Unrealized Appreciation is part of stockholders' equity. Unrealized Appreciation would then be transferred to revenue as the natural resources are sold.

A similar problem arises with resources such as growing timber, aging liquor, and maturing livestock that increase in value over time. One method is to record the increase in value as the accretion occurs as a debit to the asset account and as a credit to revenue or to an unrealized revenue account. These increases can be substantial. For example, Boise Cascade's timber resources were recently valued at $1.7 billion, whereas its book value was approximately $289 million. Accountants have been hesitant to record these increases because of the uncertainty regarding the final sales price and the problem of estimating the costs involved in getting the resources ready for sale.

**Tax Aspects of Natural Resources** The tax aspects of accounting for most natural resources have comprised some of the most controversial provisions of the Internal Revenue Code (IRC). The tax law has long provided a deduction for the greater of **cost** or **percentage** depletion against income from oil, gas, and most minerals. The percentage or statutory depletion allows a write-off ranging from 5% to 22% (depending on the natural resource) as a percentage of gross revenue received instead of as a percentage of cost. As a result, the amount of depletion may exceed the investment cost that is assigned to a given natural resource. For example, the asset may have a zero valuation, but a depletion deduction may be taken if the enterprise has gross revenue, subject to certain constraints. The significance of the percentage depletion allowance is now greatly reduced because it has been repealed for most oil and gas companies and is of only limited use in most other situations.

Note that the taxpayer may use the cost-depletion method for tax purposes if it is more favorable. For tax purposes the cost-depletion method does not have to coincide with the cost depletion taken for financial reporting purposes. For example, the IRC permits expensing certain intangible development costs that are capitalized for financial reporting purposes.[15]

**Liquidating Dividend** A company often owns as its only major asset a certain property from which it intends to extract natural resources. If the company does not expect to purchase additional properties, it distributes gradually to stockholders their capital investments by paying dividends equal to the amount of accumulated net income (after depletion) plus the amount of depletion charged. The major accounting problem is to distinguish between dividends that are a return of capital and those that are not. The company in issuing a liquidating dividend should debit Additional Paid-in Capital for that portion related to the original investment instead of Retained Earnings, because the dividend is a return of part of the investor's original contribution.

---

[15]The FASB has recently issued a standard requiring certain tax allocation procedures in such circumstances. "Accounting for Income Taxes—Oil and Gas Producing Companies," *Statement of the Financial Accounting Standards Board No. 9* (Stamford, Conn.: FASB, 1975).

## Financial Reporting of Depletion

The reporting of natural resources in a balance sheet is similar to the reporting for other assets. The following classification might be adopted:

| Properties and mineral rights | |
| --- | --- |
| Undeveloped mineral properties and rights | $xxx |
| Producing mineral properties and rights, less accumulated depletion of xxx | xxx |

Some companies do not record depletion because the number of recoverable units is considered not determinable with enough certainty to avoid distortions. In addition, it is argued that as long as resources are being discovered, there is no need for depletion. This approach has no validity in theory and should not be condoned.

In the oil and gas industry, required disclosure includes the classification and amount of costs incurred for property acquisition, exploration, development, and production. The method of accounting for these costs (successful efforts or full costing) should also be disclosed. A controversy surrounds the disclosure related to recoverable reserves. Because the most important component in assessing the future profitability of an oil and gas enterprise is its recoverable reserves, many argue that this information should be provided. Others contend that determination of these reserves is so difficult that presentation in the financial statements will only lead to confusion and distortion. *FASB Statement No. 25,* issued in 1979, recommends that the disclosure of reserve data be made **outside** the financial statements. This insures its presentation without the necessity of incurring substantive costs in obtaining independent verification of this information. As indicated earlier, the FASB is now reevaluating all the disclosures related to this industry, so that some form of value-based disclosure may be mandated.

The following excerpt from notes to financial statements taken from the 1981 annual report of NICOR Inc. illustrates the typical disclosures about oil and gas operations that are being made to investors and stockholders.

| NICOR Inc. | | | |
| --- | --- | --- | --- |
| **Oil and Gas Operations** | | | |
| The following tables summarize information concerning investment in and operation of the Company's nonutility oil and gas explorations activities: | | | |
| | | **December 31** | |
| | **1981** | 1980 | 1979 |
| | | (Millions) | |
| Capitalized costs of oil and gas properties | | | |
| Proved properties and equipment | $200.5 | $132.3 | $ 79.3 |
| Unproved properties[a] | 240.9 | 177.2 | 98.9 |
| | 441.4 | 309.5 | 178.2 |
| Accumulated depreciation and depletion | 68.5 | 34.2 | 20.8 |
| | $372.9 | $275.3 | $157.4 |

| Costs incurred in oil and gas producing activities | | | |
|---|---|---|---|
| Lease acquisition | $ 33.3 | $ 34.6 | $ 21.7 |
| Exploration | 99.8 | 54.8 | 40.4 |
| Development | 47.3 | 44.7 | 13.2 |
| Production | 13.2 | 7.1 | 3.3 |
| | $193.6 | $141.2 | $ 78.6 |
| Results of oil and gas producing activities | | | |
| Revenues | $ 68.7 | $ 35.1 | $ 16.3 |
| Production costs | 13.2 | 7.1 | 3.3 |
| Net revenues | $ 55.5 | $ 28.0 | $ 13.0 |
| Depreciation and depletion expense | $ 34.2 | $ 15.7 | $  9.4 |

[a]Unproved properties of $111 million are not being amortized as significant costs will be incurred prior to ascertaining the quantities of proved reserves attributable to the properties. These costs represent acquisition, exploration and development expenditures primarily in the Western United States. Amortization of these properties is expected to begin in 1982-1985 as the necessary geological information is obtained through additional drilling and development activities.

## QUESTIONS

1. Identify the factors that are relevant in determining the annual depreciation and explain whether these factors are determined objectively or whether they are based on judgment.

2. Distinguish between depreciation, depletion, and amortization.

3. The plant manager of a manufacturing firm suggested in a conference of the company's executives that accountants should speed up depreciation on the machinery in the finishing department because improvements were rapidly making those machines obsolcte, and a depreciation fund big enough to cover their replacement is needed. Discuss the accounting concept of depreciation and the effect on a business concern of the depreciation recorded for plant assets, paying particular attention to the issues raised by the plant manager.

4. What basic questions must be answered before the amount of the depreciation charge can be computed?

5. For what reasons are plant assets retired? Define inadequacy, supersession, and obsolescence.

6. Porter Company purchased machinery for $120,000 on January 1, 1983. It is estimated that the machinery will have a useful life of 20 years, scrap value of $16,000, production of 84,000 units, and working hours of 42,000. During 1983 the company uses the machinery for 14,300 hours, and the machinery produces 20,000 units. Compute depreciation under the straight-line, units-of-output, working-hours, sum-of-the-years'-digits, and declining-balance (use 10% as the annual rate) methods.

7. What are the major factors considered in determining what depreciation method to use?

8. What is an accelerated cost recovery system (ACRS)? Speculate as to why this system is now required.

9. It has been suggested that plant and equipment could be replaced more quickly if depreciation rates for income tax and accounting purposes were substantially increased. As a result, business operations would receive the benefit of more modern and more efficient plant facilities. Discuss the merits of this proposition.

10. A building that was purchased December 31, 1958, for $600,000 was originally estimated to have a life of 50 years with no salvage value at the end of that time. Depreciation has been recorded through 1982. During 1982 an examination of the building by an engineering firm discloses that its estimated useful life is 15 years after 1982. What should be the amount of depreciation for 1983?

11. Discuss the accounting justification for recording on the books (a) plant assets received as a gift and (b) their depreciation or depletion.

12. Under what conditions is it appropriate for a concern to use the retirement method of depreciation for plant assets? What are the advantages of this method?

13. If a business that uses the retirement method sells for $12,000 plant assets originally costing $30,000 five years ago, what entry should be made? The assets sold consist of 500 small motors, which usually last about seven years.

14. Under what conditions is it appropriate for a business to use the composite method of depreciation for its plant assets? What are the advantages and disadvantages of this method?

15. If a concern uses the composite method and its composite rate is 7.5% per year, what entry should it make when plant assets that originally cost $40,000 and have been used for 10 years are sold for $10,000?

16. List (a) the similarities and (b) the differences in the accounting treatments of depreciation and cost depletion.

17. Describe cost depletion and percentage depletion. Why is the percentage depletion method permitted?

18. In what way may the use of percentage depletion violate sound accounting theory?

19. In the extractive industries, businesses may pay dividends in excess of net income. What is the maximum permissible? How can this practice be justified?

20. Neither depreciation on replacement cost nor depreciation adjusted for changes in the purchasing power of the dollar has been recognized as generally accepted accounting practice for inclusion in the primary financial statements. Briefly present the accounting treatment that might be used to assist in the maintenance of the ability of a company to replace its productive capacity.

21. Recently the following statement appeared in a financial magazine: "RRA—or Rah-Rah, as it's sometimes dubbed—has kicked up quite a storm. Oil companies, for example, are convinced that the approach is misleading. Major accounting firms agree." What is RRA? Why might oil companies believe that this approach is misleading?

22. What are some lessons that might be learned from the current controversy concerning the proper accounting for oil and gas properties?

## CASES

**C12-1** Presented below are three different and unrelated situations involving depreciation accounting. Answer the question(s) at the end of each case situation.

### Situation I

The Rockwell Company manufactures electrical appliances, most of which are used in homes. Company engineers have designed a new type of blender which, through the use of a few attachments, will perform more functions than any blender currently on the market. Demand for the new blender can be projected with reasonable probability. In order to make the blenders, Rockwell needs a specialized machine that is not available from outside sources. It has been decided to make such a machine in Rockwell's own plant.

**Instructions**

(a) Discuss the effect of projected demand in units for the new blenders (which may be steady, decreasing, or increasing) on the determination of a depreciation method for the machine.

(b) What other matters should be considered in determining the depreciation method? Ignore income tax considerations. *useful life, salvage value*

### Situation II

Western Paper Company, a subsidiary of Northern Paper Company, operates a 300-ton-per-day kraft pulp mill and four sawmills in Wisconsin. The company is in the process of expanding its pulp mill facilities to a capacity of 1,000 tons per day and plans to replace three of its older, less efficient sawmills with an expanded facility. One of the mills to be replaced did not operate for most of 1983 (current year), and there are no plans to reopen it before the new sawmill facility becomes operational.

In reviewing the depreciation rates and in discussing the residual values of the sawmills that were to be replaced, it was noted that if present depreciation rates were not adjusted, substantial amounts of plant costs on these three mills would not be depreciated by the time the new mill came on stream.

**Instructions**

What is the proper accounting for the four sawmills at the end of 1983?

*Situation III*

Recently, Nevada Company experienced a strike that affected a number of its operating plants. The controller of this company indicated that it was not appropriate to report depreciation expense during this period because the equipment did not depreciate and an improper matching of costs and revenues would result. He based his position on the following points:

1. It is inappropriate to charge the period with costs for which there are no related revenues arising from production.

2. The basic factor of depreciation in this instance is wear and tear, and because equipment was idle no wear and tear occurred.

**Instructions**

Comment on the appropriateness of the controller's comments.

C12-2  Benjamin Manufacturing Company was organized January 1, 1984. During 1984, it has used in its reports to management the straight-line method of depreciating its plant assets.

On November 8 you are having a conference with Benjamin's officers to discuss the depreciation method to be used for income tax and stockholder reporting. The president of Benjamin has suggested the use of a new method, which he feels is more suitable than the straight-line method for the needs of the company during the period of rapid expansion of production and capacity that he foresees. Following is an example in which the proposed method is applied to a fixed asset with an original cost of $62,000, an estimated useful life of 5 years, and a scrap value of approximately $2,000.

| Year | Years of Life Used | Fraction Rate | Depreciation Expense | Accumulated Depreciation at End of Year | Book Value at End of Year |
|------|-----|------|--------|--------|--------|
| 1 | 1 | 1/15 | $ 4,000 | $ 4,000 | $58,000 |
| 2 | 2 | 2/15 | 8,000 | 12,000 | 50,000 |
| 3 | 3 | 3/15 | 12,000 | 24,000 | 38,000 |
| 4 | 4 | 4/15 | 16,000 | 40,000 | 22,000 |
| 5 | 5 | 5/15 | 20,000 | 60,000 | 2,000 |

The president favors the new method because he has heard that

1. It will increase the funds recovered during the years near the end of the assets' useful lives when maintenance and replacement disbursements are high.

2. It will result in increased write-offs in later years and thereby will reduce taxes.

**Instructions**

(a) What is the purpose of accounting for depreciation?

(b) Is the president's proposal within the scope of generally accepted accounting principles? In making your decision discuss the circumstances, if any, under which use of the method would be reasonable and those, if any, under which it would not be reasonable.

(c) The president wants your advice.
    1. Do depreciation charges recover or create funds? Explain.

2. Assume that the Internal Revenue Service accepts the proposed depreciation method in this case. If the proposed method were used for stockholder and tax reporting purposes, how would it affect the availability of funds generated by operations?

**C12-3** The certified public accountant is frequently called upon by management for advice regarding methods of computing depreciation. Of comparable importance, although it arises less frequently, is the question of whether the depreciation method should be based on consideration of the assets as units, as a group, or as having a composite life.

**Instructions**

(a) Briefly describe the depreciation methods based on treating assets as:
 1. Units.  2. A group or as having a composite life.
(b) Present the arguments for and against the use of each of the two methods.
(c) Describe how retirements are recorded under each of the two methods.

(AICPA adapted)

**C12-4** Recently, the following comments appeared in the financial press:

"RRA goes too far too fast. It leads to a high degree of imprecision and uncertainty in the income statement and balance sheet."

"Companies using full-cost tend to show higher earnings and accumulate assets faster than do companies using the successful-efforts approach."

"Congress put the problem to the SEC, which put it to the FASB, which solved it in a way the SEC didn't like. So the SEC came up with its own oil and gas industry accounting rules."

**Instructions**

(a) What is meant by the terms RRA, full-cost, and successful-efforts accounting?
(b) Why might RRA lead to imprecision and uncertainty?
(c) Why do companies show higher earnings and accumulate assets faster under full-cost accounting than under successful efforts accounting?
(d) Should Congress be directly involved in the establishment of accounting principles?

# EXERCISES

**E12-1** The Bedrock Oil Company purchased equipment for $204,000 on October 1, 1982. It is estimated that the equipment will have a useful life of 10 years and a salvage value of $6,000. Estimated production is 40,000 units and estimated working hours 60,000. During 1982 the Bedrock Oil Company uses the equipment for 2,500 hours and the equipment produces 2,000 units.

**Instructions**

Compute depreciation expense under each of the following methods. Bedrock Oil is on a calendar-year basis ending December 31.
(a) Straight-line method for 1982.
(b) Activity method (units of output) for 1982.
(c) Activity method (working hours) for 1982.
(d) Sum-of-the-years'-digits method for 1984.
(e) Double-declining balance method for 1983.

**E12-2** Kitefly Corp. purchased machinery for $112,000 on July 1, 1983. It is estimated that it will have a useful life of 10 years, scrap value of $8,000, production of 273,000 units, and working hours of 63,000. During 1984 the Kitefly Corp. uses the machinery for 7,150 hours, and the machinery produces 32,300 units.

**Instructions**

From the information given on the following page, compute the depreciation charge for 1984 under each of the following methods (round to three decimal places):

(a) Straight-line.  (d) Sum-of-the-years'-digits.
(b) Units of output.  (e) Declining-balance
(c) Working hours.  (use 20% as the annual rate).

**E12-3** Keenguy Corporation purchased a new machine for its assembly process on October 1, 1983. The cost of this machine was $111,600. The company estimated that the machine would have a trade-in value of $3,600 at the end of its service life. Its life is estimated at 5 years and its working hours are estimated at 20,000 hours. Year-end is December 31.

**Instructions**

Compute the depreciation expense under the following methods: (1) straight-line depreciation for 1983, (2) activity method for 1983, assuming that machine usage was 800 hours, (3) sum-of-the-years'-digits for 1984, and (4) double-declining balance for 1984. Each of the foregoing should be considered unrelated.

**E12-4** The Robotron Company shows the following entries in its Equipment account for 1984; all amounts are based on historical cost.

Equipment

| 1984 | | | 1984 | | |
|------|------|------|------|------|------|
| Jan. 1 | Balance | 80,000 | June 30 | Cost of equipment sold | |
| Aug. 10 | Purchases | 20,000 | | (purchased prior | |
| 12 | Freight on equipment | | | to 1984) | 8,000 |
| | purchased | 320 | | | |
| 25 | Installation costs | 800 | | | |
| Nov. 10 | Repairs | 500 | | | |

**Instructions**

(a) Prepare any correcting entries necessary.
(b) Assuming that depreciation is to be charged for a full year on the ending balance in the asset account, compute the proper depreciation charge for 1984 under each of the methods listed below. Assume an estimated life of 10 years, with no salvage value. The machinery included in the January 1, 1984, balance was purchased in 1982.
    1. Straight line.
    2. Sum-of-the-years'-digits.
    3. Declining balance (assume twice the straight-line rate).

**E12-5** Tall Tree Lumber Company owns a 5,000-acre tract of timber purchased in 1975 at a cost of $1,000 per acre. At the time of purchase the land was estimated to have a value of $150 per acre without the timber. Tall Tree Lumber Company has not logged this tract since it was purchased. In 1983, Tall Tree had the timber cruised. The cruise (appraiser) estimated that each acre contained 10,000 board feet of timber. In 1984, Tall Tree built 10 miles of roads at a cost of $5,000 per mile. After the roads were completed, Tall Tree logged 4,000 trees containing 1,000,000 board feet.

**Instructions**

(a) Determine the depletion expense for 1984.
(b) If Tall Tree depreciates the logging roads on the basis of timber cut, determine the depreciation expense for 1984.
(c) If Tall Tree plants five seedlings at a cost of $3 per seedling for each tree cut, how should Tall Tree treat the reforestation?

**E12-6** Elmira Timber Company owns 10,000 acres of timberland purchased in 1970 at a cost of $1,500 per acre. At the time of purchase the land without the timber was valued at $500 per acre. In 1971, Elmira built fire lanes and roads, with a life of 30 years, at a cost of $60,000. Every year Elmira sprays to prevent disease at a cost of $2,000 per year and spends $5,000 to maintain the fire lanes and roads. During 1972 Elmira selectively logged 500,000 board feet of timber, of the estimated 2,500,000 board feet. In 1973, Elmira planted new seedlings to replace the trees cut at a cost of $100,000.

**Instructions**

(a) Determine the depreciation expense and depletion expense for 1972.

(b) Elmira has not logged since 1972. If Elmira logged 1,000,000 board feet of timber in 1984, when the timber cruise (appraiser) estimated 5,000,000 board feet, determine the depletion expense for 1984.

**E12–7** On April 10, 1984, the Astro Company sells equipment that it purchased for $120,000 on September 25, 1970. It was originally estimated that the equipment would have a life of 15 years and a scrap value of $12,000 at the end of that time, and depreciation has been computed on that basis. The company uses the straight-line method of depreciation.

  1. Depreciation is computed for the exact period of time during which the asset is owned. (Use 365 days for base.)

  2. Depreciation is computed for the full year on the January 1 balance in the asset account.

  3. Depreciation is computed for the full year on the December 31 balance in the asset account.

  4. Depreciation for one-half year is charged on plant assets acquired or disposed of during the year.

  5. Depreciation is computed on additions from the beginning of the month following acquisition and on disposals to the beginning of the month following disposal.

  6. Depreciation is computed for a full period on all assets in use for over one-half year, and no depreciation is charged on assets in use for less than one-half year. (Use 365 days for base.)

**Instructions**

(a) Compute the depreciation charge on this equipment for 1970, for 1984, and the total charge for the period from 1970 to 1984, inclusive, under each of the six assumptions above with respect to partial periods.

(b) Briefly evaluate the methods above, considering them from the point of view of basic accounting theory as well as simplicity of application.

**E12–8** Lazy Rocker Corporation bought a machine on June 1, 1981, for $12,200, f.o.b. the place of manufacture. Freight to the point where it was set up was $200, and $250 was expended to install it. The machine's useful life was estimated at 10 years, with a scrap value of $50. In June, 1982, an essential part of the machine is replaced, at a cost of $1,500, with one designed to reduce the cost of operating the machine. On June 1, 1985, the company buys a new machine of greater capacity for $18,000, delivered, being allowed a trade-in value on the old machine of $2,000. To prepare the old machine for removal from the plant cost $75, and expenditures to install the new one were $225. It is estimated that the new machine has a useful life of 10 years, with a scrap value of $200 at the end of that time.

**Instructions**

Assuming that depreciation is to be computed on the straight-line basis, prepare schedules showing the amount of depreciation on this equipment that should be provided during the year beginning June 1, 1985. (Round to the nearest dollar.)

**E12–9** Presented below is information related to the Roxanne Corporation:

| Asset | Cost | Estimated Scrap | Estimated Life (in years) |
|-------|------|-----------------|---------------------------|
| A | $30,000 | $3,000 | 9 |
| B | 32,000 | 4,000 | 8 |
| C | 12,000 | 2,000 | 8 |
| D | 20,000 | 3,000 | 10 |
| E | 4,000 | 500 | 7 |

**Instructions**

(a) Compute the rate of depreciation per year to be applied to the plant assets under the composite method.

(b) Prepare the adjusting entry necessary at the end of the year to record depreciation for the year.

(c) Prepare the entry to record the sale of fixed asset C for cash of $5,000. It was used for six years, and depreciation was entered under the composite method.

**E12–10**  In 1984, Marlon Energy Co. replaced 23,000 utility poles at a cost of $100 each. The old poles originally cost $75 apiece.

**Instructions**

(a) Prepare the entry(ies) assuming that Marlon Energy Co. uses the retirement method for depreciating their utility poles.

(b) Prepare the entry(ies) assuming that Marlon Energy Co. uses the replacement method for depreciating their utility poles.

**E12–11**  Waubonsee Company decides to use the retirement method in accounting for house meters that it installs, because they are of small value and replaced frequently. The life of the meters is from 1 to 15 years, with the average life about 12 years.

Below are the transactions related to the house meters for 1984.

Jan. 10, 1984    Purchases 15,000 meters at $400 each.
Apr. 15, 1984    Discards 20 of the meters purchased January 10, 1984, as worthless.
June 20, 1984    Sells 50 of the meters purchased January 10, 1984, for $500.
Dec. 12, 1984    Replaces 750 meters at $420 each.

**Instructions**

Using the retirement method, prepare entries to record the transactions for 1984.

**E12–12**  Algonquin Manufacturing Company has approximately 3,000 hand tools, which it uses in its operations. Each is of relatively small value and is frequently replaced. The total cost of such tools is approximately $24,000.

Because of the characteristics of this asset, the company prefers not to keep detailed records of each tool and depreciate it. You are asked to suggest some reasonably simple method of accounting for these tools so that the asset is carried at a fair amount and operating expenses are charged with a fair amount. What do you suggest?

**Instructions**

Illustrate your suggestion with pro forma entries for the various types of transactions that might occur.

**E12–13**  Machinery purchased for $54,000 was originally estimated to have a life of 8 years with a salvage value of $6,000 at the end of that time. Depreciation has been entered for 6 years on this basis. In 1984, it is determined that the total estimated life (including 1984) should be 12 years with a salvage value of $7,500 at the end of that time. Assume straight-line depreciation.

**Instructions**

(a) Prepare the entry to correct the prior years' depreciation, if necessary.

(b) Prepare the entry to record depreciation for 1984.

**E12–14**  In 1954, Apache Company completed the construction of a building at a cost of $1,860,000 and first occupied it in January, 1955. It is estimated that the building will have a useful life of 50 years, and a salvage value of $60,000 at the end of that time.

Early in 1965, an addition to the building was constructed at a cost of $276,000. At that time it was estimated that the remaining life of the building would be, as originally estimated, an additional 40 years, and that the addition would have a life of 40 years, and a salvage value of $6,000.

In 1985, it is determined that the probable life of the building will extend to the end of 2014, or 10 years beyond the original estimate.

**Instructions**

(a) Compute the annual depreciation that would have been charged from 1955 to 1964.
(b) Compute the annual depreciation that would have been charged from 1965 to 1984.
(c) Prepare the entry, if necessary, to adjust the account balances because of the revision of the estimated life in 1985.
(d) Compute the annual depreciation to be charged beginning with 1985.

**E12–15** Comanche Company constructed a building at a cost of $1,500,000 and occupied it beginning in January, 1964. It was estimated at that time that its life would be 40 years, with no salvage value.

In January, 1984, a new roof was installed at a cost of $180,000, and it was estimated then that the building would have a useful life of 30 years from that date. The cost of the old roof was $90,000.

**Instructions**

(a) What amount of depreciation should have been charged annually from the years 1964 to 1983? (Assume straight-line depreciation.)
(b) What entry should be made in 1984 to record the replacement of the roof?
(c) Prepare the entry in January, 1984, to record the revision in the estimated life of the building, if necessary.
(d) What amount of depreciation should be charged for the year 1984?

**E12–16** Arapaho, Inc. bought a number of machines at a total cost of $90,000 during 1984. All of them qualify for the 10% investment credit. Arapaho, Inc. had income before taxes of $600,000 (tax rate 40%).

**Instructions**

(a) Prepare the entry(ies) required at December 31, 1984 to account for the investment credit. Assume that the cost reduction (deferral) method is used and that the credit is amortized over a six-year life.
(b) Prepare the entry(ies) at December 31, 1984 for the investment credit if the tax reduction (flow-through) method is used by Arapaho, Inc.

**E12–17** Chippewa, Inc. purchased machinery and equipment during 1984 amounting to $189,000, and all of these acquisitions qualify for the investment credit. Chippewa, Inc. has decided to record the investment credit in a deferred income account and amortize it over the productive life of the acquired property (seven years). The company's income before taxes was $500,000 (tax rate 45%). Assume a 10% rate for the investment credit.

**Instructions**

(a) Prepare the entry(ies) required at December 31, 1984, to account for the income tax expense and investment credit, assuming that a full year's amortization is taken in the first year.
(b) Prepare the entry(ies) required at December 31, 1984, to account for the income tax expense and investment credit, assuming that the tax reduction (flow-through) method was used.
(c) How would the journal entries under these two approaches be different in future periods?

**E12–18** You are the assistant controller for Kickapoo & Associates. On January 1, 1984, Kickapoo purchased heavy machinery with an estimated service life of 20 years. The machinery cost $400,000. This machinery qualified for a 10% investment credit. The controller believed that the cost reduction (deferral) method would be the most appropriate method for handling this transaction. Accordingly, the following entry was made:

| Jan. 1 | Machinery | 360,000 | |
| | Reserve for Investment Credit | 40,000 | |
| | Accounts Payable | | 400,000 |

Income tax expense for the year prior to any allowable credits was correctly determined to be $112,000. The controller therefore made the following entry on December 31, 1984:

| Dec. 31 | Income Tax Expense | 72,000 | |
| | Deferred Investment Credit | 40,000 | |
| | Income Taxes Payable | | 72,000 |
| | Reserve for Investment Credit | | 40,000 |

The controller, however, is unsure of the entries above and asks your opinion. Amortize investment credit over 20 years.

**Instructions**

If you believe that the cost reduction method has not been applied correctly, prepare the entry(ies) that will correct the books and bring them into proper adjustment for 1984. (Ignore any depreciation considerations.)

**E12–19** Iroquois Drilling Company has leased property on which oil has been discovered. Wells on this property produced 8,000 barrels of oil during the past year that sold at an average sales price of $30.60 per barrel. Total oil resources of this property are estimated to be 100,000 barrels.

The lease provided for an outright payment of $800,000 to the lessor before drilling could be commenced and an annual rental of $10,000. A premium of 6% of the sales price of every barrel of oil removed is to be paid annually to the lessor. In addition, the lessee is to clean up all the waste and debris from drilling and to bear the costs of reconditioning the land for farming when the wells are abandoned. It is estimated that this clean-up and reconditioning will cost no more than $6,000.

**Instructions**

From the provisions of the lease agreement, you are to compute the cost per barrel, exclusive of operating costs, to the Iroquois Drilling Company. (Round to three decimal places.)

**E12–20** Montana Mining Company purchased land on February 1, 1983, at a cost of $900,000. It estimated that a total of 66,000 tons of mineral was available for mining. After it has removed all the natural resources, the company will be required to restore the property to its previous state because of strict environmental protection laws. It estimates the cost of this restoration at $40,000. It believes it will be able to sell the property afterwards for $50,000. It incurred developmental costs of $100,000 before it was able to do any mining. In 1983, resources removed totaled 15,000 tons. It sold 10,000 tons.

**Instructions**

Compute the following information for 1983: (1) per unit material cost; (2) total material cost of 12/31/83 inventory; and (3) total material cost in cost of goods sold at 12/31/83.

# PROBLEMS

**P12–1** On January 1, 1981, Pueblo Company, a small machine-tool manufacturer, acquired for $1,500,000 a piece of new industrial equipment. The new equipment was eligible for the investment tax credit and Pueblo took full advantage of the credit and accounted for the amount using the flow-through method. The new equipment had a useful life of 5 years and the salvage value was estimated to be $150,000. Pueblo estimates that the new equipment can produce 10,000 machine tools in its first year. It estimates that production will decline by 1,000 units per year over the remaining useful life of the equipment.

The following depreciation methods may be used:

| | |
| --- | --- |
| Double-declining balance | Sum-of-the-years'-digits |
| Straight-line | Units-of-output |

**Instructions**

(a) Which depreciation method would maximize net income for financial statement reporting for the three-year period ending December 31, 1983? Prepare a schedule showing the amount of accumulated depreciation at December 31, 1983, under the method selected. Ignore present value, income tax, and deferred income tax considerations.

(b) Which depreciation method would minimize net income for income tax reporting for the three-year period ending December 31, 1983? Prepare a schedule showing the amount of accumulated depreciation at December 31, 1983, under the method selected. Ignore present value considerations.

(AICPA adapted)

**P12-2** The cost of equipment purchased by Potawatomi, Inc. on April 1, 1983 is $58,000. It is estimated that the machine will have a $2,000 salvage value at the end of its service life. Its service life is estimated at eight years; its total working hours are estimated at 32,000 and its total production is estimated at 480,000 units. During 1983, the machine was operated 3,000 hours and produced 46,000 units. During 1984, the machine was operated 4,000 hours and produced 62,000 units. (Round per hour and unit costs to three decimal places.)

**Instructions**

Compute depreciation expense on the machine for the year ending December 31, 1983, and the year ending December 31, 1984, using the following methods: (1) Straight-line; (2) units-of-output; (3) working hours; (4) sum-of-the-years'-digits; and (5) declining balance (twice the straight-line rate).

**P12-3** Navajo & Mohawk, Inc. purchased Machine #201 on April 1, 1983. The following information relating to Machine #201 was gathered at the end of April.

| | |
|---|---:|
| Price | $89,700 |
| Credit terms | 2/10, n/30 |
| Freight-in costs | $ 2,400 |
| Preparation and installation costs | $ 7,800 |
| Labor costs during regular production operations | $ 9,600 |

It was expected that the machine could be used for 10 years, after which the salvage value would be zero. Navajo & Mohawk, Inc. intends to use the machine for only 8 years, however, after which it expects to be able to sell it for $9,600. The invoice for Machine #201 was paid April 5, 1983. Navajo & Mohawk uses the calendar year as the basis for the preparation of financial statements.

**Instructions**

(a) Compute the depreciation expense for the years indicated using the following methods. (Round to the nearest cent.)
1. Straight-line method for 1983.
2. Sum-of-the-years'-digits method for 1984.
3. Double-declining balance method for 1983.

(b) Suppose the president of Navajo & Mohawk, Inc. tells you that because the company is a new organization, she expects it will be several years before production and sales are at optimum levels. She asks you to recommend a depreciation method that will allocate less of the company's depreciation expense to the early years and more to later years of the assets' lives. What method would you recommend?

**P12-4** The following data relate to the Plant Asset account of Pastrami Company at December 31, 1983:

| | | Plant Asset | | |
|---|---|---|---|---|
| | A | B | C | D |
| Original cost | $30,000 | $30,000 | $60,000 | $100,000 |
| Year purchased | 1978 | 1979 | 1980 | 1982 |
| Useful life | 10 years | 15,000 hours | 10 years | 40 years |

|  | Plant Asset | | | |
|---|---|---|---|---|
|  | A | B | C | D |
| Salvage value | $ 4,975 | $ 3,000 | $ 4,000 | $ 10,000 |
| Depreciation method | Sum-of-the-years'-digits | Activity | Straight-line | Double-declining balance |
| Accum. Depr. through 1983[a] | $18,200 | $20,000 | $16,800 | $ 5,000 |

[a]In the year an asset is purchased, Pastrami Company does not record any depreciation expense on the asset. In the year an asset is retired or traded in, Pastrimi Company takes a full year's depreciation on the asset.

The following transactions occurred during 1984:

(a) On May 5, Asset A was sold for $22,500 cash. The company's bookkeeper recorded this retirement in the following manner in the cash receipts journal:

| Cash | 22,500 | |
|---|---|---|
| Asset A | | 22,500 |

(b) On December 31, it was determined that Asset B had been used 3,000 hours during 1984.

(c) On December 31, before computing depreciation expense on Asset C, the management of Pastrami Company decided the useful life remaining from 1/1/84 was 10 years.

(d) On December 31, it was discovered that a plant asset purchased in 1983 had been expensed completely in that year. This asset cost $14,000 and has a useful life of 10 years and no salvage value. Management has decided to use the double-declining balance method for this asset, which can be referred to as "Asset E."

**Instructions**

Prepare the necessary correcting entries for the year 1984. Record the appropriate depreciation expense on the above-mentioned assets.

**P12–5** A depreciation schedule for semitrucks of the Sioux Manufacturing Company was requested by your auditor soon after December 31, 1984, showing the additions, retirements, depreciation, and other data affecting the taxable income of the company in the four-year period 1981 to 1984, inclusive. The following data were ascertained:

| Balance of Semitrucks account, Jan. 1, 1981: | |
|---|---|
| Truck No. 1 purchased Jan. 1, 1978, cost | $12,000 |
| Truck No. 2 purchased July 1, 1978, cost | 10,800 |
| Truck No. 3 purchased Jan. 1, 1980, cost | 7,200 |
| Truck No. 4 purchased July 1, 1980, cost | 6,000 |
| Balance, Jan. 1, 1981 | $36,000 |

The Semitrucks-Accumulated Depreciation account previously adjusted to January 1, 1981, and duly entered in the ledger, had a balance on that date of $14,640 (depreciation on the four trucks from the respective dates of purchase, based on a 5-year life). No charges had been made against the account before January 1, 1981.

Transactions between January 1, 1981, and December 31, 1984, and their record in the ledger were as follows:

July 1, 1981   Truck No. 3 was traded for a larger one (No. 5), the agreed purchase price of which was $9,600. The Sioux Mfg. Co. paid the automobile dealer $4,680 cash on the transaction. The entry was a debit to Semitrucks and a credit to Cash, $4,680.

Jan. 1, 1982   Truck No. 1 was sold for $3,600 cash; entry debited Cash and credited Semitrucks, $3,600.

July 1, 1983   Truck No. 4 was damaged in a wreck to such an extent that it was sold as junk for $300 cash. Sioux Mfg. Co. received $1,800 from the insurance company.

The entry made by the bookkeeper was a debit to Cash, $2,100, and credits to Miscellaneous Income, $300, and Semitrucks, $1,800.

July 1, 1983   A new truck (No. 6) was acquired for $7,200 cash and was charged at that amount to the Semitrucks account. (Assume truck No. 2 was not retired.)

Entries for depreciation had been made at the close of each year as follows: 1981, $7,200; 1982, $6,456; 1983, $6,456; 1984, $7,476.

**Instructions**

(a) For each of the four years compute separately the increase or decrease in net income arising from the company's errors in determining or entering depreciation or in recording transactions affecting trucks, ignoring income tax considerations.

(b) Prepare one compound journal entry as of December 31, 1984, for adjustment of the Semitrucks account to reflect the correct balances as revealed by your schedule, assuming that the books have not been closed for 1984.

**P12-6** The Pawnee Tool Company records depreciation annually at the end of the year. Its policy is to take a full year's depreciation on all assets used throughout the year and depreciation for one-half a year on all machines acquired or disposed of during the year. The depreciation rate for the machinery is 10% applied on a straight-line basis, with no estimated scrap value.

The balance of the Machinery account at the beginning of 1984 was $135,420; the Accumulated Depreciation on Machinery account had a balance of $51,240. The following transactions affecting the machinery accounts took place during the year.

Jan. 15   Machine No. 38, which cost $6,540 when acquired June 3, 1976, was retired and sold as scrap metal for $108.

Feb. 27   Machine No. 81 was purchased. The fair market value of this machine was $10,320. It replaces Machines No. 12 and No. 27, which were traded in on the new machine. Machine No. 12 was acquired Feb. 4, 1971, at a cost of $3,600 and is still carried in the accounts although fully depreciated and not in use; Machine No. 27 was acquired June 11, 1976, at a cost of $3,000. In addition to these two used machines, $9,240 was paid in cash. (Assume exchange of similar assets.)

Apr.  7   Machine No. 54 was equipped with electric control equipment at a cost of $420. This machine, originally equipped with simple hand controls, was purchased Dec. 11, 1980, for $1,080. The new electric controls can be attached to any one of several machines in the shop.

    12   Machine No. 24 was repaired at a cost of $660 after a fire caused by a short circuit in the wiring burned out the motor and damaged certain essential parts.

July 22   Machines No. 25, 26, and 41 are sold for $2,500 cash. The purchase dates and cost of these machines are:

|        |        |              |
|--------|--------|--------------|
| No. 25 | $2,800 | May 8, 1975  |
| No. 26 | 2,800  | May 8, 1975  |
| No. 41 | 3,600  | June 1, 1979 |

Nov. 17   Rearrangement and reinstallation of several machines to facilitate material handling and to speed up production are completed at a cost of $16,400.

**Instructions**

(a) Record each transaction in general journal entry form.

(b) Compute and record depreciation for the year. No machines now included in the balance of the account were acquired before Jan. 1, 1975.

**P12-7** The Phillips Logging and Lumber Company owns 2,000 acres of timberland on the north side of Mount St. Helens, which was purchased in 1965 at a cost of $500 per acre. In 1980, Phillips began selectively logging this timber tract. In May of 1980, Mt. St. Helens erupted, burying the timberland of Phillips under a foot of ash. All of the timber on the Phillips tract was downed. In addition, the logging roads, built at a cost of $100,000, were destroyed, as well as the logging equipment, with a net book value of $250,000.

At the time of the eruption, Phillips had logged 20% of the estimated 400,000 board feet of timber. Prior to the eruption, Phillips estimated the land to have a value of $200 per acre after the timber was harvested. Phillips depreciates logging roads on the basis of timber harvested.

Phillips estimates it will take three years to salvage the downed timber at a cost of $800,000. The timber can be sold for pulp wood at an estimated price of $3 per board foot. The value of the land is unknown, but until it will grow vegetation again, which scientists say may be as long as fifty to one hundred years, the value is nominal.

**Instructions**

(a) Determine the depletion expense per board foot for the timber harvested prior to the eruption of Mt. St. Helens.
(b) Prepare the journal entry to record the depletion expense prior to the eruption.
(c) If this tract represents approximately half of the timber holdings of Phillips, determine the amount of the estimated loss and show how the losses of roads, machinery, and timber and the salvage of the timber should be reported in the financial statements of Phillips for the year ended December 31, 1980.

**P12-8** The Mohican Mining Company has purchased a tract of mineral land for $420,000. It is estimated that this tract will yield 100,000 tons of ore with sufficient mineral content to make mining and processing profitable. It is further estimated that 5,000 tons of ore will be mined the first year and 10,000 tons each year thereafter. The land will have no residual value.

The company builds necessary structures and sheds on the site at a cost of $24,000. It is estimated that these structures can serve 15 years but, because they must be dismantled if they are to be moved, they have no scrap value. The company does not intend to use the buildings elsewhere. Mining machinery installed at the mine was purchased second-hand at a cost of $36,000. This machinery cost the former owner $38,000 and was 40% depreciated when purchased. The Mohican Mining Company estimates that about half of this machinery will still be useful when the present mineral resources have been exhausted but that dismantling and removal costs will just about offset its value at that time. The company does not intend to use the machinery elsewhere. The remaining machinery will last until about one-half the present estimated mineral ore has been removed and will then be worthless. Cost is to be allocated equally between these two classes of machinery.

**Instructions**

(a) As chief accountant for the company, you are to prepare a schedule showing estimated depletion and depreciation costs for each year of the expected life of the mine.
(b) Also draft entries in general journal entry form to record depreciation and depletion for the first year assuming actual production of 5,300 tons. Nothing occurred during the year to cause the company engineers to change their estimates of either the mineral resources or the life of the structures and equipment.

**P12-9** Ottawa Corporation, a manufacturer of steel products, began operations on October 1, 1982. The accounting department of Ottawa has started the fixed-asset and depreciation schedule presented below. You have been asked to assist in completing this schedule. In addition to ascertaining that the data already on the schedule are correct, you have obtained the following information from the company's records and personnel:

1. Depreciation is computed from the first of the month of acquisition to the first of the month of disposition.

2. Land A and Building A were acquired from a predecessor corporation. Ottawa paid $812,500 for the land and building together. At the time of acquisition, the land had an appraised value of $75,000, and the building had an appraised value of $900,000.

3. Land B was acquired on October 2, 1982, in exchange for 3,000 newly issued shares of Ottawa's common stock. At the date of acquisition, the stock had a par value of $5 per share and a fair value of $30 per share. During October 1982, Ottawa paid $10,400 to demolish an existing building on this land so it could construct a new building.

4. Construction of Building B on the newly acquired land began on October 1, 1983. By September 30, 1984, Ottawa had paid $210,000 of the estimated total construction costs of $300,000. It is estimated that the building will be completed and occupied by July, 1985.

5. Certain equipment was donated to the corporation by a local university. An independent appraisal of the equipment when donated placed the fair value at $20,000 and the salvage value at $2,000.

6. Machinery A's total cost of $110,000 includes installation expense of $550 and normal repairs and maintenance of $10,450. Salvage value is estimated as $5,500. Machinery A was sold on February 1, 1984.

7. On October 1, 1983, Machinery B was acquired with a down payment of $6,000 and the remaining payments to be made in 11 annual installments of $5,000 each beginning October 1, 1983. The prevailing interest rate was 8%. The following data were abstracted from present-value tables (rounded):

| Present value of $1.00 at 8% | | Present value of an ordinary annuity of $1.00 at 8% | |
| --- | --- | --- | --- |
| 10 years | .463 | 10 years | 6.710 |
| 11 years | .429 | 11 years | 7.139 |
| 15 years | .315 | 15 years | 8.559 |

Ottawa Corporation
FIXED ASSET AND DEPRECIATION SCHEDULE
For Fiscal Years Ended September 30, 1983, and September 30, 1984

| Assets | Acquisition Date | Cost | Salvage | Depreciation Method | Estimated Life in Years | Depreciation Expense Year Ended September 30 | |
| --- | --- | --- | --- | --- | --- | --- | --- |
| | | | | | | 1983 | 1984 |
| Land A | October 1, 1982 | $ (1) | N/A | N/A | N/A | N/A | N/A |
| Building A | October 1, 1982 | (2) | $50,000 | Straight-Line | (3) | $17,500 | (4) |
| Land B | October 2, 1982 | (5) | N/A | N/A | N/A | N/A | N/A |
| Building B | Under Construction | 210,000 to date | — | Straight-Line | 30 | — | (6) |
| Donated Equipment | October 2, 1982 | (7) | 2,000 | 150% Declining Balance | 10 | (8) | (9) |
| Machinery A | October 2, 1982 | (10) | 5,500 | Sum-of-the-Years'-Digits | 10 | (11) | (12) |
| Machinery B | October 1, 1983 | (13) | — | Straight-Line | 25 | — | (14) |

N/A—Not applicable

## Instructions

For each numbered item on the foregoing schedule, supply the correct amount. Round each answer to the nearest dollar.

(AICPA adapted)

**P12–10** You are engaged in the examination of the financial statements of the Erie Corporation for the year ended December 31, 1984. The schedules below for the property, plant and equipment, and related accumulated depreciation accounts have been prepared by the client. You have checked the opening balances to your prior year's audit workpapers.

Your examination reveals the following information:

1. All equipment is depreciated on the straight-line basis (no salvage value taken into consideration) using the following estimated lives: buildings, 25 years; all other items, 10 years. The company's policy is to take one-half year's depreciation on all asset acquisitions and disposals during the year.

2. On May 1, the company entered into a 10-year lease contract for a die-casting machine with annual rentals of $5,000 payable in advance every May 1. The lease can be canceled by either party (60 days written notice is required) and there is no option to renew the lease or buy the equipment at the end of the lease. The estimated useful life of the machine is 10 years with no salvage value. The company recorded the die-casting machine in the Machinery and Equipment account at $40,400, the present discounted value at the date of the lease, and $2,020, applicable to the machine, has been included in depreciation expense for the year. (**Hint:** leases with these conditions should not be capitalized nor should a liability be recognized.)

3. The company completed the construction of a wing on the plant building on June 30. The useful life of the building was not extended by this addition. The lowest construction bid received was $17,500, the amount recorded in the Buildings account. Company personnel were used to construct the addition at a cost of $16,500 (materials, $7,500; labor, $6,000; and overhead, $3,000).

4. On August 18, $10,000 was paid for paving and fencing a portion of land owned by the company and used as a parking lot for employees. The expenditure was charged to the Land account.

5. The amount shown in the machinery and equipment asset retirement column represents cash received on September 5 upon disposal of a machine purchased in July, 1980, for $50,000. The bookkeeper recorded depreciation expense of $3,700 on this machine in 1984.

6. Indiana City donated land and building appraised at $10,000 and $50,000, respectively, to the Erie Corporation for a plant. On September 1, the company began operating the plant. Because no costs were involved, the bookkeeper made no entry to record the transaction.

---

Erie Corp.
ANALYSIS OF PROPERTY, PLANT AND EQUIPMENT, AND
RELATED ACCUMULATED DEPRECIATION ACCOUNTS
Year Ended December 31, 1984

**Assets**

| Description | Final 12/31/83 | Additions | Retirements | Per Books 12/31/84 |
|---|---|---|---|---|
| Land | $ 32,500 | $10,000 | | $ 42,500 |
| Buildings | 120,000 | 17,500 | | 137,500 |
| Machinery and equipment | 385,000 | 40,400 | $26,000 | 399,400 |
| | $537,500 | $67,900 | $26,000 | $579,400 |

**Accumulated Depreciation**

| Description | Final 12/31/83 | Additions[a] | Retirements | Per Books 12/31/84 |
|---|---|---|---|---|
| Buildings | $ 60,000 | $ 5,150 | | $ 65,150 |
| Machinery and equipment | 173,250 | 39,220 | | 212,470 |
| | $233,250 | $44,370 | | $277,620 |

[a]Depreciation expense for the year.

**Instructions**

Prepare the formal journal entries that you would suggest at December 31, 1984, to adjust the accounts for the transactions noted above. Disregard income tax implications. The books have not been closed. Computations should be rounded off to the nearest dollar.

(AICPA adapted)

# CHAPTER 13

# Intangible Assets

Intangible assets are generally characterized by a lack of physical existence, and a high degree of uncertainty concerning future benefits. These criteria are not so clear-cut as they may seem. The following discussion by a well-noted accountant typifies some of the major problems encountered in attempting to define intangibles.

> **Q.** I infer, Mr. May, from your experience . . . that you know what in ordinary speech the word tangible means, don't you?
>
> **A.** Yes.
>
> **Q.** Well, what do you understand it to mean in ordinary speech?
>
> **A.** Something that can be touched, I imagine.
>
> **Q.** Like merchandise?
>
> **A.** Yes.
>
> **Q.** You can touch merchandise or horses?
>
> **A.** Yes.
>
> **Q.** Can you touch an account receivable?
>
> **A.** You can touch the debtor.
>
> **Q.** Is that the basis on which you include the debtor's debt as tangible?
>
> **A.** It had not occurred to me before, but possibly it is.[1]

This discussion indicates that the lack of physical existence is not by itself a satisfactory criterion for distinguishing a tangible from an intangible asset. Such assets as bank deposits, accounts receivable, and long-term investments lack physical substance, yet accountants classify them as tangible assets.

Some accountants believe that the major characteristic of an intangible asset is the high degree of uncertainty concerning the future benefits that are to be received from its employment. For example, many intangibles (1) have value only to a given enterprise, (2) have indeterminate lives, and (3) are subject to large fluctuations in value because their

---

[1] From testimony given to referee, *In the Matter of the Estate of E. P. Hatch Deceased (1912).* Reprinted in Bishop Carleton Hunt, ed., *Twenty-five Years of Accounting Responsibility,* 1911–1936 (New York: Price Waterhouse and Company, 1936), I, p. 246. Selected essays and discussions of George O. May.

benefits are based on a competitive advantage. The determination and timing of future benefits are extremely difficult and pose serious valuation problems. Tangible assets possess similar characteristics but they are not so pronounced.

Other accountants, finding the problem of defining intangibles insurmountable, prefer simply to present them in financial statements on the basis of tradition. The more common types of intangibles are patents, copyrights, franchises, goodwill, organization costs, and trademarks or trade names. These intangibles may be further subdivided on the basis of the following characteristics.

1. **IDENTIFIABILITY.** Separately identifiable or lacking specific identification.
2. **MANNER OF ACQUISITION.** Acquired singly, in groups, or in business combinations, or developed internally.
3. **EXPECTED PERIOD OF BENEFIT.** Limited by law or contract, related to human or economic factors, or indefinite or indeterminate duration.
4. **SEPARABILITY FROM AN ENTIRE ENTERPRISE.** Rights transferable without title, salable, or inseparable from the enterprise or a substantial part of it.[2]

## VALUATION OF PURCHASED INTANGIBLES

Intangibles, like tangible assets, are **recorded at cost.** Cost includes all costs of acquisition and expenditures necessary to make the intangible asset ready for its intended use. These costs are normally purchase price, legal fees, and other incidental expenses incurred in obtaining the asset.

If intangibles are acquired for stock or in exchange for other assets, **the cost of the intangible is the fair market value of the consideration given or the fair market value of the intangible received, whichever is more clearly evident.** Sometimes both the value of what is given and the value of what is received are difficult to estimate: at this point, exercise of professional judgment is required to establish an appropriate valuation. Essentially the accounting treatment closely parallels that followed for tangible assets. For example, when several intangibles, or a combination of intangibles and tangibles, are bought in a "basket purchase," the cost should be allocated on the basis of fair market values or on the basis of relative sales values.

The profession has resisted employment of some other basis of valuation, such as current replacement costs or appraisal value for these types of assets. The basic attributes of intangibles, their uncertainty as to future benefits, and their uniqueness, have discouraged valuation in excess of cost.[3]

## AMORTIZATION OF INTANGIBLE ASSETS

Intangible assets should be amortized by systematic charges to expense over their useful lives. *APB Opinion No. 17* enumerates the factors that might be considered in determining useful life.

[2]"Intangible Assets," *Opinions of the Accounting Principles Board No. 17* (New York: AICPA, 1970), par. 10.

[3]For example, Sprouse and Moonitz in *AICPA Accounting Research Study No. 3,* "A Tentative Set of Broad Accounting Principles for a Business Enterprise," advocate abandonment of historical cost in favor of replacement cost for most asset items, but suggest that intangibles should normally be carried at acquisition cost less amortization because valuation problems are so difficult.

1. Legal, regulatory, or contractual provisions may limit the maximum useful life.
2. Provisions for renewal or extension may alter a specified limit on useful life.
3. Effects of obsolescence, demand, competition, and other economic factors may reduce a useful life.
4. A useful life may parallel the service life expectancies of individuals or groups of employees.
5. Expected actions of competitors and others may restrict present competitive advantages.
6. An apparently unlimited useful life may in fact be indefinite and benefits cannot be reasonably projected.
7. An intangible asset may be a composite of many individual factors with varying effective lives.[4]

One problem relating to the amortization of intangibles is that some intangibles have indeterminable useful lives. In this case, the profession concluded that the value of an intangible asset eventually disappears and that the recorded costs of intangible assets should be amortized by systematic charges to expense over the periods estimated to be benefited. However, **intangible assets must be amortized over a period not exceeding 40 years.**[5] The 40-year requirement is based on the premise that only a few, if any, intangibles last for a lifetime. Sometimes, because it is difficult to determine useful life, a 40-year period is practical, although admittedly it is an arbitrary solution. Another reason for this 40-year limitation is simply that it ensures that companies start to write off their intangibles. There was evidence that some companies retained their intangibles (notably goodwill) indefinitely on their balance sheet for only one reason—to avoid the charge to expense that occurs when goodwill is written off.

**Intangible assets acquired from other enterprises (notably goodwill) should not be written off at acquisition.** Some accountants contend that certain intangibles should not be carried as assets on the balance sheet under any circumstances but should be written off directly to retained earnings or additional paid-in capital. The position of the profession is that the immediate write-off to retained earnings and additional paid-in capital is not acceptable because this approach denies the existence of an asset that has just been purchased.

Intangible assets are generally amortized on a straight-line basis (tax practice requires a straight-line approach), although there is no reason why another systematic approach might not be employed if the firm demonstrates that another method is more appropriate. In any case the method and period of amortization should be disclosed.

When intangible assets are amortized, the charges should be shown as expenses, reductions of income, of the years benefited, and the credits should be made either to the appropriate asset accounts or to separate accumulated amortization accounts.

## SPECIFICALLY IDENTIFIABLE INTANGIBLE ASSETS

As indicated earlier, a number of bases may be employed to differentiate one group of intangible assets from another. Originally, the accounting profession recognized two types of classification for intangibles: (a) intangibles that had a limited life and (b) intangibles that had an unlimited life.

---

[4] *APB Opinion No. 17, op. cit.,* par. 27.
[5] Ibid., par. 10.

The classification framework was subsequently changed to intangibles that are specifically identifiable, as contrasted to "goodwill type" intangible assets (unidentifiable values). **Specifically identifiable** means that costs associated with obtaining a given intangible asset can be identified as a part of the cost of that intangible asset. In contrast, **goodwill type** intangibles may create some right or privilege, but it is not specifically identifiable, it has an indeterminable life, and its cost is inherent in a continuing business. The major identifiable assets and goodwill are discussed below.

## Patents

Patents are granted by the U.S. Patent Office. A patent gives the holder exclusive right to use, manufacture, and sell a product or process **for a period of 17 years** without interference or infringement by others. If a patent is purchased from an inventor (or other owner), the purchase price represents its cost. Other costs incurred in connection with securing a patent, and attorneys' fees and other unrecovered costs of a successful legal suit to protect the patent, can be capitalized as part of the patent cost. Research and development costs related to the **development** of the product, process, or idea that is subsequently patented must be expensed as incurred, however. See pages 583–586 for a more complete presentation of accounting for research and development costs.

The cost of a patent should be amortized over its legal life or its useful life (that is, over the period benefits are received), whichever is shorter. If a patent is owned from the date it is granted, and it is expected to be useful during its entire legal life, it should be amortized over 17 years. If it appears that the patent will be useful for a shorter period of time, say, for five years, its cost should be amortized to expense over five years. Changing demand, new inventions superseding old ones, inadequacy, and other factors often limit the useful life of a patent to less than the legal life.

Legal fees and other costs incurred in successfully defending a patent suit may be charged to the Patents account because such a suit establishes the legal rights of the holder of the patent. Such costs should be amortized along with acquisition cost over the remaining useful life of the patent.

Amortization of patents may be computed on a time basis or on a basis of units produced and may be credited directly to the Patents account; it is acceptable also, although less common in practice, to credit an Accumulated Patent Amortization account. Assuming that the cost of a patent is $102,000, that it will be useful for 17 years, and that it is being amortized on a straight-line basis, the entry at the end of each year would be:

| | | |
|---|---|---|
| Patent Amortization Expense | 6,000 | |
| Patents (or Accumulated Patent Amortization) | | 6,000 |

Amortization on a units of production basis would be computed in a manner similar to that described for depreciation on property, plant, and equipment.

Royalties received from the assignment of patents to other enterprises represent revenue of the period in which the royalties are earned and should be accrued as revenue.

Although a patent's useful life should not extend beyond its legal life of 17 years, small modifications or additions may lead to a new patent. The effect may be to extend the life of the old patent, in which case it is permissible to apply the unamortized costs of the old patent to the new patent if the new patent provides essentially the same benefits. Alternatively, if a patent becomes worthless because demand drops for the product produced, the asset should be written off immediately to expense.

## Copyrights

A copyright is a federally granted right that all authors, painters, sculptors, and other artists have in their creations. A copyright is granted for the **life of the creator plus 50 years,** and gives the owner, or heirs, the exclusive right to reproduce and sell an artistic or published work. Copyrights, like patents, may be assigned or sold to other individuals. The costs of acquiring and defending a copyright may be capitalized, but the research and development costs involved must be expensed as incurred.

Generally, the useful life of the copyright is less than the legal life (life in being plus 50 years). The costs of the copyright should be allocated to the years in which the benefits are expected to be received, not to exceed 40 years. The difficulty of determining the number of years over which benefits will be received normally encourages the company to write these costs off over a fairly short period of time.

## Leaseholds

A leasehold is a contractual understanding between a lessor and a lessee that grants the lessee the right to use specific property, owned by the lessor, for a specific period of time in return for stipulated, and generally periodic, cash payments. Most lease agreements provide simply for the right of the lessee to use property of the lessor for stipulated periods. In such a case the rent is included as an expense on the books of the lessee. Special problems, however, develop in the following situations.

**Lease Prepayments**   If the rent for the period of the lease is paid in advance, of if a lump sum payment is made in advance in addition to periodic rental payments, it is necessary to allocate this prepaid rent to the proper periods. The lessee, by payment of the amount agreed upon, has purchased the exclusive right to use the property for an extended period of time. Some accountants advocate presenting this prepayment as an intangible asset; in many published financial statements, prepayments on long-term leases are classified as deferred charges.

**Capitalization of Leases**   In some cases, the lease agreement transfers substantially all of the benefits and risks incident to ownership of the property so that the economic effect on the parties is similar to that of an installment purchase. As a result, the asset value recognized when a lease is capitalized is classified as a tangible rather than an intangible asset. Such a lease is referred to as a **capital lease.** And, according to *FASB Statement No. 13,* the lessee must record a capital lease as an asset and an obligation at an amount equal to the present value of the minimum lease payments required during the lease term, excluding that portion of the payments representing executory costs such as insurance, maintenance, and taxes to be paid by the lessor.[6] Further, in such cases, it is appropriate for the lessee to depreciate the capitalized asset in a manner consistent with the lessee's normal depreciation policy for owned assets.

The FASB requires that if the lessee is party to a lease that meets one or more of the four criteria below, the lessee must classify the transaction as a capital lease and record an

---

[6]"Accounting for Leases," *Statement of Financial Accounting Standards No. 13* (Stamford, Conn.: FASB, 1976), par. 10.

asset and a liability at an amount equal to the present value of the future minimum lease payments:

1. The lease transfers ownership of the property to the lessee.
2. The lease contains a bargain purchase option.
3. The lease term (including any bargain renewal options) is equal to 75% or more of the economic life of the leased property.
4. The present value of the lease payments (excluding executory costs) equals or exceeds 90% of the fair value of the leased property.[7]

Significant provisions of material leases should be disclosed in the financial statements or in notes to the financial statements, in order that the reader may have knowledge of the financial effect of lease commitments. Chapter 22 is devoted entirely to accounting for leases.

**Leasehold Improvements** Long-term leases ordinarily provide that any improvements made to the leased property revert to the lessor at the end of the life of the lease. If the lessee constructs new buildings on leased land or reconstructs and improves existing buildings, the lessee has the right to use such facilities during the life of the lease, but they become the property of the lessor when the lease expires.

The lessee should charge the cost of the facilities to the Leasehold Improvements account and **depreciate the cost as operating expense over the remaining life of the lease, or the useful life of the improvements, whichever is shorter.** If a building with an estimated useful life of 25 years is constructed on land leased for 35 years, the cost of the building should be depreciated over 25 years. On the other hand, if the building has an estimated life of 50 years, it should be depreciated over 35 years, the life of the lease.

If the lease contains an option to renew for a period of additional years and the likelihood of renewal is too uncertain to warrant apportioning the cost over the longer period of time, the leasehold improvements are generally written off over the original term of the lease (assuming that the life of the lease is shorter than the useful life of the improvements). Leasehold improvements are generally shown in the property, plant, and equipment section, although some accountants classify them as intangible assets.

## Trademarks and Trade Names

The right to use a trademark or trade name under common law rests exclusively with the original user as long as the original user continues to use it, whether it is registered or not. The registration system provides for an indefinite number of renewals for periods of 20 years each, so a business that uses an established trademark or trade name may properly consider it to have an unlimited life. The trademark or trade name, however, must be amortized for accounting purposes over a period not to exceed 40 years.

Cost is the purchase price or, if the trademark or trade name is developed by the concern itself, cost should include attorney's fee, registration fees, design costs, and other expenditures incurred in securing it. Where the total costs of a trade name are insignificant, they are sometimes charged to expense as incurred.

[7]Ibid., par. 7.

## Organization Costs

Costs incurred in the formation of a corporation such as fees to underwriters for handling stock or bond issues, legal fees, state fees of various sorts, and promotional expenditures involving the organization of a business are classified as **organization costs.**

These items are usually charged to an account called Organization Costs and may be carried as an asset on the balance sheet as expenditures that will benefit the company over its life. Many companies amortize these costs over an arbitrary period of time (maximum 40 years), since the life of the corporation is indeterminate. Income tax regulations permit the amortization of organization costs over a period of five years or more.

It is difficult to draw a line between organization costs, normal operating expenses, and losses. Some accountants contend that **operating losses incurred in the start-up of a business** should be capitalized, since they are unavoidable and are a cost of starting a business. This approach is not sound, since this cost has no future service potential and cannot be considered an asset.

Our position that operating losses should not be capitalized during the early years is supported by the FASB in *Statement of Financial Accounting Standards No. 7,* which clarifies the accounting and reporting practices for **development stage enterprises.** The FASB concludes that the accounting practices and reporting standards should be no different for a development stage enterprise trying to establish a new business than they are for other enterprises. Except for some unique notations and disclosures, the same "generally accepted accounting principles that apply to established operating enterprises shall govern the recognition of revenue by a development stage enterprise and shall determine whether a cost incurred by a development stage enterprise is to be charged to expense when incurred or is to be capitalized or deferred."[8]

## Franchises

Franchise agreements are commonly entered into by a municipality or other governmental body and a utility or other business concern that uses public property. In such cases a privately owned enterprise is permitted to use public property in performing its services. Examples are the use of public waterways for a ferry service, the use of public land for telephone or electric lines, the use of phone lines for cable TV, or the use of city streets for a bus line. Franchises may be for a definite period of time, for an indefinite period of time, or perpetual. The company securing the franchise from the governmental unit carries a Franchise account in its records only when there are costs such as a lump sum payment in advance, or legal fees and other expenditures that are identifiable with the acquisition of the franchise. **The cost of a franchise for a limited period should be amortized as operating expense over the life of the franchise.** A franchise with an indefinite life or a perpetual franchise should be carried at cost and amortized over a reasonable period not to exceed 40 years.

If a franchise is deemed to be worthless, it should be written off immediately. For example, in 1980, Congress deregulated the trucking industry and opened to competition long-protected routes covered by franchises. Because these franchise rights were substan-

[8]"Accounting and Reporting by Development Stage Enterprises," *Statement of Financial Accounting Standards No. 7* (Stamford, Conn.: FASB, 1975), par. 10. A company is considered to be in the developing stages when its efforts are directed toward establishing a new business and either the principal operations have not started or no significant revenue has been earned.

tial, approximately 15% of the trucking industry's equity was eliminated; as a result, losses instead of profits were reported in the period of write-off.[9] For example, Roadway Express wrote off all $26.8 million worth of these assets, changing a $16.4 million profit for the quarter to a $10.4 million loss. If the present political trend toward deregulation continues, this type of situation may be encountered in other industries as well.

Annual payments made under a franchise agreement should be entered as operating expenses in the period in which they are incurred. They do not represent an asset to the concern since they do not relate to future rights to use public property.

Businesses frequently enter into similar agreements among themselves that relate to the manufacture or sale of a specific product; payments made under such agreements are properly handled as described above. Examples are the right to operate a fast food restaurant under a particular trade name (like McDonald's or Burger King) or the exclusive right to sell a particular name brand product in an area (like Omega timepieces or Sunbeam appliances).

### Property Rights

Most of the above-discussed identifiable intangibles represent **rights**—rights to use, produce, sell, or operate something. Other rights that appear to be growing in significance, and therefore in value, are water rights, mineral rights, solar and wind rights (the legal right to free flow of light and air across one's property), and other types of property rights. Although these rights have a value of their own, they are generally attached to a particular parcel of property. Therefore, the value of such property rights, if inseparable from the property, is accounted for as part of the capitalized land cost. If the right is separable from the property, as in the case of mineral rights, its cost may be capitalized separately. If minerals are later discovered or developed, the cost of the rights should be reclassified and capitalized as part of the cost of the minerals and written off as the mineral deposit is depleted.

## GOODWILL

Goodwill is undoubtedly one of the most complex and controversial assets presented in financial statements; it is often referred to as the most "intangible" of the intangibles. Goodwill is unique because unlike receivables, inventories, and patents that can be sold or exchanged individually in the marketplace, goodwill can be identified only with the business as a whole. For example, a substantial list of regular customers and an established reputation are unrecorded assets that give the enterprise a valuation greater than the sum of the fair market value of the individual identifiable assets. Numerous advantageous factors and conditions that might contribute to the value and the earning power of an enterprise can be cited; in the aggregate they represent goodwill:

| | |
|---|---|
| 1. Superior management team | 7. Outstanding credit rating |
| 2. Outstanding sales organization | 8. Top-flight training program |
| 3. Weakness in management of a competitor | 9. High standing in the community |
| 4. Effective advertising | 10. Discovery of talents or resources |
| 5. Secret process or formula | 11. Favorable tax conditions |
| 6. Good labor relations | 12. Favorable government regulation |

[9]"Accounting for Intangible Assets of Motor Carriers," *Statement of Financial Accounting Standards No. 44* (Stamford, Conn.: FASB, 1980).

**13.** Favorable association with another company

**14.** Strategic location

**15.** Unfavorable developments in the operations of a competitor[10]

**Goodwill is recorded only when an entire business is purchased because goodwill is a "going-concern" valuation and cannot be separated from the business as a whole.**[11] Goodwill generated internally should **not** be capitalized in the accounts, because measuring the components of goodwill (as listed above) is simply too complex and associating any costs with future benefits is too difficult. The future benefits of goodwill may have no relationship to the costs incurred in the development of that goodwill. To add to the mystery, goodwill may exist in the absence of specific costs to develop it. In addition, because no objective transaction with outside parties has taken place, a great deal of subjectivity might be involved, possibly even misrepresentation.

## Methods of Measuring Goodwill

The following discussion on the valuation of goodwill and of the related methods of estimation is provided not so much as the solution to an accounting problem as it is a basis for developing an acquisition price for a business enterprise. The accountant is frequently called upon to provide this information as part of the purchase negotiations.

How does one determine the value of goodwill? Conceptually, the answer is to identify the individual attributes that comprise goodwill and attempt to value them individually. This procedure is impossible at present because our measurement techniques are not sophisticated enough to measure accurately the value of a superior management team, the value of a good reputation, and so on. The methods of measuring goodwill are somewhat related to the **two basic views of the nature of goodwill:**

1. Goodwill represents intangible resources and conditions attributable to an enterprise's above-average strength in areas such as technical skill and knowledge, management, and marketing research and promotion that cannot be separately identified and valued.
2. Goodwill represents expected earnings in excess of anticipated normal earnings.[12]

One method, in accordance with the first view of goodwill, simply compares the fair market value of the net tangible and identifiable intangible assets with the bargained purchase price of the acquired business. The difference is considered goodwill, which is why goodwill is sometimes referred to as a "plug" or "gap filler" or **"master valuation"** account. **Goodwill is the residual or the excess of the cost over the fair value of the identifiable net assets acquired.**

Another view of goodwill is reflected in the second method, one that determines the earnings in excess of those that normally could be earned by the tangible and identifiable intangible assets. These excess earnings are discounted to determine the present value of this extra inflow, which is considered the amount of goodwill.

---

[10]George R. Catlett and Norman O. Olson, "Accounting for Goodwill," *Accounting Research Study No. 10* (New York: AICPA, 1968), pp. 17–18.

[11]See "Conceptual Framework for Financial Accounting and Reporting: Elements of Financial Statements and Their Measurement," *FASB Discussion Memorandum* (Stamford, Conn.: FASB, 1976), p. 235.

[12]"Accounting for Business Combinations and Purchased Intangibles," *FASB Discussion Memorandum* (Stamford, Conn.: FASB, 1976), p. 48.

## Excess of Cost over the Fair Value of Net Assets Acquired

To illustrate what is meant by the "excess of cost (purchase price) over fair value of net assets acquired (master valuation account) approach," the sequence followed in a possible merger is illustrated. Multi-Diversified, Inc. decides that it needs a parts division to supplement its existing tractor distributorship. The president of Multi-Diversified is interested in a small concern in Chicago (Tractorling Company) that has an established reputation and is seeking a merger candidate. The balance sheet of Tractorling Company is presented below.

| Tractorling Co. BALANCE SHEET as of Dec. 31, 1984 | | | |
|---|---|---|---|
| **Assets** | | **Equities** | |
| Cash | $ 25,000 | Current liabilities | $ 55,000 |
| Receivables | 35,000 | Capital stock | 100,000 |
| Inventories | 42,000 | Retained earnings | 100,000 |
| Property, plant, and equipment | 153,000 | | |
| Total assets | $255,000 | Total equities | $255,000 |

After considerable negotiation, Tractorling Company decides to accept Multi-Diversified's offer of $400,000. What then is the value of the goodwill, if any?

The answer is not quite so obvious, because the fair market values of the identifiable assets of Tractorling are not disclosed in the cost-based balance sheet above. Suppose, for example, that as the negotiations progressed, an investigation of the underlying assets of Tractorling was conducted to determine the fair market value of the assets. Such an investigation may be accomplished either through a purchase audit undertaken by Multi-Diversified's auditors in order to estimate the values of the seller's assets, or an independent appraisal from some other source. The following valuations are determined.

| FAIR MARKET VALUES | |
|---|---|
| Cash | $ 25,000 |
| Receivables | 35,000 |
| Inventories | 122,000 |
| Property, plant, and equipment | 205,000 |
| Patents | 18,000 |
| Liabilities | (55,000) |
| Fair market value of net assets | $350,000 |

Normally, differences between current fair market value and book value are more common among the long-term assets, although significant differences can also develop in the current asset category. Cash obviously poses no problems, and receivables normally are fairly close to current valuation, although at times certain adjustments need to be made because of inadequate prior provisions for uncollectible accounts. Liabilities usually are stated at their book value, although if interest rates have changed since the liabilities were incurred, a different valuation might be appropriate. Careful analysis must be made in this area to determine that no unrecorded liabilities are present.

It is not surprising to find large variances in most of the other asset areas. The difference in inventories of $80,000 ($122,000 − $42,000) could result from a number of factors, the most likely being that Tractorling Company has followed a LIFO inventory valuation. If prices have been rising for a number of years and the company is expanding, a large difference in valuation could occur. In addition, the company may not have a full cost accounting system and many of the costs of operations may not be embodied in the inventory valuation.

In many cases, the values of long-term assets such as property, plant, and equipment, and intangibles may have increased substantially over the years. This differential may be caused by inaccurate estimates of useful lives, continual expensing of small expenditures (say, less than $300), inaccurate estimates of salvage values, the discovery of some unrecorded assets, or increases in replacement cost.

Given that the fair market value of the net assets is now determined to be $350,000, how was a purchase price of $400,000 determined? Undoubtedly, the seller pointed to an established reputation, good credit rating, top management team, well-trained employees, and so on, as factors that make the value of the business greater than $350,000.[13] On the other hand, Multi-Diversified probably was attempting to assess the future earning power of these attributes as well as the basic asset structure of the enterprise today. At this point in the negotiations, price can be a function of many factors: the most important is probably sheer skill at the bargaining table. Finally, a price of $400,000 is agreed upon. The difference between the purchase price of $400,000 and the fair market value of $350,000 is labeled goodwill. Goodwill is viewed as one or a group of unidentifiable values (intangible assets) the cost of which "is measured by the difference between the cost of the group of assets or enterprise acquired and the sum of the assigned costs of individual tangible and

| DETERMINATION OF GOODWILL—MASTER VALUATION APPROACH | | |
|---|---|---|
| | Cash | $ 25,000 |
| | Receivables | 35,000 |
| | Inventories | 122,000 |
| | Property, plant, and equipment | 205,000 |
| Assigned to | Patents | 18,000 |
| purchase price | Liabilities | (55,000) |
| of $400,000 | Fair market value of net identifiable assets | $350,000 |
| | Purchase price | 400,000 |
| | Value assigned to goodwill | $ 50,000 |

[13]As another example of valuation criteria, in 1981, National Economic Research Associates of New York ranked in value "the quality of the assets" of the twenty-four U.S. based major league baseball teams: at the high end were the Detroit Tigers at $36.2 million, Philadelphia Phillies at $35.3 million, Boston Red Sox at $34.3 million; and at the low end were the Chicago Cubs and the Chicago White Sox at $20.6 million each, and the San Francisco Giants and the Oakland A's at $19 million each. Research Associates based their estimates on what the baseball franchises could be worth if they were "reasonably well managed," on the population and per-capita income of the area in which a team plays, and on the number of local professional sports franchises it competes with. Surprisingly, the valuation did not include the team's recent attendance, local radio and TV revenue, and past profits.

identifiable intangible assets acquired less liabilities assumed."[14] This procedure for valuation is referred to as a master valuation approach because goodwill is assumed to cover all the values that cannot be specifically identified with any identifiable tangible or intangible asset (see chart on page 575).

### Excess Earning Power

Conceptually, a more appealing and direct approach to valuing goodwill is to determine the total earning power that a company commands. By determining what a normal rate of return is on the tangible and identifiable intangibles in that industry, the typical earnings are computed. **The difference between what the firm earns and what is normal in the industry is referred to as the excess earning power.** This extra earning power indicates that there are unidentifiable values (intangible assets) that provide this increased earning power. Finding the value of goodwill then is a matter of discounting these excess earnings over their estimated lives.

This approach appears to be a systematic and logical way of attacking the problems for determining goodwill. Each factor necessary to compute a value under this approach is subject to question, however. Generally, the problems relate to getting answers to the following questions:

1. What is a normal rate of return?
2. How does one determine the future earnings?
3. What discount rate should be applied to the excess earnings?
4. Over what period should the excess earnings be discounted?

**Normal Rate of Return**   Determination of the normal rate of return for tangible and identifiable intangible assets means that companies similar to the enterprise in question must be analyzed. An industry average may be determined by examination of annual reports, financial services, or other related financial data. The problem with this approach is that the rate normally employed is based on the historical value of the other firms' assets, not on their fair value. Suppose, however, that a rate of 15% is decided as normal for a concern such as Tractorling. In this case, the normal earnings are calculated in the following manner.[15]

| | |
|---|---:|
| Fair market value of Tractorling's net identifiable assets | $350,000 |
| Normal rate of return | 15% |
| Normal earnings | $ 52,500 |

**Determination of Future Earnings**   The starting point for this type of analysis is normally the past earnings of the enterprise. Although estimates of future earnings are needed, the

---

[14] *APB Opinion No. 17, op. cit.,* par. 26.

[15] The fair value of Tractorling's assets (rather than historical cost) is used to compute the normal profit, because fair value is more representative of the true value of the company's assets exclusive of goodwill. To use historical cost may result in a misstatement of normal profit and an overstatement of goodwill. This illustration assumes that no significant change in assets has occurred over the past five years, that is, the current fair value of the assets approximates the average fair value for the past five years.

past often provides useful information concerning the future earnings potential of a concern. The past earnings are also useful because estimates of the future are usually overly optimistic and the hard facts of previous periods bring a sobering sense of reality to the negotiations. Generally a three- to six-year period is examined to develop past earnings data.

Tractorling's net earnings for the last five years are as follows:

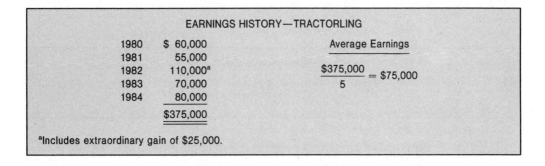

| EARNINGS HISTORY—TRACTORLING | | |
|---|---|---|
| 1980 | $ 60,000 | Average Earnings |
| 1981 | 55,000 | |
| 1982 | 110,000[a] | $\dfrac{\$375,000}{5} = \$75,000$ |
| 1983 | 70,000 | |
| 1984 | 80,000 | |
| | $375,000 | |

[a]Includes extraordinary gain of $25,000.

The average net earnings for the last five years is $75,000 or a rate of return of approximately 21.4% on the current value of the assets excluding goodwill ($75,000 ÷ $350,000). Before we go further, a question that needs answering is whether $75,000 is representative of the future earnings of this enterprise.

Often past earnings of a company to be acquired need to be adjusted because the acquirer tends to evaluate the average earnings on the basis of its own accounting procedures. Suppose, for example, that in determining earning power, Multi-Diversified measured earnings in relation to a FIFO inventory valuation figure rather than LIFO, which Tractorling employs, and that the use of LIFO reduced Tractorling's net income by $2,000 per year. In addition, Tractorling used accelerated depreciation although Multi-Diversified used a straight-line approach to estimate its earnings; the resulting earnings were lower therefore in the amount of $3,000.

Also, assets discovered on examination that might affect the earning flow should be considered. For example, the patent costs not previously recorded should be amortized, say, at the rate of $1,000 per period. Finally because the estimate of the future earnings is what we are attempting to determine, some items, like the extraordinary gain of $25,000, probably should not be considered. An analysis can now be made as follows:

| | | |
|---|---|---|
| Average net earnings per Tractorling computation | | $75,000 |
| Add | | |
| Adjustment for switch from LIFO to FIFO | $2,000 | |
| Adjustment for change from accelerated to straight-line approach | 3,000 | 5,000 |
| | | 80,000 |
| Deduct | | |
| Extraordinary gain ($25,000 ÷ 5) | 5,000 | |
| Patent amortization on straight-line basis | 1,000 | 6,000 |
| Adjusted average net earnings of Tractorling | | $74,000 |

The $74,000 is then evaluated to determine whether it represents a realistic figure for the projected earnings. Assuming that it does, the excess earnings would be determined to be $21,500, ($74,000 − $52,500).

**Choosing a Discount Rate to Apply to Excess Earnings** Determination of the discount rate is a fairly subjective estimate. The lower the discount rate, the higher the value of the goodwill. To illustrate, assume that the excess earnings are $21,500 and that these earnings will continue indefinitely. If the excess earnings are capitalized at, say, a rate of 25% in perpetuity,[16] the results are:

---

**Capitalization at 25%**

$$\frac{\text{Excess earnings}}{\text{Capitalization rate}} \quad \frac{\$21,500}{.25} = \$86,000$$

---

If the excess earnings are capitalized in perpetuity at a somewhat lower rate, say 15%, a much higher goodwill figure results.

---

**Capitalization at 15%**

$$\frac{\text{Excess earnings}}{\text{Capitalization rate}} \quad \frac{\$21,500}{.15} = \$143,333$$

---

The higher the discount rate, the lower the value of the goodwill. Normally, a rate somewhat higher than the normal rate is employed because the continuance of excess profits is uncertain. Factors that can be considered in this analysis are the stability of past earnings figures along with the speculative nature of the business. Although these factors are often difficult to crystallize into a discount rate, they do provide a basis on which a rate may be established.

**Discounting Period for Excess Earnings** Determination of the period over which the excess earnings will exist is perhaps the most difficult problem associated with computing a value for goodwill. If, for example, it is assumed that the excess earnings will last indefinitely, the superior earnings may be capitalized by the discount rate selected. If the discount rate employed is the same as the normal return (15%), then goodwill is $143,333 as computed in the previous section.

---

[16]Why do we divide by the capitalization rate to arrive at the goodwill amount? Recall that the present value of an ordinary annuity is equal to

$$P_{\overline{n}|i} = \frac{1 - \dfrac{1}{(1 + i)^n}}{i}$$

When a number is capitalized into perpetuity, $(1 + i)^n$ becomes so large that $1/(1 + i)^n$ essentially equals zero, which leaves $1/i$ or, as in the case above, $21,500/.25$.

Another method of computing goodwill that gives the same answer, using the normal return of 15%, is to discount the total average earnings of the company and subtract the fair market value of the assets as illustrated below.

| | |
|---|---|
| Average earnings capitalized at 15% in perpetuity ($74,000 ÷ 15%) | $493,333 |
| Less fair market value of assets | 350,000 |
| Present value of estimated earnings (goodwill) | $143,333 |

Frequently, however, the excess earnings are assumed to last a limited number of years, say ten, and then it is necessary to discount these earnings only over that time at a given discount rate.

To illustrate this approach, assume that Multi-Diversified believes that the excess earnings of Tractorling will last ten years and, because of the uncertainty surrounding this earning power, 25% is considered an appropriate rate of return. The present value of an annuity of $21,500 ($74,000 − $52,500) discounted at 25% for ten years is $78,941.55.[17]

## Other Methods of Valuation

Some accountants fail to discount but simply multiply the excess earnings by the number of years they believe the excess earnings will continue. This approach, often referred to as the **number of years method,** is used to provide a rough measure for what the goodwill factor should be. The approach has only the advantage of simplicity; it is sounder to recognize the discount factor.

An even simpler method is one that relies on the prices, as multiples of most recent annual earnings, that are paid for other companies in the same industry as the company to be purchased. For example, if Skyward Airlines was recently acquired for five times its average yearly earnings of $50 million, or $250 million, than Worldwide Airways, a close competitor, with $80 million in average yearly earnings would be worth $400 million. The method is simple but not very useful in those cases where historical precedents are unenlightening.

Another method (somewhat similar to discounting excess earnings) is the **discounted free cash flow method,** which involves a projection of the acquired company's free cash flow over a long period, typically ten or twenty years. The method first projects into the future a dozen or so important financial variables, including production, prices, noncash expenses (such as depreciation and amortization), taxes, and capital outlays, all adjusted for inflation. The objective is to determine the amount of cash that will accumulate over a specified number of years. The present value of the free cash flows is then computed which represents the price to be paid for the business.[18] For a simple example, if Buggert Company is expected to accumulate cash at $1 million a year for twenty years, and the buyer's rate-of-return objective is 15%, the buyer would be willing to pay about $6.26 million for Buggert

---

[17]The present value of an annuity of one dollar received in a steady stream for 10 years in the future discounted at 25% is 3.6717, (3.6717 × $21,500 = $78,941.55).

[18]Tim Metz, "Deciding How Much a Company Is Worth Often Depends on Whose Side You're On," *The Wall Street Journal* (March 18, 1981).

Company. (The present value of $1 million to be received for twenty years discounted at 15% is $6,259,330.)

In practice, prospective buyers may use all these methods and variations of their own to produce a "valuation curve" or range of prices that vary according to underlying assumptions. The buyer may have accumulated a stock of data supporting a specific price range, but the actual price paid may be more a factor of the buyer's or seller's ego and horse-trading acumen.

It seems safe to say that the valuation of goodwill is at best a highly uncertain process. As the illustrations show, the estimated value of goodwill depends on a number of factors, all of which are highly tenuous and subject to bargaining.

## Amortization of Goodwill

Once goodwill has been recognized in the accounts, the next question is: What is the proper accounting at this point? Three basic approaches have been suggested.

1. **Charge goodwill off immediately to stockholders' equity.** *Accounting Research Study No. 10,* "Accounting for Goodwill," takes the position that goodwill differs from other types of assets and demands special attention.[19] This argument is based on the proposition that goodwill, unlike other assets, is not separable and distinct from the business as a whole and therefore is not an asset in the same sense as cash, receivables, or plant assets. In other words, goodwill cannot be sold without selling the business. Furthermore, *ARS No. 10* notes that the accounting treatment for purchased goodwill and goodwill internally created should be consistent. Goodwill created internally is immediately expensed and does not appear as an asset: the same treatment should be accorded purchased goodwill. It is also contended that amortization of purchased goodwill leads to double counting, because net income is reduced by amortization of the purchased goodwill as well as by the internal expenditure made to maintain or enhance the value of the assets. Perhaps the best rationale for direct write-off is that determination of the periods over which the future benefits are to be received is so difficult that immediate charging to stockholders' equity is justified.

2. **Retain goodwill indefinitely unless reduction in value occurs.** Many accountants believe that goodwill can have an indefinite life and should be maintained as an asset until a decline in value occurs. They contend that inasmuch as internal goodwill is being expensed to maintain or enhance the purchased goodwill, some form of goodwill should always be an asset. In addition, without sufficient evidence that a decline in value has occurred, a write-off of goodwill is both arbitrary and capricious and will lead to distortions in net income.

3. **Amortize goodwill over useful life.** Still other accountants believe that goodwill as service potential eventually disappears and it is proper that the asset be charged to expense over the periods affected. This procedure provides a better matching of costs and revenues in that amortization over its useful life provides the appropriate charge to expense.

*APB Opinion No. 17* takes the position that goodwill should be written off over its useful life, its useful life being dependent on myriad factors such as regulatory restrictions, demand, competition, and obsolescence. **The profession did note that (1) goodwill should never be written off at the date of acquisition and (2) the period of amortization should not exceed 40 years.**

Immediate write-off was not considered proper, because it would lead to the untenable conclusion that all noncurrent assets should be charged off immediately. It might be noted that the profession merely prohibits the writing off of goodwill in the period of purchase and over a period exceeding 40 years; no other mention is made regarding another period.

---

[19]Catlett and Olson, *op. cit.,* pp. 89–95.

Some believe that a five-year period for amortization would be appropriate unless, depending on the specific circumstances, such as continued loss of profitability or loss of managerial talent, a shorter period is obviously justified. A single loss year or a combination of loss years does not automatically necessitate a charge-off of the goodwill.

The amortization of the goodwill should be computed using the straight-line method unless another method is deemed more appropriate, and it should be treated as a regular operating expense. Where the amortization is material, a disclosure of the charge is necessary, as well as the method and period of amortization. Goodwill amortization is not deductible for tax purposes.

### Negative Goodwill—Badwill

**Negative goodwill, often appropriately dubbed badwill, or bargain purchase, arises when the fair market value of the assets acquired is higher than the purchase price of the asset.** This situation is a result of market imperfection because the seller would be better off to sell the assets individually than in total. Situations do occur where the purchase price is less than the value of the net identifiable assets and therefore a credit develops that is referred to as negative goodwill or excess of fair value over the cost of assets acquired. Companies that have negative goodwill are in a very interesting position because the amortization of this negative goodwill to revenue increases earnings.

*APB Opinion No. 16* **takes the position that an excess of fair value over purchase price should be allocated to reduce proportionately the values assigned to noncurrent assets** (except long-term investments in marketable securities) in determining their fair values. If the allocation reduces the noncurrent assets to zero value, the remainder of the excess over cost should be classified as a deferred credit and should be amortized systematically to revenue over the period estimated to be benefited but not in excess of 40 years. The method and period of amortization should be disclosed.[20]

Negative goodwill most frequently develops in a depressed securities market when the market value of a company's stock sells at less than book value. For example, Emhart Corp. offered $23 a share (a premium over market) for U.S.M. Corp. stock which had a per-share book value of $53. Emhart Corp. (in consolidation) was able to write down its newly acquired plant assets by more than $49 million and thereby effect a reduction in annual depreciation charges of $5.8 million and add 50 cents annually to its earnings per share (on top of the $2 a share it would gain from consolidating U.S.M.'s reported profits—this extra $2.50 per share represented a 90% increase over Emhart's prior year earnings).

### Reporting of Intangibles

The reporting of intangibles differs from the reporting of property, plant, and equipment in that contra accounts are not normally shown for the intangibles. The amortization of intangibles is generally credited directly to the intangible asset.[21]

---

[20]"Business Combinations," *Opinions of the Accounting Principles Board No. 16* (New York: AICPA, 1970), par. 91.

[21]*Accounting Trends and Techniques—1981* reports that the most common type of intangible is goodwill followed by patents, trademarks, brand names, copyrights; and then licenses, franchises, and memberships.

The financial statements should disclose the method and period of amortization. Intangible assets might appear on the balance sheet as follows:

| Intangible assets (Note 3) | | |
|---|---|---|
| Patents | $ 98,000 | |
| Franchises | 115,000 | |
| Goodwill | 342,000 | $555,000 |

Note 3. The patents are amortized on a unit-of-production approach over a period of six years. The franchises are perpetual in nature, but in accordance with *APB Opinion No. 17* are being written off over the maximum period allowable (40 years) on a straight-line basis. The goodwill arose from the purchase of Multi-Media and is being amortized over a ten-year period on a straight-line basis.

The following example, taken from the 1980 annual report of Purolator, Inc., illustrates the amortization of intangibles using a contra valuation account:

| PUROLATOR, INC. | | |
|---|---|---|
| | **1980** | **1979** |
| Intangible assets (note 4) | $3,603,000 | $17,656,000 |
| Less accumulated amortization | 590,000 | 2,007,000 |
| Net intangible assets | 3,013,000 | 15,649,000 |
| *Note 4: Intangible Assets* | | |
| Intangible assets consist of the following: | | |
| December 31 | **1980** | **1979** |
| Excess of cost over underlying value of net assets of companies acquired | $2,022,000 | $13,080,000 |
| Franchise costs and other intangibles | 1,581,000 | 4,576,000 |
| | $3,603,000 | $17,656,000 |

Enactment of the Motor Carrier Act of 1980 and recent actions of the Interstate Commerce Commission and various states which regulate the motor carrier industry simplified entry by new carriers and eliminated many route, territory and commodity restrictions for existing carriers. As a result, the Financial Accounting Standards Board issued *Statement No. 44* requiring the write-off in 1980 of costs assigned to operating rights (intangible assets) which resulted in an extraordinary charge of $12,363,000.

Since there is uncertainty at this time as to the deductibility of this write-off for tax purposes, no tax benefit has been reflected in the financial statements.

Intangible assets are being amortized on a straight-line basis over their estimated lives, which periods do not exceed forty years.

Some companies follow the practice of writing their intangibles down to $1.00 to indicate that they have intangibles of which the values are uncertain. This practice is not in accord with good accounting. It would be much better to disclose the nature of the intangible, its original cost, and other relevant information such as competition, danger of obsolescence, and so on.

# RESEARCH AND DEVELOPMENT COSTS

Research and development (R & D) costs are not in themselves intangible assets but, because research and development activities frequently result in the development of something that is patented or copyrighted (such as a new product, process, idea, formula, composition, or literary work), R & D costs are presented in the intangible assets chapter.

Many businesses spend considerable sums of money on research and development to develop new products or processes, to improve present products, and to discover new knowledge that may be valuable at some future date. The following schedule shows the outlays for R & D made in 1981 by selected American companies:[22]

| Reported Research and Development Expense—1981 | | | |
|---|---|---|---|
| Company | Dollars | % of Sales | % of Profits |
| Boeing | $  844,100,000 | 8.6% | 178.5% |
| Eastman Kodak | 615,000,000 | 6.0 | 49.6 |
| General Motors | 2,249,600,000 | 3.6 | 674.7 |
| Amdahl | 75,100,000 | 17.0 | 280.7 |
| Scott Paper | 31,300,000 | 1.4 | 23.5 |
| IBM | 1,612,000,000 | 5.5 | 48.7 |

The difficulties in accounting for these research and development (R & D) expenditures are (1) identifying the costs associated with particular activities, projects, or achievements and (2) determining the magnitude of the future benefits and the length of time over which such benefits may be realized. Because of these latter uncertainties the accounting profession (through *FASB Statement No. 2*) has standardized and simplified accounting practice in this area by requiring that **all research and development costs be charged to expense when incurred.**[23]

To differentiate research and development costs from **other similar costs,** the FASB issued the following definitions:

**RESEARCH** is planned search or critical investigation aimed at discovery of new knowledge with the hope that such knowledge will be useful in developing a new product or service . . . or a new process or technique . . . or in bringing about a significant improvement to an existing product or process.

**DEVELOPMENT** is the translation of research findings or other knowledge into a plan or design for a new product or process or for a significant improvement to an existing product or process whether intended for sale or use. It includes the conceptual formulation, design, and testing of product alternatives, construction of prototypes, and operation of pilot plants. It does not include routine or periodic alterations to existing products, production lines, manufacturing processes, and other on-going operations even though those alterations may represent improvements and it does not include market research or market testing activities.[24]

---

[22]"A Research Spending Surge Defies Recession," *Business Week* (July 5, 1982), pp. 54–74.

[23]"Accounting for Research and Development Costs," *Statement of Financial Accounting Standards No. 2* (Stamford, Conn.: FASB, 1974), par. 12.

[24]Ibid., par. 8.

Many costs have characteristics similar to those of research and development costs, for instance, costs of relocation and rearrangement of facilities, start-up costs for a new plant or new retail outlet, marketing research costs, promotion costs of a new product or service, and costs of training new personnel. To further distinguish between R & D and these other similar costs, the following schedule provides (1) examples of activities that typically would be **included** in research and development, and (2) examples of activities that typically would be **excluded** from research and development.[25]

| **1. R & D Activities** | **2. Activities Not Considered R & D** |
|---|---|
| (a) Laboratory research aimed at discovery of a new knowledge. | (a) Engineering follow-through in an early phase of commercial production. |
| (b) Searching for applications of new research findings. | (b) Quality control during commercial production including routine testing. |
| (c) Conceptual formulation and design of possible product or process alternatives. | (c) Trouble-shooting breakdowns during production. |
| (d) Testing in search for or evaluation of product or process alternatives. | (d) Routine, on-going efforts to refine, enrich, or improve the qualities of an existing product. |
| (e) Modification of the design of a product or process. | (e) Adaptation of an existing capability to a particular requirement or customer's need. |
| (f) Design, construction, and testing of preproduction prototypes and models. | (f) Periodic design changes to existing products. |
| (g) Design of tools, jigs, molds, and dies involving new technology. | (g) Routine design of tools, jigs, molds, and dies. |
| (h) Design, construction, and operation of a pilot plant not useful for commercial production. | (h) Activity, including design and construction engineering related to the construction, relocation, rearrangement, or start-up of facilities or equipment. |
| (i) Engineering activity required to advance the design of a product to the manufacturing stage. | (i) Legal work on patent applications, sale, licensing, or litigation. |

## Special Problems

A special problem arises in distinguishing R & D costs from selling and administrative activities. The FASB's intent was that the acquisition, development, or improvement of a product or process by an enterprise **for use in its selling or administrative activities** be excluded from the definition of research and development activities. For example, the costs of software incurred by an airline in acquiring, developing, or improving its computerized reservation system, or the costs incurred during the development of a general management information system, are not research and development costs.[26] Conversely, an effort to develop a new or higher level of computer software intended for sale (but not under a contractual arrangement) would be considered R & D and expensed as incurred.

The costs associated with R & D activities and the accounting treatment accorded them are as follows:

---

[25]Ibid., pars. 9 and 10.

[26]"Applicability of FASB Statement No. 2 to Computer Software," *FASB Interpretation No. 6* (Stamford, Conn.: FASB, 1975), par. 4 (also see Interpretation Nos. 4 and 5).

(a) **MATERIALS, EQUIPMENT, AND FACILITIES.** Expense the entire costs, **unless the items have alternative future uses** (in other R & D projects or otherwise), then carry as inventory and allocate as consumed or capitalize and depreciate as used.

(b) **PERSONNEL.** Salaries, wages, and other related costs of personnel engaged in R & D should be expensed as incurred.

(c) **PURCHASED INTANGIBLES.** Expense the entire cost, **unless the items have alternative future uses** (in other R & D projects or otherwise), then capitalize and amortize.

(d) **CONTRACT SERVICES.** The costs of services performed by others in connection with the reporting company's R & D should be expensed as incurred.

(e) **INDIRECT COSTS.** A reasonable allocation of indirect costs shall be included in R & D costs, except for general and administrative cost, which must be clearly related to be included and expensed.[27]

Consistent with item (a) above, if an enterprise owns a research facility consisting of buildings, laboratories, and equipment which conducts R & D activities and which has alternative future uses (in other R & D projects or otherwise), the facility should be accounted for as a capitalized operational asset. The depreciation and other costs related to such research facilities are accounted for as R & D expenses.

Sometimes enterprises conduct R & D activities for other entities under a **contractual arrangement.** In this case, the contract usually specifies that all direct costs, certain specific indirect costs, plus a profit element, should be reimbursed to the enterprise performing the R & D work. Because reimbursement is expected, such R & D costs should be recorded as a receivable not R & D. It is the company for whom the work has been performed that reports these costs as R & D and expenses them as incurred.

An interesting problem has recently developed in practice regarding the financing of R & D costs through innovative financing arrangements. To illustrate, assume that Helio Netics Corp. (HNC) needs $20 million to continue research work on its photovoltaic (solar electric) cell. A limited partnership is established to raise the needed $20 million. The limited partnership is granted the right to receive royalties on the future sale of the solar panels. The accounting question is: How should HNC account for this arrangement? One view is that the limited partners simply loaned money to HNC, which subsequently used it to finance its R & D activities. If such a view is adopted, R & D is reported as an expense on HNC's books along with a liability for the loan. Conversely, others argue that the R & D activities are those of the limited partnership (a separate enterprise). In this case, HNC reports neither the R & D expense nor the related liability, but instead it provides footnote disclosure of the arrangement. From the perspective of HNC, the accounting treatment makes a substantial difference. Under one situation an expense and liability are reported; in the other, only a footnote is presented.

The SEC has taken the position that most of these arrangements should be reported as expenses with a related liability. The FASB, in its *Statement No. 68* "Research and Development Arrangements" (1982), has taken the position that to the extent that an enterprise is obligated to repay other parties for monies received, a liability and related charge to research and development expense should be recorded. As a result, many companies may no longer fund R & D costs in this manner. Thus, some contend that R & D expenditures may be reduced, which would hinder technological growth in the United States (an economic consequence argument). This example highlights both the complexity of accounting for R & D costs and the potential effect that the method of reporting these costs can have on the behavior of corporate management.

[27] FASB Statement No. 2, *op. cit.,* par. 11.

Costs of research and development activities that are unique to companies in the **extractive industries** (for example, prospecting, acquisition of mineral rights, exploration, drilling, mining, and related mineral development) and those costs discussed above which are similar to but not classified as R & D costs may be: (1) expensed as incurred, (2) capitalized and either depreciated or amortized over an appropriate period of time, or (3) accumulated as part of inventoriable costs. Choice of the appropriate accounting treatment for such costs should be guided by the degree of certainty of future benefits and the principle of matching revenues and expenses.

Acceptable accounting practice requires that disclosure be made in the financial statements (generally in the footnotes) of the total R & D costs charged to expense in each period for which an income statement is presented.

## Conceptual Questions

The requirement that all R & D costs incurred internally be expensed immediately is a conservative, practical solution which insures consistency in practice and uniformity among companies. The practice, however, of writing off against revenues of the present period expenditures made in the expectation of benefiting future periods cannot be justified on the grounds that it is good accounting theory.[28]

Defendants of immediate expensing contend that from an income statement standpoint long-run application of this standard frequently makes little difference. The amount of R & D cost charged against income each accounting period would be about the same whether there is immediate expensing or capitalization and subsequent amortization because of the ongoing nature of most companies' R & D activities. Aside from the revenue/expense mismatching, which may be minimal, critics of this practice argue that the balance sheet should report an intangible asset related to expenditures that have future benefit. To preclude capitalization of all R & D expenditures removes from the balance sheet what may be a company's most valuable asset. This standard represents one of the many trade-offs made among relevance, reliability, and cost-benefit considerations.[29]

## DEFERRED CHARGES AND LONG-TERM PREPAYMENTS

Deferred charges is a classification often used to describe a number of different items that have debit balances, among them certain types of intangibles. Intangibles sometimes classified as deferred charges include plant rearrangement costs, preoperating and start-up costs, and organization costs. How do these items happen to be classified in this section and not in a separate intangible section? Probably the major reason is that the deferred charge section often serves as a "dumping ground" for a number of small items.

---

[28]The International Accounting Standards Committee issued a standard that is in disagreement with the FASB's standard on accounting for R & D costs. The International Committee identified certain circumstances that justify the capitalization and deferral of development costs. See "Accounting for Research and Development Activities," *International Accounting Standard No. 9* (London, England: International Accounting Standards Committee, 1978), par. 17.

[29]For a discussion of the position that R & D should be capitalized in certain situations, see Harold Bierman, Jr., and Roland E. Dukes, "Accounting for Research and Development Costs, *The Journal of Accountancy* (April, 1975).

Deferred charges also include such items as long-term prepayments for insurance, rent, taxes, and other down payments. The deferred charge classification probably should be abolished because it cannot be clearly differentiated from other amortizable and depreciable assets (which also are deferred charges) and a more informative disclosure could be made of the smaller items often found in this section of the balance sheet. Such a classification has even less relevance today because the conceptual framework project establishes a definition for assets that would apparently exclude deferred charges.

## QUESTIONS

1. What are the major accounting problems related to accounting for intangibles?

2. Many accountants advocate the abandonment of historical cost for plant assets but argue that historical cost should be used in accounting for intangible assets. Are the two viewpoints inconsistent?

3. Intangible assets may be classified on a number of different bases. Indicate three different bases and illustrate how intangibles could be subdivided into these groupings.

4. Accounting authors and practitioners and this course have proposed various solutions to the problems of accounting in terms of historical cost for goodwill and similar intangibles. What problems of accounting for goodwill and similar intangibles are comparable to those of accounting for plant assets? What problems are different?

5. What are some examples of internally created intangibles? Why does the accounting profession make a distinction between internally created "goodwill type" intangibles and other intangibles?

6. State the generally accepted accounting procedures for the amortization and write-down or write-off of capitalized intangible assets.

7. It has been argued, on the grounds of conservatism, that all intangible assets should be written off immediately after acquisition. Give the accounting arguments against this treatment.

8. Indicate the period of time over which each of the following should be amortized.
   (a) Franchises.
   (b) Patents.
   (c) Leasehold improvements.
   (d) Copyrights.
   (e) Research and development costs.
   (f) Trademarks.
   (g) Goodwill.
   (h) A 20-year lease with payments of $44,000 per year on property with an estimated useful life of 50 years. The lessee has the option to renew the lease for 30 additional years at $11,000 per year.

9. What is a lease prepayment? What are property rights capitalized by the lessee? What are leasehold improvements? Should any of these items be classified as an intangible asset?

10. Recently Heublein Corporation entered into a lease agreement with Mountain Developers, Inc., to lease some land for 20 years in southwest Colorado. Heublein Corporation as lessee then built on this site a number of apartment buildings having a useful life of 35 years. The lease agreement states that the lessee has the option to renew the lease for another 20 years. Over what period should the apartments be depreciated?

11. Recently, a group of university students decided to incorporate for the purposes of selling a process to recycle the waste product from manufacturing cheese. Some of the initial costs involved were legal fees and office expenses incurred in starting the business, state incorporation fees, and stamp taxes. One student wishes to charge these costs against income in the current period; another wishes to defer these costs and amortize them in the future; and another believes these costs should be netted against common stock. Which student is correct?

12. What is goodwill? What is negative goodwill?

13. Under what circumstances is it appropriate to record goodwill in the accounts? How should

goodwill, properly recorded on the books, be amortized in order to conform with generally accepted accounting principles?

14. Explain how "average excess earnings" are determined. What is the justification for the use of this method of estimating goodwill?

15. In examining financial statements, financial analysts often write off goodwill immediately. Evaluate this procedure.

16. Discuss two methods for estimating the value of goodwill in determining the amount that should properly be paid for it.

17. What is the nature of research and development costs? What other costs have similar characteristics?

18. Research and development activities may include (a) personnel costs, (b) materials and equipment costs, and (c) indirect costs. What is the recommended accounting treatment for these three types of R & D costs?

19. During the current year Hydrostatic Railroad spent $600,000 to develop a computer program that will assist in identifying and locating all of its rolling equipment; the railroad also spent $245,000 to develop a unique software package that will be offered on a lease basis to other railroads. How should Hydrostatic account for these two expenditures?

20. Which of the following activities should be expensed currently as R & D costs:
    (a) Engineering follow-through in an early phase of commercial production.
    (b) Legal work in connection with patent applications or litigation, and the sale or licensing of patents.
    (c) Testing in search for or evaluation of product or process alternatives.
    (d) Adaptation of an existing capability to a particular requirement or customer's need as a part of continuing commercial activity.

21. In 1982, Southern Corporation developed a new product that will be marketed in 1983. In connection with the development of this product, the following costs were incurred in 1982: research and development departmental costs, $200,000; materials and supplies consumed, $50,000; compensation paid to research consultants, $60,000. It is anticipated that these costs will be recovered in 1985. What is the amount of research and development costs that Southern should record in 1982 as a charge to income?

## CASES

**C13-1** In examining the books of Imagery Mfg. Company, you find on the December 31, 1983, balance sheet, the item, "Costs of patents, $308,440."

Referring to the ledger accounts, you note the following items regarding one patent acquired in 1980.

| | |
|---|---:|
| 1980 Legal costs incurred in defending the validity of the patent | $7,200 |
| 1982 Legal costs in prosecuting an infringement suit | 9,500 |
| 1982 Legal costs (additional expenses) in the infringement suit | 3,950 |
| 1982 Cost of improvements (unpatented) on the patented device | 15,700 |

There are no credits in the account, and no allowance for amortization has been set up on the books for any of the patents. Three other patents issued in 1977, 1979, and 1980 were developed by the staff of the client. The patented articles are currently very marketable, but it is estimated that they will be in demand only for the next few years.

**Instructions**

Discuss the items included in the Patent account from an accounting standpoint.

(AICPA adapted)

**C13-2** On June 30, 1983, your client, Sparatan Corporation, was granted two patents covering plastic cartons that it has been producing and marketing profitably for the past three years. One patent covers the manufacturing process and the other covers the related products.

Sparatan executives tell you that these patents represent the most significant break-through in the industry in the past 30 years. The products have been marketed under the registered trademarks Safetainer, Duratainer, and Sealrite. Licenses under the patents have already been granted by your client to other manufacturers in the United States and abroad and are producing substantial royalties.

On July 1, Sparatan commenced patent infringement actions against several companies whose names you recognize as those of substantial and prominent competitors. Sparatan's management is optimistic that these suits will result in a permanent injunction against the manufacture and sale of the infringing products and collection of damages for loss of profits caused by the alleged infringement.

The financial vice-president has suggested that the patents be recorded at the discounted value of expected net royalty receipts.

**Instructions**

(a) What is the meaning of "discounted value of expected net receipts"? Explain.
(b) How would such a value be calculated for net royalty receipts?
(c) What basis of valuation for Sparatan's patents would be generally accepted in account-ing? Give supporting reasons for this basis.
(d) Assuming no practical problems of implementation and ignoring generally accepted ac-counting principles, what is the preferable basis of valuation for patents? Explain.
(e) What would be the preferable theoretical basis of amortization? Explain.
(f) What recognition, if any, should be made of the infringement litigation in the financial statements for the year ending September 30, 1983? Discuss.

(AICPA adapted)

C13-3 During the examination of the financial statements of Aurora Company, your assistant calls attention to significant costs incurred in the development of EDP programs (that is, software) for major segments of the sales and inventory scheduling systems.

The EDP program development costs will benefit future periods to the extent that the systems change slowly and the program instructions are compatible with new equipment acquired at three- to six-year intervals. The service value of the EDP programs is affected almost entirely by changes in the technology of systems and EDP equipment and does not decline with the number of times the program is used. Because many system changes are minor, program instructions frequently can be modified with only minor losses in program efficiency. The frequency of such changes tends to increase with the passage of time.

**Instructions**

(a) Discuss the propriety of classifying the unamortized EDP program development costs as
   1. A prepaid expense.
   2. An intangible asset.
   3. A tangible fixed asset.
(b) Discuss the propriety of amortizing the EDP program development costs by means of
   1. The straight-line method.
   2. A decreasing-charge method (for example, the sum-of-the-years'-digits method).
   3. A variable-charge method (for example, the units-of-production method).

(AICPA adapted)

C13-4 After securing lease commitments from several major stores, Fox Valley Shopping Center, Inc. was organized and built a shopping center in a growing suburb.

The shopping center would have opened on schedule on January 1, 1984, if it had not been struck by a severe tornado in December; it opened for business on October 1, 1984. All of the additional construction costs that were incurred as a result of the tornado were covered by insurance.

In July, 1983, in anticipation of the scheduled January opening, a permanent staff had been hired to promote the shopping center, obtain tenants for the uncommitted space, and manage the property.

A summary of some of the costs incurred in 1983 and the first nine months of 1984 follows.

|  | 1983 | January 1, 1984, through September 30, 1984 |
|---|---|---|
| Interest on mortgage bonds | $75,000 | $97,500 |
| Cost of obtaining tenants | 33,000 | 60,000 |
| Promotional advertising | 43,500 | 46,500 |

The promotional advertising campaign was designed to familiarize shoppers with the Center. Had it been known in time that the Center would not open until October, 1984, the 1983 expenditure for promotional advertising would not have been made. The advertising had to be repeated in 1984.

All of the tenants who had leased space in the shopping center at the time of the tornado accepted the October occupancy date on condition that the monthly rental charges for the first nine months of 1984 be canceled.

**Instructions**

Explain how each of the costs for 1983 and the first nine months of 1984 should be treated in the accounts of the shopping center corporation. Give the reasons for each treatment.

(AICPA adapted)

**C13-5** After extended negotiations Voltage Corporation bought from Igloo Company most of the latter's assets on June 30, 1984. At the time of the sale Igloo's accounts (adjusted to June 30, 1984) reflected the following descriptions and amounts for the assets transferred.

|  | Cost | Contra (Valuation) Account | Book Value |
|---|---|---|---|
| Receivables | $ 85,600 | $ 2,500 | $ 83,100 |
| Inventory | 107,000 | 5,400 | 101,600 |
| Land | 18,000 | — | 18,000 |
| Buildings | 208,600 | 73,000 | 135,600 |
| Fixtures and equipment | 203,900 | 42,000 | 161,900 |
| Goodwill | 50,000 | — | 50,000 |
|  | $673,100 | $122,900 | $550,200 |

You ascertain that the contra (valuation) accounts were allowance for doubtful accounts, allowance to reduce inventory to market, and accumulated depreciation.

During the extended negotiations Igloo held out for a consideration of approximately $625,000 (depending on the level of the receivables and inventory). As of June 30, 1984, however, Igloo agreed to accept Voltage's offer of $475,000 cash plus 1% of the net sales (as defined in the contract) of the next five years with payments at the end of each year. Igloo expects that Voltage's total net sales during this period will exceed $15,000,000.

**Instructions**

(a) How should Voltage Corporation record this transaction? Explain.

(b) Discuss the propriety of recording goodwill in the accounts of Voltage Corporation for this transaction.

(AICPA adapted)

**C13-6** Heatemup Corporation, a retail fuel oil distributor, has increased its annual sales volume to a level three times greater than the annual sales of a dealer it purchased in 1983 in order to begin operations.

The board of directors of Heatemup Corporation recently received an offer to negotiate the sale of Heatemup Corporation to a large competitor. As a result, the majority of the board wants to increase the stated value of goodwill on the balance sheet to reflect the larger sales volume developed through intensive promotion and the current market price of sales gallonage. A few of the board members, however, would prefer to eliminate goodwill altogether from the balance sheet in order to prevent "possible misinterpretations." Goodwill was recorded properly in 1983.

### Instructions

    (a) Discuss the meaning of the term "goodwill."

    (b) List the techniques used to calculate the tentative value of goodwill in negotiations to purchase a going concern.

    (c) Why are the book and market values of the goodwill of Heatemup Corporation different?

    (d) Discuss the propriety of
        1. Increasing the stated value of goodwill prior to the negotiations.
        2. Eliminating goodwill completely from the balance sheet prior to negotiations.

                                            (AICPA adapted)

**C13-7** Tinkerbell Company is in the process of developing a revolutionary new product. A new division of the company was formed to develop, manufacture, and market this new product. As of year-end (December 31, 1984) the new product has not been manufactured for resale; however, a prototype unit was built and is in operation.

    Throughout 1984 the new division incurred certain costs. These costs include design and engineering studies, prototype manufacturing costs, administrative expenses (including salaries of administrative personnel), and market research costs. In addition, approximately $600,000 in equipment (estimated useful life—10 years) was purchased for use in developing and manufacturing the new product. Approximately $240,000 of this equipment was built specifically for the design development of the new product; the remaining $360,000 of equipment was used to manufacture the pre-production prototype and will be used to manufacture the new product once it is in commercial production.

### Instructions

    (a) How are "research" and "development" defined in *Statement of Financial Accounting Standards No. 2*?

    (b) Briefly indicate the practical and conceptual reasons for the conclusion reached by the Financial Accounting Standards Board on accounting and reporting practices for research and development costs.

    (c) In accordance with *Statement of Financial Accounting Standards No. 2,* how should the various costs of Tinkerbell described above be recorded on the financial statements for the year ended December 31, 1984?

                                            (AICPA adapted)

**C13-8** R. Trendler Company operates several plants at which limestone is processed into quicklime and hydrated lime. The Batavia Plant, where most of the equipment was installed many years ago, continually deposits a dusty white substance over the surrounding countryside. Citing the unsanitary condition of the neighboring community of Geneva, the pollution of the Fox River, and the high incidence of lung disease among workers at Batavia, the state's Pollution Control Agency has ordered the installation of air pollution control equipment. Also, the Agency has assessed a substantial penalty, which will be used to clean up Geneva. After considering the costs involved (which could not have been reasonably estimated prior to the Agency's action), Trendler decides to comply with the Agency's orders, the alternative being to cease operations at Batavia at the end of the current fiscal year. The officers of Trendler agree that the air pollution control equipment should be capitalized and depreciated over its useful life, but they disagree over the period(s) to which the penalty should be charged.

### Instructions

    Discuss the conceptual merits and reporting requirements of accounting for the penalty as a

    (a) Charge to the current period.

    (b) Correction of prior periods.

    (c) Capitalizable item to be amortized over future periods.

                                            (AICPA adapted)

C13–9 Honeyall, Inc. is a large publicly held corporation. Listed below are six selected expenditures made by the company during the current fiscal year ended April 30, 1983. The proper accounting treatment of these transactions must be determined in order that Honeyall's annual financial statements will be prepared in accordance with generally accepted accounting principles.

1. Honeyall, Inc. spent $2,000,000 on a program designed to improve relations with its dealers. This project was favorably received by the dealers and Honeyall's management believes that significant future benefits should be received from this program. The program was conducted during the fourth quarter of the current fiscal year.

2. A pilot plant was constructed during 1982–83 at a cost of $4,000,000 to test a new production process. The plant will be operated for approximately five years. At that time, the company will make a decision regarding the economic value of the process. The pilot plant is too small for commercial production, so it will be dismantled when the test is over.

3. A new product will be introduced next year. The company spent $3,000,000 during the current year for design of tools, jigs, molds, and dies for this product.

4. Honeyall, Inc. purchased Merit Company for $5,000,000 in cash in early August 1982. The fair market value of the identifiable assets of Merit was $4,000,000.

5. A large advertising campaign was conducted during April 1983 to introduce a new product to be released during the first quarter of the 1983–84 fiscal year. The advertising campaign cost $2,500,000.

6. During the first six months of the 1982–83 fiscal year, $500,000 was expended for legal work in connection with a successful patent application. The patent became effective November 1, 1982. The legal life of the patent is 17 years while the economic life of the patent is expected to be approximately 10 years.

**Instructions**

For each of the six expenditures presented, determine and justify:
(a) The amount, if any, that should be capitalized and be included on Honeyall's Statement of Financial Position prepared as of April 30, 1983.
(b) The amount that should be included in Honeyall's Statement of Income for the year ended April 30, 1983.

(CMA adapted)

# EXERCISES

E13–1 Futuristic Products Company from time to time embarks on a research program when a special project seems to offer possibilities. In 1983 the company expends $300,000 on a research project, but by the end of 1983 it is impossible to determine whether any benefit will be derived from it.

**Instructions**

(a) What account should be charged for the $300,000, and how should it be shown in the financial statements?
(b) The project is completed in 1984, and a successful patent is obtained. The R & D costs to complete the project are $102,000. The administrative and legal expenses incurred in obtaining patent number 472-1001-84 in 1984 total $12,000. The patent has an expected useful life of 5 years. Record these costs in journal entry form. Also, record patent amortization (full year) in 1984.
(c) In 1985 the company successfully defends the patent in extended litigation at a cost of $36,000, thereby extending the patent life to 12/31/92. What is the proper way to account for this cost? Also, record patent amortization (full year) in 1985.
(d) Additional engineering and consulting costs incurred in 1985 to improve the quality of the patented product total $40,000. The improvements enhance the salability of the product considerably. Discuss the proper accounting treatment for this cost.

**E13-2** Cuisinart Products, Inc. has its own research department. In addition, the company purchases patents from time to time. The following statements summarize the transactions involving all patents now owned by the company.

During 1977 and 1978, $109,200 was spent developing a new process that was patented (No. 1) on March 18, 1979 at additional legal and other costs of $13,464. A patent (No. 2) developed by Philip Remmers, an inventor, was purchased for $146,850 on November 30, 1980, on which date it had 12½ years yet to run.

During 1979, 1980, and 1981, research and development activities cost $230,000. No additional patents resulted from these activities.

A patent infringement suit brought by the company against a competitor because of the manufacture of articles infringing on Patent No. 2 was successfully prosecuted at a cost of $4,970. A decision in the case was rendered in July, 1981.

A competing patent (No. 3) was purchased for $38,400 in August, 1982. This patent had 16 years yet to run. During 1983, $45,500 has been expended on patent development: $22,000 of this amount represents the cost of a device for which a patent application has been filed, but no notification of acceptance or rejection by the Patent Office has been received. The other $23,500 represents costs incurred on uncompleted development projects.

### Instructions

(a) Compute the carrying value of these patents as of December 31, 1983, assuming that the legal life and useful life of each patent is the same and that each patent is to be amortized from the first day of the month following its acquisition.
(b) Prepare a journal entry to record amortization for 1983.

**E13-3** Morley Company has provided information on intangible assets as follows:

A patent was purchased from the Doug Company for $1,800,000 on January 1, 1983. Morley estimated the remaining useful life of the patent to be 10 years. The patent was carried in Doug's accounting records at a net book value of $1,250,000 when Doug sold it to Morley.

During 1984, a franchise was purchased from the Debbie Company for $600,000. In addition, 5% of revenue from the franchise must be paid to Debbie. Revenue from the franchise for 1984 was $2,400,000. Morley estimates the useful life of the franchise to be 10 years and takes a full year's amortization in the year of purchase.

Morley incurred research and development costs in 1984 as follows:

| | |
|---|---:|
| Materials and equipment | $144,000 |
| Personnel | 168,000 |
| Indirect costs | 72,000 |
| | $384,000 |

Morley estimates that these costs will be recouped by December 31, 1987.

On January 1, 1984, Morley, because of recent events in the field, estimates that the remaining life of the patent purchased on January 1, 1983, is only 5 years from January 1, 1984.

### Instructions

(a) Prepare a schedule showing the intangibles section of Morley's balance sheet at December 31, 1984. Show supporting computations in good form.
(b) Prepare a schedule showing the income statement effect for the year ended December 31, 1984, as a result of the facts above. Show supporting computations in good form.

(AICPA adapted)

**E13-4** As the recently appointed auditor for Allan Nilsson Corporation, you have been asked to examine selected accounts before the six-month financial statements of June 30, 1983, are prepared. The controller for Allan Nilsson Corporation mentions that only one account (shown below) is kept for Intangible Assets.

**Intangible Assets**

| | | Debit | Credit | Balance |
|---|---|---|---|---|
| January 4 | Research and development costs | 930,000 | | 930,000 |
| January 5 | Legal costs to obtain patent | 70,000 | | 1,000,000 |
| January 31 | Payment of seven months rent on property leased by Nilsson | 77,000 | | 1,077,000 |
| February 1 | Stock issue costs | 53,000 | | 1,130,000 |
| February 11 | Premium on common stock | | 300,000 | 830,000 |
| March 31 | Unamortized bond discount on bonds due March 31, 2003 | 100,000 | | 930,000 |
| April 30 | Promotional expenses related to start-up of business | 300,000 | | 1,230,000 |
| June 30 | Operating losses for first six months | 270,000 | | 1,500,000 |

**Instructions**

Prepare the entry or entries necessary to correct this account. Assume that the patent has a useful life of 10 years, and that organization costs are being amortized over a 5-year period.

**E13-5** Tailwind Airlines leases an old building which it intends to improve and use as a warehouse. To obtain the lease, the company pays a bonus of $25,000. Annual rental for the 5-year lease period is $90,000. No option to renew the lease or right to purchase the property is given.

After the lease is obtained, improvements costing $139,000 are made. The building has an estimated remaining useful life of 16 years.

**Instructions**

(a) What is the annual cost of this lease to Tailwind Airlines?

(b) What amount of annual depreciation, if any, on a straight-line basis should Tailwind record?

(c) How would the annual charges stated above be changed if Tailwind had been granted as part of the lease agreement the right to purchase the building for a nominal sum at the end of the lease period?

**E13-6** The net worth of Song Kim Company excluding goodwill totals $620,000 and earnings for the last five years total $660,000. Included in the latter figure are extraordinary gains of $60,000, nonrecurring losses of $40,000, and sales commissions of $15,000. A 14% return on net worth is considered normal for the industry, and annual excess earnings are to be capitalized at 20% in arriving at goodwill in developing a sales price for the business.

**Instructions**

Compute estimated goodwill.

**E13-7** Reisling Corporation's pretax accounting income for the year 1983 was $600,000 and included the following items:

| | |
|---|---|
| Extraordinary losses | $ 75,000 |
| Extraordinary gains | 150,000 |
| Profit-sharing payments to employees | 50,000 |
| Amortization of goodwill | 33,000 |
| Amortization of identifiable intangibles | 35,000 |
| Depreciation on building | 90,000 |

Almaden Industries is seeking to purchase Reisling Corporation. In attempting to measure Reisling's normal earnings for 1983, Almaden determines that the fair value of the building is triple the book value and that the remaining economic life is double that used by Reisling. Almaden would continue the profit-sharing payments to employees; such payments are based on income before depreciation and amortization.

**Instructions**

Compute the normal earnings of Reisling Corporation for the year 1983.

**E13-8** As the president of Columbia Records Corp., you are considering purchasing Beatles Corp., whose balance sheet is summarized as follows:

| | | | |
|---|---|---|---|
| Current assets | $ 200,000 | Current liabilities | $ 200,000 |
| Fixed assets (net of depreciation) | 800,000 | Long-term liabilities | 600,000 |
| Other assets | 200,000 | Common stock | 300,000 |
| | | Retained earnings | 100,000 |
| Total | $1,200,000 | Total | $1,200,000 |

The fair market value of current assets is $400,000 because of the undervaluation of inventory. The normal rate of return on net assets for the industry is 15%. The average expected annual earnings projected for Beatles Corp. is $105,000.

**Instructions**

Assuming that the excess earnings continue for four years, how much would you be willing to pay for goodwill? (Estimate goodwill by the present-value method.)

**E13-9** Assertive Corporation is interested in acquiring Passive Company. It has determined that Passive Company's excess earnings have averaged approximately $90,000 annually over the last six years. Passive Company agrees with the computation of $90,000 as the approximate excess earnings and feels that such amount should be capitalized over an unlimited period at an 18% rate. Assertive Corporation feels that because of increased competition the excess earnings of Passive Company will continue for eight more years at best and that a 15% discount rate is appropriate.

**Instructions**

(a) How far apart are the positions of these two parties?
(b) Is there really any difference in the two approaches used by the two parties in evaluating Passive Company's goodwill? Explain.

**E13-10** Gymnastics Corporation is contemplating the purchase of Denise L. Rode Industries and evaluating the amount of goodwill to be recognized in the purchase.
Rode reported the following net incomes:

| | | |
|---|---|---|
| 1978 | — | $180,000 |
| 1979 | — | 192,000 |
| 1980 | — | 288,000 |
| 1981 | — | 300,000 |
| 1982 | — | 480,000 |

Rode has indicated that 1982 net income included the sale of one of its warehouses at a gain of $120,000 (net of tax). Net identifiable assets of Rode have a total fair market value of $900,000.

**Instructions**

Calculate goodwill in the following cases, assuming that expected income is to be a simple average of **normal income** for the past 5 years.
(a) Goodwill is determined by capitalizing average net earnings at 20%.
(b) Goodwill is determined by presuming a 15% return on identifiable net assets and capitalizing excess earnings at 25%.

**E13-11** Jon Axelson Company bought a business that would yield exactly a 20% annual rate of return on its investment. Of the total amount paid for the business, $54,000 was deemed to be goodwill, and the remaining value was attributable to the identifiable net assets.
Jon Axelson Company projected that the estimated annual future earnings of the new business would be equal to its average annual ordinary earnings over the past four years. The

total net income over the past four years was $252,000, which included an extraordinary loss of $18,000 in one year and an extraordinary gain of $54,000 in one of the other four years.

**Instructions**

Compute the fair market value of the **identifiable** net assets that Jon Axelson Company purchased in this transaction.

**E13–12** Rickety Co. has averaged its income for the past three years and finds that its average income equals $110,000. Its net assets have a fair market value of $600,000 exclusive of goodwill. The company is considering a sale of its net assets and wishes to determine an asking price that would include goodwill. Average earnings should be 15% of net assets, and earnings in excess of that amount should be capitalized at 25%.

**Instructions**

(a) What is the amount of goodwill?
(b) Compute the total value of net assets.

**E13–13** Net income figures for Gary Karsten Company are as follows:

<table>
<tr><td>1979—$54,000</td><td>1980—$30,000</td><td>1981—$66,000</td></tr>
<tr><td>1982—$48,000</td><td></td><td>1983—$36,000</td></tr>
</table>

Tangible net assets of this company are appraised at $260,000 on December 31, 1983. This business is to be acquired by Sue Graham Co. early in 1984.

**Instructions**

What amount should be paid for goodwill if:
(a) 15% is assumed to be a normal rate of return on net tangible assets, and average excess earnings for the last 5 years are to be capitalized at 24%?
(b) 12% is assumed to be a normal rate of return on net tangible assets, and payment is to be made for excess earnings for the last 4 years?

**E13–14** Mike "the Millionaire" Michaelson is considering acquiring Kroos Company in total as a going concern. He makes the following computations and conclusions:

| | |
|---|---|
| The fair value of the individual assets of Kroos Company is | $678,000 |
| The liabilities of Kroos Company are | 402,000 |
| A fair estimate of annual earnings for the indefinite future is | 72,000 per year |
| Considering the risk and potential of Kroos Company, Mike feels that he must earn a 24% return on his investment | |

**Instructions**

(a) How much should Mike be willing to pay for Kroos Company?
(b) How much (if any) of the above-noted estimates would be goodwill?

## PROBLEMS

**P13–1** The following information relates to the intangible assets of Metamorphosis Company:

| | Organization Costs | Goodwill | Purchased Patent Costs |
|---|---|---|---|
| Original cost at 1/1/1983 | $75,000 | $400,000 | $36,000 |
| Useful life at 1/1/1983 (estimated) | Indefinite[a] | 50 years | 6 years |

[a]The company has decided to write off for accounting and tax purposes the organization costs as quickly as the tax law allows.

**Instructions**

(a) Assuming straight-line amortization, compute the amount of the amortization of **each** item for 1983 in accordance with generally accepted accounting principles.

(b) Prepare the journal entries for the amortization of organization costs and goodwill for 1983.

(c) Assume that at January 1, 1984, Metamorphosis Company incurred $3,500 of legal fees in defending the rights to the patents. Prepare the entry for the year 1984 to amortize the patents.

(d) Assume that at the beginning of year 1985 the company decided that the patent costs would be applicable only for the years 1985 and 1986. (A competitor has developed a product that will eventually make Metamorphosis' obsolete.) Record the amortization of the patent costs at the end of 1985.

**P13-2** Environmental Laboratories holds a valuable patent (No. 321-1413-8A) on a precipitator that prevents certain types of air pollution. Environmental does not manufacture or sell the products and processes it develops; it conducts research and develops products and processes which it patents, and then assigns the patents to manufacturers on a royalty basis. Occasionally it sells a patent. The history of Environmental's patent number 321-1413-8A is as follows:

| Date | Activity | Cost |
|------|----------|------|
| 1973-1974 | Research conducted to develop precipitator | $585,000 |
| Jan. 1975 | Design and construction of a prototype | 111,420 |
| March 1975 | Testing of models | 43,000 |
| Jan. 1976 | Fees paid engineers and lawyers to prepare patent application; patent granted July 1, 1976 | 51,850 |
| Nov. 1977 | Engineering activity necessary to advance the design of the precipitator to the manufacturing stage | 60,000 |
| Dec. 1978 | Legal fees paid to successfully defend precipitator patent | 23,100 |
| April 1980 | Research aimed at modifying the design of the patented precipitator | 50,000 |
| July 1983 | Legal fees paid in unsuccessful patent infringement suit against a competitor | 30,440 |

Environmental assumed a useful life of 17 years when it received the initial precipitator patent. On January 1, 1981 it revised its useful life estimate downward to 5 remaining years. Amortization is computed for a full year if the cost is incurred prior to July 1, and no amortization for the year if the cost is incurred after June 30. The company's year ends December 31.

**Instructions**

Compute the carrying value of patent No. 321-1413-8A on each of the following dates (assume that *FASB Statement No. 2* applies to all years involved):

(a) December 31, 1976.

(b) December 31, 1980.

(c) December 31, 1983.

**P13-3** During 1981 Creative Company purchased a building site for its proposed research and development laboratory at a cost of $60,000. Construction of the building was started in 1981. The building was completed on December 31, 1982, at a cost of $250,000 and was placed in service on January 2, 1983. The estimated useful life of the building for depreciation purposes was 20 years; the straight-line method of depreciation was to be employed and there was no estimated net salvage value.

Management estimates that about 50% of the projects of the research and development group will result in long-term benefits (that is, at least 10 years) to the corporation. The remaining projects either benefit the current period or are abandoned before completion. A summary of the number of projects and the direct costs incurred in conjunction with the research and development activities for 1983 appears in the next column.

Upon recommendation of the research and development group Creative Company acquired a patent for manufacturing rights at a cost of $100,000. The patent was acquired on April 1, 1982 and has an economic life of 10 years.

| | Number of Projects | Salaries and Employee Benefits | Other Expenses (excluding Building Depreciation Charges) |
|---|---|---|---|
| Completed projects with long-term benefits | 15 | $ 95,000 | $45,000 |
| Abandoned projects or projects that benefit the current period | 10 | 20,000 | 10,000 |
| Projects in process—results indeterminate | 5 | 25,000 | 10,000 |
| Total | 30 | $140,000 | $65,000 |

**Instructions**

If generally accepted accounting principles were followed, how would the items above relating to research and development activities be reported on the company's
(a) income statement for 1983?
(b) balance sheet as of December 31, 1983?
Be sure to give account titles and amounts, and briefly justify your presentation.

(CMA adapted)

**P13–4** Rachael Avery Products Co., organized in 1982, has set up a single account for all intangible assets. The following summary discloses the debit entries that have been recorded during 1982 and 1983.

Intangible Assets

| | | |
|---|---|---|
| 7/1/82 | 5-year franchise; expiration date 6/30/87 | $ 36,000 |
| 10/1/82 | Advance payment on leasehold (4-year lease) | 20,000 |
| 12/31/82 | Net loss for 1982 including state incorporation fee, $1,000, and related legal fees of organizing, $5,000 (all fees incurred in 1982) | 16,000 |
| 1/2/83 | Patent purchased (8-year life) | 84,800 |
| 3/1/83 | Cost of developing a secret formula (indefinite life) | 100,000 |
| 4/1/83 | Goodwill purchased (indefinite life) | 240,000 |
| 6/1/83 | Legal fee for successful defense of patent | 14,560 |
| 9/1/83 | Research and development costs | 178,000 |

**Instructions**

Prepare the necessary entries to clear the Intangible Assets account and to set up separate accounts for distinct types of intangibles. Make the entries as of December 31, 1983, recording any necessary amortization and reflecting all balances accurately as of that date.

**P13–5** Georgia Peaches, Inc. has recently become interested in acquiring an Canadian plant to handle many of its production functions in that market. One possible candidate is Arctic, Inc., a closely held corporation, whose owners have decided to sell their business if a proper settlement can be obtained. Arctic's balance sheet appears as follows:

| | | | |
|---|---|---|---|
| Current assets | $150,000 | Current liabilities | $ 80,000 |
| Investments | 50,000 | Long-term debt | 100,000 |
| Plant assets (net) | 400,000 | Capital stock | 50,000 |
| Total assets | $600,000 | Additional paid-in capital | 170,000 |
| | | Retained earnings | 200,000 |
| | | Total equities | $600,000 |

Georgia Peaches has hired American Appraisal Corporation to determine the proper price to pay for Arctic, Inc. The appraisal firm finds that the investments have a fair market value of $150,000 and that inventory is understated by $75,000. All other assets and equities are properly stated. An examination of the company's income for the last four years indicates that the net income has steadily increased. In 1983 the company had a net operating income of $100,000, and this income should increase 20% each year over the next four years. Georgia Peaches believes that a normal return in this type of business is 18% on net assets. The asset investment in the Alaskan plant is expected to stay the same for the next four years.

**Instructions**

(a) American Appraisal Corporation has indicated that the fair value of the company can be estimated in a number of ways. Prepare an estimate of the value of the firm, assuming that any goodwill will be computed as:

1. The capitalization of the average excess earnings of Arctic, Inc. at 18%.
2. The purchase of average excess earnings over the next four years.
3. The capitalization of average excess earnings of Arctic, Inc. at 24%.
4. The present value of the average excess earnings over the next four years discounted at 15%.

(b) Arctic, Inc. is willing to sell the business for $1,000,000. How do you believe American Appraisal should advise Georgia Peaches?

(c) If Georgia Peaches were to pay $750,000 to purchase the assets and assume the liabilities of Arctic, Inc., how would this transaction be reflected on Georgia's books?

**P13-6** Presented below are financial forecasts related to Ecumenical Company for the next 10 years.

| | |
|---|---|
| Forecasted average earnings (per year) | $ 25,000 |
| Forecasted market value of net assets, exclusive of goodwill (per year) | 144,000 |

**Instructions**

You have been asked to compute goodwill under the following methods. The normal rate of return on net assets for the industry is 15%.

(a) Goodwill is equal to 5 years' excess earnings.
(b) Goodwill is equal to the present value of 5 years' excess earnings discounted at 12%.
(c) Goodwill is equal to the average excess earnings capitalized at 17%.
(d) Goodwill is equal to average excess earnings capitalized at the normal rate of return for the industry of 15%.

**P13-7** Presented below is information related to Tornado Cleaner Company for 1984, its first year of operation.

Income Summary

| | | | |
|---|---|---|---|
| Raw Material Purchased | $123,300 | Sales | $474,000 |
| Productive Labor | 38,650 | Closing Inventories | |
| Factory Overhead | 28,350 | Raw Material | 32,400 |
| Selling Expenses | 37,050 | Goods in Process | 27,000 |
| Adm. Expenses | 27,300 | Finished Goods | 39,000 |
| Interest Expense | 8,650 | Appreciation of Land | 9,000 |
| Opening Inventories | | Profit on Sale of Forfeited Stock | 3,000 |
| Raw Material | 29,100 | | |
| Goods in Process | 24,000 | | |
| Finished Goods | 30,000 | | |
| Extraordinary Loss (net) | 6,900 | | |
| Income Taxes | 81,000 | | |
| Net Income | 150,100 | | |
| | $584,400 | | $584,400 |

**Instructions**

Tornado is negotiating to sell the business after one full year of operation. Compute the amount of goodwill as 200% of the income before extraordinary items and before taxes that is in excess of $135,000; $135,000 is considered to be a normal return on investment.

**P13-8** Bombeck Corp., a high-flying conglomerate, has recently been involved in discussions with Erma, Inc. As its CPA, you have been instructed by Bombeck to conduct a purchase audit of Erma's books to determine a possible purchase price for Erma's net assets. The following information is found.

| | |
|---|---:|
| Total identifiable assets of Erma's (fair market value) | $224,000 |
| Liabilities | 32,000 |
| Average rate of return on net assets for Erma's industry | 15% |
| Forecasted earnings per year based on past earnings figures | 32,000 |

**Instructions**

(a) Bombeck asked you to determine the purchase price on the basis of the following assumptions:
  1. Goodwill is equal to 3 years' excess earnings.
  2. Goodwill is equal to the present value of excess earnings discounted at 15% for 3 years.
  3. Goodwill is equal to the capitalization of excess earnings at 15%.
  4. Goodwill is equal to the capitalization of excess earnings at 25%.

(b) Bombeck asks you which of the methods above is the most theoretically sound. Justify your answer. Any assumptions made should be clearly indicated.

**P13-9** Beringer Bros., Inc. has contracted to purchase Chablis Company including the goodwill of the latter company. The agreement between purchaser and seller on the price to be paid for goodwill is as follows: "The value of the goodwill to be paid for is to be determined by capitalizing at 18% the average annual earnings from ordinary operations for the last 5 years in excess of 15% on the net worth, which, for purposes of this computation, is to be considered to be $280,000."

The net income per books for the last 5 years is:

| | |
|---|---:|
| 1980 | $45,840 |
| 1981 | 47,280 |
| 1982 | 68,040 |
| 1983 | 39,960 |
| 1984 | 51,360 |

As assistant to the treasurer of Beringer Bros., you are instructed to review the accounts of Chablis Company and determine the amount to be paid for goodwill in accordance with the terms of the contract. In your review of the accounts you discover the following:

1. An additional assessment of federal income taxes in the amount of $15,120 for the year 1982 was made and paid in 1984. The amount was charged against Retained Earnings.

2. In 1980 the company reviewed its accounts receivable and wrote off as an expense of that year $11,220 of accounts receivable that had been carried for years and appeared very unlikely to be collected.

3. In 1981 an account for $1,080 included in the 1980 write-off above was collected and credited to "Miscellaneous Income."

4. A fire in 1983 caused a loss, charged to Income, as follows:

| | |
|---|---:|
| Book value of property destroyed | $15,360 |
| Recovery from insurance company | 9,000 |
| Net loss | $ 6,360 |

5. Expropriation of property in 1983 resulted in a gain of $5,760 credited to income.

6. Amounts paid out under the company's product guarantee plan and charged to expense in each of the 5 years were as follows:

| | |
|---|---:|
| 1980 | $ 800 |
| 1981 | 1,150 |
| 1982 | 970 |
| 1983 | 1,200 |
| 1984 | 850 |

7. In 1984 the president of the company died, and the company realized $60,000 on an insurance policy on his life. The cash surrender value of this policy had been carried on the books as an investment in the amount of $51,900. The excess of proceeds over cash surrender value was credited to income.

**Instructions**

What is the price to be paid for the goodwill in accordance with the contract agreement? Prepare your computations in good form so that you can answer any questions asked by the treasurer in regard to your conclusions.

**P13-10** Boston Bottle Corporation was incorporated on January 3, 1982. The corporation's financial statements for its first year's operations were not examined by a CPA. You have been engaged to examine the financial statements for the year ended December 31, 1983, and your examination is substantially completed. The corporation's trial balance appears below.

Boston Bottle Corporation
TRIAL BALANCE
December 31, 1983

|  | Debit | Credit |
|---|---|---|
| Cash | $  11,000 |  |
| Accounts Receivable | 42,500 |  |
| Allowance for Doubtful Accounts |  | $      500 |
| Inventories | 38,500 |  |
| Machinery | 75,000 |  |
| Equipment | 29,000 |  |
| Accumulated Depreciation |  | 10,000 |
| Patents | 98,600 |  |
| Leasehold Improvements | 26,000 |  |
| Prepaid Expenses | 10,500 |  |
| Organization Expenses | 29,000 |  |
| Goodwill | 24,000 |  |
| Licensing Agreement No. 1 | 50,000 |  |
| Licensing Agreement No. 2 | 48,500 |  |
| Accounts Payable |  | 147,500 |
| Unearned Revenue |  | 12,500 |
| Capital Stock |  | 300,000 |
| Retained Earnings, January 1, 1983 | 27,000 |  |
| Sales |  | 681,600 |
| Cost of Goods Sold | 454,000 |  |
| Selling and General Expenses | 173,000 |  |
| Interest Expense | 3,500 |  |
| Extraordinary Losses | 12,000 |  |
| Totals | $1,152,100 | $1,152,100 |

The following information relates to accounts that may yet require adjustment.

1. Patents for Boston's manufacturing process were acquired January 2, 1983, at a cost of $81,600. An additional $17,000 was spent in December, 1983, to improve machinery covered by the patents and charged to the Patents account. Depreciation on fixed assets has been properly recorded for 1983 in accordance with Boston's practice, which provides a full year's depreciation for property on hand June 30 and no depreciation otherwise. Boston uses the straight-line method for all depreciation and amortization and the legal life on its patents.

2. On January 3, 1982, Boston purchased licensing agreement No. 1, which was believed to have an unlimited useful life. The balance in the Licensing Agreement No. 1 account includes its purchase price of $48,000 and expenses of $2,000 related to the acquisition. On January 1, 1983, Boston purchases licensing agreement No. 2, which has a life expectancy of 10 years. The balance in the Licensing Agreement No. 2 account includes its $48,000 purchase price and $2,000 in acquisition expenses, but it has been reduced by a credit of $1,500 for the advance collection of 1984 revenue from the agreement.

In late December 1982 an explosion caused a permanent 70% reduction in the expected revenue-producing value of licensing agreement No. 1 and in January, 1984, a flood caused additional damage that rendered the agreement worthless.

3. The balance in the Goodwill account includes (a) $10,000 paid December 30, 1982, for an advertising program it is estimated will assist in increasing Boston's sales over a period of 4 years following the disbursement, and (b) legal expenses of $14,000 incurred for Boston's incorporation on January 3, 1982.

4. The Leasehold Improvements account includes (a) the $12,000 cost of improvements with a total estimated useful life of 12 years, which Boston, as tenant, made to leased premises in January, 1982, (b) movable assembly line equipment costing $11,500 that was installed in the leased premises in December, 1983, and (c) real estate taxes of $2,500 paid by Boston in 1983, which under the terms of the lease should have been paid by the landlord. Boston paid its rent in full during 1983. A 10-year nonrenewable lease was signed January 3, 1982, for the leased building that Boston used in manufacturing operations.

5. The balance in the Organization Expenses account properly includes costs incurred during the organizational period. The corporation has exercised its option to amortize organization costs over a 60-month period for federal income tax purposes and wishes to amortize these for accounting purposes on the same basis.

**Instructions**

Prepare an eight-column worksheet to adjust accounts that require adjustment and include columns for an income statement and a balance sheet.

A separate account should be used for the accumulation of each type of amortization and for each prior period adjustment. Formal adjusting journal entries and financial statements are **not** required. (Hint: Make sure that Licensing Agreement No. 1 is amortized over the maximum life required in *APB Opinion No. 17* before the explosion damage loss is determined.)　　　　　　　　　　　　　　　　　　　　　　　　　　　　　　　(AICPA adapted)

**P13-11** The following situations relate to accounting for intangible assets and research and development costs.

1. Deb McIntyre Co. purchased two patents directly from the inventors. Patent No. 1 can be used only in its bicycle frame development research project. Patent No. 2 can be used in many different projects and currently is being used in a research project.

2. Spats & Vests Company deferred all of its 1982 R & D costs, which totaled $420,000. In November 1983, you are hired as controller and informed that an additional $500,000 has been deferred thus far in 1983. The company wants to issue comparative financial statements in accordance with generally accepted accounting principles for the first time this year.

3. Upstart Corporation, a development stage company, deferred all its preoperating and R & D costs. Its 1983 financial statements consisted only of statements of cash receipts and disbursements, capital shares, and assets and unrecovered preoperating costs and liabilities. The officers indicate that operations should start June 30, 1984 and complete financials will be issued December 31, 1984.

4. Digital Components Corp. develops computer software to be sold to interested users. The corporation incurred $187,000 in developing a new software package to control the energy use in high-rise buildings.

5. Talent Research Company is developing a new lightweight tennis racquet under contract for Sports & Games Corp. The contract, signed January 4, requires payments to Talent Research of $200,000 on December 31 and $300,000 at the completion of the project. At December 31, Talent has recorded an account receivable of $200,000 and has deferred R & D costs of $127,000.

**Instructions**

For each of the situations above discuss the accounting treatment you recommend.

# CHAPTER 14

# Long-Term Liabilities

**Long-term debt** consists of probable future sacrifices of economic benefits arising from present obligations that are not payable within the operating cycle of the business, or within a year if there are several operating cycles within one year. Mortgages payable, bonds payable, long-term notes payable, pension obligations, lease obligations, and long-term contracts for the purchase of land or other plant assets are examples of long-term liabilities. Pension and lease obligations are discussed in Chapters 21 and 22, respectively.

## NATURE OF LONG-TERM LIABILITIES

Long-term debt, a more or less permanent means of financing growth, is used to increase the earnings available to stockholders whenever a larger rate of return can be earned on the borrowed funds than is paid out as interest. The excess represents income to the stockholders. **Long-term creditors have no vote in management affairs and receive a stated rate of interest whether the income of the firm is low, high, or nonexistent.** Incurring long-term debt is often accompanied by considerable formality. The bylaws of corporations usually require approval by the board of directors and the stockholders before bonds can be issued or other long-term debt arrangements can be contracted.

Generally, long-term debt, in whatever form, is issued subject to various **covenants or restrictions** for the protection of the lenders. The covenants and other terms of the agreement between the borrower and the lender are stated in the **bond indenture or note agreement** and may be printed on (or referred to in) the formal instrument that is evidence of the debt. Items often mentioned in the indenture or agreement include the amounts authorized to be issued, interest rate, due date or dates, property pledged as security, sinking fund requirements, working capital and dividends restrictions, and limitations concerning the assumption of additional debt. Whenever these stipulations are important for a complete understanding of the financial position and the results of operations, they should be described in the body of the financial statements or the notes thereto. In many cases, the loan instrument or contract is held by a trustee, usually a bank or trust company, who acts as an independent third party to protect the interests of the lender(s) and the borrower.

## LONG-TERM NOTES

The difference between a current and a long-term note payable is the maturity date. As indicated in Chapter 10, short-term notes payable are expected to be paid within a year or the operating cycle, whichever is longer. The most common form of long-term notes payable is a mortgage note payable. A **mortgage note payable** is a promissory note secured by a document called a mortgage that pledges title to property as security for the loan. Mortgage notes payable are used more frequently by proprietorships and partnerships than by corporations, as corporations usually find that bond issues offer advantages in obtaining large loans.

On the balance sheet, the liability should be reported using a title such as "Mortgage Notes Payable" or "Notes Payable—Secured," with a brief disclosure of the property pledged in notes to the financial statements.

The borrower usually receives cash in the face amount of the mortgage note, in which case the face amount of the note is the true liability and no discount or premium is involved. When "points" are assessed by the lender, however, the liability is different from the face amount of the note.[1] Points raise the effective interest rate above the rate specified in the note. A point is 1% of the face of the note. For example, assume that a 20-year mortgage note in the amount of $100,000 with a stated interest rate of 10.75% is given by you to Local Savings and Loan Association as part of the financing of your new house. If Local Savings demands four points to close the financing, you will receive 4% less than $100,000, or $96,000, but you will be obligated to repay the entire $100,000 at the rate of $1,015 per month. Because you received only $96,000, and must repay $100,000, your effective interest rate is increased to approximately 11.3% on the money you actually borrowed.

Mortgages may be payable in full at maturity or in installments over the life of the loan. If payable at maturity, the mortgage payable is shown as a long-term liability on the balance sheet until such time as the approaching maturity date warrants showing it as a current liability. If it is payable in installments, the current installments due are shown as current liabilities, with the remainder shown as a long-term liability.

Recently, because of unusually high, unstable interest rates and a tight money supply, the traditional **fixed-rate mortgage** has been partially supplanted with new and unique mortgage arrangements. In 1981 more than 45% of the savings and loan companies offered **variable-rate mortgages** (also called floating-rate or adjustable rate mortgages) featuring interest rates tied to changes in the fluctuating market rate. Generally the variable rate lenders adjust the interest rate at either one- or three-year intervals, pegging the adjustments to a government index that measures the going rate for mortgages nationally.[2]

Another mortgage innovation is the **shared appreciation mortgages** (SAMs) in which the lender grants a reduction in the interest rate in return for a share of the appreciation in the pledged real estate's value. SAMs, especially popular in Florida, have not gained universal favor because of the difficulty in projecting the total return on investment. Identifying and accounting for the interest element is readily accomplished, but measuring and accounting for the lender's equity in the appreciation presents practical problems.

---

[1]Points, in mortgage financing, are analogous to the original issue discount of bonds.

[2]"Adjustable-Rate Home Loans Gain Favor, but May Be Risky," *The Wall Street Journal* (September 16, 1981), p. 29.

## SHORT-TERM OBLIGATIONS EXPECTED TO BE REFINANCED

Some short-term obligations are expected to be refinanced on a long-term basis and may be excluded from current liabilities and classified as long-term debt. Such classification is permitted if an enterprise (1) **intends** to refinance the obligations on a long-term basis, and (2) **demonstrates an ability** to consummate the refinancing. The particulars of refinancing and financial agreements related to short-term obligations that may be classified as long-term debt have been discussed in Chapter 10, pages 438–441, as have the disclosure requirements pertaining to such situations.

## BONDS PAYABLE

A bond arises from a contract known as an **indenture** and represents a promise to pay: (1) a sum of money at a designated maturity date, plus (2) periodic interest at a specified rate on the face value. Individual bonds typically have a $1,000 maturity amount (face value), although some bond issues are in denominations of $50, $100, and $10,000. Bond interest payments usually are made semiannually, although the interest rate is generally expressed as an annual rate. Bonds are assumed to have a $1,000 face value unless otherwise indicated. Some of the more common types of bonds found in practice are:

> **SECURED AND UNSECURED BONDS.** Bonds may be **secured,** for example, mortgage bonds, having a claim on real estate, and collateral trust bonds, having securities of other corporations as security, or **unsecured** as to principal, such as debenture bonds.

> **TERM AND SERIAL BONDS.** Bond issues that mature on a single date are called **term bonds,** and issues that mature in installments are called **serial bonds.** Serially maturing bonds are frequently used by school or sanitary districts, municipalities, or other local taxing bodies that borrow money that will be paid back in installments to be financed through a special levy. The proper accounting for serial bonds is illustrated in Appendix I of this chapter.

> **CONVERTIBLE, COMMODITY BACKED, AND DEEP DISCOUNT BONDS.** If bonds are convertible into other securities of the corporation for a specified time after issuance, they are called **convertible bonds.** Accounting for bond conversions is discussed in Chapter 17. Two new types of bonds have been developed in an attempt to attract capital in a tight money market—commodity-backed bonds and deep discount bonds.
>
> **Commodity-backed bonds** (also called **"asset-linked bonds"**) are redeemable in measures of a commodity, such as barrels of oil, tons of coal, or ounces of rare metal. For instance, in 1980 Sunshine Mining, a silver mining producer, sold two issues of bonds redeemable with either $1,000 in cash or 50 ounces of silver (or the cash equivalent), whichever is greater at maturity. Both issues are due in 1995 and have a stated interest rate of 8½%. The accounting problem is one of projecting the maturity value, especially since silver has fluctuated between a low of $8 an ounce and a high of $50 in the last four years.
>
> In 1980, J. C. Penney Company sold the first publicly marketed long-term debt securities in the United States that do not bear interest. These **deep discount bonds,** also referred to as **"zero interest debenture bonds,"** are sold at a discount which provides the buyer's total interest payoff at maturity. An even more unique version of the "zero interest" bond is the 1982 proposal by Caesar's World Inc., a Las Vegas/Lake Tahoe gambling casino operator. Caesar's World proposed to issue 5,000 of $15,000 face amount bonds that would entitle each bondholder to spend two weeks a year at its Lake Tahoe resort in lieu of interest on the bond.[3]

---

[3]"Caesar's World May Try Bond Issue Paying in Vacations," *The Wall Street Journal* (January 22, 1982), p. 32.

**REGISTERED AND BEARER (COUPON) BONDS.** Bonds issued in the name of the owner are **registered bonds** and require surrender of the certificate and issuance of a new certificate for the investor to complete a sale. A **bearer** or **coupon** bond, however, is not recorded in the name of the owner and may be transferred from one investor to another by mere delivery.

In addition to the bonds mentioned above, **income bonds** may be issued, where interest payments are dependent upon the issuing company having income. If the issuer reserves the right to call and retire the bonds prior to maturity, they are **callable bonds.**

In short, bonds have many different features. Their main purpose is to borrow from the general public or from institutional investors for the long term when the amount of capital needed is too large for one lender to supply. By issuing bonds in $100, $1,000, or $10,000 denominations, a large amount of long-term indebtedness can be divided into many small investing units, thus enabling more than one lender to participate in the loan.

## Accounting for the Issuance of Bonds

An entire bond issue may be sold to an investment banker, who acts as a selling agent in the process of marketing the bonds. In such arrangements, investment bankers may underwrite the entire issue by guaranteeing a certain sum to the corporation, taking the risk of selling the bonds for whatever price they can get, or they may sell the bond issue for a commission to be deducted from the proceeds of the sale. Alternatively, the issuing company may choose to place privately a bond issue by selling the bonds directly to a large institution, financial or otherwise, without the aid of an underwriter.

If an entire bond issue is sold to an underwriter or another institution at par (face value), the journal entry is:

| | | |
|---|---|---|
| Cash | 800,000 | |
| Bonds Payable | | 800,000 |

If a company takes subscriptions for its bond issue and sells its own bonds, entries may be made similar to those made for capital stock sold under the subscription plan (see Chapter 15). Assume that a company authorizes a $600,000 bond issuance consisting of 600 bonds, each having a $1,000 maturity value. The entries to record the subscription, collection of cash, and issuance of bonds are:

| | | |
|---|---|---|
| Subscriptions Receivable on Bonds Payable | 600,000 | |
|   Bonds Payable Subscribed | | 600,000 |
|     (Subscriptions received on 600 bonds, at par) | | |
| Cash | 400,000 | |
|   Subscriptions Receivable on Bonds Payable | | 400,000 |
|     (Cash received in full from subscribers to 400 bonds) | | |
| Bonds Payable Subscribed | 400,000 | |
|   Bonds Payable | | 400,000 |
|     (Bonds are issued to subscribers who have paid | | |
|     subscription price in full) | | |

The Subscriptions Receivable account now has a debit balance of $200,000. If this amount is to be collected in the near future, it is shown as a current asset in the balance sheet. The other accounts relating to the bonds are shown at the top of page 607.

If the entire bond issue is not sold at one time, both the amount of the bonds authorized and the bonds issued should be disclosed on the balance sheet or in the footnotes. This

| Long-term liabilities | | |
|---|---|---|
| 10% First mortgage bonds payable due Jan. 1, 1990: | | |
| Issued and outstanding | $400,000 | |
| Subscribed | 200,000 | |
| Total amount outstanding and subscribed | | $600,000 |

disclosure is important because unissued bonds represent a source of working capital and potential indebtedness that may be incurred without securing further authorization or without pledging additional assets.

## Bonds Issued Between Interest Dates

Bond interest payments are usually made semiannually on dates specified in the bond indenture. When bonds are issued on other than the interest payment dates, buyers of the bonds will pay the seller the interest accrued from the last interest payment date to the date of issue. The purchasers of the bonds, in effect, pay the bond issuer in advance for that portion of the full six-month interest payment to which they are not entitled, not having held the bonds during this period. The purchasers will receive the full six-month interest payment on the next semiannual interest payment date.

To illustrate, if bonds of a par value of $800,000, dated January 1, 1983, and bearing interest at an annual rate of 10% payable semiannually on January 1 and July 1, are issued at par plus accrued interest on March 1, 1983, the entry on the books of the issuing corporation is:

| | | |
|---|---|---|
| Cash | 813,333 | |
| Bonds Payable | | 800,000 |
| Bond Interest Expense (or Interest Payable) | | 13,333 *(accrued interest)* |
| ($800,000 × .10 × ²⁄₁₂) | | |

The purchaser advances two months' interest, because on July 1, 1983, four months after the date of purchase, six months' interest will be received from the issuing company. The company makes the following entry on July 1, 1983:

| | | |
|---|---|---|
| Bond Interest Expense (or Interest Payable) | 40,000 | |
| Cash | | 40,000 |

The expense account now contains a debit balance of $26,666.67, which represents the proper amount of interest expense, four months at 10% on $800,000.

## Discount and Premium on Bonds Payable (Influences of the Market)

Several different terms are frequently applied to the interest element of bonds. The interest rate written in the terms of the bond issue and ordinarily appearing on the bond instrument is known as the **stated,** or **nominal,** rate. This rate, which is set by the party issuing the bonds, is expressed as a percentage of the **par value,** also called **face value** or **maturity value,** of the bonds. If bonds are sold for more than par value (at a **premium**) or less than par value (at a **discount**), the actual interest yield to the bondholder is less than or greater than the stated rate. This rate of interest actually earned by the bondholders is called the **effective, yield,** or **market** rate and is set by the supply and demand forces that operate in the investment market. If bonds are sold at a discount, the effective rate is higher than the stated rate. Conversely, if the bonds are sold at a premium, the effective rate or yield rate is lower than the stated rate.

If bonds are sold below par, it means that investors demand a rate of interest higher than the rate stated on the bonds. The investors are not satisfied with the nominal interest rate because they can earn a greater rate on alternative investments of equal risk. They cannot change the nominal rate, and so they refuse to pay par for the bond and, thus, by changing the amount invested alter the effective rate of interest. Inasmuch as the investors receive interest at the stated rate computed on the par value of the bonds, they are earning at an effective rate that is higher than the stated rate because they paid less than par for the bonds. When the issuing corporation sells bonds of a par value of $800,000 at 97, the entry is:

| | | |
|---|---|---|
| Cash ($800,000 × .97) | 776,000 | |
| Discount on Bonds Payable | 24,000 | |
| Bonds Payable | | 800,000 |

Bond discount does not represent prepaid interest but, because of its relation to the interest described above, **the discount is amortized over the period of time that the bonds are outstanding and charged to interest expense.** If the amounts involved are not material, the discount may be amortized by the straight-line method instead of the effective interest method to be described later. Assume that the bonds are due in 20 years and bear interest at the rate of 8%, payable semiannually. An entry is made at the end of each fiscal year to amortize the discount on a straight-line basis as follows:

| | | |
|---|---|---|
| Bond Interest Expense | 1,200 | |
| Discount on Bonds Payable | | 1,200 |
| ($24,000 ÷ 20 years = $1,200) | | |

Discount on Bonds Payable is credited for 1/20 of the original amount of the discount because one year represents 1/20 of the life of the bonds. If the bonds were dated and sold on October 1 and the fiscal year of the company ended on December 31, the discount amortized on December 31 of the first year is only 3/12 of 1/20 of $24,000, or $300. The $1,200 per year is amortized in each of the next 19 years, and $900 is amortized in the year in which the bonds mature.

Premium on Bonds Payable is treated in a manner similar to that described for Discount on Bonds Payable. If 20-year bonds of a par value of $800,000 are sold at 103, then the cash proceeds are $824,000 ($800,000 × 1.03) and Bonds Payable is credited for $800,000 and Premium on Bonds Payable is credited for $24,000. At the end of each year the entry to amortize premium on a straight-line basis is:

| | | |
|---|---|---|
| Premium on Bonds Payable | 1,200 | |
| Bond Interest Expense | | 1,200 |

Discount on bonds payable is not an asset because it does not provide any future economic benefit. The enterprise has the use of the borrowed funds, but for that use it must pay interest. A bond discount means that the company borrowed less than the face or maturity value of the bond and therefore is faced with an actual (effective) interest rate higher than the stated (nominal) rate. Conceptually, discount on bonds payable is a liability valuation account, that is, a reduction of the face or maturity amount of the related liability.[4]

The unamortized portion of premium on bonds payable should be reported in a similar manner. Premium on bonds payable is not itself a liability—it has no existence apart from the related debt. The lower interest cost results because the proceeds of borrowing exceed the face or maturity amount of the debt. Conceptually, premium on bonds payable is a liability valuation account, that is, an addition to the face or maturity amount of the related liability.[5] As a result, the profession requires that bond discount and bond premium be reported as a direct deduction or addition to the face amount of the bond.[6]

## Effective Interest Amortization Method

The straight-line method, as illustrated, results in an even or average allocation of the interest expense over the life of the bonds. This assumption, that the interest cost for each year is equal, is not realistic when a premium or discount is involved. A more accurate procedure is the **effective interest method** (also called **present value amortization**), because interest expense is based on the increasing (discount) or decreasing (premium) book value of the bonds. **Under this method the interest cost for each period is the effective interest rate multiplied by the carrying amount (book value) of the bonds at the start of that period (the carrying amount changing each period by the amount of the amortized discount or premium).** The amount of amortization of bond discount or premium is the difference between the effective interest expense for the period and the actual interest payments.

To illustrate, Evermaster Corporation issued $100,000 of 8% bonds on January 1, 1983, due on January 1, 1988, with interest payable each July 1 and January 1. Because the investors wished to earn effective interest of 10%, they paid $92,278 for the $100,000 of bonds, creating a $7,722 discount. The $7,722 discount is a result of the considerations noted below.

| | | |
|---|---:|---:|
| Maturity value of bonds payable | | $100,000 |
| Present value of $100,000 due in 5 years at 10%, interest payable semiannually (Table 6-2) | $61,391[7] | |
| Present value of $4,000 interest payable semiannually for 5 years at 10% annually (Table 6-4) | 30,887[7] | |
| Proceeds from sale of bonds | | 92,278 |
| Discount on bonds payable | | $   7,722 |

[4]"Elements of Financial Statements of Business Enterprises," *Statement of Financial Accounting Concepts No. 3* (Stamford, Conn.: FASB, 1980), par. 160.

[5]Ibid., par. 162.

[6]"Interest on Receivables and Payables," *Opinions of the Accounting Principles Board No. 21* (New York: AICPA, 1971), par. 16.

[7]As determined from present value tables using 5% rate for 10 periods: ($100,000 × .61391) and ($4,000 × 7.72173).

The five-year amortization schedule appears below.

| | | Debit | Credit | Carrying |
|---|---|---|---|---|
| | Credit | Interest | Bond | Value |
| Date | Cash | Expense | Discount | of Bonds |
| 1/1/83 | | | | $ 92,278 |
| 7/1/83 | $ 4,000[a] | $ 4,614[b] | $ 614[c] | 92,892[d] |
| 1/1/84 | 4,000 | 4,645 | 645 | 93,537 |
| 7/1/84 | 4,000 | 4,677 | 677 | 94,214 |
| 1/1/85 | 4,000 | 4,711 | 711 | 94,925 |
| 7/1/85 | 4,000 | 4,746 | 746 | 95,671 |
| 1/1/86 | 4,000 | 4,783 | 783 | 96,454 |
| 7/1/86 | 4,000 | 4,823 | 823 | 97,277 |
| 1/1/87 | 4,000 | 4,864 | 864 | 98,141 |
| 7/1/87 | 4,000 | 4,907 | 907 | 99,048 |
| 1/1/88 | 4,000 | 4,952 | 952 | 100,000 |
| | $40,000 | $47,722 | $7,722 | |

**SCHEDULE OF BOND DISCOUNT AMORTIZATION**
**EFFECTIVE INTEREST METHOD—SEMIANNUAL INTEREST PAYMENTS**
**8% BONDS SOLD TO YIELD 10%**

[a] $4,000 = $100,000 × .08 × 6/12

[b] $4,614 = $92,278 × .10 × 6/12

[c] $614 = $4,614 − $4,000

[d] $92,892 = $92,278 + $614

The entry to record the issuance of Evermaster Corporation's bonds at a discount on January 1, 1983, is:

| | | |
|---|---|---|
| Cash | 92,278 | |
| Discount on Bonds Payable | 7,722 | |
| Bonds Payable | | 100,000 |

The journal entry to record the first interest payment on July 1, 1983, is:

| | | |
|---|---|---|
| Bond Interest Expense | 4,614 | |
| Discount on Bonds Payable | | 614 |
| Cash | | 4,000 |

If the market had been such that the investors were willing to earn an effective interest of 6% on the bond issue described above, they would have paid $108,530 or a premium of $8,530, computed as follows:

| | | |
|---|---|---|
| Maturity value of bonds payable | | $100,000 |
| Present value of $100,000 due in 5 years at 6%, interest payable semiannually (Table 6-2) | $74,409[8] | |
| Present value of $4,000 interest payable semiannually for 5 years at 6% annually (Table 6-4) | 34,121[8] | |
| Proceeds from sale of bonds | | 108,530 |
| Premium on bonds payable | | $ 8,530 |

[8] As determined from present value tables using 3% rate for 10 periods: ($100,000 × .74409) and ($4,000 × 8.53020).

The five-year amortization schedule appears below.

| Date | Credit Cash | Debit Interest Expense | Debit Bond Premium | Carrying Value of Bonds |
|---|---|---|---|---|
| | **SCHEDULE OF BOND PREMIUM AMORTIZATION** | | | |
| | **EFFECTIVE INTEREST METHOD—SEMIANNUAL INTEREST PAYMENTS** | | | |
| | **8% BONDS SOLD TO YIELD 6%** | | | |
| 1/1/83 | | | | $108,530 |
| 7/1/83 | $ 4,000[a] | $ 3,256[b] | $ 744[c] | 107,786[d] |
| 1/1/84 | 4,000 | 3,234 | 766 | 107,020 |
| 7/1/84 | 4,000 | 3,211 | 789 | 106,231 |
| 1/1/85 | 4,000 | 3,187 | 813 | 105,418 |
| 7/1/85 | 4,000 | 3,162 | 838 | 104,580 |
| 1/1/86 | 4,000 | 3,137 | 863 | 103,717 |
| 7/1/86 | 4,000 | 3,112 | 888 | 102,829 |
| 1/1/87 | 4,000 | 3,085 | 915 | 101,914 |
| 7/1/87 | 4,000 | 3,057 | 943 | 100,971 |
| 1/1/88 | 4,000 | 3,029 | 971 | 100,000 |
| | $40,000 | $31,470 | $8,530 | |

[a]$4,000 = $100,000 × .08 × 6/12    [c]$744 = $4,000 − $3,256
[b]$3,256 = $108,530 × .06 × 6/12    [d]$107,786 = $108,530 − $744

The entry to record the issuance of the Evermaster bonds at a premium on January 1, 1983, is:

| | | |
|---|---|---|
| Cash | 108,530 | |
| Premium on Bonds Payable | | 8,530 |
| Bonds Payable | | 100,000 |

The journal entry to record the first interest payment on July 1, 1983, is:

| | | |
|---|---|---|
| Bond Interest Expense | 3,256 | |
| Premium on Bonds Payable | 744 | |
| Cash | | 4,000 |

Discount or premium should be amortized as an adjustment to interest expense over the life of the note in such a way as to result in a **constant rate of interest** when applied to the amount of debt outstanding at the beginning of any given period.[9] Although the effective interest method is recommended, other methods are permitted if the results obtained are not materially different from those produced by the effective interest method.

Until the 1950s it was common for corporations to issue bonds with low, even-percentage coupons (such as 4%) to demonstrate their financial solidity. Frequently, the result was large discounts. More recently, it has become acceptable to set the stated rate of interest on bonds in rather precise fractions (such as 10⅞%). Companies usually attempt to align the stated rate as closely as possible with the market or effective rate. While discounts and

[9]"Interest on Receivables and Payables," *op. cit.,* par. 15.

premiums continue to occur, their absolute magnitude tends to be much smaller; many times it is immaterial.

## Costs of Issuing Bonds

The issuance of bonds involves engraving and printing costs, legal and accounting fees, commissions, promotion costs, and other similar charges. According to *APB Opinion No. 21*, these items should be debited to a **deferred charge** account for Unamortized Bond Issue Costs and amortized over the life of the debt, in a manner similar to that used for discount on bonds.[10]

The FASB, however, in *Concepts Statement No. 3* takes the position that debt issue cost can be treated as either an expense or a reduction of the related debt liability. Debt issue cost is not considered an asset for the same reason that debt discount is not; that is, it provides no future economic benefit. The cost of issuing bonds in effect reduces the proceeds of the bonds issued and increases the effective interest rate and thus may be accounted for the same as the unamortized discount.

There is an obvious difference between GAAP and *Concepts Statement No. 3's* view of debt issue costs. Until a standard is issued to supersede *Opinion No. 21*, however, **acceptable GAAP for debt issue costs is to treat them as a deferred charge and amortize them over the life of the debt.**

To illustrate the accounting for costs of issuing bonds, assume that Microchip Corporation sold $20,000,000 of 10-year debenture bonds for $20,795,000 on January 1, 1984 (also the date of the bonds). Costs of issuing the bonds were $245,000. The entries at January 1, 1984 and December 31, 1984 for issuance of the bonds and amortization of the bond issue costs would be as follows:

### January 1, 1984

| | | |
|---|---|---|
| Cash | 20,550,000 | |
| Unamortized Bond Issue Costs | 245,000 | |
| Premium on Bonds Payable | | 795,000 |
| Bonds Payable | | 20,000,000 |
| (To record issuance of bonds) | | |

### December 31, 1984

| | | |
|---|---|---|
| Bond Issue Expense | 24,500 | |
| Unamortized Bond Issue Costs | | 24,500 |
| (To amortize one year of bond issue costs—straight-line method) | | |

While the bond issue costs should be amortized using the effective interest method, the straight-line method is generally used in practice because it is easier and the results are not materially different.

## Treasury Bonds

Bonds payable that have been reacquired by the issuing corporation or its agent or trustee and have not been canceled are known as treasury bonds. They should be shown on the balance sheet at their par value as a deduction from the bonds payable issued to arrive at a

---

[10]"Interest on Receivables and Payables," *op. cit.*, par. 15.

net figure representing bonds payable outstanding. When they are sold or canceled, the Treasury Bonds account should be credited.

## EARLY EXTINGUISHMENT OF DEBT

The reacquisition of bonds (or any form of debt security or instrument) before their scheduled maturity, except through conversion by the holder, is termed **early extinguishment.** Early extinguishment occurs regardless of whether the bonds are considered to be terminated or to be held as so-called "treasury bonds."

### Computing Gain or Loss

The amount paid on early extinguishment or redemption before maturity, including any call premium and expense of reacquisition, is called the **reacquisition price.** The **net carrying amount** of the bonds on any specified date is the amount payable at maturity, adjusted for unamortized premium, discount, and cost of issuance. The excess of the net carrying amount over the reacquisition price is the **gain** from early extinguishment while the excess of the reacquisition price over the net carrying amount is the **loss.**

Bonds may be issued that are **callable** by the issuer after a certain date at a stated price, so that the issuing corporation may have the opportunity to reduce its bonded indebtedness or take advantage of lower interest rates. **Noncallable** bonds may be extinguished early through purchase on the market by the issuing corporation for the same reasons. **Whether callable or noncallable, any premium or discount should be amortized over the life to maturity date** because early redemption or extinguishment is not a certainty. If the prevailing interest rates decrease after the issuance of the bonds, it is often advantageous for the issuing corporation to acquire the entire bond issue outstanding and replace it with a new bond issue bearing a lower rate of interest. The replacement of an existing issuance with a new one is called **refunding.**

**Whether the early redemption or extinguishment of outstanding bonds is a nonrefunding or a refunding situation, the difference between the reacquisition price and the net carrying amount of the redeemed bonds should be recognized currently in income of the period of redemption.**[11] In accordance with *APB Opinion No. 26,* gain or loss resulting from early extinguishment of a debt is not amortized to future periods. Differing reasons for early redemption or differing means by which the bonds are redeemed have no bearing on how to account for the loss or gain. "All extinguishments of debt before scheduled maturities are fundamentally alike."[12]

At the time of redemption, the unamortized premium or discount, and costs of issue applicable to the bonds retired should be amortized up to the acquisition date. After this amortization the balances in the accounts for bond issue costs, unamortized premium or discount, and bonds payable should be reduced in the proper amounts. For example, assume that bonds of a par value of $800,000 due in 20 years, are issued on January 1, 1984, at 97. Bond issue costs totaling $16,000 were incurred. Ten years after the issue date, the

---

[11] Amortization of a refunding loss over the remaining life of the old issue being canceled or over the life of the new issue is no longer acceptable practice.

[12] "Early Extinguishment of Debt," *Opinions of the Accounting Principles Board No. 26* (New York: AICPA, 1972), par. 20.

entire issue is redeemed at 101 and canceled. The loss on redemption is computed as follows (straight-line amortization is used for simplicity):

| | | |
|---|---:|---:|
| Reacquisition price | | $808,000 |
| Net carrying amount of bonds redeemed: | | |
| Face value | $800,000 | |
| Unamortized discount ($24,000 × 10/20) | (12,000) | |
| Unamortized issue costs ($16,000 × 10/20) | | |
| (both amortized using straight-line basis) | (8,000) | 780,000 |
| Loss on redemption | | $ 28,000 |

The entry to record the reacquisition and cancellation of the bonds is:

| | | |
|---|---:|---:|
| Bonds Payable | 800,000 | |
| Loss on Redemption of Bonds (Extraordinary) | 28,000 | |
| Discount on Bonds Payable | | 12,000 |
| Unamortized Bond Issue Costs | | 8,000 |
| Cash | | 808,000 |

The issuer of callable bonds is generally required to exercise the call on an interest date. Therefore, the amortization of any discount or premium will be up to date and there will be no accrued interest. However, early extinguishments through purchases of bonds in the open market are more likely to be on other than an interest date. If the purchase is not made on an interest date, the discount or premium must be amortized and the interest payable must be accrued from the last interest date to the date of purchase.

## Reporting Gains and Losses

Because of money market conditions in 1973–1974, and again in the early 1980s, many companies were able to buy back long-term debt securities issued in the 1960s at prices well below face value. For instance, in 1973 United Brands extinguished $125 million (face value) of 5½% convertible subordinate debentures due in 1994 (with a market value of $87.5 million in 1973) by exchanging $12.5 million in cash and $75 million in 9⅛% debenture bonds (nonconvertible) and realized a gain of approximately $37.5 million, which was taken entirely into 1973 pretax earnings. These large gains were being reported as operating income before extraordinary items. This was considered misleading. The FASB, therefore, issued *Statement No. 4*, which requires that **gains or losses from extinguishment of debt should be aggregated and, if material, classified in the income statement as an extraordinary item, net of related income tax effect.**[13] That treatment shall apply whether an extinguishment is early or at scheduled maturity date or later without regard to the criteria of "unusual nature" and "infrequency of occurrence."

The following types of extinguishment result in classification of the gains or losses as extraordinary items:

1. Early extinguishment of debt at a discount (at less than the net carrying amount).
2. Early extinguishment of debt at a premium (at more than the net carrying amount).

---

[13]"Reporting Gains and Losses from Extinguishment of Debt," *Statement of Financial Accounting Standards No. 4* (Stamford, Conn.: FASB, 1975), par. 8.

3. Early extinguishment of debt by exchanging common or preferred stock.[14]
4. Refinancing existing debt with new debt.
5. Retirement of debt maturing serially.

Only gains and losses from cash purchases of debt made to satisfy current or future sinking fund requirements are not required to be classified as extraordinary items.[15]

Gains or losses from extinguishment of debt that are reported as extraordinary items should be described in such a way that readers of the financial statements can evaluate their significance. The following disclosures are required by *Statement No. 4:*

1. A description of the extinguishment transactions, including the sources of any funds used to extinguish debt if it is practicable to identify the sources.
2. The income tax effect in the period of extinguishment.
3. The per share amount of the aggregate gain or loss net of related tax effect.[16]

The preceding information, to the extent that it is not shown separately on the face of the income statement, must be disclosed in a single footnote or adequately cross-referenced if in more than one footnote. The following illustration presents disclosure on the face of the income statement and in a footnote to the financial statements.

Digital Computer Corp. purchased for $5,000,000 cash its outstanding 5% debenture bonds having a face or maturity value, as well as net carrying amount, of $6,000,000. Disclosure was appropriately made in its annual report as follows:

| | |
|---|---:|
| Income before extraordinary item | $4,200,000 |
| Extraordinary item—gain from liquidation of debt, net of income tax effect of $480,000—Note 3 | 520,000 |
| Net income | $4,720,000 |
| Per share of common stock: | |
| Income before extraordinary item | $1.62 |
| Extraordinary item, net of tax | .20 |
| Net income | $1.82 |

Note 3. *Extraordinary Item.* The extraordinary item represents a gain of $1,000,000 less related income tax effect from the redemption and retirement of the company's outstanding 5% debenture bonds due in 1995 pursuant to an offer made by the company. The funds used to purchase the debentures represent a portion of the proceeds from the sale of 300,000 shares of the company's common stock.

[14]Gains or losses on early extinguishment that result from a conversion agreement are not reported as an extraordinary item. The reacquisition price is determined by the market value of the common or preferred stock issued, or by the market value of the debt, whichever is more clearly evident. See "Early Extinguishment of Debt through Exchange for Common or Preferred Stock," *FASB Technical Bulletin No. 80-1* (Stamford, Conn.: FASB, 1980).

[15]Some debt agreements require that the debtor periodically set aside cash in a sinking fund for the purpose of systematically accumulating funds for the eventual redemption of the debt; sinking fund accounting is presented in Chapter 18.

[16]Disclosure of earnings per share applicable to extraordinary items is optional under the provisions of *APB Opinion No. 15;* however, *FASB Statement No. 4* requires disclosure of the per-share effect of gains and losses from extinguishment of debt.

## IMPUTED INTEREST ON LONG-TERM DEBT

Business transactions often involve the exchange of notes or similar instruments (including bonds) for cash or property, goods, or services. If the note is not currently receivable, the transaction is in effect a long-term loan with interest as an inherent and natural ingredient. It is unrealistic and improbable for any business to lend money interest-free. Yet during the 1960s numerous business transactions that were material in amount were consummated either with no apparent interest or with a very low interest cost.

The accounting profession responded by issuing a standard that insures proper accounting for transactions where the form does not reflect the economic substance of the arrangement because of failure to provide for a realistic interest rate on monies payable or receivable in the future.[17] Whenever the face amount of the instrument (notes, bonds, mortgage notes, equipment obligations, and long-term accounts payable) does not reasonably represent the present value of the consideration given or received in the exchange, the accountant must evaluate the entire arrangement to determine the amounts involved for properly recording the exchange and subsequent related interest. This circumstance is most apparent when the note is noninterest-bearing or has a stated interest rate that is different from the rate of interest appropriate for the transaction at the date of issuance. Unless such notes are recorded at present value, the purchase price and cost to the buyer (issuing the note) and the sales price and profit to the seller (accepting the note) in the year of the transaction are misstated. In addition, the interest expense and interest revenue in subsequent periods are also misstated.

In discussing the appropriate accounting for long-term debt having an unrealistic stated interest rate, the following categories are important:[18]

1. Notes issued solely for cash.
2. Notes issued for cash, but with some right or privilege also being exchanged. For example, a corporation may lend a supplier cash that is receivable five years hence with no stated interest, in exchange for which the supplier agrees to make products available to the lender at lower than prevailing market prices.
3. Notes issued in a noncash exchange for property, goods, or services.

### Notes Issued Solely for Cash[19]

When the effective interest on a note is equal to its stated rate, the note sells at its face value. When the stated rate is different from the effective interest, the cash proceeds will be different from the face value of the note. As indicated earlier, the difference between the

---

[17]"Interest on Receivables and Payables," *op. cit.*

[18]According to *APB Opinion No. 21,* all payables that represent commitments to pay money at a determinable future date are subject to present value measurement techniques and interest imputation, if necessary, except for the following specifically excluded types:
  1. Normal accounts payable due within one year.
  2. Security deposits, retainages, advances, or progress payments.
  3. Transactions between parent and subsidiary.
  4. Convertible debt securities.
  5. Obligations payable at some indeterminable future date.

[19]Although the term "note" is used throughout this discussion on imputed interest, the basic principles and methodology are equally applicable to other long-term debt instruments, such as bonds.

face value and the cash proceeds received is a discount or a premium that should be amortized over the life of a note to approximate the effective interest rate.

**When a note is issued solely for cash, the interest factor is assumed to be the stated or coupon rate plus or minus the amortization of the discount or premium.** Because the note issued for cash has a present value equal to the cash proceeds, interest other than that provided by the coupon or stated rate plus or minus amortization of the discount or premium should not be imputed.

A recent example of such a transaction is Beneficial Corporation's 1982 offering of $150 million of zero-coupon notes (deep discount bonds) having a 1990 maturity date. With a face value of $1,000 each, these notes sold for $327—a deep discount of $673 each. Beneficial will amortize the discount over the eight-year life of the notes using an effective interest rate of 15%.[20] The present value of each note is the cash proceeds of $327. Rather than having to be imputed, the interest rate of 15% can be calculated by determining the interest rate which equates the amount presently paid with those amounts to be received in the future.

## Notes Exchanged for Cash and Some Right or Privilege

Sometimes when a note is issued, additional rights or privileges are given to the recipient of the note. For example, a corporation issues a noninterest-bearing note payable that is to be repaid over five years with no stated interest and in exchange agrees to sell merchandise to the lender at less than the prevailing prices of their merchandise. In this circumstance, the difference between the present value of the payable and the amount of cash received should be recorded by the issuer of the note (borrower/supplier) simultaneously as a discount (debit) on the note and as unearned revenue (credit) on the future sales. The discount should be amortized as a charge to interest expense over the life of the note. The unearned revenue, equal in amount to the discount, reflects a partial prepayment for sales transactions that will occur over the next five years. This unearned revenue should be recognized as revenue when sales are made to the lender over the next five years.

For example, assume that the face or maturity value of a five-year, noninterest bearing note is $100,000 and that the appropriate rate at which to impute interest is 10%. The conditions of the note provide that the recipient of the note (lender/customer) can purchase $500,000 of merchandise from the issuer of the note (borrower/supplier) at 90% of regular selling price over the next five years. To record the loan, the issuer of the note records a discount of $37,908, the difference between the $100,000 face amount of the loan and its present value of $62,092 ($100,000 × .62092); as the supplier of the merchandise, the issuer also records a credit to unearned revenue of $37,908. The issuer's journal entry is:

| | | |
|---|---|---|
| Cash | 100,000 | |
| Discount on Notes Payable | 37,908 | |
| Notes Payable | | 100,000 |
| Unearned Revenue | | 37,908 |

The Discount on Notes Payable is subsequently amortized to interest expense using the effective interest method. The Unearned Revenue is recognized as revenue from the sale of

---

[20]$1,000 × .32690 (from Table 6-2) = $327; see *The Wall Street Journal* (January 22, 1982), p. 32.

merchandise and is prorated on the same basis that each period's sales to the lender-customer bear to the total sales to that customer for the term of the note. In this situation the write-off of the discount and the recognition of the unearned revenue are at different rates.

### Noncash Transactions

The third type of situation involves the issuance of a note for some noncash consideration such as property, goods, or services. When the debt instrument is exchanged for property, goods, or services in a bargained transaction entered into at arm's length, the stated interest rate is presumed to be fair unless:

1. No interest rate is stated, or
2. The stated interest rate is unreasonable, or
3. The stated face amount of the debt instrument is materially different from the current cash sales price for the same or similar items or from current market value of the debt instrument.

In these circumstances the present value of the debt instrument is measured by the fair value of the property, goods, or services or by an amount that reasonably approximates the market value of the note.[21] **The interest element plus any stated rate of interest is evidenced by the difference between the face amount of the note and the fair value of the property.**

For example, assume that Scenic Development Company sold land having a cash sale price of $200,000 to Health Spa, Inc., in exchange for Health Spa's five-year, $293,860 noninterest-bearing note. The $200,000 cash sale price represents the present value of the $293,860 note discounted at 8% for five years. If the transaction is recorded on the sale date at the face amount of the note, $293,860, by both parties, Health Spa's land account and Scenic's sales would be overstated by $93,860, because the $93,860 represents the interest for five years at an effective rate of 8%. Interest revenue to Scenic and interest expense to Health Spa for the five-year period correspondingly would be understated by $93,860.

Because the difference beween the cash sale price of $200,000 and the face amount of the note, $293,860, represents interest at an effective rate of 8%, the transaction is recorded at the exchange date as follows:

| ENTRIES FOR NONCASH NOTE TRANSACTIONS | | | | |
|---|---|---|---|---|
| **Health Spa, Inc. Books** | | | **Scenic Development Company Books** | |
| Land | 200,000 | | Notes Receivable | 293,860 | |
| Discount on Notes Payable | 93,860 | | Discount on Notes Rec. | | 93,860 |
| Notes Payable | | 293,860 | Sales | | 200,000 |

During the five-year life of the note, Health Spa amortizes annually the discount of $93,860 as a charge to interest expense. Scenic Development records interest revenue totaling $93,860 over the five-year period by also amortizing the discount. The effective interest method is required, although other approaches to amortization may be used if the results obtained are not materially different from those that result from the effective interest method.

---

[21]"Interest on Receivables and Payables," *op. cit.,* par. 12.

## Imputing an Interest Rate

In each of the previously illustrated situations, the effective or real interest rate was evident or determinable by other facts involved in the exchange, such as the fair market value of what was either given or received. But, if the fair value of the property, goods, or services is not determinable and if the debt instrument has no ready market, the problem of determining the present value of the debt instrument is more difficult. To estimate the present value of a debt instrument under such circumstances, an applicable interest rate is approximated that may differ from the stated interest rate. This process of interest rate approximation is called **imputation,** and the resulting interest rate is called an **imputed interest rate.** The imputed interest rate is used to establish the present value of the debt instrument by discounting, at that rate, all future payments on the debt instrument.

The following general guidelines for imputing the appropriate interest rate have been provided:

> The prevailing rates for similar instruments of issuers with similar credit ratings will normally help determine the appropriate interest rate for determining the present value of a specific note at its date of issuance. In any event, the rate used for valuation purposes will normally be at least equal to the rate at which the debtor can obtain financing of a similar nature from other sources at the date of the transaction. The objective is to approximate the rate which would have resulted if an independent borrower and an independent lender had negotiated a similar transaction under comparable terms and conditions with the option to pay the cash price upon purchase or to give a note for the amount of the purchase which bears the prevailing rate of interest to maturity.[22]

The choice of a rate may be affected specifically by the credit standing of the issuer, restrictive covenants, the collateral, payments and other terms pertaining to the debt, and the existing prime interest rate. **Determination of the imputed interest rate is made at the time the debt instrument is issued; any subsequent changes in prevailing interest rates are ignored.**

## Accounting for Interest Imputation

On December 31, 1983, Wunderlich Company issued for architectural services a promissory note with a face value of $550,000, a due date of December 31, 1988, and bearing a stated interest rate of 2%, payable at the end of each year. The fair value of the services is not readily determinable nor is the note readily marketable. On the basis of the credit rating of Wunderlich Company, the absence of collateral, the prime interest rate at that date, and the prevailing interest on the company's other outstanding debt, an 8% interest rate is imputed as appropriate in this circumstance. The imputed interest portion of the note is determined as follows:

| | | |
|---|---:|---:|
| Maturity value of the note | | $550,000 |
| Present value of $550,000 due in 5 years at 8%— | | |
| $550,000 × .6806 (Table 6–2) | $374,330 | |
| Present value of $11,000 payable annually for | | |
| 5 years at 8% annually— | | |
| $11,000 × 3.9927 (Table 6–4) | 43,920 | |
| Present value of the note | | 418,250 |
| Discount | | $131,750 |

[22] Ibid., par. 13.

The issuance of the note and receipt of the services is recorded as follows:

**December 31, 1983**

| | | |
|---|---|---|
| Building (or Construction in Process) | 418,250 | |
| Discount on Notes Payable | 131,750 | |
| Notes Payable | | 550,000 |

The five-year amortization schedule appears below.

| SCHEDULE OF NOTE DISCOUNT AMORTIZATION EFFECTIVE INTEREST METHOD 2% NOTE DISCOUNTED AT 8% (IMPUTED) | | | | | |
|---|---|---|---|---|---|
| Date | Credit Cash | Debit Interest Expense | Credit Unamortized Discount | Unamortized Discount Balance | Present Value of Note |
| | 2% | 8% | | | |
| 12/31/83 | | | | $131,750 | $418,250 |
| 12/31/84 | $11,000[a] | $ 33,460[b] | $ 22,460[c] | 109,290[d] | 440,710[e] |
| 12/31/85 | 11,000 | 35,257 | 24,257 | 85,033 | 464,967 |
| 12/31/86 | 11,000 | 37,197 | 26,197 | 58,836 | 491,164 |
| 12/31/87 | 11,000 | 39,293 | 28,293 | 30,543 | 519,457 |
| 12/31/88 | 11,000 | 41,543[f] | 30,543[f] | -0- | 550,000 |
| | $55,000 | $186,750 | $131,750 | | |

[a]$550,000 × .02 = $11,000.
[b]$418,250 × .08 = $33,460.
[c]$33,460 − $11,000 = $22,460.
[d]$131,750 − $22,460 = $109,290.
[e]$418,250 + $22,460 = $440,710.
[f]$14 adjustment to compensate for rounding.

Payment of the first year's interest and amortization of the discount is recorded as follows:

**December 31, 1984**

| | | |
|---|---|---|
| Interest Expense | 33,460 | |
| Discount on Notes Payable | | 22,460 |
| Cash | | 11,000 |

## FINANCIAL STATEMENT PRESENTATION OF DISCOUNT OR PREMIUM

Any discount or premium resulting from the determination of present value in these trans-actions is not an asset or a liability separable from the note that produces it. Therefore, the discount or premium is reported in the balance sheet as a direct deduction from or addition to the face amount of the debt instrument. It is not classified as a deferred charge or deferred credit. The face amount of the note is disclosed in the balance sheet or in the footnotes, and the description of the note includes the effective interest rate. The balance sheet presentation of debt discount or premium may assume two different forms: (1) presentation of the discount in caption form and (2) presentation of the discount separately.[23] If we use the data from the Wunderlich Company illustration, these two forms appear as follows on December 31, 1984, one year after issuance of the note:

| Presentation of the Discount in Caption Form | | |
| --- | --- | --- |
| | 12/31/84 | 12/31/83 |
| Note payable issued for services: $550,000 face amount, due December 31, 1988, bearing 2% stated interest (less unamortized discount based on imputed interest rate of 8%— 1984, $109,290; 1983, $131,750) | $440,710 | $418,250 |

| Presentation of the Discount Separately | | |
| --- | --- | --- |
| | 12/31/84 | 12/31/83 |
| Note payable issued for services: Note due December 31, 1988, bearing stated interest of 2% | $550,000 | $550,000 |
| Less unamortized discount based on imputed interest rate of 8% | 109,290 | 131,750 |
| Note payable less unamortized discount | $440,710 | $418,250 |

If several or numerous notes are involved, the aggregate principal amount of such notes and the balance of total unamortized discount is presented in condensed form in the balance sheet and the details of each note are disclosed individually in a footnote or separate schedule to the balance sheet.

Amortization of discounts or premiums resulting from imputed interest on notes payable is reported as interest in the statement of income. Any costs of issue are reported in the balance sheet as deferred charges and are amortized to expense over the life of the debt issue.

## REPORTING LONG-TERM DEBT

Companies that have large amounts and numerous issues of long-term debt frequently report only one amount in the balance sheet and support this with comments and schedules in the accompanying notes. These footnote disclosures generally indicate the nature of the liabilities, maturity dates, interest rates, call provisions, conversion privileges, restrictions imposed by the borrower, and assets pledged as security. Any assets pledged as security for the debt should be shown in the asset section of the balance sheet. Long-term debt that matures within one year should be reported as a current liability, unless retirement is to be accomplished with other than current assets. If the debt is to be refinanced, converted into stock, or is to be retired from a bond retirement fund, it should continue to be reported as noncurrent and accompanied with a footnote explaining the method to be used in its

[23] Ibid., par. 16.

liquidation.[24] For example, Tenneco, Inc. discloses in notes to the financial statements details of its long-term debt (see pages 202–203).

In 1981, the FASB issued *Statement No. 47,* which requires disclosure at the balance sheet date of future payments for sinking fund requirements and maturity amounts of long-term debt during each of the next five years.[25] The purpose of the disclosures is to aid financial statement users in evaluating the amounts and timing of future cash flows. As an example, assume that Percy Corporation has two long-term borrowings outstanding at December 31, 1983. The first borrowing is a $50 million sinking fund debenture with annual sinking fund payments of $5 million in 1984, 1985, and 1986, $10 million in 1987 and 1988, and $15 million in 1989. The second borrowing is a $75 million bond issue which matures in 1986. Percy's disclosures would be as follows:

| Maturities and sinking fund requirements on long-term debt for the next five years are as follows: | |
|---|---|
| 1984 | $ 5,000,000 |
| 1985 | 5,000,000 |
| 1986 | 80,000,000 |
| 1987 | 10,000,000 |
| 1988 | 10,000,000 |

## UNCONDITIONAL LONG-TERM OBLIGATIONS

An issue of extreme importance to accountants is the question of "off-balance-sheet financing." **Off-balance-sheet financing** is an attempt to borrow monies to fund operations or capital projects and to do it so that the obligations are not recorded. For example, in Chapter 8 it was noted that enterprises sometimes become involved in product financing arrangements in an attempt to generate income and to borrow monies without reporting the related borrowing on the financial statement. This practice is no longer permitted; companies are now required to report this type of arrangement as a liability.[26]

In addition to product financing arrangements, companies also become involved in a variety of long-term commitments typically associated with project financing arrangements. **Project financing arrangements** arise when (1) two or more entities form another entity to construct an operating plant that will be used by both parties; (2) the new entity borrows funds to construct the project and repays the debt from the proceeds received from the project; (3) payment of the debt is guaranteed by the companies that formed the new entity. The advantage of such an arrangement is that the companies that formed the new entity do not have to report the liability on their books. To illustrate, assume that Dow Chemical and Mobil Oil each put up $1 million and form a separate company to build a chemical plant to be used by both companies. The newly formed company borrows $48 million to construct the plant. In this way neither Dow Chemical nor Mobil Oil reports the debt on their balance sheet—their only disclosure is the guarantee of the payment of

---

[24]"Balance Sheet Classification of Short-Term Obligations Expected to be Refinanced," *FASB Statement of Financial Accounting Standards No. 6* (Stamford, Conn.: FASB, 1975), par. 15.

[25]"Disclosure of Long-Term Obligations," *Statement of Financial Accounting Standards No. 47* (Stamford, Conn.: FASB, 1981), par. 10.

[26]"Accounting for Product Financing Arrangements," *Statement of Financial Accounting Standards No. 49* (Stamford, Conn.: FASB, 1981), pars. 8–9.

the debt of the new company in case the proceeds from the project are insufficient to cover the debt service requirements.[27]

In some cases, these project financing arrangements become more formalized through the use of take-or-pay contracts, through-put contracts, or similar types of contracts. In a simple **take-or-pay contract,** a purchaser of goods signs an agreement with a seller to pay specified amounts periodically in return for products or services. The purchaser must make specified minimum payments even if delivery of the contracted products or services is not taken. Often these take-or-pay contracts are associated with project financing arrangements. For example, in the illustration above, Dow Chemical and Mobil Oil sign an agreement that they will purchase products from this new plant and that they will make certain minimum payments even if they do not take delivery of the goods.

**Through-put agreements** are similar in concept to take-or-pay contracts, except that a service instead of a product is provided by the asset under construction. For example, assume that Dow and Mobil become involved in a project financing arrangement to build a pipeline (instead of a plant) to transport their various products. An agreement is signed that requires Dow and Mobil to pay specified amounts in return for the transportation of the product. In addition, these companies are obligated to provide specified minimum quantities to be transported in each period and are required to make cash payments even if they do not provide the minimum quantities to be transported.

Inconsistent methods have been used in practice to account for and disclose the unconditional obligation in a take-or-pay or through-put contract involved in a project financing arrangement. In general, most companies have attempted to develop these types of contracts to "get the debt off the balance sheet." Only in unusual situations would the acquisition of an asset and the incurrence of a liability have been reported on the balance sheet of the unconditionally obligated company.

Recognizing this situation and noting that the conceptual framework project is still in process as far as recognition of contractual rights and obligations is concerned, the FASB decided as an interim measure to issue guidelines for the disclosure of unconditional purchase obligations associated with project financing arrangements.[28]

An **"unconditional purchase obligation"** is defined as an obligation to transfer a fixed or minimum amount of funds in the future, or to transfer quantities of goods or services at fixed or minimum prices (as in take-or-pay and through-put contracts). An unconditional purchase obligation that has all of the following characteristics must be disclosed:

1. It is noncancelable, or cancelable only upon the occurrence of some remote contingency or with the permission of the other party.
2. It is part of a supplier's project financing arrangement for the facilities that are to provide the contracted goods or services.
3. It has a remaining term in excess of one year.

For those unconditional purchase obligations that are recorded on the purchaser's balance sheet, disclosure must be made of the payments to be made under the obligation for each of the next five years. In addition, the following disclosures are required for those unconditional purchase obligations that are not recorded on the purchaser's balance sheet:

---

[27]"Accounting for Contingencies," *Statement of Financial Accounting Standards No. 5,* (Stamford, Conn.: FASB, 1975), par. 12.

[28]"Disclosure of Long-Term Obligations," *op. cit.*

1. The nature and term of the obligations.
2. The total amount of the fixed and determinable portion of the obligations at the balance sheet date and for each of the next five years.
3. The nature of any variable portions of the obligations.
4. The amounts purchased under the obligations (as in take-or-pay contracts or through-put contracts) for each period for which an income statement is presented.

With respect to requirement (2) above, it is recommended, but not required, that the amount of imputed interest necessary to reduce the total amount of the obligation to its present value be disclosed.[29] The discount rate to be used should be the effective interest rate of the borrowings that financed the facility that will provide the contracted goods or services, if this rate is known by the purchaser. If not known, the discount rate should be the purchaser's incremental borrowing rate at the date the obligation is entered into. This rate is the rate the purchaser would have incurred to borrow the funds necessary to discharge the unconditional purchase obligation. An example of a through-put agreement involving a project financing arrangement is reported below for Hewlett Chemical Company:

To secure access to facilities to process chemical phenoxyethanol, the company has signed a processing agreement with a chemical company allowing Hewlett to submit 100,000 tons for processing annually for 15 years. Under the terms of the agreement, Hewlett may be required to advance funds if the chemical company is unable to meet its financial obligations. The aggregate amount of required payments at December 31, 1981 is as follows:

| | |
|---|---:|
| 1982 | $ 20,000,000 |
| 1983 | 15,000,000 |
| 1984 | 10,000,000 |
| 1985 | 9,000,000 |
| 1986 | 8,000,000 |
| Later years | 78,000,000 |
| Total | 140,000,000 |
| Less: Amount representing interest | (79,791,510) |
| Total at present value | $ 60,208,490 |

In addition, the company is required to pay a proportional share of the variable operating expenses of the plant. The company's total processing charges under the agreement for each of the preceding five years were: 1977 and 1978, $27,000,000; 1979 and 1980, $29,000,000; and 1981, $28,000,000.

These disclosure requirements help users better understand the impact that unconditional long-term purchase obligations associated with project financing arrangements have on future cash flows. However, it is imperative that the profession address the more important issue of identifying when these unconditional purchase obligations are effectively liabilities. Only by getting some of these obligations on the balance sheet instead of getting them off will sound reporting be enhanced.

---

[29]Ibid., par. 7.

# APPENDIX H

# Accounting for Troubled Debt Restructurings

During periods of depressed economic conditions or other financial hardship, some debtors have difficulty meeting their financial obligations because of serious cash flow problems. For example, New York City had a difficult time paying its interest and principal obligations on debt issued to finance its municipal operations. In addition, many real estate investment trusts, referred to as REITs (enterprises established to invest in real estate), experienced financial problems because of the general downturn in the economy in the mid-1970s, coupled with poor investment selection on their part. More recently, Chrysler Corp., International Harvester Co., and many savings and loan associations have had to restructure their debts or in some similar way be bailed out of negative cash flow situations. As a result, debt obligations are often restructured to permit the debtor either to defer or to reduce the interest or the principal obligation.

*FASB Statement No. 15,* "Accounting by Debtors and Creditors for Troubled Debt Restructurings," was issued in 1977 to clarify the proper accounting for these types of transactions. According to this statement, a troubled debt restructuring occurs when "... the creditor for economic or legal reasons related to the debtor's financial difficulties grants a concession to the debtor that it would not otherwise consider."[1] For example, a financial institution such as a bank recognizes that granting some concessions (that is, restructuring of the debt in a troubled loan situation), is a more likely way to maximize recovery than forcing the debtor into bankruptcy. *Statement No. 15* applies only to **troubled** debt restructurings in which the creditor grants some concessions; it does not apply to modifications of a debt obligation that reflect general economic conditions that dictate a reduction in interest rates. Nor does it apply to the refunding of an old debt with new debt having an effective interest rate approximately equal to that of similar debt issued by non-troubled debtors.

---

[1]"Accounting by Debtors and Creditors for Troubled Debt Restructurings," *FASB Statement of Financial Accounting Standards No. 15* (Stamford, Conn.: FASB, 1977), par. 1.

A troubled debt restructuring involves one of two basic types of transactions:

1. Settlement of debt at less than its recorded amount.
2. Continuation of debt with a modification in terms.

Whether the troubled debt restructuring is a "settlement of the debt" or a "continuation of the debt with modification in terms," the concessions granted the debtor (borrower) by the creditor (lender) generally will result in a **gain to the debtor** and a **loss to the creditor.**[2] **The gain and the loss are measured by both the debtor and creditor as the difference between the carrying amount (book value) of the obligation immediately prior to restructuring (prerestructuring value) and the undiscounted total future cash flows required after restructuring (post restructure value).** Therefore, if the carrying amount of the obligation is greater than the total future cash flows, the difference is recorded at the date of restructure as a gain to the debtor and as a loss to the creditor. And, if the carrying amount of the obligation is less than the total future cash flows, no restructure gain or loss is recognized. These are the basic principles set forth in *FASB Statement No. 15,* which attempts to achieve "accounting symmetry" between the debtor and the creditor.[3]

## SETTLEMENT OF DEBT AT LESS THAN CARRYING AMOUNT

A transfer of noncash assets (real estate, receivables, or other assets) or the issuance of the debtor's stock can be used to settle a debt obligation in a troubled debt restructuring. In these situations, **the noncash assets or equity interest given should be accounted for at their fair market value.** The debtor is required to determine the excess of the carrying amount of the payable over the fair value of the assets or equity transferred (gain), and, likewise, the creditor is required to determine the excess of the recorded investment in the receivable over the fair value of those same assets or equity interests transferred (loss). The debtor recognizes an extraordinary gain equal to the amount of the excess and the creditor normally would charge the excess (loss) against an appropriate allowance account. In addition, the debtor recognizes a gain or loss on disposition of assets to the extent that the fair value of those assets differs from their carrying amount (book value).

To illustrate a transfer of assets, assume that American City Bank has loaned $20,000,000 to Union Mortgage Company. Union Mortgage Company in turn has invested these monies in residential apartment buildings, but because of low occupancy rates it cannot meet its loan obligations. American City Bank, therefore, agrees to accept from Union Mortgage Company real estate with a fair market value of $16,000,000 in full settlement of the $20,000,000 loan obligation. The real estate has a recorded value of

---

[2]While the restructuring may result in the recognition of no gains or losses by either debtor or creditor, it is the nature of a troubled debt situation that the creditor cannot have a gain and the debtor cannot have a loss from restructuring.

[3]Although the objective of *FASB Statement No. 15* was to achieve symmetry between the entries recorded by the debtor and the creditor, this will not always be attained. The criteria specified by *Statement No. 15* must be applied separately by the debtor and the creditor to their individual facts and circumstances to determine whether a troubled debt restructuring has occurred. In order to clarify this point, the FASB indicated that when the carrying amount of the receivable on the creditor's books is different from the carrying amount of the payable on the debtor's books, it may be possible that only one of the parties will record a troubled debt restructuring. See "Classification of Debt Restructurings by Debtors and Creditors," *Technical Bulletin No. 80-2* (Stamford, Conn.: FASB, 1980).

$21,000,000 on the books of Union Mortgage Company. The entry to record this transaction on the books of American City Bank (creditor) is as follows:

| | | |
|---|---|---|
| Real Estate | 16,000,000 | |
| Allowance for Doubtful Accounts (Loss on Restructured Debt) | 4,000,000 | |
| Note Receivable from Union Mortgage Co. | | 20,000,000 |

The real estate is recorded at fair market value, and a charge is made to the Allowance for Doubtful Accounts to reflect the bad debt write-off. If no allowance were available to absorb the charge of $4,000,000, the debit would be to a loss (ordinary) account.

The entry to record this transaction on the books of Union Mortgage Company (debtor) is as follows:

| | | |
|---|---|---|
| Note Payable to American City Bank | 20,000,000 | |
| Loss on Disposition of Real Estate | 5,000,000 | |
| Real Estate | | 21,000,000 |
| Gain on Restructuring of Debt | | 4,000,000 |

Union Mortgage Company has a loss on the disposition of real estate in the amount of $5,000,000, the difference between the $21,000,000 book value and the $16,000,000 fair market value, which should be shown as an ordinary loss on the income statement in accordance with *APB Opinion No. 30*. In addition, it has a gain on restructuring of debt of $4,000,000, the difference between the $20,000,000 carrying amount of the note payable and the $16,000,000 fair market value of the real estate. **The gain on restructuring should be shown as an extraordinary item** in accordance with *FASB Statement No. 4*.

To illustrate the granting of an equity interest, assume that American City Bank had agreed to accept from Union Mortgage Company 320,000 shares of Union's common stock ($10 par) that has a fair market value of $16,000,000 in full settlement of the $20,000,000 loan obligation. The entry to record this transaction on the books of American City Bank (creditor) is as follows:

| | | |
|---|---|---|
| Investment in Marketable Equity Securities | 16,000,000 | |
| Allowance for Doubtful Accounts (Loss on Restructured Debt) | 4,000,000 | |
| Note Receivable from Union Mortgage Co. | | 20,000,000 |

The stock received by American City Bank is recorded as an investment at the fair market value at the date of restructure.

The entry to record this transaction on the books of Union Mortgage Company (debtor) is as follows:

| | | |
|---|---|---|
| Note Payable to American City Bank | 20,000,000 | |
| Common Stock | | 3,200,000 |
| Additional Paid-in Capital | | 12,800,000 |
| Gain on Restructuring of Debt | | 4,000,000 |

The stock issued by Union Mortgage Company is recorded in the normal manner with the difference between the par value and the fair market value of the stock recorded as additional paid-in capital.

## CONTINUATION OF DEBT WITH MODIFICATION OF TERMS

In some cases, a debtor will have serious short-run cash flow problems that lead the debtor to request one or a combination of the following modifications:

1. Reduction of the stated interest rate.
2. Extension of the maturity date of the face amount of the debt.
3. Reduction of the face amount of the debt.
4. Reduction or deferral of any accrued interest.

The profession takes the position that a troubled debt restructuring involving any of these modifications of terms is a continuation of an existing debt arrangement and does not transfer economic resources on the restructure date. **The effects from these types of restructurings should be accounted for prospectively (over future years) by both the debtor and the creditor.** Unless the carrying amount at the time of restructure exceeds the undiscounted total future cash flows, the debtor will not change the carrying amount of the payable and the creditor will not change the recorded investment in the receivable.[4] But, when the carrying amount of the debt at the time of restructure is greater than the undiscounted total future cash flows, both the debtor and the creditor adjust the carrying amount. The debtor recognizes a gain, the creditor recognizes a loss, and neither recognizes interest as part of the future payments or receipts.

## No Gain or Loss Recognized

The following example illustrates a restructuring in which no gain or loss is recorded. On December 31, 1983, the Morgan National Bank enters into a debt restructuring agreement with Resorts Development Company, which is experiencing financial difficulties. The bank restructures a $10,000,000 note receivable issued at par by:

1. Reducing the principal obligation from $10,000,000 to $9,000,000.
2. Forgiving $500,000 of accrued interest.
3. Extending the maturity date from December 31, 1983 to December 31, 1987, and
4. Reducing the interest rate from 12% to 8%.

The total future cash flow after restructuring of $11,880,000 ($9,000,000 of principal plus $2,880,000 of interest payments[5]) exceeds the total pre-restructure carrying amount of the debt of $10,500,000 ($10,000,000 of principal plus $500,000 of accrued interest). Consequently, no gain or loss is recorded and no adjustment is made by the debtor to the carrying amount of the payable or by the creditor to the carrying amount of the investment in the receivable.

**A new effective interest rate must be computed** by the debtor and the creditor in order to record interest expense and revenue in future periods. The new effective interest rate to be used is the discount rate that equates the present value of the future cash flows specified by the new terms with the pre-restructure carrying amount of the debt. Here, the new rate is computed by relating the pre-restructure carrying amount ($10,500,000) to the total future cash flow ($11,880,000). By trial and error and by interpolation or formula we are able to derive the rate necessary to discount the total future cash flow ($11,880,000) to a present

---

[4]"Accounting by Debtors and Creditors for Troubled Debt Restructurings," *op. cit.*, pars. 16 and 30.

[5]Total interest payments are: $9,000,000 × .08 × 4 years = $2,880,000.

value equal to the remaining balance ($10,500,000). The desired rate is 3.46613%.[6] The FASB also specifies that the effective interest method be used to compute the future interest expense of the debtor and the future interest revenue of the creditor.

On the basis of the effective rate of 3.46613%, the following interest schedule can be prepared:

| Date | Cash | Interest at Effective Rate | Reduction in Carrying Amount | Carrying Amount |
|---|---|---|---|---|
| 12/31/83 | | | | $10,500,000 |
| 12/31/84 | $ 720,000[a] | $ 363,944[b] | $ 356,056[c] | 10,143,944 |
| 12/31/85 | 720,000 | 351,602 | 368,398 | 9,775,546 |
| 12/31/86 | 720,000 | 338,833 | 381,167 | 9,394,379 |
| 12/31/87 | 720,000 | 325,621 | 394,379 | 9,000,000 |
| | $2,880,000 | $1,380,000 | $1,500,000 | |

(a) $720,000 = $9,000,000 × .08
(b) $363,944 = $10,500,000 × 3.46613%
(c) $356,056 = $720,000 − $363,944

Using the data above, the entries on the debtor's and creditor's books would be as shown on the following page:

[6]An accurate interest rate $i$ can be found by using the formulas given at the tops of Tables 6–2 and 6–4 to set up the following equation:

$$\$10,500,000 = \frac{1}{(1+i)^4} \times \$9,000,000 + \frac{1 - \frac{1}{(1+i)^4}}{i} \times \$720,000$$

(from Table 6–2)  (from Table 6–4)

Solving algebraically for $i$, it can be found that $i = 3.46613\%$.

A computer program is frequently used in practice to find the implicit interest rate.

We can also determine the approximate rate by trial and error using present value Tables 6-2 and 6-4 as follows:

| | Present value at | | |
|---|---|---|---|
| | 3% | ?% | 4% |
| *Principal (n = 4)* | | | |
| 3%—.88849 × $9,000,000 | $ 7,996,410 | | |
| ?%—(Factor from Table 6–2) × $9,000,000 | | ? | |
| 4%—.85480 × $9,000,000 | | | $ 7,693,200 |
| *Interest (n = 4)* | | | |
| 3%—3.71710 × $720,000 | 2,676,312 | | |
| ?%—(Factor from Table 6–4) × $720,000 | | ? | |
| 4%—3.62990 × $720,000 | | | 2,613,528 |
| Total present value | $10,672,722 | $10,500,000 | $10,306,278 |

Once we know that the rate is between 3% and 4%, we can interpolate to obtain an approximation of the desired rate:

$$\left(\frac{\$10,672,722 - \$10,500,000}{\$10,672,722 - \$10,306,728}\right) \times (4\% - 3\%) = .4719\%$$

$$3\% + .4719\% = 3.4719\%$$

---

### Entries for Troubled Debt Restructuring—
### No Gain or Loss Recognized

| Resorts Development Co. (Debtor) | | | Morgan National Bank (Creditor) | | |
|---|---|---|---|---|---|

**December 31, 1983 (date of restructure)[7]:**

| | | | | | |
|---|---|---|---|---|---|
| Interest Payable | 500,000 | | Notes Receivable | 500,000 | |
| Notes Payable | | 500,000 | Interest Receivable | | 500,000 |

**December 31, 1984 (date of first interest payment following restructure):**

| | | | | | |
|---|---|---|---|---|---|
| Notes Payable | 356,056 | | Cash | 720,000 | |
| Interest Expense | 363,944 | | Notes Receivable | | 356,056 |
| Cash | | 720,000 | Interest Revenue | | 363,944 |

**December 31, 1985, 1986, and 1987 (dates of 2nd, 3rd, and last interest payments):**

(Debit and credit same accounts as at 12/31/84
using applicable amounts from the interest schedule)

**December 31, 1987 (date of principal payment):**

| | | | | | |
|---|---|---|---|---|---|
| Notes Payable | 9,000,000 | | Cash | 9,000,000 | |
| Cash | | 9,000,000 | Notes Receivable | | 9,000,000 |

---

## Recognition of Gain and Loss

If the pre-restructure carrying amount exceeds the total future cash flows as a result of a modification of the terms, the debtor records a gain and the creditor records a loss at the date of restructure. To illustrate, assume the facts in the previous example except that Morgan National Bank **reduced the principal to $7,000,000** (and forgave the accrued interest of $500,000, extended the maturity date to December 31, 1987, and reduced the interest from 12% to 8%). The total future cash flow is now $9,240,000 ($7,000,000 of principal plus $2,240,000 of interest[8]), which is $1,260,000 less than the pre-restructure carrying amount of $10,500,000. Under these circumstances, Resorts Development Company (debtor) would reduce the carrying amount of its payable and Morgan National Bank (creditor) would reduce the carrying amount of its receivable by a total of $1,260,000 (accrued interest of $500,000 and principal of $760,000). Resorts would recognize an extraordinary gain and Morgan Bank would recognize an ordinary loss (or debit the allowance account) in the same amount of $1,260,000. **Because the effective interest rate is 0%, all of the future cash flows reduce the new principal balance and no interest expense or interest revenue is recognized by either the debtor or the creditor.** The following journal entries illustrate the accounting by the debtor and the creditor.

---

[7]Alternative entry at December 31, 1983 (date of restructure):

| Resorts Development Co. (Debtor) | | | Morgan National Bank (Creditor) | | |
|---|---|---|---|---|---|
| Notes Payable (12% note) | 10,000,000 | | Notes Receivable (8% note) | 9,000,000 | |
| Interest Payable | 500,000 | | Premium on Notes Rec. | 1,500,000 | |
| Notes Payable (8% note) | | 9,000,000 | Notes Receivable (12% note) | | 10,000,000 |
| Premium on Notes Payable | | 1,500,000 | Interest Receivable | | 500,000 |

[8]Total interest payments are: $7,000,000 $\times$ .08 $\times$ 4 years = $2,240,000.

| Entries for Troubled Debt Restructuring—<br>Recognition of Gain and Loss | | | | |
|---|---|---|---|---|
| **Resorts Development (Debtor)** | | **Morgan National Bank (Creditor)** | | |
| **December 31, 1983 (restructure date):** | | | | |
| Interest Payable | 500,000 | Allow. for Doubtful | | |
| Notes Payable | 760,000 | Accts. (or Loss) | 1,260,000 | |
| Gain on Restructured | | Notes Receivable | | 760,000 |
| Debt | 1,260,000 | Interest Receivable | | 500,000 |
| **December 31, 1984, 1985, 1986, and 1987 (interest payment dates):** | | | | |
| Notes Payable | 560,000 | Cash | 560,000 | |
| Cash | 560,000 | Notes Receivable | | 560,000 |
| **December 31, 1987 (principal payment date):** | | | | |
| Notes Payable | 7,000,000 | Cash | 7,000,000 | |
| Cash | 7,000,000 | Notes Receivable | | 7,000,000 |

## JUSTIFICATION FOR NOT RECOGNIZING GAIN OR LOSS

The FASB reasoned that a troubled debt restructuring involving a modification of terms is a continuation of an existing debt and is not a business transaction involving transfers of resources and obligations. Some accountants challenge this nonrecognition approach; if a company has a $1,000,000 loan receivable earning interest at 10% and the interest rate is lowered to 5% because the debtor has financial problems, they believe that a loss should be recorded immediately. In effect, this group believes that most restructurings are the result of a bargained exchange that alters the economic relationship between the creditor and debtor. Further, they believe that this change in the economic relationship should be recognized in the accounting records on the basis of the market values inherent in the restructuring. The Board contends that the creditor's primary objective of modifying the terms is to recover its investment, which is carried at the principal amount and not at principal plus future interest. The Board concluded that the effect on cash flows is essentially the same whether the modifications involve changes in amounts designated as principal amount or interest. Furthermore, accounting for restructured debt should be based on the substance of the modification—the effect on cash flows—not on the labels chosen to describe those cash flows. Therefore, to the extent that recoverability of the investment itself is not affected, no gain or loss should be recognized.[9]

In addition to the theoretical pros and cons, financial institutions lobbied hard for the nonrecognition criteria using an economic consequence argument as their rationale. For example, during the early to mid-1970s a number of financial institutions would have had to take substantial losses if the usual present value techniques had been employed in these restructuring arrangements. They argued that the recognition of these losses might cause individuals to lose confidence in the financial system, which would make it more difficult for financial institutions to raise capital. If financial institutions are unable to attract capital, the entire economy will be affected because they will be unable or unwilling to

[9]"Accounting by Debtors and Creditors for Troubled Debt Restructurings," *op. cit.*, pars. 140–155. The restructuring does not preclude the necessity for the creditor to make appropriate allowance for doubtful accounts in relation to the future collectibility of amounts from the troubled debtor.

grant credit to marginal or small borrowers. They argued that some bankruptcies, perhaps even a recession or depression, would be stimulated.

The authors believe that nonrecognition of a loss in modification of terms situations is unsound accounting. In our opinion, if an item such as the interest rate has been reduced, an economic loss has resulted and an accounting loss should be reported. The FASB has failed to recognize the change that has taken place in the present value of the receivable (obligation).

## SUMMARY OF ACCOUNTING FOR TROUBLED DEBT RESTRUCTURINGS

---

**SUMMARY OF ACCOUNTING PROCEDURES**
**FOR TROUBLED DEBT RESTRUCTURINGS**

| Form of Restructure | Accounting Procedure |
|---|---|
| **Settlement of Debt** | |
| 1. Transfer of noncash assets. | 1. Recognize gain (debtor) or loss (creditor) on restructure. Debtor—Recognize gain or loss on asset transfer. |
| 2. Granting of equity interest. | 2. Recognize gain (debtor) or loss (creditor) on restructure. |
| **Continuation of Debt with** | |
| **Modified Terms** | |
| 1. Carrying amount of debt is less than total future cash flows. | 1. Recognize no gain (loss) on restructure. Determine new effective interest rate to be used in recording interest expense (debtor) and interest revenue (creditor). |
| 2. Carrying amount of debt is greater than total future cash flows. | 2. Recognize gain (loss) on restructure.* Recognize no interest expense or revenue over remaining life of debt. |

*Recognition of gain or loss here implies that the pre-restructure carrying amount will be *reduced* to an amount equal to the total future cash flows.

---

The following disclosures for troubled debt restructurings as of the date of each balance sheet presented are required:

**Debtor**

1. A description of the changes in terms or major features of settlement.
2. The aggregate gain on restructuring and the related tax effect.
3. The per-share amount of the aggregate gain on restructuring.
4. The aggregate gain or loss on transfers of assets.
5. Information on any contingent payments.

**Creditor**

1. The aggregate recorded investment (receivable).
2. The gross interest revenue that would have been recorded in the period ignoring restructure.
3. The gross interest revenue on those receivables that was recorded in the period.
4. The amount of commitments to lend additional funds to debtors whose terms have been modified.

# Illustration of Serial Bond Amortization and Redemption Before Maturity

A serial bond issue may be sold as though each series is a separate bond issue or it may be sold as a package. Whether sold separately or as a package, one account for the total premium or discount is used in the general ledger for that serial issue. The total premium or discount to be amortized, whether computed for each series separately or for the entire issue, is entered as one amount in the Premium (or Discount) on Bonds Payable account. **The straight-line, bonds outstanding, or effective interest methods may be used to amortize the premium or discount.**

The following comprehensive illustration demonstrates (1) the amortization of premium or discount on serial bonds using the straight-line, bonds outstanding, and effective interest methods; and (2) the accounting for redemption of serial bonds before maturity under all three methods of amortization.

## AMORTIZATION OF PREMIUM OR DISCOUNT ON SERIAL BONDS

A serial bond issue in the amount of $1,000,000, dated January 1, 1982, bearing 8% interest payable at December 31 each year, is sold by Yorkville School District to yield 9% per

| | | Selling Price | Discount |
|---|---|---|---|
| Bonds due 1/1/83 (1 year away): | | | |
| Principal: $200,000 × .91743 (Table 6-2) | $183,486 | | |
| Interest: $ 16,000 × .91743 (Table 6-4) | 14,679 | | |
| | | $198,165 | $ 1,835* |
| Bonds due 1/1/84 (2 years away): | | | |
| Principal: $200,000 × .84168 (Table 6-2) | $168,336 | | |
| Interest: $ 16,000 × 1.75911 (Table 6-4) | 28,146 | 196,482 | 3,518 |
| Bonds due 1/1/85 (3 years away)   Computations | | 194,937 | 5,063 |
| Bonds due 1/1/86 (4 years away)   similar to those | | 193,522 | 6,478 |
| Bonds due 1/1/87 (5 years away)   above. | | 192,220 | 7,780 |
| Total price for all series | | $975,326 | |
| Total discount on all series | | | $24,674 |

*$1,835 = $200,000 minus $198,165

annum; the bonds mature in the amount of $200,000 on January 1 of each year beginning in 1983. The bond price and discount are computed as shown on the previous page.

## Straight-line Amortization

The straight-line method of amortization may be used if the results are not materially different from those resulting from use of the effective interest method. The total discount for the Yorkville School District issue described on page 633 would be apportioned for each series over the five years as shown in the following schedule:

| | | Amortization Schedule—Straight-line Method | | | | |
|---|---|---|---|---|---|---|
| | | | Apportioned to | | | |
| Series Due Jan. 1 | Total Discount | 1982 | 1983 | 1984 | 1985 | 1986 |
| 1983 | $ 1,835 | $1,835 | | | | |
| 1984 | 3,518 | 1,759 | $1,759 | | | |
| 1985 | 5,063 | 1,688 | 1,688 | $1,687 | | |
| 1986 | 6,478 | 1,619 | 1,619 | 1,620 | $1,620 | |
| 1987 | 7,780 | 1,556 | 1,556 | 1,556 | 1,556 | $1,556 |
| | $24,674 | $8,457 | $6,622 | $4,863 | $3,176 | $1,556 |

## Bonds Outstanding Method

When the entire issue of serial bonds is sold to underwriters at a stated price, the discount or premium is frequently amortized by the **bonds outstanding method** since the discount or premium on each series is not definitely determinable. The bonds outstanding method is an application of the straight-line method to serial bonds and assumes that the discount applicable to each bond of the issue is the same dollar amount per year.

The total discount for the Yorkville School District issue, would be apportioned over the five years as shown in the following schedule:

| | | Amortization Schedule—Bonds Outstanding Method | | |
|---|---|---|---|---|
| Year Ending Dec. 31 | Bonds Outstanding During the Year | Bonds Outstanding During the Year ÷ Total of Bonds Outstanding Column | Total Discount to be Amortized | Discount to be Amortized During Each Year |
| 1982 | $1,000,000 | 10/30 | $24,674 | $ 8,224 |
| 1983 | 800,000 | 8/30 | 24,674 | 6,580 |
| 1984 | 600,000 | 6/30 | 24,674 | 4,935 |
| 1985 | 400,000 | 4/30 | 24,674 | 3,290 |
| 1986 | 200,000 | 2/30 | 24,674 | 1,645 |
| | $3,000,000 | 30/30 | | $24,674 |

The effect of the column for "Bonds Outstanding During the Year" is to convert all the bonds into terms of bonds outstanding for one year, or a total of $3,000,000 for five years. Accordingly, during 1982 the discount to be amortized would be $1,000,000/$3,000,000 × $24,674, or $8,224. Similarly, during 1985 the discount to be amortized would be $400,000/$3,000,000 × $24,674, or $3,290.

An amortization schedule should be prepared for serial bonds in the same manner as the amortization schedule for single-maturity bonds, except that the maturity value of each series must be deducted from the total carrying amount of the bonds when the series is paid. The schedule shown below illustrates the amortization of the discount and the reduction in carrying amount for the serial bond issue described above using the bonds outstanding method.

| | | Schedule of Bond Discount Amortization—Serial Bonds | | | |
| | | Bonds Outstanding Method | | | |
| Date | Credit Cash | Credit Bond Discount | Debit Interest Expense | Debit Bonds Payable | Carrying Amount of Bonds |
|---|---|---|---|---|---|
| 1/1/82 | | | | | $975,326 |
| 12/31/82 | $ 80,000[a] | $ 8,224[b] | $ 88,224[c] | — | 983,550[d] |
| 1/1/83 | 200,000 | — | — | $ 200,000 | 783,550 |
| 12/31/83 | 64,000 | 6,580 | 70,580 | — | 790,130 |
| 1/1/84 | 200,000 | — | — | 200,000 | 590,130 |
| 12/31/84 | 48,000 | 4,935 | 52,935 | — | 595,065 |
| 1/1/85 | 200,000 | — | — | 200,000 | 395,065 |
| 12/31/85 | 32,000 | 3,290 | 35,290 | — | 398,355 |
| 1/1/86 | 200,000 | — | — | 200,000 | 198,355 |
| 12/31/86 | 16,000 | 1,645 | 17,645 | — | 200,000 |
| 1/1/87 | 200,000 | — | — | 200,000 | — |
| | $1,240,000 | $24,674 | $264,674 | $1,000,000 | |

[a]$80,000 = $1,000,000 × .08      [c]$88,224 = $80,000 + $8,224
[b]$8,224 = $1,000,000/$3,000,000 × $24,674      [d]$983,550 = $975,326 + $8,224

*Note:* Interest expense is a function of the stated interest rate plus a pro rata share of discount amortization or less a pro rata share of premium amortization.

A schedule with similar debit and credit columns could be prepared using the data from the straight-line amortization schedule. The credit to Bond Discount on December 31, 1982 would be $8,457 using the straight-line data on page 634.

## Effective Interest Method

Application of the effective interest method to serial bonds is similar to that illustrated in the section concerned with single-maturity bonds. Interest expense for the period is computed by multiplying the effective interest rate times the carrying amount of bonds outstanding during that period. The amount of amortization of bond discount or premium is the difference between the effective interest expense for the period and the actual interest payments. Under this method, the interest is at a constant rate relative to the carrying amount of the bonds outstanding. The schedule shown on page 636 illustrates the amortization of discount and the reduction in carrying amount for the Yorkville serial bond issue using the effective interest method.

The journal entries that would be recorded for the payment of the interest, amortization of the discount, and retirement of each series of bonds can be determined from the column headings in the amortization schedule.

| Date | Credit Cash | Debit Interest Expense | Credit Bond Discount | Debit Bonds Payable | Carrying Amount of Bonds |
|------|------------|------------------------|----------------------|---------------------|--------------------------|
| | | Schedule of Bond Discount Amortization—Serial Bonds Effective Interest Method 8% Bonds Sold to Yield 9% | | | |
| 1/1/82 | | | | | $975,326 |
| 12/31/82 | $ 80,000[a] | $ 87,779[b] | $ 7,779[c] | — | 983,105[d] |
| 1/1/83 | 200,000 | — | — | $ 200,000 | 783,105 |
| 12/31/83 | 64,000 | 70,479 | 6,479 | — | 789,584 |
| 1/1/84 | 200,000 | — | — | 200,000 | 589,584 |
| 12/31/84 | 48,000 | 53,063 | 5,063 | — | 594,647 |
| 1/1/85 | 200,000 | — | — | 200,000 | 394,647 |
| 12/31/85 | 32,000 | 35,518 | 3,518 | — | 398,165 |
| 1/1/86 | 200,000 | — | — | 200,000 | 198,165 |
| 12/31/86 | 16,000 | 17,835 | 1,835 | — | 200,000 |
| 1/1/87 | 200,000 | — | — | 200,000 | — |
| | $1,240,000 | $264,674 | $24,674 | $1,000,000 | |

[a]$80,000 = $1,000,000 × .08
[b]$87,779 = $975,326 × .09
[c]$7,779 = $87,779 − $80,000
[d]$983,105 = $975,326 + $7,779

*Note:* Interest expense is a function of the effective interest rate times the book carrying amount outstanding during the period.

## REDEMPTION OF SERIAL BONDS BEFORE MATURITY

If bonds of a certain series are redeemed before maturity date, it is necessary to compute the amount of unamortized discount (or premium) applicable to those bonds and to remove it from the Discount (or Premium) on Bonds Payable account.

### Straight-Line Method

Assume that on January 1, 1984, $200,000 of the Yorkville School District serial bonds due January 1, 1987 are redeemed for $201,000. The unamortized discount on the $200,000 of bonds due on January 1, 1987 is $4,668 ($1,556 + $1,556 + $1,556; the discount apportioned to 1984, 1985, and 1986, respectively) as determined from the straight-line amortization schedule on page 634. The loss on early redemption of these bonds is computed as follows:

| Purchase price of bonds redeemed | $201,000 |
|---|---|
| Carrying amount of 1/1/87 series bonds: | |
| ($200,000 − $7,780 + $1,556 + $1,556) or | |
| ($200,000 − $4,668) | 195,332 |
| Loss (extraordinary) on bond redemption | $   5,668 |

## Bonds Outstanding Method

Using the same data, the computation of the applicable unamortized discount under the bonds outstanding method is as follows:

$$\frac{3\left(\substack{\text{number of years}\\\text{before maturity}}\right) \times \$200,000 \ (\text{par of bonds}) \times \$24,674 \ (\text{total disc.})}{\$3,000,000 \ (\text{total of bonds outstanding column})} = \$4,935$$

Expressed a little differently, the discount to be amortized each year for each $200,000 of bonds is $200,000/$3,000,000 × $24,674, or $1,645. Therefore, if $200,000 of bonds are retired three years before maturity, the discount to be eliminated is 3 × $1,645, or $4,935.

Under the bonds outstanding method of amortization, the loss on early retirement of these bonds is computed as follows:

| Purchase price of bonds redeemed | $201,000 |
|---|---|
| Carrying amount of 1/1/87 series bonds: | |
| ($200,000 − $4,935) | 195,065 |
| Loss (extraordinary) on bond redemption | $   5,935 |

## Effective Interest Method

Under the effective interest method the carrying amount of all the serial bonds outstanding at the time of an early retirement must be reduced by the present value of the bonds being retired. Reference to the effective interest amortization schedule shows that the carrying amount of all the Yorkville bonds still outstanding at January 1, 1984 is $589,584. The present value of the bonds being retired is computed as follows (3 years at 9%):

| Present value of principal ($200,000 × .77218) | $154,436 |
|---|---|
| Present value of interest payments ($16,000 × 2.53130) | 40,501 |
| Present value of bonds to be retired | $194,937 |

The entry to record the early redemption using the effective interest method would be as follows on January 1, 1984.

| | | |
|---|---|---|
| Bonds Payable | 200,000 | |
| Loss (Extraordinary) on Redemption of Bonds | 6,063 | |
| Discount on Bonds Payable ($200,000 − $194,937) | | 5,063 |
| Cash | | 201,000 |

The gain or loss on redemption is the difference between the present value of the bonds ($194,937) and the cost to retire the bonds ($201,000); in this example the loss is $6,063.

**Note:** All **asterisked** Questions, Cases, Exercises, or Problems relate to material contained in the appendix to each chapter.

## QUESTIONS

1. (a) From what sources might a corporation obtain funds through long-term debt?
   (b) What is a bond indenture? What does it contain?
   (c) What is a mortgage?

2. Differentiate between a fixed-rate mortgage, a variable-rate mortgage, and a shared appreciation mortgage.

3. Under what conditions may a short-term obligation be classified as a long-term debt?

4. (a) What is the typical denomination of corporate bonds?
   (b) How often is bond interest typically payable?

5. Differentiate between term bonds, mortgage bonds, collateral trust bonds, debenture bonds, income bonds, callable bonds, registered bonds, bearer or coupon bonds, convertible bonds, commodity backed bonds, and deep discount bonds.

6. In what different ways may bonds be issued?

7. Distinguish between the following interest rates for bonds payable:
   (a) yield rate
   (b) nominal rate
   (c) stated rate
   (d) market rate
   (e) effective rate.

8. Distinguish between the following values relative to bonds payable:
   (a) par value
   (b) face value
   (c) market value
   (d) maturity value.

9. Under what conditions of bond issuance does a discount on bonds payable arise? Under what conditions of bond issuance does a premium on bonds payable arise?

10. How should unamortized discount on bonds payable be reported on the financial statements? Unamortized premium on bonds payable?

11. What are the two methods of amortizing discount and premium on bonds payable? Explain each.

12. Schwinn Company sells its bonds at a premium and applies the effective interest method in amortizing the premium. Will the annual interest expense increase or decrease over the life of the bonds? Explain.

13. How should the costs of issuing bonds be accounted for and classified in the financial statements?

14. Where should treasury bonds be shown on the balance sheet? Should treasury bonds be carried at par or at reacquisition cost?

15. What is the "call" feature of a bond issue? How does the call feature affect the amortization of bond premium or discount?

16. Why would a company wish to reduce its bond indebtedness before its bonds reach maturity? Indicate how this can be done and the correct accounting treatment for such a transaction.

17. How are gains and losses from extinguishment of debt classified in the income statement? What disclosures are required of such transactions by *FASB Statement No. 4*?

18. What must the accountant do to record properly a transaction involving the issuance of a noninterest-bearing long-term note in exchange for property?

19. How is the present value of a noninterest-bearing note computed?

20. When is the stated interest rate of a debt instrument presumed to be fair?

21. What types of payables are exempted from the provisions of *APB Opinion No. 21*?

22. What are the considerations in computing an appropriate interest rate?

23. According to *FASB Statement No. 47*, "Disclosure of Long-Term Obligations," what disclosures are required relative to long-term debt and sinking fund requirements?

24. What are project financing arrangements?

25. What are take-or-pay contracts and through-put contracts?

26. What conditions must be met in order for a contractual obligation to be disclosed as an unconditional purchase obligation?

27. What disclosures are required relative to unconditional purchase obligations that have been recognized as balance sheet liabilities?

28. What disclosures are required relative to unconditional purchase obligations that have been disclosed only in the footnotes to the financial statements?

*29. (a) In a troubled debt situation, why might the creditor grant concessions to the debtor?
(b) What type of concessions might a creditor grant the debtor in a troubled debt situation?

*30. What are the general rules for measuring and recognizing gain or loss by both the debtor and the creditor in a troubled debt restructuring?

*31. What is meant by "accounting symmetry" between the entries recorded by the debtor and the creditor in a troubled debt restructuring?

*32. Under what circumstances would a transaction be recorded as a troubled debt restructuring by only one of the two parties to the transaction?

*33. Pinot National Bank agrees to restructure Noir Company's troubled debt situation by reducing the interest rate from 14% to 8% and extending the maturity date of the debt five additional years. Explain how Noir Company should account for this modification of terms in the restructuring of its debt to Pinot National Bank.

*34. (a) Describe the bonds-outstanding method of premium or discount amortization.
(b) Describe the effective interest method of bond premium or discount amortization for serial bonds.

## CASES

**C14-1** On January 1, 1980, Cervaza Company issued for $1,075,230 its 20-year, 13% bonds that have a maturity value of $1,000,000 and pay interest semiannually on January 1 and July 1. Bond issue costs were not material in amount. Below are three presentations of the long-term liability section of the balance sheet that might be used for these bonds at the issue date:

| | |
|---|---:|
| **1.** Bonds payable (maturing January 1, 2000) | $1,000,000 |
| Unamortized premium on bonds payable | 75,230 |
| Total bond liability | $1,075,230 |

2. Bonds payable—principal (face value $1,000,000 maturing
  January 1, 2000)           $ 97,220[a]
 Bonds payable—interest (semiannual payment $65,000)  978,010[b]

  Total bond liability         $1,075,230

3. Bonds payable—principal (maturing January 1, 2000)  $1,000,000
 Bonds payable—interest ($65,000 per period for 40 periods) 2,600,000

  Total bond liability         $3,600,000

[a]The present value of $1,000,000 due at the end of 40 (six-month) periods at the yield rate of 6% per period.
[b]The present value of $65,000 per period for 40 (six-month) periods at the yield rate of 6% per period.

**Instructions**

(a) Discuss the conceptual merit(s) of each of the date-of-issue balance sheet presentations shown above for these bonds.
(b) Explain why investors would pay $1,075,239 for bonds that have a maturity value of only $1,000,000.
(c) Assuming that a discount rate is needed to compute the carrying value of the obligations arising from a bond issue at any date during the life of the bonds, discuss the conceptual merit(s) of using for this purpose:
 1. The coupon or nominal rate.
 2. The effective or yield rate at date of issue.
(d) If the obligations arising from these bonds are to be carried at their present value computed by means of the current market rate of interest, how would the bond valuation at dates subsequent to the date of issue be affected by an increase or a decrease in the market rate of interest?

                  (AICPA adapted)

**C14-2** The following article appeared in the June 19, 1979 issue of the *Wall Street Journal:*

**Bond Markets**
*Giant Commonwealth Edison Issue Hits Resale Market With $70 Million Left Over*
NEW YORK—Commonwealth Edison Co.'s slow-selling new 9¼% bonds were tossed onto the resale market at a reduced price with about $70 million still available from the $200 million offered Thursday, dealers said.
 The Chicago utility's bonds, rated double-A by Moody's and double-A-minus by Standard & Poor's, originally had been priced at 99.803, to yield 9.3% in five years. They were marked down yesterday the equivalent of about $5.50 for each $1,000 face amount, to about 99.25, where their yield jumped to 9.45%.

**Instructions**

(a) How will the development above affect the accounting for Commonwealth Edison's bond issue.
(b) Provide several possible explanations for the markdown and the slow sale of Commonwealth Edison's bonds.

**C14-3 Part I.** The appropriate method of amortizing a premium or discount on issuance of bonds is the effective interest method.

**Instructions**

(a) What is the effective interest method of amortization and how is it different from and similar to the straight-line method of amortization?
(b) How is amortization computed using the effective interest method, and why and how do amounts obtained using the effective interest method differ from amounts computed under the straight-line method?

**Part II.** Gains or losses from the early extinguishment of debt that is refunded can theoretically be accounted for in three ways:

1. Amortized over remaining life of old debt.
2. Amortized over the life of the new debt issue.
3. Recognized in the period of extinguishment.

**Instructions**

(a) Develop supporting arguments for each of the three theoretical methods of accounting for gains and losses from the early extinguishment of debt.

(b) Which of the methods above is generally accepted and how should the appropriate amount of gain or loss be shown in a company's financial statements?

(AICPA adapted)

C14-4 As the accountant for Compost Perfume Company, you have prepared the balance sheet and have presented it to the president of the company. You are asked the following questions about it:

1. Why has depreciation been charged on equipment being purchased under contract? Title has not passed to the company as yet and, therefore, they are not our assets. Why should the company not show on the left side of the balance sheet only the amount paid to date instead of showing the full contract price on the left side and the unpaid portion on the right side?

2. What is bond discount? As a debit balance, why is it not classified among the assets?

3. Bond interest payable is shown as a current liability. Did we not pay our trustee, County Trust Company, the full amount of interest due this period?

4. Treasury bonds are shown as a deduction from bonds payable issued. Why should they not be shown as an asset, since they can be sold again? Are they the same as bonds of other companies that we hold as investments?

**Instructions**

Outline your answers to these questions by writing a brief paragraph that will justify your treatment.

# EXERCISES

E14-1 Presented below are various account balances of Leslie Graham Co.:

1. Unamortized premium of bonds payable, of which $2,800 will be amortized during the next year.

2. Bank loans payable of a winery, due March 10, 1987. (The product requires aging for five years before sale.)

3. Serial bonds payable, $1,000,000, of which $200,000 are due each July 31.

4. Dividends payable in shares of stock on January 20, 1985.

5. Amounts withheld from employees' wages for income taxes.

6. Notes payable due January 15, 1986.

7. Credit balances in customers' accounts arising from returns and allowances after collection in full of account.

8. Bonds payable of $1,000,000 maturing June 30, 1985.

9. Overdraft of $500 in a bank account. (Debit balances are carried in two other accounts.)

10. Deposits made by customers who have ordered goods.

**Instructions**

Indicate whether each of the items above should be classified on December 31, 1984, as a current liability, a long-term liability, or under some other classification. Consider each one independently from all others; that is, do not assume that all of them relate to one particular business. If the classification of some of the items is doubtful, explain why in each case.

**E14-2** JoEllen King Company authorized the issuance of 14% coupon bonds in the amount of $1,000,000, with interest coupons payable semiannually, and the bonds to be dated January 1, 1984. The financial events are as follows:

1. The authorization of 1,000 bonds of $1,000 each.
2. Subscriptions received for 700 bonds, at par.
3. Cash received in full on January 1, 1984, from subscribers to 600 bonds; bonds are issued.
4. On April 1, 1984, cash is received from subscribers to 100 bonds in the amount of the par value of the bonds plus accrued interest. The bonds are issued.
5. On July 1, 1984, six months' interest is paid on the bonds outstanding.

**Instructions**

Prepare entries to record the events listed above.

**E14-3** In each of the following cases indicate whether the bond is sold at a premium or a discount and explain.

1. The stated interest rate for the bond is 16% and the effective rate is 15%.
2. The bond carries a coupon rate of 12% and is sold to yield 14%.
3. The market rate is 13% and the nominal rate of the bond is 13%.

**E14-4** On June 30, 1973, Rolling Stones Company issued 14% bonds with a par value of $700,000 due in 20 years. They were issued at 99 and were callable at 103 at any date after June 30, 1983. Because of lower interest rates and a significant change in the company's credit rating, it was decided to call the entire issue on June 30, 1984, and to issue new bonds. New 12% bonds were sold in the amount of $800,000 at 101; they mature in 20 years. Rolling Stones Company uses straight-line amortization. Interest payment dates are December 31 and June 30.

**Instructions**

(a) Prepare journal entries to record the retirement of the old issue and the sale of the new issue on June 30, 1984.
(b) Prepare the entry required on December 31, 1984, to record the payment of the first six months' interest and the amortization of premium on the bonds.

**E14-5** Fleetwood Mac Company had bonds outstanding with a maturity value of $200,000. On April 30, 1984, when these bonds had an unamortized discount of $4,000, they were called in at 106. To pay for these bonds, Fleetwood had issued other bonds a month earlier bearing a lower interest rate. The newly issued bonds had a life of 10 years. The new bonds were issued at 102 (face value $200,000). Issue costs related to the new bonds were $3,000.

**Instructions**

Ignoring interest, compute the gain or loss and record this refunding transaction.

(AICPA adapted)

**E14-6** On January 2, 1978, Supertramp Corporation issued $1,200,000 of 13% bonds at 98 due December 31, 1987. Legal and other costs of $30,000 were incurred in connection with the issue. Interest on the bonds is payable annually each December 31. The $30,000 issue costs are being deferred and amortized on a straight-line basis over the 10-year term of the bonds. The discount on the bonds is also being amortized on a straight-line basis over the 10 years (straight-line is not materially different in effect from the preferable "interest method").

The bonds are callable at 101 (that is, at 101% of face amount), and on January 2, 1983, Supertramp called $600,000 face amount of the bonds and retired them.

**Instructions**

Ignoring income taxes, compute the amount of loss, if any, to be recognized by Supertramp as a result of retiring the $600,000 of bonds in 1983 and prepare the journal entry to record the retirement.

(AICPA adapted)

**E14-7** Speedwagon, Inc. had $6,000,000 of 12% bonds (interest payable July 9 and January 9) due in 10 years outstanding. On July 1, it issued $9,600,000 of 10% 15-year bonds (interest payable July 1 and January 1) at 99. A portion of the proceeds were used to call the 12% bonds at 103 on July 10. Unamortized bond discount and issue cost applicable to the 12% bonds were $60,000 and $30,000, respectively.

**Instructions**

Prepare the journal entries necessary to record the refunding of the bonds.

**E14-8** Under the terms of its 9% bonds (interest payable June 30 and December 31), Styx Furniture Company must pay $2,000,000 to a trustee each year. The funds are to be used to retire as many bonds as possible in the open market. Hint: Establish a bond retirement fund.

On July 1, 1983, the company paid $2,000,000 to the trustee, who purchased $2,200,000 par value of bonds. Unamortized bond discount applicable to the bonds purchased was $50,000.

**Instructions**

Record the payment and purchase of the bonds on the Styx Furniture Company books.

**E14-9** On July 1, 1984, Springsteen Company makes the two following acquisitions:

1. Purchases land having a fair market value of $100,000 by issuing a 4-year noninterest-bearing promissory note in the face amount of $174,901.
2. Purchases equipment by issuing a 5%, 8-year promissory note having a maturity value of $80,000 (interest payable annually).

Springsteen Company has to pay 15% interest for funds from its bank.

**Instructions**

(a) Record the two journal entries that should be recorded by Springsteen Company for the two purchases on July 1, 1984.
(b) Record the interest at the end of the first year (July 1, 1985) on both notes using the effective interest method.

**E14-10** At December 31, 1982, C. Gregory Gardner Company has outstanding three long-term debt issues. The first is a $2,000,000 note payable which matures June 30, 1985. The second is a $10,000,000 bond issue which matures September 30, 1986. The third is a $25,000,000 sinking fund debenture with annual sinking fund payments of $5,000,000 in each of the years 1984 through 1988.

**Instructions**

Prepare the footnote disclosure required by *FASB Statement No. 47,* "Disclosure of Long-Term Obligations," for the long-term debt at December 31, 1982.

**E14-11** To secure a long-term supply, Fellerdemer Company entered into a take-or-pay contract with an aluminum recycling plant on January 1, 1982. Fellerdemer is obligated to purchase 40% of the output of the plant each period while the debt incurred to finance the plant remains outstanding. The annual cost of the aluminum to Fellerdemer will be the sum of 40% of the raw material costs, operating expenses, depreciation, interest on the debt used to finance the plant, and return on the owner's investment. The minimum amount payable to the plant under the contract, whether or not Fellerdemer is able to take delivery, is $5 million annually through December 31, 2001. Fellerdemer's total purchases under the agreement were $6 million in 1982 and $6.5 million in 1983. Funds to construct the plant were borrowed at an effective interest rate of 10%. Fellerdemer's incremental borrowing rate was 12% at January 1, 1982 and is 15% at December 31, 1983. Fellerdemer intends to disclose the contract in the footnotes to its financial statements at December 31, 1983.

**Instructions**

Assuming that the contract is an "unconditional purchase obligation" as specified by *FASB Statement No. 47*, "Disclosure of Long-Term Obligations," prepare the footnote disclosure required for the contract at December 31, 1983.

**\*E14–12** Genesis Pen Company sells 12% bonds of a serial bond issue in the amount of $3,000,000 to underwriters for $3,090,000. The bonds are dated January 1, 1980, and mature in the amount of $600,000 on January 1 of each year beginning January 1, 1982.

**Instructions**

Compute the premium to be amortized during each of the years in which any of the bonds are outstanding, using the bonds outstanding method.

**\*E14–13** Debtor owes $120,000 plus $12,000 of accrued interest to Creditor. The debt is a 10-year 5% note. Because Debtor is in financial trouble, Creditor agrees to accept some property and cancel the entire debt. The property has a cost of $60,000 and a fair market value of $84,000.

**Instructions**

(a) Prepare the journal entry on Debtor's books for debt restructure.
(b) Prepare the journal entry on Creditor's books for debt restructure.

**\*E14–14** Santana Corp. owes $150,000 plus $15,000 of accrued interest to Eagles Trust Co. The debt is a 10-year 10% note due today 12/31/83. Because Santana Corp. is in financial trouble, Eagles agrees to extend the maturity date to 12/31/85, reduce the interest rate to 3%, payable annually on 12/31 and forgive the accrued interest.

**Instructions**

(a) Prepare the journal entries on Santana's books on 12/31/83, 84, 85.
(b) Prepare the journal entries on Eagles' books on 12/31/83, 84, 85.

# PROBLEMS

**P14–1** On January 1, 1983, The Who Company sold 16% bonds having a maturity value of $100,000 for $103,353, which provides the bondholders with a 15% yield. The bonds are dated January 1, 1983, and mature January 1, 1988 with interest payable December 31 of each year. The Who Company allocates interest and unamortized discount or premium on the effective interest basis.

**Instructions**

(a) Prepare the journal entry at the date of the bond issuance.
(b) Prepare the journal entry to record the interest payment and the amortization for 1983. Preparation of a partial schedule of interest expense and bond amortization will aid in the solution.
(c) Prepare the journal entry to record the interest payment and the amortization for 1985.

**P14–2** The following amortization and interest schedule reflects the issuance of 10-year bonds by Pink Floyd Corporation on January 1, 1976, and the subsequent interest payments and charges. The company's year end is December 31, and financial statements are prepared once yearly.

| AMORTIZATION SCHEDULE | | | | |
|---|---|---|---|---|
| Year | Cash | Interest | Amount Unamortized | Book Value |
| 1/1/76 | | | $5,651 | $ 94,349 |
| 1976 | $11,000 | $11,322 | 5,329 | 94,671 |
| 1977 | 11,000 | 11,361 | 4,968 | 95,032 |
| 1978 | 11,000 | 11,404 | 4,564 | 95,436 |
| 1979 | 11,000 | 11,452 | 4,112 | 95,888 |
| 1980 | 11,000 | 11,507 | 3,605 | 96,395 |
| 1981 | 11,000 | 11,567 | 3,038 | 96,962 |
| 1982 | 11,000 | 11,635 | 2,403 | 97,597 |
| 1983 | 11,000 | 11,712 | 1,691 | 98,309 |
| 1984 | 11,000 | 11,797 | 894 | 99,106 |
| 1985 | 11,000 | 11,894 | | 100,000 |

**Instructions**

(a) Indicate whether the bonds were issued at a premium or a discount and how you can determine this fact from the schedule.

(b) Indicate whether the amortization schedule is based on the straight-line method or the effective interest method and how you can determine which method is used.

(c) On the basis of the schedule above, prepare the journal entry to record the issuance of the bonds on January 1, 1976.

(d) On the basis of the schedule above, prepare the journal entries to reflect the bond transactions and accruals for 1976.

(e) On the basis of the schedule above, prepare the journal entries to reflect the bond transactions and accruals for 1984.

**P14-3** AC-DC Company sells 14% bonds having a maturity value of $100,000 for $96,648. The bonds are dated January 1, 1983, and mature January 1, 1988. Interest is payable annually on January 1. (**Hint:** The effective interest or yield rate must be computed.)

**Instructions**

(a) Set up a schedule of interest expense and discount amortization under the straight-line method.

(b) Set up a schedule of interest expense and discount amortization under the effective interest method.

**P14-4** In 1983, Christian Sisters Winery was considering the issuance of bonds as of January 1, 1984, as follows:

Plan 1: $2,000,000 par value 12%, 1st mortgage, 20-year bonds, due Dec. 31, 2004, at 96, with interest payable annually, or

Plan 2: $2,000,000 par value 12%, 1st mortgage, 20-year bonds, due Dec. 31, 2004, at 100, with provision for payment of a 4% ($80,000) premium at maturity, interest payable annually.

Costs of issue such as printing and lawyers' fees may be ignored for the purpose of answering this question. Discount and premium are to be allocated to accounting periods on a straight-line basis.

**Instructions**

Give two separate sets of journal entries with appropriate explanations showing the accounting treatment that the foregoing bond issues would necessitate, respectively:

(a) At time of issue.

(b) Yearly thereafter.

(c) On payment at date of maturity.

**P14-5** In each of the following independent cases the company closes its books on December 31.

1. Heather Co. sells $200,000 of 14% bonds on February 1, 1983. The bonds pay interest on February 1 and August 1. The due date of the bonds is August 1, 1986. The bonds yield 16%. Give entries through December 31, 1984.

2. Dawna Co. sells $200,000 of 13% bonds on June 1, 1983. The bonds pay interest on June 1 and December 1. The due date of the bonds is June 1, 1987. The bonds yield 12%. On September 1, 1984, Dawna buys back $40,000 worth of bonds for $42,000 (includes accrued interest). Give entries through December 1, 1985.

**Instructions**

(Round to the nearest dollar.)
For the two cases above prepare all of the relevant journal entries from the time of sale until the date indicated. Use the effective interest method for discount and premium amortization (construct amortization tables where applicable). Amortize premium or discount on interest dates and at year-end. (Assume that no reversing entries were made.)

**P14-6** Presented below are selected transactions on the books of Joan Asmuth Corporation.

July 1, 1983   Bonds payable with a par value of $900,000, which are dated January 1, 1983, are sold at 102 plus accrued interest. They are coupon bonds, bear interest at 12% (payable annually at January 1), and mature January 1, 1993. (Use interest expense account for accrued interest.)

Dec. 31   Adjusting entries are made to record the accrued interest on the bonds, and the amortization of the proper amount of premium. (Use straight-line amortization.)

Jan. 1, 1984   Interest on the bonds is paid.

April 1   Bonds of par value of $450,000 are purchased at 101 plus accrued interest, and retired. (Bond premium is to be amortized only at the end of each year.)

Dec. 31   Adjusting entries are made to record the accrued interest on the bonds, and the proper amount of premium amortized.

**Instructions**

Prepare journal entries for the transactions above.

**P14-7** Asia Company issued its 11% 30-year mortgage bonds in the principal amount of $5,000,000 on January 2, 1969, at a discount of $150,000, which it proceeded to amortize by charges to expense over the life of the issue on a straight-line basis. The indenture securing the issue provided that the bonds could be called for redemption in total but not in part at any time before maturity at 104% of the principal amount, but it did not provide for any sinking fund.

On December 18, 1983, the company issued its 9% 25-year debenture bonds in the principal amount of $6,000,000 at par, and the proceeds were used to redeem the 11% 30-year mortgage bonds on January 2, 1984. The indenture securing the new issue did not provide for any sinking fund or for retirement before maturity.

**Instructions**

(a) Prepare journal entries to record the issuance of the 9% bonds and the retirement of the 11% bonds.

(b) Indicate the income statement treatment of the gain or loss from retirement and the footnote disclosure required. Assume 1984 income before extraordinary items of $3,460,000, a weighted number of shares outstanding of 1,500,000, and an income tax rate of 40%.

**P14-8** On February 1, 1983, Arch Company sold 10,000 of its 12%, 20-year, $1,000 face value bonds at 98. Interest payment dates are February 1 and August 1, and the company uses the straight-line method of bond discount amortization. On March 1, 1984, Arch took advantage of favorable prices of its stock to extinguish 1,000 of the bonds by issuing 80,000 shares of its $10 par value common stock. The company's stock was selling for $10 per share on February 1, 1983 and $13 per share on March 1, 1984.

**Instructions**

Prepare the journal entries needed on the books of Arch Company to record the following:
(a) February 1, 1983: issuance of the bonds.
(b) August 1, 1983: payment of semiannual interest.
(c) December 31, 1983: accrual of interest expense.
(d) February 1, 1984: payment of semiannual interest. (No reversing entries made.)
(e) March 1, 1984: extinguishment of 1,000 bonds.

**P14–9** On January 1, 1981, Cosmetics Products Company sold $150,000 (face value) of bonds. The bonds are dated January 1, 1981 and will mature on January 1, 1986. Interest is paid annually on December 31. The bonds are callable after December 31, 1983 at 102. Issue costs related to these bonds amounted to $1,500, and these costs are being amortized by the straight-line method. The following amortization schedule was prepared by the accountant for the first two years of the life of the bonds:

| Date | Cash | Interest | Amortization | Carrying Value of Bonds |
|---|---|---|---|---|
| 1/ 1/81 | | | | $139,186 |
| 12/31/81 | $15,000 | $16,702 | $1,702 | 140,888 |
| 12/31/82 | 15,000 | 16,907 | 1,907 | 142,795 |

**Instructions**

On the basis of the information above, answer the following questions (round your answers to the nearest dollar or percent):
(a) What is the nominal or stated rate of interest for this bond issue?
(b) What is the effective or market rate of interest for this bond issue?
(c) Present the journal entry to record the sale of the bond issue, including the issue costs.
(d) Present the appropriate entry(ies) at December 31, 1983.
(e) Present the disclosure of this bond issue on the December 31, 1983, balance sheet. Proper balance sheet subheadings must be indicated.
(f) On June 30, 1984, $75,000 of the bond issue was redeemed at the call price. Present the journal entry for this redemption. Amortization of the discount is recorded only at the end of the year.
(g) Present the effects of the bond redemption on the 1984 income statement and proper footnote disclosure. Proper income statement subheadings must be indicated. The income tax rate is 20%; 1984 income before extraordinary items is $31,023 with a weighted number of common shares outstanding during the year of 18,000. Working capital funds were used to redeem the bonds.

**P14–10** Greg Teets Company issued 10-year coupon bonds in the amount of $1,000,000 on July 1, 1982. They were issued at par and bear interest at 12%, payable semiannually on July 1 and January 1. The Sayers Bank is to act as trustee to handle the payment of interest.

On December 10, 1982, Greg Teets Company sent the Sayers Bank a check for the interest due January 1, 1983, none of which was paid to bondholders before January 1, 1983.

**Instructions**

(a) What balances will be shown in the ledger of Greg Teets Company on December 31, 1982, relating to the bonds and the interest on the bonds? How will these balances be shown in the financial statements? Establish fund account for trustee payment.
(b) Assume that in 1983 Greg Teets Company sends the Sayers Bank checks for the interest due July 1, 1983, and January 1, 1984, and that the Sayers Bank returns to the company canceled interest coupons in the amount of $114,000. Greg Teets Company sent the Sayers Bank a check for $940 to cover the trustee expenses.

What balances will be shown in the ledger of Greg Teets Company on December 31, 1983, relating to the bonds and the interest on the bonds? How will these balances be shown in financial statements?

**P14-11** Here are transactions of Led Zeppelin Company:

| | |
|---|---|
| Jan. 1, 1983 | Bonds payable (coupon bonds) in the amount of $1,000,000, and bearing interest at the rate of 12% payable semiannually on January 1 and July 1, due January 1, 2003, are issued at 96. |
| June 15 | The First Bank and Trust Co. has been engaged as trustee to handle the payment of interest to individual bondholders. A check for the interest due July 1, 1983, is sent to the trustee. |
| 30 | Record the interest expense for the first six months of 1983. Bond discount is to be amortized only at the end of each year and by the straight-line method. |
| July 20 | The trustee returns to the company canceled interest coupons paid in the amount of $56,800 and reports that trustee's expenses charged against the account amounted to $520. |
| Dec. 15 | A check for the interest due January 1, 1984, and for reported expenses is sent to the trustee. |
| 31 | Record the interest expense for the six months ended December 31, and amortize the proper amount of discount for the year. |
| Jan. 21, 1984 | The trustee returns to the company canceled interest coupons paid in the amount of $59,900. |
| Mar. 1 | Bonds of par value of $20,000 are bought on the market at 95 plus accrued interest, and retired. All interest coupons dated before July 1, 1984, have been removed. |

**Instructions**

(a) Prepare entries in journal form on the books of Led Zeppelin for the transactions given above.

(b) What will be the amount of the check to the trustee for the interest for the first six months of 1984?

(c) What will be the amount of the discount amortized on December 31, 1984?

**P14-12** Danish Inc. has been producing quality children's apparel for more than 25 years. The company's fiscal year runs from April 1 to March 31. The following information relates to the obligations of Danish as of March 31, 1984.

**Bonds Payable**

Danish issued $4,000,000 of 9% bonds on July 1, 1978 at 98, which yielded proceeds of $3,920,000. The bonds will mature on July 1, 1988. Interest is paid semi-annually on July 1 and January 1. Danish uses the straight-line method to amortize the bond discount.

**Notes Payable**

Danish has signed several long-term notes with financial institutions and insurance companies. The maturities of these notes are given in the schedule below. The total unpaid interest for all of these notes amounts to $170,000 on March 31, 1984.

| Due Date | Amount Due |
|---|---|
| April 1, 1984 | $ 150,000 |
| July 1, 1984 | 200,000 |
| October 1, 1984 | 100,000 |
| January 1, 1985 | 200,000 |
| April 1, 1985–March 31, 1986 | 600,000 |
| April 1, 1986–March 31, 1987 | 400,000 |
| April 1, 1987–March 31, 1988 | 400,000 |
| April 1, 1988–March 31, 1989 | 500,000 |
| April 1, 1989–March 31, 1990 | 700,000 |
| | $3,250,000 |

### Estimated Warranties

Danish has a one-year product warranty on some selected items in its product line. The estimated warranty liability on sales made during the 1982–83 fiscal year and still outstanding as of March 31, 1983 amounted to $55,000. The warranty costs on sales made from April 1, 1983 through March 31, 1984 are estimated at $165,000. The actual warranty costs incurred during the current 1983–84 fiscal year are as follows:

| | |
|---|---:|
| Warranty claims honored on 1982–83 sales | $ 55,000 |
| Warranty claims honored on 1983–84 sales | 75,000 |
| Total warranty claims honored | $130,000 |

### Other Information

1. *Trade payables.* Accounts payable for supplies, goods and services purchased on open account amount to $340,000 as of March 31, 1984.

2. *Payroll related items.* Outstanding obligations related to Danish's payroll as of March 31, 1984 are:

| | |
|---|---:|
| Accrued salaries and wages | $150,000 |
| FICA taxes | 18,000 |
| State and federal income taxes withheld from employees | 30,000 |
| Other payroll deductions | 3,000 |

3. *Taxes.* The following taxes incurred but not due until the next fiscal year are:

| | |
|---|---:|
| State and federal income taxes | $305,000 |
| Property taxes | 125,000 |
| Sales and use taxes | 192,000 |

4. *Miscellaneous accruals.* Other accruals not separately classified amount to $62,000 as of March 31, 1984.

5. *Dividends.* On March 15, 1984 Danish's Board of Directors declared a cash dividend of $.40 per common share and a 10% common stock dividend. Both dividends were to be distributed on April 12, 1984 to the common stockholders of record at the close of business on March 31, 1984. Data regarding Danish common stock are as follows:

| | |
|---|---|
| Par value | $5 per share |
| Number of shares issued and outstanding | 3,000,000 shares |
| Market values of common stock: | |
| March 15, 1984 | $22.00 per share |
| March 31, 1984 | 21.50 per share |
| April 12, 1984 | 22.50 per share |

### Instructions

Prepare the liability section of the balance sheet and appropriate notes to the statement for Danish Inc. as of March 31, 1984, as they should appear in its annual report to the stockholders.

(CMA adapted)

**P14–13** On December 31, 1983, Elton Company acquired a computer from John Corporation by issuing a $350,000 noninterest-bearing note, payable in full on December 31, 1986. Elton Company's credit rating permits it to borrow funds from its several lines of credit at 12%. The computer is expected to have a 6-year life and a $50,000 salvage value.

### Instructions

(a) Prepare the journal entry for the purchase on December 31, 1983.
(b) Prepare any necessary adjusting entries relative to depreciation (use straight-line) and amortization (use effective interest method) on December 31, 1984.
(c) Prepare any necessary adjusting entries relative to depreciation and amortization on December 31, 1985.

**P14–14** Stevie Wonder and Associates, Inc. purchased machinery on December 31, 1982, at a price of $80,000, paying $20,000 down and agreeing to pay the balance in four equal installments of $15,000 payable each December 31. An assumed interest of 12% is implicit in the purchase price.

**Instructions**

Prepare the journal entries that would be recorded for the purchase and for the payments and interest on the following dates:
(a) December 31, 1982.
(b) December 31, 1983.
(c) December 31, 1984.
(d) December 31, 1985.
(e) December 31, 1986.

**\*P14–15** On May 1, 1983, D. Parton Company sold a new serial bond issue with $600,000 par value for $642,000. The nominal interest rate on these bonds is 12% and the interest is payable annually on May 1. One-half of the bonds will be retired on May 1 each year for two years, beginning in 1984. D. Parton Company closes its books on December 31 each year.

**Instructions**

Prepare all of the journal entries required over the life of these bonds to record the issuance, amortization, interest accruals and payments, and retirements (assume that the reversing entries are made at the beginning of each period). Use the bonds outstanding method.

**\*P14–16** On December 31, 1979, Olivia Newton Company sold a 13% serial bond issue in the amount of $2,800,000 for $2,794,400. The bonds mature in the amount of $400,000 on December 31 of each year, beginning December 31, 1980 and interest is payable annually.

On December 31, 1982, the company retired the $400,000 of bonds due on that date and in addition purchased at 99 and retired bonds in the amount of $200,000 which were due on December 31, 1984.

**Instructions**

(a) Prepare entries to record the payment of interest for 1980, and to record the amortization of discount for the year using the bonds outstanding method.
(b) Prepare entries to record the redemption of the bonds of $600,000 which were retired on December 31, 1982.
(c) Discuss the disclosures that are required relative to the bond transactions in 1982.
(d) What amount of discount would be amortized for the year 1984?

**\*P14–17** On January 1, 1981, Clapton/McCartney Corporation issued $1,000,000 in 5-year, 10% serial bonds to be repaid in the amount of $200,000 on January 1, of 1982, 1983, 1984, 1985, and 1986. Interest is payable at the end of each year. The bonds were sold to yield a rate of 12%.

**Instructions**

(a) Prepare a schedule showing the computation of the total amount received from the issuance of the serial bonds. Show supporting computations in good form.
(b) Assume the bonds were originally sold at a discount of $46,506. Prepare a schedule of amortization of the bond discount for the first three years after issuance, using the interest (effective rate) method. Show supporting computations in good form.

(AICPA adapted)

**\*P14–18** McEllen, Inc. owes Swedish Bank a 10-year, 19% note in the amount of $220,000 plus $41,800 of accrued interest. The note is due today 12/31/84. Because McEllen, Inc. is in financial trouble, Swedish agrees to accept 80,000 shares of McEllen's $1.00 par value common stock, which is selling for $1.25, forgive the accrued interest, reduce the face amount of the note to $120,000, extend the maturity date to 12/31/87, and reduce the interest rate to 5%. Interest will continue to be due on 12/31 each year.

**Instructions**

(a) Prepare all the necessary journal entries on the books of McEllen, Inc. from restructure through maturity.
(b) Prepare all the necessary journal entries on the books of Swedish Bank from restructure through maturity.

**\*P14-19** North Corp. owes South Corp. a 10-year, 10% note in the amount of $220,000 plus $22,000 of accrued interest. The note is due today, 12/31/84. Because North Corp. is in financial trouble, South Corp. agrees to forgive the accrued interest, $20,000 of the principal, and to extend the maturity date to 12/31/87. Interest will continue to be due on 12/31 each year.

Assume the following present value factors for 3 periods:

|  | 2 1/4% | 2 3/8% | 2 1/2% | 2 5/8% | 2 3/4% | 3% |
|---|---|---|---|---|---|---|
| Amt. of 1 | .935 | .932 | .929 | .925 | .922 | .915 |
| Ord. Ann. of 1 | 2.869 | 2.863 | 2.856 | 2.850 | 2.842 | 2.829 |

**Instructions**

(a) Compute the new effective interest rate following restructure. (Hint: Find the interest rate that establishes $242,000 as the present value of the total future cash flows.)
(b) Prepare a schedule of debt (receivable) reduction and interest expense (revenue) for the years 1984 through 1987.
(c) Prepare all the necessary journal entries on the books of North Corp. for the years 1984, 1985, and 1986.
(d) Prepare all the necessary journal entries on the books of South Corp. for the years 1984, 1985, and 1986.

**\*P14-20** At December 31, 1982, D. Reeve Manufacturing Company had outstanding a $350,000, 15% note payable to Nichols National Bank. Dated January 1, 1980, the note was due December 31, 1983, with interest payable each December 31. During 1983 Reeve notified Nichols that it might be unable to meet the scheduled December 31, 1983 payment of principal and interest because of financial difficulties. On September 30, 1983, Nichols sold the note, including interest accrued since December 31, 1982, for $360,000 to Pickwick Foundry, one of Reeve's oldest and largest customers. On December 31, 1983, Pickwick agreed to accept inventory costing $250,000 and worth $385,000 from Reeve in full settlement of the note.

**Instructions**

(a) Prepare the journal entry to record the September 30, 1983 transaction on the books of Nichols, Reeve, and Pickwick. For each, indicate whether the transaction is a troubled debt restructuring.
(b) Prepare the journal entry to record the December 31, 1983 transaction on the books of Reeve and Pickwick. For each, indicate whether the transaction is a troubled debt restructuring.

PART

# STOCKHOLDERS' EQUITY, DILUTIVE SECURITIES, AND INVESTMENTS

# 4

# CHAPTER 15

# Stockholders' Equity: Issuance and Reacquisition of Capital Stock

In your first exposure to financial statements you were probably taught that the credit side of the balance sheet represents the sources of enterprise assets. Liabilities represent the amount of assets that were borrowed, and stockholders' equity represents (1) the amount that was contributed by the stockholders and (2) the portion that was earned and retained by the enterprise. While this explanation is accurate and may seem simple enough, stockholders' equity is generally the least understood section of the financial statements because of its distinctive accounting terminology and its legalistic nature.

## THE NATURE OF STOCKHOLDERS' EQUITY

The owners of an enterprise bear the ultimate risks and uncertainties and receive the benefits of enterprise operations. Their interest in the enterprise is measured by the difference between the assets and the liabilities of the enterprise. Therefore, **the owners' or stockholders' interest in a business enterprise is a residual interest.**[1] As an amount, stockholders' equity represents the cumulative net contributions by stockholders plus recorded earnings that have been retained. As a residual interest, stockholders' equity has no existence apart from the assets and liabilities of the enterprise—stockholders' equity equals net assets. Stockholders' equity is not a claim to specific assets but a claim against a portion of the total assets. Its amount is not specified or fixed; it depends on the enterprise's profitability. Stockholders' equity grows if the enterprise is profitable and shrinks or may disappear entirely if the enterprise is unprofitable.

Accounting for stockholders' equity is greatly influenced by tradition and by corporate law.[2] Although the legal aspects of equity must be respected and disclosed, legal requirements need not be the accounting basis for classifying and reporting the components of equity.[3] **The two primary sources from which equity is derived are (1) contributions by**

---

[1]"Elements of Financial Statements of Business Enterprises," *Statement of Financial Accounting Concepts No. 3* (Stamford, Conn.: FASB, 1980), pars. 43–49.

[2]Ibid., par. 48.

[3]Beatrice Melcher, "Stockholders' Equity," *Accounting Research Study No. 15* (New York: AICPA, 1973), p. 2. Ms. Melcher's study is the most comprehensive pronouncement published on this topic.

654

**stockholders paid-in capital and (2) income (earnings) retained by a corporation,** and these two components should be accounted for and reported by every corporation. The diagram shown below depicts the sources of changes in equity.[4]

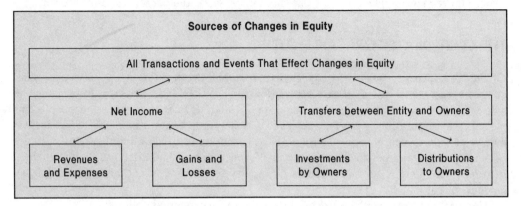

Changes in equity are also brought about by conversions of debt into equity. In addition, changes within equity are brought about by stock dividends, stock conversions, and recapitalizations (quasi reorganizations).

To this point, we have used the term stockholders' or owners' equity to denote the total capital of the enterprise. It is important to understand the many different meanings that are attached to the word **capital,** because the word often is construed differently by various user groups.

**In corporation finance,** for example, capital commonly represents the gross assets of the enterprise. **In law,** capital is considered that portion of stockholders' equity that is required by statute to be retained in the business for the protection of creditors. Generally **legal capital (stated capital)** is the par value of all capital stock issued, but when shares without par value are issued, it may be:

1. Total consideration paid in for the shares.
2. A minimum amount stated in the applicable law.
3. An arbitrary amount established by the board of directors at its discretion.

Accountants for the most part define capital more broadly than legal capital but more narrowly than total assets. **When accountants refer to capital they mean stockholders' equity or owners' equity.** They then classify stockholders' or owners' equity into two further categories—contributed capital and earned capital. **Contributed capital** (paid-in capital) is the term used to describe the total amount paid in on capital stock at any given time, or stated another way, it is the amount advanced by stockholders to the corporation for use in the business. Contributed capital includes the par value of all outstanding capital stock plus any premiums less any discounts on issuance plus the amount paid in on any subscription agreements and additional assessments. **Earned capital** is the capital that develops if the business operates profitably; it consists of all undistributed income that remains invested in the enterprise.

We have chosen to divide our coverage of stockholders' equity by discussing the accounting matters relating to contributions by stockholders in Chapter 15 and the other

---

[4]Adapted from *FASB Statement of Accounting Concepts, No. 3,* p. 23.

components, additional paid-in capital and retained earnings, in Chapter 16. Other securities that may be reported in stockholders' equity (convertible debt, stock purchase warrants, and stock options) are covered in Chapter 17, "Dilutive Securities." But first, in order to account for stockholders' equity, one must understand the corporate form of entity.

## THE CORPORATE FORM OF ENTITY

Of the three **primary forms of business organization—the proprietorship, the partnership, and the corporation**—the dominant form of business is the corporate form. In terms of the aggregate amount of resources controlled, goods and services produced, and people employed, the corporation is by far the leader. Nearly all, if not all, of the "500" largest industrial firms are corporations. Although the corporate form has a number of advantages (as well as disadvantages) over the other two forms, the principal attribute that has helped it to reach its present dominant role is its facility for attracting and accumulating large amounts of capital.

Corporations may be classified by the nature of ownership as follows:

1. **Public corporations:** governmental units or business operations owned by governmental units (such as the Federal Deposit Insurance Corporation).
2. **Private corporations.**
   a. **Nonstock:** nonprofit in nature and no stock issued (such as churches, charities, and colleges).
   b. **Stock:** companies that operate for profit and issue stock.
      (i) **Closed corporations (nonpublic enterprises):** stock held by a few stockholders (perhaps a family) and not available for public purchase.
      (ii) **Open corporations:** stock widely held and available for purchase by the public.
         (a) **Listed corporation:** stock traded on an organized stock exchange.
         (b) **Unlisted or over-the-counter corporation:** stock traded in a market in which securities dealers buy from and sell to the public.

The owners' equity accounts in a corporation are considerably different from those in a partnership or proprietorship. It is not necessary to enter into a detailed discussion of the advantages or disadvantages of the corporate form of business enterprise at this point. However, certain characteristics of the corporation do have a direct effect on what may be termed proprietorship, owners' equity, or net worth accounting, and it is helpful if these are clearly understood.

Among those special characteristics of the corporate form that affect accounting are:

1. Influence of state corporate law.
2. Use of the capital stock or share system.
3. Development of a variety of ownership interests.
4. Limited liability of stockholders.
5. Formality of profit distribution.

### State Corporate Law

Anyone desiring to establish a corporation must submit **articles of incorporation** to the proper department of the government of the state in which incorporation is desired. If the requirements are fulfilled, the corporation charter is issued, and the corporation is recognized as a legal entity subject to the laws of the state of incorporation. To some extent its actions are circumscribed by the laws of any state in which it seeks to carry on business, but, insofar as stockholders' equity accounting is concerned, the business corporation act of the state of incorporation governs.

The importance of this condition to accountants lies in the fact that **each of the 50 states has its own business corporation act.** Some of these laws are quite uniform; others vary considerably, which means that permissible transactions may vary from state to state and that accounting must reflect these differences. State laws usually prescribe the requirements for issuing stock, the treatment of proceeds of issued stock, the distributions permitted to stockholders, the effects of retiring stock, the regulations for and restrictions on acquiring treasury stock, as well as other procedures and restrictions.

Many states have adopted in their corporation laws the principles contained in the Model Business Corporation Act that was prepared in 1959 by the Committee of Corporate Laws of the American Bar Association. But other states have enacted corporate legislation with contrary features, often including elaborate and unusual provisions. The state laws are complex and vary not only in their provisions but also in their definitions of certain terms. Some laws fail to define technical terms, terms that often mean one thing in one state and another in a different state. And the problems are compounded because legal authorities often interpret the effects and restrictions of the laws differently.[5]

The laws are so diverse that there are exceptions to most generalizations we can make in regard to statutory provisions or meanings of terms. This situation somewhat complicates a discussion of stockholders' equity, but it cannot be avoided. While it is neither practical nor necessary for us to tabulate the provisions of all 50 states, we shall point out those matters on which state laws are most likely to differ.

## Capital Stock or Share System

The stockholders' equity in a corporation is generally made up of a large number of units or shares. Within a given class of stock each share is exactly equal to every other share. Each owner's interest is determined by the number of shares possessed. If a company has but one class of stock divided into 1,000 shares, a person owning 500 shares controls one-half the ownership interest of the corporation; one holding 10 shares has a one-hundredth interest.

Each share of stock has certain rights and privileges that can be restricted only by special contract at the time the shares are issued. One must examine the articles of incorporation, stock certificates, and the provisions of the state law to ascertain such restrictions on or variations from the standard rights and privileges. In the absence of restrictive provisions, each share carries the following rights:

1. To share proportionately in profits and losses.
2. To share proportionately in management (the right to vote for directors).
3. To share proportionately in corporate assets upon liquidation.
4. To share proportionately in any new issues of stock of the same class (called the preemptive right).

The first three rights are to be expected in the ownership of any business; the last may be used in a corporation to protect each stockholder's proportional interest in the enterprise. **The preemptive right protects an existing stockholder from involuntary dilution of ownership**

[5] *Accounting Research Study No. 15,* p. 8.

**interest.** Without this right stockholders with a given percentage interest might find their interest reduced by the issuance of additional stock without their knowledge and at prices that were not favorable to them. Because the preemptive right attached to existing shares makes it inconvenient for corporations to make large issuances of additional stock, as they frequently do in acquiring other companies, it has been eliminated by many corporations.

The great advantage of the share system is the ease with which an interest in the business may be transferred from one individual to another. **Individuals owning shares in a corporation may sell them to others at any time and at any price without obtaining the consent of the company or other stockholders.** Each share is personal property of the owner and may be disposed of at will. All that is required of the corporation is that it maintain a list or subsidiary ledger of stockholders as a guide to dividend payments, issuance of stock rights, voting proxies, and the like. Because shares are freely and frequently transferred, it is necessary for the corporation to revise the subsidiary ledger of stockholders periodically, generally in advance of every dividend payment or stockholders' meeting. As the number of stockholders grows, the need may develop for a more efficient system that can handle large numbers of stock transactions. Also, the major stock exchanges require controls that the typical corporation finds uneconomic to provide. Thus **registrars and transfer agents** who specialize in providing services for recording and transferring stock are usually used. The negotiability of stock certificates is governed by the Uniform Stock Transfer Act and the Uniform Commercial Code.

## Variety of Ownership Interests

In every corporation one class of stock must represent the basic ownership interest. That class is called common stock. **Common stock** is the residual corporate interest that bears the ultimate risks of loss and receives the benefits of success. It is guaranteed neither dividends nor assets upon dissolution. But common stockholders generally control the management of the corporation and tend to profit most if the company is successful. In the event that a corporation has only one authorized issue of capital stock, that issue is by definition common stock, whether so designated in the charter or not.

In an effort to appeal to all types of investors, corporations may offer two or more classes of stock with different rights or privileges attached to each class. In the preceding section it was pointed out that each share of stock of a given issue has the same rights as other shares of the same issue and that there are four rights inherent in every share. By special stock contracts between the corporation and its stockholders, certain of these rights may be sacrificed by the stockholder in return for other special rights or privileges. Thus special classes of stock are created. Because they have certain preferential rights, they are usually called **preferred stock.** In return for any special preference, the preferred stockholder is always called on to sacrifice some of the inherent rights of capital stock interests.

A common type of preference is to give the preferred stockholders a prior claim on earnings. They are assured a dividend, usually at a stated rate, before any amount may be distributed to the common stockholders. In return for this preference the preferred stock may sacrifice its right to a voice in management or its right to share in profits beyond the stated rate.

A company may accomplish much the same thing by issuing two classes of common stock, Class A stock and Class B stock. In this case one of the issues is the common stock and the other issue has some preference or restriction of basic rights. For example, DeKalb AgResearch, Inc. created two classes of common stock, Class A and Class B, when it decided to issue shares to the public a decade ago. Both Class A and Class B participate equally (per share) in all dividend payments and have the same claim on assets in dissolution. The differences are that Class A is voting and Class B is not; Class B is traded publicly over the counter while Class A, which is "family owned," must be sold privately (Class A shares are convertible, one for one, into Class B shares but not vice versa). By issuing two classes of common stock, the Class A owners of DeKalb AgResearch have obtained a ready market for the company's stock and yet provided an effective shield against outside takeover.

### Limited Liability of Stockholders

Those who "own" a corporation, that is the stockholders, contribute either property or services to the enterprise in return for ownership shares. The property or service invested in the enterprise is the extent of a stockholder's possible loss. That is, if the corporation sustains losses to such an extent that remaining assets are insufficient to pay creditors, no recourse can be had by the creditors against personal assets of the individual stockholders. In a partnership or proprietorship, personal assets of the owners can be attached to satisfy unpaid claims against the enterprise. Ownership interests in a corporation are legally protected against such a contingency; **the stockholders may lose their investment but they cannot lose more than their investment.**

Stock that has a fixed per-share amount printed on each stock certificate is called **par value stock.** Par value has but one real significance; it establishes the maximum responsibility of a stockholder in the event of insolvency or other involuntary dissolution. Par value is thus not "value" in the ordinary sense of the word. It is merely an amount per share determined by the incorporators of the company and stated in the corporation charter or certificate of incorporation. Par value establishes the nominal value per share and is the minimum amount that must be paid in by each stockholder if the stock is to be fully paid when issued. In most states, a corporation may, however, issue its capital stock either above or below par, in which case the stock is said to be issued at a **premium or a discount,** respectively.[6]

If par value stock is issued at par or at a price above par and the corporation subsequently suffers losses so that assets to repay stockholders upon dissolution are insufficient, stockholders may lose their entire investment. If, however, the stock is issued at a price below par and the losses prove to be of such magnitude as to consume not only the stockholders' investments but also a portion of the assets required to repay creditors, the creditors can force the stockholders to pay in to the corporation the amount of the discount on their capital shares. Thus the original purchasers of stock issued at a price below par are contingently liable to creditors of the corporation. In other words, stockholders may lose their entire investment in a corporation if the investments are equal to or in excess of the par value of the shares they own, or, if the investments are less than their par value, they may lose the amount of their investment plus an additional amount equal to the discount at which they purchased the stock. The limited liability feature of corporate capital stock prevents them from losing any more than the par value of their stock plus any premium paid upon purchase.

---

[6] In most states capital stock may not be issued below par; California and Maryland are among the very few that allow corporations to issue stock below par.

It should be emphasized that **the contingent liability of a stockholder for stock purchased at a price below par:**

1. Is an obligation to the corporation's creditors, not to the corporation itself.
2. Becomes a real liability only if the amount below par must be collected in order to pay the creditors upon dissolution of the company.
3. Is the responsibility of the original certificate holder at the time of dissolution unless by contract such responsibility is transferred to a subsequent holder.

While the corporate form of organization grants the protective feature of limited liability to the stockholders, the corporation must guarantee not to distribute the amount of stockholders' investment unless all prior claims on corporate assets have been paid. The corporation must maintain the corporate paid-in capital until dissolution and upon dissolution it must satisfy all prior claims before distributing any amounts to the stockholders.

In a proprietorship or partnership the owners can withdraw amounts at will because all their personal assets may be called on to protect creditors from loss. In a corporation, however, the owners cannot withdraw any amounts paid in because the only protection creditors have against loss is the amount paid in plus any discount below par.

## Formality of Profit Distribution

Essentially the owners of an enterprise may determine what is to be done with profits realized through operations. Profits may be left in the business to permit expansion or merely to provide a margin of safety, or they may be withdrawn and divided among the owners. In a proprietorship or partnership this decision is made by the owner or owners informally and requires no specific action. In a corporation, however, profit distribution is controlled by certain legal restrictions.

First of all, **no amounts may be distributed among the owners unless the corporate paid-in capital is maintained intact,** as discussed in the preceding section. State laws vary in the manner in which this specific restriction is worded and interpreted, but in general, profits determined under GAAP or standards are legally available for distribution. Some states require a cumulative profit from the inception of the corporation, that is, profits from the date of organization of the corporation must exceed the sum of any losses plus dividends already paid; others require a profit only for the period for which the dividend is to be declared.

Second, **distributions to stockholders must be formally approved by the board of directors** and recorded in the minutes of their meetings. As the top executive body in the corporation, the board of directors must make certain that no distributions are made to stockholders that are not justified by profits, and directors are generally held personally liable to creditors if liabilities cannot be paid because company assets have been illegally paid out to stockholders.

Third, **dividends must be in full agreement with the capital stock contracts as to preferences, participation, and the like.** Once the corporation has entered into contracts with various classes of stockholders, the stipulations of such contracts must be observed.

# CHARACTERISTICS OF PREFERRED STOCK

Preferred stock is a special class of shares that is designated "preferred" because it possesses certain preferences or features not possessed by the common stock.[7] The following features are those most often associated with preferred stock issues:

1. Preference as to dividends.
2. Preference as to assets in the event of liquidation.
3. Convertible into common stock.
4. Callable at the option of the corporation.
5. Nonvoting

The features that distinguish between preferred and common stock may be of a more restrictive and negative nature than preferences; for example, the preferred stock may be nonvoting, noncumulative, and nonparticipating. Unless specifically prohibited though, all of the basic rights of stock ownership apply to preferred stock.

Preferred stock is usually issued with a par value, and the dividend preference is expressed as a **percentage of the par value.** Thus, holders of 8% preferred stock with a $100 par value are entitled to an annual dividend of $8 per share. This stock is commonly referred to as 8% preferred stock. In the case of no-par preferred stock a dividend preference is expressed as a **specific dollar amount** per share, for example, $7 per share. This stock is commonly referred to as $7 preferred stock. A preference as to dividends is not assurance that dividends will be paid; it is merely assurance that the stated dividend rate or amount applicable to the preferred stock must be paid before any dividends can be paid on the common stock.

## Features of Preferred Stock

A corporation may attach whatever preferences or restrictions in whatever combination it desires to a preferred stock issue so long as it does not specifically violate its state incorporation law, and it may issue more than one class of preferred stock. For example, Bird & Son, Inc. reported the following:

> 5% cumulative preferred stock, par value $100 per share, callable at $110 per share.
>
> $2.75 convertible preference stock without par value, stated at $65 per share.

The most common features attributed to preferred stock are discussed below:

1. **Cumulative.** Dividends not paid in any year must be made up in a later year before any profits can be distributed to common stockholders. If the directors fail to declare a dividend at the normal date for dividend action, the dividend is said to have been "passed." Any passed dividend on cumulative preferred stock constitutes a **dividend in arrears.** Because no liability exists until the board of directors declares a dividend, a dividend in arrears is not recorded as a liability but is disclosed in a footnote to the financial statements. (At common law, if the

---

[7]*Accounting Trends and Techniques—1981* reports that of its 600 surveyed companies, 215 had preferred stock outstanding.

corporate charter is silent about the cumulative feature, the preferred stock is considered to be cumulative.) Noncumulative preferred stock is seldom issued because a passed dividend is lost forever to the preferred stockholder.

2. **Participating.** Holders of participating preferred stock share ratably with the common stockholders in any profit distributions beyond the prescribed rate. That is, 5% preferred stock, if fully participating, will receive not only its 5% return, but also dividends at the same rates as those paid to common stockholders if amounts in excess of 5% of par or stated value are paid to common stockholders. Also, participating preferred stock may not always be fully participating as described, but partially participating. For example, provision may be made that 5% preferred stock will be participating up to a maximum total rate of 10%, after which it ceases to participate in additional profit distributions; or 5% preferred stock may participate only in additional profit distributions that are in excess of a 9% dividend rate on the common stock. Participating preferred stocks, popular in the early 1900s, have seldom been issued in the past few decades.

3. **Convertible.** The stockholders may at their option exchange their preferred shares for common stock at a predetermined ratio. The convertible preferred stockholder not only enjoys a preferred claim on dividends but also has the option of converting into a common stockholder with unlimited participation in earnings. Convertible preferred stock has been widely used in the past two decades, especially in consummating business combinations, and is favored by investors. The accounting problems related to convertible securities are discussed in Chapter 17.

4. **Callable.** The issuing corporation can call or redeem at its option the outstanding preferred shares at specified future dates and at stipulated prices. Many preferred issues are callable. The call or redemption price is ordinarily set slightly above the original issuance price and is commonly stated in terms related to the par value. The callable feature permits the corporation to use the capital obtained through the issuance of such stock until the need has passed or it is no longer advantageous. The existence of a call price or prices tends to set a ceiling on the market value of the preferred shares unless they are convertible into common stock. When a preferred stock is called for redemption, any dividends in arrears must be paid. For many decades some preferred stock issues have contained provisions for redemption at some future date, through sinking funds or other means. More recently, some preferred stock issues have provided for mandatory redemption within five or ten years of issuance.

The motivation for issuance of preferred stock instead of debt usually lies in the existing debt to equity ratio of the issuer. As the ratio weakens because of increasing debt, an issuance of preferred stock may be used to improve upon that ratio. In other instances, issuances are made through private placements with other corporations at a lower than market dividend rate because the acquiring corporation receives dividends that are largely tax free (due to an 85% dividends received deduction).

## Debt Characteristics of Preferred Stock

With the right combination of features (that is, fixed return, no vote, redeemable), a preferred stockholder may possess more of the characteristics of a creditor than of an owner. Preferred shares generally have no maturity date, but the preferred stockholder's relationship with the company may be terminated if the corporation exercises its call privilege. At present GAAP does not distinguish between preferred stocks, not even redeemable preferred stock,[8] and other classes of capital stock for balance sheet classification

---

[8] *Redeemable preferred stock* is subject to mandatory redemption requirements or has a redemption feature that is outside the control of the issuer. It includes preferred stock that (1) has a fixed or

purposes.[9] But the FASB in *Statement No. 47* does require disclosure of any redemption features of a preferred stock issued and a schedule of redemptions required within the next five years.[10] For example, at one time Reliance Group, Inc., which might otherwise have reported only the $4 million par value of its preferred issue, is now required to disclose the $116 million redemption price due within five years.

The SEC, however, has issued a rule that prohibits companies from combining preferred stock with common stock in financial statements. Amounts have to be separately presented for redeemable preferred stock,[11] nonredeemable preferred stock, and common stock. The amounts applicable to these three categories of equity items cannot be totaled or combined for SEC reporting purposes. The general heading, stockholders' equity, is not to include **redeemable preferred stock.**

The proposal was triggered by an SEC concern about the increasing issuance of preferred stock specifying redemption over relatively short periods such as five to ten years; such stock issues are called transient preferreds. According to the SEC, such stock involves a commitment to use future resources of the company to redeem the issue, giving the holder a claim against prospective cash flows and hence a unique status different from that of holders of equity securities that represent permanent capital investments. This new type of preferred is nothing but debt thinly disguised. The roster of issuers of transient preferreds includes Eastern Airlines, National Distillers, Revlon, Inc., Westinghouse Electric, Occidental Petroleum, TWA, and Tenneco (see page 197 for an example of a separate presentation of redeemable preferred). On page 664 is an excerpt from Allied Corporation's 1981 balance sheet that is typical of how redeemable preferred stock is being reported.

Even though present GAAP does not dictate (or prohibit) separate classification, application of the FASB's qualitative characteristic of **representational faithfulness** would require that economic substance rather than the legal form or description of such securities dictate their financial statement classification.

Neither the SEC nor GAAP have addressed the possible income statement consequences (e.g., whether dividend payments should be charged to operations similar to interest expense, and how to account for extinguishments) or the conceptual question of whether redeemable preferred stock is a liability (current in the case of payments to be made in the next year).

---

determinable redemption date, (2) is redeemable at the option of the holder, or (3) has conditions for redemption that are not solely within the control of the issuer.

*Nonredeemable preferred stock* is not redeemable or is redeemable solely at the option of the issuer. *Securities and Exchange Commission Release No. 33–6097* (Washington, D.C.: SEC, July 27, 1979).

[9]Several accounting standards, however, have recognized the difference between redeemable and nonredeemable preferred stock (not necessarily using those terms). These include *FASB Statement No. 47* (which requires for capital stock redeemable at fixed or determinable prices the same disclosures required for long-term debt), *FASB Statement No. 12* (which excludes redeemable preferred stock from the definition of "equity security"), and *APB Opinion No. 16* (which requires that the cost of a company acquired by issuing senior equity securities having characteristics of redeemable preferred stock be determined on the same basis as that used in the case of debt securities).

[10]"Disclosure of Long-Term Obligations," *Statement of Financial Accounting Standards No. 47* (Stamford, Conn.: FASB, 1981), par. 10 c.

[11]*SEC Release No. 33-6097, op. cit.*

| Allied Corporation<br>(dollars in millions) | | |
| --- | --- | --- |
| | **1981** | 1980 |
| Total current liabilities | **1,373** | 1,182 |
| Long-term debt and capitalized lease obligations | **857** | 885 |
| Deferred income taxes | **335** | 311 |
| Accrued pension obligations | **89** | 103 |
| Other liabilities | **199** | 133 |
| **Preferrred redeemable stock** (1981 aggregate liquidation preference $625) | **591** | 260 |
| Common stock and other shareholders' equity: | | |
| Capital—common stock—Authorized 100,000,000 shares (par value $1 per share); issued: 1981—34,127,879 shares; 1980—33,662,621 shares | **629** | 616 |
| Common stock held in treasury, at cost: 1981—384,188 shares; 1980—174,086 shares | **(19)** | (9) |
| Retained earnings | **1,290** | 1,057 |
| Total common stock and other shareholders' equity | **1,900** | 1,664 |
| Total liabilities and shareholders' equity | **$5,344** | $4,538 |

## ACCOUNTING FOR THE ISSUANCE OF STOCK

From the preceding discussion of the special features of the corporate system it may be seen that a corporation obtains funds from its stockholders through a series of transactions that may vary considerably. First, the stock must be authorized by the state, generally in a certificate of incorporation or charter; next, shares are offered for sale and contracts to sell stock are entered into; then, amounts to be received for the stock are collected and the shares issued. The accounting problems involved in the issuance of stock are discussed under the following topics:

1. Accounting for par value stock.
2. Accounting for no-par stock.
3. Accounting for stock sold on a subscription basis.
4. Accounting for stock issued in combination with other securities (lump sum sales).
5. Accounting for stock issued in noncash transactions.
6. Accounting for assessments on stock.
7. Accounting for costs of issuing stock.

### Par Value Stock

As indicated earlier, the par value of a stock has no relationship to the fair market value of the stock. At present, the par value associated with most capital stock issuances is very low ($1, $5, $10), which contrasts dramatically with the situation in the early 1900s when practically all stock issued had a par value of $100. The reason for this change is to permit the original sale of stock at low amounts per share and at the same time to avoid the contingent liability associated with stock sold below par. Stock with a low par value is rarely, if ever, sold below par value. In addition, some states charge a transfer tax based on the par value of the stock, so a low par value may result in lower taxes.

To show the required information for issuance of par value stock, accounts must be kept for each class of stock as follows:

1. **Preferred Stock or Common Stock.** Reflects the par value of the corporation's issued shares. These accounts are credited when the shares are originally issued. No additional entries are made in this account unless additional shares are issued or shares are retired.

2. **Paid-in Capital in Excess of Par or Additional Paid-in Capital.** Indicates any excess over par value paid in by stockholders in return for the shares issued to them. Once paid in, the excess over par becomes a part of the corporation's additional paid-in capital and the individual stockholder has no greater claim on the excess paid in than all other holders of the same class of shares.

3. **Discount on Stock.** Indicates that the stock has been issued at less than par. The holder of shares issued below par may be called on to pay in the amount of the discount if necessary to prevent creditors from sustaining loss upon liquidation of the corporation.

To illustrate how these accounts are used, assume that Colonial Corporation sold, for $1,100, one hundred shares of stock with a par value of $5 per share. The entry to record the issuance is:

| | | |
|---|---|---|
| Cash | 1,100 | |
|    Common Stock | | 500 |
|    Paid-in Capital in Excess of Par (Premium on Common Stock) | | 600 |

If the stock had been issued in return for $300, the entry would have been recorded as follows:

| | | |
|---|---|---|
| Cash | 300 | |
| Paid-in Capital in Excess of Par (Discount on Common Stock) | 200 | |
|    Common Stock | | 500 |

The use of only these capital accounts assumes that no entry would be made in the general ledger accounts at the time the corporation receives its stock authorization from the state of incorporation. In case a formal journal entry is to be made for the authorization of stock, the following separate accounts would be used for authorized stock and for unissued stock:

1. **Authorized Preferred or Common Stock.** Shows the total amount of capital stock authorized. This account is credited at the time authorization from the state is received. No additional entries are made in this account unless the charter is amended to authorize the issuance of additional shares or to reduce the present authorized shares.

2. **Unissued Preferred or Common Stock.** Shows the total authorized shares not yet issued. When subtracted from the amount authorized, the stock already issued is obtained. This account is debited at the time of recording the stock authorized, and is credited for the par value of stock issued. When these accounts are kept, the amount of stock issued is determined by subtracting the balance of the unissued stock account from the balance of the authorized stock account.

## No-Par Stock

Many states permit the issuance of capital stock without par value. Shares are issued that have no per-share amount printed on the stock certificate. The reasons for issuance of no-par stock are twofold. First, issuance of no-par stock **avoids the contingent liability** that might occur if par value stock were issued at a discount. Second, some confusion still exists over the relationship (or rather the absence of a relationship) between the par value and fair market value. If shares have no par value, **the questionable treatment of using par value as a basis for value never arises.** This circumstance is particularly advantageous whenever stock is issued for property items such as tangible or intangible fixed assets. The major disadvantages of no-par stock are that some states levy a high tax on these issues and the total may be considered legal capital.

No-par stock, like par value shares, are sold for what they will bring, but unlike par value shares, they are issued without a premium or a discount and, therefore, no contingent liability accrues to the stockholders. The exact amount received represents the credit to common or preferred stock. For example, Video Electronics Corporation is organized with authorized common stock of 10,000 shares without par value. No entry, other than a memorandum entry, need be made for the authorization inasmuch as no amount is involved. If 500 shares are then issued for cash at $10 per share, the entry should be:

| | | |
|---|---|---|
| Cash | 5,000 | |
|   Common Stock—No-Par Value | | 5,000 |

If another 500 shares are issued for $11 per share the entry should be:

| | | |
|---|---|---|
| Cash | 5,500 | |
|   Common Stock—No-Par Value | | 5,500 |

**True no-par stock should be carried in the accounts at issue price without any complications due to additional paid-in capital or discount.** But some states permit the issuance of no-par stock and then proceed either to require or, in some cases, to permit such stock to have a **stated value** or minimum value below which it cannot be issued. Thus, instead of becoming no-par stock it becomes, in effect, stock with a very low par value, open to all the criticisms and abuses that first encouraged the development of no-par stock.[12]

If no-par stock is required to have a minimum issue price of $5 per share and no provision is made as to how amounts in excess of $5 per share are to be handled, the inclination is for the board of directors to declare all such amounts to be additional paid-in capital, which in many states is fully or partially available for dividends. Thus, no-par value stock with either a minimum stated value or a stated value assigned by the board of directors permits a new corporation to commence its operations with additional paid-in capital that may be in excess of its stated capital. For example, if 1,000 of the shares described above ($5 stated value) were issued at $15 per share for cash, the entry could be either

| | | |
|---|---|---|
| Cash | 15,000 | |
|   Common Stock | | 15,000 |

or

| | | |
|---|---|---|
| Cash | 15,000 | |
|   Common Stock | | 5,000 |
|   Paid-in Capital in Excess of Stated Value | | 10,000 |

In most instances the obvious advantages to the corporation of setting up an initial Additional Paid-in Capital account will influence the board of directors to require the

---

[12]*Accounting Trends and Techniques—1981* indicates that its 600 surveyed companies reported 616 issues of outstanding common stock, 541 par value issues, and 75 no-par issues; all of the no-par issues were shown at their stated (assigned) values.

latter entry. Whether for this or for other reasons, the prevailing tendency is to account for no-par stock with stated value as if it were par value stock with a par equal to the stated value.

## Stock Sold on a Subscription Basis

The preceding discussion assumed that the stock was sold for cash, but stock may also be sold on a subscription basis. Sale on a subscription basis generally occurs when new, small companies "go public" or when stock is offered to employees by corporations to obtain employee participation in the ownership of the business. When stock is sold on a subscription basis, the full price of the stock is not received initially. Normally only a partial payment is made originally and the stock is not issued until the full subscription price is received.

**Accounting for Subscribed Stock.**   Two new accounts are used when stock is sold on a subscription basis. The first, **Common or Preferred Stock Subscribed,** indicates the corporation's obligation to issue shares of its stock upon payment of final subscription balances by those who have subscribed for stock. This account thus signifies a commitment against the unissued capital stock. Once the subscription price is fully paid, the Common or Preferred Stock Subscribed account is debited and the Common or Preferred Stock account is credited. Common or Preferred Stock Subscribed is presented in the stockholders' equity section below Common or Preferred Stock.

The second account, **Subscriptions Receivable,** indicates the amount to be collected in full before stock is issued; therefore, this account indicates the amount yet to be collected before subscribed stock will be issued. It is a receivable just as ordinary trade accounts are receivable, but it differs in inception. Trade accounts receivable grow out of sales transactions in the ordinary course of business; subscriptions receivable relate to the issuance of a concern's own stock and in a sense represent capital contributions not yet paid in to the corporation.

Some controversy exists concerning the presentation of Subscriptions Receivable on the balance sheet. Most accountants place Subscriptions Receivable in the current asset section (assuming of course that payment on the receivable will be received within the operating cycle or one year whichever is longer). In some cases, Subscriptions Receivable is shown as a deduction from Common or Preferred Stock Subscribed in the stockholders' equity section, rather than as an asset, as, for example, when there is no intention to collect the balance due from subscribers in the near future, or when the receivable hinges on some event or performance related to the subscriber, or where the subscription approach is used to circumvent a state law that may prohibit the sale of capital stock at a discount.

Most states consider common or preferred stock subscribed to be similar to outstanding common or preferred stock, which means that **individuals who have signed a valid subscription contract normally have the same rights and privileges as a stockholder who holds outstanding shares of stock.**

The journal entries for handling stock sold on a subscription basis are illustrated by the following example. Pennzoil Corp. offers stock on a subscription basis to selected individuals giving them the right to purchase 10 shares of stock (par value $5) at a price of $20 per share. Fifty individuals accept the company's offer and agree to pay 50% down and to pay the remaining 50% at the end of six months.

**At date of issuance—**

| | | |
|---|---|---|
| Subscriptions Receivable | 10,000 | |
|   Common Stock Subscribed | | 2,500 |
|   Paid-in Capital in Excess of Par | | 7,500 |
|     (To record receipt of subscriptions for 500 shares) | | |
| | | |
| Cash | 5,000 | |
|   Subscriptions Receivable | | 5,000 |
|     (To record receipt of first installment representing | | |
|     50% of total due on subscribed stock) | | |

When the final payment is received and the stock is issued, the entries are:

**Six months later—**

| | | |
|---|---|---|
| Cash | 5,000 | |
|   Subscriptions Receivable | | 5,000 |
|     (To record receipt of final installment on | | |
|     subscribed stock) | | |
| | | |
| Common Stock Subscribed | 2,500 | |
|   Common Stock | | 2,500 |
|     (To record issuance of 500 shares upon receipt of | | |
|     final installment from subscribers) | | |

**Defaulted Subscription Accounts.** Sometimes a subscriber is unable to pay all installments and defaults on the agreement. The question is then raised of what to do with the balance of the subscription account as well as the amount already paid in. The solution to this problem is a function of the applicable state law. Some states permit the corporation to retain any amounts paid in on defaulted subscription accounts; other states require that any amount realized on the resale in excess of the amount due from the original subscriber be returned.

## Stock Issued in Combination with Other Securities (Lump Sum Sales)

Generally, corporations sell classes of stock separately from one another so that the proceeds relative to each class, and ordinarily even relative to each lot, are known. Occasionally, two or more classes of securities are issued for a single payment or lump sum. It is not uncommon for more than one type or class of security to be issued in the acquisition of another company. The accounting problem in a lump sum issuance is the allocation of the proceeds between the several classes of securities. The two methods of allocation available for accountants are (1) the proportional method and (2) the incremental method.

**Proportional Method.** If the fair market value or other sound basis for determining relative value is available for each class of security, the lump sum received is best allocated between the classes of securities on a proportional basis, that is, the ratio that each is to the total. For instance, if 1,000 shares of $10 stated value common stock having a market value of $20 a share and 1,000 shares of $10 par value preferred stock having a market value of $12 a share are issued for a lump sum of $30,000, the allocation of the $30,000 to the two classes would be as follows:

Fair market value of common (1,000 × $20) = $20,000
Fair market value of preferred (1,000 × $12) = 12,000

Aggregate fair market value $32,000

Allocated to common: $\dfrac{\$20,000}{\$32,000} \times \$30,000 = \$18,750$

Allocated to preferred: $\dfrac{\$12,000}{\$32,000} \times \$30,000 = \underline{\$11,250}$

Total allocation $30,000

**Incremental Method.** In instances where the fair market value of all classes of securities is not determinable, the incremental method may be used. The market value of the securities is used as a basis for those classes that are known and the remainder of the lump sum is allocated to the class for which the market value is not known. For instance, if 1,000 shares of $10 stated value common stock having a market value of $20 and 1,000 shares of $10 par value preferred stock having no established market value are issued for a lump sum of $30,000, the allocation of the $30,000 to the two classes would be as follows:

Lump-sum receipt $30,000
Allocated to common (1,000 shs. × $20 fair mkt. value) 20,000
Balance allocated to preferred $10,000

**If no fair market value is determinable for any of the classes of stock involved in a lump sum exchange, the allocation may have to be arbitrary.** If it is known that one or more of the classes of securities issued will have a determinable market value in the near future, the arbitrary basis may be used with the intent to make an adjustment when the future market value is established.

## Stock Issued in Noncash Transactions

It is not uncommon for some paid-in capital of a corporation to be the result of stock issued in exchange for property, services, or any form of asset other than cash. Accounting for the issuance of shares of stock for property or services may involve a problem of valuation. **The general rule to be applied when stock is issued for services or property other than cash is that the property or services be recorded at either its fair market value or the fair market value of the stock issued, whichever is more clearly determinable.**

If the fair market value of the property or services is readily determinable, it is used as a basis for recording the exchange. If it is not readily determinable but the fair market value of the stock issued is, the transaction is recorded at the fair market value of the stock. If both are readily determinable and the transaction is the result of an arm's-length exchange, there will probably be little difference in their fair market values. In such cases it should not matter which value is regarded as the basis for valuing the exchange. If the fair market value of the stock being issued and the property or services being received are not readily determinable, the value to be assigned is generally established by the board of directors, usually through independent appraisals. The use of the book, par, or stated values as a basis of valuation for these transactions should be avoided.

When stock is issued for personal services by employees or outsiders, the fair value of the services as of the date of the contract for such services, rather than the date of issuance of the shares (even though the date of issuance is prescribed for income tax purposes), should be the basis for valuation because the contract is viewed in an accounting sense as a subscription. In these exchanges, however, the fair market value of the shares issued is usually more readily determinable.

Unissued stock or treasury stock (issued shares that have been reacquired but not retired) may be exchanged for the property or services. If treasury shares are used, their cost should not be regarded as the decisive factor in establishing the fair market value of the property or services. The current value of the property or services, if determinable, is a better basis of valuation.

The following series of transactions illustrates the procedure for recording the issuance of 10,000 shares of $10 par value common stock for a patent:

1. The fair market value of the patent is not readily determinable but the fair market value of the stock is known to be $140,000.

| | | |
|---|---|---|
| Patent | 140,000 | |
| Common Stock | | 100,000 |
| Paid-in Capital in Excess of Par | | 40,000 |

2. The fair market value of the stock is not readily determinable, but the fair market value of the patent is determined to be $150,000.

| | | |
|---|---|---|
| Patent | 150,000 | |
| Common Stock | | 100,000 |
| Paid-in Capital in Excess of Par | | 50,000 |

3. Neither the fair market value of the stock nor the fair market value of the patent is readily determinable. An independent consultant values the patent at $125,000, and the board of directors agrees with that valuation.

| | | |
|---|---|---|
| Patent | 125,000 | |
| Common Stock | | 100,000 |
| Paid-in Capital in Excess of Par | | 25,000 |

In corporate law, the board of directors is granted the power to set the value of noncash transactions. This power has been abused. The issuance of stock for property or services has resulted in cases of overstated corporate capital through intentional overvaluation of the property or services received. The overvaluation of the stockholders' equity resulting from inflated asset values creates what is referred to as **watered stock.** The "water" can be eliminated from the corporate structure by simply writing down the overvalued assets.

If as a result of the issuance of stock for property or services the recorded assets are undervalued, **secret reserves** are created. An understated corporate structure or secret reserve may also be achieved by excessive depreciation or amortization charges, by expensing capital expenditures, excessive write-downs of inventories or receivables, or any other understatement of assets or overstatement of liabilities. An example of a liability overstatement is an excessive provision for estimated product warranties which ultimately results in an understatement of owners' equity, thereby creating a secret reserve.

## Assessments on Stock

The laws of some states provide that a corporation may assess stockholders an additional amount above their original contribution. Although this situation occurs rather infrequently, when stockholders are assessed, they must either pay or possibly forfeit their existing shares. Upon receiving the assessments from the stockholders, the corporation should determine whether the original stock was sold at a discount or a premium. If the stock was originally sold at a discount, the additional proceeds should be credited to the discount account. If the stock was originally issued at a premium, the account Additional Paid-in Capital Arising from Assessments should be credited.

## Costs of Issuing Stock

The costs associated with the acquisition of corporate capital resulting from the issuance of securities include the following:

1. Attorneys' fees.
2. Certified public accountants' fees.
3. Underwriters' fees and commissions.
4. Expenses of printing and mailing certificates and registration statements.
5. Expenses of filing with the SEC.
6. Clerical and administrative expenses of preparation.
7. Costs of advertising the issue.

In practice there are two primary methods of accounting for initial issue costs. **The first method treats issue costs as a reduction of the amounts paid in.** In effect, such costs are debited to the Paid-in Capital in Excess of Par or Stated Value. This treatment is based on the premise that issue costs are unrelated to corporate operations and thus are not properly chargeable to expense; issue costs are viewed as a reduction of proceeds of the financing activity.

**The second method treats issue costs as an organization cost** that is charged neither to expense nor to corporate capital; such costs are capitalized and classified as an intangible asset and written off over an arbitrary time period not to exceed 40 years. This treatment is based on the premise that amounts paid in as invested capital should not be violated, and that issue costs benefit the corporation over a long period of time or so long as the invested capital is utilized.

Although both treatments are applied in practice, the first method of charging issue costs to paid-in capital predominates. The Securities and Exchange Commission permits the use of either method. In addition to the costs of initial issuance of stock, corporations annually incur costs of maintaining the stockholders' records and handling ownership transfers. These recurring costs, primarily registrar and transfer agents' fees, should be charged as expense to the period in which incurred.

## REACQUISITION OF SHARES

It is not unusual to find comments in the financial media similar to the following quotations:

Northwest Industries Inc. said it will proceed with a cash tender offer to purchase five million of its common shares, which represents about 20% of its 24.9 million shares outstanding. If successful, the share repurchase at $75 per share will cost Northwest $375 million. Northwest is making the tender offer because "it believes the current price of its shares doesn't adequately reflect the value of its business."[13]

Honeywell Inc. said directors authorized the purchase of as many as one million of its common shares. The shares will be used for employee stock-option plans and general corporate purposes.[14]

Corporations purchase their outstanding stock for a variety of reasons. The major factors are (1) to have enough stock on hand to meet employee stock compensation contracts, (2) to reduce the shares outstanding in hopes of increasing earnings per share, (3) to buy out a particular ownership interest, (4) to attempt to make a market in the company's stock, (5) to contract the operations of the business, or (6) to meet the stock needs of a potential merger.

Once shares are reacquired, they may either be retired or held in the treasury for reissue. If not retired, such shares are referred to as treasury shares or treasury stock. Technically treasury stock is a corporation's own stock that has been reacquired after having been issued and fully paid. Stock originally issued at a discount and then reacquired is not properly treasury stock, but the distinction is of such little practical importance that it is commonly ignored.

**Treasury stock is not an asset.** It is inappropriate to imply that a corporation can own a part of itself. Treasury stock may be sold to obtain funds, but that possibility does not make treasury stock a balance sheet asset. When a corporation buys back some of its own outstanding stock, it has reduced its capitalization but has not acquired an asset. The possession of treasury stock does not give the corporation the right to vote, to exercise preemptive rights as a stockholder, to receive cash dividends, or to receive assets upon corporate liquidation. Treasury stock is essentially the same as unissued capital stock, and no one advocates classifying unissued capital stock as an asset in the balance sheet.[15]

## Methods of Accounting for Treasury Stock

Two general methods of handling treasury stock in the accounts are the cost method and the par value method. Both methods are considered generally acceptable and are applied in practice. The **cost method,** which enjoys more widespread use,[16] results in debiting the Treasury Stock account for the reacquisition cost and in reporting this account as a deduction from the total paid-in capital **and** retained earnings on the balance sheet. The **par** or **stated value method,** which is theoretically more justifiable, records all transactions in treasury shares at the par value of the shares and reports the treasury stock as a reduction

---

[13] *Wall Street Journal* (January 20, 1982), p. 37.

[14] *Wall Street Journal* (January 15, 1982), p. 13.

[15] In special circumstances treasury stock is presented as an asset in the balance sheet. For example, in 1980, Ford Motor Company reported treasury stock among its "Other Assets" with the following explanatory note: "At December 31, 1980, there were 300,127 shares of Common Stock of the Company, with a cost of $12 million included in other assets in the Consolidated Balance Sheet. Such shares were acquired for delivery under the deferred payment provisions of the Company's Supplemental Compensation Plan". The justification for classifying these shares as assets is based on the fact that they will be used to liquidate a specific liability that appears on the balance sheet. *Accounting Trends and Techniques—1981* reported that 6 of 408 companies disclosing treasury stock classified it among the noncurrent assets.

[16] *Accounting Trends and Techniques—1981* indicates that of its selected list of 600 companies, 352 carried common stock in treasury at cost and only 40 at par or stated value; 20 companies carried preferred stock in treasury at cost and 6 at par or stated value.

of outstanding capital stock. No matter which method is used, in most states the cost of the treasury shares acquired is considered to be a restriction on retained earnings.

**Treasury Shares Accounted for at Cost**   Under the cost method, acquisition of treasury stock is viewed as the initial step in a two-part transaction; the reissuance of the treasury stock is the second step and completes the transaction. The acquisition is a temporary contraction of total capital, and reissuance is a restoration of the total capital. Between acquisition and reissuance, treasury shares are held in suspense by the corporation. **The Treasury Stock account is debited for the cost of the shares acquired and is credited upon reissuance for this same cost** in a manner similar to that used in an inventory account. In fact, if numerous acquisitions of blocks of treasury shares are made at different prices, inventory costing methods, such as specific identification, average, or FIFO, may be used to identify the cost at date of reissuance. **Under the cost method, the price received for the stock when originally issued does not affect the entries to record the acquisition and reissuance of the treasury stock.**

If the treasury shares are reissued at a price in excess of the acquisition cost, the excess is credited to an account titled Paid-in Capital from Treasury Stock. If the treasury shares are reissued at less than acquisition cost, the deficiency is treated first as a reduction of any paid-in capital related to previous reissuances or retirements of treasury stock of the same class. If the balance in Paid-in Capital from Treasury Stock is insufficient to absorb the deficiency, the remainder is recorded as a reduction of retained earnings.[17] The following sequence of transactions with accompanying journal entries illustrates the cost method:

### COST METHOD

**1. One thousand shares of common stock of $100 par value are originally issued at 110.**

| | | |
|---|---:|---:|
| Cash | 110,000 | |
| Common Stock | | 100,000 |
| Paid-in Capital in Excess of Par | | 10,000 |

**2. One hundred shares of common are reacquired at $112.**

| | | |
|---|---:|---:|
| Treasury Stock | 11,200 | |
| Cash | | 11,200 |

**3. Ten shares of treasury stock are reissued at $112.**

| | | |
|---|---:|---:|
| Cash | 1,120 | |
| Treasury Stock (10 shares at $112 per share) | | 1,120 |

**4. Ten shares of treasury stock are reissued at $130.**

| | | |
|---|---:|---:|
| Cash | 1,300 | |
| Treasury stock (10 shares at $112 per share) | | 1,120 |
| Paid-in Capital from Treasury Stock | | 180 |

**5. Ten shares of treasury stock are reissued at $98.**

| | | |
|---|---:|---:|
| Cash | 980 | |
| Paid-in Capital from Treasury Stock | 140 | |
| Treasury Stock (10 shares at $112 per share) | | 1,120 |

---

[17]"Status of Accounting Research Bulletins," *Opinions of the Accounting Principles Board No. 6* (New York: AICPA, 1965), par. 12.

If no Paid-in Capital from Treasury Stock existed at the time of reissuance at 98, the entire $140 would be charged to Retained Earnings.

Even though the treasury stock was reissued at less than par in transaction 5 above, no consideration was given to this because the legal capital requirements were satisfied when the stock was originally issued in transaction 1. Only the difference between the *cost* of the treasury stock and its reissue price affect paid-in capital. Note also that the difference of $140 between the cost of the treasury shares and the reissue price is charged against Paid-in Capital from Treasury Stock, reducing the credit balance in that account to $40.[18]

**6. Ten shares of treasury stock are reissued at $105.**

| | | |
|---|---|---|
| Cash | 1,050 | |
| Paid-in Capital from Treasury Stock | 40 | |
| Retained Earnings | 30 | |
|   Treasury Stock (10 shares at $112 per share) | | 1,120 |

In transaction 6 the reissuance of ten additional shares at a price below cost more than eliminated the remaining balance of $40 in Paid-in Capital from Treasury Stock. When Paid-in Capital from Treasury Stock is reduced to zero, any remaining deficiency is charged against Retained Earnings. In each of the reissuing transactions illustrated above, the Treasury Stock account was credited for its reacquisition cost regardless of the reissuance price.

**Treasury Shares Accounted for at Par.**   Those who advocate accounting for treasury shares at par (or stated value) adhere to the theory that **the purchase or other acquisition of treasury shares is, in effect, a constructive retirement of those shares.** Inasmuch as the shares cannot be an asset, they must represent a retirement or at least a reduction of outstanding stock. Because shares outstanding are shown at par, the reacquired shares must be carried at par to indicate the proper reduction in stock outstanding.

Under the par value method, **the acquisition cost of treasury shares is compared with the amount received at the time of their original issue.** The Treasury Stock account is debited for the par value (or stated value) of the shares, and a pro rata amount of any excess over par (or stated value) on original issuance is charged to the related Paid-in Capital account. **Any excess of the acquisition cost over the original issue price is charged to Retained Earnings.** The amount charged to Retained Earnings may be viewed as a dividend to the retiring stockholder. **If, however, the original issue price exceeds the acquisition price of the treasury stock, this difference is credited to Paid-in Capital from Treasury Stock;** the credit to Paid-in Capital from Treasury Stock may be viewed as a capital contribution from the retiring stockholder. This accounting treatment removes all original capital balances identifiable with the treasury shares. If the treasury shares are reissued, the accounting treatment is similar to that accorded any original issuance of stock. A series of transactions with accompanying journal entries illustrates the par value method.

---

[18]Accounting practice frequently applies a slight variation to the cost treatment of the reissuance transaction. The excess of cost over the reissuance price is charged to Paid-in Capital in Excess of Par for a pro rata amount per share of any premium on the original sale of the stock, and any reissuing excess is charged to Paid-in Capital from Treasury Stock and then to Retained Earnings. For example, in transaction 5—of reissuance at 98—Paid-in Capital in Excess of Par would be debited for 100 (10 shares at original premium of $10 per share) and Paid-in Capital from Treasury Stock debited for the remainder, $40.

## PAR VALUE METHOD

**1. One thousand shares of common stock of $100 par value are originally issued at 110.**

| | | |
|---|---|---|
| Cash | 110,000 | |
| Common Stock | | 100,000 |
| Paid-in Capital in Excess of Par | | 10,000 |

**2. One hundred shares of common stock are reacquired at $112.**

| | | |
|---|---|---|
| Treasury Stock (100 shares at $100 par) | 10,000 | |
| Paid-in Capital in Excess of Par (100 at $10) | 1,000 | |
| Retained Earnings | 200 | |
| Cash | | 11,200 |

Because there was only one previous issuance of common stock (at $110 per share), the average price received is the same as the original issue price. Therefore, the $10 original excess over par per share is used to determine the total reduction in Paid-in Capital in Excess of Par. More typically, the average excess over par originally received per share is computed by dividing the total paid-in capital in excess of par from all original issuances of common stock by the number of common shares issued.

**3. One hundred shares of common stock are reacquired at $98.**

| | | |
|---|---|---|
| Treasury Stock (100 shares at $100 par) | 10,000 | |
| Paid-in Capital in Excess of Par (100 ar $10) | 1,000 | |
| Cash | | 9,800 |
| Paid-in Capital from Treasury Stock | | 1,200 |

**4. One hundred shares of common stock are reacquired at $105.**

| | | |
|---|---|---|
| Treasury Stock (100 shares at $100 par) | 10,000 | |
| Paid-in Capital in Excess of Par (100 at $10) | 1,000 | |
| Cash | | 10,500 |
| Paid-in Capital from Treasury Stock | | 500 |

**5. One hundred shares of treasury stock are reissued at $115.**

| | | |
|---|---|---|
| Cash | 11,500 | |
| Treasury Stock (100 shares at $100 par) | | 10,000 |
| Paid-in Capital in Excess of Par | | 1,500 |

**6. One hundred shares of treasury stock are reissued at $104.**

| | | |
|---|---|---|
| Cash | 10,400 | |
| Treasury Stock (100 shares at $100 par) | | 10,000 |
| Paid-in Capital in Excess of Par | | 400 |

Note that when the treasury stock is reissued, the accounting treatment is similar to that accorded any original issuance of stock. Any balance in Paid-in Capital from Treasury Stock would be reduced by any reissuances of treasury stock at less than par value; when that balance is exhausted, retained earnings would be debited. Note that a discount on capital stock account would not be debited because no contingent liability exists on the part of the new stockholders.

**Comparison of Cost and Par Value Methods.** The cost method avoids identifying and accounting for the premiums, discounts, and other amounts related to the original issue of the specific shares acquired and is the simpler, more popular method. The par method, however, maintains the integrity of the sources of the various components of capital. Thus, the par method, although more complex in application, is conceptually the superior method. The profession takes the position that the cost method is acceptable when a corporation acquires its own stock for purposes other than retirement (formal or constructive), or when ultimate disposition has not yet been decided.[19]

**Other Methods of Accounting for Treasury Stock.**   In some states the purchase of treasury stock must be handled by methods other than the two previously described. For example, the applicable state law may require a permanent reduction of retained earnings, in which case the cost of the shares purchased in excess of the stated or par value would be charged against retained earnings. Many companies use the balance in "additional paid-in capital," regardless of its source, to absorb all charges resulting from treasury stock transactions. Although not theoretically sound, this method is acceptable under *APB Opinion No. 6,* and it avoids reclassification of premiums and discounts because only one "additional paid-in capital" account is used. Care should always be exercised in recording treasury stock transactions because of the considerable variety of possible requirements. The advice of an attorney is frequently desirable in this connection.

## Retirement of Treasury Stock

A corporation may retire treasury stock held if it complies with all legal requirements that apply to it. Retired treasury shares have the status of authorized and unissued shares. The accounting treatment for retired treasury stock is dependent on whether the cost or the par value method was used to record the acquisition and whether or not retained earnings have been appropriated (set aside in a separate account) in the amount of the cost. Using data from the previous cost method and par value method illustrations, the following entries would be made for the retirement of 10 shares of common stock of $100 par value issued at 110.

| Entries to Record Retirement of Treasury Stock | | | |
|---|---|---|---|
| **Cost Method** | | **Par Value Method** | |
| **If the treasury shares were acquired at 112:** | | | |
| Common Stock | 1,000 | Common Stock | 1,000 |
| Paid-in Capital in Excess of Par | 100 | Treasury Stock | 1,000 |
| Retained Earnings | 20 | | |
| Treasury Stock | 1,120 | | |
| **If the treasury shares were acquired at 98:** | | | |
| Common Stock | 1,000 | Common Stock | 1,000 |
| Paid-in Capital in Excess of Par | 100 | Treasury Stock | 1,000 |
| Paid-in Capital from Retirement of Common Stock | 120 | | |
| Treasury Stock | 980 | | |

---

[19] *APB Opinion No. 6,* par 12.

Under the cost method, if retained earnings had been appropriated at the time of acquisition in the amount of the cost of the treasury shares, a properly titled account such as Appropriated Retained Earnings—Treasury Stock would be debited and Retained Earnings credited at the time of retirement. The debit and credit amount would be $1,120 in the first case and $980 in the second.

Under the par method, where Treasury Stock is carried at the par value of the shares held in the treasury, the entry to record the retirement is at par. If retained earnings had been appropriated at the time of retirement in the amount of the cost of the treasury shares, as under the cost method, Appropriated Retained Earnings—Treasury Stock would be debited and Retained Earnings credited, again in the same amounts—$1,120 in the first case and $980 in the second.

## Donated Treasury Stock

If stockholders donate shares of a corporation's stock back to the corporation and the corporation retires those shares, an entry would be made debiting Preferred or Common Stock for the par or stated value of the shares and crediting Donated Capital. If the shares are held by the corporation with the intention of reissuing them, they are accounted for as treasury shares under one of three different valuation methods: (1) the cost method, (2) the par value method, (3) the memo method. Regardless of the method used, **neither total assets nor total equity is changed by the donation of the stock.**

**Cost Method.** Under the cost method Treasury Stock is debited and Donated Capital is credited for the current market value of the donated shares.[20] When the donated treasury shares are reissued, they are accounted for in the same manner as other treasury stock applying the cost method.

**Par Value Method.** Under the par value method, Treasury Stock is debited for the par or stated value (or if it is true nonpar stock, the average price paid in may be used), Paid-in-Capital in excess of Par or Stated Value is debited for the original premium paid in at the time of issuance, and Donated Capital is credited. When the donated shares are reissued, they are accounted for in the same manner as other treasury stock applying the par value method, that is, as newly issued shares.

**Memo Method.** Under the memo method, the donated shares are assumed to have no cost. Only a memorandum record is made indicating the number of shares received. The entire proceeds from reissuance of the donated treasury shares would be credited to Donated Capital.

To illustrate these three methods of accounting for donated treasury shares, assume that Mrs. Whitney Lotabucks donates to New England Yarn Corp. 10,000 shares of $10 par value common stock of the corporation when the market value of the stock is $60 a share. Three months later, New England Yarn reissues the 10,000 donated treasury shares at a price of $75 a share. The original issue premium was $20 a share.

[20]"Accounting for Nonmonetary Transactions," *Opinions of the Accounting Principles Board No. 29* (New York: AICPA, 1973).

| Accounting for Donated Treasury Stock | | |
|---|---|---|
| **Cost Method** | **Par Value Method** | **Memo Method** |
| **Donation of 10,000 shares:** | | |
| Treas. Stk.　600,000 | Treas. Stk.　　100,000 | |
| 　Donated Cap.　　600,000 | Pd.-in Cap.　　　　　　　　　　　No entry | |
| | 　　in Excess | |
| | 　　of Par　　200,000 | |
| | 　　Donated Cap.　　　300,000 | |
| **Reissuance of 10,000 shares at $75 per share:** | | |
| Cash　　　　750,000 | Cash　　　　　750,000 | Cash　　　　750,000 |
| 　Treas. Stk.　　600,000 | 　Treas. Stk.　　　100,000 | 　Donated Cap.　　　750,000 |
| 　Pd.-in Cap. | 　Pd.-in Cap. in | |
| 　　Treas. Stk.　　150,000 | 　　Excess of Par　650,000 | |

If the treasury shares donated were originally issued for noncash items, attention should be directed to the original transaction, because, as was often the case in the early 1900s, an assumption of implicit discount might apply. In other words, issuance of stock for property with a donation by the stockholders was a convenient way to avoid the discount liability associated with issuing stock at a discount. Essentially the property, as well as the stockholders' equity, was overvalued initially. In this case, the proceeds received from the sale of donated shares should be credited to the overvalued assets. The approach used to avoid the discount liability is referred to as the **treasury stock subterfuge approach.** With par values so low today, this type of problem should rarely occur.

## Treasury Stock in the Balance Sheet

The two acceptable methods of reporting treasury stock in the balance sheet are related to the two bases of accounting for treasury stock. If the treasury stock is accounted for **at cost,** it is customary to report the cost as an unallocated reduction of the stockholders' equity. The cost of the treasury stock is subtracted from the total of capital stock, additional paid-in capital, and retained earnings as shown below:

| COST METHOD OF REPORTING TREASURY STOCK | |
|---|---|
| Stockholders' equity: | |
| 　Common stock, $1 par; authorized 2,000,000 shares; | |
| 　　issued 1,500,000 shares | $1,500,000 |
| 　Additional paid-in capital | 3,600,000 |
| 　　Total paid-in capital | 5,100,000 |
| 　Retained earnings (see note) | 4,781,484 |
| 　　Total paid-in capital and retained earnings | 9,881,484 |
| 　Less Cost of treasury stock (80,000 shares) | 480,000 |
| 　　Total stockholders' equity | $9,401,484 |

*Note:* Retained earnings are restricted for dividends in the amount of $480,000, the cost of the treasury stock.

Under the **par value method,** treasury stock is reported in the balance sheet as a deduction from issued shares of the same class in order to show those outstanding. An example using the same data as in the cost illustration is shown below:

| PAR VALUE METHOD OF REPORTING TREASURY STOCK | |
| --- | --: |
| Stockholders' equity: | |
| Common stock, $1 par; authorized 2,000,000 shares; | |
|    issued 1,500,000 shares | $1,500,000 |
| Less: Treasury stock (80,000 shares at par) | 80,000 |
| Common stock outstanding | 1,420,000 |
| Additional paid-in capital | 3,200,000 |
|    Total paid-in capital | 4,620,000 |
| Retained earnings (see note) | 4,781,484 |
|    Total stockholders' equity | $9,401,484 |

*Note:* Retained earnings are restricted for dividends in the amount of $480,000, the cost of the treasury stock.

Under both methods, the total stockholders' equity is the same, although the components are different in amount. Also, note that the **retained earnings is restricted in the amount of the cost of the treasury stock under both the cost and the par value methods** due to application of most state corporate laws.

## BASIC RECORDS RELATED TO STOCK

A stock certificate book and a stock transfer book are included among the special corporate records involved in accounting for stock. A stock certificate book is similar to a checkbook in that printed stock certificates are enclosed. A stock transfer book simply tells who owns the stock at a given point in time. Obviously the corporation must be able to obtain at any time a list of the current stockholders so that dividend payments, notices of annual stockholder meetings, and voting proxies may be sent to the proper persons.

Many corporations avoid the problems concerned with handling capital stock sales and transfers by engaging some organization that specializes in this type of work to serve as **registrar and transfer agent.** Banks and trust companies frequently serve in this capacity, keeping all the necessary records. The corporation is provided upon request with a registered list of stockholders for such purposes as mailing dividend checks or voting proxies.

As might be expected, certain accounts act as controlling accounts in the general ledger with subsidiary ledgers to supply necessary detail. These are:

| **General Ledger Account** | **Subsidiary Ledger** |
| --- | --- |
| Common or Preferred Stock | Stockholders' Ledger |
| Subscriptions Receivable | Subscriptions Receivable Ledger |
| Common or Preferred Stock Subscribed | Subscribed Stock Ledger |

## QUESTIONS

1. Differentiate between capital in a legal sense, capital in a corporate finance sense, and capital in an accounting sense.

2. Distinguish between the following types of corporations:
   (a) Closed vs. open.
   (b) Listed vs. unlisted.
   (c) Public vs. private.
   (d) Nonstock vs. stock.

3. Discuss the special characteristics of the corporate form of business that have a direct effect on proprietorship or owners' equity accounting.

4. In the absence of restrictive provisions, what are the basic rights of stockholders of a corporation?

5. Distinguish between common and preferred stock.

6. What features or rights may alter the character of preferred stock?

7. What is the difference between nonparticipating, partially participating, and fully participating stock?

8. (a) In what ways may preferred stock be more like a debt security than an equity security?
   (b) How should preferred stock be classified in the financial statements?

9. What is meant by par value, and what is its significance to stockholders?

10. What are the legal restrictions that control the distribution of profit of a corporation?

11. Explain each of the following terms: authorized capital stock, unissued capital stock, issued capital stock, outstanding capital stock, subscribed stock, and treasury stock.

12. Distinguish between paid-in capital and stated capital.

13. When might the Stock Subscription Receivable account be classified as a current asset? As a noncurrent asset? As a deduction in stockholders' equity section?

14. Describe the accounting for the subscription of common stock at a price in excess of the par value of the common stock.

15. Describe the accounting for the issuance for cash of no par value common stock at a price in excess of the stated value of the common stock.

16. Explain the difference between the proportional method and the incremental method of allocating the proceeds of lump sum sales of capital stock.

17. What are the different bases for stock valuation when assets other than cash are received for issued shares of stock?

18. Discuss the two methods of accounting for initial issue costs. Which do you support and why?

19. For what reasons might a corporation purchase its own stock?

20. Distinguish between the cost method and the par value method of accounting for treasury stock.

21. How is stockholders' equity affected differently by using the cost method instead of the par method for treasury stock purchases?

22. Discuss the propriety of showing:
    (a) Treasury stock as an asset.
    (b) "Gain" or "loss" on sale of treasury stock as additions to or deductions from income.
    (c) Dividends received on treasury stock as income.

23. Describe alternative methods of accounting for the receipt and immediate disposition of donated treasury stock.

## CASES

**C15-1** Graham Pencil Company is a small closely held corporation. Eighty percent of the stock is held by Joan Graham, President; of the remainder, 10% is held by members of her family and

10% by Lynn Chase, a former officer who is now retired. The balance sheet of the company at June 30, 1983 was substantially as shown below:

| Assets | | Liabilities and Capital | |
|---|---|---|---|
| Cash | $ 22,000 | Current liabilities | $150,000 |
| Other | 570,000 | Capital stock | 300,000 |
| | | Retained earnings | 142,000 |
| | $592,000 | | $592,000 |

Additional authorized capital stock of $300,000 par value had never been issued. To strengthen the cash position of the company, Ms. Graham issued capital stock of a par value of $100,000 to herself at par for cash. At the next stockholders' meeting, Ms. Chase objected and claimed that her interests had been injured.

**Instructions**

(a) Which stockholder's right was ignored in the issue of shares to Ms. Graham?
(b) How may the damage to Ms. Chase's interests be repaired most simply?
(c) If Ms. Graham offered Ms. Chase a personal cash settlement and they agreed to employ you as an impartial arbitrator to determine the amount, what settlement would you propose? Present your calculations with sufficient explanation to satisfy both parties.

**C15-2** Airfoil Boat Corporation purchased $160,000 worth of equipment in 1984 for $100,000 cash and a promise to deliver an indeterminate number of treasury shares of its $5 par common stock, with a market value of $20,000 on January 1 of each year for the next four years. Hence $80,000 in "market value" of treasury shares will be required to discharge the $60,000 balance due on the equipment.

The corporation then acquired 5,000 shares of its own stock in the expectation that the market value of the stock would increase substantially before the delivery dates.

**Instructions**

(a) Discuss the propriety of recording the equipment at
  1. $100,000 (the cash payment).
  2. $160,000 (the cash price of the equipment).
  3. $180,000 (the $100,000 cash payment + the $80,000 market value of treasury stock that must be transferred to the vendor in order to settle the obligation according to the terms of the agreement).
(b) Discuss the arguments for treating the balance due as
  1. A liability.
  2. Treasury stock subscribed.
(c) Assuming that legal requirements do not affect the decision, discuss the arguments for treating the corporation's treasury shares as
  1. An asset awaiting ultimate disposition.
  2. A capital element awaiting ultimate disposition.
(d) Compare and contrast the cost method with the par value method for each of the following:
  1. Purchase of shares at a price less than par value.
  2. Purchase of shares at a price greater than par value.
  3. Subsequent resale of treasury shares at a price less than purchase price, but more than par value.
  4. Subsequent resale of treasury shares at a price greater than both purchase price and par value.
  5. Effect on net income.

(AICPA adapted)

**C15-3** It has been said that (1) the use of the LIFO inventory method during an extended period of rising prices and (2) the expensing of all human-resource costs are among the accepted accounting practices that help create "secret reserves."

**Instructions**

(a) What is a "secret reserve"? How can "secret reserves" be created or enlarged?

(b) What is the basis for saying that the two specific practices cited above tend to create "secret reserves"?

(c) Is it possible to create a "secret reserve" in connection with accounting for a liability? If so, explain or give an example.

(d) What are the objections to the creation of "secret reserves"?

(e) It has also been said that "watered stock" is the opposite of a "secret reserve." What is "watered stock"?

(f) Describe the general circumstances in which "watered stock" can arise.

(g) What steps can be taken to eliminate "water" from a capital structure?

(AICPA adapted)

**C15–4** In connection with your first audit of Aromatic Spray Company, you note the following facts concerning its capital stock transactions:

**1.** Authorized capital consists of 8,000,000 shares of $1.00 par value common stock.

**2.** All 8,000,000 shares were issued initially in exchange for certain mineral properties, which were recorded at an amount equal to twice the par value of the shares issued.

**3.** Soon thereafter, owing to the need for additional working capital, 3,000,000 of the shares were donated to the company and immediately sold for $4,500,000 cash, which resulted in a credit to paid-in capital of this amount.

**Instructions**

(a) Describe alternative methods of accounting for the receipt and immediate disposition of donated treasury stock that was originally issued at its fair market value and had no aspect of a "treasury stock subterfuge."

(b) 1. What values should be assigned to the mineral properties and the stockholders' equity? Discuss.

2. What adjustment, if any, would you recommend?

(AICPA adapted)

# EXERCISES

**E15–1** The management of Topitout Contractors, Inc. has decided to sell capital stock to raise additional capital to allow for expansion in the rapidly growing construction industry. The corporation decides to sell this stock through a subscription basis and publicly notifies the investment world. The stock is a $5 par value issue and 18,000 shares are offered at $25 a share. The terms of the subscription are 40% down and the balance at the end of six months. All shares are subscribed for during the offering period.

**Instructions**

Give the journal entry for the original subscription, the collection of the down payments, the collection of the balance of the subscription price, and the issuance of the common stock.

**E15–2** Sportique Corp. is authorized to issue 500,000 shares of $10 par common stock. On November 30, 1984, 60,000 shares were subscribed at $14 per share. A 40% down payment was made on the subscribed stock. On January 30, 1985, the balance due on the subscribed shares was collected except for a subscriber of 8,000 shares who defaulted on his subscription. The 8,000 shares were sold on February 10, 1985, at $15 per share and the defaulting subscriber's down payment was returned.

**Instructions**

Prepare the required journal entries for the transactions above.

**E15–3** On January 1, 1983, Joan Elbert, Inc. received authorization to issue an additional 200,000 shares of $10 par value common stock. Subscribers have contracted to purchase the shares at the subscription price of $50 per share with terms of 30% down in cash and the remaining 70% at the end of six months.

**Instructions**

(a) Give Elbert's journal entry for the situation above on the date of subscription.

(b) Assume that Will Galliart has subscribed to 600 of the shares but defaults after paying his 30% down payment. Assume also that the applicable state law affords the subscriber stock on a pro rata basis. Give Elbert's journal entry for the disposition of the balances in the accounts related to Mr. Galliart.

**E15-4** Kathy Siska, Inc. issues 500 shares of $5 par value common stock and 100 shares of $100 par value preferred stock for a lump sum of $100,000.

**Instructions**

(a) Prepare the journal entry for the issuance when the market value of the common shares is $185 each and market value of the preferred is $250 each.

(b) Prepare the journal entry for the issuance when only the market value of the common stock is known and it is $150 per share.

**E15-5** Comfort Wear Company was organized with 50,000 shares of $100 par value 9% preferred stock and 100,000 shares of common stock without par value. During the first year, 1,000 shares of preferred and 1,000 shares of common were issued for a lump sum price of $170,000.

**Instructions**

What entry should be made to record this transaction under each of the following independent conditions:

(a) Shortly after the transaction described above, 500 shares of preferred stock were sold at $109.

(b) The directors have established a stated value of $80 a share for the common stock.

(c) At the date of issuance, the preferred stock had a market price of $129 per share and the common stock had a market price of $43 per share.

**E15-6** Eric Schmidt, Inc. has outstanding 50,000 shares of $10 par common stock which has been issued at $35 per share. On July 5, 1983, Schmidt repurchased 1,000 of these shares at $54 per share. Schmidt then retired the treasury shares.

**Instructions**

Give the appropriate journal entries for the acquisition and retirement of the treasury stock under:

(a) the cost method.

(b) the par value method.

**E15-7** On November 15, 1983, Jackie Remmers, a wealthy stockholder of Country Publishing Company, donates 2,000 shares of Country's $10 par common stock to the corporation. The stock was originally issued at $45 per share and is now selling for $38 in the marketplace.

**Instructions**

(a) Prepare Country's journal entry to record the donation under (1) the cost method, (2) the par value method, and (3) the memo method.

(b) Assume that Country resells the stock on December 20, 1983, when the market value is $48 per share. Prepare Country's journal entries for the resale under (1) the cost method, (2) the par value method, and (3) the memo method.

**E15-8** Rick Meier Corporation's charter authorized 100,000 shares of $10 par value common stock, and 25,000 shares of 8% cumulative and nonparticipating preferred stock, par value $100 per share. Meier engaged in the following stock transactions through December 31, 1983: 30,000 shares of common stock were issued for $380,000 and 5,000 shares of preferred stock for machinery valued at $625,000. Subscriptions for 3,000 shares of common have been taken, and 40% of the subscription price of $19 per share has been collected. The stock will be issued upon collection of the subscription price in full. Treasury stock of 500 shares of common has been purchased for $15 and accounted for under the cost method. The Retained Earnings balance is $99,000.

## Instructions

Prepare the stockholders' equity section of the balance sheet in good form. Assume that state law requires that the amount of retained earnings available for dividends be restricted by an amount equal to the cost of treasury shares acquired.

## PROBLEMS

**P15-1** On January 5, 1983, Fun & Humor Corporation received a charter granting the right to issue 5,000 shares of $100 par value, 10% cumulative and nonparticipating preferred stock and 50,000 shares of $5 par value common stock. It then completed these transactions:

Jan. 11 Accepted subscriptions to 20,000 shares of common stock at $12 per share; 20% down payments accompanied the subscription.

Feb. 1 Issued Thomas J. Nessinger Corp. 2,700 shares of preferred stock for the following assets: machinery with a fair market value of $35,000; a factory building with a fair market value of $85,000; and land with an appraised value of $175,000.

Mar. 16 Other machinery, with a fair market value of $85,000 was donated to the company.

Apr. 15 Collected the balance of the subscription price on the common shares and issued the stock.

July 29 Purchased 1,200 shares of common stock at $9 per share (use cost method).

Aug. 10 Sold 1,200 of the treasury shares at $7 per share.

Aug. 26 Declared a 10% stock dividend on the common shares. The stock was selling at $7 per share on the day of the declaration.

Sept. 15 Distributed the stock dividend.

Dec. 31 Declared a $0.10 per share cash dividend on the common stock and declared the preferred dividend.

Dec. 31 Closed the Income Summary account. There was a $61,000 net income.

## Instructions

(a) Record the journal entries for the transactions listed above.
(b) Prepare the stockholders' equity section of Fun & Humor's balance sheet as of December 31, 1983.

**P15-2** Stock transactions of Technicolor Coat Company are as follows:

Apr. 1 Subscriptions to 700 shares of its $100 par value capital stock are received, together with checks from the various subscribers to cover a 25% down payment. The stock was subscribed at 108. The remainder of the subscription price is to be paid in three equal monthly installments.

May 1 First installments are collected from all subscribers.

June 1 Second installments are received from all subscribers except Lyle McGinnis, who had subscribed for 60 shares.

5 In reply to correspondence, Mr. McGinnis states that he is unable to complete his installment payments and authorizes the company to dispose of the shares subscribed for by him.

17 The shares subscribed for by Mr. McGinnis are sold for cash at 101. Expenses of $90 were incurred in disposing of this stock. (**Hint:** Expenses and deficiencies are charged against the amount due to the subscriber.)

25 A check is mailed to Mr. McGinnis equal to the refund due him.

July 1 The final installments are collected on all open subscription accounts, and the stock is issued.

**Instructions**

Prepare entries in general journal form for the transactions above. Assume that defaulting subscribers are to receive refunds; any premium subscribed is refunded only if it is collected on resale.

**P15-3** Gadget Enterprises, Inc. (GEI) is a closely held toy manufacturer in the northeast. You have been engaged as the independent public accountant to perform the first audit of GEI. It is agreed that only current-year (1984) financial statements will be prepared.

The following stockholders' equity information has been developed from GEI records on December 31, 1983:

| | |
|---|---|
| Common stock, no par value; no stated value; | |
| authorized 10,000 shares; issued 2,000 shares | $70,000 |
| Retained earnings | 38,000 |

The following stock transactions took place during 1984:

**1.** On March 15, GEI issued 1,300 shares of common stock to Floyd Beams for $54 per share.

**2.** On March 31, GEI reacquired 825 shares of common stock from Kathy Norton (GEI's founder) for $60 per share. These shares were canceled and retired upon receipt.

For the year 1984, GEI reported net income of $37,000.

**Instructions**

(a) How should the stockholders' equity information be reported in the GEI financial statements for the year ended December 31, 1984 (1) assuming specific identification of the shares is impossible and (2) assuming application of the FIFO method?

(b) How would your answer in part (a) have been altered if GEI had treated the reacquired shares as treasury stock carried at cost rather than retired?

(c) On December 30, 1985, GEI's Board of Directors changed the common stock from no par, no stated value to no par with a $10 stated value per share. How will the stockholders' equity section be affected if comparative financial statements are prepared at December 31, 1985? (Apply the method used in (a)(1).)

**P15-4** Transactions of Sandy Clark Company are as follows:

**1.** The company is granted a charter that authorizes issuance of 12,000 shares of $100 par value preferred stock and 12,000 shares of common stock without par value.

**2.** 9,600 shares of common stock are issued to founders of the corporation for land valued by the board of directors at $506,000. The board establishes a par value of $30 a share for the common stock.

**3.** 6,000 shares of preferred stock are sold for cash at 110.

**4.** 600 shares of common stock are sold to an officer of the corporation for $60 a share.

**5.** 300 shares of outstanding preferred stock are purchased for cash at par.

**6.** 450 shares of outstanding preferred stock are purchased for cash at 98.

**7.** 600 shares of the outstanding common stock issued in No. 2 above are purchased at $62 a share.

**8.** 150 shares of repurchased preferred stock are reissued at 102.

**9.** 2,400 shares of preferred stock are issued at 99.

**10.** 300 shares of reacquired common stock are reissued for $57 a share.

**11.** 120 shares of the common stock sold in No. 10 above are repurchased for $53 a share.

**Instructions**

(a) Prepare entries in journal form to record the transactions listed above. No other transactions affecting the capital stock accounts have occurred. Treasury stock is to be entered in the Treasury Stock accounts at par.

(b) Assuming that the company has retained earnings from operations of $95,000, prepare the stockholders' equity section of its balance sheet after considering all the transactions given.

**P15-5** Before Wanda Wallace Corporation engages in the treasury stock transactions listed below, its general ledger reflects, among others, the following account balances (par value of its stock is $50 per share).

| Paid-in Capital in Excess of Par | Common Stock | Retained Earnings |
|---|---|---|
| Balance $72,000 | Balance $240,000 | Balance $60,000 |

**Instructions**

Record the treasury stock transactions (given below) under the two generally accepted methods of handling treasury stock; use the FIFO method for purchase-sale purposes.

(a) Bought 600 shares of treasury stock at $63 per share.
(b) Bought 300 shares of treasury stock at $67 per share.
(c) Sold 450 shares of treasury stock at $66 per share.
(d) Sold 240 shares of treasury stock at $62 per share.
(e) Retired the remaining shares in the treasury.

**P15-6** The accounts shown below appear in the December 31 trial balance of the Nancy Woods Company:

| | |
|---|---|
| Preferred Stock Authorized ($100 par value) | $750,000 |
| Common Stock Authorized ($10 par value) | 300,000 |
| Unissued Preferred Stock | 270,000 |
| Unissued Common Stock | 150,000 |
| Subscriptions Receivable, Common | 27,000 |
| Subscriptions Receivable, Preferred | 28,500 |
| Preferred Stock Subscribed | 45,000 |
| Common Stock Subscribed | 33,750 |
| Treasury Stock, Preferred (1050 shares at cost) | 102,900 |
| Paid-in Capital (excess of amount paid in over par value of common stock) | 131,250 |

**Instructions**

(a) Assuming that it is reasonably assured that the subscriptions will be collected, use the accounts above to determine the following:
   1. Total authorized capital stock.
   2. Total unissued capital stock.
   3. Total issued capital stock.
   4. Capital stock subscribed.
   5. Capital stock available for subscription.
   6. Net paid-in capital.

(b) What changes would occur in these six items if there is evidence that collection of the subscriptions is uncertain?

**P15-7** During May 1981 Gilroy, Inc., was organized with 3,000,000 authorized shares of $10 par value common stock, and 300,000 shares of its common stock were issued for $3,300,000. Net income through December 31, 1981, was $125,000.

On July 13, 1982, Gilroy issued 500,000 shares of its common stock for $6,250,000. A 5% stock dividend was declared on October 2, 1982, and issued on November 6, 1982, to stockholders of record on October 23, 1982. The market value of the common stock was $11 per share on the declaration date. Gilroy's net income for the year ended December 31, 1982, was $350,000. (*Hint:* Retained earnings should be reduced by the fair market value of the stock dividend.)

During 1983 Gilroy had the following transactions:

1. In February, Gilroy reacquired 30,000 shares of its common stock for $9 per share. Gilroy uses the cost method to account for treasury stock.

2. In June, Gilroy sold 15,000 shares of its treasury stock for $12 per share.

3. On December 15, 1983, Gilroy declared its first cash dividend to stockholders of $0.20 per share, payable on January 10, 1984, to stockholders of record on December 31, 1983.

4. On December 21, 1983, in accordance with the applicable state law, Gilroy formally retired 10,000 shares of its treasury stock and had them revert to an unissued basis. The market value of the common stock was $16 per share on this date.

5. Net income for 1983 was $750,000.

**Instructions**

Prepare a schedule of all transactions affecting the capital stock (shares and dollar amounts), additional paid-in capital, retained earnings, and the treasury stock (shares and dollar amounts) and the amounts that would be included in Gilroy's balance sheet at December 31, 1981, 1982, and 1983, as a result of the above facts. Show supporting computations in good form.

(AICPA adapted)

**P15–8** Entertainment Company has the following owners' equity accounts at December 31, 1982:

| | |
|---|---:|
| Common Stock—$100 par value, authorized 4,000 shares | $320,000 |
| Retained Earnings | 200,000 |

**Instructions**

(a) Prepare entries in journal form to record the following transactions, which took place during 1983. (Hint: Debit retained earnings in transaction 6.)
   1. 160 shares of outstanding stock were purchased at 96. (These are to be accounted for using the cost method.)
   2. A 10% cash dividend was declared.
   3. The dividend declared in No. 2 above was paid.
   4. The treasury shares purchased in No. 1 above were resold at 102.
   5. 400 shares of outstanding stock were purchased at 102.
   6. 80 shares of outstanding stock were purchased at 105 and retired.
   7. 240 of the shares purchased in No. 5 above were resold at 97.
(b) Prepare the stockholders' equity section of Entertainment Company's balance sheet after giving effect to these transactions, assuming that the net income for 1983 was $46,000.

**P15–9** The stockholders' equity section of Rejuvenated Company's balance sheet at December 31, 1984, was as follows:

| | |
|---|---:|
| Common stock—$100 par (authorized 50,000 shares, | |
|   issued and outstanding 12,000 shares) | $1,200,000 |
| Paid-in capital in excess of par | 240,000 |
| Retained earnings | 160,000 |
| | $1,600,000 |

On January 2, 1985, having idle cash, the company repurchased 600 shares of its stock for $75,000. During the year it sold 150 of the reacquired shares at $135 per share, another 150 at $122.50 per share, and legally retired the remaining 300 shares.

**Instructions**

(a) Discuss the possible alternatives in handling these transactions.

(b) Prepare journal entries for each transaction in accordance with the method that you believe should be applied.

**P15-10** Turnaround Corporation charter authorized issuance of 10,000 shares of $100 par value common stock and 10,000 shares of $50 preferred stock. The following transactions involving the issuance of shares of stock were completed. Each transaction is independent of the others.

1. Issued a $10,000, 5% bond payable at par and gave as a bonus one share of preferred stock, which at that time was selling for $75 a share.

2. Issued 40 shares of common stock for machinery. The machinery had been appraised at $5,100; the seller's book value was $6,000. The most recent market price of the common stock is $122 a share.

3. Voted a 5% assessment on both the 1,000 shares of outstanding common and the 500 shares of outstanding preferred. The assessment was paid in full.

4. Issued 60 shares of common and 40 shares of preferred for a lump sum amounting to $12,625. The common had been selling at $125 and the preferred at $65.

5. Issued 20 shares of common and 10 shares of preferred for furniture and fixtures. The common had a fair market value of $150 per share and the furniture and fixtures were appraised at $3,750.

**Instructions**

Record the transactions listed above in journal entry form.

**P15-11** Galactica Corporation is a publicly owned company whose shares are traded on a national stock exchange. At December 31, 1982, Galactica had 50,000,000 shares of $10 par value common stock authorized, of which 30,000,000 shares were issued and 28,000,000 shares were outstanding.

The stockholders' equity accounts at December 31, 1982, had the following balances:

| | |
|---|---|
| Common Stock | $300,000,000 |
| Additional Paid-in Capital | 160,000,000 |
| Retained Earnings | 100,000,000 |
| Treasury Stock | 36,000,000 |

During 1983, Galactica had the following transactions:

On February 1, 1983, a secondary distribution of 4,000,000 shares of $10 par value common stock was completed. The stock was sold to the public at $18 per share, net of offering costs.

On February 15, 1983, Galactica issued at $110 per share, 200,000 shares of $100 par value, 8% cumulative preferred stock.

On March 1, 1983, Galactica reacquired 40,000 shares of its common stock for $18.50 per share. Galactica uses the cost method to account for treasury stock.

On March 15, 1983, when the common stock was trading for $21 per share, a major stockholder donated 20,000 shares which are appropriately recorded as treasury stock. (Hint: use the memo method as a basis for donation.)

On March 31, 1983, Galactica declared a semiannual cash dividend on common stock of $0.10 per share, payable on April 30, 1983, to stockholders of record on April 10, 1983. The appropriate state law prohibits cash dividends on treasury stock.

On April 30, 1983, employees exercised 200,000 options that were granted in 1981 under a noncompensatory stock option plan. When the options were granted, each option had a preemptive right and entitled the employee to purchase one share of common stock for $20 per share. On April 30, 1983, the market price of the common stock was $20 per share. Galactica issued new shares to settle the transaction.

On May 31, 1983, when the market price of the common stock was $20 per share, Galactica declared a 5% stock dividend distributable on July 1, 1983, to stockholders of record on June 1, 1983. The appropriate state law prohibits stock dividends on treasury stock. The stock dividend is recorded using the market price.

On June 30, 1983, Galactica sold the 40,000 treasury shares reacquired on March 1, 1983, and an additional 560,000 treasury shares costing $11,200,000 that were on hand at the beginning of the year. The selling price was $25 per share.

On September 30, 1983, Galactica declared a semiannual cash dividend on common stock of $0.10 per share and the yearly dividend on preferred stock, both payable on October 30, 1983, to stockholders of record on October 10, 1983. The appropriate state law prohibits cash dividends on treasury stock.

Net income for 1983 was $50,000,000.

## Instructions

Prepare a work sheet to be used to summarize, for each transaction, the changes in Galactica's stockholders' equity accounts for 1983. The columns on this work sheet should have the following headings:

Date of transaction (or beginning date)

Common stock—number of shares

Common stock—amount

Preferred stock—number of shares

Preferred stock—amount

Additional paid-in capital

Retained earnings

Treasury stock—number of shares

Treasury stock—amount

Show supporting computations in good form.

(AICPA adapted)

# CHAPTER 16

# Stockholders' Equity: Additional Paid-in Capital and Retained Earnings

The following three categories normally appear as part of stockholders' equity:

1. Capital stock (legal capital).
2. Additional paid-in capital (capital in excess of par or stated value).
3. Retained earnings or deficit.

The first two categories, capital stock and additional paid-in capital, comprise **contributed (or paid-in) capital;** retained earnings represents the **earned capital** of the enterprise. The distinction between contributed capital and earned capital has a legal origin, but at present it serves the useful purpose of indicating the different sources from which the corporation has obtained its **equity capital.**

One source of the stockholders' interest in a business—capital stock—was discussed in Chapter 15. Other sources are of a very diverse nature and require careful analysis.

## ADDITIONAL PAID-IN CAPITAL

Additional paid-in capital is derived from a variety of transactions. The basic transactions affecting additional paid-in capital are expressed in account form below.

| Additional Paid-in Capital | |
|---|---|
| 1. Discounts on capital stock issued. | 1. Premiums on capital stock issued. |
| 2. Sale of treasury stock below cost. | 2. Sale of treasury stock above cost. |
| 3. Absorption of a deficit in a recapitalization (quasi reorganization). | 3. Additional capital arising in recapitalizations or revisions in the capital structure (quasi reorganizations). |
| 4. Distribution of a liquidating dividend. | 4. Additional assessments on stockholders. |
| | 5. Conversion of convertible bonds or preferred stock. |
| | 6. Distribution of a "small" stock dividend. |

In balance sheet presentation, only one amount need appear, Additional Paid-in Capital, to summarize all of these possible transactions.[1] A subsidiary ledger or separate general ledger accounts may be kept of the different sources of additional paid-in capital because certain state laws permit dividend distributions out of designated additional paid-in capital.

No operating gains or losses or extraordinary gains and losses may be debited or credited to Additional Paid-in Capital. The profession has long discouraged by-passing net income and retained earnings through the write-off of losses (for example, write-offs of bond discount, goodwill, or obsolete plant and equipment) to additional paid-in capital accounts or other capital accounts.

## DONATED AND REVALUATION CAPITAL

Two other items that may be reported in the stockholders' equity section as a form of additional capital are **donated capital** and **revaluation or unrealized appreciation capital**. Donated capital results from donations to the company by stockholders, creditors, and so on. Revaluation capital results from the write-up or write-down of assets from cost. Because of adherence to the cost principle and the concept of conservatism, assets are generally not written up from cost. Revaluation or unrealized appreciation capital having a credit balance, therefore, rarely appears on financial statements.

Because donated capital and revaluation capital (write-ups or write-downs not reported in the income statement) are such unique items, they warrant special attention when they occur. For this reason, the following stockholders' equity classifications should be distinguished.

Capital Stock
Additional Paid-in Capital
Donated Capital
Revaluation Capital
Retained Earnings

One item designated for the revaluation capital section is described in *FASB Statement No. 12* ("Accounting for Certain Marketable Securities"). It requires that the "net unrealized loss on noncurrent marketable equity securities" be reported separately as a deduction (contra item) from stockholders' equity (see Chapter 18 for a more complete discussion of this topic).

Another recent accounting standard that deals with foreign currency translations requires that, beginning in 1983, translation adjustments be "accumulated in a separate component of equity,"[2] rather than included in the determination of income. Foreign currency translations are discussed in advanced accounting.

---

[1] *Accounting Trends and Techniques—1981* reports that of its 600 surveyed companies 523 had additional paid-in capital; 187 used the caption "additional paid-in capital"; 170 used "capital in excess of par or stated value" as the caption; 62 used "capital surplus"; and 104 used some other variation or combination of those three captions.

[2] "Foreign Currency Translation," *Statement of Financial Accounting Standards No. 52* (Stamford, Conn.: FASB, 1981), par. 13.

## RETAINED EARNINGS

The basic source of retained earnings is income from operations. Stockholders assume the greatest risk in enterprise operations and stand any losses or share in any profits resulting from enterprise activities. Any income not distributed among the stockholders thus becomes additional stockholders' equity. Net income includes a considerable variety of income sources. These include the main operation of the enterprise (such as manufacturing and selling a given product), plus any ancillary activities (such as disposing of scrap or renting out unused space), plus the results of extraordinary and unusual items. All give rise to net income that increases retained earnings. The more common items that either increase or decrease retained earnings are expressed in account form below.

| Retained Earnings | |
| --- | --- |
| 1. Net loss | 1. Net income |
| 2. Prior period adjustments (error corrections) and changes in accounting principle | 2. Prior period adjustments (error corrections) and changes in accounting principle |
| 3. Cash dividends | |
| 4. Stock dividends | |
| 5. Property dividends | |
| 6. Treasury stock transactions | |

The reader may recall that Chapter 4 pointed out that under the modified all-inclusive concept of income reporting the results of irregular transactions should be reported in the income statement, not the retained earnings statement. Prior period adjustments (error corrections) should be reported as adjustments to beginning retained earnings, bypassing completely the current income statement.

## DIVIDEND POLICY

As soon as retained earnings is recorded, two alternatives exist: the credit balance can be (1) reduced by a distribution of assets (a dividend) to the stockholders, or (2) left intact and the offsetting assets used in the operations of the business. Further decisions are required under each of these alternatives, but the original decision must be whether to distribute the resources generated by profitable operations in the form of dividends to the stockholders or to retain these resources in the enterprise and use them for business purposes.

**Very few companies pay dividends in amounts equal to their retained earnings legally available for dividends.** The major reasons are as follows:

1. Agreements (bond covenants) with specific creditors to retain all or a portion of the earnings (in the form of assets) to build up additional protection against possible loss for those creditors.

2. Requirements of some state corporation laws requiring that earnings equivalent to the cost of treasury shares purchased be restricted against dividend declarations.

3. Desire to retain in the business the assets, that would otherwise be paid out as dividends, to finance growth or expansion. This is sometimes called internal financing, reinvesting earnings, or "plowing" the profits back into the business.

4. Desire to smooth out dividend payments from year to year by accumulating earnings in good years and using such accumulated earnings as a basis for dividends in bad years.

5. Desire to build up a cushion or buffer against possible losses or errors in the calculation of profits.

No particular explanation is required for any of these except the second. The laws of most states require that the corporation's stated capital (legal capital) be restricted from distribution to stockholders so that it may serve as a protection against loss to creditors. If the corporation buys its own outstanding stock, it has reduced its stated capital and distributed assets to stockholders. If this were permitted, the corporation could, by purchasing treasury stock at any price desired, return to the stockholders their investments and leave creditors with little or no protection against loss.

If a company is considering declaring a dividend, two preliminary questions must be asked:

1. Is the condition of the corporation such that a dividend is legally permissible?

2. Is the condition of the corporation such that a dividend is economically sound?

## Legality of Dividends

The legality of a dividend can be determined only by reviewing the applicable state law. Even then the law may not be clear, and a decision may require recourse to the courts. Frequently, to reduce the possibility of legal misinterpretation the company's lawyer may provide an opinion on a dividend problem. For most general dividend declarations, the following summary is adequate:

1. Retained earnings, unless legally restricted in some manner, is usually the correct basis for dividend distributions.

2. Revaluation capital is seldom the appropriate basis for dividends (except possibly stock dividends).

3. In some states, additional paid-in capital and donated capital may be used for dividends, although such dividends may be limited to preferred stock.

4. Deficits in retained earnings and debits in paid-in capital accounts must be restored before payment of any dividends.

5. Dividends in most states may not reduce retained earnings below the cost of treasury stock held.

## Financial Condition and Dividend Distributions

State laws governing dividend distributions generally require that the corporation have a credit balance in retained earnings. From the standpoint of good management attention must be given to other conditions as well. These considerations become more apparent if we assume an extreme situation such as the following.

| BALANCE SHEET | | | |
|---|---|---|---|
| Plant assets | $500,000 | Capital stock | $400,000 |
| | | Retained earnings | 100,000 |
| | $500,000 | | $500,000 |

The depicted company has a retained earnings credit balance and, unless it is restricted, legally can declare a dividend of $100,000. However, because all its assets are plant assets and used in operations, payment of a cash dividend of $100,000 requires the sale of plant assets or borrowing. Even if we assume a balance sheet showing current assets, there is still the further question of whether those assets are needed for other purposes.

| BALANCE SHEET | | | | |
|---|---|---|---|---|
| Cash | $100,000 | Current liabilities | | $ 60,000 |
| Plant assets | 460,000 | Capital stock | $400,000 | |
| | | Retained earnings | 100,000 | 500,000 |
| | $560,000 | | | $560,000 |

The existence of current liabilities implies very strongly that some of the cash is needed to meet current debts as they mature. In addition, day-by-day cash requirements for payrolls and other expenditures not included in current liabilities also require cash.

Thus, before a dividend is declared, the question of **availability of funds to pay the dividend must be considered.** Availability of funds includes more than possession of a cash balance sufficiently large to pay the dividend. Other demands for cash should perhaps be investigated by preparing a cash forecast. A dividend should not be paid unless both the present and future financial position appear to warrant the distribution.

Directors must also consider the effect of inflation on reported income. During a period of significant inflation, some costs charged to expense under historical cost accounting are understated in a comparative purchasing power sense. Income is thereby overstated because certain costs have not been adjusted for inflation. As an example, St. Regis Paper Company in 1981 reported historical cost net income of $179 million, but when it was adjusted for general inflation net income was $67.7 million. Yet St. Regis paid cash dividends of $72.3 million. Were cash dividends paid excessive? This subject is discussed in considerable depth in Chapter 25.

## TYPES OF DIVIDENDS

Dividend distributions are based either on accumulated profits, that is, retained earnings, or on some other capital item such as donated or additional capital paid-in. The natural expectation of any stockholder who receives a dividend is that the corporation has operated successfully and that he or she is receiving a share of its profits. Any dividend not based on retained earnings (a liquidating dividend) should be adequately described in the accompanying message to the stockholders so that there will be no misunderstanding of its source. Dividends are of the following types:

1. Cash dividends.
2. Property dividends.
3. Scrip dividends.
4. Liquidating dividends.
5. Stock dividends.

Dividends are commonly paid in cash but occasionally in stock, scrip, or some other asset. **All dividends, except for stock dividends, reduce the stockholders' equity in the corporation,** because the equity is reduced either through an immediate or promised future distribution of assets. When a stock dividend is declared, the corporation does not pay out assets or incur a liability. It issues additional shares of stock to each stockholder. The individual stockholder receives nothing more than additional shares of stock.

## Cash Dividends

The board of directors votes on the declaration of dividends, and if the resolution is properly approved, the dividend is declared. It cannot be paid immediately, however, because transfers of stock from one holder to another require that a current list of stockholders be prepared. For this reason the dividend resolution generally allows a short period of time before payment. A resolution approved at the January 10 (date of declaration) meeting of the board of directors might be declared payable February 5 (date of payment) to all stockholders of record January 25 (date of record).

The period from January 10 to January 25 gives time for any transfers in process to be completed and registered with the transfer agent. The time from January 25 to February 5 provides an opportunity for the transfer agent or accounting department, depending on who does this work, to prepare a list of stockholders as of January 25 and to prepare and mail dividend checks.

**A declared cash dividend is a liability and, because payment is generally required very soon, is usually a current liability.** The following entries are required to record the declaration and payment of an ordinary dividend payable in cash. For example, Roadway Freight Corp. on June 10 declared a cash dividend of 50 cents a share on 1.8 million shares payable July 16 to all stockholders of record June 24.

**At date of declaration (June 10):**

| | | |
|---|---|---|
| Retained Earnings (Cash Dividends Declared) | 900,000 | |
| Dividends Payable | | 900,000 |

**At date of record (June 24):**

No entry

**At date of payment (July 16):**

| | | |
|---|---|---|
| Dividends Payable | 900,000 | |
| Cash | | 900,000 |

To set up in the ledger an account that shows the amount of dividends declared during the year, an account called Cash Dividends Declared might be debited instead of Retained Earnings at the time of declaration. This account is then closed to Retained Earnings at the end of the year.

Dividends may be declared either as a certain percent of par, such as a 6% dividend on preferred stock, or as an amount per share, such as $0.60 per share on no-par common stock. In the first case, the rate is multiplied by the par value of the outstanding shares to get the total dividend; in the second, the amount per share is multiplied by the number of shares outstanding. **Dividends are not declared and paid on treasury stock.**

Dividend policies vary among corporations. Some older, well-established firms take pride in a long, unbroken string of quarterly dividend payments and would lower or pass the dividend only if forced to do so by a sustained decline in earnings or a critical shortage of cash. The percentage of annual earnings distributed as cash dividends ("payout ratio") is somewhat dependent on the stability and trend of earnings, with 25 to 75% of earnings being paid out by many well-established corporations. For example, Emerson Electric Co. of St. Louis continues its policy of paying dividends equivalent to 45 to 50 percent of the prior year's earnings. "Growth companies," on the other hand, pay little or no cash dividends because their policy is to expand as rapidly as internal and external financing permit. For example, neither Vicon Industries, Inc., a small growth company, nor Federal Express Corporation, a large growth company, has ever paid cash dividends to their common stockholders.

## Property Dividends

Dividends payable in assets of the corporation other than cash are called property dividends or dividends in kind. Property dividends may be in whatever form the board of directors designates, for example, merchandise, real estate, or investments. To illustrate, Ranchers Exploration and Development Corp. reported that it would pay a fourth-quarter dividend in gold bars instead of cash. Because of the obvious difficulties of divisibility of units and delivery to the stockholders, the usual property dividend is in the form of securities of other companies that the distributing corporation holds as an investment.

**A property dividend is a nonreciprocal transfer**[3] **of nonmonetary assets between an enterprise and its owners.** Prior to the issuance of *APB Opinion No. 29* in 1973, the accounting for such transfers was based on the carrying amount (book value) of the nonmonetary assets transferred. This practice was based on the rationale that there is no sale or arm's-length transaction on which to base a gain or loss and that only this method is consistent with the historical cost basis of accounting. The profession's current position is quite clear on this matter:

> A transfer of a nonmonetary asset to a stockholder or to another entity in a nonreciprocal transfer should be recorded at the fair value of the asset transferred, and a gain or loss should be recognized on the disposition of the asset.[4]

The **fair value** of the nonmonetary asset distributed is measured by the amount that would be realizable in an outright sale at or near the time of the distribution. Such amount should be determined by referring to estimated realizable values in cash transactions of the same or similar assets, quoted market prices, independent appraisals, and other available evidence.[5]

The failure to recognize the fair value of nonmonetary assets transferred may both misstate the dividend and fail to recognize gains and losses on nonmonetary assets that have already been earned or incurred by the enterprise. Recording the dividend at fair value permits future comparisons of dividend rates and, if cash must be distributed to

---

[3]A nonreciprocal transfer is a transfer of assets or services in one direction, either from an enterprise to its owners or another entity or from owners or another entity to the enterprise.

[4]"Accounting for Nonmonetary Transactions," *Opinions of the Accounting Principles Board No. 29* (New York: AICPA, 1973), par. 18.

[5]According to *APB Opinion No. 29,* accounting for the distribution of nonmonetary assets to owners of an enterprise in a spin-off or other form of reorganization or liquidation should be based on the **book value** (after reduction, if appropriate, for an indicated impairment of value) of the nonmonetary assets distributed. This is an exception to the fair value treatment prescribed for nonmonetary distributions.

stockholders in place of the nonmonetary asset, determination of the amount to be distributed is simplified. Recording fair value is especially appropriate when property dividends are given to a class of stock other than common stock. For example, preferred stock should not profit by property dividends, the market value of which exceeds the fixed dividend rate.

When the property dividend is declared, the corporation should restate at fair value the property to be distributed, recognizing any gain or loss as the difference between the fair value and carrying value of the property at date of declaration. The declared dividend may then be recorded as a debit to Retained Earnings (or Property Dividends Declared) and a credit to Property Dividends Payable at an amount equal to the fair value of the property to be distributed. Upon distribution of the dividend, Property Dividends Payable is debited, and the account containing the distributed asset (restated at fair value) is credited.

For example, Trendler, Inc., transferred some of its investments in marketable securities costing $1,250,000 to stockholders by declaring a property dividend on December 28, 1982, to be distributed on January 30, 1983, to stockholders of record on January 15, 1983. At the date of declaration the securities have a market value of $2,000,000. The entries are as below:

**At date of declaration (December 28, 1982):**

| | | |
|---|---|---|
| Investments in Securities | 750,000 | |
|   Gain on Appreciation of Securities | | 750,000 |
| Retained Earnings (Property Dividends Declared) | 2,000,000 | |
|   Property Dividends Payable | | 2,000,000 |

**At date of distribution (January 30, 1983):**

| | | |
|---|---|---|
| Property Dividends Payable | 2,000,000 | |
|   Investments in Securities | | 2,000,000 |

## Scrip Dividend

A dividend payable in scrip means that instead of paying the dividend now, the corporation has elected to pay it at some later date. **The scrip issued to stockholders as a dividend is merely a special form of note payable.** For example, the Bank of Puerto Rico issued a $9 million note as a dividend that will mature in 1990, at which time each holder of the corporation's three million common shares will receive $3 a share. Scrip dividends may be declared when the corporation has a sufficient retained earnings balance but is short of cash. The recipient of the scrip dividend may hold it until the due date, if one is specified, and collect the dividend, or possibly, may discount it to obtain immediate cash. When a scrip dividend is declared, the corporation debits Retained Earnings (or Scrip Dividend Declared) and credits Scrip Dividend Payable or Notes Payable to Stockholders, reporting the payable as a liability on the balance sheet. Upon payment, Scrip Dividend Payable is debited and Cash credited. If the scrip bears interest, the interest portion of the cash payment should be debited to Interest Expense and not treated as part of the dividend. For example, Berg Canning Company, when short of cash, avoided missing its 84th consecutive quarterly dividend by declaring on May 6, 1982 a scrip dividend in the form of two-month promissory notes amounting to 80 cents a share on 2,545,000 shares outstanding and payable at the date of record, May 27, 1982. The notes bear interest of 10% per annum and mature on July 27, 1982. The entries are as follows:

**At date of declaration (May 6, 1982):**

| | | |
|---|---|---|
| Retained Earnings (Scrip Dividends Declared) | 2,036,000 | |
|   Notes Payable to Stockholders (.80 × 2,545,000) | | 2,036,000 |

**At date of payment (July 27, 1982):**

| | | |
|---|---:|---:|
| Notes Payable to Stockholders | 2,036,000 | |
| Interest Expense ($2,036,000 $\times$ 2/12 $\times$ .10)[a] | 33,933 | |
| Cash | | 2,069,933 |

[a]The interest runs from the date of record to the date of payment.

## Liquidating Dividend

Some corporations have used paid-in capital in the early years as a basis for dividends. Without proper disclosure of this fact, stockholders may believe the corporation has been operating at a profit. A further result could be subsequent sale of additional shares at a higher price than is warranted. This type of deception, intentional or unintentional, can be avoided by requiring that a clear statement of the basis of every dividend accompany the dividend check.

Dividends based on other than retained earnings are sometimes described as liquidating dividends, thus implying that they are a return of the stockholder's investment rather than of profits. In fact, the distribution may be based on capital that resulted from donations by outsiders or other stockholders and not be a return of the given stockholder's contribution. But, in a more general sense, **any dividend not based on earnings must be a reduction of corporate paid-in capital and, to that extent, it is a liquidating dividend.** We noted in an earlier chapter that companies in the extractive industries may pay dividends equal to the total of accumulated income and depletion. The portion of these dividends in excess of accumulated income represents a return of part of the stockholder's investment.

For example, McChesney Mines, Inc., recently issued a "dividend" to its common stockholders of $100,000. The cash dividend announcement noted that $70,000 should be considered income and the remainder a return of capital. The entries are:

**At date of declaration:**

| | | |
|---|---:|---:|
| Retained Earnings | 70,000 | |
| Additional Paid-in Capital | 30,000 | |
| Dividend Payable | | 100,000 |

**At date of payment:**

| | | |
|---|---:|---:|
| Dividend Payable | 100,000 | |
| Cash | | 100,000 |

## Stock Dividends[6]

If the management wishes to capitalize part of the earnings, and thus retain earnings in the business on a permanent basis, it may issue a stock dividend. In this case, **no assets are distributed,** and each stockholder has exactly the same proportionate interest in the corporation and the same total book value after the stock dividend was issued as before it was declared. Of course, the book value per share is lower because an increased number of shares is held. While accountants agree that a *stock dividend* is the nonreciprocal issuance by a corporation of its own stock to its stockholders on a pro rata basis, they do not agree on the proper entries to be made at the time of a stock dividend. Some believe that the par

---

[6]*Accounting Trends and Techniques—1981* reported that of 600 companies surveyed, 27 issued stock dividends.

value of the stock issued as a dividend should be transferred from retained earnings to capital stock. Others believe that the fair value of the stock issued should be transferred from retained earnings to capital stock and additional paid-in capital. Ordinarily fair value is measured by the market price of the stock on the date of declaration.

The fair value position was originally adopted in this country, at least in part, in order to influence the stock dividend policies of corporations. Evidently in 1941 both the New York Stock Exchange and a majority of the Committee on Accounting Procedure regarded periodic stock dividends as objectionable. The Committee therefore acted to make it more difficult for corporations to sustain a series of such stock dividends out of their accumulated earnings by requiring the use of the fair market value when it was substantially in excess of book value.[7]

When the stock dividend is less than 20–25% of the common shares outstanding at the time of the dividend declaration, the accounting profession requires that the **fair market value** of the stock issued be transferred from retained earnings.[8] Stock dividends of less than 20–25% are often referred to as small stock dividends. This method of handling stock dividends is justified on the grounds that "many recipients of stock dividends look upon them as distributions of corporate earnings and usually in an amount equivalent to the fair value of the additional shares received."[9] We do not consider this a convincing argument. It is generally agreed that stock dividends are not income to the recipients, and, therefore, sound accounting should not recommend procedures simply because some recipients think they are income.[10]

The case against treating an ordinary stock dividend as income is supported under either an entity or proprietory assumption regarding the business enterprise. If the corporation is considered an entity separate from the stockholders, the income of the corporation is corporate income and not income to the stockholders, although the equity of the stockholders in the corporation increases. This position argues that a dividend is not income to the recipients until it is realized by them as a result of a division or severance of corporate assets. The stock dividend merely distributes the "recipient's" equity over a larger number of shares. Under this interpretation, selling the stock received as a dividend has the effect of reducing the recipient's proportionate share of the corporation's equity. Under a "proprietory" assumption, income of the corporation is considered income to the owners, and, hence, a stock dividend represents only a reclassification of equity, inasmuch as there is no change in total proprietorship.

---

[7]This represented perhaps the earliest instance of an accounting pronouncement being affected by "economic consequences," because the Committee on Accounting Procedure described its action as being required by "proper accounting and corporate policy." See *Proceedings on the Conference on the Impact of Rule Making on Intermediate Financial Accounting Textbooks,* paper presented by Stephan A. Zeff, The Ohio State University, Columbus, Ohio, June 4, 1982. Also see, Stephan A. Zeff, "The Rise of 'Economic Consequences,'" *The Journal of Accountancy* (December 1978), pp. 53–66.

[8]American Institute of Certified Public Accountants, *Accounting Research and Terminology Bulletins,* No. 43 (New York: AICPA, 1961), Ch. 7, par. 10.

[9]Ibid., par. 10.

[10]One study concluded that *small* stock dividends do not always produce significant amounts of extra value on the date after issuance (ex date) and that *large* stock dividends almost always fail to generate extra value on the ex-dividend date. Taylor W. Foster III and Don Vickrey, "The Information Content of Stock Dividend Announcements," *The Accounting Review,* Vol. LIII, No. 2 (April, 1978), pp. 360–370.

To illustrate a small stock dividend, assume that a corporation has outstanding 1,000 shares of $100 par value capital stock, and a retained earnings balance of $50,000. If it declares a 10% stock dividend, it issues 100 additional shares of stock to present stockholders. If it is assumed that the fair value of the stock at the time of the stock dividend was $130 per share, the entry is:

**At date of declaration:**

| | | |
|---|---|---|
| Retained Earnings (Stock Dividend Declared) | 13,000 | |
|    Common Stock Dividend Distributable | | 10,000 |
|    Paid-in Capital in Excess of Par | | 3,000 |

Note from the above entry that no asset nor liability has been affected. The entry merely reflects a reclassification of stockholders' equity. If a balance sheet is prepared between the dates of declaration and distribution, the common stock dividend distributable should be shown in the stockholders' equity section as an addition to capital stock (whereas cash or property dividends payable are shown as current liabilities).

When the stock is issued the entry is:

**At date of distribution:**

| | | |
|---|---|---|
| Common Stock Dividend Distributable | 10,000 | |
|    Common Stock | | 10,000 |

No matter what the fair value is at the time of the stock dividend, each stockholder retains the same proportionate interest in the corporation.

To illustrate the effect of the small stock dividend the following example is provided. Note from the detail in this illustration that the total stockholders' equity has not changed as a result of the stock dividend, and that each stockholder owns the same proportion of the total shares outstanding after as before the stock dividend.

| Small (10%) Stock Dividend | |
|---|---|
| **Before dividend:** | |
| Capital stock, 1,000 shares of $100 par | $100,000 |
| Retained earnings | 50,000 |
|    Total stockholders' equity | $150,000 |
| | |
| Stockholders' interests: | |
| A. 400 shares, 40% interest, book value | $ 60,000 |
| B. 500 shares, 50% interest, book value | 75,000 |
| C. 100 shares, 10% interest, book value | 15,000 |
| | $150,000 |
| | |
| **After declaration but before payment of 10% stock dividend:** | |
| If fair value ($130) is used as basis for entry | |
|    Capital stock, 1,000 shares at $100 par | $100,000 |
|    Common stock distributable 100 shares at $100 par | 10,000 |
|    Paid-in capital in excess of par | 3,000 |
|    Retained earnings, $50,000 − $13,000 | 37,000 |
|       Total stockholders' equity | $150,000 |

After declaration and payment of 10% stock dividend:

If fair value ($130) is used as basis for entry

| | |
|---|---:|
| Capital stock 1,100 shares at $100 par | $110,000 |
| Paid-in capital in excess of par | 3,000 |
| Retained earnings, $50,000 — $13,000 | 37,000 |
| Total stockholders' equity | $150,000 |

Stockholders' interest:

| | |
|---|---:|
| A. 440 shares, 40% interest, book value | $ 60,000 |
| B. 550 shares, 50% interest, book value | 75,000 |
| C. 110 shares, 10% interest, book value | 15,000 |
| | $150,000 |

## Stock Split

If a company has undistributed earnings each year over a long period of time so that a sizable balance in retained earnings has accumulated, the market value of its outstanding shares may increase to reflect the larger investment. Stock that was issued at prices less than $50 a share not infrequently attains a market value in excess of $200 a share. The higher the market price of a stock, the less readily it can be purchased by most people. The managements of many corporations believe that for better public relations, wider owner-ship of the corporation stock is desirable. They wish, therefore, to have a market price sufficiently low to be within range of the majority of potential investors. To reduce the market value of shares, the common device of a **stock split** is employed. For example when IBM's stock was selling at $304 a share, the company split its common stock four for one. The day after IBM's split (involving 583,268,480 shares) was effective, the stock sold for $76 a share, exactly one quarter of its price per share before the split. IBM's intent was to obtain a wider distribution of its stock by improving the marketability of the shares. From an accounting standpoint, **no entry is recorded for a stock split;** a memorandum note, however, is made to indicate that the par value of the shares has changed, and that the number of shares has increased. The lack of change in stockholders' equity is portrayed in the following illustration of a two-for-one stock split on 1,000 shares of $100 par value stock with the par being halved upon issuance of the additional shares:

| Stockholders' Equity Before 2 for 1 Split | | Stockholders' Equity After 2 for 1 Split | |
|---|---:|---|---:|
| Common stock, 1,000 shares | | Common stock, 2,000 shares | |
| at $100 par | $100,000 | at $50 par | $100,000 |
| Retained earnings | 50,000 | Retained earnings | 50,000 |
| | $150,000 | | $150,000 |

## Stock Split and Stock Dividend Differentiated

From a legal standpoint a stock split is distinguished from a stock dividend, because a stock split results in an increase (or decrease in a reverse stock split) in the number of shares outstanding and a corresponding decrease (or increase in a reverse stock split) in the par or stated value per share. A stock dividend, although it results in an increase in the number of shares outstanding, does not result in a decrease in the par value of the shares and thus it increases the total par value of outstanding shares.

The **reasons for issuing a stock dividend** are numerous and varied. Stock dividends can be more of a publicity gesture, because they are considered by many as dividends and, consequently, the corporation is not criticized for retention of profits. In addition, the corporation may simply wish to retain profits in the business by capitalizing a part of retained earnings. In such a situation, a transfer is made on declaration of a stock dividend from earned capital to contributed or permanent capital.

A stock dividend, like a stock split, also may be used to increase the marketability of the stock, although marketability is often a secondary consideration. If the stock dividend is large, it has the same effect on market price as a stock split. The profession has taken the position that **whenever additional shares are issued for the purpose of reducing the unit market price, then the distribution more closely resembles a stock split than a stock dividend. This effect usually results only if the number of shares issued is more than 20 or 25% of the number of shares previously outstanding.**[11] A stock dividend of more than 20–25% of the number of shares previously outstanding is called a large stock dividend. The profession also recommends that such a distribution not be called a stock dividend, but it might properly be called "a split-up effected in the form of a dividend" or "stock split." Also, since the par value of the outstanding shares is not altered, the transfer from retained earnings is only in the amount required by statute. Ordinarily this means a transfer from retained earnings to capital stock for the amount of the par value of the stock issued as opposed to a transfer of the market value of the shares issued as in the case of a small stock dividend.

To illustrate a large stock dividend, on November 20 Rockland Steel, Inc., declared a 30% stock dividend, payable December 29 to stockholders of record December 12. At the date of declaration, 1,000,000 shares, par value $10, are outstanding and with a fair market value of $200 per share.

The entries are:

**At date of declaration (November 20):**

| | | |
|---|---|---|
| Retained Earnings | 3,000,000 | |
|    Common Stock Dividend Distributable | | 3,000,000 |

| Computation: 1,000,000 shares | 300,000 Additional shares |
|---|---|
| × 30% | × $10 Par value |
| 300,000 | $3,000,000 |

**At date of distribution (December 29):**

| | | |
|---|---|---|
| Common Stock Dividend Distributable | 3,000,000 | |
|    Common Stock | | 3,000,000 |

## Effects of Dividend Preferences

The examples given below illustrate the effect of various provisions on dividend distributions to common and preferred stockholders. Assume that in a given year, $50,000 is to be

---

[11]*Accounting Research and Terminology Bulletin No. 43,* par. 13.

distributed as cash dividends, outstanding common stock has a par value of $400,000, and 6% preferred stock has a par value of $100,000. Dividends would be distributed to each class as shown below, employing the assumptions given.

**1.** If the preferred stock is noncumulative, nonparticipating:

|  | Preferred | Common | Total |
|---|---|---|---|
| 6% of $100,000 | $6,000 |  | $ 6,000 |
| The remainder to common |  | $44,000 | 44,000 |
| Totals | $6,000 | $44,000 | $50,000 |

**2.** If the preferred stock is cumulative and nonparticipating, and dividends were not paid on the preferred stock in the preceding two years:

|  | Preferred | Common | Total |
|---|---|---|---|
| Dividends in arrears, 6% of $100,000 for two years | $12,000 |  | $12,000 |
| Current year's dividend, 6% of $100,000 | 6,000 |  | 6,000 |
| The remainder to common |  | $32,000 | 32,000 |
| Totals | $18,000 | $32,000 | $50,000 |

**3.** If the preferred stock is noncumulative and is fully participating:[12]

|  | Preferred | Common | Total |
|---|---|---|---|
| Current year's dividend, 6% | $ 6,000 | $24,000 | $30,000 |
| Participating dividend of 4% | 4,000 | 16,000 | 20,000 |
| Totals | $10,000 | $40,000 | $50,000 |

[12]When preferred stock is participating, there may be different agreements as to how the participation feature is to be executed. However, in the absence of any specific agreement the following procedure is recommended:

**1.** After the preferred stock is assigned their current year's dividend, the common stock will receive a "like" percentage of par value outstanding. In example (3), this amounts to 6% of $400,000.

**2.** If there is a remainder of declared dividends to be participated by the preferred and common stock, this remainder will be shared in proportion to the par value dollars outstanding in each class of stock. In example (3) this proportion is:

$$\text{Preferred } \frac{\$100,000}{\$500,000} \times \$20,000 = \$4,000$$

$$\text{Common } \frac{\$400,000}{\$500,000} \times \$20,000 = \$16,000$$

The participating dividend was determined as follows:

| | |
|---|---:|
| Current year's dividend: | |
| Preferred, 6% of $100,000 = $ 6,000 | |
| Common, 6% of $400,000 = 24,000 | $ 30,000 |
| Amount available for participation ($50,000 − $30,000) | $ 20,000 |
| Par value of stock that is to participate ($100,000 + $400,000) | $500,000 |
| Rate of participation ($20,000 ÷ $500,000) | 4% |
| Participating dividend: | |
| Preferred, 4% of $100,000 | $ 4,000 |
| Common, 4% of $400,000 | 16,000 |
| | $ 20,000 |

**4.** If the preferred stock is cumulative and is fully participating, and if dividends were not paid on the preferred stock in the preceding two years (the same procedure as described in example (3) is used in this example to effect the participation feature):

| | Preferred | Common | Total |
|---|---:|---:|---:|
| Dividends in arrears, 6% of $100,000 for two years | $12,000 | | $12,000 |
| Current year's dividend, 6% | 6,000 | $24,000 | 30,000 |
| Participating dividend, 1.6% ($8,000 ÷ $500,000) | 1,600 | 6,400 | 8,000 |
| Totals | $19,600 | $30,400 | $50,000 |

## APPROPRIATIONS OF RETAINED EARNINGS

The act of appropriating retained earnings is a policy matter requiring approval by the board of directors. As soon as the action is taken by the board, the accounting department records the appropriation as approved. According to *FASB Statement No. 5,* the appropriation of retained earnings is acceptable practice, "provided that it is shown within the stockholders' equity section of the balance sheet and is clearly identified as an appropriation of retained earnings."[13]

Appropriations of retained earnings are regarded as nothing more than reclassifications of retained earnings temporarily, or perhaps even permanently, established for a given purpose. In other words, the appropriation discloses that management does not intend to distribute assets as a dividend up to the amount of the appropriation because these assets are needed by the corporation for a specified purpose. When the appropriation is no longer necessary, either because the loss has occurred or because it no longer appears as a possibility, the appropriation should be returned to retained earnings. In accordance with *FASB Statement No. 5,* "costs or losses shall not be charged to an appropriation of retained earnings, and no part of the appropriation shall be transferred to income."[14]

---

[13]"Accounting for Contingencies," *Statement of Financial Accounting Standards No. 5* (Stamford, Conn.: FASB, March 1975), par. 15.

[14]Ibid., par. 15.

Even though the retained earnings appropriation is basically a management problem, any improper use of such appropriations, or failure to properly disclose their nature, requires comment by the independent accountant.

## Reasons for Retained Earnings Appropriations

Various reasons are advanced for appropriation of retained earnings. These include:

1. **Legal restrictions.** As indicated earlier, some state laws prohibit the purchase of treasury stock by the corporation unless earnings available for dividends are present. They then restrict the retained earnings in an amount equal to the cost of any treasury stock acquired. Such laws actually require that stated capital be maintained by requiring that earnings be retained to substitute for capital stock temporarily acquired as treasury stock.

2. **Contractual restrictions.** Bond indentures frequently contain a requirement that retained earnings in specified amounts be appropriated each year during the life of the bonds. The appropriation created under such a provision is commonly called Appropriation for Sinking Fund or Appropriation for Bonded Indebtedness.

3. **Existence of possible or expected loss.** Some companies establish Appropriations for Anticipated Future Inventory Declines to reflect expected losses should a general decline in prices occur. Similar appropriations might be established for estimated losses due to lawsuits, unfavorable contractual obligations, and other contingencies.

4. **Protection of working capital position.** The board of directors may authorize the creation of an "Appropriation for Working Capital" out of retained earnings in order to indicate that the amount specified is not available for dividends because it is desirable to maintain a strong current position. Another example involves a decision made to finance a building program by internal financing. An "Appropriation for Plant Expansion" is created to indicate that retained earnings in the amount appropriated will not be considered by the directors as available for dividends.

Some corporations establish appropriations for general contingencies, or appropriate retained earnings for unspecified purposes. The real reason for the restriction may be any of those given above. The essence of the action is that the board of directors desires to reduce the amount of retained earnings **apparently** available for dividends without explaining to the stockholders exactly why. In some cases this is justified by statutory or contractual restrictions. In other cases no adequate explanation for such actions is available. The FASB does not encourage the establishment of general or unspecified appropriations.

## Recording Appropriations of Retained Earnings

As soon as the board of directors approves an appropriation of retained earnings, it becomes necessary to record the appropriation in the accounts. The unappropriated retained earnings must be reduced by the amount of the appropriation and a new account must be established to receive the amount transferred. If the appropriation merely augments a previously established amount, the account already in use should receive the credit. The appropriation is recorded as a debit to Retained Earnings and a credit to an appropriately named account that itself is just a subdivision of retained earnings. For example:

(a) An Appropriation for Plant Expansion is to be created by transfer from Retained Earnings of $400,000 a year for 5 years. The entry for each year would be:

| | | |
|---|---|---|
| Retained Earnings | 400,000 | |
| Retained Earnings Appropriated for | | |
| Plant Expansion | | 400,000 |

(b) At the end of 5 years the appropriation would have a balance of $2,000,000. If we assume that the expansion plan has been completed, the appropriation is no longer required and can be returned to retained earnings.

| | | |
|---|---|---|
| Retained Earnings Appropriated for | | |
| Plant Expansion | 2,000,000 | |
| Retained Earnings | | 2,000,000 |

Return of such an appropriation to retained earnings has the effect of increasing unappropriated retained earnings considerably without affecting the assets or current position. In effect, over the five years the company has expanded by reinvesting earnings.

### Disclosure of Restrictions on Retained Earnings

In many corporations restrictions on retained earnings or dividends exist, but no appropriation resulting in a debit to Retained Earnings and a credit to an appropriation account is recorded.[15] In such cases the accountant must weigh the significance of the restriction, and decide whether to disclose it in some manner other than through debits and credits in the equity accounts. Some bond indentures and loan agreements make appropriations of retained earnings mandatory.[16]

Most restrictions for which journal entries are not made are of a contractual nature resulting from agreements with creditors and are best disclosed by footnote. Parenthetical notations are sometimes used, but restrictions imposed by bond indentures and loan agreements commonly require an extended explanation; footnotes provide a medium for more complete explanations and free the financial statements from abbreviated notations. The footnote disclosure should reveal the source of the restriction, pertinent provisions, and the amount of retained earnings subject to restriction, or the amount not so restricted. The following example from the 1981 annual report of Federal Express Corporation illustrates a footnote disclosure relating to restrictions on retained earnings and dividends.

---

**FEDERAL EXPRESS CORPORATION**

*NOTES TO FINANCIAL STATEMENTS*

The terms of the Company's debt agreements require, among other things, the maintenance of minimum working capital, tangible net worth and certain financial ratios, all as defined. Under the most restrictive provisions of these agreements, cash dividends are limited to $5,000,000 plus 75% of cumulative consolidated net income from March 1, 1979, less amounts paid in any stock repurchases, dividends paid and certain other restricted transactions. At May 31, 1981, approximately $79,500,000 of the reported total of $117,435,000 of retained earnings was available for future dividend payments.

---

As noted in the illustrations above, restrictions may be based on the retention of a certain retained earnings balance, the corporation's ability to observe certain working capi-

---

[15]*Accounting Trends and Techniques—1981* reports that of its list of 600 selected companies 425 disclosed dividend or retained earnings restrictions.

[16]In recent years, however, the use of appropriations to indicate retained earnings restrictions has declined. In its 1950 survey of the annual report of 600 companies, the AICPA noted approximately 100 appropriations of various types; a similar survey in 1971 revealed that only 10 balance sheets contained such appropriations; and, in 1975 the AICPA ceased tabulating this bit of data.

tal requirements, additional borrowing, and on other considerations. When there is more than one type of restriction limitation, disclosure of the amount of retained earnings, so restricted, may be based on the most restrictive covenants likely to be effective in the immediate future. This is sufficient because restrictions seldom, if ever, pyramid in amount.

## Appropriations or Disclosures for Contingencies and for Self-Insurance

A **contingency** is defined as an existing condition, situation, or set of circumstances involving uncertainty as to possible gain or loss to an enterprise that will ultimately be resolved when one or more future events occur or fail to occur.[17]

At its discretion, the board of directors of a corporation may give recognition to possible future losses by directing that a portion of retained earnings be reported as restricted, or that an appropriation of retained earnings be made for a specific dollar amount. Disclosing the existence of contingencies in the notes to the financial statements is more common than appropriating a specific portion of retained earnings.[18] Shown below is an example of a disclosure taken from the annual report of Wellstone Steel Corporation.

---

**WELLSTONE STEEL CORPORATION**

*NOTES TO FINANCIAL STATEMENTS*
   *Note G (in part): Commitments and Contingencies*—On December 6, 1981, coal mines owned in whole or in part by the Corporation discontinued operations due to the United Mine Workers of America strike, which has not yet been settled.
   Although the Corporation's steel-mining operations have not been curtailed as of this date due to the strike, the strike has adversely affected profits and will continue to have an adverse effect. Management believes there are adequate coal and coke supplies to maintain steelmaking operations through mid-March, 1982.
   Utility companies supplying electricity to the Corporation have indicated that they may curtail electricity supplied and/or increase the price of electricity if their coal supplies continue to liquidate. An extended period of curtailment and/or increased electricity cost would adversely affect the Corporation's operations, employment and profitability.

---

A company may insure against many contingencies such as fire, flood, storm, and accident by taking out insurance policies and paying premiums to insurance companies. Some contingencies are, however, not insurable or the rates are prohibitive (for example, earthquakes and riots). Even though insurance is available, some businesses may adopt a policy of **self-insurance.**[19] Self-insurance appears especially valid when a company's physical or

---

[17]"Accounting for Contingencies," *op. cit.,* par. 1.

[18]*Accounting Trends and Techniques—1981* indicates just how common the disclosure of contingencies is: of the 600 companies surveyed, 747 loss contingency disclosures of varying types were reported, a total of 354 devoted to litigation alone.

[19]The American Management Association advertises its popular 2½-day course on "Self-insurance and Risk Retention" (offered several times a year) as follows: "There comes a point where sky-high insurance rates no longer make sense. The dollars you're investing in premiums could be building your corporate assets. Find out how more and more companies are using self-insurance to cut down premium costs."

operating characteristics permit application of the law of large numbers as utilized by insurance companies. Whenever the risk of loss can be spread over a large number of possible loss events that individually would be small in relation to the total potential loss, self-insurance is a temptation. It is based on the belief that the losses will be less over an extended period of time than the premiums that would be paid to insure against such losses. The company thus avoids paying the insurance company's overhead costs including the insurance agent's commission. Examples of such situations are a truck line with hundreds of trucks in different locations, or a grocery chain with hundreds of stores scattered geographically. For instance, at one time Shell Oil Company decided that it was paying a large amount for insurance while incurring few losses. Therefore, it decided against insuring its offshore drilling rigs and many of its onshore facilities as well; instead, it set up a self-insurance appropriation classified as a liability.

The accounting treatment for self-insurance can take one of three forms:

RECORD LOSSES AS INCURRED. Under this approach no accounting recognition is given to the fact that self-insurance is the mode of operation and that uninsured losses may have to be absorbed in some future period. Losses are charged to expense in the period in which "it is probable that an asset has been impaired or a liability has been incurred at the date of the financial statements" and "the amount of loss can be reasonably estimated."[20] **This approach is permitted under GAAP.**

APPROPRIATE AND RECORD LOSSES AS INCURRED. This approach treats uninsured losses in the same manner, that is, they are charged entirely to expense of the period in which they are sustained. Recognition is given to contingent losses in periods other than their incurrence, however, by appropriations of retained earnings. The amount of the annual appropriation may approximate the premium cost of adequate insurance covering the risk, or it may be a prorated allocation of an estimated and anticipated future loss. The balance of the appropriation account normally does not exceed the maximum expected loss at any one time and is never charged with actual losses. The effect of this and the first method is a varying charge for actual losses instead of a stable charge to expense that would result from premium payments to an insurance company. **This approach is also permitted under GAAP.**

ACCRUE EXPENSE.[21] This approach avoids the irregular effects on net income resulting from irregularly occurring uninsured losses and makes the income statement of a company that does not insure appear to be comparable to those of firms carrying insurance. This method accrues the estimated losses by charging operations each year with a hypothetical amount of insurance expense and crediting a similar amount to a liability account entitled Liability for Self-Insured Risks or Liability for Uninsured Losses. When the casualty losses occur, they are charged against the liability account. The liability account absorbs the impact of the loss; each year's income statement absorbs only a portion of the loss. Before 1975 the liability for self-insurance was acceptable and widely used by many large companies, especially in the airlines, insurance, and oil industries. **At present, this approach is not permitted under GAAP.**

**Self-insurance is no insurance,** and any company that assumes its own risks puts itself in the position of incurring expenses or losses as the casualties occur. The improper application of the accrual method (third method) to self-insurance obscures a fundamental difference in circumstances between companies that transfer risks to others through insurance and those that do not. There is little theoretical justification for the establishment of a

---

[20] "Accounting for Contingencies," *op. cit.,* par. 8.

[21] Although unacceptable today, this method is presented because of its previous widespread usage and appeal.

liability based on a hypothetical charge to insurance expense. This is "as if" accounting.[22] Can there be an expense, in advance of the actual occurrence of a casualty, or a liability to incur a casualty loss in the future? The FASB's answer to that question is:

> Fires, explosions, and other similar events that may cause loss or damage of an enterprise's property are random in their occurrence. With respect to events of that type, the condition for accrual is not satisfied prior to the occurrence of the event because until that time there is no diminution in the value of the property. There is no relationship of those events to the activities of the enterprise prior to their occurrence, and no asset is impaired prior to their occurrence. Further, unlike an insurance company, which has a contractual obligation under policies in force to reimburse insureds for losses, an enterprise can have no such obligation to itself, and, hence, no liability.[23]

With respect to uninsured losses that may result from injury to others, damage to the property of others, or business interruptions that may occur after the balance sheet date, premature accrual is similarly objectionable.

### Statements Presenting Changes in Retained Earnings and Paid-in Capital

Statements of retained earnings and statements of additional paid-in capital are frequently presented in the following basic format:

1. Balance at the beginning of the period.
2. Additions.
3. Deductions.
4. Balance at the end of the period.

Although a large segment of the general public (investors and creditors) has gained an elementary understanding of an appreciation for the balance sheet and income statement and, to some degree, the statement of retained earnings, only a small minority comprehend the items appearing in the statement of additional paid-in capital. The disclosure of changes in the separate accounts comprising stockholders' equity (in addition to retained earnings) is required to make the financial statements sufficiently informative.[24] Disclosure of such changes may take the form of separate statements or may be made in the basic financial statements or notes thereto.

A **columnar format** for the presentation of changes in stockholders' equity items in published annual reports is gaining in popularity; an example is St. Regis Paper Company's Statements of Shareholders' Equity as shown on page 710.

The annual report of Tenneco Inc. in Appendix E of Chapter 5, page 199 includes a comprehensive illustration of the various items that commonly appear as either additions or deductions in a "Statement of Changes in Stockholders' Equity."

---

[22] A commentary in *Forbes* (June 15, 1974, p. 42) stated its position on this matter quite succinctly: "The simple and unquestionable fact of life is this: Business is cyclical and full of unexpected surprises. Is it the role of accounting to disguise this unpleasant fact and create a fairyland of smoothly rising earnings? Or, should accounting reflect reality, warts and all—floods, expropriations and all manner of rude shocks?"

[23] "Accounting for Contingencies," *op. cit.,* par. 28.

[24] "Omnibus Opinion—1967 (Capital Changes)," *APB Opinion No. 12* (New York: AICPA, 1967), par. 10.

St. Regis Paper Company and Consolidated Subsidiaries
STATEMENTS OF SHAREHOLDERS' EQUITY

| (Thousands, except shares and per-share amounts) | Preferred Stock | Common Stock | Common Treasury Stock | Capital Surplus | Retained Earnings |
|---|---|---|---|---|---|
| **Balance at December 31, 1980** | — | 170,169 | (279) | 234,250 | 939,722 |
| Net earnings | | | | | 179,218 |
| Cash dividends: | | | | | |
| Common stock, $2.15 per share | | | | | (71,009) |
| Pooled company | | | | | (1,365) |
| Purchase of common stock, 12,830 shares | | | (428) | | |
| Issuance of common stock: | | | | | |
| Conversion of 4⅞% debentures, 8,253 shares | | 41 | | 207 | |
| Stock option plan, pooled company, 33,398 shares; conversion of debentures, pooled company, 21,517 shares | | 275 | | 989 | |
| Stock option plan, 24,508 shares | | 123 | | 578 | |
| Management incentive compensation plan, 37,319 shares, including 5,828 treasury shares | | 158 | 207 | 698 | |
| **Balance at December 31, 1981** | $— | $170,766 | $(500) | $236,722 | $1,046,566 |

Stock balances at December 31, 1980:
 common stock, 34,033,985 shares; and treasury stock, 17,992 shares.
Stock balances at December 31, 1981:
 common stock, 34,153,152 shares; and treasury stock, 24,994 shares.

The following presentation is an example of a comprehensive stockholders' equity section taken from a balance sheet that includes most of the equity items discussed in Chapters 15 and 16.

Model Corporation
STOCKHOLDERS' EQUITY
December 31, 1983

| | | |
|---|---|---|
| Capital stock: | | |
| Preferred stock, $100 par value, 7% cumulative, 30,000 shares issued and outstanding | | $3,000,000 |
| Common stock, no par, stated value $10 per share 400,000 shares issued | | 4,000,000 |
| Common stock dividend distributable, 20,000 shares | | 200,000 |
| Total capital stock | | 7,200,000 |
| Additional paid-in capital: | | |
| Excess over par—preferred | $ 150,000 | |
| Excess over stated value—common | 840,000 | 990,000 |
| Total paid-in capital | | 8,190,000 |
| Donated capital | | 100,000 |

| Retained earnings | | |
|---|---|---|
| Appropriated for plant expansion | 2,100,000 | |
| Unappropriated | 2,160,000 | 4,260,000 |
| Total capital and retained earnings | | 12,550,000 |
| Less cost of treasury stock (2,000 shares, common) | | (80,000) |
| Total stockholders' equity | | $12,470,000 |

## TRENDS IN TERMINOLOGY

As discussed in Chapter 5 the profession's recommendations relating to changes in terminology have been directed primarily to the balance sheet presentation of stockholders' equity so that words or phrases used will more accurately and more adequately describe the nature of the amounts shown.

The accounting profession has suggested discontinuance of the use of the term "surplus" in corporate accounting, particularly in financial statements. Substitute terminology is recommended for the various types of surplus because the term "surplus" connotes to many readers of the financial statements a residue or "something not needed."

The use of the term is gradually decreasing. "Retained earnings" or some modification of this term has generally replaced the term "earned surplus." Apparently, consensus regarding the terminology to replace "capital surplus" and "paid-in surplus" has not yet been reached, inasmuch as these two terms still appear in many financial statements. "Capital in excess of par (or stated value)" or "additional paid-in capital" are gaining favor over the term "paid-in surplus." But, no term having the broad connotation of "capital surplus" (all owners' equity exclusive of capital stock and retained earnings) has yet emerged.[25]

The persistent use of these "surplus" terms by many leading corporations can perhaps be attributed to the numerous state incorporation acts that still contain antiquated terminology in their provisions regulating the issuance of stock and other equity transactions.

Formerly, the term "reserve" was used in accounting to describe such diverse items as accumulated depreciation, accumulated allowances for doubtful accounts, current liabilities, and segregations of retained earnings. The profession recommends that use of the word "reserve" be confined to appropriations of retained earnings if it is to be used at all. The general adoption of this recommendation could help to clear up one of the most troublesome terminology areas in accounting.[26]

## QUASI REORGANIZATION

A corporation that consistently suffers net losses accumulates negative retained earnings, or a deficit. The laws of many states provide that no dividends may be declared and paid so

[25]*Accounting Trends and Techniques—1981* reports that the use of the term surplus is gradually declining. In its survey of 600 companies, 75 out of 523 companies reporting additional paid-in capital used either "capital surplus" or "paid-in surplus" for the caption. Only three companies used the term "earned surplus," while 474 used the caption "retained earnings."

[26]*Accounting Trends and Techniques—1981* reports that of its list of 600 selected companies, 115 continued incorrectly to use the term reserve in the asset or liability section of the balance sheet.

long as a corporation's paid-in capital has been reduced by a deficit. In these states, a corporation with a debit balance of retained earnings must first accumulate sufficient profits to offset the deficit before dividends may be paid.

This situation may be a real hardship on a corporation and its stockholders. For example, a company that has operated unsuccessfully for several years and accumulated a deficit may attain a position that gives promise of successful operation in the future. Development of new products and new markets, a new management group placed in control, or merely improved economic conditions may point to much improved operating results. But, if the state law prohibits dividends until the deficit has been replaced by earnings, the stockholders must wait until such profits have been earned, which may take a considerable period of time. Furthermore, future success may depend on obtaining additional funds through the sale of stock. If no dividends can be paid for some time, however, the market price of any new stock issue is likely to be low, if such stock can be marketed at all.

Thus, a company with every prospect of a successful future may be prevented from accomplishing its plans because of a deficit, although present management may have had nothing whatever to do with the years over which the deficit was accumulated. To permit the corporation to proceed with its plans might well be to the advantage of all interests in the enterprise; to require it to eliminate the deficit through profits might actually force it to liquidate to the possible injury of all parties at interest.

**A procedure provided for in some state laws eliminates an accumulated deficit and permits the company to proceed on much the same basis as if it had been legally reorganized, without the difficulty and expenses generally connected with a legal reorganization. This procedure, known as a "quasi reorganization," consists of the following steps:**

1. All assets are revalued at appropriate current values (generally, net realizable value) so the company will not be burdened with excessive inventory or plant asset valuations in following years. Any loss on revaluation, of course, increases the deficit.

2. Paid-in or other types of capital must be available or must be created, at least equal in amount to the deficit. If no such capital exists, it is created through donation of stock to the corporation by stockholders, by reduction of the par value of shares outstanding, or by some similar means.

3. The deficit is then charged against the paid-in capital and thus eliminated.

A series of entries given below illustrates the steps taken in a quasi reorganization of Motormatrix Corp. Motormatrix shows a deficit of $2,000,000 before the quasi reorganization of June 30, 1980, is effected.

**To revalue assets to recognize unrecorded losses:**

| | | |
|---|---|---|
| Retained Earnings | 800,000 | |
| Inventory | | 375,000 |
| Plant Assets | | 425,000 |

**To reduce par value of 60,000 shares of common stock outstanding from $100 per share to $50 per share:**

| | | |
|---|---|---|
| Common Stock | 3,000,000 | |
| Additional Paid-in Capital | | 3,000,000 |

**To charge deficit against additional paid-in capital:**

| | | |
|---|---|---|
| Additional Paid-in Capital | 2,800,000 | |
| Retained Earnings | | 2,800,000 |

The paid-in capital created at the time of the quasi reorganization may be called Reorganization Capital, Capital from Reduction in Par Value of Capital Stock, or other appropriate titles, depending on its source.

In connection with the foregoing steps, the following requirements must be fulfilled:

1. The proposed quasi reorganization procedure should be submitted to and receive the approval of the corporation stockholders before it is put into effect.

2. The new asset valuations should be fair and not deliberately understate or overstate assets, liabilities, and future earnings.

3. After the reorganization the corporation must have a zero balance of retained earnings, although it may have additional paid-in capital arising from the reorganization.

4. In subsequent reports the retained earnings must be "dated" for a period of approximately 10 years to show the fact and the date of the quasi reorganization, as illustrated in the following excerpt from the 1982 balance sheet of Motormatrix Corp.

| Stockholders' equity | | |
|---|---:|---:|
| Common stock of par value of $50 per share authorized and issued, 60,000 shares | $3,000,000 | |
| Capital arising from reduction in par value of common stock | 200,000 | |
| Earnings retained in the business (after quasi reorganization on June 30, 1980) | 103,600 | $3,303,600 |

In times of general economic or specific industry recession (such as the early 1980s) or depression the use of the quasi reorganization procedure becomes a more common occurrence as companies attempt to turn around, to get a fresh start, and make their financials more representative of the firm's changed economic status.

## QUESTIONS

1. List the possible sources of "additional paid-in capital."

2. Distinguish among: contributed capital, earned capital, and equity capital.

3. What equity accounts might conceivably have debit balances? Discuss.

4. Indicate the ways in which revaluation and donated capital originate.

5. What are some of the common items that increase or decrease retained earnings?

6. Very few companies pay dividends in amounts equal to their retained earnings legally available for dividends. Why?

7. What are the principal considerations of a board of directors in making decisions involving dividend declarations? Discuss briefly.

8. In a recent report from the FASB, it was noted that on a price-level basis (adjusted for specific prices), dividends exceeded profits. Some industries, such as primary and fabricated metals, are in effect undergoing gradual liquidation. Explain what this statement means.

9. Distinguish among: cash dividends, property dividends, scrip dividends, liquidating dividends, and stock dividends.

10. What factors influence the dividend policy of a company?

11. Describe the accounting entry for a stock dividend. Describe the accounting entry for a stock split.

12. Stock splits and stock dividends may be used by a corporation to change the number of shares of its stock outstanding.
    (a) What is meant by a stock split effected in the form of a dividend?

    (b) From an accounting viewpoint, explain how the stock split effected in the form of a dividend differs from an ordinary stock dividend.

    (c) How should a stock dividend which has been declared but not yet issued be classified in a statement of financial position? Why?

**13.** For what reasons might a company appropriate a portion of its retained earnings?

**14.** How should appropriations of retained earnings be created and written off?

**15.** Indicate the misuse and the proper use of the term "reserve."

**16.** What are some of the ways in which retained earnings may be restricted?

**17.** Is there a duplication of charges to current year's costs or expenses where a sinking fund appropriation is created for the retirement of bonds, as well as accumulated depreciation with respect to the capital assets by which such bonds are secured? Discuss briefly the point raised by this question.

**18.** What is self-insurance? What are the two acceptable forms that the accounting treatment for self-insurance may take?

**19.** Dividends are sometimes said to have been paid "out of retained earnings." What is the error in that statement?

**20.** Under what circumstances would a corporation consider submitting itself to a quasi reorganization?

**21.** Outline the accounting steps involved in accomplishing a quasi reorganization.

## CASES

**C16–1** Aeroblotka Airlines, Inc., a client, is considering the authorization of a 8% common stock dividend to common stockholders. The financial vice-president of Aeroblotka wishes to discuss the accounting implications of such an authorization with you before the next meeting of the board of directors.

**Instructions**

    (a) The first topic the vice-president wishes to discuss is the nature of the stock dividend to the recipient. Discuss the case **against** considering the stock dividend as income to the recipient.

    (b) The other topic for discussion is the propriety of issuing the stock dividend to all "stockholders of record" or to "stockholders of record exclusive of shares held in the name of the corporation as treasury stock." Discuss the case **against** issuing stock dividends on treasury shares.

                                           (AICPA adapted)

**C16–2** The directors of Iva Temper Corporation are considering the issuance of a stock dividend. They have asked you to discuss the proposed action by answering the following questions.

**Instructions**

    (a) What is a stock dividend? How is a stock dividend distinguished from a stock split-up (1) from a legal standpoint? (2) from an accounting standpoint?

    (b) For what reasons does a corporation usually declare a stock dividend? A stock split-up?

    (c) Discuss the amount, if any, of retained earnings to be capitalized in connection with a stock dividend.

                                           (AICPA adapted)

**C16–3** Paton & Littleton, a large retail chain store company, has stores throughout the United States. Because of the stores' many different locations, Paton & Littleton's president thinks it would be advantageous to self-insure the company's stores against the risk of any future loss or damage from fire or other natural causes. From past experience and by applying appropriate statistical and actuarial techniques, the president feels the amount of future losses can be predicted with reasonable accuracy.

**Instructions**

The president has asked you how Paton & Littleton should record this type of contingency and on what basis the current period should be allocated a portion of the estimated losses. What would you tell the president?

**C16-4**  After operating several years, Pacioli Publishing, Inc. showed a net worth of $750,000, of which $150,000 was represented by 1,500 shares of $100 each, and $600,000 was retained earnings. Subsequently, three additional shares were issued for each share held, which made the capital stock $600,000 and retained earnings $150,000. The operations of later years showed an aggregate loss of $420,000, leaving a deficit of $270,000.

 The corporation then reduced the par value of each share of stock to 25% of its former value, thus restoring the capital to the original amount of $150,000. The deficit was absorbed and the retained earnings shown as $180,000. It is argued that this amount represents the net operating results since organization and is, therefore, retained earnings.

**Instructions**

Give your opinion of these transactions; disregard their legal aspects.

**C16-5**  Bista & Battaglia Co., a medium-sized manufacturer, has been experiencing losses for the five years that it has been doing business. Although the operations for the year just ended resulted in a loss, several important changes resulted in a profitable fourth quarter, and the future operations of the company are expected to be profitable.

 The treasurer, Marty Larsen, suggests that there be a quasi reorganization to: (1) eliminate the accumulated deficit of $632,240, (2) write up the $702,300 cost of operating land and buildings to their fair value, and (3) set up an asset of $298,500 representing the estimated future tax benefit of the losses accumulated to date.

**Instructions**

(a) What are the characteristics of a quasi reorganization? In other words, of what does it consist?

(b) List the conditions under which a quasi reorganization generally is justified.

(c) Discuss the propriety of the treasurer's proposals to:
 1. Eliminate the deficit of $632,240.
 2. Write up the $702,300 cost of the operating land and buildings to their fair value.
 3. Set up an asset of $248,500 representing the estimated future tax benefit of the losses accumulated to date.

(AICPA adapted)

# EXERCISES

**E16-1**  Stockholders' equity on the balance sheet of Andy Morreale Corp. is composed of four major sections. They are: A. Capital stock; B. Additional paid-in capital; C. Donated capital; and D. Retained earnings.

**Instructions**

Classify each of the following items as affecting one of the four sections above or as E. an item not to be included in stockholders' equity.

| | |
|---|---|
| **1.** Net income | **7.** Retained earnings appropriated |
| **2.** Preferred stock subscribed | **8.** Allowance for Doubtful Accounts |
| **3.** Goodwill | **9.** Sinking fund |
| **4.** Donated land | **10.** Common stock |
| **5.** Cash dividends declared | **11.** Paid-in capital in excess of |
| **6.** Preferred stock | par—common |

**E16–2** The following information has been taken from the ledger accounts of Urban & Alton Corporation:

| | |
|---|---:|
| Total income since incorporation | $125,000 |
| Total cash dividends paid | 50,000 |
| Proceeds from sale of donated stock | 25,000 |
| Total value of stock dividends distributed | 15,000 |
| Gains on treasury stock transactions | 17,500 |
| Unamortized discount on bonds payable | 37,500 |
| Appropriated for plant expansion | 25,000 |

**Instructions**

Determine the current balance of unappropriated retained earnings.

**E16–3** The stockholders' equity accounts of Slezak Company have the following balances on December 31, 1984:

| | |
|---|---:|
| Common stock, $15 par, 400,000 shares issued and outstanding | $6,000,000 |
| Paid-in capital in excess of par | 1,600,000 |
| Retained earnings | 7,200,000 |

Shares of Slezak Company stock are currently selling on the Northwest Stock Exchange at $42.

**Instructions**

Prepare the appropriate journal entries for each of the following cases:
(a) A stock dividend of 10% is declared and issued.
(b) A stock dividend of 100% is declared and issued.
(c) A 4 for 1 stock split is declared and issued.

**E16–4** The following data were taken from the balance sheet accounts of Casey & Cwynar Corporation on December 31, 1983:

| | |
|---|---:|
| Current Assets | $495,000 |
| Investments | 308,250 |
| Capital Stock (par value $20) | 450,000 |
| Paid-in Capital in Excess of Par | 72,000 |
| Retained Earnings | 780,000 |

**Instructions**

Prepare the required journal entries for the following unrelated items:
(a) A 10% stock dividend is declared and distributed at a time when the market value of the shares is $30 per share.
(b) A scrip dividend of $30,000 is declared.
(c) The par value of the capital stock is reduced to $5 and the stock is split 4 for 1.
(d) A dividend is declared January 5, 1984, and paid January 25, 1984 in bonds held as an investment; the bonds have a book value of $37,000 and a fair market value of $67,500.

**E16–5** Illini Corporation, which has suffered losses for several years, has the following stockholders' equity on December 31, 1983:

| | |
|---|---:|
| Common stock, $10 par value, 20,000 shares authorized and issued | $200,000 |
| Discount on common stock | (12,000) |
| Retained earnings (deficit) | (40,000) |
| | $148,000 |

**Instructions**

Assume that, to supply badly needed cash, the company assesses the stockholders $1 per share on the shares they own.

(a) Compute: (1) The book value per share before the assessment, (2) The book value per share after the assessment.

(b) Prepare the revised stockholders' equity after the assessment.

**E16–6** The outstanding capital stock of Stoldt & Schieble Corporation consists of 1,500 shares of $100 par value, 8% preferred, and 4,000 shares of $75 par value common.

### Instructions

Assuming that the company has retained earnings of $78,000, all of which is to be paid out in dividends, and that preferred dividends were not paid during the two years preceding the current year, state how much each class of stock should receive under each of the following conditions:

(a) The preferred stock is noncumulative and nonparticipating.

(b) The preferred stock is cumulative and nonparticipating.

(c) The preferred stock is cumulative and participating.

**E16–7** Alice Congdon Company's ledger shows the following balances on December 31, 1984:

| | |
|---|---:|
| 7% Preferred stock—$15 par value, outstanding 20,000 shares | $ 300,000 |
| Common stock—$50 par value, outstanding 30,000 shares | 1,500,000 |
| Retained earnings | 540,000 |

### Instructions

Assuming that the directors decide to declare total dividends in the amount of $195,000, determine how much each class of stock should receive under each of the conditions stated below. One year's dividends are in arrears on the preferred stock.

(a) The preferred stock is cumulative and fully participating.

(b) The preferred stock is noncumulative and nonparticipating.

(c) The preferred stock is noncumulative and is participating in distributions in excess of a 10% dividend rate on the common stock.

**E16–8** Jerry Goodrich, as president of Ski Lift, Inc., has decided against purchasing casualty insurance to cover the company's four plants. Recognizing the possibility of casualty losses, he has $15,000 a year appropriated as a reserve for such contingencies; the first appropriation is made in 1983. In 1986 a fire destroys one of his plants. The plant had a 20-year life, no salvage value, and an original cost of $200,000 when it was constructed 12 years ago. After the fire in 1986, Goodrich changes his mind, buys insurance and pays an annual premium of $17,500 on January 2, 1987, and eliminates his casualty reserve.

### Instructions

Prepare the entries to journalize the insurance and casualty transactions of 1983, 1986, and 1987.

**E16–9** The following account balances are available from the ledger of Turnaround Corporation on December 31, 1983:

| | |
|---|---:|
| Capital Stock—$70 par value, 15,000 shares authorized and outstanding | $1,050,000 |
| Retained Earnings (deficit) | (315,000) |

As of January 2, 1984, the corporation gave effect to a stockholder-approved quasi reorganization by reducing the par value of the stock to $42 a share, writing down plant assets by $52,500, and eliminating the deficit.

### Instructions

Prepare the required journal entries for the quasi reorganization of Turnaround.

**E16–10** The condensed balance sheets of Snap Back Company immediately before and one year after it had completed a quasi reorganization appear below:

|  | Before Quasi | One Year After |  | Before Quasi | One Year After |
|---|---|---|---|---|---|
| Current assets | $ 300,000 | $ 420,000 | Common stock | $2,250,000 | $1,350,000 |
| Plant assets (net) | 1,500,000 | 1,050,000 | Premium on common | 150,000 | |
| | | | Retained earnings | (600,000) | 120,000 |
| | $1,800,000 | $1,470,000 | | $1,800,000 | $1,470,000 |

For the year following the quasi reorganization, the Snap Back Company reported net income of $150,000, depreciation expense of $75,000, and paid a cash dividend of $30,000. As part of the quasi reorganization, the company wrote down inventories by $75,000. No purchases or sales of plant assets and no stock transactions occurred in the year following the quasi reorganization.

**Instructions**

Prepare all the journal entries made at the time of the quasi reorganization.

## PROBLEMS

**P16-1** As the newly appointed controller in 1984 for Golf Cart Company, you are interested in analyzing the "Additional Capital" account of the company in order to present an accurate balance sheet. Your assistant, Steve Kittleson, who has analyzed the account from the inception of the company, submits the following summary:

| | Debits | Credits |
|---|---|---|
| Cash dividends—preferred | $ 135,000 | |
| Cash dividends—common | 330,000 | |
| Excess of amount paid in over par value of common stock | | 420,000 |
| Discount on preferred stock | 90,000 | |
| Net income | | 900,000 |
| Contra to appraisal increase of land | | 300,000 |
| Additional assessments of prior years' income taxes | 130,500 | |
| Extraordinary gain | | 22,500 |
| Donated treasury stock, preferred; issued and reacquired, at par | | 195,000 |
| Extraordinary loss | 172,500 | |
| Correction of a prior period error | 67,500 | |
| | 925,500 | 1,837,500 |
| Credit balance of additional capital account | 912,000 | |
| | $1,837,500 | $1,837,500 |

**Instructions**

(a) Prepare a journal entry to close the single "Additional Capital" account now used and to establish appropriately classified accounts. Indicate how you derive the balance of each new account.

(b) If generally accepted accounting principles had been followed, what amount should have been shown as total net income?

**P16-2** The balance sheet of Innovative, Inc. shows $300,000 capital stock, consisting of 3,000 shares of $100 each, and retained earnings of $225,000. As controller of the company, you find that Earl Schultz the assistant treasurer is $60,000 short in his accounts and had concealed this shortage by adding the amount to the inventory. He owns 450 shares of the company's stock and, in settlement of the shortage, offers this stock at its book value. The offer is accepted; the company pays him the excess value and distributes the 450 shares thus acquired to the other stockholders.

**Instructions**

    (a) What amount should Innovative, Inc. pay the assistant treasurer?

    (b) By what journal entries should the foregoing transactions be recorded? (Treasury stock is recorded using the cost method.)

    (c) What is the total stockholders' equity after the distribution noted above?

    (d) What would have been done if Innovative, Inc. had had a deficit of $75,000 and the 450 shares had been accepted at par?

**P16-3** The Board of Directors of Elm Corporation on December 1, 1984, declared a 2% stock dividend on the common stock of the corporation, payable on December 28, 1984, only to the holders of record at the close of business December 15, 1984. They stipulated that cash dividends were to be paid in lieu of issuing any fractional shares. They also directed that the amount to be charged against Retained Earnings should be an amount equal to the market value of the stock on the record date multiplied by the total of (a) the number of shares issued as a stock dividend, and (b) the number of shares on which cash is paid in place of the issuance of fractional shares. The following facts are given:

    **1.** At the dividend record date:

|  |  |
|---|---:|
| (a) Shares of Elm common issued | 3,048,750 |
| (b) Shares of Elm common held in treasury | 1,100 |
| (c) Shares of Elm common included in (a) above held by persons who will receive cash in lieu of fractional shares | 222,750 |
| (d) Shares of predecessor company stock that are exchangeable for Elm common at the rate of 1¼ shares of Elm common for each share of predecessor company stock (necessary number of shares of Elm common have been reserved but not issued) Provision was made for a cash dividend in lieu of fractional shares to holders of 180 of these 660 shares. | 660 |

    **2.** Values of Elm common were:

|  |  |
|---|---:|
| Par value | $ 5 |
| Market value at December 1st and 15th | $22 |
| Book value at December 1st and 15th | $16 |

**Instructions**

    Prepare entries and explanations to record the payment of the dividend.

                                             (AICPA adapted)

**P16-4** The books of Becca Diedrich Corporation carried the following account balances as of December 31, 1983:

| | |
|---|---:|
| Cash | $226,500 |
| Preferred stock, 6% cumulative, nonparticipating, $10 par | 300,000 |
| Common stock, no par value, 150,000 shares issued | 750,000 |
| Paid-in capital in excess of par (preferred) | 45,000 |
| Treasury stock (common 3,600 shares at cost) | 21,600 |
| Retained earnings | 105,000 |

    The preferred stock has dividends in arrears for the past year (1983).

    The board of directors, at their annual meeting on December 21, 1984, declared the following: "The current year dividends shall be 6% on the preferred and $.50 per share on the common; the dividends in arrears shall be paid by issuing one share of treasury stock for each ten shares of preferred held."

    The preferred is currently selling at $110 per share and the common at $6 per share. Net income for 1984 is estimated at $18,000.

**Instructions**

    (a) Prepare the journal entries required for the dividend declaration and payment, assuming that they occur simultaneously.

(b) Could Becca Diedrich Corporation give the preferred stockholders two year's dividends and common stockholders a $.50 per share dividend, all in cash?

**P16-5** Kinniry TV, Inc. has outstanding 1,500 shares of $200 par, 7% preferred stock and 4,500 shares of $20 par value common. The schedule below shows the amount of dividends paid out over the last four years.

**Instructions**

Allocate the dividends to each type of stock under assumptions (a) and (b). Express your answers in per-share amounts using the following format.

| | | Assumptions | | | |
|---|---|---|---|---|---|
| | | (a) Preferred, noncumulative, and nonparticipating | | (b) Preferred, cumulative, and fully participating | |
| Year | Paid-out | Preferred | Common | Preferred | Common |
| 1981 | $12,000 | | | | |
| 1982 | $36,000 | | | | |
| 1983 | $58,500 | | | | |
| 1984 | $78,000 | | | | |

**P16-6** Peggy Nelson, Inc., began operations in January 1980 and had the following reported net income or loss for each of its five years of operations:

| 1980 | $ 225,000 loss |
|---|---|
| 1981 | 195,000 loss |
| 1982 | 180,000 loss |
| 1983 | 375,000 income |
| 1984 | 1,500,000 income |

At December 31, 1984, Nelson capital accounts were as follows:

| | |
|---|---|
| Common stock, par value $15 per share; authorized 100,000 shares; issued and outstanding 50,000 shares | $ 750,000 |
| 4% nonparticipating noncumulative preferred stock, par value $100 per share; authorized, issued and outstanding 1,500 shares | 150,000 |
| 8% fully participating cumulative preferred stock, par value $150 per share; authorized, issued and outstanding 10,000 shares | 1,500,000 |

Nelson has never paid a cash or stock dividend. There has been no change in the capital accounts since Nelson began operations. The appropriate state law permits dividends only from retained earnings.

**Instructions**

Prepare a work sheet showing the maximum amount available for cash dividends on December 31, 1984, and how it would be distributable to the holders of the common shares and each of the preferred shares. Show supporting computations in good form.

(AICPA adapted)

**P16-7** Some of the account balances of Juan García Company at December 31, 1983, are shown below:

| | |
|---|---|
| 6% Preferred Stock ($100 par, 1,000 shares authorized) | $ 10,000 |
| Paid-in Capital in Excess of Par—Preferred Stock | 300 |
| Common Stock ($10 par, 100,000 shares authorized) | 500,000 |
| Paid-in Capital in Excess of Par—Common Stock | 50,000 |
| Unappropriated Retained Earnings | 340,500 |
| Treasury Stock—Preferred (50 shares at cost) | 5,600 |
| Treasury Stock—Common (1,000 shares at cost) | 15,000 |

| Retained Earnings Appropriated for Contingencies | 75,000 |
| Retained Earnings Appropriated for Fire Insurance | 80,000 |

The price of the company's common stock has been increasing steadily on the market; it was $23 on January 1, 1984, advanced to $27 by July 1, and to $30 at the end of the year 1984. The preferred stock is not openly traded but was appraised at $105 per share during 1984.

**Instructions**

Give the proper journal entries for each of the following:
(a) The company incurred a fire loss of $57,000 to its warehouse.
(b) The company declared a property dividend on April 1. Each common stockholder was to receive one share of Akes & Panes for every 10 shares outstanding. Juan García had 8,000 shares of Akes & Panes (2% of total outstanding stock) which was purchased in 1981 for $68,400. The market value of Akes & Panes stock was $16 per share on April 1. Record appreciation only on the shares distributed.
(c) The company resold the 50 shares of preferred stock held in the treasury for $116 per share.
(d) On July 1, the company declared a 4% stock dividend to the common stockholders.
(e) The city of Trenton, in an effort to persuade the company to expand into that city, donated to Juan García Company a plot of land with an appraised value of $26,000.
(f) At the annual board of directors meeting, the board decided to "Set up an appropriation in retained earnings for the future construction of a new plant. Such appropriation to be for $60,000 per year. Also, to increase the appropriation for possible contingencies by $25,000 and to eliminate the appropriation for fire insurance and begin purchasing such insurance from Danegeld Insurance Company."

**P16-8** The controller of Scott Fraser Paint Company presents the owners' equity section of the company's December 31, 1983 balance sheet in the following form:

Net Worth

| | |
|---|---|
| Common stock | $ 80,000 |
| Preferred stock | 220,000 |
| Retained earnings | 383,100 |
| Appraisal capital | 22,000 |
| Total net worth | $705,100 |

A study of the company records revealed the following facts:

1. The company sold 8,000 shares of no-par common stock for $13 per share at the time the firm was organized. The common stock has a stated value of $10 per share. The firm was incorporated in 1976.

2. In 1978 the company issued 2,000 shares of $100 par value, cumulative and nonparticipating, 6%, preferred stock at a price of $110 per share.

3. A common stock dividend of 800 shares was issued but not recorded in 1981, when the market value of the common stock was $21 per share.

4. The company has bought and sold its own common stock on several occasions. It has received $7,000 in excess of cost from the resale of its own common stock, which was purchased in the market.

5. At the end of 1983 the company holds 100 shares of common stock, which was acquired at a cost of $27 per share, in the treasury. The state law does not permit stated capital to be impaired as a result of treasury stock purchases. (Treasury stock recorded at cost.)

6. In 1982, certain stockholders donated 200 shares of common stock to the company; this stock was immediately sold for $24 per share. (Assume the company used the memo method to record the donation.)

7. The $22,000, which is shown as appraisal capital, represents the appraised value of land given to the firm by the local government.

8. From 1976 to the end of 1983, the company earned net income of $550,000, and distributed $200,000 of this net income in cash dividends to stockholders.

9. The total amount of the owner's equity was correctly computed by the company's accountants at the end of 1983.

**Instructions**

Prepare a revised stockholders' equity section of the balance sheet of Scott Fraser Paint Company as of December 31, 1983. (Accompany with a schedule indicating how the retained earnings balance of $383,100 was achieved.)

**P16-9** The following accounts and balances appear in Scott Spangler Company's ledger after closing but before any entries resulting from the following resolutions:

| | |
|---|---|
| Land Held for Investment | $ 76,000 dr. |
| Retained Earnings Appropriated for Possible Decline of Inventory Prices | 129,000 cr. |
| Retained Earnings Appropriated for Contingencies | 200,000 cr. |
| Retained Earnings | 540,000 cr. |
| Income Summary | 300,000 cr. |

The following resolutions were passed by the board of directors of the Scott Spangler Company at their last meeting for the year 1983:

1. A Retained Earnings Appropriated for Possible Additional Federal Income Tax Assessments of Prior Years is to be created in the amount of $35,000.

2. An amount equal to 20% of the net income for the year is to be transferred to the Retained Earnings Appropriated for Contingencies.

3. The present Retained Earnings Appropriated for Possible Decline of Inventory Prices that was set up as a charge against Retained Earnings in 1982 is to be written off as no longer required.

4. A decline in the value of land purchased for investment is to be recorded. As measured by the sales value of other property in the area, the value of the Scott Spangler Company's land has decreased 30% since date of purchase, and an equivalent write-down is to be made in the carrying value of the property.

5. A Retained Earnings Appropriated for Future Plant Expansion is to be established equal to 50% of the balance of the Retained Earnings account, after all transactions for the year noted above have been recorded.

6. A stock dividend of 8% on the capital stock (par value $100) of $500,000 is declared and issued. The market price of the stock on the date of declaration was $120 per share.

**Instructions**

(a) Prepare entries in general journal form to record the board of directors' resolutions above.
(b) What is the amount of retained earnings apparently available for dividends?
(c) What is the amount of retained earnings actually (legally) available for dividends?

**P16-10** Bedard Company has these stockholders' equity accounts:

| | Issued Shares | Amount |
|---|---|---|
| Preferred stock, $100 par value | 2,400 | $240,000 |
| Treasury shares, preferred (at cost) | 160 | 24,000 |
| Common stock without par value (at issue price) | 3,600 | 118,800 |
| Retained earnings | | 494,640 |

In view of the large retained earnings, the board of directors resolves: (1) "to pay a 100% stock dividend on all shares outstanding, capitalizing amounts of retained earnings equal to the par value and the issue price of the preferred and common stock outstanding," respectively, and thereafter (2) "to pay a cash dividend of 6% on preferred stock and a cash dividend of $3 a share on common stock."

**Instructions**

    (a) Prepare entries in journal form to record declaration of these dividends.

    (b) Prepare the stockholders' equity section of a balance sheet for Bedard Company after declaration but before distribution of these dividends.

**P16-11** The following is a summary of all relevant transactions of Rob Russell Corporation since it was organized in 1981:

    In 1981, 15,000 shares were authorized and 7,500 shares of common stock ($50 par value) were issued at a price of $55. In 1982, 1,500 shares were issued as a stock dividend when the stock was selling for $62. Three hundred shares of common stock were bought in 1983 at a cost of $66 per share. These 300 shares are still in the company treasury. (State law requires an appropriation of retained earnings equal to cost of treasury stock.)

    In 1982, 10,000 preferred shares were authorized and the company issued 3,000 of them ($100 par value) at $104. Some of the preferred stock was reacquired by the company and later reissued for $3,750 more than it cost the company. In 1983 preferred stock was donated to the company and immediately resold for $18,900. (Use memo method.)

    The corporation has earned a total of $600,000 in net income after income taxes and paid out a total of $352,500 in cash dividends since incorporation. An appropriation was made in 1983 by the board of directors from retained earnings in the amount of $75,000 for Fixed Asset Replacements.

**Instructions**

    Prepare the stockholders' equity section of the balance sheet in proper form for Rob Russell Corporation as of December 31, 1983. Account for treasury stock using the cost method.

**P16-12** Chewy Gum Corp. has outstanding 2,000,000 shares of common stock of a par value of $10 each. The balance in its retained earnings account at January 1, 1983, was $24,000,000, and it then had Additional Paid-in Capital of $5,000,000. During 1983 the company's net income was $5,400,000. A cash dividend of 40¢ a share was paid June 30, 1983, and a 10% stock dividend was distributed to stockholders of record at the close of business on December 31, 1983. You have been asked to advise on the proper accounting treatment of the stock dividend.

    The existing stock of the company is quoted on a national stock exchange. The market price of the stock has been as follows:

| | |
|---|---|
| October 31, 1983 | $22 |
| November 30, 1983 | 24 |
| December 31, 1983 | 29 |
| Average price over the two-month period | 26 |

**Instructions**

    (a) Prepare a journal entry to record the cash dividend.

    (b) Prepare a journal entry to record the stock dividend.

    (c) Prepare the stockholders' equity section (including schedules of retained earnings and additional paid-in capital) of the balance sheet of the Chewy Gum Corp. for the year 1983 on the basis of the foregoing information. Draft a note to the financial statements setting forth the basis of the accounting for the stock dividend and add separately appropriate comments or explanations regarding the basis chosen.

**P16-13** On December 15, 1983, the directors of Mike McEllen Corporation voted to appropriate $75,000 of retained earnings and to retain in the business assets equal to the appropriation for use in expanding the corporation's factory building. This was the fourth of such appropriations; after it was recorded, the stockholders' equity section of McEllen's balance sheet appeared as follows:

Stockholders' equity:

| | | |
|---|---:|---:|
| Common stock, $10 par value, 250,000 shares | | |
| authorized, 200,000 shares issued and outstanding | | $2,000,000 |
| Paid-in capital in excess of par | | 3,400,000 |
| Total paid-in capital | | 5,400,000 |
| Retained earnings— | | |
| Unappropriated | $1,300,000 | |
| Appropriated for plant expansion | 300,000 | |
| Total retained earnings | | 1,600,000 |
| Total stockholders' equity | | $7,000,000 |

On January 9, 1984, the corporation entered into a contract for the construction of the factory addition for which the retained earnings were appropriated. On November 1, 1984, the addition was completed and the contractor paid the contract price of $287,500.

On December 14, 1984, the board of directors voted to return the balance of the Retained Earnings Appropriated for Plant Expansion account to Unappropriated Retained Earnings. They also voted a 25,000 share stock dividend distributable on January 23, 1985 to the January 15, 1985 stockholders of record. The corporation's stock was selling at $34 in the market on December 14, 1984. McEllen reported net income for 1983 of $400,000 and for 1984 of $500,000.

**Instructions**

(a) Prepare the appropriate journal entries for McEllen Corporation for the information above (December 15, 1983 to January 23, 1985, inclusive).

(b) Prepare the stockholders' equity section of the balance sheet for McEllen at December 31, 1984 in proper accounting form.

**P16–14** The stockholders' equity section of Ellen Odom Mfg. Company balance sheet on January 1 of the current year is as follows:

| | | |
|---|---:|---:|
| Paid-in Capital | | |
| Common stock, par $50, 20,000 shares authorized, | | |
| 15,000 shares issued | $750,000 | |
| Paid-in capital in excess of par | 225,000 | |
| Total paid-in capital | | $ 975,000 |
| Retained Earnings: | | |
| Unappropriated | $300,000 | |
| Appropriated for plant expansion | 150,000 | |
| Appropriated for treasury stock | 70,000 | |
| Total retained earnings | | 520,000 |
| | | $1,495,000 |
| Less cost of treasury stock (1,000 shares) | | 70,000 |
| Total stockholders' equity | | $1,425,000 |

The following selected transactions occurred during the year:

1. Paid cash dividends of $1.30 per share on the common stock. The dividend had been properly recorded when declared last year. (State law prohibits cash or stock dividends on treasury shares.)

2. Declared a 5% stock dividend on the common stock when the shares were selling at $87 each in the market.

3. Made a prior period adjustment to correct an error of $70,000 (net of tax) which overstated net income in the previous year. The error was the result of an overstatement of ending inventory. The applicable tax rate was 30%.

4. Sold all of the treasury shares for $92,000.

5. Issued the certificates for the stock dividend.

6. The board appropriated $65,000 of retained earnings for plant expansion, eliminated the appropriation for treasury stock, and declared a cash dividend of $1.65 per share on the common stock.

7. The company reported net income of $162,500 for the year.

**Instructions**

(a) Prepare journal entries for the selected transactions above (ignore income taxes).

(b) Prepare a retained earnings statement for the current year.

**P16-15** The Shlee Company was formed on July 1, 1980. It was authorized to issue 200,000 shares of $5 par value common stock and 50,000 shares of 6 percent $10 par value, cumulative and nonparticipating preferred stock. Shlee Company has a July 1–June 30 fiscal year.

The following information relates to the stockholders' equity accounts of Shlee Company.

*Common Stock*

Prior to the 1982–83 fiscal year, Shlee Company had 105,000 shares of outstanding common stock issued as follows:

1. 95,000 shares were issued for cash on July 1, 1980, at $20 per share.

2. On July 24, 1980, 5,000 shares were exchanged for a plot of land which cost the seller $70,000 in 1974 and had an estimated market value of $130,000 on July 24, 1980.

3. 5,000 shares were issued on March 1, 1982; the shares had been subscribed for $32 per share on October 31, 1981.

During the 1982–83 fiscal year, the following transactions regarding common stock took place:

| | |
|---|---|
| October 1, 1982 | Subscriptions were received for 10,000 shares at $40 per share. Cash of $80,000 was received in full payment for 2,000 shares and stock certificates were issued. The remaining subscriptions for 8,000 shares were to be paid in full by September 30, 1983, at which time the certificates were to be issued. |
| November 30, 1982 | Shlee purchased 2,000 shares of its own stock on the open market at $38 per share. Shlee uses the cost method for treasury stock. |
| December 15, 1982 | Shlee declared a 2 percent stock dividend for stockholders of record on January 15, 1983, to be issued on January 31, 1983. Shlee was having a liquidity problem and could not afford a cash dividend at the time. Shlee's common stock was selling at $43 per share on December 15, 1982. |
| June 20, 1983 | Shlee sold 500 shares of its own common stock that it had purchased on November 30, 1982, for $21,000. |

*Preferred Stock*

Shlee issued 30,000 shares of preferred stock at $15 per share on July 1, 1982.

*Cash Dividends*

Shlee has followed a schedule of declaring cash dividends in December and June with payment being made to stockholders of record in the following month. The cash dividends which have been declared since inception of the company through June 30, 1983, are shown below:

| Declaration Date | Common Stock | Preferred Stock |
|---|---|---|
| 12/15/81 | $.10 per share | $.30 per share |
| 6/15/82 | $.10 per share | $.30 per share |
| 12/15/82 | — | $.30 per share |

No cash dividends were declared during June 1983 due to the company's liquidity problems.

*Retained Earnings*

As of June 30, 1982, Shlee's retained earnings account had a balance of $370,000. For the fiscal year ending June 30, 1983, Shlee reported net income of $20,000.

In March of 1982, Shlee received a term loan from Union National Bank. The bank requires Shlee to establish a sinking fund and restrict retained earnings for an amount equal to the sinking fund deposit. The annual sinking fund payment of $40,000 is due on April 30 each year; the first payment was made on schedule on April 30, 1983.

## Instructions

Prepare the stockholders' equity section of the Statement of Financial Position, including appropriate notes, for Shlee Company as of June 30, 1983, as it should appear in its annual report to the shareholders.

(CMA adapted)

**P16-16** On June 30, 1983, the stockholders' equity section of the balance sheet of Carefree Clothes Company, Inc., appears as follows:

Stockholders' equity

| | | | |
|---|---|---|---|
| 6% cumulative preferred stock | | | |
| Authorized and issued, 2,000 shares | | | |
| of $100 par value | $200,000 | | |
| Common stock | | | |
| Authorized 20,000 shares of $50 par value, | | | |
| issued, 10,400 shares | 520,000 | $720,000 | |
| Retained earnings (deficit) | | (140,000) | $580,000 |

A footnote to the balance sheet points out that preferred stock dividends are in arrears in the amount of $48,000.

At a stockholders' meeting, a new group of officers was voted into power, and a quasi reorganization plan proposed by the new officers was accepted by the stockholders. The terms of this plan are as follows:

1. Preferred stockholders to cancel their claim against the corporation for accrued dividends.
2. The par value of the common stock to be reduced from $50 a share to $20 in order to create "capital in excess of par."
3. Certain depreciable properties and inventories owned by the company to be revalued downward $100,000 and $30,000, respectively.
4. The deficit to be written off against capital in excess of par created by reduction of the par value of common stock.

## Instructions

(a) Assuming that the various steps in the reorganization plan are carried out as of June 30, prepare journal entries to record the effect of the reorganization.
(b) Assuming that the company earns a net income of $50,000 for the year ended June 30, 1984, prepare the net worth section of the balance sheet as of that date.

# CHAPTER 17

# Dilutive Securities and Earnings Per Share Calculations

The urge to merge that predominated the business scene in the 1960s has developed into merger mania in the early 1980s.[1] One consequence of heavy merger activity is an increase in the use of dilutive securities such as convertible bonds, convertible preferred stocks, stock warrants, and contingent shares. **Dilutive securities** are defined as securities that, although they are not common stock in form, enable their holders to obtain common stock upon exercise or conversion. A reduction in earnings per share often results when these securities become common stock. For example, during the sixties, corporate officers recognized that the issuance of these types of securities in a merger did not have the same immediate adverse effect on earnings per share as the issuance of common stock. In addition, many companies found that issuance of convertible securities did not seem to upset common stockholders, even though when these securities were later converted or exercised the common stockholders' interests were substantially diluted. For these reasons, different terms such as "funny money" were coined to indicate the peculiar nature of these types of securities and the unusual tricks that could be played on the uninformed investor.

The merger movement of the 1980s is somewhat different. Unlike the go-go years of the late 1960s, when mergers were often consummated as a means to increase earnings per share, the 1980 mergers appear to be based on a more substantive rationale. There are many reasons for merger mania in the 1980s. Among them the following are significant: (1) the federal government's attitude is not hostile to mergers, (2) financial institutions have developed sophisticated means of providing credit for acquisitions, (3) many owners of privately held companies wish to sell to acquire personal liquidity, and (4) it is believed that it is cheaper to buy rather than build, particularly when corporate equity securities are considered undervalued.[2]

---

[1]The late 1960s and early 1980s appear to be heavy merger periods. For example, in 1968 there were approximately 1,822 mergers; in 1981, there were 2,314 such transactions. As an illustration of the dramatic increase in the significance in merger activities in the 1980s, total dollar volume of mergers in 1975 was approximately $11.8 billion; in 1981 it was approximately $70 billion, nearly a 500% increase.

[2]For example, DuPont's stunning acquisition of Conoco, Inc. highlights some of the major incentives for mergers in the 1980s. Encouraged by the federal government's friendly attitude toward mergers, not only DuPont, but also Mobil, Seagram, and others attempted to purchase Conoco, which was considered undervalued in the stock market by these companies. Conoco's stock, which

As a consequence of this step-up in merger activity, the use of dilutive securities is again on the increase. Also increasing is the usage of certain forms of compensation packages such as stock option plans, which are dilutive in nature. These plans are used mainly to attract and retain executive talent and to provide tax relief for executives in high tax brackets.

The widespread use of different types of dilutive securities has led the accounting profession to examine the accounting in this area closely. Specifically, the profession has directed its attention to accounting for these securities at date of issuance and to the presentation of earnings per share figures that recognize the effect of these dilutive securities. The following discussion includes consideration of convertible securities, warrants, stock options, and contingent shares.

# SECTION 1 DILUTIVE SECURITIES AND COMPENSATION PLANS

## ACCOUNTING FOR CONVERTIBLE DEBT

If bonds can be converted into other securities of the corporation during some specified period of time after issuance, they are called convertible bonds. A **convertible bond** combines the benefits of a bond with the privilege of exchanging it for stock at the holder's option. This security is purchased by investors who desire the security of a bond holding, but want the added option of conversion if the value of the stock appreciates significantly.

Corporations issue convertibles for two main reasons. One is the desire to raise equity capital that, assuming conversion, will arise when the original debt is converted. To illustrate, assume that a company wants to raise $1,000,000 at a time when its common stock is selling at $45 per share. Such an issue would require sale of approximately 22,222 shares (ignoring issue costs). By selling 1,000 bonds at $1,000 par, each convertible into 20 shares of common stock, the enterprise may raise $1,000,000 by committing only 20,000 shares of its common stock. Most studies of convertible bonds indicate that the main purpose of issuing these securities has been to obtain common stock financing at cheaper rates.[3]

A second reason why companies issue convertible securities is that many enterprises could issue debt only at high interest rates unless a convertible covenant were attached. The conversion privilege entices the investor to accept a lower interest rate than would normally be the case on a straight debt issue. To illustrate, a company might have to pay 15% for a

---

was selling for less than $50 in early 1981, spurted to over $100 a share by July. In a short period of time, as much as $20 billion in standby letters of credit were arranged by the financial community to aid potential buyers. As indicated above, DuPont was the eventual winner of this sweepstakes, acquiring Conoco for over $6.82 billion.

[3]See, for example, James C. Pilcher, *Raising Capital with Convertible Debentures,* Michigan Business Studies (Ann Arbor: University of Michigan, Bureau of Business Research, 1955), pp. 60–61.

straight debt obligation but it can issue a convertible at 9%. For this lower interest rate, the investor receives the right to buy the company's common stock at a fixed price until maturity, which is often 10 to 20 years.[4]

The method for recording convertible bonds follows that used in recording straight debt issues. Any discount or premium resulting from the issuance of convertible bonds is amortized on the basis of the maturity date, because it is difficult to predict when, if at all, conversion will occur.

If bonds are converted into other securities, the principal accounting problem is the determination of the amount at which to record the securities exchanged for the bond. For example, Hilton, Inc., issued at a premium of $60 a $1,000 bond convertible into 10 shares of common stock (par value $10). At the time of conversion the unamortized premium is $50, the market value of the bond is $1,200, and the stock is quoted on the market at $120. Two possible methods of determining the issue price of the stock could be used.

1. The market price of the stocks or bonds, $1,200.
2. The book value of the bonds, $1,050.

## Market Value Approach

Recording the stock issued at the **market price** of the stock or bond offers a theoretically sound way to measure the price at which to record the transaction. If 10 shares of common stock could be sold for $1,200, paid-in capital in excess of par of $1,100 should be recorded. Since at the time of sale bonds having a book value of $1,050 are converted, a loss on the conversion of the bonds of $150 occurs. The entry would be:

| | | |
|---|---|---|
| Bonds Payable | 1,000 | |
| Premium on Bonds Payable | 50 | |
| Loss on Redemption of Bonds Payable | 150 | |
| Common Stock | | 100 |
| Paid-in Capital in Excess of Par | | 1,100 |

The use of the market price of the bonds can be supported on similar grounds. If the market price of the stock is not determinable, but the bonds can be purchased at $1,200, a good argument can be made that the stock has an issue price of $1,200.

The weakness in using the fair market value of the stock or bonds is the assumption that a gain or loss can be incurred by the corporation as a result of an equity transaction. Whereas the conversion may be favorable or unfavorable to the existing stockholder group because an increase or decrease in their equity occurs, the corporate entity, as a whole, is unaffected. Because the conversion described above is initiated by the holder of the debt instrument (rather than the issuer), it is not an "early extinguishment of debt." As a result, the gain or loss would not be classified as an extraordinary item.

## Book Value Approach

From a practical point of view, if the market price of the stock or the market price of the bonds is not determinable, the **book value** of the bonds offers the best available measure-

---

[4]Convertible bonds have suddenly become much more popular. For example, convertible issues in 1981 were more than triple the number in 1980. Major reasons are that convertibles provide a safer way to play the equity market than outright purchase of common stock and that inflation has caused investors to be gun-shy of fixed rate long-term debt.

ment of the issue price. Also, many accountants contend that even if market quotations are available, they should not be used, inasmuch as the common stock is merely substituted for the bonds and should be recorded at the carrying amount of the bonds that were converted. Under this method, no gain or loss is recorded and the entry for the foregoing transaction of Hilton, Inc. would be:

| | | |
|---|---|---|
| Bonds Payable | 1,000 | |
| Premium on Bonds Payable | 50 | |
| Common Stock | | 100 |
| Paid-in Capital in Excess of Par | | 950 |

The book value method of recording convertible bonds has received the most widespread acceptance among practitioners.

### Retirement of Convertible Debt

A special problem relates to the retirement of convertible debt for cash. The question is whether the retirement of convertible debt is a debt transaction or an equity transaction. If it is a debt transaction, the difference between the carrying amount of the retired convertible debt and the cash paid should result in a charge or credit to income; if it is an equity transaction, the difference should presumably go to additional paid-in capital.

The method for recording the **issuance** of convertible bonds follows that used in recording straight debt issues. Specifically this means that no portion of the proceeds should be attributable to the conversion feature and credited to Additional Paid-in Capital. Although theoretical objections to this approach can be raised, to be consistent, a gain or loss on **retiring** convertible debt needs to be recognized in the same way as a gain or loss on **retiring** debt that is not convertible. For this reason, the profession concluded that differences between the cash acquisition price of debt and its carrying amount should be reported **currently in income as a gain or loss.**[5] As indicated in Chapter 14, material gains or losses on extinguishment of debt are considered extraordinary items.

Failure to recognize the equity feature of convertible debt when issued creates problems upon early extinguishment. To illustrate, assume that URL issues convertible debt at a time when the investment community attaches value to the conversion feature. Subsequently the price of URL stock decreases so sharply that the conversion feature has little or no value. If URL extinguishes their convertible debt early, a large gain develops because the book value of the debt will exceed the retirement price. Many accountants consider this treatment incorrect, because the reduction in value of the convertible debt relates to its equity features, not its debt features, and therefore an adjustment to Additional Paid-in Capital should be made. As indicated earlier, however, present practice requires that an extraordinary gain or loss be recognized at the time of early extinguishment.

## CONVERTIBLE PREFERRED STOCK

Convertible preferred stock is handled at the date of issue and at conversion in the same manner as convertible debt. The major difference in accounting for a convertible bond and

---

[5]"Early Extinguishment of Debt," *Opinions of the Accounting Principles Board No. 26* (New York: AICPA, 1972).

a convertible preferred stock is in the initial recording of the security investment. Convertible bonds are considered liabilities; convertible preferreds are considered a part of stockholders' equity.

In addition, when convertible preferred stocks are exercised, there is no theoretical justification for recognition of a gain or loss. **The book value method is employed** and Preferred Stock, along with any related Additional Paid-in Capital, is debited; Common Stock and Additional Paid-in Capital (if an excess exists) are credited. A different treatment develops when the par value of the common stock issued exceeds the book value of the preferred stock. In that case, Retained Earnings is usually debited for the difference.

To illustrate, Host Enterprises issued 1,000 shares of common stock (par value $2.00) upon conversion of 1,000 shares of preferred stock (par value $1.00) that was originally issued for a $200 premium. The entry would be:

| | | |
|---|---|---|
| Convertible Preferred Stock | 1,000 | |
| Paid-in Capital in Excess of Par (Premium on Preferred Stock) | 200 | |
| Retained Earnings | 800 | |
|     Common Stock | | 2,000 |

The rationale for the debit to Retained Earnings is that the preferred stockholders are offered an additional return to facilitate their conversion to common stock. The additional return is here charged to retained earnings. In many states, however, it is required that this charge simply reduce additional paid-in capital from other sources.

## STOCK WARRANTS

**Warrants** are certificates entitling the holder to acquire shares of stock at a certain price within a stated period. This option is similar to the conversion privilege because warrants, if exercised, become common stock and have usually a dilutive effect (reduce earnings per share) similar to that of the conversion of convertible securities. A substantial difference between convertible securities and stock warrants is that upon exercise of the warrants, the holder has to pay a certain amount of money to obtain the shares.

The issuance of warrants or options to buy additional shares normally arises under three situations.

1. When issuing different types of securities, such as bonds or preferred stock, warrants are often included to make the **security more attractive,** to provide an "equity kicker."
2. Upon the issuance of additional common stock, existing stockholders have a **preemptive right to purchase common stock** first. Warrants may be issued to evidence that right.
3. Warrants, often referred to as stock options, are given as **compensation to executives and employees.**

The problems in accounting for stock warrants are complex and present many difficulties. Many of the problems remain unresolved.

### Stock Warrants Issued with Other Securities

Warrants issued with other securities are basically long-term options to buy common stock at a fixed price. Although some perpetual warrants are traded, generally their life is five years, with a few up to ten years.

Here is an illustration of the way a warrant works: Tenneco offered a unit comprised of one share of stock and one detachable warrant exercisable at $24.25 per share and good for five years. The unit sold for 22¾ ($22.75) and, since the price of the common the day before the sale was 19⅞ ($19.88), it suggests a price of 2⅞ ($2.87) for the warrants.

In this situation, the warrants had an apparent value of 2⅞ ($2.87), even though it would not be profitable at present for the purchaser to exercise the warrant and buy the stock, because the price of the stock is much below the exercise price of $24.25.[6] The investor pays for the warrant to receive a possible future call on the stock at a fixed price when the price has risen significantly. For example, if the price of the stock rises to $30, the investor has gained $2.88 ($30 minus $24.25 minus $2.87) on an investment of $2.87, a 100% increase! Obviously, if the price does not rise, the investor loses the full $2.87.[7]

The profession requires that the proceeds from the sale of debt with **detachable stock warrants** be allocated between the two securities.[8] The profession takes the position that two separable instruments are involved, that is, (1) a bond and (2) a warrant giving the holder the right to purchase common stock at a certain price. Warrants that are detachable can be traded separately from the debt and, therefore, a market value can be determined. The allocation of the sale's proceeds between the two securities would be made on the basis of their relative fair market values soon after the date of issuance.

To illustrate, AT & T's offering of detachable five-year warrants to buy one share of common stock (par value $5) at $25 (at a time when a share was selling for approximately $50) enabled it to price its offering of bonds at par with a competitive 8¾% yield. In this situation, to place a value on the two securities one would determine (1) the value of the bonds without the warrants and (2) the value of the warrants. For example, assume that AT & T's bonds (par $1,000) sold for 99 without the warrants soon after they were issued. The market value of the warrants at that time was $30. Prior to sale the warrants will not have a market value. The allocation is based on an estimate of market value, generally as established by an investment banker or on the relative market value of the bonds and the warrants soon after they are issued and traded. The price paid for 10,000, $1,000 bonds with the warrants attached was par or $10,000,000. The allocation between the bonds and warrants would be made in this manner:

$$\frac{\text{Value of bonds without warrants}}{\text{Value of bonds without warrants} + \text{Value of warrants}} \times \text{Purchase price} = \text{Value assigned to bonds}$$

$$\frac{\$9,900,000}{\$9,900,000 + \$300,000} \times \$10,000,000 = \$9,705,883$$

[6]Later in this discussion it will be shown that the value of the warrant is normally determined on the basis of a relative market value approach because of the difficulty of imputing a warrant value in any other manner.

[7]Trading in warrants is often referred to as licensed gambling. From the illustration, it is apparent that buying warrants can be an "all or nothing" proposition.

[8]A detachable warrant means that the warrant can sell separately from the bond. *APB Opinion No. 14* makes a distinction between detachable and nondetachable warrants because nondetachable warrants must be sold with the security as a complete package; thus, no allocation is permitted.

$$\frac{\text{Value of warrants}}{\text{Value of bonds without warrants}} \times \text{Purchase price} = \text{Value assigned to warrants}$$
$$+ \text{ Value of warrants}$$

$$\frac{\$300,000}{\$9,900,000 + \$300,000} \times \$10,000,000 = \$294,117$$

In this situation the entries are:

| | | |
|---|---|---|
| Cash | 9,705,883 | |
| Discount on Bonds Payable | 294,117 | |
| Bonds Payable | | 10,000,000 |
| | | |
| Cash | 294,117 | |
| Paid-in Capital—Stock Warrants | | 294,117 |

(The entries may be combined if desired; they are shown separately here to indicate that the purchaser of the bond is buying not only a bond, but also a possible claim on common stock in the future.)

Assuming that the warrants are exercised one warrant per one share of stock, the following entry would be made:

| | | |
|---|---|---|
| Cash | 250,000 | |
| Paid-in Capital—Stock Warrants | 294,117 | |
| Common Stock | | 50,000 |
| Paid-in Capital in Excess of Par | | 494,117 |

If we assume, however, that the warrants are not exercised, Paid-in Capital—Stock Warrants is debited for $294,117 and Paid-in Capital from Expired Warrants is credited for a like amount. The additional paid-in capital reverts to the old stockholders.

The question arises whether the allocation of value to the warrants is consistent with the handling accorded convertible debt in which case no value is allocated to the conversion privilege. The Board stated that the features of a convertible security are **inseparable** in the sense that choices are mutually exclusive; the holder either converts or redeems the bonds for cash, but cannot do both. No basis, therefore, exists for recognizing the conversion value in the accounts. The Board, however, indicated that the issuance of bonds with **detachable warrants** involves two securities, one a debt security, which will remain outstanding until maturity, and the other a warrant to purchase common stock. At the time of issuance, separable instruments exist, and therefore separate treatment is justified. **Nondetachable warrants,** however, do not require an allocation of the proceeds between the bonds and the warrants, i.e., the entire proceeds are recorded as debt.

Many argue that the conversion feature is not significantly different in nature from the call represented by a warrant. The question is whether, although the legal forms are different, sufficient similarities of substance exist to support the same accounting treatment. Some contend that inseparability per se is not a valid basis for restricting allocation between identifiable components of a transaction. Examples of allocation between assets of value in a single transaction are not uncommon to the accountant's experience. To illustrate, such transactions as allocation of values in basket purchases, and separation of principal and interest in capitalizing long-term leases, indicate that the accountant has attempted to allocate values in a single transaction. To deny recognition of value to the conversion feature appears to be a recourse only to the form of the instrument and does not deal with the substance of the transaction. For example, debt with stock purchase warrants can have the essential attributes of a convertible bond—the warrants can be exercised and the debentures can be used as consideration for the exercise price.

In both situations (convertible debt and debt issued with warrants), the investor has made a payment to the firm for an equity feature, that is, the right to acquire an equity instrument in the future. The only real distinction between them is that the additional payment made when the equity instrument is formally acquired takes different forms. The warrant holder pays additional cash to the issuing firm; the convertible debt holder pays for stock by foregoing the receipt of interest from conversion date until maturity date and by foregoing the receipt of the maturity value itself. Thus, it is argued that the difference is one of method or form of payment only, rather than one of substance. **Until the profession officially reverses its stand in regard to accounting for convertible debt, however, only bonds issued with detachable stock warrants will result in accounting recognition of the equity feature.**

### Rights to Subscribe to Additional Shares

If the directors of a corporation decide to issue new shares of stock, the old stockholders generally have the right (preemptive privilege) to purchase newly issued shares in proportion to their holdings. The privilege, referred to as a **stock right,** saves existing stockholders from suffering a dilution of voting rights without their consent, and it may allow them to purchase stock somewhat below its market value. The warrants issued in these situations are of short duration, unlike the warrants issued with other securities.

The certificate representing the stock right states the number of shares the holder of the right may purchase, as well as the price at which the new shares may be purchased. Each share owned ordinarily gives the owner one stock right. The price is normally less than the current market value of such shares, thereby giving the rights a value in themselves. From the time they are issued until they expire, they may be purchased and sold like any other security.

No entry is required when rights are issued to existing stockholders. Only a memorandum entry is needed to indicate the number of rights issued to existing stockholders and to insure that the company has additional unissued stock registered for issuance in case exercise of the rights occurs.

If the rights are exercised, usually a cash payment of some type is involved. If the cash received is equal to the par value, an entry crediting Common Stock at par value is made. If it is in excess of par value, a credit to Paid-in Capital in Excess of Par develops; if it is less than par value, a charge to Paid-in Capital is appropriate.

## STOCK COMPENSATION PLANS

Another form of the warrant arises in stock compensation plans used to compensate employees. Stock compensation plans are usually defined as arrangements to issue stock to officers and employees as a group or individually. A common type of warrant is a stock option plan where **selected** employees are given the option to purchase common stock at a given price over an **extended period of time.** Other types of options exist also, such as the right to receive cash or stock if certain performance criteria are met in the future. In addition, a common type of warrant develops in a stock purchase plan, where **all** employees are given the option to purchase stock at a given price over a **short period of time.**

For accounting purposes, stock option plans are usually considered compensatory—stock purchase plans are usually classified as noncompensatory.[9] **Compensatory** means that the plan was intended to compensate the employees; **noncompensatory** means that the primary purpose was not intended to compensate the employees, but rather to allow the employer to secure equity capital or to induce widespread ownership of an enterprise's common stock among employees. Specifically, the profession has concluded that non-compensatory plans have the following characteristics:

1. Participation by all employees who meet limited employment qualifications.
2. Equal offers of stock to all eligible employees.
3. Limitation of time permitted for exercise of an option or purchase right to a reasonable period.
4. Discount from the market price of the stock no greater than would be reasonable in an offer of stock to stockholders or others.[10]

For example, IBM has a stock purchase plan under which employees who meet minimal employment qualifications are entitled to purchase IBM stock at a 15% reduction from market price for a short period of time. Such a reduction from market price is not considered compensatory because the employer's objectives appear to be either to raise additional equity capital or to expand ownership of the enterprise's stock among the employees as a means of enhancing loyalty to the enterprise. This position is debatable because the employee is receiving a valuable fringe benefit. However, because it is difficult to determine the company's objectives, in practice, if the discount is in the amount of 10–15% of the market price, the foregoing type of stock purchase plan is considered noncompensatory. **It should be emphasized that plans that do not possess all of the above mentioned four characteristics are classified as compensatory.**

## Accounting for Stock Compensation Plans

Accounting for noncompensatory plans poses no practical difficulties for accountants because compensation expense is not recorded by the employer corporation. The exercise of the option to purchase shares of stock is simply accounted for as the normal issue of stock with stockholders' equity increased by the amount of the option price. Compensatory plans, however, present more difficulties. The three questions to be resolved are as follows:

1. How should compensation expense be determined?
2. Over what periods should compensation expense be allocated?
3. What types of plans are used to compensate officers and key executives?

[9]Plans in which employees pay cash, either directly or through payroll withholding, as all or a significant part of the consideration for stock they receive, are commonly referred to as stock option, stock purchase, or stock thrift or savings plans. Plans in which employees receive stock for current or future services without paying cash (or with a nominal payment) are commonly referred to as stock bonus or stock award plans. Stock bonus and award plans are invariably compensatory. Stock thrift and savings plans are compensatory to the extent of contributions of an employer corporation. Stock option and purchase plans may be either compensatory or noncompensatory.

[10]"Accounting for Stock Issued to Employees," *Opinions of the Accounting Principles Board No. 25* (New York: AICPA, 1972), par. 7.

**Determination of Compensation Expense**   Total compensation expense is computed as the difference between the market price of the stock and the option price on the **measurement date.** The measurement date is the first date on which are known both (1) the number of shares that an individual employee is entitled to receive and (2) the option or purchase price, if any. The measurement date for many plans is the date an **option is granted** to an employee. The measurement date may be later than the date of grant in plans with variable terms (either number of shares or option price or both not known) that depend on events after date of grant. Usually the measurement date for plans with variable terms is the date of exercise.

If the number of shares or the option price or both are not known, compensation expense may have to be estimated on the basis of assumptions as to what will be the final number of shares and the option price.

**Allocation of Compensation Expense**   Compensation expense is recognized in the period(s) in which the **employee performs the services.** The total compensation expense is determined at the measurement date and allocated to the appropriate periods benefited by the employee's services. In practice, it is often difficult to specify the period of service, and considerable judgment is exercised in this determination. The general rule followed is that any method that is systematic and rational is appropriate, if the periods of service cannot be clearly defined. Assuming the measurement date is the date of grant, many enterprises recognize the compensation expense over an arbitrary period; others amortize it from the grant date to the date the option may be first exercised; and others record it as a current expense.

**If the measurement date is later than the date of grant,** the employer corporation should record the compensation expense each period from date of grant to the measurement date based on the market price of the stock at the end of each period.

**Types of Plans**   Many different types of plans are used to compensate key executives. Common to all these plans is that the amount of the reward is dependent upon future events. Consequently, continued employment is a necessary element in almost all types of plans. The popularity of a given plan usually depends on prospects in the stock market and tax considerations. For example, if it appears that appreciation will occur in a company's stock, a plan that offers the option to purchase stock is attractive to an executive. Conversely, if it appears that price appreciation is unlikely, then compensation might be tied to some performance measure such as an increase in book value or earnings per share. Three common plans that illustrate different accounting issues are:

1. Stock option plans (incentive or nonqualified).
2. Stock appreciation rights plans.
3. Performance type plans.

### Stock Option Plans

A stock option plan can be either an **incentive stock option plan** or a **nonqualified (or nonstatutory) option plan.** The distinction between an incentive and a nonqualified stock option plan is based on the IRS Code and relates to the tax treatment afforded the plan.

**From the perspective of the executive,** the incentive stock option provides greater tax advantages. In these plans, an executive pays no tax on the difference between the market price of the stock and the option price when the stock is purchased. Subsequently, when the shares are sold, the executive pays only a tax of 20% (capital gains rate) on the difference between the purchase price (option price) and the sale proceeds. Conversely, an executive who receives a nonqualified stock option must pay taxes, usually at a 50% rate, on the difference between the market price of the stock and the option price at the time the stock is purchased.

**From the perspective of the company,** the nonqualified option plan provides greater tax advantages. No tax deduction is received in an incentive stock option plan, whereas in a nonqualified stock option plan the company receives a tax deduction equal to the difference between the market price and option price at the date the employee purchases the stock. To illustrate, assume that Hubbard, Inc. grants options to purchase 10,000 shares at an option price of $10 when the current market price of the stock is $10; the shares are purchased at a time when the market price is $20; and, the executive sells the shares one year later at $20. A comparison of the effect of both plans on the executive and on the company is as follows:

|  | Incentive Stock Option | Nonqualified Stock Option |
|---|---|---|
| **Effect on Executive:** | | |
| (assuming 50% tax bracket) | | |
| Profit on exercise (10,000 × ($20 − $10)) | $100,000 | $100,000 |
| Tax on exercise ($100,000 × 50%) | -0- | $ 50,000 |
| Tax on sale ($100,000 × 20%[a]) | $ 20,000 | -0- |
| After tax benefit | $ 80,000 | $ 50,000 |
| **Effect on Company:** | | |
| (assuming 40% corporate rate) | Zero tax deduction resulting in no tax benefit. | $100,000 tax deduction resulting in a $40,000 tax benefit. |
| [a]Tax rate on capital gains. | | |

In effect, the executive in Hubbard, Inc.'s case would receive an $80,000 benefit with an incentive stock option, but only a $50,000 benefit with a nonqualified plan. Conversely, the company receives no benefit from an incentive stock option, but a $100,000 tax deduction (which becomes a $40,000 tax benefit) for the nonqualified stock option.

**Incentive Stock Option Plans**   Why then would any company want to issue incentive stock options? The major reason is that they want to attract high quality personnel, and many companies believe that incentive stock options are a greater attraction. These incentive stock options are particularly helpful to smaller high technology types of enterprises that have little cash and perhaps so little taxable income that the tax deduction is therefore not helpful to the company. Granting such options helps them attract and retain key personnel for whom they must compete against larger, established companies.

In an incentive stock option plan the tax laws require that the market price of the stock and the option price at the date of grant must be equal in order for the executive to be able to take advantage of the tax benefit (that is, the 20% capital gains tax rate). The tax laws do not require this equality in nonqualified plans. **No compensation expense is, therefore, recorded for an incentive stock option** because no excess of market price over the option price exists at the date of grant (the measurement date in this case).

**Nonqualified Stock Option Plans** **Nonqualified option plans usually involve compensation** expense because the market price exceeds the option price **at the date of grant** (the measurement date). Total compensation cost is measured by this difference and then allocated to the periods benefited. The option price is set by the terms of the grant and generally remains the same throughout the option period. The market price of the shares under option, however, may vary materially in the extended period during which the option is outstanding.

To illustrate the accounting for a nonqualified plan, assume that on November 1, 1982, the stockholders of Scott Company approve a plan that grants the company's five executives options to purchase 2,000 shares each of the company's $1.00 par value common stock. The options are granted on January 1, 1983, and may be exercised at any time within the next ten years. The option price per share is $60, and the market price of the stock at the date of grant is $70 per share. The total compensation expense is computed as follows. (Note that January 1, 1983 is the measurement date because the number of shares each executive can purchase and the option price are known on this date.)

| | |
|---|---:|
| Market value of 10,000 shares at date of grant ($70 per share) | $700,000 |
| Option price of 10,000 shares at date of grant ($60 per share) | 600,000 |
| Total compensation expense | $100,000 |

As indicated earlier, the profession requires that the value of the option be recognized as an expense in the period(s) in which the employee performs services. In the case of Scott Company, assume that documents associated with issuance of the options indicate that the expected period of benefit is two years, starting with the grant date. The entry to record the total compensation expense at the date of grant is as follows:

| | | |
|---|---:|---:|
| Deferred Compensation Expense | 100,000 | |
| Paid-in Capital—Stock Options | | 100,000 |

The deferred compensation expense (a contra stockholders' equity account) then is amortized to expense over the period of service involved (two years).[11] The credit balance in the Paid-in Capital—Stock Options account is treated as an element of stockholders' equity (additional paid-in capital). An alternative to the entry above would be to record no formal entry at the date of grant, but accrue compensation expense at the end of each period as incurred. We will use the former approach for problem material because this method formalizes in the records the compensation element of these plans. On December 31, 1983, and on December 31, 1984, the following journal entry is recorded to recognize the compensation cost for the year attributable to the stock option plan.

| | | |
|---|---:|---:|
| Compensation Expense | 50,000 | |
| Deferred Compensation Expense | | 50,000 |

At December 31, 1983, the stockholders' equity section would be presented as follows, assuming that 1,000,000 shares were issued at $1.00 par value.

---

[11]The rationale for using a contra equity account is that deferred compensation expense represents an unearned compensation amount and is better reported as contra equity than as an asset.

| Stockholders' equity | | |
|---|---|---|
| Common stock, $1.00 par, 1,000,000 shares issued and outstanding | | $1,000,000 |
| Paid-in capital—stock options | $100,000 | |
| Less deferred compensation expense | 50,000 | 50,000 |
| Total stockholders' equity | | $1,050,000 |

If 20% or 2,000 of the 10,000 options were exercised on June 1, 1986 (three years and five months after date of grant), the following journal entry would be recorded:

| | | |
|---|---|---|
| Cash (2,000 × $60) | 120,000 | |
| Paid-in Capital—Stock Options (20% of $100,000) | 20,000 | |
| Common Stock (2,000 × $1.00) | | 2,000 |
| Paid-in Capital in Excess of Par | | 138,000 |

If the remaining stock options are not exercised before their expiration date, the balance in Paid-in Capital—Stock Options account should be transferred to a more properly titled paid-in capital account, such as Paid-in Capital from Expired Stock Options. The entry to record this transaction at the date of expiration would be as follows:

| | | |
|---|---|---|
| Paid-in Capital—Stock Options (80% of $100,000) | 80,000 | |
| Paid-in Capital from Expired Stock Options | | 80,000 |

The fact that a stock option is not exercised does not nullify the propriety of recording the costs of services received from the executives and attributable to the stock option plan. Under GAAP, compensation expense is, therefore, not adjusted upon expiration of the options. However, if a stock option is forfeited because **an employee fails to fulfill an obligation** (such as, leaves employment), the estimate of compensation expense recorded in current period should be adjusted (as a change in estimate). This change in estimate would be recorded by debiting Paid-in Capital–Stock Options and crediting Compensation Expense, thereby decreasing compensation expense in the period of forfeiture.

## Stock Appreciation Rights

One of the main advantages of a **nonqualified stock option** plan is that an executive may acquire shares of stock in the future having a market price substantially above the option price. A major disadvantage is that an executive must pay income tax on the difference between the market price of the stock and the option price at the **date of exercise.** This can be a big financial hardship for an executive who wishes to keep the stock (rather than sell it immediately) because the executive would have to pay not only income tax but the option price as well. Note that for **incentive stock options,** much the same problem exists; that is, the executive may have to borrow to finance the exercise price which leads to related interest costs.

One solution to this problem was the creation of **stock appreciation rights (SARs).** In this type of plan, the executive is given the right to receive **share appreciation,** which is defined as the excess of the market price of the stock at the date of exercise over a pre-established price. This share appreciation may be paid in cash, shares, or a combination of both. The major advantage of SARs is that the executive often does not have to make a cash outlay at the date of exercise, but receives a payment for the share appreciation which may be used to pay any related income taxes. Unlike a stock option plan, the shares that constitute the basis for computing the appreciation in a SARs plan are not issued; only cash or stock having a market value equivalent to the appreciation is awarded the executive.

As indicated earlier, the usual date for measuring compensation related to stock compensation plans is the date of grant. However, with SARs, the final amount of cash or shares (or a combination of the two) to be distributed is not known until the date of exercise and therefore total compensation cannot be measured until this date. Thus, the measurement date is the **date of exercise.**

How then should compensation expense be recorded during the interim periods from the date of grant to the date of exercise? Such a determination is not easy because it is impossible to know what total compensation cost will be until the date of exercise, and the service period will probably not coincide with the exercise date. In order to allocate the compensation expense to interim periods, it is necessary to assume that the best estimate of total compensation cost for the plan at any interim period is the difference between the current market price of the stock and option price multiplied by the number of stock appreciation rights outstanding. This total estimated compensation cost is then allocated over the service period to record an expense (or a decrease in expense if market price falls) in each period.[12] At the end of each interim period, total compensation expense reported to date should equal the percentage of the total service period that has elapsed multiplied by the estimated compensation cost. For example, if at an interim period the service period is 40% complete and total estimated compensation is $100,000, then total compensation expense reported to date should equal $40,000 ($100,000 times 40%).

When the exercise date is later than the service period, compensation expense should be adjusted each period in an amount sufficient to adjust total reported compensation expense to the estimated total compensation cost. In other words, after the service period elapses, compensation expense is adjusted whenever a change in the market price of the stock occurs in subsequent reporting periods until the rights expire or are exercised, whichever comes first.

Changes, either up or down, in the market value of those shares between the date of grant and the exercise date, therefore result in a change in the measure of compensation. Some periods will have credits to compensation expense if the quoted market price of the stock falls from one period to the next; the credit to compensation expense, however, cannot exceed previously recognized compensation expense. In other words, total compensation expense cannot be negative.

To illustrate, assume that American Hotels, Inc. establishes a SARs program on January 1, 1983 which entitles executives to receive cash at the date of exercise (anytime in the next five years) for the difference between the market price of the stock and the pre-established price of $10 on 10,000 SARs; the current market price of the stock is $13, and the service period runs for two years (1983–1984). The following schedule indicates the amount of compensation expense to be recorded each period, assuming that the executives hold the SARs for three years, at which time the rights are exercised.

---

[12]"Accounting for Stock Appreciation Rights and Other Variable Stock Option or Award Plans," *FASB Interpretation No. 28.* (Stamford, Conn.: FASB, 1978), par. 2.

| | | | | | | | | |
|---|---|---|---|---|---|---|---|---|
| | | **STOCK APPRECIATION RIGHTS** | | | | | | |
| | | **Schedule of Compensation Expense** | | | | | | |
| (1) | (2) | (3) | (4) | (5) | (6) | | | |
| | | Pre-established | Cumulative | | Compensation | | | |
| | Market | Price | Compensation | Percentage | Accrued | Expense | Expense | Expense |
| Date | Price | (10,000 SARs) | Recognizable[a] | Accrued[b] | to Date | 1983 | 1984 | 1985 |
| 12/31/83 | $13 | $10 | $30,000 | 50% | $ 15,000 | $15,000 | | |
| | | | | | 55,000 | | $55,000 | |
| 12/31/84 | 17 | 10 | 70,000 | 100% | 70,000 | | | |
| | | | | | (20,000) | | | $(20,000) |
| 12/31/85 | 15 | 10 | 50,000 | 100% | $ 50,000 | | | |

[a]Cumulative compensation for unexercised SARs to be allocated to periods of service.
[b]The percentage accrued is based upon a two-year service period (1983–1984).

In 1983, American Hotels would record compensation expense of $15,000 because 50% of the $30,000 total of compensation cost estimated at December 31, 1983 is allocable to 1983. In 1984, the market price increased to $17 per share; therefore, the additional compensation expense of $55,000 ($70,000 minus $15,000) was recorded. The SARs were held through 1985, during which time the stock decreased to $15. The decrease is recognized by recording a $20,000 credit to compensation expense and a debit to Liability Under Stock Appreciation Plan. Note that after the service period ends, since the rights are still outstanding, the rights are adjusted to market at December 31, 1985. Any such credit to compensation expense cannot exceed previous charges to expense attributable to that plan.

As the compensation expense is recorded each period, the corresponding credit should be to a liability account if the stock appreciation is to be paid in cash. If stock is to be issued, then a more appropriate credit would be to Paid-in Capital. The entry to record compensation expense in the first year, assuming that the SAR ultimately will be paid in cash, is as follows:

| | | |
|---|---|---|
| Compensation Expense | 15,000 | |
| Liability Under Stock Appreciation Plan | | 15,000 |

The liability account would be credited again in 1984 for $55,000 and debited for $20,000 in 1985 when the negative compensation expense is recorded. The entry to record the negative compensation expense is as follows:

| | | |
|---|---|---|
| Liability Under Stock Appreciation Plan | 20,000 | |
| Compensation Expense | | 20,000 |

At December 31, 1985 the executives receive $50,000; the entry removing the liability is as follows:

| | | |
|---|---|---|
| Liability Under Stock Appreciation Plan | 50,000 | |
| Cash | | 50,000 |

Because compensation expense is measured by the difference between market prices of the stock from period to period, multiplied by the number of SARs, compensation expense can increase or decrease substantially from one period to the next.

Many accountants are disturbed about the accounting for SARs because the amount of compensation expense to be reported each period is subject to fluctuations in the stock market. As some accountants have questioned, "Shouldn't earnings determine stock prices, rather than stock prices determine earnings?"[13] Even with this drawback, this type of plan is gaining in popularity because executives are required to make little, if any, cash outlay under these programs. For example, in the mid-1970s only about 20 top companies were using SARs; now approximately 75% of the largest 200 companies have a SARs plan and others are asking stockholders to approve these plans.

SARs are often issued in combination with compensatory stock options (referred to as **tandem** or **combination plans**) and the executive must then select which of the two sets of terms to exercise, thereby canceling the other. The existence of alternative plans running concurrently poses additional problems from an accounting standpoint because the accountant must determine, on the basis of the facts available each period, which of the two plans has the higher probability of exercise and then account for this plan, and ignore the other.

## Performance-Type Plans

Many executives have become disenchanted with stock compensation plans whose ultimate payment is a function of an increase in the market price of the common stock. This disenchantment arises because of the erratic behavior of the stock market, coupled with the belief by some executives that their level of work and the market price of the stock are not well correlated. As a result, there has been a substantial increase in the use of plans where executives receive common stock (or cash) if specified performance criteria are attained during the performance period (generally three to five years). For example, more than half of the largest 200 companies now have some type of plan that does not rely on stock price appreciation.

The **performance criteria** employed usually are increases in return on assets or equity, growth in sales, growth in earnings per share (EPS), or a combination of these factors. A good illustration of this type of plan is that of Atlantic Richfield, which offered performance units valued in excess of $700,000 to the chairman of the board. These performance units are payable in five years, contingent upon the company's meeting certain conditions regarding return on stockholders' equity and cash dividends. As another example, Honeywell uses growth in EPS as its performance criterion. When certain levels of EPS are achieved, shares of stock are issued to the executive. To illustrate, if the company achieves a cumulative average growth of 13% in annual EPS, the executive will earn 100% of the shares. The maximum allowable is 130%, which would require a 17% growth rate; below 9% the executives receive nothing.

A performance-type plan's measurement date is the date of exercise because the number of shares that will be issued or cash that will be paid out when performance is achieved are not known at the date of grant. The compensation cost is allocated to the periods involved in much the same manner as with stock appreciation rights. Tandem or combination awards are popular with these plans; that is, the executive has the choice of selecting between a performance or stock option award. For example, companies such as Bristol-

---

[13] For this reason, companies are reluctant to measure compensation expense other than at the date of grant for nonqualified option plans, because a very high compensation cost can develop that must be reported as an expense on the income statement. Few nonqualified option plans are, therefore, adopted where the measurement date is other than the date of the grant.

Myers, General Electric, Sperry, and Xerox, to name just a few, have recently adopted plans of this nature. In these cases the executive has the best of both worlds because if either the stock price increases, or the performance goal is achieved, the executive gains. In fact, in some plans the executive receives both types of plans, so that the monies received from the performance plan can finance the exercise price on the stock option plan.

## Conceptual Issues Involving Stock Compensation Plans

Much debate exists concerning the proper accounting and reporting for stock compensation plans. A number of these conceptual questions are discussed below.

**Alternate Dates**   What date should be used to measure total compensation cost? Many accountants favor the **date of grant** because the company forgoes an alternative use of shares on that date. Others believe that some other date such as the date the **option becomes exercisable** or the **date the option is exercised** is more appropriate. For example, the date the option becomes exercisable is favored by some because at that date the employee has performed the option contract, and the company is obligated to issue shares at the option price.

Others state that the excess of the market price over the option price at the date the option becomes exercisable is still an incomplete valuation that understates the value of the option, particularly when this option may be held for several years before expiring. They believe that only at the date that the option is exercised is the final value of the employee's services recognizable. In short, the commitment to transfer cash or stock to employees under a plan is only a contingency until the date of exercise, when the amount of the transfer will be known.

**Valuation**   A second issue relates to how the option should be valued, assuming the measurement date is the date of grant.

One group believes that an attempt should be made to value the **option** itself.[14] They note that an option to buy stock at a price equal to or below the market price has value and cannot be considered worthless. In addition, because there is no risk of loss to the executive and a possibility, if not a probability, of great gain, the option may possess value that is greater than the spread between the option price and the market price at the date of the grant. Similarly, others argue that although services are normally valued at the cost of the assets given in exchange for them, the **fair value of the services received** is also a proper and acceptable basis of valuation. Using this approach, an attempt is made to determine what type of cash trade-off the executives make when receiving an option for stock in lieu of a straight cash distribution. By imputing this cash trade-off, the total amount of compensation may be determined.

Others stress that the approaches described above are too subjective and argue for the approach adopted by the profession, namely, that compensation expense be measured by the difference between the market price and the option price at the **date of grant.** This argument is based on the premise that the only objective and verifiable amount that can be

---

[14] For an interesting discussion of an attempt to value options, see Clifford W. Smith, Jr. and Jerold L. Zimmerman, "Valuing Employee Stock Option Plans Using Option Pricing Models," *Journal of Accounting Research* (Autumn 1976), pp. 357–364.

determined at the date of grant is the spread between the market and option price. Many are unhappy with this latter approach because little or no compensation is recorded for many stock option plans (for example, incentive stock option plans report zero compensation expense).

Finally, it is sometimes argued that **no compensation expense should be reported** at all because no cost to the entity results from the issuance of additional shares of stock; the cost is to the stockholders in the possible dilution of their interest in the entity, and accountants should ignore this factor in their accounting. This does not appear to be a reasonable approach because a cost is involved to the existing stockholders which should be considered a cost of operating the enterprise.

**Disclosure of Compensation Plans**  The average compensation for the chief executive officers (CEOs) of the largest 800 companies was approximately $351,900 in the late 1970s. However, the compensation of some CEOs rivals the compensation paid entertainers like Burt Reynolds, Jane Fonda, Bob Hope, and so on. For example, one CEO recently received total compensation of $3,649,975 of which only $613,862 was in cash salary. As a result, it is not surprising that there is considerable interest in the amount and type of compensation paid these executives. For example, the following questions arise: Is the salary reasonable? Does the compensation package provide the proper types of incentives to executives? Will these plans lead to considerable dilution of existing stockholders' interests? Will these plans have an effect on corporate behavior?[15]

As indicated earlier, the answers to such questions are difficult because measurement of these plans is somewhat imprecise. Disclosure therefore plays an important role in helping users of the financial statements better understand these plans and their possible effects. Regardless of the basis used in valuing stock options, rights, and other types of awards, full disclosure should be made about the status of these plans at the end of the period, including the number of shares for which options or rights were exercised and are exercisable. An example on the following page taken from Bell & Howell Company's 1981 annual report illustrates how these plans are often disclosed in the financial statements.

# SECTION 2  COMPUTING EARNINGS PER SHARE

The practice of reporting earnings per share on outstanding common stock prior to the 1960s, while commonplace, was left to management's discretion. However, because of the importance of the earnings per share number, the Accounting Principles Board in *Opinion No. 15* required that earnings per share be disclosed in the statement of income.[16] In addi-

---

[15] For example, some writers have argued that management's reaction to proposed accounting standards is directly correlated to their own self-interest. If new standards would have a detrimental effect on their compensation package, the proposed standards will not be favored by this group. Ross L. Watts and Jerold L. Zimmerman, "Towards a Positive Theory of the Determination of Accounting Standards," *The Accounting Review,* January, 1978.

[16] "Earnings per Share," *Opinions of the Accounting Principles Board No. 15* (New York: AICPA, 1969).

tion, this pronouncement required two presentations of earnings per share on the income statement of companies with dilutive securities: (1) earnings per common and common equivalent shares and (2) fully diluted earnings per share.

This reporting requirement has been controversial. Some argue that the profession should not report earnings per share data. Others note that by presenting earnings per

---

**Note I—Common Stock and Incentive Stock Plans:**
Changes in Common Stock were as follows (dollars in thousands):

# Bell & Howell Company

| | 1981 | | 1980 | | 1979 | |
|---|---|---|---|---|---|---|
| | Shares | Amount | Shares | Amount | Shares | Amount |
| Issued at beginning of year | 5,837,511 | $40,726 | 5,783,478 | $39,573 | 5,769,319 | $39,358 |
| Held in treasury | (232,795) | (4,230) | (232,795) | (4,230) | (232,795) | (4,230) |
| Outstanding at beginning of year | 5,604,716 | 36,496 | 5,550,683 | 35,343 | 5,536,524 | 35,128 |
| Conversion of preferred shares | 1,681 | 115 | 132 | 9 | — | — |
| Incentive Stock Plans: | | | | | | |
| Options exercised | 14,607 | 248 | 53,901 | 886 | 14,159 | 195 |
| Federal income tax benefits and other | — | 52 | — | 258 | — | 20 |
| | 16,288 | 415 | 54,033 | 1,153 | 14,159 | 215 |
| Outstanding at end of year | 5,621,004 | $36,911 | 5,604,716 | $36,496 | 5,550,683 | $35,343 |

At the end of 1981, a total of 348,527 shares of authorized and unissued Common Stock were reserved for conversion of Preferred Stock or issuance under Incentive Stock Plans.

The Company's Incentive Stock Plans provide for stock appreciation rights along with related stock options. The rights are granted to senior executives and permit the holder, upon surrendering all or part of his related stock option, to receive cash, Common Stock, or both, of up to 100% of the difference between the market price and the option price, but not in excess of 50% of the option price. Shares covered by such surrendered stock option or portion thereof are not available for the grant of further stock options.

Proceeds from the sale of Common Stock issued under stock options granted and related federal tax benefits are credited to Common Stock at the time the option is exercised, and no charge is made against earnings with respect to stock options. Stock appreciation rights granted require a charge to earnings based upon the amount, if any, by which the fair market value of the Common Stock subject to related stock options exceeds the option price of such shares. The charges (credit) to earnings in 1981, 1980 and 1979 with respect to such rights were $(327,000), $178,000 and $374,000, respectively.

Transactions during 1981, 1980 and 1979 under Incentive Stock Plans were as follows:

| | 1981 | 1980 | 1979 |
|---|---|---|---|
| Shares under option at beginning of year | 225,262 | 271,386 | 236,754 |
| Options granted | 114,220 | 22,600 | 94,325 |
| Options and stock appreciation rights exercised | (14,607) | (53,901) | (14,159) |
| Surrendered upon exercise of stock appreciation rights | — | (6,010) | (4,240) |
| Canceled or expired | (10,300) | (8,813) | (41,294) |
| Shares under option at end of year | 314,575 | 225,262 | 271,386 |
| Shares available for future grants at end of year | 28,038 | 6,868 | 29,213 |
| Price range of shares under option at end of year (market value at date of grant) | $12.69 to $30.00 | $11.25 to $30.00 | $11.25 to $20.94 |

The 314,575 shares under option at the end of 1981 had an average exercise price of $20.69, the options were held by 222 officers and employees, and they expire at dates ranging from 1984 to 1991. Options for 122,738 shares, at prices ranging from $12.69 to $26.63 had related stock appreciation rights.

share adjusted for dilutive securities the one real fact available (earnings per outstanding shares) is not reported. In addition, many accountants are concerned that certain small companies are required to provide information not needed by those who make decisions about the companies; the required information is often costly to prepare and precludes providing other, more helpful information. As evidence of the concern, the FASB recently issued a discussion memorandum entitled "Financial Reporting by Private and Small Public Companies" in which the question of whether all enterprises should be required to report the same information is discussed. Until this study is completed, the FASB has chosen in *Statement No. 21*,[17] to suspend the reporting requirements related to earnings per share for nonpublic companies.[18]

## SIMPLE CAPITAL STRUCTURE

A corporation's capital structure is regarded as **simple** if it consists only of common stock or includes no potentially dilutive convertible securities, options, warrants, or other rights that upon conversion or exercise could in the aggregate dilute earnings per common share. A capital structure is regarded as **complex** if it includes securities that could have a dilutive effect on earnings per common share.

The appropriate presentation of earnings per share data for corporations having a simple capital structure is a **single presentation** expressed in terms such as "earnings per common share" on the face of the income statement. The computation of earnings per common share is as follows:

$$\frac{\text{Net Income} - \text{Preferred Dividends}}{\text{Weighted Average of Shares Outstanding}} = \text{Earnings Per Share}$$

**Dividends on preferred stock** (assuming it is a simple structure) should be subtracted from each of the intermediate components of income (income from continuing operations and income before extraordinary items) and finally from net income to arrive at income available to common stockholders at these various levels. If the preferred is cumulative and the dividend is not declared in the current year, an amount equal to the dividend that should have been declared for the **current year** only should be subtracted from net income. If cumulative preferred stock exists and a net loss occurs, the dividend requirement is added to the loss. Dividends in arrears for previous years should have been included in the previous years' computations.

---

[17]Suspension of the Reporting of Earnings per Share and Segment Information by Nonpublic Enterprises," *Statements of the Financial Accounting Standards Board No. 21* (Stamford, Conn.: FASB, 1978).

[18]A **nonpublic enterprise** is an enterprise other than one (1) whose debt or equity securities are traded in a public market on a foreign or domestic stock exchange or in the over-the-counter market (including securities quoted locally or regionally) or (2) that is required to file financial statements with the SEC. An enterprise is no longer considered a nonpublic enterprise when its financial statements are issued in preparation for the sale of any class of securities in a public market.

# WEIGHTED AVERAGE NUMBER OF SHARES

In all computations of earnings per share, the weighted average of shares outstanding during the period constitutes the basis for the per-share amounts reported. Shares issued or retired during a period are weighted by the fraction of the period in which they were outstanding. The weighted number of these shares is added to the number of shares outstanding for the entire period to obtain the weighted average number of shares outstanding during the period.

For example, assume that a corporation with 100,000 common shares outstanding on January 1 issued 6,000 additional common shares on March 1. The weighted average computed at different dates of the year would be as follows:

> For quarter ended March 31
> $\qquad$ 100,000 + 1/3 (6,000)    = 102,000 shares
> For six months ended June 30
> $\qquad$ 100,000 + 4/6 (6,000)    = 104,000 shares
> For nine months ended September 30
> $\qquad$ 100,000 + 7/9 (6,000)    = 104,667 shares
> For the year ended December 31
> $\qquad$ 100,000 + 10/12 (6,000) = 105,000 shares

Reacquired shares are included in the weighted average only for the time they were outstanding. For example, assume that a corporation with 100,000 shares outstanding on January 1 reacquired 6,000 shares on March 1. The weighted average at different dates of the year could be computed as follows:

> For quarter ended March 31
> $\qquad$ 94,000[a] + 2/3 (6,000) = 98,000 shares
> For six months ended June 30
> $\qquad$ 94,000 + 2/6 (6,000)   = 96,000 shares
> For nine months ended September 30
> $\qquad$ 94,000 + 2/9 (6,000)   = 95,333 shares
> For the year ended December 31
> $\qquad$ 94,000 + 2/12 (6,000) = 95,000 shares
>
> [a]100,000 − 6,000 = 94,000 shares outstanding for the full period

More complex methods of computing a weighted average may be used if the number of shares involved changes frequently. The sum of the shares outstanding each day divided by the number of days in the period would produce a precise average. The schedule on page 748 illustrates computation of a weighted average on a share-day basis. Ordinarily computations reflect outstanding shares to the nearest month.

| | COMPUTATION OF WEIGHTED AVERAGE NUMBER OF SHARES | | | |
|---|---|---|---|---|
| | Number of Shares | | | |
| Date | Increase (Decrease) | Outstanding | Days Outstanding | Share-days |
| January 1 | | 25,000 | 15[a] | 375,000 |
| January 16 | 1,000 | 26,000 | 78[b] | 2,028,000 |
| April 4 | 2,700 | 28,700 | 151 | 4,333,700 |
| September 2 | (1,500) | 27,200 | 47 | 1,278,400 |
| October 19 | 5,000 | 32,200 | 74 | 2,382,800 |
| | | | 365 | 10,397,900 |
| | | | A | B |
| | Weighted average number of shares outstanding (B ÷ A) = 28,487 | | | |

[a]Days between 1/1 and 1/16 that 25,000 shares were outstanding.
[b]Days between 1/16 and 4/4 that 26,000 shares were outstanding.

When **stock dividends, stock splits, or reverse splits** occur, computation of the weighted average number of shares requires restatement of the shares outstanding before the stock dividend or split. Stock dividends or splits are retroactive adjustments rather than transactions to be weighted by the number of days a stock dividend or split was outstanding. For example, assume that a corporation had 100,000 shares outstanding on January 1 and issued a 25% stock dividend on June 30. For purposes of computing a weighted average for the current year, the additional 25,000 shares outstanding as a result of the stock dividend are assumed to have been outstanding since the beginning of the year; the weighted average for the year would be 125,000 shares.

The issuance of a stock dividend or stock split is restated, but the issuance or repurchase of stock for cash is not. Why? The reason is that stock splits and stock dividends do not increase or decrease the net assets of the enterprise; only additional shares of stock are issued and, therefore, the weighted average shares for previous periods must be restated for comparison purposes. Conversely, the issuance or purchase of stock for cash changes the amount of net assets. As a result, the company either earns more or less in the future as a result of this change in net assets.

On a months outstanding basis a restatement due to a stock dividend is illustrated in the schedule shown at the top of page 749.

In this schedule, the month's outstanding column indicates the period of time that shares are outstanding for the year 1983. For example, from January 1 to January 31, 25,000 shares were outstanding for one month; from January 31 to April 1, 26,000 shares were outstanding for two months; from April 1 to September 1, 28,600 shares were outstanding for five months; and so on. When a stock dividend or stock split occurs, transactions prior to the dividend or split must be adjusted. In this example, the shares outstanding from January 1 to April 1 are adjusted for the stock dividend, so that these shares are stated on the same basis as shares issued subsequent to the stock dividend.

If a stock dividend or stock split occurs after the end of the year, but before the financial statements are issued, the weighted average number of shares outstanding for the prior

| | | Number of Shares | | | Share Months | |
|---|---|---|---|---|---|---|
| Date | Transaction | Increase (Decrease) | Outstanding | Months Outstanding | Original | Restated |
| January 1 | — | — | 25,000 | 1 (1/1–1/31) | 25,000 | 27,500[a] |
| January 31 | Issued for cash | 1,000 | 26,000 | 2 (1/31–4/1) | 52,000 | 57,200[a] |
| April 1 | 10% stock dividend | 2,600 | 28,600 | 5 (4/1–9/1) | | 143,000 |
| September 1 | Purchase of common stock | (1,500) | 27,100 | 2 (9/1–10/31) | | 54,200 |
| October 31 | Issued for cash | 5,000 | 32,100 | 2 (10/31–12/31) | | 64,200 |
| | | | | 12 | | 346,100 |
| | | | | A | | B |

COMPUTATION OF WEIGHTED AVERAGE NUMBER OF SHARES
WITH RESTATEMENT FOR STOCK DIVIDEND
1983

Weighted average number of shares outstanding (B ÷ A) = 28,842 (rounded)

[a]Restatement of 25,000 and 52,000 amounts by 10% stock dividend (April 1):

$$25,000 + .10(25,000) = 27,500; 27,500 \times 1 = 27,500$$
$$26,000 + .10(26,000) = 28,600; 28,600 \times 2 = 57,200$$

year (and any other years presented in comparative form) must be restated. The illustration above, for example, indicates 28,842 shares outstanding on a weighted average basis for 1983; if a 2 for 1 stock split (100% stock dividend) occurred January 10, 1984 (the next year), the shares outstanding on a weighted average basis for 1983 would be 57,684 (2 × 28,842). It should be noted that all problems in the textbook assume use of the months basis for computing weighted average rather than a weighted average on a share-day basis.

## COMPLEX CAPITAL STRUCTURES AND DILUTIVE SECURITIES

One problem with a simple EPS computation is that it fails to recognize the dilutive impact on outstanding stock when a corporation has dilutive securities in its capital structure. **Dilutive securities** present a serious problem in determining the proper earnings per share because upon conversion or exercise an adverse effect on earnings per share occurs. This adverse effect can be significant and, more importantly, unexpected unless financial statements call attention to the potential dilutive effect in some manner. Because of the increasing use of dilutive securities in the 1960s, the profession could no longer ignore the significance of these securities and, therefore, issued *APB Opinion No. 15* which developed the concept of a complex capital structure. A complex capital structure exists when a corporation has convertible securities, options, warrants or other rights that upon conversion or exercise could in the aggregate dilute earnings per share.

A complex capital structure requires a **dual presentation** of earnings per share, each with equal prominence on the face of the income statement. In accounting jargon these two presentations are referred to as "primary earnings per share" and "fully diluted earnings per share." **Primary earnings per share** is based on the number of common shares outstanding plus the shares referred to as common stock equivalents—securities that are in substance equivalent to common shares. **Fully diluted earnings per share** is a pro forma presentation that reflects the dilution of earnings per share that would have occurred if **all** contingent issuances of common stock that would have reduced earnings per share had taken place. Because of computational rules, fully diluted earnings per share will almost always be less (less income per share or more loss per share) than or equal to primary EPS.

In contrast to the formula for computing EPS for a simple capital structure, the following formula portrays the computation of EPS for a complex capital structure:

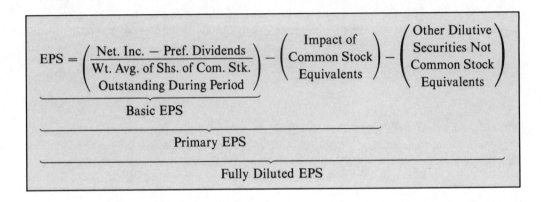

To provide relief from complex computations to corporations that have insignificant potential dilution, the profession adopted a **3% materiality test.** Any corporation whose capital structure has potential dilution of less than 3% of earnings per common share outstanding is considered to have a simple capital structure. Apparently, dilution of less than 3% is not considered to be material. To illustrate, Streeter Company has earnings per share of $2.00, ignoring all dilutive securities in its capital structure. If the possible conversion or exercise of the dilutive securities in the aggregate would reduce earnings per share to $1.94 or below (97% × $2.00), a presentation involving dilutive securities would be required. Otherwise the company reports earnings per share at $2.00 and no additional disclosure is required. In this case it is to be assumed that the weighted average number of shares is the basis and that potential dilution, if any exists, is less than 3%. **In computing the 3% dilution factor, the aggregate of all dilutive securities must be considered.** The dilutive securities are not considered individually, but in total.

### Primary Earnings Per Share

A primary earnings per share amount must be computed and presented for corporations having a complex capital structure. The basis for primary earnings per share is the outstanding common shares plus the common equivalent shares. If **no** common stock equivalents exist in a complex capital structure, the primary earnings per share is the same as the basic earnings per share for a simple capital structure; that is, net income less preferred dividends is divided by the weighted average number of common shares outstanding. For complex capital structures **with** common stock equivalents, however, an earnings per share figure that is based solely on common shares issued and outstanding is not reported.

## Common Stock Equivalents

A common stock equivalent is a security that, although not a common stock, gives its holder the right through conversion or exercise to acquire shares of common stock. Its value tends to change with changes in the value of the common stock to which it is related. Only if common stock equivalents are dilutive, as opposed to antidilutive, are they added to common shares in computing primary earnings per share. **Antidilutive securities** are securities that would create an increase in earnings per share (or a reduction in net loss per share). Once a security is classified as a common stock equivalent, it is always a common stock equivalent; it enters into the computation of primary earnings per share, however, only if it is dilutive. That is, a common stock equivalent may enter into the computation in one period and not in another, depending on whether it is dilutive or antidilutive.

## Convertible Securities

Convertible securities should be considered common stock equivalents if the cash yield to the holder at the time of issuance is significantly below what would be the yield for a similar security of the issuer without the conversion option. Therefore, a convertible security, whether bonds or preferred stock, is a common stock equivalent if, at the time of issuance it has a **cash yield of less than 66⅔%** of the current average Aa corporate bond yield.[19] The term "cash yield" refers to the ratio of cash to be received by the investor in the first year after purchasing the investment to the price paid for the investment. The rationale for the cash yield test is that **the investor would not be willing to accept a cash yield less than ⅔ of the average Aa corporate bond yield unless the convertible security contains significant common stock characteristics.** To illustrate this test, assume that Clayton Corp. had a convertible bond (face amount $1,000) with a coupon rate of 9% and a market price of $1,200. It would have a cash yield to the purchaser at **time of issuance** of 7.5% ($90/$1,200). If the average Aa corporate bond yield were 15% at the **date of issuance,** this security would be considered a common stock equivalent because the cash yield is less than ⅔ of the average Aa corporate bond yield:

$$⅔ \text{ of average Aa corporate bond yield rate of } 15\% = 10\%$$
$$\text{Cash yield} \qquad\qquad\qquad\qquad = 7.50\%$$

The cash yield test is an arbitrary rule but it provides a simple and objective criterion that is easily applied. There is a weakness in this approach, however. If market conditions change, the convertible may lose much of its apparent initial conversion value. This means that a company may have outstanding a convertible bond that has little possibility of conversion; yet, it may be classified as a common stock equivalent because at the date of issuance the investors placed a high value on the conversion option.

To be included in the computation of primary earnings per share, the conversion feature must be **exercisable within five years** of the date of the financial statement. Convertible securities initially exercisable only beyond five years but within ten years of the financial statement date and all other convertible securities not included in primary earnings per share computations (because they are not common stock equivalents) are included in fully diluted earnings per share.

---

[19]"Determining Whether a Convertible Security is a Common Stock Equivalent," *Statement of Financial Accounting Standards No. 55* (Stamford, Conn.: FASB, 1982), par. 7.

## "If Converted" Method

In computing earnings per share amounts for both the primary and the fully diluted earnings per share with convertible securities, the "if converted" method is used. The "if converted" approach computes earnings per share by assuming (1) the conversion of convertible securities at the beginning of the period (or time of issuance of the security, if issued during the period), and (2) the elimination of the related interest charges net of tax or not deducting preferred dividends in arriving at income available to common stockholders.

As an example, Marshy Field Corporation has net income for the year of $210,000 and a weighted average number of common shares outstanding during the period of 100,000 shares. The company has two convertible debenture bond issues outstanding. One is a 6% issue sold at 100 (total $1,000,000) in a prior year when the average Aa corporate bond yield was 11% and convertible into 20,000 common shares. The other is a 10% issue sold at 100 (total $1,000,000) on April 1 of the current year when the average Aa corporate bond yield was 11% and convertible into 32,000 common shares. Assume that the tax rate at present is 50%.

| COMPUTATION OF PRIMARY EARNINGS PER SHARE | | | |
|---|---|---|---|
| Net income for the year | $210,000 | Average number of shares outstanding | 100,000 |
| Add: Adjustment for interest (net of tax) on 6% debentures | 30,000 | Add: Shares assumed to be issued upon conversion of 6% debentures as of the beginning of | |
| Adjusted net income | $240,000 | the year | 20,000 |
| | A | | |
| | | Average number of common and common equivalent shares | 120,000 |
| | | | B |
| PRIMARY EARNINGS PER SHARE (A ÷ B) $2.00 | | | |

The primary earnings per share calculation includes only one dilutive security—the 6% convertible debentures. The 6% yield rate at date of issue is less than ⅔ of the average Aa corporate bond yield of 11%. The 10% convertible is not considered in the primary earnings per share calculation because the cash yield (10%) at date of issue was higher than ⅔ of the average Aa corporate bond yield (⅔ × 11% = 7⅓%). To determine the adjusted net income, interest on the "if converted" securities less the related tax effect must be added back. Because the "if converted" method assumes conversion as of the beginning of the year, it is only logical and consistent to assume that the related interest or dividends on the convertibles would not have been paid during the year. The elimination of $60,000 tax deductible interest expense would result in a $30,000 increase in income taxes, and only the net addition to income of $30,000 would have been available to common stockholders.

Note that if the dilutive 6% convertible debentures were instead dilutive 6% convertible preferreds, the preferred dividend would not be deducted from net income to arrive at income available to common stockholders. In this case it is assumed that the convertible preferred has been converted and is considered outstanding common stock for purposes of computing EPS. No tax effect would be considered because preferred dividends are not deductible for tax purposes.

Fully diluted earnings per share includes not only the 6% debentures but also the 10% debentures. The interest charges (net of tax) for both issuances are added back to arrive at adjusted net income. Note also that a weighted average determination is made of the number of shares outstanding. Because the date of issuance is subsequent to the beginning of the year in the case of the 10% convertibles, the shares assumed to have been issued on that date, April 1, are weighted as outstanding from then to the end of the period.

---

### COMPUTATION OF FULLY DILUTED EARNINGS PER SHARE

| | | | |
|---|---:|---|---:|
| Net income for the year | $210,000 | Average number of common shares outstanding | 100,000 |
| Add: Adjustment for interest (net of tax) — 6% debentures (previously computed) | 30,000 | Add: Shares assumed to be issued upon conversion of debentures | |
| 10% debentures ($1,000,000 × 10% × ¾ year × [1 − 50% tax rate]) | 37,500 | 6% (as of beginning of year) | 20,000 |
| | | 10% (as of date of issue, Apr. 1; ¾ × 32,000) | 24,000 |
| | | Average number of common and | |
| Adjusted net income | $277,500 | common equivalent shares | 144,000 |
| | A | | B |

FULLY DILUTED EARNINGS PER SHARE (A ÷ B) $1.93

---

Marshy Field Corporation would present the per-share earnings as computed above in the following manner:

---

### PRESENTATION OF EARNINGS PER SHARE[a]

| | |
|---|---:|
| (Bottom of income statement) | |
| Net income | $210,000 |
| Earnings per share: | |
| On common and common equivalent shares (Note X) | $2.00 |
| On a fully diluted basis (Note X) | $1.93 |

Note X. Earnings per common share and common equivalent share was computed by dividing net income by the weighted number of shares of common stock and common stock equivalents outstanding during the year. The 6% convertible debentures have been considered to be common stock equivalents. Consequently, the number of shares issuable assuming full conversion of these debentures as of the beginning of the year was added to the number of common shares, and net income was adjusted to eliminate the interest on these debentures, net of the applicable tax effect. Fully diluted earnings per share was computed assuming conversion of all debentures.

[a]A dual presentation is required because $1.93 is less than 97% of $2.10 ($210,000 ÷ 100,000 shares).

---

The illustration above assumes that Marshy Field's bonds were sold at face amount. If the bonds are sold at a premium or discount, interest expense must be adjusted each period to account for this occurrence. Therefore, the amount of interest expense added back to net income is the interest expense reported on the income statement, not the interest paid in cash during the period.

When the "if converted" method is employed, the conversion rate in effect during the period is used in computing primary earnings per share. It is not uncommon, however, for bond agreements to disallow conversion for at least two years after issuance followed by a conversion rate that changes over the period **the bond issue is outstanding.** In this situation, the **earliest conversion rate** is used for computation of primary earnings per share. For fully diluted earnings per share the **most advantageous conversion** rate available to the holder within ten years is used. To illustrate, assume that a convertible bond was issued January 1, 1982, with a conversion rate of 10 common shares for each bond starting January 1, 1984; beginning January 1, 1987, the conversion rate is 12 common shares for each bond, and beginning January 1, 1991, it is 15 common shares for each bond. In computing primary EPS in 1982 the conversion rate of 10 shares to one bond is used; in computing fully diluted EPS in 1982 the conversion rate of 15 shares to one bond is used.

## Options, Warrants, and Their Equivalents

Stock options and warrants outstanding and their equivalents (whether or not exercisable) are considered common stock equivalents and are included in earnings per share computations unless they are antidilutive or exercise cannot take place within five years. Stock purchase contracts, stock subscriptions not fully paid, deferred compensation packages providing for the issuance of common stock, and convertible securities that allow or require the payment of cash at issuance are treated as options and warrants for the purpose of computing earnings per share. Options, warrants, and their equivalents are included in earnings per share computations through the **treasury stock method.**

The treasury stock method assumes that the options and/or warrants are exercised at the beginning of the year (or date of issue if later) and the proceeds from the exercise of options and warrants are used to purchase common stock for the treasury. **The treasury stock method will increase the number of shares outstanding whenever the exercise price of an option or warrant is below the market price of the common stock.**[20] For example, if the exercise price of a warrant is $5.00 and the fair market value of the stock is $15, it follows that using the treasury stock method would increase the shares outstanding. Exercise of the warrant would result in one additional share outstanding, but the $5.00 received for the one share issued is not sufficient to purchase one share in the market at $15. Three warrants would have to be exercised (and three additional shares issued) to produce enough money ($15) to acquire one share in the market. Thus, an increase of two shares outstanding would result.

In terms of larger numbers, assume 1,500 options outstanding at an exercise price of $30 a common share and a common stock market price per share of $50. Through application of the treasury stock method it can be seen that there would be 600 **incremental shares** outstanding computed as shown at the top of page 755:[21]

---

[20] The opposite effect develops when the exercise price is greater than the market value of the common stock; the security is then antidilutive. The treatment accorded antidilutive securities is discussed later in this chapter.

[21] The incremental number of shares may be more simply computed:

$$\frac{\text{Market Price} - \text{Option Price}}{\text{Market Price}} \times \text{Number of Options} = \text{Number of Shares}$$

$$\frac{\$50 - \$30}{\$50} \times 1{,}500 \text{ Options} = 600 \text{ Shares}$$

| COMPUTATION OF INCREMENTAL SHARES | |
|---|---:|
| Proceeds from exercise of 1,500 options (1,500 × $30) | $45,000 |
| Shares issued upon exercise of options | 1,500 |
| Treasury shares purchasable with proceeds ($45,000 ÷ $50) | · 900 |
| Incremental shares outstanding (considered common stock equivalents) | 600 |

For both options and warrants,[22] exercise may not be assumed until the market price of the stock is above the exercise price for substantially[23] all of three consecutive months, with the latest month being the last month of the period to which earnings per share data relate. Once this three-month criterion has been satisfied, the **average market price** of the common stock for the period should be used in computing primary earnings per share. In computing fully diluted earnings per share, it is assumed that the **closing market price** (if it is higher than the average price) is used in computing the incremental shares.

To illustrate application of the treasury stock method, assume that Pauley Industries, Inc., has net income for the period of $220,000. The average number of shares outstanding for the period was 100,000 shares. The average number of shares under outstanding options (although not exercisable at this time), at an option price of $20 per share, is 5,000 shares. The average market price of the common stock during the year was $24 and the closing price at the end of the year is $28. The computation is shown on page 756.

In this example potential dilution is less than 3% for both primary and fully diluted, and, therefore, the options can be ignored. In other words, if both primary and fully diluted earnings per share are more than 97% of earnings per common share outstanding, earnings per share need be based only on the weighted average of the common shares outstanding, which would be $220,000 ÷ 100,000 shares or $2.20. In this illustration, either the primary or fully diluted would have to be $2.13 or below ($2.20 × 97%) before a dual presentation would be required. Primary earnings per share was $2.18 ($220,000 ÷ 100,834 shares) and fully diluted earnings per share was $2.17 ($220,000 ÷ 101,429 shares); therefore, a simple capital structure is assumed and a single presentation of $2.20 per share is appropriate.

If upon exercise of options and warrants, the number of shares assumed to be repurchased would exceed 20% of the already outstanding common stock, the treasury stock approach is modified. Once the proceeds have been applied to purchase common stock up to 20% of the outstanding common stock (for either primary or fully diluted EPS or both) the balance of the proceeds is assumed to be used to reduce first short-term debt and then long-term borrowings, with any remaining funds invested in government securities. The rationale for the 20% cutoff is that the purchase of this amount of stock would have a significant impact on the market price of the stock and make the use of the treasury stock method questionable.

---

[22] It might be noted that options and warrants have essentially the same assumptions and computational problems, although the warrants allow or require the tendering of some other security such as debt in lieu of cash upon exercise. In such situations, the accounting becomes quite complex, and the reader should refer to *Opinion No. 15* for its proper disposition.

[23] "Substantially" is assumed to mean 11 of 13 weeks.

**Pauley Industries, Inc.**
**COMPUTATION OF EARNINGS PER SHARE**
(Treasury Stock Method)

**Options**

|  | Primary Earnings Per Share | Fully Diluted Earnings Per Share |
|---|---|---|
| Average number of shares under options outstanding | 5,000 | 5,000 |
| Option price per share | × $20 | × $20 |
| Proceeds upon exercise of options | $100,000 | $100,000 |
| Market price of common stock: | | |
| Average | $24 | |
| Closing | | $28 |
| Treasury shares that could be repurchased with proceeds ($100,000 ÷ $24) | 4,166 | |
| ($100,000 ÷ $28) | | 3,571 |
| Excess of shares under option over treasury shares that could be repurchased (5,000 − 4,166); | 834 | |
| (5,000 − 3,571) | | 1,429 |
| Common stock equivalent shares (Incremental shares) | 834 | 1,429 |
| Average number of common shares outstanding | 100,000 | 100,000 |
| Total average number of common and common equivalent shares | 100,834 | 101,429 |
| | A | C |
| Net income for the year | $220,000 | $220,000 |
| | B | D |
| Earnings per share | $2.18 (B ÷ A) | $2.17 (D ÷ C) |

For example, assume the same facts as those in the previous illustration, except that there are also warrants outstanding to purchase 46,000 shares of common stock at $10 per share. The computation is shown on page 757.

In this case, primary and fully diluted earnings per share should be reported because dilution is greater than 3% ($2.20 minus $1.68 = dilution of 23.6%). Because there was no outstanding debt to be repurchased, it is assumed that the excess proceeds are used to purchase government securities yielding 6%. Also the ending market price was used for fully diluted earnings per share, whereas the average price was employed for primary earnings per share. Acquisition of the 20% maximum treasury shares at the ending market price (fully diluted computation) would utilize all the assumed proceeds from exercise; only the primary earnings per share computation therefore resulted in the assumed purchase of governmental securities in this example.

Pauley Industries, Inc.
COMPUTATION OF EARNINGS PER SHARE
(Treasury Stock Method)
Modification for 20% Test

**Options and Warrants**

|  | Primary Earnings Per Share | Fully Diluted Earnings Per Share |
|---|---|---|
| Proceeds upon exercise of options and warrants outstanding | | |
| Options (5,000 shares @ $20) | $100,000 | $100,000 |
| Warrants (46,000 shares @ $10) | 460,000 | 460,000 |
|  | $560,000 | $560,000 |
| Average number of shares outstanding | 100,000 | 100,000 |
| Issued shares—exercise of options | 5,000 | 5,000 |
| Issued shares—exercise of warrants | 46,000 | 46,000 |
| Shares assumed to be repurchased with proceeds from exercise (subject to 20% maximum) | (20,000)[a] | (20,000)[a] |
| Total common and common equivalent shares | 131,000 | 131,000 |
| Net income for the year | $220,000 | $220,000 |
| Add: interest revenue from purchase of government securities ([$560,000 − $480,000] × 6% × [1 − 50% tax rate]) | 2,400 | — |
| Adjusted net income | $222,400 | $220,000 |
|  | A | C |
| Total average number of common and common equivalent shares | 131,000 | 131,000 |
|  | B | D |
| Earnings per share | $1.70 (A ÷ B) | $1.68 (C ÷ D) |

[a]20,000 shares were repurchased under both the primary and fully diluted earnings per share. It took only $480,000 ($24 × 20,000) to purchase the shares under the primary earnings per share calculation, but it took $560,000 ($28 × 20,000) to purchase the shares under the fully diluted earnings per share calculation.

## Contingent Issuance Agreement

In business combinations, the acquiror may promise to issue additional shares (referred to as contingent shares) if certain conditions are met. If these shares are issuable upon the **mere passage of time or upon the attainment of a certain market price and this market price is met at the end of the year,** they should be considered as outstanding for the computation of both primary and fully diluted earnings per share.[24]

---

[24]In addition to contingent issuances of stock, other types of situations that might lead to dilution are the issuance of participating securities and two-class common. The reporting of these types of securities in EPS computation is complex and beyond the scope of this textbook.

For example, assume that Walz Corporation purchased Cardella Company and agreed to pay the stockholders of Cardella Company 20,000 additional shares in 1985 if Cardella Company's net income in 1984 is $90,000; in 1983 Cardella Company's net income is $100,000. Both primary and fully diluted earnings per share of Walz for 1983 would reflect the 20,000 contingent shares because the 1984 stipulated earnings of $90,000 are already being attained.

If attainment of increased earnings above the present level is the condition, the additional shares should be considered as outstanding only for the purpose of computing fully diluted earnings per share (but only if dilution results). For this computation, current earnings should be adjusted to give effect to the increase in earnings necessary to reach the specified level. To illustrate, assume the same facts as those above for Walz and Cardella except that the 20,000 shares are contingent upon Cardella Company's attaining a net income of $110,000 in 1984. Inasmuch as the earnings level is not being attained currently in 1983, no computation for Walz's primary earnings per share other than the traditional one need be made. In computing Walz's fully diluted earnings per share, however, the 20,000 shares would be considered outstanding. In addition, in computing fully diluted earnings per share, the 1983 net income of $100,000 would be increased by $10,000 to achieve an assumed earnings level of $110,000.

## Antidilution

In computing the 3% dilution factor, the aggregate of **all** dilutive securities must be considered. The dilutive securities are not considered individually, but in total. In addition, any security that is antidilutive should be excluded and cannot be used to offset dilutive securities. **Antidilutive** securities are securities whose inclusion in earnings per share computations would increase earnings per share (or reduce net loss per share). For example, convertible debt is antidilutive if the addition to income of the interest net of tax causes a greater percentage increase in income (numerator) than conversion of the bonds causes a percentage increase in common and common equivalent shares (denominator). With options or warrants, whenever the exercise price is higher than the market price, the security is antidilutive. **Antidilutive securities should be ignored in all calculations and should not be considered in computing either primary or fully diluted earnings per share.** This approach is reasonable because the profession's intent was to inform the investor of the possible dilution that might occur in reported earnings per share and not to be concerned with securities that, if converted or exercised, would result in an increase in earnings per share. The appendix to this chapter provides an extended example of how antidilution is considered in a complex situation.

## Earnings Per Share Presentations and Disclosures

If a corporation's capital structure is complex but contains no securities classified as common stock equivalents, the earnings per share presentation would be as follows:

| | |
|---|---|
| Earnings per common share | |
| Assuming no dilution | $3.30 |
| Assuming full dilution | $2.70 |

If common stock equivalents are present and dilutive, the earnings per share presentation should be as follows:

| | |
|---|---|
| Earnings per share | |
| On common and common equivalent share | $3.00 |
| On a fully diluted basis | $2.70 |

When the earnings of a period include special transactions, per share amounts (where applicable) should be shown for income from continuing operations, income before extraordinary items, cumulative effect of changes in accounting principles, and net income. Reporting per share amounts for gain or loss on discontinued operations and gain or loss on extraordinary items is optional. A presentation reporting extraordinary items only is presented below.

| | |
|---|---|
| Earnings per common and common equivalent share | |
| Income before extraordinary item | $3.80 |
| Extraordinary item | .80 |
| Net income | $3.00 |
| Earnings per share—assuming full dilution | |
| Income before extraordinary item | $3.35 |
| Extraordinary item | .65 |
| Net income | $2.70 |

Earnings per share amounts must be shown for all periods presented and all prior period earnings per share amounts presented should be restated for stock dividends and stock splits. When results of operations of a prior period have been restated as a result of a prior period adjustment, the earnings per share data shown for the prior periods should also be restated. The effect of the restatement should be disclosed in the year of the restatement.

Complex capital structures and dual presentation of earnings require the following additional disclosures in footnote form.

1. Description of pertinent rights and privileges of the various securities outstanding.
2. Bases on which both primary and fully diluted earnings per share were computed.
   a. Identify issues included in common stock equivalents.
   b. Identify securities included in fully diluted earnings per share computation.
   c. Describe all assumptions made.
   d. Disclose the number of shares issued upon conversion, exercise, or satisfaction of required conditions.
3. Effect of conversions subsequent to year end.

The footnote presented on the following page illustrates the use of the columnar format for disclosing the required information clearly and concisely (this is an excerpt from notes to the financial statements of Marcor, Inc.).

EARNINGS PER SHARE
Earnings per share for the year have been calculated as follows:

| | Common and Common Equivalent Shares | Assuming Full Dilution |
|---|---|---|
| Average number of common shares outstanding | 12,692,190 | 12,692,190 |
| Common stock equivalents due to assumed exercise of options | 99,636 | 114,612 |
| Average number of Series A preferred shares outstanding | — | 6,513,378 |
| Series A preferred stock equivalents due to assumed exercise of options | — | 175,154 |
| Total shares | 12,791,826 | 19,495,334 |
| Net earnings | $66,950,000 | $66,950,000 |
| Less: Preferred dividend requirements based on average number of preferred shares and preferred equivalent shares outstanding during year | 13,372,000 | — |
| Net earnings used in per share calculations | $53,578,000 | $66,950,000 |
| Net earnings per share | $4.19 | $3.43 |

## Summary

Computation of earnings per share has become a complex issue. Many accountants take strong exception to some of the arbitrary rules contained in the profession's pronouncements on EPS. The situation facing accountants in this area is a difficult one, because many securities, although technically not common stock, have many of the basic characteristics of common stock. In addition, many companies have issued these types of securities rather than common stock in order to avoid an adverse effect on the earnings per share figure. *APB Opinion No. 15* and related pronouncements were issued as an attempt to develop credibility in reporting earnings per share data.

The schematic diagram on page 761 displays graphically the elementary points of calculating earnings per share in a complex capital structure.

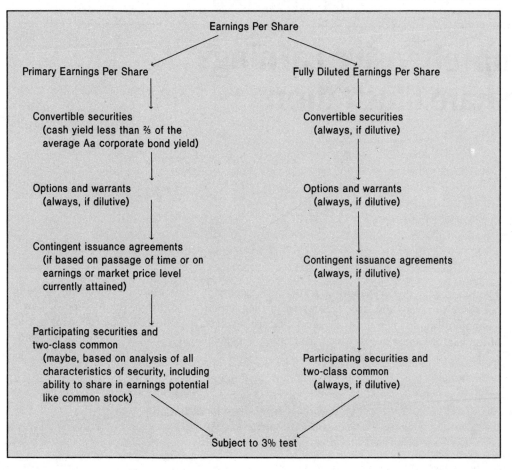

# Comprehensive Earnings Per Share Illustration

The purpose of this Appendix is to provide a complex illustration of computing earnings per share to review the issues discussed in the chapter. In addition, the method of how to compute dilution when multiple securities are involved is presented. The following section of the balance sheet of Webster Corporation is presented for analysis; assumptions related to the capital structure follow:

|  |  |
|---|---:|
| Webster Corporation<br>SELECTED BALANCE SHEET INFORMATION<br>At December 31, 1983 |  |
| **Long-term debt:** |  |
| Notes payable, 14% | $ 1,000,000 |
| 8% convertible bonds payable | 2,500,000 |
| 10% convertible bonds payable | 2,500,000 |
| Total long-term debt | $ 6,000,000 |
| **Stockholders' equity:** |  |
| 10% cumulative, convertible preferred stock, par value $100,<br>100,000 shares authorized, 25,000 shares issued and outstanding | $ 2,500,000 |
| Common stock, par value $1, 5,000,000 shares authorized,<br>500,000 shares issued and outstanding | 500,000 |
| Additional paid-in capital | 2,000,000 |
| Retained earnings | 9,000,000 |
| Total stockholders' equity | $14,000,000 |

### Notes and Assumptions
### December 31, 1983

1. Options were granted in July, 1981 to purchase 50,000 shares of common stock at $20 per share. The average market price of Webster's common stock during 1983 was $25. The market price at December 31, 1983 was $30 per share. No options were exercised during 1983.

2. Both the 8% and 10% convertible bonds were issued in 1982 at face value. The 8% issue was sold when the average Aa corporate bond yield was 13%, while the 10% issue was sold when

the average Aa corporate bond yield was 14%. Each convertible bond is convertible into 40 shares of common stock (each bond has a face value of $1,000).

3. The 10% cumulative, convertible preferred stock was issued at the beginning of 1983 at par. Each share of preferred is convertible into four shares of common stock. The average Aa bond yield was 16% when the preferred stock was issued.

4. The average income tax rate is 40%.

5. The 500,000 shares of common stock were outstanding during the entire year.

6. Preferred dividends were not declared in 1983.

7. Net income was $1,750,000 in 1983.

8. No bonds or preferred stock were converted during 1983.

The computation of primary earnings per share for 1983 starts with the amount based upon the weighted average of common shares outstanding. This is illustrated below:

| Computation of Earnings Per Share—<br>Simple Capital Structure | |
|---|---:|
| Net income | $1,750,000 |
| Less: 10% cumulative, convertible preferred stock dividend requirements | 250,000 |
| Net income applicable to common stockholders | $1,500,000 |
| Weighted average number of common shares outstanding | 500,000 |
| Earnings per common share | $3.00 |

Note the following points concerning the above calculation.

1. When preferred stock is cumulative, the preferred dividend is subtracted to arrive at net income applicable to common stock whether the dividend is declared or not.

2. The earnings per share of $3.00 must be computed because it is the per share amount that, at this point, is subject to reduction due to the existence of convertible securities and options.

3. The earnings per share of $3.00 must also be computed because, if either primary earnings per share or fully diluted earnings per share is $2.91 or less (.97 × $3.00), a dual presentation of earnings per share is required.

The steps for computing primary earnings per share follow.

1. Determine which securities are common stock equivalents.

2. Determine, for each common stock equivalent, the per share effect assuming exercise/conversion of each security.

3. Rank the results from step 2 from smallest earnings effect per share to largest earnings effect per share. That is, rank the results in order from most dilutive to least dilutive.

4. Beginning with the earnings per share based upon the weighted average of common shares outstanding ($3.00), recalculate earnings per share by adding the smallest per share effects from step 3. If the results from this recalculation are less than $3.00, proceed to the next smallest per share effect and recalculate earnings per share. This process is continued so long as each recalculated earnings per share is smaller than the previous amount. The process will end either because there are no more securities to test or a particular security maintains or increases earnings per share (is antidilutive).

The above 4 steps are now applied to the Webster Corporation.

## Primary Earnings Per Share

The Webster Corporation has four securities, that is, options, 8% and 10% convertible bonds, and the convertible preferred stock that could reduce EPS. The first step in computing primary earnings per share is to determine, for each of the above securities, whether or not each is a common stock equivalent. Exhibit 1 shows this determination for each security.

---

**Exhibit 1**
**Determination of Common Stock Equivalents**
**Primary Earnings Per Share**

| Security | Test | CSE (Yes/No) |
|---|---|---|
| Options | None | Yes (always) |
| 8% Bonds | Cash Yield = 8%<br>2/3 (13%) = 8.7% | Yes (8% < 8.7%) |
| 10% Bonds | Cash Yield = 10%<br>2/3 (14%) = 9.3% | No (10% > 9.3%) |
| 10% Preferred | Cash Yield = 10%<br>2/3 (16%) = 10.7% | Yes (10% < 10.7%) |

---

The second step in the computation of primary earnings per share is the determination of a per share effect for each common stock equivalent noted in Exhibit 1. Exhibits 2, 3, and 4 illustrate these computations.

---

**Exhibit 2**
**Per Share Effect of Options**
**(Treasury Stock Method)**
**Primary Earnings Per Share**

| | |
|---|---|
| Number of shares under options | 50,000 |
| Option price per share | × $20 |
| Proceeds upon assumed exercise of options | $1,000,000 |
| Average market price of common during 1983 | $25 |
| Treasury shares that could be acquired with proceeds ($1,000,000 ÷ $25) | 40,000 |
| Excess of shares under option over treasury shares that could be repurchased (50,000 − 40,000) | 10,000 |

Per share effect:

$$\frac{\text{Incremental Numerator Effect:} \quad \text{None}}{\text{Incremental Denominator Effect:} \quad 10,000 \text{ shares}} = \$0$$

---

---

**Exhibit 3**
**Per Share Effect of 8% Bonds**
**(If Converted Method)**
**Primary Earnings Per Share**

| | |
|---|---:|
| Interest expense for year .08 ($2,500,000) | $200,000 |
| Income tax reduction due to interest (40% × $200,000) | 80,000 |
| Interest expense avoided (net of tax) | $120,000 |
| Number of common shares issued assuming conversion of bonds (2,500 bonds × 40 shares) | 100,000 |

Per share effect:

$$\frac{\text{Incremental Numerator Effect:} \quad \$120,000}{\text{Incremental Denominator Effect:} \quad 100,000 \text{ shares}} = \$1.20$$

---

**Exhibit 4**
**Per Share Effect of 10% Convertible Preferred**
**(If Converted Method)**
**Primary Earnings Per Share**

| | |
|---|---:|
| Dividend requirement on cumulative preferred (25,000 shares × $10) | $250,000 |
| Income tax effect (dividends not an expense) | none |
| Dividend requirement avoided | $250,000 |
| Number of common shares issued assuming conversion of preferred (4 × 25,000 shares) | 100,000 |

Per share effect:

$$\frac{\text{Incremental Numerator Effect:} \quad \$250,000}{\text{Incremental Denominator Effect:} \quad 100,000 \text{ shares}} = \$2.50$$

---

The earnings per share effects for all common stock equivalents are ranked from smallest to largest in step 3. This is shown in Exhibit 5.

---

**Exhibit 5**
**Ranking of Per Share Effects—Smallest to Largest**
**Primary Earnings Per Share**

| | Effect Per Share |
|---|---:|
| 1. Options | $  0 |
| 2. 8% convertible bonds | 1.20 |
| 3. 10% convertible preferred | 2.50 |

---

The fourth step in the computation of primary earnings per share is the recalculation of earnings per share giving effect to the ranking in Exhibit 5. Starting with the earnings per share of $3 computed previously, add the incremental numerator and denominator effects of the options to the original calculation, as shown at the top of page 766.

| Options | |
|---|---:|
| Net income applicable to common | $1,500,000 |
| Add: Incremental numerator effect of options | none |
| Total | $1,500,000 |
| Weighted average number of common shares outstanding | 500,000 |
| Add: Incremental denominator effect of options | 10,000 |
| Total | 510,000 |
| Recomputed earnings per share ($1,500,000 ÷ 510,000 shares) | $2.94 |

Since the recomputed earnings per share is reduced (from $3 to $2.94), the effect of the options is dilutive. However, the dilutive effect of these options is predictable because the average market price ($25) was greater than the option price ($20). Whenever this relationship exists, the options are dilutive. Accordingly, the calculation of a per share effect (step 2) and the subsequent ranking of the options (step 3) need not have been done. However, the effect of dilutive options must be given recognition in the initial stage of step 4.

The next security to enter the primary EPS calculation is the 8% convertible bond issue. Starting with the earnings per share of $2.94 recomputed above, add the incremental numerator and denominator effects from Exhibit 3, as follows:

| 8% Convertible Bonds | |
|---|---:|
| Numerator from previous calculation | $1,500,000 |
| Add: Interest expense avoided (net of tax) | 120,000 |
| Total | $1,620,000 |
| Denominator from previous calculation (shares) | 510,000 |
| Add: Number of common shares assumed issued upon conversion of bonds | 100,000 |
| Total | 610,000 |
| Recomputed earnings per share ($1,620,000 ÷ 610,000 shares) | $2.66 |

Since the recomputed earnings per share is reduced (from $2.94 to $2.66), the effect of the 8% convertible bonds is dilutive.

The last security to enter the primary EPS computation is the 10% convertible preferred stock. Starting with the recomputed earnings per share of $2.66, add the incremental numerator and denominator effects from Exhibit 4, as shown at the top of page 767.

| Convertible 10% Preferred Stock | |
|---|---:|
| Numerator from previous calculation | $1,620,000 |
| Add: Dividend requirement avoided | 250,000 |
| Total | $1,870,000 |
| Denominator from previous calculation (shares) | 610,000 |
| Add: Number of common shares assumed issued upon conversion of preferred | 100,000 |
| Total | 710,000 |
| Recomputed earnings per share ($1,870,000 ÷ 710,000 shares) | $2.63 |

Since the recomputed earnings per share is reduced (from $2.66 to $2.63), the effect of the 10% preferred stock is dilutive. Furthermore, **since there are no more common stock equivalents to test, the $2.63 is primary earnings per share.**

Before computing fully diluted earnings per share, it is important to note what would have happened if a recomputed earnings per share would have been equal to or greater than a previously computed earnings per share number. For example, if the recomputed earnings per share, after adding the effects of the preferred stock, had been $2.66 or higher, the preferred stock would have been antidilutive. Accordingly, the primary earnings per share would have been $2.66 under this circumstance.

## Fully Diluted Earnings Per Share

The steps for computing fully diluted earnings per share follow the same approach as that for primary earnings per share. In general, most of the information gathered in the primary calculation is usable in the fully diluted computation. For example, the per share effects for the 8% bonds and the 10% preferred stock remain the same. However, a per share effect has to be determined for the 10% bonds, which were not a common stock equivalent, and the treasury stock method for the options has to be altered due to a higher end-of-period market price. Exhibits 6 and 7 show these new computations.

| Exhibit 6<br>Per Share Effect of Options<br>(Treasury Stock Method)<br>Fully Diluted Earnings Per Share | |
|---|---:|
| Number of shares under option | 50,000 |
| Option price per share | × $20 |
| Proceeds upon assumed exercise of options | $1,000,000 |
| December 31, 1983 market price of common | $30 |
| Treasury shares that could be acquired with proceeds ($1,000,000 ÷ $30) | 33,333 |
| Excess of shares under option over treasury shares<br>that could be repurchased (50,000 − 33,333) | 16,667 |
| Per share effect: | |
| Incremental Numerator Effect:    None<br>Incremental Denominator Effect:  16,667 shares = | $0 |

| Exhibit 7<br>Per Share Effect of 10% Bonds<br>(If Converted Method)<br>Fully Diluted Earnings Per Share | |
|---|---|
| Interest expense for year (10% × $2,500,000) | $250,000 |
| Income tax reduction due to interest (40% × $250,000) | 100,000 |
| Interest expense avoided (net of tax) | $150,000 |
| Number of common shares issued assuming conversion of bonds<br>(2,500 bonds × 40 shares) | 100,000 |
| Per share effect: | |
| $\dfrac{\text{Incremental Numerator Effect: \$150,000}}{\text{Incremental Denominator Effect: 100,000 shares}} =$ | $1.50 |

Exhibit 8 shows the ranking of all four potentially dilutive securities.

| Exhibit 8<br>Ranking of Per Share Effects—Smallest to Largest<br>Fully Diluted Earnings Per Share | Effect<br>Per Share |
|---|---|
| 1. Options | $  0 |
| 2. 8% convertible bonds | 1.20 |
| 3. 10% convertible bonds | 1.50 |
| 4. 10% convertible preferred | 2.50 |

The next step is to determine earnings per share giving effect to the ranking in Exhibit 8. Starting with the earnings per share of $3 computed previously, add the incremental effects of the options to the original calculation, as follows:

| Options | |
|---|---|
| Net income applicable to common | $1,500,000 |
| Add: Incremental numerator effect of options | none |
| Total | $1,500,000 |
| Weighted average number of common shares outstanding | 500,000 |
| Add: Incremental denominator effect of options—Exhibit 6 | 16,667 |
| Total | 516,667 |
| Recomputed earnings per share ($1,500,000 ÷ 516,667 shares) | $2.90 |

Since the recomputed earnings per share is reduced (from $3 to $2.90), the effect of the options is dilutive. Again, this effect could have been anticipated because the market price at year end ($30) exceeded the option price ($20).

Recomputed earnings per share, assuming the 8% bonds are converted, is as follows:

| 8% Convertible Bonds | |
|---|---|
| Numerator from previous calculation | $1,500,000 |
| Add: Interest expense avoided (net of tax) | 120,000 |
| Total | $1,620,000 |
| Denominator from previous calculation (shares) | 516,667 |
| Add: Number of common shares assumed issued upon conversion of bonds | 100,000 |
| Total | 616,667 |
| Recomputed earnings per share ($1,620,000 ÷ 616,667 shares) | $2.63 |

Since the recomputed earnings per share is reduced (from $2.90 to $2.63), the effect of the 8% bonds is dilutive.

Next, earnings per share is recomputed assuming the conversion of the 10% bonds. This is shown below:

| 10% Convertible Bonds | |
|---|---|
| Numerator from previous computation | $1,620,000 |
| Add: Interest expense avoided (net of tax) | 150,000 |
| Total | $1,770,000 |
| Denominator from previous computation (shares) | 616,667 |
| Add: Number of common shares assumed issued upon conversion of bonds | 100,000 |
| Total | 716,667 |
| Recomputed earnings per share ($1,770,000 ÷ 716,667 shares) | $2.47 |

Since the recomputed earnings per share is reduced (from $2.63 to $2.47), the effect of the 10% convertible bonds is dilutive.

The final step is the recomputation which includes the 10% preferred stock. This is shown below:

| 10% Convertible Preferred | |
|---|---|
| Numerator from previous calculation | $1,770,000 |
| Add: Dividend requirement avoided | 250,000 |
| Total | $2,020,000 |
| Denominator from previous calculation (shares) | 716,667 |
| Add: Number of common shares assumed issued upon conversion of preferred | 100,000 |
| Total | 816,667 |
| Recomputed earnings per share ($2,020,000 ÷ 816,667 shares) | $2.47 |

Since the recomputed earnings per share is not reduced, the effect of the 10% convertible preferred is antidilutive. Fully dilutive earnings per share is $2.47, and the per share effects of the preferred are not used in the computation.

Finally, the disclosure of earnings per share for Webster Corporation is shown below. Note that the 3% materiality test is satisfied because primary and fully diluted earnings per share are well below $2.91 (.97 × $3).

---

**Income Statement Presentation**

| | |
|---|---|
| Net income | $1,750,000 |
| Earnings per common share and common equivalent share (Note X) | $2.63 |
| Earnings per common share, assuming full dilution | $2.47 |

NOTE X: Earnings per common share and common equivalent share were computed by dividing net income by the weighted average number of shares of common stock and common stock equivalents outstanding during the year. The 8% convertible bonds and the 10% convertible preferred have been considered to be common stock equivalents. Consequently, the number of shares issuable, assuming full conversion of these bonds and preferred shares as of the beginning of the year, was added to the number of common shares, and net income was adjusted to eliminate the interest on these bonds (net of applicable tax) and the dividend requirement on the preferred stock. Options were also considered in the computation of earnings per common and common equivalent shares.

Fully diluted earnings per share was computed assuming conversion of all debentures and exercise of all options and warrants.

---

**Note:** All **asterisked** Questions, Cases, Exercises, or Problems relate to material contained in the appendix to each chapter.

## QUESTIONS

1. What are some of the major reasons for increased merger activity in the early 1980's? Why might this increased activity lead to the issuance of dilutive securities?

2. Discuss the similarities and the differences between convertible debt and debt issued with stock purchase warrants.

3. What accounting treatment is required for convertible debt? What accounting treatment is required for debt issued with stock purchase warrants?

4. Explain how the conversion feature of convertible debt has a value (a) to the issuer, and (b) to the purchaser.

5. What are the arguments for giving separate accounting recognition to the conversion feature of debentures?

6. Assume that no value is assigned to the conversion feature upon issue of the debentures. Assume further that four years after issue, debentures with a face value of $100,000 and book value of $96,000 are tendered for conversion into 8,000 shares of common stock immediately after an interest payment date when the market price of the debentures is 104 and the common stock is selling at $14 per share (par value $10). The company records the conversion as follows:

| | | |
|---|---|---|
| Bonds Payable | 100,000 | |
| Discount on Bonds Payable | | 4,000 |
| Common Stock | | 80,000 |
| Paid-in Capital in Excess of Par | | 16,000 |

Discuss the propriety of this accounting treatment.

7. On July 1, 1981, Harbecke Corporation issued $2,000,000 of 7% bonds payable in 10 years. The bonds include detachable warrants giving the bondholder the right to purchase for $30 one share of $1.00 par value common stock at any time during the next 10 years. The bonds were sold for $2,000,000. The value of the warrants at the time of issuance was $100,000. Prepare the journal entry to record this transaction.

8. What are stock rights? How does the issuing company account for them?

9. What are the advantages to an executive of receiving an incentive stock option? Why do some accountants believe that the present accounting for these options is inappropriate?

10. Erwin Corporation has an employee stock purchase plan which permits all full-time employees to purchase 10 shares of common stock on the third anniversary of their employment and an additional 10 shares on each subsequent anniversary date. The purchase price is set at the market price on the date purchased and no commission is charged. Discuss whether this plan would be considered compensatory.

11. What date or event does the profession believe should be used in determining the value of a stock option? What arguments support this position? What criticism may be brought against the date or event advocated by the profession?

12. What support can be offered for dates other than the date of grant on which to determine the value of a stock option?

13. What is the advantage to an executive of a stock appreciation right (SAR) plan? How is compensation expense measured in a SAR plan?

14. At December 31, 1983 the Wedgewood Company had 600,000 shares of common stock issued and outstanding, 400,000 of which had been issued and outstanding throughout the year, and 200,000 of which were issued on October 1, 1983. Net income for 1983 was $2,144,000 and dividends declared on preferred stock were $394,000. Compute Wedgewood's earnings per common share (round to the nearest penny).

15. Define the following terms.
   (a) 3% test for dilution.
   (b) Complex capital structure.
   (c) Primary earnings per share.
   (d) Common stock equivalent.
   (e) Potentially dilutive security.
   (f) Fully diluted earnings per share.

16. What are the computational guidelines for determining whether a convertible security is a common stock equivalent?

17. Discuss the reasons why securities other than common stock may be considered common stock equivalents for the computation of primary earnings per share.

18. Explain how convertible securities are determined to be common stock equivalents and how those convertible senior securities that are not considered to be common stock equivalents enter into the determination of earnings per share data.

19. Explain the treasury stock method as it applies to options and warrants in computing primary earnings per share data.

20. Earnings per share can affect market prices. Can market prices affect earnings per share? Explain.

21. What is meant by the term antidilution? Give an example.

*22. How is anti-dilution determined when multiple securities are involved?

## CASES

C17-1 Incurring long-term debt with an arrangement whereby lenders receive an option to buy common stock during all or a portion of the time the debt is outstanding is a frequent corporate financing practice. In some situations the result is achieved through the issuance of convertible bonds; in others the debt instruments and the warrants to buy stock are separate.

**Instructions**

   (a) 1. Describe the differences that exist in current accounting for original proceeds of the issuance of convertible bonds and of debt instruments with separate warrants to purchase common stock.
      2. Discuss the underlying rationale for the differences described in (a) 1. above.
      3. Summarize the arguments that have been presented in favor of accounting for convertible bonds in the same manner as for debt with separate warrants.
   (b) At the start of the year Bruce Budge Company issued $9,000,000 of 12% notes along with warrants to buy 600,000 shares of its $10 par value common stock at $18 per share. The notes mature over the next ten years starting one year from date of issuance with

annual maturities of $900,000. At the time, Budge had 4,800,000 shares of common stock outstanding and the market price was $23 per share. The company received $10,020,000 for the notes and the warrants. For Bruce Budge Company, 12% was a relatively low borrowing rate. If offered alone, at this time, the notes would have been issued at a 22 percent discount. Prepare the journal entry (or entries) for the issuance of the notes and warrants for the cash consideration received.

(AICPA adapted)

C17-2 For various reasons a corporation may issue warrants to purchase shares of its common stock at specified prices that, depending on the circumstances, may be less than, equal to, or greater than the current market price. For example, warrants may be issued:

1. To existing stockholders on a pro rata basis.

2. To certain key employees under an incentive stock option plan.

3. To purchasers of the corporation's bonds.

**Instructions**

For each of the three examples of how stock warrants are used:
(a) Explain why they are used.
(b) Discuss the significance of the price (or prices) at which the warrants are issued (or granted) in relation to (1) the current market price of the company's stock, and (2) the length of time over which they can be exercised.
(c) Describe the information that should be disclosed in financial statements, or notes thereto, that are prepared when stock warrants are outstanding in the hands of the three groups listed above.

(AICPA adapted)

C17-3 On December 12, 1981, the board of directors of Biagioni Company authorized a grant of nonqualified options to company executives for the purchase of 20,000 shares of common stock at 52 any time during 1984 if the executives still are employed by the company. The closing price of Biagioni common stock was 55 on December 12, 1981, 51 on January 2, 1984, and 49⅛ on December 31, 1984. None of the options were exercised.

**Instructions**

(a) Prepare a schedule presenting the computation of the compensation cost that should be attributed to the options of Biagioni Company.
(b) Assume that the market price of Biagioni common stock rose to 58 (instead of declining to 51) on January 2, 1984, and that all options were exercised on that date. Would the company incur a cost for executive compensation? Why?
(c) Discuss the arguments for measuring compensation from executive stock options in terms of the spread between the
  1. Market price and option price when the grant is made.
  2. Market price and option price when the options are first exercisable.
  3. Market price and option price when the options are exercised.
  4. Cash value of the executives' services estimated at date of grant and the amount of their salaries.

(AICPA adapted)

C17-4 In 1981 Smother Co. adopted a plan to give additional incentive compensation to its dealers to sell its principal product, fire extinguishers. Under the plan Smother transferred 9,000 shares of its $1.00 par value stock to a trust with the provision that Smother would have to forfeit interest in the trust and no part of the trust fund could ever revert to Smother. Shares were to be distributed to dealers on the basis of their shares of fire extinguisher purchases from Smother (above certain minimum levels) over the three-year period ending June 30, 1984.

In 1981 the stock was closely held. The book value of the stock was $6.90 per share as of June 30, 1981, and in 1981 additional shares were sold to existing stockholders for $7 per share. On the basis of this information, market value of the stock was determined to be $7 per share.

In 1981 when the shares were transferred to the trust, Smother charged prepaid expenses for $63,000 ($7 per share market value) and credited capital stock for $9,000 and additional paid-in capital for $54,000. The prepaid expense was charged to operations over a three-year period ended June 30, 1984.

Smother sold a substantial number of shares of its stock to the public in 1983 at $60 per share.

In July 1984 all shares of the stock in the trust were distributed to the dealers. The market value of the shares at date of distribution of the stock from the trust had risen to $120 per share. Smother obtained a tax deduction equal to that market value for the tax year ended June 30, 1985.

**Instructions**

(a) How much should be reported as selling expense in each of the years noted above?

(b) Smother is also considering other types of option plans. One such plan is a stock appreciation right (SAR) plan. What is a stock appreciation right plan? What is a potential disadvantage of a SAR plan from the viewpoint of the company?

**C17-5** "Earnings per share" (EPS) is the most featured single financial statistic about modern corporations. Daily published quotations of stock prices have recently been expanded to include for many securities a "times earnings" figure which is based on EPS. Stock analysts often focus their discussions on the EPS of the corporations they study.

**Instructions**

(a) Explain how dividends or dividend requirements on any class of preferred stock that may be outstanding affect the computation of EPS.

(b) One of the technical procedures applicable in EPS computations is the "treasury stock method."

   1. Briefly describe the circumstances under which it might be appropriate to apply the treasury stock method.

   2. There is a limit to the extent to which the treasury stock method is applicable. Indicate what this limit is and give a succinct summary of the procedures that should be followed beyond the treasury stock limits.

(c) Under some circumstances, convertible debentures would be considered "common stock equivalents"; under other circumstances they would not.

   1. When is it proper to treat convertible debentures as common stock equivalents? What is the effect on computation of EPS in such cases?

   2. In case convertible debentures are not considered as common stock equivalents, explain how they are handled for purposes of EPS computations.

(AICPA adapted)

**C17-6** Carol Mulligan Corporation, a new audit client of yours, has not reported earnings per share data in its annual reports to stockholders in the past. The treasurer, Richard Kinka, requested that you furnish information about the reporting of earnings per share data in the current year's annual report in accordance with generally accepted accounting principles.

**Instructions**

(a) Define the term "earnings per share" as it applies to a corporation with a capitalization structure composed of only one class of common stock and explain how earnings per share should be computed and how the information should be disclosed in the corporation's financial statements.

(b) Discuss the treatment, if any, that should be given to each of the following items in computing earnings per share of common stock for financial statement reporting.

   1. The declaration of current dividends on cumulative preferred stock.

   2. The acquisition of some of the corporation's outstanding common stock during the current fiscal year. The stock was classified as treasury stock.

   3. A 2-for-1 stock split of common stock during the current fiscal year.

   4. A provision created out of retained earnings for a contingent liability from a possible lawsuit.

5. Outstanding preferred stock issued at a premium with a par value liquidation right.
6. The exercise at a price below market value but above book value of a common stock option issued during the current fiscal year to officers of the corporation.
7. The replacement of a machine immediately prior to the close of the current fiscal year at a cost 20 percent above the original cost of the replaced machine. The new machine will perform the same function as the old machine that was sold for its book value.

## EXERCISES

**E17-1** For each of the unrelated transactions described below, present the entry(ies) required to record each transaction.

1. Teddico Corp. issued $20,000,000 par value 11% convertible bonds at 99. If the bonds had not been convertible, the company's investment banker estimates they would have been sold at 95. Expenses of issuing the bonds were $80,000.

2. Anna Company issued $20,000,000 par value 10% bonds at 98. One detachable stock purchase warrant was issued with each $100 par value bond. At the time of issuance, the warrants were selling for $4.

3. On July 1, 1983, Schmitt Company called its 11% convertible debentures for conversion. The $10,000,000 par value bonds were converted into 1,000,000 shares of $1 par value common stock. On July 1, there was $150,000 of unamortized discount applicable to the bonds, and the company incurred expenses of $75,000 in connection with the conversion of all the bonds. The company records the conversion using the book value method.

**E17-2** Maxipump, Inc. issued $6,000,000 of 10%, 10-year convertible bonds on June 1, 1983, at 98 plus accrued interest. The bonds were dated April 1, 1983, with interest payable April 1 and October 1. Bond discount is amortized semiannually on a straight-line basis.

On April 1, 1984, $1,500,000 of these bonds were converted into 1,500 shares of $20 par value common stock. Accrued interest was paid in cash at the time of conversion.

**Instructions**

(a) Prepare the entry to record the interest expense at October 1, 1983. Assume that accrued interest payable was credited when the bonds were issued. (Round to nearest dollar.)
(b) Prepare the entry(ies) to record the conversion on April 1, 1984. (Book value method is used.) Assume that the entry to record amortization of the bond discount and interest payment has been made.

**E17-3** Purdue Boiler Company has bonds payable outstanding in the amount of $500,000 and carries its account Premium on Bonds Payable in the amount of $7,500. Each $1,000 bond is convertible into 20 shares of preferred stock of par value of $50 per share.

**Instructions**

(a) Assuming that the bonds are quoted on the market at 102 and that the preferred stock may be sold on the market at $50⅞, make the entry to record the conversion of the bonds to preferred stock. (Use the market value approach.)
(b) Assuming that the book value method was used, what entry would be made?

**E17-4** On September 1, 1983, T. Campbell Company sold at 104, (plus accrued interest) four thousand of its 9%, ten-year, $1,000 face value, nonconvertible bonds with detachable stock warrants. Each bond carried two detachable warrants; each warrant was for one share of common stock, at a specified option price of $15 per share. Shortly after issuance, the warrants were quoted on the market for $3 each. No market value can be determined for the bonds above. Interest is payable on December 1, and June 1. Bond issue costs of $40,000 were incurred.

**Instructions**

Prepare in general journal format the entry to record the issuance of the bonds.

(AICPA adapted)

**E17-5** On January 1, 1982, when its $30 par value common stock was selling for $80 per share, Linda Elbert Corp. issued $10,000,000 of 8% convertible debentures due in 10 years. The conversion option allowed the holder of each $1,000 bond to convert the bond into five shares of the corporation's $30 par value common stock. The debentures were issued for $10,900,000. The present value of the bond payments at the time of issuance was $8,500,000 and the corporation believes the difference between the present value and the amount paid is attributable to the conversion feature. On January 1, 1983, the corporation's $30 par value common stock was split 2 for 1. On January 1, 1984, when the corporation's $15 par value common stock was selling for $135 per share, holders of 30% of the convertible debentures exercised their conversion options. The corporation uses the straight-line method for amortizing any bond discounts or premiums.

**Instructions**

(a) Prepare in general journal form the entry to record the original issuance of the convertible debentures.

(b) Prepare in general journal form the entry to record the exercise of the conversion option, using the book value method. Show supporting computations in good form.

**E17-6** The December 31, 1983 balance sheet of Discorama Corp. is as follows:

*not good test problem - too easy*

| | | |
|---|---:|---:|
| 8% callable, Convertible Bonds Payable (semiannual interest dates April 30 and October 31; convertible into 5 shares of $25 par value common stock per $1,000 of bond principal; maturity date April 30, 1989) | $400,000 | |
| Discount on Bonds Payable | 9,600 | $390,400 |

On March 5, 1984, Discorama Corp. called all of the bonds as of April 30 for the principal plus interest through April 30. By April 30 all bondholders had exercised their conversion to common stock as of the interest payment date. Consequently, on April 30, Discorama Corp. paid the semiannual interest and issued shares of common stock for the bonds. The discount is amortized on a straight-line basis. Discorama uses the book value method.

**Instructions**

Prepare the entry(ies) to record the interest expense and conversion on April 30, 1984. Reversing entries were made on January 1, 1984. (Round to the nearest dollar.)

**E17-7** Atlanta Inc. has decided to raise additional capital by issuing $150,000 face value of bonds with a coupon rate of 10%. In discussions with their investment bankers, it was determined that to help the sale of the bonds, detachable stock warrants should be issued at the rate of one warrant for each $100 bond sold. The value of the bonds without the warrants is considered to be $132,000, and the value of the warrants in the market is $24,000. The bonds sold in the market at issuance for $147,000.

**Instructions**

(a) What entry should be made at the time of the issuance of the bonds and warrants?

(b) If the warrants were nondetachable, would the entries be different? Discuss.

**E17-8** On January 1, 1983, Charmglo Corporation issued $4,000,000 of 10-year, 8% convertible debentures at 102. Interest is to be paid semiannually on June 30 and December 31. Each $1,000 debenture can be converted into eight shares of Charmglo Corporation $100 par value common stock after December 31, 1984.

On January 1, 1985, $400,000 of debentures are converted into common stock, which is then selling at $112. An additional $400,000 of debentures is converted on March 31, 1985. The market price of the common stock is then $115.

Bond premium is amortized on a straight-line basis.

**Instructions**

Make the necessary journal entries for:

(a) December 31, 1984.　　　　　　　　(b) January 1, 1985.

(c) March 31, 1985.        (d) June 30, 1985.

Record the conversions under both the fair market value method and the book value method.

**E17-9** On November 1, 1981, Tumbleweed Company adopted a stock option plan that granted options to key executives to purchase 45,000 shares of the company's $10 par value common stock. The options were granted on January 2, 1982, and were exercisable two years after date of grant if the grantee was still an employee of the company; the options expired six years from date of grant. The option price was set at $35; market price at the date of the grant was $47 a share.

All of the options were exercised during the year 1984; 30,000 on January 3 when the market price was $67, and 15,000 on May 1 when the market price was $77 a share.

**Instructions**

(a) Compute the value of the stock option and the corresponding amount of executive compensation.

(b) Prepare journal entries relating to the stock option plan for the years 1982, 1983, and 1984. Assume that the employee performs services equally in 1982 and 1983.

**E17-10** On November 2, 1980, the stockholders of Siska Company voted to adopt a stock option plan for Siska's key officers. According to terms of the option agreement, the officers of the company can purchase 30,000 shares of common stock during 1983 and 54,000 shares during 1984. The shares that are purchasable during 1983 represent executive compensation for 1981 and 1982, and those purchasable during 1984 represent such compensation for 1981, 1982, and 1983. If options for shares are not exercised during either year, they lapse as of the end of that year.

Options were granted to the officers of Siska on January 1, 1981, and at that time the option price was set for all shares at $30. During 1983, all options were exercised. During 1984, however, options for only 27,000 shares were exercised. The remaining options lapsed because the executives decided not to exercise. Par value of the stock is $10. The market prices of Siska common at various dates follows:

| Dates | Market Price of Siska's Common |
|---|---|
| Option agreement accepted by stockholders | $32 |
| Options granted | 35 |
| Options exercised in 1983 | 37 |
| Options exercised in 1984 | 33 |

**Instructions**

Make any necessary journal entries related to this stock option for the following years: 1980, 1981, 1983, and 1984 (Siska closes its books on December 31).

**E17-11** On January 1, 1981, Bowen, Inc., granted stock options to officers and key employees for the purchase of 20,000 shares of the company's $10 par common stock at $25 per share. The options were exercisable within a five-year period beginning January 1, 1983, by grantees still in the employ of the company, and expiring December 31, 1987. The market price of Bowen's common stock was $33 per share at the date of grant. Bowen prepares a formal journal entry to record this award. The service period for this award is two years.

On April 1, 1982, 2,000 option shares were terminated when the employees resigned from the company. The market value of the common stock was $35 per share on this date.

On March 31, 1983, 12,000 option shares were exercised when the market value of the common stock was $40 per share.

**Instructions**

Prepare journal entries to record issuance of the stock options, termination of the stock options, exercise of the stock options, and charges to compensation expense, for the years ended December 31, 1981, 1982 and 1983.

(AICPA adapted)

**E17-12** Mr. Max Rexroad has recently been elected president of ISU Company. As an incentive for Mr. Rexroad to become president, the company offered him the following pay package: (1) a salary of $85,000 per year, (2) an expense allowance of $16,000 per year, and (3) the right to purchase 5,000 shares of common stock at $10 per share; the current market price is $16 per share.

**Instructions**

(a) What entry is needed to record the granting of these stock options to Mr. Rexroad?

(b) Assume that the stock options had the following restriction attached: Mr. Rexroad must remain an employee of the company for three years before he is entitled to the stock. Consultation with investment bankers suggests that the value of these restricted shares is $14. What entry is needed to record the granting of these stock options to Mr. Rexroad?

**E17-13** On December 31, 1982, Martin Bubley Soap Company issues 150,000 stock appreciation rights to its officers entitling them to receive cash for the difference between the market price of its stock and a preestablished price of $10. The date of exercise is December 31, 1986. The market price fluctuates as follows: 12/31/83—$14; 12/31/84—$8; 12/31/85—$20; 12/31/86—$18. Rights are exercisable only if the officer is employed by the company at the date of exercise.

**Instructions**

(a) Prepare a schedule that shows the amount of compensation expense allocable to each year affected by the stock appreciation rights plan.

(b) Prepare the entry at 12/31/86 to record compensation expense, if any, in 1986.

(c) Prepare the entry on 12/31/86 assuming that all 150,000 SARs are exercised by all of the eligible officers.

**E17-14** J. Brauer Company establishes a stock appreciation rights program which entitles its new president Kay Roddick to receive cash for the difference between the market price of the stock and a preestablished price of $30 (also market price) on December 31, 1983 on 30,000 SARs. The date of grant is December 31, 1983 and the required employment (service) period is three years. President Roddick exercises all of the SARs in 1989. The market value of the stock fluctuates as follows: 12/31/84—$36; 12/31/85—$39; 12/31/86—$45; 12/31/87—$36; 12/31/88—$48.

**Instructions**

(a) Prepare a five-year (1984–1988) schedule of compensation expense pertaining to the 30,000 SARs granted President Roddick.

(b) Prepare the journal entry for compensation expense in 1984, 1987, and 1988 relative to the 30,000 SARs.

**E17-15** Sandles & Candles Co. had 100,000 shares outstanding on January 1 and reacquired 24,000 shares on March 1.

**Instructions**

What is the weighted average number of shares outstanding:

(a) For the quarter ending March 31?      (c) For the year ending December 31?

(b) For the six months ending June 30?

**E17-16** Subscription TV Company had 240,000 shares of common stock outstanding on December 31, 1984. During the year 1985 the company issued 12,000 shares on May 1 and retired 24,000 shares on October 31. For the year 1985 Subscription TV Company reported net income of $372,000 after a casualty loss of $62,000 (net of tax).

**Instructions**

What earnings per share data should be reported at the bottom of its income statement, assuming that the casualty loss is extraordinary?

**E17-17** Barrel Winery, Inc. presented the following data:

| | |
|---|---:|
| Net income | $5,700,000 |
| Preferred stock: 100,000 shares outstanding, | |
| $100 par, 7% cumulative, not convertible | 10,000,000 |
| Common stock: Shares outstanding 1/1 | 1,800,000 |
| Issued for cash, 5/1 | 900,000 |
| Acquired treasury stock for cash, 8/1 | 240,000 |
| 2-for-1 stock split, 10/1 | |

**Instructions**

Compute earnings per share.

**E17-18** A portion of the combined statement of income and retained earnings of Dorothy Swanson, Inc. for the current year follows:

| | | |
|---|---:|---:|
| Income before extraordinary item | | $ 17,000,000 |
| Extraordinary loss, net of applicable | | |
| income tax (Note 1) | | 1,700,000 |
| Net income | | 15,300,000 |
| Retained earnings at the beginning of the year | | 99,162,700 |
| | | 114,462,700 |
| Dividends declared: | | |
| On preferred stock—$6.00 per share | $ 300,000 | |
| On common stock—$1.75 per share | 14,000,000 | 14,300,000 |
| Retained earnings at the end of the year | | $100,162,700 |

*Note 1.* During the year, Swanson Inc. suffered a major casualty loss of $1,700,000 after applicable income tax reduction of $1,450,000.

At the end of the current year, Swanson, Inc. has outstanding 8,000,000 shares of $10 par common stock and 50,000 shares of 6% preferred.

On April 1 of the current year, Swanson, Inc. issued 1,000,000 shares of common stock for $32 per share to help finance the casualty.

**Instructions**

Compute the earnings per share on common stock for the current year as it should be reported to stockholders.

**E17-19** On January 1, 1984, Pelzer Industries had stock outstanding as follows:

| | |
|---|---:|
| 5% Cumulative preferred stock, $100 par value, | |
| issued and outstanding 8,000 shares. | $ 800,000 |
| Common stock, $10 par value, issued and | |
| outstanding 250,000 shares. | 2,500,000 |

To acquire the net assets of three smaller companies, Pelzer authorized the issuance of an additional 160,000 common shares. The acquisitions took place as follows:

| Date of Acquisition | | Shares Issued |
|---|---|---:|
| Company A | April 1, 1984 | 100,000 |
| Company B | July 1, 1984 | 40,000 |
| Company C | October 1, 1984 | 20,000 |

On May 14, 1984, Pelzer realized a $90,000 insurance gain on the expropriation of investments originally purchased in 1973.

On December 31, 1984, Pelzer recorded net income of $300,000 before tax and exclusive of the gain.

**Instructions**

Assuming a 50% tax rate, compute the earnings per share data that should appear on the financial statements of Pelzer Industries as of December 31, 1984. Assume that the expropriation is extraordinary.

**E17-20** At January 1, 1984 H. R. Hatfield Company's outstanding shares included:

> 150,000 shares of $100 par value, 6% cumulative preferred stock
> 1,000,000 shares of $1.00 par value common stock

Net income for 1984 was $2,584,500. No cash dividends were declared or paid during 1984. On February 15, 1985, however, all preferred dividends in arrears were paid, together with a 5% stock dividend on common shares. There were no dividends in arrears prior to 1984.

On April 1, 1984, 400,000 shares of common stock were sold for $10 per share and on October 1, 1984, 120,000 shares of common stock were purchased for $20 per share and held as treasury stock.

**Instructions**

Compute earnings per share for 1984. Assume that financial statements for 1984 were issued in March, 1985.

**E17-21** In 1983, C. Blough Enterprises issued, at par, 40, $500, 8% bonds, each convertible into 100 shares of common stock. At the time the bonds were issued, the average Aa corporate bond yield was 11%. Blough had revenues of $12,400 and expenses other than interest and taxes of $7,600 for 1984 (assume that the tax rate is 40%). Throughout 1984, 2,000 shares of common stock were outstanding; none of the bonds were converted or redeemed.

**Instructions**

(a) Compute earnings per share for 1984.
(b) Assume the same facts as those assumed for Part (a), except that the 40 bonds were issued on October 1, 1984 (rather than in 1983), and none have been converted or redeemed.
(c) Assume the same facts as assumed for Part (a), except that 20 of the 40 bonds were actually converted on July 1, 1984.

**E17-22** On June 1, 1981, Pacioli Company and Wm. Paton Company merged to form PWP Inc. A total of 900,000 shares were issued to complete the merger. The new corporation reports on a calendar-year basis.

On April 1, 1983, the company issued an additional 200,000 shares of stock for cash. All 1,100,000 shares were outstanding on December 31, 1983.

PWP Inc. also issued $500,000 of 20-year, 8 percent convertible bonds at par on July 1, 1983, when the average Aa corporate bond yield was 10 percent. Each $1,000 bond converts to 40 shares of common at any interest date. None of the bonds have been converted to date.

PWP Inc. is preparing its annual report for the fiscal year ending December 31, 1983. The annual report will show earnings per share figures based upon a reported after-tax net income of $840,000 (the tax rate is 40 percent).

**Instructions**

(a) Should PWP Inc. convertible bonds be treated as common stock equivalents for the calculation of earnings per share? Explain your answer.
(b) Without prejudice to your answer in Part a, assume that the convertible bonds are not to be treated as common stock equivalents. Determine for 1983:
    1. The number of shares to be used for calculating:
      a. Primary earnings per share.
      b. Fully diluted earnings per share.
    2. The earnings figures to be used for calculating:
      a. Primary earnings per share.
      b. Fully diluted earnings per share.

(CMA adapted)

**E17-23** A. Lowes Dickinson's net income for 1984 is $40,000. The only potentially dilutive securities outstanding were 2,000 options issued during 1983, each exercisable for one share at $5. None have been exercised, and 10,000 shares of common were outstanding during 1984. The average market price of Dickinson's stock during all quarters of 1984 was $12; the December 31, 1984, price was $22.

**Instructions**

(a) Compute the earnings per share (round to nearest cent).

(b) Assume the same facts as those assumed for Part (a), except that the 2,000 options were issued on November 1, 1984 (rather than in 1983). The average market price during the last three months of 1984 was $18. The 1984 closing price was $22.

**E17-24** Zeff Steel, Inc. indicates that its net income for 1984 is $20,100,000, which includes a gain on casualty (net of tax) of $1,800,000. Its capital structure includes some common stock reserved under employee stock options (114,000 shares). The common shares outstanding for the year remained at 6,600,000. The controller, Steve Zeff, asks your advice concerning the earnings per share figure that they should present. The common stock price has remained fairly stable during the year at $38 per share and the option price for the stock options is $32 per share.

**Instructions**

What would you tell the controller? (Assume that the gain is extraordinary.)

**E17-25** E. Koehler, Inc., recently purchased G. O. May Homes, a large midwestern prefabricated-home manufacturer. One of the terms of the merger was that if G. O. May Homes' income for 1984 was $90,000 or more, 20,000 additional shares would be paid to G. O. May Homes' stockholders in 1985. G. O. May's income for 1983 was $100,000.

**Instructions**

(a) Would the contingent shares have to be considered in E. Koehler's 1983 earnings per share computations?

(b) Assume the same facts, except that the 20,000 shares are contingent on G. O. May Homes' achieving a net income of $110,000 in 1984. Would the contingent shares have to be considered in E. Koehler's earnings per share computations?

**E17-26** Niven & Bailey Corporation earned $200,000 during a period when it had an average of 60,000 shares of common stock outstanding. The common stock sold at an average market price of $20 per share during the period and sold at $25 at the end of the period. Also outstanding were 16,000 warrants that could be exercised to purchase one share of common stock for $15 for each warrant exercised.

**Instructions**

(a) Are the warrants dilutive?

(b) Compute primary earnings per share.

(c) Compute fully diluted earnings per share.

## PROBLEMS

**P17-1** The stockholders' equity section of R. H. Montgomery, Inc. at the beginning of the current year appears below:

| | |
|---|---:|
| Common stock, $20 par value, authorized 500,000 shares, 100,000 shares issued and outstanding | $2,000,000 |
| Paid-in capital in excess of par | 400,000 |
| Retained earnings | 380,000 |

During the current year the following transactions occurred:

1. The company issued to the stockholders 100,000 rights. Ten rights are needed to buy one share of stock at $32. The rights were void after 30 days. The market price of the stock at this time was $34 per share.

**2.** The company sold to the public a $200,000, 10% bond issue at par. The company also issued with each $100 bond one detachable stock purchase warrant, which provided for the purchase of common stock at $28 per share. Shortly after issuance, similar bonds without warrants were selling at 96 and the warrants at $8.

**3.** All but 10,000 of the rights issued in (1) were exercised in 30 days.

**4.** At the end of the year, 50% of the warrants in (2) had been exercised, and the remaining were outstanding and in good standing.

**5.** During the current year, the company granted stock options for 3,000 shares of common stock to company executives. The market price of the stock on that date was $40 and the option price was $30. The options were to expire at year-end and were considered compensation for the current year.

**6.** All but 500 shares related to the stock option plan were exercised by year-end. The expiration resulted because one of the executives failed to fulfill an obligation related to the employment contract.

### Instructions

(a) Prepare general journal entries for the current year to record the transactions listed above.

(b) Prepare the stockholders' equity section of the balance sheet at the end of the current year. Assume that retained earnings at the end of the current year is $680,000.

**P17-2** A. C. Littleton Company issued $2,000,000 of convertible 10-year bonds on July 1, 1983. The bonds provide for 10% interest payable semiannually on January 1 and July 1. Expense and discount in connection with the issue was $39,000, which is being amortized monthly on a straight-line basis.

The bonds are convertible after one year into 8 shares of Littleton Company's $100 par value common stock for each $1,000 of bonds.

On August 1, 1984, $200,000 of bonds were turned in for conversion into common. Interest has been accrued monthly and paid as due. At the time of conversion any accrued interest on bonds being converted is paid in cash.

### Instructions

Prepare the journal entries to record the conversion, amortization, and interest in connection with the bonds as of:

(a) August 1, 1984.

(b) August 31, 1984.

(c) December 31, 1984, including closing entries for end of year.

(AICPA adapted)

**P17-3** Steven Elbert Company adopted a stock option plan on November 30, 1982, that provided that 60,000 shares of $5 par value stock be designated as available for the granting of options to officers of the corporation at a price of $8 a share. The market value was $12 a share on November 30, 1982.

On January 2, 1983, options to purchase 24,000 shares were granted to President Larry Mohrweis—12,000 for services to be rendered in 1983 and 12,000 for services to be rendered in 1984. Also on that date, options to purchase 12,000 shares were granted to Vice-President Karen Meiers—4,000 for services to be rendered in 1983 and 8,000 for services to be rendered in 1984. The market value of the stock was $14 a share on January 2, 1983. The options were exercisable for a period of one year following the year in which the services were rendered.

In 1984 neither the president nor the vice-president exercised their options because the market price of the stock was below the exercise price. The market value of the stock was $6 a share on December 31, 1984, when the options for 1983 services lapsed.

On December 31, 1985, both President Mohrweis and Vice-President Meiers exercised their options for 12,000 and 8,000 shares, respectively, when the market price was $16 a share.

**Instructions**

(a) Prepare the necessary journal entries in 1982 when the stock option plan was adopted, in 1983 when options were granted, in 1984 when options lapsed and in 1985 when options were exercised.

(b) What disclosure of the stock option plan should appear in the financial statements at December 31, 1982? At December 31, 1983? Assume that the stock options outstanding or exercised at any time are a significant financial item.

**P17-4** As auditor for Search & Find, you have been assigned to check Cloudy Corporation's computation of earnings per share for the current year. The controller has supplied you with the following computations:

| | |
|---|---:|
| Net income | $3,413,928 |
| Common shares issued and outstanding: | |
|   Beginning of year | 1,204,761 |
|   End of year | 1,004,901 |
|   Average | 1,104,831 |

Earnings per share
$$\frac{\$3,413,928}{1,104,831} = \$3.09 \text{ per share}$$

You have developed the following additional information:

1. There are no other equity securities in addition to the common shares.

2. There are no options or warrants outstanding to purchase common shares.

3. There are no convertible debt securities.

4. Activity in common shares during the year was as follows:

| | |
|---|---:|
| Outstanding, Jan. 1 | 1,204,761 |
| Treasury shares acquired, Oct. 1 | (300,000) |
| | 904,761 |
| Shares reissued, Dec. 1 | 100,140 |
| Outstanding, Dec. 31 | 1,004,901 |

**Instructions**

(a) On the basis of the information above, do you agree with the controller's computation of earnings per share for the year? If you disagree, prepare a revised computation of earnings per share.

(b) Assume the same facts as those in (a), except that options had been issued to purchase 150,000 shares of common stock at $10 per share. These options were outstanding at the beginning of the year and none had been exercised or canceled during the year. The average market price of the common shares during the year was $25 and the ending market price was $35. Prepare a computation of earnings per share.

**P17-5** Beams Nursery Company had the following account titles on its December 31, 1984, trial balance:

14% cumulative convertible preferred stock, $100 par value

Paid-in Capital in Excess of Par—Preferred Stock

Common stock, $1.00 stated value

Paid-in Capital in Excess of Par—Common Stock

Retained Earnings

The following additional information about the Beams Nursery Company was available for the year ended December 31, 1984:

1. 1,500,000 shares of preferred stock were authorized, of which 1,000,000 were outstanding. All 1,000,000 shares outstanding were issued on January 2, 1981, for $110 a share.

The average Aa corporate bond yield was 18% on January 2, 1981, and was 20% on December 31, 1984. The preferred stock is convertible into common stock on a one-for-one basis until December 31, 1990; thereafter the preferred stock ceases to be convertible and is callable at par value by the company. No preferred stock has been converted into common stock, and there were no dividends in arrears at December 31, 1984.

2. The common stock has been issued at amounts above stated value per share since incorporation in 1966. Of the 5,500,000 shares authorized, there were 3,900,000 shares outstanding at January 1, 1984. The market price of the outstanding common stock has increased slowly, but consistently, for the last five years.

3. The company has an employee stock option plan under which certain key employees and officers may purchase shares of common stock at 100% of the market price at the date of the option grant. All options are exercisable in installments of one-third each year, commencing one year after the date of the grant, and expire if not exercised within four years of the grant date. On January 1, 1984, options for 76,000 shares were outstanding at prices ranging from $47 to $83 a share. Options for 22,000 shares were exercised at $47 to $79 a share during 1984. No options expired during 1984 and additional options for 16,000 shares were granted at $86 a share during the year. The 70,000 options outstanding at December 31, 1984, were exercisable at $54 to $86 a share; of these, 32,500 were exercisable at that date at prices ranging from $54 to $79 a share.

4. The company also has an employee stock purchase plan under which the company pays one-half and the employee pays one-half of the market price of the stock at the date of the subscription. During 1984, employees subscribed to 65,000 shares at an average price of $87 a share. All 65,000 shares were paid for and issued late in September 1984.

5. On December 31, 1984, a total of 400,000 shares of common stock was set aside for the granting of future stock options and for future purchases under the employee stock purchase plan. The only changes in the stockholders' equity for 1984 were those described above, 1984 net income, and cash dividends paid.

**Instructions**

(a) Prepare the stockholders' equity section of the balance sheet of Beams Nursery Company at December 31, 1984; substitute, where appropriate, Xs for unknown dollar amounts. Use good form and provide full disclosure. Write appropriate footnotes as they should appear in the published financial statements.

(b) Explain how the amount of the denominator should be determined to compute primary earnings per share for presentation in the financial statements. Be specific as to the handling of each item. If additional information is needed to determine whether an item should be included or excluded or the extent to which an item should be included, identify the information needed and how the item would be handled if the information were known. Assume Beams Nursery Company had substantial net income for the year ended December 31, 1984.

(AICPA adapted)

**P17-6** The controller of Tennessee Corporation has requested assistance in determining income, primary earnings per share, and fully diluted earnings per share for presentation in the company's income statement for the year ended September 30, 1985. As currently calculated, the company's net income is $700,000 for fiscal year 1984–1985. The controller has indicated that the income figure might be adjusted for the following transactions that were recorded by charges or credits directly to retained earnings (the amounts are net of applicable income taxes):

1. The sum of $280,000, applicable to a breached 1981 contract, was received as a result of a lawsuit. Prior to the award, legal counsel was uncertain about the outcome of the suit.

2. A gain of $300,000 was realized from condemnation sale (extraordinary).

3. A "gain" of $165,000 was realized on the sale of treasury stock.

4. A special inventory write-off of $190,000 was made, of which $120,000 applied to goods manufactured prior to October 1, 1984.

Your working papers disclose the following opening balances and transactions in the company's capital stock accounts during the year:

1. Common stock (at October 1, 1984, stated value $10, authorized 450,000 shares; effective December 1, 1984, stated value $5, authorized 900,000 shares):

   Balance, October 1, 1984—issued and outstanding 90,000 shares.
   December 1, 1984—90,000 shares issued in a 2 for 1 stock split.
   December 1, 1984—420,000 shares (stated value $5) issued at $39 per share.

2. Treasury stock—common:

   March 1, 1985—purchased 60,000 shares at $37.25 per share.
   April 1, 1985—sold 60,000 shares at $40 per share.

3. Stock purchase warrants, Series A (initially, each warrant was exchangeable with $60 for one common share; effective December 1, 1984, each warrant became exchangeable for two common shares at $30 per share):

   October 1, 1984—37,500 warrants issued at $6 each.

4. Stock purchase warrants, Series B (each warrant is exchangeable with $40 for one common share):

   April 1, 1985—30,000 warrants authorized and issued at $10 each.

5. First mortgage bonds, 9%, due 2000 (nonconvertible; priced to yield 8% when issued):

   Balance, October 1, 1984—authorized, issued, and outstanding—the face value of $2,100,000.

6. Convertible debentures, 7%, due 2004 (initially, each $1,000 bond was convertible at any time until maturity into 12½ common shares; effective December 1, 1984, the conversion rate became 25 shares for each bond):

   October 1, 1984—authorized and issued at their face value (no premium or discount) of $3,600,000.

The following table shows market prices for the company's securities and the assumed average Aa corporate bond yield rate during 1984–1985:

| | Price (or Rate) at | | | |
| | 10/1/84 | 4/1/85 | 9/30/85 | Average for Year Ended 9/30/85 |
| --- | --- | --- | --- | --- |
| Common stock | 66 | 40 | 36¼ | 37½[a] |
| First mortgage bonds | 88½ | 87 | 86 | 87 |
| Convertible debentures | 100 | 120 | 119 | 115 |
| Series A Warrants | 6 | 22 | 19½ | 15 |
| Series B Warrants | — | 10 | 9 | 9½ |
| Avg. Aa corp. bond yield | 8% | 7¾% | 7½% | 7¾% |

[a]Adjusted for stock split

**Instructions**

(a) Prepare a schedule computing net income as it should be presented in the company's income statement for the year ended September 30, 1985.

(b) Assuming that net income after income taxes for the year was $1,087,200 and that there were no extraordinary items, prepare a schedule computing (1) the primary earnings per share and (2) the fully diluted earnings per share that should be presented in the company's income statement for the year ended September 30, 1985. A supporting schedule computing the numbers of shares to be used in these computations should also be prepared. (Because of the relative stability of the market price for its common shares, the annual average market price may be used where appropriate in your calculations. Assume an income tax rate of 48%.)                    (AICPA adapted)

**P17-7** On February 1, 1984, when your audit and report are nearly complete, Joan Clay, the president of Clay Toy Corporation asks you to prepare statistical schedules of comparative financial data for the past five years for inclusion in the company's annual report. Your working papers reveal the following information.

1. Income statements show net income amounts as follows:

   1979—$38,000
   1980— (40,000) (loss)
   1981— 50,000
   1982— 76,000
   1983— 98,000

2. On January 1, 1979, there were outstanding 2,000 shares of common stock, par value $100, and 1,000 shares of 6% cumulative preferred stock, par value $50.

3. A 5% dividend was paid in common stock to common stockholders on December 31, 1980. The fair market value of the stock was $145 per share at the time.

4. Eight hundred shares of common stock were issued on March 31, 1981, to purchase another company. (The transaction was accounted for as a purchase, not a pooling of interests: use weighted-average approach for purchase of a business.)

5. A dividend of cumulative preferred stock was distributed to common stockholders on July 1, 1981. One share of preferred stock was distributed for every five shares of common stock held. The fair market value of the preferred stock was $56 per share before the distribution and $54 per share immediately after the distribution.

6. The common stock was split 2-for-1 on December 31, 1982, and again on December 31, 1983.

7. Cash dividends are paid on the preferred stock on June 30 and December 31. Preferred stock dividends were paid in each year except 1980; the 1980 and 1981 dividends were paid in 1981.

8. Cash dividends on common stock are paid on June 30 and December 31. Dividends paid per share of stock outstanding at the respective dates were:

| 1979 | $ .50 | $ .50 |
|------|-------|-------|
| 1980 | None | None |
| 1981 | .75 | .75 |
| 1982 | 1.00 | .50[a] |
| 1983 | .75 | .75[b] |

[a]After 2-for-1 split.
[b]Before 2-for-1 split.

### Instructions

(a) In connection with your preparation of the statistical schedule of comparative financial data for the past five years:
   1. Prepare a schedule computing the number of shares of common stock and preferred stock outstanding as of the respective year-end dates.
   2. Prepare a schedule computing the current equivalent number of shares of common stock outstanding as of the respective year-end dates. The current equivalent shares means the weighted average number of shares outstanding in the respective prior periods after restatement for stock splits and stock dividends.
   3. Compute the total cash dividends paid to holders of preferred stock and to holders of common stock for each of the five years.
(b) Prepare a five-year summary of financial statistics to be included in the annual report. The summary should show by years "Net Income (or Loss)," "Earnings Per Share of Common Stock," and "Cash Dividends Per Share of Common Stock." The per share figures should be computed on the basis of current equivalent shares. (AICPA adapted)

**P17–8** The stockholders' equity section of Seville Company's balance sheet as of December 31, 1984, contains the following:

| | |
|---|---:|
| $2.00 cumulative convertible preferred stock (par value $25 a share; authorized 1,600,000 shares, issued 1,400,000, converted to common 750,000, and outstanding 650,000 shares; involuntary liquidation value, $30 a share, aggregating $19,500,000) | $16,250,000 |
| Common stock (par value $.25 a share; authorized 15,000,000 shares, issued and outstanding 9,200,000 shares) | 2,300,000 |
| Additional paid-in capital | 30,500,000 |
| Retained earnings | 45,050,000 |
| Total stockholders' equity | $94,100,000 |

On April 1, 1984, Seville Company acquired the business and assets and assumed the liabilities of Lockhart Corporation in a transaction accounted for as a pooling of interests. For each of Lockhart Corporation's 2,400,000 shares of $.25 par value common stock outstanding, the owner received one share of common stock of Seville Company. (**Hint:** In a pooling of interests, shares are considered outstanding for the entire year.)

Included in the liabilities of Seville Company are 10% convertible subordinated debentures issued at their face value of $20,000,000 in 1983. The debentures are due in 2000 and until then are convertible into the common stock of Seville Company at the rate of five shares of common stock for each $100 debenture. To date none of these have been converted.

On April 2, 1984, Seville Company issued 1,400,000 shares of convertible preferred stock at $40 per share. Quarterly dividends to December 31, 1984, have been paid on these shares. The preferred stock is convertible into common stock at the rate of two shares of common for each share of preferred. On October 1, 1984, 150,000 shares and on November 1, 1984, 600,000 shares of the preferred stock were converted into common stock.

During July, 1983, Seville Company granted options to its officers and key employees to purchase 600,000 shares of the company's common stock at a price of $20 a share. The options do not become exercisable until 1985.

During 1984, dividend payments and average market prices of the Seville common stock were:

| | Dividend Per Share | Average Market Price Per Share |
|---|---:|---:|
| First quarter | $.11 | $25 |
| Second quarter | .13 | 30 |
| Third quarter | .15 | 20 |
| Fourth quarter | .12 | 25 |
| Average for the year | | 25 |

The December 31, 1984 closing price of the common stock was $25 a share.

Assume that the average Aa corporate bond yield was 14% throughout 1983 and 1984. Seville Company's consolidated net income for the year ended December 31, 1984, was $11,400,000. The provision for income taxes was computed at a rate of 48%.

**Instructions**

(a) Prepare a schedule that shows the evaluation of the common stock equivalency status of the (1) convertible debentures, (2) convertible preferred stock, and (3) employee stock options.

*(b) Prepare a schedule that shows for 1984 the computation of:
  1. The weighted-average number of shares for computing primary earnings per share.
  2. The weighted-average number of shares for computing fully diluted earnings per share.

(c) Prepare a schedule that shows for 1984 the computation to the nearest cent of:
  1. Primary earnings per share.
  2. Fully diluted earnings per share.

(AICPA adapted)

*Hint: Parts (b) and (c) may be more efficiently prepared if done simultaneously.

# CHAPTER 18

# Investments in Securities and Funds

In order to engage in the production and sale of goods or services, a business enterprise must invest funds in many types of assets: monetary assets—cash and receivables; productive tangible assets—inventories, plant and equipment, and land; and intangible assets—patents, licenses, trademarks, and goodwill. In addition, some funds may be applied to the acquisition of securities of other companies. Such investments are classified as either temporary or long-term. **Temporary investments,** as discussed in Chapter 7, must be (1) readily marketable, and (2) intended to be converted into cash within one year or within the operating cycle, whichever is longer. Investments not meeting these two criteria are classified as **long-term** or **permanent.**

This chapter is devoted primarily to long-term investments in corporate securities: bonds of various types, preferred stocks, and common stocks. Numerous other items are commonly classified as long-term investments: funds for bond retirement, stock redemption, and other special purposes; investments in notes receivable, mortgages and similar debt instruments; and miscellaneous items such as advances to affiliates, cash surrender value of life insurance policies, interests in estates and trusts, equity in joint ventures and partnerships, and real estate held for appreciation or future use. Some of these items are also discussed. Long-term investments are usually presented on the balance sheet just below current assets in a separate section called Long-Term Investments, Investments and Funds, or just Investments.

Although many reasons prompt a corporation to invest in the securities of another corporation, **the primary motive is to enhance its own income.** A corporation may thus enhance its income (1) directly through the receipt of dividends or interest from the investment or through appreciation in the market value of the securities, or (2) indirectly by creating and insuring desirable operating relationships between companies to improve income performance. Frequently the most permanent of investments are those in the latter category: those for improving income performance. Benefits to the investors are derived from the influence or control that may be exercised over a major supplier, customer, or otherwise related company. As an illustration, Sears, Roebuck holds large stock interests in several of its leading suppliers: 22% of Kellwood, 31% of DeSoto, 40% of Roper, and 59% of Universal Rundle Co.

## INVESTMENTS IN BONDS

Accounting for bonds as a long-term liability was presented in Chapter 14. In this chapter our attention is on accounting for these same securities from the investor's viewpoint. The types and characteristics of bonds that may be purchased are presented on pages 605–606; you should reread that discussion as background for this chapter. The variety in these features, along with the variability in interest rates, permits investors to shop for exactly the investment that satisfies their safety, yield, and marketability preferences.

### Accounting for Bond Acquisitions

Investments in bonds should be recorded on the date of acquisition at cost, which includes brokerage fees and any other costs incidental to the purchase. **The cost or purchase price of a bond investment is its market value, which is the product of the market's appraisal of the risk involved and consideration of the stated interest rate in comparison with the prevailing market (yield) rate of interest for that type of security.** The cash amount of interest to be received periodically is fixed by the stated rate of interest on the face value (also, called principal, par, or maturity value). If the rate of return desired by the investors is exactly equal to the stated rate, **the bond will sell at its face amount.** If investors demand a higher yield than the stated rate offers, **the bond will sell at a discount.** Purchasing the bond at an amount below the face amount, or at a discount, equates the yield on the bond with the market rate of interest. If the market rate of interest is below the stated rate, **investors will pay a premium,** more than maturity value, for the bond. The relationship between bond market values and interest rates is similar to that discussed under the heading of bonds payable, pages 607–612.

If bonds are **purchased between interest payment dates,** the investor must pay the owner the market price plus the interest accrued since the last interest payment date. The investor will collect this interest plus the additional interest earned by holding the bond to the next interest date. For example, assume the purchase on June 1 of bonds having a $100,000 face value and paying 12% interest on April 1 and October 1, for 97. The entry to record purchase of the bonds and accrued interest is as follows:

| | | |
|---|---|---|
| Investments in Bonds | 97,000 | |
| Interest Revenue ($100,000 × .12 × 2/12) | 2,000 | |
| (Interest Receivable might be debited instead) | | |
| Cash | | 99,000 |

On October 1 the investor will receive interest of $6,000 consisting of $2,000 paid at date of acquisition and $4,000 earned for holding the bond for four months.

Investments acquired at par, at a discount, or at a premium are generally recorded in the accounts at cost, including brokerage and other fees but excluding the accrued interest; generally they are not recorded at maturity value. The use of a separate discount or premium account as a valuation account is acceptable procedure, but in practice it has not been widely used. This traditional exclusion of a separate discount or premium account has not yet changed even though *APB Opinion No. 21* **recommends the disclosure of unamortized discount or premium on notes and bonds receivable.**

If the discount of $3,000 were recorded separately and the bond recorded at maturity value, the entry to record the investment in bonds would be as follows:

| Investments in Bonds | 100,000 | |
|---|---|---|
| Interest Revenue | 2,000 | |
| Discount on Investment in Bonds | | 3,000 |
| Cash | | 99,000 |

When the investment is recorded net of the discount, at $97,000 as in the first example, the discount is amortized by debit entries recorded directly to the Investment in Bonds account. When the investment is recorded at maturity value, at $100,000 as in the second example, the discount is amortized by debiting the Discount on Investments in Bonds account. Both methods produce exactly the same net results on the financial statements. The following illustrations record the investment at net of discount or premium.

## Computing Prices of Bond Investments

Theoretically the market price of a bond is the present value of its maturity amount plus the present value of its interest payments, both discounted at the market rate of interest. Using this as a basis, determine the price that should be paid for $10,000 of 8% bonds, interest payable semiannually, and maturing in six years, if a 10% yield is desired. The computation is as follows:

Purchase price = PV of maturity amount plus PV of interest payments
           = $10,000 × PV of 1 for 12 periods at 5%
              + $400 × PV of annuity of 1 for 12 periods at 5%
           = ($10,000 × .55684, Table 6–2) + ($400 × 8.86325, Table 6–4)
           = $5,568.40 + $3,545.30
           = $9,113.70

## Amortization of Bond Premium and Bond Discount

As previously discussed in Chapter 14, there are two widely used methods of amortizing bond premium and bond discount: (1) **the straight-line method,** and (2) **the effective interest method** (also called the present value or compound interest or effective yield method).

Both methods of amortizing bond discount and premium on long-term investments are illustrated below. The write-off of discount on bond investments is sometimes referred to as discount "accumulation" instead of "amortization."

**Straight-line Amortization of Premium** Assume that on March 1, 1984, bonds of a face value of $50,000, bearing 8% interest payable January 1 and July 1, are purchased for $53,008 plus accrued interest. The bonds mature January 1, 1992. The entry on March 1, 1984, is:

| Investments in Bonds | 53,008.00 | |
|---|---|---|
| Interest Revenue | 666.67 | |
| Cash | | 53,674.67 |

The accrued interest of $666.67 represents interest at 8% for two months on $50,000, the par value of the bonds purchased.

When six months' interest is received on July 1, 1984, premium allocable to four months is written off under the straight-line method by a credit to the Investments account, and the revenue is reduced accordingly. The premium amortized would be 4/94 of $3,008, or $128, because the bonds have been held for four months and because there are 94 months from the date of purchase to maturity date. The entry on July 1, 1984, therefore, is:

| | | |
|---|---|---|
| Cash | 2,000 | |
| Investments in Bonds ($3,008 × 4/94) | | 128 |
| Interest Revenue | | 1,872 |

The Interest Revenue account now has a balance of $1,872 less $666.67, or $1,205.33. This represents the revenue earned on the bonds during the four months from March 1 to July 1. This amount is analyzed as follows:

| | |
|---|---|
| Interest received on July 1, 1984, 8% × $50,000 × 6/12 | $2,000.00 |
| Deduct interest accrued on Mar. 1, 1984, date of purchase of bonds, 8% × $50,000 × 2/12 | 666.67 |
| Interest received that is applicable to the 4 months from Mar. 1 to July 1 | 1,333.33 |
| Deduct premium amortized for 4 months, 4/94 × $3,008 | 128.00 |
| Revenue earned during the 4 months | $1,205.33 |

On December 31, 1984, an adjusting entry would be made to accrue six months' interest and to amortize the premium applicable to six months.

| | | |
|---|---|---|
| Interest Receivable on Bonds | 2,000 | |
| Investments in Bonds ($3,008 × 6/94) | | 192 |
| Interest Revenue | | 1,808 |

The $192 credit to the Investments account represents the premium amortization for the six months from July 1 to December 31, or 6/94 of $3,008. The credit to Interest Revenue, $1,808, represents the difference between the interest receivable of $2,000 and the premium amortized of $192, or the net amount taken up as revenue for the six months ended December 31, 1984.

During the next year and during each succeeding year, a premium of $384, representing 12/94 of the total premium paid, will be amortized. Thus, by the maturity date the entire amount of the premium will have been removed from the Investments account, and the bonds will be carried on the books at par at that time. The entry to be made at the maturity date of the bonds will therefore be:

| | | |
|---|---|---|
| Cash | 50,000 | |
| Investments in Bonds | | 50,000 |

In the entries shown above, the premium was amortized simultaneously with the interest received or accrued. They do not have to be combined in one entry, however, or entered at the same time. The entries for interest received or receivable are made at the proper times independently of the entries for premium amortization. The proper amount of premium may be amortized at the end of each fiscal year or any other designated time by debiting Interest Revenue and crediting Investments in Bonds. In the example above, the recognition of accrued interest and amortization of premium in separate entries would be as follows:

| | | |
|---|---|---|
| Interest Receivable on Bonds | 2,000 | |
| Interest Revenue | | 2,000 |

| Interest Revenue | 192 | |
| --- | --- | --- |
| Investments in Bonds | | 192 |

Separate entries are convenient when reversing entries are used because the entry for accrued interest would be reversed but no reversing entry is needed for premium amortization.

**Amortization (Accumulation) of Discount**   If bonds are purchased below par, the straight-line method of amortization is the same as that illustrated above for amortization of premium. For discount, however, the amount of discount amortized is added to the interest revenue.

Assume that bonds with a par value of $50,000, bearing 8% interest payable January 1 and July 1, and maturing January 1, 1992, are purchased on March 1, 1984, for $46,992 plus accrued interest. In other words, assume that they are purchased at a discount of $3,008 instead of a premium of $3,008, as above. Because they have 94 months yet to run, the discount to be amortized for each month is 1/94 of $3,008, or $32. The entry to record the purchase is:

| Investments in Bonds | 46,992.00 | |
| --- | --- | --- |
| Interest Revenue | 666.67 | |
| Cash | | 47,658.67 |

When six months' interest is received on July 1, 1984, the entry is:

| Cash | 2,000 | |
| --- | --- | --- |
| Investments in Bonds | 128 | |
| Interest Revenue | | 2,128 |

In this case the Investments account is debited, and the credit to Interest Revenue is the total of the interest received and the discount amortized. If bonds are purchased at a discount, the discount amortized is debited to the asset account; by maturity date the book value of the bonds will be at par.

Thus, bonds purchased at a premium are written down to par through amortization of premium, and bonds purchased at a discount are written up to par through amortization of the discount.

**Effective Interest Method**   As discussed previously under long-term debt, Chapter 14, when a premium or discount is amortized under the straight-line method, the rate of return is not the same year after year. Although the interest received is constant from period to period, the carrying amount of the bond is either increasing or decreasing by the amount of the discount or premium amortization. The straight-line method produces a constant revenue, but produces a variable rate of return on the book value of the investment. Although the effective interest method results in a varying amount being recorded as interest revenue from period to period, its virtue is that it produces a constant rate of return on the book value of the investment from period to period.

The straight-line method is the more popular method because (1) it is simple to apply; (2) it avoids the computation of the effective interest rate; and (3) it produces a close approximation of the effective interest earned, unless the maturity date is many years distant or the premium or discount is exceptionally large. *APB Opinion No. 21* specifies a preference for the effective interest method and permits other methods if the results obtained are not significantly different from those produced by the effective interest method.

The effective interest method is applied to bond investments in a fashion similar to that described for bonds payable. The effective interest rate or yield is computed at the time of investment and is applied to the beginning book value of the investment for each interest period. In each period the book value of the investment is increased by the amortized discount or decreased by the amortized premium.

To illustrate, assume that the Robinson Company is the purchaser of the Evermaster Corporation bonds discussed in Chapter 14, page 609. To restate the situation, Robinson Company purchased $100,000 of 8% bonds of Evermaster Corporation on January 1, 1983, paying $92,278. The bonds mature January 1, 1988; interest is payable each July 1 and January 1. The discount of $7,722 ($100,000 minus $92,278) provided an effective interest yield of 10%. The schedule below discloses the effect of the discount amortization on the interest revenue recorded each period using the effective interest method of amortization if the bonds are held to maturity. The investment is carried in the accounts net of the unamortized discount.

SCHEDULE OF INTEREST REVENUE AND BOND DISCOUNT
AMORTIZATION—EFFECTIVE INTEREST METHOD
8% BONDS PURCHASED TO YIELD 10%

| Date | Debit Cash | Credit Interest Revenue | Debit Bond Investment[e] | Carrying Value of Bonds |
|---|---|---|---|---|
| 1/1/83 | | | | $ 92,278 |
| 7/1/83 | $ 4,000[a] | $ 4,614[b] | $ 614[c] | 92,892[d] |
| 1/1/84 | 4,000 | 4,645 | 645 | 93,537 |
| 7/1/84 | 4,000 | 4,677 | 677 | 94,214 |
| 1/1/85 | 4,000 | 4,711 | 711 | 94,925 |
| 7/1/85 | 4,000 | 4,746 | 746 | 95,671 |
| 1/1/86 | 4,000 | 4,783 | 783 | 96,454 |
| 7/1/86 | 4,000 | 4,823 | 823 | 97,277 |
| 1/1/87 | 4,000 | 4,864 | 864 | 98,141 |
| 7/1/87 | 4,000 | 4,907 | 907 | 99,048 |
| 1/1/88 | 4,000 | 4,952 | 952 | 100,000 |
| | $40,000 | $47,722 | $7,722 | |

[a]$4,000 = $100,000 × .08 × 6/12
[b]$4,614 = $92,278 × .10 × 6/12
[c]$614 = $4,614 − $4,000
[d]$92,892 = $92,278 + $614
[e]Or, debit Discount on Investment in Bonds if the investment is carried at maturity value.

The journal entry to record the receipt of the first semiannual interest payment on July 1, 1983 (as shown on the schedule) is:

| | | |
|---|---|---|
| Cash | 4,000 | |
| Investments in Bonds | 614 | |
| Interest Revenue | | 4,614 |

## Sale of Bond Investments Before Maturity Date

If bonds carried as long-term investments are sold before maturity date, entries must be made to amortize the discount or premium to the date of sale and to remove from the Investments account the book value of bonds sold.

For example, assume that the bonds described at the bottom of page 789 are sold on April 1, 1990, at 99½ plus accrued interest. Discount has been amortized at the rate of $32 per month from March 1, 1984, through the last closing date, December 31, 1989. An entry is made to amortize discount for the three months that have expired in 1990:

| | | |
|---|---:|---:|
| Investments in Bonds | 96 | |
| Interest Revenue | | 96 |

The entry to record the sale is:

| | | |
|---|---:|---:|
| Cash | 50,750 | |
| Interest Revenue | | 1,000 |
| Investments in Bonds | | 49,328 |
| Gain on Sale of Bond Investment | | 422 |

The credit to Interest Revenue represents accrued interest for three months, for which the purchaser pays cash. The debit to Cash represents the selling price of the bonds, $49,750, plus the accrued interest of $1,000. The credit to the Investments account represents the book value of the bonds on the date of the sale, and the credit to Gain on Sale of Bonds represents the excess of the selling price over the book value of the bonds. The computation of the latter two credits is shown below:

| | | |
|---|---:|---:|
| Selling price of bonds (exclusive of accrued interest) | | $49,750 |
| Deduct book value of bonds on April 1, 1990: | | |
|   Cost | $46,992 | |
|   Add discount amortized for the period from March 1, 1984,<br>    to April 1, 1990, 73/94 × $3,008 | 2,336 | 49,328 |
| Gain on sale | | $  422 |

## INVESTMENTS IN STOCKS

Shares of stock may be acquired in the market through security exchanges or "over the counter" through stockbrokers. Stock may also be acquired directly from an issuing company or from a private investor. When stock is purchased outright for cash, the full cost includes the purchase price of the security plus brokers' commissions and other fees incidental to the purchase. If stock is **acquired "on margin"** (the margin representing borrowings from the broker), the stock purchase should be recorded at its full cost, and a liability recognized for the unpaid balance. A stock **subscription** or agreement to buy the stock of a corporation is recognized by a charge to an asset account for the security to be received and a credit to a liability account for the amount to be paid. Any interest on an obligation arising from a stock purchase should be recognized as expense.

Stock acquired in **exchange for noncash consideration** (property or services) should be recorded at (1) the fair market value of the consideration given or (2) the fair market value of the stock received, whichever is more clearly determinable. The absence of clearly determinable values for the property or services or a market price for the security acquired may force the use of appraisals or estimates to arrive at a cost.

The purchase of two or more classes of securities for a **lump sum price** calls for the allocation of the cost to the different classes in some equitable manner. If market prices are available for each class of security, the lump sum cost may be apportioned on the basis of the **relative market values.** If the market price is available for one security but not for the other, the market price may be assigned to the one and the cost excess to the other. If market prices are not available at the date of acquisition of several securities, it may be necessary to defer cost apportionment until evidence of at least one value becomes available. In some instances cost apportionment may have to wait until one of the securities is sold. In such cases, the proceeds from the sale of the one security may be subtracted from the lump sum cost, leaving the residual cost to be assigned as the cost of the other.

Accounting for numerous purchases of securities requires that information regarding the cost of individual purchases be preserved, as well as the dates of purchases and sales. If specific identification is not possible, the use of an average cost may be used for multiple purchases in close proximity to the same class of security. The first-in, first-out method of assigning costs to investments at the time of sale is also acceptable and is normally employed.

## Effect of Ownership Interest

The extent to which one corporation (**investor**) acquires an interest in the common stock in another corporation (**investee**), that is, the degree of ownership interest, generally determines the accounting treatment for the investment. Long-term investments by one corporation in the common stock of another can be classified according to the percentage of the voting stock of the investee held by the investor:

1. Holdings of more than 50% (consolidated statements).
2. Holdings between 20% and 50% (equity method).
3. Holdings of less than 20% (cost method).

When one corporation acquires a voting interest of more than 50% (**controlling interest**) in another corporation, the investor corporation is referred to as the **parent** and the investee corporation as the **subsidiary.** The investment in the common stock of the subsidiary is presented as a long-term investment on the separate financial statements of the parent.

**Consolidated financial statements** are, however, generally prepared instead of separate financial statements for the parent and the subsidiary in which the parent treats the subsidiary as an investment. Consolidated financial statements disregard the distinction between separate legal entities and treat the parent and subsidiary corporations as a single economic entity. When and how to prepare consolidated financial statements are discussed extensively in advanced accounting. Whether or not consolidated financial statements are prepared, the investment in the subsidiary is generally accounted for on the parent's books using the **equity method** as explained in this chapter.

Although an investor corporation may hold an interest of less than 50% in an investee corporation and thus not possess legal control, its "investment in voting stock gives it the ability to exercise significant influence over operating and financial policies of an investee."[1] To provide a guide for accounting for investors when 50% or less of the common voting stock is held and to develop an operational definition of "significant influence," the APB in *Opinion No. 18* submitted this statement:

> Ability to exercise that influence may be indicated in several ways, such as representation on the board of directors, participation in policy making processes, material intercompany transactions,

---

[1]"The Equity Method of Accounting for Investments in Common Stock," *Opinions of the Accounting Principles Board No. 18* (New York: AICPA, 1971), par. 17.

interchange of managerial personnel, or technological dependency. Another important consideration is the extent of ownership by an investor in relation to the concentration of other shareholdings, but substantial or majority ownership of the voting stock of an investee by another investor does not necessarily preclude the ability to exercise significant influence by the investor. The Board recognizes that determining the ability of an investor to exercise such influence is not always clear and applying judgment is necessary to assess the status of each investment.[2]

To achieve a reasonable degree of uniformity in application of the "significant influence" criterion, the profession concluded that an investment (direct or indirect) of 20% or more of the voting stock of an investee should lead to a presumption that in the absence of evidence to the contrary an investor has the ability to exercise significant influence over an investee.[3]

In instances of "significant influence" (generally an investment of 20% or more) the investor is required to account for the investment using the **equity method.** When the investor lacks significant influence over the investee, presumably less than a 20% interest, the investment is to be accounted for using either (1) **the cost method** or (2) **the lower of cost or market method,** depending upon the character of the securities as discussed later.

Judgment is frequently required in determining whether an investment of 20% or more results in "significant influence" over the policies of an investee. In the late 1970s and early 1980s an increased number of "hostile" merger and takeover attempts created situations where "significant influence" over investees was difficult to determine. The FASB therefore provided examples of cases in which an investment of 20% or more might not enable an investor to exercise "significant influence":

(a) The investee opposes the investor's acquisition of its stock. For example, the investee files suit against the investor, or files a complaint with a governmental regulatory agency.

(b) The investor and investee sign an agreement under which the investor surrenders significant shareholder rights. This commonly occurs when an investee is resisting a takeover attempt by the investor, and the investor agrees to limit its shareholding in the investee.

(c) The investor's ownership share does not result in "significant influence" because majority ownership of the investee is concentrated among a small group of shareholders who operate the investee without regard to the views of the investor.

(d) The investor needs or wants more financial information than that which is publicly issued by the investee, tries to obtain it from the investee, and fails.

(e) The investor tries and fails to obtain representation on the investee's board of directors.[4]

The FASB indicated that this list of examples is not conclusive or all-inclusive. It is meant to provide examples of the types of evidence that indicate the need for further analysis when determining whether or not an investor is able to exert "significant influence" over an investee.

In specialized industries, investments in certain securities of others are accounted for using the **market value method.** The following pages discuss and illustrate the four methods of accounting for long-term investments, namely, (1) the cost method, (2) the equity

[2]Ibid.

[3]Ibid.

[4]"Criteria for Applying the Equity Method of Accounting for Investments in Common Stock," *Interpretations of the Financial Accounting Standards Board No. 35* (Stamford, Conn.: FASB, 1981).

method, (3) the lower of cost or market method, and (4) the market value method, and their applicability.[5]

## Cost Method

Under the **cost method** a long-term investment is originally recorded and reported at cost, and it continues to be carried and reported at cost in the investment account until it is either partially or entirely disposed of, or until some fundamental change in conditions makes it clear that the value originally assigned can no longer be justified. Write-downs from cost are appropriate when the dividends received represent a distribution of earnings retained in the business prior to the acquisition of the stock by the investor (**liquidating dividend**). Ordinary cash dividends received from the investee are recorded as investment revenue.

To illustrate a liquidating dividend, assume that Semco Inc. owns 5% of the common stock of Alco Mining Company. Alco Mining declares a dividend of $200,000 and indicates that it should be considered a liquidating dividend. The entry made by Semco would be:

| | | |
|---|---|---|
| Dividend Receivable ($200,000 × .05) | 10,000 | |
|     Investment in Stock | | 10,000 |

## Equity Method

Under the **equity method** a substantive economic relationship is acknowledged between the investor and the investee. The investment is originally recorded at the cost of the shares acquired but is subsequently adjusted each period for changes in the net assets of the investee. That is, the **investment's carrying amount is periodically increased (decreased) by the investor's proportionate share of the earnings (losses) of the investee and decreased by all dividends received by the investor from the investee.** The equity method gives recognition to the fact that investee earnings increase investee net assets that underlie the investment, and that investee losses and dividends decrease these net assets.

To illustrate the cost and equity method, assume that Maxi Company purchases a 20% interest in Mini Company. For purposes of applying the cost method in this illustration, assume that Maxi does not have the ability to exercise significant influence; where the equity method is applied, assume that the 20% interest permits Maxi to exercise significant influence. The entries are shown at the top of page 797.

Note that under the cost method only the cash dividends received from Mini Company are reported as revenue by Maxi Company. Under the equity method, Maxi Company reports as revenue its share of the net income reported by Mini Company; the cash dividends received from Mini Company are recorded as a decrease in the investment carrying value. The difference between the cost and equity method can be significant. For example, McCloth Steel Corporation reported that the use of the equity method had increased its income before taxes for the year by 55% or $3.5 million. Under either method, when the underlying value of the investment is permanently impaired, that is, there appears to be no

---

[5]*Accounting Trends and Techniques—1981* reports that in 1980 of its 600 surveyed companies, 335 employed the equity method, 106 the cost method, 14 the cost less allowances for decline in value method, and 20 the lower of cost or market method as the basis for valuing investments in equity securities of other companies. The different methods resulted from differing circumstances and percentages of interest.

**Entries Under Cost and Equity Method**

| Cost Method | | Equity Method | |
|---|---|---|---|

On January 2, 1983, Maxi Company acquired 48,000 shares (20% of Mini Company common stocks) at a cost of $10 a share.

| Investment in | | | Investment in | | |
|---|---|---|---|---|---|
| Mini Company | 480,000 | | Mini Company | 480,000 | |
| Cash | | 480,000 | Cash | | 480,000 |

For the year 1983, Mini Company reported net income of $200,000; Maxi Company's share is 20% or $40,000.

| No entry | | | Investment in | | |
|---|---|---|---|---|---|
| | | | Mini Company | 40,000 | |
| | | | Revenue from Investment | | 40,000 |

On January 28, 1984, Mini Company announced and paid a cash dividend of $100,000; Maxi Company received 20% or $20,000.

| Cash | 20,000 | | Cash | 20,000 | |
|---|---|---|---|---|---|
| Revenue from | | | Investment in | | |
| Investment | | 20,000 | Mini Company | | 20,000 |

For the year 1984, Mini reported a net loss of $50,000; Maxi Company's share is 20% or $10,000.

| No entry | | | Loss on Investment | 10,000 | |
|---|---|---|---|---|---|
| | | | Investment in | | |
| | | | Mini Company | | 10,000 |

chance of recovering a portion or all of the carrying value of the investment, the carrying amount of the asset should be written down, and the writedown recognized as a loss of the period.

**Expanded Illustration of the Equity Method**   Under the equity method, periodic investor revenue consists of the investor's proportionate share of investee earnings (adjusted to eliminate intercompany gains and losses) and **amortization of the difference between the investor's initial costs and the investor's proportionate share of the underlying book value of the investee at date of acquisition.** And, if the investee's net income includes extraordinary items, the investor treats a proportionate share of the extraordinary items as an extraordinary item rather than as ordinary investment revenue before extraordinary items.

To illustrate the equity method, assume that on January 1, 1983, I. N. Vestor Company purchased 250,000 shares of Investee Company's 1,000,000 shares of outstanding common stock for $8,500,000. The book value of Investee Company's total net worth was $30,000,000 at the date of I. N. Vestor Company's 25% investment. I. N. Vestor Company thereby paid $1,000,000 [$8,500,000 minus .25($30,000,000)] in excess of book value. It was determined that $600,000 of this is attributable to its share of **undervalued depreciable assets** of Investee Company and $400,000 to **unrecorded goodwill.** I. N. Vestor Company estimated the average remaining life of the undervalued assets to be ten years and decided upon a 40-year amortization period for goodwill (the maximum length of time allowed). For the year 1983, Investee Company reported net income of $2,800,000 including an extraordinary loss of $400,000, and paid dividends at June 30, 1983 of $600,000 and at

December 31, 1983 of $800,000. The following entries would be recorded on the books of I. N. Vestor Company to report its long-term investment using the equity method:

### January 1, 1983

| | | |
|---|---|---|
| Investment in Investee Company Stock | 8,500,000 | |
| Cash | | 8,500,000 |
| (To record the acquisition of 250,000 shares of Investee Company common stock) | | |

### June 30, 1983

| | | |
|---|---|---|
| Cash | 150,000 | |
| Investment in Investee Company Stock | | 150,000 |
| [To record dividend received ($600,000 × .25) from Investee Company] | | |

### December 31, 1983

| | | |
|---|---|---|
| Investment in Investee Company Stock | 700,000 | |
| Loss from Investment (extraordinary) | 100,000 | |
| Revenue from Investment (ordinary) | | 800,000 |
| [To record share of Investee Company ordinary income ($3,200,000 × .25) and extraordinary loss ($400,000 × .25)] | | |

### December 31, 1983

| | | |
|---|---|---|
| Cash | 200,000 | |
| Investment in Investee Company Stock | | 200,000 |
| [To record dividend received ($800,000 × .25) from Investee Company] | | |

### December 31, 1983

| | | |
|---|---|---|
| Revenue from Investment (ordinary) | 70,000 | |
| Investment in Investee Company Stock | | 70,000 |
| (To record amortization of investment cost in excess of book value represented by: | | |
|    Undervalued depreciable assets—$600,000 ÷ 10 = $60,000 | | |
|    Unrecorded goodwill—$400,000 ÷ 40     = 10,000 | | |
|      Total           $70,000) | | |

The investment in Investee Company is presented in the balance sheet of I. N. Vestor Company at a carrying amount of $8,780,000 computed as follows:

| Investment in Investee Company | | |
|---|---:|---:|
| Acquisition cost, 1/1/83 | $8,500,000 | |
| Plus: Share of 1983 income before extraordinary item | 800,000 | $9,300,000 |
| Less: Share of extraordinary loss | 100,000 | |
| Dividends received 6/30 and 12/31 | 350,000 | |
| Amortization of undervalued depreciable assets | 60,000 | |
| Amortization of unrecorded goodwill | 10,000 | 520,000 |
| Carrying amount, 12/31/83 | | $8,780,000 |

In the illustration above the investment cost exceeded the underlying book value. In some cases, an investor may acquire an investment at a **cost less than the underlying book value.** In such cases specific assets are assumed to be overvalued and, if depreciable, the excess of the investee's book value over the investor's acquisition cost is amortized into investment revenue over the remaining lives of the assets. Investment revenue is increased under the presumption that the investee's net income as reported is actually understated because the investee is charging depreciation on overstated asset values.

**Investee Losses Exceed Carrying Amount**   If an investor's share of the investee's losses exceeds the carrying amount of the investment, the question arises as to whether the investor should recognize additional losses. Ordinarily the investor should discontinue applying the equity method and not recognize additional losses. If the investor's potential loss is not limited to the amount of its original investment (by guarantee of the investee's obligations or other commitment to provide further financial support), however, or if imminent return to profitable operations by the investee appears to be assured, it is appropriate for the investor to recognize additional losses.[6]

**Change in Method *from* the Equity Method**   If the investor level of influence or ownership falls below that necessary for continued use of the equity method, a change must be made to either the lower of cost or market method or the cost method, whichever is appropriate. The earnings or losses that relate to the stock retained by the investor and that were previously recognized by the investor should remain as part of the carrying amount of the investment with no retroactive restatement to the new method.

To the extent that dividends received by the investor in subsequent periods exceed its share of the investee's earnings for such periods (all periods following the change in method), they should be accounted for as a reduction of the investment carrying amount, rather than as revenue. For example, using the data from the previous illustration, assume that on January 2, 1984, Investee Company sold 1,500,000 additional shares of its own common stock to the public, thereby reducing I. N. Vestor Company's ownership from 25% to 10% and that the net income (or loss) and dividends of Investee Company for the years 1984 through 1986 were as follows:

| Year | Investor's Share of Investee Income (Loss) | Investee Dividends Received by Investor |
|------|---------------------------------------------|------------------------------------------|
| 1984 | $600,000 | $  400,000 |
| 1985 | 350,000 | 400,000 |
| 1986 | (200,000) | 300,000 |
| Totals | $750,000 | $1,100,000 |

Assuming a change from the equity method to the cost method as of January 2, 1984, I. N. Vestor Company's reported investment in Investee Company and its reported income would be as shown at the top of page 800.

Note from that illustration that when a change is made from the equity method to the cost method, the cost basis for accounting purposes is the carrying amount of the investment at the date of the change. Also, note the cessation of the amortization of the excess of acquisition price over the proportionate share of book value acquired attributable to undervalued depreciable assets and unrecorded goodwill when the change of methods occurs. In

[6]"The Equity Method of Accounting for Investments in Common Stock," *op. cit.,* par. 19(i).

| Year | Dividend Revenue Recognized | Cumulative Excess of Share of Earnings Over Dividends Received | Investment at December 31 |
|------|------|------|------|
| 1984 | $400,000 | $200,000[a] | $8,780,000 |
| 1985 | 400,000 | 150,000[b] | 8,780,000 |
| 1986 | -0- | (350,000)[c] | 8,780,000 − $350,000 = $8,430,000 |

[a]$600,000 − $400,000 = $200,000
[b]($350,000 − $400,000) + $200,000 = $150,000
[c]$150,000 − ($200,000 + $300,000) = ($350,000)

other words, the new method is applied in its entirety once the equity method is no longer appropriate.

**Change in Method *to* the Equity Method**   An investment in common stock of an investee that has been accounted for by other than the equity method may become qualified for use of the equity method by an increase in the level of ownership. At the time that an investment qualifies for use of the equity method, the investor should adopt the equity method of accounting. Such a change involves **adjusting retroactively** the carrying amount of the investment, results of operations (current and prior periods presented), and retained earnings of the investor in a step-by-step acquisition manner as if the equity method has been in effect during all of the previous periods in which this investment was held.[7]

For example, on January 2, 1980, Amsted Corp. purchased for $500,000 cash 10 percent of the outstanding shares of Cable Company common stock. On that date, the net assets of Cable Company had a book value of $3,000,000. The excess of cost over the underlying equity in net assets of Cable Company is attributed to goodwill, which is amortized over 40 years. On January 2, 1982, Amsted Corp. purchased an additional 20% of Cable Company's stock for $1,200,000 cash when the book value of Cable's net assets was $4,000,000. Now having a 30% interest, Amsted Corp. must use the equity method. The net income reported by Cable Company and the Cable Company dividends received by Amsted during the period 1980 through 1982 were as follows:

| Year | Cable Company Net Income | Cable Co. Dividends Paid to Amsted |
|------|------|------|
| 1980 | $ 500,000 | $ 20,000 |
| 1981 | 1,000,000 | 30,000 |
| 1982 | 1,200,000 | 120,000 |

The journal entries recorded from January 2, 1980, through December 31, 1982, relative to Amsted Corp's. investment in Cable Company reflecting the data above and a change from the cost method to the equity method, are as follows:[8]

[7]Ibid., par. 19(m).

[8]Adapted from Paul A. Pacter, "Applying APB Opinion No. 18—Equity Method," *Journal of Accountancy* (September 1971), pp. 59–60.

**January 2, 1980**

| | | |
|---|---|---|
| Investment in Cable Company Stock | 500,000 | |
| Cash | | 500,000 |

(To record the purchase of a 10%
interest in Cable Company)

**December 31, 1980**

| | | |
|---|---|---|
| Cash | 20,000 | |
| Dividend Revenue | | 20,000 |

(To record the receipt of cash
dividends from Cable Company)

**December 31, 1981**

| | | |
|---|---|---|
| Cash | 30,000 | |
| Dividend Revenue | | 30,000 |

(To record the receipt of cash
dividends from Cable Company)

**January 2, 1982**

| | | |
|---|---|---|
| Investment in Cable Company Stock | 1,290,000 | |
| Cash | | 1,200,000 |
| Retained Earnings | | 90,000 |

(To record the purchase of an additional
interest in Cable Company and to reflect
retroactively a change from the cost method
to the equity method of accounting for the
investment. The $90,000 adjustment is
computed as follows:

| | 1980 | 1981 | Total |
|---|---|---|---|
| Amsted Corp. equity in earnings of Cable Company 10% | $50,000 | $100,000 | $150,000 |
| Amortization of excess of acquisition price over underlying equity [$500,000 − (10% × $3,000,000)] ÷ 40 years = $5,000 per year. | (5,000) | (5,000) | (10,000) |
| Dividend received | (20,000) | (30,000) | (50,000) |
| Prior period adjustment | $25,000 | $ 65,000 | $ 90,000 |

**December 31, 1982**

| | | |
|---|---|---|
| Investment in Cable Company Stock | 345,000 | |
| Revenue from Investment | | 345,000 |

[To record equity in earnings of Cable
Company (30% of $1,200,000) less $15,000
amortization of goodwill[a]]

[a]Goodwill amortization includes $5,000 [$500,000 − (10% × $3,000,000) ÷ 40 years] from 1980 purchase of 10% interest plus $10,000 [$1,200,000 − (20% × $4,000,000) ÷ 40 years] from 1982 purchase of 20% interest.

| | | |
|---|---|---|
| Cash | 120,000 | |
| Investment in Cable Company Stock | | 120,000 |

(To record the receipt of cash
dividends from Cable Company)

Changing to the equity method is accomplished by placing the accounts related to and affected by the investment on the same basis as if the equity method has always been the basis of accounting for that investment.

**Disclosures Required Under the Equity Method**   The significance of an investment to the investor's financial position and operating results should be considered in evaluating the extent of disclosures about the investment and the investee company. According to *APB Opinion No. 18,* the following disclosures in the investor's financial statements are generally applicable to the equity method:

1. The name of each investee and the percentage of ownership of common stock.

2. The accounting policies of the investor with respect to investments in common stock.

3. The difference, if any, between the amount in the investment account and the amount of underlying equity in the net assets of the investee.

4. The aggregate value of each identified investment based on quoted market price (if available).

5. When investments of 20% or more interest are in the aggregate material in relation to the financial position and operating results of an investor, it may be necessary to present summarized information concerning assets, liabilities, and results of operations of the investees, either individually or in groups, as appropriate.

In addition, the investor is expected to disclose the reasons for **not** using the equity method in cases of 20% or more ownership interest and **for** using the equity method in cases of less than 20% ownership interest. See page 806 for examples of such disclosures from the financial statements of Borg-Warner Corporation and Insilco Corporation.

## Lower of Cost or Market Method

Whenever the investment is in "marketable equity securities" and the equity method is not appropriate (common stocks which are less than 20% interest or "lack of significant influence"), the investor is required to use the **lower of cost or market method** in accounting for the investment. The application of lower of cost or market to investments in marketable equity securities classified as current assets was discussed in considerable detail in Chapter 7. Securities qualify as "marketable equity securities" if they represent ownership shares or the right to acquire or dispose of ownership shares in an enterprise at fixed or determinable prices and there are currently available for such securities sales prices or bid and ask prices in the securities market.[9]

Under the lower of cost or market method all noncurrent marketable equity securities are grouped in a separate noncurrent portfolio for purposes of comparing the **aggregate** cost and the **aggregate** market value to determine the carrying amount at the balance sheet date. Accounting for noncurrent marketable equity securities is both similar to and different from accounting for marketable equity securities classified as current assets. Similarly, *FASB Statement No. 12* requires that the amount by which aggregate cost of the noncurrent portfolio exceeds market value (unrealized loss) be accounted for as the **valuation allowance.** Difference: Whereas changes in the valuation allowance for equity securities classified as current assets are included in the determination of income, **accumulated changes in the valuation allowance for a marketable equity securities portfolio included in noncurrent assets are included in the equity section of the balance sheet and shown separately.** In substance, the profession requires "mark to market" at each reporting date, down

---

[9]"Accounting for Certain Marketable Securities," *Statement of Financial Accounting Standards No. 12* (Stamford, Conn.: FASB, 1975), par. 7.

and up, but not in excess of original cost, and reports unrealized losses and recoveries in the equity section of the balance sheet (so long as the decline in the market value is viewed as temporary).

**Illustration of Lower of Cost or Market Method**    Bolex Company made the following long-term investments in marketable equity securities during 1983:

> January 15, 1983—Purchased 20,000 shares of Witco, Inc. common stock (a 6% interest) for $1,446,000 including brokerage commissions.
>
> July 22, 1983—Purchased 52,000 shares of Cuneo Tool Company common stock (an 11% interest) for $2,340,000 including brokerage commissions.

On December 31, 1983, Bolex determined the carrying amount of its portfolio in marketable equity securities classified as a long-term investment to be:

|  | December 31, 1983 | | |
| --- | --- | --- | --- |
| Long-Term Investments— | Cost | Market | Unrealized Gain (Loss) |
| Witco, Inc. | $1,446,000 | $1,478,000 | $ 32,000 |
| Cuneo Tool Company | 2,340,000 | 1,900,000 | (440,000)[a] |
| Total of portfolio | $3,786,000 | $3,378,000 | $(408,000) |
| Balance—valuation allowance | | | $(408,000) |

[a]This loss is assumed to be temporary.

Applying the lower of cost or market method to the Bolex portfolio at December 31, 1983, results in a carrying amount of $3,378,000. The net unrealized loss of $408,000 represents the aggregate excess of cost over the market value of the portfolio of marketable equity securities classified as noncurrent assets and is recorded in the accounts as follows:

**December 31, 1983**

| | | |
| --- | --- | --- |
| Unrealized Loss on Noncurrent Marketable Equity Securities | 408,000 | |
|     Allowance for Excess of Cost of Long-Term Equity Securities over Market Value | | 408,000 |
|     (To record excess of cost over market value of marketable equity securities portfolio classified as noncurrent assets) | | |

If the market value of the Bolex portfolio subsequently rises, the write-down would be reversed to the extent that the resulting carrying amount does not exceed cost.

**Disclosure in the Financial Statements**    The following information with respect to marketable equity securities classified as noncurrent assets should be disclosed in the body of the financial statements or in the accompanying footnotes:

1. For each balance sheet presented—the aggregate cost and aggregate market value.
2. For the latest balance sheet presented—gross unrealized gains and gross unrealized losses.
3. For each income statement presented:
   (a) Net realized gain or loss included in the determination of net income.

    (b) The basis on which cost was determined in computing realized gain or loss.

    (c) The change in the valuation allowance that has been included in the equity section of the balance sheet during the period.[10]

The data from the Bolex Company investment discussed above would be presented in the December 31, 1983, financial statements as follows:

---

### BALANCE SHEET

| | |
|---|---:|
| **Long-Term Investments** | |
| Marketable equity securities, carried at market (Note 1) | $ 3,378,000 |
| | |
| **Stockholders' Equity** | |
| Common stock | $ 9,000,000 |
| Additional paid-in capital | 2,500,000 |
| Retained earnings | 7,349,000 |
| | 18,849,000 |
| Net unrealized loss on noncurrent marketable equity securities (Note 1) | (408,000) |
|     Total stockholders' equity | $18,441,000 |

Note 1. *Marketable Equity Securities*. Marketable equity securities are carried at the lower of cost or market at the balance sheet date, with that determination made by aggregating all noncurrent marketable equity securities. Marketable equity securities included in long-term investments had a cost of $3,786,000.

    At December 31, 1983, there were gross unrealized gains of $32,000 and gross unrealized losses of $440,000 pertaining to the long-term portfolio. Because no sale of such securities occurred during the period, no gains or losses have been included in the determination of net income.

    To reduce the carrying amount of the long-term marketable equity securities portfolio to market, which was lower than cost at December 31, 1983, a valuation allowance in the amount of $408,000 was established by a charge to stockholders' equity representing the net unrealized loss.

---

Note that the charge to equity for net unrealized losses is treated as a reduction from the total equity in much the same manner as treasury stock is accounted for under the cost method.

**Decline in Market Value Other Than Temporary**   Occasionally a long-term investment in an individual marketable equity security suffers a decline in market value below cost that is other than temporary. If the decline is judged to be other than temporary, the cost basis of the individual security is written down to a new cost basis. Although the security is one for which the effect of a change in carrying amount is included in stockholders' equity, the amount of a nontemporary write-down is accounted for as a **realized loss.** The new cost basis is not changed for subsequent recoveries in market value.

In judging whether a decline in market value below cost at the balance sheet date is other than temporary, a gain or loss realized on subsequent disposition or changes in market price occurring after the date of the financial statements but prior to their issuance should be taken into consideration along with other factors.[11]

---

[10]Ibid., par. 12.

[11]"Changes in Market Value after the Balance Sheet Date," *FASB Interpretation No. 11* (Stamford, Conn.: FASB, 1976), par. 3.

**Change in Classification of a Marketable Equity Security**  If there is a change in the classification of a marketable equity security between current and noncurrent, the individual security is transferred between the portfolios at the lower of its cost or market value at the date of transfer. If market value is lower than cost, the market value becomes the new cost basis, and the difference is accounted for **as if** it were a **realized loss** and is included in the determination of net income.[12] The profession requires this treatment to reduce the incentive to change the classification of securities in order to effect changes in income.

## Market Value Method

Although not sanctioning the market value method of accounting for long-term investments, the profession did give credence to it by discussing it at considerable length in *Opinion No. 18.* Under the market value method, the investor recognizes both dividends received and changes in market prices of the stock of the investee company as earnings or losses from the investment. Dividends received are accounted for as part of revenue from the investment. In addition, the investment account is adjusted for changes in the market value of the investee's stock. The change in market value since the preceding reporting date is included in the results of operations of the investor.

Reporting of investments in common stock at market value is considered by some accountants to meet most closely the objective of reporting the economic consequences of holding the investment. Although the market value method provides the best presentation of investments in some situations, the profession has concluded that further study will be necessary before the market value method is used as the sole basis.

It is required, however, that in most cases where a 20% to 50% interest exists, a market price is available, and the equity method is employed, "the aggregate value of each identified investment based on the quoted market price usually should be disclosed."

## Applicability of Methods

In summary, application of the cost, equity, and lower of cost or market methods for long-term stock investments is as follows:

| Nature of Investment | Method |
|---|---|
| Investment in common stock in excess of 50% voting equity interest | Equity |
| Investment in common stock in excess of 20% voting equity interest, except when evidence exists of an inability to exercise significant influence | Equity |
| Investment in common stock is less than a 20% interest in the form of marketable equity securities, with no ability to exercise significant influence | Lower of Cost or Market |
| Investment in nonequity or nonmarketable securities | Cost |

---

[12]FASB Statement No. 12, *op. cit.,* par. 10. Also see "Clarification of Definitions and Accounting for Marketable Equity Securities That Become Nonmarketable," *FASB Interpretation No. 16* (Stamford, Conn.: FASB, 1977), pars. 9 & 10.

Even in cases of investments in excess of a 50% voting interest in common stock, certain conditions, for example, foreign subsidiaries operating under conditions of exchange restrictions, governmental controls, or other uncertainties, may militate against the use of the equity method. Two examples of such cases follow:

---

**Borg-Warner Corporation**

*Principles of Consolidation*—The consolidated financial statements include all subsidiaries except those in Mexico and South America, which are carried at cost due to political and economic uncertainty, and the financial services companies. Investments in the financial services companies and in affiliated companies, at least 20% owned by Borg-Warner, are carried at equity in underlying net assets.

---

**Insilco Corporation**

*Principles of Consolidation*—The consolidated financial statements include the accounts of the Company and its significant majority owned subsidiaries except its wholly-owned finance subsidiary and Times Fiber Communications, Inc., a joint venture in which the Company's 51% control is expected to be temporary. Investments in the finance subsidiary, joint ventures and other associated companies are accounted for using the equity method.

---

The following schedule compares the various methods of accounting for long-term investments in terms of their effects upon the financial statements.

---

**COMPARISON OF THE EFFECTS OF METHODS OF ACCOUNTING FOR LONG-TERM INVESTMENTS IN STOCK[13]**

| | Balance Sheet | Income Statement |
|---|---|---|
| Cost Method | Investments are carried at acquisition cost. | Dividends are recognized as revenue. |
| Equity Method | Investments are carried at cost, are periodically adjusted by the investor's share of the investee's earnings or losses, and are decreased by all dividends received from the investee. | Revenue is recognized to the extent of the investee's earnings or losses reported subsequent to the date of investment (adjusted by amortization of the difference between cost and underlying book value). |
| Lower of Cost or Market | Investments (current and noncurrent) are carried at aggregate cost or market value, whichever is lower at the balance sheet date, through use of a valuation allowance. | *Current*—excess of cost over market value and recoveries thereof are included in the determination of income. *Noncurrent*—excess of aggregate cost over market value are included in the equity section. |
| Market Value Method | Investments are carried at market value. | Cash dividends received plus or minus the changes in market price during the period are recognized as revenue. |

---

[13] Adapted and updated from Copeland, Strawser, and Binns, "Accounting for Investments in Common Stock," *Financial Executive* (February 1972), p. 37.

## Revenue from Investments in Stocks

Revenue recognized from investments, whether under the cost, lower of cost or market, or the equity methods, should be included in the income statement of the investor. Under the cost and the lower of cost or market methods, the dividends received (or receivable if declared but unpaid) are reported as investment revenue. Under the equity method, if the investee has extraordinary and prior period items reported during the period, the investor should report in a similar manner its proportionate share of the ordinary income, of the extraordinary items, and prior period adjustments unless separation into these components is considered immaterial.

The gains or losses on sales of investments also are factors in determining the net income for the period. The gain or loss resulting from the sale of long-term investments, unless it is the result of a major casualty, an expropriation, or the introduction of a new law prohibiting its ownership (which may be viewed as unusual and nonrecurring), is reported as part of current income from operations and is not an extraordinary item.

Dividends that are paid in some form of assets other than cash are called **property dividends.** In such instances, the fair market value of the property received becomes the basis for debiting an appropriate asset account and crediting Dividend Revenue.

Occasionally an investor receives a dividend that is in part, or entirely, a **liquidating dividend.** The investor should reduce the Investment account for that amount of the liquidating portion of the dividend and credit Dividend Revenue for the balance.

## Dividends Received in Stock

If the investee corporation declares a dividend payable in its own stock of the same class, instead of in cash, each stockholder owns a larger number of shares but retains the same proportionate interest in the firm as before. The issuing corporation has distributed no assets; it has merely transferred a specified amount of retained earnings to paid-in capital, thus indicating that this amount will not provide a basis in the future for cash dividends. Shares received as a result of a stock dividend or stock split-up do not constitute revenue to the recipients, because their interest in the issuing corporation is unchanged and because the issuing corporation has not distributed any of its assets.

**The recipient of such additional shares would make no formal entry,** but should make a memorandum entry and record a notation in the Investments account to show that additional shares have been received.

Although no dollar amount is entered at the time of the receipt of these shares, the fact that additional shares have been received must be considered in computing the carrying amount of any shares sold. The cost of the original shares purchased (plus the effect of any adjustments under the equity method) now constitutes the total carrying amount of both those shares plus the additional shares received, because no price was paid for the additional shares. The carrying amount per share is computed by dividing the total shares into the carrying amount of the original shares purchased.

To illustrate, assume that 100 shares of Flemal Company common stock are purchased for $9,600, and that two years later the company issues to stockholders one additional share for every two shares held; 150 shares of stock that cost a total of $9,600 are then held. Therefore, if 60 shares are sold for $4,300, the carrying amount of the 60 shares would be computed as shown at the top of page 808, assuming that the investment has been accounted for under the cost method.

| | |
|---|---:|
| Cost of 100 shares originally purchased | $9,600 |
| Cost of 50 shares received as stock dividend | 0 |
| Carrying amount of 150 shares held | $9,600 |
| Carrying amount per share is $9,600/150, or $64 | |
| Carrying amount of 60 shares sold is 60 × $64, or $3,840. | |

The entry to record the sale is:

| | | |
|---|---:|---:|
| Cash | 4,300 | |
| Investments in Stocks | | 3,840 |
| Gain on Sale of Investments | | 460 |

A total of 90 shares is still retained, and they are carried in the Investments account at $9,600 minus $3,840, or $5,760. Thus the carrying amount for those shares remaining is also $64 per share, or a total of $5,760 for the 90 shares.

## Stock Rights

When a corporation is about to offer for sale additional shares of an issue already outstanding, it may forward to present holders of that issue certificates permitting them to purchase additional shares in proportion to their present holdings. These certificates represent rights to purchase additional shares and are called **stock rights.** In rights offerings, rights generally are issued on the basis of one right per share, but it may take one or many rights to purchase one new share.

The certificate representing the stock rights, called a **warrant,** states the number of shares that the holder of the right may purchase and also the price at which they may be purchased. If this price is less than the current market value of such shares, the rights have a value in themselves, and from the time they are issued until they expire they may be purchased and sold like any other security.

Three dates are important to a proper understanding of stock rights: (1) the date the rights offering is announced, (2) the date as of which the certificates or rights are issued, and (3) the date the rights expire. From the date the right is announced until it is issued, the share of stock and the right are not separable, and the share is described as **rights-on;** after the certificate or right is received and up to the time it expires, the share and right can be sold separately. A share sold separately from an effective stock right is sold **ex-rights.**

When a right is received, the stockholders have actually received nothing that they did not have before, because the shares already owned brought them the right; they have received no distribution of the corporation assets. The carrying amount of the original shares held is now the carrying amount of those shares plus the rights and should be allocated between the two on the basis of their total market values at the time the rights are received.

**Disposition of Rights**  The investor who receives rights to purchase additional shares has three alternatives:

1. To exercise the rights by purchasing additional stock.
2. To sell the rights.
3. To permit them to expire without selling or using them.

If the investor buys additional stock, the carrying amount of the original shares allocated to the rights becomes a part of the carrying amount of the new shares purchased; if the investor sells the rights, the allocated carrying amount compared with the selling price determines the gain or loss on sale; and, if the investor permits the rights to expire, a loss is suffered, and the investment should be reduced accordingly. The following example illustrates the problem involved.

Shares owned before issuance of rights—100.
Cost of shares owned—$50 a share for a total cost of $5,000.
Rights received—one right for every share owned, or 100 rights; two
  rights are required to purchase one new share at $50.
Market values at date rights issued:

$$\text{Shares } \$60 \text{ a share}$$
$$\text{Rights } \$3 \text{ a right}$$

| | |
|---|---:|
| Total market value of shares (100 × $60) | $6,000 |
| Total market value of rights (100 × $3) | 300 |
| Combined market value | $6,300 |

Cost allocated to stock: $\dfrac{\$6,000}{\$6,300} \times \$5,000 = \$4,761.90$

Cost allocated to rights: $\dfrac{\$300}{\$6,300} \times \$5,000 = \underline{\phantom{00}238.10}$

$$\$5,000.00$$

Cost allocated to each share of stock: $\dfrac{\$4,761.90}{100} = \$47.62$

Cost allocated to each right: $\dfrac{\$238.10}{100} = \$2.38$

Note that the total cost of the stock and the rights is still $5,000 and, therefore, no entry is made in the Investments account in the general ledger at this time. The subsidiary records should reflect, however, the reduction in the carrying amount of the stock from $5,000 to $4,761.90 and the acquisition of the rights, with an allocated cost of $238.10. The general ledger account is not affected until the stock is sold, or the rights are sold or used or permitted to expire.

If some of the original shares are later sold, their cost for purposes of determining gain or loss on sale is $47.62 per share, as computed above. If 10 of the original shares are sold at $58 per share, the entry would be:

| | | |
|---|---:|---:|
| Cash | 580.00 | |
|    Investments in Stocks | | 476.20 |
|    Gain on Sale of Investments | | 103.80 |

**Entries for Stock Rights**  Rights may be sold, or used to purchase additional stock, or permitted to expire. The carrying amount allocated to the rights is a part of the Long-Term Investments account in the general ledger and, therefore, any entries made that are related to the rights are reflected in the Long-Term Investments account. For example, assume that part of the rights are sold, part are used to purchase additional stock, and part are allowed to expire.

If 40 rights to purchase 20 shares of stock are sold at $3.00 each, the entry is:

| | | |
|---|---|---|
| Cash | 120.00 | |
|    Investments in Stocks | | 95.20 |
|    Gain on Sale of Investments | | 24.80 |

The amount removed from the Long-Term Investments account is the amount allocated to 40 rights, 40 $\times$ $2.38.

If rights to purchase 20 shares of stock are exercised, and 20 additional shares are purchased at the offer price of $50, the entry is:

| | | |
|---|---|---|
| Investments in Stock | 1,000.00 | |
|    Cash | | 1,000.00 |

If these shares are sold in the future, their cost should be considered to be $1,095.20, or $54.76 per share. The price paid of $50 per share plus the amount allocated to two rights of $4.76 which is already in the Long-Term Investments account.

If the remaining 20 rights are permitted to expire, the amount allocated to these rights should be removed from the general ledger account by this entry:

| | | |
|---|---|---|
| Loss on Expiration of Stock Rights | 47.60 | |
|    Investments in Stocks | | 47.60 |

The balance of the general ledger account is now $5,381.00, as shown below.

| Investments in Stocks | | | | |
|---|---|---|---|---|
| Purchase of original 100 | | Sale of 10 shares of | | |
|   shares @ $50 per share | 5,000.00 |   original purchase | | 476.20 |
| Purchase of 20 shares by | | Sale of 40 rights | | 95.20 |
|   exercise of rights | 1,000.00 | Loss on expiration of 20 rights | | 47.60 |
| | | Balance | | 5,381.00 |
| | 6,000.00 | | | 6,000.00 |
| Balance | 5,381.00[a] | | | |
| **[a]Analysis of Balance** | | | | |
| 90 shares of original purchase, at allocated cost of $47.62 per share | | | | $4,285.80 |
| 20 shares purchased through exercise of rights, carried at $54.76 per share | | | | |
|   (cash paid of $50.00, plus $4.76 for allocated cost of two rights) | | | | 1,095.20 |
| Balance of account, as above | | | | $5,381.00 |

The balance represents 110 shares of stock, of which 90 are of the original purchase, and 20 are shares purchased through the exercise of stock rights.

## CASH SURRENDER VALUE OF LIFE INSURANCE

There are many different kinds of insurance. The kinds usually carried by businesses include (a) casualty insurance, (b) liability insurance, and (c) life insurance. Accounting for casualty insurance is discussed in Appendix G of Chapter 11. Certain types of **life in-**

**surance** constitute an investment, whereas casualty insurance and liability insurance do not. The three common types of life insurance policies that companies often carry on the lives of their principal officers are (a) **ordinary life,** (b) **limited payment,** and (c) **term insurance.** During the period that ordinary life and limited payment policies are in force, there is a cash surrender value and a loan value. Term insurance ordinarily has no cash surrender value or loan value.

If the insured officers or their heirs are the beneficiaries of the policy, the premiums paid by the company represent expense to the company and, for income tax purposes, represent income to the officer insured. In this case the cash surrender value of the policy does not represent an asset to the company.

If the company, however, is the beneficiary and has the right to cancel the policy at its own option, the cash surrender value of the policy or policies is an asset of the company. Accordingly, part of the premiums paid is not expense, because the cash surrender value increases each year. Only the difference between the premium paid and the increase in cash surrender value represents expense to the company.

For example, if Zima Corporation pays an insurance premium of $2,300 on a $100,000 policy covering its president and, as a result, the cash surrender value of the policy increases from $15,000 to $16,400 during the period, the entry to record the premium payment is:

| | | |
|---|---|---|
| Life Insurance Expense | 900 | |
| Cash Surrender Value of Life Insurance | 1,400 | |
| Cash | | 2,300 |

The cash surrender value of such life insurance policies should be reported in the balance sheet as a long-term investment, inasmuch as it is unlikely that the policies will be surrendered and canceled in the immediate future. The premium is not deductible for tax purposes, however, and the proceeds of such policies are not taxable as income.

If the insured officer died half-way through the most recent period of coverage for which the $2,300 premium payment was made, the following entry would be made (assuming cash surrender value of $15,700 and refund of a pro rata share of the premium paid):

| | | |
|---|---|---|
| Cash [$100,000 + (1/2 of $2,300)] | 101,150 | |
| Cash Surrender Value of Life Insurance | | 16,400 |
| Life Insurance Expense (1/2 × $900) | | 450 |
| Gain on Life Insurance Coverage ($100,000 − $15,700) | | 84,300 |

The gain on life insurance coverage is not reported as an extraordinary item because it is considered to be a "normal" business transaction.

## FUNDS

Assets may be set aside in special funds for specific purposes and, therefore, become unavailable for ordinary operations of the business. In this way the assets segregated in the special funds are available when needed for the intended purposes.

There are two general types of funds: (1) those in which cash is set aside to meet specific current obligations, and (2) those that are not directly related to current operations and therefore are in the nature of long-term investments.

Several funds of the first type, discussed in preceding chapters, include the following:

| **Fund** | **Purpose** |
|---|---|
| Petty Cash Fund | Payment of small expenditures, in currency |
| Payroll Cash Account | Payment of salaries and wages |
| Dividend Cash Account | Payment of dividends |
| Interest Fund | Payment of interest on long-term debt |

In general, these funds are used to handle more conveniently and more expeditiously the payments of certain current obligations, to maintain better control over such expenditures, and to divide adequately the responsibility for cash disbursements. These funds are ordinarily shown as current assets (if immaterial as part of Cash) in the balance sheet, because the obligations to which they relate are ordinarily current liabilities.

As mentioned above, funds of the second type are similar to long-term investments, as they do not relate directly to current operations. The more common funds of this type and the purpose of each are listed below:

| **Fund** | **Purpose** |
|---|---|
| Sinking Fund | Payment of long-term indebtedness |
| Plant Expansion Fund | Purchase or construction of additional plant |
| Stock Redemption Fund | Retirement of capital stock (usually preferred stock) |
| Contingency Fund | Payment of unforeseen obligations |

Because the cash set aside for purposes such as those listed above will not be needed until some time in the future, it is usually invested in securities so that revenue may be earned on the assets of the fund. The assets of a fund may or may not be placed in the hands of a trustee. If appointed, the trustee becomes the custodian of the assets, accounts to the company for them and reports revenues and expenses of the fund. Funds of this second type are ordinarily shown in the long-term investments section of the balance sheet or in a separate section if relatively large in amount.

## Entries for Funds

To account for the assets, revenues, and expenses of funds, it is desirable to keep separate accounts to accumulate such information. For example, if a fund is kept for the redemption of a preferred stock issue that was issued with a redemption provision at par after a certain date, the following accounts might be kept:

> Stock Redemption Fund Cash
> Stock Redemption Fund Investments
> Stock Redemption Fund Revenue
> Stock Redemption Fund Expense
> Gain on Sale of Stock Redemption Fund Investments
> Loss on Sale of Stock Redemption Fund Investments

When cash is transferred from the regular cash account, perhaps periodically, the entry is:

| | | |
|---|---|---|
| Stock Redemption Fund Cash | 30,000 | |
| Cash | | 30,000 |

Securities purchased by the fund are recorded at cost:

| | | |
|---|---|---|
| Stock Redemption Fund Investments | 27,000 | |
| Stock Redemption Fund Cash | | 27,000 |

If securities purchased for the fund are to be held temporarily, they would be treated in the accounts in the same manner as temporary investments, described in Chapter 7. If they are to be held for a long period of time, they are treated in accordance with the entries described for long-term investments earlier in this chapter. In both cases the securities purchased are recorded at cost when acquired, but in the case of bonds purchased as long-term investments for the fund, premium or discount should be amortized. If we assume that the entry above records the purchase at a premium of 10-year bonds of a par value of $25,000 on April 1, the issue date, and that the bonds bear interest at 8%, the entry for the receipt of semiannual interest on October 1 is:

| | | |
|---|---|---|
| Stock Redemption Fund Cash | 1,000 | |
| Stock Redemption Fund Revenue | | 1,000 |

At December 31, entries are made to record amortization of premium for nine months and to accrue interest on the bonds for three months:

| | | |
|---|---|---|
| Stock Redemption Fund Revenue | 150 | |
| Stock Redemption Fund Investments | | 150 |
| (To record amortization of premium for 9 months, 9/12 of 1/10 of $2,000) | | |
| Accrued Interest on Stock Redemption Fund Investments | 500 | |
| Stock Redemption Fund Revenue | | 500 |
| (To record accrued interest for 3 months, 3/12 of 8% of $25,000) | | |

Expenses of the fund paid are recorded by debiting Stock Redemption Fund Expenses and crediting Stock Redemption Fund Cash.

When the investments held by the fund are disposed of, the entries to record the sale are in accord with the entries illustrated earlier in the chapter, using the accounts designated as relating to the redemption fund. Any revenue and expense accounts set up to record fund transactions should be closed to Income Summary at the end of the accounting period and reflected in earnings of the current period.

The entry for retirement of the preferred stock is:

| | | |
|---|---|---|
| Preferred Capital Stock | 500,000 | |
| Stock Redemption Fund Cash | | 500,000 |

Any balance remaining in the Stock Redemption Fund Cash account is transferred back to a general cash account.

## Funds and Reserves Distinguished

Although funds and reserves (appropriations) are not similar, they are sometimes confused because they may be related and often have similar titles. **A simple distinction may be drawn: a fund is always an asset and always has a debit balance; a reserve (if used only in the limited sense recommended) is an appropriation of retained earnings, always has a credit balance, and is never an asset.**

This distinction is illustrated by reconsidering the entries made in connection with a stock redemption fund on the preceding pages.

The fund was originally established by the entry:

| | | |
|---|---|---|
| Stock Redemption Fund Cash | 30,000 | |
|    Cash | | 30,000 |

Some of this cash was used to purchase investments; the assets of the fund were then cash and investments. Ultimately the investments were sold, and the stock redemption fund cash was used to retire the preferred stock.

If the company chose to do so, it could establish an appropriation for stock redemption at the same time to reduce the retained earnings apparently available for dividends. Appropriated retained earnings is established by periodic transfers from retained earnings, as follows:

| | | |
|---|---|---|
| Retained Earnings | 30,000 | |
|    Appropriation for Stock Redemption | | 30,000 |

It will have a credit balance and will be shown in the stockholders' equity section of the balance sheet. When the stock is retired by payment of cash from the stock redemption fund, the appropriation is transferred back to retained earnings:

| | | |
|---|---|---|
| Appropriation for Stock Redemption | 500,000 | |
|    Retained Earnings | | 500,000 |

The foregoing discussion indicates that the fund was an asset accumulated to retire stock and had a debit balance; the appropriation was a subdivision of retained earnings and had a credit balance. The fund was used to redeem the stock; the appropriation was transferred back to retained earnings.

## QUESTIONS

1. Distinguish between the nature of temporary investments and long-term investments. Give two examples of each type. Is it possible for securities of the same kind to be carried by one company as a long-term investment and by the other as a short-term investment? Explain.

2. Where on the balance sheet are long-term investments customarily presented? Identify six items customarily classified as long-term investments.

3. For what reasons would a company purchase bonds and stock of another company?

4. What purpose does the variety in bond features (types and characteristics) serve?

5. Distinguish between bond maturity value, bond market value, bond face value, bond par value, and bond principal value.

6. What factors cause a difference between the stated interest rate and the yield interest rate?

7. What are the problems of accounting for bond investments between interest dates?

8. Theoretically, what is the price of a bond?

9. Distinguish between the effective-interest method and the straight-line method relative to their effect on net income over the life of a bond investment. What are the merits of each method?

10. What is the cost of a long-term investment in bonds? What is the cost of a long-term investment in stock?

11. Contrast the accounting treatment of a premium or discount on long-term bond investments with the treatment of a premium or discount on a long-term bond debt. How is the premium or discount handled relative to a temporary investment?

12. On what basis should stock acquired in exchange for noncash consideration be recorded?

13. How should the purchase of two or more classes of securities for a lump sum price be accounted for if the market price of each class is known? If the market price of only one class is known? If no market prices are known?

14. Name four methods of accounting for long-term investments in stocks subsequent to the date of acquisition. When is each method applicable?

15. What constitutes "significant influence" when an investor's financial interest is below the 50% level?

16. Distinguish between the cost and equity method of accounting for long-term investments in stocks subsequent to the date of acquisition.

17. When the equity method is applied, what disclosures should be made in the investor's financial statements?

18. Distinguish between the accounting treatment for "marketable equity securities—current" and "marketable equity securities—noncurrent."

19. Magic, Inc. gradually acquired stock in Merlin Corp. (a nonsubsidiary) until its ownership exceeded 20%. How is this investment recorded and reported after the last purchase?

20. How is a stock dividend accounted for by the recipient? How is a stock split accounted for by the recipient?

21. What three dates are significant in relation to stock rights? What are the alternatives available to the recipient of stock rights?

22. In applying the equity method what recognition, if any, does the investor give to the excess of its investment cost over its proportionate share of the investee book value at the date of acquisition? What recognition, if any, is given if the investment cost is less than the underlying book value?

23. Gigantic Corp. has an investment carrying value (equity method) on its books of $170,000 representing a 40% interest in Poquito Company, which suffered a $600,000 loss this year. How should Gigantic Corp. handle its proportionate share of Poquito's loss?

24. Distinguish between a fund and a reserve.

25. What are the two general types of funds? Give three examples of each type of fund.

## CASES

C18–1 Presented below are four unrelated situations involving marketable equity securities:

### Situation I

A noncurrent portfolio with an aggregate market value in excess of cost includes one particular security whose market value has declined to less than one-half of the original cost. The decline in value is considered to be other than temporary.

### Situation II

The statement of financial position of a company does not classify assets and liabilities as current and noncurrent. The portfolio of marketable equity securities includes securities normally considered current that have a net cost in excess of market value of $13,000. The remainder of the portfolio has a net market value in excess of cost of $32,000.

### Situation III

A marketable equity security, whose market value is currently less than cost, is classified as noncurrent but is to be reclassified as current.

### Situation IV

A company's noncurrent portfolio of marketable equity securities consists of the common stock of one company. At the end of the prior year the market value of the security was fifty percent of original cost, and this effect was properly reflected in a valuation allowance account. However, at the end of the current year the market value of the security had appreciated to twice the original cost. The security is still considered noncurrent at year end.

**Instructions**

What is the effect upon classification, carrying value, and earnings for each of the situations above? Complete your response to each situation before proceeding to the next situation.

**C18-2** The Financial Accounting Standards Board issued its *Statement No. 12* to clarify accounting methods and procedures with respect to certain marketable securities. An important part of the statement concerns the distinction between noncurrent and current classification of marketable securities.

**Instructions**

(a) Why does a company maintain an investment portfolio of current and noncurrent securities?
(b) What factors should be considered in determining whether investments in marketable equity securities should be classified as current or noncurrent, and how do these factors affect the accounting treatment for unrealized losses?

**C18-3** For the past five years Flatt, Inc. has maintained an investment (properly accounted for and reported upon) in Trumbo Co. amounting to a 10% interest in the voting common stock of Trumbo Co. The purchase price was $1,050,000 and the underlying net equity in Trumbo at the date of purchase was $930,000. On January 2 of the current year, Flatt purchased an additional 15% of the voting common stock of Trumbo for $1,800,000; the underlying net equity of the additional investment at January 2 was $1,500,000. Trumbo has been profitable and has paid dividends annually since Flatt's initial acquisition.

**Instructions**

Discuss how this increase in ownership affects the accounting for and reporting upon the investment in Trumbo Co. Include in your discussion adjustments, if any, to the amount shown prior to the increase in investment to bring the amount into conformity with generally accepted accounting principles. Also include how current and subsequent periods would be reported upon.

(AICPA adapted)

**C18-4** Beauty Cream, Inc. purchased marketable equity securities at a cost of $300,000 on February 1, 1983. When the securities were purchased, the company intended to hold the investment for more than one year. Therefore, the investment was classified as a noncurrent asset in the company's annual report for the year ended December 31, 1983 and stated at its then market value of $240,000.

On September 30, 1984 when the investment had a market value of $252,000, management reclassified the investment as a current asset because the company intended to sell the securities within the next twelve months. The market value of the investment was $270,000 on December 31, 1984.

The presentation of investments in marketable equity securities on a company's financial statement is affected by management's intentions regarding how long the investment is to be held and by the reporting requirements specified in *FASB Statement No. 12,* "Accounting for Certain Marketable Securities."

**Instructions**

(a) Explain how the difference between cost and market value of the investment in the marketable equity securities would be reflected in the financial statements of Beauty Cream, Inc. prepared for the fiscal year ending December 31, 1983, when the investment was classified as a noncurrent asset.
(b) The consequence of management's decision to recognize the investment in marketable equity securities as short-term and reclassify it as a current asset was recorded in the accounts. At what amount would the investment be recorded on September 30, 1984, the date of this decision?

(c) How would the investment in the marketable equity securities be reported in the financial statements of Beauty Cream, Inc. as of December 31, 1984 so that the company's financial position and operations for the year 1984 would reflect and report properly the reclassification of the investment from a noncurrent asset to a current asset. Be sure to indicate the affected accounts and the related dollar amounts and the note disclosures, if any.                                                                    (CMA adapted)

**C18-5** In the course of your examination of the financial statements of Relias Corporation as of December 31, 1983, the following entry came to your attention.

January 4, 1983

| | | |
|---|---|---|
| Receivable from Insurance Company | 500,000 | |
|   Cash Surrender Value of Life Insurance Policies | | 68,000 |
|   Retained Earnings | | 79,500 |
|   Donated Capital from Life Insurance Proceeds | | 352,500 |

    (Disposition of the proceeds of the life insurance policy on
    Mr. Relias' life. Mr. Relias died on January 1, 1983.)

You are aware that Mr. John Relias, an officer-stockholder in the small manufacturing firm, insisted that the corporation's board of directors authorize the purchase of an insurance policy to compensate for any loss of earning potential upon his death. The corporation paid $147,500 in premiums prior to Mr. Relias' death, and was the sole beneficiary of the policy. At the date of death there had been no premium prepayment and no rebate was due. In prior years cash surrender value in the amount of $68,000 had been recorded in the accounts.

**Instructions**

(a) What is the "cash surrender value" of a life insurance policy?
(b) How should the cash surrender value of a life insurance policy be classified in the financial statements while the policy is in force? Why?
(c) Comment on the propriety of the entry recording the insurance receivable.

**C18-6 Part A.** To manufacture and sell its products a company must invest in inventories, plant and equipment, and other operating assets. In addition, a manufacturing company often finds it desirable or necessary to invest a portion of its available resources, either directly or through the operation of special funds, in stocks, bonds, and other securities.

**Instructions**

(a) List the reasons why a manufacturing company might invest funds in stocks, bonds, and other securities.
(b) What are the criteria for classifying investments as current or noncurrent assets?

**Part B.** Because of favorable market prices, the trustee of K & P Willrett Company's bond sinking fund invested the current year's contribution to the fund in the company's own bonds. The bonds are being held in the fund without cancellation. The fund also includes cash and securities of other companies.

**Instructions**

Describe three methods of classifying the bond sinking fund on the balance sheet of K & P Willrett Company. Include a discussion of the propriety of using each method.

**C18-7** Robby Morris Inc. administers the sinking fund applicable to its own outstanding long-term bonds. The following four proposals relate to the accounting treatment of sinking fund cash and securities.

    **1.** To mingle sinking fund cash with general cash and sinking fund securities with other securities, and to show both as current assets on the balance sheet.

    **2.** To keep sinking fund cash in a separate bank account and sinking fund securities separate from other securities, but on the balance sheet to treat cash as a part of the general cash and the securities as part of general investments, both being shown as current assets.

3. To keep sinking fund cash in a separate bank account and sinking fund securities separate from other securities, but to combine the two accounts on the balance sheet under one caption, such as "Sinking Fund Cash and Investments," to be listed as a noncurrent asset.

4. To keep sinking fund cash in a separate bank account and sinking fund securities separate from other securities, and to identify each separately on the balance sheet among the current assets.

**Instructions**

Identify the proposal that is most appropriate. Give the reasons for your selection.

**C18-8** Residue Inc., a chemical processing company, has been operating profitably for many years. On March 1, 1983, Residue purchased 50,000 shares of Diversified Insurance Company stock for $2,000,000. The 50,000 shares represented 40% of Diversified's outstanding stock. Both Residue and Diversified operate on a fiscal year ending August 31.

For the fiscal year ended August 31, 1983, Diversified reported net income of $800,000 earned ratably throughout the year. During November, 1982, February, May, and August, 1983, Diversified paid its regular quarterly cash dividend of $100,000.

**Instructions**

(a) What criteria should Residue consider in determining whether its investment in Diversified should be classified as (1) a current asset (marketable security) or (2) a noncurrent asset (investment) in Residue's August 31, 1983, balance sheet? Confine your discussion to the decision criteria for determining the balance sheet classification of the investment.

(b) Assume that the investment should be classified as a long-term investment in the noncurrent asset section of Residue's balance sheet. The cost of Residue's investment equaled its equity in the recorded values of Diversified's net assets; recorded values were not materially different from fair values (individually or collectively). For the fiscal year ended August 31, 1983, how did the net income reported and dividends paid by Diversified affect the accounts of Residue (ignore income tax considerations)? Indicate each account affected, whether it increased or decreased, and explain the reason for the change in the account balance (such as Cash, Investment in Diversified, etc.). Organize your answer in the following format.

| Account Name | Increase or Decrease | Reason for Change in Account Balance |
|---|---|---|

(AICPA adapted)

## EXERCISES

**E18-1** The following data show the long-term investments of Tiptoe Shoe Company on June 30, 1983, the end of its fiscal year. These investments were purchased on the dates and at the costs shown.

| | | |
|---|---|---:|
| February 1 | Penwell Company $1,000, 11% bonds.<br>Interest payable April 1 and Oct. 1.<br>50 bonds. Due March 1, 1985. | $ 52,000 |
| March  30 | Denson Company common stock, $10 par<br>4,000 shares (5% of the outstanding shares). | 45,000 |
| May      1 | Rickety, Inc., $1,000, 10% bonds.<br>Interest payable June 1 and Dec. 1.<br>25 bonds. Due September 1, 1986. | 22,600 |
| | | $119,600 |

**Instructions**

(a) If amortization of premium or discount is recorded once a year on June 30, what entry would be necessary on June 30, 1983? (Apply the straight-line method.)

(b) What entry (if any) would be necessary if the market value of the investments was as follows on June 30:

| | |
|---|---:|
| Penwell Company | $ 51,200 |
| Denson Company | 40,800 |
| Rickety, Inc. | 25,400 |
| | $117,400 |

**E18-2** The transactions given below relate to bonds purchased by Shoestring Company:

Apr. 1, 1984  Bonds of Poe Company of a par value of $30,000 are purchased as a long-term investment at 95 plus accrued interest. The bonds bear interest at 9% payable annually on Dec. 1, and they mature Dec. 1, 1990.

Dec. 1  Interest of $2,700 is received on the Poe Company bonds. (Do not amortize discount at this time.)

Dec. 31  The proper amount of interest is accrued, and the entry is made to amortize the proper amount of discount for 1984.

June 1, 1985  Bonds of a par value of $7,500 are sold at 97 plus accrued interest. Assume that reversing entries are made January 1.

**Instructions**

Prepare journal entries required by Shoestring Company to record the transactions above using straight-line amortization.

**E18-3** On December 31, 1984, Discorama Company owns long-term investments purchased on dates and at costs shown below:

| | | |
|---|---|---:|
| Jan. 10, 1983 | A Company common stock, no par, 1,000 shares | $ 46,000 |
| Mar. 20 | B Company preferred stock, $100 par, 300 shares | 60,600 |
| Apr. 1 | C Company $1,000, 11% bonds due Apr. 1, 1993, interest payable Apr. 1 and Oct. 1, 25 bonds | 27,400 |
| June 1, 1984 | D Company $1,000, 12% bonds due June 1, 1988, interest payable Dec. 1 and June 1, 22 bonds | 20,800 |
| | | $154,800 |

**Instructions**

(a) Prepare the entry to record amortization of discount or premium on December 31, 1983. Assume that the company records amortization of discount and premium only at the end of each year using the straight-line method and records its debt securities at net cost.

(b) Prepare the entry to record amortization of discount or premium on December 31, 1984.

(c) The market value of the securities as of December 31, 1984, is as follows:

| | |
|---|---:|
| A Company common stock (representing a 2% interest) | $ 48,000 |
| B Company preferred stock (representing a 5% interest) | 52,600 |
| C Company bonds | 25,400 |
| D Company bonds | 23,000 |
| | $149,000 |

What entry, if any, would you recommend be made with respect to this information, and what disclosures, if any, should be made in the financial statements?

**E18-4** On January 1, 1984, Herbert Company purchases $200,000 of Bloyd Company 8% bonds for $154,119. The interest is payable semiannually on June 30 and December 31 and the bonds mature in 10 years. The purchase price provides a yield of 12% on the investment.

**Instructions**

(a) Prepare the journal entry on January 1, 1984, to record the purchase of the investment (record the investment at gross or maturity value).

(b) Prepare the journal entry on June 30, 1984, to record the receipt of the first interest payment and any amortization using the straight-line method.

(c) Prepare the journal entry on June 30, 1984, to record the receipt of the first interest payment and any amortization using the effective interest method.

**E18-5** On June 1, 1982, Warner, Inc., purchased as a long-term investment 800 of the $1,000 face value, 8% bonds of Universal Corporation for $738,300. The bonds were purchased to yield 10% interest. Interest is payable semiannually on December 1 and June 1. The bonds mature on June 1, 1987. Warner uses the effective interest method of amortization. On November 1, 1983, Warner sold the bonds for $785,000. This amount includes the appropriate accrued interest. (Round computations to nearest dollar.)

**Instructions**

Prepare a schedule showing the income or loss, before income taxes, from the bond investment that Warner should record for the years ended December 31, 1982, and 1983.

(CMA adapted)

**E18-6** Patriot Corp. was a 30% owner of Rebel Company, holding 300,000 shares of Rebel's common stock on December 31, 1982. The investment account had the following entries:

Investment in Rebel

| | | | |
|---|---|---|---|
| 1/1/81 Cost | $3,240,000 | 12/6/81 Dividend received | $120,000 |
| 12/31/81 Share of income | 480,000 | 12/31/81 Amortization of under- | |
| 12/31/82 Share of income | 600,000 | valued assets | 36,000 |
| | | 12/5/82 Dividend received | 240,000 |
| | | 12/31/82 Amortization of under- | |
| | | valued assets | 36,000 |

On January 2, 1983, Patriot sold 150,000 shares of Rebel for $3,000,000, thereby losing its significant influence. During the years 1983 and 1984 Rebel experienced the following results of operations and paid the following dividends to Patriot.

| | Rebel Income (Loss) | Dividends Paid to Patriot |
|---|---|---|
| 1983 | $360,000 | $48,000 |
| 1984 | (240,000) | 12,000 |

**Instructions**

(a) What effect does the January 2, 1983 transaction have upon Patriot's accounting treatment for its investment in Rebel?

(b) Compute the carrying value of the investment in Rebel as of December 31, 1984, assuming a market value of $1,800,000.

**E18-7** Fantasy Clothes Company purchased 30,000 shares (a 30% interest) of common stock of Cool-Jeans Company at $18 per share on January 2, 1983. During 1983, Cool-Jeans Company reported net income of $200,000 and paid dividends of $50,000. On January 2, 1984, Fantasy received 10,000 shares of common stock as a result of a stock split by Cool-Jeans Company.

**Instructions**

(a) Prepare the entry to record the sale of 1,000 shares at $13.75 per share by Fantasy Clothes Company on January 3, 1984, applying the lower of cost or market method in accounting for the investment (owing to lack of significant influence).

(b) Prepare the entry to record the sale of 1,000 shares at $13.75 per share on January 3, 1984, applying the equity method in accounting for the investment. Assume the acquisition cost approximated the book value acquired on January 2, 1983.

**E18-8** On July 1, 1984, Keith Bond Company purchased for cash 40% of the outstanding capital stock of Cart Company. Both Bond Company and Cart Company have a December 31 year end. Cart Company, whose common stock is actively traded in the over-the-counter market, reported its total net income for the year to Bond Company and also paid cash dividends on November 15, 1984, to Bond Company and its other stockholders.

**Instructions**

How should Keith Bond Company report the above facts in its December 31, 1984, balance sheet and its income statement for the year then ended? Discuss the rationale for your answer.

(AICPA adapted)

**E18-9** At the end of its first year of operations, Jewel Kadlec Company had a current marketable equity securities portfolio with a cost of $500,000 and a market value of $550,000. At the end of its second year of operations, Jewel Kadlec Company had a current marketable equity securities portfolio with a cost of $525,000 and a market value of $475,000. No securities were sold during the first year. One security with a cost of $80,000 and a market value of $70,000 at the end of the first year was sold for $100,000 during the second year.

**Instructions**

How should Jewel Kadlec Company report the above facts in its balance sheets and income statements for both years? Discuss the rationale for your answer.

(AICPA adapted)

**E18-10** Franzne Company pays the premiums on two insurance policies on the life of its president, Kim Franzne. Information concerning premiums paid in 1984 is given below.

| Beneficiary | Face | Prem. | Dividends Cr. to Prem. | Net Prem. | Cash Surrender Value | |
|---|---|---|---|---|---|---|
| | | | | | 1/1/84 | 12/31/84 |
| 1. Franzne Co. | $240,000 | $7,800 | $2,760 | $5,040 | $30,000 | $32,400 |
| 2. President's husband | 75,000 | 3,150 | | 3,150 | 9,000 | 9,750 |

**Instructions**

(a) Prepare entries in journal form to record the payment of premiums in 1984.
(b) If the president died in January, 1985, and the beneficiaries are paid the face amounts of the policies, what entry would the Franzne Company make?

**E18-11** Steve Robinson Inc., has $100,000 in its bonds payable account at the beginning of 1983. Interest at 12% is payable April 1 and Oct. 1. On July 17, the sinking fund trustee for Steve Robinson Inc., purchases at par $20,000 of the bonds.

**Instructions**

(a) Prepare the journal entries necessary on April 1 and October 1.
(b) What two methods may be used to disclose the holding on the balance sheet?

**E18-12** The general ledger of Jacques Company shows an account for Bonds Payable with a balance of $1,000,000. Interest is payable on these bonds semiannually. Of the $1,000,000, bonds in the amount of $200,000 were recently purchased at par by the sinking fund trustee and are held in the sinking fund as an investment of the fund. The annual rate of interest is 11%.

**Instructions**

(a) What entry or entries should be made by Jacques Company to record payment of the semiannual interest? (The company makes interest payments directly to bondholders.)
(b) Illustrate how the bonds payable and the sinking fund accounts should be shown in the balance sheet. Assume that the sinking fund investments other than Jacques Company's bonds amount to $247,000, and that the sinking fund cash amounts to $9,100.

**E18-13** The transactions given below relate to a fund being accumulated by the Mankato Rug Company over a period of 20 years for the construction of additional buildings.

1. Cash is transferred from the general cash account to the fund.
2. Preferred stock of M. Frye Company is purchased as an investment of the fund.
3. Bonds of H. Castle Corporation are purchased between interest dates at a discount as an investment of the fund.
4. Expenses of the fund are paid from the fund cash.
5. Interest is collected on H. Castle Corporation bonds.
6. Bonds held in the fund are sold at a gain between interest dates.
7. Dividends are received on M. Frye Company preferred stock.
8. Common stocks held in the fund are sold at a loss.
9. Cash is paid from the fund for building construction.
10. The cash balance remaining in the fund is transferred to general cash.

**Instructions**

Prepare journal entries to record the miscellaneous transactions listed above with amounts omitted.

## PROBLEMS

**P18-1** On December 31, 1982, Dumbo Tool Company acquired 60,000 shares of Lassie Corporation common stock at a cost of $28 a share; the purchase represented 30% of Lassie Corporation's outstanding stock.

On May 1, 1983, Lassie Corporation paid a cash dividend of $1.50 a common share.

For the year 1983, Lassie Corporation reported net income of $400,000; the market value of the investment was $1,440,000 at December 31, 1983.

On May 1, 1984, Lassie Corporation paid a dividend of $0.50 a share. For the year 1984, Lassie Corporation reported a net income of $600,000; the market value of the investment was $1,620,000 at December 31, 1984.

**Instructions**

(a) Prepare the journal entries necessary to record the transactions listed above on Dumbo Tool Company's books, assuming that the investment in Lassie Corporation does not represent a significant influence and, therefore, is carried on the lower of cost or market basis. December 31 is Dumbo Tool Company's year end.
(b) Prepare the journal entries necessary to record the transactions listed above on Dumbo Tool Company's books, assuming that the investment in Lassie Corporation is carried on the equity basis.
(c) What is the carrying value of the investment in Lassie Corporation stock on January 1, 1985 (1) under the lower of cost or market basis, and (2) under the equity method?

**P18-2** On January 1, 1981, Sherri Strain Company acquires $100,000 of Pontiff Products, Inc., 9% bonds at a price of $92,794. The interest is payable each December 31, and the bonds mature January 1, 1984. The investment will provide Sherri Strain Company a 12% yield.

**Instructions**

(a) Prepare a three-year schedule of interest revenue and bond discount amortization, applying the straight-line method.
(b) Prepare a three-year schedule of interest revenue and bond discount amortization, applying the effective interest method.
(c) Prepare the journal entry for the interest receipt of December 31, 1983, and the discount amortization under the straight-line method.
(d) Prepare the journal entry for the interest receipt of December 31, 1983, and the discount amortization under the effective interest method.

**P18-3** On January 1, 1982, Jeffries, Inc., paid $700,000 for 10,000 shares of Wolf Company's voting common stock which was a 10% interest in Wolf. At that date the net assets of Wolf totaled $6,000,000. The fair values of all of Wolf's identifiable assets and liabilities were equal to their book values. Jeffries does not have the ability to exercise significant influence over the operating and financial policies of Wolf. Jeffries received dividends of $0.90 per share from Wolf on October 1, 1982. Wolf reported net income of $400,000 for the year ended December 31, 1982.

On July 1, 1983, Jeffries paid $2,300,000 for 30,000 additional shares of Wolf Company's voting common stock which represents a 30% investment in Wolf. The fair values of all of Wolf's identifiable assets net of liabilities were equal to their book values of $6,500,000. As a result of this transaction, Jeffries has the ability to excercise significant influence over the operating and financial policies of Wolf. Jeffries received dividends of $1.10 per share from Wolf on April 1, 1983, and $1.35 per share on October 1, 1983. Wolf reported net income of $500,000 for the year ended December 31, 1983, and $200,000 for the six months ended December 31, 1983. Jeffries amortizes goodwill over a forty-year period.

**Instructions**

(a) Prepare a schedule showing the income or loss before income taxes for the year ended December 31, 1982, that Jeffries should report from its investment in Wolf in its income statement issued in March 1983.

(b) During March 1984, Jeffries issues comparative financial statements for 1982 and 1983. Prepare schedules showing the income or loss before income taxes for the years ended December 31, 1982, and 1983, that Jeffries should report from its investment in Wolf.

(AICPA adapted)

**P18-4** On January 1, 1983, Mouse Corp. bought 3,500 shares of Cat Company common stock at $12 per share. At that time Cat Company's balance sheet showed total assets of $200,000, liabilities of $20,000, common stock ($10 par value) of $100,000, and retained earnings of $80,000. The difference between book value acquired and the purchase price is attributable to assets having a remaining life of 10 years.

At the end of 1983, Cat Company reported net income of $25,000 and paid cash dividends of $7,500 on December 31, 1983. The market value of Cat Company stock was $13 per share at December 31, 1983.

On January 1, 1984, Mouse Corp. sold 875 shares of Cat Company stock at the market price of $14 per share.

**Instructions**

(a) Prepare journal entries to record the events noted above and data on the books of Mouse Corp., assuming that it is unable to exercise significant influence over Cat Company during 1983 and, therefore, applies the lower of cost or market method.

(b) Prepare journal entries to record the events above and data on the books of Mouse Corp., applying the equity method. (Round to nearest dollar.)

**P18-5** On January 3, 1981, Varsity Company purchased for $500,000 cash a 10% interest in Summerset Corp. On that date the net assets of Summerset had a book value of $3,750,000. The excess of cost over the underlying equity in net assets is attributable to undervalued depreciable assets having a remaining life of 10 years from date of Varsity purchase.

On January 2, 1983, Varsity purchased an additional 30% of Summerset's stock for $1,900,000 cash when the book value of Summerset's net assets was $5,000,000. The excess was attributable to depreciable assets having a remaining life of 8 years.

During 1981, 1982, and 1983 the following occurred:

|  | Summerset Net Income | Dividends Paid by Summerset to Varsity |
|---|---|---|
| 1981 | $375,000 | $12,500 |
| 1982 | 450,000 | 18,750 |
| 1983 | 500,000 | 37,500 |

**Instructions**

On the books of Varsity Company prepare all journal entries in 1981, 1982, and 1983 that relate to its investment in Summerset Corp., reflecting the data above and a change from the cost method to the equity method.

**P18–6** Tinkerbell Company has the following portfolio of long-term marketable equity securities at December 31, 1983.

| Security | Quantity | Percent Interest | Cost | Market |
|---|---|---|---|---|
| | | | Per Share | |
| Microtape, Inc. | 2,000 shares | 8% | $11 | $16 |
| Surley Corp. | 6,000 shares | 14% | 23 | 17 |
| Denson Company | 4,000 shares | 2% | 31 | 26 |

**Instructions**

(a) What descriptions and amounts should be reported on the face of Tinkerbell's December 31, 1983 balance sheet relative to long-term investments?

On December 31, 1984, Tinkerbell's portfolio of long-term marketable equity securities consisted of the following common stocks.

| Security | Quantity | Percent Interest | Cost | Market |
|---|---|---|---|---|
| | | | Per Share | |
| Surley Corp. | 6,000 shares | 14% | $23 | $30 |
| Denson Company | 4,000 shares | 2% | 31 | 25 |
| Denson Company | 2,000 shares | 1% | 25 | 25 |

During the year 1984, Tinkerbell Company changed its intent relative to its investment in Microtape, Inc. and reclassified the shares to current asset status when the shares were selling for $8 per share.

(b) What descriptions and amounts should be reported on the face of Tinkerbell's December 31, 1984 balance sheet relative to long-term investments? What descriptions and amounts should be reported to reflect the transactions above in Tinkerbell's 1984 income statement?

(c) Assuming that comparative financial statements for 1983 and 1984 are presented, draft the footnote necessary for full disclosure of Tinkerbell's transactions and position in marketable equity securities.

**P18–7** Kentucky Wildcats Corp. makes the following long-term investments during 1983:

| Security | Quantity | Percent Interest | Per Share Cost |
|---|---|---|---|
| Ohio Forms Company | 2,400 shares | 2% | $80 |
| Lexington Grader Corp. | 7,500 shares | 16% | 20 |
| Knoblett Development Inc. | 3,000 shares | 4% | 35 |

The following information concerning these investments relates to 1983 and 1984:

**1.** For the year 1983—Cash dividends received:

| | |
|---|---|
| Ohio Forms | $4.00 per share |
| Lexington Grader | $ .60 per share |
| Knoblett Development | $1.50 per share |

**2.** Market values per share, 12/31/83:

| | |
|---|---|
| Ohio Forms | $74 |
| Lexington Grader | $22 |
| Knoblett Development | $28 |

3. For the year 1984—Cash dividends received:

| | |
|---|---|
| Ohio Forms | $4.00 per share |
| Lexington Grader | $ .15 per share |
| Knoblett Development | $1.70 per share |

4. On Sept. 30, 1984, the investment in Lexington Grader was reclassified to current asset status when its market value per share was $15.

5. Market value per share, 12/31/84:

| | |
|---|---|
| Ohio Forms | $68 |
| Knoblett Development | $46 |

**Instructions**

(a) Prepare all of the journal entries to reflect the transactions above and data in accordance with *FASB Statement No. 12.*

(b) Prepare the descriptions and amounts that should be reported on the face of Kentucky Wildcats Corp.'s comparative financial statements for 1983 and 1984 relative to these long-term investments.

(c) Draft the footnote that should accompany the 1983–84 comparative statements relative to the noncurrent marketable equity securities.

**P18-8** Taxi Corporation carries an account in its general ledger called "Investments," which contained the following debits for investment purchases, and no credits.

| | | |
|---|---|---|
| Feb. 1, 1983 | RC Company common stock, $100 par, 200 shares | $35,200 |
| April 1 | U.S. Government bonds, 11%, due April 1, 1993, interest payable April 1 and October 1, 100 bonds of $1,000 par each (current asset) | 116,600 |
| July 1 | Noble Steel Company 12% bonds, par $50,000, dated March 1, 1983 purchased at 103 plus accrued interest, interest payable annually on March 1, due March 1, 2003 (noncurrent asset) | 53,500 |

**Instructions**

(a) Prepare entries necessary to classify the amounts into proper accounts, assuming that, of the securities held, the U.S. Government bonds are the only temporary investments.

(b) Prepare the entry to record the accrued interest and amortization of premium on December 31, 1983, using the straight-line method.

(c) The market values of the securities on December 31, 1983, were:

| | |
|---|---|
| RC Company common stock | $ 33,000 (1% interest) |
| U.S. Government bonds | 118,800 |
| Noble Steel Company bonds | 59,400 |

What entry or entries, if any, would you recommend be made?

(d) The U.S. Government bonds were sold on July 1, 1984, for $117,700 plus accrued interest. Give the proper entry.

(e) Twenty additional shares of RC Company common stock were received on July 15, 1984, as a stock dividend, and on July 31, 1984, 30 shares of RC Company common stock were sold at $176 per share. What entries would be made for these two transactions?

**P18-9** On January 10, 1983, Pontificate Company purchased 200 shares, $100 par value (a 3% interest), of common stock of Meteoric Corporation for $26,400 as a long-term investment. On July 12, 1983, Meteoric Corporation announced that one right would be issued for every two shares of stock held.

| | |
|---|---|
| July 30, 1983 | Rights to purchase 100 shares of stock at par value of $100 per share are received. The market value of the stock is $150 per share and the market value of the rights is $20 per right. |
| Aug. 10 | The rights to purchase 40 shares of stock are sold at $20 per right. |

Aug. 11      The additional 60 rights are exercised, and 60 shares of stock are purchased at $100 per share.

Nov. 15      50 shares of those purchased on January 10, 1983, are sold at $130 per share.

**Instructions**

Prepare general journal entries on the books of Pontificate Company for the foregoing transactions.

**P18-10** Discoteque Company purchases 200 shares of common stock of Gary Angotti, Inc., on February 17. The $100 par stock, costing $24,096, is to be a long-term investment for Discoteque Company.

1. On June 30, Gary Angotti, Inc., announces that rights are to be issued. One right will be received for every two shares owned.
2. The rights mentioned in (1) are received on July 15. 100 shares of $100 par stock may be purchased with these rights at par. The stock is currently selling for $118 per share. Market value of the stock rights is $15 per right.
3. On August 5, 70 rights are exercised, and 70 shares of stock are purchased at par.
4. On August 12, the remaining stock rights are sold at $17 per right.
5. On September 28, Discoteque Company sells 50 shares of those purchased February 17, at $130 a share.

**Instructions**

Prepare necessary journal entries for the five numbered items above.

**P18-11** Mountaindew Company holds 300 shares of common stock of Joe Josephson Company that it purchased for $33,867 as a long-term investment. On January 15, 1984, it is announced that one right will be issued for every 4 shares of Joe Josephson Company stock held.

**Instructions**

(a) Prepare entries on Mountaindew Company's books for the transactions below that occurred after the date of this announcement. Show all computations in good form.
     1. 100 shares of stock are sold "rights-on" for $12,300.
     2. Rights to purchase 50 additional shares of stock at par value of $100 per share are received. The market value of the stock on this date is $105 per share and the market value of the rights is $6 per right.
     3. The rights are exercised, and 50 additional shares are purchased at $100 per share.
     4. 100 shares of the stock originally held are sold at $107 per share.
(b) If the rights had not been exercised but instead had been sold at $6 per right, what would have been the amount of the gain or loss on the sale of the rights?
(c) If the stock purchased through the exercise of the rights is later sold at $107 per share, what is the amount of the gain or loss on the sale?
(d) If the rights had not been exercised, but had been allowed to expire, what would be the proper entry?

**P18-12** The transactions given below relate to a sinking fund for retirement of long-term bonds of Coed Corp.

1. In accordance with the terms of the bond indenture, cash in the amount of $125,000 is transferred at the end of the first year, from the regular cash account to the sinking fund.
2. NIU Company 10% bonds of a par value of $40,000, maturing in five years, are purchased for $37,000.
3. 400 shares of UW Company 8% preferred stock ($50 par value) are purchased at $52 per share.
4. Annual interest of $4,000 is received on NIU Company bonds. (Amortize the proper amount of discount using straight-line amortization.)

5. Sinking fund expenses of $375 are paid from sinking fund cash.

6. ISU Company 9% bonds with interest payable February 1 and August 1 are purchased on April 15 at par value of $40,000 plus accrued interest.

7. Dividends of $1,600 are received on UW Company preferred stock.

8. All the ISU Company bonds are sold on September 1 at 101 plus accrued interest. Assume interest collected August 1 was properly recorded.

9. Investments carried in the fund at $1,652,000 are sold for $1,601,000.

10. The fund contains cash of $1,611,000 after disposing of all investments and paying all expenses. $1,600,000 of this amount is used to retire the bonds payable at maturity date.

11. The remaining cash balance is returned to the general account.

## Instructions

Prepare the journal entries required by Coed Corp. for the transactions above.

**P18-13** Cheerleader Corporation has various long-term investments and maintains its books on the accrual basis. The books for the year ended December 31, 1984, have not been closed. Here is an analysis of the Investment account for the year.

Cheerleader Corporation
ANALYSIS OF INVESTMENT ACCOUNT
Year Ended December 31, 1984

| 1984 | Transactions | Fol. | Debit | Credit |
|---|---|---|---|---|
| | | | Account Per Books | |
| Jan. 1 | 5,000 shares Backand Oil Co. | | $ 5,300 | |
| | 1,000 shares General Corp. | | 34,000 | |
| | 50 shares, 9% Pfd. Grey Steel | | 6,000 | |
| | $10,000, 8% bonds, Martin Co. | | 10,270 | |
| Feb. 10 | Purchased 5,000 shares, Wash Motors | CD | 16,000 | |
| Mar. 1 | Cash dividend, Grey Steel | CR | | $  450 |
| April 1 | Interest, Martin Co. bonds | CR | | 400 |
| May 15 | Sold 800 rights, General Corp. | CR | | 1,100 |
| May 16 | Exercised 200 rights, General Corp. to purchase 50 shares, General Corp. | CD | 2,250 | |
| Aug. 5 | Sold 200 shares, Wash Motors | CR | | 2,500 |
| Sept. 18 | Sold 100 shares, General Corp. | CR | | 3,400 |
| Oct. 1 | Interest, Martin Co. bonds | | | 400 |
| | | | $73,820 | $8,250 |

Your work sheets for the year ended December 31, 1983, show these securities in the Investment account as indicated on page 828.

After inquiry the following additional data were obtained:

1. The General Corporation on May 12 issued warrants representing the right to purchase, at $45 per share, one share for every four shares held. On May 12, the market value of the stock rights-on was $50 and ex-rights was $49. Cheerleader Corporation sold 800 rights on May 15, when the market price of the stock was $51. On May 16, 200 rights were exercised.

2. On June 30, Wash Motors declared a reverse stock split of 1 for 5. One share of new $.50 par value common was exchanged for five shares of old $.10 par value common.

3. Cheerleader Corporation acquired the Martin Company bonds, which are due September 30, 1987, for $10,360. Interest is payable April 1 and October 1.

4. The sale of 100 shares of General Corporation stock was part of the 1,000 shares purchased on April 1, 1977. The stock was sold for $65 per share.

5. The government of Backand in early 1984 confiscated the assets of the Backand Oil Company and nationalized the company. Despite the protest of the United States government, the Backand government has refused to recognize any claims of the stockholders or management of the Backand Oil Company.

| Date of Acquisition | Number of Shares or Face Value of Bonds | Type of Security | Name of Issuer | Amount |
|---|---|---|---|---|
| Jan. 2, 1976 | 5,000 | Common stock, no par value | Backand Oil Co. | $ 5,300 |
| April 1, 1977 | 1,000 | Common stock, $100 par value | General Corp. | 34,000 |
| Nov. 15, 1977 | 50 | 9% preferred stock, par value $100 | Grey Steel | 6,000 |
| Oct. 1, 1982 | $10,000 | 8% bonds | Martin Co. | 10,270 |
| | | | | $55,570 |

### Instructions

Prepare a work sheet showing the adjustments to arrive at the correct balance at December 31, 1984, in the Investment account. The work sheet should include the names of other accounts affected by the adjustments or reclassifications. (Formal journal entries are not required but may be prepared to expedite and support the work sheet.)

(AICPA adapted)

**P18–14** Pacemaker, Inc., a domestic corporation having a fiscal year ending June 30, has purchased common stock in several other domestic corporations. As of June 30, 1984, the balance in Pacemaker's Investments account was $1,741,200, the total cost of stock purchased less the cost of stock sold. Pacemaker wishes to restate the Investments account to reflect the provisions of *APB Opinion No. 18, "The Equity Method of Accounting for Investments in Common Stock."*

Data concerning the investments follow:

| | Ruby, Inc. | Howat, Inc. | Jewel, Inc. |
|---|---|---|---|
| Shares of common stock outstanding | 3,000 | 32,000 | 100,000 |
| Shares purchased by Pacemaker | (a)    300 | 8,000 | 30,000 |
| | (b)    810 | | |
| Date of purchase | (a) July 1, 1981 | June 30, 1982 | June 30, 1983 |
| | (b) July 1, 1983 | | |
| Cost of shares purchased | (a) $   98,800 | $ 92,000 | $1,340,000 |
| | (b) $ 284,000 | | |
| Balance sheet at date indicated: | | | |
| Assets | July 1, 1983 | June 30, 1982 | June 30, 1983 |
| Current assets | $   724,000 | $   79,200 | $1,989,000 |
| Fixed assets, net of depreciation | 3,276,000 | 1,432,800 | 6,600,000 |
| Patent, net of amortization | | | 297,000 |
| | $4,000,000 | $1,512,000 | $8,886,000 |

Liabilities and Capital

| | | | |
|---|---|---|---|
| Liabilities | $3,000,000 | $1,144,000 | $4,989,000 |
| Common stock | 520,000 | 160,000 | 2,800,000 |
| Retained earnings | 480,000 | 208,000 | 1,097,000 |
| | $4,000,000 | $1,512,000 | $8,886,000 |

| | | | |
|---|---|---|---|
| Changes in common stock since July 1, 1981 | None | None | None |
| Average remaining life of fixed assets at date of balance sheet (above) | 12 years | 9 years | 22 years |
| Analysis of retained earnings: | | | |
| Balance, July 1, 1981 | $ 468,000 | | |
| Net income, July 1, 1981 to June 30, 1982 | 106,800 | | |
| Dividend paid—April 1, 1982 | (102,000) | | |
| Balance, June 30, 1982 | 472,800 | $ 208,000 | |
| Net income (loss), July 1, 1982 to June 30, 1983 | 111,200 | (4,000) | |
| Dividend paid—April 1, 1983 | (104,000) | | |
| Balance, June 30, 1983 | 480,000 | 204,000 | $1,097,000 |
| Net income, July 1, 1983 to June 30, 1984 | 50,000 | 36,000 | 660,000 |
| Dividends paid: | | | |
| December 28, 1983 | | | (300,000) |
| June 1, 1984 | | (11,200) | |
| Balance, June 30, 1984 | $ 530,000 | $ 228,800 | $1,457,000 |

Pacemaker's first purchase of Ruby's stock was made because of the high rate of return expected on the investment. All later purchases of stock have been made to gain substantial influence over the operations of the various companies.

In December 1983, changing market conditions caused Pacemaker to reevaluate its relation to Howat. On December 31, 1983, Pacemaker sold 6,400 shares of Howat for $108,800.

For Ruby and Howat, the fair values of the net assets did not differ materially from the book values as shown in the balance sheets above. For Jewel, fair values exceeded book values only with respect to the patent, which had a fair value of $600,000 and a remaining life of 15 years as of June 30, 1983.

**Instructions**

Prepare a work sheet to restate Pacemaker's Investments account as of June 30, 1984, and its investment income by year for the three years then ended. Transactions should be listed in chronological order and supporting computations should be in good form. **Ignore income taxes.** Amortization of goodwill, if any, is to be over a 40-year period. Use the following columnar headings for your work sheet:

| | | Investments | | | Investment Income, Year Ended June 30 | | | Other Accounts | |
|---|---|---|---|---|---|---|---|---|---|
| | | Ruby | Howat | Jewel | 1982 | 1983 | 1984 | Amount | Name |
| Date | Description | Dr. (Cr.) | Dr. (Cr.) | Dr. (Cr.) | Cr. (Dr.) | Cr. (Dr.) | Cr. (Dr.) | Dr. (Cr.) | |

(AICPA adapted)

# ISSUES RELATED TO INCOME MEASUREMENT

## 5

# CHAPTER 19

# Revenue Recognition

Revenue recognition is one of the most difficult and pressing problems facing the accounting profession. Although the profession has general guidelines to determine when revenue should be recognized, the many methods of marketing and selling products and services make it extremely difficult to develop guidelines that will apply to all situations. Significant lawsuits involving revenue recognition problems, such as those involving U.S. Financial (related party transactions), National Student Marketing (revenue that did not materialize), and Equity Funding (sales that never were) illustrate the complexity of determining when and at what amount revenue should be recognized.

As a result, there has been a significant increase in the number of professional pronouncements on accounting for revenue transactions. For example, the AICPA has published a number of industry accounting guides that deal specifically with revenue recognition problems in such areas as retail land sales, sales of real estate, franchises, construction contractors, and the motion picture industry. The AICPA's Accounting Standards Executive Committee (AcSEC) has issued Statements of Position on such issues as accounting for sales of personal property where right of return exists, recognition of profit on sales of receivables with recourse, sales of real estate, and on other specific industry revenue recognition problems in such areas as broadcasting, construction, mortgage banking, and records and music. The APB provided guidance in *APB Opinion No. 29* in handling revenue recognition problems involving nonmonetary transactions where goods and services were exchanged for other goods and services. The FASB established guidelines in *Statement No. 13*, "Accounting for Leases," to determine when a lease transaction should be considered a sale; more recently it has issued *Statements 50, 51, 53, 60,* and *63,* which provide standards for recognizing revenue in specific industries, namely: record and music, cable television, production and distribution of motion picture films, insurance, and broadcasters, respectively. In addition, the FASB issued an Invitation to Comment on "Accounting for Service Transactions" which deals primarily with revenue recognition problems in such diverse areas as health spas, mortuaries, advertising agencies, and travel agencies. All of this activity and the issuance of these pronouncements is merely evidence of the fact that determination of when a sale is a sale is a complex question that is currently being studied by the profession.

# GUIDELINES FOR REVENUE RECOGNITION[1]

Revenues are inflows or other enhancements of assets of an entity or settlements of its liabilities (or a combination of both) from delivering or producing goods, rendering services, or other earning activities that constitute the ongoing major or central operations of an enterprise during a period.[2] As an element in the income measurement process, the revenue for a period is generally determined independently of expenses by applying the revenue recognition principle.[3] The **revenue recognition principle provides that revenue is recognized when (1) the earning process is complete or virtually complete and (2) an exchange transaction has taken place.**[4] In accordance with this principle: (a) revenue from selling products is recognized at the date of sale, usually interpreted to mean the date of delivery to customers; (b) revenue from services rendered is recognized when services have been performed and are billable; (c) revenue from permitting others to use enterprise assets, such as interest, rent, and royalties, is recognized as time passes or as the assets are used; (d) revenue from disposing of assets other than products is recognized at the date of sale.

These statements describe the conceptual nature of revenue and are the basis of accounting for revenue transactions. Yet, in practice, there are departures from the revenue recognition principle, and other points in the earning process are sometimes used in recognizing revenue, owing in great measure to the considerable variety of revenue transactions. For example, many revenue recognition problems develop because the ultimate collection of the selling price is not reasonably assured or because it is difficult to determine when the earning process is complete. Real estate land sales provide a good example. To illustrate, at one time General Development recognized the entire sales price of real estate as revenue as soon as it received 5% of the purchase price or a minimum down payment and two monthly payments. Cavanaugh Industries indicated that the percentage collected need only be 3%. Dart Industries required a 10% down payment, as did Boise Cascade, yet McCulloch demanded 15%. Subsequently an industry accounting guide was issued which specified that in most instances a down payment of 25% of the sales value of the property is an adequate investment to support recognition of profit at the time of sale.

---

[1] Most of the recent accounting pronouncements on revenue recognition and much of present practice are based on *Statement of Accounting Principles Board No. 4,* "Basic Concepts and Accounting Principles Underlying Financial Statements of Business Enterprises" (AICPA, 1970). Although the FASB has published "Elements of Financial Statements of Business Enterprises" (*Concepts Statement No. 3*), which defines revenues differently than does *APB Statement No. 4,* it provides no conclusions about recognition of revenues. As part of its conceptual framework project, the FASB is still working on the recognition and measurement guidelines. Therefore, much of our discussion and explanation is based on existing pronouncements and present practice.

[2] "Elements of Financial Statements of Business Enterprises," *Statement of Financial Accounting Concepts No. 3* (Stamford, Conn.: FASB, 1980), par. 63.

[3] **Recognition** is "the process of formally recording or incorporating an item in the accounts and financial statements of an entity" (*SFAC No. 3,* par. 83). Recognition is not the same as realization, although the two are sometimes used interchangeably in accounting literature and practice. *Realization* is "the process of converting noncash resources and rights into money and is most precisely used in accounting and financial reporting to refer to sales of assets for cash or claims to cash" (*SFAC No. 3,* par. 83).

[4] "Basic Concepts and Accounting Principles Underlying Financial Statements of Business Enterprises," *Statement of the Accounting Principles Board No. 4* (New York: AICPA, 1970), pars. 148 and 150.

The profession is continually developing criteria that should be met before a departure from the sale basis is acceptable. A 1981 FASB study found some common **reasons for departures from the sale basis.**[5] One reason is a desire to **recognize earlier** in the earning process than the time of sale the effect of earning activities (revenue) if there is a high degree of certainty about the amount of revenue earned. A second reason is a desire to **delay recognition** of revenue beyond the time of sale if the degree of uncertainty concerning the amount of either revenue or costs is sufficiently high or if the sale does not represent substantial completion of the earning process.

That same FASB study concluded that there are significant inconsistencies in accounting pronouncements and, consequently, in practice for recognizing revenue. As a result similar transactions and other events are not treated similarly. Yet some "common threads" were found underlying the rationale for particular recognition methods. Recognition issues are frequently resolved by reference to concepts such as probability of collection, transfer of benefits and risks of ownership, measurability of revenues and costs, completion of the earning process, and substance over form. Unfortunately, it was found that these concepts often are applied differently.[6]

This chapter is devoted exclusively to the discussion and illustration of two of the four general types of revenue transactions described earlier, namely, (1) selling products and (2) rendering services—both of which are **sales transactions.** Accounting for the other two types of revenue transactions, (3) revenue from permitting others to use enterprise assets, and (4) revenue from disposing of assets other than products, is discussed in several other sections of the textbook. Our discussion of product sales transactions is organized around the following topics:

1. Revenue recognition at point of sale (delivery).
2. Revenue recognition before delivery.
3. Revenue recognition after delivery.
4. Revenue recognition for a special sales transaction—franchises.

Accounting for service sales transactions is presented in Appendix K of this chapter.

## REVENUE RECOGNITION AT POINT OF SALE (DELIVERY)

Many business enterprises wish to market one or more products or services: retail stores purchase many different articles they wish to sell; manufacturers market the products they have fabricated or processed; transportation companies offer to transport freight or persons; public accounting firms offer the services of their expert accountants; and so on. In return for the product or service sold, the enterprise usually receives cash or a promise of cash at some date in the future (credit sales). Thus sales transactions have two sides; on the one hand, a product or service is given; on the other, cash or a promise of cash in the future is received.

Inherent in any sales transaction is the element of gain or loss. Therefore, the enterprise does not merely record an increase in one asset and a decrease in another, but recognizes

---

[5]Henry R. Jaenicke, *Survey of Present Practices in Recognizing Revenues, Expenses, Gains, and Losses,* A Research Report (Stamford, Conn.: FASB, 1981), p. 11.

[6]Ibid., p. 16.

the transaction as involving both revenue and cost elements, each of which is recorded separately. Net income is measured when expenses are deducted from revenues.

**Cash Sales Versus Credit Sales**   Many retail sales, such as those made by grocery stores and drug stores, are made for cash. Cash is collected when goods are transferred to the customer. Cash sales differ from credit sales in that once made they are complete in themselves; no additional steps are necessary to collect cash from the customer. In a credit sale (sales on account) the seller receives a promise by the purchaser to pay cash in the future. The consideration obtained by the seller is a receivable rather than cash in hand. The accounting treatment accorded receivable transactions and related allowance for doubtful accounts was discussed in Chapter 7.

**Revenue Recognition When Right of Return Exists**   Whether cash or credit sales are involved, a special problem arises with claims for returns and allowances. In Chapter 7, the accounting treatment for normal returns and allowances was presented. However, certain companies experience such a **high ratio of returned merchandise** to sales that they find it necessary to postpone reporting sales until the return privilege has substantially expired. For example, in the publishing industry the rate of return runs up to 25% for hardcover books and 65% for some magazines. Other types of companies that experience high return rates are: perishable food dealers; rack jobbers or distributors who sell to retail outlets; record and tape companies; and some toy and sporting goods manufacturers. Returns in these industries frequently are made either through a right of contract or as a matter of practice involving "guaranteed sales" agreements or consignments.

Three alternative methods are available when the seller is exposed to continued risks of ownership through return of the product. These are: (1) not recording a sale until all return privileges have expired; (2) recording the sale, but reducing sales by an estimate of future returns; and (3) recording the sale and accounting for the returns as they occur in future periods. The FASB concluded that if a company sells its product but gives the buyer the right to return the product, revenue from the sales transaction shall be recognized at the time of sale only if **all** of the following six conditions have been met:[7]

1. The seller's price to the buyer is substantially fixed or determinable at the date of sale.
2. The buyer has paid the seller, or the buyer is obligated to pay the seller and the obligation is not contingent on resale of the product.
3. The buyer's obligation to the seller would not be changed in the event of theft or physical destruction or damage of the product.
4. The buyer acquiring the product for resale has economic substance apart from that provided by the seller.
5. The seller does not have significant obligations for future performance to directly bring about resale of the product by the buyer.
6. The amount of future returns can be reasonably estimated.

Sales revenue and cost of sales that are not recognized at the time of sale because the six conditions above are not met should be recognized either when the return privilege has substantially expired or when those six conditions subsequently are met (whichever occurs

---

[7]"Revenue Recognition When Right of Return Exists," *Statement of Financial Accounting Standards No. 48* (Stamford, Conn.: FASB, 1981), par. 6.

first). Sales revenue and cost of sales reported in the income statement should be reduced to report estimated returns.[8]

## REVENUE RECOGNITION BEFORE DELIVERY

Sometimes questions arise as to whether revenue should be recognized before the actual delivery of the product. For instance, revenue might be recognized:

1. Prior to production.
2. At completion of production.
3. During production.

**Revenue Recognition Prior to Production**   In certain types of manufacturing and in some phases of agriculture, contracting for the sale of goods well in advance of delivery is a common practice. Heavy machinery of a specialized type may be "sold" before it is even in existence; fruit, vegetable, and grain crops may be sold before maturity, with provisions for continued cultivation and harvesting by the seller; fashion goods and clothing are sometimes sold in advance of completion and delivery. Sales of this type may or may not be accompanied by deposits or advance payments, depending on trade practice in the given industry.

Proper accounting here as elsewhere requires evaluation of the facts and circumstances. The terms of the sales agreement or contract must be analyzed and then observed in recording the transaction. In general, the business community does not recognize a sale until the transaction is completed and the title passed. The Uniform Sales Act distinguishes between a **contract of sale,** whereby property is transferred from a seller to a buyer in return for a consideration called the price, and a **contract to sell,** whereby the seller and buyer agree to a future exchange of property for a price. Even in the case of a contract of sale, accountants generally record only completed transactions as sales; delivery of the product or service sold normally completes the sale. **No entries are made for contracts to sell,** other than perhaps a memorandum record. Advances made by the purchaser, under either a contract of sale or a contract to sell, are recorded by the seller as a liability when received (that is, the advance is treated as a deposit). When all conditions of the contract have been fulfilled, the sale is recorded as revenue by the seller.

For example, if $3,000 is received from a customer as an advance under a contract to sell machinery made to order at a price of $10,000, the entry should be made as follows:

| | | |
|---|---|---|
| Cash | 3,000 | |
| Customers' Advances (Liability) | | 3,000 |

When the machinery is manufactured and delivered, an entry should be made to record the sale:

| | | |
|---|---|---|
| Accounts Receivable | 7,000 | |
| Customers' Advances | 3,000 | |
| Sales | | 10,000 |

The account for Customers' Advances represents a liability, and any balance appearing in that account at the time of preparation of financial statements should ordinarily be shown

[8]Ibid., pars. 6 and 7.

in the balance sheet as a current liability. This approach is sometimes referred to as the **deposit method** of accounting for revenue recognition.

**Revenue Recognition at Completion of Production**    In certain cases revenue is recognized at the completion of production even though no sale has been made. Examples of such situations involve precious metals or agricultural products with assured prices. Revenue is recognized when these metals are mined or agricultural crops harvested because the sales price is reasonably assured, the units are interchangeable, and no significant costs are involved in distributing the product (see discussion in Chapter 9, page 395, "Valuation at Selling Price").

**Revenue Recognition During Production**    Long-term contracts such as construction-type contracts, contracts for development of military and commercial aircraft, weapons delivery systems, and space exploration hardware frequently provide that the seller (builder) may bill the purchaser at intervals as various points in the project are reached. When the project to be constructed consists of separable units such as a group of buildings or many miles of roadway, provision may be made for passage of title as well as billing at stated stages of completion, such as, with the completion of each building unit or every 10 miles of road. Such contract provisions in effect provide for delivery in installments, and the accounting records should report this by taking up sales as "delivered."

PERCENTAGE-OF-COMPLETION VERSUS COMPLETED CONTRACT    The accounting measurements associated with long-term projects are difficult because events and amounts must be estimated for a period of years. Construction companies, for example, often invest capital and labor over a considerable time. Production on one contract or job may extend over two or more accounting periods, and progress billings and collections for work performed at predetermined intervals are commonplace. Two distinctly different methods of accounting for long-term construction contracts are recognized by the accounting profession:[9]

1. PERCENTAGE OF COMPLETION METHOD. Revenues and gross profit are recognized each period based upon the progress of the construction, that is, the percentage of completion. Construction costs **plus gross profit earned to date** are accumulated in an inventory account (Construction in Process) and progress billings are accumulated in a contra inventory account (Billings on Construction in Process).

2. COMPLETED-CONTRACT METHOD. Revenues and gross profit are recognized only when the contract is completed. Construction costs are accumulated in an inventory account (Construction in Process) and progress billings are accumulated in a contra inventory account (Billings on Construction in Process).

WHEN TO USE THE PERCENTAGE-OF-COMPLETION METHOD    The rationale for using the percentage-of-completion accounting is that under most of these contracts the buyer and seller have obtained enforceable rights. The buyer has the legal right to require specific performance on the contract; the seller has the right to require progress payments that provide evidence of the buyer's ownership interest. As a result, the economics of the situa-

[9]*Accounting Trends and Techniques—1981* reports that in 1980, of the 108 of its 600 sample companies that referred to long-term construction contracts, 92 used the percentage-of-completion method and 15 used the completed-contract method (one was not determinable).

It is not uncommon for companies to use the completed-contract method for income tax purposes and the percentage-of-completion method for financial accounting purposes.

tion suggest that a continuous sale occurs as the work progresses, and revenue should be recognized accordingly.

The accounting profession has for many years considered the percentage-of-completion method preferable **"when estimates of costs to complete and extent of progress toward completion of long-term contracts are reasonably dependable."**[10]

In 1981 the AICPA recommended that the completed-contract method and the percentage-of-completion method be used in specified circumstances, and that these two methods not be viewed as acceptable alternatives in the same circumstances. The percentage-of-completion method should be used when estimates of progress toward completion, revenues, and costs are reasonably dependable and all the following conditions exist:[11]

1. The contract clearly specifies the enforceable rights regarding goods or services to be provided and received by the parties, the consideration to be exchanged, and the manner and terms of settlement.
2. The buyer can be expected to satisfy all obligations under the contract.
3. The contractor can be expected to perform the contractual obligation.

**WHEN TO USE THE COMPLETED-CONTRACT METHOD**   The completed-contract method should be used only (1) when an entity has primarily short-term contracts, or (2) when the conditions for using the percentage-of-completion method cannot be met, or (3) when there are inherent hazards in the contract beyond the normal, recurring business risks. The presumption is that percentage-of-completion is the better method and that the completed-contract method should be used only when the percentage-of-completion method is inappropriate.

## Percentage-of-Completion Method

The percentage-of-completion method recognizes revenues, costs, and gross profit as progress is made toward completion on a long-term contract. To defer recognition of these items until completion of the entire contract is to misrepresent the efforts (costs) and accomplishments (revenues), that is, the operations of the interim accounting periods. In order to apply the percentage-of-completion method, one must have some basis or standard for measuring the progress toward completion at particular interim dates.

**Measuring the Progress Toward Completion**   As one practicing accountant recently wrote, "The big problem in applying the percentage-of-completion method that cannot be demonstrated in an example has to do with the ability to make reasonably accurate estimates of completion and the final gross profit."[12]

Various methods are used in practice to determine the **extent of progress toward completion;** the most common are "cost to cost method," "efforts expended methods," and "units of work performed method." The objective of all the methods is to measure the extent of progress in terms of costs, units, or value added. The various measures (costs

---

[10]Committee on Accounting Procedure, "Long-Term Construction-Type Contracts," *Accounting Research Bulletin No. 45* (New York: AICPA, 1955), p. 7.

[11]"Accounting for Performance of Construction-Type and Certain Production Type Contracts," *Statement of Position 81-1* (New York: AICPA, 1981), par. 23.

[12]Richard S. Hickok, "New Guidance for Construction Contractors: 'A Credit Plus,'" *The Journal of Accountancy* (March 1982), p. 46.

incurred, labor hours worked, tons produced, stories completed, etc.) are identified and classified as input and output measures. **Input measures** (costs incurred, labor hours worked) are made in terms of efforts devoted to a contract. **Output measures** (tons produced, stories of a building completed, miles of a highway completed) are made in terms of results. Neither are universally applicable to all long-term projects; their use requires careful tailoring to the circumstances and the exercise of judgment.

Both input and output measures have disadvantages in certain circumstances. The input measure is based on an established relationship between a unit of input and productivity. If inefficiencies cause the productivity relationship to change, inaccurate measurements result. Another potential problem of using an input method is known as "front-end loading," which produces higher estimates of completion by virtue of incurring significant costs up front. Some early-stage construction costs should be disregarded if they do not relate to contract performance, for example, costs of uninstalled materials or costs of subcontracts not yet performed.

Output measures can result in inaccurate measures if the units used as the basis are not comparable in time, effort, or cost to complete. For example, using stories completed can be deceiving; to complete an eight-story building may require more than one-eighth the total cost to complete the first story due to the foundation and substructure construction.

One of the more popular input measures used to determine the progress toward completion is the **cost-to-cost method.** Under the cost-to-cost method, the percentage of completion is measured by comparing costs incurred to date with the most recent estimate of the total costs to complete the contract as shown in the following formula:

$$\frac{\text{Costs incurred to end of current period}}{\text{Most recent estimate of total costs}} = \text{Percent complete}$$

The percentage that costs incurred bear to total estimated costs is applied to the total revenue and the estimated total gross profit on the contract in arriving at the revenue and the gross profit amounts to be recognized to date. The amounts of revenue and gross profit recognized each year are computed using the following formula:

$$\frac{\text{Costs incurred to end of current period}}{\text{Most recent estimate of total costs}} \times \begin{array}{c}\text{Estimated total}\\ \text{revenue (or gross}\\ \text{profit) from the}\\ \text{contract}\end{array} - \begin{array}{c}\text{Total revenue}\\ \text{(or gross profit)}\\ \text{recognized}\\ \text{in prior periods}\end{array} = \begin{array}{c}\text{Current period}\\ \text{revenue}\\ \text{(or}\\ \text{gross profit)}\end{array}$$

Because the profession specifically recommends the cost-to-cost method (without excluding other bases for measuring progress toward completion), we have adopted it for use in our illustrations.[13]

---

[13]See *ARB No. 45, par. 4.*

**Illustration of the Percentage-of-Completion Method (Cost-to-Cost Basis)**    To illustrate the percentage-of-completion method, assume that the Pfeifer Construction Company has a contract starting July, 1983, to construct a $4,500,000 bridge that is expected to be completed in October, 1985, at a total cost of $4,000,000. The following data pertain to the construction period:

|  | 1983 | 1984 | 1985 |
|---|---|---|---|
| Costs to date | $1,000,000 | $2,916,000 | $4,050,000 |
| Estimated costs to complete | 3,000,000 | 1,134,000 | — |
| Progress billings during the year | 900,000 | 2,400,000 | 1,200,000 |
| Cash collected during the year | 750,000 | 1,750,000 | 2,000,000 |

The percent complete would be computed as follows:

<table>
<tr><th colspan="4" align="center">Pfeifer Construction Company<br>PERCENTAGE-OF-COMPLETION METHOD (Cost-to-Cost Basis)</th></tr>
<tr><th></th><th>1983</th><th>1984</th><th>1985</th></tr>
<tr><td>Contract price</td><td>$4,500,000</td><td>$4,500,000</td><td>$4,500,000</td></tr>
<tr><td>Less estimated cost:</td><td></td><td></td><td></td></tr>
<tr><td>  Costs to date</td><td>1,000,000</td><td>2,916,000</td><td>4,050,000</td></tr>
<tr><td>  Estimated costs to complete</td><td>3,000,000</td><td>1,134,000</td><td>—</td></tr>
<tr><td>  Estimated total costs</td><td>4,000,000</td><td>4,050,000</td><td>4,050,000</td></tr>
<tr><td>Estimated total gross profit</td><td>$ 500,000</td><td>$ 450,000</td><td>$ 450,000</td></tr>
<tr><td>Percent complete:</td><td>25%<br>$\left(\dfrac{\$1,000,000}{\$4,000,000}\right)$</td><td>72%<br>$\left(\dfrac{\$2,916,000}{\$4,050,000}\right)$</td><td>100%<br>$\left(\dfrac{\$4,050,000}{\$4,050,000}\right)$</td></tr>
</table>

On the basis of the data above, the following entries would be prepared (1) to record the costs of construction, (2) to record progress billings, and (3) to record collections (these entries appear as summaries of the many transactions that would be entered individually as they occur during the year):

| | 1983 | | 1984 | | 1985 | |
|---|---|---|---|---|---|---|
| **To record cost of construction** | | | | | | |
| Construction in Process | 1,000,000 | | 1,916,000 | | 1,134,000 | |
|   Materials, cash, | | | | | | |
|     payables, etc. | | 1,000,000 | | 1,916,000 | | 1,134,000 |
| **To record progress billings** | | | | | | |
| Accounts Receivable | 900,000 | | 2,400,000 | | 1,200,000 | |
|   Billings on Construction | | | | | | |
|     in Process | | 900,000 | | 2,400,000 | | 1,200,000 |
| **To record collections** | | | | | | |
| Cash | 750,000 | | 1,750,000 | | 2,000,000 | |
|   Accounts Receivable | | 750,000 | | 1,750,000 | | 2,000,000 |

In this illustration, the costs incurred to date as a proportion of the estimated total costs to be incurred on the project is a measure of the extent of progress toward completion. The estimated revenue and gross profit to be recognized for each year is calculated as follows:

| | 1983 | 1984 | 1985 |
|---|---|---|---|
| **Revenue recognized in:** | | | |
| 1983   $4,500,000 × 25% | $1,125,000 | | |
| 1984   $4,500,000 × 72% | | $3,240,000 | |
|     Less revenue recognized in 1983 | | 1,125,000 | |
|     Revenue in 1984 | | $2,115,000 | |
| 1985   $4,500,000 × 100% | | | $4,500,000 |
|     Less revenue recognized in 1983 and 1984 | | | 3,240,000 |
|     Revenue in 1985 | | | $1,260,000 |
| **Gross profit recognized in:** | | | |
| 1983   $500,000 × 25% | $  125,000 | | |
| 1984   $450,000 × 72% | | $  324,000 | |
|     Less gross profit recognized in 1983 | | 125,000 | |
|     Gross profit in 1984 | | $  199,000 | |
| 1985   $450,000 × 100% | | | $  450,000 |
|     Less gross profit recognized in 1983 and 1984 | | | 324,000 |
|     Gross profit in 1985 | | | $  126,000 |

The entries to recognize revenue and gross profit each year and to record completion and final approval of the contract are shown below. Note that Revenue from Long-term Contracts is credited for the amounts as computed above, while gross profit as computed above is debited to Construction in Process. The difference between the amounts recognized each year for revenue and gross profit is debited to a nominal account, Construction Expenses (similar to cost of goods sold in a manufacturing enterprise), which is reported in the income statement.

| | 1983 | 1984 | 1985 |
|---|---|---|---|
| **To recognize revenue and gross profit** | | | |
| Construction in Process (gross profit) | 125,000 | 199,000 | 126,000 |
| Construction Expenses | 1,000,000 | 1,916,000 | 1,134,000 |
|     Revenue from Long-Term Contract | 1,125,000 | 2,115,000 | 1,260,000 |
| **To record final approval of the contract** | | | |
| Billings on Construction in Process | | 4,500,000 | |
|     Construction in Process | | | 4,500,000 |

Note that the Construction in Process account is not affected by the entry to recognize construction expense. Costs must continue to be accumulated in the Construction in Process account to maintain a record of total costs incurred (plus recognized profit) to date. Although theoretically a series of "sales" takes place using the percentage-of-completion method, the inventory cost cannot be removed until the construction is completed and transferred to the new owner. The Construction in Process account would include the following summarized entries over the term of the construction project.

| Construction in Process | | | | |
|---|---|---|---|---|
| 1983 construction costs | $1,000,000 | 12/31/85 | to close | |
| 1983 recognized gross profit | 125,000 | | completed | |
| 1984 construction costs | 1,916,000 | | project | $4,500,000 |
| 1984 recognized gross profit | 199,000 | | | |
| 1985 construction costs | 1,134,000 | | | |
| 1985 recognized gross profit | 126,000 | | | |
| Total | $4,500,000 | Total | | $4,500,000 |

The Pfeifer Construction Company illustration contained a change in estimate in the second year, 1984, where the estimated total costs increased from $4,000,000 to $4,050,000. By adjusting the percent completed to the changed estimate of total costs and then deducting from revenues and gross profit computed for progress to date the amount of revenues and gross profit recognized in prior periods, the change in estimate was accounted for in a **cumulative catch-up manner.** That is, the change in estimate is accounted for in the period of change so that the balance sheet at the end of the period of change and the accounting in subsequent periods are as they would have been if the revised estimate had been the original estimate.

**Financial Statement Presentation—Percentage of Completion**    Generally when a receivable from a sale is recorded, the Inventory account is reduced. But in this case both the receivable and the inventory continue to be carried. By subtracting the balance in the Billings account from Construction in Process, double-counting the inventory is avoided.

During the life of the contract, the difference between the Construction in Process and the Billings on Construction in Process accounts is reported in the balance sheet as a current asset if a debit, and as a current liability if a credit. When the costs incurred plus the gross profit recognized to date (the balance in Construction in Process) exceed the billings, this excess is reported as a current asset entitled "Costs and Recognized Profit in Excess of Billings." The unbilled portion of a contract price can be calculated at any time by subtracting the billings to date from the revenue recognized to date as illustrated below for 1983 for Pfeifer Construction:

| Calculation of Unbilled Contract Price at 12/31/83 | |
|---|---|
| Contract revenue recognized to date: $4,500,000 $\times \dfrac{\$1,000,000}{\$4,000,000} =$ | $1,125,000 |
| Billings to date | 900,000 |
| Unbilled | $ 225,000 |

When the billings exceed costs incurred and gross profit to date, this excess is reported as a current liability entitled "Billings in Excess of Costs and Recognized Profit." When a company has a number of projects, and costs exceed billings on some contracts, and billings exceed costs on others, the contracts should be segregated so that the asset side includes only those contracts on which costs and recognized profit exceed billings, and the liability side includes only those on which billings exceed costs and recognized profit. Separate disclosures of the dollar volume of billings and costs are preferable to a presentation of the net difference only.

Using data from the previous illustration, the Pfeifer Construction Company would report the status and results of its long-term construction activities under the percentage-of-completion method as follows:

| Pfeifer Construction Company FINANCIAL STATEMENT PRESENTATION—PERCENTAGE-OF-COMPLETION METHOD | | | |
|---|---|---|---|
| | 1983 | 1984 | 1985 |
| **Income Statement** | | | |
| Revenue from long-term contracts | $1,125,000 | $2,115,000 | $1,260,000 |
| Costs of construction | 1,000,000 | 1,916,000 | 1,134,000 |
| Gross profit | $ 125,000 | $ 199,000 | $ 126,000 |
| **Balance Sheet (12/31)** | | | |
| Current assets: | | | |
| Accounts receivable | $ 150,000 | $ 800,000 | |
| Inventories | | | |
| Construction in process | 1,125,000 | | |
| Less: Billings | 900,000 | | |
| Costs and recognized profit in excess of billings | $ 225,000 | | |
| Current liabilities: | | | |
| Billings ($3,300,000) in excess of costs and recognized profit ($3,240,000) | | $ 60,000 | |

*Note 1—Summary of significant accounting policies.*
*Long-Term Construction Contracts.* The company recognizes revenues and reports profits from long-term construction contracts, its principal business, under the percentage-of-completion method of accounting. These contracts generally extend for periods in excess of one year. The amounts of revenues and profits recognized each year are based on the ratio of costs incurred to the total estimated costs. Costs included in construction in process include direct material, direct labor, and project-related overhead. Corporate general and administrative expenses are charged to the periods as incurred and are not allocated to construction contracts.

## Completed-Contract Method

Under the completed-contract method, revenue and gross profit are recognized only at point of sale, that is, when the contract is completed. Costs of long-term contracts in process and current billings are accumulated, but there are no interim charges or credits to income statement accounts for revenues, costs, and gross profit.

The principal advantage of the completed-contract method is that reported revenue is based on final results rather than on estimates of unperformed work. Its major disadvantage is that a distortion of earnings may occur; it does not reflect current performance when the period of a contract extends into more than one accounting period. Although operations may be fairly uniform during the period of the contract, revenue is not reported until the year of completion.

The **annual entries** to record costs of construction, progress billings, and collections from customers would be identical to those illustrated under the percentage-of-completion method with the significant exclusion of the recognition of revenue and gross profit. For the bridge project of Pfeifer Construction Company illustrated on the preceding pages, the following entries are made in 1985 under the completed-contract method to recognize revenue and costs and to close out the inventory and billing accounts:

| | | |
|---|---|---|
| Billings on Construction in Process | 4,500,000 | |
| Revenue from Long-Term Contracts | | 4,500,000 |
| Costs of Construction | 4,050,000 | |
| Construction in Process | | 4,050,000 |

Comparing the two methods relative to the same bridge project, the Pfeifer Construction Company would have recognized gross profit as follows:

| | Percentage-of-Completion | Completed-Contract |
|---|---|---|
| 1983 | $125,000 | $    0 |
| 1984 | 199,000 | 0 |
| 1985 | 126,000 | 450,000 |

Using the data from the illustration, the Pfeifer Construction Company would report the status and results of its long-term construction activities under the completed-contract method as follows:

**Pfeifer Construction Company**
**FINANCIAL STATEMENT PRESENTATION—COMPLETED CONTRACT METHOD**

| | 1983 | 1984 | 1985 |
|---|---|---|---|
| **Income Statement** | | | |
| Revenue from long-term contracts | — | — | $4,500,000 |
| Costs of construction | — | — | 4,050,000 |
| Gross profit | — | — | $  450,000 |
| **Balance Sheet (12/31)** | | | |
| Current assets: | | | |
| Accounts receivable | $  150,000 | $800,000 | |
| Inventories | | | |
| Construction in process | 1,000,000 | | |
| Less: Billings | 900,000 | | |
| Unbilled contract costs | $  100,000 | | |

Current liabilities:
  Billings ($3,300,000) in excess of contract
    costs ($2,916,000)                                          $384,000

*Note 1—Summary of significant accounting policies.*
*Long-Term Construction Contracts.* The company recognizes revenues and reports profits from long-term construction contracts, its principal business, under the completed-contract method. These contracts generally extend for periods in excess of one year. Contract costs and billings are accumulated during the periods of construction, but no revenues or profits are recognized until completion of the contract. Costs included in construction in process include direct material, direct labor, and project-related overhead. Corporate general and administrative expenses are charged to the periods as incurred and are not allocated to construction contracts.

## Accounting for Long-Term Contract Losses

Two types of losses can become evident under long-term contracts. First, estimates of future costs and revenues may dictate recognition of a loss in the current period, yet the contract is expected to produce a profit when it is completed. This condition arises when, during construction, there is a significant increase in the estimated total contract costs but the increase does not eliminate all profit on the contract. Under the percentage-of-completion method, the estimated cost increase may necessitate a current period adjustment of gross profit recognized on the project in prior periods. Second, cost estimates at the end of the current period may indicate that a loss will result on completion of the entire contract. In this situation, under both the percentage-of-completion and the completed-contract methods, the entire expected loss must be recognized in the current period.[14] The treatments described are consistent with accounting's conservatism custom of anticipating foreseeable losses in order to avoid overstatement of current income.

**Loss in a Year**    To illustrate a loss for the period on a contract expected to be profitable upon completion, assume that in 1984 Pfeifer Construction Company estimates the costs to complete the bridge contract at $1,468,962 instead of $1,134,000. Assuming all other data are the same, Pfeifer would compute the loss as follows:

| Computation of Recognizable Loss—1984 PERCENTAGE-OF-COMPLETION METHOD | |
| --- | --: |
| Costs to date (12/31/84) | $2,916,000 |
| Estimated costs to complete (revised) | 1,468,962 |
| Estimated total costs | $4,384,962 |
| Percent complete ($2,916,000 ÷ $4,384,962) | 66½% |
| Revenue recognized in 1984 | |
| ($4,500,000 × 66½% − $1,125,000) | $1,867,500 |
| Costs incurred in 1984 | 1,916,000 |
| Loss recognized in 1984 | $    48,500 |

[14]Sak Bhamornsiri, "Losses from Construction Contracts," *The Journal of Accountancy* (April 1982), p. 26.

Pfeifer Construction would record the loss in 1984 as follows:

| | | |
|---|---:|---:|
| Construction Expenses | 1,916,000 | |
| Construction in Process (Loss) | | 48,500 |
| Revenue from Long-Term Contract | | 1,867,500 |

The loss of $48,500 will be reported on the 1984 income statement as the difference between the reported revenues of $1,867,500 and the costs of $1,916,000.

In 1985 Pfeifer Construction will recognize the remaining 33½% of the revenue, $1,507,500, with costs of $1,468,962 as expected, and report a gross profit of $38,538. The total gross profit over the three years of the contract would be $115,038 [$125,000 (1983) − $48,500 (1984) + $38,538 (1985)], which is the difference between the total contract revenue of $4,500,000 and the total contract costs of $4,384,962. **Under the completed-contract method, no loss is recognized in 1984 because the contract is still expected to result in a profit** that will be recognized in the year of completion.

**Loss for the Entire Contract**   To illustrate an overall loss on a long-term contract, assume that in 1984 Pfeifer Construction Company estimates the costs to complete the bridge contract at $1,640,250. Total costs of $4,556,250 ($2,916,000 + $1,640,250) exceed the total contract price of $4,500,000, indicating an overall loss of $56,250. Under the percentage-of-completion method, the $125,000 of gross profit recognized in 1983 has to be offset since it is now not expected to be realized, and the cumulative loss of $56,250 must be recognized, both in 1984, for a total loss of $181,250. The revenues and costs can be computed and recorded in the normal manner with a provision for the loss that would be recognized in 1985 added to the 1984 loss as computed under the percentage-of-completion method as shown below:

---

**Computation of Recognizable Loss—1984**
**PERCENTAGE-OF-COMPLETION METHOD**

| | |
|---|---:|
| Costs to date (12/31/84) | $2,916,000 |
| Estimated costs to complete | 1,640,250 |
| Estimated total costs | $4,556,250 |
| Percent complete ($2,916,000 ÷ $4,556,250) | 64% |
| Revenue recognized in 1984 | |
| ($4,500,000 × 64% − $1,125,000) | $1,755,000 |
| Costs incurred in 1984 | 1,916,000 |
| Loss to date | 161,000 |
| Loss attributable to 1985 | 20,250[a] |
| Loss recognized in 1984 | $  181,250 |

| | | |
|---|---:|---:|
| [a]1985 Revenue: ($4,500,000 − $1,125,000 − $1,755,000) | $1,620,000 | |
| 1985 Costs: | 1,640,250 | |
| 1985 Loss (percentage-of-completion basis) | $   20,250 | |

---

Pfeifer Construction would record the loss in 1984 as follows (costs incurred in 1984 are increased by the 1985 loss recognized in 1984):

| | |
|---|---|
| Construction Expenses ($1,916,000 + $20,250) | 1,936,250[15] |
|    Construction in Process (Loss) |    181,250 |
|    Revenue from Long-Term Contracts |    1,755,000 |

At the end of 1984, Construction in Process has a balance of $2,859,750 as shown below:

| Construction in Process | | | |
|---|---|---|---|
| 1983 Construction costs | $1,000,000 | | |
| 1983 Recognized gross profit | 125,000 | | |
| 1984 Construction costs | 1,916,000 | 1984 Recognized loss | 181,250 |
|   Balance, $2,859,750 | | | |

If the costs in 1985 are $1,640,250 as projected, at the end of 1985 the Construction in Process account will have a balance of $1,640,250 + $2,859,750, or $4,500,000, equal to the contract price. When the revenue remaining to be recognized in 1985 of $1,620,000 [$4,500,000 (total contract price) − $1,125,000 (1983) − $1,755,000 (1984)] is matched with the construction expense to be recognized in 1985 of $1,620,000 [total costs of $4,556,250 less the total costs recognized in prior years of $2,936,250 (1983, $1,000,000; 1984, $1,936,250)], a zero profit results. Thus the total loss has been recognized in 1984, the year in which it first became evident.

Under the completed-contract method, the contract loss of $56,250 is also recognized in the year in which it first became evident through the following entry in 1984:

| | |
|---|---|
| Loss from Long-Term Contracts | 56,250 |
|    Construction in Process (Loss) |    56,250 |

In circumstances where the Construction in Process balance exceeds the billings, the recognized loss may be deducted on the balance sheet from such accumulated costs. That is, under both the percentage-of-completion and the completed-contract methods, the provision for the loss (the credit) may be combined with Construction in Process thereby reducing the inventory balance. In those circumstances, however, such as in the above illustration (1984), where the billings exceed the accumulated costs, the amount of the estimated loss must be reported separately on the balance sheet as a current liability. That is, under both the percentage-of-completion and the completed-contract methods, the amount of the loss of $56,250, as estimated in 1984, would be taken from the Construction in Process account and reported separately as a current liability entitled Estimated Loss from Long-Term Contracts.[16]

---

[15]The total costs to be debited to Construction Expenses in 1984, the year in which the estimated loss became evident, may alternatively be computed as follows:

| | |
|---|---|
| Estimated total cost to extent of total estimated revenue | $4,500,000 |
| Percent complete at 12/31/84 | × 64% |
| Cost to 12/31/84 before inclusion of total loss | 2,880,000 |
| Add estimated total loss | 56,250 |
| Cost to date plus loss | 2,936,250 |
| Cost recognized in prior years (1983) | 1,000,000 |
| Cost recognizable in 1984 | $1,936,250 |

[16]*Construction Contractors,* Audit and Accounting Guide (New York: AICPA, 1981), pp. 148–149.

### Disclosures in Financial Statements

In addition to making the financial statement disclosures required of all businesses, construction contractors usually make some unique disclosures. Generally these additional disclosures are made in the notes to the financial statements. For example, a construction contractor should disclose the method of recognizing revenue,[17] the basis used to classify assets and liabilities as current (the nature and length of the operating cycle), the basis for recording inventory, the effects of any revision of estimates, the amount of backlog on incompleted contracts, and the details about receivables (billed and unbilled, maturity, interest rates, and retainage provisions).

### Other Revenue Recognition Bases in Advance of Delivery

Two additional revenue recognition bases that have been suggested as appropriate in certain circumstances are: (1) the accretion basis and (2) the discovery basis. Both methods have conceptual merit, but because of practical problems and economic and tax consequences, neither the accounting profession nor the affected industries have pressed for their implementation.

**Accretion Basis**   Accretion is the increase in value resulting from natural growth or aging processes. Farmers experience accretion by growing crops and breeding animals. Timberland and nursery stock increase in value as the trees and plants grow. Some wines improve with age. Is accretion revenue? Should it be recognized as revenue? Periodic recognition of accretion as revenue has not been adopted in practice.

Accounting theoreticians are somewhat divided on the nature of accretion. Some reject recognition of accretion as revenue. They contend that while there is no doubt that assets have increased, the technical process of production remains to be undertaken, followed by conversion into liquid assets.[18] Others conclude that from an economic point of view, recognition of accretion may be justified but that the present discounted value (required to make the necessary comparative inventory valuations) is difficult to determine because it depends upon expectations of future market prices and future costs of providing growth and future costs of harvesting and getting the product ready for market.[19]

The profession permits recognition of revenue at the completion of production for certain agricultural products that possess "immediate marketability at quoted prices that cannot be influenced by the producer."[20] The accounting profession's official pronouncements, however, are silent on the possible extension of that principle to agricultural products still in the growth or production stage even if they are readily marketable at quoted prices.

**Discovery Basis**   The SEC's recent proposal for reserve recognition accounting (RRA), for oil and gas producers, as discussed in Chapter 12, has revived interest in the use of some

---

[17]Ibid., p. 30.

[18]W. A. Paton and A. C. Littleton, *An Introduction to Corporate Accounting Standards* (Sarasota, Fla.: American Accounting Association, 1940), p. 52.

[19]E. S. Hendricksen, *Accounting Theory,* 3rd ed. (Homewood, Ill.: Richard D. Irwin, 1977), p. 186.

[20]"Basic Concepts and Accounting Principles Underlying Financial Statements of Business Enterprises," *APB Statement No. 4* (New York: AICPA, 1970), par. 184.

form of discovery basis accounting in the extractive industries. As with accretion, there is no doubt that an enterprise's assets may be greatly increased and enhanced by exploration and discovery. Many contend that the financial reporting of companies in the extractive industries would be vastly improved if discovered resources were recognized as assets and changes in oil and gas reserves were included in earnings. Their arguments for the discovery basis are based on the significance of discovery in the earning process and the view that the product's market price can be reasonably estimated. The arguments against revenue recognition at the time of discovery focus on the uncertainties surrounding the assumptions needed to determine discovery values, the cost of obtaining the necessary data, and the departure from historical cost-based accounting.[21]

Except for the SEC's requirement that RRA be used in supplemental data, the discovery basis of revenue recognition is sanctioned currently neither by current practice nor by official accounting pronouncements.

## REVENUE RECOGNITION AFTER DELIVERY

In some cases, the collection of the sales price is not reasonably assured and revenue recognition is deferred. One of two methods is generally employed to defer revenue recognition until the cash is received, that is, **the cost recovery method,** or **the installment method.**[22]

**Under the cost recovery method, equal amounts of revenue and expense are recognized as collections are made until all costs have been recovered.** After all costs have been recovered, any additional cash receipts are included in income. This method is used where a high degree of uncertainty exists related to collection of receivables. **Under the installment method, emphasis is placed on collection rather than on sale, and installment sales lead to income recognition in the periods of collection rather than in the period of sale.** The installment basis of accounting is justified on the basis that when there is no reasonable basis for estimating the degree of collectibility, revenue should not be recognized until cash is collected. The exercise of professional judgment is necessary in selecting between the installment method and the cost recovery method. The resolution revolves around the degree of uncertainty in the collection of the receivable. The cost recovery method is adopted when there is a greater degree of uncertainty. Because the installment method is used extensively in certain industries, this subject is discussed in more detail in the following sections.

### Installment Sales Accounting Method

The expression "installment sales" is generally used by accountants and others to describe any type of sale for which payment is required in periodic installments over an extended

---

[21]*Survey of Present Practices in Recognizing Revenues, Expenses, Gains, and Losses, op. cit.,* p. 80.

[22]Sometimes cash is received prior to delivery of the goods and is recorded as a deposit (customer advance) because the sale transaction is incomplete. In such cases, the seller has not performed under the contract and has no claim against the purchaser. Cash received represents advances and should be accounted for using the deposit method wherein the cash received is not recognized as revenue until the contract is performed by delivery of the product. The **major difference between the cost recovery method and the deposit method** is that in the cost recovery method it is assumed that the seller has performed on the contract, but cash collection is highly uncertain. In the deposit method, the seller has not performed and no legitimate claim exists. The **deposit method** postpones recognizing a sale until a determination can be made as to whether a sale has occurred for accounting purposes.

period of time. It is used in the retail field where all types of farm and home equipment and furnishings are sold on an installment basis. It is also used to a limited degree in the heavy equipment industry where machine installations are sometimes paid for over a long period. A more recent application of the method is in the area of realty or land development sales. Because payment for the product or property sold is spread over a relatively long period, the risk of loss resulting from uncollectible accounts is greater in installment sales transactions than in ordinary sales. Consequently, various devices are used to protect the seller. In the area of merchandise, the two most common are (1) the use of a conditional sales contract that provides that title to the item sold does not pass to the purchaser until all payments have been made, and (2) use of notes secured by a chattel (personal property) mortgage on the article sold. Either of these permits the seller to "repossess" the goods sold if the purchaser defaults on one or more payments. The repossessed merchandise is then resold at whatever price it will bring to compensate the seller for the uncollected installments and the expense of repossession.

Under the installment method of accounting income recognition is deferred until the period of cash collection. Both revenues and cost of sales are recognized in the period of sale but the related gross profit is deferred to those periods in which cash is collected. Thus, instead of the sale being deferred to the future periods of anticipated collection and then related costs and expenses being deferred, only the proportional gross profit is deferred, which is equivalent to deferring both sales and cost of sales. Other expenses, that is, selling expense, administrative expense, and so on, are not deferred. **The cost of the goods sold is deferred proportionally to the deferred sales (by deferring gross profit),** but operating or financial expenses are considered as expenses in the period incurred.

Thus, the theory that cost and expenses should be matched against sales is applied in installment sales transactions through the gross profit figure but no further. Concerns operating under the installment sales method of accounting generally record operating expenses without regard to the fact that some portion of the year's gross profit is to be deferred. This practice is often justified on the basis that (1) these expenses do not follow sales as closely as does the cost of goods sold, and (2) accurate apportionment among periods would be so difficult that it could not be justified by the benefits gained.

**Acceptability of Installment Sales**    The use of the installment method as a method for revenue recognition has fluctuated widely. Until the early 1960s the installment method of accounting was widely used and accepted for installment sales transactions. As installment sales transactions increased during the sixties, somewhat paradoxically, acceptance and application of the installment method for financial accounting purposes decreased. In 1966 the APB concluded that except in special circumstances, "the installment method of recognizing revenue is not acceptable."[23]

The rationale for this position is that because the installment method of accounting recognizes no revenue until cash is collected, it is not exactly in accordance with the concept of accrual accounting. The installment method is frequently justified on the grounds that the risk of not collecting an accounts receivable may be so great that the sale itself is not sufficient evidence that recognition should occur. In some cases, this reasoning may be valid but not in a majority of cases. The general approach is that if a sale has been completed, it should be recognized; and if bad debts are expected, they should be recorded as

---

[23]"Omnibus Opinion," *Opinions of the Accounting Principles Board No. 10* (New York: AICPA, 1966), par. 12.

separate estimates of uncollectibles. Current accounting practices indicate that although collection expenses, repossession expenses, and bad debts are an unavoidable part of installment sales activities, the incurrence of these costs and the collectibility of the receivables are reasonably predictable.

**The study of this topic is justified by its widespread use as a tax accounting method, the recent increased emphasis on cash flows, and the method's acceptability in cases where a reasonable basis of estimating the degree of collectibility is deemed not to exist.** In addition, weaknesses in the sales method of revenue recognition became very apparent when the franchise and land development booms of the sixties and seventies produced many failures and disillusioned investors. Application of the sales method to **franchise and license operations** resulted in the abuse described earlier as **"front-end loading"** (recognizing revenue prematurely, that is, when the franchise is granted or the license issued rather than as it is earned or as the cash is received). Many **"land development"** ventures were susceptible to the same abuses. As a result, accounting for these transactions is now in the direction of revenue recognition on a cash basis.

**Procedure for Deferring Revenue and Cost of Sales of Merchandise** One could easily work out a procedure that deferred both the uncollected portion of the sales price and the proportionate part of the cost of the goods sold. Instead of apportioning both sales price and cost over the period of collection, however, **only the gross profit is deferred.** This procedure has exactly the same effect as deferring both sales and cost of sales but requires only one deferred account rather than two.

The steps to be used are described as follows:

**For the sales in any one year—**

1. During the year, record both sales and cost of sales in the regular way, using the special accounts described later, and compute the rate of gross profit on installment sales transactions.
2. At the end of the year, apply the rate of gross profit to the cash collections of the current year's installment sales to arrive at the realized gross profit.
3. The gross profit not realized should be deferred to future years.

**For sales made in prior years—**

1. The gross profit rate of each year's sales must be applied against cash collections of accounts receivable resulting from that year's sales to arrive at the realized gross profit.

From the preceding discussion of the general practice followed in taking up income from installment sales, it is apparent that special accounts must be used to provide certain special information required to determine the realized and unrealized gross profit in each year of operations. The requirements are as follows:

1. Installment sales transactions must be kept separate in the accounts from all other sales.
2. Gross profit on sales sold on installment must be determinable.
3. The amount of cash collected on installment sales accounts receivable must be known, and, further, the total collected on the current year's and on each preceding year's sales must be determinable.
4. Provision must be made for carrying forward each year's deferred gross profit.

In each year, the ordinary operating expenses are charged to expense accounts as under customary accounting procedure and are closed to the Income Summary account. Thus, the only peculiarity in computing net income under the installment sales method as generally applied is the deferment of gross profit until realized by collection of the accounts receivable.

To illustrate the installment sales method in accounting for the sales of merchandise, assume the following data:

| | 1983 | 1984 | 1985 |
|---|---|---|---|
| Sales (on installment) | $200,000 | $250,000 | $240,000 |
| Cost of sales | 150,000 | 190,000 | 168,000 |
| Gross profit | $ 50,000 | $ 60,000 | $ 72,000 |
| Rate of gross profit on sales | 25% | 24% | 30% |
| Cash receipts | | | |
| 1983 sales | $ 60,000 | $100,000 | $ 40,000 |
| 1984 sales | | 100,000 | 125,000 |
| 1985 sales | | | 80,000 |

To simplify the illustration, interest charges have been excluded. Summary entries in general journal form have been prepared for the transactions in the illustration. In reviewing these entries it must be remembered that as a practical matter they would not appear as summary entries, but the transactions would be entered individually as they occur. The entries as given are for purposes of illustration only. All transactions not concerned with the installment sales problem have been omitted.

**1983**

| | | |
|---|---|---|
| Installment Accounts Receivable, 1983 | 200,000 | |
|    Installment Sales | | 200,000 |
|    (To record sales made on installment in 1983) | | |
| Cash | 60,000 | |
|    Installment Accounts Receivable, 1983 | | 60,000 |
|    (To record cash collected on installment receivables) | | |
| Cost of Installment Sales | 150,000 | |
|    Inventory (or Purchases) | | 150,000 |
|    (To record cost of goods sold on installment in 1983 on either a perpetual or a periodic inventory basis) | | |
| Installment Sales | 200,000 | |
|    Cost of Installment Sales | | 150,000 |
|    Deferred Gross Profit, 1983 | | 50,000 |
|    (To close installment sales and cost of installment sales for the year) | | |
| Deferred Gross Profit, 1983 | 15,000 | |
|    Realized Gross Profit on Installment Sales | | 15,000 |
|    (To remove from deferred gross profit the profit realized through collections) | | |
| Realized Gross Profit on Installment Sales | 15,000 | |
|    Income Summary | | 15,000 |
|    (To close profits realized by collections) | | |

The realized and deferred gross profit is computed for the year 1983 as follows:

| 1983 | |
|---|---:|
| Rate of gross profit current year | 25% |
| Cash collected on current year's sales | $ 60,000 |
| Realized gross profit (25% of $60,000) | 15,000 |
| Gross profit to be deferred ($50,000 − $15,000) | 35,000 |

**1984**

| | | |
|---|---:|---:|
| Installment Accounts Receivable, 1984 | 250,000 | |
|   Installment Sales | | 250,000 |
|     (To record sales per account sales) | | |
| Cash | 200,000 | |
|   Installment Accounts Receivable, 1983 | | 100,000 |
|   Installment Accounts Receivable, 1984 | | 100,000 |
|     (To record cash collected on installment receivables) | | |
| Cost of Installment Sales | 190,000 | |
|   Inventory (or Purchases) | | 190,000 |
|     (To record cost of goods sold on installment in 1984) | | |
| Installment Sales | 250,000 | |
|   Cost of Installment Sales | | 190,000 |
|   Deferred Gross Profit, 1984 | | 60,000 |
|     (To close installment sales and cost of installment sales for the year) | | |
| Deferred Gross Profit, 1983 | 25,000 | |
| Deferred Gross Profit, 1984 | 24,000 | |
|   Realized Gross Profit on Installment Sales | | 49,000 |
|     (To remove from deferred gross profit the profit realized through collections) | | |
| Realized Gross Profit on Installment Sales | 49,000 | |
|   Income Summary | | 49,000 |
|     (To close profits realized by collections) | | |

The realized and deferred gross profit is computed for the year 1984 as follows:

| 1984 | |
|---|---:|
| **Current year's sales** | |
|   Rate of gross profit | 24% |
|   Cash collected on current year's sales | $100,000 |
|   Realized gross profit (24% of $100,000) | 24,000 |
|   Gross profit to be deferred ($60,000 − $24,000) | 36,000 |
| **Prior year's sales** | |
|   Rate of gross profit—1983 | 25% |
|   Cash collected on 1983 sales | $100,000 |
|   Gross profit realized in 1984 on 1983 sales (25% of $100,000) | 25,000 |
| **Total gross profit realized in 1984** | |
|   Realized on collections of 1983 sales | $ 25,000 |
|   Realized on collections of 1984 sales | 24,000 |
|     Total | $ 49,000 |

The entries in 1985 would be similar to those of 1984, and the total gross profit taken up or realized would be $64,000, as shown by the computations below.

| | |
|---|---:|
| **1985** | |
| **Current year's sales** | |
| Rate of gross profit | 30% |
| Cash collected on current year's sales | $ 80,000 |
| Gross profit realized on 1985 sales (30% of $80,000) | 24,000 |
| Gross profit to be deferred ($72,000 − $24,000) | 48,000 |
| **Prior year's sales** | |
| *1983 sales* | |
| Rate of gross profit | 25% |
| Cash collected | $ 40,000 |
| Gross profit realized in 1985 on 1983 sales (25% of $40,000) | 10,000 |
| *1984 sales* | |
| Rate of gross profit | 24% |
| Cash collected | $125,000 |
| Gross profit realized in 1985 on 1984 sales (24% of $125,000) | 30,000 |
| **Total gross profit realized in 1985** | |
| Realized on collections of 1983 sales | $ 10,000 |
| Realized on collections of 1984 sales | 30,000 |
| Realized on collections of 1985 sales | 24,000 |
| Total | $ 64,000 |

**Additional Problems of Installment Sales Accounting**  In addition to computing realized and deferred gross profit currently, other problems are involved in accounting for installment sales transactions. These problems are related to:

1. Interest on installment contracts.
2. Uncollectible accounts.
3. Defaults and repossessions.

INTEREST ON INSTALLMENT CONTRACTS  Because the collection of installment receivables is spread over a long period, it is customary to charge the buyer interest on the unpaid balance. Interest charges are generally provided for in setting up the schedule of payments required by the sales contract; that is, each installment payment consists of interest and principal. Generally, each payment is equal (level payment pattern) in amount to each successive payment. However, a smaller portion of each successive payment is attributable to interest and a correspondingly larger amount attributable to principal, as shown in the schedule on page 855.

When interest is involved in installment sales, it should be accounted for separately as interest revenue distinct from the gross profit recognized on the installment sales collections during the period. The interest is recognized as interest revenue at the time of the cash receipt. Also, interest accrued since the last collection date on the installment receivables should be recorded as an adjusting entry at year end.

UNCOLLECTIBLE ACCOUNTS  The problem of bad debts or uncollectible accounts receivable is somewhat different for concerns selling on an installment basis because of a repossession feature commonly incorporated in the sales agreement. This feature gives the selling company an opportunity to recoup any uncollectible accounts through repossession and resale of repossessed merchandise. If the experience of the company indicates that

| | | INSTALLMENT PAYMENT SCHEDULE | | |
|---|---|---|---|---|
| Date | Cash (Debit) | Interest Earned (Credit) | Installment Receivables (Credit) | Unpaid Balance |
| 1/2/83 | — | — | — | $3,000.00 |
| 1/2/84 | $1,164.10[a] | $240.00[b] | $ 924.10 | 2,075.90 |
| 1/2/85 | 1,164.10 | 166.07 | 998.03 | 1,077.87 |
| 1/2/86 | 1,164.10 | 86.23 | 1,077.87 | -0- |

[a]Periodic payment = Original unpaid balance ÷ PV of an annuity of $1.00 for three periods at 8%; $1,164.10 = $3,000 ÷ 2.57710.
[b]$3,000 × .08 = $240.

repossessions do not, as a rule, compensate for uncollectible balances, it may be advisable to provide for such losses through charges to a special bad debts expense account just as is done for other credit sales. This matter was covered in detail in Chapter 7.

**DEFAULTS AND REPOSSESSIONS** Depending on the terms of the sales contract and the policy of the credit department, the seller can repossess merchandise sold under an installment arrangement if the purchaser fails to meet payment requirements. Repossessed merchandise may be reconditioned before it is offered for sale, and it may be resold for cash or under a plan for installment payments.

Repossession of merchandise sold is a recognition that the related installment receivable account is not collectible and that it should be written off. Along with the account receivable, the applicable deferred gross profit must be removed from the ledger in any entry similar to the following:

| | | |
|---|---|---|
| Repossessed Merchandise (an inventory account) | xx | |
| Deferred Gross Profit | xx | |
| Installment Accounts Receivable | | xx |

The entry above assumes that the repossessed merchandise is to be recorded on the books at exactly the amount of the uncollected account less the deferred gross profit applicable. This assumption may or may not be proper. The condition of the merchandise repossessed, the cost of reconditioning, and the market for second-hand merchandise of that particular type must all be considered. **The objective should be to put any asset acquired on the books at its fair value or, when fair value is not ascertainable, at the best possible approximation of fair value.** And, if the fair value of the merchandise repossessed is less than the uncollected balance less the deferred gross profit, a "loss on repossession" should be recorded at the date of repossession.

Some accountants contend that repossessed merchandise should be entered at a valuation that will permit the company to make its regular rate of gross profit on resale. If it is entered at its approximated cost to purchase, the regular rate of gross profit is provided for, but that is completely a secondary consideration. It is more important that the asset acquired by repossession be recorded at fair value in accordance with the general practice of carrying assets at acquisition price as represented by the fair market value at the date of acquisition.

To illustrate the required entry, assume that a refrigerator was sold to Jay Hirsch for $500 on September 1, 1983. Terms require a down payment of $200 and $20 on the first of every month for 15 months thereafter. It is further assumed that the refrigerator cost $300, and is sold to provide a 40% rate of gross profit on selling price. At the year end, December 31, 1983, a total of $60 should have been collected in addition to the original down payment.

Now if Hirsch makes his January and February payments in 1984 and then defaults, the account balances applicable to Hirsch at time of default would be:

| | |
|---|---|
| Installment Account Receivable | 200 (dr.) |
| Deferred Gross Profit (40% × $240) | 96 (cr.) |

The deferred gross profit applicable to the Hirsch account still has the December 31, 1983 balance because no entry has been made to take up gross profit realized by cash collections in 1984. The regular entry at the end of 1984, however, will take up the gross profit realized by all cash collections including amounts received from Hirsch. Hence, the balance of deferred gross profit applicable to Hirsch's account may be computed by applying the gross profit rate for the year of sale to the balance of Hirsch's account receivable, 40% of $200, or $80. The account balances should therefore be considered as:

| | |
|---|---|
| Installment Account Receivable (Hirsch) | 200 (dr.) |
| Deferred Gross Profit (applicable to Hirsch after recognition of $16 of profit in January and February) | 80 (cr.) |

If the estimated fair value of the article repossessed is set at $70, the following entry would be required to record the repossession:

| | | |
|---|---|---|
| Deferred Gross Profit | 80 | |
| Repossessed Merchandise | 70 | |
| Loss on Repossession | 50 | |
| Installment Account Receivable (Hirsch) | | 200 |

The amount of the loss is determined by (1) subtracting the deferred gross profit from the amount of the account receivable to determine the unrecovered cost (or book value) of the merchandise repossessed, and (2) subtracting the estimated fair value of the merchandise repossessed from the unrecovered cost to get the amount of the loss on repossession.

| | |
|---|---|
| Balance of account receivable (representing uncollected selling price) | $200 |
| Less deferred gross profit | 80 |
| Unrecovered cost | 120 |
| Less estimated fair value of merchandise repossessed | 70 |
| Gain (or loss) on repossession | ($ 50) |

As pointed out earlier, the loss on repossession may be charged to Allowance for Doubtful Accounts if such an account is carried.

**Financial Statement Presentation of Installment Sales Transactions** If installment sales transactions represent a significant part of total sales, full disclosure of installment sales, the cost of installment sales, and any expenses allocable to installment sales is desirable. If, however, installment sales transactions constitute an insignificant part of total sales, it may be satisfactory to include only the realized gross profit in the income statement as a special item following the gross profit on sales as shown on page 857.

Health Machine Company
STATEMENT OF INCOME
For the Year Ended December 31, 1984

| | |
|---|---:|
| Sales | $620,000 |
| Cost of goods sold | 490,000 |
| Gross profit on sales | 130,000 |
| Gross profit realized on installment sales | 51,000 |
| Total gross profit on sales | $181,000 |

If more complete disclosure of installment sales transactions is desired, a presentation similar to the following may be used:

Health Machine Company
STATEMENT OF INCOME
For the Year Ended December 31, 1984

| | Installment Sales | Other Sales | Total |
|---|---:|---:|---:|
| Sales | $248,000 | $620,000 | $868,000 |
| Cost of goods sold | 182,000 | 490,000 | 672,000 |
| Gross margin on sales | 66,000 | 130,000 | 196,000 |
| Less deferred gross profit on installment sales of this year | 47,000 | | 47,000 |
| Realized gross profit on this year's sales | 19,000 | 130,000 | 149,000 |
| Add gross profit realized on installment sales of prior years | 32,000 | | 32,000 |
| Gross profit realized this year | $ 51,000 | $130,000 | $181,000 |

The apparent awkwardness of this method of presentation is difficult to avoid if full disclosure of installment sales transactions is to be provided in the income statement. One solution, of course, is to prepare a separate schedule showing installment sales transactions with only the final figure carried into the income statement.

In the balance sheet it is generally considered desirable to classify installment accounts receivable by year of collectibility. There is some question as to whether installment accounts that are not collectible for two or more years should be included in current assets. If installment sales are part of normal operations, they may be considered as current assets because they are collectible within the operating cycle of the business. Little confusion should result from this practice if maturity dates are fully disclosed as illustrated in the following example:

| Current Assets | | |
|---|---:|---:|
| Notes and accounts receivable | | |
| Trade customers | $78,800 | |
| Less allowance for doubtful accounts | 3,700 | |
| | 75,100 | |
| Installment accounts collectible in 1984 | 22,600 | |
| Installment accounts collectible in 1985 | 47,200 | $144,900 |

On the other hand, receivables from an installment contract, or contracts, resulting from a transaction **not** related to normal operations should be reported in the "other assets" section if due beyond the normal operating cycle.

Financial statement presentation of Repossessed Merchandise and of Gain or Loss on Repossessions is based on the nature of each of these items. Repossessed merchandise is a part of inventory and should be included as such in the current asset section of the balance sheet; any gain or loss on repossessions should be included in the income statement in the other revenues and gains or other expenses and losses section.

**Deferred gross profit on installment sales** is generally treated as consisting entirely of unearned revenue and classified as a current liability. Theoretically, deferred gross profit consists of three elements: (1) income tax liability to be paid when the sales are reported as realized revenue (current liability); (2) allowance for collection expense, bad debts, and repossession losses (deduction from installment accounts receivable); and (3) net income (retained earnings, restricted as to dividend availability). Because of the difficulty in allocating deferred gross profit among these three elements, however, the whole amount is frequently reported as unearned revenue. The FASB in *SFAC No. 3* states that "no matter how it is displayed in financial statements, deferred gross profit on installment sales is conceptually an asset valuation—that is, a reduction of an asset."[24] We support the FASB position but we recognize that until an official standard on this topic is issued, financial statements will probably continue to report such deferred gross profit as a current liability.

## Consignment Sales Accounting

In some sales arrangements the delivery of the goods by the manufacturer (or wholesaler) to the dealer (or retailer) is not considered to be full performance and a sale because the manufacturer retains title to the goods. This specialized method of marketing certain types of products makes use of a device known as a **consignment.** Under this arrangement, the **consignor** (manufacturer) ships merchandise to the **consignee** (dealer) who is to act as an agent for the consignor in selling the merchandise. Both consignor and consignee are interested in selling—the former to make a profit or develop a market, the latter to make a commission on the sales.

The consignee accepts the merchandise and agrees to exercise due diligence in caring for and selling the merchandise. Cash received from customers is remitted to the consignor by the consignee, after deducting a sales commission (and any chargeable expenses). A modified version of the sale basis of revenue recognition is used by the consignor. That is, revenue is recognized only after the consignor receives notification of sale and the cash remittance from the consignee. The merchandise is carried throughout the consignment as the inventory of the consignor, separately classified as Merchandise on Consignment. It is not recorded as an asset on the consignee's books. Upon sale of the merchandise, the consignee has a liability for the net amount due the consignor. The consignor periodically receives from the consignee an **account sales** that shows the merchandise received, merchandise sold, expenses chargeable to the consignment, and the cash remitted. Revenue is then recognized by the consignor.

Under the consignment arrangement, the manufacturer (consignor) accepts the risk that the merchandise might not sell and relieves the dealer (consignee) of the need to

---

[24]See *SFAC No. 3*, pars. 156–158.

commit part of its working capital to inventory. A variety of different systems and account titles are used to record consignments, but they all share the common goal of postponing the recognition of revenue until it is known that a sale to a third party has occurred.

## Summary of Product Revenue Recognition Bases

The revenue recognition bases or methods, the criteria for their use, and the reasons for departing from the sale basis are summarized in the following exhibit:

**REVENUE RECOGNITION BASES**
**OTHER THAN THE SALE BASIS FOR PRODUCTS**[25]

| Recognition Basis (or Method of Applying a Basis) | Criteria for Use of Basis | Reason(s) for Departing from Sale Basis |
|---|---|---|
| Completion-of-production basis | Immediate marketability at quoted prices; unit interchangeability; difficulty of determining costs. | Known or determinable revenues; inability to determine costs and thereby defer expense recognition until sale. |
| Percentage-of-completion method | Long-term construction of property; dependable estimates of extent of progress and cost to complete; reasonable assurance of collectibility of contract price; expectation that both contractor and buyer can meet obligations, and absence of inherent hazards that make estimates doubtful. | Availability of evidence of ultimate proceeds; better measure of periodic income; avoidance of fluctuations in revenues, expenses, and income; performance is a "continuous sale" and therefore not a departure from the sale basis. |
| Completed-contract method | Use on short-term contracts, and whenever percentage-of-completion cannot be used on long-term contracts. | Existence of inherent hazards in the contract beyond the normal, recurring business risks; conditions for using the percentage-of-completion method are absent. |
| Accretion basis | Criteria unspecified because accretion basis is not permitted by authoritative literature. | Possible support for recognizing accretion as revenue includes product marketability at known prices and desirability of recognizing changes in assets. |
| Discovery basis | Criteria unspecified because discovery basis is not permitted by authoritative literature. | Possible support for recognizing revenue at time natural resources are discovered includes the significance of discovery in the earning process and the view that sales prices can be estimated. |
| Installment method and cost recovery methods | Absence of a reasonable basis for estimating degree of collectibility. | Collectibility of the receivable is so uncertain that gross profit (or income) is not recognized until cash is actually received. |

[25] Adapted from *Survey of Present Practices in Recognizing Revenues, Expenses, Gains, and Losses, op. cit.*, pp. 12 and 13.

## REVENUE RECOGNITION FOR A SPECIAL SALES TRANSACTION—FRANCHISES

To supplement and illustrate our presentation of revenue recognition, we have chosen to cover a common yet unique type of sales transaction—**franchise sales.** Accounting for franchise sales was chosen because of its popularity, complexity, and applicability to many of the previously discussed revenue recognition bases. In accounting for franchise sales, the accountant must analyze the transaction and, considering all the circumstances, must use judgment in selecting and applying one or more of the revenue recognition bases and then, possibly, monitor the situation over a long period of time.

### The Franchise Sales Phenomenon

As indicated earlier, the accountant determines when revenue is recognized, essentially on the basis of two criteria: (1) completion or virtual completion of the earning process, and (2) occurrence of an exchange. These criteria are appropriate for most business activities, but for some sales transactions they simply are not adequate in defining when revenue should be recognized. In some situations, the accountant is forced to look to the circumstances surrounding the contract to ascertain when to recognize revenue and income. Sales transactions in some industries (for example, land development, leasing, and franchising) require closer scrutiny. The fast-growing franchise industry has given accountants special concern and challenge.

Four types of franchising arrangements have evolved: (1) manufacturer-retailer, (2) manufacturer-wholesaler, (3) service sponsor-retailer, and (4) wholesaler-retailer. The fastest growing category of franchising, and the one that caused a reexamination of appropriate accounting, has been the third category, **service sponsor-retailer.** Included in this category are such industries and businesses as:

Soft ice cream drive-ins (Tastee Freez, Dairy Queen)
Food drive-ins (McDonald's, Kentucky Fried Chicken, Burger King)
Restaurants (Perkins, Pizza Hut, Denny's)
Motels (Holiday Inns, Howard Johnson, Best Western)
Auto rentals (Avis, Hertz, National)
Part-time help (Manpower, Kelly Girl)
Others (H & R Block, Arthur Murray Studios, Seven-Eleven Stores)

Franchise companies derive their revenue from one or both of two sources: (1) from the sale of initial franchises and related assets or services, and (2) from continuing fees based on the operations of franchises. The **franchisor** (the party who grants business rights under the franchise) normally provides the **franchisee** (the party who operates the franchised business) with the following services:

1. Assistance in site selection.
   (a) Analyzing location.
   (b) Negotiating lease.
2. Evaluation of potential income.
3. Supervision of construction activity.
   (a) Obtaining financing.
   (b) Designing building.
   (c) Supervising contractor while building.
4. Assistance in the acquisition of signs, fixtures, and equipment.

**5.** Provision of bookkeeping and advisory services.
   (a) Setting up franchisee's records.
   (b) Advising on income, real estate, and other taxes.
   (c) Advising on local regulations of the franchisee's business.

**6.** Provision of employee and management training.

**7.** Provision of quality control.

**8.** Provision of advertising and promotion.[26]

During the sixties and early seventies it was standard practice for franchisors to recognize the entire franchise fee at the date of sale whether the fee was received then or was collectible over a long period of time as represented by a long-term note. Frequently, franchisors recorded the entire amount as revenue in the year of sale even though many of the services were yet to be performed and uncertainty existed regarding the collection of the entire fee. In effect the franchisors were counting their fried chickens before they were hatched. For example, a **franchise agreement** may provide for refunds to the franchisee if certain conditions are not met, and franchise fee profit can be reduced sharply by future costs of obligations and services to be rendered by the franchisor. To curb the abuses in revenue recognition that existed and to standardize the accounting and reporting practices in the franchise industry, the FASB issued *Statement No. 45* in 1981.

## Initial Franchise Fees

The initial franchise fee is consideration for establishing the franchise relationship and providing some initial services. Initial franchise fees are to be recorded as revenue only when and as the franchisor makes "substantial performance" of the services it is obligated to perform and collection of the fee is reasonably assured. **Substantial performance** occurs when the franchisor has no remaining obligation to refund any cash received or excuse any nonpayment of a note and has performed all the initial services required under the contract. "The commencement of operations by the franchisee shall be presumed to be the earliest point at which substantial performance has occurred, unless it can be demonstrated that substantial performance of all obligations, including services rendered voluntarily, has occurred before that time."[27]

## Illustration of Entries for Initial Franchise Fees

To illustrate, assume that Tum's Pizza, Inc., charges an initial franchise fee of $50,000 for the right to operate as a franchisee of Tum's Pizza. Of this amount, $10,000 is payable when the agreement is signed and the balance is payable in five annual payments of $8,000 each. In return for the initial franchise fee the franchisor will help in locating the site, negotiate the lease or purchase of the site, supervise the construction activity, and provide the bookkeeping services. The credit rating of the franchisee indicates that money can be borrowed at 8%. The present value of an ordinary annuity of five annual receipts of $8,000 each discounted at 8% is $31,941.60. The discount of $8,058.40 represents the interest revenue to be accrued by the franchisor over the payment period.

---

[26]Archibald E. MacKay, "Accounting for Initial Franchise Fee Revenue," *The Journal of Accountancy* (January 1970), pp. 66–67.

[27]"Accounting for Franchise Fee Revenue," *Statement of Financial Accounting Standards No. 45* (Stamford, Conn.: FASB, 1981), par. 5.

1. If there is reasonable expectation that the down payment may be refunded and if substantial future services remain to be performed by Tum's Pizza, Inc., the entry should be:

| | | |
|---|---|---|
| Cash | 10,000.00 | |
| Notes Receivable | 40,000.00 | |
|     Discount on Notes Receivable | | 8,058.40 |
|     Unearned Franchise Fees | | 41,941.60 |

2. If the probability of refunding the initial franchise fee is extremely low, the amount of future services to be provided to the franchisee is minimal, collectibility of the note is reasonably assured, and substantial performance has occurred, the entry should be:

| | | |
|---|---|---|
| Cash | 10,000.00 | |
| Notes Receivable | 40,000.00 | |
|     Discount on Notes Receivable | | 8,058.40 |
|     Revenue from Franchise Fees | | 41,941.60 |

3. If the initial down payment is not refundable, represents a fair measure of the services already provided, with a significant amount of services still to be performed by the franchisor in future periods, and collectibility of the note is reasonably assured, the entry should be:

| | | |
|---|---|---|
| Cash | 10,000.00 | |
| Notes Receivable | 40,000.00 | |
|     Discount on Notes Receivable | | 8,058.40 |
|     Revenue from Franchise Fees | | 10,000.00 |
|     Unearned Franchise Fees | | 31,941.60 |

4. If the initial down payment is not refundable and no future services are required by the franchisor, but collection of the note is so uncertain that recognition of the note as an asset is unwarranted, the entry should be:

| | | |
|---|---|---|
| Cash | 10,000 | |
|     Revenue from Franchise Fees | | 10,000 |

5. Under the same conditions as those listed under 4 except that the down payment is refundable or substantial services are yet to be performed, the entry should be:

| | | |
|---|---|---|
| Cash | 10,000 | |
|     Unearned Franchise Fees | | 10,000 |

In cases 4 and 5 above where collection of the note is extremely uncertain, cash collections may be recognized using the installment method or the cost recovery method.[28]

## Continuing Franchise Fees

**Continuing franchise fees** are received in return for the continuing rights granted by the franchise agreement and for providing such services as management training, advertising and promotion, legal assistance, and other support. Continuing fees should be reported as revenue when they are earned and receivable from the franchisee, unless a portion of them has been designated for a particular purpose, such as providing a specified amount for

---

[28] A study that compared four revenue recognition procedures—installment sales basis, spreading recognition over the contract life, percentage-of-completion basis, and substantial performance—for franchise sales concluded that the percentage-of-completion method is the most acceptable revenue recognition method; the substantial performance method was found sometimes to yield ultra-conservative results. (Charles H. Calhoun III, "Accounting for Initial Franchise Fees: Is It a Dead Issue?" *The Journal of Accountancy* (February 1975), pp. 60–67.)

building maintenance or local advertising. In that case, the portion deferred shall be an amount sufficient to cover the estimated cost in excess of continuing franchise fees and provide a reasonable profit on the continuing services.

## Bargain Purchases

In addition to paying continuing franchise fees, franchisees frequently purchase some or all of their equipment and supplies from the franchisor. The franchisor would account for these sales as it would for any other product sales. Sometimes, however, the franchise agreement grants the franchisee the right to make **bargain purchases** of equipment or supplies after the initial franchise fee is paid. If the bargain price is lower than the normal selling price of the same product, or if it does not provide the franchisor a reasonable profit, then a portion of the initial franchise fee should be deferred. The deferred portion would be accounted for as an adjustment of the selling price when the franchisee subsequently purchases the equipment or supplies.

## Options to Purchase

A franchise agreement may give the franchisor an **option to purchase** the franchisee's business. For example, as a matter of management policy, the franchisor may reserve the right to purchase a profitable franchised outlet, or to purchase one that is in financial difficulty. If it is probable at the time the option is given that the franchisor will ultimately purchase the outlet, then the initial franchise fee should not be recognized as revenue but should be recorded as a liability. When the option is exercised, the liability would reduce the franchisor's investment in the outlet.

## Illustration of Entries for Continuing Fees, Bargain Purchases, and Options

To illustrate these concepts, assume the facts given on page 861 in the Tum's Pizza example. In addition, assume that Tum's Pizza, Inc. charges a continuing franchise fee of $4,200 annually for services rendered during the year.

1. If 20% of the continuing franchise fee is designated specifically for building maintenance to be provided by the franchisor, the entry to record receipt of the franchise fee should be:

| | | |
|---|---|---|
| Cash | 4,200 | |
| Revenue from Continuing Franchise Fees | | 3,360 |
| Unearned Franchise Fees ($4,200 × .20) | | 840 |

When maintenance is provided, assuming that the franchisor will receive a 25% markup on selling price, the entries are:

| | | |
|---|---|---|
| Unearned Franchise Fees | 840 | |
| Revenue from Continuing Franchise Fees | | 840 |
| Maintenance Expense [$840 − ($840 × .25)] | 630 | |
| Cash (or Accounts Payable) | | 630 |

2. If during the year Tum's Pizza, Inc. sells supplies costing $3,000 to the franchisee at the normal $4,000 price, the entries are:

| | | |
|---|---|---|
| Cash (or Accounts Receivable) | 4,000 | |
| Franchise Product Sales | | 4,000 |

| | | |
|---|---|---|
| Cost of Franchise Product Sales | 3,000 | |
| Supplies Inventory | | 3,000 |

3. Collectibility of the note for the initial franchise fee is reasonably assured, and substantial performance by the franchisor has occurred. (See entry 2, page 862.) If after the initial franchise fee is paid, the franchisee has the right to purchase up to $20,000 of supplies at their cost of $15,000, the entry to record the initial franchise fee would be:

| | | |
|---|---|---|
| Cash | 10,000.00 | |
| Notes Receivable | 40,000.00 | |
| Discount on Notes Receivable | | 8,058.40 |
| Revenue from Franchise Fees | | 36,941.60 |
| Unearned Franchise Fees | | 5,000.00 |

When the franchisee subsequently purchases the supplies, the entries are:

| | | |
|---|---|---|
| Cash (or Accounts Receivable) | 15,000 | |
| Unearned Franchise Fees | 5,000 | |
| Franchise Product Sales | | 20,000 |
| Cost of Franchise Product Sales | 15,000 | |
| Supplies Inventory | | 15,000 |

4. Collectibility of the note for the initial franchise fee is reasonably assured and substantial performance by the franchisor has occurred. (See entry 2, page 862.) The franchise agreement contains an option allowing Tum's Pizza, Inc. to purchase the outlet at any time during the next five years. If it is likely that this option will ultimately be exercised, the entry to record the initial franchise would be:

| | | |
|---|---|---|
| Cash | 10,000.00 | |
| Notes Receivable | 40,000.00 | |
| Discount on Notes Receivable | | 8,058.40 |
| Deferred Franchise Purchase Option (Liability) | | 41,941.60 |

## Franchisor's Costs

Franchise accounting also involves proper accounting for the **franchisor's costs.** The objective is to match related costs and revenues by reporting them as components of income in the same accounting period. Franchisors should ordinarily defer **direct costs** (usually incremental costs) relating to specific franchise sales for which revenue has not yet been recognized. **Indirect costs** of a regular and recurring nature which are incurred irrespective of the level of franchise sales such as selling and administrative expenses (and other fixed costs) should be expensed as incurred. Costs should not be deferred, however, without reference to anticipated revenue and its realizability.[29]

## Disclosures of Franchisors

Disclosure of all significant commitments and obligations resulting from franchise agreements, including a description of services that have not yet been substantially performed, is required. Any resolution of uncertainties regarding the collectibility of franchise fees should be disclosed. Initial franchise fees should be segregated from other franchise fee revenue if they are significant. Where possible, revenues and costs related to franchisor-owned outlets should be distinguished from those related to franchised outlets.

---

[29]"Accounting for Franchise Fee Revenue," p. 17.

# APPENDIX K

# Accounting for Service Sales Transactions

To the student—

This appendix is more illustrative than authoritative because the concepts and methods presented are not official GAAP. Service sales represent a significant portion of all sales made in our economy and they are obviously being accounted for in some manner. Yet, no written official pronouncement provides specific standards of accounting for service sales transactions. Some of the methods presented on the following pages are being applied uniformly and properly in practice and to that extent (and because they do not violate any existing accounting standard) they are GAAP. But, because the profession has not issued specific guidelines, considerable variation exists in practice in accounting for revenue from service sales, even between firms in the same industry.

This section is based on the recent combined effort of the FASB and the AICPA to establish standards of accounting for certain service transactions through their issuance in 1978 of an Invitation to Comment. Like many attempts to achieve uniformity in accounting practice, this effort is being resisted and criticized by special interest groups. We present this material (1) because of its instructional value and practical applicability, (2) because it fills an area long in need of standards, and (3) because it complements so well the subject matter of this chapter.

## SERVICE INDUSTRIES AND SERVICE TRANSACTIONS

The number and variety of businesses that offer services to the public are increasing and the range of services they offer is broadening. Examples of the types of industries that offer services are listed below.

Advertising agencies
Cemetery associations
Computer service organizations
Correspondence schools
Electronic security
Employment agencies
Entertainment
Modeling agencies
Engineering firms

Equipment and office maintenance
Health spas
Mortgage banking
Perpetual care societies
Retirement homes
Transportation
Accounting
Architecture
Garbage and waste removal

| | |
|---|---|
| Interior design or decoration | Private and social clubs |
| Legal services | Public relations |
| Management consulting | Real estate brokerage |
| Medical | Research and development labs |
| Moving and storage | Travel agencies |
| Placement agencies | |

The list above is only representative of service industries; an all-inclusive list cannot be provided because the range of services is so wide.

The major accounting questions facing the types of service organizations listed above relate to when revenue should be recognized as being earned and when costs should be charged to expense. Because diverse accounting methods were being used to account for similar service transactions, the profession recently moved to narrow the range of alternative methods. The following discussion represents newly developed concepts and methods that are still in the initial stages of reception and implementation.

Service transactions are defined as transactions

> between a seller and a purchaser in which, for a mutually agreed price, the seller performs, agrees to perform at a later date, or agrees to maintain readiness to perform an act or acts, including permitting others to use enterprise resources that do not alone produce a tangible commodity or product as the principal intended result.[1]

Although this definition does not require that the act or acts to be performed be specified by a contract, in practice most service transactions performed over a period of time or requiring performance in the future are formalized by a contract. However, agreements to perform at a later date and agreements to maintain a readiness to perform an act are often only commitments or executory contracts, and commitments and executory contracts are not currently viewed as transactions to be recorded in accrual-based transaction-oriented financial statements.

Some transactions may involve both services and products. **When the sale of a product is incidental to the rendering of a service, the transaction would be accounted for as a service transaction.** For example, a fixed price equipment maintenance contract that includes parts would be considered a service transaction. Conversely, **if a service is incidental to the sale of a product, the transaction would be accounted for as a product transaction.** For example, the inclusion of a warranty or guarantee in the sale of a product is considered incidental.

Determining when a service or a product is incidental to a transaction can be difficult. An incidental nature may be indicated, however, in one of the following two ways:

1. The inclusion of a product or a service does not result in a variance in the total transaction price from what would be charged excluding that product or service.
2. A product is not sold or a service is not rendered separately in the seller's normal business.[2]

**If both the product and the service are stated separately and the total transaction price would vary because the product or the service is included or excluded, the transaction would be accounted for as both a product and a service transaction.** For example, equipment maintenance contracts in which parts are charged separately would qualify for separable product and service transaction accounting.

---

[1]"Accounting for Certain Service Transactions," *FASB Invitation to Comment* (Stamford, Conn.: FASB, 1978), p. 1.

[2]Ibid., pp. 10–11.

# REVENUE AND EXPENSE RECOGNITION FOR SERVICE TRANSACTIONS

Revenue from service transactions should be recognized on the basis of the seller's performance of the transaction. **Performance** is "the execution of a defined act or acts or occurs with the passage of time."[3]

Authoritative professional literature generally specifies that costs should be charged to expense in the period in which the revenue with which they are associated is recognized as earned. And costs should not be deferred unless they are expected to be recoverable from future revenue.[4]

For purposes of accounting for service transactions, related costs are identified as follows:[5]

1. **Initial direct costs** are costs that are directly associated with negotiating and consummating service agreements. They include, but are not necessarily limited to commissions, legal fees, costs of credit investigations, and installment paper processing fees. No portion of supervisory and administration expenses or other indirect expenses, such as rent and facilities costs, is included in initial direct costs.

2. **Direct costs** are costs that have a clearly identifiable beneficial or causal relationship (i) to the services performed or (ii) to the level of services performed for a group of customers, for example, servicemen's labor and repair parts included as part of a service agreement.

3. **Indirect costs** are all costs other than initial direct costs and direct costs. They include provisions for uncollectible accounts, general and administrative expenses, advertising expenses, and general selling expenses.

Indirect costs should be charged to expense as incurred regardless of the revenue recognition method applied to the transaction. The method of accounting for initial direct costs and direct costs is dependent upon the revenue recognition method applied to the transaction.

# METHODS OF SERVICE REVENUE RECOGNITION

Four different methods of accounting for revenues on service transactions have been proposed. The major determinant of each method's applicability is the nature and extent of performance. The four recommended methods are:

1. Specific performance method.
2. Completed performance method.
3. Proportional performance method.
4. Collection method.

## Specific Performance Method

The specific performance method is appropriate when a service transaction consists of **a single act.** Revenue should be recognized at the time the act takes place. Initial direct costs

---

[3]Ibid., p. 11.

[4]"Basic Concepts and Accounting Principles Underlying Financial Statements of Business Enterprises," *APB Statement No. 4* (New York: AICPA, 1970), par. 155.

[5]"Accounting for Certain Service Transactions," pp. 13 and 14.

and direct costs should be charged to expense at the time revenues are recognized. Thus, initial direct costs and direct costs incurred before the service is performed should be deferred until the revenue is recognized.

This method can be used by a real estate broker who would record sales commissions as revenue when the real estate transaction is consummated at the "closing." This method might also be applicable to an employment agency whose fee is contingent upon the new employee remaining at a job for a specified time period. Because the agency has rendered its services in locating and placing an employee for its client, the fee would be recorded at the time the employee is placed. However, if experience shows that there is a reasonable possibility of having to refund the fee because of the employment period contingency, it is appropriate to record an allowance based on estimates of fees that will never be collected.

## Completed Performance Method

The completed performance method is appropriate when services are performed in **more than one act** and the proportion of services to be performed in the last of a series of acts is so significant in relation to the entire service transaction that **performance cannot be deemed to have occurred until the last act occurs.** For example, for a moving company that packs, loads, and delivers goods to various locations, the act of delivery is so significant to its completing the earning process that revenue should not be recognized until delivery occurs.

Under the completed performance method, initial direct and direct costs would be expensed when revenue is recognized. Costs incurred before the service is performed should be deferred until the revenue is recognized.

## Proportional Performance Method

The proportional performance method is appropriate when services are performed in **more than one act** and revenue should be recognized as the various acts that make up the entire transaction occur, that is, in proportion to the performance of each act.[6] This method can be applied in a slightly different manner to three differing sets of circumstances:

1. **Specified number of identical or similar acts.** An equal amount of revenue would be recorded for each act expected to be performed.

   The processing of monthly mortgage payments by a mortgage banker is an appropriate application of this method.

2. **Specified number of defined but not identical acts.** Revenue is recognized in the ratio that the direct costs of performing each act have to the total estimated direct cost of the entire transaction.

   A correspondence school that provides progress evaluations, lessons, examinations, and grading might appropriately use this method.

   If the direct cost ratio is impractical or not objectively determinable as a measurement basis, a systematic and rational basis that reasonably relates revenue recognition to performance should be used. As a last resort, the straight-line method should be used.

3. **Unspecified number of identical or similar acts with a fixed period for performance.** Revenue is recognized on the straight-line method over the specified period unless there is evidence that another method is more representative of the pattern of performance.

[6]Proportional measurement is necessary only if the acts are performed in more than one financial accounting period.

A two-year club membership in which the club's facilities are available for the member's usage throughout that period is an example of appropriate application of the straight-line method.

Under the proportional performance method, **initial direct costs** are recorded as expenses in the same manner as revenue is recorded. Because there generally is a close correlation between the incurrence of **direct costs** and the extent of performance achieved, direct costs are recorded as expenses as they are incurred.

## Collection Method

If there is a significant degree of uncertainty surrounding the collectibility of service revenue, revenue should be recorded as cash is collected. Under this method, initial direct and direct costs should be recorded as expenses as incurred. The collection method is appropriate when a service is being provided to a customer whose ability to pay for those services is questionable.

## Summary of Service Revenue Recognition Methods

The four service revenue recognition methods presented above are conceptually somewhat similar to several of the product sales revenue recognition methods presented earlier in the chapter. Their similarity is portrayed below.

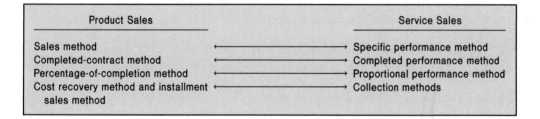

| Product Sales | | Service Sales |
|---|---|---|
| Sales method | ←——————————→ | Specific performance method |
| Completed-contract method | ←——————————→ | Completed performance method |
| Percentage-of-completion method | ←——————————→ | Proportional performance method |
| Cost recovery method and installment sales method | ←——————————→ | Collection methods |

**Note:** All **asterisked** Questions, Cases, Exercises, or Problems relate to material contained in the appendix to each chapter.

# QUESTIONS

1. What is revenue? When is revenue realized in a theoretical sense? According to the "realization principle," when is revenue realized?

2. When is revenue recognized in the following situations:
   (a) Revenue from selling products? (b) Revenue from services rendered? (c) Revenue from permitting others to use enterprise assets? (d) Revenue from disposing of assets other than products?

3. Identify several types of sales transactions and indicate the types of business for which that type of transaction is common.

4. When is revenue conventionally recognized? What conditions should exist for the recognition at date of sale of all or part of the revenue and income of any sale transaction?

5. What are the three alternative accounting methods available to a seller that is exposed to continued risks of ownership through return of the product?

6. Under what conditions may a seller who is exposed to continued risks of a high rate of return of the product sold recognize sales transactions as current revenue?

7. How does the accounting for a "contract of sale" differ from the accounting for a "contract to sell"?

8. What are the two basic methods of accounting for long-term construction contracts? Indicate the circumstances that determine when one or the other of these methods should be used.

9. For what reasons should the percentage-of-completion method be used over the completed-contract method whenever possible?

10. What methods are used in practice to determine the extent of progress toward completion? Identify some "input measures" and some "output measures" that might be used to determine the extent of progress.

11. What are the two types of losses that can become evident in accounting for long-term contracts? What is the nature of each type of loss? How is each type accounted for?

12. What is accretion? Why isn't accretion generally recognized as revenue?

13. What are the current arguments for and against using some form of discovery basis accounting in the extractive industries?

14. Identify and briefly describe the two methods generally employed to account for the cash received in situations where the collection of the sales price is not reasonably assured.

15. What is the deposit method and when might it be applied?

16. What is the nature of an installment sale? How do installment sales differ from ordinary credit sales?

17. Describe the installment sales method of accounting.

18. How are operating expenses (not included in cost of goods sold) handled under the installment method of accounting? What is the justification for such treatment?

19. When interest is involved in installment sales transactions, how should it be treated for accounting purposes?

20. How should the results of installment sales be reported on the income statement?

21. What is the nature of a sale on consignment? When is revenue recognized from a consignment sale?

22. Why in franchise arrangements may it not be proper to recognize the entire franchise fee as revenue at the date of sale?

23. How does the concept of "substantial performance" apply to accounting for franchise sales?

24. How should a franchisor account for continuing franchise fees and routine sales of equipment and supplies to franchisees?

25. What changes are made in the franchisor's recording of the initial franchise fee when the franchise agreement:
   (a) Contains an option allowing the franchisor to purchase the franchised outlet, and it is likely that the option will be exercised?
   (b) Allows the franchisee to purchase equipment and supplies from the franchisor at bargain prices?

26. At what time is it proper to recognize income in the following cases:
   (a) installment sales with no reasonable basis for estimating the degree of collectibility;
   (b) sales for future delivery; (c) merchandise shipped on consignment; (d) profit on incomplete construction contracts; and (e) subscriptions to publications?

*27. When should revenue from service transactions be recognized?

*28. Identify and differentiate between the three types of service costs. What is the guideline for expensing costs in general? What are the general guidelines for recognizing the three types of service costs?

*29. What are the four methods of accounting for service transactions that have been recommended by the profession? Which product sales revenue recognition bases are each of these service revenue recognition methods most similar to in effect on revenue timing?

# CASES

**C19-1** Revenue is usually recognized at the point of sale. Under special circumstances, however, bases other than the point of sale are used for the timing of revenue recognition.

**Instructions**

(a) Why is the point of sale usually used as the basis for the timing of revenue recognition?
(b) Disregarding the special circumstances when bases other than the point of sale are used, discuss the merits of each of the following objections to the sales basis of revenue recognition:
    1. It is too conservative because revenue is earned throughout the entire process of production.
    2. It is not conservative enough because accounts receivable do not represent disposable funds, sales returns and allowances may be made, and collection and bad debt expenses may be incurred in a later period.
(c) Revenue may also be recognized (1) during production and (2) when cash is received. For each of these two bases of timing revenue recognition give an example of the circumstances in which it is properly used and discuss the accounting merits of its use in lieu of the sales basis.

(AICPA adapted)

**C19-2** The earning of revenue by a business enterprise is recognized for accounting purposes when the transaction is recorded. In some situations, revenue is recognized approximately as it is earned in the economic sense. In other situations, however, accountants have developed guidelines for recognizing revenue by other criteria, for example, such as, at the point of sale.

**Instructions**

(Ignore income taxes.)
(a) Explain and justify why revenue is often recognized as earned at time of sale.
(b) Explain in what situations it would be appropriate to recognize revenue as the productive activity takes place.
(c) At what times, other than those included in (a) and (b) above, may it be appropriate to recognize revenue? Explain.

**C19-3** H & S Blue Stamps, Inc., was formed early this year to sell trading stamps throughout the Southwest to retailers who distribute the stamps free to their customers. Books for accumulating the stamps and catalogs illustrating the merchandise for which the stamps may be exchanged are given free to retailers for distribution to stamp recipients. Centers with inventories of merchandise premiums have been established for redemption of the stamps. Retailers may not return unused stamps to H & S.

The following schedule expresses H & S's expectations as to percentages of a normal month's activity that will be attained. For this purpose, a "normal month's activity" is defined as the level of operations expected when expansion of activities ceases or tapers off to a stable rate. The company expects that this level will be attained in the third year and that sales of stamps will average $4,000,000 per month throughout the third year.

| Month | Actual Stamp Sales Percent | Merchandise Premium Purchases Percent | Stamp Redemptions Percent |
|---|---|---|---|
| 6th | 30% | 40% | 10% |
| 12th | 60 | 60 | 45 |
| 18th | 80 | 80 | 70 |
| 24th | 90 | 90 | 80 |
| 30th | 100 | 100 | 95 |

H & S plans to adopt an annual closing date at the end of each 12 months of operation.

**Instructions**

    (a) Discuss the factors to be considered in determining when revenue should be recognized in measuring the income of a business enterprise.

    (b) Discuss the accounting alternatives that should be considered by H & S Blue Stamps, Inc., for the recognition of its revenues and related expenses.

    (c) For each accounting alternative discussed in (b), give balance sheet accounts that should be used and indicate how each should be classified.

(AICPA adapted)

**\*C19-4** Planetary Products Inc. is a large conglomerate consisting of forty-four subsidiary companies with plants and offices throughout the United States and the world. Arthur Ross, Pricewhinney, Coopersells, and Peat Co. is the international public accounting firm engaged to design and install a computerized total information, accounting, and cost control system in each of Planetary's subsidiaries. The CPA firm is given three years to complete the engagement; it intends to work continuously on the project but will assign the largest number of its staff to the project during its least busy period each year (May to October). Arthur Ross, Pricewhinney, Coopersells, and Peat Co. obtained this consulting engagement after much study, planning, an elaborate presentation, and a bid of $5,200,000.

**Instructions**

    (a) Name and describe four different methods of accounting for the revenues from service-type engagements, indicating when revenue is recognized.

    (b) For each of the four types of methods of accounting for revenues from a service type engagement, describe how initial direct costs and direct costs should be expensed.

    (c) Discuss the manner or method of revenue recognition and expensing of initial indirect costs and direct costs that you believe is appropriate for the CPA firm in its performance of the engagement described above.

    (d) How does the receipt of cash for payment of services affect revenue recognition in this and other service transactions?

**C19-5** Artichoke Heaven Inc. sells franchises to independent operators throughout the southeastern part of the United States. The contract with the franchisee includes the following provisions:

    **1.** The franchisee is charged an initial fee of $50,000. Of this amount $10,000 is payable when the agreement is signed and an $8,000 noninterest-bearing note is payable at the end of each of the five subsequent years.

    **2.** All of the initial franchise fee collected by Artichoke Heaven Inc. is to be refunded and the remaining obligation canceled if, for any reason, the franchisee fails to open his franchise.

    **3.** In return for the initial franchise fee Artichoke Heaven Inc. agrees to (a) assist the franchisee in selecting the location for his business, (b) negotiate the lease for the land, (c) obtain financing and assist with building design, (d) supervise construction, (e) establish accounting and tax records, and (f) provide expert advice over a five-year period relating to such matters as employee and management training, quality control, and promotion.

    **4.** In addition to the initial franchise fee the franchisee is required to pay to Artichoke Heaven Inc. a monthly fee of 2% of sales for menu planning, recipe innovations, and the privilege of purchasing ingredients from Artichoke Heaven Inc. at or below prevailing market prices.

Management of Artichoke Heaven Inc. estimates that the value of the services rendered to the franchisee at the time the contract is signed amounts to at least $10,000. All franchisees to date have opened their locations at the scheduled time and none has defaulted on any of the notes receivable.

    The credit ratings of all franchisees would entitle them to borrow at the current interest rate of 10%. The present value of an ordinary annuity of five annual receipts of $8,000 each discounted at 10% is $30,326.

## Instructions

(a) Discuss the alternatives that Artichoke Heaven Inc. might use to account for the initial franchise fee, evaluate each by applying generally accepted accounting principles to this situation, and give illustrative entries for each alternative.

(b) Given the nature of Artichoke Heaven Inc.'s agreement with its franchisees, when should revenue be recognized? Discuss the question of revenue recognition for both the initial franchise fee and the additional monthly fee of 2% of sales and give illustrative entries for both types of revenue.

(c) Assuming that Artichoke Heaven Inc. sells some franchises for $70,000, which includes a charge of $20,000 for the rental of equipment for its useful life of 10 years, that $30,000 of the fee is payable immediately and the balance on noninterest-bearing notes at $8,000 per year, that no portion of the $20,000 rental payment is refundable in case the franchisee goes out of business, and that title to the equipment remains with the franchisor, what would be the preferable method of accounting for the rental portion of the initial franchise fee? Explain. (AICPA adapted)

# EXERCISES

**E19-1** On June 3, Huskie Company sold to Denise Rode merchandise having a sale price of $4,500 with terms of 2/10, n/60, f.o.b. shipping point. An invoice totaling $135, terms n/30, was received by Denise Rode on June 8 from the Messenger Transport Service for the freight cost. Upon receipt of the goods, June 5, Denise Rode notified Huskie Company that merchandise costing $300 contained flaws that rendered it worthless; the same day Huskie Company issued a credit memo covering the worthless merchandise and asked that it be returned at company expense. The freight on the returned merchandise was $24, paid by Huskie Company on June 7. On June 12, the company received a check for the balance due from Denise Rode.

## Instructions

(a) Prepare journal entries on Huskie Company books to record all the events noted above under each of the following bases:
1. Sales and receivables are entered at gross selling price.
2. Sales and receivables are entered net of cash discounts.
(b) Prepare the journal entry under basis 2, assuming that Denise Rode did not remit payment until July 29.

**E19-2** In 1983, Mountain Tunnel Corp. began construction work under a three-year contract. The contract price was $1,000,000. Mountain uses the percentage-of-completion method for financial accounting purposes. The income to be recognized each year is based on the proportion of cost incurred to total estimated costs for completing the contract. The financial statement presentations relating to this contract at December 31, 1983, follow:

| Balance Sheet | | |
|---|---|---|
| Accounts receivable—construction contract billings | | $18,750 |
| Construction in progress | $62,500 | |
| Less contract billings | 58,750 | |
| Cost of uncompleted contract in excess of billings | | 3,750 |
| Income Statement | | |
| Income (before tax) on the contract recognized in 1983 | | $12,500 |

## Instructions

(a) How much cash was collected in 1983 on this contract?
(b) What was the initial estimated total income before tax on this contract?
c. What was the % of completion for 1983 (AICPA adapted)

**E19-3** On April 1, 1983, Faivre, Inc., entered into a cost-plus-fixed-fee contract to construct an electric generator for Dalton Corporation. At the contract date, Faivre estimated that it would take two years to complete the project at a cost of $2,000,000. The fixed fee stipulated in the contract is $300,000. Faivre appropriately accounts for this contract under the percentage-of-completion method. During 1983 Faivre incurred costs of $700,000 related to the project, and the estimated cost at December 31, 1983, to complete the contract is $1,400,000. Dalton was billed $500,000 under the contract.

**Instructions**

Prepare a schedule to compute the amount of gross profit to be recognized by Faivre under the contract for the year ended December 31, 1983. Show supporting computations in good form.

(AICPA adapted)

**E19-4** Tough Construction Company uses the percentage-of-completion method of accounting. In 1983, Tough began work under contract #E2-D2, which provided for a contract price of $2,100,000. Other details follow:

|  | 1983 | 1984 |
|---|---|---|
| Costs incurred during the year | $ 300,000 | $1,375,000 |
| Estimated costs to complete, as of December 31 | 1,200,000 | -0- |
| Billings during the year | 360,000 | 1,740,000 |
| Collections during the year | 250,000 | 1,600,000 |

**Instructions**

(a) What portion of the total contract price would be recognized as revenue in 1983? 1984?
(b) Assuming the same facts as those above except that Tough uses the completed-contract method of accounting, what portion of the total contract price would be recognized as revenue in 1984?
(c) Prepare a complete set of journal entries for 1983.

**E19-5** In 1983, Sissy Construction Company agreed to construct an apartment building at a price of $1,050,000. The information relating to the costs and billings for this contract is as follows:

|  | 1983 | 1984 | 1985 |
|---|---|---|---|
| Costs incurred to date | $240,000 | $440,000 | $ 840,000 |
| Estimated costs yet to be incurred | 560,000 | 360,000 | -0- |
| Customer billings to date | 100,000 | 360,000 | 1,050,000 |
| Collection of billings to date | 80,000 | 300,000 | 940,000 |

**Instructions**

(a) Assuming that the percentage-of-completion method is used, compute the amount of gross profit to be recognized in 1983 and 1984. Prepare journal entries for 1984.
(b) For 1984, show how the details related to this construction contract would be disclosed on the balance sheet and on the income statement.

**E19-6** Barrington Construction Company began operations in 1983. Construction activity for the first year is shown below. All contracts are with different customers, and any work remaining at December 31, 1983 is expected to be completed in 1984.

| Project | Total Contract Price | Billings Through 12/31/83 | Cash Collections Through 12/31/83 | Contract Costs Incurred Through 12/31/83 | Estimated Additional Costs to Complete |
|---|---|---|---|---|---|
| 1 | $ 520,000 | $ 350,000 | $310,000 | $424,000 | $106,000 |
| 2 | 670,000 | 210,000 | 210,000 | 126,000 | 504,000 |
| 3 | 475,000 | 475,000 | 395,000 | 315,000 | -0- |
|  | $1,665,000 | $1,035,000 | $915,000 | $865,000 | $610,000 |

**Instructions**

Prepare a partial income statement and balance sheet to indicate how the above information would be reported for financial statement purposes. Barrington uses the completed-contract method.

**E19–7** Delicate Construction Company began operations January 1, 1983. During the year, Delicate entered into a contract with Silo & Shed Corporation to construct a manufacturing facility. At that time, Delicate estimated that it would take five years to complete the facility at a total cost of $4,800,000. The total contract price for construction of the facility is $6,200,000. During the year, Delicate incurred $1,250,000 in construction costs related to the construction project. The estimated cost to complete the contract is $3,750,000. Silo & Shed was billed and paid 30% of the contract price.

**Instructions**

Prepare schedules to compute the amount of gross profit to be recognized for the year ended December 31, 1983, and the amount to be shown as "cost of uncompleted contract in excess of related billings" or "billings on uncompleted contract in excess of related costs" at December 31, 1983, under each of the following methods:
(a) Completed-contract method.
(b) Percentage-of-completion method.
Show supporting computations in good form.                    (AICPA adapted)

**E19–8** On May 3, 1983, Don Ford Company consigned 60 freezers, costing $500 each to Diana Company. The cost of shipping the freezers amounted to $600, and was paid by Don Ford Company. On December 30, 1983, an account sales was received from the consignee, reporting that 40 freezers had been sold for $600 each. Remittance was made by the consignee for the amount due, after deducting a commission of 10%, advertising of $100, and total installation costs of $200 on the freezers sold.

**Instructions**

(a) Compute the inventory value of the units unsold in the hands of the consignee.
(b) Compute the profit for the consignor for the units sold.
(c) Compute the amount of cash that will be remitted by the consignee.

**E19–9** Linda Leise Co. appropriately uses the installment sales method of accounting. On December 31, 1985, the books show balances as follows:

| Installment Receivables | | Deferred Gross Profit | | Gross Profit on Sales | |
|---|---|---|---|---|---|
| 1983 | $10,000 | 1983 | $ 7,000 | 1983 | 35% |
| 1984 | 40,000 | 1984 | 26,000 | 1984 | 34% |
| 1985 | 90,000 | 1985 | 105,000 | 1985 | 32% |

**Instructions**

(a) Prepare the adjusting entry or entries required on December 31, 1985 to recognize 1985 realized gross profit. (Cash receipts entries have already been made.)
(b) Compute the amount of cash collected in 1985 on accounts receivable of each year.

**E19–10** Frank Lovell Corporation, which began business on January 1, 1983, appropriately uses the installment sales method of accounting. The following data were obtained for the years 1983 and 1984:

|  | 1983 | 1984 |
|---|---|---|
| Installment sales | $700,000 | $840,000 |
| Cost of installment sales | 560,000 | 630,000 |
| General & administrative expenses | 70,000 | 84,000 |
| Cash collections on sales of 1983 | 300,000 | 250,000 |
| Cash collections on sales of 1984 | -0- | 400,000 |

**Instructions**

(a) Compute the balance in the deferred gross profit accounts on December 31, 1983 and on December 31, 1984.

(b) A 1983 sale resulted in default in 1985. At the date of default, the balance on the installment receivable was $12,000, and the repossessed merchandise had a fair value of $8,200. Prepare the entry to record the repossession.

(AICPA adapted)

**E19–11** Sandy Schultz Corporation sells farm machinery on the installment plan. On July 1, 1983, Schultz entered into an installment sale contract with Agriculture, Inc., for an eight-year period. Equal annual payments under the installment sale are $100,000 and are due on July 1. The first payment was made on July 1, 1983.

Additional information is as follows.

1. The amount that would be realized on an outright sale of similar farm machinery is $556,000.

2. The cost of the farm machinery sold to Agriculture is $417,000.

3. The finance charges relating to the installment period are $244,000 based on a stated interest rate of 12%, which is appropriate.

4. Circumstances are such that the collection of the installments due under the contract is reasonably assured.

**Instructions**

What income or loss before income taxes should Schultz record for the year ended December 31, 1983, as a result of the above transaction?

(AICPA adapted)

**E19–12** Lowprice Outlet, Inc. was involved in two default and repossession cases during the year:

1. A refrigerator was sold to Ms. Alice Congdon for $1,800, including a 40% markup on selling price. Ms. Congdon made a down payment of 20%, four of the remaining 24 equal payments, and then defaulted on further payments. The refrigerator was repossessed, at which time the fair value was determined to be $800.

**Instructions**

Prepare the journal entry to record the repossession.

2. An oven which cost $1,200 was sold to Mr. Chuck Ehrlich for $1,600 on the installment basis. Mr. Ehrlich made a down payment of $240 and paid $80 a month for six months, after which he defaulted. The oven was repossessed and the estimated value at time of repossession was determined to be $720.

**Instructions**

Prepare the journal entry to record the repossession.

**E19–13** Semi-Trailer Company uses the installment sales method in accounting for its installment sales. On January 1, 1984, Semi-Trailer Company had an installment account receivable from Elaine Wunderlich with a balance of $1,250. During 1984, $200 was collected from Wunderlich. When no further collection could be made, the merchandise sold to Wunderlich was repossessed. The merchandise, when repossessed, had a fair market value of $400. The company spent $50 for reconditioning of the merchandise. The merchandise was originally sold with a gross profit rate of 40%.

**Instructions**

Prepare the entries on the books of Semi-Trailer Company to record all transactions related to Wunderlich during 1984.

**E19–14** Herb Huskie Hamburgers, Inc., charges an initial franchise fee of $60,000. Upon the signing of the agreement, a payment of $30,000 is due; thereafter, three annual payments of

$10,000 are required. The credit rating of the franchisee is such that it would have to pay interest at 10% to borrow money.

**Instructions**

Prepare the entries to record the initial franchise fee on the books of the franchisor under the following assumptions:
(a) The down payment is not refundable, no future services are required by the franchisor, and collection of the note is reasonably assured.
(b) The franchisor has substantial services to perform, and the collection of the note is very uncertain.
(c) The down payment is not refundable, collection of the note is reasonably certain, the franchisor has yet to perform a substantial amount of services, and the down payment represents a fair measure of the services already performed.

**E19-15** On January 1, 1983, Andrew Franklin signed an agreement to operate as a franchisee of Sickbay Hospital Supplies, Inc., for an initial franchise fee of $40,000. The amount of $15,000 was paid when the agreement was signed, and the balance is payable in five annual payments of $5,000 each beginning January 1, 1984. The agreement provides that the down payment is not refundable and that no future services are required of the franchisor. Franklin's credit rating indicates that he can borrow money at 12% for a loan of this type.

**Instructions**

(a) How much should Sickbay record as revenue from franchise fees on January 1, 1983? At what amount should Franklin record the acquisition cost of the franchise on January 1, 1983?
(b) What entry would be made by Sickbay on January 1, 1983, if the down payment were refundable and substantial future services remain to be performed by Sickbay?
(c) How much revenue from franchise fees would be recorded by Sickbay on January 1, 1983, if:
   1. The initial down payment was not refundable, it represented a fair measure of the services already provided, with a significant amount of services still to be performed by Sickbay in future periods, and collectibility of the note is reasonably assured?
   2. The initial down payment is not refundable and no future services are required by the franchisor, but collection of the note is so uncertain that recognition of the note as an asset is unwarranted?
   3. The initial down payment has not been earned and collection of the note is so uncertain that recognition of the note as an asset is unwarranted?

# PROBLEMS

**P19-1** Highrise Construction Company has entered into a contract beginning January 1, 1983, to build a parking complex. It has been estimated that the complex will cost $700,000 and will take three years to construct. The complex will be billed to the purchasing company at $1,000,000. The following data pertain to the construction period.

|                             | 1983      | 1984      | 1985      |
|-----------------------------|-----------|-----------|-----------|
| Costs to date               | $350,000  | $490,000  | $700,000  |
| Estimated costs to complete | 350,000   | 210,000   | —         |
| Progress billings to date   | 300,000   | 650,000   | 1,000,000 |
| Cash collected to date      | 250,000   | 600,000   | 1,000,000 |

**Instructions**

(a) Using the percentage-of-completion method, compute the estimated gross profit that would be recognized during each year of the construction period.
(b) Using the completed-contract method, compute the estimated gross profit that would be recognized during each year of the construction period.

**P19-2** Hardhat Construction Company has contracted to build an office building. The construction is scheduled to begin on January 1, 1983, and the estimated time of completion is July 1, 1986. The building cost is estimated to be $50,000,000 and will be billed at $56,000,000. The following data relate to the construction period.

|  | 1983 | 1984 | 1985 | 1986 |
|---|---|---|---|---|
| Costs to date | $15,000,000 | $25,000,000 | $35,000,000 | $50,000,000 |
| Estimated cost to complete | 35,000,000 | 25,000,000 | 15,000,000 | — |
| Progress billings to date | 7,000,000 | 20,000,000 | 35,000,000 | 56,000,000 |
| Cash collected to date | 7,000,000 | 18,000,000 | 30,000,000 | 56,000,000 |

**Instructions**

(a) Compute the estimated gross profit for 1983, 1984, 1985, and 1986, assuming that the percentage-of-completion method is used. (Ignore income taxes.)

(b) Prepare the necessary journal entries for Hardhat Construction Company for the years 1985 and 1986.

**P19-3** On February 1, 1983, Dainty Construction Company obtained a contract to build an athletic stadium. The stadium was to be built at a total cost of $4,500,000 and was scheduled for completion by September 1, 1985. One clause of the contract stated that Dainty was to deduct $10,000 from the $6,200,000 billing price for each week that completion was delayed. Completion was delayed five weeks, which resulted in a $50,000 penalty. Below are the data pertaining to the construction period.

|  | 1983 | 1984 | 1985 |
|---|---|---|---|
| Costs to date | $1,500,000 | $3,220,000 | $4,600,000 |
| Estimated costs to complete | 3,000,000 | 1,380,000 | — |
| Progress billings to date | 1,000,000 | 2,500,000 | 6,150,000 |
| Cash collected to date | 800,000 | 2,300,000 | 6,150,000 |

**Instructions**

(a) Using the percentage-of-completion method, compute the estimated gross profit recognized in the years 1983-1984.

(b) Prepare a partial balance sheet for December 31, 1984, showing the balances in the receivable and inventory accounts.

**P19-4** On March 1, 1983, Concordia Construction Company contracted to construct a factory building for Montgomery Manufacturing, Inc., for a total contract price of $5,000,000. The building was completed by October 31, 1985. The annual contract costs incurred, estimated costs to complete the contract, and accumulated billings to Montgomery for 1983, 1984, and 1985 are given below:

|  | At 12/31/83 | At 12/31/84 | At 12/31/85 |
|---|---|---|---|
| Contract costs incurred | $1,000,000 | $2,840,000 | $ 960,000 |
| Estimated costs to complete the contract | 3,000,000 | 960,000 | -0- |
| Billings to Montgomery | 800,000 | 3,000,000 | 1,200,000 |

**Instructions**

(a) Using the percentage-of-completion method, prepare schedules to complete the profit or loss to be recognized as a result of this contract for the years ended December 31, 1983, 1984, and 1985. Ignore income taxes.

(b) Using the completed contract method, prepare schedules to compute the profit or loss to be recognized as a result of this contract for the years ended December 1983, 1984, and 1985. Ignore income taxes.

**P19-5** Hartwick Construction Company commenced doing business on January 1, 1983. Construction activities for the first year of operations are shown in the table below. All contract costs are with different customers, and any work remaining at December 31, 1983 is expected to be completed in 1984.

| Project | Total Contract Price | Billings Through 12/31/83 | Cash Collections Through 12/31/83 | Contract Costs Incurred Through 12/31/83 | Estimated Additional Costs to Complete |
|---|---|---|---|---|---|
| A | $ 260,000 | $175,000 | $155,000 | $212,000 | $ 53,000 |
| B | 335,000 | 105,000 | 105,000 | 63,000 | 252,000 |
| C | 237,500 | 237,500 | 197,500 | 157,500 | -0- |
| D | 100,000 | 35,000 | 25,000 | 56,375 | 46,125 |
| E | 230,000 | 200,000 | 200,000 | 185,000 | 15,000 |
| | $1,162,500 | $752,500 | $682,500 | $673,875 | $366,125 |

**Instructions**

(a) Prepare a schedule to compute income to be reported, unbilled contract costs and recognized profit, and billings in excess of costs and recognized profit using the percentage-of-completion method.

(b) Prepare a partial income statement and balance sheet to indicate how the information would be reported for financial statement purposes.

**P19-6** On July 1, 1983, Compton Construction Company, Inc., contracted to build an office building for Dorothy Swanson for a total contract price of $4,000,000. On July 1, Compton estimated that it would take between two and three years to complete the building. On December 31, 1985, the building was deemed substantially completed. Following are accumulated contract costs incurred, estimated costs to complete the contract, and accumulated billings to Ashland for 1983, 1984, and 1985.

| | At 12/31/83 | At 12/31/84 | At 12/31/85 |
|---|---|---|---|
| Contract costs incurred | $ 350,000 | $2,500,000 | $4,250,000 |
| Estimated costs to complete the contract | 3,150,000 | 1,700,000 | -0- |
| Billings to Ashland | 720,000 | 2,160,000 | 3,600,000 |

**Instructions**

(a) Using the percentage-of-completion method, prepare schedules to compute the profit or loss to be recognized as a result of this contract for the years ended December 31, 1983, 1984, and 1985. Ignore income taxes.

(b) Using the completed contract method, prepare schedules to compute the profit or loss to be recognized as a result of this contract for the years ended December 1983, 1984, and 1985. Ignore income taxes.

**P19-7** Presented below is summarized information for Hazard Appliance Co., which sells merchandise on the installment basis:

| | 1983 | 1984 | 1985 |
|---|---|---|---|
| Sales (on installment plan) | $200,000 | $240,000 | $200,000 |
| Cost of sales | 120,000 | 151,200 | 130,000 |
| Gross profit | $ 80,000 | $ 88,800 | $ 70,000 |
| Collections from customers on: | | | |
| 1983 installment sales | $ 60,000 | $110,000 | $ 20,000 |
| 1984 installment sales | | 80,000 | 120,000 |
| 1985 installment sales | | | 70,000 |

**Instructions**

    (a) Compute the realized gross profit for each of the years 1983, 1984, and 1985.

    (b) Prepare in journal form all entries required in 1985, applying the installment method of accounting.

**P19-8** Royal Stores sells merchandise on open account as well as on installment terms.

|  | 1983 | 1984 | 1985 |
|---|---|---|---|
| Sales on account | $417,000 | $389,000 | $510,000 |
| Installment sales | 240,000 | 320,000 | 380,000 |
| Collections on installment sales |  |  |  |
|   Made in 1983 | 80,000 | 120,000 | 40,000 |
|   Made in 1984 |  | 110,000 | 160,000 |
|   Made in 1985 |  |  | 125,000 |
| Cost of sales |  |  |  |
|   Sold on account | 291,900 | 268,410 | 351,900 |
|   Sold on installment | 151,200 | 192,000 | 224,200 |
| Selling expenses | 87,000 | 84,500 | 110,000 |
| Administrative expenses | 42,000 | 48,000 | 54,000 |

**Instructions**

    From the data above, which cover the three years since Royal Stores commenced operations, determine the net income for each year, applying the installment method of accounting.

**P19-9** Cutrate Company sells appliances for cash and also on the installment plan. Entries to record cost of sales are made monthly.

Cutrate Company
TRIAL BALANCE
December 31, 1985

| | | |
|---|---:|---:|
| Cash | $ 145,200 | |
| Installment Accounts Receivable, 1984 | 48,000 | |
| Installment Accounts Receivable, 1985 | 152,000 | |
| Inventory—New Merchandise | 124,000 | |
| Inventory—Repossessed Merchandise | 24,000 | |
| Accounts Payable | | $ 96,600 |
| Deferred Gross Profit, 1984 | | 45,600 |
| Capital Stock | | 200,000 |
| Retained Earnings | | 84,800 |
| Sales | | 424,000 |
| Installment Sales | | 300,000 |
| Cost of Sales | 330,000 | |
| Cost of Installment Sales | 195,000 | |
| Gain or Loss on Repossessions | 800 | |
| Selling and Administrative Expenses | 132,000 | |
| | $1,151,000 | $1,151,000 |

    The accounting department has prepared the following analysis of cash receipts for the year:

| | |
|---|---:|
| Cash sales (including repossessed merchandise) | $424,000 |
| Installment accounts receivable, 1984 | 104,000 |
| Installment accounts receivable, 1985 | 148,000 |
| Other | 36,000 |
| Total | $712,000 |

Repossessions recorded during the year are summarized as follows:

| | 1984 |
|---|---|
| Uncollected balance | $8,000 |
| Loss on repossession | 800 |
| Repossessed merchandise | 4,800 |

**Instructions**

From the trial balance and accompanying information:

(a) Compute the rate of gross profit for 1984 and 1985.

(b) Prepare closing entries as of December 31, 1985 under the installment method of accounting.

(c) Prepare a statement of income for the year ended December 31, 1985. Include only the realized gross profit in the income statement.

**P19-10** Selected transactions of Threedee TV Sales Company are presented below:

1. A television set costing $560 is sold to John Engstrom on November 1, 1984 for $800. Engstrom makes a down payment of $200 and agrees to pay $25 on the first of each month for 24 months thereafter.

2. Engstrom pays the $25 installment due December 1, 1984.

3. On December 31, 1984, the appropriate entries are made to record profit realized on the installment sales.

4. The first seven 1985 installments of $25 each are paid by Engstrom. (Make one entry.)

5. In August 1985 the set is repossessed, after Engstrom fails to pay the August 1 installment and indicates that he will be unable to continue the payments. The estimated fair value of the repossessed set is $130.

**Instructions**

Prepare journal entries to record on the books of Threedee TV Sales Company the transactions above.

**P19-11** The following summarized information relates to the installment sales activity of Allabuy Stores, Inc. for the year 1983:

| | |
|---|---|
| Installment sales during 1983 | $600,000 |
| Cost of goods sold on installment basis | 348,000 |
| Collections from customers | 170,000 |
| Unpaid balances on merchandise repossessed | 20,000 |
| Estimated value of merchandise repossessed | 6,600 |

**Instructions**

(a) Prepare journal entries at the end of 1983 to record on the books of Allabuy Stores, Inc. the summarized data above.

(b) Prepare the entry to record the gross profit realized during 1983.

**P19-12** Cottonco Inc. sells merchandise for cash and also on the installment plan. Entries to record cost of goods sold are made at the end of each year.

Repossessions of merchandise (sold in 1984) were made in 1985 and were recorded correctly as follows:

| | | |
|---|---|---|
| Deferred Gross Profit, 1984 | 4,200 | |
| Repossessed Merchandise | 6,000 | |
| Loss on Repossessions | 1,800 | |
| Installment Accounts Receivable, 1984 | | 12,000 |

Part of this repossessed merchandise was sold for cash during 1985, and the sale was recorded by a debit to Cash and a credit to Sales.

The inventory of repossessed merchandise on hand December 31, 1985, is $4,000; of new merchandise, $100,000. There was no repossessed merchandise on hand January 1, 1985. Collections on accounts receivable during 1985 were:

| | |
|---|---|
| Installment Accounts Receivable, 1984 | $80,000 |
| Installment Accounts Receivable, 1985 | 50,000 |

The cost of the merchandise sold under the installment plan during 1985 was $108,800. The rate of gross profit on 1984 and on 1985 installment sales can be computed from the information given above.

---

Cottonco Inc.
TRIAL BALANCE
December 31, 1985

| | Dr. | Cr. |
|---|---|---|
| Cash | $101,400 | |
| Installment Accounts Receivable, 1984 | 72,000 | |
| Installment Accounts Receivable, 1985 | 110,000 | |
| Inventory, Jan. 1, 1985 | 120,000 | |
| Repossessed Merchandise | 6,000 | |
| Accounts Payable | | $ 24,000 |
| Deferred Gross Profit, 1984 | | 53,200 |
| Capital Stock, Common | | 200,000 |
| Retained Earnings | | 40,000 |
| Sales | | 400,000 |
| Installment Sales | | 160,000 |
| Purchases | 360,000 | |
| Loss on Repossessions | 1,800 | |
| Operating Expenses | 106,000 | |
| | $877,200 | $877,200 |

**Instructions**

(a) From the trial balance and other information given above, prepare adjusting and closing entries as of December 31, 1985.

(b) Prepare an income statement for the year ended December 31, 1985. Include only the realized gross profit in the income statement.

**P19-13** On January 1, 1983, Limbo's Restaurants, Inc., entered into a franchise agreement granting the franchisee the right to do business under Limbo's name. According to the terms of the franchise agreement, Limbo has an option to purchase the restaurant at any time within the next five years. It is probable that this option will be exercised. The initial franchise fee is $75,000. The franchisee paid $45,000 down and gave a $30,000 4-year note payable, on which interest should be imputed at 10%. Straight-line interest amortization is used. Collectibility of the note is reasonably assured, and Limbo's had substantially performed all services by January 1, 1983. Their terms of the franchise agreement provide that the franchisee must pay a continuing annual fee of $20,000. Half of this is for the purchase of food and supplies from Limbo's at the normal sales price. During 1983, Limbo's provided services costing $4,000 to the franchisee and provided food and supplies costing $7,000. At December 31, 1983, Limbo's purchased the restaurant from the franchisee, paying $100,000 and canceling the franchisee's note.

**Instructions**

Prepare the journal entries needed on the books of Limbo's Restaurants, Inc. to record each of the following:

(a) January 1, 1983: receipt of the initial franchise fee.

(b) During 1983: receipt of the continuing franchise fee and provision of food, supplies, and services to the franchisee.

(c) December 31, 1983: amortization of discount on the note and the purchase of the restaurant. The straight-line method of discount amortization is used.

**P19-14** On January 1, 1983, Vacation QuikFoto, Inc., entered into a franchise agreement with a local business, allowing the business (franchisee) to open an outlet under Vacation's name. The franchisee paid 40% of the initial $15,000 franchise fee, and gave a $9,000, 2-year, 12% note payable for the difference. Interest on the note is due annually on December 31. In return for the initial franchise fee, Vacation located a site in a shopping mall, negotiated the lease, and installed photo-processing equipment. According to the franchise agreement, the franchisee is to pay a $7,000 continuing annual franchise fee, of which 5% must be spent by Vacation on local advertising. When the initial franchise fee is paid, the franchisee has an option to purchase the photo-processing equipment at 50% of its fair market value. It is estimated that the equipment will be worth $10,000 on January 1, 1983. At January 1, 1983, collectibility of the franchisee's note was reasonably assured, and Vacation had substantially performed all contracted services. During 1983 and 1984, Vacation fulfilled its obligation to provide local advertising services, and incurred other annual costs of $2,500. On January 1, 1985, the franchisee paid the note and exercised its bargain purchase option on the equipment.

**Instructions**

Prepare the journal entries needed on the books of Vacation QuikFoto, Inc. to record each of the following:

(a) January 1, 1983: receipt of the initial franchise fee.

(b) During 1983: receipt of the continuing franchise fee and incurrence of advertising and other costs.

(c) December 31, 1983: receipt of annual interest on the note.

(d) During 1984: receipt of the continuing franchise fee and incurrence of advertising and other costs.

(e) December 31, 1984: receipt of annual interest on the note.

(f) January 1, 1985: collection of the note and sale of the photo-processing equipment.

**P19-15** Curtiss Construction Company, Inc., entered into a firm fixed-price contract with Mellissa Packard Associates on July 1, 1981, to construct a four-story office building. At that time, Curtiss estimated that it would take between two and three years to complete the project. The total contract price for construction of the building is $4,000,000. Curtiss appropriately accounts for this contract under the completed-contract method in its financial statements and for income tax reporting. The building was deemed substantially completed on December 31, 1983. Estimated percentage of completion, accumulated contract costs incurred, estimated costs to complete the contract, and accumulated billings to Packard under the contract were as follows:

| | At December 31, 1981 | At December 31, 1982 | At December 31, 1983 |
|---|---|---|---|
| Percentage of completion | 10% | 60% | 100% |
| Contract costs incurred | $ 350,000 | $2,500,000 | $4,250,000 |
| Estimated costs to complete the contract | $3,150,000 | $1,700,000 | -0- |
| Billings to Packard | $ 720,000 | $2,160,000 | $3,600,000 |

**Instructions**

(a) Prepare schedules to compute the amount to be shown as "cost of uncompleted contract in excess of related billings" or "billings on uncompleted contract in excess of related costs" at December 31, 1981, 1982, and 1983. Ignore income taxes. Show supporting computations in good form.

(b) Prepare schedules to compute the profit or loss to be recognized as a result of this contract for the years ended December 31, 1981, 1982, and 1983. Ignore income taxes. Show supporting computations in good form. (AICPA adapted)

**P19–16** Frigidtemp Company, on January 2, 1983, entered into a contract with a manufacturing company to purchase room-size air conditioners and to sell the units on an installment plan with collections over approximately 30 months with no carrying charge.

For income tax purposes Frigidtemp elected to report income from its sales of air conditioners according to the installment method.

Purchases and sales of new units were as follows:

| | Units Purchased | | Units Sold | |
| Year | Quantity | Price Each | Quantity | Price Each |
| --- | --- | --- | --- | --- |
| 1983 | 1,200 | $120 | 1,000 | $180 |
| 1984 | 1,800 | 108 | 2,000 | 168 |
| 1985 | 800 | 126 | 700 | 171.60 |

Collections on installment sales were as follows:

| | Collections Received | | |
| | 1983 | 1984 | 1985 |
| --- | --- | --- | --- |
| 1983 sales | $36,000 | $72,000 | $ 72,000 |
| 1984 sales | | 84,000 | 138,000 |
| 1985 sales | | | 25,200 |

In 1985, 40 units from the 1984 sales were repossessed and sold for $87 each on the installment plan. At the time of repossession $1,440 had been collected from the original purchasers and the units had a fair value of $3,024.

General and administrative expenses for 1985 were $60,000. No charge has been made against current income for the applicable insurance expense from a three-year policy expiring June 30, 1986 costing $3,600, and for an advance payment of $12,000 on a new contract to purchase air conditioners beginning January 2, 1986.

**Instructions**

Assuming that the weighted-average method is used for determining the inventory cost, including repossessed merchandise, prepare schedules computing for 1983, 1984 and 1985:
(a) 1. The cost of goods sold on installments.
    2. The average unit cost of goods sold on installments for each year.
(b) The gross profit percentages for 1983, 1984 and 1985.
(c) The gain or loss on repossessions in 1985.
(d) The net income from installment sales for 1985 (ignore income taxes).

(AICPA adapted)

**P19–17** After a two-year search for a buyer, Hobson, Inc., sold its idle plant facility to Jackson Company for $700,000 on January 1, 1980. On this date the plant had a depreciated cost on Hobson's books of $500,000. Under the agreement Jackson paid $100,000 cash on January 1, 1980, and signed a $600,000 note bearing interest at 10%. The note was payable in installments of $100,000, $200,000, and $300,000 on January 1, 1981, 1982 and 1983, respectively. The note was secured by a mortgage on the property sold. Hobson appropriately accounted for the sale under the cost recovery method since there was no reasonable basis for estimating the degree of collectibility of the note receivable. Jackson repaid the note with three late installment payments, which were accepted by Hobson, as follows:

| Date of Payment | Principal | Interest |
| --- | --- | --- |
| July 1, 1981 | $100,000 | $90,000 |
| December 31, 1982 | 200,000 | 75,000 |
| February 1, 1984 | 300,000 | 32,500 |

On April 1, 1984, Hobson exchanged a tract of land, which it had acquired for $105,000 as a potential future building site, for a used printing press of Tyler Company, and paid a cash difference of $30,000. The fair value of the land was $190,000 on the exchange date based on a recent appraisal. The fair value of the printing press was not reasonably determinable, but it had a depreciated cost of $210,000 on Tyler's books at April 1, 1984.

**Instructions**

(a) Prepare a schedule (using the format shown below) to record the initial transaction for the sale of the idle plant facility, the application of subsequent cash collections on the note, and the necessary journal entry on the date the transaction is complete.

| Date | Cash Received | Note Receivable | Idle Plant (Net) | Deferred Income | Income Recognized |
|---|---|---|---|---|---|
|  | Debit | Dr. (Cr.) | (Credit) | Dr. (Cr.) | (Credit) |
| January 1, 1980 | $100,000 |  |  |  |  |
| July 1, 1981 | 190,000 |  |  |  |  |
| December 31, 1982 | 275,000 |  |  |  |  |
| February 1, 1984 | 332,500 |  |  |  |  |
| February 1, 1984 |  |  |  |  |  |

(b) Prepare the journal entry on Hobson's books to record the exchange transaction with Tyler. Show supporting computations in good form.

(AICPA adapted)

# CHAPTER 20

# Accounting for Income Taxes

Business income is generally subject to federal and state income taxes. In computing income taxes, businesses must complete tax returns including a statement showing the amount of income subject to tax. In general, the form and content of the tax return income statement are similar to the form and content of the accounting income statement. **Taxable income** in the tax return, however, is computed in accordance with prescribed tax regulations and rules, while **accounting income** is measured in accordance with generally accepted accounting principles. And, because the basic objectives of measuring taxable income are different from the objectives of measuring accounting income, tax rules are frequently different from accounting principles. Therefore, differences between taxable income and accounting income exist.

The differences between taxable income and accounting income give rise to **tax differences,** some of which must be recognized in the accounting records and in the resultant financial statements. Our interest in analyzing these tax differences is to determine their effect on the measurement of income tax expense for corporations. This chapter deals primarily with the accounting for tax differences between periods (**interperiod tax allocation**). The accounting requirements for tax allocation within a period (**intraperiod tax allocation**) were discussed in Chapter 4.

## PRINCIPLES OF TAX ALLOCATION

Accountants generally view the income tax as an expense that should be matched with the income to which it relates. The process of associating income tax expense with related income is known as **tax allocation.** Both interperiod tax allocation and intraperiod tax allocation are applications of the concept, "Let the tax follow the income."

### Interperiod Tax Allocation

Before 1954, the amount of income tax expense reported in external financial statements was almost always equal to the amount of income tax shown as payable in the tax return. Beginning in 1954, the Internal Revenue Code permitted use of accelerated depreciation methods for tax purposes even if the straight-line method was used for financial reporting purposes. Since then, a variety of provisions in the tax law have generated differences between the amount of income taxes currently payable and the amount of income tax expense currently recognizable in the income statement. For example, to induce companies to expand their investment in property, plant, and equipment, the Economic Recovery Tax Act of 1981 permits companies to use an accelerated cost recovery system (ACRS) that permits write-offs over periods as short as three years. These recovery periods are generally unrelated to and shorter than the useful lives that are appropriate for financial reporting.[1] To illustrate, assume that Nichols Real Estate purchased an apartment building on January 1, 1982 at a cost of $360,000, of which $300,000 is related to the building. The building is being depreciated for tax purposes over a 15-year period using the straight-line method. For accounting purposes, the useful life of the building is thirty years and it is also depreciated on a straight-line basis. Depreciation for tax purposes is $20,000 ($300,000 ÷ 15), whereas for financial reporting purposes it is $10,000 ($300,000 ÷ 30).

To illustrate the computation of taxes payable and tax expense (without interperiod tax allocation), assume that Nichols Real Estate has annual gross revenues of $200,000, annual operating expenses other than depreciation of $150,000, and is subject to an income tax rate of 40% of its income before tax. The computation of its income tax liability for each of the thirty years of the building's life is computed below.

|  | Each of the First 15 Years | Each of the Remaining 15 Years |
|---|---|---|
| **Nichols Real Estate COMPUTATION OF INCOME TAX LIABILITY** | | |
| Gross revenues | $200,000 | $200,000 |
| Operating expenses: | | |
| Other than depreciation | (150,000) | (150,000) |
| Depreciation | (20,000) | -0- |
| Taxable income | $ 30,000 | $ 50,000 |
| Income taxes payable (40%) | $ 12,000 | $ 20,000 |

Without interperiod tax allocation, the income tax expense reported on the accounting income statements would be the same as the income tax payable computed on the tax returns. The accounting income statements, **without interperiod tax allocation,** appear on the top of page 888.

Because income tax expense and the income taxes payable are the same, the journal entry to record the tax expense for 1982 is as follows:

| | | |
|---|---|---|
| Income Tax Expense | 12,000 | |
| Income Tax Payable | | 12,000 |

During the first fifteen years, the income statements on page 888 show net income of $28,000 a year and an effective tax rate of only 30% ($12,000/$40,000) on income before taxes (pretax accounting income). This situation occurs because the company is temporarily enjoying a substantial tax advantage. After the fifteen-year period the company will continue to depreciate the building for accounting purposes but will not be entitled to

---

[1] A short discussion of ACRS and its treatment of depreciation was provided in Chapter 12. A more detailed discussion is presented later in this chapter.

| | Nichols Real Estate PARTIAL INCOME STATEMENTS (Without Interperiod Tax Allocation) | |
|---|---|---|
| | Each of the First 15 Years | Each of the Remaining 15 Years |
| Gross revenues | $200,000 | $200,000 |
| Operating expenses: | | |
|   Other than depreciation | (150,000) | (150,000) |
|   Depreciation | (10,000) | (10,000) |
| Income before taxes (pretax accounting income) | 40,000 | 40,000 |
|   Income taxes | (12,000) | (20,000) |
|     Net income | $ 28,000 | $ 20,000 |

depreciation on it for taxation purposes. The result will be to increase income tax expense and decrease net income, so that the effective tax rate in the remaining fifteen years is 50% ($20,000/$40,000).

## Reasons for Interperiod Tax Allocation

Many accountants believe that the income presentation for Nichols Real Estate shown above gives an unrealistic view of the company's activities and is misleading to financial statement users. This is because depreciation expense for accounting purposes is based on a thirty-year asset life, whereas the income tax expense computed without allocation is determined as if a fifteen-year asset life had been used. Consequently, reported tax expense is not matched with reported income before taxes.

For Nichols Real Estate, although total depreciation is the same, the use of an accelerated method of depreciation for tax purposes results in a timing difference for expense recognition. To avoid distortion of the income statement, many argue that reported income tax expense should be adjusted for timing differences such as the one described. Interperiod tax allocation is the accepted and required adjustment process that relates tax expense to pretax accounting income when such tax expense is different from actual taxes paid because of differences in the timing of revenue or expense recognition. Nichols' income statements with interperiod tax allocation appear on page 889.

Note that the only difference between the illustrations without and with tax allocation procedures relates to the reporting of income tax expense and net income. Without allocation, $12,000 income tax expense is reported in each of the first fifteen years and $20,000 in the last fifteen years. With allocation, $16,000 income tax expense is reported in each of the thirty years for a total reported tax expense of $480,000. As indicated above, many believe that income tax allocation is appropriate because the income tax expense follows the reported pretax accounting income. Thus, a constant 40% rate is employed over the thirty-year period. Without interperiod income tax allocation, the effective income tax rate changed from 30% to 50% at the end of the first fifteen years.

## Deferred Income Taxes

As indicated earlier, if interperiod allocation procedures are not employed, the amounts of income tax expense and income taxes currently payable are the same, and a single entry is

| Nichols Real Estate PARTIAL INCOME STATEMENTS (With Interperiod Tax Allocation) | Each of the First 15 Years | Each of the Remaining 15 Years |
|---|---|---|
| Gross revenues | $200,000 | $200,000 |
| Operating expenses: | | |
| Other than depreciation | (150,000) | (150,000) |
| Depreciation | (10,000) | (10,000) |
| Income before taxes (pretax accounting income) | 40,000 | 40,000 |
| Income tax expense | (16,000) | (16,000) |
| Net income | $ 24,000 | $ 24,000 |

adequate to journalize the income tax accrual. Such is not the case with interperiod tax allocation because the amounts reported for income tax expense and income taxes payable are different. As a result, when interperiod tax allocation procedures are employed, accounting tax expense is debited to Income Tax Expense, the taxes due and payable are credited to Income Taxes Payable, and the difference between these two amounts is debited (or credited) to an account entitled Deferred Income Taxes. In the period in which a timing difference reverses, the amount accumulated in Deferred Income Taxes is reduced, as it absorbs the difference between reported tax expense and the tax actually payable for those later years.

To illustrate, for Nichols Real Estate during each of the first fifteen years, income tax expense, based on pretax accounting income, is $16,000 (40% × $40,000). Income tax payable, based on taxable income, is $12,000 (40% × $30,000). The $4,000 difference between the two amounts is due to **the tax effect of the timing difference** in reporting depreciation ([$20,000 − $10,000] × 40%). This would be recorded with the following entry:

| | | |
|---|---|---|
| Income Tax Expense | 16,000 | |
| Income Tax Payable | | 12,000 |
| Deferred Income Taxes | | 4,000 |

At the end of fifteen years the Deferred Income Taxes account would have fifteen credits of $4,000 each as follows:

| Deferred Income Taxes | |
|---|---|
| 1982 | 4,000 |
| ⸾ | ⸾ |
| 1996 | 4,000 |
| Total (15 yrs. × 4,000) | 60,000 |

Deferred Income Taxes are presented in the liability section of the balance sheet if the account has a credit balance and as an asset if it has a debit balance.

During the next fifteen years, the income tax actually payable each year will be $20,000 (40% × $50,000). The income statement would continue to report income tax expense of $16,000. For each of the last fifteen years of the building's life, a charge of $4,000 should be made to the Deferred Income Taxes account as follows:

| | | |
|---|---|---|
| Income Tax Expense | 16,000 | |
| Deferred Income Taxes | 4,000 | |
| Income Tax Payable | | 20,000 |

The Deferred Income Taxes account as it would appear at the end of the asset's life is shown below.

| Deferred Income Taxes | | | |
|---|---|---|---|
| 1997 | 4,000 | 1982 | 4,000 |
| 2011 | 4,000 | 1996 | 4,000 |
| Total | 60,000 | Total | 60,000 |

Note that a zero balance in deferred income taxes results at the end of the asset's useful life.

### Intraperiod Tax Allocation

Refer to pages 142–144, where income statements with and without intraperiod tax allocation were presented. You should refer to that discussion at this point, and recall that intraperiod tax allocation involves apportioning reported tax expense among the following reported items: (1) income from continuing operations, (2) discontinued operations, (3) extraordinary items, (4) changes in accounting principle, and (5) prior period adjustments.

Frequently, to provide informative disclosure to financial statement users, both intraperiod and interperiod tax allocation are applied. To illustrate, assume that Nichols Real Estate has $150,000 of operating expenses for 1982 including an extraordinary loss, before taxes, of $50,000. GAAP requires that the extraordinary loss be reported, net of tax effect, in a separate section of the income statement. The separate disclosure of the loss, along with intraperiod allocation of the tax effect associated with it, helps financial statement users evaluate earnings trends and the impact of taxes on a company's operations. In the Nichols Real Estate example, although taxes paid in 1982 are $12,000, the annual tax expense to be reported on the income statement is $16,000, as determined previously. With intraperiod tax allocation, the total $16,000 tax expense for 1982 would be reported in two components: (1) as a $36,000 tax expense associated with the $90,000 ($40,000 + $50,000) income before taxes and extraordinary items, and (2) as a $20,000 tax saving associated with the $50,000 extraordinary loss.[2] The company's income statement for 1982 as it should appear with both interperiod tax allocation and intraperiod tax allocation, is shown at the top of page 891.

---

[2]This assumes that the 40% tax rate is applicable to the extraordinary loss as well as to the other items of revenue and expense. In practice, special tax rates are frequently applicable to items classified as "extraordinary" for accounting purposes.

Nichols Real Estate
PARTIAL INCOME STATEMENTS
(With Interperiod and Intraperiod Tax Allocation)

|  |  | The First Year (1982) |
|---|---|---|
| Gross revenues |  | $200,000 |
| Operating expenses: |  |  |
| Other than depreciation |  | (100,000) |
| Depreciation |  | (10,000) |
| Income before taxes and extraordinary loss |  | 90,000 |
| Income tax expense |  | (36,000) |
| Income before extraordinary loss |  | 54,000 |
| Extraordinary loss | $50,000 |  |
| Less tax saving | 20,000 | (30,000) |
| Net income |  | $ 24,000 |

Tax allocation then is the process of associating (matching) reported tax expense with reported income. **Interperiod** tax allocation involves determination of the **amount** of tax expense to be reported in a particular accounting period; this is done by matching tax expense to accounting income. **Intraperiod** tax allocation involves determination of the **format** to be used in disclosing tax expense within a particular period; this is done by apportioning reported tax expense to the related components of reported earnings.

### Interperiod Tax Allocation—Specific Differences

Numerous items create differences between taxable income and pretax accounting income. For purposes of accounting recognition these differences are of two types: (1) timing differences and (2) permanent differences.

**Timing Differences**    **Timing differences** arise when items of revenue and expense are included in the computation of accounting income in one period and in the computation of taxable income in a different period. Timing differences originate in one period and reverse or "turn around" in one or more subsequent periods. When they originate, some timing differences result in reporting less tax expense than the amount of taxes currently payable; when these timing differences reverse, the accounting tax expense is greater than the taxes paid. For other timing differences, accounting tax expense exceeds taxes payable in the period the timing differences originate, and is less than taxes payable in the period of reversal. **The profession concluded that interperiod tax allocation is required "to account for the tax effects of transactions which involve timing differences."**[3] Examples of items that result in timing differences are classified on the top of page 892.[4]

[3] "Accounting for Income Taxes," *Opinions of the Accounting Principles Board No. 11* (New York: AICPA, 1967), par. 16.

[4] In addition to the typical problems associated with deferred income taxes, a number of professional pronouncements have been issued involving special areas. See "Accounting for Income Taxes—Special Areas," *Opinions of the Accounting Principles Board No. 23* (New York: AICPA, 1972); "Accounting for Income Taxes—Investments in Common Stock Accounted for by the Equity

---

**EXAMPLES OF TIMING DIFFERENCES**

1. Revenues or gains that are included in taxable income **later** than in accounting income (these give rise to initial credits to Deferred Income Taxes):
   a. Gross profit on installment sales.
   b. Gross profit from long-term construction contracts, where the completed-contract method is used for tax purposes and the percentage-of-completion method is used for accounting purposes.
   c. Earnings from investments in stock, where income is recognized according to the equity method for accounting purposes and when dividends are later received for tax purposes.

2. Revenues or gains that are included in taxable income **earlier** than in accounting income (these give rise to initial debits to Deferred Income Taxes):
   a. Rents, royalties, service fees, and interest revenue collected in advance.

3. Expenses or losses that are deducted for taxable income **later** than for accounting income (these give rise to initial debits to Deferred Income Taxes):
   a. Estimated costs of guarantees and warranties.
   b. Estimated losses on inventories, purchase commitments, uncollectible receivables, and short-term marketable securities.
   c. Estimated losses on pending lawsuits and claims.

4. Expenses or losses that are deducted for taxable income determination **earlier** than for accounting income (these give rise to initial credits to Deferred Income Taxes):
   a. Use of accelerated depreciation for tax purposes and straight-line depreciation for accounting purposes.
   b. Use of shorter asset lives for tax purposes than for accounting purposes.
   c. Interest and taxes during construction that are deducted when incurred for tax purposes and capitalized for accounting purposes.

---

**Permanent Differences**   Some differences between taxable income and accounting income are permanent. **Permanent differences** are items that (1) enter into accounting income but **never** into taxable income or (2) enter into taxable income but **never** into accounting income. Congress has enacted a variety of tax law provisions in an effort to attain certain political, economic, and social objectives. Some of these provisions exclude certain revenues from taxation, limit the deductibility of certain expenses, and permit the deduction of certain other expenses in excess of costs incurred. A corporation that has tax-free income, nondeductible expenses, or allowable deductions in excess of cost has an effective tax rate that is different from the statutory tax rate. The apparent discrepancy between the reported tax and the "normal" tax is not allocated between accounting periods. Since permanent differences affect only the period in which they occur, they are not reversed or offset by corresponding differences in subsequent periods. **The profession concluded that interperiod tax allocation is not appropriate for permanent differences.** Examples of common items that result in permanent differences are provided at the top of page 893.

---

Method," *Opinions of the Accounting Principles Board No. 24* (New York: AICPA, 1972); "Accounting for Income Taxes—Oil and Gas," *Statement of Financial Accounting Standards No. 9* (Stamford, Conn.: FASB, 1974); "Applicability of Indefinite Reversal Criteria to Timing Differences," *FASB Interpretation No. 22* (Stamford, Conn.: FASB, 1978); "Accounting for Unused Investment Credit," *FASB Interpretation No. 25* (Stamford, Conn.: FASB, 1978); "Accounting for Tax Benefits Releated to U.K. Tax Legislation Concerning Stock Relief," *Statement of Financial Accounting Standards No. 31* (Stamford, Conn.: FASB, 1979); "Application of Percentage Limitations in Recognizing Investment Tax Credit," *Statement of Financial Accounting Standards No. 32* (Stamford, Conn.: FASB, 1980). In addition, a number of *FASB Technical Bulletins* address special problems associated with deferred income taxes.

---

**EXAMPLES OF PERMANENT DIFFERENCES**

**1.** Items recognized for accounting purposes but **not** for tax purposes:
   a. Interest received on state and municipal obligations.
   b. Proceeds from life insurance carried by the company on key officers or employees.
   c. Compensation expense associated with certain employee stock options.
   d. Premiums paid for life insurance carried by the company on key officers or employees (company is beneficiary).
   e. Fines and expenses resulting from a violation of law.
   f. Amortization of goodwill.
   g. Charitable contributions in excess of the tax limitation (10% of taxable income).
   h. Expenses incurred in obtaining tax-exempt income.

**2.** Items recognized for tax purposes but **not** for accounting purposes:
   a. "Percentage depletion" of natural resources in excess of their cost.
   b. Net operating loss deduction. This special feature of tax law is designed to give taxpayers who suffer a loss in a bad year some relief from taxes paid in the three years immediately preceding and/or the 15 years following the loss year.
   c. The 85% deduction for dividends received from U.S. corporations.

---

## Timing and Permanent Differences Illustrated

Interperiod tax allocation procedures require separate computations of income tax expense, income taxes payable, and the tax effects of timing differences. When income taxes are recorded, the taxes due and payable are credited to Income Tax Payable, the appropriate deferred income taxes (either a debit or credit amount) are determined, and the accounting tax expense is debited to Income Tax Expense. In the period(s) a timing difference reverses, the amount accumulated in Deferred Income Taxes is reduced, as it absorbs the difference between reported tax expense and the tax actually payable for those later years.

Depending on whether taxable income exceeds pretax accounting income or vice versa in the year of origination, an originating difference may result in either a debit or credit to Deferred Income Taxes. An **originating difference** is the initial timing difference between pretax accounting income and taxable income, whether the pretax accounting income exceeds, or is exceeded by, taxable income. A **reversing difference,** on the other hand, occurs when timing differences that originated in prior periods are eliminated and the tax effect is removed from the Deferred Income Taxes account. As a result, a reversing difference may result in a debit or credit depending on the originating difference. In short, an originating and reversing difference may be in either direction depending upon the circumstances.

To illustrate the computations used when both timing and permanent differences exist, assume that the Bio-Tech Company reported pretax accounting income of $200,000 in each of the years 1982, 1983, and 1984. The company was subject to a 30% tax rate, and has the following differences between pretax accounting income and taxable income:

**1.** Gross profit in 1983 on installment receivables, $18,000, was reported for tax purposes over an 18-month period at a constant amount per month beginning January 1, 1983. The original sale occurred in 1982.

**2.** Goodwill amortization was $5,000 in 1983 and 1984. This was not deductible for tax purposes.

The first item above is a timing difference and the second is a permanent difference. The reconciliation of Bio-Tech Company's pretax accounting income to taxable income and the computation of taxes payable appear at the top of page 894.

| Bio-Tech Company RECONCILIATION AND COMPUTATION OF INCOME TAX PAYABLE | | | |
|---|---|---|---|
| | 1982 | 1983 | 1984 |
| Pretax accounting income | $200,000 | $200,000 | $200,000 |
| **Permanent difference** | | | |
| Goodwill amortization | | 5,000 | 5,000 |
| **Timing difference** | | | |
| Originating | (18,000) | | |
| Reversing | | 12,000 | 6,000 |
| Taxable income | 182,000 | 217,000 | 211,000 |
| × Tax rate | .30 | .30 | .30 |
| Income tax payable | $ 54,600 | $ 65,100 | $ 63,300 |

Notice that differences causing pretax accounting income to exceed taxable income are deducted from pretax accounting income when determining taxable income, and vice versa.

Computations necessary for recording income taxes would be as follows:

| Bio-Tech Company COMPUTATION OF DEFERRED TAXES AND INCOME TAX EXPENSE | | | |
|---|---|---|---|
| | 1982 | 1983 | 1984 |
| **Income tax payable** | $54,600 cr. | $65,100 cr. | $63,300 cr. |
| Tax effects of timing differences | | | |
| Originating | 18,000 | | |
| Reversing | | 12,000 | 6,000 |
| × Tax rate | .30 | .30 | .30 |
| **Deferred income taxes** | $ 5,400 cr. | $ 3,600 dr. | $ 1,800 dr. |
| **Income tax expense** (to balance) | $60,000 dr. | $61,500 dr. | $61,500 dr. |

Deferred Income Taxes is **debited** whenever taxable income exceeds pretax accounting income adjusted for permanent differences. Similarly, Deferred Income Taxes is **credited** whenever taxable income is less than pretax accounting income adjusted for permanent differences. The latter is the usual situation encountered in practice, because of company policies that dictate use of tax methods that postpone recognition of taxable income. **The tax effects of permanent differences have no impact on the Deferred Income Taxes account,** because interperiod tax allocation is not used for permanent differences. Consequently, whenever permanent differences exist, accounting tax expense cannot be computed directly by multiplying pretax accounting income by the statutory tax rate, as was done previously in the Nichols Real Estate example. A company with permanent differences has an effective tax rate that is different from the statutory tax rate. In this example, although the statutory tax rate is 30%, Bio-Tech Company's effective tax rate for 1983 and 1984 is

30.75% ($61,500 ÷ $200,000). The debit to Income Tax Expense is equal to the amount needed to balance the entry when recording taxes. It is essentially a "plug" figure.[5]

Bio-Tech Company would make the following entries to record income taxes:

**December 31, 1982**

| | | |
|---|---|---|
| Income Tax Expense | 60,000 | |
| Income Tax Payable | | 54,600 |
| Deferred Income Taxes | | 5,400 |

**December 31, 1983**

| | | |
|---|---|---|
| Income Tax Expense | 61,500 | |
| Deferred Income Taxes | 3,600 | |
| Income Tax Payable | | 65,100 |

**December 31, 1984**

| | | |
|---|---|---|
| Income Tax Expense | 61,500 | |
| Deferred Income Taxes | 1,800 | |
| Income Tax Payable | | 63,300 |

At the end of 1984, after the timing difference has reversed, the balance in the Deferred Income Taxes account is zero.

## Financial Statement Presentation

**Deferred income tax credit** is the excess of the accounting income tax expense relative to certain transactions over the income tax payable applicable to those same transactions, and **deferred income tax debit** is the excess of the income tax payable applicable to certain transactions over the accounting income tax expense relative to those same transactions. Classification of deferred income tax credits on the balance sheet as a liability is seriously questioned by some accountants. These individuals argue that no present obligation exists because it is contingent upon having future taxable income. Other accountants believe that the term "deferred" is a misnomer when used in relation to tax effect credits resulting from tax allocation, because these items have the characteristics of accruals instead of deferrals. Deferred income tax credits are reported as either current or noncurrent liabilities, although some companies report the long-term portion of them on the balance sheet between the long-term debt and the stockholders' equity sections. Deferred income tax debits, which are not as common as the credits, are reported as either current or noncurrent assets.

**GAAP Disclosures**    Relative to these problems, the profession concluded that deferred income tax debits (charges) and credits do not represent receivables or payables in the usual economic sense. They should be classified on the balance sheet as current or noncurrent depending on the classification of the balance sheet asset or liability to which the deferral relates. A deferred tax charge or credit is considered to be related to an asset or liability if reduction[6] of the asset or liability will cause the timing difference to reverse or turn around. Some timing differences, however, are not related to specific assets or liabilities, either because there is no associated asset or liability account, or because reduc-

---

[5]This statement somewhat oversimplifies the problem. The income tax expense amount can be proven by adjusting for the permanent difference. Also, the "with and without method" discussed in the appendix to this chapter provides an approach to computing tax expense.

[6]The term "reduction" includes amortization, sale, or other realization of an asset and amortization, payment, or other satisfaction of a liability.

tion of the associated asset or liability will not cause the timing difference to reverse. In these cases, the timing difference should be classified as current or noncurrent "based on the expected reversal date of the specific timing difference."[7]

To illustrate, assume that Morgan, Inc. records bad debt expense using the allowance method for accounting purposes and the direct write-off method for tax purposes. The company currently has Accounts Receivable and Allowance for Doubtful Accounts balances of $2 million and $100,000, respectively. In addition, given a 50% tax rate, it has a debit balance in Deferred Income Taxes of $50,000 (50% $\times$ $100,000). The $50,000 debit balance in Deferred Income Taxes is considered to be related to the Accounts Receivable and the Allowance for Doubtful Accounts balances because collection or write-off of the receivables will cause the deferred income taxes to reverse. Therefore, the Deferred Income Taxes account is classified as current, the same as the Accounts Receivable and Allowance for Doubtful Accounts balances.

To illustrate the classification when the timing difference is not related to a particular asset or liability account, assume that Morgan, Inc. decides to change to the allowance method for tax purposes, so that the same method of recording bad debts will be employed for both accounting and tax purposes. As a result, Morgan will now have an additional $100,000 deductible expense for tax purposes because of the switch to the allowance method. Furthermore, assume that the IRS will permit the favorable tax treatment that results to Morgan only if it is phased in evenly over a five-year period. That is, Morgan is entitled to a $50,000 ($100,000 $\times$ 50%) refund (or tax savings) to be received at the rate of $10,000 per year for five years, this year and the next four. The deferred income taxes do not relate to Accounts Receivable or Allowance for Doubtful Accounts because collection or write-off of the receivables will not cause the timing differences to reverse; the timing differences will reverse over time. At the date of change, since, $10,000 of the deferred income taxes would be realized immediately in the form of a refund (or tax savings), $10,000 would be classified as a current (receivable) item, and $30,000 would be classified as a noncurrent receivable.

In practice, most companies engage in a large number of transactions that give rise to deferred taxes. The balance in the deferred taxes account should be analyzed into its components and classified on the balance sheet in two categories: one for the **net** current amount and one for the **net** noncurrent amount. This procedure is summarized as indicated below.

1. Classify the amounts as current or noncurrent. If they are related to a specific asset or liability, they should be classified in the same manner as the related asset or liability. If not so related, they should be classified on the basis of the expected reversal date.

2. Determine the net current amount by summing the various debits and credits classified as current. If the net result is a debit, report on the balance sheet as a current asset; if a credit, report as a current liability.

3. Determine the net noncurrent amount by summing the various debits and credits classified as noncurrent. If the net result is a debit, report on the balance sheet as a noncurrent asset; if a credit, report as a long-term liability.

To illustrate, assume that K. Scott Company's Deferred Taxes account has a $205,000 credit balance at December 31, 1983. Analysis of the account reveals the following:

---

[7]"Balance Sheet Classification of Deferred Income Taxes," *Statement of Financial Accounting Standards No. 37* (Stamford, Conn.: FASB, 1980), par. 4.

### K. Scott Company
### CLASSIFICATION OF TIMING DIFFERENCES AS CURRENT OR NONCURRENT

| Timing Difference | Resulting Balance in Deferred Taxes | Related Balance Sheet Account | Classification |
|---|---|---|---|
| 1. Rent collected in advance: recognized when earned for accounting purposes and when received for tax purposes. | $ 42,000 dr. | Unearned Rent | current |
| 2. Use of straight-line depreciation for accounting purposes and accelerated depreciation for tax purposes. | 214,000 cr. | Equipment | noncurrent |
| 3. Recognition of profits on installment sales during period of sale for accounting purposes and during period of collection for tax purposes. | 45,000 cr. | Installment Accounts Receivable | current |
| 4. Warranty liabilities: recognized for accounting purposes at time of sale; for tax purposes at time paid. | 12,000 dr. | Estimated Liability Under Warranties | current |
| Total | $205,000 cr. | | |

The net current timing differences are $9,000 debit, and the net noncurrent timing differences are $214,000 credit. Consequently, deferred taxes would appear as follows on K. Scott's December 31, 1983 balance sheet:

| | |
|---|---|
| **Current Assets** | |
| Deferred Income Taxes | $  9,000 |
| **Long-term Liabilities** | |
| Deferred Income Taxes | $214,000 |

**SEC Disclosures**   For companies reporting to the SEC, the components of **income tax expense** must be segregated into (1) the current and noncurrent components, (2) the tax effects of current period timing differences, and (3) a reconciliation between the effective tax rate indicated by the book income and the statutory income tax rate.

The reason for this disclosure is twofold: first, when the oil companies in the mid-seventies were considered to have earned excess profits, many politicians and other interested parties attempted to determine the effective tax rates of these companies. Because this information was not available in published financial reports, pressure was exerted on the SEC to require this type of disclosure. Second, many investors are interested in the reconciliation of the book income to taxable income to assess the quality of the company's earnings. Earnings that are enhanced by a favorable tax effect should be examined carefully, particularly if the tax effect is nonrecurring. For example, one year Wang Laboratories reported net income of $3.3 million, or 82 cents a share, versus $3.1 million, or 77 cents, in the preceding period. All of the increase in net income and then some resulted from a tax rate that was lower in the current year than in the preceding year (32.6% versus 39%). The difference in the rates was due primarily to the investment tax credit.

In compliance with the SEC's disclosure requirements, Burlington Northern Inc. presented the components of income tax expense in its 1981 annual report as follows:

---

### Burlington Northern Inc.

**(4) INCOME TAXES**

The provision (credit) for income taxes consists of the following:

(Thousands of Dollars)

| | 1981 | 1980 | 1979 |
|---|---|---|---|
| **Currently Payable:** | | | |
| Federal | $ (1,214) | $29,500 | $ 7,577 |
| State | 6,663 | 12,637 | 5,645 |
| Total | 5,449 | 42,137 | 13,222 |
| **Deferred:** | | | |
| Federal | 129,291 | 40,212 | (16,403) |
| State | 12,072 | 2,420 | 2,931 |
| Total | 141,363 | 42,632 | (13,472) |
| TOTAL—NET | $(146,812) | $84,769 | $ (250) |

The Federal income tax rate was 46% for each year. The difference between such rate and our effective tax rates, which are computed by dividing total tax expense by income before income taxes, were:

| | 1981 | 1980 | 1979 |
|---|---|---|---|
| Statutory rate | 46.0% | 46.0% | 46.0% |
| Reduction in taxes resulting from investment tax credit | (8.6) | (17.4) | (43.5) |
| Reduction in taxes relating to capital gains tax rates on certain sales of real estate and investments, timber and other natural resource income | (2.7) | (3.7) | (6.7) |
| State income taxes net of Federal tax return benefit | 2.4 | 2.6 | 2.6 |
| Other | (2.1) | .1 | 1.5 |
| Effective Rate | 35.0% | 27.6% | (.1)% |

Deferred income taxes are the part of total income tax expense which are not payable on the current year's tax return. Deferred taxes result from certain expenses being deductible and certain income being taxable in different years for income tax and accounting purposes. The most significant of these items and the tax effect of each are as follows:

| Description: | Tax Effect (Thousands of Dollars) | | |
|---|---|---|---|
| | 1981 | 1980 | 1979 |
| Excess of tax over book depreciation | $ 36,265 | $ 21,077 | $ 15,839 |
| Ratable depreciation of railroad track structure | 203,179 | | |
| Sale of tax benefits | (8,100) | | |
| Asset depreciation range adjustment— expenses capitalized for tax purposes—net | 3,600 | 5,208 | 6,074 |
| Revenues and gains taxable in other years | 21,661 | 14,606 | 6,573 |
| Accruals for casualties and claims and other expenses not deductible in the current year | (40,674) | (21,646) | (16,645) |
| Amortization of railroad grading and tunnel bores allowed for tax purposes | 2,873 | 3,747 | 3,427 |
| Net operating loss carryover | (48,179) | | |
| Other | 6,819 | (2,493) | 2,195 |
| Investment credit applicable to deferred taxes | (36,081) | 22,133 | (30,935) |
| Total | $141,363 | $ 42,632 | $(13,472) |

---

For another example refer to the Tenneco Inc. annual report (see pages 201 and 202) footnotes, which contain a comprehensive presentation of the components of income tax expense and the variation in tax rates.

## INTERPERIOD TAX ALLOCATION—PRACTICAL PROBLEMS

Each of the preceding computations of deferred income taxes involved a single timing difference between taxable income and pretax accounting income. It was relatively easy to determine the exact tax effect, the build-up of the deferral, and the reversal or turnaround. This method is called the **individual item basis.** In practice, however, it is typical for a corporation to have a multitude of items handled differently for tax purposes and accounting purposes. Because of the volume of records which must be kept, it becomes impractical to identify, follow, and account for each individual transaction. To simplify computation of the tax effects of numerous timing differences, one of two acceptable alternatives to the individual item basis may be employed. These two methods are called (1) the "group-of-similar-items, gross change basis," and (2) the "group-of-similar-items, net change basis," or simply the "gross change method" and the "net change method."

In addition, it was assumed in the preceding illustrations that the tax rate remained constant over several periods, and that the same tax rate was applicable to all components of income. In practice, however, these assumptions would not be valid. The tax rates experienced by a particular company vary because of legislative changes in the tax law, and because of changes in the company's amount of taxable income. Further, special tax rates may be applicable to the various components of income reported in a particular year. The **gross change method** and the **net change method** are alternative computational approaches that deal with the accounting problems arising from changes in tax rates. The **with and without technique** is a computational approach that deals with the accounting problems arising from such tax provisions as graduated rate schedules, special capital gains tax rates, investment tax credits, foreign tax credits, and carryovers of certain losses and expenses. This procedure is discussed in the appendix to this chapter.

## Gross Change Method

Under the gross change method, the tax effects of timing differences originating in the current period are computed at current tax rates. Reversals of timing differences that originated in prior periods are removed from the Deferred Income Taxes account at the applicable prior tax rates. To facilitate the computations, the following steps are used:

1. Separate all timing differences, whether originating or reversing, into groups of similar items. For example, group all installment sales transactions, or all depreciation items.
2. Classify the items within each group as either originating or reversing.
3. Determine the tax effect of the aggregate originating differences within a particular group by using the current tax rates.
4. Determine the tax effect of the aggregate reversing differences in the group by using the applicable prior tax rates (that is, the rates in effect when the differences originated).
5. For each group, the difference between (3) and (4) constitutes the amount of change in the Deferred Income Taxes account for the period.

Under this method, when a group of similar timing differences reverses, the balance in deferred taxes is written down (amortized) at the same tax rates that were in effect when the timing differences originated. Since it is unlikely that all of the reversing timing differences within a particular group originated at the same tax rates, it is necessary to select an appropriate tax rate to be applied to these timing differences in the periods they reverse. In practice, either a FIFO flow assumption or an average rate assumption may be used to determine the tax effect of the reversing differences within a particular group. If the **FIFO basis** is employed, a record must be maintained of all the originating differences and the rates at which they originated. As these timing differences reverse, the first-in differences are the amounts first reversed. If an **average rate basis** is used, the amount of the reduction in deferred taxes is determined by multiplying the aggregate reversing differences within a particular group by the weighted-average tax rate in effect during prior periods. For each group, a different weighted-average tax rate may be appropriate. This weighted-average tax rate is equal to the ratio of aggregate deferred taxes to aggregate timing differences at the beginning of the period.

The gross change basis is similar to the individual item basis in that the tax effects of timing differences are reversed (drawn down) at the same tax rate at which they originated. The two bases are different in that **the gross change method groups similar timing differences and the individual item basis does not.** The gross change method is a practical extension of the individual item basis.

### Net Change Method

Under the net change method, the tax effect associated with a particular group of net timing differences is determined by using the current tax rates. The net change method is similar to the gross change method in that all timing differences are separated into groups of similar items. It is different in that tax effects are not computed separately for the originating items and the reversing items within a particular group. Reversing differences within a group are first offset against originating differences. The tax effect of the entire group of timing differences is then computed by applying **current** tax rates to the **net change in the aggregate timing differences** within the group.

### Illustration of Gross Change and Net Change Methods

To illustrate the differing effect of the gross change method and the net change method on deferred taxes, assume that in 1984 the Byrd Company reported pretax accounting income of $500,000. It was subject to a 46% tax rate, and reported the following differences between pretax accounting income and taxable income:

1. Municipal bond interest revenue, not subject to tax, was $7,000 in 1984. This is a permanent difference.
2. Asset lives used for tax purposes are shorter than those used for accounting purposes. In 1984, depreciation of certain recently acquired assets was $232,000 for accounting purposes and $400,000 for tax purposes. This is an originating timing difference of $168,000. For certain other assets which are no longer being depreciated for tax purposes, accounting depreciation expense was $110,000. This is a reversing timing difference of $110,000.

The reconciliation of Byrd Company's pretax accounting income to taxable income and the computation of taxes payable are provided at the top of page 901.

Byrd Company
RECONCILIATION AND COMPUTATION OF INCOME TAXES PAYABLE—1984

| | |
|---|---:|
| Pretax accounting income | $500,000 |
| **Permanent differences:** | |
| Municipal bond interest | (7,000) |
| **Depreciation timing differences:** | |
| Originating | (168,000) |
| Reversing | 110,000 |
| Taxable income | 435,000 |
| × Tax rate | .46 |
| Income tax payable | $200,100 |

Byrd Company has maintained the following record of timing differences and deferred taxes for prior years:

Bryd Company
SUMMARY OF DEPRECIATION TIMING DIFFERENCES
(Assume all were originating differences)

| Year | Timing Difference | Tax Rate | Deferred Income Tax |
|---|---|---|---|
| 1981 | $100,000 | 50% | $ 50,000 |
| 1982 | 40,000 | 48% | 19,200 |
| 1983 | 60,000 | 52% | 31,200 |
| | $200,000 | | $100,400 |

The average tax rate in prior years was 50.2% ($100,400 ÷ $200,000).

Computations of deferred income taxes and tax expense for 1984 under the gross change method and the net change method are shown at the top of page 902.

The **income tax payable** is unaffected whether the gross change or the net change method is employed. If the tax rate were the same in all periods, the tax expense and the deferred income tax amounts would also be unaffected by the choice of methods. But because of tax rate changes, the methods produce different results. Under both the gross change method and the net change method, the tax effects of originating differences are computed at current tax rates. **The tax effects of reversing differences, however, are computed at applicable prior tax rates under the gross change method, and at current tax rates under the net change method.** When tax rates change, this difference in approach yields different results.

Under the net change method, during periods in which net timing differences **increase,** an amount equal to the tax effect of the net increase in timing differences is added to the deferred tax account. During each period in which net timing differences **decrease,** deferred taxes are amortized, but never in excess of the amounts previously provided. In a period when reversal of all timing differences of a particular type occurs, the entire related

| | Gross Change Method | | Net Change |
|---|---|---|---|
| **Byrd Company**<br>COMPUTATION OF DEFERRED TAXES AND TAX EXPENSE—1984 | (FIFO) | (Average) | Method |
| **Income tax payable** | $200,100 cr. | $200,100 cr. | $200,100 cr. |
| Tax effects of timing differences:<br>Originating:<br>   $168,000 × 46% | $ 77,280 cr. | $ 77,280 cr. | |
| Reversing:<br>   $100,000 × 50% (from 1981) | 50,000 dr. | | |
|    $ 10,000 × 48% (from 1982) | 4,800 dr. | | |
|    $110,000 × 50.2% | | $ 55,220 dr. | |
| Net:<br>   ($168,000 − $110,000) × 46% | | | $ 26,680 cr. |
| **Deferred income taxes** | $ 22,480 cr. | $ 22,060 cr. | $ 26,680 cr. |
| **Income tax expense** (to balance) | $222,580 dr. | $222,160 cr. | $226,780 dr. |

deferred tax account should be amortized regardless of the amount determined under the net change computation. For example, if a company that has been using the installment method for tax purposes abandons that method by selling or collecting all installment receivables, then the entire amount of deferred tax credits relative to installment sales that was carried over from the preceding period should be amortized in the current period.[8]

## Criteria for Choosing Between Methods

As long as cumulative timing differences are not expected to reverse, both the net change method and the gross change method represent a consistent approach to the computation of income tax expense. Since the net change method is the easier to apply, it appears more desirable in these circumstances.

On the other hand, when cumulative timing differences are expected to reverse, the net change method may not be appropriate. The entire deferred tax account must be amortized in the periods of reversal, regardless of the amount that would have been determined currently. This can result in the reporting of tax expense that is considerably more (or less) than the current effective tax rate. This is not consistent with the approach used under the net change method during the periods when cumulative timing differences are increasing. Therefore, reported tax expense in the period of reversal would not be comparable to amounts computed in previous years. In these cases, the gross change method (or individual item basis) appears more appropriate.

When the gross change method is used where individual groupings of originating differences can be identified by year, the FIFO basis is usually considered more appropriate than the average rate basis. An example would be the establishment of a liability for warranties

---

[8]Donald J. Bevis and Raymond E. Perry, "Accounting for Income Taxes, *An Interpretation of APB Opinion No. 11* (New York: AICPA, 1969), p. 20.

with losses recognized in subsequent periods for tax purposes. When it is difficult to identify individual items or groupings, as it is with a great number of depreciable assets, the average basis is generally selected.

Although the net change method is more widely used in practice, the gross change method is considered theoretically preferable.

## INTERPERIOD TAX ALLOCATION AND DEPRECIATION DEDUCTIONS

The illustrations involving depreciation up to this point have been simplified to allow you to focus on the concept of interperiod tax allocation. As a result of the tax legislation passed in 1981 (the Economic Recovery Tax Act of 1981), however, companies are required to use an accelerated cost recovery system (ACRS) of depreciation for tax purposes. The ACRS approach is a major departure for tax accounting related to capital expenditures that will probably increase the differences between taxable income and accounting income. The reasons why Congress legislated the ACRS approach are: (1) to help companies achieve a faster write-off of their capital investment, which should provide them with additional tax benefits and, it was hoped, stimulate new investment, and (2) to eliminate the controversy about the useful life of an asset by adopting required recovery periods for most capital investments.

Under the ACRS approach, capital expenditures are generally recovered over 3-, 5-, 10-, or 15-year periods, depending upon the type of property involved. The different types of classes are as follows:

---

### CLASSES OF PROPERTY

**THREE-YEAR PROPERTY**—Automobiles, light-duty trucks, machinery and equipment used in research and development activities, and certain special tools.

**FIVE-YEAR PROPERTY**—Primarily all machinery and equipment that does not fall into the three-year class.

**TEN-YEAR PROPERTY**—Primarily public utility property and certain real estate such as amusement park structures.

**FIFTEEN-YEAR PROPERTY**—All public utility property and depreciable real estate not permitted to be written off over ten years.

---

The deduction under ACRS is determined by multiplying the cost of the asset by a certain percentage. The percentage for each class of recovery property is published in tables developed by the government. The percentages vary from year to year during the recovery period. For 3-, 5-, and 10-year property, the full first-year percentage applies no matter when in the tax year the property is placed in service. For 15-year property, the percentage depends on whether the property is personal property (for example, equipment) or real property (for example, apartment buildings). The rates employed for 3-, 5-, and 10-year property apply to personal property while special rules apply to real property. The tax rates are shown on page 904 (excluding fifteen-year real property):

| TAX RATES FOR ACRS PROPERTY[a] | | | | |
|---|---|---|---|---|
| Recovery Year | 3-Year | 5-Year | 10-Year | 15-Year (public utility property) |
| 1 | 25% | 15% | 8% | 5% |
| 2 | 38 | 22 | 14 | 10 |
| 3 | 37 | 21 | 12 | 9 |
| 4 | | 21 | 10 | 8 |
| 5 | | 21 | 10 | 7 |
| 6 | | | 10 | 7 |
| 7 to 10 | | | 9 | 6 |
| 11 to 15 | | | | 6 |

[a]NOTE: These tables approximate a 150% declining balance, changing to straight-line when the straight-line method provides a greater deduction than the declining balance method. The reason the rate is lower in the first year is that only a half-year depreciation is built into the allowable percentage for the first year.

To illustrate how these rates are applied, assume that Harmon, Inc. purchases research equipment on April 3, 1982 at a cost of $120,000. Harmon's depreciation deduction for tax purposes over the three-year period using the table above is as follows:

| Year | Depreciation | |
|---|---|---|
| 1982 | $30,000 | ($120,000 × 25%) |
| 1983 | $45,600 | ($120,000 × 38%) |
| 1984 | $44,400 | ($120,000 × 37%) |

Note that even if Harmon's research equipment had salvage value, it would be ignored. For example, if the research equipment had a salvage value of $10,000, the depreciation deduction would be the same as above.

An **alternate ACRS method** to determine depreciation deductions is based on the straight-line method. Often referred to as the **optional straight-line method,** it applies to all the classes of property described earlier. If the optional straight-line method is adopted, deductions may be taken over the class life or over a longer period of time. The reason an enterprise may choose a longer life is that it may not have the income currently to take advantage of higher depreciation deductions permitted under the ACRS method using the cost recovery tables. The optional periods are shown below:

| OPTIONAL STRAIGHT-LINE CLASS LIVES | |
|---|---|
| Class of Property | Recovery Period Permitted |
| 3 Year | 3, 5, or 12 years |
| 5 Year | 5, 12, or 25 years |
| 10 Year | 10, 25, or 35 years |
| 15-year (personal property) | 15, 35, or 45 years |

Under the alternate ACRS method, in the first year the property is placed in service, half of the amount of depreciation that would be permitted for a full year may be deducted. This is referred to as the half-year convention (as indicated earlier, the half-year convention is built into the cost recovery tables, and it does not apply to 15-year real estate). Also, salvage value is ignored in the optional straight-line method. For example, Harmon, Inc.'s research equipment would be depreciated as follows, assuming a three-year class life is selected:

| OPTIONAL STRAIGHT-LINE—3-YEAR LIFE | | |
|---|---|---|
| Year | Depreciation | |
| 1982 | $20,000 | ($120,000 ÷ 3) ÷ 2 |
| 1983 | $40,000 | ($120,000 ÷ 3) |
| 1984 | $40,000 | ($120,000 ÷ 3) |
| 1985 | $20,000 | ($120,000 ÷ 3) ÷ 2 |

This discussion provides a brief overview of the ACRS method. A basic understanding of this system is needed because this method must be employed for tax purposes. Deferred income tax balances will undoubtedly increase as a result of this legislation because depreciation deductions for tax purposes will usually exceed depreciation charges for accounting purposes.

## A COMPREHENSIVE ILLUSTRATION

Provided below and on pages 906–907 is a comprehensive illustration of a deferred income tax problem with several timing and permanent differences. Study it carefully. It should help you understand the concepts and methods presented so far in this chapter.

The Tonge Company, which was organized in 1981, manufactures and constructs special elevator systems for nuclear power plants. Each contract generates a gross profit of $90,000. The company completed 3 contracts in 1981, 10 in 1982, 12 in 1983, and 19 in 1984.

Additional information:

1. One-third of contract revenue is collected in the year a contract is completed and one-third is collected in each of the following two years. Gross profit is recognized in the year of completion for accounting purposes and in the year cash is collected for tax purposes (installment basis).

2. Product warranty liability accrued for accounting purposes was $20,000 in 1981, $80,000 in 1982, $100,000 in 1983, and $160,000 in 1984. 50% of the warranty claims are paid in the year they are accrued, and 50% in the following year.

3. In 1984, nondeductible compensation expense associated with employee stock options was $40,000.

4. In 1984, nontaxable municipal bond interest revenue was $20,000.

5. The weighted average tax rate in prior years was 42%. The tax rate for 1984 is 45%.

6. Pretax accounting income for 1984 is $900,000, which includes an extraordinary gain (taxed at 45%) on early bond retirement, $90,000.

7. Before recording income taxes for 1984, the balance in deferred taxes is $407,400 credit. Of this amount, $428,400 credit relates to gross profit on installment sales, and $21,000 debit relates to warranty liability. The company classifies both of these as current items.

## COMPUTATION OF TIMING DIFFERENCES FOR 1984

### Gross Profit on Installment Sales

| | | |
|---|---|---:|
| Accounting (1984 contracts): | 19 × $90,000 | $1,710,000 |
| Less Tax (1984 contracts): | 1/3 × 19 × $90,000 | (570,000) |
| (1983 contracts): | 1/3 × 12 × $90,000 | (360,000) |
| (1982 contracts): | 1/3 × 10 × $90,000 | (300,000) |
| Net timing differences | | $ 480,000 |

**Originating differences**

(excess of accounting over tax gross profit on 1984 contracts:
$1,710,000 − $570,000)  $1,140,000

**Reversing differences**

(excess of tax over accounting gross profit on 1983 and 1982 contracts:
$360,000 + $300,000 − $0)  $ 660,000

### Product Warranty Liability

| | |
|---|---:|
| Accounting (expense in 1984 for 1984 contracts) | $160,000 |
| Less Tax (claims paid in 1984 on 1984 contracts) | (80,000) |
| (claims paid in 1984 on 1983 contracts) | (50,000) |
| Net timing differences | $ 30,000 |

**Originating differences**

(for 1984 contracts, excess of accounting expense recognized currently over
claims paid currently: $160,000 − $80,000)  $ 80,000

**Reversing differences**

(for 1983 contracts, excess of claims paid currently over accounting expense
recognized currently: $50,000 − $0)  $ 50,000

## COMPUTATION OF INCOME TAX PAYABLE, DEFERRED INCOME TAXES, AND INCOME TAX EXPENSE FOR 1984

### Reconciliation and Computation of Income Tax Payable

| | |
|---|---:|
| Pretax accounting income | $ 900,000 |
| Permanent differences | |
| Employee stock options | 40,000 |
| Municipal bond interest revenue | (20,000) |
| Timing differences | |
| Installment sales gross profit | |
| Originating | (1,140,000) |
| Reversing | 660,000 |
| Warranty liability | |
| Originating | 80,000 |
| Reversing | (50,000) |
| Taxable income | $ 470,000 |
| × Tax rate | .45 |
| Income tax payable | $ 211,500 |

| Computation of Deferred Income Taxes | | |
|---|---|---|
| | Gross Change Method (Average Rate) | Net Change Method |
| Income tax payable | $211,500 cr. | $211,500 cr. |
| Tax effects of timing differences: | | |
| Installment sales gross profit | | |
| Originating: $1,140,000 × 45% | $513,000 cr. | |
| Reversing: $ 660,000 × 42% | 277,200 dr. | |
| Net: $ 480,000 × 45% | | $216,000 cr. |
| Warranty liability | | |
| Originating: $ 80,000 × 45% | 36,000 dr. | |
| Reversing: $ 50,000 × 42% | 21,000 cr. | |
| Net: $ 30,000 × 45% | | 13,500 dr. |
| Deferred income taxes | $220,800 cr. | $202,500 cr. |
| Income tax expense (to balance) | $432,300 dr. | $414,000 dr. |

The amount of income tax expense should be reported on the income statement, properly allocated to the extraordinary gain and other items. The amounts of income tax payable and deferred income taxes should be reported on the balance sheet, properly classified as current. Assuming that the net change method is used, the financial statements would appear as follows:

| Partial Income Statement for 1984 | | |
|---|---|---|
| Income before tax and extraordinary item | | $810,000 |
| Income taxes | | 373,500[a] |
| Income before extraordinary item | | 436,500 |
| Extraordinary gain on bond retirement | $90,000 | |
| Less tax effect (45%) | (40,500) | 49,500 |
| Net income | | $486,000 |

| Partial Balance Sheet, December 31, 1984 | | |
|---|---|---|
| Current Liabilities | | |
| Income tax payable | | $211,500 |
| Deferred income taxes | | 609,900[b] |

[a]($414,000 − $40,500)
[b]($407,400 + $202,500)

## APPROPRIATENESS OF INTERPERIOD TAX ALLOCATION

The desirability of using the deferred income tax procedure is not unanimously agreed upon. Some believe that the appropriate tax to be reported on the income statement is the tax actually levied in that year. In short, this group, often referred to as the **nonallocation** (or flow-through) proponents, does not believe that the allocation of income taxes provides useful information to users of the financial statements or at least benefits in excess of cost.

They note that the nature of the credit balance in the Deferred Income Taxes account is not clear. They contend that it is not a liability at the time the account is established because it is not payable to anyone. The payment of additional tax in the future is contingent upon the earning of future taxable income. Further, the balance in Deferred Income Taxes is not representative of the actual amount of additional future tax to be paid unless tax rates remain the same.

Despite these arguments, the profession justified interperiod tax allocation on the basis of the going concern assumption and the matching principle. Income taxes are seldom paid completely in the period to which they relate. However, the operations of a business entity are expected to continue on a going-concern basis in the absence of evidence to the contrary, and income taxes are expected to continue to be assessed in the future. Income taxes represent a periodic expense of business enterprises and they should be recognized under the accrual basis rather than the cash basis of accounting. This requires application of accrual, deferral, and estimation concepts in the same manner as these would be applied to other items of expense. Consequently interperiod tax allocation is required to match reported income tax expense with reported pretax accounting income.

Although the predominant view holds that interperiod tax allocation is appropriate, there are two concepts regarding the extent to which it should be applied: (1) comprehensive allocation and (2) partial allocation.

### Comprehensive Allocation Versus Partial Allocation

Under **comprehensive allocation,** interperiod tax allocation is applied to **all timing differences.** Supporters of this view believe that reported income tax expense should reflect the tax effects of all timing differences included in pretax accounting income, regardless of the period in which the related income taxes are actually paid. This view recognizes that the amount of income tax currently payable is not necessarily the income tax reported in the financial statements relating to the current period. Consequently, deferred taxes should be recognized when timing differences originate, even if it is virtually certain that their reversal in future periods will be offset by new originating differences at that time. As a practical matter, therefore, recurring differences between taxable income and pretax accounting income would give rise to an indefinite postponement of tax. An example of a recurring timing difference is the use of accelerated depreciation for tax purposes by a company which uses straight-line depreciation for accounting purposes. This results in the accumulation of deferred tax credits which will not be paid as long as the company is acquiring depreciable assets faster than it is retiring them. Although the deferred taxes associated with specific assets do indeed reverse, the aggregate balance in deferred taxes remains stable or continues to grow because of the recurring purchases of additional assets.

Supporters of **partial allocation** contend that unless deferred tax amounts are expected to be paid or recovered within a relevant period of time, they should not affect reported income. Consequently, interperiod tax allocation is not appropriate for recurring timing differences that result in an indefinite postponement of tax. Under this view, the presumption is that reported tax expense for a period should be the same as the tax payable for the period. Accordingly, only **nonrecurring,** material differences between taxes payable and accounting tax expense should be recognized. These should be recognized and allocated between periods only if they are reasonably expected to be paid or recovered within a relatively short period of time not exceeding, for example, three years. An example is an

**isolated** installment sale in which the gross profit is reported for accounting purposes at the date of sale and for tax purposes when collected.

The supporters of comprehensive allocation contend that partial allocation is a departure from accrual accounting because it emphasizes cash outlays, whereas comprehensive allocation results in a more thorough and consistent matching of revenues and expenses. **Present GAAP requires application of comprehensive allocation.**

## Conceptual Approaches to Deferred Income Taxes

The preceding viewpoints involving no allocation, partial allocation, and comprehensive allocation represent different approaches to the problem of identifying those transactions for which interperiod tax allocation is appropriate. The three views differ as to **whether accounting recognition should be given to the tax effects of timing differences.** Because tax rates change over time, additional questions relate to what method of tax allocation should be used in accounting for tax effects and how those effects should be presented in the financial statements. Three different methods of tax allocation have been proposed: (1) the deferred method, (2) the liability method, and (3) the net of tax method.

**Deferred Method     Under the deferred method the amount of deferred income tax is based on tax rates in effect when timing differences originate.** The balance in deferred taxes is not adjusted to reflect subsequent changes in tax rates or the imposition of new taxes. Consequently the balance in deferred taxes may not be representative of the actual amount of additional taxes payable or receivable in the periods that timing differences reverse. In *Opinion No. 11* the profession specified that under this method deferred charges and credits relating to timing differences "represent the cumulative recognition given to their tax effects and as such do not represent receivables or payables" in the usual economic sense.[9] This method is an income statement-oriented approach that emphasizes proper matching of expenses with revenue in the periods that timing differences originate. The gross change and net change methods previously discussed are practical applications of the deferred method. **Present GAAP requires that the deferred method be used for interperiod tax allocation.**

**Liability Method     Under the liability method the amount of deferred income tax is based on the tax rates expected to be in effect during the periods in which the timing differences reverse.** Advocates of this method believe that the initial computation of deferred taxes is a tentative estimate which is subject to future adjustment if the tax rate changes or new taxes are imposed. Ordinarily, the most reasonable assumption about future tax rates is that the current tax rate will continue. However, if a rate change is known or reasonably certain at the time of the initial computation, the anticipated rate would be used under the liability method. Under this method deferred taxes are viewed as economic liabilities for taxes payable or assets for prepaid tax. Therefore it would be appropriate to discount them to the present value of the amounts ultimately expected to be paid or received. This method is a balance sheet-oriented approach that emphasizes the usefulness of financial statements in evaluating financial position and predicting future cash flows. **This method is not accepted currently for financial accounting purposes.**

---

[9]"Accounting for Income Taxes," *Opinions of the Accounting Principles Board No. 11* (New York: AICPA, 1967), par. 56.

**Net-of-Tax Method**    Under the net-of-tax method no Deferred Income Taxes account is reported on the balance sheet. Further, the amount of income tax expense reported on the income statement is the same as the taxes currently payable. The tax effects of timing differences (determined by either the deferred or liability methods) are not reported separately. Instead, they are reported as **adjustments to the carrying amounts of specific assets or liabilities and the related revenues or expenses.** This view recognizes that future taxability and tax deductibility are important factors in the valuation of individual assets and liabilities. For example, depreciation is said to reduce the value of an asset both because of a decline in economic usefulness and because of the loss of a portion of future tax deductibility; accelerated depreciation uses up this portion of the asset value more rapidly than does straight-line depreciation. Under this view, depreciation expense reported on the income statement would include, in addition to an amount for straight-line depreciation, an amount equal to the current tax effect of the excess of tax depreciation over accounting depreciation. On the balance sheet the related cumulative tax effect would be reported as a reduction of the specific asset rather than as a credit balance in a Deferred Income Taxes account. Under this method the asset, liability, revenue, or expense accounts would be presented "net-of-tax." **This method is not acceptable currently for financial accounting purposes.**

## Continued Debate and Future Prospects

The profession adopted the **deferred** method of **comprehensive** interperiod tax allocation as the acceptable accounting method, considering it "an integral part of the determination of income tax expense." The adoption of *APB Opinion No. 11,* however, did not end the controversy over interperiod tax allocation. Significant developments taking place since then have led a growing number of accountants to challenge the deferred method of comprehensive allocation.

**Continued Growth in the Amount of Deferred Taxes**    Recent trends in tax law provisions have accelerated the growth of deferred income tax credits reported on the balance sheet. For example, Burlington Northern, Inc. reported pretax accounting income of $478.1 million in 1981. This amount is expected to grow substantially over the 1982–1986 period. However, the company expects to pay little or no tax over this period, primarily because of the accelerated depreciation (ACRS) permitted by the Economic Recovery Tax Act of 1981. As a result, virtually the entire amount of accounting tax expense, which is expected to exceed one billion dollars over the next several years, will be credited to deferred taxes rather than to taxes payable. The problem is especially significant in this case because of the extremely long periods expected to elapse before the timing differences reverse. Many companies are experiencing the same phenomenon. For example, a recent study showed that over 10% of the largest 250 companies in the United States have deferred income tax credit balances in excess of 20% of stockholders' equity.[10] As another writer has noted, "For many companies, deferred income tax credits have increased considerably more than retained earnings in the last decade."[11]

---

[10]"Rollover," *Forbes* (January 18, 1982).

[11]J. T. Ball, "Accounting for Income Taxes," *Accountants Handbook,* Lee J. Seidler and D. R. Carmichael, eds. (New York: John Wiley & Sons, 1981), ch. 13.

**Cost/Benefit Considerations**   Since *APB Opinion No. 11* was adopted, differences between pretax accounting income and taxable income have proliferated. The computations required can become very complex and give rise to varying interpretations when numerous timing differences are involved. A considerable amount of analysis is required to determine that the allocations are made properly. For these reasons, many accountants believe that the information benefits provided by the present method of interperiod tax allocation are more than outweighed by the considerable accounting costs involved. In addition, many users of financial statements complain that it is difficult to understand the concept of deferred income taxes and its significance for financial reporting purposes.

**Decreased Importance of Matching**   The profession justified comprehensive allocation on the basis of the matching principle. However, matching is coming under increasing attack. One writer noted that matching is "too often an attractive but empty slogan rather than a meaningful concept one can look to for guidance" and that "what consitutes proper matching . . . is very much in the eyes of the beholders." Thus some believe that comprehensive allocation results in (1) amounts carried as assets that have no demonstrable value and that are never expected to be realized, (2) amounts carried as liabilities that are more in the nature of contingencies, and (3) corresponding charges or credits to income for contingent amounts. Apparently the FASB agrees. In *Concepts Statement No. 3,* the FASB indicates that the deferred method of tax allocation does not fit the definition of an asset or liability.

In summary, much discussion involving the proper accounting for deferred income taxes is occurring. For example, the FASB is currently in the process of developing a discussion memorandum on the entire issue. It appears likely, therefore, that accounting for deferred income taxes may change in the future.

## ACCOUNTING FOR NET OPERATING LOSSES

A **net operating loss** occurs for tax purposes in a year when tax-deductible expenses exceed taxable revenues. An inequitable tax burden would result if companies were taxed during profitable periods without receiving any tax relief during periods of net operating losses. Under certain circumstances, therefore, the federal tax laws permit taxpayers to use the losses of one year to offset the profits of other years. This income-averaging provision is accomplished through the **carryback and carryforward of net operating losses.** Under this provision, a company pays no income taxes for a year in which it incurs a net operating loss. In addition, it may elect one of the two following options:

1. It may carry the loss back three years, receiving refunds for income taxes paid in those years. The remaining loss is carried forward for up to fifteen years. The carryforward is used to offset future taxable income.
2. It may choose to carry the loss forward only, offsetting future taxable income for up to fifteen years.[12]

---

[12]The election to forego the three-year carryback period might be advantageous where a taxpayer had investment tax credit carryovers that might be wiped out and lost because of the carryback of the net operating loss. However, election of the carryback option provides an immediate inflow of cash at a time when alternate sources of cash may not be available. For this reason many companies with net operating losses, including companies that do not expect to return to profitable operations for a period of time, elect to carry their losses back. Cash refunds from loss carrybacks can be significant. In 1980, for example, International Harvester reported a pretax accounting loss of $891 million, and received a refund for $387 million of taxes paid in the three preceding years.

Operating losses can be substantial. For example, Chrysler Corporation's total losses exceeded three billion dollars for the years 1978, 1979, and 1980. Companies that have suffered substantial losses are often attractive merger candidates because in certain cases the acquirer may use these losses to reduce its income taxes.

## Loss Carryback

To illustrate the accounting procedures for net operating loss carrybacks, assume that Groh, Inc. experienced the following:

| Year | Taxable Income or Loss | Tax Rate | Tax Paid |
|------|------------------------|----------|----------|
| 1979 | $ 75,000 | 30% | $22,500 |
| 1980 | 50,000 | 35% | 17,500 |
| 1981 | 100,000 | 30% | 30,000 |
| 1982 | 200,000 | 40% | 80,000 |
| 1983 | (500,000) | — | -0- |

The taxable incomes or loss were the same as the pretax accounting amounts reported each year; that is, there were no timing differences. In 1983, Groh, Inc. incurs a net operating loss which it elects to carry back. Under the law, the carryback must be applied first to the **third year preceding the loss year.** Therefore the loss would be carried back first to 1980. Any unused loss would then be carried back to 1981; the remainder would finally be applied against 1982. Accordingly Groh would file amended tax returns for each of the years 1980, 1981, and 1982, receiving refunds for the $127,500 ($17,500 + $30,000 + $80,000) of taxes paid in those years. For accounting purposes, the $127,500 represents the **tax effect of the loss carryback.** This tax effect should be recognized in 1983, the loss year. The APB specified in *Opinion No. 11* that since the tax loss gives rise to a refund that is both measurable and currently realizable, the associated tax benefit should be recognized in the loss period.

The following journal entry is appropriate for 1983:

| | | |
|---|---|---|
| Income Tax Refund Receivable | 127,500 | |
| Refund of Income Taxes Due to Loss Carryback | | 127,500 |

The account debited would be reported on the balance sheet as a current asset at December 31, 1983. The account credited is a contra-expense item which would be reported on the income statement for 1983 as follows:

| Groh, Inc.<br>PARTIAL INCOME STATEMENT FOR 1983<br>(Recognition of Loss Carryback in the Loss Year) | |
|---|---|
| Operating loss before income taxes | $(500,000) |
| Less: refund of income taxes due to loss carryback | 127,500 |
| Net loss | $(372,500) |

Since the $500,000 operating loss for 1983 exceeds the $350,000 total taxable income from the three preceding years, the remaining $150,000 loss is to be carried forward.

## Loss Carryforward

If a net operating loss is not fully absorbed through a carryback or if it is decided not to carry the loss back, it can be carried forward for up to fifteen years.[13] Because carryforwards are used to offset future taxable incomes, the **tax effect of a loss carryforward** represents **future tax savings.** Realization of the future tax benefit is dependent upon future earnings, the prospect of which may be highly uncertain.[14]

The accounting issue, then, is whether the tax effect of a loss carryforward should be recognized in the loss year when the potential benefits arise, or in future years when the benefits are actually realized. The profession concluded that "the tax benefits of loss carryforwards should not be recognized until they are actually realized, except in **unusual circumstances** when realization is **assured beyond any reasonable doubt** at the time the loss carryforwards arise."[15]

Future earnings prospects for companies with unfavorable earnings histories are often highly uncertain. These companies frequently experience great difficulty in returning to profitable operations. They may be unable to raise additional needed capital because they cannot borrow at attractive rates or find investors willing to purchase their stock. For these reasons, the potential future tax savings arising from loss carryforwards are not recognized during the loss year, unless there is "assurance beyond any reasonable doubt" that they will actually be realized. This requirement would be met when **both** of the following conditions exist:

1. The loss results from an identifiable, isolated and nonrecurring cause and the company either has been continuously profitable over a long period or has suffered occasional losses which were more than offset by taxable income in subsequent years, and

2. Future taxable income is virtually certain to be large enough to offset the loss carryforward and will occur soon enough to provide realization during the carryforward period.[16]

**Realization Not Assured**    In most cases, therefore, no journal entry is made in the loss year to record the tax benefits of loss carryforwards. *APB Opinion No. 11* specified that they are to be recorded as **extraordinary items** in the period(s) they are ultimately realized. To illustrate, assume that Groh, Inc. of the preceding example returned to profitable operations in 1984, when it earned a taxable income of $200,000, subject to a 40% tax rate. In 1983, the loss year, the company records only the tax benefits associated with the loss carryback, as described previously. For 1984, assuming that pretax accounting income was the same as taxable income, the company would make the following entry:

| | | |
|---|---|---|
| Income Tax Expense | 80,000 | |
| Tax Reduction Due to Loss Carryforward—Extraordinary Item | | 60,000 |
| Income Taxes Payable | | 20,000 |

[13]The length of the carryforward period has varied. It was increased from seven years to fifteen years by the Economic Recovery Tax Act of 1981.

[14]For example, Chrysler Corporation estimates that its loss carryforward, which exceeds three billion dollars, represents approximately one billion dollars in potential future tax savings.

[15]"Accounting for Income Taxes," *op. cit.,* par. 45.

[16]Ibid., par. 47.

The $60,000 extraordinary credit is equal to the $150,000 loss carryforward multiplied by the 40% 1984 tax rate. It reduces the taxes that otherwise would have been payable for 1984. This would be reported as follows on the 1984 income statement:

| Groh, Inc.<br>PARTIAL INCOME STATEMENT FOR 1984<br>(Recognition of Loss Carryforward When Realized) | |
|---|---:|
| Income before income taxes | $200,000 |
| Income taxes | (80,000) |
| Income before extraordinary item | 120,000 |
| Extraordinary item: | |
|   Tax reduction due to loss carryforward | 60,000 |
| Net income | $180,000 |

**Realization Assured**  To illustrate the accounting when realization is assured, return to the Groh, Inc. example of the preceding sections. Assume that realization of future tax savings from carryforward of the 1983 loss is assured beyond any reasonable doubt. For 1983 the company would record the tax effects of the $350,000 loss carryback as described previously. It would also record the tax effects of the $150,000 loss carryforward as an **asset** (future tax benefit). The amount of the future tax benefit would be determined by using the **estimated future tax rate** expected to be in effect in the period(s) the carryforward is realized. Assuming that the company expects a 40% future tax rate, the following journal entries would be appropriate for 1983:

| | | |
|---|---:|---:|
| Income Tax Refund Receivable | 127,500 | |
|   Refund of Income Taxes Due to Loss Carryback | | 127,500 |
| | | |
| Estimated Future Tax Benefits—Loss Carryforward | 60,000 | |
|   Tax Reduction Due to Loss Carryforward | | 60,000 |

The two accounts debited are both assets. The Income Tax Refund Receivable will be realized immediately as a refund of taxes paid in the past. The Estimated Future Tax Benefits will be realized in the future as a reduction of taxes payable in later years. The two accounts credited are contra expense items which would be presented on the 1983 statement as follows:

| Groh, Inc.<br>PARTIAL INCOME STATEMENT FOR 1983<br>(Recognition of Loss Carryback and Carryforward in the Loss Year) | |
|---|---:|
| Operating loss before income taxes | $(500,000) |
| Less: Refund of income taxes due to loss carryback | 127,500 |
|      Tax reduction due to loss carryforward | 60,000 |
| Net loss | $(312,500) |

In 1984, when the company returns to profitable operations, the following entry would be recorded, assuming a 40% tax rate:

| | | |
|---|---|---|
| Income Tax Expense | 80,000 | |
| Estimated Future Tax Benefits—Loss Carryforward | | 60,000 |
| Income Taxes Payable | | 20,000 |

The 1984 income statement, which appears below, would not report the tax effects of either the loss carryback or the loss carryforward, since these had been reported previously in 1983. It should be emphasized that recognition of the carryforward in the loss year is confined to those relatively rare cases where realization of the carryforward is assured beyond any reasonable doubt. For example, one recent survey of over 4,000 companies found only one company, Aetna Life & Casualty, that was recognizing future tax benefits in current income in 1981.[17]

---

**Groh, Inc.**
**PARTIAL INCOME STATEMENT FOR 1984**

| | |
|---|---|
| Income before taxes | $200,000 |
| Income taxes | (80,000) |
| Net income | $120,000 |

---

Notice in this example that the decision to recognize the carryforward in the loss year affects only the timing, and not the total amount, of income reported in the 1983–1984 period. Whether the carryforward is recognized in 1983 when the loss is incurred, or in 1984 when the tax benefits are realized, the total loss reported for the two-year period is $192,500 ($372,500 minus $180,000, or $312,500 minus $120,000).

## Concluding Comments

Interperiod tax allocation is one of the most challenging and complex areas in accounting practice. Many complications encountered in actual practice have not been discussed in this chapter, in the hope that comprehension of the basic theory along with some of the mechanics may be obtained readily. In the discussion of net operating losses, for example, it was assumed that the amount of taxable income or loss was the same as the pretax accounting amount for all years involved; that is, there were no timing differences that would further complicate recognition of loss carrybacks and carryforwards. In practice, however, it is common for loss carrybacks and carryforwards to occur when net deferred tax debits or credits exist. Under these circumstances it would be necessary to adjust the net deferred tax balance. In addition, it was assumed that when the tax effect of a loss carryforward is recognized in the loss year by using estimated future tax rates, the actual future tax rates were the same as the estimated rates used.

---

[17]Carol J. Loomis, "Behind the Profits Glow at Aetna," *Fortune*, Nov. 15, 1982, p. 56.

# APPENDIX L

# The With and Without Technique

The presentation thus far in this chapter has illustrated the deferred tax computation as simply the current tax rate multiplied by the timing differential. This is referred to as the **"short-cut method."** In practice, however, owing to the interplay of such items as graduated tax rates, special capital gains rates, investment tax credits, foreign tax credits, and operating losses, the deferred tax is frequently computed using the **"with and without timing differences technique."** The with and without technique is not an alternative to the gross change or the net change methods, but is used in conjunction with one of these methods. When the net change method is used, the following steps are involved in applying this technique:

1. Compute the **income tax payable** on taxable income. Taxable income is equal to pretax accounting income adjusted for any permanent differences and for **all timing differences.** All special tax rates and credits are applied in the determination of income tax payable. This represents the "with" portion of the computation (that is, **with** adjustment for timing differences).

2. Compute the income tax that would have been paid on "adjusted pretax income." Adjusted pretax income is equal to pretax accounting income adjusted for any permanent differences but without adjustment for timing differences. All special tax rates and credits are applied to adjusted pretax income **as if it were taxable income** on which tax would be paid. This represents the "without" portion of the computation (that is, **without** adjustment for timing differences).

3. The difference between (1) the income tax payable **with** adjustment for timing differences and (2) the pro forma tax **without** adjustment for timing differences represents the current tax effect of net timing differences. It is debited (or credited) to the deferred tax account.

To illustrate, assume that in 1984 the Archer Company reported pretax accounting income of $90,000. As a consequence it was subject to the graduated corporate tax rate schedule starting at 15% and ending at 46%. The following items were reported differently for accounting and tax purposes:

1. Life insurance premiums paid on policies covering executive officers were $5,000. The company is the beneficiary of the policies. The increase in cash surrender value of the policies was $3,000.

2. Unearned rental fees collected in advance were $28,000. 1984 pretax income included $18,000 of fees received in prior years.

Application of the with and without technique, using the net change method, would be as follows:

| Archer Company<br>INCOME TAX COMPUTATION FOR 1984—WITH AND WITHOUT TECHNIQUE<br>Net Change Method | | |
| --- | --- | --- |
| | With | Without |
| Pretax accounting income | $ 90,000 | $90,000 |
| Permanent differences | | |
|   Life insurance premiums paid | 5,000 | 5,000 |
|   Increase in cash surrender value | (3,000) | (3,000) |
| Timing differences | | |
|   Originating: Receipts of unearned rents | 28,000 | — |
|   Reversing: Rents earned currently | (18,000) | — |
| Taxable income | $102,000 | |
| Adjusted pretax income | | $92,000 |
| Tax: 15% on 1st $25,000 | $ 3,750 | $ 3,750 |
|     18% on 2nd $25,000 | 4,500 | 4,500 |
|     30% on 3rd $25,000 | 7,500 | 7,500 |
|     40% on 4th $25,000 (40% × $17,000 = $6,800) | 10,000 | 6,800 |
|     46% on remainder | 920 | — |
| Income tax payable | $ 26,670 cr. | |
| Tax on adjusted pretax income | | $22,550 dr. |
| Deferred income taxes (to balance) | | $ 4,120 dr. |

Under the short-cut method the deferred tax would have been computed as $4,600 ([$28,000 minus $18,000] × 46%). Owing to the interplay of the graduated tax rate schedule, however, the amount deferred is not equal to the 46% marginal tax rate multiplied by the $10,000 net timing difference. This illustrates that the "short-cut method" of applying the current tax rate to the amount of timing differences should be used only when there is no possibility that special tax rates or credits will apply.

**Note:** All **asterisked** Questions, Cases, Exercises, or Problems relate to material contained in the appendix to each chapter.

## QUESTIONS

1. In what basic ways do the objectives of determining taxable income differ from the objectives of measuring accounting income?
2. It is sometimes contended that the federal income tax is not an expense but a sharing of profits with the government. Do you agree? Why or why not?

3. As controller for Genuine Products Company, you are asked to meet with the board of directors to discuss the company's income tax situation. Several members of the board express concern over the fact that the company is reporting a larger amount of income tax expense on its published income statements than is to be paid to the federal government with the company's income tax return for that same year.
   (a) Explain to the board members the accounting rationale for this discrepancy.
   (b) How might this difference between tax paid and tax expense have arisen?

4. Describe two items that account for taxable income being higher than accounting income.

5. Describe two items that account for accounting income being higher than taxable income.

6. Explain what a permanent difference is in the interperiod allocation of income taxes. Give three examples.

7. Explain what a timing difference is in the interperiod allocation of income taxes. Give three examples.

8. How are deferred charges and deferred credits, arising from income tax allocation, treated on the balance sheet?

9. Explain the "individual-item basis" of interperiod tax allocation.

10. What are the steps that are involved in applying the "gross-change method"?

11. What is the basic difference between the "gross change method" and the "net change method"?

12. In what circumstances is application of the "gross change method" more desirable than application of the "net change method"? In what circumstances is it less desirable?

13. What are the three conceptual approaches to interperiod tax allocation? Explain each and identify the one adopted by the profession.

14. What is the theoretical rationale for allocating income taxes between periods?

15. What three views exist as to whether accounting recognition should be given to the tax effects of timing differences? Elaborate briefly on each view.

16. What method of interperiod income tax allocation has the accounting profession adopted and why?

17. What is the accelerated cost recovery system? Of what relevance is the accelerated cost recovery system to financial reporting?

18. Olympic Products purchases a plant asset for $100,000 and uses the optional straight-line class life of five years. What is the depreciation for tax purposes in Year 1 and Year 5?

19. How is it determined whether deferred tax amounts are considered to be "related" to specific asset or liability accounts?

20. Describe the procedures involved in segregating various deferred tax amounts into current and noncurrent categories.

21. What is the tax effect of a sustained large operating loss to a corporation after it has operated profitably for several consecutive years?

22. Differentiate between "carrybacks" and "carryforwards." Which can be accounted for with the greater certainty when they arise? Why?

23. What are the alternatives in accounting for a loss carryforward? What are the circumstances that determine the alternative to be applied?

## CASES

**C20-1** Income tax allocation is an integral part of generally accepted accounting principles. The applications of intraperiod tax allocation (within a period) and interperiod tax allocation (among periods) are both required.

**Instructions**

(a) Explain the need for intraperiod tax allocation (covered in Chapter 4).

(b) Indicate and explain whether each of the following independent situations should be treated as a timing difference or a permanent difference.

    1. Estimated warranty costs (covering a three-year warranty) are expensed for accounting purposes at the time of sale but deducted for income tax purposes when incurred.

    2. Depreciation for accounting and income tax purposes differs because of different bases of carrying the related property which was acquired in a trade-in. The different bases are a result of different rules used for accounting and tax purposes to compute the basis of property acquired in a trade-in.

    3. A company properly uses the equity method to account for its 30% investment in another company. The investee pays dividends that are about 10% of its annual earnings.

(c) Discuss the nature of the deferred income tax accounts and possible classifications in a company's statement of financial position. Indicate the manner in which these accounts are to be reported.

**C20–2** Listed below are 17 of the more common items that are treated differently for accounting and tax purposes.

    **1.** Charitable contributions—excess of accounting expense over tax limitation. The amount not currently deductible for tax purposes may be carried forward and deducted in later years.

    **2.** Fine for polluting.

    **3.** Income discovered after closing but included in the tax return.

    **4.** Excess of tax depreciation over accounting depreciation.

    **5.** Tax-exempt interest revenue.

    **6.** Excess of percentage depletion over cost depletion.

    **7.** Excess of charge to accounting records (allowance method) over charge to tax return (direct write-off method) for uncollectible receivables.

    **8.** Excess of accrued pension expense over amount paid.

    **9.** Excess of fair market value of a charitable contribution (deductible for taxes) over cost (charged to expense).

    **10.** Installment sales income for accounting purposes exceeds tax income.

    **11.** Expenses incurred in obtaining tax-exempt income.

    **12.** A trademark acquired directly from the government is capitalized and amortized over subsequent periods for tax purposes and expensed for accounting purposes in this period.

    **13.** Prepaid advertising expense deferred for accounting purposes and deducted as an expense for tax purposes.

    **14.** Premiums paid on life insurance of officers (corporation beneficiary).

    **15.** Amortization of goodwill.

    **16.** Proceeds of life insurance policies on lives of officers.

    **17.** Estimated future warranty costs.

**Instructions**

Indicate whether the items are permanent differences or timing differences and whether the originating difference will result in a debit to deferred taxes or a credit to deferred taxes.

**C20–3** In its financial statements for 1983 the Hyperopia Company reports an item—Deferred Federal Income Tax, $310,500. The president states that this is in connection with a five-year accelerated cost recovery system (ACRS depreciation) allowed by the federal government. (Assume full year's depreciation permitted for tax purposes in each year.)

**Instructions**

(a) Explain the nature of this item on the financial statement, and the accounting theory involved in this procedure.

(b) Assuming straight-line depreciation with no salvage value, give the journal entries that were probably made to record this item, and the entries that will affect this account in future years. Entries that will be repeated over a number of years may be so labeled. (Assume a 20-year life for accounting purposes, a cost of $4,500,000 for the assets involved, and a flat 46% corporation tax rate.)

**C20-4 Part a.** This year Lorac Company has each of the following items in its income statement:

1. Gross profits on installment sales.
2. Revenues on long-term construction contracts.
3. Estimated costs of product warranty contracts.
4. Premiums on officers' life insurance with Lorac as beneficiary.

**Instructions**

(a) Under what conditions would deferred income taxes need to be reported in the financial statements?
(b) Specify when deferred income taxes would need to be recognized for each of the items above, and indicate the rationale for such recognition.

**Part b.** Eneri Company's president has heard that deferred income taxes can be variously classified in the balance sheet.

**Instructions**

Identify the conditions under which deferred income taxes would be classified as a non-current item in the balance sheet. What justification exists for such classification?

(AICPA adapted)

**C20-5** During 1983, the Beck Company incurred interest cost of $600,000 during construction of a new office building, which was completed on December 31. For tax purposes, the interest cost is deductible in 1983. For accounting purposes, the interest must be capitalized and depreciated over the 15-year life of the building. Based on a 1983 tax rate of 40%, Beck's accountant estimates that the company will enjoy an immediate tax saving of $240,000. He contends that recognition of an immediate deferred tax liability for the full $240,000 will distort the company's debt ratios, since payment of any additional future taxes depends on such uncertain factors as the company's future earnings and tax rates. He believes that use of the deferred method of interperiod tax allocation would be misleading to financial statement users, since the $600,000 timing difference is a "semipermanent difference" which will take 15 years to reverse fully. He believes that the liability method is more appropriate for "semipermanent" differences such as this, and that the tax effect should be discounted to its present value.

**Instructions**

(a) Describe the difference between the deferred method and the liability method of interperiod tax allocation.
(b) Assuming pretax accounting income of $2,000,000, prepare the journal entry needed to record income taxes for 1983 under the deferred method.
(c) Assuming annual pretax accounting income of $2,000,000 and a 40% tax rate, prepare the journal entry needed annually to record income taxes during the 15 years subsequent to 1983 under the deferred method.
(d) Assuming that the liability method of interperiod tax allocation was appropriate, what journal entry might be prepared in 1983 to record income taxes? Assume that a 10% discount factor is used, a 40% tax rate is appropriate, and pretax accounting income is $2,000,000.

## EXERCISES

**E20-1** The pretax accounting income of Appalachian Company has differed from that of its taxable income throughout each of the last four years as follows:

| Year | Pretax Accounting Income | Taxable Income | Tax Rate |
|------|-------------------------|----------------|----------|
| 1982 | $270,000 | $180,000 | 50% |
| 1983 | 300,000 | 225,000 | 40% |
| 1984 | 330,000 | 270,000 | 40% |
| 1985 | 360,000 | 480,000 | 40% |

Pretax accounting income for each year includes an expense of $10,000 from the amortization of goodwill, which is not deductible for tax purposes.

**Instructions**

Prepare journal entries to reflect income tax allocation in all four years using the individual item basis. Assume that the reversing differences in 1985 originated in 1982 and 1983.

**E20-2** Because of a timing difference in an expense item, Cascada, Inc., reported the following tax and accounting income:

| | 1982 | 1983 | 1984 |
|--|------|------|------|
| Taxable income | $ 90,000 | $135,000 | $225,000 |
| Pretax accounting income | 150,000 | 120,000 | 180,000 |

The company's income is taxed at a 46% rate.

**Instructions**

Prepare the year-end journal entries to accrue its income tax liability and to reflect tax allocation at the end of each of the three years. All differences between taxable income and pretax accounting income are the result of timing differences.

**E20-3** The income statements of Andirondak, Inc. for a three-year period provide the following data:

| | 1983 | 1984 | 1985 |
|--|------|------|------|
| Income before depreciation | 150,000 | 170,000 | 190,000 |
| Depreciation (asset with 3-year life) | 30,000 | 30,000 | 30,000 |
| Pretax income after depreciation | 120,000 | 140,000 | 160,000 |

A 45% tax rate is applicable to all three years. For tax purposes the company uses the accelerated cost recovery system (ACRS). The recovery percentages are used for a three-year life.

**Instructions**

Prepare the journal entry for each year to record the income tax expense and the income tax payable.

**E20-4** The following information about Wiggley Gum Co. is provided:

| | 1983 | 1984 | 1985 |
|--|------|------|------|
| Pretax Accounting Income | $70,000 | $90,000 | $55,000 |
| Taxable Income | 60,000 | 65,000 | 75,000 |

**Instructions**

(a) Assuming a tax rate of 40% and that the differences in income are entirely the result of timing differences, prepare the journal entries at the end of each year to reflect income tax allocation.

(b) Assume the same facts as in (a) except that in 1984, $10,000 of the income reflected in pretax accounting income is from interest on municipal bonds (tax exempt). Prepare any journal entries that would change from what they were in part (a).

**E20-5** At December 31, 1982, Norris Company's Deferred Income Taxes account had a $469,000 credit balance, consisting of the following items:

| Timing Difference | Resulting Balance in Deferred Taxes |
|---|---|
| 1. Excess of tax depreciation over accounting depreciation. | $490,000 cr. |
| 2. Accrual, for accounting purposes, of estimated loss contingency from pending lawsuit that is not expected to be settled before 1984. The loss will be deducted on the tax return when paid. | 95,000 dr. |
| 3. Capitalization, for accounting purposes, of interest and property taxes incurred during construction of a building in 1982. The expenditures were deducted on the 1982 tax return. | 74,000 cr. |
| Total | $469,000 cr. |

**Instructions**

Indicate the manner in which deferred taxes should be presented on Norris Company's December 31, 1982 balance sheet.

**E20-6** African Imports Co., an installment seller of furniture, records sales on the accrual basis for financial reporting purposes but on the installment method for tax purposes. As a result, $75,000 of deferred income taxes have been accrued at December 31, 1984. In accordance with trade practice, installment accounts receivable from customers are shown as current assets, although the average collection period is approximately three years.

At December 31, 1984, African Imports Co. has recorded a $30,000 deferred income tax debit arising from a book accrual of noncurrent deferred compensation expense which is **not** currently tax deductible.

Also, at December 31, 1984, African Imports has accrued $22,500 of deferred income taxes resulting from the use of accelerated depreciation for tax purposes and straight-line depreciation for financial reporting purposes.

**Instructions**

How should the deferred income taxes be classified on African Imports' December 31, 1984, balance sheet?

(AICPA adapted)

**E20-7** Executone Corporation has an item costing $45,000 that was expensed for tax purposes but is amortized over three years for accounting purposes. The tax rate is 40% in the year of origination, 1983, and 30% in the years of "turn around," 1984 and 1985. The accounting and tax data for the three years is shown below.

| | Financial Accounting | Tax Return |
|---|---|---|
| **1983 (40% tax rate)** | | |
| Income before timing difference | $50,000 | $50,000 |
| Timing difference | 15,000 | 45,000 |
| Income after timing difference | $35,000 | $ 5,000 |
| **1984 (30% tax rate)** | | |
| Income before timing difference | $50,000 | $50,000 |
| Timing difference | 15,000 | –0– |
| Income after timing difference | $35,000 | $50,000 |
| **1985 (30% tax rate)** | | |
| Income before timing difference | $50,000 | $50,000 |
| Timing difference | 15,000 | –0– |
| Income after timing difference | $35,000 | $50,000 |

**Instructions**

Prepare the journal entries to record the income tax expense and the income tax payable at the end of each year applying the individual item basis.

**E20-8** Airport Limo Company uses accelerated cost recovery system for tax purposes and straight-line depreciation for accounting purposes. In the current year 1984 the tax rate increased to 45%. The tax rate in all prior years was 35%. Pretax accounting income is $750,000 in 1984, originating timing differences are $200,000, and reversing timing differences are $84,000.

**Instructions**

(a) Compute the amount entered in the deferred tax account under (1) the gross change method and (2) the net change method.

(b) Prepare the journal entry to record the taxes payable, the tax expense, and the deferred taxes for 1984 under (1) the gross change method and (2) the net change method.

**E20-9** During your audit of Darrel Grover Company, the following information was disclosed:

1.

| Year | Amount Due per Tax Return |
|------|---------------------------|
| 1983 | $80,000 |
| 1984 | 65,000 |

2. On January 1, 1983, equipment costing $100,000 was purchased. For accounting purposes, the company uses straight-line depreciation over a ten-year life. For tax purposes, the company uses the accelerated cost recovery system (ACRS) over a five-year life. Annual tax depreciation is based on the following percentages of asset cost:

1st year: 15%
2nd year: 22%
3rd through 5th year: 21%

3. In January 1984, $75,000 was collected in advance rental of a building for a three-year period. The entire $75,000 was reported as taxable income in 1984, but $50,000 of the $75,000 was reported as unearned revenue in 1984 for accounting purposes.

4. The tax rate is 40% in both 1983 and 1984.

5. The client company used the accepted deferred method of income tax allocation.

**Instructions**

(a) Determine the amount entered in the deferred tax account for 1983 and 1984, and whether the amount is a debit or a credit.

(b) Determine the balance in the deferred tax account at December 31, 1984, and whether it is a debit or a credit balance.

**E20-10** Istanbul Rug Company purchased fixed assets costing $1,500,000 on January 1, 1982. For tax purposes, the company uses the optional straight-line depreciation over an accelerated cost recovery period of three years. For accounting purposes the company uses straight-line depreciation over six years. The tax rates for the years involved are: 1982, 40%; 1983, 40%; 1984, 50%; 1985, 50%; 1986, 50%; and 1987, 50%.

**Instructions**

Assume that depreciation is the only timing difference involved and that the deferred method using the gross change method is applied.

(a) For each year involved, use the FIFO basis to determine:

1. The tax rate applicable to the originating or reversing differences.

2. The amount entered in the deferred tax account, and whether the amount is a debit or a credit.

3. The balance in the deferred tax account at year-end, and whether the balance is a debit or a credit.

(b) For each year involved, use the average rate basis to determine the three items indicated in part (a).

**E20–11** Mike Moluf Company leases equipment to customers under leases which require each year's rent to be paid in advance. At the beginning of the year, there was $200,000 of deferred rental income which for accounting purposes was earned during the year. During the year, $500,000 of taxable rent was collected, of which $150,000 was earned, leaving a balance of $350,000 in the deferred rental income account. The tax rate in the current year was 40%; in prior years it had been 48%.

**Instructions**

Pretax accounting income for the current year was $1,000,000.
(a) Compute the taxable income and the income tax payable.
(b) Compute the income tax expense for the current year and the ending balance in deferred taxes using (1) the gross change method and (2) the net change method.

**E20–12** Taxable income and pretax accounting income would be identical for Erin Lobb Corp. except for its treatments of gross profits on installment sales and estimated costs of warranties. The following income computations have been prepared:

| Taxable Income | 1983 | 1984 | 1985 |
|---|---|---|---|
| Excess of Revenues over Expenses | $100,000 | $140,000 | $50,000 |
| Installment Gross Profit Collected | 16,000 | 16,000 | 16,000 |
| Cost of Warranties | (5,000) | (5,000) | (5,000) |
| Taxable Income | $111,000 | $151,000 | $61,000 |

| Pretax Accounting Income | 1983 | 1984 | 1985 |
|---|---|---|---|
| Excess of Revenues over Expenses | $100,000 | $140,000 | $50,000 |
| Installment Gross Profit Earned | 48,000 | -0- | -0- |
| Estimated Cost of Warranties | (15,000) | -0- | -0- |
| Income Before Taxes | $133,000 | $140,000 | $50,000 |

The tax rates in effect were: 1983, 40%; 1984 and 1985, 50%.

**Instructions**

Prepare the journal entries to reflect income tax expense and payable for each of the years under:
(a) The net change method.
(b) The gross change method (FIFO basis).

**\*E20–13** Assume the following for Religious Films Company:

| | |
|---|---|
| Pretax accounting income | $200,000 |
| Taxable income | 90,000 |

Tax rates:
| | |
|---|---|
| $0–$100,000 | 22% |
| Over $100,000 | 46% |

Pretax accounting income includes $30,000 of interest on tax-exempt municipal bonds. Depreciation expense computed using the accelerated cost recovery system for tax purposes exceeds the amount computed under the straight-line method (used for financial accounting purposes) by $80,000.

**Instructions**

Compute the amount of income tax expense that will be reported on the income statement, differentiating between the portion that is current and that which is deferred. Compute the tax using the "with and without" technique. (Ignore all investment credit considerations.)

**\*E20–14** The income of the Motts Juice Company for the year is as follows:

| | |
|---|---|
| Pretax accounting income | $120,000 |
| Taxable income | 147,000 |

The income figures above include a $25,000 gain on the sale of land; this gain is taxed at a special capital gain rate of 30%. The difference between pretax accounting income and taxable income is a result of accruing warranty expense for accounting purposes, but recording the expense when paid for tax purposes.

The following tax rates are in effect for the non-capital gain income:

| | |
|---|---|
| $0–$100,000 | 22% |
| Over $100,000 | 46% |

**Instructions**

(a) Prepare the journal entry to record the tax payable, tax expense, and deferred tax for the year using the "with and without technique."
(b) What is the amount of the deferred tax that would have been arrived at applying the short-cut method?

**E20–15** The pretax income (or loss) figures for the Cola Pepsi Company are as follows:

| | |
|---|---|
| 1979 | $100,000 |
| 1980 | 120,000 |
| 1981 | 60,000 |
| 1982 | (100,000) |
| 1983 | (200,000) |
| 1984 | 80,000 |
| 1985 | 80,000 |

Pretax accounting income and taxable income were the same for all years involved. Assume a 50% tax rate for 1979 and 1980, and a 40% rate for the remaining years. In 1982 and 1983, the company is not assured of future earnings against which to offset the loss.

**Instructions**

Prepare the journal entries for the years 1981 to 1985 to reflect income tax expense and the effects of the loss carrybacks and carryforwards assuming Cola Pepsi Company elects the carryback and the carryforward.

**E20–16** Bible Publishing Corporation experienced pretax accounting income (or loss) and taxable income (or loss) from 1976 through 1984 as follows:

| | Income (Loss) | Tax Rate |
|---|---|---|
| 1976 | $15,000 | 20% |
| 1977 | 30,000 | 40% |
| 1978 | 12,000 | 40% |
| 1979 | 48,000 | 50% |
| 1980 | (120,000) | 30% |
| 1981 | 60,000 | 30% |
| 1982 | 30,000 | 40% |
| 1983 | 105,000 | 50% |
| 1984 | (60,000) | 46% |

**Instructions**

(a) What entry for income taxes should have been recorded in 1980 if there was no assurance at that time that taxable income would be reported in the next fifteen years?
(b) What entry for income taxes should have been recorded in 1980 if taxable income was assured beyond any reasonable doubt in the next fifteen years? (Expected rate 30%.)
(c) Indicate what the bottom portion of the income statement in 1981 would look like, assuming that the situation as stated in part (b) above existed in 1980.

**E20–17** Diego Restaurants Inc. reports the following pretax income (loss) for both accounting purposes and tax purposes:

| Year | Pretax Income (Loss) | Tax Rate |
|------|---------------------|----------|
| 1982 | $120,000 | 50% |
| 1983 | 60,000 | 50% |
| 1984 | (240,000) | 40% |
| 1985 | 180,000 | 40% |

**Instructions**

(a) Prepare the journal entries for the years 1982 to 1985 to reflect tax expense and the allocation of loss carrybacks and carryforwards, assuming that in 1984 Diego Restaurants Inc. is not assured of future earnings against which to offset the loss.

(b) Prepare the journal entries for 1984 and 1985, assuming that Diego Restaurants Inc. is assured beyond any reasonable doubt of future earnings against which to offset the loss.

## PROBLEMS

**P20–1** The Circle Line Company reported taxable income of $145,000 for the year ended December 31, 1983. For tax purposes, the company depreciates its fixed assets by the optional straight-line method over an accelerated cost recovery period of 5 years. For accounting purposes, the company uses the straight-line method for the following assets:

| Asset | Date of Purchase | Original Cost | Estimated Useful Life |
|-------|-----------------|---------------|----------------------|
| Machinery | January, 1976 | $100,000 | 10 years |
| Equipment | January, 1982 | 200,000 | 8 years |

The tax rate for 1983 is 46%. It was 50% for all prior years.

**Instructions**

(Assume ACRS applicable to all years.)

(a) Compute the amount of pretax accounting income reported in 1983.

(b) Prepare computations of income tax payable, income tax expense, and deferred income taxes for 1983:
  1. Using the gross change method.
  2. Using the net change method.

**P20–2** The following facts apply to the Tailend Company, for the calendar year 1983.

1. Assets are purchased at the beginning of 1983 at a cost of $60,000. For accounting purposes, straight-line depreciation over an eight-year life is used. For tax purposes, accelerated cost recovery system (ACRS) depreciation over a five-year life is used, under which the company may deduct 15% of the asset cost during 1983.

2. Warranty liability of $8,400 provided for accounting purposes is not deductible for tax purposes until warranty costs are incurred.

3. Accounting income before taxes includes $12,000 related to construction-type contracts still in process which are accounted for on the percentage-of-completion method for accounting purposes and on the completed contract method for tax purposes.

4. Amortization of goodwill of $2,400 is not deductible for tax purposes.

5. Included in pretax accounting income is $4,500 of interest on tax-exempt municipal bonds.

6. Pretax accounting income is $73,200.

**Instructions**

Prepare the journal entry to record the income taxes payable, income tax expense, and deferred income taxes for the year 1983. Assume that the federal income tax rate is 48%.

**P20-3** The following information is obtained from the records of C & M Hankes Company:

| Year | Pretax Accounting Income | Tax Depr. over (under) Book Depr. | Taxable Income | Tax Paid at 46% |
|------|------|------|------|------|
| 1979 | $ 20,000 | $ 20,000 | -0- | -0- |
| 1980 | 60,000 | 20,000 | $ 40,000 | $ 18,400 |
| 1981 | 120,000 | 100,000 | 20,000 | 9,200 |
| 1982 | 180,000 | 120,000 | 60,000 | 27,600 |
| 1983 | 80,000 | (60,000) | 140,000 | 64,400 |
| 1984 | 20,000 | (200,000) | 220,000 | 101,200 |
| | $480,000 | $ -0- | $480,000 | $220,800 |

**Instructions**

Prepare a schedule that provides for each of the years above the amount for each of the following column heads:

| Income Tax Expense | Income Tax Payable | Increase (Decrease) in Deferred Tax | Debit or Credit Balance in Deferred Tax |
|------|------|------|------|

**P20-4** Crop-Keep Corp. manufactures, constructs, and sells huge silos. The company was organized and began operations on January 1, 1982. The silo sells for a gross profit of $75,000. One-third of the total sale is collected in the first year and one-third in each of the following two years. Twelve silos were sold in 1982, 18 in 1983, and 20 in 1984. There have been no bad debts and none are expected. Gross profit is recognized in the year of sale for accounting purposes but is recognized in the year cash is received for tax purposes. Installment accounts receivable are considered a current asset.

The company's plant and equipment, acquired on January 1, 1982, cost $2,250,000. For accounting purposes, straight-line depreciation over a nine-year life is used. For tax purposes, straight-line depreciation over an accelerated cost recovery period of five years is used.

The company owns $125,000 of 10% municipal bonds, the interest on which is nontaxable. Pretax accounting income for 1984 is $512,000.

**Instructions**

(a) Prepare the necessary journal entry to record income taxes for 1984 under the deferred method. The tax rate has been 40% since the company was organized.

(b) Assume that there was a $720,000 credit balance in the deferred income tax account at December 31, 1983. Of this amount, $480,000 credit relates to the installment sales and the remainder to the depreciation. Compute the balance in deferred income taxes at December 31, 1984, and indicate the section(s) of the balance sheet where it would be shown.

(c) Prepare the necessary journal entry to record income taxes for 1984 under the deferred method, assuming that the tax rate changed to 30% for 1984. The gross change method should be used.

**P20-5** The following data represent the differences between accounting and tax income for Oriental Import, Inc., whose pretax accounting income is $860,000 for the current year.

1. The company uses accelerated cost recovery system (ACRS) depreciation for tax purposes, and the straight-line method for accounting purposes. Tax depreciation expense exceeded accounting depreciation expense by $102,500.

2. Officer life insurance expense was $5,200 for the year and you have determined that this expense is not deductible for tax purposes. The expense amount represents the difference between the premium paid ($7,400) and the increase in the cash value of the policy ($2,200).

3. Rents of $5,000, applicable to next year, had been collected in December and deferred for financial statement purposes.

4. In a previous year, the company established an allowance for product warranty expense. A summary of the current year's transactions appears below:

| | |
|---|---:|
| Balance at January 1 | $ 96,300 |
| Provision for the year | 35,600 |
| | 131,900 |
| Payments made on product warranties | 26,000 |
| Balance at December 31 | $105,900 |

**Instructions**

(a) Compute the current and deferred, if any, federal income tax provision. (Assume a 40% tax rate and apply the individual item basis.)

(b) Draft the income statement for the current year, beginning with "income before taxes" and identifying "taxes currently payable" and "deferred" (net tax effect of timing differences).

**P20-6** Bouquet Perfume Co. recognizes gross margin on installment sales for accounting purposes at the time of sale and defers such gross margin for tax purposes until subsequent periods when the receivables arising from the installment sales are collected. Bouquet Perfume Co. uses the accelerated cost recovery system for tax purposes.

Additional information:

| | |
|---|---:|
| Property | |
| 1983 tax depreciation in excess of accounting depreciation | $105,000 |
| All depreciable property acquired in 1981; estimated useful life | 10 years |
| Installment sales | |
| Gross margin on 1983 installment sales uncollected at year end | $180,000 |
| Gross margin on prior-years' installment sales collected during 1983 | $150,000 |
| Taxes | |
| Pretax accounting income for 1983 | $300,000 |
| Tax rate for 1983 | 50% |
| Average rate for all prior deferred income taxes | 48% |
| Ignore graduated tax rates and assume no investment credit | |

**Instructions**

Compute taxable income and the tax payable in 1983, and summarize the 1983 changes in the deferred income tax account balance.

(a) Using the gross change method.

(b) Using the net change method.

**P20-7** The Jaspule Company began operations on January 3, 1984. Taxable income and pretax accounting income would be identical except for the following items:

| Item | Revenue (Expense) Reported on 1984 Income Statement | Revenue (Expense) Reported on 1984 Tax Return |
|---|---:|---:|
| 1. Depreciation: Building is written off over a fifteen-year period for tax purposes and a thirty-year period for accounting purposes. | $(60,000) | $(120,000) |
| 2. Rental fees collected in advance: Recognized in entirety on 1984 tax return. $90,000 will be earned in 1985. | 160,000 | 250,000 |
| 3. Prepaid advertising expenditures for 1985 ad campaign: Deferred for accounting purposes and deducted as an expense in 1984 for tax purposes. | -0- | (15,000) |

The income tax rate was 40% during 1984.

**Instructions**

    (a) Compute the balance in Jaspule Company's Deferred Income Taxes account at December 31, 1984.

    (b) Indicate the manner in which the deferred taxes should be presented on Jaspule's December 31, 1984 balance sheet.

**P20-8** The following information about Nature Products Company is provided to you:

    **1.** In 1983, $60,000 was collected in rent; for book purposes the entire amount was reported as revenue in 1984. In 1984, $75,000 was collected in rent; of this amount, $30,000 was reported as unearned revenue in 1984. For tax purposes, the rent is reported as revenue in the year of collection.

    **2.** On January 1, 1980, the company purchased a machine costing $120,000. The machine has a salvage value of $7,500, and has a useful life of 5 years. The straight-line method of depreciation is used for book purposes, and the sum-of-the-years'-digits method is used for income tax purposes. (Because the asset was purchased in 1980, the new ACRS for tax purposes does not apply.)

    **3.** On January 1, 1984, equipment was purchased which had a cost of $180,000. The equipment has no salvage value, and has a useful life of 4 years. The straight-line method of depreciation is used for book purposes, and the optional straight-line method using a ten-year life is employed for tax purposes. (Hint: Half year depreciation in 1984.)

    **4.** The tax rate for years prior to 1984 is 40%; for 1984, the tax rate is 50%.

    **5.** Pretax accounting income of $322,500 for 1984 includes interest revenue of $22,500 from tax-exempt municipal obligations.

    **6.** On the 1984 tax return, the company reported $45,000 of gross profit from installment sales. This profit was reported in 1983 for book purposes.

    **7.** The balance (credit) in the Deferred Tax account as of December 31, 1983 is $90,000.

**Instructions**

    (a) Using the gross change method, compute the tax expense for 1984, and the balance in the Deferred Tax account at December 31, 1984.

    (b) Using the net change method, compute the tax expense for 1984, and the balance in the Deferred Tax account at December 31, 1984.

**P20-9** You have been assigned to make a computation of Pickaberry Company's provision for income taxes for 1983 and 1984. On the basis of your review of the working papers, you have developed the following information.

| Reconciliation of Book Income to Taxable Income | 1983 | 1984 |
|---|---|---|
| | (dollars in thousands) | |
| Pretax book income | $130 | $ 910 |
| Permanent book/tax differentials: | | |
|   Amortization of goodwill | 70 | 80 |
| Pretax book income after adjustment for permanent tax differentials | 200 | 990 |
| Book/tax timing differences: | | |
|   Excess for tax depreciation over book | (400) | (200) |
|   Provision for loss on sale of plant—booked in 1983 but sold in 1984 | 200 | (200) |
|   Provision for warranties: | | |
|     Provided during year | 500 | |
|     Paid during year | | (300) |
| Taxable income | $500 | $ 290 |
| Federal income tax rates | 38% | 50% |

**Instructions**

Assuming that only federal income taxes are payable, compute the provision for income taxes and net income for both years by drafting the lower portion of the comparative income statement beginning with "income before taxes" and presenting the portion of the tax "currently payable" and the amount due to increase or decrease in the deferral (net tax effect of timing differences). Apply the gross change method.

**P20-10** Suntan Lotion Corp. sustained a $110,000 net operating loss during the first year of operations when the applicable tax rate was 42%.

**Instructions**

(a) Assuming that the corporation is not confident it will have future earnings against which it can offset the loss carryforward, prepare the entries for income taxes in the year of loss and in the succeeding year (assume a $140,000 pretax income and a 42% rate in the succeeding year).

(b) Assuming that the corporation is assured beyond a reasonable doubt of earnings in the succeeding periods to cover the loss, prepare the entries for income taxes in the year of the loss and in the succeeding year (assume a $140,000 pretax income and a 42% tax rate in the succeeding year).

(c) For both the loss year and the succeeding year, present the lower portion of the income statement (pretax accounting income or loss and below) for assumptions (a) and (b).

**P20-11** On January 2, 1983, Don & Diana Cafes Inc. commenced operations. The company had an accounting loss of $580,000 for that year. There were no timing differences during 1983. The loss carryforward cannot be assured beyond a reasonable doubt, because 1983 was the company's first year of operations. During 1984, the company had taxable income (equal to its accounting income) of $800,000. Assume the tax rate for 1983 and 1984 was 46%.

**Instructions**

(a) Prepare the comparative partial statement of income (loss) for Don & Diana Cafes Inc. for the year ended December 31, 1984, with comparative figures for 1983. The statement will start with "Income (loss) before income taxes and extraordinary item."

(b) Assume that Don & Diana Cafes Inc. has been in existence since January 1, 1978, and had taxable income (loss) as follows (use the carryback elective):

| Year ended December 31 | Taxable income (loss) |
|---|---|
| 1978 | $ (60,000) |
| 1979 | 70,000 |
| 1980 | (10,000) |
| 1981 | 70,000 |
| 1982 | 200,000 |

**Instructions**

Prepare the partial statement of income (loss) for the years ended December 31, 1983 and 1984. Explain how the tax refund, if any, should be treated. Assume the tax rate for all previous periods is 46%.

**P20-12** Your firm has been appointed to examine the financial statements of Chyron Energy, Inc. (CEI) for the two years ended December 31, 1984 in conjunction with an application for a bank loan. CEI was formed on January 2, 1973.

Early in the engagement you learned that the controller was unfamiliar with income tax accounting and that no tax allocations had been recorded.

During the examination, considerable information was gathered from the accounting records and client employees regarding interperiod tax allocation. This information, which has been audited, is as follows (with dollar amounts rounded to the nearest $100):

**1.** CEI uses a bad debt write-off method for tax purposes and a full accrual method for book purposes. The balance of the Allowance for Doubtful Receivables account at December 31, 1982 was $124,000. Following is a schedule of accounts written off and the corresponding year(s) in which the related sales were made.

| Year(s) in Which Sales Were Made | Year in Which Accounts Written Off | |
|---|---|---|
| | 1984 | 1983 |
| 1982 and prior | $39,600 | $58,000 |
| 1983 | 14,400 | |
| 1984 | | |
| | $54,000 | $58,000 |

The following is a schedule of changes in the Allowance for Doubtful Receivables account for the two years ended December 31, 1984:

| | Year Ended December 31 | |
|---|---|---|
| | 1984 | 1983 |
| Balance at beginning of year | $132,000 | $124,000 |
| Accounts written off during the year | (54,000) | (58,000) |
| Bad debt expense for the year | 76,000 | 66,000 |
| Balance at end of year | $154,000 | $132,000 |

2. Following is a reconciliation between net income per books and taxable income:

| | Year Ended December 31 | |
|---|---|---|
| | 1984 | 1983 |
| (1) Net income per books | $ 666,200 | $ 525,600 |
| (2) Federal income tax payable during year | 364,600 | 473,600 |
| (3) Taxable income not recorded on the books this year: | | |
| Deferred sales commissions | 20,000 | |
| (4) Expenses recorded on the books this year not deducted on the tax return: | | |
| (a) Allowance for doubtful receivables | 22,000 | 8,000 |
| (b) Amortization of goodwill | 16,000 | 16,000 |
| (5) Total of lines 1 through 4 | 1,088,800 | 1,023,200 |
| (6) Income recorded on the books this year not included on the tax return: | | |
| Tax exempt interest—Belleville 5% Municipal Bonds | 10,000 | |
| (7) Deductions on the tax return not charged against accounting income this year: | | |
| Depreciation | 167,400 | 76,000 |
| (8) Total of lines 6 and 7 | 177,400 | 76,000 |
| (9) Taxable income (line 5 less line 8) | $ 911,400 | $ 947,200 |

3. Assume that the effective tax rates are as follows:

   1982 and prior years:    60%        1983:    50%        1984:    40%

4. In December 1984 CEI entered into a contract to serve as distributor for Brown Manufacturer, Inc.'s engineering products. The contract became effective December 31, 1984, and $20,000 of advance commissions on the contract were received and deposited on December 31, 1984. Because the commissions had not been earned, they were accounted for as a deferred credit to income on the balance sheet at December 31, 1984.

5. Goodwill represents the excess of cost over fair value of the net tangible assets of a

retiring competitor that were acquired for cash on January 2, 1979. The original balance was $160,000.

**Instructions**

(a) Prepare a schedule calculating (1) the balance of deferred income taxes at December 31, 1983 and 1984, and (2) the amount of the timing differences between actual income tax payable and financial income tax expense for 1983 and 1984. Round all calculations to the nearest $100. (Use the gross change technique.)

(b) Independently of your solution to part (a) and assuming data shown below, prepare the section of the income statement beginning with pretax accounting income to disclose properly income tax expense for the years ended December 31, 1984 and 1983.

|  | 1984 | 1983 |
|---|---|---|
| Pretax accounting income | $960,800 | $931,200 |
| Taxes payable currently | 364,600 | 473,600 |
| Deferred tax account change—Dr. (Cr.) | (56,200) | 49,000 |
| Balance of deferred tax at end of year—Dr. (Cr.) | (88,400) | (32,200) |

(AICPA adapted)

# CHAPTER 21

# Accounting for Pension Costs

Many business organizations have been concerned with providing for the retirement of employees since the late 1800s. During recent decades a marked increase in this concern has resulted in the establishment of private pension plans in most large companies and in many medium- and small-sized ones.

The substantial growth of these plans, both in numbers of employees covered and in amounts of retirement benefits, has increased the significance of pension cost in relation to the financial position and the results of operations of many companies. For example, in 1975 private pension plans covered 27.7 million individuals, paid benefits of $16 billion, and had assets of $211 billion; in 1995 it is estimated that such plans will cover 44.5 million individuals, pay benefits of $106 billion, and have assets in excess of $2.5 trillion.

Generally accepted accounting principles for accounting by employers for pensions are provided in *APB Opinion No. 8*, "Accounting for the Cost of Pension Plans,"[1] issued in 1966. In 1980 *FASB Statement No. 36*, "Disclosure of Pension Information,"[2] was issued as an amendment to *Opinion No. 8*, requiring disclosure of additional information related to pension plans. Nevertheless, there are still frequent expressions of concern related to accounting practices in this area. This should not be surprising because of the complex array of social concepts, legal considerations, actuarial techniques, income tax regulations, and varying business philosophies that characterize the environment in which pension plans have developed. For example, the administration of pensions has been significantly influenced by ERISA (Employee Retirement Income Security Act), commonly referred to as the Pension Reform Act of 1974, and a related amendment, the Multiemployers Pension Plan Amendments Act of 1980. As a result, the profession is in the process of reevaluating certain aspects of accounting for pension plans.[3]

---

[1] "Accounting for the Cost of Pension Plans," *Opinions of the Accounting Principles Board No. 8* (New York: AICPA, 1966).

[2] "Disclosure of Pension Information," *FASB Statement of Financial Accounting Standards No. 36* (Stamford, Conn.: FASB, 1980).

[3] For example, in 1981 the profession issued an FASB Discussion Memorandum entitled "Employers' Accounting for Pensions and the Postemployment Benefits." This undoubtedly will lead to some changes in pension plan accounting and reporting. Other discussion memorandums will also be issued, discussing specialized problems in this area.

## THE NATURE OF PENSION PLANS

A **private pension plan** is an arrangement under which a company undertakes to provide its retired employees with benefits (ordinarily, monthly payments) that can be determined or estimated in advance from the provisions of a document or from the company's practices (commonly called a **defined-benefit plan**). Some pension plans are **funded,** that is, the company sets funds aside for future pension benefits by making payments to a funding agency that is responsible for accumulating the assets of the pension fund and for making payments to the recipients as the benefits become due. In an insured plan, the funding agency is an insurance company; in a trust fund plan, the funding agency is a trustee. The process of making the cash payments to a funding agency is called **funding.** Some plans are **unfunded,** that is, the fund is under the control of the company instead of an independent funding agency; pension payments to retired employees are made directly by the company as they become due.

Some plans are **contributory;** the employees bear part of the cost of the stated benefits or voluntarily make payments to increase their benefits. Other plans are **noncontributory,** because the employer bears the entire cost. Companies generally design **qualified pension plans** in accord with federal income tax requirements that permit deductibility of the employer's contributions to the pension fund (within certain limits) and tax-free status of the earnings of the pension fund assets.

The above-mentioned differences, together with differences in eligibility requirements, specified retirement ages, levels of benefits, and disability options, result in an almost infinite variety of plans. In all pension plans, however, the three primary accounting problems are (1) **measuring the amount** of pension obligation resulting from the plan, (2) **allocating the cost** of the plan to the proper accounting periods, and (3) **disclosing the status and effects** of the plan in the financial statements and the accompanying footnotes. Because the first problem involves complicated actuarial considerations, **actuaries** are engaged to measure the amount of the pension obligation.[4] Actuaries also play a leading role in allocating pension costs to accounting periods.

### Employer Versus Plan (Fund) Accounting

The subject of pension accounting may be divided and separately treated as **accounting for the employer** and **accounting for the pension fund.** The company or employer is the organization sponsoring the pension plan; the employer incurs the cost and makes contributions to the pension fund. The fund or plan is the entity that receives the contributions from the employer, administers the pension assets, and makes the benefit payments to the pension recipients (retired employees). The diagram at the top of page 935 shows the three distinct entities involved in a pension plan and indicates the flow of cash between them.

---

[4]An actuary's primary purpose is to ensure that the company has established an appropriate funding pattern to meet its pension obligations. This computation entails the development of a set of assumptions and continued monitoring of these assumptions to assure their realism. That the general public has little understanding of what an actuary does is illustrated by the following excerpt from *The Wall Street Journal:* "A polling organization once asked the general public what an actuary was and received among its more coherent responses the opinion that it was a place where you put dead actors."

The need for proper administration of and sound accounting for pension funds becomes apparent when one appreciates the absolute as well as the relative size of these funds. For example, the following companies recently had pension fund assets and related stockholders' equity as follows:

| Company | Size of the Pension Fund | Total Stockholder Equity |
|---|---|---|
| General Electric | $6,580,000,000 | $8,200,000,000 |
| Lockheed | 1,900,000,000 | 349,000,000 |
| Ford Motor | 6,200,000,000 | 8,567,500,000 |
| K Mart | 261,000,000 | 2,343,200,000 |

Pension expense as a percent of total labor expense is substantial for many companies. For example, Bethlehem Steel's percentage recently was 11.1%, Exxon's 12.8%, and General Motors 10.8%.[5]

An unfunded pension plan is administered by the employer, while a funded plan is administered by a trustee. In either case, however, the fund should have separate legal and accounting identity for which a set of books is maintained and financial statements are prepared. Maintaining books and records and preparing financial statements for the fund, known as "accounting for employee benefit plans," is not the subject of this chapter.[6] This chapter is devoted to the pension accounting and reporting problems of the employer as the sponsor of a pension plan.

The company as the employer records pension cost on its books in accordance with management policy within the standards prescribed by *APB Opinion No. 8* and subsequent statements of the FASB. Contributions in the form of cash payments are made by the company to the pension fund in accordance with policies established jointly by the com-

---

[5]Some have suggested that pension funds are the new owners of America's giant corporations. At the beginning of 1980, pension funds (private and governmental) held or owned 43% of all corporate bonds outstanding, 15% of the market value of corporate stock, 14% of U.S. government securities, and 4% of all mortgages outstanding. The enormous size (and the social significance) of these funds is staggering. Understandably, labor unions are taking an increased interest in how these funds are invested and they have expressed interest in investing pension assets for such social purposes as rebuilding the industrial base of the Northeast and the Midwest.

[6]The FASB issued a standard covering the accounting and reporting for employee benefit plans. "Accounting and Reporting by Defined Benefit Plans," *Statement of Financial Accounting Standards No. 35* (Stamford, Conn.: FASB, 1979).

pany and the trustees of the pension plan and the Pension Reform Act of 1974. Measurement of the pension cost and determination of the amount to be funded are separate, independent functions. If the recorded pension expense exceeds the cash contributions to the pension fund, the excess is reported as a pension liability on the company's balance sheet. Correspondingly, if the payments exceed the expense, the excess is reported as a prepaid asset.

The pension fund administrator invests the contributions received from the employer, reinvests earnings therefrom, and pays pension benefits to retired employees. At any time the expected present value of future pension payments (the pension liability) may be actuarially computed. This liability represents the amount that the pension fund must equal now (assuming no further contributions by the employer) in order for earnings from the fund and the gradual reductions in the fund itself to exactly cover all expected future payments to present and expected future retirees over their expected lifetimes for employment services rendered to date. If the pension fund assets equal or exceed the expected pension liability, the plan is **fully funded.**[7]

**Pension liability** has one meaning in reference to the pension fund and another in reference to the employer company. The expected pension liability of the pension fund is an actuarial concept representing an economic liability under the pension plan for future cash payments to retirees. The pension liability that frequently appears on company balance sheets represents an accounting credit that results from an excess of amounts expensed over amounts contributed to the pension fund; it does not represent the economic obligations under the plan and usually does not represent amounts legally owed to the pension fund.

## Cash Basis Versus Accrual Basis

Until the mid-1960s, with few exceptions, companies applied the **cash basis** of accounting to pension plans by recognizing the amount paid in a particular accounting period for pension benefits as the pension expense for the period. The amount paid or funded in a fiscal period is dependent upon financial management and may be discretionary; however, funding may be based on the availability of cash, the level of earnings, or other factors unrelated to accounting considerations. Application of the cash basis permits the manipulation of the amount of pension cost appearing in the income statement simply by varying the cash paid to the pension fund. Two once-common funding methods, **"pay-as-you-go"** (recognize pension costs only when benefits are paid directly to the retired employee) and **"terminal funding"** (recognize pension costs when annuity is purchased or contribution is made to the trust for retired employees), are no longer considered acceptable because they are cash basis-oriented and do not recognize pension costs prior to the retirement of employees.

There is now broad agreement that pension cost should be accounted for on the **accrual basis.** Most accountants and an increasing number of business managers recognize that **accounting for pension plans requires measurement of the cost and its identification with the appropriate time periods,** which involves application of accrual, deferral, and estimation

---

[7]As used in this context, the term "funding" refers to the relationship between pension fund assets and the present value of expected future pension benefit payments. This usage is in contrast to the use of "funding" to mean the contributions made by the employer to the pension fund. Thus, it is possible, and generally accurate, to say that a company is "fully funding" its accrued pension expense as recorded on the books and yet state that the pension fund is "under funded" in an actuarial sense.

concepts in the same manner that they are applied in the measurement and the time-period identification of other costs and expenses. The going-concern, matching, and consistency assumptions are all applicable and relevant to pension plan accounting.

## Past Service Cost and Normal Pension Cost

In determining future retirement benefits, many pension plans give employees credit for their years of service prior to adoption of the plan. For example, if on January 1, 1983, a company adopted a pension plan that granted benefits to employees on the basis of their total years of service to the company, an employee who had been an employee since January 1, 1973, would already have 10 years of service toward pension credit. Some of the actuarial methods frequently used to determine pension cost compute separately the cost associated with the years prior to the date of adoption (this is called **past service cost**) and the cost associated with the years after the date of adoption or amendment (this is called **normal cost**). The diagram below identifies past service cost and normal cost as they relate to the adoption date of a pension plan.

**Past service cost** arises from the granting of service credits to employees for years of service prior to adoption of a pension plan. The amount of past service cost is an actuarial estimate derived from a complicated actuarial method that takes into consideration such factors as life expectancy of employees, retirement age, employee turnover, future salary levels, interest rates, gains and losses of the fund, administrative costs, and pension benefits.

**Normal pension cost** is the cost assigned annually for the service credits earned by the employees during a given year. Normal cost also involves a complicated determination based on service credits for the current year with a separate determination made annually because of changes in the number of employees, salaries, and terms of the plan.

If a pension plan is initiated when a company is organized, no past service cost is recognized; only normal pension cost is incurred. Similarly, if no credits are given for service prior to inception of a pension plan, no past service cost arises.

Accountants generally agree that, although past service cost results from consideration given to years of service prior to adoption of the pension plan, this cost is related to periods subsequent to the adoption. Therefore, it should be treated as an expense of the years following adoption of the plan and should not be charged against retained earnings as something applicable to the past.

To illustrate these points, assume that the actuarial firm of Rowe and Satter Co. is hired by Boston Corp. to prepare a report on a proposed pension plan that Boston Corp. is considering. Boston Corp. wishes to determine the past service cost and the normal cost that would be incurred for the typical employee. The following basic assumptions have been made by the actuary:

1. The plan is noncontributory and plan assets will earn 6% interest.
2. The typical employee will receive at retirement $200 per year for each year employed by Boston Corp.

3. Mortality table—1978 is used.

4. The typical employee is 50 years old, will retire at age 65, and has worked for the company for 10 years.

Boston Corp. indicates that it will give credit for past service prior to adoption of the plan. **To compute the past service cost** the actuary first determines the expected life of the employee after retirement; the mortality table indicates that it is 13 years. Because the employee has already worked 10 years, the company has a future obligation of $2,000 ($200 × 10) for 13 years. The computation to determine the amount of monies the pension fund must have on hand at the date of this employee's retirement to meet the pension cost attributable to the period of past service is as follows:

| (Attributable to 10 Years of Past Service) | | |
|---|---|---|
| Amount to be paid each period | | $ 2,000 |
| Present value of ordinary annuity for 13 periods at 6% (Table 6-4) | × | 8.85268 |
| Amount needed at retirement | | $17,705 |

Because the employee still has 15 years to go before retirement, the amount needed at retirement is discounted as follows:

| Amount needed at retirement | | $17,705 |
|---|---|---|
| Present value of $1 for 15 periods at 6% interest (Table 6-2) | × | .41727 |
| Past service cost | | $ 7,388 |

The present value of the past service cost pension obligation of $2,000 per year beginning in fifteen years and continuing for 13 years is $7,388. The past service cost of $7,388 may be funded immediately or over some period of years that may or may not coincide with the amortization period.

**To compute the normal cost,** the actuary must determine the cost of the pension plan at the date of the employee's retirement for the service credits earned by the employee after adoption of the plan. This employee will work for 15 more years before retirement and will be entitled to receive $3,000 ($200 × 15) for each year of expected life after the age of 65, which in this case is 13 years. The following computation is made to determine the amount that the pension fund must have on hand at the date of the employee's retirement:

| (Attributable to 15 Years of Future Service) | | |
|---|---|---|
| Amount to be paid each period | | $ 3,000 |
| Present value of ordinary annuity for 13 periods at 6% (Table 6-4) | × | 8.85268 |
| Amount needed at retirement | | $26,558 |

Assuming that Boston Corp. desires a constant normal cost from year to year, the amount needed at retirement is divided by the amount of an ordinary annuity of 1 for 15 years at 6% to arrive at the normal cost per year: $1,141 = $26,558 ÷ 23.27597.[8] On the basis of the facts and assumptions given, normal cost each period is $1,141 for Boston Corp. As illustrated later, other patterns for allocating the normal cost to each year may have been employed. This decision usually depends on the preferences of the company as to the earnings and funding patterns it wishes to follow. Also, to keep the illustration simple, we used data for one typical employee, whereas in practice pension costs are computed for groups of employees.

## Amendments to Pension Plans and Prior Service Cost

Pension plans are frequently amended to increase retirement benefits. A change in benefits requires an actuarial valuation of the plan. Ordinarily, these amendments recognize years of service prior to the date of the amendment and also the years thereafter. The period of service prior to the date of the amendment, or any actuarial valuation of the plan, is labeled the prior service period. Similarly, **prior service cost** refers to the portion of the total pension cost that, under the actuarial cost method in use, is identified with all periods prior to the date of an actuarial valuation of the plan (date of amendment). Therefore, as of the date of its computation, prior service cost includes (1) the past service cost, (2) the normal cost for years prior to that date, and (3) the increases in pension cost arising from any amendment and attributable to years prior to that date. **Essentially, prior service cost is computed at any time in the same way that past service cost would be computed if the plan were being put into effect for the first time.** The diagram below identifies the prior service period.

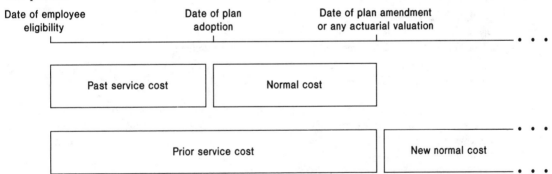

*APB Opinion No. 8* makes reference to a **specific part** of prior service cost, that is, any increases or decreases in prior service cost arising as a result of an amendment to the plan. Because this cost is accounted for in a manner similar to that used for past service cost, the term **past service cost** is used to refer to both types of cost.

One question that arises is whether a liability and a related expense should be reported at the time a plan is initiated or is amended to increase benefits. The profession takes the

---

[8]An alternative computation is to find the amount needed at the date of the adoption of the plan to fund the normal cost. This value then should be divided by the present value of an ordinary annuity to arrive at the normal cost, as indicated below:

$$\$26,558 \times .41727 = \$11,082$$
$$\$11,082 \div 9.71225 = \$1,141$$

position that **no liability or expense** should be reported for these benefits at this point, because the employer would not increase benefits retroactively unless it expected to receive benefits in the future. As a result, the liability and related expense should be recognized in the future. This highly debatable point is one of the major issues confronting the FASB in its reevaluation of accounting for pensions.

## Actuarial Cost Methods

The major difficulties in estimating pension cost are in selecting the pertinent data relating to the employee group (employee age, years of service, compensation, etc.), designing the actuarial computations, and formulating the assumptions regarding future events (employee turnover and mortality, and pension fund earnings). Having made the necessary assumptions, the actuary would make a valuation using one of several actuarial cost methods to determine the periodic contributions the employer is to make to the pension fund. Recall that in our previous illustration with Boston Corp., we arrived at a normal cost of $1,141 per year. In other words, if $1,141 were invested in the pension fund each year and earned 6%, the amount needed at retirement, $26,558, would be achieved.

Other approaches could be employed to fund this amount. For example, Boston Corp. may wish to fund as a constant percentage of salaries each year. Such a procedure would lead to lower funding earlier and higher funding later as the salaries increased. Conversely, Boston Corp. may wish to develop a funding procedure that maximizes the funding earlier. Although the actuarial methods are used primarily to determine the amounts to be funded, they may also be used to measure periodic pension expense. Five actuarial cost methods are acceptable for assigning pension costs to accounting periods; they are:[9]

1. Accrued benefit cost method.
2. Individual level cost method (without supplemental liability).
3. Individual level cost method (with supplemental liability).
4. Aggregate level cost method (without supplemental liability).
5. Aggregate level cost method (with supplemental liability).

Just as different depreciation methods result in different amounts of periodic depreciation expense, so the actuarial cost methods above produce different amounts of periodic pension expense. The diagrams on page 941 illustrate the annual cost patterns produced by these five actuarial cost methods.[10]

---

[9]The terms in parentheses are the related terms that were most commonly employed in practice until 1966, when the new terminology was proposed by the actuarial profession. "Supplemental liability" means past service cost or prior service cost.

[10]Source: William A. Dreher, "Alternatives Available Under APB Opinion No. 8: An Actuary's View," *Journal of Accountancy* (September 1967), p. 41. In examining these diagrams, note that the accrued benefit, individual level (with liability), and the aggregate cost (with liability) amortize the past service cost independently over a twenty-year period. At the end of twenty years, the contribution rate drops substantially. Conversely, the individual level (without liability) and aggregate cost (without liability) include the past service cost as part of the normal cost; therefore the past service cost is spread over a longer period. After about twenty-five years the pension fund and related expense are approximately the same under any accepted actuarial cost method, assuming a stabilized labor force.

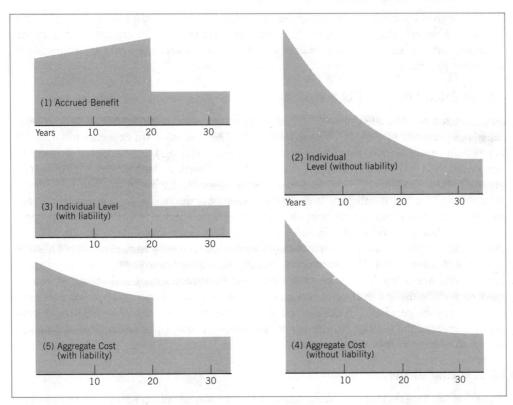

The **two major reasons why these actuarial cost methods differ relate to how the past service cost is handled and whether present or future salary levels are employed to determine the normal cost.** For example, the individual level cost method *without* supplemental liability includes the amortization of past service cost in its computation of normal cost. Conversely, the individual level cost method *with* supplemental liability does not include past service cost in its computation. In addition the accrued benefit cost method accrues normal cost on the basis of today's employee salary level. Under this approach, assuming that salary levels increase, more cost will be reported in later years than in earlier years. Conversely, all of the individual and aggregate level cost methods attempt to allocate the normal cost more evenly over the periods involved by projecting the future salary levels and normalizing these costs over the entire period affected.

All of these actuarial cost methods are considered acceptable to provide pension costs consistent with the objectives of accrual accounting. The actuarial cost method chosen for accounting purposes does not have to be the same as the method used to fund the pension plan. The selection of the funding pattern is based on a number of considerations. For example, some companies employ shorter periods to fund in order to maximize tax deductions and build funds for increased future benefits. Others choose a longer period to fund in order to retain working capital. Where funding and pension expense are the same, companies that fund over a shorter period of time sometimes receive criticism from labor because lower pension expense is reported later in the plan. Acceptable accounting merely requires that the method be rational and systematic, be applied consistently, and result in a reasonable measure of pension cost from year to year.

Although the technical aspects of pension cost determination require the skill, experience, and judgment of an actuary, accountants must be familiar enough with actuarial methods and concepts to reach their own conclusions about the reasonableness of the estimated provision.

## Accumulated Plan Benefits and Vesting

Accumulated plan benefits are those future benefit payments that are attributable under the plan's provision to employees' service to date. These **benefits** are expected to be paid to (1) retired or terminated employees or their beneficiaries, (2) beneficiaries of deceased employees, and (3) present employees or their beneficiaries. Accumulated plan benefits may be divided in terms of vested and unvested benefits. **Vested benefits** are earned pension benefits that are not contingent upon the employee continuing in the service of the employer. Thus, to the extent that benefits vest, a present employee is entitled at some specified future date (normally retirement age) to benefits earned, even if the employee leaves the company before retirement. If payments for benefits already earned are contingent on staying with the same employer until retirement, the plan is "nonvesting." As long as prior service costs are being funded, vested benefits need not be accrued and recorded, but the amount must be disclosed. If prior service costs are not being funded, a provision for vested benefits may be required.[11] Because the Pension Reform Act of 1974 (ERISA) significantly increased the vesting requirements of company pension plans, this area is receiving increased attention from accountants.

## Interest Equivalents

A pension fund is established and maintained for the purpose of accumulating the amounts necessary to pay retirement benefits as they come due. The primary source of pension funds is, of course, the periodic contributions of the employer. Another source of funds assumed in actuarially determining the amount of the employer's contributions and expense is the **earnings** on the pension fund assets. If the employer does not fund or underfunds the pension plan, earnings do not materialize in the amount actuarially assumed or necessary to meet the expected benefit payments. Therefore, when the amounts of the actuarially determined pension expense vary from the amounts funded, the annual accounting pension provision is adjusted by "an amount equivalent to interest" on the accumulated difference. The annual pension expense is **increased** by an amount equivalent to interest on the prior years' expense provisions not funded, or it is **decreased** by an amount equivalent to interest on prior years' funding in excess of expense provisions.

# ACCOUNTING FOR PENSION COSTS

The amount of pension expense recognized during a particular accounting period depends on the factors listed below.

1. **The amount of past or prior service cost.** The amount of past or prior service cost is determined by an actuary and represents the present value of the future obligations resulting from

---

[11]At this point, a reasonable question to ask is, "What is the difference between accumulated benefits and prior service costs (defined in a broad context)?" Accumulated plan benefits are earned benefits to date; prior service cost is not necessarily the same. Prior service cost is a function of the

the cost of credits for employee services rendered prior to the adoption or amendment of the pension plan.

2. **The funding or nonfunding of past or prior service cost.** The funding or nonfunding of the past or prior service cost is a financial decision of the employer subject to laws such as ERISA. As a minimum, the annual pension expense should include an amount equivalent to interest on any unfunded past or prior service cost.

3. **The periods over which past or prior service cost is amortized.**[12] The amortization of past or prior service cost is also the decision of the employer. The acceptable rate of amortization may range from no amortization at all to a maximum of 10% a year.

4. **The amount of normal cost.** The amount of normal cost is determined by an actuary on the basis of employee service credits for the current year.

5. **The interest rate appropriate to the pension fund.** The interest rate determined by the actuary to be appropriate to the pension fund operation affects all computations of pension cost. Interest is an integral part of pension cost because time and annuity factors are inherent in pension concepts.

6. **The amounts funded annually.** The amounts funded annually are frequently a financial decision of the employer and need not parallel the amounts expensed annually. Interest equivalents on the difference between the amounts expensed and the amounts funded can increase or decrease the periodic pension expense.

7. **The amount of vested benefits.** Pension expenses must include a provision for vested benefits only if prior service costs are not being amortized over 40 years or less. Even then a provision may not be required except in limited circumstances.[13]

Each of the foregoing factors must be considered and resolved before an accounting entry can be recorded to recognize annual pension cost.

To illustrate the accounting entries that result under different circumstances, assume that on January 1, 1980, the Odom Corporation, in business since 1966, adopts a funded pension plan for the benefit of its employees. The plan is noncontributory and provides for vesting after 15 years of service by each eligible employee. A local bank is engaged as the trustee for the pension fund. An actuarial consulting firm recommends a 5% interest rate as appropriate and, applying an acceptable actuarial method, determines that the past service cost at the date of adoption (January 1, 1980) is $240,000 and that the normal (current) pension cost for the year 1980 is $50,000, which is to be funded fully each year.

The management of Odom Corporation must now formulate an **amortization** policy and a **funding** policy for past service cost.

## Case A—Amortization and Funding Periods the Same

Management decides to amortize and fund the past service cost of $240,000 over 15 years; equal payments are to be made to the pension fund trustee at the end of each year. The annual amortization of past service cost and the annual payment to the pension fund trustee are identical and computed as follows:

---

actuarial cost method selected and therefore may be higher or lower than accumulated plan benefits at any time. The implications of this difference are discussed later in this chapter.

[12]The 1981 issue of *Accounting Trends and Techniques*, p. 277, reported that of 482 pension plans, 478 amortize prior service costs; only 4 do not amortize these costs.

[13]The amount of the vested benefit provision would be the lesser of (1) the amount, if any, by which 5% of such excess of vested benefits at the beginning of the year exceeds any reduction in vested benefits during the year, or (2) the amount needed to amortize all prior service costs over 40 years.

$$\$240,000 \div \begin{array}{c}\text{PV of an ordinary annuity} \\ \text{of 1 for 15 periods at 5\%}\end{array} = \begin{array}{c}\text{Periodic amortization} \\ \text{and funding payment}\end{array}$$

$$\$240,000 \div 10.37966 \text{ (Table 6–4)} \qquad = \$23,122$$

The entry on December 31, 1980 to recognize the annual pension expense and to record the Odom Corporation contributions to the pension fund trustee would appear as follows:

| | | |
|---|---|---|
| Pension Expense (normal cost) | 50,000 | |
| Pension Expense (past service cost) | 23,122 | |
|     Cash | | 73,122 |

(Normal and past service costs are recorded separately merely for illustration purposes. These two amounts are generally combined and recorded in one pension expense account.)

The following schedule (first three years only) shows the relationship of the past service cost amortization and funding policies to the amount charged annually to pension expense.

Odom Corporation—Case A
SCHEDULE OF AMORTIZATION AND FUNDING OF PAST SERVICE COST

| | Amortization—15 Years | | | Funding 15 Years | Balance Sheet Deferred Expense/Liability | |
|---|---|---|---|---|---|---|
| Year | 15-Year Annual Amount | Interest Reduction/ Increase | Pension Expense Debit | Cash Credit | Debit/ (Credit) | 12/31 Balance |
| | (a) | (b) | (c) | (d) | (e) | (f) |
| 1980 | $23,122 | -0- | $23,122 | $23,122 | -0- | -0- |
| 1981 | 23,122 | -0- | 23,122 | 23,122 | -0- | -0- |
| 1982 | 23,122 | -0- | 23,122 | 23,122 | -0- | -0- |

(a) $240,000 ÷ 10.37966.
(b) 5% of the preceding balance of (f).
(c) (a) plus (or minus) (b).
(d) $240,000 ÷ 10.37966.
(e) (d) minus (c).
(f) Preceding balance plus (or minus) (e).

Because the current provisions for pension expense, normal cost, and past service cost are fully funded each year, the balance sheet would report neither a debit for deferred pension cost nor a credit for pension liability. At the end of 15 years when the past service cost is fully amortized and funded, only the normal pension cost would be expensed and funded each year.

It should be noted that it is difficult to understand what is being amortized because the principal amount to be amortized is **unrecorded.** Generally, amortization involves the write-off of an amount that has been recorded on the books as a debit or a credit. The past or prior service cost that is amortized may be likened to an unrecorded deferred charge. In fact, if all past service costs were funded at the initiation of the pension plan, they might be recorded as a deferred charge, and the amortization could then be related to the write-off of the unamortized amount which would appear on the balance sheet.

## Case B—Amortization Period Longer than Funding Period

Management decides to amortize past service cost of $240,000 over 15 years and to fund this cost by making equal payments at the end of each of the first 10 years. The annual amortization and funding payments are computed as follows:

Amortization:

$$\$240,000 \div \frac{\text{PV of an ordinary annuity}}{\text{of 1 for 15 periods at 5\%}} = \text{Periodic amortization}$$

$$\$240,000 \div 10.37966 \ (\text{Table 6-4}) \quad = \$23,122$$

Funding:

$$\$240,000 \div \frac{\text{PV of an ordinary annuity}}{\text{of 1 for 10 periods at 5\%}} = \text{Periodic funding payment}$$

$$\$240,000 \div 7.72173 \ (\text{Table 6-4}) \quad = \$31,081$$

The following schedule shows the results from funding past service cost over a shorter period than the period of amortizing that cost. A deferred charge accumulates during the first 10 years and is depleted during the next 5 years. Also, the periodic amortization is reduced by the interest on the cumulative amount funded in excess of the amounts amortized.

| | Amortization—15 Years | | | Funding 10 Years | Balance Sheet Deferred Charge | |
|---|---|---|---|---|---|---|
| Year | 15-Year Annual Amount | Interest Reduction | Pension Expense Debit | Cash Credit | Debit/ (Credit) | Debit Balance |
| | (a) | (b) | (c) | (d) | (e) | (f) |
| 1980 | $23,122 | -0- | $ 23,122 | $ 31,081 | $ 7,959 | $ 7,959 |
| 1981 | 23,122 | $ 398 | 22,724 | 31,081 | 8,357 | 16,316 |
| 1982 | 23,122 | 816 | 22,306 | 31,081 | 8,775 | 25,091 |
| 1983 | 23,122 | 1,255 | 21,867 | 31,081 | 9,214 | 34,305 |
| 1984 | 23,122 | 1,715 | 21,407 | 31,081 | 9,674 | 43,979 |
| 1985 | 23,122 | 2,199 | 20,923 | 31,081 | 10,158 | 54,137 |
| 1986 | 23,122 | 2,707 | 20,415 | 31,081 | 10,666 | 64,803 |
| 1987 | 23,122 | 3,240 | 19,882 | 31,081 | 11,199 | 76,002 |
| 1988 | 23,122 | 3,800 | 19,322 | 31,081 | 11,759 | 87,761 |
| 1989 | 23,122 | 4,388 | 18,734 | 31,081 | 12,347 | 100,108 |
| 1990 | 23,122 | 5,005 | 18,117 | -0- | (18,117) | 81,991 |
| 1991 | 23,122 | 4,100 | 19,022 | -0- | (19,022) | 62,969 |
| 1992 | 23,122 | 3,148 | 19,974 | -0- | (19,974) | 42,995 |
| 1993 | 23,122 | 2,150 | 20,972 | -0- | (20,972) | 22,023 |
| 1994 | 23,122 | 1,099* | 22,023 | -0- | (22,023) | -0- |
| 1995 | -0- | -0- | -0- | -0- | -0- | -0- |
| | | | $310,810 | $310,810 | | |

Odom Corporation—Case B
SCHEDULE OF AMORTIZATION AND FUNDING OF PAST SERVICE COST

\* Adjusted for $2 discrepancy due to rounding of computations.
(a) $240,000 ÷ 10.37966.
(b) 5% of the preceding balance of (f).
(c) (a) minus (b).
(d) $240,000 ÷ 7.72173.
(e) (d) minus (c).
(f) Preceding balance plus (e).

Using data from the schedule on page 945, the entries to recognize the annual pension expense (normal cost assumed to be $50,000 for all years, although it generally changes from year to year in actual practice) and to record Odom Corporation's annual contribution to the pension fund trustee would appear as follows for 1980, 1991, and 1995:

**December 31, 1980**

| | | |
|---|---|---|
| Pension Expense (normal cost) | 50,000 | |
| Pension Expense (past service cost) | 23,122 | |
| Deferred Pension Expense | 7,959 | |
| Cash ($50,000 + $31,081) | | 81,081 |

**December 31, 1991**

| | | |
|---|---|---|
| Pension Expense (normal cost) | 50,000 | |
| Pension Expense (past service cost) | 19,022 | |
| Deferred Pension Expense | | 19,022 |
| Cash | | 50,000 |

**December 31, 1995**

| | | |
|---|---|---|
| Pension Expense (normal cost) | 50,000 | |
| Cash | | 50,000 |

## Case C—Amortization Period Shorter than Funding Period

Management decides to amortize past service cost of $240,000 over 15 years and to fund past service cost by making equal payments at the end of each of the first 20 years. The annual amortization and funding payments are computed as follows:

$$\text{Amortization} = \$240,000 \div 10.37966 = \$23,122$$
$$\text{Funding} = \$240,000 \div 12.46221 = \$19,258$$

The schedule at the top of page 947 shows the results from funding past service cost over a longer period than the period of amortizing that cost. A liability for the excess of the annual pension cost over the amount funded accumulates during the first 15 years and is eliminated during the next 5 years. Also, the periodic amortization is increased by the interest on the cumulative amount amortized in excess of the amounts funded.

Using data from the schedule at the top of page 947, the entries to recognize the annual pension expense (normal cost assumed to be $50,000 for all years) and to record Odom Corporation's annual contribution to the pension fund trustee would appear as follows for 1980, 1994, 1995, and 2000:

**December 31, 1980**

| | | |
|---|---|---|
| Pension Expense (normal cost) | 50,000 | |
| Pension Expense (past service cost) | 23,122 | |
| Liability for Pension Expense Not Funded | | 3,864 |
| Cash ($50,000 + $19,258) | | 69,258 |

**December 31, 1994**

| | | |
|---|---|---|
| Pension Expense (normal cost) | 50,000 | |
| Pension Expense (past service cost) | 26,907 | |
| Liability for Pension Expense Not Funded | | 7,649 |
| Cash | | 69,258 |

| | Odom Corporation—Case C SCHEDULE OF AMORTIZATION AND FUNDING OF PAST SERVICE COST | | | | | |
|---|---|---|---|---|---|---|
| | Amortization—15 Years | | | Funding 20 Years | Balance Sheet Pension Liability | |
| Year | 15-Year Annual Amount | Interest Increase | Pension Expense Debit | Cash Credit | (Debit)/ Credit | Credit Balance |
| | (a) | (b) | (c) | (d) | (e) | (f) |
| 1980 | $23,122 | -0- | $ 23,122 | $ 19,258 | $ 3,864 | $ 3,864 |
| 1981 | 23,122 | $ 193 | 23,315 | 19,258 | 4,057 | 7,921 |
| 1982 | 23,122 | 396 | 23,518 | 19,258 | 4,260 | 12,181 |
| 1994 | 23,122 | 3,785 | 26,907 | 19,258 | 7,649 | 83,346 |
| 1995 | -0- | 4,167 | 4,167 | 19,258 | (15,091) | 68,255 |
| 1999 | -0- | 915 | 915 | 19,258 | (18,343) | -0- |
| 2000 | -0- | -0- | -0- | -0- | -0- | -0- |
| | | | $385,160 | $385,160 | | |

(a) $240,000 ÷ 10.37966.
(b) 5% of preceding balance of (f).
(c) (a) plus (b).

(d) $240,000 ÷ 12.46221.
(e) (c) minus (d).
(f) Preceding balance plus (e).

**December 31, 1995**

| | | |
|---|---|---|
| Pension Expense (normal cost) | 50,000 | |
| Pension Expense (past service cost) | 4,167 | |
| Liability for Pension Expense Not Funded | 15,091 | |
| Cash | | 69,258 |

**December 31, 2000**

| | | |
|---|---|---|
| Pension Expense (normal cost) | 50,000 | |
| Cash | | 50,000 |

As indicated in the foregoing illustrations, the typical elements of periodic pension expense are (1) normal cost, (2) an amortized amount of past service cost, and (3) an amount equivalent to interest on the difference between amounts recorded for accounting purposes and the amounts funded.

The amortization and funding schedules above were presented to illustrate the effect on the annual expense provisions of differences in the amounts funded and the amounts amortized for past service cost. These differences occur in practice and are justifiable because the amortization or write-off of the past or prior service cost is independent of the funding of that same amount, just as the depreciation of an asset is separate from the retirement of the liability incurred when the asset was acquired.

The preceding schedules are unrealistic in that the real world pension situation seldom remains so constant and unaltered for such long periods of time. It is not uncommon for pension plans to be amended as frequently as every three years. Therefore, computations for pension expense and minimum and maximum provisions (explained in the following section) are made on a year-to-year basis and are dependent upon the amounts funded and accrued in the previous year.

## TWO VIEWS OF PENSION COST

Adoption of the accrual basis of accounting does not resolve a major controversy that exists relating to pension plan accounting. The question that still must be resolved is: What cost must be accounted for? And that question begs the question: What is the nature of pension cost? Two opposing views of the nature of pension cost exist among accountants.

Some accountants argue that pension cost is related to **the plan or the continuing employee group as a whole.** They believe that it is unnecessary to make specific expense charges for prior service cost if all future benefit payments can be met by annual provisions representing normal cost plus an amount equivalent to interest[14] on the unfunded prior service cost. The justification given for this treatment is that actuarial assumptions are a function of the mass of employees moving through the pension plan over the years and are not based on particular people at a particular time. In addition, they claim that an employer obtains diverse advantages of indefinite duration as a result of granting past service credits under a pension plan. The past service cost is, therefore, an intangible that does not diminish in value and thus does not need to be amortized.[15]

This approach, often referred to as the **minimum method,** holds that pension cost should not be less than the total of:

1. Normal cost.
2. An amount equivalent to interest on any unfunded prior service cost.
3. A provision for vested benefits, if any is indicated.

Other accountants believe that the annual expense of a pension plan is related to **the cost of specific pension benefits payable in the future to specific persons.** Proponents of this view advocate recognition of the past service cost over a period related to the remaining years of service of the employee group that is to receive credit for working years before adoption of the plan. Their argument is supported by the fact that past service cost is part of the cost of providing pensions for the employees initially covered. And, although it may be true that the future periods benefited by the past service element of the plan are indefinite in length, by far the greatest part of the benefit is related to the service lives of the employees who will receive pensions measured in part by past service. Therefore, past service cost should be charged to expense over the remaining service lives of such employees.[16]

This approach, often referred to as the **maximum method,** holds that pension cost should not be more than the total of:

1. Normal cost.
2. Ten percent (10%) of the past service cost (until fully amortized).
3. Ten percent (10%) of any increase or decrease in prior service cost arising from amendments of the plan (until fully amortized).
4. Interest equivalents on any differences between the amounts expensed and the amounts funded.

The major difference between these two approaches is essentially in the accounting for prior service cost. Under the minimum method, only interest on the unfunded prior service

---

[14]Such interest is necessary to keep the unfunded cost from growing, that is, to maintain the original size of unfunded past service cost stated at present value relative to the future benefits applicable to that past period.

[15]Ernest L. Hicks, "Accounting for the Cost of Pension Plans," *Accounting Research Study No. 8* (New York: AICPA, 1965), pp. 31–55.

[16]Ibid.

cost is considered. Under the maximum, 10% of the past service cost and 10% of any increase or decrease in prior service cost arising from amendments of the plan are included in current pension expense.

In examining the elements of the minimum computation, note that a provision for vested benefits may be needed. This provision is generally required under the minimum method when the present value of the vested benefits exceeds the value of the assets in the fund plus any accrued pension liability currently reported on the balance sheet. For example, assume that Sloan Inc. has $2 million of net assets in a pension fund and an accrued pension liability of $500,000. If the present value of the vested benefits payable is $2,800,000, should $300,000 [$2,800,000 − ($2,000,000 + $500,000)] be reported on the balance sheet as a liability with a related expense? Under the minimum method, the general approach is to recognize this amount as additional pension expense by means of a complex formula. The formula essentially limits the amount to be added to expense by spreading these costs over future periods. In many cases the vested liability is not recognized because the normal cost allocation covers this liability. This problem does not arise under the maximum approach because the normal cost plus the rapid write-off of past or prior service costs more than offset the vested liability.

## Additional Points on Minimum-Maximum Computations

The minimum and maximum computations represent the floor and the ceiling for periodic charges of pension costs to expense. The profession does not specify the method to be used in computing pension expense. It merely advocates the consistent application of any accounting method that uses an acceptable actuarial cost method and that results in an expense provision that falls between the defined minimum and maximum.

The minimum and the maximum do not exist per se; rather, they relate to the particular policies adopted by the employer. In other words, you can test for a minimum and a maximum only if given a particular amortization and funding policy. That is, each year should be tested because the minimum and maximum depend upon the actual amortization and funding practices that have occurred prior to and during the year.

Under actuarial cost methods that do not recognize past service cost separately, the maximum and the minimum are the same. In the maximum, the 10% limitation applies separately to **past** service cost on the initiation of a pension plan and to changes in **prior** service cost resulting from plan amendments. For example, if the initial past service cost is $1,000,000 and an amendment at the end of the fifth year results in an additional $500,000 of prior service cost, the amortization amounts might be as follows:

| | |
|---|---|
| Years  1– 5 | $100,000 (10% × $1,000,000) |
| Years  6–10 | 150,000 (10% × $1,500,000) |
| Years 11–15 | 50,000 (10% × $500,000) |

## Minimum and Maximum Illustrated

Using the data from Case A (pages 943–944), in which the amortization and funding periods are the same, results in the minimum computations and the maximum computations for selected years as shown on page 950.

### Computation of Minimum Provision—Case A

| Year | Normal Cost | Past Service Cost Unfunded Bal. 1/1 | Past Service Cost 5% Interest on Unfunded PSC | Past Service Cost Funded 12/31 | Past Service Cost Unfunded Bal. 12/31 | Minimum Pension Provision |
|---|---|---|---|---|---|---|
| | (a) | (b) | (c) | (d) | (e) | (f) |
| 1980 | $50,000 | $240,000 | $12,000 | $23,122 | $228,878 | $62,000 |
| 1981 | 50,000 | 228,878 | 11,444 | 23,122 | 217,200 | 61,444 |
| 1982 | 50,000 | 217,200 | 10,860 | 23,122 | 204,938 | 60,860 |
| 1991 | 50,000 | 81,991 | 4,100 | 23,122 | 62,969 | 54,100 |
| 1995 | 50,000 | -0- | -0- | -0- | -0- | 50,000 |

(a) Actuarially determined.
(b) Balance in (e) in preceding year.
(c) 5% of (b).
(d) PSC funded in current year (15 years).
(e) (b) plus (c) minus (d).
(f) (a) plus (c).

### Computation of Maximum Provision—Case A

| Year | Normal Cost | PSC Amortization 10% | Def. Charge or Liability Bal. 1/1 | Interest Equivalent at 5% | Maximum Pension Provision |
|---|---|---|---|---|---|
| | (a) | (b) | (c) | (d) | (e) |
| 1980 | $50,000 | $24,000 | -0- | -0- | $74,000 |
| 1981 | 50,000 | 24,000 | -0- | -0- | 74,000 |
| 1982 | 50,000 | 24,000 | -0- | -0- | 74,000 |
| 1993 | 50,000 | 24,000 | -0- | -0- | 74,000 |
| 1994 | 50,000 | 24,000 | -0- | -0- | 74,000 |
| 1995 | 50,000 | -0- | -0- | -0- | 50,000 |

(a) Actuarially determined.
(b) 10% of past service cost (until fully amortized).
(c) Cumulative difference between expense accrued and amounts funded.
(d) 5% of (c).
(e) (a) plus (b) minus (d), if deferred charge, or plus (d), if liability.

A comparison of Odom Corporation's practice in Case A of amortizing and funding past service cost over 15 years with the computed minimum and maximum provisions indicates that the amounts expensed are acceptable because they fall between the minimum and maximum each year. For example, in 1980 the maximum is $74,000 and the minimum is $62,000. Because $73,122 is between these limits, this amount is expensed in the current period.

Using the data from Case B (pages 944–945), in which the amortization period is longer than the funding period, results in the minimum computations and the maximum computations as shown on page 951.

### Computation of Minimum Provision—Case B

| Year | Normal Cost | Past Service Cost Unfunded Bal. 1/1 | Past Service Cost 5% Interest on Unfunded PSC | Past Service Cost Funded 12/31 | Past Service Cost Unfunded Bal. 12/31 | Minimum Pension Provision |
|------|------|------|------|------|------|------|
|      | (a)  | (b)  | (c)  | (d)  | (e)  | (f)  |
| 1980 | $50,000 | $240,000 | $12,000 | $31,081 | $220,919 | $62,000 |
| 1981 | 50,000 | 220,919 | 11,046 | 31,081 | 200,884 | 61,046 |
| 1982 | 50,000 | 200,884 | 10,044 | 31,081 | 179,847 | 60,044 |
| 1991 | 50,000 | -0- | -0- | -0- | -0- | 50,000 |
| 1995 | 50,000 | -0- | -0- | -0- | -0- | 50,000 |

(a) Actuarially determined.
(b) Balance in (e) in preceding year.
(c) 5% of (b).

(d) PSC funded in current year (10 years).
(e) (b) plus (c) minus (d).
(f) (a) plus (c).

### Computation of Minimum Expense—1981

| | |
|---|---:|
| Normal cost | $50,000 |
| Interest on unfunded PSC (5% × $220,919) | 11,046 |
| Vested benefits provision | -0- |
| Minimum expense, 1981 | $61,046 |

### Computation of Maximum Provision—Case B

| Year | Normal Cost | PSC Amortization 10% | Deferred Charge Bal. 1/1 | Interest Equivalent at 5% | Maximum Pension Provision |
|------|------|------|------|------|------|
|      | (a)  | (b)  | (c)  | (d)  | (e)  |
| 1980 | $50,000 | $24,000 | -0- | -0- | $74,000 |
| 1981 | 50,000 | 24,000 | $ 7,959 | $ 398 | 73,602 |
| 1982 | 50,000 | 24,000 | 16,316 | 816 | 73,184 |
| 1991 | 50,000 | 24,000 | 81,991 | 4,100 | 69,900 |
| 1992 | 50,000 | 24,000 | 62,969 | 3,148 | 70,852 |
| 1993 | 50,000 | 24,000 | 42,995 | 2,150 | 71,850 |
| 1994 | 50,000 | 24,000 | 22,023 | 1,099 | 72,901 |
| 1995 | 50,000 | -0- | -0- | -0- | 50,000 |

(a) Actuarially determined.
(b) 10% of past service cost (until fully amortized).
(c) Cumulative difference between expense accrued and amounts funded.

(d) 5% of (c).
(e) (a) plus (b) minus (d).

### Computation of Maximum Expense—1981

| | |
|---|---:|
| Normal cost | $50,000 |
| Amortization of PSC (10% × $240,000) | 24,000 |
| Interest equivalent—deduction (5% × $7,959) | (398) |
| Maximum expense, 1981 | $73,602 |

A comparison of Odom Corporation's practice in Case B of amortizing the past service cost over 15 years and funding it over 10 years with the computed minimum and maximum provisions indicates that the amounts expensed are acceptable because they fall between the minimum and maximum each year.

Using the data from Case C (pages 946–947), in which the amortization period is shorter than the funding period, results in the following minimum and maximum computations as shown on page 953.

A comparison of Odom Corporation's practice in Case C of amortizing the past service cost over 15 years and funding it over 20 years with the computed minimum and maximum provisions indicates that the amounts expensed are acceptable because they fall between the minimum and maximum each year.

In all of the three cases above the periodic pension expense fell between the minimum and maximum limits and, therefore, was an acceptable provision. **If the pension expense falls outside the minimum and maximum limits, the closest limit would be recorded as pension expense;** an adjustment in the deferred balance would be required, together with a recomputation of the defined maximum in succeeding years.[17]

In these illustrations the minimum and maximum did not change over the 15 years. As long as the company's pension expense falls between these two constraints, these lower and upper boundaries may not be affected. It is sometimes difficult to understand why the maximum can be applied for 15 years, when the past service cost and prior service cost increments should be amortized over 10 years. However, it should be remembered that in the cases illustrated here the maximum is not being used as the amount of the pension expense; rather, it is being used only as an upper boundary.

## EXPERIENCE (ACTUARIAL) GAINS OR LOSSES

As discussed earlier, actuaries deal with several uncertainties in estimating the cost of a pension plan. In tentatively resolving these uncertainties, actuaries make assumptions. Assumptions, for example, usually have to be made about such items as the interest rate, mortality rate, retirement rate, turnover rate, disability rate, and salary amounts. Seldom does actual experience coincide with estimated results. Consequently, **adjustments may need to be made to reflect (1) deviations between estimated conditions and actual experience, and (2) revisions in the underlying assumptions.** These adjustments are referred to as "experience gains and losses" in the Pension Reform Act of 1974 and as "actuarial gains and losses" in *APB Opinion No. 8.* If the experience is favorable (actual earnings rate exceeds assumed earnings rate) or if the new assumptions are more optimistic, the adjustments that result are gains; if experience has been unfavorable (actual salary rates of employees higher than assumed salary rates) or if the new assumptions are less optimistic, the adjustments are losses. The net effect of the gains and losses determined in a particular valuation is ordinarily dealt with as a single amount.

---

[17]Also, in all of the illustrations the defined maximum exceeded the defined minimum in amount. **It is possible for the minimum to exceed the maximum,** generally in cases when prior service cost is unfunded and the interest rate (used in computing the interest equivalents for both the minimum and the maximum) exceeds the rate of prior service cost amortization under the maximum. When the minimum exceeds the maximum, the minimum should be used as the basis for recognizing the accrued pension expense. The fact that the minimum can exceed the maximum (as both are defined in *Opinion No. 8*) is a result of the deficiencies in the maximum concept approved by the APB. Because of the mandatory funding now required under ERISA, this situation is unlikely to occur.

## Computation of Minimum Provision—Case C

| Year | Normal Cost | Past Service Cost | | | | Minimum Pension Provision |
| | | Unfunded Bal. 1/1 | 5% Interest on Unfunded PSC | Funded 12/31 | Unfunded Bal. 12/31 | |
|---|---|---|---|---|---|---|
| | (a) | (b) | (c) | (d) | (e) | (f) |
| 1980 | $50,000 | $240,000 | $12,000 | $19,258 | $232,742 | $62,000 |
| 1981 | 50,000 | 232,742 | 11,637 | 19,258 | 225,121 | 61,637 |
| 1982 | 50,000 | 225,121 | 11,256 | 19,258 | 217,119 | 61,256 |
| ⟨ | ⟨ | ⟨ | ⟨ | ⟨ | ⟨ | ⟨ |
| 1995 | 50,000 | 83,371 | 4,169 | 19,258 | 68,282 | 54,169 |
| ⟨ | ⟨ | ⟨ | ⟨ | ⟨ | ⟨ | ⟨ |
| 1999 | 50,000 | 18,341 | 917 | 19,258 | -0- | 50,917 |
| 2000 | 50,000 | -0- | -0- | -0- | -0- | 50,000 |

(a) Actuarially determined.
(b) Balance in (e) in preceding year.
(c) 5% of (b).
(d) PSC funded in current year (10 years).
(e) (b) plus (c) minus (d).
(f) (a) plus (c).

## Computation of Maximum Provision—Case C

| Year | Normal Cost | PSC Amortization 10% | Liability Balance 1/1 | Interest Equivalent at 5% | Maximum Pension Provision |
|---|---|---|---|---|---|
| | (a) | (b) | (c) | (d) | (e) |
| 1980 | $50,000 | $24,000 | -0- | -0- | $74,000 |
| 1981 | 50,000 | 24,000 | $ 3,864 | $ 193 | 74,193 |
| 1982 | 50,000 | 24,000 | 7,921 | 396 | 74,396 |
| ⟨ | ⟨ | ⟨ | ⟨ | ⟨ | ⟨ |
| 1994 | 50,000 | 24,000 | 75,697 | 3,785 | 77,785 |
| 1995 | 50,000 | -0- | 83,346 | 4,167 | 54,167 |
| ⟨ | ⟨ | ⟨ | ⟨ | ⟨ | ⟨ |
| 1999 | 50,000 | -0- | 18,304 | 915 | 50,915 |
| 2000 | 50,000 | -0- | -0- | -0- | 50,000 |

(a) Actuarially determined.
(b) 10% of past service cost (until fully amortized).
(c) Cumulative difference between expense accrued and amounts funded.
(d) 5% of (c).
(e) (a) plus (b) plus (d).

Once the gains and losses have been identified and measured, the problem becomes one of timing their recognition in providing for pension expense: the familiar problem of allocating gains and losses to accounting periods. To eliminate wide fluctuations in pension costs caused by these gains and losses, the profession requires that **these gains and losses usually should be spread or averaged over the current and future periods.** The time period considered reasonable for spreading or averaging is from 10 to 20 years. In practice, therefore, one of the following methods is usually applied:

1. **Spreading method.** Net gains and losses are applied to current and future cost, either through the normal cost or through the past service cost (or prior service cost on amendment); a future period of 10 to 20 years is considered reasonable.

2. **Averaging method.** An average of annual net gains and losses, developed from knowledge of those that occurred in the past and consideration of those expected to occur in the future, is applied either to the normal cost or through the past service cost (or prior service cost on amendment).

The accountant must be careful to determine whether normal cost has already been adjusted for the actuarial gain or loss. For example, some actuarial cost methods automatically spread the actuarial gains or losses and therefore double accounting might occur if a separate adjustment were made. Other actuarial cost methods recognize the actuarial gain immediately but spread or average the loss.

Note also that there is a major exception to the two approaches mentioned above. Actuarial gains and losses should be recognized immediately if they arise from a single occurrence not directly related to the operation of the pension plan and not in the ordinary course of the employer's business. Examples of **single occurrence gains or losses** are effects of a plant closing and a merger or acquisition of another whole business. To illustrate, in the late seventies Bethlehem Steel reported a third-quarter loss of $477 million, one of the largest quarterly deficits ever recorded by a U.S. corporation. A great part of this loss was attributable to future estimated benefits payable to workers who were permanently laid off. In this situation, the actuarial loss should be treated as an adjustment to the gain or loss on the plant closing, and should not affect pension cost for the current or future periods.

To illustrate the spreading method, assume that Harden Co.'s actuarial reports indicate that actuarial gains and losses are computed separately, are not a part of normal cost, and are spread over 10 years. The information relative to normal cost and actuarial gains and losses for Harden Co. is as follows:

| Year | Normal Cost | Actuarial Gain or (Loss) | Cumulative Actuarial Gain or (Loss) |
|------|-------------|--------------------------|-------------------------------------|
| 1973 | $83,000 | $ 7,000 | $ 7,000 |
| 1974 | 85,000 | 32,000 | 39,000 |
| 1975 | 86,000 | (7,000) | 32,000 |
| 1976 | 86,000 | (21,000)[a] | 11,000 |
| 1977 | 87,000 | 18,000 | 29,000 |
| 1978 | 88,000 | (73,000)[b] | (44,000) |
| 1979 | 90,000 | 6,000 | (38,000) |
| 1980 | 91,000 | 9,000 | (29,000) |
| 1981 | 90,000 | 15,000 | (14,000) |
| 1982 | 92,000 | (8,000) | (22,000) |
| 1983 | 94,000 | 12,000 | (10,000) |

[a]Changed interest rate assumption from 7% to 6½%.
[b]Plant closing resulted in a $69,000 actuarial loss.

The total pension cost for 1982 and 1983, assuming that actuarial gains and losses (excluding single occurrence loss of $69,000 due to plant closing) are spread, is as follows:

---

Computation of Pension Expense—1982

| | |
|---|---|
| Normal cost | $92,000 |
| Adjustment for actuarial gain | 4,700[a] |
| Total pension expense | $87,300 |

[a][($22,000) + $69,000] ÷ 10 = $4,700 Gain

Computation of Pension Expense—1983

| | |
|---|---|
| Normal cost | $94,000 |
| Adjustment for actuarial gain | 5,200[a] |
| Total pension expense | $88,800 |

[a][($10,000) + $69,000 − $7,000] ÷ 10 = $5,200 Gain

---

In 1983, the computation of the cumulative actuarial gain or loss is again adjusted for the single occurrence actuarial loss and the actuarial gain of $7,000 related to 1973 (now outside the 10-year period) is eliminated because it is fully amortized.

The profession further recommends recognizing **unrealized appreciation and depreciation** on investments to determine annual pension expense on a rational and systematic basis that avoids giving unjustified weight to short-term market fluctuations. Appreciation and depreciation ordinarily need not be recognized, however, for debt securities expected to be held to maturity and redeemed at face value.

The Pension Reform Act of 1974 requires that actuarial gains and losses be amortized over a period not to exceed 15 years for a single employer plan and 20 years for a multi-employer plan. Actuarial gains decrease the contributions of the employer, whereas losses increase the amount the employer must contribute to meet funding requirements.

## REPORTING OF PENSIONS IN FINANCIAL STATEMENTS

**Within the Financial Statements**    The existence of a pension plan may result in recording not only an annual provision for pension expense, which is reported on the income statement, but also accrued or deferred pension costs that are reported in the body of the balance sheet. As already indicated, if the amount paid (credit to Cash) by the employer to the pension trust is less than the annual provision (debit to Pension Expense), a credit balance accrual in the amount of the difference arises. This accrued pension cost usually appears in the long-term liability section and might be described as Liability for Pension Expense Not Funded, Provisions for Pension Cost in Excess of Payments, or Pension Costs Charged to Expense But Not Funded, or Due to Pension Fund. Classification as a current liability occurs when the liability requires the disbursement of cash within the next year.

If the cash paid (amount funded) to the pension trust during the period is greater than the amount charged to expense, a deferred charge equal to the difference arises. This deferral should be reported as Prepaid Pension Expense in the current asset section if it is current in nature, and as Deferred Pension Expense in the other assets section if it is long-term in nature.

Under present GAAP unfunded prior service cost and past service cost are not reported as liabilities. Prior service cost in general and past service cost in particular, although measured by employee service in years prior to incurrence of the cost, are considered an expense of subsequent years. Neither prior nor past service are considered to have accounting significance until recognized as expense under appropriate accrual accounting. Only if the prior or past service cost is a part of the accrual or the deferral discussed in the two preceding paragraphs would this cost appear in the employer's balance sheet.

If employees have legally enforceable claims against the employer, **vested pension rights** exist, and any excess of the actuarial present value of such rights over the amount funded or accrued might be reported as a liability. This circumstance arises occasionally in the early years of a pension plan that creates significant unfunded vested pension obligations. The unfunded vested pension right is a legal obligation that would be reported as a long-term liability (unless payment within the year appears likely) with other pension cost accruals but should be described as Pension Benefits Payable But Not Funded or Expensed. The debit side of this entry should not be charged to expense but should be carried forward as a deferred charge to the operations of future years and reported in the other assets section as Deferred Pension Expense.[18]

**Footnote Disclosure**  Because company pension plans are frequently important to an understanding of financial position and the results of operations, the following information, if not disclosed in the body of the financial statements, should be disclosed in footnotes:[19]

1. A brief statement that a pension plan exists, identifying the employee groups covered.
2. A brief statement of the company's accounting and funding policies.
3. The provision for pension cost for the period.
4. Information regarding the following:
   (a) The actuarial present value of accumulated plan benefits, separated between vested benefits and nonvested benefits.
   (b) The plan's net assets available for benefits.
   (c) The assumed rates of return used in determining the actuarial present value of accumulated plan benefits.
   (d) The date as of which the benefit information was determined.
5. The nature and effect of significant matters affecting comparability for all periods presented, such as changes in accounting methods, changes in circumstances, or significant amendments.

The footnote on the top of page 957 taken from the annual report of National Distillers and Chemicals Corporation is an example of what the profession considers appropriate pension cost disclosure.

## The Pension Reform Act of 1974

The Employee Retirement Income Security Act of 1974 (ERISA) affects virtually every private retirement plan in the United States. It attempts to safeguard employees' pension rights by mandating many pension plan requirements, including minimum funding, participation, and vesting. These requirements can influence the employers' costs significantly.

---

[18]For example, at one time IBM transferred $150 million to its pension trust because the vested benefits exceeded the market value of the fund and balance sheet accruals by $340 million. IBM classified the transfer as a prepaid expense.

[19]"Disclosure of Pension Information," *Statement of Financial Accounting Standards No. 36* (Stamford, Conn.: FASB, 1980), pars. 7 and 8.

---

### NATIONAL DISTILLERS AND CHEMICALS CORPORATION

Note 13—Pension Plans          (000 omitted)

The Company and its subsidiaries have pension plans covering substantially all of their domestic employees and employees in certain foreign countries. The total pension expense (including amortization of prior service costs over varying periods up to 40 years) was $20,260 in 1980, $19,630 in 1979 and $16,194 in 1978. The Company makes annual contributions to the plans equal to the amounts accrued for pension expense. The actuarial present value of accumulated plan benefits and net assets available for benefits at the latest valuation dates (principally January 1, 1980) is as follows:

| Actuarial present value of accumulated plan benefits: | |
|---|---|
| Vested | $184,400 |
| Nonvested | 13,800 |
| | $198,200 |
| Net assets available for benefits | $202,400 |

For approximately 90 percent of the plans, the assumed rate of return used in determining the actuarial present value of accumulated plan benefits was 10 percent, which was the approximate equivalent rate of interest for U.S. government bonds as of the valuation date having a duration equivalent to the average duration over which benefit payments will be deferred. The other plans used a 6 or 6½ percent rate of return.

---

An important part of this legislation is that annual funding is no longer discretionary; an employer must fund the plan in accordance with an actuarial cost method which over time will be sufficient to pay for all pension obligations. If funding does not occur in a reasonable manner, fines may be imposed and tax deductions denied. Plan administrators are required to publish a comprehensive description and summary of the plan and detailed annual reports accompanied by many supplementary schedules and statements relating to the plan. ERISA further mandates that the required reports, statements, and supplementary schedules be subjected to audit by qualified independent public accountants.

Another important part of the Act is the creation of the Pension Benefit Guaranty Corporation (PBGC). **The PBGC's purpose is to administer terminated plans** and to impose liens on the employer's assets for certain unfunded pension liabilities. If a plan is terminated, the PBGC can effectively impose a lien against the employer's assets for the excess of the present value of guaranteed vested benefits over the pension fund assets. This lien has the status of a tax lien and, therefore, takes priority over most other creditorship claims. An interesting aspect of this section of the Act is that the PBGC has the power to force an involuntary termination of a pension plan whenever the risks related to nonpayment of the pension obligation seem unreasonable. Because ERISA restricts the lien that the PBGC can impose to 30% of net worth, the PBGC must monitor all plans to insure that net worth is sufficient to meet the pension benefit obligations.

A large number of terminated plans have resulted in the PBGC paying approximately $57 million in benefits since 1974 to more than 39,000 participants of the failed plans. Already the PBGC is in a deficit position, and with large bankruptcies such as Braniff's (possible benefit payments as much as $70 million), the agency needs additional funds. Currently the PBGC receives its funding from employers who contribute a certain dollar amount for each employee covered under the plan (at present more than 28 million employees).[20]

An interesting accounting problem relates to the manner of disclosing the possible termination of a plan. When, for example, should a contingent liability be disclosed, given that the company is experiencing financial difficulty and may have difficulty meeting its pension obligations if its plan is terminated? At present this issue is unresolved, and considerable judgment would have to be exercised in assessing the proper accounting for these contingent liabilities.

In response to the 1974 Pension Reform Act, the FASB concluded that **no change is required in the minimum and maximum limits for the annual pension provision for pension cost as set forth in** *APB Opinion No. 8.* (Because the provisions of the 1974 Act support the maximum amount as pension cost, however, the maximum and minimum distinction loses some of its significance.) If a change in pension cost results from compliance with the 1974 Act, it must enter into the determination of periodic provisions for pension expense **after** the date the plan becomes subject to the Act.

Also, on the basis of its analysis of the 1974 Act, the Board does not believe that the Act creates a legal obligation for unfunded pension costs that warrants accounting recognition as a liability except in the following two respects: (1) In the event of the termination of a pension plan, the Act imposes a liability on an enterprise. When there is convincing evidence that a plan will be terminated, and the liability on termination will exceed fund assets and related prior accruals, the excess liability must be accrued. If the amount of the excess liability cannot be reasonably determined, disclosure of the circumstances and an estimate of the possible range of the liability must be disclosed in notes to the financial statements. (2) The employer must fund a minimum amount annually unless a waiver is obtained from the government; without a waiver, the amount currently required to be funded must be recognized as a liability by a charge to pension expense for the period, by a deferred charge, or by a combination of the two as appropriate.[21]

## MULTIEMPLOYER PLANS

Multiemployer pension plans are plans sponsored by two or more different employers. They are often negotiated as part of workers' labor union contracts in the trucking, coal mining, construction, and entertainment industries.[22] ERISA created an incentive for financially troubled companies to withdraw without penalty from multiemployer plans and shift their liability for paying pension benefits to the federal PBGC. Withdrawal by a substantial number of employers could have triggered widespread bankruptcies of these plans, as the burden of funding them fell on the remaining participating employers. To remedy this

---

[20] It appears likely that some increase in the premiums PBGC charges will be needed. For example, if Chrysler, Uniroyal, Wheeling-Pittsburgh Steel, and International Harvester were to declare that they could not pay their pension benefits, the PBGC would have a liability in excess of $1 billion. Given recent bankruptcies, such as White Motor and Rath Packing, the PBGC might not be able to meet these commitments without increased funding. See Geoffrey Colvin, "How Sick Companies Are Endangering the Pension System," *Fortune* (October 4, 1982).

[21] "Accounting for the Cost of Pension Plans Subject to the Employee Retirement Income Security Act of 1974," *FASB Interpretation No. 3* (Stamford, Conn.: FASB, 1974), pars. 3 and 5.

[22] Today there are 2,000 multiemployer pension plans covering eight million workers in the United States.

situation, Congress recently passed the Multiemployer Pension Plan Amendments Act of 1980, amending ERISA. It provides PBGC coverage only for insolvent plans, not for terminated plans, and it imposes substantial obligations for a part of the plan's unfunded vested benefits on those companies that withdraw from multiemployer plans.[23] In response to this law, the FASB issued *Technical Bulletin No. 81-3,* "Multiemployer Pension Plan Amendments Act of 1980." In it the FASB staff concluded that no changes in pension accounting would be required as a result of the new law. However, it is apparent that certain employers' contingent liabilities have significantly increased as a result of this amendment to ERISA.

## PENSION ACCOUNTING—THE CONTROVERSY

The environment related to pension reporting has changed dramatically since the issuance of *APB Opinion No. 8.* The number and size of pension plans have grown enormously, the rate of inflation has hit double digits, laws and regulations have changed, and some companies now have large amounts of unfunded accumulated benefits that will have to be paid in the future. As a consequence, some question whether disclosure requirements will suffice to rectify what some believe to be deficiencies in the present reporting of pension information. The major accounting issues are grouped under the following topics: liability recognition, expense recognition, interest rate and future salary levels, and postemployment benefits.

**Liability Recognition**   Many accountants challenge the present reporting for pension liabilities. Perhaps the most important issue relates to plans that have unfunded accumulated benefits arising from initiating the plan and from amendments giving retroactive benefit increases.[24]

Two schools of thought exist on this matter. One view is that this item meets the definition of a liability in that it arises from a past transaction, it is a present obligation, and it requires payment in the future. A modification of this argument is that only the

---

[23] This amendment has come under severe attack by many because it encourages unprofitable companies to stay in business as long as they can. For example, in the trucking industry, many companies would like to shut down losing operations or liquidate entirely. However, a company that follows one of these options may become liable for a pension liability that is in excess of the proceeds it will receive in the liquidation. As an illustration, Republic Industries purchased Johnson Motor Lines in 1979. Subsequently, Johnson Motor Lines closed, making Johnson liable for withdrawal penalties. This resulted in claims from five different multiemployer funds totaling $17.7 million, a figure not only in excess of the net worth of Johnson and Republic, but also in excess of the cumulative net income of Johnson since its inception in 1945. See, for example, Shirley Hobbs Scheible, "Erisa Eraser," *Barrons,* April 12, 1982.

[24] Note that the terms past or prior service cost were not used here. Neither does the FASB in its new disclosure requirements (*FASB No. 36*) require information to be reported on unfunded past or prior service cost. The reason is that the use of the term is somewhat misleading. That is, one company that selects an actuarial cost method that amortizes past or prior service cost as part of normal cost would not report unfunded past or prior service cost. An identical company that uses an actuarial cost method that does not amortize its costs as part of normal cost but does it separately would have to disclose these costs. For example, American Telephone and Telegraph reported more than $200 million in unfunded vested benefits in a recent annual report, but no funded prior service cost was reported because the actuarial method used did not recognize such a liability.

unfunded vested portion of the accumulated benefits is a liability. This latter argument is based on a more legalistic interpretation of what is a liability.

The other view is that pension arrangements are executory contracts (contracts in which neither party has performed), and therefore a liability does not arise until the services are received. In this case, even though prior service credit may be given, it is future benefits that the employer expects to receive from the employee. As the future benefits are received, the employee earns the pension and at this point a liability should be recognized. As an additional point, supporters of the second view might acknowledge that unfunded vested benefits are liabilities, but would be reluctant to report them in the financial statements because of their inherent subjectivity. This inherent subjectivity results from the many assumptions and estimates that need to be made to arrive at this number. In effect, the trade-off between relevance and reliability would have to be considered.

Which of these two views, or related modifications, will prevail is difficult to answer. Reporting additional liabilities in the financial statements (if it happens) would undoubtedly have a significant impact on many enterprises' reported capital structure.

**Expense Recognition**  For the most part, accountants have used one of the actuarial cost methods as a basis for recognizing expenses. Two objections exist to this approach. First, the actuarial cost methods were devised by actuaries to insure that monies were available at retirement to meet pension claims. These methods were not developed to meet the objectives of financial reporting. Some, therefore, contend that the cost of services received and the present obligation to make future pension payments will not be accurately reported in the financial statements. Second, some argue that to achieve a consistent approach to expense recognition, only one method should be approved. For example, some who hold this view believe that a constant percentage of salaries should be the basis used to determine pension expense. Others argue that comparability would not be served by requiring one method. No two companies are the same in that they have different work forces, different plans, and are subject to different economic considerations.

**Interest Rate and Future Salary Levels**  Actuaries usually can develop reasonably accurate statistics on mortality, turnover, and disability. However, economically related indicators such as interest rates and future salary levels (in effect, inflation) are more difficult to predict. The difficulty of developing accurate assumptions regarding interest rate and future salary levels leads to problems and potential abuses. At present the profession requires that the actuarial present value of accumulated plan benefits be disclosed. In measuring these accumulated plan benefits future salary increases are not taken into consideration. However, the interest rate normally used to arrive at the actuarial present value of accumulated plan benefits does take inflation into account. As a result of these measurement techniques, the benefits are understated, which may lead to misleading financial statements. A few companies attempt to overcome this measurement deficiency by providing information as to how their computation for the actuarial present value of accumulated benefits would be affected if future salaries were considered. Du Pont, for example, indicates that a $1.6 billion surplus (assets over accumulated benefits) under FASB assumptions would become a $100 million unfunded liability if future salary increases were considered. For General Electric, a small surplus would turn into an $800 million net liability.

In addition to this problem of future salary increases, the selection of an interest rate is highly subjective. A recent survey indicated that the average interest rate used by companies in the pension area was 6.3%, but many companies exceeded this average by a good margin. For example, Aluminum Company of America, Bethlehem Steel, and LTV all recently used rates of 10%. The variance in interest rates used lessens comparability among pension plans of enterprises. In addition, it should be emphasized that seemingly small changes in these rates can have substantial effects on the reported net income. For example, Chrysler in the late 1970s changed its interest rate from 6% to 7%, which added $50 million to net income.

**Postemployment Benefits**   Postemployment benefits (other than pensions) can be defined as all forms of benefits, such as health insurance, life insurance, and disability benefits, provided to a former employee. Although these types of costs have generally been charged on a pay-as-you-go basis, some argue that these benefits are similar to pensions and should be accrued and funded prior to the time the employee retires. With the escalating cost of medical benefits to retirees, these costs can be substantial. For example, in one study using reasonable assumptions, postemployment benefits expense would be approximately 44% of the amount reported as pension expense.[25] Although it is difficult to predict what the FASB will mandate in this area, conceptually these costs appear to have the same attributes as pensions; therefore similar accounting would appear appropriate.

## FUTURE ACCOUNTING STANDARDS

Whether or not there will be changes in the present reporting standard for pension costs is difficult to predict. Recently, the FASB indicated its current thinking. Their tentative conclusions were that pension obligations would be recognizable as a balance sheet liability, net of the fair value of the plan assets. The pension obligation would include consideration of future salary levels in its computation. Also reported would be the liability arising from the introduction of a new plan, or changes in existing plans, that reward past service. At the same time, an intangible asset representing enhanced future employee services would be reported as an asset and amortized to expense in future periods.

## QUESTIONS

1. Define a private pension plan. Differentiate between a funded and an unfunded pension plan. How does a contributory pension plan differ from a noncontributory plan?
2. Differentiate between "accounting for the employer" and "accounting for the pension fund."
3. Explain the term "funded" as it relates to (1) the pension fund and (2) the employer. Explain the meaning of "pension liability" as it relates to (1) the pension fund and (2) the employer.
4. Explain how cash basis accounting for pension plans differs from accrual basis accounting for pension plans.
5. Why is cash basis accounting generally considered unacceptable for pension plan accounting?
6. Why might a company select a shorter period to fund its pension plan?
7. Distinguish among (a) normal cost, (b) past service cost, and (c) prior service cost as they relate to pension plans.

---

[25]See, for example, "Employers' Accounting for Pensions and Other Postemployment Benefits" (Stamford, Conn.: FASB, 1981), par. 364. In another study, it was estimated that these costs are currently 1% of payroll, but by the year 2020 they will be 6% of payroll. See Paul A. Gewirtz, Marvin H. Green, and William Napoli, Jr., "The Unexpected Benefit Obligations," *The Financial Executive* (January 1982).

8. A partial footnote to the financial statement of the Dryer Soap Company discloses the existence of the company's employee pension plan:

   **Pension Plan.** The company has a pension plan covering all employees. Total pension expense for the year was $528,400, which includes normal cost, and the amortization of "past service cost," which originally totaled $1,400,000 (unamortized balance at year end being $1,033,826), over a 20-year period at 6%. The company's policy is to fund the pension cost accrued with the trustee of the pension plan.

   (a) What is meant by "past service cost"?

   (b) Of the total annual pension expense, what amount is normal cost?

   (c) What amount was paid to the pension fund trustee during the year?

   (d) On the basis of the footnote above, what amounts appear in the body of the balance sheet relative to the pension plan?

9. What are accumulated plan benefits? What are "vested benefits" and under what circumstances must they be accrued?

10. Upon what factors is the amount of pension expense recognized during a particular accounting period dependent?

11. What is the nature of "interest equivalents" and what is the justification for including them in the determination of pension cost?

12. Accountants currently are divided in their opinions of the nature of pension cost. Two primary views are supported.

    (a) What are these two views?

    (b) Indicate which of these views you support and explain your view.

13. What is the minimum annual provision for pension cost that may be provided under *APB Opinion No. 8*? What is the maximum annual provision?

14. Which method results in the more appropriate pension cost provision: the minimum provision or the maximum provision? Support your view.

15. If accounting charges for past service costs exceed funding payments, what kind of account arises and how should it be reported in the financial statements? If the reverse occurs, that is, payments exceed charges, what kind of account arises and how should it be reported?

16. What are actuarial gains and losses as related to pension plans? What methods are applied in practice to account for actuarial gains or losses?

17. In what situations should actuarial gains and losses be recognized immediately?

18. What disclosures should be made in financial statements or their related footnotes for pension plans?

19. (a) What are the arguments in favor of accruing past service cost only to the extent funded?

    (b) What are the arguments in favor of accruing past service cost regardless of the amount funded?

20. What is a multiemployer plan and what accounting questions arise when a company is involved with one of these plans?

21. One of the most controversial issues related to pension plan reporting is how to account for unfunded accumulated benefits arising from plan initiation and plan amendments that give retroactive benefit increases. What is accounting practice in this area? What other approach is advocated?

22. What problems do interest rates and future salaries create in accounting for pension plans? Why are interest rates of such importance in accounting for pension plans?

## CASES

**C21-1** The following items frequently appear on financial statements.

   (a) Under the caption Deferred Charges:
   Deferred Pension Cost (attributable to Funding of Past Service Liability).

(b) Under the caption Retained Earnings Appropriated:
Reserve for Past Service Pension Cost (after deducting the related anticipated tax reduction).

(c) On the Income Statement:
Current Service Cost (Normal Cost)
Past Service Cost
Trustee's Fees.

**Instructions**

With regard to "accounting for pension cost," explain the significance of each of the items above on corporate financial statements. Show how each is consistent with generally accepted accounting principles. (Note: all items set forth above are not necessarily to be found on the statements of a single company.)

(AICPA adapted)

**C21-2** In examining the costs of pension plans, a CPA encounters certain terms. The elements of pension costs that the terms represent must be dealt with appropriately if generally accepted accounting principles are to be reflected in the financial statements of entities with pension plans.

**Instructions**

(a) 1. Discuss the theoretical justification for accrual recognition of pension costs.
2. Discuss the relative objectivity of the measurement process of accrual versus cash (pay-as-you-go) accounting for annual pension costs.
(b) Explain the following terms as they apply to accounting for pension plans:
1. Actuarial valuations.
2. Actuarial cost methods.
3. Vested benefits.
(c) What information should be disclosed about a company's pension plans in its financial statements and its notes?

(AICPA adapted)

**C21-3** Lahey Inc. has just acquired all of the capital stock of Golf Cart Corporation and has asked you to audit the balance sheet of the latter as of the date of acquisition. In the course of your examination you determine that the company has a noncontributory pension plan and has charged to income all payments made to the pension trust. There is no special provision in the pension plan that limits the company liability to an amount equal to assets in trust. The independent actuaries employed by the company have furnished you with the following summary of past service liability as of the audit date.

|  | Accrued Liability | Assets in Trust | Net Liability |
|---|---|---|---|
| For employees already retired | $1,307,900 | $467,500 | $ 840,400 |
| For employees eligible to retire at their own option | 524,700 |  | 524,700 |
| For employees under retirement age | 1,725,900 |  | 1,725,900 |
|  | $3,558,500 | $467,500 | $3,091,000 |

**Instructions**

Discuss the factors to be considered in making adjustments to properly set forth the financial position disclosed by the statements under audit. Lahey Inc. is in the 48% tax bracket.

(AICPA adapted)

**C21-4** Sigma Oopsalon, Inc., was organized in 1963 and established a formal pension plan on January 1, 1979, to provide retirement benefits for all employees. The plan is noncontributory and is funded through a trustee, the Corner National Bank, which invests all funds and pays all benefits as they become due. Vesting occurs when the employee retires at age sixty-five. Original past service cost of $220,000 is being amortized over 15 years and funded over 10 years. The company also funds an amount equal to current normal cost net of actuarial gains and losses. There have been no amendments to the plan since its inception. Portions of the independent actuary's report follows:

---

**Sigma Oopsalon, Inc.**
**BASIC NONCONTRIBUTORY PENSION PLAN**
Actuarial Report as of June 30, 1983

---

I. Current Year's Funding and Pension Cost

| | | |
|---|---:|---:|
| Normal cost (before adjustment for actuarial gains) computed under the individual level cost method (with liability) | | $ 68,300 |
| Actuarial gains: | | |
| Investment gains (losses): | | |
| Excess of expected dividend revenue over actual dividend revenue | | (700) |
| Gain on sale of investments | | 8,100 |
| Gains in actuarial assumptions for: | | |
| Mortality | | 6,800 |
| Employee turnover | | 10,100 |
| Reduction in pension cost from closing of plant | | 16,000 |
| Net actuarial gains | | 40,300 |
| Normal cost (funded currently) | $28,000 | 28,000 |
| Past service costs: | | |
| Funding | 28,490 | |
| Amortization | | 21,194 |
| Total funded | $56,490 | |
| Total pension cost for financial statement purposes | | $ 49,194 |

II. Fund Assets (all available for benefits)

| | | |
|---|---:|---:|
| Cash | | $ 8,400 |
| Dividends receivable | | 3,050 |
| Investment in common stocks, at cost (market value, $355,600) | | 325,500 |
| | | $ 336,950 |

III. Actuarial Liabilities (nonvested as of June 30, 1983)

| | |
|---|---:|
| Number of employees | 92 |
| Number of employees retired | 0 |
| Yearly earnings of employees | $1,196,000 |
| Actuarial liability (present value of accumulated plan benefits) | $ 290,000 |

---

**Instructions**

(a) What interest rate is being used in the amortization and funding of the past service cost?

(b) On the basis of requirements for accounting for the cost of pension plans, evaluate the (1) treatment of actuarial gains and losses and (2) computation of pension cost for financial statement purposes. Ignore income tax considerations.

(c) Independently of your answer to part (a), assume that the total amount to be funded is $65,326, the total pension cost for financial statement purposes is $58,030, and all amounts presented in the actuary's report are correct. In accordance with professional pronouncements what type of information would be presented in the footnote to the financial statements of Sigma Oopsalon, Inc., for the year ended June 30, 1983.

(AICPA adapted)

# EXERCISES

**E21-1** On January 1, 1983, Taco Still Company adopts an employee pension plan. The following data relate to the operation of the plan for the year 1983:

1. Normal pension cost was actuarially computed to be $84,000 for 1983 and $89,000 for 1984 and is being funded annually.
2. The past service cost of $360,000 is to be amortized over 10 years.
3. It is estimated that investments of the pension fund will earn 10%.
4. The past service cost is being funded over 15 years with end-of-year payments.

**Instructions**

(Round to the nearest dollar and ignore the minimum and maximum limits.)
(a) Prepare the journal entry to record the payment to the pension trust and the provision for pension cost for 1983.
(b) Assuming that the same facts exist in 1984, prepare the journal entry to record the payment to the pension trust and the provision for pension cost for 1984.

**E21-2** On January 2, 1983, Refrigfry Corp. adopted a pension plan covering all its employees. The plan's actuary estimated past service costs at $300,000. Refrigfry funds the entire amount of past service cost plus interest at the end of the first year of the plan, and each year funds normal cost in full at the end of the year. For accounting purposes, Refrigfry has chosen to record as annual pension expense 10% of past service cost, plus normal cost, plus (or minus) interest on any differences between amounts expensed and amounts funded. Normal cost is as follows: 1983, $60,000; 1984, $60,000; 1985, $70,000; and 1986, $80,000. The actuary recommends the use of a 9% rate for discounting.

**Instructions**

(Round to the nearest dollar.)
(a) Prepare the journal entry to record the pension expense and the amount funded in 1983.
(b) Prepare the journal entry to record the pension expense and the amount funded in 1986.

**E21-3** On January 1, 1983, Mustafa Rug Co. adopted a noncontributory pension plan. An actuary determined that the past service cost at the date of adoption was $650,000, and that the normal pension cost is $200,000. The actuary also indicated that the appropriate interest rate was 8%.

Management plans to fund the normal cost fully each year, and to fund the past service cost by making equal payments at the end of each of the first 5 years. The past service cost is to be amortized over 20 years.

**Instructions**

(Round to the nearest dollar and ignore the minimum and maximum limits.)
Prepare the journal entries to recognize the annual pension expense and to record the annual contribution to the pension fund for the years 1983, 1984, and 1985.

**E21-4** Gooie Bakeries, Inc. adopted a pension plan for its employees on January 1, 1982. The pertinent data relative to the cost of the plan are as follows:

1. Cost allocated to past service, $700,000.
2. Period of past service cost amortization: 20 years.
3. Normal cost, $75,000.
4. Amount funded annually, $100,000.
5. Rate of earnings on pension fund investments, 8%.

**Instructions**

(a) Prepare a five-year schedule that discloses for each year, beginning with the year of adoption, the amounts of (1) normal cost, (2) amortized past service cost, (3) interest equivalent on difference between prior years' provisions and amounts funded, (4) total annual charge to expense, (5) amount funded, and (6) cumulative difference between provisions and amounts funded (round to the nearest dollar and ignore the minimum and maximum limits).

(b) Using the data from part (a), prepare the journal entry to record the amount funded in the fifth year and the provision for pension expense.

**E21-5** As a result of labor negotiations, Camel Fur Co. adopts a pension plan for its employees. An actuarial firm estimates past service cost at $400,000 and normal cost for the first year of $50,000. Camel Fur Co. will amortize the past service cost at the rate of 10% per year and fund it over 20 years with end-of-the-year payments. Only half of each year's normal cost will be funded during the first three years. The company's intent is to expense the maximum allowable for acceptable accounting purposes. The actuary recommends the use of a 9% discounting rate.

**Instructions**

(Round to the nearest dollar.)
(a) Prepare the journal entry to record the pension provision and the amount funded during the first year.
(b) Prepare the journal entry to record the pension provision and the amount funded during the third year. Normal cost is $60,000 in the second year and $80,000 in the third year.
(c) What is reported on Camel Fur's balance sheet at the end of the third year?

**E21-6** Cimple Energy Corp. adopts a pension plan on January 1, 1983. The following information relates to the operation of the plan for 1983 and 1984:

1. Normal pension cost was actuarially computed to be $44,000 for both years. Normal cost is funded annually.

2. The past service cost of $270,000 is to be funded by making equal payments at the end of each of the first 20 years, and is to be amortized over 10 years.

3. It is estimated that investments of the pension fund will earn a 12% return.

**Instructions**

Compute the minimum provision allowed under *APB Opinion No. 8* for the years 1983 and 1984.

**E21-7** Gunsmoke Chemicals, Inc. fully funds the normal portion of its pension expense. When the company started its pension plan early in 1983, it adopted a 16-year amortization period and a 20-year funding period for the past service cost of $350,000. The data below relate to the pension plan for 1983–85.

|  | 1983 | 1984 | 1985 |
|---|---|---|---|
| Normal cost | $100,000 | $103,900 | $110,100 |
| Past service cost: |  |  |  |
| Amortization on 16-year basis | 30,037 | 30,037 | 30,037 |
| Interest at 4% on accrued pension liability | -0- | 171 | 349 |
| Annual year-end payments to pension fund | 25,754 | 25,754 | 25,754 |

**Instructions**

(Round to the nearest dollar.)
(a) Prepare the journal entries to recognize the annual pension expense and the annual contribution to the pension fund for 1983–85.
(b) Compute the accrued pension liability at the end of 1985.
(c) Compute the minimum and maximum pension expense for 1984.

**E21-8** On January 1, 1981, Tonge Company adopted a noncontributory pension plan covering all of its employees. An actuary determined that the past service cost at the date of adoption was

$800,000; the normal cost is $150,000 annually; and the appropriate interest rate is 8%. Tonge's accountant indicates that the past service cost is to be amortized over 15 years. Tonge has chosen Byrd National Bank as the trustee of the plan. According to the trust agreement, Tonge is to fund the normal cost fully at the end of each year, and to fund the past service cost by making equal payments at the end of each of the first 10 years. Reports issued by the trustee indicated the following:

|  | 12/31/81 | 12/31/82 |
|---|---|---|
| Fund Assets | $269,225 | $ 561,790 |
| Fund Liabilities | -0- | 1,800 |
| Actuarial Present Value of Accumulated Plan Benefits: |  |  |
| Vested | 100,000 | 150,000 |
| Nonvested | 900,000 | 1,000,000 |

**Instructions**

(a) Indicate the amounts that would be reflected on Tonge's income statement and balance sheet for 1981 and 1982.

(b) Prepare the footnote disclosure needed in Tonge's financial statements at December 31, 1982 relative to its pension plan.

**E21-9** The notes to the financial statements of Gregory Company at December 31, 1982 include the following:

**Pension Plan:** On January 1, 1981, the company adopted a pension plan covering all of its employees. The total pension expense for 1982 was $248,714, which includes normal cost, $150,000, amortization of past service cost over 15 years, $97,815, and an amount equivalent to interest (6%) on the excess of provisions over amounts funded. The company funds normal cost fully each year and is funding the past service cost in equal amounts over 20 years. A comparison of accumulated plan benefits and plan net assets for the company's pension plan is presented below:

|  | At December 31, 1982 |
|---|---|
| Actuarial Present Value of Accumulated Plan Benefits: |  |
| Vested | $ 201,000 |
| Nonvested | 1,167,420 |
|  | $1,368,420 |
| Net Assets | $ 479,620 |

The weighted average assumed rate of return used in determining the actuarial present value of accumulated plan benefits was 6%.

**Instructions**

(a) Determine the amounts of the following:
  1. Past service cost at January 1, 1981. (Round to nearest dollar.)
  2. Amount of past service cost which is funded each year.

(b) Provide a brief explanation of each of the following amounts:
  1. $248,714.
  2. $97,815.
  3. $1,368,420.
  4. $479,620.
  5. What does the difference between $1,368,420 and $479,620 represent?

**E21-10** DuPage Corporation, a calendar-year company, adopted a noncontributory defined benefit pension plan on January 1, 1983. DuPage's actuarial consulting firm recommended a 6% interest rate as appropriate and, applying an acceptable actuarial method, determined that the past service cost at the date of adoption of the plan is $300,000. Management decided to amortize the past service cost over 16 years and to fund the past service cost by making equal payments to the pension fund trustee at the end of each of the first 20 years. As of December 31, 1984, no benefits have vested. The normal (current) pension cost is to be funded fully each year. Information provided by the actuarial consultant relating to the pension plan for the years 1983 and 1984 is as follows:

|  | 1983 | 1984 |
|---|---|---|
| Amortization of past service cost | $29,686 | $29,686 |
| Funding of past service cost | 26,155 | 26,155 |
| Normal pension cost | 60,000 | 65,000 |

**Instructions**

(a) Prepare schedules to compute the amounts relating to the pension plan that DuPage should report on its income statement and balance sheet for 1983 and 1984. Show supporting computations in good form.

(b) Compute the minimum and maximum pension cost limits allowable under generally accepted accounting principles for 1983. Show supporting computations in good form.

(AICPA adapted)

**E21-11** Rozanna Dana Inc. adopts a pension plan on January 1, 1983. According to actuarial computations, the past service cost is $1,350,000, and the normal cost for 1983 and 1984 is $400,000. The past service cost is completely funded on January 1, 1983; normal cost is funded each year. The pension fund is able to earn 6% on its investments.

**Instructions**

Assuming that the defined maximum limit is recognized as pension expense, prepare the journal entries for 1983 and 1984 to record pension expense and to record the payment to the pension fund. Support your entries with labeled computations.

**E21-12** Current pronouncements on pension accounting advocate the consistent application of an accounting method that uses an acceptable actuarial cost method and that results in annual pension provisions that lie between the minimum and maximum. Interest equivalents are a part of both minimum and maximum annual pension provisions.

Presented below are data related to the employee's pension plan of the Pretzel Chip Corporation:

| | |
|---|---|
| Past service cost | $750,000 |
| Normal cost | 65,000 |
| Cash deposited in the fund during 1984 | 100,000 |
| Pension expense not funded or deferred pension expense, 1/1/84 | –0– |
| Funded portion of past service cost, 1/1/84 | 200,000 |
| Pension expense for 1984 as computed by the firm's accountants | 125,000 |
| Rate of return earned on pension fund investment | 8% |

**Instructions**

(a) What would the 1984 interest equivalent be under the minimum annual provision for the case above?

(b) What would the 1984 interest equivalent be under the maximum annual provision for the case above?

**E21-13** Cathedral Filmstrips Co., a calendar-year corporation, adopted a company pension plan at the beginning of 1983. This plan is to be funded and noncontributory. Cathedral used an appropriate actuarial cost method to determine its normal annual pension cost for 1983 and 1984 as $15,000 and $16,000, respectively, which was paid in the appropriate year.

Cathedral's actuarially determined past service costs were funded on January 1, 1983, at an amount properly computed as $118,000. These past service costs are to be amortized at the maximum amount permitted by generally accepted accounting principles. The interest factor assumed by the actuary is 9%.

## Instructions

Prepare journal entries to record the funding of past service costs on December 31, 1983, and the pension expenses for the years 1983 and 1984. Under each journal entry give the explanation or computation to support your entry. Round to the nearest dollar.

(AICPA adapted)

# PROBLEMS

**P21-1** Pine Oaks Company initiated a funded, noncontributory pension plan and gave employees credit for prior employment. The actuary estimated the past service cost at date of inception of the plan to be $120,000. Management decides to amortize past service cost over three years and to fund past service cost over four years using an 8% interest rate. (A less than 10-year amortization period is assumed only to keep the problem short.) Normal cost is actuarially determined to be $18,000 for year 1, $22,000 for year 2, $25,000 for year 3, and $27,000 for year 4; normal cost is fully funded each year.

## Instructions

(Round all amounts to the nearest dollar and ignore the minimum and maximum limits.)
(a) Prepare an amortization, funding, and expense schedule for the first four years.
(b) Prepare the entries for each of the first four years of the plan.
(c) Indicate the amounts that would be reflected on the income statement and the balance sheet for the first four years.

**P21-2** Carefree Hospital Corp. initiated a funded, noncontributory pension plan and gave employees credit for prior employment (assume no vested benefits). The past service cost was actuarially estimated at the date of inception of the plan to be $840,000. To keep the problem short, assume the past service cost is to be amortized over four years and funded over three years in equal amounts. Normal cost is actuarially determined to be $300,000 each year for the first two years and $380,000 for the next two years; normal cost is fully funded each year. The actuary recommends a 10% interest rate.

## Instructions

(Round amounts to the nearest dollar and ignore the minimum and maximum limits.)
(a) Prepare an amortization, funding, and expense schedule for the first four years.
(b) Prepare the entries for each of the first four years of the pension plan.
(c) Indicate the amounts that are reflected on the income statement and the balance sheet for the first four years.

**P21-3** The notes to the financial statements of New Rose's Company, for the year ended December 31, 1983, include the following:
**Retirement Plan:** The charge to operations for pension expense of $2,373,858 includes normal cost of $2,000,000, past service cost amortization of $360,900, and interest (9%) equivalents of $12,958 on the excess of provisions over amounts funded. Normal cost is funded annually and, although the company's plan (adopted January 1, 1981) does not require funding of past service cost, this cost is currently being funded over 30 years. For accounting purposes the past service cost is being amortized over a 16-year period. As of the balance sheet date the unamortized past service cost allocable to future periods was $2,702,020.

## Instructions

(Round all amounts to the nearest dollar.)
(a) Differentiate "normal cost" from "past service cost."
(b) What justification is there for allocating past service cost to future periods?
(c) What amounts relative to the company's pension plan appear in the body of the balance sheet at December 31, 1983? Assume normal cost is $2,000,000 each year.
(d) Prepare the journal entry, with explanation, to record the amount funded in 1983 and the pension provision for the year.

**P21-4** Don Walker Piano Company is contemplating the adoption of a pension plan for its employees. President Walker wishes to know the effect such a plan might have on the company's earnings. An actuarial consulting firm has indicated that the cost of the proposed plan allocated to past service would be $800,000 and that normal cost would be $120,000. President Walker had indicated that the company will not fund the past service cost, but each year the company will pay to the pension trustee an amount equal to normal cost and interest at 8% on the unfunded past service cost.

**Instructions**

(a) Compute for President Walker (1) the minimum provision and (2) the maximum provision allowable in the first year under the stipulations and data relative to the company's pension plan.

(b) Compute for President Walker (1) the minimum provision and (2) the maximum provision allowable in the fifth year of the plan assuming no change in actuarial method or the funding policies of the company (round computations to the nearest dollar).

**P21-5** Several years after incorporation Wingtip Airlines Company initiated a funded, noncontributory pension plan. The past service cost at the date of inception of the plan was actuarially estimated to be $354,595. The past service cost is to be amortized over four years and funded over three years.

**Instructions**

(Ignore the minimum and maximum limits.)

(a) Prepare a schedule that reflects the amortization and funding of the past service cost using a 12% interest rate.

(b) Assuming the actuary determined the normal pension cost to be $75,000 for year 1 and $80,000 for year 2, prepare the entries with respect to the pension plan for both years.

(c) Indicate the amounts that are reflected on the income statement and the balance sheet for each of the first two years.

**P21-6** Vertigo Ladder Co. initiated a funded, noncontributory pension plan several years after incorporation. The actuary estimated the past service cost at the date of inception of the plan to be $188,609. To keep the problem short, assume the company decides to amortize the past service over three years and to fund past service cost over two years.

**Instructions**

(Ignore the minimum and maximum limits.)

(a) Prepare a schedule that reflects the amortization and funding of the past service cost using a 10% interest rate.

(b) Assuming that the actuary determined the normal pension cost to be $70,000 for year 1 and $73,000 for year 2, prepare the entries with respect to the pension plan for both years.

(c) Indicate the amounts that are reflected on the income statement and the balance sheet for each of the first two years.

**P21-7** Rittenberg Enterprises, which started operations in 1978, instituted a pension plan on January 1, 1983. The insurance company which is administering the pension plan has computed the present value of past service costs at $100,000 for the five years of operations through December 31, 1982. The pension plan provides for fully vested benefits when employees have completed ten years of service. Therefore, there will be no vested benefits until December 31, 1987.

The insurance company proposed that Rittenberg Enterprises fund the past service cost in equal installments over 25 years calculated by the present value method. Using an interest rate of 8%, the annual payment for past service cost would be $9,368. The company's treasurer agreed to this payment schedule. In addition, the controller concluded that a 25-year period was a reasonable period for amortizing the past service costs for book purposes. Consequently, the past service costs will also be amortized at the annual rate of $9,368 for 25 years.

The normal cost for the pension fund is estimated to be $30,000 each year for the next four years. The annual payment to the insurance company covering the current year's normal cost and the annual installment on the past service cost is payable on December 31 each year, the end of Rittenberg Enterprises' fiscal year. The insurance company was paid $39,368 ($30,000 + $9,368) on December 31, 1983, to cover the company's pension obligations for 1983.

**Instructions**

(a) Calculate and label the components of the maximum and minimum 1983 financial statement pension expense limits in accordance with generally accepted accounting principles for Rittenberg Enterprises.

(b) Assume Rittenberg Enterprises will be unable to remit the full pension payment ($39,368) in 1984 and will submit only $30,000 (the normal cost) to the insurance company. If Rittenberg Enterprises can recognize $39,368 as pension expense in 1984, show the entry required. If the company cannot recognize the $39,368 as pension expense in 1984, explain why not.

(CMA adapted)

**P21–8** Aroma Winery Inc. adopts a pension plan on January 1, 1983. An actuarial firm advises that an 8% interest rate is appropriate, and determines that the past service cost as of January 1, 1983 is $525,000, and the normal cost for 1983 is $76,000. The plan provides for vesting after 30 years of service by employees.

Management decides to fund the normal cost fully each year and to fund the past service cost over 30 years. Past service cost is to be amortized over 25 years.

**Instructions**

Assuming that the normal cost remains the same for 1984 and 1985, prepare the following for the years 1983, 1984, and 1985.

(a) A schedule that reflects the amortization and funding of past service cost, and the amounts to be reflected in the balance sheet.

(b) A schedule showing the computation of the minimum provision.

(c) A schedule showing the computation of the maximum provision.

(d) Journal entries at each year end to recognize the annual pension expense and to record the contribution to the pension fund.

**P21–9** Kathy Crabtree Ad Agency initiated a pension plan several years after incorporation. The amount of the past service cost was computed at the date of adoption of the plan to be $730,000. Management decides to amortize the past service cost over four years and to fund it each year end over three years. The normal cost is computed to be $40,000 for the first four years of the plan; normal cost is completely funded each year. An interest rate of 9% is appropriate for the pension fund. Assume that there are no vested benefits.

**Instructions**

(a) Prepare a schedule that reflects the amortization and funding of past service cost and the amounts reflected on the balance sheet at the end of the first four years.

(b) Prepare a schedule showing the computation of the minimum provision.

(c) Prepare a schedule showing the computation of the maximum provision.

(d) For financial accounting reporting purposes, will the company be allowed to amortize past service cost over four years?

**P21–10** On January 1, 1983, Gary Borling Publishing Co. adopts a funded, noncontributory pension plan. An actuarial firm computes the normal cost to be $54,000 for 1983 and 1984 and determines that the past service cost amounts to $440,000 at the date of the plan adoption. An interest rate of 9% is appropriate to the pension fund. Normal cost is fully funded each year. Past service cost is to be funded by equal payments at the end of each of the first 30 years.

**Instructions**

(a) Assuming that management decides to amortize past service costs over 30 years, prepare a schedule to reflect the amortization and funding of past service cost for 1983 and 1984. Also compute the maximum and minimum provisions under these policies.

(b) Prepare the journal entries to record the pension expense and the contribution to the pension fund for the years 1983 and 1984 under each of the following situations using the funding information above:

1. Past service cost is amortized over 30 years.
2. Management desires to record the minimum acceptable pension expense.
3. Management desires to record the maximum acceptable pension expense.

**P21-11** Yogi Mattress Co., through labor negotiations has been encouraged to amend as of January 1, 1984, its employee pension plan, which has been in operation for 4 years, having been adopted on January 1, 1980. At the time the plan was adopted, the past service cost was actuarially computed to be $800,000 with normal cost set at $100,000 annually. Since the inception of the plan, the company has been funding in amounts equal to the annual provisions. The annual provisions for pension costs have included normal cost and amortization of past service cost over 25 years at a 6% interest rate.

As a result of the amendment, retirement benefits are to be increased. And, because credit has been given for years of service prior to the date of amendment, prior service cost has increased $420,000, and normal cost has increased to $145,000. The increase in prior service cost is to be amortized over 21 years, but the company will continue to fund annually the same amount it funded during the first 4 years of the plan.

Annual provisions for pension cost from January 1, 1984, include normal cost, amortization of past service cost (until fully amortized), amortization of the increase in prior service cost, and interest equivalents at 6% on any difference between prior years' provisions and amounts funded.

**Instructions**

(a) Compute the amount of prior service cost as of the amendment date, January 1, 1984.
(b) What amounts relative to the pension plan appeared in the body of the December 31, 1983, balance sheet?
(c) Prepare the journal entry that was recorded in 1983 for the amount funded and the provision for pension cost. Show computations in your explanation.
(d) Prepare the journal entry, with explanation, to record the amount funded in 1984 and the provision for pension cost for that year.
(e) What amounts relative to the pension plan would appear in the body of the December 31, 1984, balance sheet?
(f) Prepare the journal entry, with explanation, to record the amount funded in 1985 (assume no change in actuarial method or funding policy from 1984) and the provision for pension cost for 1985.

**P21-12** Meditation Corporation, which has been in operation for the past 23 years, decided late in 1983 to adopt, beginning on January 1, 1984, a funded pension plan for its employees. The pension plan is to be noncontributory and will provide for vesting after 5 years of service by each eligible employee. A trust agreement has been entered into whereby a large national insurance company will receive the yearly pension fund contributions and administer the fund.

Management, through extended consultation with the fund trustee, internal accountants, and independent actuaries, arrived at the following conclusions:

1. The normal pension cost for 1984 will be $30,000.
2. The present value of the past service cost at date of inception of the pension plan (January 1, 1984) is $200,000.
3. Because of the large sum of money involved, the past service costs will be funded at a rate of $17,765 per year for the next 30 years. The first payment will not be due until January 1, 1985.
4. In accordance with *APB Opinion No. 8*, the "unit credit method" of accounting for the pension costs will be followed. Pension costs will be amortized over a 25-year period.

The 25-year accrual factor is $18,736 per year. Neither the maximum nor minimum amortization amounts as prescribed by *APB Opinion No. 8* will be violated.

5. Where applicable, an 8% interest rate was assumed.

**Instructions**

(a) Define: Normal pension costs, past service costs.
(b) What amounts (use xxx if amount can't be calculated) will be reported in the company's
 1. Income statement for 1984?
 2. Balance sheet as of December 31, 1984?
 3. Notes to the statements?
 Give account titles with the amounts.
(c) What amounts (use xxx if amount can't be calculated) will be reported in the company's
 1. Income statement for 1985?
 2. Balance sheet as of December 31, 1985?
 3. Notes to the statements?
 Give account titles with the amounts.

(CMA adapted)

**P21–13** The following information has been obtained from the actuarial reports for the Fiedler Music Company. Assume that the market value of the securities in the pension fund is equal to book value, and that there is no past or prior service cost.

| Year | Current Cost | Actuarial Gains (Losses) | Net Contribution |
|------|------|------|------|
| 1974 | $ 33,266 | $    998 | $32,268 |
| 1975 | 39,113 | 6,609 | 32,504 |
| 1976 | 41,770 | 10,827 | 30,943 |
| 1977 | 51,548 | (180) | 51,728 |
| 1978 | 58,101 | 7,876 | 50,225 |
| 1979 | 50,940 | 50,940[a] | -0- |
| 1980 | 64,063 | 28,701[b] | 35,362 |
| 1981 | 69,948 | 27,552 | 42,396 |
| 1982 | 86,520 | 19,441 | 67,079 |
| 1983 | 96,900 | 25,624 | 71,276 |
| 1984 | 108,150 | 173,542[c] | -0- |

[a]Includes $35,025 gain as a result of change in interest assumption from 6% to 6½%.
[b]Includes $6,021 of gain carried over from 1976.
[c]Includes:
 1. $27,000 gain due to withdrawal of 2 officers of the Company.
 2. $65,600 gain as result of change in interest assumption from 6½% to 7½%.
 3. $51,200 gain from withdrawals in connection with a plant closing 2/20/84.

**Instructions**

Fiedler Music Company uses the spreading method to allocate its actuarial gains and losses over a period of 10 years. Compute the amount of pension expense for the years 1983 and 1984 giving proper consideration to the separately noted items in a, b, and c.

**P21–14** In December 1973 a noncontributory employee group-retirement plan was adopted by the Vitesse Cycle Company. Assume that the market value of the securities in the fund is equal to book value. The following information has been obtained from the actuary's reports.

| Year | Current Cost | Actuarial Gains (Losses) | Net Contribution |
|------|------|------|------|
| 1974 | $133,064 | $ 3,994 | $129,070 |
| 1975 | 156,452 | 46,998 | 109,454 |
| 1976 | 167,078 | 43,306 | 123,772 |
| 1977 | 206,192 | (720) | 206,912 |
| 1978 | 232,404 | 22,614 | 209,790 |
| 1979 | 203,758 | 203,758[a] | -0- |
| 1980 | 256,250 | 114,806[b] | 141,444 |
| 1981 | 279,794 | 110,210 | 169,584 |
| 1982 | 346,078 | 77,764 | 268,314 |
| 1983 | 390,180 | 102,498 | 287,682 |
| 1984 | 394,501 | 272,878[c] | 121,623 |

[a]Includes $170,112 gain from change in interest assumption from 5 to 5½%.
[b]Includes $24,084 of gain carried over from 1979.
[c]Includes $85,000 gain due to withdrawal of 2 officers of the company.

**Instructions**

Vitesse Cycle Company uses the spreading method to allocate actuarial gains and losses. The company has adopted a 10-year period for allocation.
(a) Compute the pension expense for 1983 and 1984.
(b) What alternative methods could be used to allocate the actuarial gains and losses?

# CHAPTER 22

# Accounting for Leases

A **lease** is a contractual agreement between a **lessor** and a **lessee** that conveys to the lessee the right to use specific property (real or personal), owned by the lessor, for a specific period of time in return for stipulated, and generally periodic, cash payments (rents). An essential element of the lease agreement is that the lessor conveys less than the total interest in the property. Because of the financial, operating, and risk advantages that the lease arrangement provides, many businesses lease substantial amounts of property, both real and personal, as an alternative to ownership.

Prior to 1960, leasing chiefly affected retailing companies, which frequently lease their premises. Over the past two decades, leasing has grown tremendously in popularity; instead of borrowing money to buy an airplane, a computer, a nuclear core, or a satellite, a company leases it. Even the gambling casinos lease their slot machines. Airlines and railroads lease huge amounts of equipment; many hotel and motel chains lease their facilities; and most retail chains lease the bulk of their retail premises and warehouses. Increasingly, utilities have turned to leasing, as it has become harder for them to borrow money. The increased significance and prevalence of lease arrangements in recent years have intensified the need for uniform accounting and complete informative reporting of these transactions.[1]

## ADVANTAGES OF LEASING

Although the lease arrangement is not without its disadvantages, the growth in its use suggests that leasing often has a genuine advantage over owning property. Some of the commonly discussed advantages of leasing are:

1. Leasing permits 100% financing versus 60 to 80% under purchasing, thus conserving cash and working capital.

---

[1]The popularity and general applicability of leasing are evidenced by the fact that 548 of 600 companies surveyed by the AICPA in 1980 disclosed either capitalized or noncapitalized lease data (*Accounting Trends and Techniques*—1981).

2. Leasing permits rapid changes in equipment, reduces risk of obsolescence, and in many cases passes the risk in residual value to the lessor.

3. Leasing permits write-off of the full cost of the asset (including land and residual values) and provides additional tax advantages through acceleration of deductions, investment tax credits, or the shifting of tax advantages to the party in the higher tax bracket.

4. Leasing may be more flexible, because lease agreements may contain less restrictive provisions than other debt agreements.

5. Leasing in a certain manner leads to junior claims, does not add debt on a balance sheet, and does not affect financial ratios; hence it may add to borrowing capacity.[2]

The last point, commonly referred to as "off-balance-sheet financing," is critical to some companies. For instance, the 1981 balance sheet of Chart House, Inc., a restaurateur operating 500 restaurants nationwide, showed long-term debt of $127 million and total stockholders' equity of $88 million. Therefore, Chart House's debt-to-equity ratio was a high but manageable 1.4 to 1. But the company also was obligated under leases, chiefly for restaurant land; the future rental payments related to those noncancelable operating leases was $125 million. Add the capitalized value of these payments to the long-term debt and Chart House's debt-to-equity ratio climbs well over 2 to 1. In the late seventies, Safeway Stores was first required to capitalize lease commitments with a present value of $748 million on a balance sheet showing only $131 million in long-term debt. Or, consider what the situation of Glosser Bros., Inc., a retail store chain, would be if it had to capitalize its future minimum lease commitments on noncancelable leases of $72 million on its 1982 balance sheet showing less than $3 million of long-term debt and $24 million of equity.

The existence or nonexistence of these advantages depends a great deal on the type and use required of the asset, the period of time involved, the financial condition of the company, and the future tax and economic conditions. Therefore, the decision to lease or to purchase deserves thorough individual analysis.

## LEASE PROVISIONS

Because a lease is a contract, the provisions agreed to by the lessor and lessee may vary widely and be limited only by their ingenuity and the peculiarities of the asset. The **duration** (lease term) of the lease may be from a few moments to the entire expected economic life of the asset. The **rental payments** may be level from year to year, increasing in amount, or decreasing; the rents may be predetermined or may vary with sales, the prime interest rate, the consumer price index or some other factor; in most cases the rent is set to enable the lessor to recover the cost of the asset plus a fair return over the life of the lease. The **obligations for taxes, insurance, and maintenance** (executory costs) may be assumed by either the lessor or the lessee, or they may be divided between the lessor and the lessee. **Restrictions** somewhat comparable to those in bond indentures may limit the lessee's activities relative to dividend payments, or incurrence of further debt and lease obligations. The lease contract may be **noncancelable** or may grant the right to **early termination** on pay-

---

[2]As demonstrated later in this chapter, certain types of lease arrangements need not be capitalized on the balance sheet. The liability section is frequently relieved of large future lease commitments which if recorded would adversely affect the debt-to-equity ratio. The reluctance to record lease obligations as liabilities is one of the primary reasons capitalized lease accounting is resisted and circumvented by lessees.

ment of a set scale of prices (prices often representing the unrecovered cost of the lessor) plus a penalty. In case of **default** the lessee may be liable for all future payments at once, receiving title to the property in exchange; or the lessor may enjoy the prerogative to sell and to collect from the lessee all or a portion of the difference between the sale price and the lessor's unrecovered cost. **Alternatives of the lessee at termination** of the lease may range from none, to the right to purchase the leased asset at the fair market value, or the right to renew or buy at a nominal price.[3]

In practice, any combination of provisions on these different points may be used, ranging from provisions that approach the purchase of a current service through the traditional short-term rental lease to those that seem to be purely financing devices for purchase/sale transactions. These different transactions call for different accounting methods to portray properly the substance of each situation.

## CONCEPTUAL NATURE OF A LEASE

If United Airlines borrows $47,000,000 on a 10-year note from National City Bank to purchase a Boeing 757 jet plane, it is clear that an asset and related liability should be reported on United's balance sheet at that amount. If United purchases the 757 for $47,000,000 directly from Boeing through an installment purchase over 10 years, it is equally clear that an asset and related liability should be reported. However, if United leases the Boeing 757 for 10 years through a noncancelable lease transaction with payments of the same amount as the installment purchase transaction, differences of opinion start to develop over how this and other types of lease transactions should be reported. The various views of accounting for leases are as follows:

**Do Not Capitalize Any Leased Assets** Because the lessee does not have ownership of the property, capitalization under this view is considered inappropriate. Furthermore, a lease is an executory contract requiring continuing performance by both parties. Because executory contracts (such as purchase commitments and employment contracts) are not capitalized at present, this view contends that leases also should not be capitalized.

**Capitalize Those Leases Similar to Installment Purchases** Accountants should report transactions in accordance with their economic substance; therefore, if installment purchases are capitalized, so also should leases that have the same characteristics as installment purchases. For example, in the illustration above United is committed to the same payments over a 10-year period for either a lease or installment purchase; lessees simply make rental payments while owners make mortgage payments. Why shouldn't the financial statements report these transactions in the same manner?

**Capitalize All Long-Term Leases** Under this approach, the only requirement for capitalization is the long-term right to use the property. Often referred to as the property rights approach, it would lead to the capitalization of all long-term leases.[4]

**Capitalize Firm Leases Where the Penalty for Nonperformance is Substantial** A final approach is to capitalize only firm (noncancelable) contractual rights and obligations. "Firm" means that it is unlikely that performance under the lease can be avoided without a severe penalty.[5]

---

[3] John H. Myers, "Reporting of Leases in Financial Statements," *Accounting Research Study No. 4* (New York: AICPA, 1964), pp. 10–11.

[4] See, for example, *Accounting Research Study No. 4,* which advocated this position.

[5] Yuji Ijiri, *Recognition of Contractual Rights and Obligations,* Research Report (Stamford, Conn.: FASB, 1980).

## To Capitalize or Not to Capitalize

In short, the various viewpoints range from no capitalization to capitalization of all leases. The FASB apparently agrees with the capitalization approach when it is similar to an installment purchase situation, noting that a lease which transfers substantially all of the benefits and risks of ownership of property should be capitalized. This viewpoint leads to three basic conclusions: (1) the characteristics which indicate that substantially all of the benefits and risks of ownership have been transferred must be identified. Such transactions are capital leases which should be recorded as purchases and sales of assets. (2) For consistency, the same characteristics should apply to the lessee and the lessor. (3) Those leases that do not transfer substantially all the benefits and risks of ownership are operating leases and should not be capitalized but rather accounted for simply as rental payments and receipts.

## If Capitalization, What Amount?

In stipulating the number, timing, and amounts of the rental payments, the lease provides the basis for measuring the asset and the liability involved. By capitalizing the present value of the future rental payments, **the lessee** records an asset and a liability at an amount generally representative of the asset's market value or purchase price. Having capitalized the asset, the lessee records the depreciation. **The lessor,** having transferred substantially all the benefits and risks of ownership, recognizes a sale matching the cost of the asset against the sale and records a receivable in the amount of the future rentals. The lease rental payments are accounted for by both the lessee and the lessor as periodic payments consisting of interest and principal.

The remainder of the chapter presents the different types of leases and the specific criteria, accounting rules, and disclosure requirements set forth by the FASB in accounting for leases.

# ACCOUNTING FOR LEASES—A BRIEF BACKGROUND

As indicated above, the FASB adopted the installment purchase approach as far as determining when lease transactions should be capitalized. This approach is much the same as that used by the profession earlier, when in 1965 the APB required that leases that were in substance "installment purchases" be capitalized by the lessee as asset purchases with a related obligation. The accounting criteria set forth for capitalization or noncapitalization of lease arrangements, however, were readily circumvented by lessees. Furthermore, the earlier standards did not require symmetry in the classification of and accounting for the lease by both the lessee and the lessor as parties to the same lease.

In 1976 the FASB issued *Statement No. 13,* "Accounting for Leases," which superseded all previous official pronouncements on lease accounting. The Board believed that *Statement No. 13* would remove "most, if not all, of the conceptual differences in lease classification as between lessors and lessees and that it provides criteria for such classification that are more explicit and less susceptible to varied interpretation than those in previous literature."[6]

---

[6]"Accounting for Leases," *Statement of Financial Accounting Standards No. 13* (Stamford, Conn.: FASB, 1976), par. 62.

# ACCOUNTING BY LESSEES

## Classification of Leases by the Lessee

In attempting to standardize accounting for leases, the FASB tried to determine when the risks and benefits of ownership transferred. If conditions were similar to an installment purchase, in effect, the lessee should capitalize the lease and the lessor should remove the asset from its balance sheet. If the transaction did not meet certain criteria, the lease should not be capitalized. Therefore, from the standpoint of the **lessee** all leases may be classified for accounting purposes as follows:

(a) Operating leases (noncapitalization method).
(b) Capital leases (capitalization method).

If at the date of the lease agreement (inception of the lease[7]) the lessee is party to a non-cancelable lease that meets **one or more** of the following four criteria, the lessee shall classify and account for the arrangement as a **capital lease:**

1. The lease transfers ownership of the property to the lessee.
2. The lease contains a bargain purchase option.[8]
3. The lease term is equal to 75% or more of the estimated economic life of the leased property.[9]
4. The present value of the minimum lease payments (excluding executory costs) equals or exceeds 90% of the fair value of the leased property.[10]

Leases that do not meet any of the four criteria above are classified and accounted for by the lessee as **operating leases.**

The flowchart on page 980 shows that a lease meeting any one of the four criteria results in the lessee having a capital lease.

In keeping with the FASB's reasoning that a significant portion of the value of the asset is consumed in the first 75% of its life, neither the third nor the fourth criterion is to be applied when the inception of the lease occurs during the last 25 percent of the life of the asset.

## Operating Method (Lessee)

Under the **operating method,** rent expense (and a compensating liability) accrues day by day to the lessee as the property is used. The lessee assigns rent to the periods benefiting from the use of the asset and ignores, in the accounting, any commitments to make future payments. Appropriate accruals are made if the accounting period ends between cash payment dates. For example, if on January 1, 1984, a company leases an asset for four

[7]For purposes of classifying the lease transaction, inception is the date of the lease agreement or commitment, if earlier. See "Inception of the Lease," *Statement of Financial Accounting Standards No. 23* (Stamford, Conn.: FASB, 1978), par. 7.

[8]A **bargain purchase option** is a provision allowing the lessee to purchase the leased property for a price that is lower than the expected fair value of the property at the date the option becomes exercisable; the difference between the purchase price and the expected fair market value must be large enough to make exercise of the option reasonably assured at the inception of the lease.

[9]However, this criterion as well as criterion four cannot be used for a lease that begins within the last 25% of the total estimated economic life of the leased property, including earlier years of use.

[10]"Accounting for Leases," *op. cit.,* par. 7.

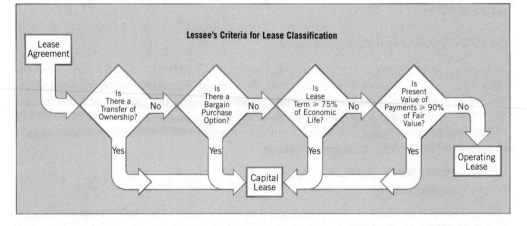

years at an annual rental of $80,000 payable at the beginning of each year, the following journal entry is recorded annually for four years:

| | | |
|---|---:|---:|
| Rent Expense | 80,000 | |
| Cash (or Rent Payable) | | 80,000 |

The rented asset, as well as any long-term liability for future rental payments, is not reported on the balance sheet. Rent expense would be reported on the income statement. In addition, footnote disclosure is required for all operating leases that have noncancelable lease terms in excess of one year. An illustration of the type of footnote disclosure required for an operating lease (as well as other types of leases) is provided in Appendix M of this chapter.

### Capital Lease Method (Lessee)

Under the **capital lease method** the lessee treats the lease transaction as if an asset were being purchased on time, that is, like a financing transaction in which an asset is acquired and an obligation is created. **The lessee records a capital lease as an asset and a liability at the lower of (1) the present value of the minimum lease payments (excluding executory costs) during the lease term**[11] **or (2) the fair market value of the leased asset at the inception of the lease.**[12]

[11]The **lease term** is the sum of all the following periods, but not beyond the date a bargain purchase option becomes exercisable:
1. The fixed noncancelable term.
2. Any periods covered by a bargain renewal option.*
3. Renewal periods in which penalties are imposed in an amount that reasonably assures the renewal of the lease.
4. Renewal periods during which a lessee's guarantee of the lessor's debt is expected to be in effect.
5. Renewal periods preceding the date a bargain purchase becomes exercisable.
6. Periods for which the *lessor* has the option to renew or extend the lease term.
   * A **bargain renewal option** is a provision allowing the lessee to renew the lease for a rental that is lower than the expected fair rental of the property at the date the option becomes exercisable; the difference between the renewal rental and the expected fair rental must be great enough to make exercise of the option to renew reasonably assured at the inception of the lease.

[12]"Accounting for Leases," *op. cit.*, par. 10.

The special terms related to accounting for capital leases are discussed below:

**Minimum Lease Payments**   The amount of minimum lease payments for the lessee is the sum of:

1. The minimum rental payments required during the lease term.
2. The amount of any bargain purchase option, or if there is no such option:
   a. The amount of any guarantee by the lessee of the residual value.
   b. The amount payable for failure to renew or extend the lease.

Contingent rentals and executory costs (defined below) are not included in the lessee's computation of the present value of the minimum lease payments.

**Discount Rate**   The lessee computes the present value of the minimum lease payments using the **lessee's incremental borrowing rate,** which is defined as: "The rate that, at the inception of the lease, the lessee would have incurred to borrow the funds necessary to buy the leased asset on a secured loan with repayment terms similar to the payment schedule called for in the lease."[13]

If, however, the lessee (1) knows the **implicit rate computed by the lessor** and (2) the implicit rate computed by the lessor is less than the lessee's incremental borrowing rate, then the lessee must use the implicit rate. The interest rate implicit in the lease is the discount rate that, when applied to the minimum lease payments and the unguaranteed residual value accruing to the lessor, causes the aggregate present value to be equal to the fair value of the leased property to the lessor.[14] In practice, the lessee frequently does not know the implicit rate. Because **the lessee may not capitalize the leased property at more than its fair value,** the lessee is prevented from using an excessively low discount rate.

In a capital lease transaction the lessee is using the lease as a source of financing. The lessor finances the transaction (provides the investment capital) through the leased asset and the lessee makes rent payments which actually are installment payments. Therefore, over the life of the property rented, the rental payments to the lessor constitute a payment of principal plus interest.

**Executory Costs**   Like most assets, leased tangible assets require the incurrence of insurance, maintenance, and tax expenses (called **executory costs**) during their economic life. If the lessor retains responsibility for the payment of these "ownership-type costs," a portion of each lease payment that represents executory costs should be excluded in computing the present value of the minimum lease payments because it does not represent payment on or reduction of the obligation. If the portion of the minimum lease payments representing executory costs is not determinable from the provisions of the lease, an estimate of such amount must be made. Many lease agreements, however, specify that these executory costs be assumed by the lessee; in these cases the rental payment can be used without adjustment in the present value computation.

**Residual Value**   The residual value is the estimated fair (market) value of the leased property at the end of the lease term.[15] The lessor often transfers the risk of loss to the lessee or

---

[13]Ibid., par. 5 (l).

[14]Ibid., par. 5 (k).

[15]"Lessee Guarantee of the Residual Value of Leased Property," *FASB Interpretation No. 19* (Stamford, Conn.: FASB, 1977), par. 3.

to a third party through a guarantee of the estimated residual value. The amount of a **guaranteed residual value** is (1) the certain or determinable amount at which the lessor has the right to require the lessee to purchase the asset, or (2) the amount the lessee or the third-party guarantor guarantees will be realized. If it is not guaranteed in full, the **unguaranteed residual value** is the estimated residual value exclusive of any portion guaranteed. According to *FASB Interpretation No. 19,* a lease provision requiring the lessee to make up a residual value deficiency that is attributable to damage, extraordinary wear and tear, or excessive usage is not included in the minimum lease payments. Such costs are similar to contingent rentals in that the amount is not determinable at the inception of the lease. Like **contingent rentals,** such costs are recognized as period costs when incurred.[16]

**Accounting Separately for the Asset and the Liability**  If the lease agreement satisfies either criterion (1) or (2), that is, transfers ownership of the asset to the lessee or contains a bargain purchase option, the leased asset is depreciated in a manner consistent with the lessee's normal depreciation policy for owned assets, using the economic life of the asset and any estimated salvage value. If the lease does not transfer ownership of the asset to the lessee or contain a bargain purchase option, the leased asset is amortized over the term of the lease.

Throughout the term of the lease, **the effective interest method** is used to allocate each lease payment between a reduction of the lease obligation and interest expense. This method produces a constant rate of interest in each period on the outstanding balance of the obligation.

Whichever discount rate is used by the lessee in determining the present value of the minimum lease payments, that rate usually must be used by the lessee in applying the effective interest method to capital leases.

Although the amount capitalized as an asset and the amount recorded as an obligation at the inception of the lease are computed at the same present value, the amortization of the asset and the discharge of the obligation are **independent accounting processes** during the term of the lease. The lessee should amortize the leased asset by applying the conventional depreciation methods: straight-line, sum-of-the-years'-digits, declining balance, units of production, etc. The selection of a depreciation method should be more in line with the objectives of income measurement and asset valuation.

The FASB uses the term "amortization" more frequently than the term "depreciation" in recognition of intangible leased property rights. The authors prefer the term "depreciation" as a description of the write-off of the costs of the expired services of a tangible asset.

## Capitalized Lease Method Illustrated (Lessee)

The preceding section was a discussion of the theory and rules underlying the accounting treatment used by the lessee in recording capitalized lease transactions. The following presentation illustrates the accounting involved in applying the capitalized lease method.

Lessor Company and Lessee Company sign a lease agreement dated January 1, 1984, that calls for Lessor Company to lease equipment to Lessee Company beginning January 1, 1984. The lease agreement contains the following terms and provisions:

---

[16]For a discussion of contingent rentals, see *FASB Statement No. 29,* "Determining Contingent Rentals" (Stamford, Conn.: FASB, 1979).

1. The term of the lease is five years, and the lease agreement is noncancelable, requiring equal rental payments of $25,981.62 at the beginning of each year (annuity due basis).

2. The equipment has a fair value at the inception of the lease of $100,000, an estimated economic life of five years, and no residual value.

3. Lessee Company pays all of the executory costs except for the property taxes of $2,000 per year, which are included in the annual payments.

4. The lease contains no renewal options and the equipment reverts to Lessor Company at the termination of the lease.

5. Lessee Company's incremental borrowing rate is 11% per year.

6. Lessee Company depreciates similar equipment that it owns on a straight-line basis.

7. Lessor Company set the annual rental to earn a rate of return on its investment of 10% per year; this fact is known to Lessee Company.

The lease meets the criteria for classification as a capital lease because (1) the lease term of five years, being equal to the equipment's estimated economic life of five years, satisfies the 75% test, and (2) the present value of the minimum lease payments ($100,000 as computed below) exceeds 90% of the fair value of the property ($100,000).

The minimum lease payments are $119,908.10 ($23,981.62 × 5) and the amount capitalized as leased assets is computed as the present value of the minimum lease payments (excluding executory costs—property taxes of $2,000) as follows:

> Capitalized amount = ($25,981.62 − $2,000) × present value of an annuity due
> of 1 for 5 periods at 10%
> (Table 6–5)
>
>    = $23,981.62 × 4.16986
>    = $100,000

The lessor's implicit interest rate of 10% is used instead of the lessee's incremental borrowing rate of 11%, because (1) it is lower, and (2) the lessee has knowledge of it.

The entry to record the signing of the lease and the capitalization of the present value of the minimum lease payments net of executory costs (i.e., the recorded value of the asset and the liability) on Lessee Company's books on January 1, 1984, is:

| | | |
|---|---|---|
| Leased Equipment Under Capital Leases | 100,000 | |
| Obligations Under Capital Leases | | 100,000 |

Note that the preceding entry records the obligation at the net amount of $100,000 (the present value of the future rental payments) rather than at the gross amount of $119,908.10 ($23,981.62 × 5).

The journal entry to record the **first lease payment on January 1, 1984** is as follows:

| | | |
|---|---|---|
| Property Tax Expense | 2,000.00 | |
| Obligations Under Capital Leases | 23,981.62 | |
| Cash | | 25,981.62 |

Recording the annual lease payment in subsequent periods results in the recognition of additional expenses relative to the leased equipment, because in this case each lease payment of $25,981.62 consists of three elements: (1) a reduction in the lease obligation, (2) a financing cost (interest expense), and (3) executory costs (property taxes). The total financing cost (interest expense), over the term of the lease, is the difference between the present value ($100,000) of the lease payments and the actual cash disbursed, net of executory costs, ($119,908.10), or $19,908.10. The annual interest should be computed by applying the effective interest method. Therefore, the annual interest expense is a function of the outstanding obligation, as illustrated in the following schedule:

**LESSEE COMPANY**
**Lease Amortization Schedule**
**(Annuity due basis)**

| Date | Annual Lease Payment | Executory Costs | Interest (10%) on Unpaid Obligation | Reduction of Lease Obligation | Lease Obligation |
|------|------|------|------|------|------|
| | (a) | (b) | (c) | (d) | (e) |
| 1/1/84 | | | | | $100,000.00 |
| 1/1/84 | $ 25,981.62 | $ 2,000 | $  -0- | $ 23,981.62 | 76,018.38 |
| 1/1/85 | 25,981.62 | 2,000 | 7,601.84 | 16,379.78 | 59,638.60 |
| 1/1/86 | 25,981.62 | 2,000 | 5,963.86 | 18,017.76 | 41,620.84 |
| 1/1/87 | 25,981.62 | 2,000 | 4,162.08 | 19,819.54 | 21,801.30 |
| 1/1/88 | 25,981.62 | 2,000 | 2,180.32* | 21,801.30 | -0- |
| | $129,908.10 | $10,000 | $19,908.10 | $100,000.00 | |

(a) Lease payment as required by lease.
(b) Executory costs included in rental payment.
(c) Ten percent of the preceding balance of (e) except for 1/1/84; since this is an annuity due, no time has elapsed at the date of the first payment and no interest has accrued.
(d) (a) minus (b) and (c).
(e) Preceding balance minus (d).
*Rounded by 19 cents.

At December 31, 1984, Lessee Company's fiscal year end, **accrued interest** is recorded as follows (if reversing entries are used, this entry would be reversed at 1/1/85):

| | | |
|------|------|------|
| Interest Expense | 7,601.84 | |
| Interest Payable | | 7,601.84 |

Depreciation of the leased equipment over its lease term of five years applying Lessee Company's normal depreciation policy (straight-line method) results in the following entry on December 31, 1984:

| | | |
|------|------|------|
| Depreciation Expense—Capital Leases | 20,000 | |
| Accumulated Depreciation—Capital Leases | | 20,000 |
| ($100,000 ÷ 5 years) | | |

At December 31, 1984, the assets recorded under capital leases are separately identified on the lessee's balance sheet. Similarly the related obligations are separately identified with the portion due within one year or the operating cycle, whichever is longer, classified with current liabilities and the balance with noncurrent liabilities. For example, the current portion of the 12/31/84 total obligation of $76,018.38 in the lessee's amortization schedule is the amount of the reduction in the obligation in 1985, or $16,379.78. The liability section as it relates to lease transactions at 12/31/84 would appear as follows:

| Current Liabilities | |
| --- | --- |
| Interest Payable | $ 7,601.84 |
| Obligations Under Capital Leases | 16,379.78 |
| Noncurrent Liabilities | |
| Obligations Under Capital Leases | $59,638.60 |

The journal entry to record the lease payment of January 1, 1985, is as follows:

| | | |
| --- | --- | --- |
| Property Tax Expense | 2,000.00 | |
| Interest Expense (or Interest Payable) | 7,601.84 | |
| Obligations Under Capital Leases | 16,379.78 | |
| Cash | | 25,981.62 |

Entries through 1988 would follow the pattern above. Other executory costs (insurance and maintenance) assumed by Lessee Company would be recorded in a manner similar to that used to record any other operating costs incurred on assets owned by Lessee Company.

**Upon expiration of the lease,** the amount capitalized as leased equipment is fully amortized and the lease obligation is fully discharged. If not purchased, the equipment would be returned to the lessor, and the leased equipment and related accumulated depreciation accounts would be removed from the books.[17] If the equipment is purchased at termination of the lease at a price of $5,000, and the estimated life of the equipment is changed from five to seven years, the following entry might be made:

| | | |
| --- | --- | --- |
| Equipment ($100,000 + $5,000) | 105,000 | |
| Accumulated Depreciation—Capital Leases | 100,000 | |
| Leased Equipment Under Capital Leases | | 100,000 |
| Accumulated Depreciation—Equipment | | 100,000 |
| Cash | | 5,000 |

## COMPARISON OF CAPITAL LEASE WITH OPERATING LEASE

If the lease illustrated above had been accounted for as an operating lease, the first-year charge to operations would have been $25,981.62, the amount of the rental payment. Treating the transaction as a capital lease, however, resulted in a first-year charge of $29,601.84: depreciation of $20,000 (assuming straight-line), interest expense of $7,601.84 (per schedule on page 984), and executory costs of $2,000. The schedule on page 986 shows that while the total charges to operations are the same over the lease term whether the lease is accounted for as a capital lease or as an operating lease, under the capital lease treatment the charges are higher in the earlier years and lower in the later years.[18]

---

[17]If the lessee purchases a leased asset *during the term of a "capital lease,"* it is accounted for like a renewal or extension of a capital lease, that is, "any difference between the purchase price and the carrying amount of the lease obligation shall be recorded as an adjustment of the carrying amount of the asset." See "Accounting for Purchase of a Leased Asset by the Lessee During the Term of the Lease," *FASB Interpretation No. 26* (Stamford, Conn.: FASB, 1978), par. 5.

[18]The higher charges in the early years is one reason lessees are reluctant to adopt the capital lease accounting method. Lessees (especially those of real estate) claim that it is really no more costly to operate the leased asset in the early years than in the later years; thus, they advocate an even charge similar to that produced by the operating method.

**LESSEE COMPANY**
Schedule of Charges to Operations
Capital Lease Versus Operating Lease

| Year | Capital Lease | | | | Operating Lease Charge | Difference |
|---|---|---|---|---|---|---|
| | Depreciation | Executory Costs | Interest | Total Charge | | |
| 1984 | $ 20,000 | $ 2,000 | $ 7,601.84 | $ 29,601.84 | $ 25,981.62 | $ 3,620.22 |
| 1985 | 20,000 | 2,000 | 5,963.86 | 27,963.86 | 25,981.62 | 1,982.24 |
| 1986 | 20,000 | 2,000 | 4,162.08 | 26,162.08 | 25,981.62 | 180.46 |
| 1987 | 20,000 | 2,000 | 2,180.32 | 24,180.32 | 25,981.62 | (1,801.30) |
| 1988 | 20,000 | 2,000 | — | 22,000.00 | 25,981.62 | (3,981.62) |
| | $100,000 | $10,000 | $19,908.10 | $129,908.10 | $129,908.10 | $  –0– |

If an accelerated method of depreciation is used, the differences between the amounts charged to operations under the two methods would be even larger in the earlier and later years.

In addition, using the capital lease approach would have resulted in an asset and related liability of $100,000 initially reported on the balance sheet; no such assset or liability would be reported under the operating method. Therefore, the following occurs if a capital lease instead of an operating lease is employed: (a) an increase in the amount of reported debt (both short-term and long-term), (b) an increase in the amount of total assets (specifically long-lived assets), and (c) a lower income early in the life of the lease and, therefore, lower retained earnings. Thus many companies believe that capital leases have a detrimental impact on their financial position as their debt to total equity ratio increases and their rate of return on total assets decreases. As a result, the business community resists capitalizing leases.

Whether their resistance is well founded is a matter of conjecture. From a cash flow point of view, the company is in the same position whether the lease is accounted for as an operating or a capital lease. The reason why managers often argue against capitalization is that it can more easily lead to violation of loan covenants, can affect the amount of compensation received by owners (for example, a stock compensation plan tied to earnings), and finally can lower rates of return and increase debt to equity relationships, thus making the company less attractive to present and potential investors.[19]

---

[19]A recent study indicates that management's behavior did change as a result of *FASB No. 13*. For example, many companies restructure their leases to avoid capitalization; others increase their purchases of assets instead of leasing; and others, faced with capitalization, postpone their debt offerings or issue stock instead. However, it is interesting to note that the study found no significant effect on stock or bond prices as a result of capitalization of leases. A. Rashad Abdel-khalik, "The Economic Effects on Lessees of FASB Statement No. 13, Accounting for Leases," *Research Report* (Stamford, Conn.: FASB, 1981).

# ACCOUNTING BY LESSORS

## Classification of Leases by the Lessor

From the standpoint of the **lessor,** all leases may be classified for accounting purposes as follows:

(a) Operating leases.

(b) Direct financing leases.

(c) Sales-type leases.

If at the date of the lease agreement (inception) the lessor is party to a lease that meets **one or more** of the following Group I criteria (1, 2, 3, and 4) and **both** of the following Group II criteria (1 and 2), the lessor shall classify and account for the arrangement as a **direct financing lease** or a **sales-type lease.**[20] (Note that the Group I criteria are identical to the criteria that must be met for a lease to be classified as a capital lease by a lessee, per page 979.)

### Group I

1. The lease transfers ownership of the property to the lessee.
2. The lease contains a bargain purchase option.
3. The lease term is equal to 75% or more of the estimated economic life of the leased property.
4. The present value of the minimum lease payments (excluding executory costs) equals or exceeds 90% of the fair value of the leased property.

### Group II

1. Collectibility of the payments required from the lessee is reasonably predictable.
2. No important uncertainties surround the amount of unreimbursable costs yet to be incurred by the lessor under the lease (lessor's performance is substantially complete).

Why the Group II requirements? The answer is that the profession wants to make sure that the lessor has really transferred the risks and benefits of ownership. If collectibility of payments is not predictable, or if performance by the lessor is incomplete, then it is inappropriate to remove this leased asset from the lessor's books. As an illustration, computer leasing companies at one time used to buy IBM equipment, lease it, and remove the leased assets from their balance sheets. In leasing the asset, the computer leasing companies stated that they would be willing to substitute new IBM equipment if obsolescence occurred. However, when IBM introduced a new computer line, IBM refused to sell it to the computer leasing companies. As a result, a number of computer leasing companies could not meet their contracts with their customers and were forced to take back the old equipment. What the computer leasing companies had taken off the books now had to be reinstated. Such a case demonstrates one reason for the Group II requirements.

**The distinction for the lessor between a direct financing lease and a sales-type lease is the presence or absence of a manufacturer's or dealer's profit (or loss).** A sales-type lease involves a manufacturer's or dealer's profit, and a direct financing lease does not. The profit (or loss) to the lessor is evidenced by the difference between the fair value of the leased property at the inception of the lease and the lessor's cost or carrying amount (book value). Normally, sales-type leases arise when manufacturers or dealers use leasing as a

---

[20]*FASB Statement No. 13, op. cit.,* pars. 6, 7, and 8.

means of marketing their products. For example, a computer manufacturer will lease its computer equipment to businesses and institutions. Direct financing leases generally result from arrangements with lessors that are primarily engaged in financing operations, such as lease-finance companies, banks, insurance companies, and pension trusts. However, a lessor need not be a manufacturer or dealer to recognize a profit (or loss) at the inception of the lease that requires application of the sales-type lease accounting.

**All leases that do not qualify as direct financing or sales-type leases are classified and accounted for by the lessors as operating leases.** The following flowchart shows the circumstances under which a lease is classified as operating, direct financing, or sales-type for the lessor.

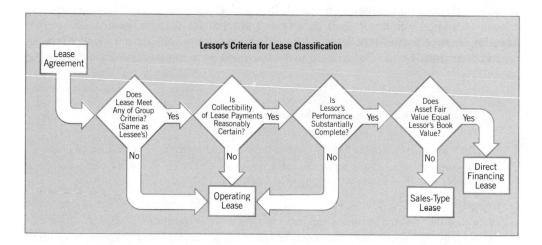

As a consequence of the additional Group II criteria for lessors, it is possible that a lessor having not met both criteria will classify a lease as an **operating** lease while the lessee will classify the same lease as a **capital** lease. In such an event, both the lessor and lessee will carry the asset on their books and both will depreciate the capitalized asset.

For purposes of comparison with the lessee's accounting, only the operating and direct financing leases will be illustrated in the following section. The more complex sales-type lease will be discussed later in the chapter.

**Operating Method (Lessor)**   Under the **operating method** each rental receipt of the lessor is recorded as rental revenue for the use of an item carried as a plant asset. The plant asset is depreciated in the normal manner, with the depreciation expense of the period matched against the rental revenue. The amount of revenue recognized in each accounting period is a level amount (straight-line basis) regardless of the lease provisions, unless another systematic and rational basis is more representative of the time pattern in which the benefit is derived from the leased asset. In addition to the depreciation charge, maintenance costs and the cost of any other services rendered under the provisions of the lease that pertain to the current accounting period are charged to expense. To illustrate the operating method, assume that Mayo, Inc., as owner-operator of a medical arts building having a cost of $2,000,000 and a depreciable life of 40 years (no salvage value), earned gross rentals of $460,000 during the year from its three-year leases with various doctors and dentists. The earned gross rentals of $460,000 are recorded in a straightforward manner:

| Cash (or Rent Receivable) | 460,000 | |
| Rental Revenue | | 460,000 |

Depreciation is simply recorded (using the straight-line method) as follows:

| Depreciation Expense—Leased Buildings | 50,000 | |
| Accumulated Depreciation—Leased Buildings | | 50,000 |

If $240,000 in real estate taxes, insurance, maintenance, and other operating costs during the year are the obligation of the lessor, they are recorded as expenses chargeable against the gross rental revenues. All the revenues and expenses of the leased building would be conventionally recorded by Mayo, Inc., with income before interest and taxes of $170,000 resulting from the rental activity (revenue of $460,000 less expenses of $290,000).

If Mayo, Inc., owned plant assets that it used in addition to those leased to others, the leased building would be separately classified with or near property, plant, and equipment in an appropriately titled account such as Building Leased to Others or Investment in Leased Property; Accumulated Depreciation is conventionally shown as a deduction from the investment. If significant in amount or in terms of activity, the rental revenues and accompanying expenses are separated in the income statement from sales revenue and cost of goods sold.

Rent is reported as revenue over the lease term as it becomes receivable according to the provisions of the lease. Generally, rentals under an operating lease are receivable on a straight-line basis, that is, in equal amounts at equal intervals. However, if the rentals depart from a straight-line basis, the revenue still should be recognized on a straight-line basis unless another basis more accurately reflects a decline in the service potential of the asset.

**Direct Financing Method (Lessor)**    Leases that are in substance the financing of an asset purchase by a lessee require the lessor to substitute a "lease payments receivable" for the leased asset. The information necessary to record a direct financing lease is as follows:

1. **GROSS INVESTMENT ("LEASE PAYMENTS RECEIVABLE").** The minimum lease payments plus the unguaranteed residual value accruing to the lessor at the end of the lease term.[21]
2. **UNEARNED INTEREST REVENUE.** The difference between the gross investment (the receivable) and the cost or carrying amount (book value) of the property.
3. **NET INVESTMENT.** The gross investment (the receivable) less the unearned interest revenue included therein.

**The minimum lease payments (net of executory costs paid by lessor) plus the unguaranteed residual value accruing to the benefit of the lessor (labeled "gross investment" by the FASB) are recorded as the "lease payments receivable."** The unearned interest revenue is amortized to revenue over the lease term by applying the effective interest method. Thus, a constant rate of return is produced on the net investment in the lease. Any contingent rentals, including rentals based on variables such as machine hours of use or sales volume, are credited to revenue when they become receivable.[22]

---

[21] Ibid., par. 17. Initially the unguaranteed residual value could be classified in a separate account. If the unguaranteed residual value is included in the Lease Payments Receivable account, it would be reclassified by the lessor at the end of the lease term if not purchased by the lessee.

[22] See amendment of *FASB Statement No. 13:* "Determining Contingent Rentals," *Statement of Financial Accounting Standards No. 29* (Stamford, Conn.: FASB, 1979).

The following presentation, utilizing the data from the preceding Lessor Company/Lessee Company illustration on page 983, illustrates the accounting treatment accorded a direct financing lease. The information relevant to Lessor Company in accounting for this lease transaction is repeated below.

1. The term of the lease is five years beginning January 1, 1984, noncancelable, and requires equal rental payments of $25,981.62 at the beginning of each year; payments include $2,000 of executory costs (property taxes).

2. The equipment has a cost of $100,000 to Lessor Company, a fair value at the inception of the lease of $100,000, an estimated economic life of five years, and no residual value.

3. No initial direct costs were incurred in negotiating and closing the lease transaction.

4. The lease contains no renewable options and the equipment reverts to Lessor Company at the termination of the lease.

5. Collectibility is reasonably assured and no additional costs (with the exception of the property taxes being collected from the lessee) are to be incurred by Lessor Company.

6. Lessor Company set the annual rentals to insure a rate of return of 10% (implicit rate) on its investment as follows:

| | |
|---|---|
| Cost of leased asset | $100,000.00 |
| Less: Present value of residual value | -0- |
| Amount to be recovered by lessor through lease payments | $100,000.00 |
| Five periodic lease payments: $100,000 ÷ 4.16986[a] | $ 23,981.62 |

[a]PV of an annuity due of 1 for 5 years at 10% (Table 6-5)

The lease meets the criteria for classification as a direct financing lease because (1) the lease term exceeds 75% of the equipment's estimated economic life, (2) the present value of the minimum lease payments exceeds 90% of the equipment's fair value, (3) collectibility of the payments is reasonably assured, and (4) there are no further costs to be incurred by Lessor Company. It is not a sales-type lease because there is no difference between the fair value ($100,000) of the equipment and the lessor's cost ($100,000).

The lease payments receivable (gross investment) is calculated as follows:

Lease payments receivable = Minimum lease payments minus executory costs paid by lessor plus unguaranteed residual value
= [($25,981.62–$2,000) × 5] + $0
= $119,909.10

The unearned interest revenue is computed as the difference between the lease payments receivable and the lessor's cost or carrying amount of the leased asset:

Unearned interest revenue = Lease payments receivable
minus asset cost or carrying amount
= $119,908.10 − $100,000
= $19,908.10

The net investment in direct financing leases is $100,000, that is, the gross investment of $119,908.10 minus the unearned interest revenue of $19,908.10.

The lease of the asset, the resulting receivable, and the unearned interest revenue are recorded January 1, 1984 (the inception of the lease) as follows:

| | | |
|---|---|---|
| Lease Payments Receivable | 119,908.10 | |
|   Equipment | | 100,000.00 |
|   Unearned Interest Revenue—Leases | | 19,908.10 |

The unearned interest revenue is classified on the balance sheet as a deduction from the lease payments receivable if the receivable is reported gross. Generally, the lease payments receivable, although **recorded** at the gross investment amount, is **reported** in the balance sheet at the "net investment" amount (gross investment less unearned interest revenue) and entitled "Net investment in capital leases," classified either as current or noncurrent, depending upon when the net investment is recovered.

The leased equipment with a cost of $100,000, which represents Lessor Company's investment, is replaced with a lease receivable that includes the interest receivable. In a manner similar to the lessee's treatment of interest, Lessor Company applies the effective interest method and recognizes interest revenue as a function of the unrecovered net investment, as illustrated in the following schedule:

| | | | | | |
|---|---|---|---|---|---|
| | | **LESSOR COMPANY** | | | |
| | | Lease Amortization Schedule | | | |
| | | (Annuity due basis) | | | |
| Date | Annual Lease Payment | Executory Costs | Interest (10%) on Net Investment | Net Investment Recovery | Net Investment |
| | (a) | (b) | (c) | (d) | (e) |
| 1/1/84 | | | | | $100,000.00 |
| 1/1/84 | $ 25,981.62 | $ 2,000.00 | -0- | $ 23,981.62 | 76,018.38 |
| 1/1/85 | 25,981.62 | 2,000.00 | $ 7,601.84 | 16,379.78 | 59,638.60 |
| 1/1/86 | 25,981.62 | 2,000.00 | 5,963.86 | 18,017.76 | 41,620.84 |
| 1/1/87 | 25,981.62 | 2,000.00 | 4,162.08 | 19,819.54 | 21,801.30 |
| 1/1/88 | 25,981.62 | 2,000.00 | 2,180.32* | 21,801.30 | — |
| | $129,908.10 | $10,000.00 | $19,908.10 | $100,000.00 | |

(a) Annual rental that provides a 10% return on net investment.
(b) Executory costs included in rental payment.
(c) Ten percent of the preceding balance of (e) except for 1/1/84.
(d) (a) minus (b) and (c).
(e) Preceding balance minus (d).
*Rounded by 19 cents.

On January 1, 1984, the journal entry to record receipt of the first year's lease payment is as follows:

| | | |
|---|---|---|
| Cash | 25,981.62 | |
|   Lease Payments Receivable | | 23,981.62 |
|   Property Tax Expense/Property Taxes Payable | | 2,000.00 |

On 12/31/84 the interest revenue earned during the first year and included in the receipt above is recognized through the following entry:

| | | |
|---|---|---|
| Unearned Interest Revenue—Leases | 7,601.84 | |
| Interest Revenue—Leases | | 7,601.84 |

At December 31, 1984, the net investment under capital leases is reported in the lessor's balance sheet among current assets and/or noncurrent assets. The portion due within one year or the operating cycle, whichever is longer, is classified as a current asset and the balance with noncurrent assets. The total net investment at 12/31/84 is equal to $83,620.22 (the balance at 1/1/84, $76,018.38 plus interest receivable for 1984 of $7,601.84). The current portion of the 12/31/84 balance of $83,620.22 is the net investment to be received in 1985, $16,379.78, plus the interest of $7,601.84. The remainder, $59,638.60 (Lease Payments Receivable of $71,944.86 [$23,981.62 × 3] minus Unearned Interest Revenue of $12,306.26 [$5,963.86 + $4,162.08 + $2,180.32]) should be reported in the noncurrent asset section. The asset section as it relates to lease transactions at 12/31/84 would appear as follows:

| | |
|---|---|
| Current assets: | |
| Net investment in capital leases | $23,981.62 |
| Noncurrent assets: | |
| Net investment in capital leases | $59,638.60 |

The following entries record receipt of the second year's lease payment and accrual of the interest earned:

**January 1, 1985**

| | | |
|---|---|---|
| Cash | 25,981.62 | |
| Lease Payments Receivable | | 23,981.62 |
| Property Tax Expense/Property Taxes Payable | | 2,000.00 |

**December 31, 1985**

| | | |
|---|---|---|
| Unearned Interest Revenue—Leases | 5,963.86 | |
| Interest Revenue—Leases | | 5,963.86 |

Journal entries through 1988 would follow the same pattern except that no entry would be recorded in 1988 (the last year) for accrued interest. Because the receivable is fully collected by 1/1/88, no balance (investment) is outstanding during 1988 to which Lessor Company could attribute any interest. Upon expiration of the lease (whether an ordinary annuity or an annuity due situation), the gross receivable and the unearned interest revenue would be fully written off. **Lessor Company recorded no depreciation.** If the equipment is sold to Lessee Company for $5,000 upon expiration of the lease, Lessor Company would recognize disposition of the equipment as follows:

| | | |
|---|---|---|
| Cash | 5,000 | |
| Gain on Sale of Leased Equipment | | 5,000 |

## SPECIAL ACCOUNTING PROBLEMS

The features of lease arrangements that provide unique accounting problems are:

1. Residual values.
2. Sales-type leases.
3. Bargain purchase options.
4. Initial direct costs.
5. Sale leasebacks.

### Residual Values

The residual value is the **estimated fair value** of the leased asset at the end of the lease term. Frequently, a significant residual value exists at the end of the lease term, especially when the economic life of the leased asset exceeds the lease term. If title does not pass automatically to the lessee (criterion 1) and a bargain purchase option does not exist (criterion 2), the lessee returns physical custody of the asset to the lessor at the end of the lease term. The residual value may be unguaranteed or guaranteed by the lessee. If the lessee, for example, agrees to make up any deficiency below a stated amount that the lessor realizes in residual value at the end of the lease term, that stated amount is the **guaranteed residual value.**

The guaranteed residual value is employed in lease arrangements for two reasons. One is a business reason: it protects the lessor against any loss in estimated residual value, thereby insuring the lessor of the desired rate of return on investment. The second is an accounting reason that has given added significance to the guaranteed residual value: as you will learn from the discussion at the end of this chapter, the guaranteed residual value is one of the devices frequently used to circumvent certain accounting rules.

The fact that the residual value is guaranteed or unguaranteed is of economic risk consequence to the lessor (that is, a guaranteed residual value has more assurance of realization than does an unguaranteed residual value). As a result, some adjustment in rental rates may take place because the certainty of recovery has been increased for the lessor. After this rate is established, then it makes no difference from an accounting point of view whether the residual value is guaranteed or unguaranteed from the lessor's perspective. The net investment to be recorded by the lessor (once the rate is set) will be the same whether the residual value is guaranteed or unguaranteed. For example, assume the same data as in the Lessee Company/Lessor Company illustrations except that a residual value of $5,000 is estimated at the end of the five-year lease term. With an estimated residual value of $5,000 and an objective of earning a 10% return on investment (ROI),[23] whether the residual value is guaranteed or unguaranteed, Lessor Company would compute the amount of the lease payments as follows:

---

[23]Technically the rate of return demanded by the lessor would be different depending upon whether the residual value was guaranteed or unguaranteed. We are ignoring this difference in subsequent sections to simplify the illustrations.

| LESSOR'S COMPUTATION OF LEASE PAYMENTS (10% ROI)<br>(Annuity due basis, including residual value)<br>Guaranteed or Unguaranteed Residual Value | |
| --- | --- |
| Cost of leased asset to lessor | $100,000.00 |
| Less: Present value of residual value ($5,000 × .62092, Table 6-2) | 3,104.60 |
| Amount to be recovered by lessor through lease payments | $ 96,895.40 |
| Five periodic lease payments ($96,895.40 ÷ 4.16986, Table 6-5) | $ 23,237.09 |

The foregoing lease payment amount should be contrasted to the lease payments of $23,981.62 as computed on page 990 where no residual value existed. The payments are less because the lessor's recoverable amount is less by the present value of the residual value.

**Lessee Accounting for Residual Value**  Whether the estimated residual value is guaranteed or unguaranteed is of both economic and accounting consequence to the lessee. The accounting difference is in the fact that the term "minimum lease payments," the basis for capitalization, includes the guaranteed residual value but excludes the unguaranteed residual value, as illustrated in the next two sections.

GUARANTEED RESIDUAL VALUE (LESSEE ACCOUNTING)  A guaranteed residual value affects the lessee's computation of the minimum lease payments and, therefore, the amounts capitalized as a leased asset and a lease obligation. In effect, the guaranteed residual value is an additional lease payment that will be paid in property or cash, or both, at the end of the lease term. Using the rental payments as computed by the lessor above, the minimum lease payments are $121,185.45 ([$23,237.09 × 5] + $5,000). The capitalized present value of the minimum lease payments (excluding executory costs) is computed as follows:

| LESSEE'S CAPITALIZED AMOUNT (10% RATE)<br>(Annuity due basis; including **guaranteed** residual value) | |
| --- | --- |
| Present value of five annual rental payments<br>($23,237.09 × 4.16986, Table 6-5) | $ 96,895.40 |
| Present value of guaranteed residual value of $5,000<br>due five years after date of inception: ($5,000 × .62092, Table 6-2) | 3,104.60 |
| Lessee's capitalized amount | $100,000.00 |

A schedule of interest expense and amortization of the lease obligation of $100,000 that produces a final guaranteed residual value payment of $5,000 at the end of five years is prepared by Lessee Company as follows:

**LESSEE COMPANY**
**Lease Amortization Schedule**
**(Annuity due basis, guaranteed residual value—GRV)**

| Date | Annual Lease Payment Plus GRV | Executory Costs | Interest (10%) on Unpaid Obligation | Reduction of Lease Obligation | Lease Obligation |
|---|---|---|---|---|---|
| | (a) | (b) | (c) | (d) | (e) |
| 1/1/84 | | | | | $100,000.00 |
| 1/1/84 | $ 25,237.09 | $ 2,000 | -0- | $ 23,237.09 | 76,762.91 |
| 1/1/85 | 25,237.09 | 2,000 | $ 7,676.29 | 15,560.80 | 61,202.11 |
| 1/1/86 | 25,237.09 | 2,000 | 6,120.21 | 17,116.88 | 44,085.23 |
| 1/1/87 | 25,237.09 | 2,000 | 4,408.52 | 18,828.57 | 25,256.66 |
| 1/1/88 | 25,237.09 | 2,000 | 2,525.67 | 20,711.42 | 4,545.24 |
| 12/31/88 | 5,000.00* | | 454.76** | 4,545.24 | -0- |
| | $131,185.45 | $10,000 | $21,185.45 | $100,000.00 | |

(a) Annual lease payment as required by lease.
(b) Executory costs included in rental payment.
(c) Preceding balance of (e) $\times$ 10%, except 1/1/84.
(d) (a) minus (b) and (c).
(e) Preceding balance minus (d).
*Represents the guaranteed residual value; this amount or any part of it will be paid if the residual value is less than $5,000 at 12/31/88.
**Rounded by 24 cents.

If, at the end of the lease, the fair market value of the residual value is less than $5,000, Lessee Company may have to record a loss. For example, assume that Lessee Company depreciated the leased asset down to its residual value of $5,000 but that the fair market value of the residual value at 12/31/88 was $3,000. In this case, the Lessee Company would have to report a loss of $2,000. The following journal entry would be made (assuming cash was paid to make up the residual value deficiency):

| | | |
|---|---|---|
| Loss on Capital Lease | 2,000 | |
| Obligations Under Capital Leases | 5,000 | |
| Accumulated Depreciation—Capital Leases | 95,000 | |
|    Leased Equipment Under Capital Leases | | 100,000 |
|    Cash | | 2,000 |

If the fair market value exceeds $5,000, a gain may be recognized. Gains on guaranteed residual values may be apportioned to the lessor and lessee in whatever ratio the parties initially agree.

UNGUARANTEED RESIDUAL VALUE (LESSEE ACCOUNTING) An unguaranteed residual value from the lessee's viewpoint is the same as no residual value in terms of its effect upon the lessee's method of computing the minimum lease payments and the capitalization of the leased asset and the lease obligation. For example, assume the same facts as those above except that the $5,000 residual value is **unguaranteed instead of guaranteed.** The amount of the annual lease payments would be the same, $23,237.09, because whether the residual value is guaranteed or unguaranteed, Lessor Company's amount to be recovered through lease rentals is the same, that is, $96,895.40. The minimum lease payments are $116,185.45 ($23,237.09 × 5). Lessee Company would capitalize the following amount:

| LESSEE'S CAPITALIZED AMOUNT (10% RATE) |
|---|
| (Annuity due basis, including **unguaranteed** residual value) |

| | |
|---|---:|
| Present value of five annual rental payments of $23,237.09 × 4.16986 | |
|   (Table 6-5) | $96,895.40 |
| Unguaranteed residual value of $5,000 (Not capitalized by lessee) | -0- |
| Lessee's capitalized amount | $96,895.40 |

The Lessee Company's schedule of interest expense and amortization of the lease obligation of $96,895.40, assuming an unguaranteed residual value of $5,000 at the end of five years, is as follows:

| | | | | | |
|---|---|---|---|---|---|
| | | **LESSEE COMPANY** | | | |
| | | Lease Amortization Schedule (10%) | | | |
| | | (Annuity due basis, **unguaranteed** residual value) | | | |

| Date | Annual Lease Payments | Executory Costs | Interest (10%) on Unpaid Obligation | Reduction of Lease Obligation | Lease Obligation |
|---|---|---|---|---|---|
| | (a) | (b) | (c) | (d) | (e) |
| 1/1/84 | | | | | $96,895.40 |
| 1/1/84 | $ 25,237.09 | $ 2,000 | -0- | $23,237.09 | 73,658.31 |
| 1/1/85 | 25,237.09 | 2,000 | $ 7,365.83 | 15,871.26 | 57,787.05 |
| 1/1/86 | 25,237.09 | 2,000 | 5,778.71 | 17,458.38 | 40,328.67 |
| 1/1/87 | 25,237.09 | 2,000 | 4,032.87 | 19,204.22 | 21,124.45 |
| 1/1/88 | 25,237.09 | 2,000 | 2,112.64* | 21,124.45 | -0- |
| | $126,185.45 | $10,000 | $19,290.05 | $96,895.40 | |

(a) Annual lease payment as required by lease.
(b) Executory costs included in rental payment.
(c) Preceding balance of (e) × 10%.
(d) (a) minus (b) and (c).
(e) Preceding balance minus (d).
*Rounded by 19 cents.

Assuming that the residual had a fair market value of $3,000, no loss would be reported in this situation. Assuming that the leased asset has been fully depreciated and that the lease obligation has been fully amortized (as shown in the amortization schedule), no entry is required at the end of the lease term, except to remove the asset from the books.

If we continue the assumption that the fair value of the leased asset is $100,000, this lease still satisfies the 90% of fair value criterion (because the present value of the minimum lease payments, $96,895.40, is approximately 97% of the fair value of $100,000). Note that if the unguaranteed residual value is sufficiently large, thereby reducing the minimum lease payments, the present value of the minimum lease payments can be less than 90% of the fair value of the leased asset, thereby disqualifying the transaction from capital lease status **for the lessee and the lessor** (assuming that the transaction did not qualify under any of the other three criteria). If, however, **the residual value is guaranteed by a third party,** it is treated by the lessee as an unguaranteed residual value but by the lessor as a guaranteed residual value. This anomaly in lease accounting has been used extensively in the business world to undermine the FASB's intent to maintain accounting **symmetry** between the lessee and the lessor (see the last section of this chapter for a more extended discussion of these attempts at circumvention).

**LESSEE ENTRIES INVOLVING RESIDUAL VALUES**   The entries by Lessee Company for both a guaranteed and an unguaranteed residual value are shown below in comparative form.

| LESSEE COMPANY | | | | |
|---|---|---|---|---|
| **Entries for Guaranteed and Unguaranteed Residual Values** | | | | |
| Guaranteed Residual Value | | | Unguaranteed Residual Value | |
| **Capitalization of Lease 1/1/84:** | | | | |
| Leased Equipment under | | | Leased Equipment under | |
| Capital Leases | 100,000.00 | | Capital Leases | 96,895.40 | |
| Obligations under | | | Obligations under | |
| Capital Leases | | 100,000.00 | Capital Leases | | 96,895.40 |
| **First Payment 1/1/84:** | | | | |
| Property Tax Expense | 2,000.00 | | Property Tax Expense | 2,000.00 | |
| Obligations under | | | Obligations under | |
| Capital Leases | 23,237.09 | | Capital Leases | 23,237.09 | |
| Cash | | 25,237.09 | Cash | | 25,237.09 |
| **Adjusting Entry for Accrued Interest 12/31/84:** | | | | |
| Interest Expense | 7,676.29 | | Interest Expense | 7,365.83 | |
| Interest Payable | | 7,676.29 | Interest Payable | | 7,365.83 |
| **Entry to Record Depreciation 12/31/84:** | | | | |
| Depreciation Expense— | | | Depreciation Expense— | |
| Capital Leases | 19,000.00 | | Capital Leases | 19,379.08 | |
| Accumulated Deprecia- | | | Accumulated Deprecia- | |
| tion—Capital Leases | | 19,000.00 | tion—Capital Leases | | 19,379.08 |
| ([$100,000 − $5,000] ÷ 5 years) | | | ($96,895.40 ÷ 5 years) | |
| **Second Payment 1/1/85:** | | | | |
| Property Tax Expense | 2,000.00 | | Property Tax Expense | 2,000.00 | |
| Obligations under | | | Obligations under | |
| Capital Leases | 15,560.80 | | Capital Leases | 15,871.26 | |
| Interest Expense | | | Interest Expense | |
| (or Interest Payable) | 7,676.29 | | (or Interest Payable) | 7,365.83 | |
| Cash | | 25,237.09 | Cash | | 25,237.09 |

**Lessor Accounting for Residual Value**   As indicated earlier, the net investment to be recovered by the lessor is the same whether the residual value is guaranteed or unguaranteed. The lessor works on the assumption that the residual value will be realized at the end of the lease term whether guaranteed or unguaranteed. Therefore, as shown on page 998 the lease payments required by the lessor to earn a certain return on investment are the same ($23,237.09) whether the residual value is guaranteed or unguaranteed. Lessor accounting for residual values varies only slightly for direct financing and sales-type leases, as discussed below and on pages 999 and 1000.

**DIRECT FINANCING LEASE** Using the Lessee Company/Lessor Company data and assuming a residual value (either guaranteed or unguaranteed) of $5,000 and classification of the lease as a direct financing lease, the following necessary amounts are computed:

> Gross investment = ($23,237.09 × 5) + $5,000 = $121,185.45
> Unearned interest revenue = $121,185.45 − $100,000 = $21,185.45
> Net investment = $121,185.45 − $21,185.45 = $100,000

The schedule for amortization of guaranteed and unguaranteed residual value is the same:

**LESSOR COMPANY**
**Lease Amortization Schedule**
**(Annuity due basis, guaranteed or unguaranteed residual value)**

| Date | Annual Lease Payment Plus Residual Value | Executory Costs | Interest (10%) on Net Investment | Net Investment Recovery | Net Investment |
|------|------|------|------|------|------|
| | (a) | (b) | (c) | (d) | (e) |
| 1/1/84 | — | — | — | — | $100,000.00 |
| 1/1/84 | $ 25,237.09 | $ 2,000.00 | — | $ 23,237.09 | 76,762.91 |
| 1/1/85 | 25,237.09 | 2,000.00 | $ 7,676.29 | 15,560.80 | 61,202.11 |
| 1/1/86 | 25,237.09 | 2,000.00 | 6,120.21 | 17,116.88 | 44,085.23 |
| 1/1/87 | 25,237.09 | 2,000.00 | 4,408.52 | 18,828.57 | 25,256.66 |
| 1/1/88 | 25,237.09 | 2,000.00 | 2,525.67 | 20,711.42 | 4,545.24 |
| 12/31/88 | 5,000.00 | — | 454.76* | 4,545.24 | -0- |
| | $131,185.45 | $10,000.00 | $21,185.45 | $100,000.00 | |

(a) Annual lease payment as required by lease.
(b) Executory costs included in rental payment.
(c) Preceding balance of (e) × 10%, except 1/1/84.
(d) (a) minus (b) and (c).
(e) Preceding balance minus (d).
*Rounded by 24 cents.

Using the amounts computed above, the following entries would be made by Lessor Company during the first year for this direct financing lease:

**Lessor Entries for Either Guaranteed or Unguaranteed Residual Value**

**Inception of Lease 1/1/84:**

| | | |
|------|------|------|
| Lease Payments Receivable | 121,185.45 | |
| Equipment | | 100,000.00 |
| Unearned Interest Revenue—Leases | | 21,185.45 |

**First Payment Received 1/1/84:**

| | | |
|---|---|---|
| Cash | 25,237.09 | |
| Lease Payments Receivable | | 23,237.09 |
| Property Tax Expense/Property Taxes Payable | | 2,000.00 |

**Adjusting Entry for Accrued Interest 12/31/84:**

| | | |
|---|---|---|
| Unearned Interest Revenue—Leases | 7,676.29 | |
| Interest Revenue—Leases | | 7,676.29 |

The entries above may be compared to those of Lessee Company on page 997.

## Sales-Type Lease (Lessor)

As already indicated, the primary difference between a direct financing lease and a sales-type lease is the manufacturer's or dealer's gross profit (or loss). The information necessary to record the sales-type lease is as follows:

1. **Gross investment** (also "lease payments receivable"). The minimum lease payments plus the unguaranteed residual value accruing to the lessor at the end of the lease term.
2. **Unearned interest revenue.** The gross investment less the sum of the present values of the two components of gross investment.
3. **Sales price of the asset.** The present value of the minimum lease payments.
4. **Cost of goods sold.** The cost of the asset to the lessor, less the present value of any unguaranteed residual value.

From the above, note that the gross investment and the unearned interest revenue account are the same whether a guaranteed or an unguaranteed residual value is involved. If the residual value is guaranteed, it is part of the minimum lease payment; if not guaranteed, it is still included as dictated by the definition. A difference does exist, however, in the accounting for guaranteed and unguaranteed residual values relative to the amount recorded for both sales revenue and cost of goods sold. In the case of a guaranteed residual value, the residual value can be considered part of sales revenue because the lessor knows this amount will be received. In the case of an unguaranteed residual value, however, the residual value is not sold, so cost of goods sold is reduced. However, the gross profit on the sale of the asset is the same whether a guaranteed or unguaranteed residual value is involved. The difference in the two methods relates to the amounts recorded as sales and cost of goods sold.

To illustrate a sales-type lease with a guaranteed and unguaranteed residual value, assume the same facts as in the preceding direct financing lease situation (page 998). The estimated residual value is $5,000 (the present value of which is $3,104.60) and the leased equipment has an $85,000 cost to the dealer, Lessor Company. At the end of the lease term assume that the fair market value of the residual value is $3,000.

The amounts relevant to a sales-type lease are computed as follows:

| | Sales-Type Lease | |
|---|---|---|
| | Guaranteed Residual Value | Unguaranteed Residual Value |
| Gross investment | $121,185.45 ([$23,237.09 × 5] + $5,000) | Same |

| | Guaranteed Residual Value | Unguaranteed Residual Value |
|---|---|---|
| Unearned interest revenue | $ 21,185.45 ($121,185.45 − $100,000) | Same |
| Sales price of the asset | $100,000 ($96,895.40 + $3,104.60) | $96,895.40 |
| Cost of goods sold | $ 85,000 | $81,895.40 ($85,000 − $3,104.60) |
| Gross profit | $ 15,000 ($100,000 − $85,000) | $15,000 ($96,895.40 − $81,895.40) |

The entries to record this transaction on January 1, 1984 and the receipt of the residual value at the end of the lease term are as follows:

### LESSOR COMPANY
#### Entries for Guaranteed and Unguaranteed Residual Values

| Guaranteed Residual Values | | | Unguaranteed Residual Values | | |
|---|---|---|---|---|---|

**To record sales-type lease at inception (January 1, 1984):**

| | | | | | |
|---|---|---|---|---|---|
| Cost of Goods Sold | 85,000.00 | | Cost of Goods Sold | 81,895.40 | |
| Lease Payments Receivable | 121,185.45 | | Lease Payments Receivable | 121,185.45 | |
| Sales Revenue | | 100,000.00 | Sales Revenue | | 96,895.40 |
| Unearned Interest Revenue | | 21,185.45 | Unearned Interest Revenue | | 21,185.45 |
| Inventory | | 85,000.00 | Inventory | | 85,000.00 |

**To record receipt of the first lease payment (January 1, 1984):**

| | | | | | |
|---|---|---|---|---|---|
| Cash | 25,237.09 | | Cash | 25,237.09 | |
| Lease Payments Receivable | | 23,237.09 | Lease Payments Receivable | | 23,237.09 |
| Prop. Tax Exp./Prop. Tax Pay. | | 2,000.00 | Prop. Tax Exp./Prop. Tax Pay. | | 2,000.00 |

**To recognize interest revenue earned during the first year (December 31, 1984):**

| | | | | | |
|---|---|---|---|---|---|
| Unearned Interest Revenue | 7,676.29 | | Unearned Interest Revenue | 7,676.29 | |
| Interest Revenue | | 7,676.29 | Interest Revenue | | 7,676.29 |
| (see lease amortization schedule, page 998.) | | | | | |

**To record receipt of the second lease payment (January 1, 1985):**

| | | | | | |
|---|---|---|---|---|---|
| Cash | 25,237.09 | | Cash | 25,237.09 | |
| Lease Payments Receivable | | 23,237.09 | Lease Payments Receivable | | 23,237.09 |
| Prop. Tax Exp./Prop. Tax Pay. | | 2,000.00 | Prop. Tax Exp./Prop. Tax Pay. | | 2,000.00 |

**To recognize interest revenue earned during the second year (December 31, 1985):**

| | | | | | |
|---|---|---|---|---|---|
| Unearned Interest Revenue | 6,120.21 | | Unearned Interest Revenue | 6,120.21 | |
| Interest Revenue | | 6,120.21 | Interest Revenue | | 6,120.21 |

**To record receipt of residual value at end of leased term (December 31, 1988):**

| | | | | | |
|---|---|---|---|---|---|
| Inventory | 3,000 | | Inventory | 3,000 | |
| Cash | 2,000 | | Loss on Capital Lease | 2,000 | |
| Lease Payments Receivable | | 5,000 | Lease Payments Receivable | | 5,000 |

The profit recorded by Lessor company at the point of sale is the same, $15,000, whether the residual value is guaranteed or unguaranteed, but the sales revenue and cost of goods sold amounts are different.

The **estimated unguaranteed residual value** in a sales-type lease (and a financing-type lease) must be reviewed periodically. If the estimate of the unguaranteed residual value declines, the accounting for the transaction must be revised using the changed estimate. The decline represents a reduction in the lessor's net investment and is recognized as a loss in the period in which the residual estimate is reduced. Upward adjustments in estimated residual value are not recognized.

## Bargain Purchase Option (Lessee)

A bargain purchase option allows the lessee to purchase the leased property for a future price that is so much lower than the expected future fair value of the property that at the inception of the lease the future exercise of the option appears to be reasonably assured. If a bargain purchase option exists, **the lessee must increase the present value of the minimum lease payments by the present value of the option price.**

For example, assume that Lessee Company in the illustration on page 998 had an option to buy the leased equipment for $5,000 at the end of the five-year lease term when the fair value is expected to be $18,000. The significant difference between the option price and the fair value creates a bargain purchase option, the exercise of which is reasonably assured. The computations of (1) the amount of the five lease payments necessary for the lessor to earn a 10% return on net investment, (2) the amount of the minimum lease payments, (3) the amount capitalized as leased assets and lease obligation, and (4) the amortization of the lease obligation are affected by a bargain purchase option in the same manner that they are by a guaranteed residual value. Therefore, the computations, amortization schedule, and entries that would be prepared for this $5,000 bargain purchase option are identical to those shown on pages 994–997 for the $5,000 guaranteed residual value.

The only difference between the accounting treatment given a bargain purchase option and a guaranteed residual value of identical amounts and circumstances is in the computation of the annual depreciation. In the case of a guaranteed residual value the lessee depreciates the asset over the lease life while in the case of a bargain purchase option the lessee uses the economic life of the asset.

## Initial Direct Costs (Lessor)

The incremental costs incurred by the lessor that are directly associated with negotiating, consummating, and initially processing leasing transactions are called **initial direct costs.** Examples of initial direct costs are: commissions, legal fees, costs of investigating the lessee's financial status, costs of preparing and processing documents, and that portion of salespersons' and other employees' compensation that is applicable to time spent on **completed** lease transactions.[24]

For **operating leases,** the lessor should defer initial direct costs and allocate them over the lease term in proportion to the recognition of rental income. In a **sales-type lease** transaction, the lessor expenses the initial direct costs in the year of incurrence, that is, the period in which the profit on the sale is recognized. In a **direct financing lease,** however, initial direct costs should be allocated over the term of the lease by charging any initial direct costs to expense as such costs are incurred and recognizing as revenue in the same

---

[24]"Accounting for Leases—Initial Direct Costs," *Statement of Financial Accounting Standards No. 17* (Stamford, Conn.: FASB, 1977), par. 8.

period a portion of the unearned revenue equal to the initial direct costs. To illustrate, if Lessor Corp. incurred $4,900 of initial direct costs in consummating the lease with Lessee Corp., Lessor would make the following two entries:

| | | |
|---|---|---|
| Various expenses, e.g., Sales Commissions, Legal Expense, | | |
| Office Salaries, Travel Expense, etc. | 4,900 | |
| Cash and Accounts Payable | | 4,900 |
| Unearned Interest Revenue | 4,900 | |
| Interest Revenue | | 4,900 |

The remaining unearned interest revenue is amortized over the lease term applying the effective interest method. Because the unearned interest revenue is reduced by the amount of the initial direct costs, a new implicit interest rate must be computed to amortize the remaining unearned interest revenue. This dual entry method of allocating initial direct costs over the lease term is recommended by the FASB because it is the method that has been used for some years throughout the leasing industry.

## Sale-Leaseback

The term "sale-leaseback" describes a transaction in which the owner of property (seller-lessee) sells the property to another and simultaneously leases it back from the new owner. The use of the property is continued without interruption. For example, a company buys land, constructs a building to its specifications, sells the property to an investor, and then immediately leases it back.

Generally, in such a transaction the property is sold at a price equal to or greater than current market value and is leased back for a term approximating the property's useful life and for lease payments sufficient to repay the buyer for the cash invested plus a reasonable return on investment. In addition, the lessee pays all executory costs (maintenance, insurance, and taxes), just as if title had passed. The sale price and the amount of the rents are related. The tax advantage for the seller-lessee is the deductibility of the entire lease payment, which may include interest and amortization of the cost of land and already partially depreciated other real property. Thus, the tax deduction under the lease arrangement may exceed allowable depreciation had title been retained. The sale-leaseback mechanism is used frequently where financing is a problem.

LESSEE   If the lease meets one of the four criteria for treatment as a capital lease (see page 979), the **seller-lessee accounts for the transaction as a sale and the lease as a capital lease.** If none of the criteria is satisfied, the seller-lessee accounts for the transaction as a sale and the lease as an operating lease. Any profit or loss experienced by the seller-lessee from the sale of the assets that are leased back under a capital lease should be deferred and amortized over the lease term (or the economic life if either criterion (1) or (2) is satisfied) in proportion to the amortization of the leased assets.[25] For example, if Lessee, Inc. sells equipment having a book value of $580,000 and a fair value of $623,110 to Lessor, Inc. for $623,110 and leases the equipment back for $50,000 a year for 20 years, the profit of $43,110 should be amortized over the 20-year period at the same rate that the $623,110 is

[25] *Statement of Financial Accounting Standards No. 28,* "Accounting for Sales with Leasebacks" (Stamford, Conn.: FASB, 1979), however, requires the seller to recognize some profit or loss in certain limited circumstances.

depreciated. Under an operating lease such profit or loss should be deferred and amortized in proportion to the rental payments over the period of time the assets are expected to be used by the lessee. If the leased asset is land only, the amortization shall be on a straight-line basis over the lease term.

The profession requires, however, that when the fair value of the asset is **less** than the book value (carrying amount), a loss must be recognized immediately up to the amount of the difference between the book value and fair value. For example, if Lessee, Inc. sells equipment having a book value of $650,000 and a fair value of $623,110, the difference of $26,890 should be charged to a loss account.

**LESSOR**    If the lease meets one of the criteria in Group I and both of the criteria in Group II (see page 987), the **purchaser-lessor** records the transaction as a purchase and a direct financing lease. If the lease does not meet the criteria, the purchaser-lessor records the transaction as a purchase and an operating lease.

**Sale-Leaseback Illustration**    To illustrate the accounting treatment accorded a sale-leaseback transaction, assume that Lessee Corp. on January 1, 1984, sells a used Boeing 747 having a carrying amount on its books of $75,500,000, to Lessor Corp. for $80,000,000, and immediately leases the aircraft back under the following conditions:

1. The term of the lease is 15 years, noncancelable, requiring equal rental payments of $10,487,443 at the beginning of each year.
2. The aircraft has a fair value of $80,000,000 on January 1, 1984, and an estimated economic life of 15 years.
3. Lessee Corp. has the option to renew the lease, one year at a time, at the same rental payments upon expiration of the original lease.
4. Lessee Corp. pays all executory costs.
5. Lessee Corp. depreciates similar aircraft that it owns on a straight-line basis over 15 years.
6. The annual payments assure the lessor a 12% return.
7. The incremental borrowing rate of Lessee Corp. is 12%.

This lease is a capital lease to Lessee Corp. because the lease term exceeds 75% of the estimated life of the aircraft and because the present value of the lease payments exceeds 90% of the fair value of the aircraft to the lessor. Assuming that collectibility of the lease payments is reasonably predictable, and that no important uncertainties exist in relation to unreimbursable costs yet to be incurred by the lessor, Lessor Corp. should classify this lease as a direct financing lease.

The typical journal entries to record the transactions relating to this lease for both Lessee Corp. and Lessor Corp. for the first year are presented on page 1004.

## LEASE ACCOUNTING—THE UNSOLVED PROBLEM

As indicated at the beginning of this chapter, lease accounting is a much abused area in which strenuous efforts are being made to circumvent *Statement No. 13*. In practice, the accounting rules for capitalizing leases have been rendered partially ineffective by the strong desires of lessees to resist capitalization. Leasing generally involves large dollar amounts which when capitalized materially increase reported liabilities and adversely affect the debt-to-equity ratio. Lease capitalization is also resisted because charges to expense made in the early years of the lease term are higher under the capital lease method

## Entries for Sale-Leaseback

| Lessee Corp. | | | Lessor Corp. | | |
|---|---|---|---|---|---|

**Sale of Aircraft by Lessee to Lessor Corp., January 1, 1984:**

| | | | | | |
|---|---|---|---|---|---|
| Cash | 80,000,000 | | Aircraft | 80,000,000 | |
| Aircraft | | 75,500,000 | Cash | | 80,000,000 |
| Unearned Profit on | | | Lease Payments | | |
| Sale-Leaseback | | 4,500,000 | Receivable | 157,311,645 | |
| | | | Aircraft | | 80,000,000 |
| Leased Aircraft Under | | | Unearned Interest | | |
| Capital Leases | 80,000,000 | | Revenue | | 77,311,645 |
| Obligations Under | | | ($10,487,443 × 15 = $157,311,645) | | |
| Capital Leases | | 80,000,000 | | | |

**First Lease Payment, January 1, 1984:**

| | | | | | |
|---|---|---|---|---|---|
| Obligations Under | | | Cash | 10,487,443 | |
| Capital Leases | 10,487,443 | | Lease Payments | | |
| Cash | | 10,487,443 | Receivable | | 10,487,443 |

**Incurrence and Payment of Executory Costs by Lessee Corp. throughout 1984:**

(No entry)

| | | |
|---|---|---|
| Insurance, Maintenance, | | |
| Taxes, etc. | XXX | |
| Cash or Accounts | | |
| Payable | | XXX |

**Depreciation Expense on the Aircraft, December 31, 1984:**

(No entry)

| | | |
|---|---|---|
| Depreciation Expense | 5,333,333 | |
| Accumulated Depr.— | | |
| Capital Leases | | 5,333,333 |
| ($80,000,000 ÷ 15) | | |

**Amortization of Profit on Sale-Leaseback by Lessee Corp., December 31, 1984:**

(No entry)

| | | |
|---|---|---|
| Unearned Profit on | | |
| Sale-Leaseback | 300,000 | |
| Depreciation Expense | | 300,000 |
| ($4,500,000 ÷ 15) | | |

Note: A case might be made for crediting Revenue instead of Depreciation Expense.

**Interest for 1984, December 31, 1984:**

| | | | | | |
|---|---|---|---|---|---|
| Interest Expense | 8,341,507[a] | | Unearned Interest Revenue | 8,341,507 | |
| Interest Payable | | 8,341,507 | Interest Revenue | | 8,341,507[a] |

**[a]Partial Lease Amortization Schedule:**

| Date | Annual Rental Payment | Interest 12% | Reduction of Balance | Balance |
|---|---|---|---|---|
| 1/1/84 | | | | $80,000,000 |
| 1/1/84 | $10,487,443 | — | $10,487,443 | 69,512,557 |
| 1/1/85 | 10,487,443 | $8,341,507 | 2,145,936 | 67,366,621 |

than under the operating method, frequently without tax benefit. As a consequence, "let's beat *Statement No. 13*" has become one of the most popular games in town.[26]

[26]Richard Dieter, "Is Lessee Accounting Working?" *The CPA Journal* (August 1979), pp. 13–19. This article provides interesting examples of abuses of *Statement No. 13,* discusses the circumstances that led to the current situation, and proposes a solution for the confusion.

To avoid leased asset capitalization, lease agreements are designed, written, and interpreted so that none of the four capitalized lease criteria is satisfied from the lessee's viewpoint. Devising lease agreements in such a way has not been too difficult when the following specifications are met.

1. Make certain that the lease does not specify the transfer of title to the property to the lessee.
2. Do not write in a bargain purchase option.
3. Set the lease term at something less than 75% of the estimated economic life of the leased property.
4. Arrange for the present value of the minimum lease payments to be less than 90% of the fair value of the leased property.

But the real challenge lies in disqualifying the lease as a capital lease to the lessee while having the same lease qualify as a capital (sales or financing) lease to the lessor. Unlike lessees, lessors try to avoid having lease arrangements classified as operating leases.

Avoiding the first three criteria is relatively simple, but it takes a little ingenuity to avoid the "90% recovery test" for the lessee while satisfying it for the lessor. Two of the factors involved in this effort are: (1) the use of the incremental borrowing rate by the lessee when it is higher than the implicit interest rate of the lessor, by making information about the implicit rate unavailable to the lessee; and (2) residual value guarantees.

The lessee's use of the higher interest rate is probably the more popular subterfuge. While lessees are knowledgeable about the fair value of the leased property and, of course, the rental payments, they generally are not aware of the estimated residual value used by the lessor. Therefore the lessee does not know exactly the lessor's implicit interest rate and therefore is free to use the incremental borrowing rate.

The residual value guarantee is the other unique, yet popular device used by lessees and lessors. In fact, a whole new industry has emerged to circumvent symmetry between the lessee and the lessor in accounting for leases. The residual value guarantee has spawned numerous companies whose principal, or even sole, function is to guarantee the residual value of leased assets. These "third-party guarantors" (insurers), for a fee, assume the risk of deficiencies in leased asset residual value.[27]

Because the guaranteed residual value is included in the minimum lease payments for the lessor, the 90% recovery of fair market value test is satisfied and the lease is a nonoperating lease to the lessor. Because the residual value is guaranteed by a third party, the minimum lease payments of the lessee do not include the guarantee. Thus, by merely transferring some of the risk to a third party, lessees can alter substantially the accounting treatment by converting what would otherwise be capital leases to operating leases.

Much of this circumvention is encouraged by the nature of the criteria which stem from weaknesses in the basic objective of *Statement No. 13.* Accounting standard-setting bodies continue to have poor experience with arbitrary break points or other size and percentage criteria, i.e., rules like "90% of," "75% of," etc. As indicated earlier, some accountants

---

[27] As an aside, third-party guarantors have experienced some difficulty. Lloyd's of London, for example, insured the fast growing U.S. computer-leasing industry in the amount of $2 billion against revenue losses and losses in residual value if leases were cancelled. Because of "overnight" technological improvements and the successive introductions of more efficient and less expensive computers by IBM, lessees in abundance cancelled their leases. As the market for second-hand computers became flooded and residual values plummeted, third-party guarantor Lloyd's of London projected a loss of $400 million. Much of the third-party guarantee business was stimulated by the lessees' and lessors' desire to circumvent *FASB No. 13.*

believe that a more workable solution would be to require capitalization of all leases that extend for some defined period (such as one year) on the basis that the lessee has acquired an asset (a property right) and a corresponding liability rather than on the basis that the lease transfers substantially all the risks and rewards of ownership. Others take a less stringent stand, but nonetheless call for the capitalization of more lease transactions.

Three years after it issued *Statement No. 13,* a majority of the FASB expressed "the tentative view that, if *Statement 13* were to be reconsidered, they would support a property right approach in which all leases are included as 'rights to use property' and as 'lease obligations' in the lessee's balance sheet."[28] So we will have come full circle, since that is the accounting view that was recommended by AICPA *Accounting Research Study No. 4* in 1962.

## REPORTING LEASE DATA IN FINANCIAL STATEMENTS

### Disclosures Required of the Lessee

The FASB requires that the following information with respect to leases be disclosed in the **lessee's** financial statements or in the footnotes:[29]

---

**Lessee's Disclosures**

(a) For **capital leases:**

  i. The gross amount of assets recorded under capital leases as of the date of each balance sheet presented by major classes according to nature or function. This information may be combined with the comparable information for owned assets.

  ii. Future *minimum lease payments* as of the date of the latest balance sheet presented, in the aggregate and for each of the five succeeding fiscal years, with separate deductions from the total for the amount representing *executory costs,* including any profit thereon, included in the *minimum lease payments* and for the amount of the imputed interest necessary to reduce the net *minimum lease payments* to present value.

  iii. The total of minimum sublease rentals to be received in the future under noncancelable subleases as of the date of the latest balance sheet presented.

  iv. Total *contingent rentals* actually incurred

for each period for which an income statement is presented.

  v. Assets recorded under capital leases and the accumulated amortization thereof shall be separately identified in the lessee's balance sheet or in footnotes thereto. Likewise, the related obligations shall be separately identified in the balance sheet as obligations under capital leases and shall be subject to the same considerations as other obligations in classifying them with current and noncurrent liabilities in classified balance sheets. The amount of depreciation on capitalized leased assets should be separately disclosed.

(b) For **operating leases** having initial or remaining noncancelable *lease terms* in excess of one year:

  i. Future minimum rental payments required as of the date of the latest balance sheet presented, in the aggregate and for each of the five succeeding fiscal years.

  ii. The total of minimum rentals to be r

---

[28]"Is Lessee Accounting Working?" *op. cit.,* p. 19.

[29]"Accounting for Leases," *FASB Statement No. 13,* as amended and interpreted through May 1980 (Stamford, Conn.: FASB, 1980), par. 16.

ceived in the future under noncancelable subleases as of the date of the latest balance sheet presented.

(c) For **all operating leases,** rental expense for each period for which an income statement is presented, with separate amounts for minimum rentals, *contingent rentals,* and sublease rentals. Rental payments under leases with *terms* of a month or less that were not renewed need not be included.

(d) A **general description** of the lessee's leasing arrangements including, but not limited to, the following:
   i. The basis on which *contingent rental* payments are determined.
   ii. The existence and terms of renewal or purchase options and escalation clauses.
   iii. Restrictions imposed by lease agreements, such as those concerning dividends, additional debt, and further leasing.

## Disclosures Required of the Lessor

The FASB requires that **lessors** disclose in the financial statements or in the footnotes the following information when leasing "is a significant part of the lessor's business activities in terms of revenue, net income, or assets."[30]

---

**Lessor's Disclosures**

(a) For **sales-type and direct financing leases:**
   i. The components of the net investment in sales-type and direct financing leases as of the date of each balance sheet presented:
      a. Future *minimum lease payments* to be received, with separate deductions for (i) amounts representing *executory costs,* including any profit thereon, included in the minimum lease payments and (ii) the accumulated allowance for uncollectible *minimum lease payments* receivable.
      b. The *unguaranteed residual values* accruing to the benefit of the lessor.
      c. Unearned revenue.
   ii. Future *minimum lease payments* to be received for each of the five succeeding fiscal years as of the date of the latest balance sheet presented.
   iii. The amount of unearned revenue included in income to offset *initial direct costs* charged against income for each period for which an income statement is presented. (For direct financing leases only.)
   iv. Total *contingent rentals* included in income for each period for which an income statement is presented.

(b) For **operating leases:**
   i. The cost and carrying amount, if different, of property on lease or held for leasing by major classes of property according to nature or function, and the amount of accumulated depreciation in total as of the date of the latest balance sheet presented.
   ii. Minimum future rentals on noncancelable leases as of the date of the latest balance sheet presented, in the aggregate and for each of the five succeeding fiscal years.
   iii. Total *contingent rentals* included in income for each period for which an income statement is presented.

(c) A **general description** of the lessor's leasing arrangements.

---

## Illustrated Disclosures

The financial statement excerpts from the 1980 annual report of Kroger Co. which follow present the statement and note disclosures typical of a lessee having capital leases.

---

[30]Ibid., par. 23.

| KROEGER CO. | 1980 | 1979 |
|---|---|---|
| | ($000) | |
| **Property, Plant and Equipment:** | | |
| Land ........................................... | $  32,811 | $  28,059 |
| Buildings and land improvements ........................... | 158,662 | 149,573 |
| Equipment ........................................ | 793,754 | 650,035 |
| Leaseholds and leasehold improvements ..................... | 237,321 | 205,107 |
| **Leased property under capital leases** ................... | **152,866** | **137,270** |
| | 1,375,414 | 1,170,044 |
| Allowance for depreciation and amortization ................. | (490,797) | (444,824) |
| Property, plant and equipment, net ....................... | $ 884,617 | $ 725,220 |
| **Current Liabilities:** | | |
| **Current portion of obligations under capital leases** ...... | $  **3,741** | $  **3,057** |
| **Noncurrent Liabilities:** | | |
| **Obligations under capital leases** ...................... | **117,819** | **106,055** |

*NOTES TO CONSOLIDATED FINANCIAL STATEMENTS*

**Accounting Policies (in part)**

*Leases*

The Company operates principally in leased premises. Lease terms generally range from ten to twenty-five years with options of renewal for additional periods.

Options provide in some cases for reduced rentals and/or the right to purchase. Certain of the leases provide for contingent rental based on a percent of sales.

Rent expense (under operating leases) consists of:

| (000 omitted) | 1980 | 1979 | 1978 |
|---|---|---|---|
| Minimum rentals, net of minor sublease rentals ......... | $118,404 | $101,904 | $91,065 |
| Contingent rentals ................................ | 12,228 | 10,623 | 8,720 |
| Total ........................................... | $130,632 | $112,527 | $99,785 |

Assets recorded under capital leases include:

| (000 omitted) | 1980 | 1979 |
|---|---|---|
| Distribution and manufacturing facilities ........................... | $ 97,213 | $ 96,579 |
| Store facilities ................................................ | 55,653 | 40,691 |
| Less accumulated amortization .................................. | (41,486) | (36,884) |
| | $111,380 | $100,386 |

Minimum annual rentals, net of subleased rentals which are minor in amount, for the five years subsequent to 1980 and in the aggregate are:

| (000 omitted) | Capital Leases | Operating Leases |
|---|---|---|
| 1981 ......................................................... | $ 16,013 | $ 123,076 |
| 1982 ......................................................... | 15,988 | 119,427 |
| 1983 ......................................................... | 15,729 | 115,434 |
| 1984 ......................................................... | 15,318 | 112,511 |
| 1985 ......................................................... | 14,744 | 109,298 |
| 1986 and thereafter ......................................... | 221,779 | 1,152,310 |
| | $299,571 | $1,732,056 |
| Less estimated executory costs included in capital leases ........... | (13,792) | |
| Net minimum lease payments under capital leases ................. | $285,779 | |
| Less amount representing interest ............................. | (164,219) | |
| Present value of net minimum lease payments under capital leases ................................ | $121,560 | |

For another illustration of lease disclosure by a lessee, see Tenneco's note 10 under "Lease Commitments" on page 205.

The following note from the 1982 annual report of Glosser Bros. Inc. illustrates the disclosures of a lessee having only operating leases:

---

### OPERATING LEASE DISCLOSURES

Glosser Bros., Inc. (Lessee)

*NOTE E—LEASING ARRANGEMENTS*

The company conducts its retail store operations primarily from leased facilities. Substantially all leases contain provisions for multiple renewal options. Leases are primarily net leases which require the payment of executory costs such as real estate taxes, insurance, common area maintenance and other operating costs in addition to minimum rentals. The remaining leases are gross leases which provide for minimum rentals that include executory costs. Certain leases require additional rentals based on percentages of sales exceeding specified amounts.

Following is a schedule by fiscal year of future minimum rental payments required under operating leases that have initial or remaining noncancelable lease terms in excess of one year as of January 30, 1982:

| | |
|---|---|
| 1982 | $ 4,182,000 |
| 1983 | 3,996,000 |
| 1984 | 3,845,000 |
| 1985 | 3,714,000 |
| 1986 | 3,629,000 |
| Later years | 53,452,000 |
| Total minimum payments required | $72,818,000 |

Rental expense is comprised as follows:

| | 1981 | 1980 | 1979 |
|---|---|---|---|
| Minimum rentals | $3,708,000 | $3,423,000 | $2,882,000 |
| Additional rentals | 194,000 | 222,000 | 270,000 |
| Total | $3,902,000 | $3,645,000 | $3,152,000 |

Rental expense under leases from affiliated lessors approximated $516,000, $520,000 and $519,000 in 1981, 1980 and 1979.

# APPENDIX M

# Real Estate Leases and Leveraged Leases

Presented in this appendix are these additional lease accounting topics:

1. Leases Involving Real Estate.
2. Leveraged Leases.

## LEASES INVOLVING REAL ESTATE[1]

Special problems can arise when leases involve land, or land and buildings, or equipment as well as real estate.

### Land

If land is the sole item of property leased, the **lessee** should account for the lease as a capital lease only if criteria (1) or (2) are met, that is, if the lease transfers ownership of the property or contains a bargain purchase option; otherwise it is accounted for as an operating lease. Because ownership of the land is expected to pass to the lessee when the lease is classified as a capital lease, the asset is not normally depreciated. The **lessor** accounts for a land lease either as a sales-type or direct financing lease, whichever is appropriate, if the lease transfers ownership or contains a bargain purchase option and meets both the collectibility and uncertainties tests; otherwise the operating method is used.

### Land and Building

If both land and building are involved and the lease transfers ownership or contains a bargain purchase option, the land and the building should be separately classified by the **lessee**. The present value of the minimum lease payments is allocated between land and building in proportion to their fair values at the inception of the lease. The **lessor** accounts for the lease as a single unit either as a sales-type, direct financing, or operating lease, as appropriate.

[1]Ibid., pars. 24–26.

When both land and building are involved and the lease does not transfer ownership or contain a bargain purchase option, the accounting treatment is dependent upon the proportion of land to building. If the fair value of the land is less than 25% of the total fair value of the leased property, both the lessee and the lessor consider the land and the building as a single unit. The land is then amortized along with the building by the lessee. If the fair value of the land is 25% or more of the total fair value, the land and building are considered separately by both the lessee and the lessor. The lessee accounts for the building as a capital lease and the land as an operating lease if one of the two remaining criteria (3 or 4) is met. If none of the criteria are met, the lessee uses the operating method on the land and building. The lessor accounts for the building as a sales-type or direct financing lease as appropriate and the land element separately as an operating lease.

## Real Estate and Equipment

If a lease involves both real estate and equipment, the portion of the lease payments applicable to the equipment should be estimated by whatever means are appropriate and reasonable. The equipment then should be treated separately for purposes of applying the criteria and accounted for separately according to its classification by both lessees and lessors.

When the leased property is part of a larger whole, for example, an office or a floor of a building or a store in a shopping center, "reasonable estimates of the leased property's fair value might be objectively determined by referring to an independent appraisal of the leased property or to estimated replacement cost information."[2]

# LEVERAGED LEASES

Leveraged leasing began in the late sixties and grew during the seventies. It has been estimated that more than $5 billion worth of capital equipment is financed annually through the use of leveraged leases, and there is every expectation that the use of this type of lease will continue in popularity.

Under a properly structured lease arrangement the lessor has the tax benefits of the asset to use as a basis to shield taxable income. In addition, the lessor can concentrate the tax benefits by **leveraging** the lease. That is, the lessor of the property may finance a small percentage of the purchase price (with 100% ownership of the asset) and find debt participants who will finance the balance. The leveraged lease arrangement generally involves the following:

1. It meets the definition of a direct financing lease, except that the 90% of fair value criterion is not applicable.
2. Three participants in the lease arrangement—
   a. An owner-lessor (equity participant).
   b. A lessee (user of the asset).
   c. A third-party long-term creditor (debt participant).
3. The owner-lessor provides a portion of the cost of the property to be leased, generally 20% to 40%.
4. Long-term creditors (generally financial institutions) provide the remaining portion (60 to 80%) of the cost of the equipment. The amount provided by these third-party creditors is

---

[2]"Leases Involving Only Part of a Building," *FASB Interpretation No. 24* (Stamford, Conn.: FASB, 1978), par. 6.

generally called the **leveraged debt.** The leveraged debt is structured **without recourse** to the owner-lessor; it is secured by a pledge of lease payments or by a security interest in the property. For this reason, the interest rate obtained by the long-term creditors for the leveraged debt is based, in part, on the lessee's credit rating.

5. The asset is then purchased from the manufacturer or contractor by the lessor-owner and leased to the lessee. In return, the lessor-owner receives the rental payments, makes debt service payments (principal and interest) to the long-term creditors, and retains any difference. The residual value from the disposition of the asset at the end of the lease term is retained by the lessor. Generally, the lessor's net investment declines during the early years and rises during the later years of the lease. The lessor's return and early net cash inflow results from several sources: (1) lease rentals; (2) investment tax credit; and (3) income tax benefits such as depreciation (often accelerated) on the total cost of the property, interest expense on the debt, and possibly others.

The following diagram illustrates the relationship of the parties involved in a leveraged lease transaction.

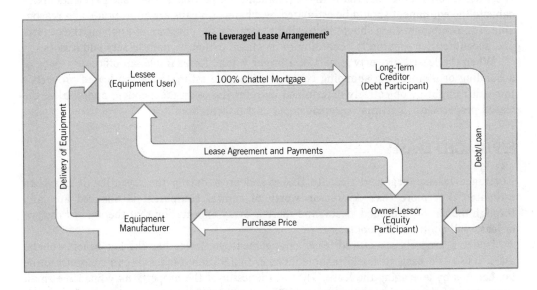

The accounting for a leveraged lease by the lessee is not distinguishable from the accounting for an unleveraged one. The FASB requires that the lessor classify leveraged leases as direct financing leases with the lessor's liability to the third-party creditor offset against its lease receivables from the lessee. Thus, the lessor reports an asset only if the lease receivable is greater than its debt. And, the lessor reports income from the lease only in those years when the receivable exceeds the debt.

Because the accounting for leveraged leases by lessors can be quite complex and unique to the specific tailored lease, it is not illustrated in this chapter.[4]

---

[3]Taken from "A Straightforward Approach to Leveraged Leasing," by Pierce R. Smith, *The Journal of Commercial Bank Lending* (July 1973), pp. 40–47.

[4]For an illustration of the accounting and financial statement disclosures related to leveraged leases, see *FASB Statement No. 13,* Appendix E, par. 123.

**Note:** All **asterisked** Questions, Cases, Exercises, or Problems relate to material contained in the appendix to each chapter.

## QUESTIONS

1. Identify the two recognized lease accounting methods for lessees and distinguish between them.

2. Allservice Inc. is expanding its operations and is in the process of selecting the method of financing this program. After some investigation, the company determines that it may (1) issue bonds and with the proceeds purchase the needed assets, or (2) lease the assets on a long-term basis.

   Without knowing the comparative costs involved, answer these questions:
   (a) What might be the advantages of leasing the assets instead of owning them?
   (b) What might be the disadvantages of leasing the assets instead of owning them?
   (c) In what way will the balance sheet be differently affected by leasing the assets as opposed to issuing bonds and purchasing the assets?

3. McHenry Corp. is considering leasing a significant amount of assets. The President, Joan Robinson, is attending an informal meeting in the afternoon with a potential lessor. Because her legal advisor cannot be reached, she has called on you, the controller, to brief her on the general provisions of lease agreements to which she should give consideration in such preliminary discussions with a possible lessor.

   Identify the general provisions of the lease agreement that the president should be told to include in her discussion with the potential lessor.

4. M. Wickers Company rents a warehouse on a month-to-month basis for the storage of its excess inventory. The company periodically must rent space whenever its production greatly exceeds actual sales. For several years the company officials have discussed building their own storage facility, but this enthusiasm wavers when sales increase sufficiently to absorb the excess inventory.

   What is the nature of this type of lease arrangement, and what accounting treatment should be accorded it?

5. Differentiate between the "lessee's incremental borrowing rate" and the "lessor's implicit rate" in accounting for leases indicating when one or the other should be used.

6. Outline the accounting procedures involved in applying the operating method by a lessee.

7. Outline the accounting procedures involved in applying the capital lease method by a lessee.

8. Identify the lease classifications for lessors and the criteria that must be met for each classification.

9. Outline the accounting procedures involved in applying the direct financing method.

10. Outline the accounting procedures involved in applying the operating method by a lessor.

11. M. Moluf Company is a manufacturer and lessor of computer equipment. What should be the nature of its lease arrangements with lessees if the company wishes to account for its lease transactions as sales-type leases?

12. Burt & Reynolds Corporation's lease arrangements qualify as sales-type leases at the time of entering into the transactions. How should the corporation recognize revenues and costs in these situations?

13. Why are present-value concepts appropriate and applicable in accounting for financing-type lease arrangements?

14. Mellissa Packard, M.D. (lessee) has a noncancelable 20-year lease with Izykowski Realty, Inc., (lessor) for the use of a medical building. Taxes, insurance, and maintenance are paid by the lessee in addition to the fixed annual payments, of which the present value is equal to the fair market value of the leased property. At the end of the lease period, title becomes the lessee's at a nominal price.

   Considering the terms of the lease described above, comment on the nature of the lease transaction and the accounting treatment that should be accorded it by the lessee.

15. The residual value is the estimated fair value of the leased property at the end of the lease term.
    (a) Of what significance is (1) an unguaranteed and (2) a guaranteed residual value in the lessee's accounting for a capitalized lease transaction?
    (b) Of what significance is (1) an unguaranteed and (2) a guaranteed residual value in the lessor's accounting for a direct financing lease transaction?

16. How should changes in the estimated residual value be handled by the lessor?

17. Describe the effect of a "bargain purchase option" on accounting for a capital lease transaction by a lessee.

18. What are "initial direct costs" and how are they accounted for?

19. What is the nature of a "sale-leaseback" transaction?

20. What disclosures should be made by a lessee if the leased assets and the related obligation are not capitalized?

*21. Assume that Hargrove Inc. leases land for agricultural purposes; what criteria are applied to determine whether capital or operating lease treatment is applied?

*22. What distinguishes a leveraged lease from all other lease arrangements?

*23. What is the cash flow that the lessor realizes in a normal leveraged lease transaction?

# CASES

**C22–1** The Davids Corporation is a diversified company with nationwide interests in commercial real estate developments, banking, copper mining, and metal fabrication. The company has offices and operating locations in major cities throughout the United States. Corporate headquarters for Davids Corporation is located in a metropolitan area of a midwestern state, and executives connected with various phases of company operations travel extensively. Corporate management is presently evaluating the feasibility of acquiring a business aircraft that can be used by company executives to expedite business travel to areas not adequately served by commercial airlines. Proposals for either leasing or purchasing a suitable aircraft have been analyzed, and the leasing proposal was considered to be more desirable.

The proposed lease agreement involves a twin-engine turboprop Viking that has a fair market value of $900,000. This plane would be leased for a period of 10 years beginning January 1, 1983. The lease agreement is cancelable only upon accidental destruction of the plane. An annual lease payment of $127,600 is due on January 1 of each year; the first payment is to be made on January 1, 1983. Maintenance operations are strictly scheduled by the lessor, and Davids Corporation will pay for these services as they are performed. Estimated annual maintenance costs are $6,200. The lessor will pay all insurance premiums and local property taxes, which amount to a combined total of $3,600 annually and are included in the annual lease payment of $127,600. Upon expiration of the 10-year lease, Davids Corporation can purchase the Viking for $40,000. The estimated useful life of the plane is 15 years, and its salvage value in the used plane market is estimated to be $100,000 after 10 years. The salvage value probably will never be less than $75,000 if the engines are overhauled and maintained as prescribed by the manufacturer. If the purchase option is not exercised, possession of the plane will revert to the lessor, and there is no provision for renewing the lease agreement beyond its termination on December 31, 1992.

Davids Corporation can borrow $900,000 under a 10-year term loan agreement at an annual interest rate of 12%. The lessor's implicit interest rate is not expressly stated in the lease agreement, but this rate appears to be approximately 8% based on ten net rental payments of $124,000 per year and the initial market value of $900,000 for the plane. On January 1, 1983, the present value of all net rental payments and the purchase option of $40,000 is $800,000 using the 12% interest rate. The present value of all net rental payments and the $40,000 purchase option on January 1, 1983 is $920,000 using the 8% interest rate implicit in the lease agreement. The financial vice-president of Davids Corporation has established that this lease agreement is a capital lease as defined in *Statement of Financial Accounting Standard No. 13,* "Accounting for Leases."

## Instructions

(a) What is the appropriate amount that Davids Corporation should recognize for the leased aircraft on its Balance Sheet after the lease is signed?

(b) Without prejudice to your answer in part (a), assume that the annual lease payment is $127,600 as stated in the question, that the appropriate capitalized amount for the leased aircraft is $1,000,000 on January 1, 1983, and that the interest rate is 9%. How will the lease be reported in the December 31, 1983 Balance Sheet and related Income Statement? (Ignore any income tax implications.)

(CMA adapted)

**C22-2** Oakwood Corp. entered into a lease arrangement with Thing Leasing Corporation for a certain machine. Thing's primary business is leasing and it is not a manufacturer or dealer. Oakwood will lease the machine for a period of three years which is 50% of the machine's economic life. Thing will take possession of the machine at the end of the initial three-year lease and lease it to another smaller company that does not need the most current version of the machine. Oakwood does not guarantee any residual value for the machine and will not purchase the machine at the end of the lease term.

Oakwood's incremental borrowing rate is 16% and the implicit rate in the lease is 14½%. Oakwood has no way of knowing the implicit rate used by Thing. Using either rate, the present value of the minimum lease payments is between 90% and 100% of the fair value of the machine at the date of the lease agreement.

Oakwood has agreed to pay all executory costs directly and no allowance for these costs is included in the lease payments.

Thing is reasonably certain that Oakwood will pay all lease payments, and, because Oakwood has agreed to pay all executory costs, there are no important uncertainties regarding costs to be incurred by Thing. Assume that no indirect costs are involved.

## Instructions

(a) With respect to Oakwood (the lessee) answer the following:
  1. What type of lease has been entered into? Explain the reason for your answer.
  2. How should Oakwood compute the appropriate amount to be recorded for the lease or asset acquired?
  3. What accounts will be created or affected by this transaction and how will the lease or asset and other costs related to the transaction be matched with earnings?
  4. What disclosures must Oakwood make regarding this leased asset?

(b) With respect to Thing (the lessor) answer the following:
  1. What type of leasing arrangement has been entered into? Explain the reason for your answer.
  2. How should this lease be recorded by Thing and how are the appropriate amounts determined?
  3. How should Thing determine the appropriate amount of earnings to be recognized from each lease payment?
  4. What disclosures must Thing make regarding this lease?

(AICPA adapted)

**C22-3 Part 1.** Capital leases and operating leases are the two classifications of leases described in FASB pronouncements, from the standpoint of the **lessee.**

## Instructions

(a) Describe how a capital lease would be accounted for by the lessee both at the inception of the lease and during the first year of the lease, assuming the lease transfers ownership of the property to the lessee by the end of the lease.

(b) Describe how an operating lease would be accounted for by the lessee both at the inception of the lease and during the first year of the lease, assuming equal monthly payments are made by the lessee at the beginning of each month of the lease. Describe the change in accounting, if any, when rental payments are not made on a straight-line basis.

Do **not** discuss the criteria for distinguishing between capital leases and operating leases.

**Part 2.** Sales-type leases and direct financing leases are two of the classifications of leases described in FASB pronouncements, from the standpoint of the **lessor.**

**Instructions**

Compare and contrast a sales-type lease with a direct financing lease as follows:
(a) Gross investment in the lease.
(b) Amortization of unearned interest revenue.
(c) Manufacturer's or dealer's profit.
    Do **not** discuss the criteria for distinguishing between the leases described above and operating leases.

(AICPA adapted)

## EXERCISES

**E22–1** Fresno Leasing Company leases a new machine that cost $36,000 to Wesylian Corporation on a three-year noncancelable contract. Wesylian Corporation agrees to assume all risks of normal ownership including such costs as insurance, taxes, and maintenance. The machine has a three-year useful life and no residual value. The lease was signed on January 1, 1984; Fresno Leasing Company expects to earn a 10% return on its investment. The annual rentals are payable on each December 31.

**Instructions**

(a) Discuss the nature of the lease arrangement and the accounting method each party to the lease should apply.
(b) Prepare an amortization schedule that would be suitable for both the lessor and the lessee and covers all the years involved.

**E22–2** Chautauqua Company enters into a lease agreement on July 1, 1984 for the purpose of leasing a machine to be used in its manufacturing operations. The following data pertain to this agreement:

1. The term of the noncancelable lease is 3 years, with no renewal option, and no residual value at the end of the lease term. Payments of $92,935.08 are due on July 1 of each year, beginning July 1, 1984.
2. The fair value of the machine on July 1, 1984 is $265,000. The machine has a remaining economic life of 5 years, with no salvage value. The machine reverts to the lessor upon the termination of the lease.
3. Chautauqua Company elects to depreciate the machine on the straight-line method.
4. Chautauqua Company's incremental borrowing rate is 12% per year. Chautauqua does not have knowledge of the implicit rate computed by the lessor.

**Instructions**

Prepare the journal entries on the books of the lessee that relate to the lease agreement through June 30, 1986. The accounting period of Chautauqua Company ends on December 31. (Assume that reversing entries are made.)

**E22–3** On January 1, 1984, Scratch Paper Co. signs a 10-year noncancelable lease agreement to lease a storage building from Mozart Storage Company. The following information pertains to this lease agreement:

1. The agreement requires equal rental payments of $135,000 beginning on January 1, 1984.
2. The fair value of the building on January 1, 1984 is $800,000.
3. The building has an estimated economic life of 12 years, with an unguaranteed residual value of $10,000. Scratch Paper Co. depreciates similar buildings on the straight-line method.

4. The lease is nonrenewable. At the termination of the lease, the building reverts to the lessor.

5. Scratch Paper's incremental borrowing rate is 12% per year. The lessor's implicit rate is not known by Scratch Paper Co.

6. The yearly rental payment includes $8,583.74 of executory costs related to taxes on the property.

**Instructions**

Prepare the journal entries on the lessee's books to reflect the signing of the lease agreement and to record the payments and expenses related to this lease for the years 1984 and 1985. Scratch Paper's corporate year end is December 31.

**E22-4** Burke Travel Company leases an automobile with a fair value of $6,430 from Judy Nolan Motors, Inc. on the following terms:

1. Noncancelable term of 50 months.

2. Rental of $150 per month (at end of each month; present value at 1% per month is $5,877).

3. Estimated residual value after 50 months is $910 (the present value at 1% per month is $553). Burke Travel Company guarantees the residual value of $910.

4. Estimated economic life of the automobile is 60 months.

5. Burke Travel Company's incremental borrowing rate is 12% a year (1% a month). Nolan's implicit rate is unknown.

**Instructions**

(a) What is the nature of this lease to Burke Travel Company?
(b) What is the present value of the minimum lease payments?
(c) Record the lease on Burke Travel Company's books at the date of inception.
(d) Record the first month's depreciation on Burke Travel Company's books (assume straight-line).
(e) Record the first month's lease payment.

**E22-5** Bach Horn Company leases a car at fair value to a salesman on January 1, 1984. The term of the noncancelable lease is four years. The following information about the lease is provided:

1. Title to the car passes to the lessee upon the termination of the lease when residual value is estimated at $1,000.

2. The fair value of the car is $10,000. The cost of the car to Bach Horn Company is $6,000. The car has an economic life of five years.

3. Bach Horn Company desires a rate of return of 15% on its investment.

4. Collectibility of the lease payments is reasonably predictable. There are no important uncertainties surrounding the amount of costs yet to be incurred by the lessor.

5. Equal annual lease payments are due at the beginning of each lease year.

**Instructions**

(a) Prepare a lease amortization schedule for Bach Horn Company for the four-year lease term.
(b) What type of lease is this? Discuss.
(c) Prepare the journal entries in 1984, 1985, and 1986 to record the lease agreement, the receipt of lease payments, and the recognition of income.

**E22-6** Holistic Leasing Company signs a lease agreement on January 1, 1984 to lease electronic equipment to Hamsmith Company at cost. The term of the noncancelable lease is two years and payments are required at the end of each year. The following information relates to this agreement:

1. Hamsmith Company has the option to purchase the equipment for $10,000 upon the termination of the lease.

2. The equipment has a cost of $60,000 to Holistic Leasing Company; the useful economic life is two years, with a salvage value of $10,000.

3. Hamsmith Company is required to pay $5,000 each year to the lessor for executory costs.

4. Holistic Leasing Company desires to earn a return of 12% on its investment.

5. Collectibility of the payments is reasonably predictable, and there are no important uncertainties surrounding the costs yet to be incurred by the lessor.

**Instructions**

(a) Prepare the journal entries on the books of Holistic Leasing to reflect the payments received under the lease, and to recognize income, for the years 1984 and 1985.

(b) Assuming that Hamsmith Company exercises its option to purchase the equipment on December 31, 1985, prepare the journal entry to reflect the sale on Holistic's books.

**E22–7** On February 20, 1983, Riley, Inc., purchased a machine for $1,200,000 for the purpose of leasing it. The machine is expected to have a ten-year life, no residual value, and will be depreciated on the straight-line basis. The machine was leased to Sutter Company on March 1, 1983, for a four-year period at a monthly rental of $18,000. There is no provision for the renewal of the lease or purchase of the machine by the lessee at the expiration of the lease term. Riley paid $60,000 of commissions associated with negotiating the lease in February 1983.

**Instructions**

(a) What expense should Sutter record as a result of the above facts for the year ended December 31, 1983? Show supporting computations in good form.

(b) What income or loss before income taxes should Riley record as a result of the above facts for the year ended December 31, 1983? (Hint: Amortize commissions over the life of the lease.)

(AICPA adapted)

**E22–8** On January 1, 1983, Karnak Corporation sells a computer to Liquidity Finance Co. for $1,000,000, and immediately leases the computer back. The relevant information is as follows:

1. The computer was carried on Karnak's books at a value of $750,000.

2. The term of the noncancelable lease is 20 years; title will transfer to Karnak.

3. The lease agreement requires equal rental payments of $101,852.18 at the end of each year.

4. The incremental borrowing rate of Karnak Corporation is 10%. Karnak is aware that Liquidity Finance Co. set the annual rental to insure a rate of return of 8%.

5. The computer has a fair value of $1,000,000 on January 1, 1983.

6. Karnak pays executory costs of $5,000 per year.

**Instructions**

Prepare the journal entries for both the lessee and the lessor for 1983 to reflect the sale and leaseback agreement. No uncertainties exist and collectibility is reasonably certain.

**\*E22–9** On January 1, 1984, Briarpatch Corporation sells land to Ski-Daddle Corporation for $1,100,000, and immediately leases the land back. The relevant information is as follows:

1. The land was carried on Briarpatch's books at a value of $800,000.

2. The term of the noncancelable lease is 20 years; title will pass to Briarpatch at the end of the lease term.

3. The lease agreement requires equal rental payments of $112,037.40 at the end of each year.

4. The incremental borrowing rate of Briarpatch Corporation is 10%. Briarpatch is aware that Ski-Daddle Corporation set the annual rental to insure a rate of return of 8%.

5. The land has a fair value of $1,100,000 on January 1, 1984.

6. Briarpatch pays all executory costs. These costs consist of insurance and taxes amounting to $11,000 per year.

**Instructions**

Prepare the journal entries for both the lessee and the lessor for 1984 to reflect the sale and leaseback agreement. No uncertainties exist and collectibility is reasonably certain.

# PROBLEMS

**P22-1** We-lease-it, Inc., agrees to rent Napa Winery Corporation the equipment that it requires to expand its production capacity to meet customers' demands for its products. The lease agreement calls for five annual lease payments of $200,000 at the end of each year. On the date the capital lease begins, the lessee recognizes the existence of leased assets and the related lease obligation at the present value of the five annual payments discounted at a rate of 15%, $670,432. The lessee uses the effective-interest method of reducing lease obligations. The leased equipment has an estimated useful life of five years and no residual value; Napa Winery uses the sum-of-the-years'-digits method on similar equipment that it owns.

**Instructions**

(a) What would be the total amount of the reduction in the lease obligation of the lessee during the first year? The second year?

(b) Prepare the journal entry made by Napa Winery Corporation (lessee) on the date the lease begins.

(c) Prepare the journal entries to record the lease payment and interest expense for the first year; the second year.

(d) Prepare the journal entry at the end of the first full year to recognize depreciation of the leased equipment.

**P22-2** Wheelit Company leased a new crane to Foxy Lady Company under a 5-year noncancelable contract starting January 1, 1984. Terms of the lease require payments of $11,000 each January 1, starting January 1, 1984. Wheelit will pay insurance, taxes, and maintenance charges on the crane, which has an estimated life of 12 years, a fair value of $80,000, and a cost to Wheelit Company of $80,000. The estimated fair value of the crane is expected to be $10,000 at the end of the lease term. No bargain purchase or renewal options are included in the contract. Both Wheelit and Foxy Lady adjust and close books annually at December 31. Collectibility is reasonably certain and no uncertainties exist relative to unreimbursable lessor costs. Foxy Lady's incremental borrowing rate is 7% and Wheelit's implicit interest rate of 6% is unknown to Foxy.

**Instructions**

(a) Identify the type of lease involved and give reasons for your classification. Discuss the accounting treatment that should be applied by both the lessee and the lessor.

(b) Prepare all the entries related to the lease contract and leased asset for the year 1984 for the lessee and lessor, assuming:
1. Insurance $160.
2. Taxes $80.
3. Maintenance $490.
4. Straight-line depreciation and salvage value of $2,000.

(c) Discuss what should be presented in the balance sheet and income statement and related footnotes of both the lessee and the lessor at December 31, 1984.

**P22-3** Burlington Railroad and Electro-Motive Corporation enter into an agreement that requires Electro-Motive to build three diesel-electric engines to Burlington's specifications. Upon completion of the engines, Burlington has agreed to lease them for a period of 12 years and to assume all costs and risks of ownership. The lease is noncancelable, becomes effective on

January 1, 1984, and requires annual rental payments of $280,000 each January 1, starting January 1, 1984.

Burlington's incremental borrowing rate is 13%, and the implicit interest rate used by Electro-Motive and known to Burlington is 12%. The total cost of building the three engines is $1,550,000. The economic life of the engines is estimated to be 12 years with residual value set at zero. The railroad depreciates similar equipment on a straight-line basis. At the end of the lease, the railroad assumes title to the engines. Collectibility is reasonably certain and no uncertainties exist relative to unreimbursable lessor costs.

**Instructions**

(Round all numbers to the nearest dollar.)

(a) Discuss the nature of this lease transaction from the viewpoints of both lessee and lessor.

(b) Prepare the journal entry or entries to record the transaction on January 1, 1984 on the books of the Burlington Railroad.

(c) Prepare the journal entry or entries to record the transaction on January 1, 1984 on the books of the Electro-Motive Corporation.

(d) Prepare the journal entries for both the lessee and lessor to record the first rental payment on January 1, 1984.

(e) Prepare the journal entries for both the lessee and lessor to record interest expense (revenue) at December 31, 1984. (Prepare a lease amortization schedule for two years.)

(f) Show the items and amounts that would be reported on the balance sheet (not footnotes) at December 31, 1984 for both the lessee and the lessor.

**P22-4** On January 1, 1984, Aroma Cheese Company contracts to lease equipment for five years, agreeing to make a payment of $70,000 (including the executory costs of $10,000) at the beginning of each year, starting January 1, 1984. The taxes, the insurance, and the maintenance, estimated at $10,000 a year, are the obligations of the lessee. The leased equipment is to be capitalized at $267,906. The asset is to be amortized on a straight-line basis while the obligation is to be reduced on an effective-interest basis. Aroma's incremental borrowing rate is 8%, and the implicit rate in the lease is 6%, which is known by Aroma. Title to the equipment transfers to Aroma when the lease expires. The asset has an estimated useful life of five years and no residual value.

**Instructions**

(Round all numbers to the nearest dollar.)

(a) Explain the probable relationship of the $267,906 amount to the lease arrangement.

(b) Prepare the journal entry or entries that should be recorded on January 1, 1984 by Aroma Cheese Company.

(c) Prepare the journal entry to record depreciation of the leased asset for the year 1984.

(d) Prepare the journal entry to record the interest expense for the year 1984.

(e) Prepare the journal entry to record the lease payment of January 1, 1985 assuming reversing entries are not made.

(f) What amounts will appear on the lessee's December 31, 1984 balance sheet relative to the lease contract?

**P22-5** Atlas Steel Company as lessee signed a lease agreement for equipment for 5 years, beginning December 31, 1983. Annual rental payments of $30,000 are to be made at the beginning of each lease year (December 31). The taxes, insurance, and the maintenance costs are the obligation of the lessee. The interest rate used by the lessor in setting the payment schedule is 11%; Atlas' incremental borrowing rate is 12%. Atlas is unaware of the rate being used by the lessor. At the end of the lease, Atlas has the option to buy the equipment for $1, considerably below its then estimated fair value. The equipment has an estimated useful life of 8 years. Atlas uses the straight-line method of depreciation on similar owned equipment.

**Instructions**

(Round all numbers to the nearest dollar.)

(a) Prepare the journal entry or entries, with explanations, that should be recorded on December 31, 1983 by Atlas. (Assume no residual value.)

(b) Prepare the journal entry or entries, with explanations, that should be recorded on December 31, 1984 by Atlas (prepare the lease amortization schedule for all five payments).

(c) Prepare the journal entry or entries, with explanations, that should be recorded on December 31, 1985 by Atlas.

(d) What amounts would appear on the December 31, 1985 balance sheet of Atlas relative to the lease arrangement?

**P22-6** Melton Weaving, Inc., was incorporated in 1982 to operate as a computer software service firm with an accounting fiscal year ending August 31. Melton's primary product is a sophisticated on-line inventory-control system; its customers pay a fixed fee plus a usage charge for using the system.

Melton has leased a large, BIG-I computer system from the manufacturer. The lease calls for a monthly rental of $31,000 for the 144 months (12 years) of the lease term. The estimated useful life of the computer is 15 years.

Each scheduled monthly rental payment includes $5,000 for full-service maintenance on the computer to be performed by the manufacturer. All rentals are payable on the first day of the month beginning with August 1, 1983, the date the computer was installed and the lease agreement was signed.

The lease is noncancelable for its 12-year term, and it is secured only by the manufacturer's chattel lien on the BIG-I system. On any anniversary date of the lease after August 1988, Melton can purchase the BIG-I system from the manufacturer at 75% of the then current fair value of the computer.

This lease is to be accounted for as a capital lease by Melton, and it will be depreciated by the straight-line method with no expected salvage value. Borrowed funds for this type of transaction would cost Melton 12% per year (1% per month). Following is a schedule of the present value of $1 for selected periods discounted at 1% per period when payments are made at the beginning of each period.

| Periods (months) | Present Value of $1 per Period Discounted at 1% per Period |
|:---:|:---:|
| 1 | 1.000 |
| 2 | 1.990 |
| 3 | 2.970 |
| 143 | 76.658 |
| 144 | 76.899 |

**Instructions**

Prepare, in general journal form, all entries Melton should have made in its accounting records during August 1983 relating to this lease. Give full explanations and show supporting computations for each entry. Remember, August 31, 1983, is the end of Melton's fiscal accounting period and it will be preparing financial statements on that date. Do not prepare closing entries.

(AICPA adapted)

**P22-7** Steve Dairy leases its milking equipment from Zeff Finance Company under the following lease terms:

1. The lease term is five years, noncancelable, and requires equal rental payments of $46,500 due at the beginning of each year starting January 1, 1984.

2. The equipment has a fair value and cost at the inception of the lease (January 1, 1984) of $200,100, an estimated economic life of five years, and a residual value (which is guaranteed by Steve Dairy) of $10,000.

3. The lease contains no renewable options and the equipment reverts to Zeff Finance Company upon termination of the lease.

4. Steve Dairy's incremental borrowing rate is 10% per year; the implicit rate is also 10%.

5. Steve Dairy depreciates similar equipment that it owns on a straight-line basis.

**6.** Collectibility of the payments is reasonably predictable, and there are no important uncertainties surrounding the costs yet to be incurred by the lessor.

**Instructions**

(a) Describe the nature of the lease and in general discuss how the lessor and lessee should account for the lease transaction.

(b) Prepare the journal entries at January 1, 1984 for the lessee and the lessor.

(c) Prepare the journal entries at December 31, 1984 (the lessee's and lessor's year-end).

(d) Prepare the journal entry at January 1, 1985 for the lessee and the lessor. (Assume no reversing entries.)

(e) What would have been the amount to be capitalized by the lessee upon the inception of the lease if

1. The residual value of $10,000 had been guaranteed by a third party, not the lessee.

2. The residual value of $10,000 had not been guaranteed at all.

(f) On the lessor's books, what would be the amount recorded as the Net Investment at the inception of the lease, assuming

1. The residual value of $10,000 had been guaranteed by a third party.

2. The residual value of $10,000 had not been guaranteed at all.

(g) Suppose the useful life of the milking equipment had been nine years. How large would the residual value have had to be in order for the lessee to qualify for the operating method? (Assume that the residual value would be guaranteed by a third party.)

**P22-8** Itaree Company manufactures a desk-type computer with an estimated economic life of 12 years and leases it to Tailwind Airlines for a period of 10 years. The normal selling price of the equipment is $259,569, and its unguaranteed residual value at the end of the lease term is estimated to be $20,000. Tailwind will pay annual payments of $40,000 at the beginning of each year and all maintenance, insurance, and taxes. Itaree incurred costs of $200,000 in manufacturing the equipment and $7,000 in negotiating and closing the lease. Itaree has determined that the collectibility of the lease payments is reasonably predictable, that there will be no additional costs incurred, and that the implicit interest rate is 12%.

**Instructions**

(Round all numbers to the nearest dollar.)

(a) Discuss the nature of this lease in relation to the lessor and compute the amount of each of the following items:

1. Gross investment.

2. Unearned income.

3. Sales price.

4. Cost of sales.

(b) Prepare a 10-year lease amortization schedule.

(c) Prepare all of the lessor's journal entries for the first year.

**P22-9** In 1981 Intervalley Express Company negotiated and closed a long-term lease contract for newly constructed truck terminals and freight storage facilities. The buildings were erected to the company's specifications on land owned by the company. On January 1, 1982, Intervalley Express Company took possession of the leased properties. On January 1, 1982 and 1983, the company made cash payments of $1,440,000 that were recorded as rental expenses.

Although the terminals have a composite useful life of 40 years, the noncancelable lease runs for 20 years from January 1, 1982, with a bargain purchase option available upon expiration of the lease.

The 20-year lease is effective for the period January 1, 1982 through December 31, 2001. Advance rental payments of $1,200,000 are payable to the lessor on January 1 of each of the first 10 years of the lease term. Advance rental payments of $360,000 are due on January 1 for each of the last 10 years of the lease. The company has an option to purchase all of these leased facilities for $1 on December 31, 2001. It also must make annual payments to the lessor of $90,000 for property taxes and $150,000 for insurance. The lease was negotiated to assure the lessor a 6% rate of return.

**Instructions**

(Round all computations to the nearest dollar.)

(a) Prepare a schedule to compute for Intervalley Express Company the discounted present value of the terminal facilities and related obligation at January 1, 1982.

(b) Assuming that the discounted present value of terminal facilities and related obligation at January 1, 1982, was $12,000,000, prepare journal entries for Intervalley Express Company to record the:

1. Cash payment to the lessor on January 1, 1984.

2. Amortization of the cost of the leased properties for 1984 using the straight-line method and assuming a zero salvage value.

3. Accrual of interest expense at December 31, 1984.

Selected present value factors are as follows:

| Periods | For an Ordinary Annuity of $1 at 6% | For $1 at 6% |
|---------|-------------------------------------|--------------|
| 1 | .943396 | .943396 |
| 2 | 1.833393 | .889996 |
| 8 | 6.209794 | .627412 |
| 9 | 6.801692 | .591898 |
| 10 | 7.360087 | .558395 |
| 19 | 11.158117 | .330513 |
| 20 | 11.469921 | .311805 |

(AICPA adapted)

**P22–10** During 1984, Lowrent Leasing Co. began leasing equipment to small manufacturers. Below is information regarding leasing arrangements.

1. Lowrent Leasing Co. leases equipment with terms from 3 to 5 years depending upon the useful life of the equipment. At the expiration of the lease, the equipment will be sold to the lessee at 10% of the lessor's cost, the expected salvage value of the equipment.

2. The amount of the lessee's monthly payment is computed by multiplying the lessor's cost of the equipment by the payment factor applicable to the term of lease.

| Term of Lease | Payment Factor |
|---------------|----------------|
| 3 years | 3.32% |
| 4 years | 2.63% |
| 5 years | 2.22% |

3. The excess of the gross contract receivable for equipment rentals over the cost (reduced by the estimated salvage value at the termination of the lease) is recognized as revenue over the term of the lease under the sum-of-the-years'-digits method computed on a monthly basis.

4. The following leases were entered into during 1984:

| Machine | Dates of Lease | Period of Lease | Machine Cost |
|---------|----------------|-----------------|--------------|
| Die | 7/1/84–6/30/88 | 4 years | $90,000 |
| Press | 9/1/84–8/31/87 | 3 years | $60,000 |

**Instructions**

(a) Prepare a schedule of gross contracts receivable for equipment rentals at the dates of the lease for the die and press machines.

(b) Prepare a schedule of unearned lease income at December 31, 1984 for each machine lease.

(c) Prepare a schedule computing the present dollar value of lease payments receivable (gross investment) for equipment rentals at December 31, 1984. (The present dollar value of the "lease receivables for equipment rentals" is the outstanding amount of the gross lease receivables less the unearned lease income included therein.) Without prejudice to your solution to part (b), assume that the unearned lease income at December 31, 1984, was $29,000.

(AICPA adapted)

**P22-11** Dumont Corporation, a lessor of office machines, purchased a new machine for $500,000 on December 31, 1983, which was delivered the same day (by prior arrangement) to Finley Company, the lessee. The following information relating to the lease transaction is available:

1. The leased asset has an estimated useful life of seven years which coincides with the lease term.

2. At the end of the lease term, the machine will revert to Dumont, at which time it is expected to have a residual value of $60,000 (none of which is guaranteed by Finley).

3. Dumont's implicit interest rate (on its net investment) is 12%, which is known by Finley.

4. Finley's incremental borrowing rate is 14% at December 31, 1983.

5. Lease rental consists of seven equal annual payments, the first of which was paid on December 31, 1983.

6. The lease is appropriately accounted for as a direct financing lease by Dumont and as a capital lease by Finley. Both lessor and lessee are calendar-year corporations and depreciate all fixed assets on the straight-line basis.

**Instructions**

(Round all amounts to the nearest dollar.)
(a) Compute the annual rental under the lease.
(b) Compute the amounts of the gross lease rentals receivable and the unearned interest revenue that Dumont should disclose at the inception of the lease on December 31, 1983.
(c) What expense should Finley record for the year ended December 31, 1984?

(AICPA adapted)

**\*P22-12** On February 1, 1981, Willie Company buys land costing $300,000 and on that site has a large shopping center constructed to its specifications at a cost of $2,700,000. The center is completed on December 27, 1983. On January 1, 1984, Willie Company sells the shopping center property to Stargell Development Corporation for $3,000,000 cash and immediately signs an agreement to lease the entire property for 40 years, making annual payments of $278,870 on January 1, starting on January 1, 1984. These payments are sufficient to repay the Stargell Development Corporation its cash outlay and to provide a 10% return on the investment. Title to the property will revert to Willie Company at the termination of the lease. All maintenance and other services, and the cost of insurance, taxes, and utilities, are the responsibility of the lessee. The Willie Company has decided to amortize the property on a straight-line basis.

**Instructions**

(Round all numbers to the nearest dollar.)
(a) From the information above, prepare for Willie Company the journal entries (on an annual basis), with explanations, relative to the leased property for the year 1984.
(b) What accounts and amounts will appear in the December 31, 1984 financial statements of Willie Company relative to the leased property?
(c) From the information above, prepare for Stargell Development Corporation books journal entries relative to the leased property for the year 1984.

**\*P22-13** Storit Company owns land having a cost basis of $56,000 on which it constructs a warehouse that is completed on January 1, 1984, at a cost of $404,799. On that date Storit sells the warehouse and the land to Robert Morris Realty Inc. for $504,799 and simultaneously signs a lease under the following conditions:

1. Ten-years and noncancelable.

2. Fair values at 1/1/84—land $100,000; warehouse $404,799.

3. Estimated life of the warehouse is 20 years with no residual value.

**4.** Lease payments are $82,154 payable each December 31.

**5.** Storit Company's incremental borrowing rate is 10%; the lessor uses it to compute the annual payments.

**6.** Lessee has the option to buy the warehouse for $1 at the end of the lease term.

**7.** Lessee depreciates similar assets using the straight-line method.

**8.** Lessee assumes responsibility for executory costs.

**9.** Collectibility of the payments is reasonably certain and no uncertainties exist relative to unreimbursable lessor costs.

**Instructions** (Round all amounts to the nearest dollar.)

(a) Prepare a lease amortization schedule usable by both lessee and lessor through 1986 to record interest and reduction of principal.
(b) Prepare entries for the books of both the lessee and the lessor on January 1, 1984.
(c) Prepare entries for the books of both the lessee and the lessor for 1984 amortization and the first rental payment on December 31, 1984.
(d) Indicate the amounts and accounts that should appear on the December 31, 1984 balance sheet of both the lessee and the lessor.
(e) Prepare the footnotes that should accompany the December 31, 1984 financial statements of the lessee and the lessor.

**P22-14** Bambi Hora Inc. manufactures an X-ray machine with an estimated life of 12 years and leases it to Community Hospital for a period of 10-years. The normal selling price of the machine is $259,569, and its guaranteed residual value at the end of the lease term is estimated to be $20,000. The hospital will pay rents of $40,000 at the beginning of each year and all maintenance, insurance, and taxes. Hora Inc. incurred costs of $200,000 in manufacturing the machine and $7,000 in negotiating and closing the lease. Hora Inc. has determined that the collectibility of the lease payments is reasonably predictable, that there will be no additional costs incurred, and that the implicit interest rate is 12%.

**Instructions** (Round all numbers to the nearest dollar.)

(a) Discuss the nature of this lease in relation to the lessor and compute the amount of each of the following items:

    1. Gross investment.     3. Sales price.
    2. Unearned interest revenue.     4. Cost of sales.

(b) Prepare a 10-year lease amortization schedule.
(c) Prepare all of the lessor's journal entries for the first year.

**P22-15** Assume the same data as in Problem 22–8 with Tailwind Airlines having an incremental borrowing rate of 12%.

**Instructions** (Round all numbers to the nearest dollar.)

(a) Discuss the nature of this lease in relation to the lessee and compute the amount of the initial obligation under capital leases.
(b) Prepare a 10-year lease amortization schedule.
(c) Prepare all of the lessee's journal entries for the first year.

**P22-16** Assume the same data as in Problem 22–14 with Community Hospital having an incremental borrowing rate of 12%.

**Instructions** (Round all numbers to the nearest dollar.)

(a) Discuss the nature of this lease in relation to the lessee and compute the amount of the initial obligation under capital leases.
(b) Prepare a 10-year lease amortization schedule.
(c) Prepare all of the lessee's journal entries for the first year.

# CHAPTER 23

# Accounting Changes
and Error Analysis

Headlines such as the following often appear in the financial press:

"McCormick lowers its profit, probes accounting methods."

"J. P. Stevens, Inc. changes to LIFO method of determining inventory cost."

"Aeronautical company revises estimates of service lives of Boeing 747s."

"Deficit would have been $20 million more if firm hadn't altered accounting."

"Change in reporting land sales of unit cited for $8.2 million deficit despite operating net."

Why do these changes in accounting occur? The primary reasons are that (1) companies often believe that a different method better reports the financial results of the enterprise; (2) future events or conditions that were uncertain are now clarified; or (3) companies wish to change their financial statements to be more attractive to investors and
creditors. Accountants face the difficult problem of determining whether such changes are
appropriate and how changes in accounting should be reported in the accounting records to
facilitate analysis and understanding of financial statements. Trends shown in comparative
financial statements and historical summaries are particularly affected by the manner in
which changes in accounting are disclosed. This chapter discusses the different procedures
used to account for (1) accounting changes and (2) error corrections.

## ACCOUNTING CHANGES

Before the issuance of *APB Opinion No. 20,* "Accounting Changes," companies had considerable flexibility in reporting changes affecting comparability in accounting reports.
This flexibility was evidenced by alternative accounting treatments that were developed
and used in essentially equivalent situations. For example, when the steel companies changed
their methods of depreciating plant assets from accelerated depreciation to straight-line
depreciation, the effect of the change was presented in different ways by different companies. The cumulative difference between the depreciation charges that had been recorded
and what would have been recorded could have been reported in the income statement of
the period of the change. Similarly, the change could have been ignored, and the undepreciated asset balance simply depreciated on a straight-line basis in the future. Or companies could simply have restated the prior periods on the basis that the straight-line

approach had always been used. When such alternatives exist, comparability of the statements between periods and between companies is diminished and useful historical trend data are obscured.

The profession's first step in this area was to establish categories for the different types of changes and corrections that occur in practice:[1]

## A. Types of Accounting Changes:

1. **Change in accounting principle.** A change from one generally accepted accounting principle to another generally accepted accounting principle: for example, a change in the method of depreciation from double-declining to straight-line depreciation of plant assets.

2. **Change in accounting estimate.** A change that occurs as the result of new information or as additional experience is acquired. An example is a change in the estimate of the useful lives of depreciable assets.

3. **Change in reporting entity.** A change from reporting as one type of entity to another type of entity: for example, changing specific subsidiaries comprising the group of companies for which consolidated financial statements are prepared.

## B. Correction of an Error in Previously Issued Financial Statements (not an accounting change)

Errors in financial statements that occur as a result of mathematical mistakes, mistakes in the application of accounting principles, or oversight or misuse of facts that existed at the time financial statements were prepared: for example, the incorrect application of the retail inventory method for determining the final inventory value.

Changes were classified in these categories because the individual characteristics of each category necessitate different methods of recognizing these changes in the financial statements. Each of these items is discussed separately to investigate its unusual characteristics and to determine how each item should be reported in the accounts and how the information should be disclosed in comparative statements.

## CHANGES IN ACCOUNTING PRINCIPLE

**A change in accounting principle involves a change from one generally accepted accounting principle to another generally accepted accounting principle.** The term "accounting principle" is defined to include changes in the method of application of an accounting principle. Below are examples of changes in accounting principles.

1. Changing the basis of inventory pricing from average cost to LIFO.

2. Changing the method of depreciation on plant assets from accelerated to straight-line or vice versa.

3. Changing the method of accounting for construction contracts from the completed contract to the percentage of completion.

A careful examination must be made in each circumstance to insure that a change in principle has occurred. **A change in accounting principle is not considered to result from the adoption of a new principle in recognition of events that have occurred for the first time or**

[1]"Accounting Changes," *Opinions of the Accounting Principles Board No. 20* (New York: AICPA, 1971).

**that were previously immaterial.** For example, when a depreciation method that is adopted for newly acquired plant assets is different from the method or methods used for previously recorded assets of a similar class, this is not considered a change in accounting principle. Certain marketing expenditures that were previously immaterial and expensed in the period incurred may now be material and acceptably deferred and amortized without being considered a change in accounting principle. Finally, **if the accounting principle previously followed was not acceptable, or if the principle was applied incorrectly, a change to a generally accepted accounting principle is considered a correction of an error.** For example, a switch from the cash basis of accounting to the accrual basis is considered a correction of an error. If the company deducted salvage value when computing double-declining depreciation on plant assets and later recomputed depreciation without deduction of estimated salvage, an error is corrected.

Three approaches have been suggested for reporting changes in accounting principles in the accounts:

**RETROACTIVELY.** The cumulative effect of the use of the new method on the financial statements at the beginning of the period is computed. A retroactive adjustment of the financial statements is then made, recasting the financial statements of prior years on a basis consistent with the newly adopted principle. Advocates of this position argue that only by restatement of prior periods can changes in accounting principles lead to comparable financial statements. If this approach is not used, the year previous to the change will be on the old method; the year of the change will report the entire cumulative adjustment in income; and the following year will present financial statements on the new basis without the cumulative effect of the change. The question is how can public confidence in financial statements be maintained when the periods are not on a comparable basis? Consistency is considered essential to providing meaningful earnings-trend data and other financial relationships necessary to evaluate the business.

**CURRENTLY.** The cumulative effect of the use of the new method on the financial statements at the beginning of the period is computed. This adjustment is then reported in the current year's income statement as a special item between the captions "Extraordinary items" and "Net income." Advocates of this position argue that restating financial statements for prior years results in a loss of confidence by investors in financial reports. How will a present or prospective investor react when told that the earnings computed five years ago are now entirely different? Restatement, if permitted, also might upset many contractual and other arrangements that were based on the old figures. For example, profit-sharing arrangements computed on the old basis might have to be recomputed and completely new distributions made, which might create numerous legal problems. Many practical difficulties also exist; the cost of restatement may be excessive, or restatement may be impossible on the basis of data available. Finally, some individuals argue that restatement permits possible manipulation of earnings, because changes having a favorable effect on income might be handled currently or in the future, but changes having an unfavorable effect might be handled retroactively.

**PROSPECTIVELY.** No change is made in previously reported results. Opening balances are not adjusted, and no attempt is made to allocate charges or credits for prior events. Advocates of this position argue that once management presents to investors and to others financial statements based on acceptable accounting principles, they are final, because management cannot change prior periods by adopting a new principle. According to this line of reasoning, the cumulative adjustment in the current year is not appropriate, because this approach reports in net income an amount that has little or no relationship to the current year's income or economic events.

Before the adoption of *APB Opinion No. 20,* all three of the approaches above were used. *APB Opinion No. 20,* however, settled this issue by establishing guidelines that are to be used, depending on the type of change in accounting principle involved. We have classified these changes in accounting principle into three categories:

1. Cumulative-Effect Type Accounting Change.

**2.** Retroactive-Effect Type Accounting Change.

**3.** Change to the LIFO Method of Inventory.

## Cumulative-Effect Type Accounting Change

The general requirement established by the profession was that the **current or catch-up method should be used to account for changes in accounting principles.** The basic requirements are as follows:

1. The current or catch-up approach should be employed. The cumulative effect of the adjustment should be reported in the income statement between the captions "extraordinary items" and "net income." The cumulative effect is not an extraordinary item but should be reported on a net-of-tax basis in a manner similar to that used for an extraordinary item.

2. Financial statements for prior periods included for comparative purposes should be presented as previously reported.

3. Income before extraordinary items and net income computed on a **pro forma (as if)** basis should be shown on the face of the income statement for all periods presented as if the newly adopted principle had been applied during all periods affected. Related earnings per share data should also be reported. The reader, then, has some understanding of how restated financial statements appear.[2] The pro forma amounts should include both (1) the direct effects of a change and (2) nondiscretionary adjustments in items based on income before taxes or net income (such as profit-sharing expense and certain royalties) that would have been recognized if the newly adopted principle had been followed in prior periods; related income tax effects should be recognized for both (1) and (2). If an income statement is presented for the current period only, the actual and pro forma amounts (including earnings per share) for the immediately preceding period should be disclosed.

To illustrate, assume that Lang, Inc. decided at the beginning of 1984 to change from the sum-of-the-years'-digits method of depreciation to the straight-line method for financial reporting for its buildings. For tax purposes, the company has employed the elective straight-line method and will continue to do so. The assets originally cost $120,000 in 1982 and have an estimated useful life of fifteen years. The data assumed for this illustration are:

| Year | Sum-of-the-Years' Digits Depreciation | Straight-Line Depreciation | Difference | Tax Effect 40% | Effect on Income (net of tax) |
|------|---------------------------------------|----------------------------|------------|----------------|-------------------------------|
| 1982 | $15,000[a] | $ 8,000[b] | $ 7,000 | $2,800 | $4,200 |
| 1983 | 14,000 | 8,000 | 6,000 | 2,400 | 3,600 |
| | $29,000 | $16,000 | $13,000 | $5,200 | $7,800 |

[a]$120,000 \times \dfrac{15}{120} = $15,000.    [b]$120,000 \div 15 = $8,000.

The entry made to record this change in 1984 should be:

| | | |
|---|---|---|
| Accumulated Depreciation | 13,000 | |
|    Deferred Income Taxes | | 5,200 |
|    Cumulative Effect of Change in Accounting | | |
|      Principle—Depreciation | | 7,800 |

[2]Ibid., par. 21.

The debit of $13,000 to Accumulated Depreciation is the excess of the sum-of-the-years'-digits depreciation over the straight-line depreciation. The credit to Deferred Income Taxes of $5,200 is recorded to eliminate this account from the financial statements. Prior to the change in accounting principle, sum-of-the-years'-digits was used for book but not tax purposes, which gave rise to a debit balance in the Deferred Income Taxes account of $5,200. Now that the Company intends to use the straight-line method for both tax and book purposes, interperiod tax allocation procedures are not necessary and the Deferred Income Tax account should be eliminated. The cumulative effect on income resulting from the difference between sum-of-the-years'-digits depreciation and straight-line depreciation is reduced by the tax effect on that difference.

The information is reported in comparative statements as follows:

### CUMULATIVE-EFFECT TYPE ACCOUNTING CHANGE
Reporting the Change in Two-Year Comparative Statements

| | 1984 | 1983 |
|---|---|---|
| Income before extraordinary item and cumulative effect of a change in accounting principles (assumed) | $120,000 | $111,000 |
| Extraordinary item, net of tax (assumed) | (30,000) | 10,000 |
| Cumulative effect on prior years of retroactive application of new depreciation method, net of tax (Note A) | 7,800 | |
| Net income | $ 97,800 | $121,000 |
| Per-share amounts | | |
| Earnings per share (10,000 shares) | | |
| Income before extraordinary item and cumulative effect of a change in accounting principle | $12.00 | $11.10 |
| Extraordinary item | (3.00) | 1.00 |
| Cumulative effect on prior years of retroactive application of new depreciation method | .78 | |
| Net income | $ 9.78 | $12.10 |

*Pro forma* (as if) *amounts,* assuming retroactive application of new depreciation method:

| | 1984 | 1983 |
|---|---|---|
| Income before extraordinary item | $120,000 | $114,600[a] |
| Earnings per common share | $12.00 | $11.46 |
| Net income | $ 90,000[b] | $124,600[b] |
| Earnings per common share | $ 9.00 | $12.46 |

Note A. *Change in Depreciation Method for Plant Assets.* In 1984 depreciation of plant assets is computed by use of the straight-line method. In prior years, beginning in 1982, depreciation of buildings was computed by the sum-of-the-years'-digits. The new method of depreciation was adopted in recognition of . . . (state justification for the change of depreciation method) . . . and has been applied retroactively to building acquisitions of prior years. The effect of the change in 1984 was to increase income before extraordinary item by approximately $3,000 (or thirty cents per share). The adjustment necessary for retroactive application of the new method, amounting to $7,800, is included in income of 1984. The pro forma amounts shown on the income statement have been adjusted for the effect of retroactive application on depreciation, and the pro forma effect for related income taxes.

aThe pro forma income before extraordinary item is computed as follows:

| | |
|---|---:|
| Income before extraordinary item (1983) not restated | $111,000 |
| Excess of accelerated depreciation over straight-line depreciation (1983), net of tax | 3,600 |
| Pro forma income before extraordinary item (restated) | $114,600 |

bNet income is computed after adding or subtracting extraordinary items as follows:

| | 1984 | 1983 |
|---|---:|---:|
| Income before extraordinary item | $120,000 | $114,600 |
| Extraordinary item | (30,000) | 10,000 |
| Net income | $ 90,000 | $124,600 |

It should be understood that the pro forma (as if) amounts are presented only as supplementary information. **Pro forma amounts permit financial statement users to determine the net income that would have been shown if the newly adopted principle had been in effect in the earlier periods.** This type of data provides useful information to an individual who is interested in assessing the trend in earnings over a period of time. If space does not permit disclosure on the face of the income statement, the pro forma amounts may be shown in separate schedules or in notes.

### Retroactive-Effect Type Accounting Change

In certain circumstances, a change in accounting principle may be handled retroactively. Under the retroactive treatment the cumulative effect of the new method on the financial statements at the beginning of the period is computed. A retroactive adjustment of the financial statements presented is made by recasting the statements of prior years on a basis consistent with the newly adopted principle. Any part of the cumulative effect attibutable to years prior to those presented is treated as an adjustment of beginning retained earnings of the earliest year presented. In such situations, the nature of and justification for the change and the effect on net income and related per-share amounts should be disclosed for each period presented. The five situations that require the restatement of all prior period financial statements are:

1. A change from the LIFO inventory valuation method to another method.
2. A change in the method of accounting for long-term construction-type contracts.
3. A change to or from the "full-cost" method of accounting in the extractive industries.
4. Issuance of financial statements by a company for the first time to obtain additional equity capital, to effect a business combination, or to register securities. (This procedure may be used once and only once by closely held companies.)
5. A professional pronouncement recommends that a change in accounting principle be treated retroactively. For example, *FASB No. 11* requires that retroactive treatment be given for changes in "Accounting for Contingencies."[3]

---

[3]"Accounting for Contingencies—Transition Method," *Statement of the Financial Accounting Standards Board No. 11* (Stamford, Conn.: FASB, 1975). It is interesting to note that all recent professional pronouncements have required that any new standard adopted be applied retroactively. For example, see P. Jacque Grinnell and Corine T. Norgaard, *The Journal of Accountancy* (December 1979), who discuss the implications of this trend and its possible ramifications.

Why did the profession provide for these exceptions? The reasons are varied. The major one is that reflecting the cumulative adjustment in the period of the change might have such a large effect on net income that the income figure would be misleading. A perfect illustration is the experience of Chrysler Corporation when it changed its inventory accounting from LIFO to FIFO in 1970. If the change had been handled currently, Chrysler would have had to report a $53,500,000 adjustment to net income for 1970, which would have resulted in net income of $45,900,000 instead of a net loss of $7,600,000.

As another illustration, the railroad industry has recently switched from the retirement-replacement method of depreciating railroad equipment to a more generally used method such as straight-line depreciation. Such treatment means that a substantial adjustment to income in the period of change is required. Many in the railroad industry argue that the adjustment is so large that to include the cumulative effect in the current year instead of restating prior periods distorts the information and makes it less useful. Such situations lend support to restatement so that comparability is not seriously affected.

To illustrate the retroactive method, assume that Madsen Construction Co. has accounted for its income from long-term construction contracts using the completed-contract method. In 1984, the company changed to the percentage-of-completion method because the management believes that this approach provides a more appropriate measure of the income earned. For tax purposes (assume a 40% rate), the company has employed the completed-contract method and plans to continue using this method in the future.

The following information is available for analysis:

| Year | Pretax Income from Percentage-of-Completion | Pretax Income from Completed-Contract | Difference in Income Difference | Difference in Income Tax Effect 40% | Difference in Income Income Effect (net of tax) |
|---|---|---|---|---|---|
| Prior to 1983 | $600,000 | $400,000 | $200,000 | $80,000 | $120,000 |
| In 1983 | 180,000 | 160,000 | 20,000 | 8,000 | 12,000 |
| Total at beginning of 1984 | $780,000 | $560,000 | $220,000 | $88,000 | $132,000 |
| In 1984 | $200,000 | $190,000 | $ 10,000 | $ 4,000 | $ 6,000 |

The entry to record the change in 1984 would be:

| | | |
|---|---|---|
| Construction in Process | 220,000 | |
| Deferred Income Taxes | | 88,000 |
| Retained Earnings | | 132,000 |

The Construction in Process account is increased by $220,000, representing the adjustment in prior years' income of $132,000 and the adjustment in prior years' tax expense of $88,000. The Deferred Income Taxes account is used to recognize interperiod tax allocation. If, in previous years, the percentage-of-completion method had been employed for accounting purposes while the completed-contract method was used for tax purposes, a difference of $220,000 between book income and taxable income would have developed, on which $88,000 of tax would have been deferred.

The bottom portion of the income statement for Madsen Construction Co., giving effect to the retroactive change in accounting principle, would be as follows:

---

**RETROACTIVE-EFFECT TYPE ACCOUNTING CHANGE**
Reporting the Change in Two-Year Comparative Statements

| Income Statement | 1984 | 1983 |
|---|---|---|
| Net income | $120,000[a] | $108,000[a] |
| Per Share Amounts | | |
| Earnings per share (100,000 shares) | $1.20 | $1.08 |

[a]The net income for the two periods is computed as follows:
1984     $200,000 − .40 ($200,000) = $120,000
1983     $180,000 − .40 ($180,000) = $108,000

---

The adjustment for the cumulative effect of the accounting change would be reported in the statement of retained earnings in comparative form as follows:

---

**STATEMENT OF RETAINED EARNINGS**

| | 1984 | 1983 |
|---|---|---|
| Balance at beginning of year, as previously reported | $1,696,000 | $1,600,000 |
| Add adjustment for the cumulative effect on prior years of applying retroactively the new method of accounting for long-term contracts (Note A) | 132,000 | 120,000 |
| Balance at beginning of year, as adjusted | 1,828,000 | 1,720,000 |
| Net income | 120,000 | 108,000 |
| | $1,948,000 | $1,828,000 |

Note A. *Change in Method of Accounting for Long-Term Contracts.* The company has accounted for revenue and costs for long-term construction contracts by the percentage-of-completion method in 1984, whereas in all prior years revenue and costs were determined by the completed-contract method. The new method of accounting for long-term contracts was adopted to recognize . . . [state justification for change in accounting principle] . . . and financial statements of prior years have been restated to apply the new method retroactively. For income tax purposes, the completed-contract method has been continued. The effect of the accounting change on income of 1984 was an increase of $6,000 net of related taxes and on income of 1983 as previously reported was an increase of $12,000 net of related taxes. The balances of retained earnings for 1983 and 1984 have been adjusted for the effect of applying retroactively the new method of accounting.

---

Note that the foregoing two-year comparative statement has major differences from the earlier two-year comparative statement (pages 1030–1031). First, no pro forma information is necessary when changes in accounting principles are handled retroactively, because the income numbers for previous periods are restated. In other words, the pro forma method described in the previous section provides the same type of information as the retroactive method of this section. Second, a retained earnings statement was included in this two-year comparative statement to indicate the type of adjustment that is needed to restate the beginning balance of retained earnings. In 1983, the beginning balance was adjusted for the excess of the percentage-of-completion income over the completed-contract income prior to 1983 ($120,000). In 1984, the beginning balance was adjusted for the $120,000 plus the additional $12,000 for 1983.

No such adjustments are necessary when the current or catch-up method is employed, because the cumulative effect of the change on net income is reported in the income statement of the current year and no prior period reports are restated. It is ordinarily appropriate to prepare a retained earnings statement when presenting comparative statements regardless of what type of accounting change is involved; an illustration was provided for the retroactive method only to explain the additional computations required.

### Change to the LIFO Method of Inventory

The profession generally requires that the cumulative effect of any accounting change should be shown in the income statement between "extraordinary items" and "net income," except for the conditions mentioned in the preceding section. In addition, this rule does not apply when a company changes to the LIFO method of inventory valuation. In such a situation, **the base-year inventory for all subsequent LIFO calculations is the opening inventory in the year the method is adopted. There is no restatement of prior years' income because it is just too impractical.** A restatement to LIFO would be subject to assumptions as to the different years that the layers were established, and these assumptions would ordinarily result in the computation of a number of different earnings figures. The only adjustment necessary may be to restate the beginning inventory to a cost basis from a lower of cost or market approach. This type of adjustment was discussed in Appendix F of Chapter 9.

Disclosure then is limited to showing the effect of the change on the results of operations in the period of change. Also the reasons for omitting the computations of the cumulative effect and the pro forma amounts for prior years should be explained. Finally, the company should disclose the justification for the change to LIFO. A recent annual report of Bell & Howell Company indicates the type of disclosure necessary.

---

**BELL & HOWELL COMPANY**

*Notes to Consolidated Financial Statements*

*Inventories.* Beginning in 1980, the Company changed the method of valuing substantially all of the domestic inventories of the Learning Systems & Materials line of business from the first-in, first-out (FIFO) method to the last-in, first-out (LIFO) method, which is not in excess of market. The Company plans to adopt the LIFO method of valuation for the domestic inventories of the Specialized Business Equipment line of business beginning in 1981. The change is being made over two years to provide adequate time for implementation. The change to the LIFO method provides a better matching of current costs with current revenues in the determination of net earnings. The effect of this change was to reduce net earnings for 1980 by $613,000, or $.11 per share. There is no cumulative effect of this change on prior years' reported earnings. At the end of 1980, $22,953,000 of inventories were valued using the LIFO method; if the FIFO method had been used, they would have been valued $1,246,000 higher than reported.

---

In practice, many companies defer the formal adoption of LIFO until year end. Management thus has an opportunity to assess the impact that a change to LIFO will have on the financial statements and to evaluate the desirability of a change for tax purposes. As indicated in Chapter 8, many companies have changed to LIFO in recent years because of the advantages of this inventory valuation method in a period of inflation.

## CHANGE IN ACCOUNTING ESTIMATE

The preparation of financial statements requires estimating the effects of future conditions and events. Future conditions and events and their effects cannot be perceived with certainty; therefore, estimating requires the exercise of judgment. Accounting estimates will change as new events occur, as more experience is acquired, or as additional information is obtained. The following are examples of items that require estimates:

1. Uncollectible receivables.
2. Inventory obsolescence.
3. Useful lives and salvage values of assets.
4. Periods benefited by deferred costs.
5. Liabilities for warranty costs and income taxes.
6. Recoverable mineral reserves.

**Changes in estimates must be handled prospectively;** that is, no changes should be made in previously reported results. Opening balances are not adjusted, and no attempt is made to "catch-up" for prior periods. Financial statements of prior periods are not restated and pro forma amounts for prior periods are not reported. Instead, the effects of all changes in estimate are accounted for in (1) the period of change if the change affects that period only or (2) the period of change and future periods if the change affects both. As a result changes in estimates are viewed as normal recurring corrections and adjustments, the natural result of the accounting process, and retroactive treatment is prohibited.

The circumstances related to a change in estimate appear to be very different from those surrounding a change in accounting principle. If changes in estimates were handled on a retroactive basis, or catch-up basis, continual adjustments of prior years' income would occur. It seems proper to accept the view that because new conditions or circumstances exist, the revision fits the new situation and should be handled in the current and future periods.

To illustrate, Winckler, Inc. purchased a building for $300,000 which was originally estimated to have a useful life of 15 years and no salvage value. Depreciation has been recorded for five years on a straight-line basis. On January 1, 1984, the estimate of the useful life is revised so that the asset is considered to have a total life of 25 years. Assume that the useful life for financial reporting and tax purposes is the same. The accounts at the beginning of the sixth year are as follows:

| | |
|---|---:|
| Building | $300,000 |
| Less: Accumulated Depreciation—Building (5 yrs. × $20,000) | 100,000 |
| Book value of building | $200,000 |

The entry to record depreciation for the year 1984 is:

| | | |
|---|---|---|
| Depreciation Expense | 10,000 | |
| Accumulated Depreciation—Building | | 10,000 |

The $10,000 depreciation charge is computed as follows:

$$\text{Depreciation charge} = \frac{\text{book value of asset}}{\text{remaining service life}} = \frac{\$200,000}{25 \text{ years} - 5 \text{ years}}$$

Differentiating between a change in an estimate and a change in an accounting principle is sometimes difficult. When, for example, a company changes from deferring and amortizing certain marketing costs to recording them as an expense as incurred because future benefits of the cost have become doubtful, is it a change in principle or a change in estimate? In such a case, **whenever it is impossible to determine whether a change in principle or a change in estimate has occurred, the change should be considered a change in estimate.**

A similar problem occurs in differentiating between a change in estimate and a correction of an error, although the answer is more clear cut. How do we determine whether the information was overlooked in earlier periods (an error) or whether the information is now available for the first time (change in estimate)? Proper classification is important because corrections of errors have a different accounting treatment from that given changes in estimates. The general rule is that **careful estimates that later prove to be incorrect should be considered changes in estimate.** Only when the estimate was obviously computed incorrectly because of lack of expertise or in bad faith should the adjustment be considered an error. There is no clear demarcation line here and the accountant must use good judgment in light of all the circumstances.

## REPORTING A CHANGE IN ENTITY

An accounting change that results in financial statements that are actually the statements of a different entity should be reported by **restating** the financial statements of all prior periods presented to show the financial information for the new reporting entity for all periods.

Examples of a change in reporting entity are:

1. Presenting consolidated statements in place of statements of individual companies.
2. Changing specific subsidiaries comprising the group of companies for which consolidated financial statements are presented.
3. Changing the companies included in combined financial statements.
4. Accounting for a pooling of interests.
5. A change in the cost, equity, or consolidation method of accounting for subsidiaries and investments. A change in the reporting entity does not result from creation, cessation, purchase, or disposition of a subsidiary or other business unit.

The financial statements of the year in which the change in reporting entity is made should describe the nature of the change and the reason for it. The effect of the change on income before extraordinary items, net income, and earnings per share amounts should be disclosed for all periods presented. These disclosures need not be repeated in subsequent period financial statements. These situations are not illustrated in this textbook, but are presented in advanced accounting.

# REPORTING A CORRECTION OF AN ERROR

*APB Opinion No. 20* also discussed how a correction of an error should be handled in the financial statements, because no authoritative guidelines existed previously in this area. The conclusions of *APB Opinion No. 20* were reaffirmed in *FASB Statement No. 16,* issued in 1977.[4] No business, large or small, is immune from errors. The risk of material errors, however, may be reduced through the installation of good internal control and the application of sound accounting procedures.

The following are examples of accounting errors:

1. A change from an accounting principle that is **not** generally accepted to an accounting principle that is acceptable. The rationale adopted is that the prior periods were incorrectly presented because of the application of an improper accounting principle; for example, a change from the cash basis of accounting to the accrual basis.

2. Mathematical mistakes that result from adding, subtracting, and so on. An illustration is the totaling of the inventory count sheets incorrectly in computing the inventory value.

3. Changes in estimate that occur because the estimates are not prepared in good faith, for example, the adoption of a clearly unrealistic depreciation rate.

4. An oversight such as the failure to accrue or defer certain assets and liabilities at the end of the period.

5. A misuse of facts such as the failure to use salvage value in computing the depreciation base for the straight-line approach.

6. The incorrect classification of a cost as an expense instead of an asset and vice versa.

As soon as they are discovered, errors must be corrected by proper entries in the accounts and reported in the financial statements. **The profession requires that corrections of errors be treated as prior period adjustments,** be recorded in the year in which the error was discovered, and be reported in the financial statements as an adjustment to the beginning balance of retained earnings. If comparative statements are presented, the prior statements affected should be restated to correct for the error. The disclosures need not be repeated in the financial statements of subsequent periods.

To illustrate, in 1985 the bookkeeper for Werner Company discovered that in 1984 the company failed to record in the accounts $20,000 of depreciation expense on a newly constructed building. The depreciation is correctly included in the tax return. Because of numerous timing differences, reported net income for 1984 was $150,000 and taxable income was $110,000. The following entry was made for income taxes (assume a 40% effective tax rate in 1984):

| | | |
|---|---|---|
| Income Tax Expense | 60,000 | |
|   Income Tax Payable | | 44,000 |
|   Deferred Income Taxes | | 16,000 |

As a result of the $20,000 omission error in 1984:

| | |
|---|---|
| Depreciation expense (1984) **was** understated | $20,000 |
| Accumulated depreciation **is** understated | 20,000 |
| Income tax expense (1984) **was** overstated ($20,000 × 40%) | 8,000 |
| Net income (1984) **was** overstated | 12,000 |
| Deferred income taxes **is** overstated ($20,000 × 40%) | 8,000 |

---

[4]"Prior Period Adjustments," *Statements of Financial Accounting Standards No. 16* (Stamford, Conn.: FASB, 1977), p. 5.

The entry made in 1985 to correct the omission of $20,000 of depreciation in 1984 would be:

**1985 Correcting Entry**

| | | |
|---|---|---|
| Retained Earnings | 12,000 | |
| Deferred Income Taxes | 8,000 | |
|    Accumulated Depreciation—Buildings | | 20,000 |

The journal entry to record the correction of the error is the same whether single-period or comparative financial statements are prepared; however, presentation on the financial statements will differ. If single-period (noncomparative) statements are presented, the error should be reported as an adjustment to the opening balance of retained earnings of the period in which the error is discovered, as shown below:

| | | |
|---|---|---|
| Retained earnings, January 1, 1985: | | |
|   As previously reported | | $350,000 |
|   Correction of an error (depreciation) | $20,000 | |
|   Less applicable income tax reduction | 8,000 | (12,000) |
| Adjusted balance of retained earnings, January 1, 1985 | | 338,000 |
| Add net income 1985 | | 400,000 |
| Retained earnings, December 31, 1985 | | $738,000 |

If comparative financial statements are prepared, adjustments should be made to correct the amounts for all affected accounts reported in the statements for all periods reported. The data for each year being presented should be restated to the correct basis, and any catch-up adjustment should be shown as a prior period adjustment to retained earnings for the earliest period being reported. For example, in the case of Werner Company, the error of omitting the depreciation of $20,000 in 1984, which was discovered in 1985, results in the restatement of the 1984 financial statements when presented in comparison with those of 1985. The following accounts in the 1984 financial statements (presented in comparison with those of 1985) would have been restated:

In the balance sheet:

| | |
|---|---|
| Accumulated depreciation—buildings | $20,000 increase |
| Deferred income taxes | $ 8,000 decrease |
| Retained earnings, ending balance | $12,000 decrease |

In the income statement:

| | |
|---|---|
| Depreciation expense—buildings | $20,000 increase |
| Tax expense | $ 8,000 decrease |
| Net income | $12,000 decrease |

In the statement of retained earnings:

| | |
|---|---|
| Retained earnings, ending balance (due to lower net income for the period) | $12,000 decrease |

The 1985 financial statements in comparative form with those of 1984 are prepared as if the error had not occurred. As a minimum, such comparative statements in 1985 would include a footnote calling attention to restatement of the 1984 statements and disclosing the effect of the correction on income before extraordinary items, net income, and the related per share amounts.

## SUMMARY OF ACCOUNTING CHANGES AND CORRECTIONS OF ERRORS

The development of guidelines in reporting accounting changes and corrections has helped in resolving several significant and long-standing accounting problems. Yet, because of diversity in situations and characteristics of the items encountered in practice, the application of professional judgment is of paramount importance. In applying these guides, the primary objective is to serve the user of the financial statements; achieving such service requires accuracy, full disclosure,[5] and an absence of misleading inferences. The principal distinction and treatments presented in the earlier discussion are summarized below.

1. **Changes in accounting principle** (General Rule).
   Employ the current or catch-up approach by:
   a. Reporting current results on the new basis.
   b. Reporting the cumulative effect of the adjustment in the current income statement between the captions "extraordinary items" and "net income."
   c. Presenting prior period financial statements as previously reported.
   d. Presenting pro forma data on income and earnings per share data for all prior periods presented.

2. **Changes in accounting principle** (Exceptions).
   Employ the retroactive approach by:
   a. Restating the financial statements of all prior periods presented.
   b. Disclosing in the year of the change the effect on net income and earnings per share for all prior periods presented.
   Employ the change to LIFO approach by:
   a. Not restating prior years' income.
   b. Using opening inventory in the year the method is adopted as the base-year inventory for all subsequent LIFO computations.
   c. Disclosing the effect of the change on the current year, and the reasons for omitting the computation of the cumulative effect and pro forma amounts for prior years.

3. **Changes in estimate.**
   Employ the current and prospective approach by:
   a. Reporting current and future financial statements on the new basis.
   b. Presenting prior period financial statements as previously reported.
   c. Making no adjustments to current period opening balances for purposes of catch-up, and making no pro forma presentations.

---

[5]"Reporting on Consistency and Accounting Changes," *Statement on Auditing Procedure No. 53,* discusses the various disclosure requirements related to changes in accounting. A change in accounting principle, a change in the reporting entity (special type of change in accounting principle), and a correction of an error involving a change in accounting principle require recognition in the auditor's report relative to consistency. A change in accounting estimate does not affect the auditor's opinion relative to consistency; however, if the estimate change has a material effect on the financial statements, disclosure may be required in a note to the financial statements. Error correction not involving a change in accounting principle does not require disclosure relative to consistency (New York: AICPA, 1972).

4. **Changes in entity.**
   Employ the retroactive approach by:
   a. Restating the financial statements of all prior periods presented.
   b. Disclosing in the year of change the effect on net income and earnings per share data for all prior periods presented.

5. **Changes due to error.**
   Employ the retroactive approach by:
   a. Correcting all prior period statements presented.
   b. Restating the beginning balance of retained earnings for the first period presented when the error effects extend to a period prior to that one.

Changes in accounting principle are considered appropriate only when the enterprise demonstrates that the alternative generally accepted accounting principle that is adopted is **preferable** to the existing one. In applying the profession's guidelines, preferability among accounting principles should be determined on the basis of whether the new principle constitutes an improvement in financial reporting, not on the basis of the income tax effect alone. For example, Bell and Howell recently changed to the LIFO method because it "provides a better matching of current costs with current revenues in the determination of net earnings" (see note to financial statement on page 1034). But it is not always easy to determine what is an improvement in financial reporting. **How does one measure preferability or improvement?** Bell and Howell, for example, argues that a change in accounting principle from FIFO to LIFO inventory valuation better matches current costs and current revenues. Conversely, another enterprise might change from LIFO to FIFO because it wishes to report a more realistic balance sheet amount for inventory. How does an accountant determine which is the better of these two arguments? It appears that the auditor must have some "standard" or "objective" as a basis for determining the method that is preferable. Because no universal standard or objective is generally accepted, the problem of determining preferability continues to be a difficult one.

Initially the SEC took the position that the public accountant in the role of auditor should indicate whether a change in accounting principle was preferable. The SEC has modified this approach, noting that greater reliance may be placed on management's judgment in assessing preferability. Even though the criterion of preferability is difficult to apply, the general guidelines established have acted as a deterrent to capricious changes in accounting principles. **If an FASB standard creates a new principle or expresses preference for or rejects a specific accounting principle, a change is considered clearly acceptable.** Similarly, other authoritative documents, such as AcSEC's statements of position and AICPA industry audit guides, are considered preferable accounting when a change in accounting principles is contemplated.[6]

## ERROR ANALYSIS

As indicated earlier, material errors are unusual in large corporations because internal control procedures coupled with the diligence of the accounting staff are ordinarily sufficient to find any major errors in the system. Smaller businesses may face a different

---

[6]"Specialized Accounting and Reporting Principles and Practices in AICPA Statements of Position and Guides on Accounting and Auditing Matters," *Statement of Financial Accounting Standards No. 32* (Stamford, Conn.: FASB, 1979).

problem. These enterprises may not be able to afford an internal audit staff, nor implement the necessary control procedures to insure that accounting data are always recorded accurately. The following discussion, therefore, applies primarily to smaller firms whose internal control systems are inappropriate or inefficient for processing the accounting data.

In practice, firms do not correct for errors discovered that do not have a significant effect on the presentation of the financial statements. For example, the failure to record accrued wages of $5,000 when the total payroll for the year is $1,750,000 and net income is $940,000 is not considered significant, and no correction is made. Obviously, defining materiality is difficult, and accountants must rely on their experience and judgment to determine whether adjustment is necessary for a given error. **All errors discussed in this section are assumed to be material and to require adjustment.** Also, all of the tax effects are ignored in this section.

The accountant must answer three questions in error analysis:

1. What type of error is involved?
2. What entries are needed to correct for the error?
3. How are financial statements to be restated once the error is discovered?

## Type of Error Involved

As indicated earlier, the profession requires that errors be treated as prior period adjustments and be reported in the current year as adjustments to the beginning balance of Retained Earnings. If comparative statements are presented, the prior statements affected should be restated to correct for the error.

Three types of errors can occur; because each error has its own peculiarities, differentiation among the types is important.

## Balance Sheet Errors

These errors affect only the presentation of the real accounts, that is, the improper classification of an asset, liability, or stockholders' equity account. Examples are the classification of a short-term receivable as part of the investment section; the classification of a note payable as an account payable; and the classification of plant assets as inventory. Reclassification of the item to its proper position is needed when the error is discovered. If comparative statements that include the error year are prepared, the balance sheet for the error year is restated correctly.

## Income Statement Errors

These errors affect only the presentation of the nominal accounts presented in the income statement. Errors involve the improper classification of revenues or expenses, such as recording interest revenue as part of sales; purchases as bad debt expense; and depreciation expense as interest expense. An income statement classification error has no effect on the balance sheet and no effect on net income; a reclassification entry is needed when the error is discovered, if it is discovered in the year it is made. If the error occurred in prior periods, no entry is needed at the date of discovery because the accounts for the current year are correctly stated. If comparative statements that include the error year are prepared, the income statement for the error year is restated correctly.

## Balance Sheet and Income Statement Effect

The third type of error involves both the balance sheet and income statement. For example, assume that accrued wages payable were overlooked by the bookkeeper at the end of the accounting period. The effect of this error is to understate expenses, understate liabilities, and overstate net income for that period of time. This type of error affects both the balance sheet and the income statement and is classified in the following two ways—counterbalancing and noncounterbalancing.

**Counterbalancing errors** are errors that will be offset or corrected over two periods. In the previous illustration, the failure to record accrued wages is considered a counterbalancing error because over a two-year period the error will no longer be present. In other words the failure to record accrued wages in the previous period means: (1) net income for the first period is overstated; (2) accrued wages payable (a liability) is understated, and (3) wages expense is understated. In the next period, net income is understated; accrued wages payable (a liability) is correctly stated; and wages expense is overstated. For the **two years combined:** (1) net income is correct; (2) wages expense is correct; and (3) accrued wages payable at the end of the second year is correct. Most errors in accounting that affect both the balance sheet and income statement are counterbalancing errors.

**Noncounterbalancing errors** are errors that are not offset in the next accounting period; for example, the failure to capitalize equipment that has a useful life of five years. If we expense this asset immediately, expenses will be overstated in the first period but understated in the next four periods. At the end of the second period, the effect of the error is not fully offset. Net income is correct in the aggregate only at the end of five years, because the asset is fully depreciated at this point. Only in rare instances is an error never reversed, for example, when land is initially expensed. Because land is not depreciable, theoretically the error is never offset unless the land is sold.

**Accountants define counterbalancing errors as errors that correct themselves over two periods, whereas noncounterbalancing errors are those that take longer than two periods to correct themselves.** How these errors are handled in the accounting records is illustrated in the following sections.

## Counterbalancing Errors

The usual types of counterbalancing errors are illustrated on the following pages. In studying these illustrations, a number of points should be remembered. First, determine whether or not the books have been closed for the period in which the error is found:

1. **The books have been closed.**
   a. If the error is already counterbalanced, no entry is necessary.
   b. If the error is not yet counterbalanced, an entry is necessary to adjust the present balance of retained earnings.
2. **The books have not been closed.**
   a. If the error is already counterbalanced and we are in the second year, an entry is necessary to correct the current period and to adjust the beginning balance of Retained Earnings.

b. If the error is not yet counterbalanced, an entry is necessary to adjust the beginning balance of Retained Earnings and correct the current period.

Second, if comparative statements are presented, restatement of the amounts for comparative purposes is necessary. This situation occurs even if a correcting journal entry is not required. To illustrate, assume that Sanford's Cement Co. failed to accrue income in 1982 when earned, but recorded the income in 1983 when received. The error was discovered in 1985. No entry is necessary to correct for this error because the effects have been counterbalanced by the time the error is discovered in 1985. However, if comparative financial statements for 1982 through 1985 are presented, the accounts and related amounts for the years 1982 and 1983 should be restated correctly for financial reporting purposes.

**Failure to Record Accrued Wages**　On December 31, 1984, accrued wages in the amount of $1,500 were not recognized. The entry in 1985 to correct this error, assuming that the books have not been closed for 1985, is:

| | | |
|---|---|---|
| Retained Earnings | 1,500 | |
| Wages Expense | | 1,500 |

The rationale for this entry is as follows: (1) When the accrued wages of 1984 are paid in 1985, an additional debit of $1,500 is made to the 1985 Wages Expense. (2) Wages Expense—1985 is overstated by $1,500. (3) Because 1984 accrued wages were not recorded as Wages Expense—1984, the net income for 1984 was overstated by $1,500. (4) Because 1984 net income is overstated by $1,500, the Retained Earnings account is overstated by $1,500 because net income is closed to Retained Earnings.

If the books have been closed for 1985, no entry is made because the error is counterbalanced.

**Failure to Record Prepaid Expenses**　In January, 1984, Hurley Enterprises purchased a two-year insurance policy costing $1,000; Insurance Expense was debited, and Cash was credited. No adjusting entries were made at the end of 1984.

The entry on December 31, 1985, to correct this error, assuming that the books have not been closed for 1985, is:

| | | |
|---|---|---|
| Insurance Expense | 500 | |
| Retained Earnings | | 500 |

If the books have been closed for 1985, no entry is made because the error is counterbalanced.

**Overstatement of Prepaid Revenue**　On December 31, 1984, Hurley Enterprises received $50,000 as a prepayment for renting certain office space for the following year. The entry made at the time of receipt of the rent payment was a debit to Cash and a credit to Rent Revenue. No adjusting entry was made as of December 31, 1984. The entry on December 31, 1985, to correct for this error, assuming that the books have not been closed for 1985, is:

| | | |
|---|---|---|
| Retained Earnings | 50,000 | |
| Rent Revenue | | 50,000 |

If the books have been closed for 1985, no entry is made because the error is counterbalanced.

**Overstatement of Accrued Revenue**  On December 31, 1984, Hurley Enterprises accrued as interest revenue $8,000 that applied to 1985. The entry made on December 31, 1984, was to debit Accrued Interest Receivable and credit Interest Revenue. The entry on December 31, 1985, to correct for this error, assuming that the books have not been closed for 1985, is:

| | | |
|---|---|---|
| Retained Earnings | 8,000 | |
| Interest Revenue | | 8,000 |

If the books have been closed for 1985, no entry is made because the error is counterbalanced.

**Understatement of Ending Inventory**  On December 31, 1984, the physical count of the inventory was understated by $25,000 because the inventory crew failed to count one warehouse of merchandise. The entry on December 31, 1985, to correct for this error, assuming that the books have not been closed for 1985, is:

| | | |
|---|---|---|
| Inventory (beginning) | 25,000 | |
| Retained Earnings | | 25,000 |

If the books have been closed for 1985, no entry is made because the error is counterbalanced.

**Overstatement of Purchases**  Hurley Enterprise's accountant recorded a purchase of merchandise for $9,000 in 1984 that applied to 1985. The physical inventory for 1984 was correctly stated. The entry on December 31, 1985, to correct for this error, assuming that the books have not been closed for 1985, is:

| | | |
|---|---|---|
| Purchases | 9,000 | |
| Retained Earnings | | 9,000 |

If the books have been closed for 1985, no entry is made because the error is counterbalanced.

**Overstatement of Purchases and Inventories**  Sometimes both the physical inventory and the purchases are incorrectly stated. Assume, as in the previous illustration, that purchases for 1984 are overstated by $9,000 and that inventory is overstated by the same amount. The entry on December 31, 1985, to correct for this error, assuming that the books have not been closed for 1985, is:

| | | |
|---|---|---|
| Purchases | 9,000 | |
| Inventory | | 9,000[a] |

[a]The net income for 1984 is correctly computed because the overstatement of purchases was offset by the overstatement of ending inventory in the cost of goods sold computation.

If the books have been closed for 1985, no entry is made because the error is counterbalanced.

## Noncounterbalancing Errors

Because such errors do not counterbalance over a two-year period, the entries are more complex and correcting entries are needed, even if the books have been closed.

**Failure to Record Depreciation**    Assume that Hurley Enterprises purchased a machine for $10,000 on January 1, 1984, that had an estimated useful life of five years. The accountant incorrectly expensed this machine in 1984. The error was discovered in 1985. If we assume that the company desires to use straight-line depreciation on this asset, the entry on December 31, 1985, to correct for this error, given that the books have not been closed, is:

| | | |
|---|---|---|
| Machinery | 10,000 | |
| Depreciation Expense | 2,000 | |
|   Retained Earnings | | 8,000[a] |
|   Accumulated Depreciation | | 4,000[a] |

[a]Computations:

**Retained Earnings**

| | |
|---|---|
| Overstatement of expense in 1984 | $10,000 |
| Proper depreciation for 1984 (20% × $10,000) | (2,000) |
| Retained earnings understated as of Dec. 31, 1984 | $ 8,000 |

**Accumulated Depreciation**

| | |
|---|---|
| Accumulated depreciation (20% × $10,000 × 2) | $ 4,000 |

If the books have been closed for 1985, the entry is:

| | | |
|---|---|---|
| Machinery | 10,000 | |
|   Retained Earnings | | 6,000[a] |
|   Accumulated Depreciation | | 4,000 |

[a]Computations:

**Retained Earnings**

| | |
|---|---|
| Retained earnings understated as of Dec. 31, 1984 | $ 8,000 |
| Proper depreciation for 1985 (20% × $10,000) | (2,000) |
| Retained earnings understated as of Dec. 31, 1985 | $ 6,000 |

**Failure to Adjust for Bad Debts**    Companies sometimes use a specific charge-off method in accounting for bad debt expense when a percentage of sales is more appropriate. Adjustments are often made to change from the specific write-off to some type of allowance method. For example, assume that Hurley Enterprises has recognized bad debt expense when the debts have actually become uncollectible as follows:

| | 1984 | 1985 |
|---|---|---|
| From 1984 sales | $550 | $690 |
| From 1985 sales | | 700 |

Hurley estimates that an additional $1,400 will be charged off in 1986; $300 applicable to 1984 Sales and $1,100 to 1985 Sales. The entry on December 31, 1985, assuming that the **books have not been closed for 1985,** is:

| | | |
|---|---|---|
| Bad Debt Expense | 410[a] | |
| Retained Earnings | 990[a] | |
|   Allowance for Doubtful Accounts | | 1,400 |

[a]Computations:
  **Allowance for doubtful accounts**—additional $300 for 1984 sales and $1,100 for 1985 sales.
  **Bad debts and retained earnings balance:**

|                                        | 1984    | 1985     |
|----------------------------------------|---------|----------|
| Bad debts charged for                  | $1,240  | $ 700    |
| Additional bad debts anticipated       | 300     | 1,100    |
| Proper bad debt expense                | 1,540   | 1,800    |
| Charges currently made to each period  | (550)   | (1,390)  |
| Bad debt adjustment                    | $ 990   | $ 410    |

If the **books have been closed for 1985,** the entry is:

| | | |
|---|---|---|
| Retained Earnings | 1,400 | |
| Allowance for Doubtful Accounts | | 1,400 |

## Comprehensive Illustration: Numerous Errors

In some circumstances not one but a combination of errors occurs. A work sheet is therefore prepared to facilitate the analysis. To demonstrate the use of a work sheet, the following problem is presented for solution. The mechanics of the work sheet preparation should be obvious from the solution format.

The income statements of the Hudson Company for the years ended December 31, 1983, 1984, and 1985 indicate the following net incomes.

| | |
|---|---|
| 1983 | $17,400 |
| 1984 | 20,200 |
| 1985 | 11,300 |

An examination of the accounting records of the Hudson Company for these years indicates that several errors were made in arriving at the net income amounts reported. The following errors were discovered:

(a) Wages earned by workers but not paid at December 31 were consistently omitted from the records. The amounts omitted were

| | |
|---|---|
| December 31, 1983 | $1,000 |
| December 31, 1984 | 1,400 |
| December 31, 1985 | 1,600 |

These amounts were recorded as expenses when paid in the year following that in which they were earned.

(b) The merchandise inventory on December 31, 1983, was overstated by $1,900 as the result of errors made in the footings and extensions on the inventory sheets.

(c) Unexpired insurance of $1,200, applicable to 1985, was expensed on December 31, 1984.

(d) Interest receivable in the amount of $240 was not recorded on December 31, 1984.

(e) On January 2, 1984, a piece of equipment costing $3,900 was sold for $1,800. At the date of sale the equipment had accumulated depreciation pertaining to it of $2,400. The cash received was recorded as Miscellaneous Income in 1984. In addition, depreciation was recorded for this equipment in both 1984 and 1985 at the rate of 10% of cost.

**INSTRUCTIONS**  Prepare a schedule showing the corrected net income amounts for the years ended December 31, 1983, 1984, and 1985. Each correction of the amount originally reported should be clearly labeled. In addition, indicate the balance sheet accounts affected as of December 31, 1985 (see pages 1047–1048).

Correcting entries **if the books have not been closed** on December 31, 1985 are:

| | | |
|---|---:|---:|
| Retained Earnings | 1,400 | |
|   Wages Expense | | 1,400 |
|   (To correct improper charge to wages expense for 1985) | | |
| Wages Expense | 1,600 | |
|   Wages Payable | | 1,600 |
|   (To record proper wages expense for 1985) | | |
| Insurance Expense | 1,200 | |
|   Retained Earnings | | 1,200 |
|   (To record proper insurance expense for 1985) | | |
| Interest Revenue | 240 | |
|   Retained Earnings | | 240 |
|   (To correct improper credit to interest revenue in 1985) | | |
| Retained Earnings | 1,500 | |
| Accumulated Depreciation | 2,400 | |
|   Machinery | | 3,900 |
|   (To record write-off of machinery in 1984 and adjustment of retained earnings) | | |
| Accumulated Depreciation | 780 | |
|   Depreciation Expense | | 390 |
|   Retained Earnings | | 390 |
|   (To correct improper charge for depreciation expense in 1984 and 1985) | | |

**If the books have been closed:**

| | | |
|---|---:|---:|
| Retained Earnings | 1,600 | |
|   Wages Payable | | 1,600 |
|   (To record proper wage expense for 1985) | | |
| Retained Earnings | 1,500 | |
| Accumulated Depreciation | 2,400 | |
|   Machinery | | 3,900 |
|   (To record write-off of machinery in 1984 and adjustment of retained earnings) | | |
| Accumulated Depreciation | 780 | |
|   Retained Earnings | | 780 |
|   (To correct improper charge for depreciation expense in 1984 and 1985) | | |

| Solution: | Work Sheet Analysis of Changes in Net Income | | | | Balance Sheet Correction at December 31, 1985 | | |
|---|---|---|---|---|---|---|---|
| **•** | 1983 | 1984 | 1985 | Totals | Debit | Credit | Account |
| Net income as reported | $17,400 | $20,200 | $11,300 | $48,900 | | | |
| Wages unpaid, 12/31/83 | (1,000) | 1,000 | | -0- | | | |
| Wages unpaid, 12/31/84 | | (1,400) | 1,400 | -0- | | | |
| Wages unpaid, 12/31/85 | | | (1,600) | (1,600) | | $1,600 | Wages Payable |
| Inventory overstatement, 12/31/83 | (1,900) | 1,900 | | -0- | | | |
| Unexpired insurance, 12/31/84 | | 1,200 | (1,200) | -0- | | | |

| | 1983 | 1984 | 1985 | Totals | Debit | Credit | Account |
|---|---|---|---|---|---|---|---|
| Interest receivable, 12/31/84 | | 240 | (240) | -0- | | | |
| Correction for entry made upon sale of equipment, 1/2/84[a] | | (1,500) | | (1,500) | $2,400 | 3,900 | Accumulated Depreciation Machinery |
| Overcharge of depreciation, 1984 | | 390 | | 390 | 390 | | Accumulated Depreciation |
| Overcharge of depreciation, 1985 | | | 390 | 390 | 390 | | Accumulated Depreciation |
| Corrected net income | $14,500 | $22,030 | $10,050 | $46,580 | | | |

| [a]Cost | $ 3,900 |
|---|---|
| Accumulated depreciation | 2,400 |
| Book value | 1,500 |
| Proceeds from sale | 1,800 |
| Gain on sale | 300 |
| Income reported | (1,800) |
| Adjustment | $(1,500) |

## Preparation of Financial Statements

Discussion of error analysis up to now has been concerned with the identification of the type of error involved and the accounting for its correction in the accounting records. The correction of the error should be presented on comparative financial statements. In addition, five- or ten-year summaries are given for the interested financial reader. The work sheet on page 1049 (Table 23–1) illustrates how a typical year's financial statements are restated given many different errors. The resulting balance sheet, income statement, and the correcting entries are not presented because they should be self-explanatory.

To illustrate, Reynolds and Sons operate a small retail outlet in the town of Prescott. Lacking expertise in accounting, they did not keep adequate records; as a result, many errors occurred in recording the accounting information. Presented on page 1049 is a work sheet that begins with the unadjusted trial balance of Reynolds and Sons; the correcting entries and their effect on the financial statements can be determined by examining the work sheet. Supplementary information related to the correction of errors appears below and at the top of page 1049.

1. The bookkeeper inadvertently failed to record a cash receipt of $1,000 on the sale of merchandise in 1985.

2. Accrued wages expense at the end of 1984 was $2,500; at the end of 1985, $3,200. The company did not accrue for wages; all wages are charged to administrative expense.

3. The beginning inventory was understated by $5,400 because goods in transit at the end of last year were not counted. The proper purchase entry had been made.

4. No allowance had been set up for estimated uncollectible receivables. It is decided to set up such an allowance for the estimated probable losses as of December 31, 1985 for 1984 accounts of $700, and for 1985 accounts of $1,500. It is also decided to correct the charge against each year so that it shows the losses (actual and estimated) relating to that year's sales. Accounts have been written off to bad debt expense (selling expense) as follows:

|                | In 1984 | In 1985 |
|----------------|---------|---------|
| 1985 Accounts  |         | $1,600  |
| 1984 Accounts  | $400    | 2,000   |

5. Unexpired insurance not recorded at the end of 1984, $600; at the end of 1985, $400. All insurance expense is charged to Administrative Expense.

6. An account payable of $6,000 should have been a note payable.

7. During 1984, an asset that cost $10,000 and had a book value of $4,000 was sold for $7,000. At the time of sale Cash was debited and Miscellaneous Income was credited for $7,000.

8. As a result of the last transaction, the company overstated depreciation expense (an administrative expense) in 1984 by $800 and in 1985 by $1,200.

9. In a physical count, the company determined the final inventory to be $40,000.

**TABLE 23-1** WORK SHEET ANALYSIS TO ADJUST FINANCIAL STATEMENTS FOR THE YEAR 1985

|  | Trial Balance Unadjusted Debit | Trial Balance Unadjusted Credit | Adjustments Debit | | Adjustments Credit | | Income Statement Adjusted Debit | Income Statement Adjusted Credit | Balance Sheet Adjusted Debit | Balance Sheet Adjusted Credit |
|---|---|---|---|---|---|---|---|---|---|---|
| Cash | 3,100 | | (1) | 1,000 | | | | | 4,100 | |
| Accounts Receivable | 17,600 | | | | | | | | 17,600 | |
| Notes Receivable | 8,500 | | | | | | | | 8,500 | |
| Inventories, Jan. 1, 1985 | 34,000 | | (3) | 5,400 | | | 39,400 | | | |
| Property, Plant & Equip. | 112,000 | | | | (7) | 10,000ª | | | 102,000 | |
| Accumulated Depreciation | | 83,500 | (7) | 6,000ª | | | | | | 75,500 |
|  |  |  | (8) | 2,000 | | | | | | |
| Investments | 24,300 | | | | | | | | 24,300 | |
| Accounts Payable | | 14,500 | (6) | 6,000 | | | | | | 8,500 |
| Notes Payable | | 10,000 | | | (6) | 6,000 | | | | 16,000 |
| Capital Stock | | 43,500 | | | | | | | | 43,500 |
| Retained Earnings | | 20,000 | (4) | 2,700ᵇ | (3) | 5,400 | | | | 17,600 |
|  |  |  | (7) | 4,000ª | (5) | 600 | | | | |
|  |  |  | (2) | 2,500 | (8) | 800 | | | | |
| Sales | | 94,000 | | | (1) | 1,000 | | 95,000 | | |
| Purchases | 21,000 | | | | | | 21,000 | | | |
| Selling Expenses | 22,000 | | | | (4) | 500ᵇ | 21,500 | | | |
| Administrative Expenses | 23,000 | | (2) | 700 | (5) | 400 | 22,700 | | | |
|  |  |  | (5) | 600 | (8) | 1,200 | | | | |
| Totals | 265,500 | 265,500 | | | | | | | | |
| Wages Payable | | | | | (2) | 3,200 | | | | 3,200 |
| Allowance for Doubtful Accounts | | | | | (4) | 2,200ᵇ | | | | 2,200 |
| Unexpired Insurance | | | (5) | 400 | | | | | 400 | |
| Inventory, Dec. 31, 1985 | | | | | | | | (9) 40,000 | (9) 40,000 | |
| Net Income | | | | | | | 30,400 | | | 30,400 |
| Totals | | | | 31,300 | | 31,300 | 135,000 | 135,000 | 196,900 | 196,900 |

Computations for a and b on page 1050.

Computations:

| ªMachinery | | ᵇBad Debts | 1984 | 1985 |
|---|---|---|---|---|
| Proceeds from sale | $7,000 | Bad debts charged for | $2,400 | $1,600 |
| Book value of machinery | 4,000 | Additional bad debts anticipated | 700 | 1,500 |
| Gain on sale | 3,000 | | 3,100 | 3,100 |
| Income credited | 7,000 | Charges currently made to each year | (400) | (3,600) |
| Retained earnings adjustment | $4,000 | Bad debt adjustment | $2,700 | $ (500) |

## QUESTIONS

1. In recent years, *The Wall Street Journal* has indicated that many companies have changed their accounting principles. What are the major reasons why companies change accounting methods?

2. What are the advantages of employing the current or catch-up method for handling changes in accounting principle?

3. Define a change in estimate and provide an illustration. When is a change in accounting estimate effected by a change in accounting principle?

4. Discuss and illustrate how a correction of an error in previously issued financial statements should be handled.

5. State how each of the following items is reflected in the financial statements:
   (a) Charge for failure to record depreciation in a previous period.
   (b) Change from straight-line method of depreciation to sum-of-the-years'-digits.
   (c) Change from FIFO to LIFO method for inventory valuation purposes.
   (d) Litigation won in current year, related to prior period.
   (e) Change in the realizability of certain receivables.
   (f) Write-off of receivables.
   (g) Change from the percentage-of-completion to the completed-contract method for reporting net income.

6. Indicate how the following items are recorded in the accounting records in the current year.
   (a) Change from the cash basis to accrual basis of accounting.
   (b) Change from LIFO to FIFO method for inventory valuation purposes.
   (c) Change in the estimate of service lives for plant assets.
   (d) Large write-off of goodwill.
   (e) A change in depreciating plant assets from accelerated to the straight-line method.
   (f) Large write-off of inventories because of obsolescence.

7. Nebit, Inc. has followed the practice of capitalizing certain marketing costs and amortizing these costs over their expected life. In the current year, the company determined that the future benefits from these costs were doubtful. Consequently, the company adopted the policy of expensing these costs as incurred. How should this accounting change be reported in the comparative financial statements?

8. Jackson Construction Co. had followed the practice of expensing all materials assigned to a construction job without recognizing any salvage inventory. On December 31, 1983, it was determined that salvage inventory should be valued at $41,500. Of this amount, $20,000 arose during the current year. How should this change in accounting principle be reflected in the financial statements?

9. Londondary, Inc. wishes to change from the sum-of-the-years'-digits to the straight-line depreciation method for financial reporting purposes. The auditor indicates that a change would be permitted only if it is to a preferable method. What difficulties develop in assessing preferability?

10. How should consolidated financial statements be reported this year when statements of individual companies were presented last year?

11. Spruce Enterprises controlled four domestic subsidiaries and one foreign subsidiary. Prior to the current year, Spruce Enterprises had excluded the foreign subsidiary from consolidation. During the current year, the foreign subsidiary was included in the financial statements. How should this change in accounting principle be reflected in the financial statements?

12. Winkler Co., a closely held corporation, is in the process of preparing financial statements to accompany an offering of its common stock. The company at this time has decided to switch from the accelerated depreciation to the straight-line method of depreciation to better present its financial operations. How should this change in accounting principle be reported in the financial statements?

13. Prior to 1984, Deacon Inc. excluded manufacturing overhead costs from work in process and finished goods inventory. These costs have been expensed as incurred. In 1984, the company decided to change its accounting methods for manufacturing inventories to full costing by including these costs as product costs. Assuming that these costs are material, how should this change be reflected in the financial statements for 1983 and 1984?

14. Kirkland Corp. failed to record accrued salaries for 1981, $1,800; 1982, $2,100; and 1983, $4,200. What is the amount of the overstatement or understatement of Retained Earnings at December 31, 1984?

15. In January, 1983, installation costs of $7,000 on new machinery were charged to Repair Expense. Other costs of this machinery of $30,000 were correctly recorded and have been depreciated using the straight-line method with an estimated life of 10 years and no salvage value. At December 31, 1984, it is decided that the machinery has a useful life of 20 years, starting with January 1, 1984. What entry(ies) should be made in 1984 to correctly record transactions related to machinery, assuming the machinery has no salvage value? The books have not been closed for 1984.

16. On January 2, 1983, $100,000 of 10%, 20-year bonds were issued for $98,000. The $2,000 discount was charged to Interest Expense. The bookkeeper records interest only on the interest payment dates of January 1 and July 1. What is the effect on reported net income for 1983 of this error, assuming straight-line amortization of the discount? What entry is necessary to correct for this error, assuming that the books are not closed for 1983?

17. Equipment was purchased on January 2, 1983 for $14,000, but no portion of the cost has been charged to depreciation. The corporation wishes to use the straight-line method for these assets, which have been estimated to have a life of 10 years and no salvage value. What effect does this error have on net income in 1983? What entry is necessary to correct for this error, assuming that the books are not closed for 1983?

18. An account payable of $9,000 for merchandise purchased on December 23, 1983 was recorded in January 1984. This merchandise was not included in inventory at December 31, 1983. What effect does this error have on reported net income for 1983? What entry should be made to correct for this error, assuming that the books are not closed for 1983?

# CASES

C23-1 Rickshaw Inc. has recently hired a new independent auditor who says she wants "to get everything straightened out." Consequently, she has proposed the following accounting changes in connection with the client's 1983 financial statements:

1. In the past, the client has spread preproduction costs in its furniture division over 5 years. Because its latest furniture is of the "fad" type, it appears that the largest volume of sales will occur during the first two years after introduction. Consequently, the client proposes to amortize preproduction costs on a per-unit basis, which will result in expensing most of such costs during the first 2 years after the furniture's introduction. If the new accounting method had been used prior to 1983, retained earnings at December 31, 1982, would have been $300,000 less.

2. For the nursery division the client proposes to switch from FIFO to LIFO inventories as it is believed that LIFO will provide a better matching of current costs with revenues.

The effect of making this change on 1983 earnings will be an increase of $270,000. The client says that the effect of the change on December 31, 1982, retained earnings cannot be determined.

3. To achieve a better matching of revenues and expenses in its building construction division, the client proposes to switch from the completed-contract method of accounting to the percentage-of-completion method. Had the percentage-of-completion method been employed in all prior years, retained earnings at December 31, 1982, would have been $1,237,500 greater.

4. At December 31, 1982, the client had a receivable of $787,500 from Blakely, Inc. on its balance sheet. Blakely, Inc. has gone bankrupt, and no recovery is expected. The client proposes to write off the receivable as a prior period item.

5. The client proposes the following changes in depreciation policies:
   (a) For office furniture and fixtures it proposes to change from a 10-year useful life to an 8-year life. If this change had been made in prior years, retained earnings at December 31, 1982 would have been $150,000 less. The effect of the change on 1983 income alone is a reduction of $15,000.
   (b) For its manufacturing assets the client proposes to change from double-declining balance depreciation to straight line. If straight-line depreciation had been used for all prior periods, retained earnings would have been $285,000 greater at December 31, 1982. The effect of the change on 1983 income alone is a reduction of $18,000.
   (c) For its equipment in the leasing division the client proposes to adopt the sum-of-the-years'-digits depreciation method. The client had never used SYD before. The first year the client operated a leasing division was 1983. If straight-line depreciation were used, 1983 income would be $60,000 greater.

6. In preparing its 1982 statements, one of the client's bookkeepers overstated ending inventory by $172,500 because of a mathematical error. The client proposes to treat this item as a prior period adjustment.

## Instructions

(a) For each of the changes described above decide whether:
   1. The change involves an accounting principle, accounting estimate, or correction of an error.
   2. Restatement of opening retained earnings is required.
(b) Do any of the changes require presentation of pro forma amounts?
(c) What would be the proper adjustment to the December 31, 1982, retained earnings? What would be the "cumulative effect" shown separately in the 1983 income statement?

**C23–2** Listed below are three independent, unrelated sets of facts relating to accounting changes.

### Situation I

A company decides in January 1983 to adopt the straight-line method of depreciation for plant equipment. The straight-line method will be used for new acquisitions as well as for previously acquired plant equipment for which depreciation had been provided on an accelerated basis.

### Situation II

A company determined that the depreciable lives of its fixed assets are too long at present to fairly match the cost of the fixed assets with the revenue produced. The company decided at the beginning of the current year to reduce the depreciable lives of all of its existing fixed assets by five years.

### Situation III

Cavanaugh Company is in the process of having its first audit. The company's policy with regard to recognition of revenue is to use the installment method. However, *APB No. 10* states that the installment method of revenue recognition is not a generally accepted accounting principle except in certain circumstances, which are not present here. Ms. Laura Cavanaugh, the president, is willing to change to an acceptable method.

**Instructions**

For each of the situations described, provide the information indicated below.
(a) Type of accounting change.
(b) Manner of reporting the change under current generally accepted accounting principles including a discussion, where applicable, of how amounts are computed.
(c) Effect of the change on the balance sheet and income statement.

**C23–3** Melissa Melton, controller of Tuttle Corp., is aware that an opinion on accounting changes has been issued. After reading the opinion, she is confused and is not sure what action should be taken on the following items related to the Tuttle Corp. for the year 1983:

1. All equipment sold by Tuttle is subject to a three-year warranty. It has been estimated that the expense ultimately to be incurred on these machines is 1% of sales. In 1983, because of a production breakthrough, it is now estimated that ½ of 1% of sales is sufficient. In 1981 and 1982, warranty expense was computed as $40,000 and $50,000, respectively. The company now believes that these warranty costs should be reduced by 50%.

2. In 1983, the company decided to change its method of inventory pricing from average cost to the FIFO method. The effect of this change on prior years is to increase 1981 income by $60,000 and decrease 1982 income by $20,000.

3. In 1983, Tuttle decided to change its policy on accounting for certain marketing costs. Previously, the company had chosen to defer and amortize all marketing costs over at least five years because Tuttle believed that a return on these expenditures did not occur immediately. Recently, however, the time differential has considerably shortened, and Tuttle is now expensing the marketing costs as incurred.

4. In 1983, the company examined its entire policy relating to the depreciation of plant equipment. Plant equipment had normally been depreciated over a 15-year period, but recent experience has indicated that the company was incorrect in its estimates and that the assets should be depreciated over a 20-year period.

5. One division of Tuttle Corp., Forbes, Inc., has consistently shown an increasing net income from period to period. On closer examination of their operating statement, it is noted that bad debt expense and inventory obsolescence charges are much lower than in other divisions. In discussing this with the controller of this division, it has been learned that the controller has increased his net income each period by knowingly making low estimates related to the write-off of receivables and inventory.

6. In 1983, the company purchased new machinery that should increase production dramatically. The company has decided to depreciate this machinery on an accelerated basis, even though other machinery is depreciated on a straight-line basis.

**Instructions**

Melissa Melton has come to you, as her CPA, for advice about the situations above. Indicate the appropriate accounting treatment that should be given each of these situations.

**C23–4** Various types of accounting changes can affect the financial statements of a business enterprise differently. Assume that the following list describes changes that have a material effect on the financial statements for the current year of your business enterprise.

1. Correction of a mathematical error in inventory pricing made in a prior period.

2. A change from prime costing to full absorption costing for inventory valuation.

3. A change from presentation of statements of individual companies to presentation of consolidated statements.

4. A change in the method of accounting for leases for tax purposes to conform with the

financial accounting method. As a result, both deferred and current taxes payable changed substantially.

**5.** A change from the FIFO method of inventory pricing to the LIFO method of inventory pricing.

**6.** A change from the completed-contract method to the percentage-of-completion method of accounting for long-term construction-type contracts.

**7.** A change in the estimated useful life of previously recorded fixed assets based on newly acquired information.

**8.** A change from deferring and amortizing preproduction costs to recording such costs as an expense when incurred because future benefits of the costs have become doubtful. The new accounting method was adopted in recognition of the change in estimated future benefits.

**9.** A change from including the employer share of FICA taxes with Payroll Tax Expenses to including it with "Retirement benefits" on the income statement.

#### Instructions

Identify the type of change that is described in each item above and indicate whether the prior year's financial statements should be restated when presented in comparative form with the current year's statements. Ignore possible pro forma effects.

## EXERCISES

**E23-1** Resurrection Inc. purchased equipment for $232,000 which was estimated to have a useful life of 8 years with a salvage value of $8,000 at the end of that time. Depreciation has been entered for 5 years on a straight-line basis. In 1984 it is determined that the total estimated life should be 12 years with a salvage value of $4,500 at the end of that time.

#### Instructions

(a) Prepare the entry (if any) to correct the prior years' depreciation.

(b) Prepare the entry to record depreciation for 1984.

**E23-2** R. J. Schmidt Corporation owns equipment that originally cost $300,000 and had an estimated useful life of 10 years. The equipment had no expected salvage value.

The two requirements below are independent and must be considered as entirely separate from each other.

#### Instructions

(a) After using the double-declining balance method for two years, the company decided to switch to the straight-line method of depreciation. Prepare the general journal entry(ies) necessary in the third year to properly account for (1) the change in accounting principle and (2) depreciation expense.

(b) After using the straight-line method for 2 years, the company determined that the useful life of the equipment is 12 years (2 more than the original estimate). Prepare the general journal entry(ies) necessary to properly account for the depreciation expense in the third year.

**E23-3** Mendelsohn Co. purchased equipment on January 1, 1981 for $385,000. At that time it was estimated that the machine would have a 10-year life and no salvage value. On December 31, 1984, the firm's accountant found that the entry for depreciation expense had been omitted in 1982. In addition, management has informed the accountant that they plan to switch to straight-line depreciation, starting with the year 1984. At present, the company uses the sum-of-the-years'-digits method for depreciating equipment.

#### Instructions

Prepare the general journal entries the accountant should make at December 31, 1984.

**E23-4** Theta Chi Enterprises changed from the double-declining balance to the straight-line method in 1984 on all its plant assets. For tax purposes, assume that the amount of the ACRS depreciation is higher than the double-declining balance depreciation for each of the three years. The appropriate information related to this change is as follows:

| Year | Double-Declining Balance Depreciation | Straight-Line Depreciation | Difference |
|------|---------------------------------------|----------------------------|------------|
| 1982 | $300,000 | $150,000 | $150,000 |
| 1983 | 240,000 | 150,000 | 90,000 |
| 1984 | 192,000 | 150,000 | 42,000 |

Net income for 1983 was reported at $380,000; net income for 1984 was reported at $395,000, excluding any adjustment for the cumulative effect of a change in depreciation methods. The straight-line method of depreciation was employed in computing net income for 1984.

**Instructions**

(a) Assuming a tax rate of 45%, what is the amount of the cumulative effect adjustment in 1984?

(b) Prepare the journal entry(ies) to record the cumulative effect adjustment in the accounting records.

(c) Starting with income before cumulative effect of change in accounting principle, prepare the remaining portion of the income statement for 1983 and 1984. Indicate the pro forma net income that should be reported. Ignore per-share computations and footnote disclosures.

**E23-5** R. W. Hill Company changed from the completed-contract to the percentage-of-completion method of accounting for long-term construction contracts during 1984. For tax purposes, the company employs the completed-contract method and will continue this approach in the future. The appropriate information related to this change is as follows:

|      | Pretax Income from: | | |
|------|---------------------|--|--|
|      | Percentage-of-Completion | Completed-Contract | Difference |
| 1983 | $1,500,000 | $1,270,000 | $230,000 |
| 1984 | 1,410,000 | 1,100,000 | 310,000 |

**Instructions**

(a) Assuming that the tax rate is 40%, what is the amount of net income that would be reported in 1984?

(b) What entry(ies) are necessary to adjust the accounting records for the change in accounting principle?

**E23-6** Below is the net income of the Braniff Company, a private corporation, computed under the three inventory methods using a periodic system.

|      | FIFO | Average Cost | LIFO |
|------|------|--------------|------|
| 1981 | $22,000 | $20,000 | $18,000 |
| 1982 | 25,000 | 22,000 | 21,000 |
| 1983 | 24,000 | 24,000 | 23,000 |
| 1984 | 30,000 | 27,000 | 26,000 |

**Instructions**

(a) Assume that in 1984 Braniff decided to change from the FIFO method to the average cost method of pricing inventories. Prepare the journal entry necessary for the change that took place during 1984, and show all the appropriate information needed for reporting on a comparative basis.

(b) Assume that in 1984 Braniff, which had been using the LIFO method since incorporation in 1978, changed to the FIFO method of pricing inventories. Prepare the journal entry necessary for the change, and show all the appropriate information needed for reporting on a comparative basis.

(c) Assume that in 1984 Braniff, which had been using the FIFO method, changed to the LIFO method of pricing inventories. Prepare the journal entry necessary for the change, and show all appropriate information needed for reporting on a comparative basis.

**E23-7** Furniture Industries utilizes periodic inventory procedures and on Dec. 31, 1984 decides to change from FIFO to LIFO. The following information is available in the company records:

|  |  | Units | Unit Cost |
|---|---|---|---|
| 1983: | Beginning Inventory | 3,000 | $20 |
| | Purchases:   #1 | 5,000 | 24 |
| |          #2 | 4,000 | 28 |
| |          #3 | 6,000 | 32 |
| |          #4 | 5,000 | 36 |
| |          #5 | 5,000 | 39 |
| | Ending Inventory | 6,000 | |
| 1984: | Beginning Inventory | 6,000 | |
| | Purchases:   #1 | 2,000 | 44 |
| |          #2 | 5,000 | 47 |
| |          #3 | 5,000 | 53 |
| |          #4 | 7,000 | 56 |
| |          #5 | 3,000 | 60 |
| | Ending Inventory | 11,000 | |

**Instructions**

(a) State the value at which Furniture Industries reports the ending inventory for 1984.
(b) Indicate what additional disclosures are necessary for this change (both within the body of the financial statements and in footnotes). Assume a 40% tax rate.

**E23-8** Dottie Linens, Inc. acquired the following assets in January of 1981:

| | |
|---|---|
| Equipment, estimated service life, 5 years; salvage value, $45,000 | $495,000 |
| Building, estimated service life, 30 years; no salvage value | $693,000 |

The equipment has been depreciated using the sum-of-the-years'-digits method for the first 3 years, for financial reporting purposes. In 1984, the company decided to change the method of computing depreciation to the straight-line method for the equipment, but no change was made in the estimated service life or salvage value. It was also decided to change the total estimated service life of the building from 30 years to 39 years, with no change in the estimated salvage value. The building is depreciated on the straight-line method.

The company has 100,000 shares of capital stock outstanding. Results of operations for 1984 and 1983 are shown below:

| | 1984 | 1983 |
|---|---|---|
| Income before cumulative effect of change in computing depreciation for 1984: depreciation for 1984 has been computed on the straight-line basis for both the equipment and building[a] | $406,000 | $400,000 |
| Income per share before cumulative effect of change in computing depreciation for 1984 | $4.06 | $4.00 |

[a]It should be noted that the computation for depreciation expense for 1984 and 1983 for the building was based on the original estimate of service life of 30 years.

**Instructions**

(a) Compute the cumulative effect of the change in accounting principle to be reported in the income statement for 1984, and prepare the journal entry to record the change. (Ignore tax effects.)

(b) Present comparative data for the years 1983 and 1984, starting with income before cumulative effect of accounting change. Prepare pro forma data. Do not prepare the footnote. (Ignore tax effects.)

**E23–9** The first audit of the books of Seattle Company was made for the year ended December 31, 1984. In examining the books, the auditor found that certain items had been overlooked or incorrectly handled in the last three years. These items are:

1. The Seattle Company purchased another company early in 1982 and recorded goodwill of $150,000. Seattle had not amortized goodwill since its value had not diminished.

2. In 1984, the company changed its basis of inventory pricing from FIFO to LIFO. The cumulative effect of this change was to decrease net income by $43,000. The company debited this cumulative effect to Retained Earnings. LIFO was used in computing income in 1984.

3. In 1984, the company wrote off $175,000 of inventory considered to be obsolete; this loss was charged directly to Retained Earnings.

4. At the beginning of 1982, the company purchased a machine for $72,000 (salvage value of $9,000) that had a useful life of six years. The bookkeeper used straight-line depreciation, but failed to deduct the salvage value in computing the depreciation base for the three years.

5. At the end of 1983, the company failed to accrue sales salaries of $77,000.

6. A tax lawsuit that involved the year 1982 was settled late in 1984. It was determined that the company owed an additional $75,000 in taxes related to 1982. The company did not record a liability in 1982 or 1983 because the possibility of loss was considered remote, and charged the $75,000 to a loss account in 1984.

**Instructions**

Prepare the journal entries necessary in 1984 to correct the books, assuming that the books have not been closed. The proper amortization period for goodwill is 40 years. Disregard effects of corrections on income tax.

**E23–10** Presented below are the comparative statements for Dalmation, Inc.

|  | 1984 | 1983 |
|---|---|---|
| Sales | $300,000 | $250,000 |
| Cost of sales | 180,000 | 142,000 |
| Gross profit | 120,000 | 108,000 |
| Expenses | 77,000 | 68,000 |
| Net income | $ 43,000 | $ 40,000 |
| Retained earnings (Jan. 1) | $150,000 | $130,000 |
| Net income | 43,000 | 40,000 |
| Dividends | (25,000) | (20,000) |
| Retained earnings (Dec. 31) | $168,000 | $150,000 |

The following additional information is provided:

1. In 1984, Dalmation decided to switch its depreciation method from sum-of-the-years'-digits to the straight-line method. The differences in the two depreciation methods for the assets involved are:

|  | 1983 | 1984 |
|---|---|---|
| Sum-of-the-years'-digits | $50,000 | $40,000ᵃ |
| Straight-line | 30,000 | 30,000 |

ᵃThe 1984 income statement contains depreciation expense of $40,000.

2. In 1984, the company discovered that the ending inventory for 1983 was overstated by $25,000; ending inventory for 1984 is correctly stated.

**Instructions**

(a) Prepare the revised income and retained earnings statement for 1983 and 1984, assuming comparative statements (ignore income tax effects). Do not prepare footnotes or pro forma amounts.

(b) Prepare the revised income and retained earnings statement for 1984, assuming a noncomparative presentation (ignore income tax effects). Do not prepare footnotes or pro forma amounts.

**E23-11** The reported net incomes for the first two years of Medical Products, Inc. were as follows: 1983—$147,000; 1984—$185,000. Early in 1985, the following errors were discovered:

1. Depreciation of equipment for 1983 was overstated $7,500.

2. Depreciation of equipment for 1984 was understated $28,500.

3. December 31, 1983 inventory was understated $60,000.

4. December 31, 1984 inventory was overstated $15,000.

**Instructions**

Prepare the correcting entry necessary when these errors are discovered. Assume that the books are closed.

**E23-12** Bombay Tool Company's December 31 year-end financial statements contained the following errors:

|  | December 31, 1983 | December 31, 1984 |
|---|---|---|
| Ending inventory | $6,000 understated | $5,400 overstated |
| Depreciation expense | $1,200 understated | — |

An insurance premium of $45,000 was prepaid in 1983 covering the years 1983, 1984, and 1985. The entire amount was charged to expense in 1983. In addition, on December 31, 1984, fully depreciated machinery was sold for $9,600 cash, but the entry was not recorded until 1985. There were no other errors during 1983 or 1984, and no corrections have been made for any of the errors. Ignore income tax considerations.

**Instructions**

(a) Compute the total effect of the errors on 1984 net income.

(b) Compute the total effect of the errors on the amount of Bombay's working capital at December 31, 1984.

(c) Compute the total effect of the errors on the balance of Bombay's retained earnings at December 31, 1984.

**E23-13** When the records of Rainbow Corporation were reviewed at the close of 1984, the errors listed below were discovered. For each item indicate by a check mark in the appropriate column whether the error resulted in an overstatement, an understatement, or had no effect on net income for the years 1983 and 1984.

| Item | 1983 | | | 1984 | | |
|---|---|---|---|---|---|---|
| | Over-statement | Under-statement | No Effect | Over-statement | Under-statement | No Effect |
| **1.** Failure to record the correct amount of ending 1983 inventory. The amount was overstated because of an error in calculation. | | | | | | |
| **2.** Failure to record merchandise purchased in 1983. Merchandise was also omitted from ending inventory in 1983 but was not yet sold. | | | | | | |
| **3.** Failure to record amortization of patent in 1983. | | | | | | |
| **4.** Failure to record accrued interest on notes payable in 1983; amount was recorded when paid in 1984. | | | | | | |
| **5.** Failure to reflect supplies on hand on balance sheet at end of 1983. | | | | | | |

**E23–14** A partial trial balance of Whirlitzur Corporation is as follows on December 31, 1984:

| | Dr. | Cr. |
|---|---|---|
| Supplies on hand | $ 2,000 | |
| Accrued salaries and wages | | $ 2,000 |
| Accrued interest on investments | 4,000 | |
| Prepaid insurance | 100,000 | |
| Unearned rental income | | -0- |
| Accrued interest payable | | 12,000 |

Additional adjusting data:

1. A physical count of supplies on hand on December 31, 1984 totaled $1,200.

2. Through oversight, the accrued salaries and wages account was not changed during 1984. Accrued salaries and wages on 12/31/84 amounted to $3,300.

3. The accrued interest on investments account was also left unchanged during 1984. Accrued interest on investments amounts to $3,700 on 12/31/84.

4. The unexpired portions of the insurance policies totaled $72,800 as of December 31, 1984.

5. $12,000 was received on January 1, 1984 for the rent of a building for both 1984 and 1985. The entire amount was credited to rental income.

6. Depreciation for the year was erroneously recorded as $3,000 rather than the correct figure of $30,000.

7. A further review of depreciation calculations of prior years revealed that depreciation of $7,200 was not recorded. It was decided that this oversight should be corrected by a prior period adjustment.

**Instructions**

(a) Assuming that the books have not been closed, what are the adjusting entries necessary at December 31, 1984?

(b) Assuming that the books have been closed, what are the adjusting entries necessary at December 31, 1984?

**E23–15** The reported net income for Sherri Strain Inc. for 1983 was $60,700 and $50,000 for 1984. However, the accountant noted that the following errors had been made:

1. Sales for 1983 included amounts of $22,000 which had been received in cash during 1983, but for which the related products were delivered in 1984. Title did not pass to the purchaser until 1984.

2. The inventory on December 31, 1983 was understated by $4,950.

3. The bookkeeper in recording interest expense for both 1983 and 1984 on bonds payable made the following entry on an annual basis:

| Interest Expense | 13,200 | |
| Cash | | 13,200 |

The bonds have a face value of $220,000 and pay a stated interest rate of 6%. They were issued at a discount of $11,000 on January 1, 1983 to yield an effective interest rate of 7%. (Assume that the effective yield method should be used.)

4. Ordinary repairs to equipment had been erroneously charged to the Equipment account during 1983 and 1984. Repairs in the amount of $7,800 in 1983 and $7,200 in 1984 were so charged. The company applies a rate of 12½% to the balance in the Equipment account at the end of the year in its determination of depreciation charges.

**Instructions**

Prepare a schedule showing the determination of corrected net income for 1983 and 1984.

**E23–16** Presented below is the net income related to J. Borke, Inc.:

| 1984 | 1983 | 1982 |
| --- | --- | --- |
| $147,000 | $117,000 | $210,000 |

Assume that depreciation entries for 1984 have not been recorded. The following information is also available.

1. Borke purchased a truck on January 1, 1981 for $19,000 with a $1,000 salvage value and a six-year life. The company debited an expense account and credited cash on the purchase date.

2. During 1984, Borke changed from the straight-line method of depreciation for its building to the double-declining method. The following computations present depreciation on both bases:

| | 1984 | 1983 | 1982 |
| --- | --- | --- | --- |
| Straight-line | $50,000 | $50,000 | $ 50,000 |
| Double-declining | 81,000 | 90,000 | 100,000 |

**3.** Early in 1984, Borke determined that a piece of equipment purchased in January 1981 at a cost of $16,500 with an estimated life of five years and salvage of $1,500, is now estimated to continue in use until December 31, 1988 and will have a $750 salvage value. J. Borke, Inc. has been using straight-line depreciation.

**4.** Borke won a court case in 1984 related to a patent infringement in 1981. Borke will collect its $8,720 settlement of the suit in 1985. The company had not recorded any entries related to this suit in previous periods.

**5.** Borke, in reviewing its provision for uncollectibles during 1984, has determined that 1% of sales is the appropriate amount of bad debt expense to be charged to operations. The company had used ½ of 1% as its rate in 1983 and 1982 when the expense had been $9,000 and $6,000, respectively. The company would have recorded $12,000 of bad debt expense on December 31, 1984 under the old rate. An entry for bad debt expense in 1984 has not been recorded.

**Instructions**

For each of the foregoing accounting changes, errors, or prior period adjustments, present the journal entry(ies) Borke would have made to record them during 1984, assuming that the books have not been closed. If no entry is required, write "none."

**E23–17** Monet, Inc. purchases a computer for $100,000 on January 1, 1982. For financial reporting purposes, it is estimated that the computer will have a useful life of four years with no salvage value. For tax purposes, the computer is depreciated as three-year property using the cost recovery rates of 25%, 38%, and 37%, respectively. For book purposes, the company has used the sum-of-the-years'-digits depreciation method for 1982 and 1983, but decides to change to the straight-line method in 1984. The tax rate for all periods involved is 40%.

**Instructions**

(a) Prepare the journal entry to record the change in accounting method in 1984.
(b) Compute the amount of deferred income taxes that would be reported on the December 31, 1984, balance sheet and whether it would have a debit or credit balance.

**E23–18** Hirley Enterprises purchases on January 1, 1982, a number of light-duty trucks costing $200,000. For book purposes, the company depreciates these assets on a straight-line basis over five years. For tax purposes, the company uses the elective straight-line method for three-year property and selects the three-year period. At the beginning of the second year, the company decides to change to the double-declining balance method of depreciation for book purposes. The tax rate for all periods involved is 30%.

**Instructions**

(a) Prepare the journal entry to record the change in accounting method in 1983.
(b) Compute the balance in deferred income taxes at the end of 1983.

# PROBLEMS

**P23–1** Gamm Products was organized in late 1980 to manufacture and sell hosiery. At the end of its fourth year of operation, the company has been fairly successful, as indicated by the following reported net incomes.

| | | | |
|---|---|---|---|
| 1981 | $150,000[a] | 1983 | 230,000 |
| 1982 | 195,000[b] | 1984 | 300,000 |

[a]Includes a $14,000 increase because of change in bad debt experience rate.
[b]Includes extraordinary gain of $30,000.

The company has decided to expand operations and has applied for a sizable bank loan. The bank officer has indicated that the records should be audited and presented in comparative statements to facilitate analysis by the bank. Gamm, therefore, hired the auditing firm of Mary Sepaniak Co. and has provided the following additional information.

1. In early 1982, Gamm changed their estimate from 2 to 1% on the amount of bad debt expense to be charged to operations. Bad debt expense for 1981, if a 1% rate had been used, would have been $14,000. The company, therefore, restated its net income of 1981.

2. In 1984, the auditor discovered that the company had changed its method of inventory pricing from LIFO to FIFO. The effect on the income statements for the previous years is as follows:

| | 1981 | 1982 | 1983 | 1984 |
|---|---|---|---|---|
| Net income unadjusted-LIFO basis | $150,000 | $195,000 | $230,000 | $300,000 |
| Net income unadjusted-FIFO basis | 160,000 | 200,000 | 255,000 | 295,000 |
| | $ 10,000 | $ 5,000 | $ 25,000 | ($ 5,000) |

3. In 1982, the company changed its method of depreciation from the accelerated method to the straight-line approach. The company used the straight-line method in 1982. The effect on the income statement for the previous year is as follows:

| | 1981 |
|---|---|
| Net income unadjusted (accelerated method) | $150,000 |
| Net income unadjusted (straight-line method) | 156,000 |
| | $ 6,000 |

4. In 1984, the auditor discovered that:
   a. The company incorrectly overstated the ending inventory by $19,000 in 1983.

   b. A dispute developed in 1982 with the Internal Revenue Service over the deductibility of entertainment expenses. In 1981, the company was not permitted these deductions, but a tax settlement was reached in 1984 that allowed these expenses. As a result of the court's finding, tax expenses in 1984 were reduced by $8,000.

**Instructions**

(a) Indicate how each of these changes or corrections should be handled in the accounting records.

(b) Present comparative income statements for the years 1981 to 1984, starting with income before extraordinary items. Do not prepare pro forma amounts.

**P23-2** On December 31, 1984, before the books were closed, the management and accountants of Cemetery Stones, Inc. made the following determinations about three depreciable assets:

1. Depreciable asset A was purchased January 2, 1981. It originally cost $165,000 and, for depreciation purposes, the straight-line method was originally chosen. The asset was originally expected to be useful for 10 years and have a zero salvage value. In 1984, the decision was made to change the depreciation method from straight-line to sum-of-the-years'-digits, and the estimates relating to useful life and salvage value remained unchanged.

2. Depreciable asset B was purchased January 3, 1980. It originally cost $90,000 and, for depreciation purposes, the straight-line method was chosen. The asset was originally expected to be useful for 10 years and have a zero salvage value. In 1984, the decision was made to shorten the total life of this asset to 8 years and to estimate the salvage value at $3,000.

3. Depreciable asset C was purchased January 5, 1979. The asset's original cost was $30,000, and this amount was entirely expensed in 1979. This particular asset has a 10-year useful life and no salvage value. The straight-line method was chosen for depreciation purposes.

Additional data:

1. Income in 1984 before depreciation expense amounted to $200,000.

2. Depreciation expense on assets other than A, B, and C totaled $40,000 in 1984.

3. Income in 1983 was reported at $400,000.

4. Ignore all income tax effects.

5. 100,000 shares of common stock were outstanding in 1983 and 1984.

**Instructions**

(a) Prepare all necessary entries in 1984 to record these determinations.

(b) Prepare comparative income statements for Cemetery Stones, Inc. for 1983 and 1984, starting with income before the cumulative effects of any change in accounting principle.

(c) Prepare comparative retained earnings statements for Cemetery Stones, Inc. for 1983 and 1984. The company had retained earnings of $200,000 at December 31, 1982.

**P23-3** Beyer Company reported net income of $750,000 for 1982. Its preliminary calculation of net income for 1983 shows $900,000. The books are still open for 1983. Additional information is as follows:

1. On January 1, 1982, Beyer purchased equipment for $1,100,000. Beyer estimated its useful life to be 10 years with a zero salvage value. Beyer uses sum-of-the-years'-digits depreciation. Based on new information available at the end of 1983, Beyer now estimates the asset's useful life should total 8 years. Depreciation expense based on a 10-year useful life has already been recorded in 1983.

2. In reviewing the December 31, 1983 inventory, Beyer discovered errors in its inventory-taking procedures which have caused inventories for the last 3 years to be incorrect. Inventory at the end of 1981 was overstated $7,000; at the end of 1982, it was overstated $9,000; and at the end of 1983, it was understated $3,000. Beyer uses a periodic inventory system and does not have a Cost of Goods Sold account. All information used to compute cost of goods sold is compiled in the Income Summary account. At the end of 1983, entries were made to remove the beginning inventory amount from the Inventory account (with a corresponding debit to Income Summary) and to establish the ending inventory amount in the Inventory account (with a corresponding credit to Income Summary). The Income Summary account is still open.

3. Beyer has failed to accrue wages payable at the end of each of the last 3 years, as follows:

| December 31, 1981 | $1,500 |
|---|---|
| December 31, 1982 | 2,500 |
| December 31, 1983 | 2,000 |

4. Beyer has two large blast furnaces that it uses in its manufacturing process. These furnaces must be periodically relined. Furnace A was relined in January 1977 at a cost of $300,000 and again in January 1982 at a cost of $400,000. Furnace B was relined for the first time in January 1983 at a cost of $450,000. All these costs were charged to Maintenance Expense as incurred.

5. Since a relining will last for five years, a better matching of revenues and expenses would have resulted if the cost of the relining was capitalized and depreciated over 5 years. Beyer has decided to make a change in accounting principle from expensing relining costs as incurred to capitalizing them and depreciating them over 5 years on a straight-line basis. A full year's depreciation will be taken in the year of relining. This change meets the requirements for a change in accounting principle.

**Instructions**

(a) Prepare the journal entries necessary at December 31, 1983 to record the above corrections and changes. The books are still open for 1983. Income tax effects may be ignored.

(b) Beyer plans to issue comparative (1983 and 1982) financial statements. Starting with $900,000 for 1983 and $750,000 for 1982, prepare a schedule to derive the correct net incomes for 1983 and 1982 to be shown in these statements. Income tax effects may be ignored.

(c) What are the pro forma net incomes for 1983 and 1982 that would be reported in the comparative financial statements? Income tax effects may be ignored.

**P23-4** The management of Santgria Corporation has concluded, with the concurrence of its independent auditors, that results of operations would be more fairly presented if Santgria changed its method of pricing inventory from last-in, first-out (LIFO) to average cost in 1983. Given below is the five-year summary of income and a schedule of what the inventories might have been if stated on the average cost method.

### Santgria Corporation
### STATEMENT OF INCOME AND RETAINED EARNINGS
### For the Years Ended May 31

|  | 1979 | 1980 | 1981 | 1982 | 1983 |
|---|---|---|---|---|---|
| Sales—net | $13,964 | $15,506 | $16,673 | $18,221 | $18,898 |
| Cost of goods sold |  |  |  |  |  |
| Beginning inventory | 1,000 | 1,100 | 1,000 | 1,115 | 1,237 |
| Purchases | 13,000 | 13,900 | 15,000 | 15,900 | 17,100 |
| Ending inventory | (1,100) | (1,000) | (1,115) | (1,237) | (1,369) |
| Total | 12,900 | 14,000 | 14,885 | 15,778 | 16,968 |
| Gross profit | 1,064 | 1,506 | 1,788 | 2,443 | 1,930 |
| Administrative expenses | 700 | 763 | 832 | 907 | 989 |
| Income before taxes | 364 | 743 | 956 | 1,536 | 941 |
| Income taxes (50%) | 182 | 372 | 478 | 768 | 471 |
| Net income | 182 | 371 | 478 | 768 | 470 |
| Retained earnings—beginning | 1,206 | 1,388 | 1,759 | 2,237 | 3,005 |
| Retained earnings—ending | $ 1,388 | $ 1,759 | $ 2,237 | $ 3,005 | $ 3,475 |
| Earnings per share | $ 1.82 | $ 3.71 | $ 4.78 | $ 7.68 | $ 4.70 |

### Schedule of Inventory Balances Using Average Cost Method

#### Year Ended May 31

| 1978 | 1979 | 1980 | 1981 | 1982 | 1983 |
|---|---|---|---|---|---|
| $950 | $1,124 | $1,101 | $1,270 | $1,490 | $1,699 |

**Instructions**

Prepare comparative statements for the five years, assuming that Santgria changed its method of inventory pricing to average cost. Indicate the effects on net income and earnings per share for the years involved. (All amounts except EPS are rounded up to the nearest dollar.)

**P23-5** Minoso Corporation has decided that in the preparation of its 1984 financial statements two changes will be made from the methods used in prior years:

1. *Depreciation.* Minoso has always used an accelerated method for tax and financial reporting purposes but has decided to change during 1984 to the straight-line method for financial reporting only. Assume that the accelerated method for tax and reporting purposes has been the same in the past. The effect of this change is as follows:

| | Excess of Accelerated Depreciation Over Straight-line Depreciation |
|---|---|
| Prior to 1983 | $1,365,000 |
| 1983 | 106,050 |
| 1984 | 103,950 |
| | $1,575,000 |

Depreciation is charged to cost of sales and to selling, general, and administrative expenses on the basis of 75% and 25%, respectively.

**2.** *Bad debt expense.* In the past Minoso has recognized bad debt expense equal to 1.5% of net sales. After careful review it has been decided that a rate of 1.75% is more appropriate for 1984. Bad debt expense is charged to selling, general, and administrative expenses.

The following information is taken from preliminary financial statements, prepared before giving effect to the two changes:

Minoso Corporation
CONDENSED BALANCE SHEET
December 31, 1984
With Comparative Figures for 1983

|  | 1984 | 1983 |
|---|---|---|
| **Assets** | | |
| Current assets | $43,561,000 | $43,900,000 |
| Plant assets, at cost | 45,792,000 | 43,974,000 |
| Less accumulated depreciation | 23,761,000 | 22,946,000 |
|  | $65,592,000 | $64,928,000 |
| **Liabilities and Stockholders' Equity** | | |
| Current liabilities | $21,124,000 | $23,650,000 |
| Long-term debt | 15,154,000 | 14,097,000 |
| Capital stock | 11,620,000 | 11,620,000 |
| Retained earnings | 17,694,000 | 15,561,000 |
|  | $65,592,000 | $64,928,000 |

Minoso Corporation
INCOME STATEMENT
For the Year Ended December 31, 1984
With Comparative Figures for 1983

|  | 1984 | 1983 |
|---|---|---|
| Net sales | $80,520,000 | $78,920,000 |
| Cost of goods sold | 54,847,000 | 53,074,000 |
|  | 25,673,000 | 25,846,000 |
| Selling, general, and administrative expenses | 19,540,000 | 18,411,000 |
|  | 6,133,000 | 7,435,000 |
| Other income (expense), net | (1,198,000) | (1,079,000) |
| Income before income taxes | 4,935,000 | 6,356,000 |
| Income taxes | 2,368,800 | 3,050,880 |
| Net income | $ 2,566,200 | $ 3,305,120 |

There have been no timing differences between any book and tax items prior to the changes above. The effective tax rate is 48%.

**Instructions**

For the items listed below compute the amounts that would appear on the comparative (1984 and 1983) financial statements of Minoso Corporation after adjustment for the two accounting changes. Show amounts for both 1984 and 1983 and prepare supporting schedules as necessary.

(a) Accumulated depreciation.
(b) Deferred income taxes (cumulative).
(c) Selling, general, and administrative expenses.
(d) Current portion of federal income tax expense.
(e) Deferred portion of federal income tax expense.
(f) Retained earnings.
(g) Pro forma net income.

(AICPA adapted)

**P23-6** Rose Widolf Corporation has used the accrual basis of accounting for several years. A review of the records, however, indicates that some expenses and revenues have been handled on a cash basis because of errors made by an inexperienced bookkeeper. Income statements prepared by the bookkeeper reported $18,000 net income for 1983 and $20,000 net income for 1984. Further examination of the records reveals that the following items were handled improperly.

1. Rent was received from a tenant in December 1983; the amount, $725, was recorded as income at that time even though the rental pertained to 1984.

2. Wages payable on December 31 have been consistently omitted from the records of that date and have been entered as expenses when paid in the following year. The amounts of the accruals recorded in this manner were:

| | |
|---|---|
| December 31, 1982 | $ 850 |
| December 31, 1983 | 1,200 |
| December 31, 1984 | 780 |

3. Invoices for office supplies purchased have been charged to expense accounts when received. Inventories of supplies on hand at the end of each year have been ignored, and no entry has been made for them.

| | |
|---|---|
| December 31, 1982 | $1,000 |
| December 31, 1983 | 625 |
| December 31, 1984 | 1,140 |

**Instructions**

Prepare a schedule that will show the corrected net income for the years 1983 and 1984. All items listed should be labeled clearly.

**P23-7** Reding Coat Corporation is in the process of negotiating a loan for expansion purposes. The books and records have never been audited and the bank has requested that an audit be performed. Reding has prepared the following comparative financial statements for the years ended December 31, 1984, and 1983:

---

**BALANCE SHEET**
As of December 31, 1984 and 1983

| | 1984 | 1983 |
|---|---|---|
| **Assets** | | |
| Current assets | | |
| Cash | $ 163,000 | $ 82,000 |
| Accounts receivable | 392,000 | 296,000 |
| Allowance for doubtful accounts | (37,000) | (18,000) |
| Marketable securities, at cost | 78,000 | 78,000 |
| Merchandise inventory | 207,000 | 202,000 |
| Total current assets | 803,000 | 640,000 |

| Plant assets | | |
|---|---:|---:|
| Property, plant, and equipment | 167,000 | 169,500 |
| Accumulated depreciation | (121,600) | (106,400) |
| Total fixed assets | 45,400 | 63,100 |
| Total assets | $ 848,400 | $703,100 |

Liabilities and Stockholders' Equity

| Liabilities | | |
|---|---:|---:|
| Accounts payable | $ 121,400 | $196,100 |

| Stockholders' equity | | |
|---|---:|---:|
| Common stock, par value $10, authorized 50,000 shares, issued and outstanding 20,000 shares | 260,000 | 260,000 |
| Retained earnings | 467,000 | 247,000 |
| Total stockholders' equity | 727,000 | 507,000 |
| Total liabilities and stockholders' equity | $ 848,400 | $703,100 |

### STATEMENT OF INCOME
### For the Years Ended December 31, 1984 and 1983

| | 1984 | 1983 |
|---|---:|---:|
| Sales | $1,000,000 | $900,000 |
| Cost of sales | 430,000 | 395,000 |
| Gross profit | 570,000 | 505,000 |
| Operating expenses | 210,000 | 205,000 |
| Administrative expenses | 140,000 | 105,000 |
| | 350,000 | 310,000 |
| Net income | $ 220,000 | $195,000 |

During the course of the audit, the following additional facts were determined:

1. An analysis of collections and losses on accounts receivable during the past two years indicates a drop in anticipated losses due to bad debts. After consultation with management it was agreed that the loss experience rate on sales should be reduced from the recorded 2% to 1½%, beginning with the year ended December 31, 1984.

2. An analysis of marketable securities revealed that this investment portfolio consisted entirely of short-term investments in marketable equity securities that were acquired in 1983. The total market valuation for these investments as of the end of each year was as follows:

       December 31, 1983     $81,000
       December 31, 1984     $63,400

3. The merchandise inventory at December 31, 1983, was overstated by $4,200 and the merchandise inventory at December 31, 1984, was overstated by $6,400.

4. On January 2, 1983, equipment costing $12,000 (estimated useful life of 10 years and residual value of $2,000) was incorrectly charged to operating expenses. Reding records depreciation on the straight-line method. In 1984 fully depreciated equipment (with no residual value) that originally cost $17,500 was sold as scrap for $2,800. Reding credited the proceeds of $2,800 to property and equipment.

5. An analysis of 1983 operating expenses revealed that Reding charged to expense a three-year insurance premium of $2,970 on January 15, 1983.

**Instructions**

(a) Prepare the journal entries to correct the books at December 31, 1984. The books for 1984 have not been closed. Ignore income taxes.

(b) Prepare a schedule showing the computation of corrected net income for the years ended December 31, 1984 and 1983, assuming that any adjustments are to be reported on comparative statements for the two years. The first items on your schedule should be the net income for each year. Ignore income taxes. (Do not prepare financial statements.)

(AICPA adapted)

**P23–8** You have been asked by a client to review the records of Bonnie Buczek Company, a small manufacturer of precision tools and machines. Your client is interested in buying the business, and arrangements have been made for you to review the accounting records.

Your examination reveals the following:

1. Bonnie Buczek Company commenced business on April 1, 1981, and has been reporting on a fiscal year ending March 31. The company has never been audited, but the annual statements prepared by the bookkeeper reflect the following income before closing and before deducting income taxes:

| Year Ended March 31 | Income Before Taxes |
|---|---|
| 1982 | $ 73,600 |
| 1983 | 114,400 |
| 1984 | 107,580 |

2. A relatively small number of machines have been shipped on consignment. These transactions have been recorded as ordinary sales and billed as such. On March 31 of each year, machines billed and in the hands of consignees amounted to:

| 1982 | $ 6,500 |
|---|---|
| 1983 | none |
| 1984 | 5,590 |

Sales price was determined by adding 30% to cost. Assume that the consigned machines are sold the following year.

3. On March 30, 1983, two machines were shipped to a customer on a C.O.D. basis. The sale was not entered until April 5, 1983, when cash was received for $6,100. The machines were not included in the inventory at March 31, 1983. (Title passed on March 30, 1983.)

4. All machines are sold subject to a five-year warranty. It is estimated that the expense ultimately to be incurred in connection with the warranty will amount to ½ of 1% of sales. The company has charged an expense account for warranty costs incurred.

Sales per books and warranty costs were:

| Year Ended March 31 | Sales | Warranty Expense for Sales Made In 1982 | 1983 | 1984 | Total |
|---|---|---|---|---|---|
| 1982 | $ 940,000 | $760 | | | $ 760 |
| 1983 | 1,010,000 | 360 | $1,310 | | 1,670 |
| 1984 | 1,795,000 | 320 | 1,620 | $1,910 | 3,850 |

5. A review of the corporate minutes reveals the manager is entitled to a bonus of ½ of 1% of the income before deducting income taxes and the bonus. The bonuses have never been recorded or paid.

6. Bad debts have been recorded on a direct write-off basis. Experience of similar enterprises indicates that losses will approximate ¼ of 1% of sales. Bad debts written off were:

Bad Debts Incurred on Sales Made In

|        | 1982   | 1983     | 1984     | Total   |
|--------|--------|----------|----------|---------|
| 1982   | $750   |          |          | $ 750   |
| 1983   | 800    | $ 520    |          | 1,320   |
| 1984   | 350    | 1,800    | $1,700   | 3,850   |

7. The bank deducts 6% on all contracts financed. Of this amount ½% is placed in a reserve to the credit of Bonnie Buczek Company that is refunded to Buczek as finance contracts are paid in full. The reserve established by the bank has not been reflected in the books of Buczek. The excess of credits over debits (net increase) to the reserve account with Buczek on the books of the bank for each fiscal year were as follows:

| 1982 | $ 3,000 |
|------|---------|
| 1983 | 3,900   |
| 1984 | 5,100   |
|      | $12,000 |

8. Commissions on sales have been entered when paid. Commissions payable on March 31 of each year were:

| 1982 | $ 1,400 |
|------|---------|
| 1983 | 800     |
| 1984 | 1,120   |

**Instructions**

(a) Present a schedule showing the revised income before income taxes for each of the years ended March 31, 1982, 1983, and 1984. Make computations to the nearest whole dollar.

(b) Prepare the journal entry or entries you would give the bookkeeper to correct the books. Assume the books have not yet been closed for the fiscal year ended March 31, 1984. Disregard correction of income taxes.

(AICPA adapted)

**P23–9** Askew Company is in the process of adjusting and correcting its books at the end of 1984. In reviewing its records, the following information is compiled.

1. On January 1, 1983, Askew implemented a stock appreciation right (SAR) plan for its top executives. The plan was to run from January 1, 1982 to December 31, 1984. This period was the intended service period and the date of exercise was December 31, 1984. At December 31, 1984 (the measurement date), the executives were to receive in cash the appreciation in the market value of the stock over the 3-year period. Using the market prices of the stock at the end of 1982 and 1983, respectively, Askew estimated compensation expense of $17,000 for 1982 and $21,000 for 1983. At December 31, however, the market price of the stock was below its price at January 1, 1982.

2. Askew has failed to accrue sales commissions payable at the end of each of the last 2 years, as follows:

| December 31, 1983 | $3,000 |
|-------------------|--------|
| December 31, 1984 | $1,800 |

3. In reviewing the December 31, 1984, inventory, Askew discovered errors in its inventory-taking procedures which have caused inventories for the last 3 years to be incorrect, as follows:

| December 31, 1982 | Understated | $7,000—Physical |
|-------------------|-------------|-----------------|
| December 31, 1983 | Understated | $9,000—Physical |
| December 31, 1984 | Overstated  | $3,000          |

Askew has already made an entry to establish the incorrect December 31, 1984, inventory amount.

4. At December 31, 1984, Askew decided to change its depreciation method on its office equipment from double-declining balance to straight line. Assume that the ACRS depre-

ciation is higher than the double-declining depreciation taken for each period. The following information is available (the tax rate is 30%):

| | Double-Declining Balance | Straight Line | Pre-Tax Difference | Tax Effect | Difference, Net of Tax |
|---|---|---|---|---|---|
| Prior to 1984 | $70,000 | $40,000 | $30,000 | $9,000 | $21,000 |
| 1984 | 12,000 | 10,000 | 2,000 | 600 | 1,400 |

Askew has already recorded the 1984 depreciation expense using the double-declining balance method.

5. Before 1984, Askew accounted for its income from long-term construction contracts on the percentage of completion basis (while using the completed contract method for tax purposes). Early in 1984, Askew changed *to* the completed contract basis on its books so it would be using the same method for its books as it uses for tax purposes. Income for 1984 has been recorded using the completed contract method. The income tax rate is 30%. The following information is available:

| | Pre-Tax Income | |
|---|---|---|
| | Percentage of Completion | Completed Contract |
| Prior to 1984 | $150,000 | $100,000 |
| 1984 | 60,000 | 20,000 |

**Instructions**

Prepare the journal entries necessary at December 31, 1984 to record the above corrections and changes. The books are still open for 1984. Askew has not yet recorded its 1984 income tax expense and payable amounts so current year tax effects may be ignored. Prior year tax effects must be considered in items 4 and 5.

# PREPARATION AND ANALYSIS OF FINANCIAL STATEMENTS

## 6

# CHAPTER 24

# Statement of Changes in Financial Position

How did Atlantic Richfield finance the large investment it made to drill for oil in the North Slope of Alaska? How will Boeing Aircraft finance the new B-757 and B-767 jet aircraft that it is building for the airline industry? How was Sears Industries Inc. able to purchase long-term assets recently in the same year that it sustained a net loss? How much of the proposed expansion by Marriott Hotels will be financed through cash provided by operations? These types of questions are often asked by investors, creditors, and internal management who are interested in the financial operations of a business enterprise. However, an examination of the balance sheet, income statement, and statement of retained earnings often fails to provide ready answers to questions of this type.

The balance sheet presents the status of the assets and equities as of a specific date; the income statement presents a summary of the nature and results of transactions affecting net income. The statement of retained earnings provides an analysis of changes in retained earnings. These statements present to a limited extent and in a fragmented manner information about the financial activities of an enterprise during the period. Comparative balance sheets help to show what new assets have been acquired or disposed of and what liabilities have been incurred or liquidated. The income statement provides information as to resources provided by operations. The statement of retained earnings provides information as to the resources used to pay dividends. None of these statements, however, presents a detailed summary of all the resources provided during the period and the uses to which they were put.

## EVOLUTION OF A NEW STATEMENT

A statement specifically designed to furnish this information is now issued by all major business enterprises as one of the primary financial statements. This statement, the **Statement of Changes in Financial Position,** is designed to present information on the financing and investing activities of a business enterprise. The evolution of this statement provides an interesting example of how the needs of financial statement users are met.

The statement originated in a simple analysis called the "Where-Got and Where-Gone Statement" that consisted of nothing more than a listing of the increases or decreases in the company's balance sheet items. After some years, the title of this statement was changed to "the funds statement." In 1961, the AICPA, recognizing the significance of this statement, sponsored research in this area that resulted in the publication of *Accounting Research Study No. 2,* entitled " 'Cash Flow' Analysis and the Funds Statements."[1] This study recommended that the funds statement be included in all annual reports to the stockholders and that it be covered by the auditor's opinion.

In 1963, *APB Opinion No. 3* was issued to provide some standards for the preparation and presentation of such statements. The Board recommended that the name be changed to "Statement of Source and Application of Funds" and said "that a statement of source and application of funds should be presented as supplementary information in financial reports. The inclusion of such information is not mandatory, and it is optional as to whether it should be covered in the report of the independent accountant."[2]

After the issuance of *APB Opinion No. 3,* support by the business community, the stock exchanges, and the SEC resulted in a substantial increase in the number of companies that presented statements of source and applications of funds.[3] The value of and demand for this type of information resulted in the issuance in 1971 of *APB Opinion No. 19,* which made it mandatory that a "statement of changes in financial position" be presented as an integral part of the financial statements and that it be covered by the auditor's opinion. The Board concluded

> . . . that information concerning the financing and investing activities of a business enterprise and the changes in its financial position for a period is essential for financial statement users, particularly owners and creditors, in making economic decisions. When financial statements purporting to present both financial position (balance sheet) and results of operations (statement of income and retained earnings) are issued, a statement summarizing changes in financial position should also be presented as a basic financial statement for each period for which an income statement is presented. These conclusions apply to all profit-oriented business entities, whether or not the reporting entity normally classifies its assets and liabilities as current and noncurrent.[4]

The Board recommended that the new title be "Statement of Changes in Financial Position," a title that has rapidly gained popularity.

## WHAT IS MEANT BY CHANGES IN FINANCIAL POSITION?

The changes that occur in financial position from one period to another can be measured in several different ways. The more common approaches are discussed below.

### Cash

Under this concept the changes in the cash balance that occur over a period of time are summarized. Any transaction that either increases or decreases cash is considered in preparing the final statement. For example, the purchase of land for cash is considered a change in financial position because it decreases cash. A transaction that has no effect on

---

[1] Perry Mason, " 'Cash Flow' Analysis and the Funds Statement," *Accounting Research Study No. 2* (New York: AICPA, 1961).

[2] "The Statement of Source and Application of Funds," *Opinions of the Accounting Principles Board No. 3* (New York: AICPA, 1963), par. 8.

[3] *Accounting Trends and Techniques—1981,* for example, indicates that all 600 companies surveyed presented a statement of changes in financial position in 1980.

[4] "Reporting Changes in Financial Position," *Opinions of the Accounting Principles Board No. 19* (New York: AICPA, 1971), par. 7.

cash such as the purchase of land on credit is not reported. Using cash to measure changes in financial position has limitations, because many important transactions resulting in changes in financial position are of a noncash variety and are excluded from this statement.

An approach that is similar to cash and is becoming more popular is "cash and temporary investments" (often referred to as cash and cash equivalents). Many believe that the distinction between cash and surplus cash temporarily invested is not substantive enough to warrant separation. Concepts similar to cash and temporary investments such as (1) cash, temporary investments, and receivables (monetary assets); and (2) cash, temporary investments, and receivables minus current liabilities (net monetary assets), are sometimes suggested as means of measuring changes in financial position, but these concepts are not extensively employed in practice.[5]

## Working Capital

Changes in financial position are often measured in terms of working capital (current assets minus current liabilities). Any transaction that increases or decreases working capital is shown in the statement. For example, the purchase of land for cash or on short-term credit is reported in the changes statement because a change in working capital occurs. The use of working capital as the basis permits the exclusion of many routine transactions such as cash collections on accounts receivable and the purchase of inventory on credit. All of these transactions are summarized in the amount reported as "resources (working capital) provided by operations."

## All Financial Resources

If cash or working capital alone is used in measuring changes in financial position, some major financial transactions may be omitted. For example, issuing common stock for buildings or machinery has no effect on cash or working capital, but it is a significant financial transaction that should be disclosed. For this reason the definition of changes in financial position was expanded to include **any change that significantly affects the financing and investing aspects of the enterprise.** This approach, called the **all financial resources concept,** expands the definition of resources beyond cash or working capital to cover all significant financial occurrences. The profession requires the use of the all financial resources concept, indicating that a company may explain its changes in resources using a concept such as cash, cash and temporary investments, or working capital, but that whatever concept is followed, it must be adjusted to disclose significant financial transactions that would otherwise be omitted under this concept.

**The statement of changes in financial position must be based upon the all financial resources concept;** at the same time, statements that employ a cash or working capital approach disclose the change in cash or working capital. To accomplish these two objectives, the statement (using working capital as an illustration) must identify and analyze

---

[5]*Accounting Trends and Techniques—1981* indicates that in 1980 only 59 out of 600 companies surveyed used cash and cash equivalent approaches in measuring changes in financial position while 541 of the companies surveyed analyzed the change in terms of working capital. It appears, however, that many companies will change to a cash or cash and cash equivalent approach in the near future.

two categories of items: (1) sources of working capital (inflows) and applications of working capital (outflows), and (2) sources and applications of resources that did not affect (flow through) working capital.

# SECTION 1   WORKING CAPITAL APPROACH

Working capital is the difference between current assets and current liabilities. As a fund, working capital is viewed as containing all current assets (increases in working capital) and all current liabilities (decreases in working capital). **Any transaction that results in a net increase in working capital is a "source" of working capital;** that is, it provides working capital. **Any transaction that results in a net decrease in working capital is a "use" of working capital;** that is, it applies working capital. Some transactions merely rearrange the internal content of working capital; that is, they neither increase nor decrease working capital. For example, the collection of cash from an account receivable, the write-off of an accounts receivable (under the allowance method), the payment of an account payable, and the purchase of inventory for cash or on short-term credit, are neither sources nor applications of working capital, because the net balance does not change. Thus, **in the analysis of working capital we must separate the transactions that cause changes (increases or decreases) in working capital from those that merely change the composition but not the total of working capital. It is the change in the working capital balance, along with other significant (nonworking capital) changes in resources, that the statement of changes in financial position reports.**

The diagram below illustrates the type of events and transactions that result in working capital being provided and applied.

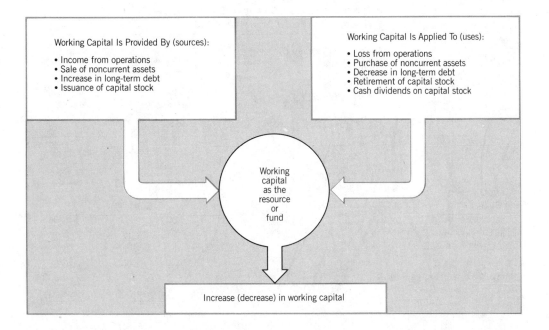

Working Capital Is Provided By (sources):

- Income from operations
- Sale of noncurrent assets
- Increase in long-term debt
- Issuance of capital stock

Working Capital Is Applied To (uses):

- Loss from operations
- Purchase of noncurrent assets
- Decrease in long-term debt
- Retirement of capital stock
- Cash dividends on capital stock

Working capital as the resource or fund

Increase (decrease) in working capital

## ILLUSTRATIONS OF WORKING CAPITAL APPROACH

### First Illustration

To illustrate the preparation of a statement of changes in financial position, let us assume a very simple situation. The comparative account balances and the differences in account balances for Potter, Inc. are:

|  | Dec. 31, 1984 | Dec. 31, 1983 | Differences Dr. | Differences Cr. |
|---|---|---|---|---|
| Cash | $15,000 | $10,000 | $ 5,000 | |
| Accounts receivable | 65,000 | 80,000 | | $15,000 |
|  | $80,000 | $90,000 | | |
|  |  |  |  | |
| Accounts payable | $ 4,000 | $20,000 | 16,000 | |
| Common stock | 50,000 | 50,000 | | |
| Retained earnings | 26,000 | 20,000 | | 6,000 |
|  | $80,000 | $90,000 | $21,000 | $21,000 |

Potter, Inc.

Assume that no dividends were declared or paid during the year and that the net income for the year was $6,000.

Presented below is a statement of changes in financial position and a supporting schedule of working capital changes, prepared from the information presented above.

Potter, Inc.
STATEMENT OF CHANGES IN FINANCIAL POSITION
For the Year Ended December 31, 1984

| Resources provided by Operations | $6,000 |
|---|---|
| Resources applied to Increase in working capital | $6,000 |

SCHEDULE OF WORKING CAPITAL CHANGES

|  | Working Capital Change Increase | Working Capital Change Decrease |
|---|---|---|
| Current assets |  |  |
| Cash | $ 5,000 |  |
| Accounts receivable |  | $15,000 |
| Current liabilities |  |  |
| Accounts payable | 16,000 |  |
| Totals | 21,000 | 15,000 |
| Increase in working capital |  | 6,000 |
|  | $21,000 | $21,000 |

Net income for the year was $6,000, and the additional resources provided by that source were applied to increase working capital by that same amount. As shown in the comparative balance sheets, however, the total assets decreased $10,000 during the year. The schedule of working capital changes indicates that the decrease in current assets of $10,000 was more than offset by a decrease in accounts payable of $16,000; thus, the net result is an increase in working capital of $6,000. The profession requires that changes in the elements of working capital be analyzed in appropriate detail in a tabulation or schedule accompanying the statement or in the statement itself. This approach is mandatory because significant information often found in the **schedule of working capital changes** is not provided in the basic statement. To illustrate, assume that a company shifted its current assets from marketable securities into short-term receivables and that the assets involved were significant in relation to the total asset structure of the enterprise. This change in the composition of current assets should be described in the lower part of the statement of changes in financial position, or in supplemental information.

## Second Illustration

Net income usually must be adjusted to arrive at resources provided by operations because certain expenses do not decrease working capital and some items of revenue and gain do not increase working capital. Depreciation expense, for example, does not cause a decrease in working capital during the current period. To direct attention to the effect of depreciation on the preparation of this statement, the information presented below has been condensed somewhat and the schedule of working capital changes has been omitted.

| Information Processing, Inc. | | | | |
|---|---|---|---|---|
| Accounts | Dec. 31, 1984 | Dec. 31, 1983 | Differences Dr. | Cr. |
| Current assets | $ 25,000 | $ 20,000 | $5,000 | |
| Plant assets | 80,000 | 80,000 | | |
| | $105,000 | $100,000 | | |
| | | | | |
| Accumulated depreciation | $ 11,000 | $ 10,000 | | $1,000 |
| Current liabilities | 12,000 | 15,000 | 3,000 | |
| Common stock | 50,000 | 50,000 | | |
| Retained earnings | 32,000 | 25,000 | | 7,000 |
| | $105,000 | $100,000 | $8,000 | $8,000 |

Assume that no dividends were declared or paid during the year and that the net income for the year was $7,000. Examination of the columns for differences indicates that working capital increased $8,000 during the year as evidenced by an increase of $5,000 in current assets and a decrease of $3,000 in current liabilities. Where did this $8,000 increase in working capital come from? The other two items appearing in the differences columns above are $7,000 of net income for the year and a $1,000 increase in the accumulated depreciation; these two items total $8,000. The recording of depreciation, however, did not provide resources. A more accurate statement is that **the charge for depreciation**

**expense that reduced net income did not require any current expenditure during the period.**
Therefore, net income must be adjusted for such noncash or nonworking capital charges in
order to disclose the total cash or working capital provided by operations. Total working
capital provided by operations is $8,000. The statement below reports this information.

| Information Processing, Inc. STATEMENT OF CHANGES IN FINANCIAL POSITION For the Year Ended December 31, 1984 | |
|---|---:|
| Resources provided by | |
| Operations: | |
| Net income for the year | $7,000 |
| Add (or deduct) item not affecting working capital | |
| Depreciation on plant assets | 1,000 |
| | $8,000 |
| Resources applied to | |
| Increase in working capital | $8,000 |

The statement usually begins with net income or loss and adds back or deducts items
that did not use or provide working capital during the period. Items added or deducted in
accordance with this procedure are not sources or uses of working capital, and the related
caption should make that clear. An acceptable alternative that produces the same result is
to start with total revenue that provided working capital and deduct operating costs and
expenses that required the outlay of working capital during the period. In either case, the
final amount should be appropriately described as resources provided by operations.

Other charges to expense for the period that do not require the use of working capital
may be treated in the same manner as depreciation. Bond discount amortized, amortization
of patents or goodwill, and changes in deferred income taxes are examples of such charges
that are illustrated later in this chapter.

## Third Illustration

The preceding two illustrations were made very simple to illustrate specific points. A more
comprehensive example follows:

| | Doral, Inc. | | | |
|---|---|---|---|---|
| | | | Differences | |
| Accounts | Dec. 31, 1984 | Dec. 31, 1983 | Dr. | Cr. |
| Cash | $ 4,600 | $ 3,000 | $ 1,600 | |
| Accounts receivable (net) | 11,300 | 15,000 | | $ 3,700 |
| Inventories | 11,500 | 25,000 | | 13,500 |
| Prepaid expenses | 1,200 | 1,000 | 200 | |
| Land | 34,000 | 40,000 | | 6,000 |
| Equipment | 95,000 | 60,000 | 35,000 | |
| | $157,600 | $144,000 | | |

| | | | | |
|---|---|---|---|---|
| Accumulated depreciation—equipment | $ 23,000 | $ 20,000 | | $ 3,000 |
| Accounts payable | 4,000 | 10,000 | 6,000 | |
| Dividends payable | 5,500 | 5,000 | | 500 |
| Bonds payable (long-term) | 13,500 | 6,000 | | 7,500 |
| Common stock | 80,000 | 80,000 | | |
| Retained earnings | 31,600 | 23,000 | | 8,600 |
| | $157,600 | $144,000 | $42,800 | $42,800 |

Additional information concerning some of the differences:

1. Land carried at $6,000 was sold for $7,000 during the year; the gain of $1,000 was not considered an extraordinary item.

2. Equipment costing $40,000 was purchased during the year; equipment with a cost of $5,000 was sold at its book value of $1,500. Depreciation expense for the year was $6,500.

3. Bonds payable in the amount of $7,500 were issued for cash.

4. Net income for the year was $19,600; cash dividends of $11,000 were declared.

In preparing a statement of changes in financial position, a work sheet, described later, could be used, although it is possible to prepare the statement without using one. To prepare the statement without the use of a work sheet, it is necessary to analyze the differences that occur in the accounts from one period to the next.

The starting point in the development of the statement of changes in financial position is computation of the working capital change. The working capital change is computed as shown below.

Doral, Inc.
SCHEDULE OF WORKING CAPITAL CHANGES
For the Year Ended December 31, 1984

| | Working Capital Change | |
|---|---|---|
| Current Assets | Increase | Decrease |
| Increase in cash | $ 1,600 | |
| Decrease in accounts receivable (net) | | $ 3,700 |
| Decrease in inventories | | 13,500 |
| Increase in prepaid expenses | 200 | |
| Current Liabilities | | |
| Decrease in accounts payable | 6,000 | |
| Increase in dividends payable | | 500 |
| | 7,800 | 17,700 |
| Decrease in working capital | 9,900 | |
| | $17,700 | $17,700 |

The schedule of working capital changes shown above is somewhat different from the one used in the first illustration on page 1076. The repetition of the words "increase" or "decrease" in the left-hand margin may be monotonous in this example, but it provides another example of how this schedule might be shown. This format should be used for problem material unless another approach is specifically requested.

After the change in working capital is computed, an analysis of the nonworking capital accounts is performed. **An analysis of the retained earnings account is a good starting point** because the net income is the first item reported on a statement of changes in financial position. Then the noncurrent assets, liabilities, and other stockholders' equity accounts should be analyzed.

**Increase in Retained Earnings**   Retained earnings increased $8,600 for Doral, Inc. as a result of net income of $19,600 less cash dividends of $11,000. The net income amount would be reported as follows:

| | |
|---|---|
| Resources provided by<br>  Operations:<br>    Net income | $19,600 |

The cash dividends are reported as a use of resources as follows:

| | |
|---|---|
| Resources applied to<br>  Cash dividends | $11,000 |

The appropriate time to indicate that resources are applied is at the time the cash dividend is declared. At the declaration date, the equity of the stockholders is decreased and a current obligation of the same amount is established. The subsequent payment of the dividend to the stockholders has no effect on working capital because the current liability and cash are reduced by the same amount.

**Decrease in Land**   The decrease in the balance of the land account from the beginning to the end of the year is $6,000. The resources provided by the sale of the land are $7,000; the gain of $1,000 is included in net income for the year. On the statement of changes in financial position, the following information is reported:

| | |
|---|---|
| Resources provided by<br>  Sale of land | $7,000 |

The total proceeds from the sale of the land is reported as resources provided by sale of land. Note that the $1,000 gain on sale of the land is included in net income. This gain of $1,000 must be deducted from net income when computing working capital provided by operations to avoid double counting.

**Equipment and Related Depreciation**   Equipment costing $40,000 was purchased during the year; this purchase would be reported as follows:

| | |
|---|---|
| Resources applied to<br>  Purchase of equipment | $40,000 |

In addition, equipment costing $5,000 was sold at its book value of $1,500. This transaction would be reported as follows:

| | |
|---|---|
| Resources provided by<br>    Sale of equipment | $1,500 |

Depreciation expense for the year is $6,500 and would be reported as an item added back to net income to show working capital provided by operations. The difference of $3,000 in the Accumulated Depreciation—Equipment account is the net result of the increase of $6,500 from 1984 depreciation expense and the decrease of $3,500 from the sale of equipment.

**Issuance of Bonds Payable**   Bonds in the amount of $7,500 were issued during the year. This transaction would be reported as follows:

| | |
|---|---|
| Resources provided by<br>    Issuance of bonds payable | $7,500 |

**Completed Statement—Third Illustration**   Combining the foregoing items that were illustrated separately, a complete statement of changes in financial position would be presented as shown on page 1082.

## SOURCES OF INFORMATION FOR STATEMENT

Listed below are important points to remember in the preparation of the statement of changes in financial position.

1. Comparative balance sheets provide the basic information from which the report is prepared. Additional information obtained from analyses of specific accounts is also included.

2. The increase or decrease in working capital (current assets less current liabilities) is shown in one amount in the statement. As this is sometimes the most significant item in the report, increases or decreases in the individual items comprising working capital are shown in a separate (supporting) schedule of changes in working capital, or included in the body of the statement, as illustrated later in this chapter.

3. Both increases and decreases of plant assets, investments, long-term debt, and contributed capital stock are shown in the statement. This requires supplementary information obtained by analysis of related accounts.

4. An analysis of the Retained Earnings account is necessary to derive data relative to resources provided and applied. The net increase or decrease in Retained Earnings without any explanation is a meaningless amount in the statement, because it might represent the effect of net income, dividends declared, appropriations of retained earnings, and "prior period" adjustments.

5. The statement includes all changes that have passed through working capital or have resulted in an increase or decrease in working capital and in addition, some significant financial transactions discussed later.

6. Write-downs, amortization charges, and similar "book" entries, such as depreciation of plant assets, are considered as neither sources nor applications of resources, because they have no

effect on working capital. To the extent that they have entered into the determination of net income, however, they must be added back to or subtracted from net income to arrive at working capital provided by operations.

| Doral, Inc. STATEMENT OF CHANGES IN FINANCIAL POSITION For the Year Ended December 31, 1984 | | |
|---|---|---|
| Resources provided by | | |
| Operations: | | |
| Net income | | $19,600 |
| Add or (deduct) items not affecting working capital | | |
| Gain on sale of land | $(1,000) | |
| Depreciation expense | 6,500 | 5,500 |
| Working capital provided by operations | | 25,100 |
| Sale of land | | 7,000 |
| Sale of equipment | | 1,500 |
| Issuance of bonds payable | | 7,500 |
| Total resources provided | | 41,100 |
| Resources applied to | | |
| Cash dividends | 11,000 | |
| Purchase of equipment | 40,000 | |
| Total resources applied | | 51,000 |
| Decrease in working capital | | $ 9,900 |

SCHEDULE OF WORKING CAPITAL CHANGES

| | Working Capital Change | |
|---|---|---|
| Current Assets | Increase | Decrease |
| Increase in cash | $ 1,600 | |
| Decrease in accounts receivable (net) | | $ 3,700 |
| Decrease in inventories | | 13,500 |
| Increase in prepaid expenses | 200 | |
| Current Liabilities | | |
| Decrease in accounts payable | 6,000 | |
| Increase in dividends payable | | 500 |
| | 7,800 | 17,700 |
| Decrease in working capital | 9,900 | |
| | $17,700 | $17,700 |

# SPECIAL PROBLEMS IN STATEMENT ANALYSIS

Some of the special problems related to preparing the statement of changes in financial position were discussed in connection with the preceding illustrations. Other problems that arise with some frequency in the preparation of this statement may be categorized as follows:

1. Adjustments similar to depreciation.
2. Nonworking capital (all financial resources) transactions.
3. Extraordinary items.
4. Net losses.
5. Reclassification of current and noncurrent items.

## Adjustments Similar to Depreciation

Depreciation expense is the adjustment to net income that is made most commonly to arrive at working capital provided by operations. But there are numerous other expense or revenue items that do not affect working capital. Examples of expense items that must be added back to net income are the **amortization of intangible assets** such as goodwill and patents, and the **amortization of deferred charges** such as bond issue costs. These charges to expense involve expenditures made in prior periods that are being amortized currently and reduce net income without affecting working capital in the current period. Also, **amortization of bond discount or premium** on long-term bonds payable affects the amount of interest expense, but neither affects working capital. As a result, amortization of these items should be added back to or subtracted from net income to arrive at working capital provided from operations.

In similar manner, **changes in deferred income taxes and deferred investment credit** accounts affect net income but have no effect on working capital. For example, Martin Marietta Corporation recently experienced an increase in its liability for deferred taxes of approximately $26,000,000. Tax expense was increased and net income was decreased by this amount, but working capital was not affected; therefore, $26,000,000 was added back to net income. Conversely, Outboard Marine Corporation recently had a decrease in its liability for deferred taxes of $3,890,000 and subtracted this amount from net income to arrive at working capital provided from operations.

**A change related to an investment in common stock** when the income or loss is accrued under the equity method is another common adjustment to net income. For example, Johns-Manville Corporation's equity in earnings of foreign subsidiaries recently increased by approximately 127 million dollars. Such an increase, however, is not represented by a working capital flow, so it was deducted from net income to arrive at working capital provided by operations. Similarly, Dictaphone Corporation's equity in the net losses of its foreign subsidiaries was $132,000, and this amount was added back to net income. If the company receives a dividend from its equity investee, resources provided from a cash dividend should be reported.

The diagram at the top of page 1084 illustrates the common types of adjustments that are made to net income to arrive at working capital provided by operations.

Some current asset adjustments such as the allocation of prepaid expenses are similar to depreciation in that they involve an allocation to expense during the current period but represent an expenditure made in a prior period. They are treated differently in the statement, however, because prepaid expenses are part of working capital, and the net increase or decrease in working capital is reported in the statement in one amount, whereas changes in long-term assets are shown separately.

The same holds true for any other charge or credit that might occur in the current asset or current liability section. For example, an increase in the allowance for doubtful accounts is a part of the computation of an increase or decrease in working capital without adjustment or special treatment. Similarly, a decrease in a current liability such as unearned revenue would be shown in the schedule of working capital changes but not as a separate adjustment to net income to arrive at working capital provided by operations.

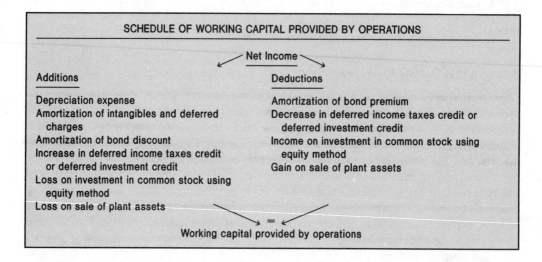

## Nonworking Capital Transactions

Up to now, we have concentrated on those items that flow through, or effect a change in, working capital. Under the all financial resources concept, the statement of changes in financial position must also include nonworking capital transactions that are considered significant financing and investing activities of an enterprise.

**Nonworking Capital Transactions Reported** The types of nonworking capital transactions that are commonly reported in the statement of changes in financial position are: (1) the issuance of long-term debt or equity securities to purchase noncurrent assets; (2) the conversion of long-term debt or preferred stock to common stock; (3) the acquisition of long-term assets through gift or donation or the forgiveness of a long-term obligation; and (4) the retirement of debt through a sinking fund classified as long-term. To illustrate, assume that Posture Furniture Company acquired a $200,000 warehouse in exchange for a long-term $200,000 mortgage note on the property. This transaction does not affect cash or working capital but it has a significant impact on resources and would be reported in the statement of changes in financial position as follows:

| | |
|---|---|
| Resources provided by<br>    Issuance of mortgage note for building | $200,000 |
| Resources applied to<br>    Purchase of building in exchange for long-term note | $200,000 |

For another illustration, assume that Houston, Inc. converted bonds having a par and book value of $50,000 for 50,000 shares of common stock ($1 par). In a statement of changes in financial position, this information would be reported as shown on page 1085.

| Resources provided by | |
|---|---|
| Issuance of common stock for retirement of debt | $50,000 |
| Resources applied to | |
| Retirement of debt through issuance of common stock | $50,000 |

This transaction resulted in the issuance of additional common stock and the retirement of long-term debt with no effect upon working capital or cash.

**Nonworking Capital Transactions Not Reported**   Certain financial transactions that affect only nonworking capital accounts do not require reporting in the statement of changes in financial position because they do not provide or use resources. Examples of these types of transactions are **stock dividends, stock splits, and appropriations of retained earnings.** To illustrate, when a corporation declares a dividend distributable in **stock** instead of in **cash,** a transfer from Retained Earnings to Capital Stock and to Additional Paid-in Capital is usually made. This type of dividend should not be disclosed in the statement of changes in financial position, because no change has occurred either in the amount or in the composition of stockholders' equity that has an effect on the resources of the enterprise.

Similarly, stock splits and appropriations of retained earnings do not represent either resources provided or resources applied; therefore, they should not be reported in a statement of changes in financial position.

## Extraordinary Items

The statement of changes in financial position ordinarily begins with net income. Whenever extraordinary gains or losses are involved, the statement starts with income before extraordinary items. To this amount are added back or deducted items recognized in determining income or loss that did not use or provide working capital. These items should be subtotaled and appropriately labeled "working capital provided by operations for the year, exclusive of extraordinary item." This subtotal should be followed by the extraordinary item.

To illustrate, assume that Tandem Bike Company reported net income of $39,000, which included an extraordinary gain of $9,000 (net of $3,000 tax) resulting from the sale of their only investment in equity securities (book value $16,000). Depreciation expense was $4,000 for the period. In the statement of changes in financial position the following information would be reported:

| Tandem Bike Company<br>PARTIAL STATEMENT OF CHANGES IN FINANCIAL POSITION | |
|---|---|
| Resources provided by | |
| Operations: | |
| Income before extraordinary item | $30,000 |
| Add (or deduct) items not affecting working capital | |
| Depreciation expense | 4,000 |
| Working capital provided by operations, exclusive of extraordinary item | 34,000 |
| Extraordinary item—gain on sale of investment (net of $3,000 tax) | 9,000 |
| | 43,000 |
| Book value of investment sold | 16,000 |

Note that the extraordinary gain of $9,000 (net of $3,000 tax) is shown in a separate section as an extraordinary item. The book value of the investment ($16,000) is shown as an additional source to arrive at a total resources provided by sale of investment of $25,000.

Some accountants consider this type of presentation cumbersome. In practice the extraordinary gain and the proceeds of sale are often shown as one source item after "working capital provided by operations, exclusive of extraordinary item," as reported below:

| | |
|---|---|
| **Tandem Bike Company** | |
| **PARTIAL STATEMENT OF CHANGES IN FINANCIAL POSITION** | |
| Resources provided by | |
| Operations: | |
| Income before extraordinary item | $30,000 |
| Add (or deduct) items not affecting working capital | |
| Depreciation expense | 4,000 |
| Working capital provided by operations, exclusive of extraordinary item | 34,000 |
| Extraordinary item—sale of investment, including | |
| extraordinary gain of $9,000 (net of $3,000 tax) | 25,000 |

In the latter illustration, the entire transaction is reported in one section of the statement. Because of its simplicity and ease of understanding, **this format should be used for problem material for both gains and losses unless another approach is requested.** This format is also widely used in practice.

## Net Losses

If an enterprise reports a net loss instead of a net income, the net loss must be adjusted for those items that do not result in a working capital inflow or outflow. The presentation in the statement of changes in financial position differs depending on whether the net loss after adjusting for the charges or credits not affecting working capital results in negative or positive working capital from operations. For example, if the net loss was $50,000 and the total amount of charges to be added back was $60,000, then resources are provided by operations in the amount of $10,000, as shown in the computation below:

| COMPUTATION OF WORKING CAPITAL **PROVIDED** BY OPERATIONS | | |
|---|---|---|
| Net loss | | $(50,000) |
| Add (or deduct) items not affecting working capital | | |
| Depreciation of plant assets | $55,000 | |
| Amortization of patents | 5,000 | 60,000 |
| Working capital provided by operations | | $ 10,000 |

A presentation similar to the one above would appear in the resources **provided** section of the statement of changes in financial position. If the company experienced a net loss of $80,000 and the total amount of the charges to be added back is $25,000, the presentation might appear in the resources **applied** section as illustrated on page 1087.

| COMPUTATION OF WORKING CAPITAL **APPLIED** TO OPERATIONS | |
|---|---|
| Net loss | $(80,000) |
| Add (or deduct) items not affecting working capital | |
| Depreciation of plant assets | 25,000 |
| Working capital applied to operations | ($55,000) |

Alternatively, the negative $55,000 is often reported in the resources provided section. This approach is illustrated on page 1099 and should be used for homework assignments.

### Reclassifications

A change that sometimes occurs in the long-term liability section is the reclassification of a part of the long-term debt obligation to the current liability section. In this situation, the transfer should be examined to determine its effect on working capital. Because a decrease in working capital occurs, working capital is considered to have been applied to retire long-term debt. For example, United Merchants and Manufacturers at one time reported in their resources applied section approximately $10 million related to the reclassification of a long-term debt to a short-term obligation. In such cases, resources are considered applied to the retirement of long-term debt in the amount of $10 million. Similarly, if a long-term asset such as a sinking fund investment is transferred from long-term assets to short-term assets, working capital is considered to have been provided. The same principle would apply if marketable securities were reclassified from noncurrent to current assets. If a current asset such as a receivable is reclassified as long-term, resources are applied because working capital has decreased.

## COMPREHENSIVE ILLUSTRATION—USE OF A WORK SHEET

If numerous adjustments are necessary or if other complicating factors are present, many accountants prefer to use a work sheet to assemble and classify the data that will appear on the statement of changes in financial position. The work sheet is merely a device to aid in the preparation of the statement; its use is not required. The use of T-accounts or even the use of supplementary computations will often serve as suitable substitutes, and they may prove less time-consuming to anyone experienced in preparing such statements. The T-account approach is illustrated in the appendix to this chapter.

A work sheet for Hanes Corporation is presented on page 1095. **The important items to note as you study the illustration are:**

1. A working capital summary account is prepared to identify the working capital balance at both the beginning and the end of the year. (See the first item in the debits section of the work sheet.) A major purpose of the work sheet is to identify and organize the changes in working capital.

2. The other (nonworking capital) account balances listed on the work sheet are separated into those with debit balances and those with credit balances. The first column (far left) contains the beginning of the year balances and the last column (far right) contains the end of the year balances. The transactions that effected the changes in these accounts during the period are the reconciling items that appear between these two columns.

3. The transactions for the current year are then examined to determine whether they affected resources provided or applied. After the transactions are analyzed and entered in the work sheet, all the differences between the beginning and ending balances should be reconciled.

4. The adjustments shown on the work sheet are not entered in any journal or posted to any account. They are not adjustments to correct accounts; they are merely adjustments for this work sheet to facilitate the preparation of a statement of changes in financial position. The totals of the reconciling transaction debit and credit columns should balance.

5. The bottom portion of the work sheet provides the information necessary to prepare the formal statement of changes in financial position (excluding the analysis of the changes in working capital).

To illustrate procedures for preparation of the work sheet, the financial statements and other data related to the Hanes Corporation are presented with the balance sheet shown below, the statement of income and retained earnings on page 1089, and the schedule of

|  | 1984 | 1983 | Difference Incr. or Decr. |
|---|---|---|---|
| **Hanes Corporation** **COMPARATIVE BALANCE SHEET** **December 31, 1984 and 1983** | | | |
| **Assets** | | | |
| Cash | $ 59,000 | $ 66,000 | 7,000 Decr. |
| Accounts receivable (net) | 104,000 | 51,000 | 53,000 Incr. |
| Inventories | 493,000 | 341,000 | 152,000 Incr. |
| Prepaid expenses | 16,500 | 17,000 | 500 Decr. |
| Investments in stock of Porter Co. | | | |
| (equity method) | 18,500 | 15,000 | 3,500 Incr. |
| Land | 131,500 | 82,000 | 49,500 Incr. |
| Equipment | 187,000 | 142,000 | 45,000 Incr. |
| Accumulated depreciation—equipment | (29,000) | (31,000) | 2,000 Decr. |
| Buildings | 262,000 | 262,000 | — |
| Accumulated depreciation—buildings | (74,100) | (71,000) | 3,100 Incr. |
| Goodwill | 7,600 | 10,000 | 2,400 Decr. |
| Total Assets | $1,176,000 | $884,000 | |
| **Liabilities** | | | |
| Accounts payable | $ 132,000 | $131,000 | 1,000 Incr. |
| Accrued liabilities | 40,500 | 38,000 | 2,500 Incr. |
| Dividends payable | 2,500 | 1,000 | 1,500 Incr. |
| Income taxes payable | 3,000 | 16,000 | 13,000 Decr. |
| Notes payable (long-term) | 60,000 | — | 60,000 Incr. |
| Bonds payable | 100,000 | 100,000 | — |
| Premium on bonds payable | 7,000 | 8,000 | 1,000 Decr. |
| Deferred income taxes (long-term) | 9,000 | 6,000 | 3,000 Incr. |
| Total Liabilities | 354,000 | 300,000 | |
| **Stockholders' Equity** | | | |
| Common stock ($1.00 par) | 60,000 | 50,000 | 10,000 Incr. |
| Additional paid-in capital | 187,000 | 38,000 | 149,000 Incr. |
| Retained earnings | 592,000 | 496,000 | 96,000 Incr. |
| Treasury stock | (17,000) | — | 17,000 Incr. |
| Total stockholders' equity | 822,000 | 584,000 | |
| Total Liabilities and Stockholders' Equity | $1,176,000 | $884,000 | |

working capital changes on page 1090. Additional explanations related to preparation of the work sheet are provided throughout the discussion presented on pages 1091–1094.

---

### Hanes Corporation
### COMBINED STATEMENT OF INCOME AND RETAINED EARNINGS
### For the Year Ended 1984

| | |
|---|---:|
| Net sales | $524,500 |
| Other income | 3,500 |
| Total revenues | 528,000 |
| Expense | |
| Cost of goods sold | 310,000 |
| Selling and administrative expense | 47,000 |
| Other expense and losses | 12,000 |
| Total expenses | 369,000 |
| Income before income tax and extraordinary item | 159,000 |
| Income Tax | |
| Current | 47,000 |
| Deferred | 3,000 |
| Income before extraordinary item | 109,000 |
| Gain on condemnation of land (net of $2,500 tax) | 8,000 |
| Net income | 117,000 |
| Retained earnings, January 1 | 496,000 |
| Less: | |
| Cash dividends | 6,000 |
| Stock dividend | 15,000 |
| Retained earnings, December 31 | $592,000 |
| Per Share: | |
| Income before extraordinary items | $1.98 |
| Extraordinary item | .15 |
| Net income | $2.13 |

### Additional Information

(a) Other income of $3,500, represents Hanes Corporation's equity share in the net income of Porter Company, an equity investee. Hanes Corporation owns 22% of Porter Company.

(b) Land in the amount of $60,000 was purchased through the issuance of a long-term note; in addition, certain parcels of land were condemned, resulting in an $8,000 gain, net of $2,500 tax.

(c) An analysis of the equipment account and related accumulated depreciation indicates the following:

| | Equipment Dr./(Cr.) | Accum. Dep. Dr./(Cr.) | Gain or Loss |
|---|---:|---:|---:|
| Balance at end of 1983 | $142,000 | $(31,000) | |
| Purchases of equipment | 53,000 | | |
| Sale of equipment | (8,000) | 2,500 | 1,500L |
| Depreciation for the period | | (11,500) | |
| Major repair charged to accumulated depreciation | | 11,000 | |
| Balance at end of 1984 | $187,000 | $(29,000) | |

(d) The change in the accumulated depreciation—building, goodwill, premium on bonds payable, and deferred income tax accounts resulted from depreciation and amortization entries.

(e) An analysis of the paid-in capital accounts in stockholders' equity discloses the following:

| | Common Stock | Additional Paid-In Capital |
|---|---|---|
| Balance at end of 1983 | $50,000 | $ 38,000 |
| Issuance of 2% stock dividend | 1,000 | 14,000 |
| Sale of stock for cash | 9,000 | 135,000 |
| Balance at end of 1984 | $60,000 | $187,000 |

**Hanes Corporation**
**SCHEDULE OF WORKING CAPITAL CHANGES**
**For the Year Ended 1984**

| | Working Capital Change | |
|---|---|---|
| Current Assets | Increase | Decrease |
| Decrease in cash | | $ 7,000 |
| Increase in accounts receivable (net) | $ 53,000 | |
| Increase in inventories | 152,000 | |
| Decrease in prepaid expenses | | 500 |
| Current Liabilities | | |
| Increase in accounts payable | | 1,000 |
| Increase in accrued liabilities | | 2,500 |
| Increase in dividends payable | | 1,500 |
| Decrease in income taxes payable | 13,000 | |
| Totals | 218,000 | 12,500 |
| Increase in working capital | | 205,500 |
| | $218,000 | $218,000 |

## Analysis of Working Capital Changes

As indicated earlier, the first step in the preparation of a statement of changes in financial position is to compute the increase or decrease in working capital for the year. The schedule of working capital changes for Hanes Corporation is presented above. A major purpose of the statement of changes in financial position is to report the investing and financing activities that caused this increase in working capital of $205,500.

If a work sheet is employed, the beginning and ending balances of working capital are determined and entered on the work sheet. To illustrate, Hanes Corporation has $289,000 of working capital at the beginning of 1984 and $494,500 at the end of 1984 (as computed from the current items on the comparative balance sheet on page 1088). These two working capital amounts ($289,000 and $494,500) should be entered at the top of the work sheet as illustrated on page 1095.

## Analysis of Work Sheet Transactions

The following discussion (from page 1091 through page 1094) provides an explanation of the individual adjustments that appear on the work sheet on page 1095.

**Change in Retained Earnings**   Net income for the period is comprised of "income before extraordinary item" and an "extraordinary gain." Income before the extraordinary item is $109,000 and the extraordinary gain is $8,000 (net of $2,500 tax) from condemnation of land that has a book value of $10,500. The entry on the work sheet for certain items affecting retained earnings would be as follows:

(1)

| | | |
|---|---|---|
| Resources Provided by Income before Extraordinary Item | 109,000 | |
| Resources Provided by Condemnation of Land (Gain) | 8,000 | |
|     Retained Earnings | | 117,000 |

The resources provided by income before extraordinary item is reported at the bottom of the work sheet and is the starting point for preparation of the statement of changes in financial position. The resources provided by the condemnation of the land, gain of $8,000 (net of $2,500 tax), is entered separately at the bottom of the work sheet as a resource provided item. The book value ($10,500) part of this extraordinary item transaction is handled separately in preparing the work sheet.

Retained earnings was also affected by a stock dividend and a cash dividend. The retained earnings statement reports a stock dividend of $15,000. The work sheet entry for this transaction is as follows:

(2)

| | | |
|---|---|---|
| Retained Earnings | 15,000 | |
|     Common Stock | | 1,000 |
|     Additional Paid-in Capital | | 14,000 |

The issuance of stock dividends is not considered to be either resources provided or resources applied; therefore, although this transaction is entered on the work sheet for reconciling purposes, it is not reported in the statement of changes.

The cash dividend of $6,000 requires the use of resources and is recorded in the work sheet by the following entry:

(3)

| | | |
|---|---|---|
| Retained Earnings | 6,000 | |
|     Resources Applied to Cash Dividends | | 6,000 |

The beginning and ending balances of retained earnings are reconciled by the entry of the three items above.

**Investment in Stock of Porter Co.**   The investment in the stock of Porter Co. increased $3,500, which reflects Hanes Corporation's share of the income earned by its equity investee during the current year. Although revenue, and therefore income per the income statement, was increased $3,500 by the accounting entry that recorded Hanes' share of Porter Co.'s net income, no working capital or resources were provided. The following work sheet entry is made:

(4)

| | | |
|---|---|---|
| Investment in Stock of Porter Co. | 3,500 | |
|     Income before Extraordinary Item— | | |
|         Equity in Earnings of Porter Co. | | 3,500 |

**Land**   Land in the amount of $60,000 was purchased through the issuance of a long-term note payable. Although this transaction did not affect working capital, it is considered a significant financial resource transaction that should be reported because both resources provided and resources applied are affected. Two entries are necessary to record this transaction on the work sheet.

(5)

| | | |
|---|---|---|
| Land | 60,000 | |
|   Resources Applied to Purchase of Land— | | |
|     Issuance of Long-term Note | | 60,000 |
| | | |
| Resources Provided by Issuance of Long-term Note— | | |
|   Purchase of Land | 60,000 | |
|     Note Payable | | 60,000 |

In addition to the all financial resources transactions involving the issuance of a note to purchase land, the land account was decreased by the condemnation proceedings. The work sheet entry to record the book value portion of this transaction is as follows:

(6)

| | | |
|---|---|---|
| Resources Provided by Condemnation of Land (Book Value) | 10,500 | |
|   Land | | 10,500 |

The $10,500 of resources provided by condemnation plus the $8,000 gain recorded earlier constitute the total resources of $18,500 related to the condemnation. The land account balances are now reconciled.

**Equipment and Accumulated Depreciation**   An analysis of the equipment account and its related accumulated depreciation account shows that a number of financial transactions have affected these accounts. Equipment in the amount of $53,000 was purchased during the year. The entry to record this transaction on the work sheet is as follows:

(7)

| | | |
|---|---|---|
| Equipment | 53,000 | |
|   Resources Applied to the Purchase of Equipment | | 53,000 |

In addition, equipment with a book value of $5,500 was sold at a loss of $1,500. The entry to record this transaction on the work sheet is as follows:

(8)

| | | |
|---|---|---|
| Resources Provided by Sale of Equipment | 4,000 | |
| Income before Extraordinary Item—Loss on | | |
|   Sale of Equipment | 1,500 | |
| Accumulated Depreciation—Equipment | 2,500 | |
|   Equipment | | 8,000 |

The proceeds from the sale of the equipment provide working capital of $4,000. In addition, the loss on the sale of the equipment has reduced the income before extraordinary item, but has not affected working capital; therefore, it must be added back to income before extraordinary item to report accurately working capital provided by operations.

Depreciation on the equipment was reported at $11,500 and should be presented on the work sheet in the following manner:

(9)

| | | |
|---|---|---|
| Income before Extraordinary Item— | | |
|   Depreciation Expense | 11,500 | |
|     Accumulated Depreciation—Equipment | | 11,500 |

The depreciation expense is added back to the income before extraordinary item because it reduced income but did not affect working capital.

Finally, a major repair to the equipment in the amount of $11,000 was charged to Accumulated Depreciation—Equipment. Because this expenditure required working capital, the following work sheet entry is made:

**(10)**

| | | |
|---|---|---|
| Accumulated Depreciation—Equipment | 11,000 | |
|   Resources Applied to Major Repairs of Equipment | | 11,000 |

The balances in the equipment and related accumulated depreciation accounts are reconciled after adjustment for the foregoing items.

**Other Nonworking Capital Charges or Credits** An analysis of the remaining accounts indicates that changes in the Accumulated Depreciation—Building, Goodwill, Premium on Bonds Payable, and Deferred Income Taxes balances resulted from charges or credits not affecting working capital. The following compound entry to the work sheet could be made for these nonworking capital, income-related items:

**(11)**

| | | |
|---|---|---|
| Income before Extraordinary Item—Depreciation Expense | 3,100 | |
| Income before Extraordinary Item—Amortization of Goodwill | 2,400 | |
| Income before Extraordinary Item—Deferred Income Taxes | 3,000 | |
| Premium on Bonds Payable | 1,000 | |
|   Accumulated Depreciation—Buildings | | 3,100 |
|   Goodwill | | 2,400 |
|   Deferred Income Taxes | | 3,000 |
|   Income before Extraordinary Item— | | |
|     Bond Premium Amortization | | 1,000 |

**Common Stock and Related Accounts** A comparison of the common stock balances and the additional paid-in capital balances shows that transactions during the year affected these accounts. First, a stock dividend of 2% was issued to stockholders. As indicated in the discussion of work sheet entry (2), no resources were provided or applied by the stock dividend transaction. In addition to the shares issued via the stock dividend, the Hanes Corporation sold shares of common stock at $16 per share. The work sheet entry to record this transaction is as follows:

**(12)**

| | | |
|---|---|---|
| Resources Provided by Sale of Common Stock | 144,000 | |
|   Common Stock | | 9,000 |
|   Additional Paid-in Capital | | 135,000 |

Also, the company purchased shares of its common stock in the amount of $17,000. The work sheet entry to record this transaction is as follows:

**(13)**

| | | |
|---|---|---|
| Treasury Stock | 17,000 | |
|   Resources Applied to Purchase of Treasury Stock | | 17,000 |

**Final Summary Entry** The final entry to reconcile the change in working capital and to balance the work sheet is shown on page 1094.

**(14)**

| | | |
|---|---|---|
| Working Capital Summary | 205,500 | |
| Increase in Working Capital | | 205,500 |

The $205,500 amount is the difference between the beginning of the year and the end of the year working capital balance. That amount also appears on the schedule of working capital changes on page 1090.

Once it has been determined that the differences between the beginning and ending balances per the work sheet columns have been accounted for, the reconciling transactions columns can be totaled, and they should balance. The statement of changes in financial position can be prepared entirely from the items and amounts that appear at the bottom of the work sheet in the form of "resources provided by" and "resources applied to." The difference between the resources provided and the resources applied should equal the change in working capital. This reconciliation provides evidence that the posting of the transactions during the period was performed accurately. However, the statement may still be incorrect if certain transactions were improperly analyzed.

## Preparation of Statement

Presented below is a formal statement of changes in financial position. The schedule of working capital changes that appears on page 1090 may be incorporated into the statement by showing it at the bottom, or as a separate schedule accompanying the statement.

| Hanes Corporation<br>STATEMENT OF CHANGES IN FINANCIAL POSITION<br>For the Year Ended December 31, 1984 | | |
|---|---|---|
| Resources provided by | | |
| Operations: | | |
| Income before extraordinary item | | $109,000 |
| Add (or deduct) items not affecting working capital | | |
| Equity in earnings of Porter Co. | $(3,500) | |
| Loss on sale of equipment | 1,500 | |
| Depreciation expense | 14,600 | |
| Amortization of goodwill | 2,400 | |
| Deferred income taxes | 3,000 | |
| Amortization of bond premium | (1,000) | 17,000 |
| Working capital provided by operations, exclusive of extraordinary item | | 126,000 |
| Extraordinary item—Condemnation of land, including extraordinary gain | | |
| of $8,000 (net of $2,500 tax) | | 18,500 |
| Issuance of note payable to purchase land | | 60,000 |
| Sale of equipment | | 4,000 |
| Sale of common stock | | 144,000 |
| Total resources provided | | 352,500 |
| Resources applied to | | |
| Cash dividends | 6,000 | |
| Purchase of land through issuance of note payable | 60,000 | |
| Purchase of equipment | 53,000 | |
| Major repairs of equipment | 11,000 | |
| Purchase of treasury stock | 17,000 | |
| Total resources applied | | 147,000 |
| Increase in working capital | | $205,500 |

Hanes Corporation
**WORK SHEET FOR PREPARATION OF STATEMENT OF CHANGES IN FINANCIAL POSITION**
For the Year Ended 1984

| | Balance 1/1/84 | Reconciling Items—1984 Debit | | Reconciling Items—1984 Credit | | Balance 12/31/84 |
|---|---|---|---|---|---|---|
| **Debits** | | | | | | |
| Working capital summary | $289,000 | (14) | 205,500 | | | $ 494,500 |
| Investments (equity method) | 15,000 | (4) | 3,500 | | | 18,500 |
| Land | 82,000 | (5) | 60,000 | (6) | 10,500 | 131,500 |
| Equipment | 142,000 | (7) | 53,000 | (8) | 8,000 | 187,000 |
| Buildings | 262,000 | | | | | 262,000 |
| Goodwill | 10,000 | | | (11) | 2,400 | 7,600 |
| Treasury stock | -0- | (13) | 17,000 | | | 17,000 |
| Total debits | $800,000 | | | | | $1,118,100 |
| **Credits** | | (8) | 2,500 | | | |
| Accum. depr.—equip. | $ 31,000 | (10) | 11,000 | (9) | 11,500 | 29,000 |
| Accum. depr.—bldgs. | 71,000 | | | (11) | 3,100 | 74,100 |
| Notes payable (long-term) | -0- | | | (5) | 60,000 | 60,000 |
| Bonds payable | 100,000 | | | | | 100,000 |
| Premium on bonds payable | 8,000 | (11) | 1,000 | | | 7,000 |
| Deferred income taxes | 6,000 | | | (11) | 3,000 | 9,000 |
| Common stock | 50,000 | | | (2) | 1,000 | |
| | | | | (12) | 9,000 | 60,000 |
| Additional paid-in capital | 38,000 | | | (2) | 14,000 | |
| | | | | (12) | 135,000 | 187,000 |
| Retained earnings | 496,000 | (2) | 15,000 | | | |
| | | (3) | 6,000 | (1) | 117,000 | 592,000 |
| Total credits | $800,000 | | $374,500 | | $374,500 | $1,118,100 |
| **Resources provided by Operations:** | | | | | | |
| Income before extraordinary item | | (1) | 109,000 | | | |
| Equity in earnings of Porter Co. | | | | (4) | 3,500 | Total |
| Loss on sale of equipment | | (8) | 1,500 | | | resources |
| Depr. exp.—equip. | | (9) | 11,500 | | | provided |
| Depr. exp.—bldgs. | | (11) | 3,100 | | | by |
| Amortization of goodwill | | (11) | 2,400 | | | operations |
| Deferred income taxes | | (11) | 3,000 | | | $126,000 |
| Amortization of bond premium | | | | (11) | 1,000 | |
| Condemnation of land (gain) | | (1) | 8,000 | | | |
| Condemnation of land (book value) | | (6) | 10,500 | | | |
| Issuance of note to purchase land | | (5) | 60,000 | | | |
| Sale of equipment | | (8) | 4,000 | | | |
| Sale of common stock | | (12) | 144,000 | | | |
| **Resources applied to** | | | | | | |
| Declaration of cash dividend | | | | (3) | 6,000 | |
| Purchase of land for note | | | | (5) | 60,000 | |
| Purchase of equipment | | | | (7) | 53,000 | |
| Major repairs of equipment | | | | (10) | 11,000 | |
| Purchase of treasury stock | | | | (13) | 17,000 | |
| Increase in working capital | | | | (14) | 205,500 | |
| | | | $357,000 | | $357,000 | |

The Tenneco Inc. financial statements on page 198 contain a comprehensive statement of changes in financial position prepared on a working capital basis.

# SECTION 2  CASH APPROACH

## APPEAL OF THE CASH BASIS APPROACH

The working capital format is the one most often used in preparing a statement of changes in financial position. The financial reporting environment, however, is changing dramatically in this area. For example, in a recently proposed concepts statement, the FASB tentatively indicated that meaningful components of cash flow are generally more useful than reporting changes in working capital. Furthermore, the Financial Executives Institute has recommended that companies use the cash (or cash and cash equivalent) approach instead of a working capital basis in preparing this statement. Also many practitioners and academics have recently argued for a more cash basis orientation to the statement of changes in financial position.[6] It is not surprising therefore that a recent survey reported that a number of companies are voluntarily changing to a cash basis, and it appears that many more will do so in the near future.

Why the sudden change in the financial reporting environment? One major reason is that investors and analysts are concerned that **accrual accounting has become too far removed from the underlying cash flows of the enterprise.** They contend that accountants are using too many arbitrary allocation devices (deferred taxes, depreciation, amortization of intangibles, accrual of revenues, etc.) and are therefore computing a net income figure that no longer provides an acceptable indicator of the earning power of the enterprise. Similarly, **because financial statements take no cognizance of the inflation besetting the economy today, many look for a more concrete standard like cash flow to evaluate operating success or failure.** In addition, others contend that the **working capital concept does not provide as useful information about liquidity and financial flexibility as does the cash approach.** For example, information on receivable and inventory financing is important; frequently receivable and inventory mismanagement leads to a lack of liquidity and other financial problems. The classic illustration of such a problem is W. T. Grant, which reported reasonable amounts of working capital being provided by operations but apparently too much of its working capital was tied up in receivables and inventories. A review of its cash flow from operations, however, would have shown the significant lack of liquidity and financial inflexibility that eventually caused the company's bankruptcy. Finally, a statement of changes in financial position emphasizing a cash basis approach is useful to management and short-term creditors in **assessing the enterprise's ability to meet cash operating needs.** As Walter Wriston, chairman of the board of Citibank, recently noted, "Well, assets give you a warm feeling, but they don't generate cash. The first question I would ask any

---

[6]For example, one writer has recommended that the statement of changes in financial position as currently prepared should be discontinued and replaced with three required statements: a statement of cash receipts and payments, a statement of financing activities, and a statement of investing activities. See Loyd C. Heath, *Accounting Research Monograph No. 3: Financial Reporting and the Evaluation of Solvency* (New York: AICPA, 1978).

borrower these days is, 'What is your breakeven cash flow?' That's the one thing we can't find out from your audit reports and it is the single most important question we ask."

If the emphasis is on a statement of changes in financial position employing a cash basis approach, **changes in the elements of working capital (e.g., receivables, inventories, and payables) constitute sources and uses of cash and should be disclosed in appropriate detail in the body of the statement.** This approach is different from the working capital approach, in which changes in working capital are reported separately in a tabulation accompanying the statement; the cash basis approach presents the cash provided by operations, not the working capital provided by operations.

## CHANGING FROM ACCRUAL TO CASH BASIS—INDIRECT APPROACH

Adaptation to a cash basis approach from a working capital approach is relatively simple. Each working capital item is adjusted to show its effect on the income figure as if a cash basis instead of an accrual basis of income determination were employed.

For example, if an increase in receivables has occurred this year, it must be deducted from working capital provided by operations to arrive at cash provided by operations. An increase in receivables increases working capital but does not increase cash flow. Similarly, an increase in inventories also increases working capital but decreases cash flow because cash was used to increase this asset. The general rule is that **all increases in current assets (other than cash) decrease cash, and all decreases in current assets increase cash.** The opposite effect occurs with liabilities. For example, a decrease in accounts payable increases working capital but decreases cash because cash is used to reduce this liability. Thus **all increases in current liabilities increase cash and all decreases reduce cash.** The following diagram illustrates the common types of adjustments that are made to working capital provided by operations to arrive at cash provided by operations.

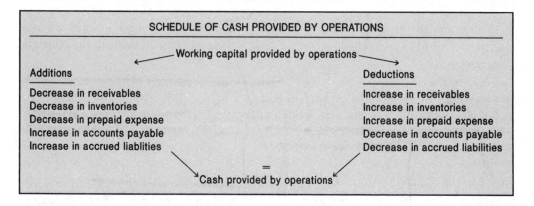

SCHEDULE OF CASH PROVIDED BY OPERATIONS

Working capital provided by operations

| Additions | Deductions |
|---|---|
| Decrease in receivables | Increase in receivables |
| Decrease in inventories | Increase in inventories |
| Decrease in prepaid expense | Increase in prepaid expense |
| Increase in accounts payable | Decrease in accounts payable |
| Increase in accrued liablities | Decrease in accrued liabilities |

= Cash provided by operations

Certain changes in current assets and current liabilities do not affect **cash provided by operations.** For example, changes in temporary investments should have no effect on operations and should be reported as either cash provided or cash applied. Similarly, changes in notes receivable and payable may not directly affect operations. In these cases, a separate resource applied or cash provided amount should also be reported. Changes in dividends payable are ignored in computing cash provided by operations and are reported as cash applied to dividends in a separate section of the statement.

To illustrate these concepts, Hanes Corporation would make the conversion in the manner shown in the schedule below. All other changes (depreciation, amortization of goodwill, etc.) are handled the same whether a working capital or a cash basis is employed.

| Hanes Corporation<br>SCHEDULE OF CHANGE FROM ACCRUAL TO CASH BASIS | | |
|---|---|---|
| Operations | Working Capital<br>Provided | Cash Provided |
| Income before extraordinary item | $109,000 | $109,000 |
| Add items providing or not requiring<br>working capital or cash | | |
| Loss on sale of equipment | 1,500 | 1,500 |
| Depreciation expense | 14,600 | 14,600 |
| Amortization of goodwill | 2,400 | 2,400 |
| Deferred income taxes | 3,000 | 3,000 |
| Decrease in prepaid expenses | | 500 |
| Increase in accounts payable | | 1,000 |
| Increase in accrued liabilities | | 2,500 |
| Deduct items requiring or not providing<br>working capital or cash | | |
| Equity in earnings of Porter Co. | (3,500) | (3,500) |
| Amortization of bond premium | (1,000) | (1,000) |
| Increase in accounts receivable (net) | | (53,000) |
| Increase in inventories | | (152,000) |
| Decrease in income taxes payable | | (13,000) |
| Working capital and cash provided by<br>operations, exclusive of<br>extraordinary item | $126,000 | $ (88,000) |

Conversion to the cash basis of accounting requires that changes in each working capital item except cash be included along with nonworking capital items in the schedule.

**Increase in Accounts Receivable (net)**   When accounts receivable (net) increased during the current year, revenues on an accrual basis are higher than revenues on a cash basis, because goods sold on account are reported as revenues. To convert income on an accrual basis to income on a cash basis, the increase of $53,000 in accounts receivable must be deducted from income on an accrual basis.

**Increase in Inventories**   When inventory purchased exceeds inventory sold, cost of goods sold on an accrual basis is lower than cost of goods sold on a cash basis, because the cost of inventory on hand is deferred to the subsequent period. To convert income on an accrual basis to income on a cash basis, the increase of $152,000 in inventory must be deducted from income on an accrual basis.

**Decrease in Prepaid Expenses**   When prepaid expenses decrease during a period, expenses on an accrual basis income statement are higher than they are on a cash basis income statement, because prepaid expenses of a previous period have been amortized as a charge to expense. To convert income on an accrual basis to income on a cash basis, the decrease of $500 in prepaid expenses must be added to income on the accrual basis.

**Increase in Accounts Payable and Accrued Liabilities**  When accounts payable and accrued liabilities increase during a period, cost of goods sold and expenses on an accrual basis are higher than they are on a cash basis, because goods are purchased and expenses are incurred for which payment has not taken place. To convert income on an accrual basis to income on a cash basis, the increases of $1,000 in accounts payable and $2,500 in accrued liabilities must be added to income on the accrual basis.

**Decrease in Income Taxes Payable**  When income tax payable decreased during a period, expenses on an accrual basis are lower than expenses on a cash basis, because payment for income taxes exceeded the cost incurred for income taxes during the current period. To convert income on an accrual basis to income on a cash basis, the $13,000 decrease in income tax payable must be deducted from income on an accrual basis.

| Hanes Corporation STATEMENT OF CHANGES IN FINANCIAL POSITION (CASH BASIS) For the Year Ended December 31, 1984 | | |
|---|---:|---:|
| Resources provided by | | |
| Operations: | | |
| Income before extraordinary item | | $109,000 |
| Add (or deduct) items not affecting cash | | |
| Equity in earnings of Porter Co. | $ (3,500) | |
| Loss on sale of equipment | 1,500 | |
| Depreciation expense | 14,600 | |
| Amortization of goodwill | 2,400 | |
| Deferred income taxes | 3,000 | |
| Amortization of bond premium | (1,000) | |
| Decrease in prepaid expenses | 500 | |
| Increase in accounts payable | 1,000 | |
| Increase in accrued liabilities | 2,500 | |
| Increase in accounts receivable (net) | (53,000) | |
| Increase in inventories | (152,000) | |
| Decrease in income taxes payable | (13,000) | (197,000) |
| Cash provided by operations, exclusive of extraordinary item | | (88,000) |
| Extraordinary item—Condemnation of land, including extraordinary gain of $8,000 (net of $2,500 tax) | | 18,500 |
| Issuance of note payable to purchase land | | 60,000 |
| Sale of equipment | | 4,000 |
| Sale of common stock | | 144,000 |
| Total resources provided | | 138,500 |
| Resources applied to | | |
| Cash dividends | 4,500 | |
| Purchase of land through issuance of note payable | 60,000 | |
| Purchase of equipment | 53,000 | |
| Major repairs of equipment | 11,000 | |
| Purchase of treasury stock | 17,000 | |
| Total resources applied | | 145,500 |
| Decrease in cash | | $ 7,000 |

The increase in the dividends payable account is ignored in computing cash provided by operations since it is not a determinant of net income. Because the dividend payable account increased $1,500, dividends must have been declared that have not been paid. As a result, only $4,500 (not $6,000) of dividends was paid and should be reported as a separate resource applied under the cash basis.

The statement of changes in financial position for Hanes Corporation emphasizing a cash basis approach is shown on page 1099.

## CHANGING FROM ACCRUAL TO CASH BASIS—DIRECT APPROACH

Some refer to the method just presented to compute cash provided by operations as the **indirect method** or **reconciliation approach.** It is referred to in this manner because cash revenues and cash expenses are not computed; instead, a reconciliation is made between income provided by operations (accrual basis) and cash provided by operations.

Another approach is the **direct method,** which computes cash revenues and cash expenses directly. To illustrate this method, a portion of the Hanes Corporation acccrual basis income statement is adjusted to a cash basis. For purposes of this illustration, the increase in accounts payable is related to cost of goods sold; depreciation expense, prepaid expense, and accrued liabilities are related to selling and administrative expenses; and amortization of goodwill and bond premium are related to other expenses and losses. Other relationships should be apparent. This illustration is presented on page 1101.

If a cash basis statement of changes in financial position is employed, should the indirect (reconciliation approach) or direct method be employed? Those who favor the indirect approach argue that by providing a reconciliation between net income and cash provided from operations, the differences are highlighted; such is not the case with the direct approach. Furthermore, some contend that the direct approach is nothing more than a cash basis income statement, which will confuse and create uncertainty for financial statement users who are familiar with accrual-based income statements. Finally, some question whether the direct approach is cost/benefit justified. They maintain that additional preparation costs would probably be required because the financial records are not maintained on a cash basis.

Conversely, others argue that by reporting the actual sources and uses of cash, the direct method will be more helpful to users in understanding past trends and in estimating future cash flows. Furthermore, it is argued that a better understanding of the relationship between net income and cash flows is achieved through the use of the direct method. Only by reporting the cash revenues and cash expenses can one understand how the cash is generated. Use of the indirect approach implies that net income and certain expenses (for example, depreciation, amortization of intangibles) are sources of cash, which is misleading.

## FLEXIBILITY IN DISCLOSURE AND FORMAT

The statement of changes in financial position has not been standardized in form and content to as great an extent as the balance sheet and income statement, except that certain major categories are normally included. The arrangement of items is usually kept flexible so that any significant changes that might develop in a particular year can be highlighted. Consequently many variations in content and form appear. Generally the statement is pre-

Hanes Corporation
SCHEDULE OF CHANGE FROM ACCRUAL TO CASH
BASIS INCOME STATEMENT (Partial)

| | Accrual Basis | Adjustment | Add (Subtract) | Cash Basis |
|---|---|---|---|---|
| Net sales | $524,500 | − Increase in accounts receivable | ($53,000) | $471,500 |
| Other income | 3,500 | − Equity in earnings of Porter, Co. | (3,500) | -0- |
| Total revenues | 528,000 | | | 471,500 |
| Expenses | | | | |
| Cost of goods sold | 310,000 | − Increase in accounts payable | (1,000) | |
| | | + Increase in inventories | 152,000 | 461,000 |
| Selling and administrative expense | 47,000 | − Depreciation expense | (14,600) | |
| | | − Decrease in prepaid expenses | (500) | 29,400 |
| | | − Increase in accrued liabilities | (2,500) | |
| Other expenses and losses | 12,000 | − Loss on sale of equipment | (1,500) | |
| | | − Amortization of goodwill | (2,400) | |
| | | + Amortization of bond premium | 1,000 | 9,100 |
| Total expenses | 369,000 | | | 499,500 |
| Income (loss) before income tax | 159,000 | | | (28,000) |
| Income tax | | | | |
| Current | 47,000 | + Decrease in Income Taxes Payable | 13,000 | 60,000 |
| Deferred | 3,000 | − Increase in Deferred Income Taxes | (3,000) | -0- |
| Net income (loss) | $109,000 | | | ($88,000)[a] |

[a]Note that the cash provided (applied) by operations computed here, a negative $88,000, equals the amount computed earlier using the reconciliation format.

sented either in a balanced form (total sources equal applications) or in a form that high-lights the change in working capital or cash.

*APB Opinion No. 19* indicates that the statement may take the form that most usefully portrays the financing and investing aspects of the reporting entity. The opinion, however, specifies the following provisions:

1. A statement summarizing changes in financial position should be presented as a basic finan-cial statement along with the balance sheet and statement of income.

2. The statement summarizing changes in financial position should be based on a broad concept embracing all changes in financial position (all financial resources).

3. The title to be used for summarizing changes in financial position is Statement of Changes in Financial Position.

4. The statement should prominently disclose working capital or cash provided from or used in operations for the period. Disclosure is considered most informative if the effect of extraordi-nary items is reported separately from the effects of ordinary items.

5. The statement should begin with income or loss before extraordinary items, if any, and add back (or deduct) items that did not use (or provide) working capital.

6. A schedule of changes in working capital should be in a tabulation accompanying the state-ment or in the statement itself.

7. Effects of financing and investing activities should be disclosed individually when material. For example, both outlays for acquisitions and proceeds from retirements of property should be reported; both long-term borrowings and repayments of long-term debt should be reported; and outlays for purchases of consolidated subsidiaries should be summarized by major assets obtained and obligations assumed.

8. Related items should be presented together where the result contributes to clarity. To illustrate, we might associate the retirement or sale of the old property with the purchase of new property. The proper approach is to deduct the proceeds from the sale of the old property from the cost of the new. It is not considered proper to show the net amount, unless it is immaterial or unless it is part of a normal trade-in cycle to replace equipment.

## USEFULNESS OF STATEMENT OF CHANGES IN FINANCIAL POSITION

Some of the benefits of a statement of changes in financial position are as follows.

**Assessing Future Cash Flows** *FASB Concepts Statement No. 1* indicates that a primary objective of financial reporting is to predict the amount, timing, and uncertainty of future cash flows. Income data when augmented with data from a statement of changes in financial position provides a better basis for assessing future cash flows.

**Assessing Quality of Income** Some believe that fund flow information is more reliable than income information because income involves a number of assumptions, estimates, and valuations. Fund flow data are considered more concrete, closer to cash. As a result, the higher the proportion that funds generated by operations is to net income, the more confidence users have in the income number.

**Assessing Operating Capability** Operating capability is the ability of an enterprise to maintain a given physical level of operations. Whether an enterprise is able to maintain its operating capability, provide for future growth, and distribute dividends to the owners depends on whether adequate funds are being or will be generated.

**Assessing Financial Flexibility and Liquidity** Financial flexibility is the ability of an enterprise to take effective actions to alter the amounts and timing of cash flows so it can respond to unexpected needs and opportunities. Information on fund flow data (particularly funds provided by operation) should be useful in determining whether a company will be able to survive adverse operating conditions. The term "liquidity" is used to describe the amount of time that is expected to elapse until an asset is realized or otherwise converted into cash or until a liability has to be paid. Information on the enterprise's ability to generate funds from operations is important because it indicates whether a company might have difficulty in meeting obligations as they fall due, paying dividends and meeting other recurring costs.

**Providing Information on Financing and Investing Activities** The statement of changes in financial position can provide answers to questions such as:

How was it possible to distribute dividends in excess of current earnings or in the presence of a net loss for the period?

How did cash (working capital) increase even though there was a net loss for the period?

Why was money borrowed during the period?

How was the expansion in plant and equipment financed?

What happened to the proceeds from the sale of plant and equipment?

How was the retirement of debt accomplished?

What became of the assets derived from the increase in outstanding capital stock?

What became of the proceeds of the bond issue?

How was the increase in cash or working capital financed?

In addition, many meaningful relationships can be established such as funds provided by operations to debt, to capital expenditures, to dividends, or a combination of these items. In addition, this statement provides insight into changes occurring in the company that cannot be determined from examination of a balance sheet and income statement.

# APPENDIX N

# The T-Account Approach to Preparation of the Statement of Changes in Financial Position

Many accountants find the work sheet approach to preparing a statement of changes in financial position time-consuming and cumbersome. In some cases, the detail of a work sheet is not needed, and there is not enough time to prepare a work sheet. Therefore, the **T-account approach** for preparing a statement of changes in financial position has been devised. This procedure provides a quick and systematic method of accumulating the appropriate information to be presented in the formal statement of changes in financial position. The T-accounts used in this approach are not part of the general ledger or any other ledger; they are developed only for use in this process.

## ILLUSTRATION

To illustrate the T-account approach, we will use the information of the Hanes Corp. example presented on pages 1088–1090. When the T-account approach is employed, the net change in working capital for the period is computed by comparing the beginning and ending balances of the working capital accounts. After the net change is computed, a T-account for working capital is prepared and the net change in working capital is entered at the top of this account on the left if working capital increased, and on the right if it decreased (see illustration of T-account on page 1107). The T-account is then structured into four separate classifications: (1) Sources—Operations and (2) Sources—Other, both on the left; and (3) Applications—Operations and (4) Applications—Other, on the right. T-accounts are then set up for all nonworking capital items that have had activity during the period, with the net change entered at the top of each account. The objective of the T-account approach is to explain the net change in working capital through the various changes that have occurred in the nonworking capital accounts. The working capital T-account acts as a summarizing account. Most of the changes in the nonworking capital items are explained through the working capital account. Significant financial transactions that did not affect working capital are assumed to provide and apply working capital and are entered in this summary account to insure their inclusion in the final statement. To illustrate, a complete version of the T-account approach is presented on the following pages.

The following items caused the change in working capital (you should trace each entry to the accounts that are presented beginning on page 1107):

ILLUSTRATION **1105**

**1.** Net income for the period, comprised of income before extraordinary item of $109,000 and an extraordinary gain of $8,000 (net of tax), increased retained earnings $117,000. To avoid the detail of nonworking capital revenues and expenses, we employ a short-cut by starting with income before extraordinary item and then in subsequent entries adjust it to reflect resources provided by operations, exclusive of extraordinary item. In general journal form, the entry to report this increase and the extraordinary item would be:

| | | |
|---|---|---|
| Working Capital—Operations | 109,000 | |
| Working Capital—Other | 8,000 | |
|    Retained Earnings | | 117,000 |

**2.** The retained earnings account also discloses stock dividends of $15,000. Because this transaction is not considered a significant investing or financing activity, the working capital account is not affected, and the following entry would be made:

| | | |
|---|---|---|
| Retained Earnings | 15,000 | |
|    Common Stock | | 1,000 |
|    Additional Paid-in Capital | | 14,000 |

**3.** Further analysis of the retained earnings account indicates that a cash dividend of $6,000 was declared during the current period. The entry to record the transaction would be:

| | | |
|---|---|---|
| Retained Earnings | 6,000 | |
|    Working Capital—Other | | 6,000 |

Note that the net change in the retained earnings balance of $96,000 is now reconciled. This reconciliation procedure is basic to the T-account approach because it insures that all appropriate transactions have been considered.

**4.** The equity in the earnings of Porter Co. must be subtracted from income before extraordinary item because this income item does not increase working capital. The journal entry to recognize this equity in the earnings of Porter Co. is as follows:

| | | |
|---|---|---|
| Investment in Stock of Porter Co. | 3,500 | |
|    Working Capital—Operations | | 3,500 |

**5.** A note of $60,000 was issued to purchase land. Although this transaction did not affect working capital, it is a significant financial transaction that should be reported. The transaction is therefore assumed both to have increased working capital and to have decreased working capital in order to report this amount in the net working capital account. The following entry would be made:

| | | |
|---|---|---|
| Land | 60,000 | |
|    Working Capital—Other | | 60,000 |
| Working Capital—Other | 60,000 | |
|    Note Payable | | 60,000 |

An alternative to this approach is simply to adjust the Land and Note Payable account, noting that in a formal preparation of a statement of changes in financial position, this transaction must be reported.

**6.** In addition, land with a book value of $10,500 was condemned. The entry to record this transaction is as follows:

| | | |
|---|---|---|
| Working Capital—Other | 10,500 | |
|    Land | | 10,500 |

Note that adding the $10,500 book value of this condemnation to the $8,000 extraordinary gain net of $2,500 tax determined earlier provides total resources of $18,500 related to the condemnation.

**7.** Equipment and the related Accumulated Depreciation account indicate that a number of financial transactions affected these accounts. The first transaction is the purchase of equipment, which is recorded as follows:

| | | |
|---|---|---|
| Equipment | 53,000 | |
| Working Capital—Other | | 53,000 |

**8.** In addition, equipment with a book value of $5,500 was sold at a loss of $1,500. The entry to record this transaction is as follows:

| | | |
|---|---|---|
| Working Capital—Other | 4,000 | |
| Working Capital—Operations | 1,500 | |
| Accumulated Depreciation—Equipment | 2,500 | |
| Equipment | | 8,000 |

Note that the loss on the sale of the equipment has reduced the income before extraordinary item, but has not affected working capital. The loss must therefore be added back to income before extraordinary item to report accurately resources provided by operations.

**9.** Depreciation on the equipment of $11,500 must be recorded as follows:

| | | |
|---|---|---|
| Working Capital—Operations | 11,500 | |
| Accumulated Depreciation—Equipment | | 11,500 |

**10.** The major repair reduced working capital, so the necessary journal entry is as follows:

| | | |
|---|---|---|
| Accumulated Depreciation—Equipment | 11,000 | |
| Working Capital—Other | | 11,000 |

The equipment account and related accumulated depreciation account are now reconciled.

**11.** Analysis of the remaining accounts indicates changes in Accumulated Depreciation—Building, Premium on Bonds Payable, and Deferred Income Taxes that must be accounted for in determining the resources provided by operations, exclusive of extraordinary item. The entry to record these transactions is as follows:

| | | |
|---|---|---|
| Working Capital—Operations | 3,100 | |
| Working Capital—Operations | 2,400 | |
| Working Capital—Operations | 3,000 | |
| Premium on Bonds Payable | 1,000 | |
| Accumulated Depreciation—Buildings | | 3,100 |
| Goodwill | | 2,400 |
| Deferred Income Taxes | | 3,000 |
| Working Capital—Operations | | 1,000 |

**12.** Examination of the common stock account indicates that in addition to the stock dividend (transaction 2), common stock was issued at $16 per share. The entry to record this transaction is as follows:

| | | |
|---|---|---|
| Working Capital—Other | 144,000 | |
| Common Stock | | 9,000 |
| Additional Paid-in Capital | | 135,000 |

**13.** The company also purchased treasury stock, which is recorded as follows:

| | | |
|---|---|---|
| Treasury Stock | 17,000 | |
| Working Capital—Other | | 17,000 |

After the entries above are posted to the appropriate accounts, the working capital account (shown on page 1107) is used as the basis for preparing the statement of changes

ILLUSTRATION  **1107**

in financial position. The debit side of the working capital account contains the resources provided and the credit side contains the resources applied. The difference between the two sides of the working capital account should reconcile to the increase or decrease in working capital. The completed statement of changes in financial position is presented on page 1094.

### Working Capital

| Increases | | Decreases | |
|---|---|---|---|
| Net change | $205,500 | | |
| **Sources—Operations:** | | **Applications—Operations:** | |
| 1. Income before extraordinary item | 109,000 | 4. Equity in earnings of Porter Co. | 3,500 |
| 8. Loss on sale of equipment | 1,500 | 11. Bond premium amortization | 1,000 |
| 9. Depreciation expense | 11,500 | | 4,500 |
| 11. Depreciation expense | 3,100 | | |
| 11. Goodwill amortization | 2,400 | | |
| 11. Deferred income taxes | 3,000 | | |
| | 130,500 | | |
| **Sources—Other:** | | **Applications—Other:** | |
| 1. Condemnation of land | 8,000 | 3. Cash dividends | 6,000 |
| 5. Issuance of note | 60,000 | 5. Purchase of land | 60,000 |
| 6. Condemnation of land | 10,500 | 7. Purchase of equipment | 53,000 |
| 8. Sale of equipment | 4,000 | 10. Major repair of equipment | 11,000 |
| 12. Sale of common stock | 144,000 | 13. Purchase of treasury stock | 17,000 |
| | 226,500 | | 147,000 |

### Investment in Stock of Porter Co. (equity method)

| | | | |
|---|---|---|---|
| Net change | $ 3,500 | | |
| 4. Equity in earnings | 3,500 | | |

### Land

| | | | |
|---|---|---|---|
| Net change | $ 49,500 | | |
| 5. Purchase of land | 60,000 | 6. Condemnation | 10,500 |

### Equipment

| | | | |
|---|---|---|---|
| Net change | $ 45,000 | | |
| 7. Purchase | 53,000 | 8. Sale of equipment | 8,000 |

### Accumulated Depreciation Equipment

| | | | |
|---|---|---|---|
| Net change | $ 2,000 | | |
| 8. Sale of equipment | 2,500 | 9. Depreciation expense | 11,500 |
| 10. Major repair | 11,000 | | |

### Accumulated Depreciation—Buildings

| | | | |
|---|---|---|---|
| | | Net change | $ 3,100 |
| | | 11. Depreciation expense | 3,100 |

### Goodwill

| | | | |
|---|---|---|---|
| | | Net change | $ 2,400 |
| | | 11. Amortization of goodwill | 2,400 |

### Notes Payable

|  |  | Net change | $ 60,000 |
|---|---|---|---|
|  |  | 5. Issuance of Note | 60,000 |

### Premium on Bonds Payable

| Net change | $ 1,000 |  |  |
|---|---|---|---|
| 11. Bond premium amortization | 1,000 |  |  |

### Deferred Income Taxes

|  |  | Net change | $ 3,000 |
|---|---|---|---|
|  |  | 11. Increase | 3,000 |

### Common Stock

|  |  | Net change | $ 10,000 |
|---|---|---|---|
|  |  | 2. Stock dividend | 1,000 |
|  |  | 12. Sale of common stock | 9,000 |

### Additional Paid-In Capital

|  |  | Net change | $149,000 |
|---|---|---|---|
|  |  | 2. Stock dividend | 14,000 |
|  |  | 12. Sale of common stock | 135,000 |

### Retained Earnings

|  |  | Net change | $ 96,000 |
|---|---|---|---|
| 2. Stock dividend | 15,000 | 1. Net Income | 117,000 |
| 3. Cash dividend | 6,000 |  |  |

### Treasury Stock

| Net change | $ 17,000 |  |  |
|---|---|---|---|
| 13. Purchase of treasury stock | 17,000 |  |  |

## SUMMARY OF T-ACCOUNT APPROACH

Short-cut approaches are often used with the T-account approach. For example, the journal entries may not be prepared because the transactions are obvious. Also, only the nonworking capital T-accounts that have a number of changes, such as Equipment, Accumulated Depreciation—Equipment, and Retained Earnings, need be presented in T-account form. Other more obvious changes in nonworking capital items can be determined simply by examining the comparative balance sheet and other related data. The T-account approach provides certain advantages over the work sheet method in that (1) a statement usually can be prepared much faster using the T-account method, and (2) the use of the T-account method helps in understanding the relationship between working capital and nonworking capital items. Conversely, the work sheet on highly complex problems provides a more orderly and systematic approach to preparing the statement of changes in financial position. In addition, in practice the work sheet is used extensively to insure that all items are properly accounted for.

The following steps are used in the T-account approach:

1. Determine the increase or decrease in working capital for the year.

2. Post the increase or decrease to the working capital T-account and establish four classifications within this account: Sources—Operations, Sources—Other, Applications—Operations, and Applications—Other.

3. Determine the increase or decrease in each nonworking capital account. Accounts that have no change can be ignored unless two transactions have occurred in the same account of the same amount, which is highly unlikely. A short-cut approach is to prepare T-accounts only for nonworking capital accounts that have a number of transactions. All other changes can be immediately posted to the working capital account after examining the additional information related to the changes in the balance sheet for a period.

4. Reconstruct entries in nonworking capital accounts and post them to the nonworking capital account affected and to the working capital T-account.

5. Using the postings from the working capital T-account, prepare the formal statement of changes in financial position.

One word of caution: the T-account approach will have to be modified if an all financial resources transaction occurs, such as the issuance of bonds to purchase a building. Although these transactions do not affect the working capital T-accounts directly, an assumption may be made that they affect working capital indirectly and can be reported in the working capital account as sources and uses. An alternative is simply to adjust the two accounts affected, remembering that these transactions must be reported on a formal statement of changes in financial position.

# QUESTIONS

1. What is the purpose of the statement of changes in financial position? How does it differ from a balance sheet or income statement?

2. What are the common funds or approaches that are used as the basis in preparing a statement of changes in financial position? Which approach is recommended by *APB Opinion No. 19*? Why?

3. The following differences result from comparing the amounts in two successive balance sheets. Do the following items represent resources provided, resources applied, or neither?

| | Differences | | |
| --- | --- | --- | --- |
| | Debit | Credit | Explanation |
| (a) Equipment | $82,000 | | Equipment purchased |
| (b) Goodwill | | $12,000 | Amortization of goodwill |
| (c) Common stock distributable | | 40,000 | Declaration of stock dividend |
| (d) Common stock | 16,000 | | Purchase of treasury stock |
| (e) Retained earnings | 7,000 | | Net income of $15,000 and dividends of $22,000 |

4. The net income for the year for Polytech, Inc., is $231,000, but the statement of changes in financial position indicates that the resources provided by operations is $296,000. What might account for the difference?

5. Give three examples of financial transactions that would be omitted if a working capital concept not including all financial resources were used as the basis for preparing a statement of changes in financial position.

6. On a statement of changes in financial position, why is the amortization of prepaid expenses treated differently than the depreciation taken on a plant asset?

7. Give four examples of changes in the capital structure that do not appear on the statement of changes in financial position.

8. Give four examples of items added back to income before extraordinary items to arrive at working capital provided by operations.

9. The working capital provided by operations in Seattle, Inc.'s statement of changes in financial position for 1983 was $8,000,000. For 1983, depreciation on plant assets was $3,800,000, amortization of goodwill was $100,000, and dividends on common stock were $2,000,000. Compute Seattle's net income for 1983.

10. Each of the following items must be considered in preparing a statement of changes in financial position for Steel Plate, Inc. for the year ended December 31, 1984. For each item state where it is to be shown in the statement, if at all.
    (a) Plant assets that had cost $20,000 six and one-half years before and were being depreciated on a straight-line basis over 10 years with no estimated scrap value were sold for $6,000.
    (b) During the year 1,000 shares of common stock with a stated value of $20 a share were issued for $40 a share.
    (c) Uncollectible accounts receivable in the amount of $22,000 were written off against the Allowance for Doubtful Accounts.
    (d) The company sustained a net loss for the year of $5,000. Depreciation amounted to $2,000 and patent amortization to $1,000.

11. Master Loan Inc. has a net income for the year of $650,000. Included in this net income are: a gain on casualty (extraordinary item), net of tax of $60,000; depreciation expense of $130,000; and amortization of bond premium of $10,000. What amount should Master Loan Inc. report on its statement of changes in financial position for resources provided by operations, exclusive of extraordinary item?

12. Chris Lahey, a student in intermediate accounting, decided that he would have no difficulty in preparing a statement of changes in financial position on the next exam if the problem were straightforward. He still, however, has difficulty understanding the following items. Explain how these items should be treated in a statement of changes in financial position.
    (a) The maturing portion of a long-term serial bond.
    (b) A long-term note given for the purchase of inventory.
    (c) Gain on the sale of marketable securities (current).
    (d) A common stock split.

13. Why are more business enterprises switching to a cash basis approach in preparing a statement of changes in financial position?

14. Harbecke, Inc., reported net income of $2 million in 1983. Depreciation for the year was $210,000, receivables increased $300,000, and accounts payable increased $160,000. Compute cash provided from operations, assuming the receivable and payable increases related to operations.

15. Nair, Inc., reported sales on an accrual basis of $100,000. If gross receivables increased $80,000, and the allowance for bad debts $12,000 after a write-off of $6,000, compute cash sales.

16. Does a separate schedule of working capital have to be included if a cash approach is adopted? Discuss.

17. What are some of the arguments in favor of using the indirect (reconciliation approach) as opposed to the direct approach for reporting a cash basis statement of changes in financial position?

18. Of what use is the statement of changes in financial position?

## CASES

**C24–1 Part A.** After considerable discussion and research in recent years concerning the reporting of changes in financial position (sources and applications of funds), *Accounting Principles Board Opinion No. 19* concluded:

*... That the statement summarizing changes in financial position should be based on a broad concept embracing all changes in financial position and that the title of the statement should reflect this broad concept. The Board therefore recommends that the title be Statement of Changes in Financial Position.*

**Instructions**

(a) What are the two common meanings of "funds" as used when preparing the statement of changes in financial position? Explain.

(b) What is meant by "... a broad concept embracing all changes in financial position ..." as used by the Accounting Principles Board in its *Opinion No. 19*? Explain.

**Part B.** R. Ace Company is a young and growing producer of electronic measuring instruments and technical equipment. You have been retained by Ace to advise it in the preparation of a statement of changes in financial position. For the fiscal year ended October 31, 1984, you have obtained the following information concerning certain events and transactions of Ace.

1. The board of directors declared a $400,000 cash dividend on October 20, 1984, payable on November 18, 1984, to stockholders of record on November 5, 1984.

2. The amount of reported earnings for the fiscal year was $800,000, which included a deduction for an extraordinary loss of $83,000 (see item 6 below).

3. Depreciation expense of $350,000 was included in the earnings statement.

4. Uncollectible accounts receivable of $38,000 was written off against the allowance for doubtful accounts. Also, $45,000 of bad debts expense was included in determining income for the fiscal year, and the same amount was added to the allowance for doubtful accounts.

5. A gain of $5,200 was realized on the sale of a machine; it originally cost $75,000, of which $30,000 was undepreciated on the date of sale.

6. On April 1, 1984, a freak flood caused an uninsured inventory loss of $83,000 ($170,000 loss, less reduction in income taxes of $87,000). This extraordinary loss was included in determining income as indicated in 2 above.

7. On July 3, 1984, building and land were purchased for $600,000; Ace gave in payment $75,000 cash, $200,000 market value of its unissued common stock, and a $325,000 purchase-money mortgage.

8. On August 3, 1984, $750,000 face value of Ace's 10% convertible debentures were converted into $140,000 par value of its common stock. The bonds were originally issued at face value.

**Instructions**

Explain whether each of the 8 numbered items above is a source or use of working capital and explain how it should be disclosed in Ace's statement of changes in financial position for the fiscal year ended October 31, 1984. If any item is neither a source nor a use of working capital, explain why it is not and indicate the disclosure, if any, that should be made of the item in Ace's statement of changes in financial position for the fiscal year ended October 31, 1984.

**C24–2** Presented below is the financial statement related to Shakespeare Book Co.:

Shakespeare Book Co.
STATEMENT SHOWING CAUSES
OF NET CHANGE IN WORKING CAPITAL

| | |
|---|---|
| Funds were obtained from: | |
| Operations (net income transferred to retained earnings) | $185,220.40 |

| | | |
|---|---:|---:|
| Current assets used up in year's operations: | | |
| Cash on hand and in banks | $ 35,627.25 | |
| Postal stamps | 20.00 | 35,647.25 |
| Increase in common stock outstanding | 10,000.00 | |
| Increase in paid-in capital in excess of par | 21,000.00 | 31,000.00 |
| | | $251,867.65 |
| | | |
| Funds were applied to: | | |
| Payments of cash dividends | | $ 35,331.00 |
| Declaration of stock dividends (not yet issued) | | 26,400.00 |
| Investment in additions to | | |
| Accounts receivable—trade | $ 12,504.83 | |
| Notes receivable—trade | 2,500.00 | |
| Inventories | 103,742.51 | |
| Marketable securities | 10,600.01 | |
| Cash surrender value of life insurance | 1,141.25 | |
| Fixed assets (net increase) | 15,450.52 | |
| Patents | 20,000.00 | |
| Prepaid expense | 2,502.04 | 168,441.16 |
| Payments of serial bond maturities | | 10,000.00 |
| Reduction in current liabilities | | 11,695.49 |
| | | $251,867.65 |

**Instructions**

You are to criticize the statement above, considering mainly its **function** and **content.** (There are differences of opinion concerning the general form of such a statement and the terminology used. You need not concern yourself with these matters in your criticism except where you believe them to be essential to the accomplishment of the statement's function.) Mention in your discussion specific items that the data supplied lead you to believe (1) may have been omitted incorrectly from the statement or (2) should have been excluded from the statement. For each item that you mention, give your reason for inclusion or deletion and state how you would treat the item. You need not prepare a revised statement.

**C24-3** The following statement was prepared by Solar Corporation's accountant:

Solar Corporation
STATEMENT OF SOURCE AND APPLICATION OF FUNDS
For the Year Ended September 30, 1984

| | |
|---|---:|
| Source of funds | |
| Net income | $ 72,000 |
| Depreciation and depletion | 61,000 |
| Increase in long-term debt | 189,000 |
| Common stock issued under employee option plans | 16,000 |
| Changes in current receivables and inventories, less current | |
| liabilities (excluding current maturities of long-term debt) | 14,000 |
| | $352,000 |
| | |
| Application of funds | |
| Cash dividends | $ 44,000 |
| Expenditures for property, plant, and equipment | 224,000 |
| Investments and other uses | 20,000 |
| Change in cash | 64,000 |
| | $352,000 |

The following additional information relating to Solar Corporation is available for the year ended September 30, 1984:

1. The corporation received $16,000 in cash from its employees on its employee stock option plans, and wage and salary expense attributable to the option plans was an additional $22,000.

2.

| | |
|---|---:|
| Expenditures for property, plant, and equipment | $242,000 |
| Proceeds from retirements of property, plant, and equipment | 18,000 |
| Net expenditures | $224,000 |

3. A stock dividend of 10,000 shares of Solar Corporation common stock was distributed to common stockholders on April 1, 1984, when the per-share market price was $7 and par value was $1.

4. On July 1, 1984, when its market price was $6 per share, 16,000 shares of Solar Corporation common stock were issued in exchange for 4,000 shares of preferred stock.

5. The balance sheet of Solar Corporation distinguishes between current and noncurrent assets and liabilities.

6.

| | |
|---|---:|
| Depreciation expense | $ 58,000 |
| Depletion expense | 3,000 |
| | $ 61,000 |

7.

| | |
|---|---:|
| Increase in long-term debt | $610,000 |
| Retirement of debt | 421,000 |
| Net increase | $189,000 |

**Instructions**

(a) In general, what are the objectives of a statement of the type shown above for the Solar Corporation? Explain.

(b) Identify the weaknesses in the form and format of the Solar Corporation's statement of changes in financial position without reference to the additional information.

(c) For each of the seven items of additional information for the statement of changes in financial position indicate the preferable treatment and explain why the suggested treatment is preferable.

(AICPA adapted)

**C24-4** The statement of changes in financial position is normally a required basic financial statement for each period for which an earnings statement is presented. The reporting entity has flexibility in form, content and terminology of this statement to meet the objectives of differing circumstances. For example, the concept of "funds" may be interpreted to mean, among other things, cash or working capital. However, the statement should be prepared based on the "all financial resources" concept.

**Instructions**

(a) What is the "all financial resources" concept?

(b) What are two types of financial transactions which would be disclosed under the "all financial resources" concept that would not be disclosed without this concept?

(c) What effect, if any, would each of the following seven items have upon the preparation of a statement of changes in financial position prepared in accordance with generally accepted accounting principles using the cash concept of funds?

1. Accounts receivable—trade.
2. Inventory.
3. Depreciation.
4. Deferred income tax credit from interperiod allocation.
5. Issuance of long-term debt in payment for a building.
6. Payoff of current portion of debt.
7. Sale of a fixed asset resulting in a loss.

(AICPA adapted)

**C24–5** Each of the following items must be considered in preparing a statement of changes in financial position for Denson Originals, Inc. for the year ended December 31, 1984.

1. Fixed assets that had cost $10,000 six and one-half years before and were being depreciated on a 10-year basis, with no estimated scrap value, were sold for $3,125.

2. During the year, goodwill of $100,000 was completely written off to expense.

3. During the year, 500 shares of common capital stock with a stated value of $25 a share were issued for $31 a share.

4. The company sustained a net loss for the year of $2,100. Depreciation amounted to $900 and patent amortization was $400.

5. An Appropriation for Contingencies in the amount of $80,000 was created by a charge against Retained Earnings.

6. Uncollectible accounts receivable in the amount of $2,000 were written off against the Allowance for Doubtful Accounts.

7. Investments that cost $12,000 when purchased four years earlier were sold for $11,000. The loss was considered ordinary.

8. Bonds payable with a par value of $24,000 on which there was an unamortized bond premium of $1,800 were redeemed at 102. The gain was credited to income.

### Instructions

For each item, state first where it is to be shown in the statement and then illustrate how you would present the necessary information, including the amount. Consider each item to be independent of the others. Assume that correct entries were made for all transactions as they took place.

## EXERCISES

**E24–1** Don and Diana are equal partners in the Five Flys Restaurant. Don withdraws from the partnership at the end of 1984, terminating the partnership. Below you are given comparative financial data and other pertinent information.

| | Dec. 31, 1983 | Dec. 31, 1984 | Increase or (Decrease) |
|---|---|---|---|
| Cash | $ 5,700 | $ 7,400 | $1,700 |
| Receivables | 7,800 | 10,300 | 2,500 |
| Allowance for doubtful accounts | (900) | (1,000) | 100 |
| Marketable securities | 5,000 | 5,000 | — |
| Prepaid expenses | 1,300 | 1,100 | (200) |
| Land | 10,000 | 10,000 | — |
| Building and equipment | 31,600 | 35,600 | 4,000 |
| Accumulated depreciation | (3,700) | (5,300) | 1,600 |
| | $56,800 | $63,100 | |
| Accounts payable | $ 3,000 | $ 2,600 | (400) |
| Notes payable (short-term) | 1,700 | 1,000 | (700) |
| Accrued expenses | 1,500 | 1,800 | 300 |
| Mortgage payable | 22,100 | 20,000 | (2,100) |
| Don, capital | 17,400 | 22,500 | 5,100 |
| Diana, capital | 11,100 | 15,200 | 4,100 |
| | $56,800 | $63,100 | |

1. Equipment for $4,000 was purchased in 1984.

**2.** At the time of the termination, Don makes withdrawals totaling $1,700; Diana has withdrawn $4,000.

**Instructions**

Prepare a statement of changes in financial position (working capital approach) for the year 1984.

**E24-2** Condensed financial data of Tennyson Company for the years ended December 31, 1983 and December 31, 1984, are presented below:

Tennyson Company
COMPARATIVE POSITION STATEMENT DATA
as of December 31, 1983 and 1984

|  | 1983 | 1984 |
|---|---|---|
| Cash | $ 38,400 | $124,800 |
| Receivables, net | 49,000 | 83,200 |
| Inventories | 61,900 | 92,500 |
| Investments | 97,000 | 90,000 |
| Plant assets | 212,500 | 240,000 |
|  | $458,800 | $630,500 |
| Accounts payable | $ 67,300 | $100,000 |
| Mortgage payable | 74,900 | 50,000 |
| Accumulated depreciation | 52,000 | 30,000 |
| Common stock | 131,100 | 175,000 |
| Retained earnings | 133,500 | 275,500 |
|  | $458,800 | $630,500 |

Tennyson Company
INCOME STATEMENT
For the Year Ended December 31, 1984

| | | |
|---|---|---|
| Sales | $320,000 | |
| Interest and other revenue | 20,000 | $340,000 |
| Less: | | |
| Cost of goods sold | 130,000 | |
| Selling and administrative expenses | 10,000 | |
| Depreciation | 24,000 | |
| Income taxes | 5,000 | |
| Interest charges | 3,000 | |
| Loss on sale of plant assets | 6,000 | 178,000 |
| Net income | | 162,000 |
| Dividends | | 20,000 |
| Income retained in business | | $142,000 |

**Additional information:**

New plant assets costing $80,000 were purchased during the year. Investments were sold at book value.

**Instructions**

From the foregoing information, prepare a statement of changes in financial position (working capital approach).

**E24-3** Comparative adjusted trial balances for Lisa Herrington, Inc., are presented below:

Lisa Herrington, Inc.
ADJUSTED TRIAL BALANCE

| | Dec. 31, 1983 | | Dec. 31, 1984 | |
| --- | --- | --- | --- | --- |
| | Dr. | Cr. | Dr. | Cr. |
| Cash | $ 5,400 | | $ 8,200 | |
| Marketable securities | 20,000 | | 22,000 | |
| Receivables (net) | 60,000 | | 66,800 | |
| Inventories | 64,000 | | 72,000 | |
| Delivery equipment | 29,000 | | 33,500 | |
| Accumulated depreciation— delivery equipment | | $ 17,000 | | $ 20,000 |
| Machinery | 14,500 | | 17,500 | |
| Accumulated depreciation— machinery | | 8,500 | | 10,500 |
| Building | 55,000 | | 55,000 | |
| Accumulated depreciation— buildings | | 7,000 | | 15,000 |
| Land | 15,000 | | 15,000 | |
| Accounts payable | | 47,500 | | 43,000 |
| Accrued expenses | | 8,000 | | 9,500 |
| Long-term notes payable | | 11,000 | | 5,000 |
| Bonds payable | | 50,000 | | 50,000 |
| Common stock | | 65,000 | | 65,000 |
| Retained earnings | | 38,000 | | 48,900 |
| Sales | | 294,900 | | 335,100 |
| Cost of goods sold | 220,000 | | 245,000 | |
| Operating expenses | 48,000 | | 51,000 | |
| Income taxes | 16,000 | | 16,000 | |
| | $546,900 | $546,900 | $602,000 | $602,000 |

**Instructions**

Using the information above, prepare a statement of changes in financial position (working capital approach).

**E24-4** Condensed financial data of Covaleski Company for 1983 and 1984 are presented below:

Covaleski Company
COMPARATIVE BALANCE SHEET DATA
As of December 31, 1983 and 1984

| | 1983 | 1984 |
| --- | --- | --- |
| Cash | $1,150 | $1,200 |
| Receivables, net | 1,300 | 1,600 |
| Inventory | 1,700 | 1,600 |
| Plant assets | 1,700 | 1,900 |
| Accumulated depreciation | (1,150) | (1,200) |
| Long-term investments | 1,400 | 1,300 |
| | $6,100 | $6,400 |

| | | |
|---|---|---|
| Accounts payable | $ 900 | $1,300 |
| Taxes payable | 600 | 550 |
| Bonds payable | 1,500 | 1,150 |
| Capital stock | 1,700 | 1,800 |
| Retained earnings | 1,400 | 1,600 |
| | $6,100 | $6,400 |

Covaleski Company
INCOME STATEMENT
For the Year Ended 1984

| | | |
|---|---|---|
| Sales | | $6,900 |
| Cost of goods sold | | 5,200 |
| Gross margin | | $1,700 |
| Operating expenses: | | |
| Selling expense | $600 | |
| Administrative expense | 650 | |
| Depreciation expense | 50 | 1,300 |
| Net income | | $ 400 |
| Cash dividends | | 200 |
| Income retained in business | | $ 200 |

**Additional information:**
There were no gains or losses in any noncurrent transactions during 1984.

**Instructions**

(a) Prepare a statement of changes in financial position (cash basis) using the indirect approach.

(b) Prepare a statement of changes in financial position using the direct approach.

**E24-5** Presented below are data taken from the records of S. Kopp Company.

| | December 31, 1983 | December 31, 1984 |
|---|---|---|
| Current assets | $ 47,000 | $ 80,000 |
| Long-term investments | 58,000 | 10,000 |
| Plant assets | 237,000 | 396,000 |
| | $342,000 | $486,000 |
| Accumulated depreciation | $ 40,000 | $ 30,000 |
| Current liabilities | 32,000 | 35,000 |
| Bonds payable | -0- | 105,000 |
| Capital stock | 250,000 | 250,000 |
| Donated capital | -0- | 31,000 |
| Retained earnings | 20,000 | 35,000 |
| | $342,000 | $486,000 |

1. Securities carried at a cost of $48,000 on December 31, 1983, were sold during 1984 for $39,000. The loss (not extraordinary) was incorrectly charged directly to Retained Earnings.

2. Plant assets that cost $50,000 and were 70% depreciated were sold during the year for $8,000. The loss (not extraordinary) was incorrectly charged directly to Retained Earnings.

3. Net income as reported on the income statement for the year was $45,000.

4. Dividends paid amounted to $14,000.

5. Depreciation charged for the year was $25,000.

6. Land was donated to S. Kopp Company by the city. The land was worth $31,000. (Assume credit to Donated Capital is correct.)

**Instructions**

Prepare a statement of changes in financial position (working capital concept). No schedule of working capital changes is required.

**E24-6** Comparative balance sheets at December 31, 1983 and 1984, for Melton Brick Company follow.

|  | 1983 | 1984 |
|---|---|---|
| Cash | $ 48,000 | $ 54,000 |
| Receivables | 66,000 | 60,000 |
| Inventory | 112,000 | 110,000 |
| Prepaid expenses | 8,000 | 9,000 |
| Plant assets | 220,000 | 312,000 |
| Accumulated depreciation | (61,000) | (86,000) |
| Patents | 40,000 | 35,000 |
|  | $433,000 | $494,000 |
| Accounts payable | $ 87,000 | $ 75,000 |
| Taxes payable | 66,000 | 68,000 |
| Mortgage payable | 95,000 | — |
| Preferred stock | — | 150,000 |
| Additional paid-in capital—preferred | — | 6,000 |
| Common stock | 150,000 | 150,000 |
| Retained earnings | 35,000 | 45,000 |
|  | $433,000 | $494,000 |

1. The only entries in the Retained Earnings account are for dividends paid in the amount of $20,000 and for the net income for the year.

2. The income statement for 1984 is as follows:

| Sales | | $132,000 |
|---|---|---|
| Cost of sales | | 94,000 |
| Gross profit | | 38,000 |
| Operating expenses | | 8,000 |
| Net income | | $ 30,000 |

3. The only entry in the Accumulated Depreciation account is the depreciation expense for the period.

**Instructions**

(a) From the information above, prepare a statement of changes in financial position (working capital approach).

(b) From the information above, prepare a statement of changes in financial position (cash approach). Use the indirect approach.

**E24-7** Candice Urbanak, Inc., had the following condensed balance sheet at the end of operations for 1983.

Candice Urbanak, Inc.
BALANCE SHEET
December 31, 1983

| | | | |
|---|---|---|---|
| Current assets | $ 37,500 | Current liabilities | $ 15,000 |
| Investments | 20,000 | Long-term notes payable | 25,500 |
| Plant assets (net) | 67,500 | Bonds payable | 25,000 |
| Land | 40,000 | Capital stock | 75,000 |
| | | Retained earnings | 24,500 |
| | $165,000 | | $165,000 |

During 1984 the following occurred:

1. A tract of land was purchased for $7,750.
2. Bonds payable in the amount of $6,000 were retired at par.
3. An additional $12,500 in capital stock was issued at par.
4. Dividends totaling $9,375 were paid to stockholders.
5. Net income for 1984 was $26,250 after allowing depreciation of $11,250.
6. Land was purchased through the issuance of $22,500 in bonds.
7. Candice Urbanak, Inc., sold part of its investment portfolio for $12,875. This transaction resulted in a gain of $375 for the firm. The company often sells and buys securities of this nature.

**Instructions**

(a) Prepare a statement of changes in financial position for 1984. A supporting schedule of working capital changes need not be prepared.
(b) Prepare the condensed balance sheet for Candice Urbanak, Inc., as it would appear at December 31, 1984. Assume that current liabilities remained at $15,000.

**E24-8** The accounts below appear in the ledger of Chaucer Company.

| | Retained Earnings | Dr. | Cr. | Bal. |
|---|---|---|---|---|
| Jan. 1, 1984 | Credit Balance | | | $ 42,000 |
| Aug. 15 | Dividends (cash) | $19,600 | | 22,400 |
| Dec. 31 | Net Income for 1984 | | $12,000 | 34,400 |

| | Machinery | Dr. | Cr. | Bal. |
|---|---|---|---|---|
| Jan. 1, 1984 | Debit Balance | | | $140,000 |
| Aug. 3 | Purchases of Machinery | $42,000 | | 182,000 |
| Sept. 10 | Cost of Machinery Constructed | 28,000 | | 210,000 |
| Nov. 15 | Machinery Sold | | $56,000 | 154,000 |

| | Accumulated Depreciation— Machinery | Dr. | Cr. | Bal. |
|---|---|---|---|---|
| Jan. 1, 1984 | Credit Balance | | | $ 84,000 |
| Apr. 8 | Extraordinary Repairs | $21,000 | | 63,000 |
| Nov. 15 | Accum. Depreciation of Machinery Sold | 25,200 | | 37,800 |
| Dec. 31 | Depreciation for 1984 | | $11,200 | 49,000 |

**Instructions**

From the information given, prepare all adjustments that should be made on a work sheet for a statement of changes in financial position (working capital concept). The loss on sale of equipment (Nov. 15) was $12,600.

**E24-9** Presented below is some information related to Browning International:

1. Convertible bonds payable of a par value of $400,000 were exchanged for unissued common stock of a par value of $400,000. The market price of both types of securities was par.

2. The net income for the year was $60,000.

3. Depreciation charged on the building was $16,000.

4. Organization costs in the amount of $10,000 was written off during the year as a charge to expense.

5. Some old office equipment was traded in on the purchase of some dissimilar office equipment and the following entry was made:

| | | |
|---|---|---|
| Office Equipment | 5,000 | |
| Accum. Depreciation—Office Equipment | 3,000 | |
| Office Equipment | | 4,000 |
| Cash | | 3,400 |
| Gain on Disposal of Plant Assets | | 600 |

The Gain on Disposal of Plant Assets was credited to current operations as ordinary income.

6. Dividends in the amount of $24,000, payable in cash, were declared near the end of the year, and an entry was made to record them. They are payable in January of next year.

7. The Appropriations for Bonded Indebtedness in the amount of $240,000 was returned to Retained Earnings during the year, because the bonds were retired during the year.

**Instructions**

Show by journal entries the adjustments that would be made on a work sheet for a statement of changes in financial position.

**E24-10** Below is the comparative balance sheet for Yeats Printing Corporation.

| | Dec. 31, 1983 | Dec. 31, 1984 |
|---|---|---|
| Cash | $ 20,000 | $ 15,500 |
| Short-term investments | 20,000 | 25,000 |
| Accounts receivable | 45,000 | 43,000 |
| Allowance for doubtful accounts | (2,000) | (1,800) |
| Prepaid expenses | 2,500 | 3,200 |
| Inventories | 65,000 | 73,000 |
| Land | 50,000 | 50,000 |
| Buildings | 73,500 | 100,000 |
| Accumulated depreciation—buildings | (21,000) | (30,000) |
| Equipment | 47,000 | 53,000 |
| Accumulated depreciation—equipment | (16,500) | (19,000) |
| Delivery equipment | 39,000 | 39,000 |
| Accumulated depreciation—delivery equipment | (20,500) | (24,000) |
| Patents | -0- | 10,000 |
| | $302,000 | $336,900 |

| | | |
|---|---:|---:|
| Accounts payable | $ 18,000 | $ 26,000 |
| Short-term notes payable | 6,000 | 4,000 |
| Accrued payables | 5,000 | 3,000 |
| Mortgage payable | 53,000 | 65,000 |
| Bonds payable | 62,500 | 50,000 |
| Capital stock | 102,000 | 110,000 |
| Additional paid-in capital | 4,000 | 5,500 |
| Retained earnings | 51,500 | 73,400 |
| | $302,000 | $336,900 |

Dividends in the amount of $5,000 were declared and paid in 1984.

**Instructions**

From this information, prepare a work sheet for a statement of changes in financial position (working capital approach). Make reasonable assumptions as appropriate. Do not prepare a schedule of working capital changes.

**E24–11** Presented below is information related to G. Ohlendorf, Inc. for the years 1983 and 1984 to aid in preparing a statement of changes in financial position (cash concept).

G. Ohlendorf, Inc.
BALANCE SHEETS

| | December 31, | |
|---|---:|---:|
| Assets | 1984 | 1983 |
| Current assets: | | |
| Cash | $ 128,000 | $100,000 |
| Marketable securities | 62,000 | |
| Accounts receivable—net | 415,000 | 290,000 |
| Merchandise inventory | 345,000 | 210,000 |
| Prepaid expenses | 50,000 | 25,000 |
| | 1,000,000 | 625,000 |
| Property, plant, and equipment | 565,000 | 300,000 |
| Less accumulated depreciation | 55,000 | 25,000 |
| | 510,000 | 275,000 |
| | $1,510,000 | $900,000 |
| Equities | | |
| Current liabilities: | | |
| Accounts payable | $ 272,000 | $220,000 |
| Accrued expenses | 70,000 | 65,000 |
| Dividends payable | 40,000 | |
| | 382,000 | 285,000 |
| Note payable—due 1987 | 245,000 | |
| Stockholders' equity: | | |
| Common stock | 600,000 | 450,000 |
| Retained earnings | 283,000 | 165,000 |
| | 883,000 | 615,000 |
| | $1,510,000 | $900,000 |

G. Ohlendorf, Inc.
INCOME STATEMENTS

| | Year Ended December 31, | |
|---|---|---|
| | 1984 | 1983 |
| Net sales—including service charges | $3,275,000 | $2,000,000 |
| Cost of goods sold | 2,525,000 | 1,600,000 |
| Gross profit | 750,000 | 400,000 |
| Expenses (including income taxes) | 500,000 | 260,000 |
| Net income | $ 250,000 | $ 140,000 |

Additional information available included the following:

Although Ohlendorf will report all changes in financial position, management has adopted a format emphasizing the flow of cash.

All accounts receivable and accounts payable relate to trade merchandise. Cash discounts are not allowed to customers but a service charge is added to an account for late payment. Accounts payable are recorded net and always are paid to take all of the discount allowed. The Allowance for Doubtful Accounts at the end of 1984 was the same as at the end of 1983; no receivables were charged against the Allowance during 1984.

The proceeds from the note payable were used to finance a new store building. Capital stock was sold to provide additional working capital.

**Instructions**

Compute the following for the year 1984:
(a) Cash collected from accounts receivable, assuming that all sales are on account.
(b) Cash payments made on accounts payable to suppliers, assuming that all purchases of inventory are on account.
(c) Cash dividend payment.
(d) Cash receipts that were not provided by operations.
(e) Cash payments for assets that were not reflected in operations.

**E24-12** Fresno Canning Co. has recently decided to go public and has hired you as the independent CPA. One statement that the enterprise is anxious to have prepared is a statement of changes in financial position. Financial statements of Fresno Canning Co., for 1983 and 1984 are provided below.

| | 12/31/83 | | 12/31/84 | |
|---|---|---|---|---|
| Cash | | $ 13,000 | | $ 21,000 |
| Accounts receivable | | 14,000 | | 33,000 |
| Merchandise inventory | | 35,000 | | 22,000 |
| Property, plant, and equipment | $78,000 | | $60,000 | |
| Less accumulated depreciation | (24,000) | 54,000 | (22,000) | 38,000 |
| | | $116,000 | | $114,000 |
| Accounts payable | | 23,000 | | 30,000 |
| Federal income taxes payable | | 30,000 | | 25,000 |
| Bonds payable | | 33,000 | | 35,000 |
| Common stock | | 14,000 | | 6,000 |
| Retained earnings | | 16,000 | | 18,000 |
| | | $116,000 | | $114,000 |

INCOME STATEMENT
For the Year Ended December 31, 1984

| | | |
|---|---:|---:|
| Sales | | $220,000 |
| Cost of sales | | 180,000 |
| Gross profit | | 40,000 |
| Selling expenses | $ 18,000 | |
| Administrative expenses | 6,000 | 24,000 |
| Income from operations | | 16,000 |
| Interest expense | | 5,000 |
| Income before taxes | | 11,000 |
| Income taxes | | 2,000 |
| Net income | | $  9,000 |

The following additional data were provided:

1. Dividends for the year 1984 were $5,000.
2. During the year equipment was sold for $10,000. This equipment cost $18,000 originally and had a book value of $12,000 at the time of sale. The loss on sale was incorrectly charged to retained earnings.
3. All depreciation expense is in the selling expense category.

**Instructions**

(a) Prepare a statement of changes in financial position using a working capital approach.
(b) Prepare a statement of changes in financial position emphasizing a cash approach using the indirect approach. All sales and purchases are on account.

**E24-13** Clarence Hankes Co. reported $210,000 of net income for 1984. The accountant, in preparing the statement of changes in financial position on a working capital basis, noted several items that might offset working capital provided by operations. These items are listed below:

1. During 1984, Hankes purchased 100 shares of treasury stock at a cost of $20 per share. These shares were then resold at $25 per share.
2. During 1984, Hankes sold 100 shares of IBM common at $250 per share. Acquisition cost of these shares was $150 per share. This investment was shown on Hankes' December 31, 1983 balance sheet as a current asset.
3. During 1984, Hankes changed from the straight-line method to the double-declining balance method of depreciation for its machinery. The debit to the Cumulative Effect account was for $19,000 net of tax.
4. During 1984, Hankes revised its estimate for bad debts. Before 1984, Hankes' bad debts expense was 1% of its net sales. In 1984, this percentage was increased to 1½%. Net sales for 1984 were $500,000.
5. During 1984, Hankes issued 500 shares of its $10 par common stock for a patent. The market value of the shares on the date of the transaction was $23 per share.
6. Depreciation expense for 1984 is $23,000.
7. Hankes Co. holds 40% of the Seabrook Company's common stock as a long-term investment. Seabrook Company reported $14,000 of net income for 1984.
8. Seabrook Company paid a total of $2,000 of cash dividends in 1984.

9. A comparison of Hankes' December 31, 1983 and December 31, 1984 balance sheets indicates that the credit balance in Deferred Income Taxes (classified as a long-term liability) decreased $4,000.

10. During 1984, Hankes declared a 10% stock dividend. One thousand shares of $10 par common stock were distributed. The market price at date of issuance was $20 per share.

**Instructions**

Prepare a schedule that shows working capital provided by operations.

**E24–14** Odon Company has not yet prepared a formal Statement of Changes in Financial Position for the 1983 fiscal year. Comparative Statements of Financial Position as of December 31, 1982 and 1983, and a Statement of Income and Retained Earnings for the year ended December 31, 1983 are presented below.

Odon Company
STATEMENT OF INCOME AND RETAINED EARNINGS
Year Ended December 31, 1983
(000 omitted)

| | | |
|---|---:|---:|
| Sales | | $2,408 |
| Expenses | | |
| Cost of goods sold | $1,100 | |
| Salaries and benefits | 850 | |
| Heat, light, and power | 75 | |
| Depreciation | 60 | |
| Property taxes | 18 | |
| Patent amortization | 25 | |
| Miscellaneous expense | 10 | |
| Interest | 55 | 2,193 |
| Income before income taxes | | 215 |
| Income taxes | | 105 |
| Net income | | 110 |
| Retained earnings—Jan. 1, 1983 | | 310 |
| | | 420 |
| Stock dividend declared and issued | | 130 |
| Retained earnings—Dec. 31, 1983 | | $ 290 |

Odon Company
STATEMENT OF FINANCIAL POSITION
December 31
(000 omitted)

| Assets | 1982 | 1983 |
|---|---:|---:|
| Current assets | | |
| Cash | $ 100 | $ 60 |
| U.S. treasury notes | 50 | -0- |
| Accounts receivable | 500 | 610 |
| Inventory | 600 | 720 |
| Total current assets | 1,250 | 1,390 |

| Long-term assets | | |
|---|---|---|
| Land | 70 | 80 |
| Buildings and equipment | 600 | 710 |
| Accumulated depreciation | (120) | (180) |
| Patents (less amortization) | 130 | 105 |
| Total long-term assets | 680 | 715 |
| Total assets | $1,930 | $2,105 |

| **Liabilities and Stockholders' Equity** | | |
|---|---|---|
| Current liabilities | | |
| Accounts payable | $ 300 | $ 360 |
| Taxes payable | 20 | 25 |
| Notes payable | 400 | 400 |
| Total current liabilities | 720 | 785 |
| Term notes payable—due 1988 | 200 | 200 |
| Total liabilities | 920 | 985 |
| Owners' equity | | |
| Common stock outstanding | 700 | 830 |
| Retained earnings | 310 | 290 |
| Total stockholders' equity | 1,010 | 1,120 |
| Total liabilities and stockholders' equity | $1,930 | $2,105 |

**Instructions**

Prepare a Statement of Changes in Financial Position which reconciles the change in cash balance. Use the direct approach. Changes in accounts receivable and accounts payable relate to sales and cost of sales. Taxes payable relates only to income taxes.

(CMA adapted)

**E24–15** Presented below are comparative balance sheets for El Matador, Incorporated.

| | December 31 | |
|---|---|---|
| | 1984 | 1983 |
| Cash | $ 450,000 | $ 500,000 |
| Accounts receivable, net | 1,150,000 | 900,000 |
| Inventory | 3,100,000 | 2,175,000 |
| Prepaid expenses | 50,000 | 75,000 |
| Land | 500,000 | 200,000 |
| Plant and equipment | 5,500,000 | 4,890,000 |
| Accumulated depreciation | (1,900,000) | (1,500,000) |
| Investments in other companies | 350,000 | 160,000 |
| Total assets | $9,200,000 | $7,400,000 |
| Accounts payable | $1,775,000 | $1,210,000 |
| Income taxes payable | 200,000 | 250,000 |
| Notes payable—current portion | 500,000 | — |
| Long-term notes | 1,250,000 | 1,750,000 |
| Deferred taxes | 400,000 | 250,000 |
| Common stock | 3,500,000 | 2,800,000 |
| Retained earnings | 1,575,000 | 1,140,000 |
| Total liabilities and equities | $9,200,000 | $7,400,000 |

The 1984 income statement follows.

| | |
|---|---:|
| Sales | $8,000,000 |
| Cost of goods sold | 3,820,000 |
| Gross margin | 4,180,000 |
| Operating expenses | 2,900,000 |
| Operating income | 1,280,000 |
| Gain on sale of equipment | 120,000 |
| Income before taxes | 1,400,000 |
| Income tax expense | 500,000 |
| Net income | $ 900,000 |

The following additional information is available.

1. The company issued $190,000 of its own stock in exchange for 10% of the stock of another company.
2. Fully depreciated equipment costing $100,000 new was retired and removed from the books.
3. A stock dividend of $200,000 was declared and issued during the year; a cash dividend was also declared and paid.
4. A $300,000 fabricating plant was acquired during 1984 by giving $200,000 in common stock and $100,000 in cash.
5. Depreciation expense totaled $650,000; $550,000 included in cost of goods sold and $100,000 included in operating expenses.
6. Unneeded equipment with an original cost of $350,000 and a book value of $200,000 was sold for $320,000.
7. Five thousand shares of common stock were issued at $22 per share.
8. $500,000 in long-term notes were reclassified to current status.

**Instructions**

(a) Prepare a statement of changes in financial position (cash basis), using the indirect approach.
(b) Prepare a statement of changes in financial position (cash basis), using the direct approach. Assume that the accounts receivable and accounts payable relate solely to sales and cost of sales. Amortization of prepaid expenses relates to operating expenses.

# PROBLEMS

**P24–1** The comparative balance sheets for Railway Car Corporation show the following information:

| | December 31 | |
|---|---:|---:|
| | 1984 | 1983 |
| Cash | $ 38,500 | $ 7,000 |
| Accounts receivable | 12,000 | 10,000 |
| Inventory | 12,000 | 6,000 |
| Investments | — | 2,000 |
| Building | — | 29,750 |
| Equipment | 50,000 | 35,000 |
| Patent | 5,000 | 6,250 |
| Totals | $117,500 | $96,000 |

| | | |
|---|---:|---:|
| Allowance for doubtful accounts | $ 3,000 | $ 4,500 |
| Accumulated depreciation on equipment | 2,000 | 4,500 |
| Accumulated depreciation on building | — | 11,000 |
| Accounts payable | 5,000 | 3,000 |
| Dividends payable | — | 6,000 |
| Notes payable, short-term (nontrade) | 3,000 | 4,000 |
| Long-term notes payable | 36,000 | 25,000 |
| Common stock | 38,000 | 33,000 |
| Retained earnings | 30,500 | 5,000 |
| | $117,500 | $96,000 |

Additional data related to 1984 are as follows:

1. Equipment that had cost $7,000 and was 50% depreciated at time of disposal was sold for $2,500 (net of tax).
2. $5,000 of the long-term note payable was paid by issuing common stock.
3. The only cash dividends paid were $6,000.
4. On January 1, 1984 the building was completely destroyed by a flood. Insurance proceeds on the building were $29,750 (net of tax).
5. Investments (long-term) were sold at $3,700 (net of tax) above their cost. The company has made similar sales and investments in the past.
6. Cash of $6,000 was paid for the acquisition of equipment.
7. A long-term note for $16,000 was issued for the acquisition of equipment.

**Instructions**

Prepare a statement of changes in financial position (working capital approach). No work sheet or schedule of working capital changes is required. Flood damage is unusual and infrequent in that part of the country.

**P24-2** The following schedule showing net changes in balance sheet accounts at December 31, 1984, compared to December 31, 1983, was prepared from the records of The Omaha Company. The statement of changes in financial position for the year ended December 31, 1984, has not yet been prepared.

| Assets | Net Change Increase (Decrease) |
|---|---:|
| Cash | $ 70,000 |
| Accounts receivable, net | 66,000 |
| Inventories | 37,000 |
| Prepaid expenses | 1,000 |
| Property, plant, and equipment, net | 54,000 |
| Total assets | $228,000 |
| | |
| **Liabilities** | |
| Accounts payable | $ (50,500) |
| Notes payable—current | (15,000) |
| Accrued expenses | 28,000 |
| Bonds payable | (29,000) |
| Less decrease in unamortized bond discount | 2,200 |
| Total liabilities | (64,300) |

Stockholders' Equity

| | |
|---|---:|
| Common stock, $10 par value | 500,000 |
| Capital contributed in excess of par value | 200,000 |
| Retained earnings | (437,700) |
| Appropriation of retained earnings for possible future inventory price decline | 30,000 |
| Total stockholders' equity | 292,300 |
| Total liabilities and stockholders' equity | $228,000 |

Additional Information:

1. The net income for the year ended December 31, 1984, was $198,800. There were no extraordinary items.

2. During the year ended December 31, 1984, uncollectible accounts receivable of $26,400 were written off by a charge to allowance for doubtful accounts.

3. A comparison of property, plant and equipment as of the end of each year follows:

| | December 31, 1984 | December 31, 1983 | Net Increase (Decrease) |
|---|---:|---:|---:|
| Property, plant, and equipment | $565,500 | $510,000 | $55,500 |
| Less: Accumulated depreciation | 229,500 | 228,000 | (1,500) |
| Property, plant, and equipment, net | $336,000 | $282,000 | $54,000 |

During 1984, machinery was purchased at a cost of $47,000. In addition, machinery that was acquired in 1977 at a cost of $48,000 was sold for $5,400. At the date of sale, the machinery had an undepreciated cost of $8,400. The remaining increase in property, plant, and equipment resulted from the acquisition of a tract of land for a new plant site.

4. The bonds payable mature at the rate of $29,000 every year.

5. In January 1984, the company issued an additional 18,000 shares of its common stock at $14 per share upon the exercise of outstanding stock options held by key employees. In May 1984 (market price $14), the company declared and issued a 4% stock dividend on its outstanding stock. During the year, a cash dividend was paid on the common stock. On December 31, 1984, there were 832,000 shares of common stock outstanding.

6. The appropriation of retained earnings for possible future inventory price decline was provided by a charge against retained earnings, in anticipation of an expected future drop in the market related to goods in inventory.

**Instructions**

(a) Prepare a statement of changes in financial position for the year ended December 31, 1984, based upon the information presented above. The statement should be prepared using a working capital format.

(b) Prepare a schedule of changes in working capital for the year 1984.

(AICPA adapted)

**P24-3** You have completed the field work in connection with your audit of Garfield Corporation for the year ended December 31, 1984. The following schedule shows the balance sheet accounts at the beginning and end of the year:

| | Dec. 31, 1984 | Dec. 31, 1983 | Increase or (Decrease) |
|---|---|---|---|
| Cash | $ 287,900 | $ 320,000 | $ (32,100) |
| Accounts receivable | 487,800 | 410,000 | 77,800 |
| Inventory | 691,700 | 660,000 | 31,700 |
| Prepaid expenses | 12,000 | 8,000 | 4,000 |
| Investment in subsidiary | 106,800 | — | 106,800 |
| Cash surrender value of life insurance | 2,304 | 1,800 | 504 |
| Machinery | 187,000 | 190,000 | (3,000) |
| Buildings | 566,500 | 407,900 | 158,600 |
| Land | 52,500 | 52,500 | — |
| Patents | 69,000 | 60,000 | 9,000 |
| Goodwill | 40,000 | 50,000 | (10,000) |
| Bond discount and expense | 3,276 | — | 3,276 |
| | $2,506,780 | $2,160,200 | $346,580 |

| | Dec. 31, 1984 | Dec. 31, 1983 | Increase or (Decrease) |
|---|---|---|---|
| Accrued taxes payable | $ 94,000 | $ 79,600 | $ 14,400 |
| Accounts payable | 299,280 | 280,000 | 19,280 |
| Dividends payable | 70,000 | — | 70,000 |
| Bonds payable—8% | 125,000 | — | 125,000 |
| Bonds payable—12% | — | 100,000 | (100,000) |
| Allowance for doubtful accounts | 35,300 | 40,000 | (4,700) |
| Accumulated depreciation—building | 407,000 | 400,000 | 7,000 |
| Accumulated depreciation—machinery | 141,000 | 130,000 | 11,000 |
| Premium on bonds payable | — | 2,400 | (2,400) |
| Capital stock—no par | 1,301,200 | 1,453,200 | (152,000) |
| Additional paid-in capital | 14,000 | — | 14,000 |
| Appropriation for plant expansion | 10,000 | — | 10,000 |
| Retained earnings—unappropriated | 10,000 | (325,000) | 335,000 |
| | $2,506,780 | $2,160,200 | $346,580 |

### STATEMENT OF RETAINED EARNINGS

| | | | |
|---|---|---|---|
| January | 1, 1984 | Balance (deficit) | $(325,000) |
| March | 31, 1984 | Net income for first quarter of 1984 | 25,000 |
| April | 1, 1984 | Transfer from paid-in capital | 300,000 |
| | | Balance | 0 |
| December 31, 1984 | | Net income for last three quarters of 1984 | 90,000 |
| | | Dividend declared—payable January 20, 1985 | (70,000) |
| | | Appropriation for plant expansion | (10,000) |
| | | Balance | $ 10,000 |

Your working papers contain the following information:

1. On April 1, 1984, the existing deficit was written off against capital stock created by reducing the stated value of the no-par stock.

2. On November 1, 1984, 29,600 shares of no-par stock were sold for $162,000. The board of directors voted to regard $5 per share as stated capital.

3. A patent was purchased for $15,000.

4. Machinery was purchased for $5,000 and installed in December, 1984. A check for this amount was sent to the vendor in January, 1985.

5. During the year, machinery that had a cost basis of $8,000 and on which there was accumulated depreciation of $5,200 was sold for $1,000. No other plant assets were sold during the year.

6. The 12%, 20-year bonds were dated and issued on January 2, 1972. Interest was payable on June 30 and December 31. They were sold originally at 106. These bonds were retired at 101 (net of tax) plus accrued interest on March 31, 1984.

7. The 8%, 40-year bonds were dated January 1, 1984, and were sold on March 31 at 98 plus accrued interest. Interest is payable semianually on June 30 and December 31. Expense of issuance was $839.

8. Garfield Corporation acquired 80% control in the Subsidiary Company on January 2, 1984, for $100,000. The income statement of the Subsidiary Company for 1984, shows a net income of $8,500.

9. Extraordinary repairs to buildings of $7,200 were charged to Accumulated Depreciation—Building.

### Instructions

From the information above prepare a statement of changes in financial position (working capital approach). A work sheet is not necessary, but the principal computations should be supported by schedules or skeleton ledger accounts.

**P24-4** The manager of Yummy Cookie Company has reviewed the annual financial statements for the year 1984 and is unable to determine from a reading of the balance sheet the reasons for the changes in working capital during the year. You are given the following balance sheets of Yummy Cookie Company.

| | 12/31/84 | 12/31/83 | Increase (Decrease) |
|---|---|---|---|
| Land | $ 138,000 | $ 150,000 | $ (12,000) |
| Machinery | 335,000 | 200,000 | 135,000 |
| Tools | 40,000 | 70,000 | (30,000) |
| Bond investment | 17,000 | 15,000 | 2,000 |
| Inventories | 210,000 | 218,000 | (8,000) |
| Goodwill | -0- | 210,000 | (210,000) |
| Buildings | 810,000 | 550,000 | 260,000 |
| Accounts receivable | 178,000 | 92,000 | 86,000 |
| Notes receivable—trade | 21,000 | 27,000 | (6,000) |
| Cash in bank | -0- | 8,000 | (8,000) |
| Cash on hand | 2,600 | 1,000 | 1,600 |
| Unexpired insurance—machinery | 700 | 1,400 | (700) |
| Unamortized bond discount | 2,000 | 2,500 | (500) |
| | $1,754,300 | $1,544,900 | $ 209,400 |
| Capital stock ($100 par) | $ 700,000 | $ 400,000 | $ 300,000 |
| Bonds payable | 160,000 | 100,000 | 60,000 |
| Accounts payable | 56,000 | 52,000 | 4,000 |
| Bank overdraft | 3,000 | -0- | 3,000 |
| Notes payable—trade | 7,000 | 10,000 | (3,000) |
| Bank loans—short term | 4,500 | 6,800 | (2,300) |
| Accrued interest | 9,000 | 6,000 | 3,000 |
| Accrued taxes | 4,000 | 3,000 | 1,000 |
| Allowance for doubtful accounts | 4,700 | 2,300 | 2,400 |
| Accumulated depreciation | 269,000 | 181,000 | 88,000 |
| Retained earnings | 537,100 | 783,800 | (246,700) |
| | $1,754,300 | $1,544,900 | $ 209,400 |

You are advised that the following transactions took place during the year:

1. The income statement for the year 1984 was:

| | | |
|---|---:|---:|
| Sales (net) | | $1,271,300 |
| Operating charges: | | |
|   Material and supplies | $250,000 | |
|   Direct labor | 210,000 | |
|   Manufacturing overhead | 181,500 | |
|   Depreciation | 120,900 | |
|   Selling expenses | 245,000 | |
|   General expenses | 230,000 | |
|   Interest expense (net) | 15,000 | |
| Unusual items: | | |
|   Write-off of goodwill | 240,000 | |
|   Write-off of land | 12,000 | |
|   Loss on machinery | 1,600 | 1,506,000 |
| Net loss | | $ 234,700 |

2. A 3% cash dividend was declared and paid on the outstanding capital stock at 1/1/84.

3. There were no purchases or sales of tools. The cost of tools used is in depreciation.

4. Stock was sold during the year at $90; the discount was charged to Goodwill.

5. Old machinery that cost $4,500 was scrapped and written off the books. Accumulated depreciation on such equipment was $2,900.

**Instructions**

(a) Prepare a statement of changes in financial position using a working capital approach.

(b) Prepare a statement of changes in financial position using a cash basis approach. Use the indirect approach. Assume that the bank loan—short term and bank overdraft were related to transactions involving the purchase of materials and supplies. All sales and purchases of inventory are made on account.

**P24–5** The balance sheet of Vaccum Pack Company at December 31, 1983, is as follows:

Vaccum Pack Company
BALANCE SHEET
December 31, 1983

| | | | |
|---|---:|---:|---:|
| Cash | | | $ 42,000 |
| Receivables | | | 108,000 |
| Inventories | | | 214,000 |
| Prepaid expenses | | | 28,000 |
|   Total current assets | | | 392,000 |
| Investments (long-term) | | | 84,000 |
| Land | | $ 45,000 | |
| Buildings | $570,000 | | |
|   Less accumulated depreciation | 110,000 | 460,000 | |
| Equipment | 385,000 | | |
|   Less accumulated depreciation | 180,000 | 205,000 | 710,000 |
| Patents | | | 122,000 |
| | | | $1,308,000 |
| Accounts payable | | | $ 85,000 |
| Notes payable | | | 120,000 |
| Taxes payable | | | 188,000 |
|   Total current liabilities | | | 393,000 |

| | | |
|---|---:|---:|
| Bonds payable | | 500,000 |
| Preferred stock | $200,000 | |
| Common stock | 200,000 | |
| Retained earnings | 15,000 | 415,000 |
| | | $1,308,000 |

Vaccum Pack Company's management predicts the following transactions for the coming year:

| | |
|---|---:|
| Sales (accrual basis) | $4,840,000 |
| Payments for salaries, purchases, interest, taxes, etc. (cash basis) | 4,486,000 |
| Decrease in prepaid expenses | 5,500 |
| Increase in receivables | 110,000 |
| Increase in inventories | 35,000 |
| Depreciation: | |
|   Buildings | 33,000 |
|   Equipment | 55,000 |
| Patent amortization | 11,000 |
| Increase in accounts payable | 22,000 |
| Increase in taxes payable | 99,000 |
| Reduction in bonds payable | 500,000 |
| Sales of investments (all those held 12/31/83) | 110,000 |
| Issuance of common stock at par | 220,000 |

**Instructions**

(a) Prepare a balance sheet as it will appear December 31, 1984, if all the anticipated transactions work out as expected.

(b) Prepare a statement of changes in financial position (working capital approach) for 1984, assuming that the expected 1984 transactions are all completed. Assume that the sale of investments is not an extraordinary item.

(c) Prepare a statement of changes in financial position (cash approach) for 1984, assuming that the expected 1984 transactions are all completed. Use the indirect approach.

(d) Compute cash provided by operations, using the direct approach.

**P24–6** The following financial data were furnished to you by Cunico Corporation:

1. A six-months note payable for $55,000 was issued toward the purchase of new equipment.

2. The long-term note payable requires the payment of $16,000 per year plus interest until paid.

3. Treasury stock was sold for $1,000 more than its cost.

4. All dividends were paid by cash.

5. All purchases and sales were on account.

6. The sinking fund will be used to retire the long-term bonds.

7. Equipment with an original cost of $15,000 was sold for $6,000.

8. Selling and General Expenses includes the following expenses:

| | |
|---|---:|
| Expired insurance | $ 2,000 |
| Building depreciation | 7,500 |
| Equipment depreciation | 15,500 |
| Bad debts expense | 7,000 |
| Interest expense | 18,000 |

Cunico Corporation
COMPARATIVE TRIAL BALANCES
At Beginning and End of Fiscal Year Ended October 31, 1984

| | October 31, 1984 | Increase | Decrease | November 1, 1983 |
|---|---|---|---|---|
| Cash | $ 228,000 | $178,000 | | $ 50,000 |
| Accounts receivable | 146,000 | 46,000 | | 100,000 |
| Inventories | 291,000 | | $ 9,000 | 300,000 |
| Unexpired insurance | 2,500 | 500 | | 2,000 |
| Long-term investments at cost | 10,000 | | 30,000 | 40,000 |
| Sinking fund | 90,000 | 10,000 | | 80,000 |
| Land and building | 195,000 | | | 195,000 |
| Equipment | 215,000 | 125,000 | | 90,000 |
| Discount on bonds payable | 8,400 | | 600 | 9,000 |
| Treasury stock at cost | 5,100 | | 4,900 | 10,000 |
| Cost of goods sold | 530,000 | | | |
| Selling and general expenses | 296,000 | | | |
| Income tax | 31,000 | | | |
| Loss on sale of equipment | 2,000 | | | |
| Capital gains tax | 3,000 | | | |
| Total debits | $2,053,000 | | | $876,000 |
| Allowance for doubtful accounts | $ 8,000 | $ 3,000 | | $ 5,000 |
| Accumulated depreciation—building | 30,000 | 7,500 | | 22,500 |
| Accumulated depreciation—equipment | 36,000 | 8,500 | | 27,500 |
| Accounts payable | 50,000 | | 10,000 | 60,000 |
| Notes payable—current | 75,000 | 55,000 | | 20,000 |
| Accrued expenses payable | 20,000 | 5,000 | | 15,000 |
| Taxes payable | 33,000 | 23,000 | | 10,000 |
| Unearned revenue | 3,000 | | 6,000 | 9,000 |
| Note payable—long-term | 44,000 | | 16,000 | 60,000 |
| Bonds payable—long-term | 250,000 | | | 250,000 |
| Common stock | 300,000 | 100,000 | | 200,000 |
| Appropriation for sinking fund | 90,000 | 10,000 | | 80,000 |
| Unappropriated retained earnings | 90,000 | | 22,000 | 112,000 |
| Paid-in capital in excess of par value | 101,000 | 96,000 | | 5,000 |
| Sales | 912,000 | | | |
| Gain on sale of investments (ordinary) | 11,000 | | | |
| Total credits | $2,053,000 | | | $876,000 |

**Instructions**

(a) Prepare schedules computing
   1. Collections of accounts receivable.
   2. Payments of accounts payable.
(b) Prepare a statement of changes in financial position—cash approach for Cunico Corporation. Use the indirect approach.

(AICPA adapted)

**P24-7** Tampa Drilling Company has prepared its financial statements for the year ended December 31, 1983, and for the three months ended March 31, 1984. You have been asked to prepare a statement of changes in financial position on a working capital basis for the three months ended March 31, 1984. The company's balance sheet data at December 31, 1983, and March 31, 1984, and its income statement data for the three months ended March 31, 1984, follow. You have previously satisfied yourself as to the correctness of the amounts presented.

| | Balance Sheet | |
| --- | --- | --- |
| | December 31, 1983 | March 31, 1984 |
| Cash | $ 24,400 | $ 87,400 |
| Marketable investments | 17,600 | 7,300 |
| Accounts receivable, net | 24,620 | 49,320 |
| Inventory | 29,590 | 48,590 |
| Total current assets | 96,210 | 192,610 |
| Land | 41,300 | 18,700 |
| Building | 250,000 | 250,000 |
| Equipment | — | 83,000 |
| Accumulated depreciation | (15,000) | (17,750) |
| Investment in 30%-owned company | 60,920 | 67,100 |
| Other assets | 15,100 | 15,100 |
| Total | $448,530 | $608,760 |
| Accounts payable | $ 21,220 | $ 16,000 |
| Dividend payable | — | 9,000 |
| Income taxes payable | — | 34,946 |
| Total current liabilities | 21,220 | 59,946 |
| Other liabilities | 186,000 | 186,000 |
| Bonds payable | 45,000 | 115,000 |
| Discount on bonds payable | (2,400) | (2,150) |
| Deferred income taxes | 5,610 | 846 |
| Preferred stock | 30,000 | — |
| Common stock | 80,000 | 110,000 |
| Dividends declared | — | (9,000) |
| Retained earnings | 83,100 | 148,118 |
| Total | $448,530 | $608,760 |

| | Income Statement Data for the Three Months Ended March 31, 1984 |
| --- | --- |
| Sales | $242,807 |
| Gain on sale of marketable investments | 3,400 |
| Equity in earnings of 30%-owned company | 6,180 |
| Gain on condemnation of land (extraordinary) | 10,400 |
| | $262,787 |
| Cost of sales | $138,407 |
| General and administrative expenses | 22,010 |
| Depreciation | 2,750 |
| Interest expense | 1,150 |
| Income taxes | 33,452 |
| | 197,769 |
| Net income | $ 65,018 |

Your discussion with the company's controller and a review of the financial records have revealed the following information:

1. On January 8, 1984, the company sold marketable securities for cash.

2. The company's preferred stock is convertible into common stock at a rate of one share of preferred for two shares of common. The preferred stock and common stock have par values of $2 and $1, respectively.

3. On January 17, 1984, three acres of land were condemned. An award of $33,000 in cash was received on March 22, 1984. Purchase of additional land as a replacement is not contemplated by the company. (Treated as a capital gain for tax purposes.)

4. On March 25, 1984, the company purchased equipment for cash.

5. On March 29, 1984, bonds payable were issued by the company at par for cash.

6. The company's tax rate is 40% for regular income and 20% for capital gains.

**Instructions**

Prepare in good form a statement of changes in financial position, including any supporting schedules needed, on a working capital basis for Tampa Drilling Company for the three months ended March 31, 1984.

(AICPA adapted)

# CHAPTER 25

# Financial Reporting and Changing Prices

It has often been said that only two things in life are certain—death and taxes. However, a third could probably now be added—inflation, that is, the value of every currency in the world steadily decreases. For example, during the decade of the 1970s, the compound annual inflation rate (the average) was 6.7% in the United States, 9% in France, 13.2% in Great Britain, 15% in Mexico, 28.3% in Brazil, 117.2% in Argentina, and 163.6% in Chile. Each of these increases in prices has been accompanied with a comparable decrease in the value of that country's currency.

In the United States prior to 1970 it was easy to ignore inflation's impact because the changes from year to year were considered insignificant. With the general price level doubling between 1970 and 1980, and 1981 and 1982 having continued inflation, this is no longer the case. In fact, as the diagram on page 1137 illustrates, we have been experiencing a significant decline in the purchasing power of the U.S. dollar over the period 1949–1981 when the rate of inflation is compounded. The effects of this phenomenon are substantial. Many companies are experiencing liquidity problems, even though they are reporting record net income figures, because they lack the necessary funds to replace their inventories and productive capacity. As one study recently noted, some companies (such as Ford Motor Company and Polaroid) are paying out dividends in excess of net income after the income has been adjusted for price-level changes.[1]

As a consequence, the accounting and financial world is presented with challenges, decisions, and opportunities. Accountants and others are becoming receptive to imaginative proposals for improvements in financial reporting. A difficult, exciting, and extensive experimental and educational process lies ahead. Before we have consensus on which changes to make and which new approaches to adopt, all of the parties concerned need to understand the alternatives and grasp what the new information is intended to portray. Such is the purpose of this chapter.

## ALTERNATIVE FINANCIAL REPORTING APPROACHES

As indicated in Chapter 2, a long-standing principle of accounting holds that transactions should be recorded at historical cost. However, many accountants are unhappy with the present reporting model, noting that historical cost financial statements have severe limita-

[1]"Living Off Capital," *Forbes* (November 10, 1980), p. 232.

### INFLATION IN THE UNITED STATES
### (Based on the Consumer Price Index)

| Year | Consumer Price Index 1967 = 100[a] | Purchasing Power of Dollar 1982 = $1.00 | Rate of Inflation[c] |
|---|---|---|---|
| 1960 | 88.7 | 3.32 | 1.6% |
| 1961 | 89.6 | 3.28 | 1.0 |
| 1962 | 90.6 | 3.25 | 1.1 |
| 1963 | 91.7 | 3.21 | 1.2 |
| 1964 | 92.9 | 3.17 | 1.3 |
| 1965 | 94.5 | 3.11 | 1.7 |
| 1966 | 97.2 | 3.03 | 2.9 |
| 1967 | 100.0 | 2.94 | 2.9 |
| 1968 | 104.2 | 2.82 | 4.2 |
| 1969 | 109.8 | 2.68 | 5.4 |
| 1970 | 116.3 | 2.53 | 5.9 |
| 1971 | 121.3 | 2.43 | 3.7 |
| 1972 | 125.3 | 2.35 | 3.3 |
| 1973 | 133.1 | 2.21 | 6.2 |
| 1974 | 147.4 | 2.00 | 10.7 |
| 1975 | 161.2 | 1.83 | 9.4 |
| 1976 | 170.5 | 1.73 | 5.7 |
| 1977 | 181.5 | 1.62 | 6.4 |
| 1978 | 195.4 | 1.51 | 7.7 |
| 1979 | 217.4 | 1.35 | 11.3 |
| 1980 | 246.8 | 1.19 | 13.5 |
| 1981 | 272.4 | 1.08 | 10.4 |
| 1982 | 294.2[b] | 1.00 (Est.) | 8.0 |

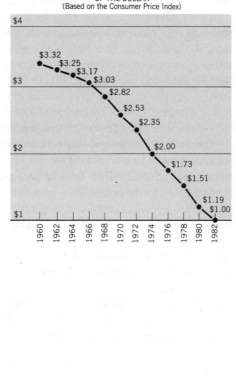

DECLINE IN THE PURCHASING POWER
OF THE DOLLAR
(Based on the Consumer Price Index)

[a]Source: *Handbook on Basic Economic Statistics,* Bureau of Economic Statistics, Inc., Economic Statistics Bureau of Washington, D.C., April 1982, Vol. XXXVI, No. 4.
[b]Estimated. Source: *Business Forecasts—1982,* Federal Reserve Bank of Richmond, p. 4.
[c]Rate of inflation $= \dfrac{CPI_t - CPI_{t-1}}{CPI_{t-1}}$

tions. Criticism is especially strong when one perceives the effects of double-digit inflation in the United States in recent years. At such times cost is no longer adequate because the cost figures of a year ago are not comparable to current cost levels. To meet these criticisms, three different solutions have been offered.

1. **CONSTANT DOLLAR ACCOUNTING.** Change the measuring unit but retain the historical cost reporting model.
2. **CURRENT VALUE ACCOUNTING.** Retain the measuring unit but depart from the historical cost reporting model.
3. **CURRENT VALUE/CONSTANT DOLLAR ACCOUNTING.** Change the measuring unit and depart from the historical cost reporting model.

**Constant Dollar Accounting (General Price-Level Model)**   A dollar is valued in terms of its ability to purchase "a number of items in general," or more appropriately, its "purchasing power." If a dollar today cannot buy the same bundle of goods that a dollar bought a number of years ago, then inflation has occurred. This phenomenon has great relevance to accountants because we assume that our measuring unit (the dollar) is stable; unfortunately, the truth is that our measuring unit changes, and as it changes, distortions develop.

Those who advocate the adjustment of accounting data for changes in the purchasing power of the dollar, referred to as **constant dollar accounting** or **general price-level accounting,** ask the question: Is it possible to add 1963 dollars, 1975 dollars, and 1983 dollars and arrive at any meaningful sum because of the differences in their purchasing power? Adding 20,000, 1963 dollars, with 30,000, 1975 dollars and 40,000, 1983 dollars may total 90,000 dollars, but the sum may have no more economic significance than the addition of 20,000 U.S. dollars to 30,000 French francs and 40,000 German marks for a total of 90,000 monetary units. The monetary units are just not equivalent.

Constant dollar accounting is historical cost data adjusted for changes in the unit of measurement. The advantages of this approach are that it is simple to compute, objective in nature, and reasonably easy to understand. If general price-level fluctuations are extreme enough to make cost data less useful than desired, financial statements adjusted for general price-level changes can be prepared from the historical cost data and used together with, or in place of, the cost-based statements.

**Current Value Accounting**   A second approach called current value accounting abandons historical cost as a basis for financial statements and shifts to some measure of current value. Proponents of this approach argue that the problem is not with the unit of measure but rather with the historical cost model.

Their position is that users of financial statements are primarily interested in what the business is worth now, rather than what costs were incurred at some point in the past. Their argument is based on the notion of economic asset value, which conceptually is the present value of the future net receipts from the particular asset in question.

Recognizing the practical problems of determining the present value of future cash flows, many contend that any objective approximation of economic value is more useful to financial statement readers than are historical cost figures. For many assets, current value figures are available on an objective basis, and it is argued that they are sufficiently close approximations to economic value to be useful. Investments in stocks and bonds quoted on a securities exchange, for example, provide current value information that is reliable. Various staple commodities are also quoted on an open market price basis, and these prices could be used for valuing inventories. Some contend that there is a second-hand market for machinery and equipment sufficient to provide objective prices for many of these items. Where there are no quoted market prices, appraisals or specific index numbers may be used. Thus, for many assets an approximation of current value is available.

**Current Value/Constant Dollar Accounting**   A third group contends that both the unit of measurement and the historical cost model should be changed. As two writers noted in discussing constant dollar accounting: "We feel that the modification is a necessary one, but hope that the doctor, having cured the hangnail, does not fail to diagnose the pneumonia."[2] Advocates of this approach argue that the unit of measurement must be standardized (else we are using "a rubber ruler" in measuring dollars) and that after standardiza-

---

[2]Edgar O. Edwards and Philip W. Bell, *The Theory and Measurement of Business Income* (Berkeley: University of California Press, 1961), p. 16.

tion some form of current value accounting should be employed. Only under this combined approach will the effects of real changes in enterprise wealth and earning power be determined.[3]

## PROFESSIONAL PRONOUNCEMENTS

In 1963, the AICPA published *Accounting Research Study No. 6,* "Reporting the Financial Effects of Price-Level Changes," which recommended that constant dollar accounting information be reported on a supplemental basis.[4] Subsequently, the APB in 1969 noted that "general price-level adjusted financial statements present useful information that is not available from historical dollar statements" and therefore encouraged their use. However, the APB indicated that general price-level information was not required for fair presentation of financial position and results of operations.[5]

Owing to the relatively high rate of inflation experienced worldwide during the seventies and the expectation of continued significant inflation, several other countries undertook studies to find better ways to report financial position, earning power, and cash flows. In May 1974 the Accounting Standards Steering Committee in the United Kingdom issued a proposal for constant dollar financial statements. It was followed in December 1974 by the Financial Accounting Standards Board in the United States and the Institute of Chartered Accountants in Australia, both of whom similarly proposed adoption of financial reporting in units of general purchasing power.[6] The Canadian Institute of Chartered Accountants issued a similar proposal in July 1975.

Just when it appeared that the business world was about to adopt constant dollar accounting, several fast-moving developments occurred. The Institute of Chartered Accountants in Australia in June 1975 took a different tack in a second proposal. It suggested a current value approach to the valuation of assets in the balance sheet and a profit measurement based on matching revenue and expense, both expressed in current cost. Then in 1976, the Securities and Exchange Commission issued *ASR No. 190,* which required a modified form of current value accounting. Large publicly held companies were required to disclose the cost of replacing inventories and plant and equipment and to show what their cost of goods sold and depreciation expense would be if computed on a current replacement cost basis.[7]

Upon issuance of *ASR No. 190,* the FASB began to reevaluate its position concerning accounting for price-level changes. Many believed that it was important for the Board to take decisive action in this area; otherwise the entire standard setting related to this issue would be developed by the SEC. In 1979 the FASB issued *Statement No. 33,* "Financial

---

[3]For discussion that supports this approach, see Robert R. Sterling, "Relevant Financial Reporting in a Period of Changing Prices," *Journal of Accountancy* (February 1975).

[4]Staff of the Accounting Research Division, "Reporting the Financial Effects of Price-Level Changes," *Accounting Research Study No. 6* (New York: AICPA, 1963).

[5]"Financial Statements Restated for General Price-Level Changes," *APB Statement No. 3* (New York: AICPA, 1969).

[6]"Financial Reporting in Units of General Purchasing Power," *Exposure Draft* (Stamford, Conn.: FASB, 1974).

[7]"Disclosure of Certain Replacement Cost Data," *Accounting Series Release No. 190* (Washington: SEC, 1976). The requirement was eliminated after issuance of *FASB Statement No. 33.*

Reporting and Changing Prices," which requires certain large, publicly held enterprises to disclose supplementary information on both a constant dollar basis and a current cost basis.[8] In order to encourage experimentation in the development of techniques for accumulating, reporting, and analyzing data on the effects of price changes, the requirements of *Statement No. 33* are more flexible than is customary in Board statements.

## ORGANIZATION OF THIS CHAPTER

To help you in understanding accounting for changing prices, this chapter is divided into three main sections as follows:

**Constant Dollar Accounting**—Preparation of comprehensive financial statements on a constant dollar basis is explained and illustrated.

**Current Cost Accounting**—Preparation of comprehensive financial statements on a current cost basis is explained and illustrated.

*FASB Statement No. 33* **Accounting**—Comprehensive financial statements, adjusted for changing prices, are not required; however, a partial restatement on both a constant dollar and current cost basis is mandated. These supplementary schedules and disclosures are illustrated.

We believe that it is important that you master each of these three topics to fully understand accounting for changing prices. In addition, we have provided in the appendix to this chapter a detailed explanation and illustration of accounting for changing prices on a combined current cost/constant dollar basis.

## CONSTANT DOLLAR ACCOUNTING

In addition to being a medium of exchange, the dollar has a "real" value that is determined by the amount of goods and services for which it can be exchanged. **This real value is commonly called purchasing power.** As the economy experiences periods of inflation (rising price levels) or deflation (declining price levels), the amount of goods and services for which a dollar can be exchanged changes; that is, the purchasing power of the dollar changes from one time period to the next.

For example, in 1969 ten gallons of regular gasoline cost $3.48. In 1982, ten gallons of regular gasoline cost approximately $12.50. Similarly, thirteen years ago the median price of a new house was $25,000; today it is $88,400. Changes in the prices of gasoline and houses are examples of changes in the prices of specific items. The aggregation of specific prices at any particular time constitutes a **general price level.** A general price level change recognizes the change in the value of money in all its uses (often referred to as **general inflation**).

Fortunately, the need to measure purchasing power is neither new nor restricted to accounting. Various agencies of the United States government, like those of many foreign countries, publish indexes designed to measure changes in the general price level. When such indexes provide acceptable measures of general price-level changes, they can be used in accounting to adjust historical costs for changes in general purchasing power.

---

[8]"Financial Reporting and Changing Prices," *Statement of Financial Accounting Standards No. 33* (Stamford, Conn.: FASB, 1979).

## Measuring General Price-Level Changes

A price index is a weighted-average relation between money and a given set of goods and services. Constructing a price index that measures the change in purchasing power of the dollar is a complex problem; it involves the exercise of judgment in accumulating and appraising data.

It is fair to say, however, that the general indexes now available are reasonably useful to most persons and business managers as gauges of the change in the purchasing power of the dollar. The more widely used indexes of price change that are computed regularly by agencies of the U.S. government are:

1. The Gross National Product Implicit Price Deflator (GNP Deflator).
2. The Consumer Price Index for all Urban Consumers (CPI-U).
3. The Wholesale Price Index.
4. The Composite Construction Cost Index.
5. The 22 Commodity Spot Price Index.

The CPI-U reflects the average change in the retail prices of a fairly broad but select "basket" of consumer goods. It has been the most popular index because it is reported monthly (as opposed to the quarterly publication of the GNP Deflator) and it is not revised after its initial publication. As a result, **the FASB requires that the index used in constant dollar accounting be the CPI-U.**[9]

## Restatement in Common Dollars

The procedure for restating the dollars of varying purchasing power reported in historical cost financial statements in dollars of current purchasing power is mathematically a simple, although sometimes time-consuming, process. The restatement (frequently called translation or conversion) is accomplished by multiplying the amount to be restated by a fraction, the numerator of which is the index for current prices and the denominator of which is the index for prices that prevailed at the date related to the amount being restated. For example, the cost of an asset acquired for $1,000 on June 30, 1973, is restated in terms of December 31, 1983, dollars as follows:

$$\frac{1983 \text{ index}}{1973 \text{ index}} \times \$1000 = \text{cost of asset in terms of 1983 dollars}$$

Technically, the index at date of acquisition, June 30, 1973, should be used for the denominator. Because daily price-level indexes are not available, the average index for June 1973 may be used. The average annual index may be used with satisfactory results in the absence of rampant inflation or deflation and, particularly, in the initial restatement when price-level adjustments are being made for the first time, a large number of amounts are to be adjusted, and the amounts to be restated are several years removed.

To further illustrate the method of restating historical dollars to current dollars, assume the facts presented on page 1142 relative to acquired assets and the preparation of financial statements in 1983:

[9]Ibid., par. 39.

| Year | Acquisition Cost | CPI-U Price Index |
|------|------------------|-------------------|
| 1959 | $10,000 | 87 |
| 1967 | $10,000 | 99 |
| 1974 | $10,000 | 140 |
| 1983 | $10,000 | 308 (Estimated) |

To express all of these acquisition costs in terms of one year's prices, say 1983, the restatement process to restate all dollars to the dollar in existence in 1983 is:

| | | |
|------|------------------|--------|
| 1959 | $10,000 × 308/87, or | $35,402 |
| 1967 | 10,000 × 308/99, or | 31,111 |
| 1974 | 10,000 × 308/140, or | 22,000 |
| 1983 | 10,000 × 308/308, or | 10,000 |
| | Total in terms of 1983 dollars | $98,513 |

Thus, the total acquisition cost of the assets, $40,000, is modified on a constant dollar basis to $98,513 in terms of year 1983 prices.

## Monetary and Nonmonetary Classifications

In preparing constant dollar financial statements, it is essential to distinguish between (1) the amounts that are by their nature already stated in current dollars and, therefore, require no restatement, and (2) the amounts that require restatement in order to be stated in terms of current dollars. The former are classified as **monetary items,** the latter as **nonmonetary items.**

Monetary assets include cash, contractual claims to a fixed amount of cash in the future, such as accounts and notes receivable, and investments that pay a fixed amount of interest or dividends and will be repaid at a fixed amount in the future (the date of repayment, however, need not be specified—as for an investment in preferred stock). **Monetary liabilities** include accounts and notes payable, accruals such as wages and interest payable, and long-term obligations payable in a fixed sum (including preferred stockholders' equity).

All assets and liabilities not classified as monetary items are classified as "nonmonetary" for constant dollar accounting purposes. **Nonmonetary assets** are the items whose prices in terms of the monetary unit may change over time: for example, inventories, investments in common stocks, property, plant, and equipment, and deferred charges that represent costs expended in the past. **Nonmonetary liabilities** are obligations to provide given amounts of goods and services or an equivalent amount of purchasing power (even though the payment may be in the form of cash): for example, advances received on sales contracts, liabilities for rent collected in advance, and deferred credits that represent reductions of prior expense.

The importance of distinguishing between monetary and nonmonetary items in reporting the impact of changing price levels is demonstrated by Raymond J. Chambers:

The importance of the distinction lies in the fact that monetary assets and nonmonetary assets are subject to quite different risks. Holdings of monetary assets are subject to the risk of changes in the purchasing power of money. If for whatever reasons, the general level of prices rises, the purchasing power of a unit of money tends to fall; a greater number of units is required to buy a given good. Clearly then, nonmonetary assets are subject to the same influences, but in the opposite direction. If the price level is expected to rise, it is clearly preferable to hold goods and to incur fixed obligations than it is to hold monetary assets.[10]

A list of the more common monetary and nonmonetary items is presented on page 1144. Note that inventories, property, plant, and equipment, and intangibles are nonmonetary in nature. Conversely, most liabilities are monetary because they involve a fixed claim to pay cash, except for liabilities that are liquidated through the exchange of goods or services. Stockholders' equity accounts such as common stock and additional paid-in capital are nonmonetary in nature. Retained earnings is computed separately each period by adding constant dollar net income less any dividends to the beginning balance of retained earnings.

## Effects of Holding Monetary and Nonmonetary Items

Holders of money lose general purchasing power during inflation because a given amount of money buys progressively fewer goods and services. This same loss in purchasing power occurs when any "monetary" asset is held during a period of inflation. For instance, in the case of accounts or notes receivable, or any claim to a fixed amount of money, the amount of money expected to be received represents a diminishing amount of general purchasing power simply as a result of inflation. Similarly, accounts, notes, and bonds payable, or any fixed amount of money payable in the future becomes less burdensome during inflation because they are payable in dollars of reduced general purchasing power.

The resulting gains and losses have been variously described as "inflation gains or losses," "monetary gains or losses," "purchasing power gains and losses," and "general price-level gains or losses." **The FASB in *Statement No. 33* calls them "purchasing power gains or losses on net monetary items."**[11] Whatever their name, these explicit measurements of the gains and losses resulting from monetary assets and liabilities are the unique product of constant dollar adjustments of historical amounts.

To illustrate the effects of holding a monetary asset during a period of inflation, assume that you have the following balance sheet at the beginning of the period.

| **Balance Sheet**<br>(Beginning of Period) | | | |
|---|---|---|---|
| Cash | $100 | Owners' equity | $100 |

If the general price level doubles during the year, and no transactions take place, then to be in the same economic position you should have the balance sheet shown on page 1145 at the end of the year.

---

[10]Raymond J. Chambers, *Accounting, Evaluation and Economic Behavior* (Englewood Cliffs, N.J.: Prentice-Hall, 1966), p. 196.

[11]"Financial Reporting and Changing Prices," *op. cit.*

## CLASSIFICATION OF MONETARY AND NONMONETARY ITEMS[a]

**Monetary Items:**

Assets

Cash on hand and demand bank deposits
Time deposits
Preferred stock (nonconvertible and nonparticipating)
Bonds (other than convertible)
Accounts and notes receivable
Allowance for doubtful accounts
Loans to employees
Long-term receivables
Refundable deposits
Advances to unconsolidated subsidiaries
Cash surrender value of life insurance
Advances to suppliers (not on a fixed price contract)
Deferred income tax charges

Liabilities

Accounts and notes payable
Accrued expenses payable
Cash dividends payable
Advances from customers (not on a fixed price contract)
Accrued losses on firm purchase commitments
Refundable deposits
Bonds payable and long-term debt
Unamortized premium or discount on bonds or notes payable
Convertible bonds payable
Deferred income tax credits

**Nonmonetary Items:**

Assets

Inventory (other than inventories used on contracts)
Investment in common stocks in most situations
Property, plant, and equipment
Accumulated depreciation of property, plant, and equipment
Purchase commitments (portion paid on fixed price contracts)
Patents, trademarks, licenses, and formulas
Goodwill
Deferred property acquisition costs
Other intangible assets and deferred charges

Liabilities

Sales commitments (portion collected on fixed price contracts)
Obligations under warranties
Deferred investment tax credit

### Items Requiring Individual Analysis:

Assets

*Investment in preferred stock (convertible or participating) and convertible bonds*
If the market values the security primarily as a bond, it is monetary; if it values the security primarily as a stock, it is nonmonetary.

*Inventories*
If the future cash receipts will not vary because of future changes in prices, they are monetary. Goods priced at market upon delivery are nonmonetary.

*Prepaid insurance, advertising, rents and other prepayments*
Claims to future services are nonmonetary. Prepayments that are deposits, advance payments or receivables are monetary because the prepayment does not obtain a given quantity of future services but rather is a fixed money offset.

*Pension, sinking and other funds under enterprise control*
The specific assets in the fund should be classified as monetary or nonmonetary.

Liabilities

*Accrued vacation pay*
If it is paid at the wage rates as of the vacation dates and if those rates may vary, it is nonmonetary. If they do not vary, then it is monetary.

*Deferred revenue*
Nonmonetary if an obligation to furnish goods or services is involved.

*Accrued pension obligations*
Fixed amounts payable to a fund are monetary; all other amounts are nonmonetary.

Special Items

*Deferred income tax charges and credits*
Deferred income tax charges and credits are considered monetary by the FASB. The position is inconsistent with *APB Opinion No. 11* which requires the deferred method instead of the liability approach. Because of practical difficulties of computing various layers at which deferred income taxes originated, the Board classified these items as monetary.

*Preferred stock (stockholders' equity)*
If, as is commonly the case, the preferred stockholders' equity is fixed in terms of the number of dollars to be paid in liquidation, then the aggregate par or stated value of the preferred stock may be treated (from the viewpoint of common stockholders' equity) as a monetary item.

---

[a]Adapted from "Financial Reporting and Changing Prices," *Statement of Financial Accounting Standards No. 33* (Stamford, Conn.: FASB, 1979).

| Balance Sheet (End of Period) | | | |
|---|---|---|---|
| Cash | $200 | Owners' equity | $200 |

However, the fact is that you have only $100 and have experienced a purchasing power loss in holding monetary items in a period of inflation. Your balance sheet would be presented as follows on a constant dollar basis.

| Balance Sheet (End of Period) | | | |
|---|---|---|---|
| Cash | $100 | Owners' equity | $200 |
| | | Retained earnings | (100) |
| | | | $100 |

In summary, you have lost $100 in end-of-year dollars.

Nonmonetary items, on the other hand do not represent a fixed claim to receive or pay cash. If, for example, the price level doubles, and you hold inventory, the cost of the inventory should be adjusted because, like other nonmonetary items, it retains its purchasing power. To illustrate the effects of holding a nonmonetary asset during a period of inflation, assume that you have the following balance sheet at the beginning of the period.

| Balance Sheet (Beginning of Period) | | | |
|---|---|---|---|
| Inventory | $100 | Owners' equity | $100 |

If the price level doubles and the inventory was purchased at the beginning of the period, then your balance sheet in constant dollars is as follows.

| Balance Sheet (End of Period) | | | |
|---|---|---|---|
| Inventory | $200 | Owners' equity | $200 |

In summary, monetary assets and liabilities are stated in dollars of current purchasing power in the historical dollar balance sheet; consequently, they will appear at the same amounts in current general price-level statements without being adjusted. The fact that the end of the current year amounts are the same in historical dollars as in constant dollar statements does not obscure the fact, however, that purchasing power gains or losses result from holding them during a period of general price-level change. Conversely, nonmonetary items are reported at different amounts in the constant dollar statements than they are in the historical cost statements, assuming a change in the general price level.

## Constant Dollar Accounting—Lia Corporation

When financial statements are being adjusted to constant dollars for the first time, it is necessary to analyze completely the amounts in each account to determine their year of origin. The initial adjustment process involves considerably more work than subsequent adjustments. When comparative financial statements are being adjusted, the previous period's amounts must be restated in terms of the price level at the latest statement date. If adjusted statements have been prepared for the previous year, the restatement of that year can be accomplished by multiplying each amount in the previous year's adjusted statements by the ratio of the current index to the index of the immediately preceding year.

To illustrate the procedures peculiar to constant dollar accounting, the accounts of Lia Corporation are presented on a historical cost basis in the form of abbreviated comparative balance sheets and an intervening income statement on page 1147 (Exhibit 1). Price-level changes are magnified to illustrate their effects. Only the first six items of additional information have relevance in computing a constant dollar set of financial statements. Assume that Lia Corporation started business on January 1, 1984.

## Adjustment of Balance Sheet Items

**Monetary Items**   The amounts of the monetary items at the end of the year 12/31/84 do not need to be restated because they are reported in end-of-year dollars. The amounts at the beginning of the period, however, must be restated in order to express them in terms of purchasing power at the end of the year. These computations are shown below.

| | | |
|---|---|---:|
| **Cash, receivables, and other monetary assets** | | |
| 12/31/84 | $325,000 × 200/200 | $ 325,000 |
| 1/1/84 | $200,000 × 200/100 | $ 400,000 |
| **Current liabilities (all monetary)** | | |
| 12/31/84 | $200,000 × 200/200 | $ 200,000 |
| 1/1/84 | $100,000 × 200/100 | $ 200,000 |
| **Long-term liabilities (all monetary)** | | |
| 12/31/84 | $650,000 × 200/200 | $ 650,000 |
| 1/1/84 | $650,000 × 200/100 | $1,300,000 |

The balances of the monetary items at 12/31/84 are stated in terms of the price level on 12/31/84 and remain the same. The cash, receivables, and other monetary items had greater purchasing power on 1/1/84 than they now have on 12/31/84. Therefore, the 1/1/84 balances must be increased to 12/31/84 dollars to restate the beginning balances in end-of-year dollars. The current and long-term liabilities at 1/1/84 must also be converted to 12/31/84 dollars.

**Inventories**   Inventories can present a special problem because restatement in terms of the current price level requires knowledge of the dates of acquisition and the historical cost. If the specific identification method is used, the identified number of historical dollars is multiplied by a fraction, the numerator of which is the current index and the denominator of which is the index for the date of acquisition. Typically, however, a FIFO, LIFO, or

## Exhibit 1
## Lia Corporation
### COMPARATIVE BALANCE SHEETS
As of January 1, 1984 and December 31, 1984 (Historical Cost Basis)

| | January 1, 1984 | December 31, 1984 |
|---|---|---|
| Cash, receivables, and other monetary assets | $ 200,000 | $ 325,000 |
| Inventories | 250,000 | 300,000 |
| Equipment (net) | 150,000 | 140,000 |
| Land | 450,000 | 450,000 |
| Total assets | $1,050,000 | $1,215,000 |
| Current liabilities (all monetary) | $ 100,000 | $ 200,000 |
| Long-term liabilities (all monetary) | 650,000 | 650,000 |
| Total liabilities | 750,000 | 850,000 |
| Common stock | 300,000 | 300,000 |
| Retained earnings | -0- | 65,000 |
| Total stockholders' equity | 300,000 | 365,000 |
| Total liabilities and stockholders' equity | $1,050,000 | $1,215,000 |

## Lia Corporation
### STATEMENT OF INCOME AND RETAINED EARNINGS
For the Year Ended December 31, 1984 (Historical Cost Basis)

| | | |
|---|---|---|
| Sales | | $800,000 |
| Cost of goods sold: | | |
| Inventory, January 1, 1984 | $250,000 | |
| Purchases | 520,000 | |
| Goods available for sale | 770,000 | |
| Inventory, December 31, 1984 | 300,000 | 470,000 |
| Gross profit | | 330,000 |
| Selling and administrative expenses | | 170,000 |
| Depreciation expense | | 10,000 |
| Income before income taxes | | 150,000 |
| Income taxes | | 75,000 |
| Net income | | 75,000 |
| Retained earnings, January 1, 1984 | | -0- |
| | | 75,000 |
| Cash dividends | | 10,000 |
| Retained earnings, December 31, 1984 | | $ 65,000 |

**Additional related information:** (Only the first six items have relevance in computing a constant dollar set of financial statements.)

### Constant Dollar Information

1. The following CPI-U index numbers are assumed for use in the illustration:

| | | |
|---|---|---|
| 1/1/84 | Opening of the business | 100 |
| 1984 | First-year average | 160 |
| 12/31/84 | Year end | 200 |

2. The inventory is priced on a first-in, first-out (FIFO) basis. The beginning inventory was purchased at the opening of the business. The ending inventory was acquired in November and December at a price level of 180.

3. Acquisition of the equipment and land took place at the opening of the business.

4. The equipment has a useful life of 15 years and is depreciated on a straight-line basis with no salvage value.

5. All revenue and expenses, except for that portion of the cost of goods sold represented by the beginning inventory are earned or incurred evenly throughout the year.

6. Dividends are declared and paid at the end of the year.

### Current Cost Information

7. Cost of goods sold on a current cost basis at different dates during the year is $760,000 (assume incurred evenly). Current cost of the inventory at the end of 1984 is $500,000.

8. Current cost of the equipment at the end of 1984 excluding accumulated depreciation is $180,000. Net current cost is $168,000.

9. Current cost of the land at the end of 1984 is $900,000.

10. Historical cost and current cost are identical for the inventory, equipment, and land at the beginning of the year 1/1/84.

11. Selling and administrative expenses and income taxes are the same on both an historical and current cost basis.

average-cost assumption is utilized. The price-level restatement should be consistent with that assumption. In this case it is assumed that the FIFO method is applied and that the year-end inventory consists of goods acquired during the last two months at an average index of 180 for those months:

| | | |
|---|---|---|
| 12/31/84 | Inventories—ending $300,000 × 200/180 | $333,333 |
| 1/1/84 | Inventories—beginning $250,000 × 200/100 | $500,000 |

**Equipment**  The equipment would be restated in end-of-year dollars as follows:

| | | |
|---|---|---|
| 12/31/84 | Equipment (net)—$140,000 × 200/100 | $280,000 |
| 1/1/84 | Equipment (net)—$150,000 × 200/100 | $300,000 |

**Land**  The restatement of the land in end-of-year dollars is the same on both balance sheets:

| | | |
|---|---|---|
| 12/31/84 | Land—$450,000 × 200/100 | $900,000 |
| 1/1/84 | Land—$450,000 × 200/100 | $900,000 |

The computations above illustrate that while price-level restatements for equipment and land are straightforward, the initial restatement process can be tedious when a large number of items and acquisition dates are involved.

**Common Stock and Retained Earnings**  The common stock account balances at 12/31/84 and at 1/1/84 are converted to end-of-year dollars as follows:

| | | |
|---|---|---|
| 12/31/84 | Common stock—$300,000 × 200/100 | $600,000 |
| 1/1/84 | Common stock—$300,000 × 200/100 | $600,000 |

Retained earnings is computed as the amount needed to balance the balance sheet. The following balances are reported:

| | | |
|---|---|---|
| 12/31/84 | Retained earnings | $388,333 |
| 1/1/84 | Retained earnings | -0- |

Note that the amount of retained earnings at 12/31/84 should be reconcilable to the amount of restated income for the year 1984 taking into consideration dividends paid during the year (see Exhibit 2 page 1152).

In preparing constant dollar financial statements, common stock, additional paid-in capital, and retained earnings may all be viewed as stockholders' equity and treated as one residual, inseparable sum. Price-level adjusted common stockholders' equity may then be measured as the difference between (1) total **restated** assets and (2) total **restated** liabilities plus preferred stockholders' equity (if any):

| | | |
|---|---|---|
| 12/31/84 | Common stockholders' equity—$1,838,333 (assets) — $850,000 (liabilities) = | $988,333 |
| 1/1/84 | Common stockholders' equity—$2,100,000 (assets) — $1,500,000 (liabilities) = | $600,000 |

The abbreviated comparative balance sheet of Lia Corporation prepared on a comprehensive constant dollar basis is presented on page 1152 (Exhibit 2).

## Adjustment of Combined Income and Retained Earnings Statement Items

**Sales**   Because sales were spread evenly over the year, the average index for 1984 may be used to restate sales to end-of-year dollars:

$$\$800,000 \times 200/160 = \$1,000,000$$

If sales (or other operating items) are seasonal or if the price-level changes are not reasonably constant during the year, quarterly sales (or other operating items) are restated using quarterly indexes.

**Cost of Goods Sold**   The cost of goods sold can be restated in 12/31/84 dollars as follows (purchases are assumed to be made evenly over the year and therefore the average index for 1984 is used):

| | | |
|---|---|---|
| Beginning inventory | $250,000 × 200/100 = | $   500,000 |
| Purchases | 520,000 × 200/160 = | 650,000 |
| Goods available for sale | 770,000 | 1,150,000 |
| Ending inventory | 300,000 × 200/180 = | 333,333 |
| Cost of goods sold | $470,000 | $   816,667 |

**Selling and Administrative Expenses**   Assuming that these expenses were incurred evenly throughout the period, they would be restated as follows:

$$\$170,000 \times 200/160 = \$212,500$$

**Depreciation Expense**   The equipment was purchased at the beginning of the year; depreciation expense should be restated to end-of-year dollars as follows:

$$\$10,000 \times 200/100 = \$20,000$$

**Income Taxes**    Assuming that these expenses were incurred evenly throughout the period, they would be restated as follows:

$$\$75,000 \times 200/160 = \$93,750$$

**Cash Dividends**    Cash dividends were paid to common stockholders at the end of the year when the index was 200. No adjustment is necessary, as the following computation illustrates:

$$\$10,000 \times 200/200 = \$10,000$$

### Purchasing Power Gain or Loss

Analyzing the effects of price-level changes on monetary items reveals management's effectiveness in coping with such changes. The computation of the purchasing power gain or loss on net monetary items involves preparing a detailed **statement of sources and uses of monetary items** for the period under consideration, restated item by item. The first step in such a procedure is to compute the total net monetary items at the beginning of the period. These net monetary items are restated to end-of-year dollars to insure that all monetary items are stated on the same price-level basis. That is, whenever monetary items of an earlier period are compared to a current period, the earlier monetary item must be restated to the current price level for comparison purposes. **Current period monetary items are already stated in end-of-year dollars as indicated earlier.** The sources (such as revenues) and uses (such as purchases) are then restated to end-of-year dollars. Because most of these items occur continuously during the year, an average index for the denominator of the restatement ratio is used. Because the dividends occur at the end of the year, the denominator for the restatement ratio is the end-of-year index. Items that do not occur continuously during the year are restated using as the denominator the appropriate index at the time the event takes place.

The net monetary items at the end of the year on an historical cost basis are equal to the beginning monetary items plus the sources of monetary items minus the uses of monetary items during the period. The net monetary items on a restated basis are then compared to the monetary items on an historical cost basis to determine whether a purchasing power gain or loss occurs. Thus restatement of monetary items is made only for purposes of computing the gain or loss from holding net monetary items. The restated monetary items are not reported on financial statements. As indicated earlier, holding monetary assets during a period of rising prices results in a loss in purchasing power, whereas holding monetary liabilities results in a gain in purchasing power. In the Lia Corporation illustration shown at the top of page 1151, on a restated basis, the net monetary liabilities exceed the net monetary assets by $1,066,250 whereas on an historical cost basis the net monetary liabilities exceed the net monetary assets by $525,000. The company recognizes a purchas-

Lia Corporation
COMPUTATION OF PURCHASING POWER GAIN OR LOSS—1984
(End-of-Year Dollars)

| | 1984 Historical | Restatement Ratio | Restated to 12/31/84 Dollars |
|---|---|---|---|
| Net monetary items historical—1/1/84: | | | |
| Cash, receivables, and other monetary assets | $ 200,000 | | |
| Current liabilities (all monetary) | (100,000) | | |
| Long-term liabilities (all monetary) | (650,000)  $(550,000) | × 200/100 | $(1,100,000) |
| Add (sources of monetary items): | | | |
| Sales | 800,000 | × 200/160 | 1,000,000 |
| | 250,000 | | (100,000) |
| Deduct (uses of monetary items): | | | |
| Purchases | 520,000 | × 200/160 | 650,000 |
| Selling and administrative expense | 170,000 | × 200/160 | 212,500 |
| Income taxes | 75,000 | × 200/160 | 93,750 |
| Cash dividends | 10,000 | × 200/200 | 10,000 |
| Total uses | 775,000 | | 966,250 |
| Net monetary items historical—12/31/84: | | | |
| Cash, receivables and other monetary assets | 325,000 | | |
| Current liabilities (all monetary) | (200,000) | | |
| Long-term liabilities (all monetary) | (650,000)  $(525,000) | | |
| Net monetary items restated | | | (1,066,250) |
| Net monetary items historical | | | (525,000) |
| Purchasing power gain on net monetary items | | | $   541,250 |

ing power gain in this situation because it is in a better financial position on an historical cost basis. That is, it is better to have a $525,000 excess of liabilities over assets than a $1,066,250 excess of liabilities over assets. Whenever a company is in a better financial position on an historical cost basis than on a restated price-level basis regarding net monetary items, a gain results. Conversely, if Lia Corporation were to have net monetary assets of $100,000 on an historical cost basis and net monetary assets on a restated price-level basis of $300,000, a purchasing power loss of $200,000 results.

The statement of income and retained earnings on a constant dollar basis is illustrated on page 1152 (Exhibit 2).

## Advantages and Disadvantages of Constant Dollar Accounting

Constant dollar financial statements have been discussed widely within both the accounting profession and the business and financial community and lauded by many as a means of overcoming the reporting problems during periods of inflation or deflation. The following arguments have been submitted in support of preparing such statements:

1. Constant dollar accounting provides management with an **objectively** determined quantification of the impact of inflation on its business operations.

Exhibit 2
Lia Corporation
COMPARATIVE BALANCE SHEETS
As of January 1, 1984 and December 31, 1984
(Constant Dollar Basis)

|  | January 1, 1984 | December 31, 1984 |
|---|---|---|
| Cash, receivables and other monetary assets | $ 400,000 | $ 325,000 |
| Inventories | 500,000 | 333,333 |
| Equipment (net) | 300,000 | 280,000 |
| Land | 900,000 | 900,000 |
| Total assets | $2,100,000 | $1,838,333 |
| Current liabilities (all monetary) | $ 200,000 | $ 200,000 |
| Long-term liabilities (all monetary) | 1,300,000 | 650,000 |
| Total liabilities | 1,500,000 | 850,000 |
| Common stock | 600,000 | 600,000 |
| Retained earnings | -0- | 388,333 |
| Total stockholders' equity | 600,000 | 988,333 |
| Total liabilities and stockholders' equity | $2,100,000 | $1,838,333 |

Lia Corporation
STATEMENT OF INCOME AND RETAINED EARNINGS
For the Year Ended December 31, 1984
(Constant Dollar Basis)

| | | |
|---|---|---|
| Sales | | $1,000,000 |
| Cost of goods sold | | |
| Inventory, January 1, 1984 | $ 500,000 | |
| Purchases | 650,000 | |
| Goods available for sale | 1,150,000 | |
| Inventory, December 31, 1984 | 333,333 | 816,667 |
| Gross profit | | 183,333 |
| Selling and administrative expenses | | 212,500 |
| Depreciation expense | | 20,000 |
| Loss before income taxes | | (49,167) |
| Income taxes | | 93,750 |
| Loss before purchasing power gain on net monetary items | | (142,917) |
| Purchasing power gain on net monetary items | | 541,250 |
| Constant dollar net income | | 398,333 |
| Retained earnings, January 1, 1984 | | -0- |
| Cash dividends | | (10,000) |
| Retained earnings, December 31, 1984 | | $ 388,333 |

2. Constant dollar accounting eliminates the effects of inflation from financial information by requiring each enterprise to follow the same objective procedure and use the same price-level index, thereby **preserving comparability of financial statements between firms.**

3. Constant dollar accounting **enhances comparability between the financial statements of a single firm** by eliminating differences due to price-level changes and thereby improves trend analysis.

4. Constant dollar accounting eliminates the effects of price-level changes without having to develop a new structure of accounting; that is, it **preserves the historical cost-based accounting system** that is currently used and understood.

5. Constant dollar accounting **eliminates the necessity of and attraction to the "piecemeal" approaches** used in combating the effects of inflation on financial statements, namely, LIFO inventory costing and accelerated depreciation of property, plant, and equipment.

In spite of widespread publicity, discussion, and authoritative support both inside and outside the accounting profession, the preparation and public issuance of constant dollar financial statements up to this point has been negligible, probably because of the following disadvantages said to be associated with constant dollar financial statements.

1. The additional **cost** of preparing constant dollar statements is not offset by the benefit of receiving sufficient relevant information.

2. Constant dollar financial statements will cause **confusion** and be misunderstood by users.

3. Restating the "value" of nonmonetary items at historical cost adjusted for general price-level changes **is no more meaningful than historical cost alone,** that is, it suffers all the shortcomings of the historical cost method.

4. The reported purchasing power gain from monetary items is **misleading** because it does not necessarily represent successful management or provide funds for dividends, plant expansion, or other purposes.

5. Constant dollar accounting **assumes that the impact of inflation falls equally** on all businesses and on all classes of assets and costs, which is not true.

Probably the greatest deterrent to widespread and mandatory adoption of constant dollar accounting in the past has been **what it is not;** constant dollar accounting is not present value, net realizable value, or current cost accounting, and therein lies much of the opposition to its use.

## CURRENT VALUE ACCOUNTING

There is no single definition of value. **The value of anything is dependent upon answers to questions like: Value to whom? and Value for what purpose?** The determination of one value can be responsive at best to only one type of problem. Assets, defined as "things of value," cannot be represented by one number from which all types of economic decisions can be made. Value is what assets are worth to a particular person, for a particular purpose, at a particular point in time. Hence, the word is generally preceded by a descriptive adjective, such as going-concern value, resale value, liquidation value, market value, present value, current value, fair value, book value, net realizable value, exit value, appraisal value, and others.

Value should not be confused with valuation, which in accounting is the assignment of dollar amounts to assets and liabilities. Value and valuation, however, are interrelated in that the accounting process of valuation results in the assignment of an amount that represents a value, generally either historical entry exchange value or historical exit exchange value, which in conventional accounting is cost and selling price, respectively. The point is, that the accounting process of valuation, because of its preoccupation with historical exchange prices, has contributed only a small portion of its information potential. Begging to be tapped at a time when inflation makes the existing historical basis of valuation obsolete are the other bases of valuation, namely, current value, replacement value, present value, reproduction value, net realizable value, appraisal value, etc. Determining which basis of valuation to adopt depends largely on the answers to the question: What is the objective of financial statements? Multiple answers may require multiple disclosures of values.

## The Current Value Approach

The term **current value** has recently been adopted as the generic term representative of the process that reports an entity's resources and obligations on the basis of "present worth," using any of several means or techniques of evaluation. The three most commonly advocated **concepts of current value** are: (1) present value (discounted future cash flows), (2) net realizable value (current cash equivalents) and (3) current cost. The current value approach merely describes the objective that is accomplished through the application of selected techniques and methods to the individual items to be measured and reported. In similar manner the term "historical cost approach" merely represents the many concepts, methods, and techniques applied in preparing cost-based financial statements.

**Present Value**    Present value (often referred to as **value in use**) relates to the future cash inflows and outflows that can be attributed to or related to the specific item or group of items being measured. As discussed in Chapter 6, present value is measured by discounting at an appropriate interest rate the future estimated net cash inflows, or cost savings, of the item being valued. Present value is frequently viewed as the ideal basis for current valuation of resources and obligations because it is most consistent with the user's objective of predicting future cash flows.[12] In most cases, however, except for monetary items, the direct measurement of present value is not feasible, owing perhaps to the lack of cash flow data or to complex interactions among several resources and obligations that invalidate cash flows as valuation tools for individual items.

**Net Realizable Value**    A net realizable value model is based on the premise that **the value of the asset is the selling price of the asset in the market less cost of disposal,** instead of its purchase price or replacement cost.[13] Proponents of this approach believe that the market value or current cash equivalent is the best means available for measuring the value of enterprise assets and that changes in market value should be reported in net income immediately. The criticisms of this model are that some assets do not have a ready market price, that the computation of value is subjective, and that many assets are held for use, not sale, so that market value is not useful information. It should be noted that this approach generally assumes no forced or distress sale; "liquidation value" implies a forced or distressed sale value.

**Current Cost**    Current cost[14] is the cost of replacing the identical asset owned, that is, one

---

[12]See, for example, George J. Staubus, *A Theory of Accounting to Investors* (Berkeley: University of California Press, 1961), for an excellent exposition of this valuation system.

[13]See, for example, Chambers, *op. cit.*

[14]Although they are used interchangeably, a subtle but important distinction exists between current cost and replacement cost. Current cost is the current purchase price of an asset owned, whereas replacement cost is the current purchase price of assets which will replace existing assets. In many cases, such as inventories, current cost and replacement cost are the same, because replacement will be with similar assets. However, with long-term assets, significant differences can develop. For

of the same age and of the same operating capacity.[15] Current cost may be approximated in a variety of ways but often is computed by applying a **specific price index** to the historical cost or book value of assets. Specific price indexes are available for specific industries and for broad classifications of equipment and other plant assets. The application of specific price indexes to assets is computationally similar to the application of general price indexes. Because the current cost method is conceptually appealing, and because the FASB requires supplementary information on a current cost basis, our discussion of current cost procedures is extensive.

## Current Cost—Simplified Illustration

To illustrate the current cost accounting model, assume that Andrea Co. purchased inventory at the beginning of Period 1 for $100,000; the current cost of the inventory at the end of Period 1 is $125,000; at the end of Period 2 the current cost is $155,000; and the inventory is sold in Period 3 for $170,000 when the inventory has a current cost of $160,000. Net income under the current cost and historical cost models for the three periods would be reported as shown below.

| Andrea Co.<br>COMPARISON OF CURRENT COST AND HISTORICAL COST | | | |
|---|---|---|---|
| **Current Cost Model** | | | |
| | Period 1 | Period 2 | Period 3 |
| Revenues | $ -0- | $ -0- | $170,000 |
| Cost of goods sold | -0- | -0- | 160,000 |
| Current cost income from continuing operations | -0- | -0- | 10,000 |
| Holding gain | 25,000 | 30,000 | 5,000 |
| Current cost net income | $25,000 | $30,000 | $ 15,000 |
| **Historical Cost Model** | | | |
| Revenue | $ -0- | $ -0- | $170,000 |
| Cost of goods sold | -0- | -0- | 100,000 |
| Historical cost net income | $ -0- | $ -0- | $ 70,000 |

The total net income is the same over the three years using either the current cost or the historical cost approach. The current cost approach recognizes the income as the inventory increases in value, whereas the historical cost approach delays recognition until the inventory is sold. In this illustration, the term **holding gain is employed to measure the increase in current cost that arises from holding the inventory from period to period.**

---

example, assume that a Boeing 727 aircraft is going to be replaced with a new Boeing 767. In computing the current cost of the Boeing 727, we would take the cost of the Boeing 767 and adjust that cost for the value of the differences in service potential due to differences in life, output capacity, and nature of service, including any operating cost savings associated with the new aircraft. However, under replacement cost only the difference in output capacity is considered and no allowances are made for differences in useful life or operating costs.

[15]For a complete discussion of current cost, see Lawrence Revsine, *Replacement Cost Accounting* (Englewood Cliffs, N.J.: Prentice-Hall, 1973); Edgar O. Edwards and Phillip W. Bell, *The Theory*

## Current Cost—Complex Illustration

In a comprehensive current cost model, holding gains and losses are usually segregated between those that are realized and those that are unrealized. **Realized holding gains and losses** are the difference between the current cost and the historical cost of the asset sold or consumed during the period. **Unrealized holding gains and losses** relate to assets on hand at the end of the year. These gains and losses are the total increase in the current cost of the assets from the date they were acquired to the end of the current year. **The total holding gain recognized for any period will then be as follows:**

1. **the holding gains and losses realized during the year, and**
2. **the change in the unrealized holding gain or loss between the beginning and the end of the year.**

To illustrate, assume the same information as in the Andrea Co. in the preceding illustration. A current cost accounting system would report the following:

| Andrea Co. COMPREHENSIVE APPROACH | | | |
|---|---|---|---|
| **Current Cost Model** | | | |
| | Period 1 | Period 2 | Period 3 |
| Revenues | $ -0- | $ -0- | $170,000 |
| Cost of goods sold | -0- | -0- | 160,000 |
| Current cost income from continuing operations | -0- | -0- | 10,000 |
| Realized holding gain | -0- | -0- | 60,000 |
| Realized income | -0- | -0- | 70,000 |
| Unrealized holding gain (loss) | 25,000 | 30,000 | (55,000) |
| Current cost net income | $25,000 | $30,000 | $ 15,000 |

The realized holding gain in Period 3 is $60,000, the difference between the current cost of inventory ($160,000) and the historical cost of inventory ($100,000); it is reported when the asset is sold. The unrealized holding gain or loss reported in each period is the change in the total unrealized holding gain from one period to the next. For example in Period 2, the total unrealized holding gain at the beginning of the period is $25,000 and at the end of the period is $55,000. The unrealized holding gain reported in Period 2 is therefore $30,000 ($55,000 minus $25,000). In Period 3 the total unrealized holding gain at the beginning of the period is $55,000 and at the end of the period is zero because the inventory is sold. As a result, an unrealized holding loss of $55,000 ($55,000 minus $0) is reported in the third period.[16]

---

*and Measurement of Business Income* (Berkeley: University of California Press, 1961); and James A. Largay, III, and John Leslie Livingstone, *Accounting for Changing Prices* (Santa Barbara, Calif.: Wiley/Hamilton, 1976).

[16]This system is basically the approach adopted by Edwards and Bell (see footnote 15). Note that only the change in the unrealized holding gain is considered in computing current cost net income. If current cost net income included realized holding gains and total unrealized holding gains, you could be double counting because the realized holding gain would recognize unrealized holding gains of prior periods.

In the current cost model, three different income numbers are reported. **Current cost income from continuing operations** reflects current cost margins—sales revenues less the current cost of inputs. **Realized income** measures the total income realized during the year. Realized income and historical cost income are always the same. Classification within the income statement is different however, because the current cost model subdivides historical cost income into two components—current cost income from continuing operations and realized holding gains. **Current cost net income** measures the total income of the enterprise for one period and takes into account both realized and unrealized holding gains. Many consider this income number to provide the most appropriate measure of whether an enterprise is successful from one period to the next.

## Current Cost Accounting—Lia Corporation

To illustrate the current cost approach, assume the same historical information for Lia Corporation as that reported on page 1147 (Exhibit 1). The additional related information, **numbers 7–11,** is relevant for preparing current cost financial statements.

## Adjustment of Balance Sheet Items

Preparation of the balance sheet on a current cost basis is relatively straightforward. The current cost of each item is reported without adjustment for any general price-level changes. The abbreviated comparative balance sheets for Lia Corporation would be presented as indicated on page 1160 (Exhibit 3).

All the monetary items are stated at face value. No adjustments to the beginning-of-the-year balances are necessary because they are not being reported on a constant dollar basis. The inventory, equipment, and land in both balance sheets are reported at their current cost. Common stock is not adjusted because changes in the purchasing power of the dollar are not considered. The retained earnings is simply the difference between the assets and liabilities less the common stock. Retained earnings also can be computed by adding the beginning balance to the current cost net income less dividends for 1984. Dividends are not adjusted in a current cost system.

## Adjustment of Income Statement Items

As indicated earlier, the current cost income statement usually reports three types of income: current cost income (loss) from continuing operations, realized income (loss), and current cost net income (loss). If the data from the Lia Corporation are used, the following would be reported on the income statement.

**Sales** Because revenues are stated at their current price when sold, their amount is the same in either an historical cost or a current cost system.

| Sales | $800,000 |
|---|---|

**Cost of Goods Sold** Current cost of goods sold as given in the additional information in Exhibit 1 is the result of adjusting the historical cost of goods sold to the current cost of these items at the date of sale.

| | |
|---|---|
| Cost of goods sold | $760,000 |

**Selling and Administrative Expenses**  These expenses are reported at their current cost, which in this case is the same as their historical cost.

| | |
|---|---|
| Selling and administrative expenses | $170,000 |

**Depreciation Expense**  In a current cost accounting system, it is appropriate to assume that depreciation expense is incurred evenly through the year. As a result, average current cost balances should be used as the basis for computing depreciation:[17] In this case, depreciation expense on the equipment is computed and reported as follows:

$$\text{Average current cost balance} = \frac{\$150,000 + \$180,000}{2} = \$165,000$$

$$\text{Depreciation expense} = \$165,000 \div 15 = \$11,000$$

**Income Taxes**  These expenses are reported at their current cost, which is the same as their historical cost:

| | |
|---|---|
| Income taxes | $75,000 |

**Realized and Unrealized Holding Gains**  The computation of the unrealized, realized, and total holding gain is shown at the top of page 1159.

An explanation of the unrealized and realized holding gains follows:

**INVENTORY, COST OF GOODS SOLD, AND PURCHASES**  During the period, the company experienced an unrealized holding gain on its ending inventory of $200,000 ($500,000 minus $300,000). In addition, a realized holding gain of $290,000 ($760,000 minus $470,000) on the sale of products occurred. A holding gain on the purchases does not take place because at the date of purchase the historical cost and current cost are the same.

**EQUIPMENT AND DEPRECIATION EXPENSE**  The computation for the holding gains involving the equipment and related depreciation expense is complex. As indicated earlier, the current cost depreciation for the period is $11,000 computed on the average current cost balance for the year. The difference of $1,000 ($11,000 minus $10,000) between the current cost depreciation and the historical cost depreciation is reported as a realized holding gain. A portion of the equipment which has appreciated in value is now consumed (depreciated), and a holding gain should be realized.

---

[17]Note that some theorists would argue for depreciation expense to be reported on the basis of the ending balance. Our presentation is in accordance with *FASB Statement No. 33*.

Exhibit 3-A
Lia Corporation
UNREALIZED AND REALIZED HOLDING GAINS

| | Historical Cost | Current Cost | Unrealized Holding Gain (Loss) | Realized Holding Gain (Loss) |
|---|---|---|---|---|
| Inventory 12/31/84[a] | $300,000 | $500,000 | $200,000 | $ -0- |
| Cost of goods sold | 470,000 | 760,000 | -0- | 290,000 |
| Purchases | 520,000 | 520,000 | -0- | -0- |
| Equipment (net) 12/31/84 | 140,000 | 168,000 | 28,000 | -0- |
| Depreciation expense | 10,000 | 11,000 | -0- | 1,000 |
| Land 12/31/84 | 450,000 | 900,000 | 450,000 | -0- |
| Total unrealized holding gain | | | $678,000 | |
| Total realized holding gain | | | | $291,000 |
| Increase (decrease) in current cost of assets held during the year (total holding gain) | ($678,000 + $291,000) | | | $969,000 |

[a]Note that beginning inventory, equipment (net) and land are ignored here because historical cost and current cost are the same.

An additional complication, however, arises in relation to depreciation because the 12/31/84 balance sheet reports the equipment at a total current cost of $180,000 (per current cost information at bottom of page 1147), not $165,000 (average balance of current cost). In order to report the proper accumulated depreciation balance of $12,000 ($180,000 ÷ 15 years), a **catch-up depreciation charge** (often referred to as **backlog depreciation**) must be made. This catch-up depreciation charge is reported as a reduction of the unrealized holding gain on the equipment. The entry to record this catch-up depreciation is as follows:

| | | |
|---|---|---|
| Unrealized Holding Gain | 1,000 | |
|    Accumulated Depreciation | | 1,000 |
|    ($12,000 − $11,000) | | |

The problem of catch-up depreciation will arise whenever an average is used to compute depreciation and the year-end current cost is higher than the average.

In addition to the realized holding gain, an unrealized holding gain of $28,000, after deducting catch-up depreciation, must be recognized. This unrealized holding gain is the difference between the current cost of the equipment at the end of the year minus the current cost of the equipment at the beginning of the year adjusted for depreciation. No unrealized holding gains exist from previous periods.

Note that in Exhibit 3–A above we assume that the catch-up depreciation entry is recorded and is incorporated into the reported financial information. As a result, the equipment (net) on a current cost basis was stated at $168,000 ($180,000 minus $12,000) on 12/31/84. Another way to compute the unrealized holding gain is to assume that the catch-up depreciation entry has not been recorded. In this case, the unrealized holding gain is computed at $29,000 ($169,000 minus $140,000). Therefore, it would be necessary to reduce the unrealized holding gain by the catch-up depreciation adjustment in a separate computation. In either approach, the unrealized holding gain should be the same.

**Land** The current cost of the land has increased $450,000 ($900,000 minus $450,000), and an unrealized holding gain in this amount should be recognized.

The current cost income statement for Lia Corporation is presented below.

Exhibit 3
Lia Corporation
COMPARATIVE BALANCE SHEETS
As of January 1 and December 31, 1984
(Current Cost Basis)

|  | January 1, 1984 | December 31, 1984 |
|---|---|---|
| Cash, receivables, and other monetary assets | $ 200,000 | $ 325,000 |
| Inventories | 250,000 | 500,000 |
| Equipment (net) | 150,000 | 168,000 |
| Land | 450,000 | 900,000 |
| Total assets | $1,050,000 | $1,893,000 |
| Current liabilities (all monetary) | 100,000 | 200,000 |
| Long-term liabilities (all monetary) | 650,000 | 650,000 |
| Total liabilities | 750,000 | 850,000 |
| Common stock | 300,000 | 300,000 |
| Retained earnings | -0- | 743,000 |
| Total stockholders' equity | 300,000 | 1,043,000 |
| Total liabilities and stockholders' equity | $1,050,000 | $1,893,000 |

Lia Corporation
STATEMENT OF INCOME AND RETAINED EARNINGS
For the Year Ended December 31, 1984
(Current Cost Basis)

|  |  |
|---|---|
| Sales | $ 800,000 |
| Cost of goods sold | 760,000 |
| Gross profit | 40,000 |
| Selling and administrative expenses | 170,000 |
| Depreciation expense | 11,000 |
| Loss before income taxes | (141,000) |
| Income taxes | 75,000 |
| Current cost loss from continuing operations | (216,000) |
| Realized holding gain | 291,000 |
| Realized income | 75,000 |
| Unrealized holding gain | 678,000 |
| Current cost net income | 753,000 |
| Retained earnings, January 1, 1984 | -0- |
|  | 753,000 |
| Cash dividends | 10,000 |
| Retained earnings, December 31, 1984 | $ 743,000 |

The current cost loss from continuing operations and the realized holding gain when added together equal historical cost net income. An advantage of the current cost over the historical cost income statement is the segregation of income into these two components.

## Comparison of Constant Dollar and Current Cost

The heading of this section was intentionally not worded "Constant Dollar **versus** Current Cost" because these two different bases of reporting financial information are not per se competing or conflicting methods. They are competing approaches only in the minds of their staunch proponents, who feel the adoption of one approach precludes the adoption of the other. This need not be so because constant dollar accounting and current cost accounting are complementary responses to different measurement problems.

Public confusion about the differences between and merits of these two approaches begins when accountants or other writers lump them together or discuss them on the implicit assumption that a choice has to be made between the two and that the real problem is deciding which to choose. A common misconception is that, because it is the less drastic departure from present historical cost accounting, constant dollar accounting is merely the first step toward current cost accounting. Conceptually, neither is an approximation of the other or a first step toward the other.

The basis of both constant dollar accounting and current cost accounting is the **theory of capital maintenance,** that is, that income is recognized only after capital is kept intact. Both recognize that when prices rise, the degree of capital maintenance may not be readily discernible unless some allowance is made for changes in prices. But the similarities cease at this point, because the two approaches view capital maintenance differently and, therefore, offer different treatments for the price change problem.[18]

The **objective of constant dollar accounting** is to maintain capital in terms of constant purchasing power as measured by a general index of the level of prices. This concept implies that the business must maintain at a constant level its ability to purchase a wide variety of goods and services throughout the economy. In the operation of a business, a certain amount of purchasing power is given up through the process of acquiring, producing, and selling goods over a period of time. The investors in and the managers of the business need to know whether the purchasing power sacrificed is being restored and maintained.

The **objective of current cost accounting** is to maintain capital in terms of operating capacity or the ability to provide goods and services at the same level at the end of a period as at the beginning. This approach assumes that all resources consumed or sold will be replaced with resources performing a similar function at the same or better level of production. This approach implies (1) the use of replacement or reproduction cost (using specific price-level indexes) for nonmonetary assets revalued at their specific current cost and (2) matching with revenues the sacrifice value of resources sold or consumed.

In summary, constant dollar accounting does not rest on the assumption that when a producer parts with a product, the assets and services consumed in producing it must be replaced in order to maintain the continuity of production. Instead, it relates the purchasing power of cash invested in assets to the purchasing power generated by those assets; it views replacement of the assets as new investment decisions that are not affected by decisions made in the past.[19]

---

[18] For a more complete discussion of the effect of price-level adjustments on capital maintenance, see Norman S. Featherson, "Inflation Accounting," *World* (New York: Peat, Marwick, Mitchell & Co., Summer 1975).

[19] Ibid.

## Advantages and Disadvantages of Current Cost

A distinct advantage that current cost has over both historical cost and constant dollar accounting is that the specific changes (up and down) in individual items are considered. While the general level of prices may be increasing, specific items may be decreasing. Such items as calculators, tennis balls, watches, microwave ovens, and television sets, for example, have decreased in price, whereas the general level of prices has increased. Constant dollar accounting using a general price index does not make an allowance for these changes in prices as effectively as a current cost system does.

The major arguments for the use of a current cost approach are:

1. **Current cost provides a better measure of efficiency.** If, for example, depreciation is based on current costs, not historical costs, a better measure of operating efficiencies is obtained. For example, assume that you are a new manager in an operation that includes a number of assets purchased recently at current prices, and your performance is compared with that of someone in a similar job elsewhere who is using similar assets that were purchased five years ago when the price was substantially lower. You probably would contend that the five-year-old assets should be revalued because the other manager will show a lower depreciation charge and higher net income than you will.

2. **Current cost is an approximation of the service potential of the asset.** It is difficult if not impossible to determine the present discounted values of specific cash flows that will occur from the use of certain assets; but current cost frequently is a reasonable approximation of this value. As the current cost increases, the implication is that the enterprise has a holding gain (an increase from one period to another in the current cost of that item) because the aggregate value of the asset's service potential has increased.

3. **Current cost provides for the maintenance of physical capital.** Assume that an asset is purchased for one dollar, sold for two dollars, and replaced for two dollars. How much income should be reported and how much tax should be paid? Under traditional accounting procedures, one dollar of income would be earned (which is subject to tax and a claim for dividend distribution). If current cost is used, however, no income exists to be taxed and claims for dividend distributions would probably be fewer.

4. **Current cost provides an assessment of future cash flows.** Information on current cost margins may be useful for assessing future cash flows when the selling price of a product is closely related to its current cost. In addition, reporting holding gains (losses) may provide help in assessing future cash flows.

The major arguments against current cost adjustments are:

1. **The use of current cost is subjective because it is difficult to determine the exact current cost of all items at any point in time.** A good second-hand market for all types of assets does not exist. In most cases, the asset is not replaced with an identical asset; it is replaced with a better one, a faster one, an improved one, an altogether different one, or not replaced at all.

2. **The maintenance of physical capital is not the accountant's function.** It is generally conceded that it is management's function to ensure that capital is not impaired.

3. **Current cost is not always an approximation of the fair market value.** An asset's value is a function of the future cash flows generated by it. Current cost, however, does not necessarily measure an increase in the service potential of that asset.

## CURRENT COST/CONSTANT DOLLAR

Some accountants contend that neither a current cost system nor a constant dollar system alone is appropriate. Although current cost accounting measures changes in the current cost of assets held, it does nothing to reveal the extent to which the changes in the holding gains are real or fictitious if the purchasing power of the dollar is changing. To illustrate, assume that you purchased marketable securities for $100 and their current cost is now $180. Under current cost accounting, an unrealized holding gain of $80 is recognized. But suppose that the general price level increased 60% during the period of time you held these marketable securities. How much is your gain, net of inflation? Current cost/constant dollar proponents would argue that your gain is $20, as computed below.

| | |
|---|---|
| Current cost (end of period) | $180 |
| Historical cost (adjusted to constant dollars)—$100 $\times \dfrac{160}{100}$ | 160 |
| Holding gain, net of inflation | $\underline{\underline{\$\ 20}}$ |

The final number is often referred to as **holding gain, net of inflation** because the gain reported is stated in real dollars, instead of dollars unadjusted for general inflation.

## Advantages and Disadvantages of Current Cost/Constant Dollar Accounting

Many of the arguments indicated earlier for and against current cost and constant dollar accounting apply here. Some arguments that have particular relevance are presented below:

Arguments for current cost/constant dollar accounting:

1. Current cost/constant dollar accounting both **stabilizes the measuring unit and provides current, comparable data.**
2. A current cost/constant dollar system provides **more information** than either system alone. Holding gains and losses adjusted for inflation and deflation are reported, as well as the purchasing power gain or loss on net monetary items.
3. Because it is not certain what is the most useful income figure, by providing these additional disclosures, users through **experimentation** will identify the most useful data.

Arguments against current cost/constant dollar accounting:

1. The **cost** to prepare this information is significant and is perhaps not justified by the benefits received.
2. Very few people will understand the new data. Providing this additional information may be more harmful than helpful. More information is not always better information, because it **may confuse readers or lead to information overload.**
3. The conceptual superiority of the current cost/constant dollar accounting system is **untested and unproven.** For example, there is no body of literature that indicates that the information might lead to better predictions of cash flow.

A detailed analysis of current cost/constant dollar accounting for Lia Corporation is provided in Appendix O of this chapter.

## FASB POSITION

In late 1979, the long-awaited *FASB Statement No. 33* on "Financial Reporting and Changing Prices" was issued. The Board indicated that **no major changes should be made to the primary financial statements at the present time** but that something must be done to augment them with information about the effects of price changes. **The statement requires two different types of disclosure—one on a constant dollar basis and the other on a current cost basis.** Balance sheets and complete statements of income on either a current cost or a constant dollar basis are not required, although their presentation is encouraged. Certain enterprises are required to report the following:[20]

(a) Income from continuing operations on a constant dollar basis.
(b) The purchasing power gain or loss on net monetary items.

### AND

(a) Income from continuing operations on a current cost basis.
(b) Current cost amounts of inventory and property, plant, and equipment at the end of the year.
(c) Increases or decreases in current cost amounts of inventory and property, plant, and equipment, net of inflation (same as total holding gain, net of inflation).

In addition, a five-year summary of selected financial data, including information on income, sales and other operating revenues, net assets, dividends per common share, and market price per share must be reported. In the computation of net assets, only inventory and property, plant, and equipment need be adjusted for the effects of changing prices.

Because of the costs involved in preparing this information, only certain large public companies are required to present this information on a supplementary basis, although others are encouraged to do so.[21] Information related to changing prices is to be presented in supplementary statements, schedules, or supplementary notes in the financial reports along with the primary financial statements.

In summary, the Board is requiring companies to report both constant dollar and current cost information. What is proposed is a set of disclosures that fall short of requiring comprehensive financial statements of either of these approaches. Many will argue that the Board went too far; others will argue that the Board did not go far enough. Actually, the FASB had little choice. Some current cost disclosure was necessary to cause the SEC rescission of *ASR No. 190*.[22] In addition, given the continued inflation, some form of constant dollar accounting has become imperative.

### Partial Restatement Required

*FASB Statement No. 33* does not require the preparation of comprehensive financial statements on a constant dollar or current cost basis. However, the Board encourages companies to experiment and to present financial statements on a comprehensive basis. If comprehen-

---

[20]"Financial Reporting and Changing Prices," *Statement of Financial Accounting Standards No. 33* (Stamford, Conn.: FASB, 1979).

[21]Large public companies are defined as enterprises having inventories and property, plant, and equipment (before deducting accumulated depreciation, depletion and amortization) amounting to more than $125 million or total assets amounting to more than $1 billion (after deducting accumulated depreciation).

[22]The SEC voted to delete its replacement cost disclosure requirements when *FASB Statement No. 33* became effective.

sive financial statements are prepared, we believe that the financial statements presented earlier provide an appropriate basis for reporting this information. Little guidance is provided in *Statement No. 33* for companies that wish to present comprehensive financial statements, except that the minimum disclosures required for partial restatement should be included if comprehensive restatement occurs.

Because accounting for changing prices is a complex issue, the Board simplifies the analysis in a number of ways. First, **restatement is necessary only for inventory, property, plant, and equipment, cost of goods sold, and depreciation and depletion expense;** sales and other revenues, and other expenses do not have to be adjusted. In addition, investments in subsidiaries, intangibles, and deferred charges and credits do not have to be restated. The Board takes this approach because the differences between historical cost and constant dollar or current cost amounts for inventories, property, plant, and equipment are likely to be great.[23]

Second, the Board requires this limited information be reported in **average-for-the-year dollars** instead of year-end dollars. This approach has significant computational advantages in that revenues and expenses assumed to occur evenly throughout the year will be the same in historical as well as constant dollars. Current cost measures of cost of goods sold and depreciation expense also approximate measures in average-for-the-year dollars without further adjustment.[24] If comprehensive financial statements are prepared, they may be prepared in average-for-the-year dollars or end-of-year dollars. The problem with the use of average-for-the-year dollars when comprehensive financial statements are prepared is that the monetary items must be adjusted to average-for-the-year dollars and, therefore, will not be stated at the same amount as the historical cost balances.

Third, **no distinction is made between realized and unrealized holding gains and losses.** Only a total holding gain or loss, net of inflation, referred to in the statement as the excess of the increase in specific prices over the increase in the general price level, need be presented.

## FASB Position—Lia Corporation

To illustrate the constant dollar and current cost approach required by the FASB, assume the information for Lia Corporation on page 1147 (Exhibit 1). When a partial income statement is prepared in constant dollars, average-for-the-year dollars must be used. It should be emphasized that even if revenues and other expenses are not incurred evenly throughout the year, the profession assumes an even incurrence to simplify the computations.

## Adjustments to Income Statement Items

**Sales**  Because sales are spread evenly through the year, they are incurred in average-for-the-year dollars. Therefore no adjustment is necessary on a constant dollar basis or on a current cost basis. Sales are reported as follows:

| | |
|---|---|
| Constant Dollar | $800,000 |
| Current Cost | $800,000 |

[23] *Statement No. 33, op. cit.,* par. 202.
[24] Ibid., par. 189.

**Cost of Goods Sold**  The cost of goods sold can be restated in average-for-the-year dollars as follows:

| | | |
|---|---|---|
| Beginning inventory | $250,000 × 160/100 = | $400,000 |
| Purchases | 520,000 × 160/160 = | 520,000 |
| Goods available for sale | 770,000 | 920,000 |
| Ending inventory | 300,000 × 160/180 = | 266,667 |
| Cost of goods sold | $470,000 | $653,333 |

The current cost of goods sold of $760,000 was incurred in average-for-the-year dollars. The following two amounts would be reported for cost of goods sold:

| | |
|---|---|
| Constant Dollar | $653,333 |
| Current Cost | $760,000 |

**Selling and Administrative Expenses**  These expenses are incurred evenly throughout the year, and no adjustment is necessary on a constant dollar or current cost basis. These amounts are reported as follows:

| | |
|---|---|
| Constant Dollar | $170,000 |
| Current Cost | $170,000 |

**Depreciation Expense**  The equipment was purchased at the beginning of the year, and depreciation expense is restated to average-for-the-year dollars as follows:

$$\$10,000 \times 160/100 = \$16,000$$

As indicated earlier, the depreciation expense on a current cost basis was computed as follows:

$$\text{Average current cost balance} = \frac{\$150,000 + \$180,000}{2} = \$165,000$$

$$\text{Depreciation expense} = \$165,000 \div 15 = \$11,000$$

The following two amounts would then be reported as depreciation expense:

| | |
|---|---|
| Constant Dollar | $16,000 |
| Current Cost | $11,000 |

**Income Taxes**  These expenses were incurred evenly throughout the year and are reported as follows:

| | |
|---|---|
| Constant Dollar | $75,000 |
| Current Cost | $75,000 |

To compute the purchasing power gain or loss, the beginning net monetary items are restated to average-for-the-year dollars. The sources and uses of monetary items are then determined. Because most of the sources and uses occur continuously throughout the period (dividends excepted), no restatement of these balances is necessary. **Note that the ending monetary items on an historical cost basis are adjusted to average-for-the-year dollars to determine the purchasing power gain or loss on net monetary items.**

Lia Corporation
COMPUTATION OF PURCHASING POWER GAIN OR LOSS—1984
(Average-for-the-Year Dollars)

| | 1984 Historical | Restatement Ratio | Restated to Average Dollars |
|---|---|---|---|
| Net monetary items historical— 1/1/84: | | | |
| Cash, receivables, and other monetary assets | $200,000 | | |
| Current liabilities (all monetary) | (100,000) | | |
| Long-term liabilities (all monetary) | (650,000)  $(550,000) | × 160/100 | $(880,000) |
| Add (sources of monetary items): | | | |
| Sales | 800,000 | × 160/160 | 800,000 |
| | 250,000 | | (80,000) |
| Deduct (uses of monetary items): | | | |
| Purchases | 520,000 | × 160/160 | 520,000 |
| Selling and administrative expenses | 170,000 | × 160/160 | 170,000 |
| Income taxes | 75,000 | × 160/160 | 75,000 |
| Cash dividends | 10,000 | × 160/200 | 8,000 |
| Total uses | 775,000 | | 773,000 |
| Net monetary items historical— 12/31/84: | | | |
| Cash, receivables, and other monetary assets | $325,000 | | |
| Current liabilities (all monetary) | (200,000) | | |
| Long-term liabilities (all monetary) | (650,000)  $(525,000) | | |
| Net monetary items—restated | | | (853,000) |
| Net monetary items—historical adjusted to average-for-the-year dollars | $(525,000) | × 160/200 | (420,000) |
| Purchasing power gain on net monetary items | | | $ 433,000 |

As indicated, Lia Corporation has a purchasing power gain of $433,000. This gain results because on a constant dollar basis the company would have net monetary liabilities of $853,000, whereas on an historical cost basis it has net monetary liabilities of $420,000.

Note that use of the average-for-the-year dollar method simplifies the computation of the income from continuing operations and the purchasing power gain or loss on net monetary items because many items are not adjusted.

## Adjustments of Balance Sheet Items

Although the FASB does not require a balance sheet, to compute the excess of the increase in specific prices over the increase in the general price level (total holding gain, net of inflation), a number of balance sheet items must be adjusted. Note that the FASB current cost approach states current cost in average-for-the-year dollars. The current cost of assets on hand at the end of the year must therefore be deflated to average-for-the-year dollars.

**Inventory**   The inventory at the beginning of the year on an historical cost and inventory at the beginning of the year on a current cost basis are the same. As a result, the beginning inventory is restated as follows:

| | |
|---|---|
| Constant Dollar | $250,000 \times 160/100 = \$400,000$ |
| Current Cost (FASB) | $250,000 \times 160/100 = \$400,000$ |

The ending inventory on an historical cost basis ($300,000) and ending inventory on a current cost basis ($500,000) are not the same and are reported as follows:

| | |
|---|---|
| Constant Dollar | $300,000 \times 160/180 = \$266,667$ |
| Current Cost (FASB) | $500,000 \times 160/200 = \$400,000$ |

**Equipment**   The equipment at the beginning of the year on an historical cost basis and equipment at the beginning of the year on a current cost basis are identical. As a result, the beginning equipment is restated as follows:

| | |
|---|---|
| Constant Dollar | $150,000 \times 160/100 = \$240,000$ |
| Current Cost (FASB) | $150,000 \times 160/100 = \$240,000$ |

The equipment at the end of the year on an historical cost basis ($140,000) and equipment at the end of the year on a current cost basis ($168,000) are different and are restated as follows:

| | |
|---|---|
| Constant Dollar | $140,000 \times 160/100 = \$224,000$ |
| Current Cost (FASB) | $168,000 \times 160/200 = \$134,400$ |

**Land** At the beginning of the year land on an historical cost basis and land on a current cost basis are identical. As a result, the land is restated as follows:

| | |
|---|---|
| Constant Dollar | $450,000 × 160/100 = $720,000 |
| Current Cost (FASB) | $450,000 × 160/100 = $720,000 |

At the end of the year land on an historical cost basis ($450,000) and land on a current cost basis ($900,000) are different. These items are restated as follows:

| | |
|---|---|
| Constant Dollar | $450,000 × 160/100 = $720,000 |
| Current Cost (FASB) | $900,000 × 160/200 = $720,000 |

**Total Holding Gain** The computation of the total holding gain, net of inflation, is as follows:

Exhibit 4-A
Lia Corporation
UNREALIZED AND REALIZED HOLDING GAINS

| | Constant Dollar | Current Cost (FASB) | Unrealized Holding Gain (Loss) | Realized Holding Gain (Loss) |
|---|---|---|---|---|
| Inventory 12/31/84[a] | $266,667 | $400,000 | $133,333 | $ -0- |
| Cost of goods sold | 653,333 | 760,000 | -0- | 106,667 |
| Purchases | 520,000 | 520,000 | -0- | -0- |
| Equipment (net) 12/31/84 | 224,000 | 134,400 | (89,600) | -0- |
| Depreciation expense | 16,000 | 11,000 | -0- | (5,000) |
| Land 12/31/84 | 720,000 | 720,000 | -0- | -0- |
| Total unrealized holding gain | | | $ 43,733 | |
| Total realized holding gain | | | | $101,667 |
| Increase (decrease) in current cost of assets held during the year, net of inflation (total holding gain, net of inflation) | ($43,733 + $101,667) | | | $145,400 |

[a]Note that beginning inventory, equipment (net) and land are ignored here because historical cost and current cost are the same.

Note that if the total holding gain is $969,000 (Exhibit 3–A) and the total holding gain (net of inflation) is $145,400 (Exhibit 4–A), the effect of inflation can then be determined as follows:

| | |
|---|---|
| Increase in current cost (total holding gain) | $969,000 |
| Increase in current cost (FASB) | 145,400 |
| Effect of inflation | $823,600 |

Conceptually, this computation is somewhat misleading. The increase in current cost (total holding gain) in Exhibit 3–A is computed in end-of-year dollars, whereas the increase in current cost (FASB) is computed in average-for-the-year dollars. As a result, the inflation adjustment is misleading because the computation uses data from two different price levels. Unfortunately, this computation is based on cost/benefit considerations; that is, to determine current cost in the middle of the year, another computation of current cost is necessitated. Thus, the current cost at the end of the year is used, which leads to a misstatement of the effect of inflation.

The partial income statement reporting constant dollar and current cost income from continuing operations is shown on page 1171 (Exhibit 4) with the information required in the five-year summary. Note that the purchasing power gain or loss on net monetary items, as well as the excess of the specific increase in inventory, equipment, and land over the increase in the general price level (total holding gain, net of inflation) are not added to income from continuing operations to arrive at total income. The reason is that some believe these items should be credited or debited directly to stockholders' equity. Others argue that these gains and losses should be reported as the last element in or immediately following net income. And still others argue that one of the two items should be income, but not the other. As a consequence, the Board decided that disclosure was the most important consideration and did not attempt to classify these items as either income or capital.

Information on changing prices may be presented in an **income statement format** (Exhibit 4) or a **reconciliation format** as shown below. The reconciliation format is provided below and shows the adjustments to historical cost income from continuing operations to arrive at the inflation-adjusted amounts. The computations are provided in the statement to indicate how the individual amounts are determined.

---

**Lia Corporation**
**STATEMENT OF INCOME FROM CONTINUING OPERATIONS**
**ADJUSTED FOR CHANGING PRICES**
For the Year Ended December 31, 1984

| | | |
|---|---:|---:|
| Income from continuing operations, as reported in the income statement | | $ 75,000 |
| Adjustments to restate costs for the effect of general inflation | | |
|    Cost of goods sold ($653,333 − $470,000) | $183,333 | |
|    Depreciation expense ($16,000 − $10,000) | 6,000 | 189,333 |
| Loss from continuing operations adjusted for general inflation | | 114,333 |
| Adjustments to reflect the difference between general inflation and | | |
|     changes in specific prices (current costs) | | |
|    Cost of goods sold ($760,000 − $653,333) | $106,667 | |
|    Depreciation expense ($11,000 − $16,000) | (5,000) | 101,667 |
| Loss from continuing operations adjusted for changes in specific prices | | $216,000 |

(The remainder of the reconciliation would provide the same information as Exhibit 4 starting with purchasing power gain on net monetary items.)

---

## Five-Year Summary

In addition to reporting the constant dollar and current cost information for the current year, a five-year comparison of selected financial data adjusted for the effects of changing prices is required. The purpose of this summary is to provide the user of the financial

Exhibit 4
Lia Corporation
STATEMENT OF INCOME FROM CONTINUING OPERATIONS
ADJUSTED FOR CHANGING PRICES
For the Year Ended December 31, 1984

|  | Historical Cost | Constant Dollar | Current Cost |
|---|---|---|---|
| Sales | $800,000 | $ 800,000 | $ 800,000 |
| Cost of goods sold | 470,000 | 653,333 | 760,000 |
| Selling and administrative expense | 170,000 | 170,000 | 170,000 |
| Depreciation expense | 10,000 | 16,000 | 11,000 |
| Income taxes | 75,000 | 75,000 | 75,000 |
|  | 725,000 | 914,333 | 1,016,000 |
| Income (loss) from continuing operations | $ 75,000 | $(114,333) | $ (216,000) |
| Purchasing power gain on net monetary items |  | $ 433,000 | $ 433,000 |
| Increase in specific prices (current cost) of inventories, equipment and land held during the year[a] |  |  | $ 969,000 |
| Effect of increase in general price-level[b] |  |  | $ 823,600 |
| Excess of increase in specific price over increase in the general price-level |  |  | $ 145,400 |

[a]At December 31, 1984 current cost of the inventory was $500,000, equipment $168,000 and land $900,000.
[b]Presentation is not required by FASB Statement No. 33.

FIVE-YEAR COMPARISON OF SELECTED
SUPPLEMENTARY FINANCIAL DATA ADJUSTED FOR EFFECTS OF CHANGING PRICES
(In Average 1984 Dollars)

|  | Years Ended December 31,[a] | | | | |
|---|---|---|---|---|---|
|  | 1980 | 1981 | 1982 | 1983 | 1984 |
| Net sales and other operating revenues | XX | XX | XX | XX | $ 800,000 |
| Historical cost information adjusted for general inflation: |  |  |  |  |  |
| Income (loss) from continuing operations |  |  |  |  | $(114,333) |
| Income (loss) from continuing operations per common share |  |  |  |  | $(1.14) |
| Net assets at year-end |  |  |  |  | $790,666 |
| Current cost information: |  |  |  |  |  |
| Income (loss) from continuing operations |  |  |  |  | $(216,000) |
| Income (loss) from continuing operations per common share |  |  |  |  | $(2.16) |
| Excess of increase in specific prices over increase in the general price level |  |  |  |  | $145,400 |
| Net assets at year-end |  |  |  |  | $834,400 |
| Purchasing power gain on net monetary items |  |  |  |  | $433,000 |
| Cash dividends declared per common share |  |  |  |  | .10 |
| Market price per common share at year-end |  |  |  |  | Not given |
| Average consumer price index |  |  |  |  | 160 |

[a]Note that Lia Corporation started operations in 1984 and therefore prior changing price information is not available.

statements with some idea of the trend in such items as earnings, dividends, and consumer prices. Using the Lia Corporation illustration, most of the information for this report has already been computed or is easily computed. The only additional computation that is necessary is the balance in net assets on a constant dollar and current cost basis. To determine the required amounts, (a) constant dollar and historical cost and (b) current cost and historical cost for inventories, property, plant, and equipment must be computed. These amounts are added to net assets (stockholders' equity) and then converted to average-for-the-year dollars. This computation is shown below:

Lia Corporation
COMPUTATION OF NET ASSETS
As of December 31, 1984

|  | Historical Cost Exhibit 1 | Constant Dollar Exhibit 2 | Current Cost Exhibit 3 |
|---|---|---|---|
| Inventory | $300,000 | $ 333,333 | $ 500,000 |
| Equipment (net) | 140,000 | 280,000 | 168,000 |
| Land | 450,000 | 900,000 | 900,000 |
|  | $890,000 | $1,513,333 | $1,568,000 |
| Net assets (stockholders' equity), 12/31/84, as stated in the financial statements (historical cost) |  | $365,000 | $ 365,000 |
| Inventory, equipment (net) and land |  |  |  |
| Constant dollar amount |  | $1,513,333 |  |
| Historical cost amount |  | 890,000 | 623,333 |
| Current cost amount |  | $1,568,000 |  |
| Historical cost amount |  | 890,000 | 678,000 |
| Net assets 12/31/84—as stated in year-end dollars |  |  |  |
| Constant dollar |  | $988,333 |  |
| Current cost |  |  | $1,043,000 |
| Adjustment to average dollars |  |  |  |
| Constant dollar $988,333 × 160/200 |  | $790,666 |  |
| Current cost $1,043,000 × 160/200 |  |  | $ 834,400 |

For purposes of the five-year summary it is assumed that 100,000 shares were outstanding for the year. This information is presented at the bottom of page 1171 (Exhibit 4).

## Additional Highlights

Other matters of importance are as follows:

1. Use of recoverable amount
2. Income taxes
3. Determination of current costs.

**Recoverable Amount** The term recoverable amount means net realizable value or the present value (value in use) expected to be recoverable from the sale or use of the asset. When the recoverable amount of an asset is **permanently lower** than historical cost in constant dollars or current cost, the recoverable amount should be used as the measure of the assets and of the expense associated with the use or sale of the assets for that measure of income. This concept is similar to that used for historical cost statements (lower of cost or market for inventories as an illustration). To state assets at a cost figure that is in excess of its recoverable amounts is inappropriate. A better approach is to recognize the loss immediately.

**Income Taxes** Total income tax is based on historical cost and is charged as an expense in arriving at income from continuing operations. The Board wishes to highlight the impact of the income taxes on overstated profits and thereby inform users of the excessive taxation that often occurs in a period of inflation. Others disagree with this approach and argue that a portion of the income taxes should be allocated to the realized holding gain. Still others contend that income taxes should be imputed on the unrealized holding gain as well. If the purpose is to disclose the economic change from one period to another, then many argue that the unrealized holding gain should have a tax effect associated with it.

The Board requires the reporting company to disclose that it made no adjustments to income tax expense for any timing differences that might arise as a result of restatement on a current cost basis. In addition, it must be disclosed that income tax expense has not been allocated between income from continuing operations and the increases or decreases in the current cost amounts of inventory and property, plant, and equipment.

**Determination of Current Costs** The following bases for determining the current cost of inventories and property, plant, and equipment may be used.

DIRECT PRICING Current invoice prices and vendors' price lists or other quotations or estimates are acceptable methods of valuing both inventories and property, plant, and equipment.

INDEXATION Either external or specific internal indexes might be used to value both inventories and property, plant, and equipment.

STANDARD COSTS If these costs reflect current costs, they may be used to determine the current cost of inventories.

Keeping with the Board's attempt to simplify the computations, cost of goods sold measured on a LIFO basis is assumed to provide an acceptable approximation of cost of goods sold on a current cost basis if the effect of any decrease in inventory layers is excluded.

## Comparative Analysis

Presented as Exhibit 5 (page 1175) is a comparative set of the financial statements prepared under the different valuation approaches illustrated in this chapter. Note that for **balance sheet** purposes, the current year's monetary balances are unaffected, regardless of the valuation method employed, if reported in end-of-year dollars. However, the nonmonetary items are adjusted, depending upon the method selected.

Examination of the **income statement** shows that Lia Corporation's profitability is the result of a purchasing power gain on net monetary items due principally to holding a large amount of debt during a period of price inflation. During a period of inflation, companies with large real estate holdings and large fixed-rate loans outstanding report higher income under constant dollar and current cost/constant dollar statements.

Note also that Lia Corporation would report a loss from continuing operations on a constant dollar, current cost, and the FASB approach, but would still be paying income taxes. This presentation illustrates why many have contended that the historical cost income numbers are an illusion which vanish after phantom inventory profits are considered and depreciation expense is adjusted for the cost of replacing aging assets.

Finally, note that historical cost net income, $75,000, equals current cost realized income, $75,000. This occurrence in our illustration is not a coincidence; it demonstrates that the current cost approach segregates the historical cost income into two components—income (loss) from continuing operations and realized holding gain (loss).

## CONCLUDING OBSERVATIONS

Now that certain enterprises are required to report price-level information, the interested parties will be able to determine the effects of changing prices on an enterprise's operating performance. One recent survey, for example, which included all 800 industrial companies required to provide information on changing prices, found the following.[25]

**Income from Continuing Operations Decreases**    When historical cost numbers are restated to constant dollars, constant dollar income (excluding purchasing power gains or losses) was half the historical cost net income. When restated to a current cost basis, income from continuing operations was 34% of historical cost income. The extent of the decrease varies by industry. As indicated earlier, inflation hits hardest those industries that have the oldest assets. Conversely, companies experiencing technological growth are not affected as much. For example, the transportation and communications industries (including railroads) had a current cost to historical cost net income of 11%; the industry group that included computers had a current cost to historical cost net income of 68%.

**Taxes Increased**    On an average basis, the effective tax rate has increased approximately 61%, from an effective rate of 42.4% on an historical cost basis to 68.2% on a current cost basis (on a constant dollar basis, the effective tax rate is 60.8%). For example, in a recent annual report, R. J. Reynolds Industries had increases in effective tax rates from historical cost to current cost of 49.7% and to a constant dollar of 75.3%. In fact, some companies, particularly utilities had effective tax rates on a current cost basis of approximately 100%.

**Capital Depletion**    On the basis of historical cost financial statements, after dividend payments, net assets increased approximately 6% because income exceeded dividends by this amount. On a current cost basis, however, dividends exceeded income, resulting in a disinvestment rate of 2.4%. Therefore American industry on an aggregate basis is in the process of gradual liquidation, using current cost numbers. Again the effect varies greatly by industry. For example, transportation and communication equipment and utilities are particularly hard hit.

[25]Anthony Phillips and Beverly Welch, "The Real News Behind Those Cheerful Headlines," *Highlights of Financial Reporting Issues* (Stamford, Conn.: FASB, October 14, 1981).

Exhibit 5
Lia Corporation
COMPARATIVE ANALYSIS OF DIFFERENT REPORTING SYSTEMS
December 31, 1984

| Balance Sheet | Historical Cost (Exhibit 1) | Constant Dollar (Exhibit 2) | Current Cost (Exhibit 3) | FASB Approach (Exhibit 4) (Partial) |
|---|---|---|---|---|
| Cash, receivables and other monetary assets | $ 325,000 | $ 325,000 | $ 325,000 | NA |
| Inventories | 300,000 | 333,333 | 500,000 | 500,000[a] |
| Equipment (net) | 140,000 | 280,000 | 168,000 | 168,000 |
| Land | 450,000 | 900,000 | 900,000 | 900,000 |
| Total assets | $1,215,000 | $1,838,333 | $1,893,000 | |
| Current liabilities (all monetary) | 200,000 | 200,000 | 200,000 | NA |
| Long-term liabilities (all monetary) | 650,000 | 650,000 | 650,000 | NA |
| Total liabilities | 850,000 | 850,000 | 850,000 | NA |
| Common stock | 300,000 | 600,000 | 300,000 | NA |
| Retained earnings | 65,000 | 388,333 | 743,000 | NA |
| Total stockholders' equity | 365,000 | 988,333 | 1,043,000 | NA |
| Total liabilities and stockholders' equity | $1,215,000 | $1,838,333 | $1,893,000 | |

[a]The current cost of inventories and property, plant, and equipment must be disclosed.

| Income Statement | Historical Cost (Exhibit 1) | Constant Dollar (Exhibit 2) | Current Cost (Exhibit 3) | FASB Approach Constant Dollar (Exhibit 4) (Partial) | FASB Approach Current Cost |
|---|---|---|---|---|---|
| Sales | $800,000 | $1,000,000 | $800,000 | $ 800,000 | $ 800,000 |
| Cost of goods sold | 470,000 | 816,667 | 760,000 | 653,333 | 760,000 |
| Gross profit | 330,000 | 183,333 | 40,000 | 146,667 | 40,000 |
| Selling and administrative expenses | 170,000 | 212,500 | 170,000 | 170,000 | 170,000 |
| Depreciation expense | 10,000 | 20,000 | 11,000 | 16,000 | 11,000 |
| Income taxes | 75,000 | 93,750 | 75,000 | 75,000 | 75,000 |
| Income (loss) from continuing operations | 75,000 | (142,917) | (216,000) | $(114,333) | $(216,000) |
| Realized holding gain (loss) | NA | NA | 291,000 | | |
| Realized income (loss) | NA | NA | 75,000 | | |
| Unrealized holding gain | NA | NA | 678,000 | | |
| Specific increase (decrease) in inventories, equipment, land, net of inflation | NA | NA | NA | | $ 145,400 |
| Purchasing power gain or (loss) on net monetary items | NA | 541,250 | NA | $ 433,000 | $ 433,000 |
| Net income | 75,000 | 398,333 | 753,000 | | |
| Beginning retained earnings | -0- | -0- | -0- | | |
| | 75,000 | 398,333 | 753,000 | | |
| Cash dividends | 10,000 | 10,000 | 10,000 | | |
| Ending retained earnings | $ 65,000 | $ 388,333 | $743,000 | | |

**Rate of Return on Investment Decreased**    At the same time that income is declining when adjusted for changing prices, net assets (stockholders' equity) is increasing. As a result, rate of return on investment decreases substantially. To illustrate, when current cost income is divided by stockholders' equity on a current cost basis to indicate a real return, it becomes apparent that U.S. industry is not achieving an adequate rate of return. For example, on an historical basis, the machinery industry is earning 16.3%, mining and construction 20.5%, and primary and fabricated metals 12.1%; on a current cost basis, these percentages are 8.1%, 4.1%, and .5%, respectively.

These data suggest that the information on changing prices may be relevant. This information provides insights that historical cost financial data cannot provide. The important question at this point is how useful these disclosures are to users of the financial statements. For example, are analysts currently using these disclosures? Does the information on changing prices affect their decision process, their costs of analysis, their techniques of financial analysis, and so on? What are the costs of preparing this information? How reliable is the information? What are the economic consequences of reporting price-level information? The accounting profession is attempting to answer these questions through research.

# APPENDIX O

# Current Cost/Constant Dollar Accounting

If current cost/constant dollar financial statements are prepared, all amounts in the financial statements are generally stated at current cost in year-end dollars. The following illustration is based on Lia Corporation data on page 1147 (Exhibit 1) and all of the related additional information (**numbers 1–11**).

## Adjustment of Balance Sheet Items

Because assets and liabilities are stated at current cost in year-end dollars on a current cost balance sheet, these items appear at the same amounts on a current cost/constant dollar balance sheet. The items that make up stockholders' equity will differ because under a current cost system common stock is not adjusted to end-of-year dollars, whereas under a current cost/constant dollar system, common stock is restated. In addition, retained earnings must be restated for current cost/constant dollar net income which includes a purchasing power gain or loss on net monetary items. The amounts reported on the comparative balance sheet on page 1179 (Exhibit A) should be compared with the amounts on the balance sheets in Exhibits 2 and 3 in this chapter.

The 1/1/84 balance sheet is restated to end-of-year dollars. The balance sheet at 12/31/84 (Exhibit A) is the same as the current cost balance sheet shown on page 1160 (Exhibit 3) with the exception of common stock and retained earnings. Common stock must be restated to 12/31/84 dollars and the retained earnings balance is determined by subtracting the liabilities and common stock balances from total assets. The retained earnings balance can also be determined by adding the current cost/constant dollar net income less dividends to beginning retained earnings.

## Adjustment of Income Statement Items

To arrive at a current cost/constant dollar income statement, the current cost income statement must be adjusted to year-end dollars.

**Sales and Related Expenses** Sales, cost of goods sold, selling and administrative expenses, depreciation expense and income taxes are adjusted to year-end dollars as follows:

| | |
|---|---:|
| Sales $800,000 × 200/160 = | $1,000,000 |
| Cost of goods sold $760,000 × 200/160 = | 950,000 |
| Selling and administrative expenses $170,000 × 200/160 = | 212,500 |
| Depreciation expense $11,000 × 200/160 = | 13,750 |
| Income taxes $75,000 × 200/160 = | 93,750 |

Note. All of the items above were stated in average dollars and must be adjusted to year-end dollars.

**Realized and Unrealized Holding Gains** The computation of the total holding gain, net of inflation, is as follows:

Exhibit B
Lia Corporation
UNREALIZED AND REALIZED HOLDING GAINS

| | Constant Dollar[a] | Current Cost/ Constant Dollar[b] | Unrealized Holding Gain (Loss) | Realized Holding Gain (Loss) |
|---|---:|---:|---:|---:|
| Inventory 12/31/84* | $333,333 | $500,000 | $166,667 | $ -0- |
| Cost of goods sold | 816,667 | 950,000 | -0- | 133,333 |
| Purchases | 650,000 | 650,000 | -0- | -0- |
| Equipment (net) 12/31/84 | 280,000 | 168,000 | (112,000) | -0- |
| Depreciation expense | 20,000 | 13,750 | -0- | (6,250) |
| Land 12/31/84 | 900,000 | 900,000 | -0- | -0- |
| Total unrealized holding gain | | | $ 54,667 | |
| Total realized holding gain | | | | $127,083 |
| Increase (decrease) in current cost of assets held during the year, net of inflation (total holding gains, net of inflation) | | ($54,667 + $127,083) | | $181,750[1] |

*Note that beginning inventory, equipment (net), and land are ignored here because historical cost and current cost are the same.
[a]All amounts taken from Exhibit 2 in chapter.
[b]All amounts in this column are adjusted to year-end dollars.

An explanation of the unrealized and realized holding gains follows:

INVENTORY, COST OF GOODS SOLD AND PURCHASES The beginning inventory is the same under both a constant dollar and current cost/constant dollar accounting system because the historical cost and current cost amounts were identical at the start of the business. An unrealized holding gain of $166,667 ($500,000 minus $333,333) must be recognized on the ending inventory because the current cost/constant dollar basis exceeds the constant dollar basis. A realized holding gain of $133,333 must also be recognized for the difference between the current cost/constant dollar cost of goods sold $950,000 and the constant dollar cost of goods sold of $816,667. No holding gains result on the purchases because the historical cost and current cost amounts are identical.

[1]Note that another way to compute the $181,750 is to restate the total holding gain (net of inflation) from Exhibit 4-A to end-of-year dollars ($145,400 × $\frac{200}{160}$ = $181,750).

Exhibit A
Lia Corporation
COMPARATIVE BALANCE SHEETS
As of January 1 and December 31, 1984
(Current Cost/Constant Dollar Basis)

|  | January 1, 1984 | December 31, 1984 |
|---|---|---|
| Cash, receivables, and other monetary assets | $    400,000 | $    325,000 |
| Inventories | 500,000 | 500,000 |
| Equipment (net) | 300,000 | 168,000 |
| Land | 900,000 | 900,000 |
| Total assets | $2,100,000 | $1,893,000 |
| Current liabilities (all monetary) | $    200,000 | $    200,000 |
| Long-term liabilities (all monetary) | 1,300,000 | 650,000 |
| Total liabilities | 1,500,000 | 850,000 |
| Common stock | 600,000 | 600,000 |
| Retained earnings | –0– | 443,000 |
| Total stockholders' equity | 600,000 | 1,043,000 |
| Total liabilities and stockholders' equity | $2,100,000 | $1,893,000 |

Lia Corporation
STATEMENT OF INCOME AND RETAINED EARNINGS
For the Year Ended December 31, 1984
(Current Cost/Constant Dollar Basis)

| | |
|---|---|
| Sales | $1,000,000 |
| Cost of goods sold | 950,000 |
| Gross profit | 50,000 |
| Selling and administrative expenses | 212,500 |
| Depreciation expense | 13,750 |
| Loss before income taxes | (176,250) |
| Income taxes | 93,750 |
| Loss from continuing operations | (270,000) |
| Realized holding gain, net of inflation | 127,083 |
| Realized loss | (142,917) |
| Unrealized holding gain, net of inflation | 54,667 |
|  | (88,250) |
| Purchasing power gain on net monetary items | 541,250 |
| Current cost/constant dollar net income | 453,000 |
| Retained earnings, January 1, 1984 | –0– |
|  | 453,000 |
| Cash dividends | 10,000 |
| Retained earnings, December 31, 1984 | $    443,000 |

**DEPRECIATION EXPENSE AND EQUIPMENT**    Depreciation expense on a constant dollar basis is $20,000, and on a current cost/constant dollar is $13,750 ($11,000 × 200/160). A realized holding loss, net of inflation would therefore be recognized in the amount of $6,250 ($20,000 minus $13,750). Because the current cost/constant dollar basis of the equipment at the end of the year is less than the constant dollar basis of the equipment at the end of the year by $112,000 ($280,000 minus $168,000), an unrealized holding loss (net of inflation), of that amount must be recognized. No unrealized holding gain exists at the beginning of the year.

LAND  The current cost of the land has increased $450,000 to $900,000. The land restated on a constant dollar basis is also $900,000. As a result, no holding gain or loss is recognized.

**Purchasing Power Gain or Loss**  The purchasing power gain on net monetary items of $541,250 as computed on page 1151 is already stated in year-end dollars and need not be adjusted. This purchasing power gain on net monetary items is added to the current cost/constant dollar loss from continuing operations to arrive at the final net income on a current cost/constant dollar basis.

**Note:** All **asterisked** Questions, Cases, Exercises, or Problems relate to material contained in the appendix to each chapter.

## QUESTIONS

1. What is a price index? How does a general price index differ from a specific price index?

2. What is constant dollar accounting? How does constant dollar accounting differ from current cost accounting?

3. Assume that the Consumer Price Index for Urban Consumers has increased to 155 from 100 six years ago. How many end-of-year dollars are needed today to purchase what $30,000 purchased three years ago?

4. Distinguish between monetary and nonmonetary items. What is a purchasing power gain or loss on net monetary items?

5. If the general price level is rising steadily, which of the following would be most realistically valued for balance sheet purposes: (a) equipment, (b) cash, or (c) real estate?

6. Jenny Van Alstyne purchased a 10-year, 16% bond at par for $1,000, collected interest annually during the life of the bond, and realized the principal amount of the bond at maturity. If the price level were half as high at maturity date as it was at the date of purchase, how did Jenny fare?

7. Mark DeFlippo purchased a 20-year, 10% bond at par for $1,000, collected interest annually during the life of the bond, and realized the principal amount of the bond at maturity. If the price level were twice as high at maturity date as it was at the date of purchase, how did Mark fare?

8. Assume a decade of rising prices. Would the following items give rise to (a) purchasing power gains, (b) purchasing power losses, or (c) neither purchasing power gains or losses?
   (a) Owning land during the period.
   (b) Holding a long-term note payable.
   (c) Holding cash in a pension fund.
   (d) Having preferred stock outstanding during the period.
   (e) Holding a note receivable.
   (f) Having patents during the period.
   (g) Having an investment in common stocks.

9. Classify each of the following as monetary or nonmonetary items:
   (a) Equipment
   (b) Premium on bonds payable
   (c) Common stock
   (d) Bonds

(e) Preferred stock (par value to be paid in liquidation)
(f) Investment in common stock
(g) Refundable deposits
(h) Accumulated depreciation—equipment
(i) Accounts receivable
(j) Deferred income taxes

10. Indicate whether a company gains or loses under each of the following conditions:
    (a) A company maintains equal amounts of monetary assets and monetary liabilities during a period of price-level increases.
    (b) A company maintains an excess of liabilities over monetary assets during a period of price-level increases.
    (c) A company maintains an excess of monetary assets over monetary liabilities during a period of price-level increases.
    (d) A company maintains an excess of monetary assets over monetary liabilities during a period of price-level decrease.

11. What are the major arguments in opposition to modifying financial statements for general price-level changes?

12. Explain three commonly advocated concepts of current value.

13. Some theorists have argued that the present value of future discounted cash flows should be used as the basis for measuring assets and liabilities. What are the major disadvantages to this approach?

14. Many have noted that the major difference between constant dollar and current cost accounting is related to the view of capital maintenance. What is the theory of capital maintenance and how does the constant dollar approach differ from the current cost approach in this regard?

15. A comprehensive current cost model emphasizes three different income numbers. Explain the rationale for these three income numbers.

16. At the beginning of 1983, a company purchased inventory for $60,000. During the year, the company sold half this inventory for $70,000 at a time when the current cost of the inventory sold was $45,000. At the end of the year, the remaining inventory had a current cost of $65,000. Compute the current cost income from continuing operations, the realized holding gain, the unrealized holding gain and the current cost net income.

17. MacDonald and Robertson has decided that it wishes to report current cost information related to its inventories. What approaches might be utilized to find the current cost for inventories?

18. Tam Bridges Inc. purchased equipment at the beginning of the year for $100,000 that had an estimated life of 10 years and no salvage value. The current cost of the equipment at the end of the year was $120,000. Assuming straight-line depreciation on a current cost basis, how much depreciation would be reported as a charge to current cost income from continuing operations? How much should be charged to the unrealized holding gain?

19. Many believe that if a partial or complete current cost income statement is prepared, income taxes should not be allocated to the realized or unrealized holding gain. Explain the rationale for this approach. Indicate the FASB position on this matter.

20. What are the major advantages of current cost accounting? Explain the difference between current cost accounting and replacement cost accounting.

21. Why might the use of specific price-level adjustments (current cost) produce a better indicator of disposable wealth than constant dollar accounting?

22. Some argue that a current cost approach is not acceptable, unless the historical cost numbers are adjusted to a constant dollar basis. Explain the rationale for this approach.

23. On January 1, 1983, Pritchett, Inc. had cash of $20,000 and inventories whose historical cost and current cost were $28,000. During the year, the general price level increased 10% on an even basis throughout the period, and the current cost of the inventories at the end of the year was $36,000. Assuming that the company held these assets for the entire year, compute the unrealized holding gain if a current cost/constant dollar approach were employed and reported in (1) end-of-year dollars and (2) average-for-the-year dollars.

**\*24.** What are the major differences between the current cost/constant dollar approach and the current cost approach?

**25.** Why do you believe the FASB required a dual presentation (constant dollar and current cost) for reporting price-level effects?

**26.** *FASB Statement No. 33,* "Financial Reporting and Changing Prices," was issued in 1979. Indicate the major reporting requirements of this statement.

**\*27.** What are the major advantages of the current cost/constant dollar approach?

## CASES

**C25-1** A business entity's financial statements could be prepared by using historical cost or current value as a basis. In addition, the basis could be stated in terms of unadjusted dollars or dollars restated for changes in purchasing power. The various permutations of these two separate and distinct areas are shown in the following matrix:

|  | Unadjusted Dollars | Dollars Restated for Changes in Purchasing Power |
|---|:---:|:---:|
| Historical cost | 1 | 2 |
| Current value | 3 | 4 |

Block number 1 of the matrix represents the traditional method of accounting for transactions in accounting today, wherein the absolute (unadjusted) amount of dollars given up or received is recorded for the asset or liability obtained (**relationship between resources**). Amounts recorded in the method described in block number 1 reflect the original cost of the asset or liability and do not give effect to any change in value of the unit of measure (**standard of comparison**). This method assumes the validity of the accounting concepts of going concern and stable monetary unit. Any gain or loss (including holding and purchasing power gains or losses) resulting from the sale or satisfaction of amounts recorded under this method is deferred in its entirety until sale or satisfaction.

**Instructions**

For each of the remaining matrix blocks (2, 3, and 4) respond to the following questions. **Limit your discussion to nonmonetary assets only.**

(a) How will this method of recording assets affect the relationship between resources and the standard of comparison?

(b) What is the theoretical justification for using each method?

(c) How will each method of asset valuation affect the recognition of gain or loss during the life of the asset and ultimately from the sale or abandonment of the asset? Your response should include a discussion of the timing and magnitude of the gain or loss and conceptual reasons for any difference from the gain or loss computed using the traditional method.

(AICPA adapted)

**C25-2** Shipman Corp., a wholesaler with large investments in plant and equipment, began operations in 1944. The company's history has been one of expansion in sales, production, and physical facilities. Recently, some concern has been expressed that the conventional financial statements do not provide sufficient information for decisions by investors. After consideration of proposals for various types of supplementary financial statements to be included in the 1983 annual report, management has decided to present a balance sheet as of December 31, 1983, and a statement of income and retained earnings for 1983, both restated for changes in the general price level.

**Instructions**

(a) On what basis can it be contended that Shipman's conventional statements should be restated for changes in the general price level?

(b) Distinguish between financial statements restated for general price-level changes and current value financial statements.

(c) Distinguish between monetary and nonmonetary assets and liabilities as the terms are used in constant dollar accounting. Give examples of each.

(d) Outline the procedures Shipman should follow in preparing the proposed supplementary statements. (Assume statements are computed in year-end dollars.)

(e) Indicate the major similarities and differences between the proposed supplementary statements and the corresponding conventional statements.

(f) Assuming that in the future Shipman will want to present comparative supplementary statements, can the 1983 supplementary statements be presented in 1984 without adjustment? Explain.

(AICPA adapted)

**C25-3** The general purchasing power of the dollar has declined considerably because of inflation in recent years. To account for this changing value of the dollar, many accountants suggest that financial statements be adjusted for general price-level changes. Three independent, unrelated statements regarding general price-level adjusted financial statements follow. Each statement contains some fallacious reasoning.

### Statement I

When adjusting financial data for general price-level changes, a distinction must be made between monetary and nonmonetary assets and liabilities, which, under the historical cost basis of accounting, have been identified as "current" and "noncurrent." When using the historical cost basis of accounting, no purchasing power gain or loss is recognized in the accounting process, but when financial statements are adjusted for general price-level changes, a purchasing power gain or loss will be recognized on monetary and nonmonetary items.

### Statement II

The accounting profession has not seriously considered price-level adjusted financial statements before because the rate of inflation usually has been so small from year to year that the adjustments would have been immaterial in amount. Price-level adjusted financial statements represent a departure from the historical cost basis of accounting. Financial statements should be prepared on the basis of facts, not estimates.

### Statement III

If financial statements were adjusted for general price-level changes, depreciation charges in the income statement would permit the recovery of dollars of current purchasing power and, thereby, equal the cost of new assets to replace the old ones. General price-level adjusted data would yield statement-of-financial-position amounts closely approximating current values. Furthermore, management can make better decisions if constant dollar financial statements are published.

**Instructions**

Evaluate each of the independent statements and identify the areas of fallacious reasoning in each and explain why the reasoning is incorrect. Complete your discussion of each statement before proceeding to the next statement.

(AICPA adapted)

**C25-4** The controller for Trophy, Inc. has recently hired you as assistant controller. Recognizing that you should be quite familiar with the recent pronouncement on accounting for changing prices, the controller shows you supplementary information that the auditors recommend be reported as supplementary data for the year. Part of the information is as follows:

Trophy, Inc.
STATEMENT OF INCOME FROM CONTINUING
OPERATIONS ADJUSTED FOR CHANGING PRICES
For the Year Ended December 31, 1983

(In (000s) of Average 1983 Dollars)

| | | |
|---|---:|---:|
| Income from continuing operations, as reported in the income statement | | $ 27,000 |
| Adjustments to restate costs for the effect of general inflation | | |
| Cost of goods sold | (22,152) | |
| Depreciation and amortization expense | (12,390) | (34,542) |
| Loss from continuing operations adjusted for general inflation | | (7,542) |
| Adjustments to reflect the difference between general inflation and changes in specific prices (current costs) | | |
| Cost of goods sold | (3,072) | |
| Depreciation and amortization expense | (16,110) | (19,182) |
| Loss from continuing operations adjusted for changes in specific prices | | $(26,724) |
| Purchasing power gain on net monetary items | | $ 23,187 |
| Increase in specific prices (current cost) of inventories and property, plant, and equipment held during the year[a] | | $ 73,824 |
| Effect of increase in general price level | | 56,877 |
| Excess of increase in specific prices over increase in the general price level | | $ 16,947 |

[a]At December 31, 1983 current cost of inventory was $197,100 and current cost of property, plant, and equipment, net of accumulated depreciation was $255,300.

**Instructions**

The controller is interested in the answer to the following questions:
(a) Why is the statement presented in average 1983 dollars?
(b) What is meant by general inflation?
(c) What is the difference in the two losses from continuing operations?
(d) Why are the other expenses such as officers' salaries not reported on this statement?
(e) What is the purchasing power gain on net monetary items? (Explain.)
(f) Why are taxes not allocated to the increase in specific prices of inventories and property, plant, and equipment?
(g) Must Trophy, Inc. report this information in this manner, or are other alternatives available? (Assume that the company is required to present supplementary price-level data.)

C25-5 In September 1979 *Statement of Financial Accounting Standards No. 33,* "Financial Reporting and Changing Prices," (*FASB 33*) was released. This statement applies to public enterprises that have either (1) inventories and property, plant, and equipment (before deducting accumulated depreciation) of more than $125 million or (2) total assets amounting to more than $1 billion (after deducting accumulated depreciation). No changes are required in the basic financial statements, but information required by *FASB No. 33* is to be presented in supplementary statements, schedules, or notes in the financial reports.

**Instructions**

(a) A number of terms are defined and used in *FASB 33*.
   1. Differentiate between the terms constant dollar and current cost.
   2. Explain what is meant by current cost/constant dollar accounting and how it differs from historical cost accounting.
(b) Identify the accounts for which an enterprise must measure the effects of changing prices in order to present the supplementary information required by *FASB No. 33*.

(c) *FASB No. 33* is based upon *FASB Concepts Statement No. 1,* "Objectives of Financial Reporting by Business Enterprises," which concludes that financial reporting should provide information to help investors, creditors, and other financial statement users assess the amounts, timing, and uncertainty of prospective net cash inflows to the enterprise.

1. Explain how *FASB No. 33* may help in attaining this objective.
2. Identify and discuss two ways in which the information required by *FASB No. 33* may be useful for internal management decisions.

(CMA adapted)

# EXERCISES

**E25-1** Excerpts from the trial balance of Power Equipment Company as of December 31, 1984, when the price index was 150 include the following accounts.

| | |
|---|---:|
| Bonds payable (due 1991) | $300,000 |
| Depreciation expense—building | 11,000 |
| Inventory (LIFO basis) | 60,000 |
| Sales (made evenly throughout the year) | 400,000 |
| Cash | 40,000 |
| Notes receivable | 60,000 |
| Land | 100,000 |
| Building | 440,000 |
| Accounts payable | 30,000 |

During 1984, the average price index was 135. The land was purchased in 1976 when the price index was 105, and the building was constructed in 1980 when the index was 120. The bonds were issued November, 1979, when the index was 115. The LIFO inventory was built up during 1981 when the average index was 125.

**Instructions**

At what amounts would these accounts be presented in constant dollar financial statements in (1) end-of-year dollars and (2) average-for-the-year dollars?

**E25-2** You have been asked to prepare constant dollar financial statements for Kitchen Products Company. At the end of the period for which statements are being prepared, the price index being used stands at 180. The index values prevailing when each item (amount) was first recorded on the books is shown below.

| Item | Index | Item | Index |
|---|---|---|---|
| 1. Equipment | 160 | 5. Bonds payable (long-term) | 175 |
| 2. Accounts payable | 135 | 6. Insurance expense | 140 |
| 3. Land | 180 | 7. Notes receivable (short-term) | 130 and 150 |
| 4. Depreciation on equipment | 160 | 8. Rent income | 178 |

**Instructions**

Indicate which of the items above would be raised, lowered, or remain unchanged on constant dollar statements as compared to the historical cost statements.

**E25-3** Presented below are selected price indices for specific dates or periods:

| | |
|---|---|
| Dec. 31, 1956—100 | June 30, 1983—204 |
| Feb. 15, 1957—106 | Dec. 31, 1983—215 |
| Mar. 21, 1957—108 | Average 1983—206 |
| May  1, 1972—169 | June 19, 1984—220 |
| Sept. 23, 1976—190 | Dec. 31, 1984—233 |
| Dec. 31, 1979—197 | Average 1984—222 |

1. Cash (on hand Dec. 31, 1984).
2. Equipment (purchased Mar. 21, 1957).
3. Common stock, $100 par, issued Dec. 31, 1956.
4. Land (acquired Feb. 15, 1957).
5. Preferred stock, 6% (issued Sept. 23, 1976).
6. Accounts receivable (balance Dec. 31, 1984).
7. Inventory (LIFO accumulated throughout 1983).
8. Depreciation expense for 1984 (on equipment purchased March 21, 1957).
9. Sales made during 1984.
10. Investments in common stocks (purchased May 1, 1972).
11. Accounts payable (balance Dec. 31, 1984).
12. Bonds payable (issued Dec. 31, 1979, maturing Dec. 31, 1996).
13. Purchases made during 1984.
14. Interest expense (incurred evenly through 1984).
15. Allowance for doubtful accounts (balance Dec. 31, 1984).

**Instructions**

Given the dates and respective price indices above, indicate what the numerator and the denominator would be to adjust the following items for price-level changes for presentation in a December 31, 1984, constant dollar balance sheet, in end-of-year dollars.

**E25-4** Express Transport Co. purchased equipment for $60,000 on January 1, 1983, when the price index was 120. The equipment has an estimated life of 10 years with no scrap value. At December 31, 1983, the price index was 140 and at December 31, 1984, it was 150.

**Instructions**

(a) At what amounts is the equipment carried on constant dollar balance sheets at December 31, 1983, and December 31, 1984? (Assume amounts reported in end-of-year dollars.) Round answers to nearest dollar.
(b) What is the amount of depreciation expense (use the straight-line method) on the constant dollar income statements for the years ended December 31, 1983 and December 31, 1984? (Assume amounts reported in end-of-year dollars.)
(c) Assuming that the average price level in 1983 was 130 and in 1984 was 144, indicate the amount at which equipment and the related depreciation would be reported on the related financial statements for each of these years. (Assume average-for-the-year dollars is employed.)

**E25-5** Earlville Grain Company began operations on January 1, 1984. At that time merchandise was purchased for $40,000. Additional merchandise was purchased uniformly throughout the year for $210,000. The inventory at December 31, 1984 consists of goods purchased throughout December, at a cost of $29,000. Earlville utilized a FIFO cost assumption. Assume the following price-level indices:

| | |
|---|---|
| January 1, 1984 | 126 |
| 1984 Year Average | 144 |
| December, 1984, Average | 150 |
| December 31, 1984 | 153 |

**Instructions**

Compute the cost of goods sold as it would appear in a constant dollar income statement for 1984 in (1) end-of-year dollars and (2) average-for-the-year dollars.

**E25-6** At the beginning of 1983, Cortland Carmel Co. had net monetary assets of $80,000. During the period, the following items increased or decreased this balance:

1. Equipment was purchased in the first quarter for $11,000 and dividends were paid on December 31 of $6,000.

2. Sales of $230,000 were made evenly throughout the period.

3. Purchases of $150,000 were made evenly throughout the period.

4. Selling expenses (excluding depreciation) of $40,000 were incurred in the first quarter.

The Consumer Price Index for all Urban Consumers was as follows:

| | |
|---|---|
| January 1, 1983 | 100 |
| First quarter, 1983 | 105 |
| Average 1983 | 110 |
| December 31, 1983 | 120 |

**Instructions**

(a) Compute the purchasing power gain or loss on net monetary items for 1983 in end-of-year dollars.

(b) Compute the purchasing power gain or loss on net monetary items for 1983 in average-for-the-year dollars as required in *FASB Statement No. 33*.

**E25-7** The books of New Glarus Company carried the following selected items on December 31.

| | 1984 | 1983 |
|---|---|---|
| Plant and equipment | $125,500 | $225,500 |
| Accumulated depreciation—plant and equipment | 30,000 | 85,000 |
| Common stock, $10 par | 100,000 | 100,000 |
| Net monetary items | 42,700 | 30,500 |
| Inventory (FIFO) | 66,600 | 50,000 |

Other relevant information:

1. The following Consumer Price Indices for all Urban Consumers existed

| | |
|---|---|
| December 31, 1983 | 115 |
| April 15, 1984 | 110 |
| June 15, 1984 | 115 |
| December 15, 1984 | 130 |
| December 31, 1984 | 130 |
| Average for 1984 | 120 |

2. Equipment costing $100,000 and having $60,000 of accumulated depreciation was sold on April 15, 1984 for its book value.

3. The company paid a $.10/share cash dividend on June 15, 1984 and December 15, 1984.

4. Assume that all other transactions that affect net monetary items such as sales occur evenly through 1984.

**Instructions**

(a) Compute the purchasing power gain or loss on net monetary items for 1984 in end-of-year dollars.

(b) Compute the purchasing power gain or loss on net monetary items for 1984 in average-for-the-year dollars as required by *FASB Statement No. 33*.

**E25-8** Porosity Foundry Co. owns a patent for a milling device. The device has a remaining life of four years. Salem estimates the future cash flows from the patent to be as follows:

| Year | Cash Receipts Received at the End of Each Year | Cash Disbursements Made at the End of Each Year | Net Cash Inflows |
|---|---|---|---|
| 1 | $50,000 | $22,000 | $28,000 |
| 2 | 40,000 | 18,000 | 22,000 |
| 3 | 25,000 | 14,000 | 11,000 |
| 4 | 21,000 | 14,000 | 7,000 |

**Instructions**

(a) Assuming a 10% discount factor, determine the present value of the patent. (Round to nearest dollar.)

(b) Many contend that the present value of future cash flows is the proper method for valuation purposes. Speculate as to why this approach was not adopted in *FASB Statement No. 33*.

**E25-9** Memphis Poultry, Inc. adopted a current cost system in its first year of operation. At the start of the first year, 1983, the company purchased $24,000 of inventory, and at the end of the year had an inventory of $14,400 on an historical cost basis and $22,800 on a current cost basis. At the time the inventory was sold, the current cost of the inventory was $13,200. Sales for the year were $18,000. Ignore all tax effects and assume that the Consumers Price Index for all Urban Consumers did not change over this period. Other expenses were $1,200 on both historical cost and current cost bases.

**Instructions**

(a) Prepare a current cost income statement.

(b) Prepare a current cost income statement in accordance with *FASB Statement No. 33*.

**E25-10** Assume the same information as Exercise 25-9, and that the Consumer Price Index for all Urban Consumers was as follows:

| | |
|---|---|
| Beginning of 1983 | 100 |
| Average for 1983 | 130 |
| End of 1983 | 160 |

**Instructions**

Compute the increase (decrease) in the current cost of inventory, less the effect of the increase in the general price level. Assume that the current cost of goods sold was sold at the time when the general price level was at the average for the year. The beginning inventory was acquired at the beginning price level. The company is presenting only a partial income statement in accordance with *FASB Statement No. 33*.

**E25-11** Silo Mfg. Co. is considering the adoption of a current cost system. Presented below is the enterprise's balance sheet at the end of the first year based on historical cost.

Silo Mfg. Co.
BALANCE SHEET
as of December 31, 19xx

| Cash | $25,000 | Accounts Payable | $ 9,000 |
|---|---|---|---|
| Inventory | 42,000 | Capital Stock | 50,000 |
| Land | 16,000 | Retained Earnings | 24,000 |
| | $83,000 | | $83,000 |

The following additional information is presented:

1. Cost of goods sold on an historical cost basis is $60,000; on a current cost basis $68,000.

2. No dividends were paid in the first year of operation.

3. Ending inventory on a current cost basis is $47,000; land on a current basis is $24,000 at the end of the year.

4. Operating expenses for the first year were $20,000.

**Instructions**

(a) Prepare an income statement for the current year on a (1) historical cost basis; (2) current cost basis. No unrealized holding gains exist at the beginning of the year.

(b) Prepare a balance sheet for the current year on a current cost basis.

**E25–12**

|  | Cindy Ubl, Inc.<br>INCOME STATEMENT<br>For the Year Ended December 31, 1984 |  |  |
|---|---|---|---|
|  |  |  | Historical |
| Sales |  |  | $1,000,000 |
| Cost of goods sold: |  |  |  |
|   Inventory 1/1/84 |  | $ 40,000 |  |
|   Purchases |  | 500,000 |  |
|  |  | 540,000 |  |
|   Inventory 12/31/84 |  | 100,000 |  |
|   Cost of goods sold |  |  | 440,000 |
| Gross profit |  |  | 560,000 |
| Depreciation |  | 400,000 |  |
| Operating expenses |  | 190,000 |  |
| Total expenses |  |  | 590,000 |
| Net loss |  |  | $ (30,000) |

Additional information:

1. Revenues are earned and operating expenses are incurred evenly throughout the year.
2. Inventory was acquired during the last week of the year (FIFO basis).
3. Depreciable assets have a 5-year life and were acquired as follows:

      January 1, 1981—$1,500,000    January 1, 1983—   500,000

4. The Consumer Price Index for all Urban Consumers was as follows:

| | |
|---|---|
| 1/1/81 | 175 |
| Average, 1981 | 160 |
| 1/1/83 | 140 |
| Average, 1983 | 130 |
| 1/1/84 | 115 |
| Average, 1984 | 105 |
| 12/31/84 | 80 |

5. The purchasing power loss on net monetary items was $29,000.

**Instructions**

(a) Using the data provided above, prepare a comprehensive constant dollar income statement in year-end dollars.
(b) What are the major differences between a comprehensive income statement on a constant dollar basis and a partial income statement on a constant dollar basis prepared in accordance with the provisions of *FASB Statement No. 33*?

**E25–13** Presented below is the historical cost income statement of Cutlass, Inc.

| | |
|---|---|
| Sales | $37,500 |
| Cost of goods sold | 15,000 |
| Gross profit | 22,500 |
| Depreciation expense | 2,500 |
| Other expenses | 7,500 |
| Income before taxes | 12,500 |
| Income taxes (50%) | 6,250 |
| Net income | $ 6,250 |

Assume that the current cost of goods sold was $18,750 and that depreciation on a current cost basis was $6,250. Current cost and historical cost are the same on all other items. The general price level has not changed.

**Instructions**

(a) Prepare a current cost partial income statement per *FASB Statement No. 33*. Use the income statement format and assume that no unrealized holding gains exist.

(b) If a portion of the income tax were allocated to the realized holding gain, how would the income statement differ?

(c) What might be the rationale of the FASB for not allocating the income tax?

**E25-14** Hydrants & Plugs Co. purchased 100 bolts of cloth for $520 each on July 1, 1983. On December 15, 50 bolts were sold for $650 each, the current cost to replace the sold bolts was $585 each. On March 31, 1984, the remaining bolts were sold for $715 each; their current cost had risen to $663.

**Instructions**

Compute the current cost net income in 1983 and 1984. Indicate the realized and unrealized holding gains (losses) reported in each year. Ignore income taxes.

**E25-15** Presented below is information related to equipment purchased by Chocolate Company.

| | |
|---|---:|
| Historical cost (acquired 7/1/83) | $18,000 |
| Current cost 1/1/85 (gross) | 21,600 |
| Current cost 12/31/85 (25% increase in specific price index) | 27,000 |
| Accumulated depreciation 1/1/85: | |
|   Historical cost | 5,400 |
|   Current cost | 6,480 |
| Life of asset | 5 years |
| Depreciation method | Straight-line |

**Instructions**

(a) Compute the amount of depreciation expense that would be reported in arriving at income from continuing operations on a current cost basis per *FASB Statement No. 33*. (One-half year's depreciation was taken in the year of acquisition.)

(b) Compute the increase in current cost of equipment (holding gain) that will be reported per *FASB Statement No. 33*.

# PROBLEMS

**P25-1** Retail Showcase Mart was organized on December 15, 1983. The company's initial Statement of Financial Position is presented below.

Retail Showcase Mart
STATEMENT OF FINANCIAL POSITION
December 31, 1983

**Assets**

| | |
|---|---:|
| Cash | $200,000 |
| Inventory (at historical cost which equals market value; FIFO; periodic) | 400,000 |
| Furniture and fixtures | 200,000 |
| Land (held for future store site) | 100,000 |
|     Total assets | $900,000 |

**Liabilities and Stockholders' Equity**

| | |
|---|---|
| Accounts payable | $300,000 |
| Capital stock ($5 par, 200,000 shares authorized; 120,000 issued and outstanding) | 600,000 |
| Total liabilities and stockholders' equity | $900,000 |

The Statement of Income and the Statement of Financial Position prepared at the close of business on December 31, 1984 are presented below.

Retail Showcase Mart
STATEMENT OF INCOME
For the Year Ended December 31, 1984

| | | |
|---|---|---|
| Sales | | $1,100,000 |
| Cost of goods sold: | | |
| Inventory 1/1/84 | $ 400,000 | |
| Purchases | 1,000,000 | |
| Goods available | $1,400,000 | |
| Inventory 12/31/84 | 600,000 | 800,000 |
| Gross profit | | $ 300,000 |
| Operating expenses | | |
| Rent | $ 36,000 | |
| Depreciation | 20,000 | |
| Other (all required cash expenditures) | 44,000 | 100,000 |
| Income before taxes | | $ 200,000 |
| Income tax expense | | 80,000 |
| Net income | | $ 120,000 |
| Earnings per share | | $1.00 |

Retail Showcase Mart
STATEMENT OF FINANCIAL POSITION
December 31, 1984

**Assets**

| | |
|---|---|
| Cash | $ 240,000 |
| Accounts receivable | 400,000 |
| Inventory (at historical cost; FIFO; periodic) | 600,000 |
| Furniture and fixtures (net) | 180,000 |
| Land (held for future store site) | 100,000 |
| Total assets | $1,520,000 |

**Liabilities and Stockholders' Equity**

| | |
|---|---|
| Accounts payable | $ 800,000 |
| Capital stock ($5 par, 200,000 shares authorized; 120,000 issued and outstanding) | 600,000 |
| Retained earnings | 120,000 |
| Total liabilities and stockholders' equity | $1,520,000 |

Retail Showcase Mart rents its showroom facilities on an operating lease basis at a cost of $3,000 per month. The rent would be $5,000 per month if it were based on the current cost of the facility. All sales and cash outlays for costs and expenses occur uniformly throughout the year.

The following information is indicative of the changing prices since Retail Showcase Mart began its operations.

1. The Consumer Price Index for All Urban Consumers for the following times is:

| | |
|---|---|
| December 31, 1983 | 200 |
| October 1, 1984 | 216 |
| December 31, 1984 | 220 |
| Average for 1984 | 212 |

2. The ending inventory was acquired on October 1, 1984.

3. Inventory at current cost on December 31, 1984, is $700,000.

4. Cost of goods sold at current cost as of date of sale is $875,000.

5. Current cost of the land on December 31, 1984, is $150,000.

6. The sales and purchases occurred uniformly throughout 1984.

7. The "net recoverable amounts" for inventories and fixed assets have been determined by management to be in excess of the net current costs.

The accounting manager of Retail Showcase Mart has decided to comply voluntarily with the reporting requirements presented in the *Statement of Financial Accounting Standards No. 33,* "Financial Reporting and Changing Prices."

**Instructions**

(a) Compute Retail Showcase Mart's purchasing power gain or loss for 1984 in terms of December 31, 1984 dollars. Round all computations to the nearest $100.

(b) Prepare a constant dollar income statement for 1984 for Retail Showcase Mart in terms of December 31, 1984 dollars. Round all computations to the nearest $100.

(c) Identify and explain the advantages and disadvantages of constant dollar financial statements.

(CMA adapted)

**P25-2** The following information is taken from the historical cost income statement of Batavia Electronics:

| | |
|---|---|
| Sales revenue | $1,000,000 |
| Cost of goods sold | 600,000 |
| Selling and administrative expenses | 29,000 |
| Depreciation expense | 91,000 |
| Interest expense | 64,000 |
| Income taxes | 16,000 |

The historical cost balance sheet for Batavia Electronics is as follows:

| Assets | 12/31/82 | 12/31/83 |
|---|---|---|
| Cash and accounts receivable | $ 80,000 | $ 190,000 |
| Inventory | 500,000 | 520,000 |
| Equipment | 130,000 | 250,000 |
| Accumulated depreciation—equipment | (11,500) | (30,500) |
| Building | 800,000 | 800,000 |
| Accumulated depreciation—building | (80,000) | (152,000) |
| | $1,418,500 | $1,577,500 |

Liabilities and Owners' Equity

| | | |
|---|---:|---:|
| Accounts payable | $ 40,000 | $ 50,000 |
| 8% bonds payable | 600,000 | 650,000 |
| Preferred stock | 100,000 | 100,000 |
| Common stock | 300,000 | 300,000 |
| Retained earnings | 378,500 | 477,500 |
| | $1,418,500 | $1,577,500 |

The following additional information is provided:

1. The general price-level index at December 31, 1982 is 160; the average index for the year 1983 is 170; the index at December 31, 1983 is 180.

2. Sales revenues and material purchases occurred uniformly throughout the year. The expenses, other than depreciation, were paid uniformly throughout the year.

3. The inventories utilize a FIFO cost assumption. The December 31, 1982 inventory consists of goods acquired during the last three months of the year; the average index during those three months was 150. The December 31, 1983 inventory consists of goods acquired during the last month of 1983; the average index for that month was 176.

4. The equipment account consists of the following:

| Acquisition date | Amount | Index |
|:---:|---:|:---:|
| 6/ 5/81 | $ 50,000 | 120 |
| 10/27/82 | 80,000 | 148 |
| 10/ 9/83 | 120,000 | 174 |
| | $250,000 | |

Depreciation is calculated using the straight-line method, a useful life of 10 years, and no expected salvage value. Company policy is to take ½ year's depreciation in the year of acquisition or retirement.

5. The building was acquired in 1982, when the index was 135. The building has a 20-year life, with an estimated salvage value of $50,000. Depreciation is calculated using the double-declining balance method. Company policy with respect to buildings is to take a full year's depreciation in the year of acquisition.

6. Bonds with a face value of $600,000 were issued in 1965, when the company was organized. Bonds with a face value of $50,000 were issued in 1983, when the index was 171.

7. The preferred stock has a par value of $100, and a fixed liquidation value of $110.

8. Dividends of $101,000 were paid uniformly throughout the year.

9. The common stock was issued when the company was organized in 1965, when the index was 95.

**Instructions**

(a) Prepare a schedule computing the purchasing power gain or loss on net monetary items in end-of-year dollars.

(b) Prepare a constant dollar income statement in end-of-year dollars.

(c) Prepare a constant dollar balance sheet for 1983 in end-of-year dollars, and restate the 1982 balance sheet to the current end-of-year price level.

(d) Prepare a schedule computing the purchasing power gain or loss on net monetary items in average-for-the-year dollars as required by *FASB Statement No. 33*.

**P25–3** Flack Records, Inc. is discussing the possibility of reporting its cost of goods sold and ending inventory on an historical cost, constant dollar, current cost, and current cost/constant dollar basis. Assume that you are given the following information with respect to Flack Records, Inc.

| | Historical Cost | Current Cost | Consumer Price Index for Urban Consumers |
|---|---|---|---|
| Beginning inventory | $ 40,000 | $40,000 | 100 |
| Purchases | 160,000 | a | 125 (average) |
| Ending inventory | 50,000 | 65,000 | 150 |

aNote: the current cost of goods sold is $192,000 (incurred evenly through the year).

Assume that the beginning and ending inventory were purchased when the general price-level indexes were 100 and 150, respectively. Purchases were made evenly throughout the year.

**Instructions**

(a) Compute the cost of goods sold and ending inventory under an historical cost, constant dollar, and current cost, in year-end dollars.
(b) At what amount would cost of goods sold and inventory be reported in accordance with *FASB Statement No. 33,* assuming that comprehensive financial statements are not prepared. (Hint: the conversion factor for 125/150 to be used is .833.)
(c) Compute the increase in current cost of inventory, net of general inflation effects. Indicate the realized and unrealized holding gain, net of inflation. Compute in average-for-the-year dollars.

**P25-4** Presented below is information related to Osco Stores, Inc., at the beginning of the year 1984:

Osco Stores, Inc.
BALANCE SHEET
January 1, 1984

| Assets | | Equities | |
|---|---|---|---|
| Cash | $ 10,000 | Long-term Debt | $ 40,000 |
| Inventory | 20,000 | | |
| Land | 15,000 | Common Stock | 35,000 |
| Building | 55,000 | Retained Earnings | 25,000 |
| Total assets | $100,000 | Total equities | $100,000 |

Additional information related to transactions occurring in 1984 follows:

| | |
|---|---|
| Sales | $100,000 |
| Purchases of inventory in 1984 | 60,000 |
| Ending inventory, 12/31/84, historical cost | 22,000 |
| Ending inventory, 12/31/84, current cost | 26,000 |
| Cost of goods sold on current cost basis at different dates during the year (average current cost of goods sold the same) | 65,000 |

Land's current cost increased to $19,000 during the year.
Building's current cost is $70,000, excluding accumulated depreciation.
Operating expenses on both an historical cost and current cost basis were $20,000.
All applicable transactions were on a cash basis.
The company uses a perpetual system for recording inventories.
The building has an estimated useful life of 25 years and is being depreciated on the straight-line basis.
Current cost and historical cost for inventory, land, and buildings are identical at the beginning of the period.

**Instructions**

(a) Prepare an income statement and balance sheet on an historical cost basis for 1984.
(b) Prepare an income statement and balance sheet on a current cost basis for 1984.

(c) Prepare the income statement information that is required to be presented under *FASB Statement No. 33* for current cost data in an income statement format for 1984. Assume no change in the Consumer Price Index for all Urban Consumers during the year.

(d) Prepare the income statement information that is required to be presented under *FASB Statement No. 33* for current cost data for 1984 in a reconciliation format. Assume no change in the Consumer Price Index for all Urban Consumers during the year.

**P25-5** Assume the same information as Problem 25–4 and that the following changes occurred in the Consumers Price Index for all Urban Consumers:

| | |
|---|---|
| Beginning of 1984 | 100 |
| Average | 130 |
| End of 1984 | 180 |

**Instructions**

(a) Prepare an income statement and balance sheet on a constant dollar basis in end-of-year dollars. Assume that sales, purchases, and operating expenses were incurred evenly throughout the year. Land, building, and beginning inventory were acquired when the general price-level index was at 100. Ending inventory was comprised of goods purchased when the general price level was 130. (Hint: use the conversion factor of 1.3846 for the 180/130; do not use the fraction approach.) Round to nearest dollar.

(b) Assume the same information as (a) and prepare the partial income statement that is required to be presented under *FASB Statement No. 33* for constant dollar data in an (1) income statement format and (2) a reconciliation format. (Hint: use the conversion factor of .7222 for 130/180; do not use the fraction approach.)

(c) Assume the same information as (a) and prepare the partial income statement that is required to be presented under *FASB Statement No. 33* for current cost data in an income statement format.

(d) Assume the same information as (a) and using the data in (c), prepare a partial income statement in a reconciliation format, starting with income from continuing operations as reported in the historical cost income statement.

**\*P25-6** Assume the same information as presented in Problems 25–4 and 25–5.

**Instructions**

Prepare an income statement and a balance sheet on a current cost/constant dollar basis in end-of-the-year dollars. (Hint: Make certain the data from instruction (a) of Problem 25–5 is used.)

**P25-7** Presented below is information related to Moyer Development Corp.

1981  Purchased land for $80,000 cash on December 31.
Current cost at year end was $80,000.

1982  Held this land all year.
Current cost at year end was $104,000.

1983  October 31—sold this land for $136,000. Current cost of land at date of sale is $130,000.

General price-level index:

| | |
|---|---|
| December 31, 1981 | 100 |
| December 31, 1982 | 110 |
| October 31, 1983 | 120 |

**Instructions**

(a) Determine the amount that the land would be stated on a balance sheet at December 31, 1981 and 1982 under the following assumptions (end-of-year dollars):
1. Constant dollar accounting
2. Current cost accounting

(b) Determine the following items:
   1. Constant dollar income for 1981, 1982, and 1983 (end-of-year dollars).
   2. Unrealized holding gain (loss) on current cost basis for 1982, unadjusted for inflation.
   3. Income from continuing operations on a current cost basis for 1983.
   4. Realized holding gain (loss) on a current cost basis in 1983, unadjusted for inflation.
(c) Indicate the amount of income from continuing operations that would be reported under *FASB Statement No. 33* for 1981, 1982, and 1983. Assume that the general indexes presented above also reflect the average index for the year; that is 1981 average index equals 100; 1982 average index equals 110; 1983 average index equals 120.

**\*P25–8** Assume the same information as in Problem 25–7.

**Instructions**

(a) Determine the amount at which the land would be stated on a balance sheet at December 31, 1981 and 1982, assuming current cost/constant dollar accounting in end-of-year dollars.
(b) Determine the realized holding gain (loss) on a current cost/constant dollar basis for 1983.
(c) Determine the unrealized holding gain (loss) on a current cost/constant dollar basis for 1983.

**P25–9** Pockets & Cuffs Inc. started operations on January 1, 1983 with the following balance sheet:

Pockets & Cuffs Inc.
BALANCE SHEET
as of January 1, 1983

| | | | |
|---|---|---|---|
| Cash | $15,000 | Common stock | $60,000 |
| Inventories | 45,000 | Paid-in capital | 30,000 |
| Equipment | 30,000 | | |
| Total assets | $90,000 | | $90,000 |

Transaction data for 1983 were as follows:

| | |
|---|---|
| Current cost of ending inventory at year end | $ 75,000 |
| Current cost of equipment at year end (5-year life—straight-line depreciation) | 37,500 |
| Income taxes (50% rate) | |
| Sales (cash) | 157,500 |
| Purchases (cash) | 90,000 |
| Ending inventory, historical cost | 67,500 |
| Cash operating expenses (excludes depreciation) | 30,000 |
| Current cost of goods sold (incurred evenly through year) | 82,500 |

**Instructions**

(a) Prepare an historical cost income statement and balance sheet for Pockets & Cuffs Inc. for 1983.
(b) Prepare a comprehensive current cost income statement and balance sheet for Pockets & Cuffs Inc. for 1983. Assume that the historical cost of the inventory and equipment is the same as its current cost at the beginning of 1983. Depreciation expense is computed on the average current cost asset balances. Charge catch-up depreciation to the unrealized holding gain. Operating expenses on an historical and current cost basis are the same.

**P25–10** Assume the same data as Problem 25–9, and that the Consumer Price Index for all Urban Consumers is as follows:

| | |
|---|---|
| Beginning of 1983 | 100 |
| Average | 120 |
| End of 1983 | 150 |

Assume that all revenues, purchases, and expenses (excluding depreciation) and the ending inventory were incurred at the average price level.

**Instructions**

    (a) Prepare a constant dollar income statement and balance sheet for Pockets & Cuffs Inc. for 1983 in end-of-year dollars.

    (b) Prepare a constant dollar income statement and balance sheet for Pockets & Cuffs Inc. in average-for-the-year dollars.

    (c) Prepare a partial income statement in the reconciliation format as required by *FASB Statement No. 33*. (Ignore the computation for the increase in specific prices, net of inflation, that appears at the bottom of this statement.)

**\*P25–11** Assume the same data as Problems 25–9 and 25–10.

**Instructions**

    (a) Prepare a current cost/constant dollar income statement and balance sheet for Pockets & Cuffs Inc., for 1983 in end-of-year dollars.

    (b) Prepare a current cost/constant dollar income statement and balance sheet for Pockets & Cuffs Inc., for 1983 in average-for-the-year dollars.

**P25–12** Denver Drilling Inc. is experimenting with the use of current cost in its accounting. At the beginning of 1983, the company purchased inventory that had a cost of $60,000, of which $36,000 was sold evenly during the year end at a sales price of $54,000. The general price level was 100 at the beginning of 1983 and 150 at the end of the period. The average price level for the period was 120. It is estimated that the current cost of the inventory at the date of sale was $39,600 and the current cost of the ending inventory at December 31, 1983 is $26,400. Assume that the company has no other beginning inventory or purchases and uses a perpetual system. (Ignore income taxes.)

**Instructions**

    (a) Prepare an income statement on an historical cost basis for the year 1983.

    (b) Prepare an income statement on a constant dollar basis for the year 1983 in end-of-year dollars.

    (c) Prepare a comprehensive income statement on a current cost basis for the year 1983.

    (d) Prepare, in an income statement format, income from continuing operations in accordance with *FASB Statement No. 33* and other related disclosures, where possible, for the year 1983.

    (e) Prepare, in a reconciliation format, income from continuing operations in accordance with *FASB Statement No. 33* and other related disclosures, where possible, for the year 1983.

**\*P25–13** Assume the same data as presented in Problem 25–12.

**Instructions**

    Prepare a comprehensive income statement on a current cost/constant dollar basis for the year 1983 in end-of-year dollars.

**P25–14** The balance sheet of Red Rock, Inc., appeared as follows on December 31, 1984:

Red Rock, Inc.
BALANCE SHEET
December 31, 1984
(in millions)

| Assets | | Equities | |
|---|---|---|---|
| Cash | $ 100 | Liabilities | |
| | | Long-term note payable | $ 600 |
| Inventory, at FIFO cost | 200 | Shareholders' Equity | |
| Equipment | 700 | Capital stock (100 shares) | 400 |
| Total assets | $1,000 | Total equities | $1,000 |

At December 31, 1984, the historical cost and current cost of the inventory were the same. The equipment was purchased new on December 31, 1984. Red Rock uses straight-line depreciation and estimates the equipment will have a useful life of five years with no salvage value.

Financial and economic events experienced by Red Rock, Inc. during 1985, the first year of operations, included:

| | |
|---|---|
| Sales, all on account | $1,100 |
| Cash purchases of inventory | 500 |
| Accounts receivable, December 31, 1985 | 300 |
| Inventory at historical cost, December 31, 1985 | 100 |
| Inventory at current cost, December 31, 1985 | 130 |
| Cost of goods sold at current cost as of date of sale | 675 |
| Equipment at current cost, December 31, 1985 | 850 |

The general price level index was 100 at the end of 1984, 200 at the end of 1985, with an average of 160 for 1985. The price shifts occurred uniformly throughout 1985. The index at the time ending inventory was acquired was 175. The "net recoverable amounts" for inventory and equipment have been determined by management to be in excess of net current costs. All sales and purchases occurred evenly throughout the year.

### Instructions

(All computations should be to the nearest dollar.)

(a) Prepare an income statement for the year ended 1985 and comparative balance sheets as of December 31, 1984 and 1985, using each of the following measurements:
  1. Historical cost.
  2. Constant dollar, in 1985 year-end dollars.
  3. Current cost (disclose realized and unrealized holding gains separately).

(b) Prepare an income statement for the year ended 1985 in accordance with the disclosure requirements of *FASB No. 33,* using a reconciliation format including the purchasing power gain or loss and the increases or decreases for the current year in the current cost amounts of inventory and equipment, net of inflation. Also, prepare the five-year summary information for 1984 and 1985.

# CHAPTER 26

# Basic Financial Statement Analysis

The interpretation and evaluation of financial statement data require familiarity with the basic tools of financial statement analysis. Naturally, the type of financial analysis that takes place depends on the particular interest that the analyst (whether creditor, stockholder, potential investor, manager, government agency, or labor leader) has in the enterprise. For example, **short-term creditors,** such as banks, are primarily interested in the ability of the firm to pay its currently maturing obligations. The composition of the current assets and their relation to short-term liabilities are examined closely to evaluate the short-run solvency of the firm. **Bondholders,** on the other hand, look more to long-term indicators, such as the enterprise's capital structure, past and projected earnings, and changes in financial position. **Stockholders,** present or prospective, also are interested in many of the features considered by a long-term creditor. Their examination is focused on the earnings picture, because changes in it greatly affect the market price of their investment. Stockholders also are concerned with the financial position of the firm, because it affects indirectly the stability of the earnings.

The **management** of a company is of necessity concerned about the composition of its capital structure and about the changes and trends in earnings. This financial information has a direct influence on the type, amount, and cost of external financing that the company may obtain. In addition, the company finds financial information useful on a day-to-day operating basis in such areas as capital budgeting, breakeven analysis, variance analysis, gross margin analysis, and for internal control purposes.

The accountant's function is twofold: (1) to measure economic events and transactions and (2) to communicate economic information about them to interested parties. Thus far in this textbook we have discussed the measurement and reporting functions of accounting. But communication in accounting means more than just preparing the reports; accountants must also analyze and interpret financial statements.

## A GENERAL PERSPECTIVE ON FINANCIAL STATEMENT ANALYSIS

Expertise in financial statement analysis reflects a skill that one acquires primarily by experience. Nevertheless, in order to develop this skill, one must have an idea of the techniques used in financial statement analysis and how to interpret the results. These aspects can be examined in a textbook and serve as a basis for building the skill required to conduct a useful analysis.

Information from financial statements can be gathered by examining relationships between items on the statements (ratios, percentages) and identifying trends in these relationships (comparative analysis). A problem with learning how to analyze statements is that the means may become an end in itself. There are thousands of possible relationships that could be calculated and trends identified. If one knows only how to calculate ratios and trends without realizing how such information can be used, little is accomplished. Therefore, a logical approach to financial statement analysis is necessary. Such an approach may consist of the following steps:

1. **Know the questions for which you want to find answers.** As indicated at the beginning of this chapter, there are various groups with different types of interests in a company. Depending on the perspective of the user, particular questions of interest to them can be identified.

2. **Know the questions that particular ratios and comparisons are able to help answer.** These will be discussed in the remainder of this chapter.

3. **Match 1 and 2 above.** By such a matching, the statement analysis will have a logical direction and purpose.

Several caveats must be mentioned. Financial statements report on the past. As such, analysis of this data is an examination of the past. Whenever such information is incorporated into a decision-making (future-oriented) process, a critical assumption is that the past is a reasonable basis for predicting the future. This is usually a reasonable approach, but the limitations associated with it should be recognized. Also, ratio and trend analyses will help identify present strengths and weaknesses of a company. In many cases, however, such analyses will not reveal why things are as they are. As such, ratios and trends may serve as "red flags" indicating problem areas. Finding answers about "why" usually requires an in-depth analysis and an awareness of many factors about a company that are not reported in the financial statements—for instance, the impact of inflation, actions of competitors, technological developments, a strike at a major supplier's or buyer's operations.

Another point is that a single ratio by itself it not likely to be very useful. For example, a current ratio of two times (current assets are twice current liabilities) may be viewed as satisfactory. If, however, the industry average is three times, such a conclusion may be questioned. Even given this industry average, one may conclude that the particular company is doing well if the ratio last year was 1.5 times. Consequently, to derive meaning from ratios, some standard against which to compare them is needed. Such a standard may come from industry averages, past years' amounts, a particular competitor, or planned levels.

Finally, awareness of the limitations of accounting numbers used in an analysis is important. Some of these limitations and their consequences will be discussed in this chapter. Understanding the many accounting issues and alternatives presented throughout this book provides a background against which the limitations of accounting numbers can be more fully appreciated.

## BASIC MEASURES OF FINANCIAL ANALYSIS

Various devices are used in the analysis of financial statement data to bring out the comparative and relative significance of the financial information presented. These devices include ratio analysis, comparative analysis, percentage analysis, and examination of related data. It is difficult to say that one device is more useful than another because every situation faced by the investment analyst is different, and the answers needed are often obtained only upon close examination of the interrelationships among all the data provided.

## RATIO ANALYSIS

Ratio analysis is the starting point in developing the information desired by the analyst. Ratios (summary indicators)[1] can be classified as follows:

**LIQUIDITY RATIOS.** Measures of the short-run ability of the enterprise to pay its maturing obligations.

**ACTIVITY RATIOS.** Measures of how effectively the enterprise is using the assets employed.

**PROFITABILITY RATIOS.** Measures of the degree of success or failure of a given enterprise or division for a given period of time.

**COVERAGE RATIOS.** Measures of the degree of protection for long-term creditors and investors.

---

**Anetek Chemical Corporation**
**INCOME STATEMENT**
**For the Year Ended December 31**
**(000 Omitted)**

|  | 1984 | 1983 |
|---|---|---|
| Sales and other revenue: | | |
| Net sales | $1,600,000 | $1,350,000 |
| Interest revenue | 25,000 | 20,000 |
| Other revenue | 50,000 | 30,000 |
| Total revenue | 1,675,000 | 1,400,000 |
| Cost and other charges: | | |
| Cost of goods sold | 1,000,000 | 850,000 |
| Depreciation and amortization | 150,000 | 150,000 |
| Selling and administrative expenses | 225,000 | 150,000 |
| Interest expense | 50,000 | 25,000 |
| Total | 1,425,000 | 1,175,000 |
| Income before taxes | 250,000 | 225,000 |
| Income taxes | 100,000 | 75,000 |
| Net income | $ 150,000 | $ 150,000 |
| Earnings per share[a] | $5.00 | $4.50 |

[a]Additional information:
Number of shares outstanding in 1984 is thirty million shares.
Market price of Anetek's stock at end of 1984 is $60.
Cash dividend per share in 1984 is $2.25.
Correction of error in prior period $4.5 million.

---

[1]Summary indicators might be defined as amounts, ratios, or other computations that distill some key information about the business enterprise. For example, a proposed FASB concepts statement uses this terminology to describe ratios, and a recent research report of the FASB uses this term in the same connection. Paul Frishkoff, "Reporting of Summary Indicators: An Investigation of Research and Practice," *Research Report* (Stamford, Conn.: FASB, 1981).

Anetek Chemical
CONSOLIDATED BALANCE SHEET[a]
December 31
(000 omitted)

|  | 1984 | 1983 |
|---|---|---|
| **Assets** | | |
| Current assets: | | |
| Cash | $ 40,000 | $ 25,000 |
| Marketable securities (at cost) | 100,000 | 75,000 |
| Accounts receivable | 350,000 | 300,000 |
| Inventories (at lower of cost or market) | 310,000 | 250,000 |
| Total current assets | 800,000 | 650,000 |
| Investments (at cost) | 300,000 | 325,000 |
| Fixed assets: | | |
| Property, plant and equipment (at cost) | 2,000,000 | 1,900,000 |
| Less—accumulated depreciation | (900,000) | (800,000) |
| | 1,100,000 | 1,100,000 |
| Goodwill | 50,000 | 25,000 |
| Total assets | $2,250,000 | $2,100,000 |
| **Debt and Equity** | | |
| Current liabilities: | | |
| Accounts payable | $ 125,000 | $ 100,000 |
| Notes payable | 250,000 | 200,000 |
| Accrued and other liabilities | 200,000 | 150,000 |
| Total current liabilities | 575,000 | 450,000 |
| Long-term debt: | | |
| Bonds and notes payable | 725,000 | 550,000 |
| Total liabilities | 1,300,000 | 1,000,000 |
| Stockholders' equity: | | |
| Common stock | 150,000 | 150,000 |
| Additional paid-in capital | 550,000 | 650,000 |
| Retained earnings | 250,000 | 300,000 |
| Total equity | 950,000 | 1,100,000 |
| Total debt and equity | $2,250,000 | $2,100,000 |

[a]The footnotes and some detail that accompanied this statement are excluded for purposes of simplicity and brevity.

The use of these ratios is illustrated through an actual case example adopted from the annual report of a large chemical concern that we have disguised under the name of Anetek Chemical Corporation.

Anetek Chemical Corporation is a worldwide enterprise offering more than 1,400 products and services in the following major classifications: chemicals, plasters, pharmaceuticals, metals, agricultural chemicals, packaging, and industrial chemical cleaning. Anetek products are manufactured through the recovery and upgrading of chemicals found in underground mines, salt deposits, petroleum, and seawater. Production is accomplished through the intensive application of technology developed in large part by the company's own research organization. "Anetek" people number some 50,000 in 48 nations. The comparative financial statements of Anetek (pages 1201–1202) are the basis for all of the ratios. **The ratios, like the financial statements, are computed with the last three digits (000) omitted.**

## Liquidity Ratios

The ability of a firm to meet its current debts is important in evaluating its financial position. For example, Anetek Chemical has current liabilities of $575,000. Can these current obligations be met when due? Certain basic ratios can be computed that provide some guides for determining the enterprise's short-term debt-paying ability.

**1. Current Ratio** The current ratio is the ratio of total current assets to total current liabilities. Although the quotient is the dollars of current assets available to cover each dollar of current debt, it is most frequently expressed as a coverage of so many times. Sometimes it is called the working capital ratio, because working capital is the excess of current assets over current liabilities. The computation of the current ratio for Anetek is:

$$\text{Current Ratio} = \frac{\text{Current Assets}}{\text{Current Liabilities}} = \frac{\$800,000}{\$575,000} = 1.39 \text{ times}$$

$$\text{Industry Average}^2 = 2.30 \text{ times}$$

The current ratio of 1.39 to 1 compared with the industry average of 2.30 to 1 indicates that Anetek's safety factor to meet maturing short-term obligations is noticeably low. Does the relatively low current ratio indicate the existence of a liquidity problem? Or considering that the ratio is greater than 1 to 1, is the situation well in hand? The current ratio is only one measure of determining liquidity, and it does not answer all of the liquidity questions. How liquid are the receivables and inventory? What effect does the omission of the inventory have on the analysis of liquidity? To answer these and other questions, additional analysis of other related data is required.

**2. Acid-Test Ratio** A satisfactory current ratio does not disclose the fact that a portion of the current assets may be tied up in slow-moving inventories. With inventories, especially raw material and work in process, there is a question of how long it will take to transform them into the finished product and what ultimately will be realized on the sale of the merchandise. Elimination of the inventories, along with any prepaid expenses, from the current assets might provide better information for the short-term creditor. Many analysts

---

[2]The industry average ratios are taken from Dun and Bradstreet, Inc., *Key Business Ratios in 25 Lines,* and Leo Troy's *The Almanac of Business and Industrial Financial Ratios.* The standard ratios provide some basis for comparison with other companies in the same industry.

favor a "quick" or "acid-test" ratio that relates total current liabilities to cash, marketable securities, and receivables. The acid-test ratio is computed for Anetek as follows:

$$\text{Acid-test Ratio} = \frac{\text{Cash} + \text{Marketable Securities} + \text{Net Receivables}}{\text{Current Liabilities}} = \frac{\$490,000}{\$575,000} = .85 \text{ times}$$

$$\text{Industry Average} = 1.20 \text{ times}$$

The acid-test ratio for Anetek as compared with the industry average is low. This means that Anetek may have difficulty in meeting its short-term needs unless the firm is able to obtain additional current assets through conversion of some of its long-term assets, through additional financing, or through profitable operating results.

**3. Defensive-Interval Ratio**   Neither the current ratio nor the acid-test ratio gives a complete explanation of the current debt-paying ability of the company. The matching of current assets with current liabilities assumes that the current assets will be employed to pay off the current liabilities. Some investors argue that a better measure of liquidity is provided by the defensive-interval ratio. The defensive-interval ratio is computed by dividing defensive assets (cash, marketable securities, and net receivables) by projected daily expenditures from operations. This ratio measures the time span a firm can operate on present liquid assets without resorting to revenues from next year's sources. Projected daily expenditures are computed by dividing cost of goods sold plus selling and administrative expenses and other ordinary cash expenses by 365 days.[3]

The defensive-interval measure for Anetek is:

$$\text{Defensive-Interval Measure} = \frac{\text{Defensive Assets}}{\text{Projected Daily Operational Expenditures (based on past expenditures) minus Noncash Charges}}$$

$$= \$490,000 \div \frac{\$1,525,000 - \$150,000}{365}$$

$$= 130 \text{ days}$$

$$\text{Industry Average} = 80 \text{ days}$$

Whether this ratio provides a better measure of liquidity than the current ratio or acid-test ratio is difficult to evaluate, but it does provide another useful tool for analyzing the liquidity position of the enterprise.[4] This ratio establishes a safety factor or margin for the

---

[3]The only necessary adjustments to the total expense figure are deductions of any noncash charges such as depreciation and provisions for any known changes in planned operations from previous periods.

[4]For other approaches to measuring short-term liquidity, see Harold Bierman, "Measuring Financial Liquidity," *The Accounting Review* (October 1960), pp. 628–632, where he argues for the ratio

investor in determining the capability of the company to meet its basic operational costs.[5] It would appear that 130 days provides the company with a relatively high degree of protection, and tends to offset the weakness indicated by the low current and acid-test ratios.

## Activity Ratios

Another way of evaluating liquidity is to determine how quickly certain assets can be turned into cash. How liquid, for example, are the receivables and inventory? In addition, this type of calculation provides information related to how efficiently the enterprise utilizes its assets. Activity ratios are computed for Anetek Chemical on the basis of receivables, inventories, and total assets.

**4. Receivables Turnover** The receivables turnover ratio is computed by dividing net sales by average receivables outstanding during the year. Theoretically, the numerator should include only net credit sales. This information is frequently not available, however, and if the relative amounts of charge and cash sales remain fairly constant, the trend indicated by the ratio will still be valid. Unless seasonal factors are significant, average receivables outstanding can be computed from the beginning and ending balance of the trade receivables. Net receivables instead of gross receivables are used for the computation.

$$\text{Accounts Receivable Turnover} = \frac{\text{Net Sales}}{\text{Average Trade Receivables (net)}}$$

$$= \$1,600,000 \div \frac{\$350,000 + \$300,000}{2}$$

$$= 4.92 \text{ or every 74 days (365 days} \div 4.92)$$

$$\text{Industry Average}^6 = 7.15 \text{ or every 51 days}$$

This information provides some indication of the quality of the receivables, and also an idea of how successful the firm is in collecting its outstanding receivables. The faster this turnover, the more credence the current ratio and acid-test ratio have in the financial analysis. If possible, an aging schedule should also be prepared to determine how long the receivables have been outstanding. It is possible that the receivables turnover is quite satisfactory, but this situation may have resulted because certain receivables have been collected

---

of net working capital to resources provided by operations; and James Walter, "Determination of Technical Solvency," *Journal of Business* (January 1957), pp. 30–43, where he uses the ratio of resources provided by operations to current debt.

[5]See George H. Sorter and George Benston, "Appraising the Defensive Position of the Firm: The Interval Measure," *Accounting Review* (October 1960), pp. 633–640; and Sidney Davidson, George H. Sorter, and Hemu Kalle, "Measuring the Defensive Position of a Firm," *Financial Analyst's Journal* (January-February 1964), pp. 23–29.

[6]Often the receivables turnover is transformed to an average collection period. In this case, 4.92 is divided into 365 days to obtain 74 days. Several figures other than 365 could be used here; a most common alternative is 360 days. Because our industry average was based on 365, we used this figure in our computations.

quickly whereas others have been outstanding for a relatively long period. In Anetek's case, the receivables turnover appears low. The general rule used is that the time allowed for payment by the selling terms should not be exceeded by more than 10 or 15 days. Dividing 365 days by the turnover provides a measure (74 days for Anetek) of the average number of days to collect accounts receivable. Therefore, the higher the turnover, the shorter this period of time.

**5. Inventory Turnover** Inventory turnover is computed by dividing the average inventory into the cost of goods sold. The inventory turnover ratio for Anetek Chemical is:

$$\text{Inventory Turnover} = \frac{\text{Cost of Goods Sold}}{\text{Average Inventory}} = \frac{\$1,000,000}{\dfrac{\$310,000 + \$250,000}{2}}$$

$$= 3.57 \text{ times or every 102 days (365 days} \div 3.57)$$

$$\text{Industry Average} = 4.62 \text{ or every 79 days}$$

The inventory turnover measures how quickly inventory is sold. Dividing 365 days by the inventory turnover indicates the average number of days it takes to sell inventory (or average number of days' sales for which inventory is on hand).

Generally, the higher the inventory turnover, the better the enterprise is performing. It is possible, however, that the enterprise is incurring high "stockout costs" because not enough inventory is available. The ratio is useful because it provides a basis for determining whether obsolete inventory is present or pricing problems exist. In Anetek's case, the turnover ratio is lower than the industry average, indicating that some slow-moving inventory exists. Remember that this ratio is an average, which means that many goods may be turning over quite rapidly, whereas others may have failed to sell at all. In addition, it was assumed that an average of the beginning and ending inventory was representative of the average for the year. If this situation is not correct, additional computations must be made.

Because inventory is stated at cost, it must be divided into cost of sales (a cost figure) instead of into sales, which includes some margin of profit. Occasionally analysts use sales instead of cost of goods sold as a substitute, but this practice has no theoretical support unless inventories are valued at retail prices.

The method of inventory valuation can affect the computed turnover and the current ratio. The analyst should be aware of the different valuations that can be used in costing inventory (for example, FIFO, LIFO, etc.) and the effect these different valuation procedures might have on the ratio.

From the accounts receivable and inventory turnover information, a **total conversion period** can be determined. The total conversion period is the average number of days it takes from acquiring inventory to collecting cash from its sale. It is calculated by adding the average number of days it takes to sell inventory to the average number of days to collect accounts receivable. For Anetek, the total conversion period is 176 days (102 + 74). Examining the conversion period and its two components can be useful in identifying differences between companies or between years for the same company to evaluate the effectiveness of marketing, credit granting, and collection policies.

**6. Asset Turnover**   The asset turnover ratio is determined by dividing average total assets into net sales for the period. The asset turnover for Anetek is:

$$\text{Asset Turnover} = \frac{\text{Net Sales}}{\text{Average Total Assets}} = \frac{\$1,600,000}{\dfrac{\$2,250,000 + \$2,100,000}{2}} = .74$$

$$\text{Industry Average} = .94$$

This ratio supposedly indicates how efficiently the company utilizes its assets. If the turnover ratio is high, the implication is that the company is using its assets effectively to generate sales. If the turnover ratio is low, the company either has to use its assets more efficiently or dispose of them. The problem with this turnover calculation is that it places a premium on using old assets because their book value is low. In addition, this ratio is affected by the depreciation method employed by the company. For example, a company that employs an accelerated method of depreciation will have a higher turnover than a company using straight-line, all other factors being equal. For these reasons, the ratio should not be the only one considered in evaluating the efficiency of the company in this area.

## Profitability Ratios

Profitability ratios indicate how well the enterprise has operated during the year. These ratios answer such questions as: Was the net income adequate? What rate of return does it represent? What is the rate of net income by activities? What amount was paid in dividends? What amount was earned by different equity claimants? Generally, the ratios are either computed on the basis of sales or on an investment base such as total assets. Profitability is frequently used as the ultimate test of management effectiveness.

**7. Profit Margin on Sales**   The profit margin on sales is computed by dividing net income by net sales for the period. Anetek's ratio is:

$$\text{Profit Margin on Sales} = \frac{\text{Net Income}}{\text{Net Sales}} = \frac{\$150,000}{\$1,600,000} = 9.4\%$$

$$\text{Industry Average} = 6\%$$

This ratio indicates that Anetek is achieving an above-average rate of profit on each sales dollar received. It provides some indication of the buffer available in case of higher costs or lower sales in the future. Employment of this ratio in conjunction with the asset turnover ratio offers an interplay that leads to a rate of return on total assets. This relationship is expressed as follows:

$$\text{Rate of Return on Assets} = \text{Profit Margin on Sales} \times \text{Asset Turnover}$$

$$\text{Rate of Return on Assets} = \frac{\text{Net Income}}{\text{Net Sales}} \times \frac{\text{Net Sales}}{\text{Average Total Assets}}$$

$$= \frac{\$150,000}{\$1,600,000} \times \frac{\$1,600,000}{\dfrac{\$2,250,000 + \$2,100,000}{2}}$$

$$= 6.9\%$$

$$\text{Industry Average} = 5.6\%$$

The profit margin on sales does not answer the question of how profitable the enterprise was for a given time period. Only by determining how many times the assets turned over during a period of time is it possible to ascertain the amount of net income earned on the total assets.

Many enterprises have a small profit margin on sales and a high turnover (grocery and discount stores), whereas other enterprises have a relatively high profit margin but a low inventory turnover (jewelry and furniture stores).

One of the most interesting applications of this is called the du Pont system of financial control.[7] The basic components in the du Pont system are presented in the following diagram.

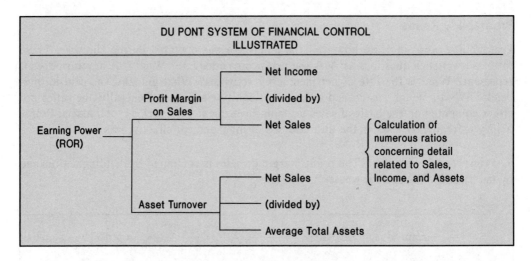

In this system, ratios can be defined in enough detail to give the analyst the information desired. The significant point is that all ratios can help explain the different effects leading to the rate of return on invested capital.

---

[7]Descriptions of this system are available in T. C. Davis, *How the du Pont Organization Appraises Its Performance,* Financial Management Series, No. 94 (New York: American Management Association Treasurer's Dept., 1950); and C. A. Kline, Jr. and H. L. Hissler, "The du Pont Chart System for Appraising Operating Performance," *N.A.C.A. Bulletin* (August 1953), pp. 1595–1619.

**8. Rate of Return on Assets** As just indicated, this ratio is computed by using as a numerator net income and as a denominator average total assets. The ratio for Anetek is:

$$
\text{Rate of Return on Assets} = \frac{\text{Net Income}}{\text{Average Total Assets}}
$$

$$
= \$150,000 \div \frac{\$2,250,000 + \$2,100,000}{2}
$$

$$
= 6.9\%
$$

$$
\text{Industry Average} = 5.6\%
$$

Anetek's rate of return is slightly above the average of the industry and is a result of Anetek's relatively high profit margin on sales.

Many contend that a better measure of the rate earned on the assets results from the use of net income before subtraction of the interest charge.[8] This ratio is computed by dividing net income plus interest expense (net of tax effect) by average total assets. Interest expense (net of tax effect), including discount amortization, is added back to income because the interest represents a cost of securing additional assets and, therefore, should not be considered as a deduction in arriving at the amount of return on assets. The ratio for Anetek is:

$$
\text{Rate of Return on Assets} = \frac{\text{Net Income} + \text{Interest Expense} - \text{Tax Savings}^9}{\text{Average Total Assets}}
$$

$$
= \frac{\$150,000 + \$50,000 - .40\,(\$50,000)}{\dfrac{\$2,250,000 + \$2,100,000}{2}}
$$

$$
= 8.3\%
$$

**9. Rate of Return on Common Stock Equity** This ratio is defined as net income after interest, taxes, and preferred dividends divided by average common stockholders' equity. Anetek's ratio is computed in this manner:

$$
\text{Rate of Return on Common Stock Equity} = \frac{\text{Net Income minus Preferred Dividends}}{\text{Average Common Stockholders' Equity}}
$$

$$
= \$150,000 \div \frac{\$950,000 + \$1,100,000}{2}
$$

$$
= 14.6\%
$$

$$
\text{Industry Average} = 9.5\%
$$

[8] For example, public utilities compute their rate of return on the basis of this approach.

[9] The tax savings is computed by multiplying the interest expense by the effective tax rate. The effective tax rate is determined by dividing the provision for income taxes by income before taxes.

When the rate of return on total assets is lower than the rate of return on the common stockholders' investment, the enterprise is said to be trading on the equity at a gain. Trading on the equity increases the company's financial risk, but it enhances residual earnings whenever the rate of return on assets exceeds the cost of debt capital.

Whether the rate of return on total assets or the rate of return on common stock equity is a better measure of performance is difficult to evaluate. For example, when *Forbes* (a popular financial magazine) is asked to provide basic guidelines for profitability, it computes both ratios. The three companies listed below all rank fairly close in return on equity; however, they are not as close in rate of return on total assets.

| COMPARISONS OF DIFFERENT TYPES PROFITABILITY INDEXES | | | | |
| --- | --- | --- | --- | --- |
| Company | 5-Year Return on Common Equity | | 5-Year Return on Total Assets | |
| | Rank[a] | Percent | Rank | Percent |
| Teledyne | 24 | 35.4 | 34 | 34.2 |
| Superior Oil | 26 | 34.8 | 418 | 12.2 |
| Pioneer | 33 | 32.9 | 152 | 17.4 |
| [a]Rank amongst 500 publicly owned U.S. companies. | | | | |

When these three companies are evaluated, Superior Oil stands out as a company that is highly leveraged; that is, a great deal of debt is in its capital structure. Leveraging per se is not wrong, but in an economic downturn chances are that Superior Oil would turn less profitable more quickly than the other two companies.

On the other hand, there are companies such as Avon Products and Petrie Stores that had leveraged very little; can they be considered less profitable? For example, Avon Products has a rate of return on assets of 30.0% (Rank 11) and rate of return on common equity of 30.8% (Rank 42). Is Avon more or less profitable than Superior Oil? It is a difficult question to evaluate and both ratios should be considered in the analysis.

**Trading on the Equity**   The expression "trading on the equity" describes the practice of using borrowed money at fixed interest rates or issuing preferred stock with constant dividend rates in hopes of obtaining a higher rate of return on the money used than the interest or preferred dividends paid. Because these issues must be given a prior claim on some or all of the corporate assets, the advantage to common stockholders must come from borrowing at a lower rate of interest than the rate of return obtained by the corporation on the assets borrowed. If this can be done, the capital obtained from bondholders or preferred stockholders earns enough to pay the interest or preferred dividends, and to leave a margin for the common stockholders. When this condition exists, trading on the equity is profitable. A comparison of the rate of return on total assets with the rate paid to other than common stock claimants indicates the profitability of trading on the equity in any given case. To illustrate, Anetek's rate of return on total assets is 6.9%, whereas the rate of return on the stockholders' equity is 14.6%. Anetek traded on the equity at a gain. In essence, the liability claimants were paid a lower rate than 6.9%. Anetek is a very highly leveraged company which has achieved an excellent rate of return on common equity by using its debt effectively. A word of caution—trading on the equity is a two-way street: just as a company's gains can be magnified, so also can losses be magnified.

**10. Earnings Per Share**   The earnings per share figure is one of the most important ratios used by investment analysts, yet it is one of the most deceptive. If no dilutive securities are present in the capital structure, then earnings per share is simply computed by dividing net income minus preferred dividends by the average number of shares of outstanding common stock. If, however, convertible securities, stock options, warrants, or other dilutive securities are included in the capital structure, (1) earnings per common and common equivalent shares and (2) fully diluted earnings per share figures may have to be used.[10] The computation for Anetek is:

$$\text{Earnings Per Share} = \frac{\text{Net Income Minus Preferred Dividends}}{\text{Weighted Shares Outstanding}} = \frac{\$150,000}{30,000} = \$5.00$$

Because no dilutive securities that are common stock equivalents or potentially dilutive securities are present in Anetek's capital structure, primary earnings per share and fully diluted earnings per share amounts need not be reported.

Certain problems exist when the earnings per share ratio is computed. Often earnings per share can be increased simply by reducing the number of shares outstanding through the purchase of treasury stock. In addition, the earnings per share figure fails to recognize the probable increasing base of the stockholders' investment. That is, earnings per share, all other factors being equal, will probably increase year after year if the corporation reinvests earnings in the business because a larger earnings figure is generated without a corresponding increase in the number of shares outstanding. Because even the well-informed element of the public attaches such importance to earnings per share, caution must be exercised, and it should not be given more emphasis than it deserves. The common problem is that the per-share figure draws the investor's attention from the enterprise as a whole—which involves differing magnitudes of sales, costs, volumes, and invested capital—and concentrates too much attention on the single share of stock.

**11. Price Earnings Ratio**   The price earnings (P/E) ratio is an oft-quoted statistic used by analysts in discussing the investment possibility of a given enterprise. It is computed by dividing the market price of the stock by its earnings per share. For Anetek, the ratio is:

$$\text{Price Earnings Ratio} = \frac{\text{Market Price of Stock}}{\text{Earnings Per Share}} = \frac{\$60}{\$5} = 12.0$$

The average price earnings ratio for the thirty stocks that comprise the Dow Jones industrial average in mid-1982 was 8.2. A steady drop in a company's price earnings ratio

[10]See Chapter 17 for a discussion of how dilutive securities should be handled to compute earnings per share.

indicates that investors are wary of the firm's growth potential. Some companies have high P/E multiples, while others have low multiples. For instance, Allied Products in 1982 enjoyed a P/E ratio of 28 while Bendix had a low P/E ratio of 5. The reason for this difference is linked to several factors: relative risk, stability of earnings, trends in earnings, and the market's perception of the growth potential of the stock. Analysts who believe a company will be able to generate future earnings at even higher levels than at present may value the stock higher than its present earnings may warrant and vice versa.

**12. Payout Ratio** The payout ratio is the ratio of cash dividends to net income. If preferred stock is outstanding, this ratio is computed for common stockholders by dividing cash dividends paid to common stock by income available to common stockholders. Assuming that the cash dividends are $67,500, the payout ratio for Anetek is:

$$\text{Payout Ratio} = \frac{\text{Cash Dividends}}{\text{Net Income}} = \frac{\$67,500}{\$150,000} = 45\%$$

It is important to many investors that a fairly substantial payout ratio exist; however, speculators view appreciation in the value of the stock as more important. Generally, growth companies are characterized by low payout ratios because they reinvest most of their earnings. For example, Anetek has a rather high payout ratio when compared with Dresser Industries, which normally pays out approximately 16% of earnings, but a relatively low payout ratio when compared with Commonwealth Edison Co., which normally pays out 70%.

Another closely related ratio that is often used is the dividend yield; it is simply the cash dividend per share divided by the market price of the stock. The cash dividend per share for Anetek is $2.25, so the dividend yield is 3.75% ($2.25/ $60.00). This ratio affords investors some idea of the rate of return that will be received in cash dividends in the short run from their investment. In 1982, International Business Machines (IBM) stockholders experienced a modest yield of approximately 5.6%, while American Telephone and Telegraph (AT & T) stockholders experienced a dividend yield of approximately 11%.

## Coverage Ratios

The coverage ratios are computed to help in predicting the long-run solvency of the firm. These ratios are of interest primarily to bondholders who need some indication of the measure of protection available to them. In addition, they indicate part of the risk involved in investing in common stock because the more debt that is added to the capital structure, the more uncertain is the return on common stock.

**13. Debt to Total Assets** This ratio provides the creditors with some idea of the corporation's ability to withstand losses without impairing the interests of creditors. The lower this ratio is, the more "buffer" there is available to creditors before the corporation becomes insolvent. From the creditor's point of view a low ratio of debt to total assets is desirable. The ratio for Anetek is:

$$\text{Debt to Total Assets} = \frac{\text{Debt}}{\text{Total Assets or Equities}} = \frac{\$1,300,000}{\$2,250,000} = 58\%$$

$$\text{Industry Average} = 38\%$$

There are other ways of expressing this ratio, such as the ratio of debt to stockholders' equity, the ratio of stockholders' equity to the sum of debt and stockholders' equity. Essentially, these ratios all provide the same answer to the question: How well protected are the creditors in the case of possible insolvency of the enterprise?[11] This ratio has a very definite effect on the company's ability to obtain additional financing. Anetek is highly leveraged; further growth through debt financing may not be possible.

**14. Times Interest Earned**   The times interest earned ratio is computed by dividing income before interest charges and taxes by the interest charge. This ratio stresses the importance of a company covering all interest charges. Note that the times interest earned ratio uses income before interest and income taxes because this amount represents the amount of income available to cover interest. Income taxes are paid only after interest charges have been met. The ratio for Anetek is:

$$\text{Times Interest Earned} = \frac{\substack{\text{Income Before Taxes} \\ \text{and Interest Charges}}}{\text{Interest Charges}} = \frac{\$300,000}{\$50,000} = 6 \text{ times}$$

In this case Anetek's interest coverage is adequate.

If a company pays preferred dividends, the number of times the preferred dividends were earned is computed by dividing the net income for the year by the annual preferred dividend requirements.

**15. Book Value Per Share**   A much-used basis for evaluating the net worth and any changes in it from year to year is found in the book value or equity value per share of stock. Book value per share of stock is the amount each share would receive if the company were liquidated **on the basis of amounts reported on the balance sheet.** The figure loses much of its relevance if the valuations on the balance sheet do not approximate fair market value of the assets. It is computed by allocating the stockholders' equity items among the various classes of stock and then dividing the total so allocated to each class of stock by the number of shares outstanding.

The book value per common share for Anetek is:

$$\text{Book Value Per Share} = \frac{\text{Common Stockholders' Equity}}{\text{Outstanding Shares}} = \frac{\$950,000}{30,000} = \$31.67$$

---

[11] Additional protection, of course, is afforded through specified liens and collateral and through contractual restrictive covenants.

Preferred stock is not a part of the capital structure of Anetek. When this type of security is present, an analysis of the covenants involving the preferred shares should be studied. If preferred dividends are in arrears, the preferred stock is participating, or if preferred stock has a redemption or liquidating value higher than its carrying amount, retained earnings must be allocated between the preferred and common stockholders.

To illustrate, assume that the following situation exists:

| Stockholders' equity | Preferred | Common |
|---|---|---|
| Preferred stock, 5% | $300,000.00 | |
| Common stock | | $400,000.00 |
| Excess of issue price over par of common stock | | 37,500.00 |
| Retained earnings | | 162,582.00 |
| Totals | $300,000.00 | $600,082.00 |
| Shares outstanding | 3,000 | 4,000 |
| Book value per share | $ 100.00 | $ 150.02 |

In the computation above it is assumed that no preferred dividends are in arrears and that the preferred is not participating. Now assume that the same facts exist except that the 5% preferred is cumulative, participating up to 8%, and that dividends for three years before the current year are in arrears. The book value of each class of stock is then computed as follows, assuming that no action has yet been taken concerning dividends for the current year:

| Stockholders' equity | Preferred | Common |
|---|---|---|
| Preferred stock[12], 5% | $300,000.00 | |
| Common stock | | $400,000.00 |
| Excess of issue price over par of common stock | | 37,500.00 |
| Retained earnings: | | |
|   Dividends in arrears (3 years at 5% a year) | 45,000.00 | |
|   Current year requirement at 5% | 15,000.00 | 20,000.00 |
|   Participating—additional 3% | 9,000.00 | 12,000.00 |
|   Remainder to common | | 61,582.00 |
| Totals | $369,000.00 | $531,082.00 |
| Shares outstanding | 3,000 | 4,000 |
| Book value per share | $ 123.00 | $ 132.77 |

In connection with the book value computation, the analyst must know how to handle such items as the number of authorized and unissued shares, the number of treasury shares on hand, any commitments with respect to the issuance of unissued shares or the reissuance of treasury shares, and the relative rights and privileges of the various types of stock authorized. Although the book value per share figure is useful in some cases, in many instances it is not meaningful for decision-making purposes.

[12]If the preferred stock has a liquidating preference as to assets, this is considered in determining book value. For example, if the preferred stockholder receives $360,000 at liquidation instead of $300,000, an additional $60,000 is allocated to the preferred.

**16. Cash Flow Per Share**   One of the most popular yet least understood ratios used today is cash flow per share. It is computed by dividing net income plus noncash charges (such as depreciation and amortization) by the number of shares of common stock outstanding. The cash flow per share for Anetek is:

$$\text{Cash Flow Per Share} = \frac{\text{Net Income} + \text{Noncash Adjustments}}{\text{Outstanding Shares}}$$

$$= \frac{\$150,000 + \$150,000}{30,000} = \$10.00$$

This amount represents neither the flow of cash through the enterprise nor the residual of the cash received minus the cash disbursed divided by the outstanding shares of stock. It is frequently used to determine approximately the amount of cash generated internally.

At present, the profession strongly recommends that isolated statistics of working capital or cash provided from operations, especially per-share amounts, not be presented in annual reports to stockholders.[13] The profession's concern has been that cash flow per share can be misleading and may be used as a measure of profitability.

## LIMITATIONS OF RATIO ANALYSIS

Because a ratio can be computed precisely, it is easy to attach a high degree of reliability or significance to it. Financial analysis involves many alternative approaches though, and ratio analysis is only one of several means of gaining an understanding about a business enterprise from the financial data. Different and supplementary approaches such as careful investigation of footnotes, examination of the company's accounting policies, analysis of product-line breakdowns, and inspection of interim data are discussed in the next chapter.

The reader of financial statements must understand the basic limitations associated with ratio analysis when evaluating an enterprise. As analytical tools, ratios are attractive because they are simple and convenient. Frequently decisions are based on only these simple computations involving relationships between financial data. The ratios are only as good as the data upon which they are based.

One important limitation of ratios is that they are **based on historical cost which can lead to distortions in measuring performance.** By failing to incorporate changing price information, many believe that inaccurate assessments of the enterprise's financial condition and performance result. To illustrate, Superior Oil Company at one time owned 1.4% of Texaco, Inc., which it carried at the cost of approximately 64 million dollars, although the fair market value of the investment was almost twice that figure or approximately $118 million. Such significant information tends to be obscured by the enthusiasm for computing precise ratios.

---

[13]"Reporting Changes in Financial Position," *APB Opinion No. 19* (New York: AICPA, 1971), par. 15. As indicated in Chapter 24, whether the profession's position will continue is uncertain because increasing emphasis is being placed on cash flow (given our numerous credit crunches over the last ten years) by financial analysts. Note that the cash flow discussed above is highly simplified because it does not adjust for changes in receivables, payables, and other current assets and liabilities affecting operations.

## Anetek Chemical Corporation
### SUMMARY OF FINANCIAL RATIOS

| Ratio | Formula for Computation | Computation |
|---|---|---|
| **I. Liquidity** | | |
| 1. Current ratio | $\dfrac{\text{Current assets}}{\text{Current liabilities}}$ | $\dfrac{\$800,000}{\$575,000} = 1.39 \text{ times}$ |
| 2. Quick, or acid-test | $\dfrac{\text{Cash, marketable securities, and receivables}}{\text{Current liabilities}}$ | $\dfrac{\$490,000}{\$575,000} = .85 \text{ times}$ |
| 3. Defensive-interval measure | $\dfrac{\text{Defensive assets}}{\text{Projected daily expenditures minus noncash expenditures}}$ | $\dfrac{\$490,000}{\dfrac{\$1,525,000 - \$150,000}{365}} = 130 \text{ days}$ |
| **II. Activity** | | |
| 4. Receivable turnover | $\dfrac{\text{Net sales}}{\text{Average trade receivables (net)}}$ | $\dfrac{\$1,600,000}{\dfrac{\$350,000 + \$300,000}{2}} = $ 4.92 times, every 74 days |
| 5. Inventory turnover | $\dfrac{\text{Cost of goods sold}}{\text{Average inventory}}$ | $\dfrac{\$1,000,000}{\dfrac{\$310,000 + \$250,000}{2}} = $ 3.57 times, every 102 days |
| 6. Asset turnover | $\dfrac{\text{Net sales}}{\text{Average total assets}}$ | $\dfrac{\$1,600,000}{\dfrac{\$2,250,000 + \$2,100,000}{2}} = .74 \text{ times}$ |
| **III. Profitability** | | |
| 7. Profit margin on sales | $\dfrac{\text{Net income}}{\text{Net sales}}$ | $\dfrac{\$150,000}{\$1,600,000} = 9.4\%$ |
| 8. Rate of return on assets | $\dfrac{\text{Net income}}{\text{Average total assets}}$ | $\dfrac{\$150,000}{\dfrac{\$2,250,000 + \$2,100,000}{2}} = 6.9\%$ |
| 9. Rate of return on common stock equity | $\dfrac{\text{Net income minus preferred dividends}}{\text{Average common stockholders' equity}}$ | $\dfrac{\$150,000}{\dfrac{\$950,000 + \$1,100,000}{2}} = 14.6\%$ |
| 10. Earnings per share | $\dfrac{\text{Net income}}{\text{Weighted shares outstanding}}$ | $\dfrac{\$150,000}{30,000} = \$5.00$ |
| 11. Price earnings ratio | $\dfrac{\text{Market price of stock}}{\text{Earnings per share}}$ | $\dfrac{\$60}{\$5} = 12 \text{ times}$ |
| 12. Payout ratio | $\dfrac{\text{Cash dividends}}{\text{Net income}}$ | $\dfrac{\$67,500}{\$150,000} = 45\%$ |
| **IV. Coverage** | | |
| 13. Debt to total assets | $\dfrac{\text{Debt}}{\text{Total assets or equities}}$ | $\dfrac{\$1,300,000}{\$2,250,000} = 58\%$ |
| 14. Times interest earned | $\dfrac{\text{Income before interest charges and taxes}}{\text{Interest charges}}$ | $\dfrac{\$300,000}{\$50,000} = 6 \text{ times}$ |
| 15. Book value per share | $\dfrac{\text{Common stockholders' equity}}{\text{Outstanding shares}}$ | $\dfrac{\$950,000}{30,000} = \$31.67$ |
| 16. Cash flow per share | $\dfrac{\text{Income plus noncash adjustments}}{\text{Outstanding shares}}$ | $\dfrac{\$150,000 + \$150,000}{30,000} = \$10.00$ |

Also, investors must remember that **where estimated items (such as depreciation and amortization) are significant, income ratios lose some of their credibility.** Income recognized before the termination of the life of the business is an approximation. In analyzing the income statement, the user should be cognizant of the uncertainty surrounding the computation of net income. "The physicist has long since conceded that the location of an electron is best expressed by a probability curve. Surely an abstraction like earnings per share is even more subject to the rules of probability and risk."[14]

Probably the greatest criticism of ratio analysis is the **difficult problem of achieving comparability among firms in a given industry.** Achieving comparability among firms that apply different accounting procedures is difficult and requires that the analyst (1) identify basic differences existing in their accounting and (2) adjust the balances to achieve comparability.

Basic differences in accounting usually involve one of the following areas:

1. Inventory valuation (FIFO, LIFO, average cost).
2. Depreciation methods, particularly the use of straight-line versus accelerated depreciation.
3. Capitalization versus expense of certain costs, particularly costs involved in developing natural resources.
4. Pooling versus purchase in accounting for business combinations.
5. Capitalization of leases versus noncapitalization.
6. Investments in common stock carried at cost, equity, and sometimes market.
7. Differing treatments of pension costs.
8. Questionable practices of defining discontinued operations and extraordinary items.

The use of these different alternatives can make quite a significant difference in the ratios computed. For example, in the brewing industry, at one time Anheuser-Busch noted that if it had used average cost for inventory valuation instead of LIFO, inventories would have increased approximately $33,000,000; such an increase would have a substantive impact on the current ratio. Several studies have already been made analyzing the impact of different accounting methods on financial statement analysis. The differences in income that can develop are staggering in some cases, depending on the company's accounting policies.[15] The average investor may find it difficult to grasp all these differences, but investors must be aware of the potential pitfalls if they are to be able to make the proper adjustments.

Finally, it must be recognized that a substantial amount of important information about a company is not in its financial statements. Events involving such things as industry changes, management changes, competitors' actions, technological developments, government actions, and union activities are often critical to the successful operation of a company. These events occur continuously and information regarding them must come from careful analysis of financial reports in the media and other sources. Indeed many would argue, under what is known as the **efficient market hypothesis,** that financial statements

---

[14] Richard E. Cheney, "How Dependable Is the Bottom Line?" *The Financial Executive* (January 1971), p. 12.

[15] Examples of such descriptive studies are: Curtis L. Norton and Ralph E. Smith, "A Comparison of General Price Level and Historical Cost Financial Statements in the Prediction of Bankruptcy, *The Accounting Review* (January 1979), pp. 72–87. Robert Alan Cerf, "Price Level Changes and Financial Ratios," *Journal of Business* (July 1957), pp. 180–192, and Thomas A. Nelson, "Capitalizing Leases—The Effect on Financial Ratios," *Journal of Accountancy* (July 1963), pp. 49–58.

should contain "no surprises" to those engaged in market activities because the effect of these events should be known before the issuance of such reports. Appendix P elaborates on some of these events.

## PRICE-LEVEL DATA AND RATIOS

The analyst must recognize that traditional financial statements are based on historical cost. Depending upon the type and age of the assets involved, inflation or deflation can greatly affect financial data. As a result, some users restate historical cost based financial statements to determine whether there has been any real increase from year to year in the elements of the financial statements. As one individual stated in a recent research study on the use of price-level data: "The use of constant dollars helps management unclutter its thinking .... The effect of inflation at even 7 to 8 percent per year boggles the mind."[16]

Alternatively, many believe that current cost data provide a better measure for determining the overall performance of the enterprise. To illustrate how current cost information might be used in ratio analysis, certain selected ratios have been developed from a recent annual report of Borg-Warner Corporation.[17] The ratios and their significance are provided below.

| SELECTED RATES ON CURRENT COST BASIS (millions of dollars) | | |
|---|---|---|
| Formula | Computation | Significance |
| $\dfrac{\text{Current Cost Income}}{\text{Historical Cost Income}}$ | $= \dfrac{\$76}{\$126} = 60.3\%$ | The lower the ratio, the higher the impact of inflation. |
| $\dfrac{\text{Income Taxes}}{\text{Income before Income Taxes (current cost)}}$ | $= \dfrac{\$47}{\$52} = 90.4\%$ | Shows the tax on capital that results if higher than historical rate. |
| $\dfrac{\text{Holding Gains}}{\text{Physical Assets}}$ | $= \dfrac{\$57}{\$1,381} = 4.1\%$ | Indicates whether the company has assets that are appreciating in value. |

These ratios are simply examples of the type of information that can be developed from current cost data. As the investment community becomes familiar with this data, and more companies internalize it in their decision-making process, these ratios and variants thereof will take on added significance to many users of the financial statements.

---

[16]Adapted from an article by Allen H. Seed, "Measuring Financial Performance in an Inflationary Environment," *Financial Executive* (January 1982), pp. 41–46.

[17]Ibid.

# REPORTING RATIOS—SOME ISSUES

A proposed FASB concepts statement indicates that financial reporting should provide enough information to compute ratios that are used frequently. For example, because rate of return on assets or equity is commonly computed, it follows that data should be provided in the financial reports to prepare this information. In fact, some argue that the FASB should simply require the reporting of the more common ratios in the financial statements.

Whether the FASB should establish standards for the reporting of ratios is debatable. Some argue that the FASB is already involved in requiring standards in this area, given its requirement that EPS information be disclosed on the face of the income statement for publicly held companies. Furthermore, because EPS is the only ratio required, many believe undue emphasis is given to it. To discourage this emphasis, some argue that additional ratio information should be presented, such as rate of return on assets and equity.

Others, however, believe that the FASB should not be involved in developing standards related to the presentation of ratios. A basic concern expressed by this group is: how far should the FASB go? That is, where does financial reporting end and financial analysis begin? Furthermore, we know so little concerning which ratios are used and in what combinations that attempting to require disclosure of certain ratios in this area would not be helpful.[18] One reason for the profession's reluctance to mandate disclosures is that research regarding the use and usefulness of summary indicators is still limited and inconclusive. Some of the major findings to date are as follows:

**Predictability Studies**    One interesting approach using ratios has been the use of prediction models to determine whether a company is headed for bankruptcy or increased profitability. Several studies have been partially successful in using a combination of ratios to predict a possible bankruptcy situation, whereas attempts to determine profitability have met with dismal failure. For example, one study found the ratio of cash flow to total debt was the best predictor of bankruptcy. This study showed how financial ratios can be used to predict failure five years prior to its actual occurrence.[19] Ratios also have been used to predict other types of events, such as bank lending decisions, credit ratings, mergers and acquisitions, and so on, although success has been limited in these areas.

**Survey and Interview Studies**    These studies generally attempt to determine what financial statement users believe are the most appropriate ratios for analysis purposes. One of the most significant studies suggests that information on return on investment, cash flows, changes in financial position, effects of inflation, and components of earnings are considered more important than earnings per share.[20]

---

[18] For an expanded discussion of these points, see Frishkoff, *op. cit.*

[19] William H. Beaver, "Financial Ratios as Predictors of Failure," Empirical Research in Accounting, Selected Studies, 1966, *Journal of Accounting Research,* pp. 71–127; and William H. Beaver, "Alternative Accounting Measures as Predictors of Failures," *The Accounting Review* (January 1968), pp. 113–122. See also E. B. Deakin, "Discriminate Analysis of Predictors of Business Failure," *Journal of Accounting Research* (Spring 1972), pp. 167–179.

[20] Louis Harris and Associates, Inc., "A Study of the Attitudes Toward an Assessment of the Financial Accounting Standards Board" (Stamford, Conn.: Financial Accounting Foundation, 1980).

Anetek Chemical Corporation
CONDENSED COMPARATIVE STATEMENTS
(000,000 omitted)

| Income (000 omitted) | 1984 | 1983 | 1982 | 1981 | 1980 | 10 Years Ago 1974 | 20 Years Ago 1964 |
|---|---|---|---|---|---|---|---|
| **Sales and other revenue:** | | | | | | | |
| Net sales | $1,600.0 | $1,350.0 | $1,309.7 | $1,176.2 | $1,077.5 | $636.2 | $170.7 |
| Other revenue | 75.0 | 50.0 | 39.4 | 34.1 | 24.6 | 9.0 | 3.7 |
| Total | 1,675.0 | 1,400.0 | 1,349.1 | 1,210.3 | 1,102.1 | 645.2 | 174.4 |
| **Costs and other charges:** | | | | | | | |
| Cost of sales | 1,000.0 | 850.0 | 827.4 | 737.6 | 684.2 | 386.8 | 111.0 |
| Depreciation and depletion | 150.0 | 150.0 | 122.6 | 115.6 | 98.7 | 82.4 | 14.2 |
| Selling and administrative expenses | 225.0 | 150.0 | 144.2 | 133.7 | 126.7 | 66.7 | 10.7 |
| Interest expense | 50.0 | 25.0 | 28.5 | 20.7 | 9.4 | 8.9 | 1.8 |
| Taxes on income | 100.0 | 75.0 | 79.5 | 73.5 | 68.3 | 42.4 | 12.4 |
| Total | 1,525.0 | 1,250.0 | 1,202.2 | 1,081.1 | 987.3 | 587.2 | 150.1 |
| Net income for the year | 150.0 | 150.0 | 146.9 | 129.2 | 114.8 | 58.0 | 24.3 |
| **Other Statistics** | | | | | | | |
| Earnings per share on common stock (in dollars)[a] | $ 5.00 | $ 4.50 | $ 4.09 | $ 3.58 | $ 3.11 | $ 1.66 | $ 1.06 |
| Cash dividends per share paid to stockholders on common stock (in dollars)[a] | 2.25 | 2.15 | 1.95 | 1.79 | 1.71 | 1.11 | .25 |
| Cash dividends declared on common stock | 67.5 | 66.1 | 59.9 | 54.1 | 53.3 | 30.8 | 5.0 |
| Stock dividend at approximate market value | | | | 46.8 | | 27.3 | |
| Taxes (major) | 144.5 | 125.9 | 116.5 | 105.6 | 97.8 | 59.8 | 17.0 |
| Wages paid | 389.3 | 325.6 | 302.1 | 279.6 | 263.2 | 183.2 | 48.6 |
| Cost of employee benefits | 50.8 | 36.2 | 32.9 | 28.7 | 27.2 | 18.4 | 4.4 |
| Number of employees at year end (thousands) | 47.4 | 36.4 | 35.0 | 33.8 | 33.2 | 26.6 | 14.6 |
| Additions to property | 306.3 | 192.3 | 241.5 | 248.3 | 166.1 | 185.0 | 49.0 |

[a]Adjusted for stock splits and stock dividends.

**Behavioral Research**   Experiments that examine the decision-making process given the use of certain information (often referred to as behavioral research) are few and limited in scope. In short, we do not know how information is used, except in a very controlled environment. Some limited evidence on credit granting activities by bank loan officers suggests that reasonable predictions of business failure can be made using only certain key ratios.[21]

Such studies indicate the potential that ratio analysis holds. Although this type of analysis has many limitations, the merits of ratio analysis as a method for analyzing a business situation should be recognized.

## COMPARATIVE ANALYSIS

In comparative analysis the same reports or data are presented for two or more different dates or periods so that like items may be compared. Ratio analysis provides only a single snapshot, the analysis being for one given point or period in time. In a comparative analy-

---

[21]See, for example, Robert Libby, "Accounting Ratios and the Prediction of Failure: Some Behavioral Evidence," *Journal of Accounting Research* (Spring 1975), pp. 150–161.

sis, an investment analyst can concentrate on a given item and determine whether it appears to be growing or diminishing year by year and the proportion of such change to related items. Generally, companies present comparative financial statements.[22]

In addition, many companies include in their annual reports 5- or 10-year summaries of pertinent data that permit the reader to examine and analyze trends. *ARB No. 43* concluded that "the presentation of comparative financial statements in annual and other reports enhances the usefulness of such reports and brings out more clearly the nature and trends of current changes affecting the enterprise." An illustration of a 5-year condensed statement with additional supporting data as presented by Anetek Chemical Corporation is presented on page 1220.

## PERCENTAGE ANALYSIS

Analysts also use percentage analysis to help them evaluate an enterprise. Percentage analysis consists of reducing a series of related amounts to a series of percentages of a given base. All items in an income statement are frequently expressed as a percentage of sales or sometimes as a percentage of cost of goods sold; a balance sheet may be analyzed on the basis of total assets. This analysis facilitates comparison and is helpful in evaluating the relative size of items or the relative change in items. A reduction of absolute dollar amounts to percentages may also facilitate comparison between companies of different size. To illustrate, here is a comparative analysis of the expense section of Anetek for the last two years.

| Anetek Chemical | | | | |
|---|---|---|---|---|
| | 1984 | 1983 | Difference | % Change Inc. (dec.) |
| Cost of sales | $1,000.0 | $850.0 | $150.0 | 17.6 |
| Depreciation and depletion | 150.0 | 150.0 | 0 | 0 |
| Selling and administrative expenses | 225.0 | 150.0 | 75.0 | 50.0 |
| Interest expense | 50.0 | 25.0 | 25.0 | 100.0 |
| Taxes | 100.0 | 75.0 | 25.0 | 33.3 |

This approach, normally called **horizontal analysis,** indicates the proportionate change over a period of time. It is especially useful in evaluating a trend situation, because absolute changes are often deceiving.

Another approach, called **vertical analysis,** is the expression of each item on a financial statement in a given period to a base figure. For example, Anetek Chemical's income statement using this approach appears on page 1222.

---

[22]In 1981 all 600 companies surveyed in *Accounting Trends and Techniques* presented comparative 1979 amounts in their 1980 balance sheets and income statements.

| Anetek Chemical<br>INCOME STATEMENT<br>(000,000 omitted) | | |
| --- | --- | --- |
| | Amount | Percentage of<br>Total Revenue |
| Net sales | $1,600.0 | 96% |
| Other revenue | 75.0 | 4 |
|    Total revenue | 1,675.0 | 100 |
| Less | | |
|   Cost of goods sold | 1,000.0 | 60 |
|   Depreciation and depletion | 150.0 | 9 |
|   Selling and administrative expenses | 225.0 | 13 |
|   Interest expense | 50.0 | 3 |
|   Income tax | 100.0 | 6 |
| Total expenses | 1,525.0 | 91 |
|    Net income | $ 150.0 | 9 |

A variation in vertical analysis, referred to as **common-size analysis,** is the presentation of percentages without the dollar amounts given.

# Fundamental Analysis Versus Capital Market Analysis

The approach presented in this chapter assumes that a present or potential stockholder analyzes financial information to determine whether a common stock is under- or over-valued. This approach, often referred to as **fundamental analysis,** attempts to find the **intrinsic value** of the security, which is defined as "that value which is justified by the facts, e.g., assets, earnings, dividends, definite prospects including the factor of management."[1] An investor who, therefore, finds a common stock that has an intrinsic value higher than the current market price will buy or continue to hold this security. Conversely, if the intrinsic value of the common stock is lower than the current market price, the investor will sell or not purchase the stock. The assumption of fundamental analysis is that by careful investigation, under- and overvalued common stocks may be detected and appropriate investment decisions made.

To illustrate, Del Monte Corporation's stock at one time dropped from $29 to $23 per share—this drop was attributed to the fact that its most recent earnings per share had dropped from $2.16 to $1.65. However, certain analysts concluded after careful investigation that Del Monte's income would have increased 48 cents instead of declining 51 cents if not for some nonrecurring charges that had little to do with the operations of the business. Apparently many other investors arrived at the same conclusion because the stock price increased 87% to $44 a share a short time later. This example demonstrates that many believe that fundamental analysis is the most useful technique in analyzing financial statements.

Proponents of **capital market analysis** (efficient market hypothesis) believe that the current market price of the common stock at any given point in time reflects all available public information and, therefore, analysis of financial statements will not enable an investor to find an under- or overvalued security. The implication of this approach is that attempts to "beat the market" through fundamental analysis are fruitless because the market is efficient with respect to incorporating publicly available information into the common stock price. It should be emphasized that capital market analysis in its most common form states only that the current price reflects publicly available information such as that

---

[1]Benjamin Graham, David L. Dodd, and Sidney Cottle, *Security Analysis: Principles and Techniques,* 4th ed. (New York: McGraw-Hill Book Co., 1962), p. 28.

found in financial statements; if you happen to have inside information, you may be able to use it advantageously.

What then does an investor do who believes that the capital market is efficient with respect to publicly available information? To answer this question, we have to recognize that **an investor in common stock is interested in determining the return that would be received and the risk level that would be assumed if the common stock were purchased.** The return on each share of common stock is measured by the change in the market price plus the dividend payment received; the risk level is computed by assessing the probability of achieving a desired return. It follows that the higher the return, the greater the risk and vice versa. A rational investor will attempt to achieve the highest return possible, given the risk level assumed.

In fundamental analysis, it is extremely difficult to determine the risk level that an investor is assuming. Although an analysis of the financial condition of the business enterprise provides indications as to the possible variability in the returns from the common stock, no theory of risk measurement has been well formulated. This is not the case in capital market analysis. A capital market advocate notes that the risk (variability) associated with the return on a common stock is comprised of two components, a **systematic risk** and an **unsystematic risk.** The systematic risk, often referred to as **beta,** measures the average change in a common stock's return for each change in the return on the market as a whole. For example, if a common stock has a beta of one, a 10 percent increase in the market would mean that a 10 percent increase in the return on that common stock should be expected. Conversely, if a common stock has a beta of a negative one, the return on the security moves directly opposite to changes in the overall market. The nonsystematic risk, however, cannot be correlated with any factor and is considered random. By acquiring a portfolio of stocks, the investor can avoid this unsystematic risk entirely because over a number of stocks this risk component cancels and is eliminated from consideration.

The implication of capital market analysis is that an investor should be concerned with the acquisition of a portfolio of common stocks and not with the purchase of an individual security. Purchase of a number of stocks provides two important advantages. First, the investor can eliminate the unsystematic risk because this component cancels out for a number of stocks. Second, the investor can determine the risk level desired and, hopefully, can attain this level. If an investor prefers less risk, the investor should establish a portfolio of common stocks with a low beta; if a higher return is desired, a higher beta portfolio should be selected.

To illustrate the difference between fundamental analysis and capital market analysis, assume that you are interested in purchasing some shares of General Motors stock. Adherents of fundamental analysis would suggest that you analyze the financial statements of General Motors to determine its intrinsic value or what you think "the stock is worth." Comparison of the present price to its intrinsic value will then provide the answer as to whether this stock should be purchased. Proponents of capital market analysis, however, would argue that you should determine the beta of General Motors stock and how this beta interacts with the other stocks held in your portfolio. If the purchase of General Motors stock increases the beta in your portfolio, and if you desire this additional risk, then the appropriate investment decision is evident.

What implications does capital market analysis have for financial analysis? Some might argue that analyzing the financial statements is useless because the information is already incorporated in the market price of the stock. One should recognize, however, that for the market to be efficient, someone must analyze the information. Thus, some form of analysis is needed to make the market efficient. Second, even if the market is efficient regarding the stock price, information for users other than present and potential stockholders is needed. For example, credit grantors will need to analyze the financial statements carefully to insure that proper loan decisions are made.

It should be emphasized that capital market analysis is highly controversial in the investment community. Only after continual experimentation will the financial community be able to determine its conceptual validity.

**Note:** All **asterisked** questions, cases, exercises, or problems relate to material contained in the appendix to each chapter.

## QUESTIONS

1. "The significance of financial statement data is not in the amount alone." Discuss the meaning of this statement.

2. Distinguish between ratio analysis and percentage analysis relative to the interpretation of financial statements. What is the value of these two types of analysis?

3. A close friend of yours, who is a Psychology major and who has not had any college courses or any experience in business, is receiving the financial statements from companies in which he has minor investments (acquired for him by his now deceased father). He asks you what he needs to know to interpret and to evaluate the financial statement data that he is receiving. What would you tell him?

4. The controller of a *Fortune* 500 chemical company has requested you to include in your report certain balance sheet and income statement ratios so that comparisons may be made. Indicate the types or categories of ratios that might be provided and explain their significance.

5. Of what significance is the current ratio? If this ratio is too low, what may it signify? Can this ratio be too high? Explain.

6. How does the acid-test ratio differ from the current ratio? How are they similar? Of what benefit is the defensive interval ratio?

7. Answer each of the questions in the following unrelated situations:
   (a) A company has current assets of $90,000 (of which $40,000 is inventory and prepaid items) and current liabilities of $30,000. What is the current ratio? What is the acid-test ratio? If the company borrows $15,000 cash from a bank on a 120-day loan, what will its current ratio be? What will the acid-test ratio be?
   (b) A company has current assets of $600,000 and current liabilities of $240,000. The board of directors declares a cash dividend of $160,000. What is the current ratio after the declaration, but before payment? What is the current ratio after the payment of the dividend?
   (c) The current ratio of a company is 5:1 and its acid-test ratio is 1:1. If the inventories and prepaid items amount to $500,000, what is the amount of current liabilities?
   (d) A company had an average inventory last year of $190,000 and its inventory turnover was 4.2. If sales volume and unit cost remain the same this year as last and inventory turnover is 7.0 this year, what will average inventory have to be during the current year?

8. In calculating inventory turnover, why is cost of goods sold used as the numerator? As the inventory turnover increases, what increasing risk does the business assume?

9. What is the relationship of the asset turnover ratio to the rate of return on assets?

10. One member of the board of directors suggests that the corporation maximize trading on equity, that is, using stockholders' equity as a basis for borrowing additional funds at a lower rate of interest than the expected earnings from the use of the borrowed funds.
    (a) Explain how a change in income tax rates affects trading on equity.
    (b) Explain how trading on equity affects earnings per share of common stock.
    (c) Under what circumstances should a corporation seek to trade on equity to a substantial degree?

11. Explain the meaning of the following terms:
    (a) Dividend yield.
    (b) Price-earnings ratio.
    (c) Payout ratio.
    (d) Earnings per share.

12. What is meant by book value? Of what significance is preferred stock in the computation of book value?

13. Of what importance are the following ratios in financial analysis?
    (a) Stockholders' equity to total assets or equity.
    (b) Debt to total assets or equities.
    (c) Times interest earned.
    (d) Ratio of plant assets to long-term liabilities.

14. Discuss the inherent limitations of single-year statements for purposes of analysis and interpretation. Include in your discussion the extent to which these limitations are overcome by the use of comparative statements.

15. Comparative balance sheets and comparative income statements that show a firm's financial history for each of the last 10 years may be misleading. Discuss the factors or conditions that might contribute to misinterpretations. Include a discussion of the additional information and supplementary data that might be included in or provided with the statements to prevent misinterpretations.

16. Explain the meaning of the following terms: (a) common-size analysis, (b) vertical analysis, (c) horizontal analysis, (d) percentage analysis.

17. Presently, the profession requires that earnings per share be disclosed on the face of the income statement. What are some disadvantages of reporting ratios on the financial statements?

18. A student who just completed his first finance course commented, "We didn't use ratio analysis; our instructor indicated that ratio analysis was no longer fashionable." Discuss.

*19. Some believe that the stock market is efficient with respect to incorporating publicly available information into the stock price. What implication does this statement have for financial statement analysis?

## CASES

**C26-1** The transactions listed below relate to Demco, Inc. You are to assume that on the date on which each of the transactions occurred the corporation's accounts showed only common stock ($100 par) outstanding, a current ratio of 2.7:1 and a substantial net income for the year to date (before giving effect to the transaction concerned). On that date the book value per share of stock was $151.53.

Each numbered transaction is to be considered completely independent of the others, and its related answer should be based on the effect(s) of that transaction alone. Assume that all numbered transactions occurred during 1984 and that the amount involved in each case is sufficiently material to distort reported net income if improperly included in the determination of net income. Assume further that each transaction was recorded in accordance with generally accepted accounting principles and, where applicable, in conformity with the all-inclusive concept of the income statement.

For each of the lettered transactions you are to decide whether it:

A. Increased the corporation's 1984 net income.

B. Decreased the corporation's 1984 net income.

C. Increased the corporation's total retained earnings directly (i.e., not via net income).

D. Decreased the corporation's total retained earnings directly.

E. Increased the corporation's current ratio.

F. Decreased the corporation's current ratio.

G. Increased each stockholder's proportionate share of total owner's equity.

**H.** Decreased each stockholder's proportionate share of total owner's equity.

**I.** Increased each stockholder's equity per share of stock (book value).

**J.** Decreased each stockholder's equity per share of stock (book value).

**K.** Had none of the foregoing effects.

**Instructions**

List the numbers 1 through 10. Select as many letters as you deem appropriate to reflect the effect(s) of each transaction as of the date of the transaction by printing beside the transaction number the letter(s) that identifies that transaction's effect(s).

*Transactions*

1. In January the board directed the write-off of certain patent rights that had suddenly and unexpectedly become worthless.

2. The corporation wrote off all of the unamortized discount and issue expense applicable to bonds that it refinanced in 1984.

3. Treasury stock originally repurchased and carried at $103 per share was sold for cash at $106 per share.

4. The corporation sold at a profit land and a building that had been idle for some time. Under the terms of the sale, the corporation received a portion of the sales price in cash immediately, the balance maturing at six-month intervals.

5. The board of directors authorized the write-up of certain fixed assets to values established in a competent appraisal.

6. The corporation called in all its outstanding shares of stock and exchanged them for new shares on a 2-for-1 basis, reducing the par value at the same time to $50 per share.

7. The corporation paid a cash dividend which had been recorded in the accounts at time of declaration.

8. Litigation involving Demco, Inc., as defendant was settled in the corporation's favor, with the plaintiff paying all court costs and legal fees. The corporation had appropriated retained earnings in 1978 as a special contingency appropriation for this court action, and the board directs abolition of the appropriation.

9. The corporation received a check for the proceeds of an insurance policy from the company with which it is insured against theft of trucks. No entries concerning the theft had been made previously, and the proceeds reduce but do not cover completely the loss.

10. Treasury stock, which had been repurchased at and carried at $104 per share, was issued as a stock dividend. In connection with this distribution, the board of directors of Demco, Inc. had authorized a transfer from retained earnings to permanent capital of an amount equal to the aggregate market value ($106 per share) of the shares issued. No entries relating to this dividend had been made previously.

(AICPA adapted)

C26-2 As the CPA for Badger Meters Inc., you have been requested to develop some key ratios from the comparative financial statements. This information is to be used to convince creditors that Badger Meters Inc. is solvent and to support the use of going-concern valuation procedures in the financial statements.

The data requested and the computations developed from the financial statements follow:

|  | 1984 | 1983 |
|---|---|---|
| Current ratio | 2.6 times | 2.1 times |
| Acid-test ratio | .8 times | 1.3 times |
| Property, plant, and equipment to stockholders' equity | 2.5 times | 2.2 times |
| Sales to stockholders' equity | 2.4 times | 2.7 times |
| Net income | Up 32% | Down 9% |
| Earnings per share | $3.30 | $2.50 |
| Book value per share | Up 6% | Up 9% |

**Instructions**

(a) Badger Meters asks you to prepare a list of brief comments stating how each of these items supports the solvency and going concern potential of the business. The company wishes to use these comments to support its presentation of data to its creditors. You are to prepare the comments as requested, giving the implications and the limitations of each item separately, and then the collective inference that may be drawn from them about Badger's solvency and going-concern potential.

(b) Having done as the client requested in part (a), prepare a brief listing of additional ratio-analysis-type data for this client which you think its creditors are going to ask for to supplement the data provided in part (a). Explain why you think the additional data will be helpful to these creditors in evaluating the client's solvency.

(c) What warnings should you offer these creditors about the limitations of ratio analysis for the purposes stated here?

**C26-3** Antique Furniture, Inc. went public three years ago. The board of directors will be meeting shortly after the end of the year to decide on a dividend policy. In the past, growth has been financed primarily through the retention of earnings. A stock or a cash dividend has never been declared. Presented below is a brief financial summary of Antique Furniture, Inc. operations.

| | ($000 omitted) | | | | |
| | 1984 | 1983 | 1982 | 1981 | 1980 |
|---|---|---|---|---|---|
| Sales | $20,000 | $16,000 | $14,000 | $6,000 | $4,000 |
| Net income | $ 3,000 | $ 1,600 | $ 800 | $1,000 | $ 200 |
| Average total assets | $22,000 | $19,000 | $11,500 | $4,200 | $3,000 |
| Current assets | $ 8,000 | $ 6,000 | $ 3,000 | $1,200 | $1,000 |
| Working capital | $ 3,600 | $ 3,200 | $ 1,200 | $ 500 | $ 400 |
| Common shares: | | | | | |
| Number of shares | | | | | |
| outstanding (000) | 2,000 | 2,000 | 2,000 | 20 | 20 |
| Average market price | $9 | $6 | $4 | — | — |

**Instructions**

(a) Suggest factors to be considered by the board of directors in establishing a dividend policy.

(b) Compute the rate of return on assets, profit margin on sales, earnings per share, and price-earnings ratio for each of the five years for Antique Furniture, Inc.

(c) Comment on the appropriateness of declaring a cash dividend at this time, using the ratios computed in part (b) as a major factor in your analysis.

**C26-4** The owners of Fermi Labs, Inc., a closely held corporation, have offered to sell their 100% interest in the company's common stock at an amount equal to the book value of the common stock. They will retain their interest in the company's preferred stock.

The president of Trendler Corporation, your client, would like to combine the operations of Fermi Labs with the Metal Products Division, and she is seriously considering having Trendler Corporation buy the common stock of Fermi Labs. She questions the use of "book value" as a basis for the sale, however, and has come to you for advice.

**Instructions**

Draft a report to your client. Your report should cover the following points:

(a) Define book value. Explain its significance in establishing a value for a business that is expected to continue in operation indefinitely.

(b) Describe the procedure for computing book values of ownership equities.

(c) Why should your client consider the Fermi Labs Inc. accounting policies and methods in her evaluation of the company's reported book value? List the areas of accounting policy and method relevant to this evaluation.

(d) What factors, other than book value, should your client recognize in determining a basis for the sale?

(AICPA adapted)

**C26–5** The Finance Committee of the Farnsworth Corporation was established to appraise and screen departmental requests for plant expansions and improvements at a time when these requests totaled $11,200,000. The committee then sought your professional advice and help in establishing the minimum performance standards that it should demand of these projects in the way of anticipated rates of return before interest and taxes.

Farnsworth Corporation is a closely held family corporation in which the stockholders exert an active and unified influence on the management. At this date, the company has no long-term debt and has 1,000,000 shares of common capital stock outstanding which were sold at $20 per share. It is currently earning $5 million (income before interest and taxes) per year. The applicable tax rate is 50%.

If the projects under consideration are approved, management is confident that the $11,200,000 of required funds can be obtained either:

1. **By Borrowing:** via the medium of an issue of $11,200,000, 11%, 20-year bonds.

2. **By Equity Financing:** via the medium of an issue of 560,000 shares of common stock to the general public. It is expected and anticipated that the ownership of these 560,000 shares will be widely dispersed and scattered.

The company has been earning a 14% return after taxes. The management and the dominant stockholders consider this rate of earnings to be a fair price-earnings ratio (8 times earnings) as long as the company remains free of long-term debt. A lowering of the price-earnings ratio to six and two-thirds times earnings constitutes an adequate adjustment to compensate for the risk of carrying $11,200,000 of long-term debt. They believe that this reflects, and is consistent with, current market appraisals.

### Instructions

(a) Prepare columnar schedules comparing minimum returns, considering interest, taxes, and earnings ratio, which should be produced by each alternative to maintain the present capitalized value per share (of $20).

(b) What minimum rate of return on new investment is necessary for each alternative to maintain the present capitalized value per share (of $20)?

(AICPA adapted)

**\*C26–6** Two students are discussing the merits of ratio analysis as a basis for financial analysis. In discussing the valuation of common stock, one student notes that many securities sell too high in normal markets. These stocks, often referred to as "blue chip" stocks—the prosperous leaders of the industry—have a popularity that is not supported by their assets and earnings. It seems that certain companies and certain industries attract a bullishness that overvalues the stock. Through fundamental analysis, therefore, we can determine whether this stock is overvalued in relation to its intrinsic value.

The second student argues that this type of analysis is no longer used in the investment community for evaluating common stocks. The student notes that a new theory of investment selection based on capital market analysis is now used extensively. Unfortunately, the student cannot explain this concept except to indicate that it has something to do with "beta" and a "portfolio of stocks."

### Instructions

(a) Define the term "intrinsic value" and explain why an investment analyst would be interested in finding this value.

(b) Explain the term "beta" and its importance to the theory of capital market analysis.

(c) Why is a portfolio of stocks necessary in the capital market analysis approach to selection of common stocks?

## EXERCISES

**E26–1** Presented below is information related to Media Network Inc.:

Media Network Inc.
BALANCE SHEET
December 31, 1984

| | | | | | |
|---|---|---|---|---|---|
| Cash | | $ 40,000 | Notes payable (short-term) | | $ 60,000 |
| Receivables | $110,000 | | Accounts payable | | 26,000 |
| less allowance | 10,000 | 100,000 | Accrued liabilities | | 5,000 |
| Inventories | | 150,000 | Capital stock (par $5) | | 250,000 |
| Prepaid insurance | | 3,000 | Retained earnings | | 132,000 |
| Land | | 20,000 | | | |
| Equipment (net) | | 160,000 | | | |
| | | $473,000 | | | $473,000 |

STATEMENT OF INCOME
Year Ended December 31, 1984

| | | |
|---|---|---|
| Sales | | $1,100,000 |
| Cost of Sales | | |
| Inventory, Jan. 1, 1984 | $100,000 | |
| Purchases | 790,000 | |
| Cost of goods available for sale | 890,000 | |
| Inventory, Dec. 31, 1984 | 150,000 | |
| Cost of goods sold | | 740,000 |
| Gross Profit on Sales | | 360,000 |
| Operating Expenses | | 170,000 |
| Net Income | | $ 190,000 |

**Instructions**

(a) Compute the following ratios or relationships of Media Network Inc.. Assume that the ending account balances are representative unless the information provided indicates differently.
1. Current ratio.
2. Inventory turnover.
3. Receivables turnover.
4. Earnings per share.
5. Profit margin on sales.
6. Rate of return on common stock equity on December 31, 1984.

(b) Indicate for each of the following transactions whether the transaction would improve, weaken, or have no effect on the current ratio of Media Network Inc. at December 31, 1984.
1. Write off an uncollectible account receivable, $2,200.
2. Purchase additional capital stock for cash.
3. Pay $24,000 on notes payable (short-term).
4. Collect $23,000 on accounts receivable.
5. Buy equipment on account.
6. Give an existing creditor a short-term note in settlement of account.

**E26-2** Expandabelt Company has been operating for several years, and on December 31, 1984, presented the following balance sheet:

Expandabelt Company
BALANCE SHEET
December 31, 1984

| Cash | $ 20,000 | Accounts payable | $ 70,000 |
|---|---|---|---|
| Receivables | 70,000 | Mortgage payable | 130,000 |
| Inventories | 80,000 | Common stock ($1.00 par) | 120,000 |
| Plant assets (net) | 180,000 | Retained earnings | 30,000 |
| | $350,000 | | $350,000 |

The net income for 1984 was $20,000. Projected annual operational expenditures (based on past data) exclusive of depreciation are $45,000. Assume that total assets are the same in 1983 and 1984.

**Instructions**

Compute each of the following ratios. For each of the five indicate the manner in which it is computed and its significance as a tool in the analysis of the financial soundness of the company.
(a) Current ratio.
(b) Acid-test ratio.
(c) Defensive interval measure.
(d) Debt to total assets.
(e) Rate of return on assets.

**E26-3** Financial information for Airtrain Company is presented below.

| Assets | 12/31/84 | 12/31/83 |
|---|---|---|
| Cash | $ 140,000 | $ 142,000 |
| Receivables (net) | 270,000 | 198,000 |
| Inventories | 1,200,000 | 1,050,000 |
| Short-term investments | 200,000 | 400,000 |
| Prepaid items | 60,000 | 80,000 |
| Land | 300,000 | 300,000 |
| Building and equipment (net) | 2,000,000 | 1,760,000 |
| | $4,170,000 | $3,930,000 |

| Equities | | |
|---|---|---|
| Accounts payable | $ 630,000 | $ 430,000 |
| Notes payable | 200,000 | 200,000 |
| Accrued liabilities | 100,000 | 100,000 |
| Bonds payable due 1989 | 700,000 | 800,000 |
| Common stock | 2,000,000 | 2,000,000 |
| Retained earnings | 540,000 | 400,000 |
| | $4,170,000 | $3,930,000 |

Airtrain Company
COMPARATIVE INCOME STATEMENT
Years Ended December 31, 1984 and 1983

|  | 1984 | 1983 |
|---|---|---|
| Sales | $4,200,000 | $3,900,000 |
| Cost of goods sold | 3,400,000 | 3,100,000 |
| Gross profit | 800,000 | 800,000 |
| Operating expenses | 480,000 | 400,000 |
| Net income | $ 320,000 | $ 400,000 |

**Instructions**

From these data compute as many ratios presented in the chapter, for both years, as possible. Assume that the ending account balances for 1983 are representative unless the information provided indicates differently. The beginning inventory for 1983 was $800,000.

**E26-4** Shown below is the equity section of the balance sheet for Sampson Company and Dehlila Company. Each has assets totaling $4,200,000.

| Sampson Co. | | Dehlila Co. | |
|---|---|---|---|
| Current liabilities | $ 300,000 | Current liabilities | $ 500,000 |
| Long-term debt, 10% | 1,500,000 | Common stock ($20 par) | 3,000,000 |
| Common stock ($20 par) | 1,800,000 | Retained earnings | 700,000 |
| Retained earnings | 600,000 | | |
| | $4,200,000 | | $4,200,000 |

For the last two years each company has earned the same income before interest and taxes.

|  | Sampson Co. | Dehlila Co. |
|---|---|---|
| Income before interest and taxes | $820,000 | $820,000 |
| Interest expense | 150,000 | -0- |
| | 670,000 | 820,000 |
| Income taxes (40%) | 268,000 | 328,000 |
| Net income | $402,000 | $492,000 |

**Instructions**

(a) Which company is more profitable in terms of return on total assets?
(b) Which company is more profitable in terms of return on stockholders' equity?
(c) Which company has the greater net income per share of stock? Why?
(d) From the point of view of income, is it advantageous to the stockholders of Sampson Co. to have the long-term debt outstanding? Why?

**E26-5** The controller of Anapolis Sail Company finds that, although the company continues to earn about the same net income year after year, the rate of return on stockholders' equity is decreasing. Most of the profits are permitted to remain in the business so that total assets are increasing year by year, but there is very little increase in net income. As the recently hired chief accountant, you are requested to assist the controller in locating the difficulty and to suggest remedial measures.

Among the matters of interest that you find is the following:

| | Inventory Dec. 31 | Cost of Goods Sold |
|---|---|---|
| 1981 | $283,000 | $2,850,000 |
| 1982 | 321,000 | 2,650,000 |
| 1983 | 402,000 | 2,800,000 |
| 1984 | 448,000 | 2,980,000 |

**Instructions**

(a) What conclusions can be reached on the basis of this information only?
(b) What further investigation does it suggest? State exactly how you would proceed.
(c) If your conclusions are confirmed in the additional investigation, what recommendations would you make concerning remedial measures?

**E26-6** Presented below is information related to Serveyou Inc.

| | |
|---|---|
| Operating income | $ 498,750 |
| Bond interest expense | 180,000 |
| | 318,750 |
| Income taxes | 165,750 |
| Net income | $ 153,000 |
| Bonds payable | $1,500,000 |
| Common stock | 525,000 |
| Appropriation for contingencies | 75,000 |
| Retained earnings, unappropriated | 300,000 |

**Instructions**

Is Serveyou Inc. trading on the equity successfully? Explain.

**E26-7** Hardy Luggage Company's condensed financial statements provide the following information:

| BALANCE SHEET | | |
|---|---|---|
| | Dec. 31, 1984 | Dec. 31, 1983 |
| Cash | $ 40,000 | $ 60,000 |
| Accounts receivable (net) | 130,000 | 80,000 |
| Marketable securities (short-term) | 80,000 | 40,000 |
| Inventories | 460,000 | 360,000 |
| Prepaid expenses | 3,000 | 7,000 |
| Total current assets | $ 713,000 | $ 547,000 |
| Property, plant, and equipment (net) | 637,000 | 653,000 |
| Total assets | $1,350,000 | $1,200,000 |
| Current liabilities | 200,000 | 160,000 |
| Bonds payable | 400,000 | 400,000 |
| Common stockholders' equity | 750,000 | 640,000 |
| Total liabilities and stockholders' equity | $1,350,000 | $1,200,000 |

**INCOME STATEMENT**
For the Year Ended 1984

| | |
|---|---:|
| Sales | $1,100,000 |
| Cost of goods sold | (700,000) |
| Gross profit | 400,000 |
| Selling and administrative expense | (106,000) |
| Interest expense | (40,000) |
| Net income | $ 254,000 |

**Instructions**

(a) Determine the following:
1. Current ratio at December 31, 1984.
2. Acid-test ratio at December 31, 1984.
3. Accounts receivable turnover for 1984.
4. Inventory turnover for 1984.
5. Rate of return on assets for 1984.
6. Rate of return on common stock equity for 1984.

(b) Prepare a brief evaluation of the financial condition of Hardy Luggage Company and of the adequacy of its profits.

**E26-8** As loan analyst for Kansas Statewide Bank, you have been presented the following information:

**Assets**

| | Howat Co. | Kadlac Co. |
|---|---:|---:|
| Cash | $ 80,000 | $ 255,000 |
| Receivables | 152,000 | 222,000 |
| Inventories | 455,000 | 460,000 |
| Total current assets | 687,000 | 937,000 |
| Other assets | 500,000 | 612,000 |
| Total assets | $1,187,000 | $1,549,000 |

**Liabilities and Capital**

| | Howat Co. | Kadlac Co. |
|---|---:|---:|
| Current liabilities | $ 280,000 | $ 320,000 |
| Long-term liabilities | 400,000 | 500,000 |
| Capital stock and retained earnings | 507,000 | 729,000 |
| Total liabilities and capital | $1,187,000 | $1,549,000 |
| Annual sales | $1,050,000 | $1,500,000 |
| Rate of gross profit on sales | 30% | 41% |

Each of these companies has requested a loan of $50,000 for six months with no collateral offered. Inasmuch as your bank has reached its quota for loans of this type, only one of these requests is to be granted.

**Instructions**

Which of the two companies, as judged by the information given above, would you recommend as the better risk and why? Assume that the ending account balances are representative of the entire year.

**E26-9** Presented below is information related to Fishery Company for 1984:

| | |
|---|---:|
| Sales | $720,000 |
| Net income | 60,000 |

| Average total assets | 360,000 |
| Average stockholders' equity | 200,000 |
| Market price of stock at year-end | $70 per share |
| Cash dividend per share | $1.60 |
| Earnings per share | $2.40 |

**Instructions**

(a) Compute the following ratios for 1984:
1. Profit margin on sales.
2. Rate of return on stockholders' equity.
3. Rate of return on total assets.
4. Dividend yield.
5. Price-earnings ratio.

(b) Compute the following for 1985, assuming that all other factors remain constant:
1. Total sales if the profit margin on sales is 10%.
2. Average total assets if the asset turnover is two times.
3. Net income if the earnings per share is $3.50.
4. Rate of return on stockholders' equity, assuming that stockholders' equity increases 10 percent.
5. Asset turnover, assuming that average total assets increase $40,000.

**E26-10** Wingtip Company is a wholesale distributor of professional equipment and supplies. The company's sales have averaged about $900,000 annually for the three-year period 1981–1983. The firm's total assets at the end of 1983 amounted to $850,000.

The president of Wingtip Company has asked the controller to prepare a report that summarizes the financial aspects of the company's operations for the past three years. This report will be presented to the Board of Directors at their next meeting.

In addition to comparative financial statements, the controller has decided to present a number of relevant financial ratios which can assist in the identification and interpretation of trends. At the request of the controller, the accounting staff has calculated the following ratios for the three-year period 1981–1983:

| | 1981 | 1982 | 1983 |
| --- | --- | --- | --- |
| Current ratio | 1.80 | 1.92 | 1.96 |
| Acid-test (quick) ratio | 1.08 | 0.99 | 0.87 |
| Accounts receivable turnover | 8.75 | 7.71 | 6.42 |
| Inventory turnover | 4.73 | 4.32 | 3.42 |
| Percent of total debt to total assets | 48 | 45 | 42 |
| Percent of long-term debt to total assets | 28 | 24 | 21 |
| Sales to fixed assets (fixed asset turnover) | 1.58 | 1.69 | 1.79 |
| Sales as a percent of 1981 sales | 1.00 | 1.03 | 1.05 |
| Gross margin percentage | 36.0 | 34.7 | 34.6 |
| Net income to sales | 7.0% | 7.0% | 7.2% |
| Return on total assets | 7.7% | 7.7% | 7.8% |
| Return on stockholders' equity | 13.6% | 13.1% | 12.7% |

In the preparation of his report, the controller has decided first to examine the financial ratios independently of any other data to determine if the ratios themselves reveal any significant trends over the three-year period.

**Instructions**

(a) The current ratio is increasing while the acid-test (quick) ratio is decreasing. Using the ratios provided, identify and explain the contributing factor(s) for this apparently divergent trend.

(b) In terms of the ratios provided, what conclusion(s) can be drawn regarding the company's use of financial leverage during the 1981–1983 period?

(c) Using the ratios provided, what conclusion(s) can be drawn regarding the company's net investment in plant and equipment? (CMA adapted)

**E26-11** Gerhardt Gears, Inc. began operations in January 1982 and reported the following results for each of its three years of operations:

| | |
|---|---|
| 1982 | $ 320,000 net loss |
| 1983 | $ 40,000 net loss |
| 1984 | $1,200,000 net income |

At December 31, 1984, Gerhardt Gears, Inc. capital accounts were as follows:

| | |
|---|---|
| 12% cumulative preferred stock, par value $100; authorized, issued, and outstanding 10,000 shares | $1,000,000 |
| Common stock, par value $1.00; authorized 2,000,000 shares; issued and outstanding 1,000,000 shares | $1,000,000 |

Gerhardt Gears, Inc. has never paid a cash or stock dividend. There has been no change in the capital accounts since Gerhardt began operations. The appropriate state law permits dividends only from retained earnings.

**Instructions**

(a) Compute the book value of the common stock and preferred stock at December 31, 1984.

(b) Compute the book value of the common stock and preferred stock at December 31, 1984, assuming that the preferred stock has a liquidating value of $106 per share.

## PROBLEMS

**P26-1** Dakota Bros. Corporation's management is concerned over the corporation's current financial position and return on investment. They request your assistance in analyzing their financial statements, and furnish the following statements:

Dakota Bros. Corporation
STATEMENT OF WORKING CAPITAL DEFICIT
December 31, 1984

| | | |
|---|---:|---:|
| Current liabilities | | $224,500 |
| Less current assets: | | |
| Cash | $ 10,000 | |
| Accounts receivable (net) | 75,600 | |
| Inventory | 109,098 | 194,698 |
| Working capital deficit | | $ 29,802 |

Dakota Bros. Corporation
INCOME STATEMENT
For the Year Ended December 31, 1984

| | |
|---|---:|
| Sales (90,500 units) | $778,300 |
| Cost of goods sold | 452,500 |
| Gross profit | 325,800 |
| Selling and administrative expenses, including $24,860 depreciation | 155,660 |
| Income before income taxes | 170,140 |
| Income taxes | 74,000 |
| Net income | $ 96,140 |

Additional information:

Assets other than current assets consist of land, building, and equipment with a book value of $377,000 on December 31, 1984. Assume that ending account balances are representative of amounts existing throughout the year.

**Instructions**

Assuming that Dakota Bros. Corporation operates 300 days per year, compute the following (use 300 days in all computations):

(a) Accounts receivable turnover.

(b) Inventory turnover.

(c) Number of days' operations (working capital provided by operations) to cover the working capital deficit.

(d) Return on total assets as a product of asset turnover and the profit margin on sales (profit margin ratio).

**P26-2** Kentuc Company is listed on the New York Stock Exchange. The market value of its common stock was quoted at $19 per share at December 31, 1984, and 1983. Kentuc's balance sheet at December 31, 1984, and 1983, and statement of income and retained earnings for the years then ended are presented below:

Kentuc Company
BALANCE SHEET

| | December 31, | |
| --- | --- | --- |
| **Assets** | 1984 | 1983 |
| Current assets: | | |
| Cash | $ 3,500,000 | $ 3,600,000 |
| Marketable securities, at cost which approximates market | 13,000,000 | 11,000,000 |
| Accounts receivable, net of allowance for doubtful accounts | 120,000,000 | 95,000,000 |
| Inventories, lower of cost or market | 134,000,000 | 154,000,000 |
| Prepaid expenses | 2,500,000 | 2,400,000 |
| Total current assets | 273,000,000 | 266,000,000 |
| Property, plant, and equipment, net of accumulated depreciation | 311,000,000 | 308,000,000 |
| Investments, at equity | 2,000,000 | 3,000,000 |
| Long-term receivables | 14,000,000 | 16,000,000 |
| Goodwill and patents, net of accumulated amortization | 6,000,000 | 6,500,000 |
| Other assets | 7,000,000 | 8,500,000 |
| Total assets | $613,000,000 | $608,000,000 |
| **Liabilities and Stockholders' Equity** | | |
| Current liabilities: | | |
| Notes payable | $ 5,000,000 | $ 15,000,000 |
| Accounts payable | 38,000,000 | 48,000,000 |
| Accrued expenses | 24,500,000 | 27,000,000 |
| Income taxes payable | 1,000,000 | 1,000,000 |
| Payments due within one year on long-term debt | 6,500,000 | 7,000,000 |
| Total current liabilities | 75,000,000 | 98,000,000 |
| Long-term debt | 169,000,000 | 180,000,000 |
| Deferred income taxes | 74,000,000 | 67,000,000 |
| Other liabilities | 9,000,000 | 8,000,000 |

Stockholders' equity:

| | | |
|---|---|---|
| Common stock, par value $1.00 per share; authorized 20,000,000 shares; issued and outstanding 12,000,000 shares | 12,000,000 | 10,000,000 |
| 10% cumulative preferred stock, par value $100.00 per share; $100.00 liquidating value; authorized 50,000 shares; issued and outstanding 40,000 shares | 4,000,000 | 4,000,000 |
| Additional paid-in capital | 107,000,000 | 107,000,000 |
| Retained earnings | 163,000,000 | 134,000,000 |
| Total stockholders' equity | 286,000,000 | 255,000,000 |
| Total liabilities and stockholders' equity | $613,000,000 | $608,000,000 |

Kentuc Company
STATEMENT OF INCOME AND RETAINED EARNINGS

| | Year ended December 31, | |
|---|---|---|
| | 1984 | 1983 |
| Net sales | $700,000,000 | $500,000,000 |
| Costs and expenses: | | |
| Cost of goods sold | 540,000,000 | 400,000,000 |
| Selling, general, and administrative expenses | 66,000,000 | 60,000,000 |
| Other, net | 7,000,000 | 6,000,000 |
| Total costs and expenses | 613,000,000 | 466,000,000 |
| Income before income taxes | 87,000,000 | 34,000,000 |
| Income taxes | 35,000,000 | 15,600,000 |
| Net income | 52,000,000 | 18,400,000 |
| Retained earnings at beginning of period | 134,000,000 | 126,000,000 |
| Dividends on common stock | 22,600,000 | 10,000,000 |
| Dividends on preferred stock | 400,000 | 400,000 |
| Retained earnings at end of period | $163,000,000 | $134,000,000 |

**Instructions**

On the basis of the information above, compute the following for 1984 only:
(a) Current (working capital) ratio.
(b) Quick (acid-test) ratio.
(c) Number of days' sales in average receivables, assuming a business year consisting of 300 days and all sales on account.
(d) Inventory turnover.
(e) Book value per share of common stock, assuming that there is no dividend arrearage on the preferred stock.
(f) Earnings per share on common stock.
(g) Price-earnings ratio on common stock.
(h) Dividend-payout ratio on common stock.

**P26–3** Warford Corporation was formed five years ago through a public subscription of common stock. Lucinda Street, who owns 15 percent of the common stock, was one of the organizers of Warford and is its current president. The company has been successful, but currently is experiencing a shortage of funds. On June 10, Street approached the Bell National Bank, asking for a 24-month extension on two $30,000 notes, which are due on June 30, 1983 and September 30, 1983. Another note of $7,000 is due on December 31, 1983, but she expects no difficulty in paying this note on its due date. Street explained that Warford's cash flow problems are due primarily to the company's desire to finance a $300,000 plant expansion over the next two fiscal years through internally generated funds.

The Commercial Loan Officer of Bell National Bank requested financial reports for the last two fiscal years. These reports are reproduced below.

Warford Corporation
STATEMENT OF FINANCIAL POSITION
March 31

| Assets | 1982 | 1983 |
|---|---|---|
| Cash | $ 12,500 | $ 16,400 |
| Notes receivable | 104,000 | 112,000 |
| Accounts receivable (net) | 68,500 | 81,600 |
| Inventories (at cost) | 50,000 | 80,000 |
| Plant & equipment (net of depreciation) | 646,000 | 680,000 |
| Total assets | $881,000 | $970,000 |
| **Liabilities and Owners' Equity** | | |
| Accounts payable | $ 72,000 | $ 69,000 |
| Notes payable | 54,500 | 67,000 |
| Accrued liabilities | 6,000 | 9,000 |
| Common stock (60,000 shares, $10 par) | 600,000 | 600,000 |
| Retained earnings[a] | 148,500 | 225,000 |
| Total liabilities and owners' equity | $881,000 | $970,000 |

[a]Cash dividends were paid at the rate of $1.00 per share in fiscal year 1982 and $1.25 per share in fiscal year 1983.

Warford Corporation
INCOME STATEMENT
For the Fiscal Years Ended March 31

| | 1982 | 1983 |
|---|---|---|
| Sales | $2,700,000 | $3,000,000 |
| Cost of goods sold[a] | 1,720,000 | 1,902,500 |
| Gross margin | $ 980,000 | $1,097,500 |
| Operating expenses | 780,000 | 845,000 |
| Income before income taxes | $ 200,000 | $ 252,500 |
| Income taxes (40%) | 80,000 | 101,000 |
| Net income | $ 120,000 | $ 151,500 |

[a]Depreciation charges on the plant and equipment of $100,000 and $102,500 for fiscal years ended March 31, 1982 and 1983, respectively, are included in cost of goods sold.

### Instructions

(a) Compute the following items for Warford Corporation:
1. Current ratio for fiscal years 1982 and 1983.
2. Acid test (quick) ratio for fiscal years 1982 and 1983.

    3. Inventory turnover for fiscal year 1983.

    4. Return on assets for fiscal years 1982 and 1983.

    5. Percentage change in sales, cost of goods sold, gross margin, and net income after taxes from fiscal year 1982 to 1983.

(b) Identify and explain what other financial reports and/or financial analyses might be helpful to the commercial loan officer of Bell National Bank in evaluating Street's request for a time extension on Warford's notes.

(c) Assume that the percentage changes experienced in fiscal year 1983 as compared with fiscal year 1982 for sales, cost of goods sold gross margin, and net income after taxes will be repeated in each of the next two years. Is Warford's desire to finance the plant expansion from internally generated funds realistic? Discuss.

(d) Should Bell National Bank grant the extension on Warford's notes considering Street's statement about financing the plant expansion through internally generated funds? Discuss.

(CIA adapted)

**P26-4** Optima Corporation has in recent years maintained the following relationships among the data on its financial statements:

| | |
|---|---|
| 1. Gross profit rate on net sales | 40% |
| 2. Net profit margin on net sales | 10% |
| 3. Rate of selling expenses to net sales | 20% |
| 4. Accounts receivable turnover | 8 per year |
| 5. Inventory turnover | 6 per year |
| 6. Acid-test ratio | 2 to 1 |
| 7. Current ratio | 3 to 1 |
| 8. Quick asset composition: 8% cash, 32% marketable securities, 60% accounts receivable | |
| 9. Asset turnover | 2 per year |
| 10. Ratio of total assets to intangible assets | 20 to 1 |
| 11. Ratio of accumulated depreciation to cost of fixed assets | 1 to 3 |
| 12. Ratio of accounts receivable to accounts payable | 1.5 to 1 |
| 13. Ratio of working capital to stockholders' equity | 1 to 1.6 |
| 14. Ratio of total debt to stockholders' equity | 1 to 2 |

The corporation had a net income of $240,000 for 1984 which resulted in earnings of $9.38 per share of common stock. Additional information includes the following:

1. Capital stock authorized, issued (all in 1976), and outstanding:
   Common, $10 per share par value, issued at 10% premium
   Preferred, 11% nonparticipating, $100 per share par value, issued at a 10% premium

2. Market value per share of common at December 31, 1984: $112.56

3. Preferred dividends paid in 1984: $5,500

4. Times interest earned in 1984: 17

5. The amounts of the following were the same at December 31, 1984, as at January 1, 1984: inventory, accounts receivable, 10% bonds payable—due 1986, and total stockholders' equity

6. All purchases and sales were "on account."

**Instructions**

(a) Prepare in good form the condensed (1) balance sheet and (2) income statement for the year ending December 31, 1984, presenting the amounts you would expect to appear on Optima's financial statements (ignoring income taxes). Major captions appearing on Optima's balance sheet are: Current Assets, Property, plant, and equipment, Intangible Assets, Current Liabilities, Long-Term Liabilities, and Stockholders' Equity. In addition to the accounts divulged in the problem, you should include accounts for Prepaid Expenses, Accrued Expenses, and Administrative Expenses.

(b) Compute the following for 1984 (show your computations):

1. Rate of return on common stockholders' equity.
2. Price-earnings ratio for common stock.
3. Dividends paid per share of common stock.
4. Dividends paid per share of preferred stock.
5. Dividend yield on common stock. (AICPA adapted)

**P26-5** Heartland Incorporated has been operating successfully for a number of years. The balance sheet of the company as of December 31 is presented below.

Heartland Incorporated
BALANCE SHEET
December 31, 1984

| Assets | | | Equities | | |
|---|---|---|---|---|---|
| Current assets | | | Current liabilities | | |
| Cash | | $ 50,000 | Notes payable | | $ 80,000 |
| Accounts receivable (net) | | 140,000 | Accounts payable | | 77,000 |
| Notes receivable | | 80,000 | Taxes payable | | 61,000 |
| Inventories | | 270,000 | Total current liabilities | | 218,000 |
| Prepaid items | | 20,000 | | | |
| Total current assets | | 560,000 | Long-term bank loan, due in | | |
| Fixed assets | | | 1987, 9% interest | | 140,000 |
| Land | $ 30,000 | | Stockholders' equity | | |
| Building (net) | 165,000 | | Common stock | | |
| Equipment (net) | 330,000 | | ($10 par) | $350,000 | |
| Total fixed assets | | 525,000 | Retained | | |
| | | $1,085,000 | earnings | 377,000 | 727,000 |
| | | | | | $1,085,000 |

This balance sheet indicates that the bulk of the company's growth has been financed by the common stockholders, because more than $377,000 of past net income of the company has been retained and is now invested in various operating assets. For the last three years the company has earned an average net income of $110,000 after interest ($15,000) and taxes ($61,000).

The board of directors has been considering an expansion of operations. Estimations indicate that the company can double its volume of operations with an additional investment of about $800,000. Of this amount $600,000 would be used to add to the present building, to purchase new equipment, and to reorganize certain operations. The remaining amount would be needed for working capital—inventories and higher receivables. Competitive conditions are such that the added volume can probably be sold at the existing prices and that income before taxes and interest will total $350,000. The tax rate of about 36% on income after interest will continue.

Three alternative plans for financing the expansion are under consideration:

1. Sell enough additional stock to raise $800,000. For this purpose it is estimated the stock would sell at $32 per share.

2. Sell 20-year bonds at 12% interest, totaling $620,000. In addition, sell 10,000 shares of additional stock at a price of $32 per share. Use part of the proceeds to pay off the present long-term bank loan.

3. Sell 20-year bonds at 12% interest, totaling $730,000. Use part of the proceeds to pay off present long-term bank loans. The remaining funds are to be provided by short-term creditors. The cost of these funds (in interest and discounts not taken) is estimated at $27,000 a year.

Assume that the financing alternative selected will take place immediately.

**Instructions**

(a) Compute the current ratio under each plan and compare it with the present current ratio.

(b) Compute earnings per share under each plan and compare with the present earnings per share.

(c) Compute the rate of return on common stock equity under each plan and compare with the present return.

(d) Compute the ratio of debt to total equity under each plan and compare it with the present ratio.

**P26-6** The stockholders' equity in Ranchero Manufacturing, Inc. is as follows:

| | | | |
|---|---|---|---|
| Preferred stock—12% cumulative, nonparticipating, $100 par value | | | |
| Authorized 10,000 shares; issued 5,000 shares | $500,000 | | |
| Less 500 shares in treasury | 50,000 | | |
| Outstanding, 4,500 shares | 450,000 | | |
| Common stock, $1.00 par value | | | |
| Authorized 1,000,000 shares; issued 900,000 shares | 900,000 | | |
| Capital in excess of par | 210,000 | $1,560,000 | |
| Capital arising from the acquisition of preferred stock below par value | | 3,000 | |
| Retained earnings | | | |
| Appropriation for contingencies | 46,000 | | |
| Appropriation for sinking fund | 280,000 | | |
| Appropriation for possible inventory decline | 75,000 | | |
| Unrestricted | 516,000 | 917,000 | $2,480,000 |

**Instructions**

Compute the book value per share of the common and preferred stock under each of the following conditions:

(a) As stated above, assume that there are no preferred stock dividends in arrears.

(b) Assume the same situation as stated above except that preferred stock dividends are $108,000 in arrears including the current year.

(c) Assume the same situation as in (a) except that the preferred stock is fully participating, based on the ratio of the total par value of the respective stocks outstanding.

(d) Assume the same situation as in (a) except that, instead of retained earnings, the company has a deficit of $300,000.

**P26-7** Presented below are comparative balance sheets for the Eversonic Company.

Eversonic Company
COMPARATIVE BALANCE SHEET
December 31, 1984 and 1983

| | December 31 | |
|---|---|---|
| Assets | 1984 | 1983 |
| Cash | $ 150,000 | $ 230,000 |
| Accounts receivable (net) | 220,000 | 160,000 |
| Investments | 160,000 | 150,000 |
| Inventories | 860,000 | 930,000 |
| Prepaid expense | 25,000 | 20,000 |
| Fixed assets | 2,400,000 | 1,800,000 |
| Accumulated depreciation | (1,000,000) | (700,000) |
| | $2,815,000 | $2,590,000 |

Liabilities and Stockholders' Equity

| | | |
|---|---:|---:|
| Accounts payable | $    50,000 | $    30,000 |
| Accrued expenses | 150,000 | 200,000 |
| Bonds payable | 300,000 | 200,000 |
| Capital stock | 2,000,000 | 1,770,000 |
| Retained earnings | 315,000 | 390,000 |
| | $2,815,000 | $2,590,000 |

**Instructions**

(a) Prepare a comparative balance sheet of Eversonic Company showing the percent each item is of the total.

(b) Prepare a comparative balance sheet of Eversonic Company showing the dollar change and the percent change for each item.

(c) Of what value is the additional information provided in part (a)?

(d) Of what value is the additional information provided in part (b)?

**P26–8** Compustatic Company is planning to invest $10,000,000 in an expansion program which is expected to increase income before interest and taxes by $2,300,000. The company currently is earning $4 per share on 1,000,000 shares of common stock outstanding. The capital structure prior to the investment is:

| | |
|---|---:|
| Debt | $10,000,000 |
| Equity | 30,000,000 |
| | $40,000,000 |

The expansion can be financed by sale of 250,000 shares at $40 net each, or by issuing long-term debt at a 10% interest cost. The firm's recent income statement was as follows:

| | |
|---|---:|
| Sales | $100,000,000 |
| Variable cost | $ 60,000,000 |
| Fixed cost | 31,000,000 |
| | $ 91,000,000 |
| Income before interest and taxes | $  9,000,000 |
| Interest | 1,000,000 |
| Income before income taxes | $  8,000,000 |
| Income taxes (50%) | 4,000,000 |
| Net income | $  4,000,000 |

**Instructions**

(a) Assuming that the firm maintains its current income and achieves the anticipated income from the expansion, what will be the earnings per share (1) if the expansion is financed by debt? (2) if the expansion is financed by equity?

(b) At what level of income before interest and taxes will the earnings per share under either alternative be the same amount?

(c) The choice of financing alternatives influences the earnings per share. The choice might also influence the earnings multiple used by the "market." Discuss the factors inherent in choice between the debt and equity alternatives that might influence the earnings multiple. Be sure to indicate the direction in which these factors might influence the earnings multiple.

(CMA adapted)

# CHAPTER 27

# Full Disclosure in Financial Reporting

Accountants have long recognized that attempting to present all essential information about an enterprise in a balance sheet, income statement, and statement of changes in financial position is an extremely difficult if not impossible task.

For example, *FASB Concepts No. 1* notes that although financial reporting and financial statements have essentially the same objectives, some useful information is better provided in the financial statements and some is better provided by means of financial reporting other than financial statements. As indicated in Chapter 2, the profession has adopted a full disclosure principle that calls for financial reporting of any financial facts significant enough to influence the judgment of an informed reader. But such a principle can be difficult to put into operation. In some situations the benefits of disclosure may be apparent but the costs uncertain, while in other instances the costs may be certain but the benefits of disclosure not so apparent.

The costs of disclosure cannot be dismissed. For example, *The Wall Street Journal* indicated that if governmental reporting rules in segmented reporting were adopted, a company like Fruehauf would have to increase its accounting staff 50%, from 300 to 450 individuals. Many accountants and managers believe that the present reporting requirements are so substantial that users have a difficult time absorbing the information; they charge the profession with engaging in **information overload.** Conversely, others contend that even more information is needed to assess an enterprise's financial position and earnings potential.

The complexity of this situation is highlighted by such financial disasters as Braniff Airlines, W. T. Grant, Franklin National Bank, and Penn Square Bank. Was the information presented about these companies not comprehensible? Was it buried? Was it too technical? Or was it simply not there? No easy answers are forthcoming. One problem is that the profession is still in the process of developing the guidelines that tell whether a given transaction should be disclosed and what format this disclosure should take. Different users want different information, and it becomes exceedingly difficult to develop disclosure policies that meet their varied objectives.[1]

---

[1]See, for example, Stephen Buzby, "The Nature of Adequate Disclosure," *The Journal of Accountancy* (April 1974) for an interesting discussion of issues related to disclosure.

## INCREASE IN REPORTING REQUIREMENTS

Disclosure requirements have increased substantially in recent years. For example, one survey showed that in a sample of 10 of the largest industrial companies in the United States, the average number of pages of notes to the financial statements increased from 2½ to 8½ pages, and the average number of pages of financial information from 9 to 17 pages over a recent 10-year period. This result is not surprising because as illustrated throughout this textbook, the FASB has issued many standards in the last ten years that have substantial disclosure provisions. The reasons for this increase in disclosure requirements are varied; some of them are listed below.

**Complexity of the Business Environment**  The difficulty of distilling economic events into summarized reports has been magnified by the increasing complexity of business operations in such areas as leasing, business combinations, pensions, financing arrangements, revenue recognition, and deferred taxes. As a result, **footnotes** are used extensively to explain these transactions and their future effects.

**Necessity for Timely Information**  Today, more than ever before, information that is current and predictive is being demanded. For example, more complete **interim data** are required. And published financial forecasts, long avoided and even feared by some accountants, are recommended by the SEC.

**Accounting as a Control and Monitoring Device**  The government has recently sought more information and public disclosure of such phenomena as **management compensation, environmental pollution, related party transactions, errors and irregularities,** and **illegal activities.** A "post-Watergate" concern is expressed in many of these newer disclosure requirements, and accountants and auditors have been selected as the agents to assist in controlling and monitoring these concerns. A trend toward **differential disclosure** also is occurring. For example, the SEC requires that certain substantive information be reported to it that is not found in annual reports to stockholders. And the FASB, recognizing that certain disclosure requirements are costly and unnecessary for certain companies, has eliminated reporting requirements for nonpublic enterprises in such areas as earnings per share and segmental reporting.

In general, the major areas of interest to the profession other than the financial statements include (1) footnotes to the financial statements, and (2) supplementary financial information.

## FOOTNOTES TO THE FINANCIAL STATEMENTS

Footnotes are an integral part of the financial statements of a business enterprise, but they are often overlooked because they are highly technical and often appear in small print. Footnotes are the accountant's means of amplifying or explaining the items presented in the main body of the statements. Information pertinent to specific financial statement items can be explained in qualitative terms, and supplementary data of a quantitative nature can be provided to expand the information in the financial statements. Restrictions imposed by financial arrangements or basic contractual agreements also can be explained in footnotes. It is generally conceded that, although footnotes may be technical and difficult to understand, they provide meaningful information for the user of the financial statements.

## Accounting Policies

Accounting policies of a given entity are the specific accounting principles and methods currently employed and considered most appropriate to present fairly the financial statements of the enterprise. The profession in *APB Opinion No. 22,* "Disclosure of Accounting Policies," concluded that information about the accounting policies adopted and followed by a reporting entity is essential for financial statement users in making economic decisions. It recommended that when financial statements are issued, a statement identifying the accounting policies adopted and followed by the reporting entity should also be presented as an integral part of the financial statements. The disclosure should be given in a separate Summary of Significant Accounting Policies preceding the notes to the financial statements or as the initial note. The Summary of Significant Accounting Principles answers such questions as: What method of depreciation is used on plant assets? What valuation method is employed on inventories? What amortization policy is followed in regard to intangible assets? How is the investment credit handled for plant assets? How are marketing costs handled for financial reporting purposes?

Refer to Appendix D, pages 200–201, Chapter 5 for an illustration of footnote disclosure of accounting policies (Note 1) and other footnotes accompanying the audited financial statements of Tenneco Inc.

Some of the excerpts from Anetek Chemical Corporation's Summary of Accounting Policies are used for illustration purposes. Following the quoted footnote is an analysis of the information provided by the footnote.

---

*Principles of Consolidation*—The financial statements include all significant subsidiaries on a full consolidation basis. During 1984, several minor acquisitions were consummated. One acquisition was accounted for as a pooling of interests; the others were accounted for as purchases. The effect of these acquisitions on the results of operations was not material.

---

**Analysis**    This footnote discloses that the company acquired several other businesses during the year. Because the acquisitions are acknowledged not to be material, it is not important that the differing effects of the "purchase" and "pooling of interests" method be understood. When the mergers or acquisitions during the period are material, the difference between "purchase" accounting and "pooling of interests" accounting could have significant effects on the balance sheet and income statement. The general subject of accounting for combinations is covered in advanced accounting. From this footnote the reader can determine that a part of the company's growth is attributable to external growth through business combinations as opposed to internal growth.

---

*Goodwill*—The excess of the cost of investments in consolidated subsidiaries over their net assets at dates of acquisition is carried as goodwill. All goodwill is amortized over a five-year period on a straight-line basis.

**Analysis**   Anetek is apparently taking a fairly conservative policy regarding amortization of goodwill. Comparison of this amortization policy with that of other chemical companies might provide some interesting insights into the accounting philosophy and policies employed by Anetek. Is the income of a company that amortizes goodwill over a 40-year period comparable with the income of a company that amortizes goodwill over a 5-year period?

## Disclosure of Gain or Loss Contingencies

In some cases, enterprises have either gain or loss contingencies that are not disclosed in the body of the financial statements. As indicated in earlier chapters, these contingencies may take a variety of forms such as pending lawsuits, either favorable or unfavorable, a contingent liability on an accommodation endorsement, and possible renegotiation refunds on government contracts. A footnote from Anetek's balance sheet is presented below:

---

*Loss Contingencies*—In February 1981, when the United States Resources Commission reported finding mercury residues in fish, Anetek Chemical launched a "crash" program to make sure of emission control related to mercury emission. Several damage suits related to mercury have been lodged against Anetek. Anetek Chemical feels they are not legally liable and, therefore, is contesting these suits.

Other suits have been started against the company and certain subsidiaries because of alleged product damage and other claims. All suits are being contested and the amount of uninsured liability thereunder, if any, is considered to be immaterial.

---

**Analysis**   The nature of various suits in relation to ecological matters is explained to the investor. The opinion of the company regarding possible damages is also considered. In addition, other litigative matters at this time do not seem to be material and do not have a substantially adverse effect on Anetek's financial position. The investor should read this section carefully, reading even between the lines, to measure the potential impact of contingencies.

## Examination of Credit Claims

An investor normally finds it extremely useful to determine the nature and cost of creditorship claims. The liability section in the balance sheet can provide the major types of liabilities outstanding only in the aggregate. Footnote schedules regarding such obligations provide additional information about how the company is financing its operations, the costs that will have to be borne in future periods, and the timing of future cash outflows as shown on page 1248.

**Analysis**   The footnote discloses the composition and details of the outstanding long-term debt. For example, the company has promissory notes, debentures, convertible debentures, and other notes payable, ranging in cost from 6% to 16%. In addition, the amount of debt to be retired in installments is disclosed. The interest rates represent a fixed annual cost. The maturity dates indicate when large cash outlays will have to be made or refinancing will have to take place.

## LONG-TERM DEBT & AVAILABLE CREDIT FACILITIES

**(a) Details of long-term debt:**

| | (000 omitted) December 31, | |
| --- | --- | --- |
| | 1984 | 1983 |
| Promissory notes | | |
| 13%, final maturity 1998 | $ 50,000 | $ 85,000 |
| 16%, final maturity 1999 | 45,000 | 150,000 |
| Debentures | | |
| 9.35%, final maturity 1996 | 50,000 | 60,000 |
| 11.70%, final maturity 2006 | 100,000 | 100,000 |
| 12.75%, final maturity 2007 | 100,000 | 100,000 |
| 13.875%, final maturity 2008 | 100,000 | |
| 13.90%, final maturity 2008 | 100,000 | |
| Debentures, subordinate convertible, 6% due 1993 | | |
| (1984—22,184 common shares reserved) | 5,000 | 5,000 |
| Notes payable under revolving credit agreements | | |
| Due 1987 (total available facility $225,000,000) | 50,000 | 50,000 |
| Due 1989 (total available facility $110,000,000) | 50,000 | 50,000 |
| Other (various rates and maturities): | | |
| Foreign currency loans | 50,000 | 35,000 |
| Dollar loans | 25,000 | 15,000 |
| Total | $725,000 | $650,000 |

The promissory notes and debentures are payable generally in annual installments beginning at various dates.

Agreements relating to the issuance of the 13.875% and 13.90% debentures provide for delivery of $8,000,000 and $18,000,000 principal amounts, respectively, subsequent to December 31, 1984. The debentures are recorded as debt when proceeds are received.

Installments (stated in millions) due on long-term debt in the five years after 1984 are: 1985, $62.0; 1986, $31.6; 1987, $46.2; 1988, $39.5; 1989, $83.6.

**(b) Available credit at year end:**

In addition to the revolving credit agreements referenced above, the company had a 1.0 billion Deutsche mark agreement with a group of major German banks exercisable through 1989. Of the German credit facility, 30.0 million Deutsche marks were in use at December 31, 1984.

## Claims of Equity Holders

Many companies present in the body of the balance sheet the number of shares authorized, issued, and outstanding and the par value for each type of equity security. Such data may also be presented in a footnote. Beyond that, the most common type of equity footnote disclosure relates to contracts and senior securities outstanding that might affect the various claims of the residual equity holders: for example, the existence of outstanding stock options, outstanding convertible debt, and convertible preferred stock. In addition, it is necessary to disclose to equity claimants certain types of restrictions currently in force. Generally, these types of restrictions involve the amount of earnings available for dividend distribution. The footnote on page 1249 illustrates the type of data often presented for stockholders' equity.

### Stockholders' Equity

At December 31, 1984 authorized capital stock consisted of 100,000,000 common shares and 25,000,000 preferred shares of $5 par and $1 par per share, respectively.

The changes in the number and amount of issued shares of common stock during 1984 were:

|  | Shares | Amount |
|---|---|---|
| Issued January 1 | 29,812,750 | $157,152,870 |
| Sold to employees | 166,583 | 832,915 |
| Awarded as restricted stock | 18,705 | 93,525 |
| Conversion of debentures | 1,962 | 9,810 |
| Issued December 31 | 30,000,000 | $158,089,120 |

At December 31, 1984, there were 30,000,000 shares of common stock outstanding. None of the preferred shares have been issued.

In May 1984, the company made an offering of common stock to its employees at $57.75 a share, payable generally through payroll deductions. At December 31, 1984, there were unfilled subscriptions for 151,541 shares which may be cancelled at the option of the employee. Partial payments on these subscriptions aggregating $4,814,000 are included in current liabilities.

The stockholders authorized in 1983 an Award Plan providing for the granting, during the ensuing 10-year period, of 350,000 shares of Restricted or Deferred Stock, or a combination thereof, to selected employees in lieu of cash for services. During 1984, 18,705 shares of Restricted Stock were issued and 745 shares of Deferred Stock were awarded. At December 31, 1984, there were 312,635 shares available for grant. The Plan also extended to May 1990 the previous authority for granting dividend units.

The stockholders previously authorized plans for granting options to purchase common stock at the fair market value at the date of grant to officers and key employees. The options must be exercised within five years from the date of issuance. Changes during 1984 in the number of shares under option were:

|  | 1984 Option Plan | 1984 Incentive Plan | Dividend Units[a] |
|---|---|---|---|
| Options: |  |  |  |
|   Outstanding January 1 | 300,247 | 82,350 | 61,420 |
|   Granted | 30,000 |  |  |
|   Expired or terminated | 1,500 | 15,600 |  |
|   Outstanding December 31 | 328,747 | 66,750 | 61,420 |
| Not optional: |  |  |  |
|   December 31 | 71,253 |  | 188,580 |
| Price range on |  |  |  |
|   Outstanding options | $61.44 to | $60.00 to |  |
|     at December 31 | 87.99 | 76.25 |  |

[a] A dividend unit is the right to receive for a specified period cash payments equivalent in value to cash dividends paid during such period on one share of common stock.

In computing earnings per share, no adjustment was made for common shares issuable under stock purchase and option plans or upon conversion of 6% debentures because there would be no material dilutive effect.

**Analysis**    This footnote provides information about (1) the capital changes during the year and (2) the compensation plans related to employees, officers, and key executives. This footnote indicates the magnitude of the changes that occurred in the equity section during the year and also the potential changes that may develop from existing contractual arrangements. For example, the number of shares outstanding during the year changed very little, even though some shares were sold to employees and some conversion of debentures occurred. In addition, at present the dilutive effect of existing contractual arrangements outstanding in the form of convertible debenture bonds and stock options is not material (less than 3%).

## Executory Commitments

An enterprise often becomes involved in several executory contracts. When two parties commit themselves to some undertaking on the basis of a signed contract but neither party has yet performed, the contract is executory. Examples in accounting are pension agreements, lease arrangements, and purchase commitments. Most companies do not recognize these items in the accounts, although many accountants believe that these items should be recorded, notwithstanding the difficult valuation problems. Everyone agrees that some type of disclosure is necessary because these commitments will affect the cash flow of the enterprise in the future. An example of Anetek's commitments is as follows:

---

*Retirement Plans and Other Commitments*—The company and certain subsidiaries have plans to provide retirement benefits for eligible employees. The company's plan was amended effective January 1, 1984 to extend coverage to substantially all full-time employees and to provide additional benefits. The cost of the plan was $14,398,000 in 1984 and $13,634,000 in 1983. The company's policy is to accrue and fund pension cost as computed by its actuary.

A comparison of accumulated plan benefits and plan net assets for the company's U.S. defined benefit plans is presented below:

| January 1 | 1984 | 1983 |
|---|---|---|
| (In thousands) | | |
| Actuarial present value of accumulated plan benefits: | | |
| Vested | $169,838 | $149,606 |
| Nonvested | 20,638 | 18,860 |
| Total | $190,476 | $168,466 |
| Net assets available for benefits | $196,274 | $168,587 |

The weighted average assumed rate of return used in determining the actuarial present value of accumulated plan benefits was 6.5% for both 1984 and 1983. For the company's pension plans outside the United States the actuarially computed value of vested benefits as of January 1, 1984 and 1983 approximated the total of those plans' pension funds and balance sheet accruals.

The total cost of pension plans for all companies in the consolidated group in 1984 and 1983 was $17,177,000 and $14,987,000 respectively.

At December 31, 1984, the company and its subsidiaries were lessees under various lease agreements. While the majority of these leases will expire during the next eight years, it is expected that they will be renewed or replaced by leases on other properties and facilities. The rental payments (stated in millions) due in cash five years after 1984 are: 1985, $36.3; 1986, $31.9; 1987, $30.5; 1988, $28.1; 1989, $25.9.

---

**Analysis**  Examination indicates that the company is computing pension expense on an actuarial basis instead of on a pay-as-you-go basis. In addition, the fact that pension assets exceed the computed value of vested and nonvested benefits suggests that pension obligations may not be a problem at this point. In addition, it should be noted that the company uses a conservative rate of interest which indicates that the pension plan is relatively stable (given the other factors mentioned earlier).

The company also discloses in this footnote that certain fixed assets have been leased and sets out the payment amounts and due dates over the next five years. This information is valuable to a credit grantor, because a lease is similar to a liability in that the future payments on a lease represent future obligations.

## Disclosure of Special Transactions or Events

Related party transactions, errors and irregularities, and illegal acts pose especially sensitive and difficult problems for the accountant. The accountant/auditor who has responsibility for reporting on these types of transactions has to be extremely careful that the rights of the reporting company and the needs of users of the financial statements are properly balanced.

**Related party transactions** arise when a business enterprise engages in transactions in which one of the transacting parties has the ability to influence significantly the policies of the other, or in which a nontransacting party has the ability to influence the policies of the two transacting parties.[2]

Transactions involving related parties cannot be presumed to be carried out on an arm's-length basis because the requisite conditions of competitive, free-market dealings may not exist. Transactions such as borrowing or lending money at abnormally low or high interest rates, real estate sales at amounts that differ significantly from appraised value, exchanges of nonmonetary assets, and transactions involving enterprises that have no economic substance ("shell corporations") suggest that related parties may be involved. The accountant is expected to report the economic substance rather than the legal form of these transactions and to make adequate disclosures. *FASB Statement No. 57* requires the following disclosures of material related party transactions:

(a)  The nature of the relationship(s) involved.

(b)  A description of the transactions (including transactions to which no amounts or nominal amounts were ascribed) for each of the periods for which income statements are presented.

(c)  The dollar amounts of transactions for each of the periods for which income statements are presented.

(d)  Amounts due from or to related parties as of the date of each balance sheet presented.

An example of the disclosure of related party transactions is taken from the 1981 Annual Report of Chart House Inc. (see top of page 1252).

---

[2]Examples of related party transactions include transactions between (a) a parent company and its subsidiaries; (b) subsidiaries of a common parent; (c) an enterprise and trusts for the benefit of employees (controlled or managed by the enterprise); (d) an enterprise and its principal owners, management, or members of immediate families; and affiliates.

---

**Chart House Inc.**

(7) *Related Party Transactions*—The Company provides computer services to the First National Bank of Lafayette, of which William E. Trotter, II, Chairman of the Board, and Braxton I. Moody, III, Vice Chairman of the Board, are substantial shareholders. During 1981, 1980, and 1979, respectively, the Company received $553,000 and $446,000, and $310,000 for computer services rendered to the First National Bank of Lafayette.

The Company has various leases for office space with an entity owned by Messrs. Moody and Trotter for terms of up to five years (renewable through 1995) requiring rental payments of approximately $298,000 per year.

In May, 1981, the Company purchased four restaurants for $1,550,000 from Universal Restaurants, Inc., a company of which a director of Chart House Inc. was a principal shareholder, director, and officer.

---

**Errors** are defined as unintentional mistakes, whereas **irregularities** are intentional distortions of financial statements.[3] As indicated in earlier sections of this textbook, when errors are discovered, the financial statements should be corrected. The same treatment should be given irregularities. The discovery of irregularities, however, gives rise to a whole different set of suspicions, procedures, and responsibilities on the part of the accountant/ auditor.

**Illegal acts** encompass such items as illegal political contributions, bribes, kickbacks, and other violations of laws and regulations.[4] In these situations, the accountant/auditor must evaluate the adequacy of disclosure in the financial statements. For example, if revenue is derived from an illegal act that is considered material in relation to the financial statements, this information should be disclosed. Passage of the Foreign Corrupt Practices Act of 1977 has had a significant impact upon the accounting profession, and its implications are not yet completely clear.

Many companies are involved in related party transactions; errors and irregularities, and illegal acts, however, are the exception rather than the rule. Disclosure plays a very important role in these areas because the transaction or event is more qualitative than quantitative and involves more subjective than objective evaluation. The users of the financial statements, however, must be provided with some indication of the existence and nature of these transactions where material. These items are generally revealed through disclosures, modifications in the auditor's report, or in reports of changes in auditors.

## Reporting for Diversified (Conglomerate) Companies

In the last two decades business enterprises have evidenced an increasing tendency to diversify their operations. As a result, investors and investment analysts have sought more information concerning the details behind conglomerate financial statements. Particularly, they are requesting revenue and income information on the **individual** segments that comprise the **total** business income figure. In addition, some attention has also been given to the segmentation of the balance sheet and statement of changes in financial position for the various divisions or subsidiaries comprising the consolidated group.

---

[3]"The Independent Auditor's Responsibility for the Detection of Errors and Irregularities," *Codification of Statements on Auditing Standards* (New York: AICPA, 1979), pp. 117–124.

[4]"Illegal Acts of Clients," *Statement on Auditing Standards No. 17* (New York: AICPA, 1977).

An illustration of segmentation is presented in the following example of an office equipment and auto parts company.

| | Consolidated | Office Equipment | Auto Parts |
|---|---|---|---|
| **Office Equipment and Auto Parts Company** | | | |
| **INCOME STATEMENT DATA** | | | |
| **(in millions)** | | | |
| Net sales | $78.8 | $18.0 | $60.8 |
| Manufacturing costs: | | | |
| Inventories, beginning | 12.3 | 4.0 | 8.3 |
| Materials and services | 38.9 | 10.8 | 28.1 |
| Wages | 12.9 | 3.8 | 9.1 |
| Inventories, ending | (13.3) | (3.9) | (9.4) |
| | 50.8 | 14.7 | 36.1 |
| Selling and administrative expense | 12.1 | 1.6 | 10.5 |
| Total operating expenses | 62.9 | 16.3 | 46.6 |
| Income before taxes | 15.9 | 1.7 | 14.2 |
| Income taxes | (9.3) | (1.0) | (8.3) |
| Net income | $ 6.6 | $ .7 | $ 5.9 |

If only the consolidated figures are available to the analyst, much information regarding the composition of these figures is hidden in aggregated figures. There is no way to tell from the consolidated data the extent to which the differing product lines **contribute to the company's profitability, risk, and growth potential.**[5] For example, in the illustration above, if the office equipment segment is deemed a risky venture, the segmentation provides useful information for purposes of making an informed investment decision.

Companies have been somewhat hesitant to disclose segmented data for the reasons listed below.

1. Without a thorough knowledge of the business and an understanding of such important factors as the competitive environment and capital investment requirements, the investor may find the segment information meaningless or even draw improper conclusions about the reported earnings of the segments.

2. Additional disclosure may harm reporting firms because it may be helpful to competitors, labor unions, suppliers, and certain government regulatory agencies.

3. Additional disclosure may discourage management from taking intelligent business risks because segments reporting losses or unsatisfactory earnings may cause stockholder dissatisfaction with management.

4. The wide variation among firms in the choice of segments, cost allocation, and other accounting problems limits the usefulness of segment information.

[5]One writer has shown that data provided on a segmental basis allows an analyst to predict future total sales and earnings better than data presented on a nonsegmental basis. See D. W. Collins, "Predicting Earnings with Sub-Entity Data: Some Further Evidence," *Journal of Accounting Research* (Spring 1976).

5. The investor is investing in the company as a whole and not in the particular segments, and it should not matter how any single segment is performing if the overall performance is satisfactory.

6. Certain technical problems, such as classification of segments and allocation of segment revenues and cost (especially "common costs"), are formidable.

On the other hand, the advocates of segmented disclosures offer these reasons:

1. Segment information is needed by the investor to make an intelligent investment decision regarding a diversified company.

   (a) Sales and earnings of individual segments are needed to forecast consolidated profits because of the differences between segments in growth rate, risk, and profitability.

   (b) Segment reports disclose the nature of a company's businesses and the relative size of the components as an aid in evaluating the company's investment worth.

2. The absence of segmented reporting by a diversified company may put its unsegmented, single product-line competitors at a competitive disadvantage because the conglomerate may obscure information that its competitors must disclose.

Since the issuance of *FASB Statement No. 14* however, enterprises that issue a complete set of financial statements have been required to disclose as part of those statements certain information relating to: the enterprise's operations in different industries, its foreign operations, its export sales, and its major customers.[6] The basic requirements of the statement are as follows:

1. Information required to be reported is to be prepared on the same accounting basis and by the same accounting principles used in the enterprise's consolidated financial statements.

2. A number of methods might be used to identify industry segments such as the Standard Industrial Classification manual, currently existing profit centers, or relating common risk factors to products or product groups. The Board concluded that none of these methods by itself is suitable and that management should exercise its judgment in determining industry segments. Industry segments should be determined on a worldwide basis where practicable.

3. Each industry segment that is significant to the enterprise as a whole must report certain information. It is significant if it satisfies **one or more** of the following tests in each period for which financial statements are presented:

   (a) Its revenues are 10% or more of the combined revenues of all industry segments.

   (b) Its operating profit or loss is 10% or more of the **greater,** in absolute amount, of either:

       (i) the combined operating profit of all industry segments that did not incur a loss; or

       (ii) the combined operating loss of all industry segments that did incur a loss; or

---

[6]"Financial Reporting for Segments of a Business Enterprise," *Statement of Financial Accounting Standards No. 14* (Stamford, Conn.: FASB, 1976), par. 3. A number of pronouncements have been issued since 1976 that modify certain disclosure requirements. "Financial Reporting for Segments of a Business Enterprise—Interim Financial Statements," *Statement of Financial Accounting Standards No. 18* (Stamford, Conn.: FASB, 1977) indicates that segment information need not be presented in interim reports. "Suspension of the Reporting of Earnings per Share and Segment Information by Nonpublic Enterprises," *Statement of Financial Accounting Standards No. 21* (Stamford, Conn.: FASB, 1978) states that a nonpublic company is not required to disclose segmental data. "Reporting Segment Information in Financial Statements that are Presented in Another Enterprise's Financial Report," *Statement of Financial Accounting Standards No. 24* (Stamford, Conn.: FASB, 1978) eliminates the requirement for the disclosure of segmental data in the separate financial statements of a parent company or affiliate that also presents consolidated or combined financial statements. "Disclosure of Information About Major Customers," *Statement of Financial Accounting Standards No. 30* (Stamford, Conn.: FASB, 1979) requires that the amount of sales to an individual domestic government or foreign government be disclosed when those revenues are 10 percent or more of the enterprise's revenues.

(c) Its identifiable assets are 10% or more of the combined identifiable assets of all industry segments.

**4.** The statement requires that the following information be presented for each reportable segment and in the aggregate for the remaining industry segments:

**Revenues**—Sales to unaffiliated customers and to other industry segments are to be separately disclosed. The basis of accounting for intersegment sales or transfers must be described and consistently applied.

**Profitability**—Operating profit or loss must be disclosed for each reportable segment. To the extent that an unusual amount of income or expense or an unusual or infrequently occurring item *(APB Opinion No. 30)* is included in the industry segment profitability, the nature and amount shall be explained. Disclosure of changes in accounting principles *(APB Opinion No. 20)* should be explained and attributed to the reportable segment.

**Identifiable Assets**—Identifiable assets of an industry segment must be disclosed for each reportable segment. Disclosure of additional information on certain assets may be desirable for some reportable segments.

Such information may be included within the body of the financial statements, in the notes to the financial statements, or in a separate schedule included as an integral part of the financial statements. At a minimum, revenues and operating profit or loss must be reconciled to corresponding amounts in the consolidated statement of operations and identifiable assets reconciled to consolidated total assets.

The trend is toward greater segmented financial disclosure when an enterprise consists of two or more segments in distinctly different lines of business or otherwise clearly subject to different trends and risks. Certain accounting problems do exist, however, which still have not been resolved completely.

**Definition of a Segment**    The first major problem in accounting for a diversified enterprise is to define the reporting basis. For example, **should the company provide information on a legal-entity basis, a geographical basis, an organizational-units basis, type-of-customer basis, or an industry-grouping basis?** Each of these approaches has certain benefits, yet all of them have disadvantages as well.

For example, setting the divisions up on the basis of legal entities has the advantage of providing a fairly clean and defined set of entities. Often these entities are set up merely to hold properties, meet certain governmental regulations, or provide tax shelters, however. In these situations, the corporation operates the businesses on a much different basis and uses the legal entities only for questions of form rather than substance.

A second possible alternative is in terms of geographical distribution. This approach has some validity, particularly in comparing national and international business but, in general, it appears that more appropriate bases might be selected. A very similar approach is by type of customer, normally government versus nongovernment. Again, such information is valuable in certain circumstances, but its application appears to be relatively restricted to a small number of companies.

A general view that seems to prevail among accountants is that the enterprise should be free to select the breakdown that best represents the underlying activities of the business. An organizational unit approach probably reflects this point of view, because enterprises normally devise some way of relating responsibilities to various segments of the business. The problem with using this procedure is that the organizational unit is continually changing as operations are expanded or contracted. A problem of comparability between periods can develop.

In addition to the problem of determining the basis for identifying the segments, there is the question of what percentage to use. As indicated earlier, a 10% factor is applied to one of the following items: revenue, income or loss, or identifiable assets. But these criteria are still subject to interpretation. For example, at one time Weyerhaeuser Co. indicated that except for certain real estate ventures, everything else related to paper production, so no additional disclosure was necessary. Other timber companies have broken down their segments into such categories as pulp and paper, packaging products, and wood products and have provided operating data. In general, however, the disclosure requirements associated with *FASB Statement No. 14* appear quite reasonable and the flexibility afforded management seems desirable. Management is in the best position to judge which is the most meaningful breakdown of its divisional data, and with experimentation useful information should be forthcoming.

**Allocation of Common Costs**   One of the critical problems in providing segmented income statements for conglomerate companies is the allocation of common costs. Common costs are those incurred for the benefit of more than one segment and whose interrelated nature prevents a completely objective division of costs among segments. For example, the president's salary is very difficult to allocate to various segments. The significance of common costs is indicated by a Financial Executive Research Foundation survey that shows that the average ratio of common costs to net sales is greater than that of net income to net sales.

Many different bases for allocation have been suggested, such as sales, gross profit, assets employed, investment, and marginal income. The choice of basis is important because it can materially influence the relative profitability of the segments.

The use of a **defined profit** concept has been suggested. Defined profit is the excess of segment revenues over directly chargeable segment expense. Common costs in this framework are charged against total company defined profits but not against any individual segments. This approach is not used at present and it is unlikely that this concept will be implemented because no final earnings figures ever occur for separate divisions.

**Transfer Pricing Problems**   Transfer pricing is the practice of charging a price for goods "sold" between divisions or subsidiaries of a company, commonly called intracompany transfers. A transfer price system is used for several reasons, but the primary objective is to measure the performance and profitability of a given segment of the business in relation to other segments. In addition, a pricing system is needed to insure control over the flow of goods through the enterprise.

Transfer pricing is not a problem of the same magnitude as common costs, but it still is very significant in many business enterprises. At present, different approaches to transfer pricing are used. Some firms transfer the goods at market prices; others use cost plus a fixed fee; and some use variable cost. In some situations, the company lets the division bargain for the price of the item in question.

In evaluating a specific division, we must consider the transfer pricing problem. If, for example, Division A sells certain goods to Division B using a market price instead of cost, the operating results of both divisions are affected. Transfer pricing in many situations does not occur on an arm's-length basis and, therefore, the final results of a given division must be suspect. In practice, there are at present no defined guides in regard to a company's disclosure of its method of transfer pricing for external reporting purposes.

## ILLUSTRATION OF SEGMENTED REPORTING

Although many problems exist with segmented reporting, the information provided by revenue and profit breakdowns is considered useful by most investors. A sample schedule taken from Crown Zellerbach's corporate report shows the different product-line breakdowns disclosed.

| | Timber and Wood Products | Pulp and Paper | Containers and Packaging | Distribution | Energy | Eliminations and Other | Total |
|---|---|---|---|---|---|---|---|
| **Crown Zellerbach** 1980 (In millions of dollars) | | | | | | | |
| **Sales and transfers** | | | | | | | |
| To unaffiliated customers | $522.7 | $1,047.8 | $522.8 | $950.0 | $23.3 | $ — | $3,066.6 |
| To other segments | 77.1 | 191.1 | 38.7 | 3.9 | — | (310.8) | — |
| | $599.8 | $1,238.9 | $561.5 | $953.9 | $23.3 | $(310.8) | $3,066.6 |
| Operating earnings | $ 39.4 | $ 104.8 | $ (6.3) | $ 30.6 | $17.8 | $ (81.6) | $ 104.7 |
| Assets | $557.2 | $ 927.0 | $461.0 | $235.4 | $15.0 | $ 177.1 | $2,372.7 |
| Depreciation, amortization, depletion, and cost of timber harvested | $ 45.8 | $ 42.0 | $ 20.8 | $ 3.0 | $ 1.2 | $ 3.3 | $ 116.1 |
| Capital expenditures | $ 57.3 | $ 127.0 | $ 78.1 | $ 8.8 | $ 3.2 | $ 7.2 | $ 281.6 |

## Interim Reports

One further source of information for the investor is interim reports, which are reports that cover periods of less than one year. At one time, interim reports were referred to as the forgotten reports; such is no longer the case. The stock exchanges, the SEC, and the accounting profession have taken an active role in developing guidelines for the presentation of interim information. The SEC mandates that certain companies file a Form 10Q, which requires a company to disclose quarterly data similar to that disclosed in the annual report. It also requires those companies to disclose selected quarterly information in notes to the annual financial statements.[7] A recent annual report of Pitney Bowes illustrates the disclosure of selected quarterly data (in millions of dollars except for per-share amounts), see presentation at the top of page 1258.

In addition to this requirement, the APB issued *Opinion No. 28,* which attempted to narrow the reporting alternatives related to interim reports.[8]

Because of the short-term nature of these reports, however, there is considerable controversy as to the general approach that should be employed. One group (**discrete view**) believes that each interim period should be treated as a separate accounting period; deferrals and accruals would therefore follow the principles employed for annual reports. Accounting transactions should be reported as they occur, and expense recognition should not change

---

[7]"Disclosure of Interim Results for Registrants," *ASR No. 177* (Washington: SEC, 1975).

[8]"Interim Financial Reporting," *Opinions of the Accounting Principles Board No. 28* (New York: AICPA, 1973).

| Pitney Bowes, Inc. | | | | |
|---|---|---|---|---|
| | | Three months ended | | |
| 1981 | March 31 | June 30 | Sept. 30 | Dec. 31 |
| Sales and rentals | $279.0 | $306.7 | $295.3 | $348.1 |
| Service | 43.3 | 46.0 | 47.1 | 48.9 |
| Total revenue | $322.3 | $352.7 | $342.4 | $397.0 |
| Cost of sales and rentals | $127.6 | $139.2 | $135.5 | $152.7 |
| Net income | $ 10.9 | $ 17.1 | $ 14.7 | $ 26.8 |
| Net income per common and common equivalent share | $ .61 | $ .95 | $ .79 | $ 1.40 |

with the period of time covered. Conversely, another group (**integral view**) believes that the interim report is an integral part of the annual report and that deferrals and accruals should take into consideration what will happen for the entire year. In this approach, estimated expenses are assigned to parts of a year on the basis of sales volume or some other activity base. At present, many companies follow the discrete approach for certain types of expenses and the integral approach for others because the standards currently employed in practice are vague and lead to differing interpretations.

## Interim Reporting Requirements

*APB Opinion No. 28* indicates that the same acounting principles used for annual reports should be employed for interim reports. Revenues should be recognized in interim periods on the same basis as they are for annual periods. For example, if the installment sales method is used as the basis for recognizing revenue on an annual basis, then the installment basis should also be applied to interim reports as well. Also, cost directly associated with revenues (product costs), such as materials, labor and related fringe benefits, and manufacturing overhead should be treated in the same manner for interim reports as for annual reports.

Companies generally should use the same inventory pricing methods (FIFO, LIFO, etc.) for interim reports that they use for annual reports. However, the following exceptions are appropriate at interim reporting periods:

1. Companies may use the gross profit method for interim inventory pricing, but disclosure of the method and adjustments to reconcile with annual inventory are necessary.
2. When LIFO inventories are liquidated at an interim date and expected to be replaced by year end, cost of goods sold should include the expected cost of replacing the liquidated LIFO base and not give effect to the interim liquidation.
3. Inventory market declines should not be deferred beyond the interim period unless they are temporary and no loss is expected for the fiscal year.
4. Planned variances under a standard cost system which are expected to be absorbed by year end ordinarily should be deferred.

Costs and expenses other than product costs, often referred to as *period costs,* are often charged to the interim period as incurred, but may be allocated among interim periods on the basis of an estimate of time expired, benefit received, or activity associated with the periods. Considerable latitude is exercised in accounting for these costs in interim periods, and many believe more definitive guidelines are needed.

Regarding disclosure, the following interim data should be reported as a minimum:

1. Sales or gross revenues, provision for income taxes, extraordinary items, cumulative effect of a change in accounting principles or practices, and net income.
2. Primary and fully diluted earnings per share where appropriate.
3. Seasonal revenue, cost, or expenses.
4. Significant changes in estimates or provisions for income taxes.
5. Disposal of a segment of a business and extraordinary, unusual, or infrequently occurring items.
6. Contingent items.
7. Changes in accounting principles or estimates.
8. Significant changes in financial position.

The profession also encourages but does not require companies to publish a balance sheet and a statement of changes in financial position. When this information is not presented, significant changes in such items as liquid assets, net working capital, long-term liabilities, and stockholders' equity should be disclosed. To illustrate the type of summarized disclosure presented, the interim report for Emerson Electric Co. for the second quarter and first six months of 1982 are presented on page 1260.

## Unique Problems of Interim Reporting

In *APB Opinion No. 28,* the Board indicated that it favored the integral approach. However, within this broad guideline, a number of unique reporting problems develop related to the following items.

**Advertising and Similar Costs**   The general guidelines are that costs such as advertising should be deferred in an interim period if the benefits extend beyond that period; otherwise they should be expensed as incurred. But such a determination is difficult, and even if they are deferred, how should they be allocated between quarters? Because of the vague guidelines in this area, accounting for advertising varies widely. Some companies in the food industry, such as Nabisco and Pillsbury, charge advertising costs as a percentage of sales and adjust to actual at year end, whereas General Foods and Kellogg's expense these costs as incurred.

The same type of problem relates to such items as social security taxes, research and development costs, and major repairs. For example, should the company expense social security costs (payroll taxes) on the highly paid personnel early in the year or allocate and spread them to subsequent quarters? Should a major repair that occurs later in the year be anticipated and allocated proportionately to earlier periods?

**Expenses Subject to Year-End Adjustment**   Allowance for bad debts, executive bonuses, pension costs, and inventory shrinkage are often not known with a great deal of certainty until year end. **These costs should be estimated and allocated in the best possible way to interim periods.** It should be emphasized that companies use a variety of allocation techniques to accomplish this objective.

**Income Taxes**   Not every dollar of corporate taxable income is assessed at the same tax rate. For example, in 1983 the following corporate tax rate structure was applicable:

| Taxable Income | Tax Rate |
|---|---|
| $0—$25,000 | 15% |
| $25,000—$50,000 | 18% |
| $50,000—$75,000 | 30% |
| $75,000—$100,000 | 40% |
| Over $100,000 | 46% |

# Emerson Electric Co.

## Condensed Consolidated Operating Results
(Thousands of dollars except per share data; **unaudited**)

Report on Results for
Second Quarter and
First Six Months of
Fiscal 1982

| | Three Months Ended March 31, | | 1982 Over 1981 |
|---|---|---|---|
| | **1982** | 1981 | |
| Net sales | **$ 919,863** | $ 911,093 | 1.0% |
| Earnings before income taxes | **$ 139,586** | $ 132,057 | 5.7% |
| Income taxes | **$ 61,227** | $ 58,379 | 4.9% |
| Net earnings | **$ 78,359** | $ 73,678 | 6.4% |
| Earnings per common share | **$ 1.14** | $ 1.07 | 6.5% |

| | Six Months Ended March 31, | | |
|---|---|---|---|
| | **1982** | 1981 | |
| Net sales | **$1,761,815** | $1,707,710 | 3.2% |
| Earnings before income taxes | **$ 267,308** | $ 250,132 | 6.9% |
| Income taxes | **$ 117,100** | $ 110,189 | 6.3% |
| Net earnings | **$ 150,208** | $ 139,943 | 7.3% |
| Earnings per common share | **$ 2.18** | $ 2.04 | 6.9% |

## Condensed Consolidated Balance Sheets
(Thousands of dollars; **unaudited**)

| | March 31, | |
|---|---|---|
| Assets | **1982** | 1981 |
| Cash and short-term investments | **$ 63,779** | $ 45,265 |
| Receivables and unbilled costs, net | **578,875** | 577,430 |
| Inventories | **925,021** | 898,198 |
| Other current assets | **99,515** | 54,892 |
| Total current assets | **1,667,190** | 1,575,785 |
| Property, plant & equipment, net | **573,382** | 553,780 |
| Other assets | **81,465** | 62,461 |
| | **$2,322,037** | $2,192,026 |
| **Liabilities and Stockholders' Equity** | | |
| Current liabilities | **$ 664,389** | $ 632,490 |
| Long-term debt, less current maturities | **156,666** | 193,204 |
| Stockholders' equity | **1,500,982** | 1,366,332 |
| | **$2,322,037** | $2,192,026 |

This progressive aspect of business income taxes poses a problem in preparing **interim financial statements.** Should the income to date be annualized and the proportionate income tax accrued for the period to date? Or should the first amount of income earned be taxed at the lower rate of tax applicable to such income? Prior to 1974, companies generally followed the marginal principle and accrued the tax applicable to each additional dollar of income. The marginal principle was especially applied to businesses having a seasonal or uneven income pattern on the justification that the interim accrual of tax is based on the actual results to date. As a result of this diversity, the profession requires that "at the end of each interim period the company should make its best estimate of the effective tax rate expected to be applicable for the full fiscal year. The rate so determined should be used in providing for income taxes on a current year-to-date basis."[9]

Because businesses did not similarly apply this general guideline in accounting for similar situations, the FASB issued *Interpretation No. 18.* This interpretation requires that the **estimated annual effective tax rate** be applied to the year-to-date "ordinary" income at the end of each interim period to compute the year-to-date tax. Further, the **interim period tax** related to "ordinary" income shall be the difference between the amount so computed and the amounts reported for previous interim periods of the fiscal period.[10]

**Extraordinary Items**   Extraordinary items consist of unusual and nonrecurring material gains and losses. In the past, they were handled in interim reports in one of three ways: (1) absorbed entirely in the quarter in which they occurred; (2) prorated over the four quarters; or (3) disclosed only by footnote. **The required approach is to charge or credit the loss or gain in the quarter that it occurs instead of attempting some arbitrary multiple-period allocation.** This approach is consistent with the way in which extraordinary items are currently handled on an annual basis; no attempt is made to prorate the extraordinary items over several years. Some accountants favor the omission of extraordinary items from the quarterly net income because they believe that inclusion of extraordinary items that may be large in proportion to interim results naturally distorts the predictive value of interim reports. Many accountants, however, consider this approach inappropriate because it deviates from the actual situation.

**Changes in Accounting**   What happens if a company decides to change an accounting principle in the third quarter of a fiscal year? Should the cumulative effect adjustment be charged or credited to that quarter? Presentation of a cumulative effect in the third quarter may be misleading because of the inherent subjectivity associated with the first two quarters' reported income. In addition, a question arises as to whether such a change might not be used to manipulate a given quarter's income. As a result, *FASB Statement No. 3* was issued indicating that **if a cumulative effect change occurs in other than the first quarter, no**

---

[9]"Interim Financial Reporting," *Opinions of the Accounting Principles Board No. 28* (New York: AICPA, 1973), par. 19. The estimated annual effective tax rate should reflect anticipated investment tax credits, foreign tax rates, percentage depletion, capital gains rates, and other available tax planning alternatives.

[10]"Accounting for Income Taxes in Interim Periods," *FASB Interpretation No. 18* (Stamford, Conn.: FASB, March 1977), par. 9. "Ordinary" income (or loss) refers to "income (or loss) from continuing operations before income taxes (or benefits)" excluding extraordinary items, discontinued operations, and cumulative effects of changes in accounting principles.

**cumulative effect should be recognized in those quarters.**[11] **Rather, the cumulative effect at the beginning of the year should be computed and the first quarter restated.** Subsequent quarters would not report a cumulative effect adjustment.

**Earnings Per Share**  Interim reporting of earnings per share has all the problems inherent in computing and presenting annual earnings per share, and then some. If shares are issued in the third period, EPS for the first two periods will not be indicative of year-end EPS. If an extraordinary item is present in one period and new equity shares are sold in another period, the EPS figure for the extraordinary item will change for the year. On an annual basis only one EPS figure is associated with an extraordinary item and that figure does not change; the interim figure is subject to change. **For purposes of computing earnings per share and making the required disclosure determinations, each interim period should stand alone, that is, all applicable tests should be made for that single period.**

**Seasonality**  Seasonality occurs when sales are compressed into one short period of the year while certain costs are fairly evenly spread throughout the year. For example, the natural gas industry has its heavy sales in the winter months, as contrasted with the beverage industry, which has its heavy sales in the summer months.

The problem of seasonality is related to the matching concept in accounting. Expenses should be matched against the revenues they create. In a seasonal business, wide fluctuations in profits occur because off-season sales do not absorb the company's fixed costs (for example, manufacturing, selling, and administrative costs that tend to remain fairly constant regardless of sales or production).

To illustrate why seasonality is a problem, assume the following information:

| | |
|---|---|
| Selling price per unit | $1 |
| Annual sales for the period (projected and actual) | |
| 100,000 units @ $1.00 | $100,000 |
| Manufacturing costs: | |
| Variable | 10¢ per unit |
| Fixed | 20¢ per unit or $20,000 for the year |
| Nonmanufacturing costs: | |
| Variable | 10¢ per unit |
| Fixed | 30¢ per unit or $30,000 for the year |

Sales for four quarters and the year (projected and actual) were:

| | | Percent of Sales |
|---|---|---|
| 1st Quarter | $ 20,000 | 20 |
| 2nd Quarter | 5,000 | 5 |
| 3rd Quarter | 10,000 | 10 |
| 4th Quarter | 65,000 | 65 |
| Total for the Year | $100,000 | 100% |

---

[11]"Reporting Accounting Changes in Interim Financial Statements," *Statement of the Financial Accounting Standards Board No. 3* (Stamford, Conn.: FASB, 1974). This standard also provides guidance related to a LIFO change and accounting changes made in the fourth quarter of a fiscal year where interim data are not presented.

Under the present accounting framework, the income statements for the quarters might be as presented as follows:

| | 1st Qtr | 2nd Qtr | 3rd Qtr | 4th Qtr | Year |
|---|---|---|---|---|---|
| Sales | $20,000 | $ 5,000 | $10,000 | $65,000 | $100,000 |
| Manufacturing costs | | | | | |
| Variable | ( 2,000) | ( 500) | ( 1,000) | ( 6,500) | ( 10,000) |
| Fixed[a] | ( 4,000) | ( 1,000) | ( 2,000) | ( 13,000) | ( 20,000) |
| | 14,000 | 3,500 | 7,000 | 45,500 | 70,000 |
| Nonmanufacturing costs | | | | | |
| Variable | ( 2,000) | ( 500) | ( 1,000) | ( 6,500) | ( 10,000) |
| Fixed[b] | ( 7,500) | ( 7,500) | ( 7,500) | ( 7,500) | ( 30,000) |
| Net income | $ 4,500 | ($ 4,500) | ($ 1,500) | $31,500 | $ 30,000 |

[a]The fixed manufacturing costs are inventoried, so that equal amounts of fixed costs do not appear during each quarter.
[b]The fixed nonmanufacturing costs are not inventoried so that equal amounts of fixed costs appear during each quarter.

An investor who uses the first quarter's results can be misled. If the first quarter's earnings are $4,500, should this figure be multiplied by four to predict annual earnings of $18,000? Or, as the analysis suggests, inasmuch as $20,000 in sales is 20% of the predicted sales for the year, net income for the year should be $22,500 ($4,500 × 5). Either figure is obviously wrong, and after the second quarter's results occur, the investor may become even more confused.

The problem with the conventional approach is that the fixed nonmanufacturing costs are not charged in proportion to sales. Some enterprises have adopted a way of avoiding this problem by making all fixed nonmanufacturing costs follow the sales pattern, as shown below:

| | 1st Qtr | 2nd Qtr | 3rd Qtr | 4th Qtr | Year |
|---|---|---|---|---|---|
| Sales | $20,000 | $ 5,000 | $10,000 | $65,000 | $100,000 |
| Manufacturing costs | | | | | |
| Variable | ( 2,000) | ( 500) | ( 1,000) | ( 6,500) | ( 10,000) |
| Fixed | ( 4,000) | ( 1,000) | ( 2,000) | ( 13,000) | ( 20,000) |
| | 14,000 | 3,500 | 7,000 | 45,500 | 70,000 |
| Nonmanufacturing costs | | | | | |
| Variable | ( 2,000) | ( 500) | ( 1,000) | ( 6,500) | ( 10,000) |
| Fixed | ( 6,000) | ( 1,500) | ( 3,000) | ( 19,500) | ( 30,000) |
| Net income | $ 6,000 | $ 1,500 | $ 3,000 | $19,500 | $ 30,000 |

This approach solves some of the problems of interim reporting; sales in the first quarter are 20% of total sales for the year, and net income in the first quarter is 20% of total income. In this case, as in the previous example, the investor cannot rely on multiplying any given quarter by four, but can use comparative data or rely on some estimate of sales in relation to income for a given period.

The greater the degree of seasonality experienced by a company, the greater the possibility for distortion. Because no definitive guidelines are available for handling such items as the fixed nonmanufacturing costs, variability in income can be substantial. To alleviate this problem, the profession recommends that companies subject to material seasonal variations disclose the seasonal nature of their business and consider supplementing their interim reports with information for 12-month periods ended at the interim date for the current and preceding years.

The two illustrations above highlight the difference between the **discrete** and **integral** viewpoint. The fixed nonmanufacturing expenses would be expensed as incurred under the discrete viewpoint, but under the integral method they would be charged to expense on the basis of some measure of activity.

**Continuing Controversy**   The profession has developed some standards for interim reporting. But much still has to be done. As yet, it is unclear whether the discrete, integral, or some combination of these two methods will be proposed.

Discussion also persists concerning the independent auditor's involvement in interim reports. Many auditors are reluctant to express an opinion on interim financial information, arguing that the data are too tentative and subjective. Conversely, an increasing number of individuals advocate some type of examination of interim reports. A compromise may be a limited review of interim reports that provides some assurance that an examination has been conducted by an outside party and that the published information appears to be in accord with generally accepted accounting principles.[12]

## SUPPLEMENTARY INFORMATION

Supplementary information may include information that presents a different perspective from that adopted in the financial statements. This may be quantifiable information that is high in relevance but low in reliability, or information that is helpful, but not essential. The major supplementary information required is the data and schedules that must be provided by certain companies on the effects of changing prices (constant dollar and current cost information). In addition, certain disclosures related to the oil and gas industry may be required as supplementary information, although these may be part of the footnotes. Supplementary information related to many other matters may also be reported. Some of the more important are discussed and illustrated in the following sections.

### Management's Responsibilities for Financial Statements

The public accounting profession has attempted for many years to educate the public to the fact that a company's management has the primary responsibility for the preparation, integrity, and objectivity of the company's financial statements. Only recently have management letters acknowledging such responsibility appeared in annual reports to stockholders. Presented at the top of page 1265 is the management letter that served as a prelude to the 1981 financial statements of General Motors Corporation.

---

[12]For example, the AICPA has been involved in developing guidelines for the review of interim reports. "Limited Review of Interim Financial Statements," *Statement on Auditing Standards No. 24* (New York: AICPA, 1979) sets standards for the review of interim reports.

**GENERAL MOTORS CORPORATION**

**CONSOLIDATED FINANCIAL STATEMENTS**

### Responsibilities for Financial Statements

The following financial statements of General Motors Corporation and consolidated subsidiaries were prepared by the management which is responsible for their integrity and objectivity. The statements have been prepared in conformity with generally accepted accounting principles and, as such, include amounts based on judgments of management. Financial information elsewhere in this Annual Report is consistent with that in the financial statements.

Management is further responsible for maintaining a system of internal accounting controls, designed to provide reasonable assurance that the books and records reflect the transactions of the companies and that its established policies and procedures are carefully followed. From a stockholder's point of view, perhaps the most important feature in the system of control is that it is continually reviewed for its effectiveness and is augmented by written policies and guidelines, the careful selection and training of qualified personnel, and a strong program of internal audit.

Deloitte Haskins & Sells, independent certified public accountants, are engaged to examine the financial statements of General Motors Corporation and its subsidiaries and issue reports thereon. Their examination is conducted in accordance with generally accepted auditing standards which comprehend a review of internal controls and a test of transactions. The Accountants' Report appears on page 26.

The Board of Directors, through the Audit Committee (composed entirely of non-employee Directors), is responsible for assuring that management fulfills its responsibilities in the preparation of the financial statements. The Committee selects the independent public accountants annually in advance of the Annual Meeting of Stockholders and submits the selection for ratification at the Meeting. In addition, the Committee reviews the scope of the audits and the accounting principles being applied in financial reporting. The independent public accountants, representatives of management, and the internal auditors meet regularly (separately and jointly) with the Committee to review the activities of each and to ensure that each is properly discharging its responsibilities. To ensure complete independence, Deloitte Haskins & Sells have full and free access to meet with the Committee, without management representatives present, to discuss the results of their examination, the adequacy of internal accounting controls, and the quality of the financial reporting.

*Roger B Smith*
Chairman

*F. Alan Smith*
Chief Financial Officer

## Disclosure of Social Responsibility

The social responsibility of business has received a great deal of public attention in recent years. The public and local, state, and federal governments have urged that businesses make a more adequate response to current issues of social concern than they have in the past. For example, the SEC has already required listed corporations to file a report if pollution expenditures have a material effect on earnings. Some investment funds, such as Dreyfus Third Century Fund, have been incorporated to invest only in "socially responsible" companies. The Council on Economic Priorities has been established as an independent research organization to inquire into the social activities of private enterprises. The United Church of Christ uses various criteria for determining the social consciousness of a corporation before investing church funds.

The information related to social expenditures as presented in current financial reports is haphazard. Expenditures for the following types of items are generally considered "social awareness expenditures":

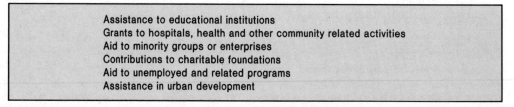

Assistance to educational institutions
Grants to hospitals, health and other community related activities
Aid to minority groups or enterprises
Contributions to charitable foundations
Aid to unemployed and related programs
Assistance in urban development

The following diagram illustrates the extent of disclosure for the Fortune 500 companies:[13]

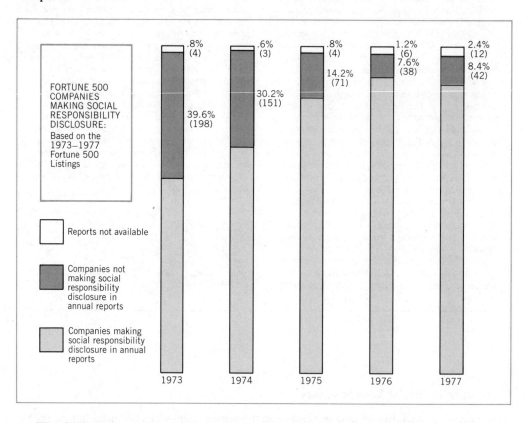

The SEC requires that the following types of environmental information should be disclosed in filings with their agency:

1. The material effects that compliance with federal, state, and local environmental protection laws may have upon capital expenditures, earnings, and competitive position.

2. Litigation commenced or known to be contemplated against registrants by a government authority pursuant to federal, state, and local environmental regulatory provisions.

3. All other environmental information of which the average, prudent investor ought reasonably to be informed.

As yet, no standards or requirements have been proposed for the measurement and reporting of the social responsibilities assumed by individual enterprises by the FASB. To some investors, it is a matter of importance whether a company is adopting affirmative policies

[13]Ernst & Whinney, *Social Responsibility Disclosure—1978 Survey*, p. 3.

with regard to environmental matters or is simply doing the minimum to assure legal compliance.

## Management Discussion and Analysis

The management discussion and analysis section covers three financial aspects of an enterprise's business—liquidity, capital resources, and results of operations. It requires management to highlight favorable or unfavorable trends and to identify significant events and uncertainties that affect these three factors. This approach obviously involves a number of subjective estimates, opinions, and soft data; however, the SEC, which has mandated this disclosure, believes the relevance of this information exceeds the potential lack of reliability. This disclosure is also in concert with *FASB Concepts Statement No. 1,* which notes that management knows more about the enterprise than users and therefore can increase the usefulness of financial information by identifying significant transactions that affect the enterprise and by explaining their financial impact.

The management discussion and analysis section of Mark Controls Corporation's 1981 annual report is presented on page 1268.

## Reporting on Forecasts

In recent years, the investing public's demand for more and better information has focused on disclosure of corporate expectations for the future through publication of earnings forecasts. Financial forecasts have therefore become the subject of intensive discussion with journalists, corporate executives, the SEC, financial analysts, accountants, and others making their views known. Predictably, there are strong arguments on either side. Listed below are some of the arguments.

Arguments for requiring published forecasts:

1. Investment decisions are based on future expectations; therefore, information about the future facilitates better decisions.
2. Forecasts are already circulated informally, but are uncontrolled, frequently misleading, and not available equally to all investors. This confused situation should be brought under control.
3. Circumstances now change so rapidly that historical information is no longer adequate for prediction.

Arguments against requiring published forecasts:

1. No one can foretell the future. Therefore forecasts, while conveying an impression of precision about the future, will inevitably be wrong.
2. Organizations will strive only to meet their published forecasts, not to produce results that are in the stockholders' best interest.
3. When forecasts are not proved to be accurate, there will be recriminations and probably legal actions.
4. Disclosure of forecasts will be detrimental to organizations, because it will fully inform not only investors, but also competitors (foreign and domestic).[14]

In 1978, the SEC indicated that companies are **permitted** (not required) to include profit projections in reports filed with that agency.[15] The SEC guidelines indicate that:

---

[14]Joseph P. Cummings, *Financial Forecasts and the Certified Public Accountant* (New York: Peat, Marwick, Mitchell & Co., November 30, 1972).

[15]"Guides for Disclosure of Projections of Future Economic Performance," *Release No. 5992* (Washington: SEC, November 7, 1978).

**mcc** **MARK CONTROLS**
CORPORATION

MANAGEMENT'S DISCUSSION AND ANALYSIS OF RESULTS OF OPERATIONS AND FINANCIAL CONDITION

### 1981 Compared to 1980

**RESULTS OF OPERATIONS**

Consolidated net sales in 1981 were 4% higher than in 1980. The Company's two major business segments (flow control products and building control systems) accounted for essentially all of the increase. Sales of the flow control products segment increased 1% over 1980 levels. All operating units within this segment posted sales gains with the exception of the engineered steel gate valve unit—Pacific Valves. Sales of ball and butterfly valves and water systems products showed the most improvement. As anticipated, engineered steel gate valve shipments were below 1980 levels. This decline was principally due to a slowdown in orders for process industry projects, particularly for refinery reconfiguration and modification. Major engineering contractors and their oil industry customers continue to cite current economic uncertainties, high interest rates, low refinery utilization, and improved availability of light/sweet crude oil as the primary reasons for delaying many of the projects. The building control systems segment posted a sales increase of 7% in 1981. This improvement reflects a continued improved order rate for MCC Powers' System 600 computer-based energy management system. In addition, the servicing of existing building control systems showed good growth in 1981 compared to 1980. Because a substantial portion of Mark Controls' output is built to specification, it is not practicable to determine the portion of a year's sales increases attributable to price and volume factors.

Consolidated gross profits increased 10% in 1981 over 1980. The flow control products segment experienced a 4% decline due to lower sales and gross margins at the engineered steel gate valve unit. Operating expenses of this segment increased 18% primarily as the result of inflation and higher selling expenses in support of increased sales of most product lines. Increased gross profits of the building control systems segment more than offset the decline in the flow control products segment. The 21% increase in 1981 was the result of a higher sales volume, a more favorable product mix, and improved operating efficiencies. Operating expenses of this segment increased 24% primarily as a result of inflation, increased systems development spending and higher field selling, and engineering expenditures.

Consolidated interest expense increased 12% in 1981 over 1980 due to an increase in average outstanding borrowings and continued high interest rates on the Company's prime rate denominated debt.

Consolidated net income decreased 37% in 1981 as compared to 1980. Earnings for 1981 include an after tax provision of $1.6 million relating to the possible sale of the Company's home building products unit, Fiat Products, Inc. (See Note 7 to the consolidated financial statements.) Excluding this loss, 1981 net income would have been $6.5 million, down 17% from 1980 net income of $7.8 million. This decline was primarily attributable to the lower sales volume and margins at the Pacific Valves unit.

**LIQUIDITY AND CAPITAL RESOURCES**

Working capital increased $11.6 million during 1981. Additional working capital requirements were financed by earnings, deferral of income taxes and higher short-term and long-term bank borrowings. Total debt represented 46% of total capitalization at the end of 1981 compared to 40% at the end of 1980. As discussed in Note 7 to the consolidated financial statements, the Company hopes to realize from the sale of its home building products unit about $8.5 million in cash which will be used to reduce short-term bank borrowings. The Company's bank credit lines at year-end included long-term revolving credit lines and short-term credit lines of $15 million each. The Company continues to devote significant efforts to accounts receivable collections and inventory turnover improvements, which should contribute favorably to the Company's liquidity position. Available borrowing capacity, sound asset management and earnings should be adequate to finance anticipated working capital requirements during 1982.

Capital expenditures were $9.3 million in 1981, slightly lower than the record 1980 level of $9.6 million. The expenditures were concentrated in the flow control products segment which is more capital intensive than the building control systems segment. Most of the expenditures were made to increase the production capacity of existing facilities and to implement cost reduction programs. The Company's earnings and credit lines were used to finance these expenditures in 1981. At December 31, 1981, the Company was not bound by any material capital expenditure commitments.

---

**1.** Management has the option to provide good-faith projections, provided it has some reasonable basis for the projection. Disclosure of the assumptions used to prepare the forecast would be helpful. The most probable amount or the most reasonable range for the items projected should be used.

2. Projections should include at least these financial items: revenues, net income, and earnings per share, although disclosure is not limited to these items. Management should select the period over which the items should be projected. It is recommended that management indicate whether updates will be furnished.

3. Outside reviews of the projections may be included. If a review is included, the qualifications of the reviewer, extent of the review, and relationship between the reviewer and the company should be described.

To encourage management to disclose this type of information, the SEC has issued a "safe harbor" rule. The safe harbor rule provides protection to an enterprise that presents an erroneous projection as long as the projections were prepared on a reasonable basis and were disclosed in good faith.[16]

**Experience in Great Britain**    Great Britain has permitted financial forecasts for years, and the results have been fairly successful. Some significant differences exist between the English and the American business and legal environment,[17] but probably none that could not be overcome if influential interests in this country cooperated to produce an atmosphere conducive to quality forecasting. A typical British forecast adapted from a construction company's report to support a public offering of stock is as follows:

---

Profits have grown substantially over the past 10 years and directors are confident of being able to continue this expansion. . . . While the rate of expansion will be dependent on the level of economic activity in Ireland and in England, the group is well structured to avail itself of opportunities as they arise, particularly in the field of property development, which is expected to play an increasingly important role in the group's future expansion.

Profits before taxation for the half year ended 30th June 1981 was 402,000 pounds. On the basis of trading experiences since that date and the present level of sales and completions, the directors expect that in the absence of unforeseen circumstances, the group's profits before taxation for the year to 31st December 1981 will be not less than 960,000 pounds. . . .

No dividends will be paid in respect of the year December 31, 1981. In a full financial year, on the basis of above forecasts (not including full year profits) it would be the intention of the board, assuming current rates of tax, to recommend dividends totaling 40% (of after-tax profits), of which 15% payable would be as an interest dividend in November 1982 and 25% as a final dividend in June 1983.

---

A general narrative-type forecast issued by a U.S. corporation might appear as follows:

---

On the basis of promotions planned by the company for the second half of fiscal 1984, net earnings for that period are expected to be approximately the same as those for the first half of fiscal 1984, with net earnings for the third quarter expected to make the predominant contribution to net earnings for the second half of fiscal 1984.

---

[16]"Safe-Harbor Rule for Projections," *Release No. 5993* (Washington: SEC, 1979).

[17]The British system, for example, does not permit litigation on forecasted information, and the solicitor (lawyer) is not permitted to work on a contingent fee basis. See "A Case for Forecasting—The British Have Tried It and Find That It Works," *World* (New York: Peat, Marwick, Mitchell & Co., Autumn 1978), pp. 10–13.

**Questions of Liability**   What happens if a company does not meet its forecasts? Are the company and the auditor going to be sued? If a company, for example, projects an earnings increase of 15% and achieves only 5%, should the stockholder be permitted to have some judicial recourse against the company? One court case involving Monsanto Chemical Corporation has provided some guidelines. In this case, Monsanto predicted that sales would increase 8 to 9% and that earnings would rise 4 to 5%. In the last part of the year, the demand for Monsanto's products dropped as a result of a business turndown and, therefore, the company's earnings declined instead of increasing. The company was sued because the projected earnings figure was erroneous, but the judge dismissed the suit because the forecasts were the best estimates of qualified people whose intents were honest.

As indicated earlier, the SEC's "safe harbor" rules are intended to protect enterprises that provide good-faith projections. However, much concern exists as to how the SEC and the courts will interpret such terms as "good faith" and "reasonable assumptions" when erroneous projections mislead users of this information.

**Many Unresolved Problems**   In addition to the question of liability, several other issues must be resolved before earnings projections should be made mandatory. The role and responsibility of the CPA as an attestor of forecasts must be determined. Should forecasts consist of general expectations or detailed disclosures? Should a single value ($1.50) or a range of values ($1.50 ± $.20) be presented? What should be the length of the period to be forecasted?[18]

Financial forecasts provide such highly relevant investment information that the demand for them will not subside. Although there are some disadvantages to requiring forecasts, they are outweighed by the advantages. We believe that the publication of forecasts is a natural and inevitable extension of corporate disclosure.

## EXAMINATION OF THE AUDITOR'S REPORT

Another important source of information that is often overlooked by investors in their examination of the financial statements is the auditor's report. An **auditor** is a professional who conducts an independent examination of the accounting data presented by the business enterprise. If the auditor is satisfied that the financial statements represent the financial position and results of operations, an **opinion** is expressed on audited statements as indicated at the top of page 1271.

---

[18]It might be noted that AcSEC has issued a statement of position on financial forecasts, providing guidance to those who choose to issue information related to the future. "Presentation and Disclosure of Financial Forecasts," *AcSEC Statement of Position 75-4* (New York: AICPA, 1975). The AICPA's Management Advisory Services Division has also issued a statement dealing with guidelines for systems to prepare financial forecasts: "Guidelines for Systems for the Preparation of Financial Forecasts," Management Advisory Services Executive Committee, *Guideline Series No. 3* (New York: AICPA, 1975). In addition, the AICPA issued a guide which covers a CPA's review of, and reporting on reviews of, financial forecasts, *Review of Financial Forecasts* (New York: AICPA, 1980).

We have examined the Consolidated Balance Sheet of Anetek Chemical Corporation and consolidated subsidiaries as of December 31, 1984 and 1983 and the related Statements of Consolidated Income and Changes in Consolidated Financial Position for each of the three years in the period ended December 31, 1984. Our examinations were made in accordance with generally accepted auditing standards and, accordingly, included such tests of the accounting records and such other auditing procedures as we considered necessary in the circumstances.

In our opinion, these financial statements present fairly the financial position of the companies at December 31, 1984 and 1983 and the results of their operations and the changes in their financial position for each of the three years in the period ended December 31, 1984, in conformity with generally accepted accounting principles applied on a consistent basis.

In preparing this report, the auditor follows these reporting standards:

1. The report shall state whether the financial statements are presented in accordance with generally accepted accounting principles.

2. The report shall state whether such principles have been consistently observed in the current period in relation to the preceding period.

3. Informative disclosures in the financial statements are to be regarded as reasonably adequate unless otherwise stated in the report.

4. The report shall contain either an expression of opinion regarding the financial statements taken as a whole or an assertion to the effect that an opinion cannot be expressed. When an overall opinion cannot be expressed, the reasons therefore should be stated. In all cases where an auditor's name is associated with financial statements, the report should contain a clear-cut indication of the character of the auditor's examination, if any, and the degree of responsibility being taken.

In short, these standards require that an auditor state in the opinion that generally accepted accounting principles have been followed and that they have been applied on a basis consistent with that of the preceding year. In most cases, the auditor issues a standard **unqualified** or **"clean"** opinion; that is, the auditor believes that the financial statements do present fairly the financial statements on a basis consistent with that used in the preceding year. There are situations in which the auditor, however, is required to (1) express a **qualified** opinion, (2) express an **adverse** opinion, or (3) **disclaim** an opinion.

A qualified opinion contains an exception to the standard opinion; ordinarily the exception is not of sufficient magnitude to invalidate the statements as a whole; if it were, an adverse opinion would be rendered. The usual circumstances in which the auditor may deviate from the standard unqualified short-form report on financial statements are as follows:

1. The scope of the examination is limited or affected by conditions or restrictions.

2. The statements do not fairly present financial position or results of operations because of:
   (a) Lack of conformity with generally accepted accounting principles and standards.
   (b) Inadequate disclosure.

3. Accounting principles and standards are not consistently applied.

4. Unusual uncertainties exist concerning future developments, the effects of which cannot be reasonably estimated or otherwise resolved satisfactorily.

If the auditor is confronted with one of the situations noted above, the opinion must be qualified. A qualification is one of two types, a "subject to" or an "except for." A **subject to** qualification is used when the qualification results from an uncertainty that would materially affect the financial statements, such as serious deficiencies in working capital, litigation in which the company is a defendant, and threatened expropriation. An **except for** qualification is used in all other cases mentioned above.

An adverse opinion is required in any report in which the exceptions to fair presentation are so material that in the independent auditor's judgment a qualified opinion is not justified. In such a case, the financial statements taken as a whole are not presented in accordance with generally accepted accounting principles. Adverse opinions are rare, because most enterprises change their accounting to conform with the auditor's desires. A disclaimer of an opinion is normally issued for one of two reasons: (1) the auditor has gathered so little information on the financial statements that no opinion can be expressed, or (2) the auditor concludes on the basis of the evaluation that the ability of the company to continue on a going-concern basis is highly questionable because of financing or operating problems.

The qualified (subject to) opinion shown below was issued because of the concern about "the realization of excimer laser costs."

---

**Report of Independent Public Accountants**

To the Shareholders and the Board of Directors of Helionetics, Inc.:

We have examined the balance sheets of HELIONETICS, INC. (the "Company"), a California corporation, as of December 31, 1981 and 1980, and the related statements of operations, shareholders' investment and changes in financial position for each of the three years in the period ended December 31, 1981. Our examinations were made in accordance with generally accepted auditing standards and, accordingly, included such tests of the accounting records and such other auditing procedures as we considered necessary in the circumstances.

The Company has incurred costs amounting to $792,400 at December 31, 1981 and $179,400 at December 31, 1980 in connection with the construction of an excimer laser. As explained in Note 11 to the financial statements, the realization of these costs is dependent upon the success of the Laser Division's future operations.

In our auditors' report dated April 7, 1981, our opinion on the 1980 financial statements expressed a qualification with respect to realization of costs incurred in connection with the Company's proposed underwritten public offering. As explained in Note 4 to the financial statements, the Company completed the public offering on June 23, 1981 and realized the related costs incurred. Accordingly, our present opinion on the 1980 financial statements, as presented herein, is different from that expressed in our previous report.

In our opinion, subject to the realization of the excimer laser costs discussed in the second paragraph, the financial statements referred to above present fairly the financial position of Helionetics, Inc. as of December 31, 1981 and 1980, and the results of its operations and the changes in its financial position for each of the three years in the period ended December 31, 1981, in conformity with generally accepted accounting principles applied on a consistent basis.

Los Angeles, California
March 15, 1982

*Arthur Andersen & Co*
ARTHUR ANDERSEN & CO.

---

Another illustration of how a close reading of the auditor's report can warn the investor of possible disaster in the future is an annual report of Lockheed Aircraft that stated:

---

In our opinion, subject to the realization of the work-in-process inventories and accounts receivable described in Note 2, the statements mentioned above present fairly, . . . except for the change in accounting for administrative and general expenses and independent research and development costs described in Note 1.

The change in accounting in Note 1 increased earnings by $22 million out of a total of $44 million reported as net income for the year. Note 2 had to do with the costs associated with the C-5 aircraft. Essentially, the question revolved around the ultimate realizability of receivables and inventory related to construction of this aircraft. If Lockheed could not collect on these claims, the company would be in financial difficulty running into hundreds of millions of dollars.

The auditor's report stated in part:

> As discussed in Notes 2 and 3, the company is faced with contingencies of extraordinary magnitudes arising from disputes with, and claims against, the U.S. Government as well as uncertainty as to its commercial TriStar program. These items are material to both the financial position and the results of the operations of the company, and their resolution may significantly affect its future. In our opinion, subject to the effect of the matters referred to in the preceding paragraph. . . .

Our point should be clear: the sophisticated analyst should examine closely the auditor's report in conjunction with the examination of the other financial data. Although the information usually can be found in other parts of the financial statements, the auditor's report can be a convenient and useful source of highly pertinent information.

## CRITERIA FOR MAKING ACCOUNTING AND REPORTING CHOICES

Throughout this textbook, and especially in this chapter, we have stressed the need to provide information that is useful to predict the amount, timing, and uncertainty of future cash flows. To achieve this objective, the accountant must make judicial choices between alternative accounting concepts, methods, and means of disclosure. You are probably surprised and even discouraged at the large number of choices among acceptable alternatives that accountants are required to make.

You should recognize, however, as indicated in Chapter 1, that accounting is greatly influenced by its environment. Because it does not exist in a vacuum, it seems unrealistic to assume that alternative presentations to certain transactions and events will be eliminated entirely. Nevertheless, we are hopeful that the profession, through the development of a conceptual framework, will be able to focus on the needs of financial statement users and eliminate diversity where appropriate. The FASB concepts statement on objectives of financial reporting, elements of financial statements, qualitative characteristics of accounting information, and potential statements on reporting, recognition, and measurement are important steps in the right direction. Nevertheless, the profession must continue its efforts to develop a sound foundation upon which accounting standards and practice can be built. As Aristotle said: "The correct beginning is more than half the whole."

## QUESTIONS

1. A recent annual report of a major steel company states: "Income tax expense includes provision for deferred income taxes of 8.8 million in 1982 and 13.1 million in 1981. Tax expense was reduced by a flow-through of the allowable investment credit of 7.3 million in 1982 and 3.1 million in 1981." What does this footnote mean?

2. Some financial writers have described the 1970s as the age of disclosure. What is the full disclosure principle in accounting? Why has disclosure increased substantially in the last ten years?

3. What are the major advantages of footnotes? What type of items are usually reported in footnotes?

4. The auditor for Sandab, Inc. is debating whether the major categories of property, plant, and equipment and related accumulated depreciation should be reported in a footnote or in the summary of significant accounting policies. What would be your recommendation? Why?

5. Dublin Co. is liable for a 7% mortgage payable of $24,600, secured by land and buildings, which is payable in semiannual installments (including principal and interest) of $4,500. Indicate the balance sheet presentation of long-term debt, current maturities, and indicate in general terms the necessary disclosure.

6. The SEC requires a reconciliation between the effective tax rate and the federal government's statutory rate. Of what benefit is such a disclosure requirement?

7. At the beginning of 1983, Pagliais' Inc. entered into an eight-year nonrenewable lease agreement. Provisions in the lease require the client to make substantial reconditioning and restoration expenditures at the end of the lease. What type of disclosure do you believe is necessary for this type of situation?

8. A recent annual report of Cocina Industries states: "The company and its subsidiaries have long-term leases expiring on various dates after December 31, 1984. Amounts payable under such commitments, without reduction for related rental income, are expected to average approximately $5,711,000 annually for the next three years. Related rental income from certain subleases to others is estimated to average $3,094,000 annually for the next three years." What information is provided by this footnote?

9. An annual report of Ford Motor Corporation states: "Net income a share is computed based upon the average number of shares of capital stock of all classes outstanding. Additional shares of common stock may be issued or delivered in the future on conversion of outstanding convertible debentures, exercise of outstanding employee stock options, and for payment of defined supplemental compensation. Had such additional shares been outstanding, net income a share would have been reduced by 10¢ in the current year and 3¢ in the previous year.

"As a result of capital stock transactions by the company during the current year, (primarily the purchase of Class A Stock from Ford Foundation), net income a share was increased by 6¢." What information is provided by this footnote?

10. What type of disclosure or accounting do you believe is necessary for the following items:
   (a) The client reports an extraordinary item (net of tax) correctly on the income statement. No other mention is made of this item in the annual report.
   (b) The client expects to recover a substantial amount in connection with a pending refund claim for a prior year's taxes. Although the claim is being contested, counsel for the company has confirmed the client's expectation of recovery.
   (c) Because of a general increase in the number of labor disputes and strikes, both within and outside the industry, there is an increased likelihood that the client will suffer a costly strike in the near future.

11. The following information was described in a footnote of Rochelle Packing Co. "During August 1981 Halco Products Corporation purchased 311,003 shares of the Company's common stock which constitutes approximately 35% of the stock outstanding. Halco has since obtained representation on the Board of Directors.

"An affiliate of Halco Products Corporation acts as a food broker for the Company in the greater New York City marketing area. The commissions for such services after August 1981 amounted to approximately $20,000." Why is this information disclosed?

12. What approaches might be employed to disclose "social awareness" expenditures?

13. What is the difference between a CPA's unqualified opinion or "clean" opinion and a qualified one?

14. When does a CPA render a "subject to" qualified opinion? When does a CPA render an adverse opinion?

15. What are diversified companies? What accounting problems are related to diversified companies?

16. Explain the following terms:
    (a) Identifiable assets.
    (b) Defined profit.
    (c) Industry segment.
    (d) Common cost.

17. The controller for Unity, Inc. recently commented: "If I have to disclose our segments individually, the only people who will gain are our competitors and the only people that will lose are our present stockholders." Evaluate this comment.

18. An article in the financial press entitled "What is New in Annual Reports This Year" noted that annual reports would include an expanded discussion and analysis section. What would this expanded section contain?

19. "The financial statements of a company are management's, not the accountant's." Discuss the implications of this statement.

20. One student of Intermediate Accounting was heard to remark after a class discussion on diversified reporting: "All this is very confusing to me. First we are told that there is merit in presenting the consolidated results and now we are told that it is better to show segmental results. I wish they would make up their minds." Evaluate this comment.

21. A financial writer noted recently: "There are substantial arguments for including earnings projections in annual reports and the like. The most compelling is that it would give anyone interested something now available to only a relatively select few—like large shareholders, creditors, and attentive bartenders." Identify some arguments against providing earnings projections.

22. An article discussing the negative aspects of forecasts noted: "What if Ford had made official projections early last year of 1979 and 1980 earnings. Did it correctly foresee OPEC's running amok and estimate billion dollar losses in each of these years for its North American automobile operations?" Identify some arguments for providing earnings forecasts.

23. What are interim reports? Why are balance sheets often not provided with interim data?

24. What are the accounting problems related to the presentation of interim data?

25. Sport Wear, Inc., a closely held corporation, has decided to go public. The controller, Robby Morrley, is concerned with presenting interim data when a LIFO inventory valuation is used. What problems are encountered with LIFO inventories when quarterly data are presented?

26. What approaches have been suggested to overcome the seasonal problem related to interim reporting?

# CASES

**C27-1** Presented below are three independent situations.

### Situation I

A company has adopted a policy of recording self-insurance for any possible losses resulting from injury to others by the company's vehicles. The premium for an insurance policy for the same risk from an independent insurance company would have an annual cost of $3,000. During the period covered by the financial statements, there were no accidents involving the company's vehicles that resulted in injury to others.

### Situation II

A company offers a one-year warranty for the product that it manufactures. A history of warranty claims has been compiled and the probable amount of claims related to sales for a given period can be determined.

*Situation III*

Subsequent to the date of a set of financial statements, but prior to the issuance of the financial statements, a company enters into a contract that will probably result in a significant loss to the company. The amount of the loss can be reasonably estimated.

**Instructions**

Discuss the accrual or type of disclosure necessary (if any) and the reason(s) why such disclosure is appropriate for each of the three independent sets of facts above.

(AICPA adapted)

**C27-2** Pacific Inc. produces electronic components for sale to manufacturers of radios, television sets, and phonographic systems. In connection with her examination of Pacific's financial statements for the year ended December 31, 1984, Melissa Melton, CPA, completed field work two weeks ago. Ms. Melton now is evaluating the significance of the following items prior to preparing her auditor's report. Except as noted, none of these items have been disclosed in the financial statements or footnotes.

*Item 1*

A major electronics firm has introduced a line of products that will compete directly with Pacific's primary line, now being produced in the specially designed new plant. Because of manufacturing innovations, the competitor's line will be of comparable quality but priced 50% below Pacific's line. The competitor announced its new line during the week following completion of field work. Ms. Melton read the announcement in the newspaper and discussed the situation by telephone with Pacific executives. Pacific will meet the lower prices that are high enough to cover variable manufacturing and selling expenses but will permit recovery of only a portion of fixed costs.

*Item 2*

The company's new manufacturing plant building, which cost $1,200,000 and has an estimated life of 25 years, is leased from Corner National Bank at an annual rental of $240,000. The company is obligated to pay property taxes, insurance, and maintenance. At the conclusion of its 10-year noncancellable lease, the company has the option of purchasing the property for $1.00. In Pacific's income statement the rental payment is reported on a separate line.

*Item 3*

A 10-year loan agreement, which the company entered into three years ago, provides that dividend payments may not exceed net income earned after taxes subsequent to the date of the agreement. The balance of retained earnings at the date of the loan agreement was $317,000. From that date through December 31, 1984, net income after taxes has totaled $450,000 and cash dividends have totaled $220,000. On the basis of these data the staff auditor assigned to this review concluded that there was no retained earnings restriction at December 31, 1984.

*Item 4*

Recently Pacific interrupted its policy of paying cash dividends quarterly to its stockholders. Dividends were paid regularly through 1983, discontinued for all of 1984 to finance equipment for the company's new plant, and resumed in the first quarter of 1985. In the annual report dividend policy is to be discussed in the president's letter to stockholders.

**Instructions**

For each of the items above discuss any additional disclosures in the financial statements and footnotes that the auditor should recommend to her client. (The cumulative effect of the four items should not be considered.)

**C27-3** Spify Container Corporation is in the process of preparing its annual financial statements for the fiscal year ended April 30, 1983. Because all of Spify's shares are traded intrastate, the company does not have to file any reports with the Securities and Exchange Commission. The company manufactures plastic, glass, and paper containers for sale to food and drink manufacturers and distributors.

Spify Container Corporation maintains separate control accounts for its raw materials, work-in-process, and finished goods inventories for each of the three types of containers. The inventories are valued at the lower of cost or market.

The company's property, plant, and equipment are classified in the following major categories: land, office buildings, furniture and fixtures, manufacturing facilities, manufacturing equipment, leasehold improvements. All fixed assets are carried at cost. The depreciation methods employed depend upon the type of asset (its classification) and when it was acquired.

Spify Container Corporation plans to present the inventory and fixed asset amounts in its April 30, 1983, balance sheet as shown below.

| | |
|---|---|
| Inventories | $2,956,906 |
| Property, plant, and equipment (net of depreciation) | $4,875,574 |

**Instructions**

What information regarding inventories and property, plant, and equipment must be disclosed by Spify Container Corporation in the audited financial statements issued to stockholders, either in the body or the notes, for the 1982–1983 fiscal year?

(CMA adapted)

**C27-4** You are completing an examination of the financial statements of Cabinet Manufacturing Corporation for the year ended February 28, 1984. Cabinet's financial statements have not been examined previously. The controller of Cabinet has given you the following draft of proposed footnotes to the financial statements:

---

Cabinet Manufacturing Corporation
NOTES TO FINANCIAL STATEMENTS
Year Ended February 28, 1984

---

*Note 1.* With the approval of the Commissioner of Internal Revenue, the company changed its method of accounting for inventories from the first-in first-out method to the last-in first-out method on March 1, 1983. In the opinion of the company the effects of this change on the pricing of inventories and cost of goods manufactured were not material in the current year but are expected to be material in future years.

*Note 2.* The investment property was recorded at cost until December, 1983, when it was written up to its appraisal value. The company plans to sell the property in 1984, and an independent real estate agent in the area has indicated that the appraisal price can be realized. Pending completion of the sale the amount of the expected gain on the sale has been recorded in an unearned income account.

*Note 3.* The stock dividend described in our May 24, 1983, letter to stockholders has been recorded as a 110 for 100 stock split-up. Accordingly, there were no changes in the stockholders' equity account balances from this transaction.

---

**Instructions**

For each of the notes above discuss the note's adequacy and needed revisions, if any, of the financial statements or the note.

**C27-5** You have completed your audit of Van Buren Iron Ware Inc. and its consolidated subsidiaries for the year ended December 31, 1984, and were satisfied with the results of your examination. You have examined the financial statements of Van Buren for the past three years. The corporation is now preparing its annual report to stockholders. The report will include the consolidated financial statements of Van Buren and its subsidiaries and your short-form auditor's report. During your audit the following matters came to your attention:

1. In 1984 the corporation changed its method of accounting for the investment credit. An investment credit of $161,000 deferred in prior years was credited to income and the full 1984 investment credit of $62,000 was recorded as a reduction of income tax expense. As a result, net income after taxes for 1984 was increased by $223,000. You approved of this change as an acceptable alternative accounting treatment.

2. The Internal Revenue Service is currently examining the corporation's 1981 federal income tax return and is questioning the amount of a deduction claimed by the corporation's domestic subsidiary for a loss sustained in 1981. The examination is still in process, and any additional tax liability is indeterminable at this time. The corporation's tax counsel believes that there will be no substantial additional tax liability.

3. A vice-president who is also a stockholder resigned on December 31, 1984, after an argument with the president. The vice-president is soliciting proxies from stockholders and expects to obtain sufficient proxies to gain control of the board of directors so that a new president will be appointed. The president plans to have a footnote prepared that would include information of the pending proxy fight, management's accomplishments over the years, and an appeal by management for the support of stockholders.

**Instructions**

(a) Prepare the footnotes, if any, that you would suggest for the items listed above.
(b) State your reasons for not making disclosure by footnote for each of the listed items for which you did not prepare a footnote.

(AICPA adapted)

**C27-6** In an annual report of Republic Steel, the following was reported:

"In the Cleveland District, a major improvement in air emission control was made possible by the completion of the first phase of construction of a giant suppressed combustion pollution control system for the basic oxygen furnaces.

"The system, believed to be the first of its type ever installed on an existing steelmaking complex, replaces a bank of electrostatic precipitators which will be used to control other emissions that occur in the steelmaking process. The total system is expected to become fully operational this spring."

**Instructions**

(a) Do you believe that Republic should disclose information of this nature?
(b) How might an enterprise measure its socially responsible activities?

**C27-7** Musketeer Enterprises acquired a large tract of land in a small town approximately 10 miles from Capital City. The company executed a firm contract on November 15, 1983, for the construction of a one-mile race track, together with related facilities. The track and facilities were completed December 15, 1984. On December 31, 1984, a 15% installment note of $150,000 was issued along with other consideration in settlement of the construction contract. Installments of $50,000 fall due on December 31 of each of the next three years. The company planned to pay the notes from cash received from operations and from sale of additional capital stock.

The company adopted the double-declining balance method of computing depreciation. No depreciation was taken in 1984 because all racing equipment was received in December after the completion of the track and facilities.

The land on which the racing circuit was constructed was acquired at various dates for a total of $61,000, and its approximate market value on December 31, 1984, is $78,000.

Through the sale of tickets to spectators, parking fees, concession income, and income from betting, the company officials anticipated that approximately $275,000 is taken in during the typical year's racing season. Cash expenses for a racing season were estimated at $173,000.

You have made an examination of the financial condition of Musketeer Enterprises as of December 31, 1984. The balance sheet as of that date and statement of operations follow.

Musketeer Enterprises
BALANCE SHEET
December 31, 1984

### Assets

| | | |
|---|---:|---:|
| Cash | | $ 14,500 |
| Accounts receivable | | 1,000 |
| Prepaid expenses | | 7,500 |
| Property (at cost) | | |
|   Land | $ 61,000 | |
|   Grading and track improvements | 80,200 | |
|   Grandstand | 110,000 | |
|   Buildings | 65,000 | |
|   Racing equipment | 45,000 | 361,200 |
| Organization costs | | 300 |
|     Total assets | | $384,500 |

### Liabilities and Stockholders' Equity

| | |
|---|---:|
| Accounts payable | $ 22,000 |
| Installment note payable—15% | 150,000 |
| Stockholders' equity | |
|   Capital stock, par value $1.00 per share, authorized | |
|     200,000, issued and outstanding 47,800 shares | 47,800 |
|   Capital in excess of par, representing amounts paid | |
|     in over par value of capital stock | 174,700 |
|   Retained earnings (deficit) | (10,000) |
|     Total liabilities and stockholders' equity | $384,500 |

Musketeer Enterprises
STATEMENT OF INCOME
For the Period from Inception, December 1, 1981
to December 31, 1984

| | |
|---|---:|
| Income | |
|   Profit on sales of land | $ 8,000 |
|   Other | 200 |
| | 8,200 |
| General and administrative expenses | 24,300 |
| Net loss for the period | $16,100 |

On January 15, 1985, legislation that declared betting to be illegal was enacted by the state legislature and was signed by the governor. A discussion with management on January 17 about the effect of the legislation revealed that it is now estimated that revenue will be reduced to approximately $80,000 and cash expenses will be reduced to one-third the original estimate.

### Instructions

(Disregard federal income tax implications.)
(a) Prepare the explanatory notes to accompany the balance sheet.

(b) What opinion do you believe the auditor should render? Discuss.

(AICPA adapted)

**C27-8** Boxit Corporation, a publicly traded company, is preparing the interim financial data which it will issue to its stockholders and the Securities and Exchance Commission (SEC) at the end of the first quarter of the 1983–1984 fiscal year. Boxit's financial accounting department has compiled the following summarized revenue and expense data for the first quarter of the year:

| | |
|---|---|
| Sales | $15,000,000 |
| Cost of goods sold | 9,000,000 |
| Variable selling expenses | 450,000 |
| Fixed selling expenses | 750,000 |

Included in the fixed selling expenses was the single lump sum payment of $600,000 for television advertisements for the entire year.

**Instructions**

(a) Boxit Corporation must issue its quarterly financial statements in accordance with generally accepted accounting principles regarding interim financial reporting.
   1. Explain whether Boxit should report its operating results for the quarter as if the quarter were a separate reporting period in and of itself or if the quarter were an integral part of the annual reporting period.
   2. State how the sales, cost of goods sold, and fixed selling expenses would be reflected in Boxit Corporation's quarterly report prepared for the first quarter of the 1983–1984 fiscal year. Briefly justify your presentation.
(b) What financial information, as a minimum, must Boxit Corporation disclose to its stockholders in its quarterly reports?

(CMA adapted)

**C27-9** The following statement is an excerpt from Paragraphs 9 and 10 of *Accounting Principles Board (APB) Opinion No. 28,* "Interim Financial Reporting":

> Interim financial information is essential to provide investors and others with timely information as to the progress of the enterprise. The usefulness of such information rests on the relationship that it has to the annual results of operations. Accordingly, the Board has concluded that each interim period should be viewed primarily as an integral part of an annual period.

> In general, the results for each interim period should be based on the accounting principles and practices used by an enterprise in the preparation of its latest annual financial statements unless a change in an accounting practice or policy has been adopted in the current year. The Board has concluded, however, that certain accounting principles and practices followed for annual reporting purposes may require modification at interim reporting dates so that the reported results for the interim period may better relate to the results of operations for the annual period.

**Instructions**

Listed below are six (6) independent cases on how accounting facts might be reported on an individual company's interim financial reports. For each of these cases, state whether the method proposed to be used for interim reporting would be acceptable under generally accepted accounting principles applicable to interim financial data. Support each answer with a brief explanation.

1. Morris Company wrote inventory down to reflect lower of cost or market in the first quarter of 1983. At year end the market exceeds the original acquisition cost of this inventory. Consequently, management plans to write the inventory back up to its original cost as a year-end adjustment.

2. Marbella Company realized a large gain on the sale of investments at the beginning of the second quarter. The company wants to report one-third of the gain in each of the remaining quarters.

3. Engstrom Company has estimated its annual audit fee. They plan to prorate this expense equally over all four quarters.

4. Baker Company was reasonably certain they would have an employee strike in the third quarter. As a result, they shipped heavily during the second quarter but plan to defer the recognition of the sales in excess of the normal sales volume. The deferred sales will be recognized as sales in the third quarter when the strike is in progress. Baker Company management thinks this is more nearly representative of normal second- and third-quarter operations.

5. Iliff Company takes a physical inventory at year end for annual financial statement purposes. Inventory and cost of sales reported in the interim quarterly statements are based on estimated gross profit rates, because a physical inventory would result in a cessation of operations. Iliff Company does have reliable perpetual inventory records.

6. Zima Company is planning to report one-fourth of its pension expense each quarter.

(CMA adapted)

**C27–10** Magneto Manufacturing Company, a California corporation listed on the Pacific Coast Stock Exchange, budgeted activities for 1984 as follows:

|  | Amount | Units |
|---|---|---|
| Net sales | $9,000,000 | 1,000,000 |
| Cost of goods sold | 5,400,000 | 1,000,000 |
| Gross margin | $3,600,000 | |
| Selling, general, and administrative expenses | 2,100,000 | |
| Operating income | $1,500,000 | |
| Nonoperating revenues and expenses | –0– | |
| Income before income taxes | $1,500,000 | |
| Estimated income taxes (current and deferred) | 825,000 | |
| Net income | $ 675,000 | |
| Earnings per share of common stock | $6.75 | |

Magneto has operated profitably for many years and has experienced a seasonal pattern of sales volume and production similar to those below forecasted for 1984. Sales volume is expected to follow a quarterly pattern of 10%, 20%, 35%, 35%, respectively, because of the seasonality of the industry. Also, owing to production and storage capacity limitations, it is expected that production will follow a pattern of 20%, 25%, 30%, 25%, per quarter, respectively.

At the conclusion of the first quarter of 1984, the controller of Magneto has prepared and issued the following interim report for public release:

|  | Amount | Units |
|---|---|---|
| Net sales | $ 900,000 | 100,000 |
| Cost of goods sold | 540,000 | 100,000 |
| Gross margin | $ 360,000 | |
| Selling, general, and administrative expenses | 412,500 | |
| Operating loss | $ (52,500) | |
| Loss from warehouse fire | (262,500) | |
| Loss before income taxes | $(315,000) | |
| Estimated income taxes | –0– | |
| Net loss | $(315,000) | |
| Loss per share of common stock | $(3.15) | |

The following additional information is available for the first quarter just completed, but was not included in the public information released:

1. Assume that the warehouse fire loss met the conditions of an extraordinary loss. The warehouse had an undepreciated cost of $480,000; $217,500 was recovered from insurance on the warehouse. No other gains or losses are anticipated this year from similar events or transactions, and Magneto had no similar losses in preceding years; thus, the full loss will be deductible as an ordinary loss for income tax purposes.

2. The company uses a standard cost system in which standards are set at currently attainable levels on an annual basis. At the end of the first quarter there was underapplied fixed factory overhead (volume variance) of $75,000 that was treated as an asset at the end of the quarter. Production during the quarter was 200,000 units, of which 100,000 were sold.

3. The selling, general, and administrative expenses were budgeted on a basis of $1,350,000 fixed expenses for the year plus $0.75 variable expenses per unit of sales.

4. The effective income tax rate, for federal and state taxes combined, is expected to average 55% of earnings before income taxes during 1984. There are no permanent differences between pretax accounting earnings and taxable income.

5. Earnings per share were computed on the basis of 100,000 shares of capital stock outstanding. Magneto has only one class of stock issued, no long-term debt outstanding, and no stock option plan.

**Instructions**

(a) Without reference to the specific situation described above, what are the standards of disclosure for interim financial data (published interim financial reports) for publicly traded companies? Explain.

(b) Identify the weaknesses in form and content of Magneto's interim report without reference to the additional information.

(c) For each of the five items of additional information, indicate the preferable treatment for each item for interim reporting purposes and explain why that treatment is preferable.
(AICPA adapted)

**C27-11** An article in *Barron's* noted:

Okay. Last fall, someone with a long memory and an even longer arm reached into that bureau drawer and came out with a moldy cheese sandwich and the equally moldy notion of corporate forecasts. We tried to find out what happened to the cheese sandwich—but, rats!, even recourse to the Freedom of Information Act didn't help. However, the forecast proposal was dusted off, polished up and found quite serviceable. The SEC, indeed, lost no time in running it up the old flagpole—but no one was very eager to salute. Even after some of the more objectionable features—compulsory corrections and detailed explanations of why the estimates went awry—were peeled off the original proposal.

Seemingly, despite the Commission's smiles and sweet talk, those craven corporations were still afraid that an honest mistake would lead down the primrose path to consent decrees and class action suits. To lay to rest such qualms, the Commission last week approved a "Safe Harbor" rule that, providing the forecasts were made on a reasonable basis and in good faith, protected corporations from litigation should the projections prove wide of the mark (as only about 99% are apt to do).

**Instructions**

(a) What are the arguments for preparing profit forecasts?
(b) What is the purpose of the "safe harbor" rule?
(c) Why are corporations concerned about presenting profit forecasts?

**C27-12** The following article appeared in *The Wall Street Journal*:

WASHINGTON—The Securities and Exchange Commission staff issued guidelines for companies grappling with the problem of dividing up their business into industry segments for their annual reports.

An industry segment is defined by the Financial Accounting Standards Board as a part of an enterprise engaged in providing a product or service or a group of related products or services primarily to unaffiliated customers for a profit.

Although conceding that the process is a "subjective task" that "to a considerable extent, depends on the judgment of management," the SEC staff said companies should consider the nature of the products, the nature of their production and their markets and marketing methods to determine whether products and services should be grouped together or in separate industry segments.

**Instructions**

(a) What does financial reporting for segments of a business enterprise involve?
(b) Identify the reasons for requiring financial data to be reported by segments.
(c) Identify the possible disadvantages of requiring financial data to be reported by segments.
(d) Identify the accounting difficulties inherent in segment reporting.

**C27-13** The most recently published statement of consolidated income of Jersey Industries, Inc., appears below:

Ginger Baumgartner, a representative of a firm of security analysts, visited the central headquarters of Jersey Industries to obtain more information about the company's operations.

In the annual report Jersey's president stated that Jersey was engaged in the pharmaceutical, food-processing, toy-manufacturing, and metal-working industries. Ms. Baumgartner complained that the published income statement was of limited utility in her analysis of the firm's operations. She said that Jersey should have disclosed separately the profit earned in each of its component industries. Further, she maintained that several items appearing on the statement of consolidated retained earnings should have been included on the income statement; a gain of $950,100 on the sale of the furniture division in early March of the current year and an assesment for additional income taxes of $247,350 resulting from an examination of the returns covering the years ended March 31, 1980 and 1981 (normally recurring).

---

**Jersey Industries, Inc.**
**STATEMENT OF CONSOLIDATED INCOME**
**For the Year Ended March 31, 1983**

| | |
|---|---:|
| Net sales | $57,061,800 |
| Other revenue | 611,100 |
| Total revenue | 57,672,900 |
| Cost of products sold | 40,759,950 |
| Selling and administrative expenses | 13,031,250 |
| Interest expense | 445,350 |
| Total cost and expenses | 54,236,550 |
| Income before income taxes | 3,436,350 |
| Income taxes | 1,507,800 |
| Net income | $ 1,928,550 |

---

**Instructions**

(a) Explain what is meant by a "conglomerate" company.
(b) 1. Discuss the accounting problems involved in measuring net profit by industry segments within a company.
2. With reference to Jersey Industries' statement of consolidated income, identify the specific items where difficulty might be encountered in measuring profit by each of its industry segments, and explain the nature of the difficulty.

(c) 1. What criteria should be applied in determining whether a gain or loss should be excluded from the determination of net income?

2. What criteria should be applied in determining whether a gain or loss that is properly includable in the determination of net income should be included in the results of ordinary operations or shown separately as an extraordinary item after all other items of revenue and expense?

3. How should the gain on the sale of the furniture division and the assessment of additional taxes each be presented in Jersey's financial statements?

(AICPA adapted)

# Index